McDougal Littell
CLASSZONE

Visit **classzone.com** and get connected.

ClassZone resources provide instruction, practice and learning support for students and parents.

 Animated Geography

- Brings geography to life with interactive activities and visuals
- Provides interactive maps, charts, and graphs

Current Events

- Takes you beyond the text and keeps you up-to-date on world events
- Reflects the most recent political, economic, and social issues
- Provides weekly current events quizzes to help check comprehension

Interactive Review

- Provides a unique way to review key concepts and events
- Includes geography games, crossword puzzles, and matching games
- Helps ensure lesson comprehension through graphic organizers, animated flipcards, and review/study notes

Research and Writing

- Includes research links chapter resources, and state-specific resources
- Provides support for your writing assignments through complete writing models, rubrics, and research guides

Access the online version of your textbook at classzone.com

Your complete text, along with animated maps, charts and infographics, is available for immediate use!

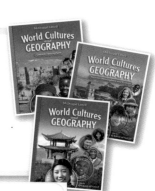

McDougal Littell
Where Great Lessons Begin

McDougal Littell

World Cultures
and
GEOGRAPHY

Sarah Bednarz

Marci Smith Deal

Inés Miyares

Donna Ogle

Charles White

Senior Consultants

Sarah Witham Bednarz is associate professor of geography at Texas A&M University, where she has taught since 1988. She earned a Ph.D. in Educational Curriculum and Instruction specializing in geography in 1992 from Texas A&M University and has written extensively about geography literacy and education. Dr. Bednarz was an author of *Geography for Life: National Geography Standards, 1994.* In 2005 she received the prestigious George J. Miller Award from the National Council for Geographic Education.

Marci Smith Deal is the K–12 Social Studies Curriculum Coordinator for Hurst-Euless-Bedford Independent School District in Texas. She received the 2000 Distinguished Geographer Award for the State of Texas, and was one of the honorees of the 2001 National Council for Geographic Education Distinguished Teacher Award. She has served as president for the Texas Council for Social Studies Supervisors and as vice-president for the Texas Council for Social Studies. She currently serves as a teacher consultant for National Geographic Society.

Inés M. Miyares is professor of geography at Hunter College-City University of New York. Born in Havana, Cuba, and fluent in Spanish, Dr. Miyares has focused much of her scholarship on Latin America, immigration and refugee policy, and urban ethnic geography. She holds a Ph.D. in geography from Arizona State University. In 1999 Dr. Miyares was the recipient of the Hunter College Performance Excellence Award for excellence in teaching, research, scholarly writing, and service. She has just published a co-edited book on contemporary ethnic geographies in the United States.

ISBN-13: 978-0-618-59664-5   ISBN-10: 0-618-59664-X

Printed in the United States of America

07 08 09— 1421 —12 11 10

Internet Web Site: http://www.mcdougallittell.com

Senior Consultants

Donna Ogle is professor of Reading and Language at National-Louis University in Chicago, Illinois, and is a specialist in reading in the content areas, with an interest in social studies. She is past president of the International Reading Association and a former social studies teacher. Dr. Ogle is currently directing two content literacy projects in Chicago schools and is Senior Consultant to the Striving Readers Research Project. She continues to explore applications of the K-W-L strategy she developed and is adding a Partner Reading component—PRC2 (Partner Reading and Content 2).

Charles S. White is associate professor in the School of Education at Boston University, where he teaches methods of instruction in social studies. Dr. White has written and spoken extensively on the importance of civic education, both in the United States and overseas. He has worked in Russia since 1997 on curriculum reform and teacher preparation in education for democracy. Dr. White has received numerous awards for his scholarship, including the 1995 Federal Design Achievement Award from the National Endowment for the Arts, for the Teaching with Historic Places project. In 1997, Dr. White taught his Models of Teaching doctoral course at the Universidad San Francisco de Quito, Ecuador.

Middle School Teacher Consultant

Judith K. Bock earned a B.A. in Elementary Education and an M.A. in Geography and Environmental Sciences from Northeastern Illinois University. She taught as a middle school educator in gifted education for 33 years and is currently an adjunct geography professor in college geography departments in metropolitan Chicago. Ms. Bock serves on several local, state, and national geography education committees, writes geography lesson plans and curriculum, and facilitates geography workshops and institutes. She received the Distinguished Teaching Award from NCGE and was awarded the Outstanding Geographer in Illinois–2004 from the Illinois Geographical Society.

Consultants and Reviewers

Regional Reviewers

Edwin Bryant
Professor of Hinduism
Rutgers University
New Brunswick, New Jersey

Gary S. Elbow
Associate Dean of the Honors College
and Professor of Geography
Texas Tech University
Lubbock, Texas

Ibipo Johnston-Anumonwo
Professor of Geography
State University of New York College
at Cortland
Cortland, New York

James A. Millward
Associate Professor of History
Georgetown University
Washington, D.C.

Mark Peterson
Associate Professor of Korean
Brigham Young University
Provo, Utah

Teacher Reviewers

Erik Branch
James C. Wright
Middle School
Madison, Wisconsin

Ann Christianson
John Muir Middle School
Wausau, Wisconsin

Jim Easton
Roscoe Middle School
Roscoe, Illinois

Ed Felton
Coopersville
Middle School
Coopersville, Michigan

Greta Frensley
Knox Doss Middle School
Gallatin, Tennessee

Todd Harrison
Hardin County
Middle School
Savannah, Tennessee

Esther Howse
Byron Center West Middle School
Byron Center, Michigan

Amber McVey
Antioch Middle School
Gladstone, Missouri

Ken Metz
Glacier Creek
Middle School
Cross Plains, Wisconsin

Suzanne Moen
DeForest Middle School
DeForest, Wisconsin

Tim Mortenson
Patrick Marsh Middle School
Sun Prairie, Wisconsin

Matt Parker
Eastgate Middle School
Kansas City, Missouri

Terry Rhodes
McNair Middle School
Fayetteville, Arkansas

Matthew J. Scheidler
Wayzata East Middle School
Plymouth, Minnesota

Don Stringfellow
Mobile City Public
School System
Mobile, Alabama

Student Panel

The following Middle School Student Panel reviewed textbook materials and technology products for this program.

Jessica Baker
Nelly Benitez
Ameer Cannon
Katie Conley
Murad Dajani
Will DiFrancesca
Tom Foydel
Philippa Gillette
Jenny Gorelick
Michael Grassle
Danielle Jackson
DeJauna Jackson
Mark Johnson
David Lenz
Andrew Mack

Madelaine Martin
Jabari McIntyre
Victoria Meliska
Sarah Peters
Brianna Ransom
Andrés Rivera-Thompson
Simone Samuels
Ben Shoaf
Gabriel Siegal
Kyle Siegal
Brock Snider
Hank Strickler
Jasmine Wright
Hannah Wyler

CONTENTS IN BRIEF

Resources

Online Activities
@ ClassZone.com

Animated GEOGRAPHY
Amazon Rain Forest

Explore life in a rain forest—the Yanomamo people, plants, animals, and the scientists who study them.

Interactive Review

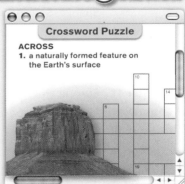

Solve a crossword of key terms and names related to Earth's physical geography.

Online Test Practice

Review test-taking strategies and practice for your test at the end of every chapter.

UNIT 2 The United States and Canada

Online Activities
@ ClassZone.com

Worldster
Kirima's Web Page

Visit Kirima's Web page to experience the sights and sounds of her world.

Interactive Review

Play the GeoGame to test your knowledge of the geography of the United States.

Online Test Practice
Review test-taking strategies and practice for your test at the end of every chapter.

UNIT 3 Latin America

Online Activities
@ ClassZone.com

Pedro's Web Page

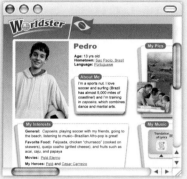

Visit Pedro's Web page to experience the sights and sounds of his world.

Interactive Review

Use interactive Flip Cards to review key terms and names related to Mexico.

Online Test Practice

Review test-taking strategies and practice for your test at the end of every chapter.

UNIT 4 Europe

Online Activities
@ ClassZone.com

Animated GEOGRAPHY
Victorian London

Enter the world of Victorian London and visit homes, shops, parks, and an underground railway.

Interactive Review

Play the GeoGame to test your knowledge of the geography of Western Europe.

Online Test Practice

Review test-taking strategies and practice for your test at the end of every chapter.

UNIT 5
Russia and the Eurasian Republics

Online Activities
@ ClassZone.com

Zuhura's Web Page

Visit Zuhura's Web page to experience the sights and sounds of her world.

Play the Name Game to test your knowledge of the Eurasian Republics.

Online Test Practice

Review test-taking strategies and practice for your test at the end of every chapter.

UNIT 6 Africa

Online Activities
@ ClassZone.com

Animated GEOGRAPHY
The Great Pyramid

Enter the world of ancient Egypt to see how the pyramids were built.

Interactive Review

Play the GeoGame to test your knowledge of Egypt and North Africa.

Online Test Practice
Review test-taking strategies and practice for your test at the end of every chapter.

UNIT 7
Southwest Asia and South Asia

Online Activities
@ ClassZone.com

Animated GEOGRAPHY
Monsoons

Discover the life-giving and life-destroying effects of a monsoon. Hear news accounts of flooded villages.

Interactive Review

Solve a crossword of key terms and names related to Southwest Asia.

Online Test Practice

Review test-taking strategies and practice for your test at the end of every chapter.

UNIT 8 East Asia and Southeast Asia

Online Activities
@ ClassZone.com

Cheng's Web Page

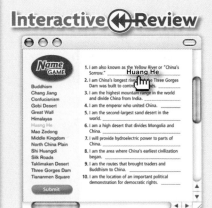

Visit Cheng's Web page to experience the sights and sounds of his world.

Interactive Review

Play the Name Game to test your knowledge of China.

Online Test Practice
Review test-taking strategies and practice for your test at the end of every chapter.

UNIT 9
Oceania and Antarctica

Online Activities
@ ClassZone.com

Animated GEOGRAPHY
The Great Barrier Reef

Dive into Australia's waters and explore life on the reef.

Interactive Review

Use interactive Flip Cards to review key terms and names related to Oceania and Antarctica.

Online Test Practice

Review test-taking strategies and practice for your test at the end of every chapter.

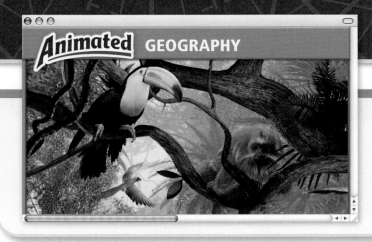

FEATURES

Animated GEOGRAPHY

CONNECT

GEOGRAPHY

HISTORY

CULTURE

ECONOMICS

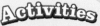

Activities

FEATURES

Worldster

COMPARING

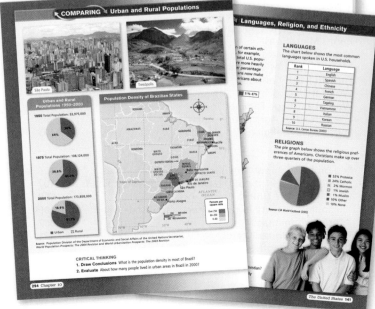

MAPS

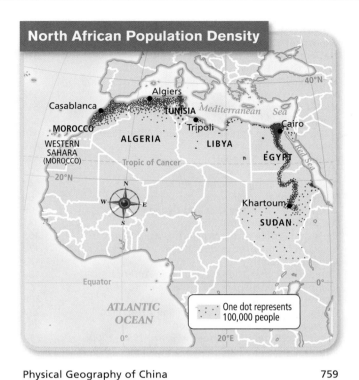

North African Population Density

One dot represents 100,000 people

GRAPHS, TABLES, AND CHARTS

Economic Activities of Kenya *2004*

- 2% —
- 11%
- 12%
- 49%
- 26%

- Services, Government
- Agriculture, Fishing
- Tourism
- Manufacturing
- Mining, Forestry

Source: Central Bank of Kenya Statistical Bulletin

"Say cheetah" A photographer gets a close-up view of a cheetah at Masai Mara National Reserve.

INFOGRAPHICS

Egyptian Social Roles

Pharaoh

Priests The priests cared for the temples and held religious ceremonies.

Priests and Nobles

Scribes and Government Officials

Craftspeople and Merchants

Farmers

Laborers and Slaves Slaves might be prisoners of war, or people who owed debts or had committed crimes. In general, slaves were eventually freed.

Laborers and Slaves

Four Steps to Being a Strategic Reader

These pages explain how *World Cultures and Geography* chapters are organized. By using the four key strategies below, you'll become a more successful reader of geography.

1 Set a Purpose for Reading

2 Build Your Social Studies Vocabulary

3 Use Active Reading Strategies

4 Check Your Understanding

Can you find it?
Find the following items on this and the next three pages.
- **one** chapter Essential Question
- **two** places where important words are defined
- **three** online games
- **four** key strategies for reading

1 Set a Purpose for Reading

Key features at the beginning of each chapter and section help you set a purpose for reading.

A **Essential Question** This key question sets the main purpose for reading.

B **Connect Geography & History** This feature helps you to consider the relationship between geography and history.

C **Animated Geography** identifies the region or country you'll be studying.

D **Before, You Learned** and **Now You Will Learn** This information helps you to connect what you've studied before to what you'll study next.

E **Key Question** Each topic covered in the chapter is followed by a Key Question that sets your purpose for reading about that topic.

2 Build Your Social Studies Vocabulary

The Reading for Understanding pages provide three important ways to build your vocabulary.

A **Terms & Names** cover the most important events, people, places, and social studies concepts in the section.

B **Background Vocabulary** lists words you need to know in order to understand the basic concepts and ideas discussed in the section.

C **Visual Vocabulary** features provide visual support for some definitions.

D **Terms & Names** and **Background Vocabulary** are highlighted and defined in the main text so that you'll understand them as you read.

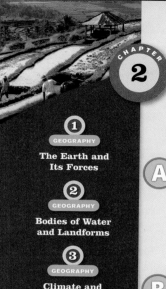

A ⊕ **ESSENTIAL QUESTION**

How do Earth's physical systems make life on Earth possible?

B **CONNECT** ⟶ **Geography & History**

Use the map and the time line to answer the following questions.
1. On which plate does most of the United States sit...
2. Which event on the time line is supported by the ... evidence on this map?

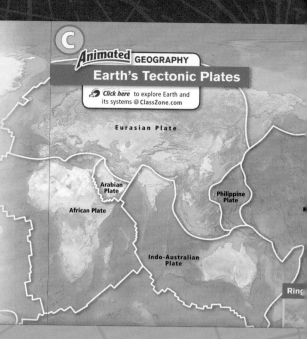

Animated GEOGRAPHY

Earth's Tectonic Plates

⟳ **Click here** to explore Earth and its systems @ ClassZone.com

Eurasian Plate

Arabian Plate

African Plate

Philippine Plate

Indo-Australian Plate

Ring

External Forces Shaping the Earth

E ▼ **KEY QUESTION** What external forces shape the Earth?

External forces also reshape the Earth's surface. The two main external forces are weathering and erosion. **Weathering** is the gradual physical and chemical breakdown of rocks near or on the Earth's surface. **Erosion** is the wearing away and movement of weathered materials from one place to another by the action of water, wind, or ice. As you can see, weathering and erosion work together to shape the Earth.

D **Weathering** Weathering occurs slowly, over many years or even centuries. The two types of weathering are mechanical weathering and chemical weathering. Mechanical weathering is a process in which rocks are broken down into smaller pieces by physical means. It takes place when ice, extremes of hot and cold, or even tree roots cause rocks to split apart. It also occurs when hard objects, such as other rocks or sand, scrape or rub against a rock, and pieces of the rock break off.

Chemical weathering is caused by chemical reactions between the minerals in the rock and elements in the air or water. This process changes the make-up of the rock itself. For example, most rocks contain iron. When iron comes in contact with water, it rusts, which helps to break down the rock. Water and elements in the air can cause other minerals in rocks to dissolve.

The Grand Canyon The Grand Canyon is located on the Colorado River in Arizona. It is an example of both weathering and erosion caused by wind and water.

UNITED STATES
Grand Canyon
ARIZONA
MEXICO

SECTION 2 Reading for Understanding

▶ **Key Ideas**

D **BEFORE, YOU LEARNED**
Internal and external forces shape the surface of the Earth.

NOW YOU WILL LEARN
Interaction between landfo... of water makes life on Earth...

▶ **Vocabulary**

A **TERMS & NAMES**

drainage basin the area drained by a major river

ground water water found beneath the Earth's surface

hydrologic cycle the circulation of water between the Earth, the oceans, and the atmosphere

landform a feature on the Earth's surface formed by physical force

plateau a broad, flat area of land higher than the surrounding land

relief the difference in the elevation of a landform from its lowest point to its highest point

B **continental shelf** the subme... at the edge of a continent

BACKGROUND VOCABU...

atmosphere the layer of gas... surround the Earth

C Visual Vocabulary landform

▶ **Reading Strategy**

Re-create the web diagram shown at right. As you read and respond to the **KEY QUESTIONS**, use the diagram to organize important details about the Earth's landforms and bodies of water.

📖 See Skillbuilder Handbook, page R4

FIND MAIN IDEAS

WATER BODIES

⟳ **GRAPHIC ORGANIZERS**
Go to **Interactive Review** @ Class...

③ Use Active Reading Strategies

Active reading strategies help you note the most important information in each section.

Ⓐ Reading Strategy Each Reading for Understanding page contains a Reading Strategy diagram to help you track and organize the information you read.

Ⓑ Skillbuilder Handbook Every Reading Strategy is supported by a corresponding lesson in the Skillbuilder Handbook section at the back of this book.

Ⓒ Active Reading Strategies in the Skillbuilder Handbook will help you to read and study *World Cultures and Geography*.

---

drainage basin the area drained by a major river

ground water water found beneath the Earth's surface

hydrologic cycle the circulation of water between the Earth, the oceans, and the atmosphere

landform a feature on the Earth's surface formed by physical force

plateau a broad, flat area of land higher than the surrounding land

relief the difference in the elevation of a landform from its lowest point to its highest point

continental shelf the submerged l... at the edge of a continent

BACKGROUND VOCABULARY

atmosphere the layer of gases that surround the Earth

Visual Vocabulary landform

▷ Reading Strategy Ⓐ

Re-create the web diagram shown at right. As you read and respond to the **KEY QUESTIONS**, use the diagram to organize important details about the Earth's landforms and bodies of water.

See Skillbuilder Handbook, page R4

34 Chapter 2

FIND MAIN IDEAS

WATER BODIES   LANDF...

GRAPHIC ORGANIZERS
Go to **Interactive Review @ ClassZone.com**

Skillbuilder Handbook

Ⓒ Contents

Reading and Critical Thinking Skills

Ⓑ 1.2 Finding Main Ideas

Defining the Skill

A **main idea** is a statement that summarizes the subject of a speech, an article, a section of a book, or a paragraph. Main ideas can be stated or unstated. The main idea of a paragraph is often stated in the first or last sentence. If it is the first sentence, it is followed by sentences that support that main idea. If it is the last sentence, the details build up to the main idea. To find an unstated idea, use the details of the paragraph as clues.

Applying the Skill

The following paragraph provides reasons why Japan and Australia make such good trading partners. Use the strategies listed below to help you identify the main idea.

How to Find the Main Idea

Strategy ❶ Identify what you think may be the stated main idea. Check the first and last sentences of the paragraph to see if either could be the stated main idea.

Strategy ❷ Identify details that support the main idea. Some details explain that idea. Others give examples of what is stated in the main idea.

TRADING PARTNERS

Australia is an island. Japan is also an island, though much smaller than Australia. Australia is not as densely populated as Japan. ❷ In Japan, an average of 881 people live in each square mile. Australia averages 7 people per square mile. ❷ Australia has wide-open lands available for agriculture, ranching, and mining. ❷ Japan buys wool from Australian ranches, wheat from Australian farms, and iron ore from Australian mines. To provide jobs for its many workers, ❷ Japan developed industries. Those industries ❷ sell electronics and cars to Australia. ❶ Australia and Japan are trading partners because each has something the other needs.

Make a Chart

Making a chart can help you identify the main idea and details in a passage or paragraph. The chart below identifies the main idea and details in the paragraph you just read.

Main Idea: Australia and Japan are good trading partners because each supplies something the other needs.

Detail: Japan's population density is 881 people per square mile; Australia's is 7 per square mile.

Detail: Australia has land, natural resources, and agricultural products.

Detail: Japan buys wool, wheat, and iron ore from Australia.

Detail: Japan has many industries.

Detail: Australia buys electronics and cars from Japanese industries.

④ Check Your Understanding

One of the most important things you'll do as you study *World Cultures and Geography* is to check your understanding of events, people, places, and issues as you read.

Ⓐ Interactive Review includes a Name Game and provides online activities to test your knowledge of the geography you just studied.

Ⓑ Section Assessment reviews the section Terms & Names, revisits your Reading Strategy notes, and provides key questions about the section.

Interactive Review

Ⓐ CHAPTER SUMMARY

Key Idea 1
The Earth is composed of many layers, and its surface continually changes because of the drifting of the continents.

Key Idea 2
Interaction between landforms and bodies of water makes life on Earth possible.

Key Idea 3
The Earth's rotation and revolution influence weather, climate, and living conditions on Earth.

Key Idea 4
Human interference with physical systems causes problems with the environment.

For **Review and Study Notes**, go to Interactive Review @ ClassZone.com

NAME GAME

Use the Terms & Names list to complete each s on paper or online.

1. I am the hot metal center of the Earth. <u>core</u>

2. I am a naturally formed feature on the Earth's surface. _____

3. I fall in the form of rain, snow, sleet, or hail. _____

4. I am an increase in the Earth's temperature. _____

5. I move weathered materials from one place to another. _____

6. I am the trapping of the sun's heat by gases in the atmosphere. _____

7. I am a large rigid piece of the Earth's crust that is in motion. _____

8. I am typical weather conditions over a period of time. _____

9. I circulate water between the Earth, oceans, and atmosphere. _____

10. I am plants that grow in a region. _____

Activities

Flip Cards

Use the online flip cards to quiz yourself on terms and names introduced in this chapter.

magma

melted or liquid rock

Crossword

Complete an online cross your knowledge of Earth

ACROSS

1. a naturally formed fe Earth's surface

Erosion New landforms and new soil are formed by erosion. It occurs when materials loosened by weathering are moved by water, wind, or ice to new locations. Currents in streams and rivers pick up loose materials and deposit them downstream or carry them out to sea. These tiny pieces of rock, deposited by water, wind, or ice are called **sediment**. Sediment can be sand, stone, or finely ground particles called silt.

Wave action along coastlines carries rocks and sand from one place to another. Waves also pound boulders into smaller rocks. Wind erosion lifts particles from the Earth's surface and blows them great distances. The wind's actions can reshape rock s Arizona's Grand Canyon is a result of both wind and water

Another type of erosion is caused by glaciers. **Glaciers** slow-moving masses of ice. They grind rocks and boulders un the ice and leave behind the rock when the ice melts. Pa central United States have been shaped by glacial erosion.

▲ **SYNTHESIZE** Explain how external forces shape the Eart surface.

ONLINE QUIZ
For test practice, go to Interactive Review @ClassZone.com

Ⓑ Section ① Assessment

TERMS & NAMES

1. **Explain the importance of**
   • continent
   • tectonic plate
   • weathering
   • erosion

USE YOUR READING NOTES

2. **Categorize** Use your completed chart to answer the following question:

Are external or internal forces responsible for volcanoes? Explain your answer.

INTERNAL FORCES	EXTERNAL FORCES
1.	1.
2.	2.
3.	3.
4.	4.

KEY IDEAS

3. What are the five layers that make up the Earth's interior and exterior?

4. How were the continents formed?

5. What are the two major external forces reshaping the Earth?

CRITICAL THINKING

6. **Draw Conclusions** How does the movement of wind, water, or ice reshape the Earth's surface?

7. **Analyze Causes and Effects** What is the relationship between plate movement, volcanoes, and earthquakes?

8. **CONNECT to Today** In which parts of the United States are external forces shaping the landscape?

9. **ART Create a Puzzle** Make a copy of a map of the world. Cut out the continents. Use the continents as puzzle pieces to form the continent of Pangaea. When you have finished putting the pieces together, draw an outline around the entire supercontinent.

33

Exploring Geography Online

World Cultures and Geography provides a variety of tools to help you explore geography online. See geography come to life in the Animation Center. Find help for your research projects in the Research and Writing Center. Review for tests with the Interactive Review, or create your own activities in the Activity Center. Go to ClassZone.com to make *World Cultures and Geography* interactive!

ClassZone.com

is your gateway to exploring geography. Explore the different **ClassZone Centers** to help you study and have fun with geography.

A **Interactive Review**
provides you with flip cards, a crossword puzzle, section quizzes, drag-and-drop map activities, and more.

B **Activity Center**
lets you explore world cultures through a **Worldster** community and participate in **WebQuests** and geography games.

C **Activity Maker**
lets you create your own activities so that you can focus on what *you* need to review.

Animation Center

A rich collection of interactive features and maps on a wide variety of geographical topics at **ClassZone.com**

 Roll-overs
Explore the illustration by clicking on areas you'd like to know more about. This Amazon Rain Forest animation includes features about biodiversity, life in the rain forest, and more.

 Video and Photo Gallery
Explore the rain forest and the scientists who study it.

Review Game

- Create your own review game to study geography *your* way in the Activity Maker at **ClassZone.com**

- Select your own topics from any chapter to help you focus on specific regions, people, or events to review.

- Help your friends to explore geography online. Challenge them to play a review game that you create and modify!

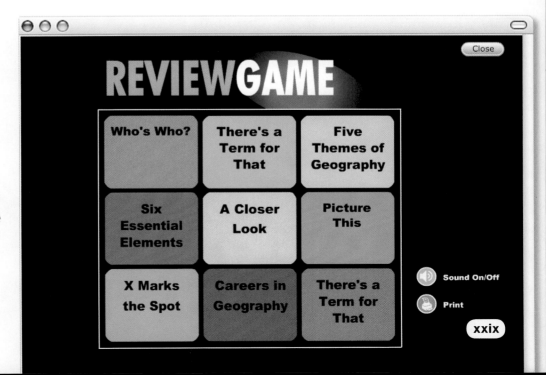

Guide to
Test-Taking Strategies and Practice

This section will help you develop and practice the skills you need to take standardized tests. Strategies are provided to help you answer the different kinds of questions that appear on standardized tests. Each strategy is followed by a set of questions you can use for practice.

CONTENTS for Test-Taking Strategies and Practice

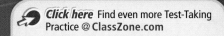
Click here Find even more Test-Taking Practice @ ClassZone.com

The chart below provides a guide to the test-taking strategies that will help prepare you for the standards-based assessments.

- Learn each strategy by reviewing the numbered steps on the pages listed in the column.

- Practice the strategy on the following page.

- Apply the strategies you learned on the pages of the chapters listed in the column.

STRATEGY	LEARN	PRACTICE	APPLY
Multiple Choice	p. S2	p. S3	p. 85, Chapter 3 p. 493, Chapter 15
Primary and Secondary Sources	p. S4	p. S5	p. 311, Chapter 10 p. 519, Chapter 16
Political Cartoons	p. S6	p. S7	p. 508, Chapter 16 p. 639, Chapter 20
Charts	p. S8	p. S9	p. 55, Chapter 2 p. 909, Chapter 29
Line and Bar Graphs	p. S10	p. S11	p. 227, Chapter 7 p. 447, Chapter 14
Pie Graphs	p. S12	p. S13	p. 251, Chapter 8 p. 849, Chapter 27
Political Maps	p. S14	p. S15	p. 23, Chapter 1 pp. 324–325, Chapter 11
Thematic Maps	p. S16	p. S17	p. 55, Chapter 2 p. 397, Chapter 12
Time Lines	p. S18	p. S19	p. 166, Chapter 6 p. 405, Chapter 13
Constructed Response	p. S20	p. S21	p. 85, Chapter 3 p. 551, Chapter 17
Extended Response	p. S22	p. S23	p. 54, Chapter 2 p. 358, Chapter 11
Document-Based Questions	pp. S24–S25	pp. S26–S27	p. 12, Chapter 1 p. 515, Chapter 16

Test-Taking Strategies and Practice

Use the strategies in this section to improve your test-taking skills. First, read the tips on the left page. Then use them to help you with the practice items on the right page.

Multiple Choice

A multiple-choice question is a question or incomplete sentence and a set of choices. One of the choices correctly answers the question or completes the sentence.

1 Read the question or incomplete sentence carefully. Try to answer the question before looking at the choices.

2 Look for key words in the question. They may help you figure out the correct answer.

3 Read each choice with the question. Don't decide on your final answer until you have read all the choices.

4 Rule out any choices that you know are wrong.

5 Watch answers with words like *all*, *never*, and *only*. These answers are often incorrect.

6 Sometimes the last choice is *All of the above*. Make sure that the other choices are all correct before you pick this answer.

7 Be careful with questions that include the word *not*.

1 1. The Sahara is (mostly)

A. sand, rocks, and gravel.

3 choices
B. boulders and sand.

C. cliffs and gulleys.

D. grasses and bushes.

2 Words like *mostly* or *partly* are key words in multiple choice. Look for answers that are mostly true or partly true about the subject.

4 You know that if the Sahara is a desert, **D** is incorrect. A desert cannot be mostly covered with grass and bushes.

2. Over hundreds of years, Bantu-speaking people migrated from West Africa to

A. South and Southwest Asia.

B. (every) continent on earth.

C. East and South Africa.

D. (all) of North Africa and Arabia.

5 Watch for answers that have words like *all*, *never*, *always*, *every*, and *only*. These answers are often incorrect.

3. The people of West Africa passed on their history by

A. painting pictures.

B. telling stories.

C. creating dances.

6 D. all of the above

4. Which of the following is (not) one of the nations in southern Africa?

A. Zimbabwe

B. Nigeria

C. Mozambique

D. Namibia

7 First rule out all the answers that name southern African countries. The answer that remains is the correct choice.

answers: 1 (A); 2 (C); 3 (D); 4 (B)

Directions: Read each question carefully. Choose the best answer from the four choices.

1. Which of the following was *not* a result of the bubonic plague?

   A. Cities worked together during the plague.

   B. Europe lost one-third of its population.

   C. The Church lost its prestige among the people.

   D. The economies of many countries were ruined.

2. Martin Luther started a reform movement when he

   A. published the New Testament in German.

   B. criticized some of the Church's practices.

   C. wrote his 95 Theses and made them public.

   D. all of the above

3. The Ottoman Empire reached its greatest size and glory under the rule of

   A. Mehmet II.

   B. Selim the Grim.

   C. Suleiman the Lawgiver.

   D. Timur the Lame.

4. During the 1700s, England controlled which of the following?

   A. the sugar trade

   B. the Atlantic slave trade

   C. the cotton trade

   D. the coconut trade

Primary and Secondary Sources

Sometimes you will need to study a document to answer a question. Documents can be either primary sources or secondary sources. Primary sources are written or created by people who either saw an event or were actually part of the event. A primary source can be a photograph, letter, diary, speech, or autobiography.

A secondary source is an account of events by a person who did not actually experience them. Newspaper articles and history books are some examples of secondary sources.

① Look at the source line to learn about the document and its author. If the author is well known and has been quoted often, the information is likely true.

② Skim the article to get an idea of what it is about.

③ Note special punctuation. For example, ellipses (. . .) indicate that words have been left out.

④ Ask yourself questions about the document as you read.

⑤ Review the questions to see what information you will need to find. Then reread the document.

Good Government

Chap. 2.20 Lord Ji Kang asked, "What should I do in order to make the people respectful, loyal, and zealous [hard-working]?" The Master said: "Approach them with dignity and they will be respectful. Be yourself a good son and kind father, and they will be loyal. Raise the good and train the incompetent, and they will be zealous."

Chap. 13.2 Ran Yong . . . asked about government. The Master said: "Guide the officials. Forgive small mistakes. Promote [people] of talent." "How does one recognize that a [person] has talent and deserves to be promoted?" The Master said: "Promote those you know. Those whom you do not know will hardly remain ignored."

The *Analects* is a book of thoughts and ideas by Confucius. He was a scholar and teacher in ancient China.

① —*The Analects of Confucius*

1. Confucius is giving advice on how to

    A. be a gentleman.

    B. be a good ruler.

    C. become wealthy.

    D. raise a good family.

2. Which sentence *best* expresses the idea of these paragraphs?

    A. The wise ruler governs people through fear.

    B. People should obey their rulers no matter what.

    C. A good ruler gives a lot of orders to people.

    D. If rulers do things well, people will follow them.

answers: 1 (B); 2 (D)

Directions: Read this passage. Use the passage and your knowledge of world cultures and geography to answer questions 1 and 2.

Before World War I

In 1892, France and Russia had become military allies. Later, Germany signed an agreement to protect Austria. If any nation attacked Austria, Germany would fight on its side. France and Russia had to support each other as well. For instance, if France got into a war with Germany, Russia had to fight Germany, too. This meant that in any war, Germany would have to fight on two fronts: France on the west and Russia on the east.

If a war broke out, what part would Great Britain play? No one knew. It might remain neutral, like Belgium. It might, if given a reason, fight against Germany.

1. If Russia and Germany went to war, which country had to help Russia?

   A. Great Britain
   B. Belgium
   C. Austria
   D. France

2. What was a result of the military alliance formed between France and Russia?

   A. Belgium would have to fight a war on the side of Germany.
   B. Great Britain would remain neutral.
   C. Germany would have to fight a war on two fronts.
   D. France and Russia would support Germany in a war.

Political Cartoons

Cartoonists who draw political cartoons use both words and art to express opinions about political issues.

1 Try to figure out what the cartoon is about. Titles and captions may give clues.

2 Use labels to help identify the people, places, and events represented in the cartoon.

3 Note when and where the cartoon was published.

4 Look for symbols—that is, people, places, or objects that stand for something else.

5 The cartoonist often exaggerates the physical features of people and objects. This technique will give you clues as to how the cartoonist feels about the subject.

6 Try to figure out the cartoonist's message and summarize it in a sentence.

1 NEXT!

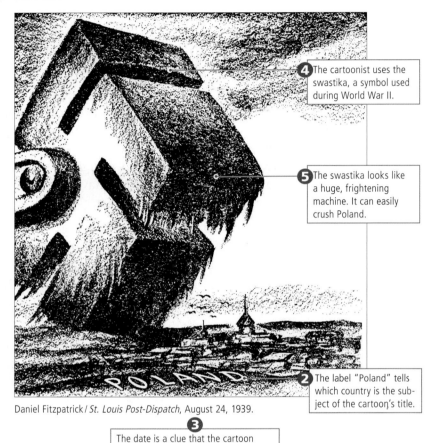

4 The cartoonist uses the swastika, a symbol used during World War II.

5 The swastika looks like a huge, frightening machine. It can easily crush Poland.

2 The label "Poland" tells which country is the subject of the cartoon's title.

Daniel Fitzpatrick / *St. Louis Post-Dispatch*, August 24, 1939.

3 The date is a clue that the cartoon refers to the beginning of World War II.

1. What does the swastika in the cartoon stand for?

    A. the Soviet Union

    B. Nazi Germany

    C. the Polish army

    D. Great Britain

6 2. Which sentence best summarizes the cartoonist's message?

    A. Germany will attack Poland next.

    B. Poland should stop Germany.

    C. Germany will lose this battle.

    D. Poland will fight a civil war.

answers: 1 (B); 2 (A)

Directions: Study this cartoon. Use the cartoon and your knowledge of world cultures and geography to answer questions 1 and 2.

Steve Sack, *Minneapolis Star-Tribune*, January 1, 1992.

1. How has the cartoonist drawn Saddam Hussein?

   A. as Count Dracula

   B. as Darth Vader

   C. as Frankenstein's monster

   D. as a military leader

2. Notice all the "MADE IN" labels on Saddam Hussein. The best title for the cartoon would be

   A. "A Monster Never Sleeps."

   B. "The Monster of Iraq."

   C. "They've Made a Mistake."

   D. "They've Created a Monster."

Charts

Charts present facts in a visual form. History textbooks use several different types of charts. The chart that is most often found on standardized tests is the table. A table organizes information in columns and rows.

1 Read the title of the chart to find out what information is represented.

2 Read the headings at the top of each column. Then read the headings at the left of each row.

3 Notice how the information in the chart is organized.

4 Notice that information from different years is used for different countries.

5 Of all the countries listed, six took in the most immigrants. Think about what these countries have in common.

6 Read the questions and then study the chart again.

1 This chart is about the number of people who immigrated to different countries.

4 Notice that information from different years is used for different countries.

Immigration to Selected Countries

Country	Years	Number of Immigrants
Argentina	1856–1932	6,405,000
Australia	1861–1932	2,913,000
Brazil	1821–1932	4,431,000
British West Indies	1836–1932	1,587,000
Canada	1821–1932	5,206,000
Cuba	1901–1932	857,000
Mexico	1911–1931	226,000
New Zealand	1851–1932	594,000
South Africa	1881–1932	852,000
United States	1821–1932	34,244,000
Uruguay	1836–1932	713,000

Source: Alfred W. Crosby, Jr. *The Columbian Exchange: Biological and Cultural Consequences of 1492*

3 This chart lists countries in alphabetical order. Other charts organize information by years or by numbers.

5 Of all the countries listed, six took in the most immigrants. Think about what these countries have in common.

1. The country that received the most immigrants was

A. Canada.

B. the British West Indies.

C. the United States.

D. Brazil.

2. Different countries received immigrants in different years. According to the chart, which countries received immigrants the earliest?

A. Argentina, New Zealand, and Canada

B. Canada, Brazil, and United States

C. Mexico, United States, and British West Indies

D. Brazil, South Africa, and Cuba

answers: 1 (C); 2 (B)

Directions: Read the chart carefully. Use the chart and your knowledge of world cultures and geography to answer questions 1 and 2.

Ancient Civilizations				
Feature	**China**	**Egypt**	**Indus Valley**	**Mesopotamia**
Location	River valley	River valley	River valley	River valley
Period	2000 B.C.–400 B.C.	3100 B.C.–332 B.C.	2500 B.C.–1500 B.C.	3500 B.C.–500 B.C.
Specialized workers	Priests; government workers, soldiers; workers in bronze, silk; farmers	Priests; government workers, scribes, soldiers; workers in pottery, stone; farmers	Priests; government officials; workers in pottery, bricks; farmers	Priests; government officials, scribes, soldiers; workers in pottery, textiles; farmers
Institutions	Walled cities; oracle-bone reading	Ruling class of priests, nobles; education system	Ruling class of priests	Ruling class of priests and nobles; education for scribes
Record keeping	Pictographic writing	Hieroglyphic writing	Pictographic writing	Cuneiform writing
Advanced technology and artifacts	Writing; making bronze and silk; irrigation systems	Papyrus; mathematics; astronomy, engineering; pyramids; mummification; medicine	Irrigation systems; indoor plumbing; seals	Wheel; plow; sailboat; bronze weapons

1. Which civilization appeared first?

A. China

B. Egypt

C. Indus Valley

D. Mesopotamia

2. The Indus Valley civilization did not have

A. irrigation systems.

B. walled cities.

C. government officials.

D. indoor plumbing.

Line and Bar Graphs

Graphs are often used to show numbers. Line graphs often show changes over time. Bar graphs make it easy to compare numbers.

1 Read the title of the graph to find out what information is represented.

2 Study the labels on the graph.

3 Look at the source line that tells where the graph is from. Decide whether you can depend on the source to provide reliable information.

4 See if you can make any generalizations about the information in the graph. Note whether the numbers change over time.

5 Read the questions carefully and then study the graph again.

1 Exports of English Manufactured Goods, 1699–1774

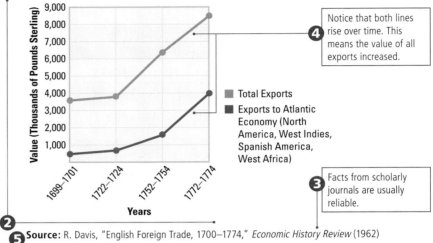

Notice that both lines **4** rise over time. This means the value of all exports increased.

Facts from scholarly **3** journals are usually reliable.

2
5 **Source:** R. Davis, "English Foreign Trade, 1700–1774," *Economic History Review* (1962)

1. Which of the following is a true statement?

    A. Exports to the Atlantic economy declined over time.

    B. Total exports stayed the same over time.

    C. Total exports rose sharply after 1724.

    D. Exports to the Atlantic economy fell sharply after 1754.

1 Nations with High Foreign Debt, 2003

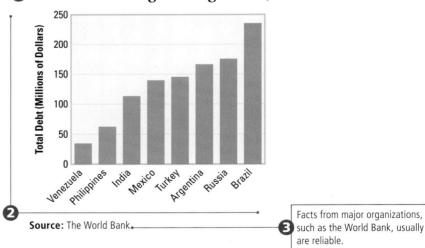

2
Source: The World Bank.

Facts from major organizations, **3** such as the World Bank, usually are reliable.

5 **2.** The nation with the second largest foreign debt is

    A. Brazil.   **C.** Russia.

    B. Argentina.   **D.** Mexico.

answers: 1 (C); 2 (C)

Directions: Study the graphs carefully. Use the graphs and your knowledge of world cultures and geography to answer questions 1 and 2.

Japan: Gross Domestic Product, 1984–2002

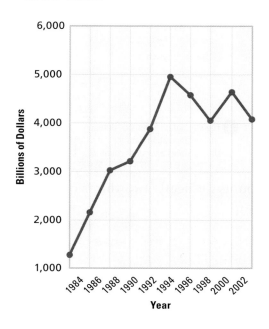

Source: Annual Report on National Accounts 2005, Cabinet Office of the Government of Japan

Unemployment Rates for Selected Countries, 2005

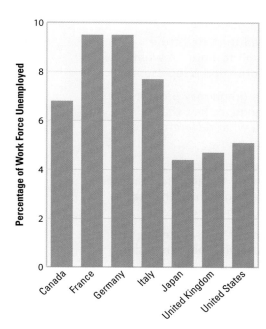

Source: Organization for Economic Cooperation and Development

1. Japan's gross domestic product increased the most between

   A. 1986 and 1990.

   B. 1990 and 1994.

   C. 1994 and 1998.

   D. 1998 and 2002.

2. Which country had the lowest unemployment rate in 2005?

   A. Japan

   B. Germany

   C. United States

   D. United Kingdom

Pie Graphs

A pie, or circle, graph shows the relationship among parts of a whole. These parts look like slices of a pie. Each slice is shown as a percentage of the whole pie.

1 Read the title of the graph to find out what information is represented.

2 The graph may provide a legend, or key, that tells you what different slices represent.

3 The size of the slice is related to the percentage. The larger the percentage, the larger the slice.

4 Look at the source line that tells where the graph is from. Ask yourself if you can depend on this source to provide reliable information.

5 Read the questions carefully, and study the graph again.

1 **World Population by Region, 2006**

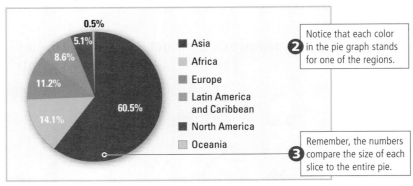

2 Notice that each color in the pie graph stands for one of the regions.

3 Remember, the numbers compare the size of each slice to the entire pie.

Source: Population Reference Bureau

4 The Population Reference Bureau studies population data for the United States and other countries.

1. Which region accounts for nearly two-thirds of the world's population?

A. Africa

B. North America

C. Europe

D. Asia

2. A greater share of the world's population lives in Latin America and the Caribbean than lives in

A. Africa

B. Europe

C. North America

D. Asia

For this question, find the "pie slices" for each of the regions listed in the alternatives. Compare each one to the "pie slice" for Latin America and the Caribbean.

answers: 1 (D); 2 (C)

Directions: Study the pie graph. Use the graph and your knowledge of world cultures and geography to answer questions 1 and 2.

World Energy Consumption by Region

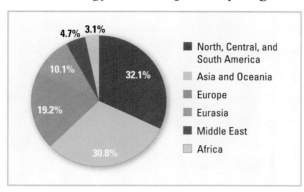

Source: Energy Information Administration/Annual Energy Review 2005

1. Which region uses the least energy?

   A. Europe

   B. Asia and Oceania

   C. Africa

   D. Middle East

2. North, Central, and South America are grouped together because

   A. they are in the same part of the world.

   B. all three have about the same number of people.

   C. all three are roughly the same size.

   D. they use the same power sources.

Political Maps

Political maps show the divisions within countries. A country may be divided into states, provinces, or other kinds of segments. The maps also show where major cities are. They may also show mountains, oceans, seas, lakes, and rivers.

1 Read the title of the map. This will give you the subject and purpose of the map.

2 Read the labels on the map. They also give information about the map's subject and purpose.

3 Study the key or legend to help you understand the symbols on the map.

4 Use the scale to estimate distances between places shown on the map. Maps usually show the distance in both miles and kilometers.

5 Use the compass rose to figure out directions on the map.

6 Read the questions. Carefully study the map to find the answers.

3 The legend gives symbols for the nation's capital and the states' capitals.

1 Present-Day United States

2 The labels identify the states of the United States.

1. What state extends farthest east?

A. Oregon

B. Maine

C. Georgia

D. Alaska

2. About how many miles is it from the western end of the Great Lakes to the Pacific Ocean along the United States–Canada border?

A. 1,000

B. 1,500

C. 2,000

D. 2,500

answers: 1 (B); 2 (B)

Directions: Study the map carefully. Use the map and your knowledge of world cultures and geography to answer questions 1 and 2.

Present-Day Europe

1. What body of water borders Poland on the north?

A. North Sea

B. Norwegian Sea

C. Baltic Sea

D. Adriatic Sea

2. The northernmost country in Europe is

A. Ireland.

B. Denmark.

C. Iceland.

D. Norway.

Thematic Maps

Thematic maps focus on special topics. For example, a thematic map might show a country's natural resources or major battles in a war.

1 Read the title of the map. This will give you the subject and purpose of the map.

2 Read the labels on the map. They give information about the map's subject and purpose.

3 Study the key or legend to help you understand the symbols on the map.

4 Ask yourself whether the symbols show a pattern.

5 Read the questions. Carefully study the map to find the answers.

1 The Spread of Buddhism

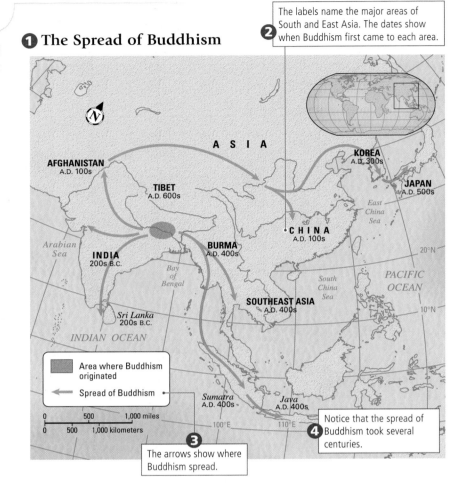

2 The labels name the major areas of South and East Asia. The dates show when Buddhism first came to each area.

Area where Buddhism originated

Spread of Buddhism

3 The arrows show where Buddhism spread.

4 Notice that the spread of Buddhism took several centuries.

1. Where did Buddhism start?

    A. Japan

    B. India

5   **C.** China

    D. Afghanistan

2. Buddhism spread from China to

    A. Japan and Tibet.

    B. Tibet and Korea.

    C. Korea and Japan.

    D. all of the above

answers: 1 (B); 2 (C)

Directions: Study the map carefully. Use the map and your knowledge of world cultures and geography to answer questions 1 and 2.

The Roman Empire, A.D. 400

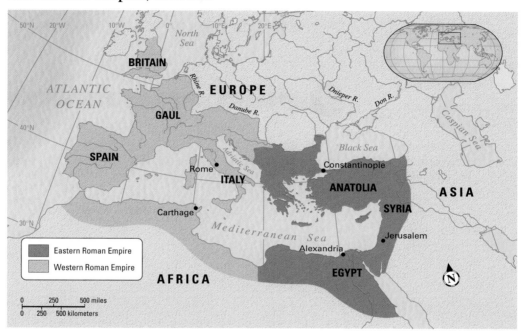

1. Which area was part of the Eastern Roman Empire?

   A. Spain

   B. Gaul

   C. Anatolia

   D. all of the above

2. The northernmost region in the Western Roman Empire was

   A. Syria.

   B. Gaul.

   C. Spain.

   D. Britain.

Time Lines

A time line is a chart that lists events in the order in which they occurred. Time lines can be vertical or horizontal.

1 Read the title to learn what period of time the time line covers.

2 Note the dates when the time line begins and ends.

3 Read the events in the order they occurred.

4 Think about what else was going on in the world on these dates. Try to make connections.

5 Read the questions. Then carefully study the time line to find the answers.

1 Dates of Independence in African Countries

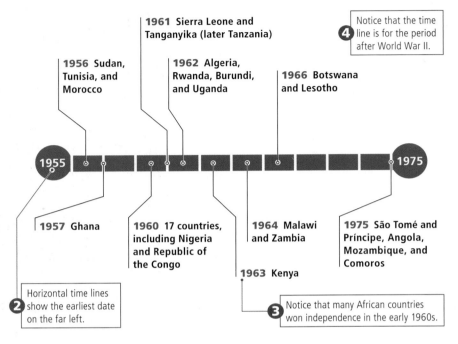

1961 Sierra Leone and Tanganyika (later Tanzania)

4 Notice that the time line is for the period after World War II.

1956 Sudan, Tunisia, and Morocco

1962 Algeria, Rwanda, Burundi, and Uganda

1966 Botswana and Lesotho

1955

1975

1957 Ghana

1960 17 countries, including Nigeria and Republic of the Congo

1964 Malawi and Zambia

1975 São Tomé and Príncipe, Angola, Mozambique, and Comoros

1963 Kenya

2 Horizontal time lines show the earliest date on the far left.

3 Notice that many African countries won independence in the early 1960s.

1. How many countries gained independence from 1961 to 1966?

A. 7

B. 9

C. 11

D. 13

2. Why do you think so many countries won their independence after World War II?

A. European nations were weaker after the war.

B. All Europeans in Africa moved back to Europe.

C. Europe no longer wanted to own colonies.

D. Europe gave each colony its own army after the war.

answers: 1 (C), 2 (A)

Directions: Study the time line. Use the information shown and your knowledge of world cultures and geography to answer questions 1 and 2.

The Breakup of the Soviet Union

1985 Mikhail Gorbachev becomes leader of Soviet Union.

1989 In Soviet elections, many Communist candidates are defeated.

1991 Boris Yeltsin is elected president of Russia.

1991 Communist and army hardliners seize power; Yeltsin leads resistance that defeats them.

1991 Soviet Union ceases to exist. Over the next several months, 14 other republics become independent.

1986 Gorbachev starts economic and political reforms.

1988 New Soviet constitutional amendments allow for open elections.

1990 Lithuania declares independence.

1985   1991

1. What happened after Lithuania declared independence?

   A. Gorbachev started economic and political reforms.

   B. Many other republics became independent.

   C. New constitutional amendments allowed for open elections.

   D. Gorbachev defeated Yeltsin in a new election.

2. In which year did Communist and army hardliners try to seize power?

   A. 1985

   B. 1988

   C. 1990

   D. 1991

Constructed Response

Constructed-response questions focus on a document, such as a photograph, cartoon, chart, graph, or time line. Instead of picking one answer from a set of choices, you write a short response. Sometimes, you can find the answer in the document. Other times, you will use what you already know about a subject to answer the question.

❶ Read the title of the document to get an idea of what it is about.

❷ Study the document (including any caption, if it is an image).

❸ Read the questions carefully. Study the document again to find the answers.

❹ Write your answers. You don't need to use complete sentences unless the directions say so.

❶ The Salt March

Copyright © Hulton Archive

Mohandas Gandhi and poet Sarojini Naidu lead Indians in a march down the west coast of India. They are protesting the Salt Acts of 1930.

❷ This document is a photograph showing Mohandas K. Gandhi leading a demonstration.

1. Mohandas Gandhi was an important leader in what country?

❹ *India*

2. Read the title of the photograph. What was the Salt March?

It was a protest against the Salt Acts. These acts said that Indians could buy salt only from the British. They also had to pay sales taxes when they bought salt.

3. What principle did Gandhi follow to win independence for India? Describe the (ways) he put this principle into action.

❸ The question uses the plural "ways." Your answer must include more than one way.

passive resistance, civil disobedience, or nonviolence. He led peaceful marches against unjust laws. He organized boycotts of British goods. He also told people not to cooperate with the British government.

Directions: Read the following passage from *Zlata's Diary*, a diary kept by Zlata, a 12-year-old girl. Use the passage and your knowledge of world cultures and geography to answer questions 1 and 2. You do not need to use complete sentences.

Saturday, May 2, 1992

Dear Mimmy,

Today was truly, absolutely the worst day ever in Sarajevo. The shooting started around noon. Mommy and I moved into the hall. Daddy was in his office, under our apartment, at the time. We told him on the intercom to run quickly to the downstairs lobby where we'd meet him . . . The gunfire was getting worse, and we couldn't get over the wall to the Bobars', so we ran down to our own cellar.

The cellar is ugly, dark, smelly. Mommy, who's terrified of mice, had two fears to cope with. The three of us were in the same corner as the other day. We listened to the pounding shells, the shooting, the thundering noise overhead. We even heard planes. At one moment I realized that this awful cellar was the only place that could save our lives. Suddenly, it started to look almost warm and nice. It was the only way we could defend ourselves against all this terrible shooting. We heard glass shattering in our street. Horrible. I put my fingers in my ears to block out the terrible sounds. I was worried about Cicko. We had left him behind in the lobby. Would he catch cold there? Would something hit him? I was terribly hungry and thirsty. We had left our half-cooked lunch in the kitchen.

—Zlata Filipovic, *Zlata's Diary: A Child's Life in Sarajevo* (1994)

1. What does Zlata say is happening in the city of Sarajevo?

2. How does the war affect Zlata and her family?

Extended Response

Extended-response questions, like constructed-response questions, focus on a document of some kind. However, they are more complicated and require more time to complete.

Some extended-response questions ask you to present the information in the document in a different form. You might be asked to present the information in a chart in graph form, for example. Other questions ask you to complete a document such as a chart or graph. Still others require you to apply your knowledge to information in the document to write an essay.

1 Read the title of the document to get an idea of what it is about.

2 Carefully read directions and questions.

3 Study the document.

4 Sometimes the question and/or example may give you part of the answer. (The answer given tells how inventions were used and what effects they had on society. Your answers should have the same kind of information.)

5 The question may require you to write an essay. Write down some ideas to use in an outline. Then use your outline to write the essay. (A good essay will contain the ideas shown in the rubric to the right.)

> Read the column heads carefully. They offer important clues about the subject of the chart. For instance, the column head "Impact" is a clue about why these inventions were so important.

1 Inventions of the Industrial Revolution **3**

Invention	Impact
Flying shuttle, spinning jenny, water frame, spinning mule, power loom	Spun thread and wove cloth faster; more factories were built and more people were hired **4**
Cotton gin	Cleaned seeds from cotton faster; companies produced more cotton
Macadam road, steamboat, locomotive	Made travel over land and water faster; could carry larger, heavier loads; railroads needed more coal and iron
Mechanical reaper	Made harvesting easier; increased wheat production

2 **1.** Read the list of inventions in the left-hand column. In the right-hand column, briefly state what the inventions meant to industry. The first item has been filled in for you.

2. The chart shows how some inventions helped create the Industrial Revolution. Write a short essay describing how the Industrial Revolution changed people's lives.

5 **Essay Rubric:** The best essays will point out that progress in agriculture meant that fewer people were needed to work the farms. As a result, many farm workers went to the city looking for work in factories. As cities grew, poor sanitation and poor housing made them unhealthy and dangerous places to live. Life for factory workers was hard. They worked long hours under bad conditions. At first, the Industrial Revolution produced three classes of people: an upper class of landowners and aristocrats; a middle class of merchants and factory owners; and a large lower class of poor people, including factory workers. Eventually, conditions improved even for the lower class. This was partly because factory goods could be sold at a lower cost. In time, even the poorer people could afford to buy many goods and services.

Directions: Use the drawing and passage below and your knowledge of world cultures and geography to answer question 1.

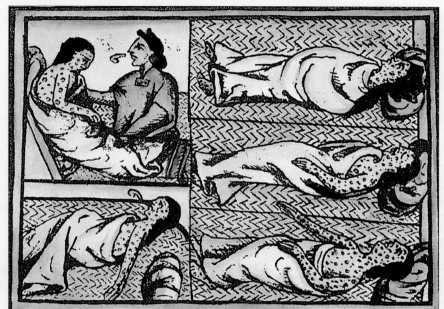

Smallpox Spreads Among the Aztecs

European diseases were like a second "army" of conquerors. Native people had no way to treat diseases like smallpox, typhoid fever, or measles. This "army" was more deadly than swords or guns.

—Based on P. M. Ashburn, *The Ranks of Death* (1947)

The Granger Collection, New York.

1. What role did disease play in the Spanish conquest of the Aztec and Inca?

Document-Based Questions

To answer a document-based question, you have to study more than one document. First you answer questions about each document. Then you use those answers and information from the documents, as well as your own knowledge of world cultures and geography, to write an essay.

1 Read the "Historical Context" section. It will give you an idea of the topic that will be covered in the question.

2 Read the "Task" section carefully. It gives you the topic for your essay.

3 Study each document. Think about the connection the documents have to the topic in the "Task" section.

4 Read and answer the questions about each document. Think about how your answers connect to the "Task" section.

1 **Introduction**

Historical Context: By the 8th century B.C., Mongol nomads lived in different tribes. They sometimes fought among themselves. In the early 1200s, a new leader—Genghis Khan—united these tribes. He turned the Mongols into a powerful fighting army.

2 **Task:** Discuss how the Mongols conquered Central and East Asia and how their rule affected Europeans' lives.

Part 1: Short Answer

Study each document carefully. Answer the questions that follow.

3 **Document 1: Mongol Warrior**

Victoria & Albert Museum, London/Art Resource, New York.

4 **1.** What were the characteristics of a Mongol warrior?

The Mongols were great horsemen who could ride a long way without rest. They attacked without warning and showed no mercy. They used clever tricks to frighten their enemies. Also, they borrowed or invented new weapons of war.

③ Document 2: The Mongol Empire

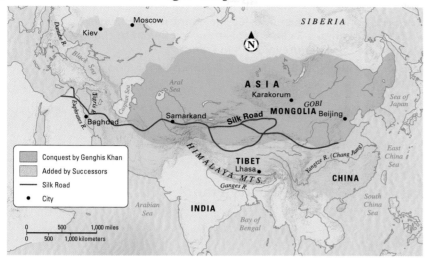

④ 2. What route linked the Mongol Empire to Europe? What was the main purpose of this route?

Silk Road; as a trade route between Asia and Europe

③ Document 3: The Great Khan's Wealth

. . . All those who have gems and pearls and gold and silver must bring them to the Great Khan's mint . . . By this means the Great Khan acquires all the gold and silver and pearls and precious stones of all his territories [lands] . . .

. . . The Great Khan must have, as indeed he has, more treasure than anyone else in the world . . . All the world's great [rulers] put together have not such riches as belong to the Great Khan alone.

—Marco Polo, *The Travels of Marco Polo* (c. 1300)

④ 3. Why do you think Marco Polo's travels made Europeans want to see East Asia?

Europeans were interested in the treasure of the Great Khan and East Asia.

⑤ Part 2: Essay

Write an essay discussing how the Mongols conquered Central and East Asia and how their rule affected Europeans' lives. Use information from the documents, your short answers, and your knowledge of world cultures and geography to write your essay. **⑥**

⑤ Read the essay question carefully. Then write a brief outline for your essay.

⑥ Write your essay. The first paragraph should introduce your topic. The middle paragraphs should explain it. The closing paragraph should restate the topic and your conclusion. Support your ideas with quotations or details from the documents. Add other supporting facts or details from your knowledge of world cultures and geography.

⑦ A good essay will contain the ideas in the rubric below.

⑦

Essay Rubric: The best essays will describe how the Mongols' tactics, fierce will, and strong military organization enabled them to conquer Central and East Asia (Documents 1 and 2). The essays will also state that Mongol rule brought a period of peace and unity to regions that had been divided. This peace allowed trade to start again along the Silk Road (Document 2). This trade brought new ideas and products to Europe. Stories of the immense wealth in Mongol lands made Europeans want to tap into those riches (Document 3).

TEST-TAKING STRATEGIES AND PRACTICE

Introduction

Historical Context: For many centuries, kings and queens ruled the countries of Europe. Their power was supported by nobles and armies. Then European society began to change. In the late 1700s, those changes produced a violent revolution in France.

Task: Discuss how social conflict and new ideas contributed to the French Revolution and why the Revolution turned radical.

Part 1: Short Answer

Study each document carefully. Answer the questions that follow.

Document 1: Social Classes in Pre-Revolutionary France

LE GRAND ABUS

1. This cartoon shows a peasant woman carrying women of nobility and the Church. What does the cartoon say about the lives of the poor before the revolution?

_____

_____

_____

Le Grand Abus. Engraving of a cartoon held in the collection of M. de baron de Vinck d'Orp of Brussels/Mary Evans Picture Library, London.

Document 2: A Declaration of Rights

1. Men are born and remain free and equal in rights . . .

2. The aim of all political association is the preservation of the natural and [unlimited] rights of man. These rights are liberty, property, security, and resistance to oppression . . .

—*Declaration of the Rights of Man and of the Citizen* (1789)

2. According to this document, which rights belong to all people?

_____

Document 3: The French Revolution—Major Events

July 1789 Crowd storms the Bastille.

Aug. 1789 National Assembly abolishes feudalism, approves *Declaration of the Rights of Man and of the Citizen.*

June 1791 Royal family is arrested in escape attempt.

Sep. 1791 France is made a constitutional monarchy.

Jan. 1793 King is executed.

July 1793 Robespierre and allies gain control of government, begin to arrest rivals.

1793–1794 Reign of Terror: about 300,000 are arrested and 17,000 are executed.

1789 —————————————————————————— 1794

July 1790 Church is put under control of government. National Assembly seizes lands of Catholic Church.

Aug. 1792 Paris mob captures King Louis XVI.

Sep. 1792 Crowds kill priests, nobles in September Massacres; monarchy is abolished.

July 1794 Robespierre is executed, Reign of Terror ends.

3. Over time, the revolution became more violent. How does the information in the time line show this?

_____

Part 2: Essay

Write an essay discussing how social conflict and new ideas led to the French Revolution and why it became so violent. Use information from the documents, your short answers, and your knowledge of world cultures and geography to write your essay.

Map Basics

Maps are an important tool for studying the use of space on Earth. This handbook covers the basic map skills and information that geographers rely on as they investigate the world—and the skills you will need as you study geography.

Mapmaking depends on surveying, or measuring and recording the features of Earth's surface. Until recently, this could be undertaken only on land or sea. Today, aerial photography and satellite imaging are the most popular ways to gather data.

Satellite Imagery A satellite image is a photograph taken from a satellite. This image shows Africa. The color of the land indicates whether it is desert, forest, farmland, or mountains.

Reading a Map Most maps have these parts, which help you to read and understand the information presented.

Ⓐ **Title** The title indicates the subject of the map and tells you what information it contains.

Ⓑ **Symbols** Symbols may stand for capital cities, economic activities, or natural resources. Check the map legend for more details.

Ⓒ **Labels** Labels are words or phrases that name features on the map.

Ⓓ **Colors** Colors show a variety of information on a map. The map legend tells what the colors mean.

Ⓔ **Lines of Longitude** These are imaginary lines that show distances east or west of the prime meridian.

Ⓕ **Lines of Latitude** These are imaginary lines that show distances north or south of the equator.

Ⓖ **Compass Rose** The compass rose shows you north (N), south (S), east (E), and west (W) on the map. Sometimes only north is shown.

Ⓗ **Locator Globe** The box shows where the area on the map is located in the world.

Ⓘ **Scale** A scale compares a unit of length on the map and a unit of distance on Earth.

Ⓙ **Legend** A legend, or key, lists and explains the symbols and colors used on the map.

A Economic Activity of Africa

FRANCE
SWITZ.
HUNGARY
ROMANIA
CRO.
SERBIA
ITALY MONT.
ALB.
BULGARIA
GREECE
TURKEY
CYPRUS
SYRIA
LEBANON
ISRAEL
JORDAN
IRAN
IRAQ
KUWAIT
QATAR
U.A.E.
SAUDI ARABIA
OMAN
YEMEN

SPAIN
PORTUGAL
*Madeira Is.
(PORT.)*
Casablanca
*Canary Is.
(SPAIN)*
MOROCCO
WESTERN SAHARA
(MOROCCO)
Algiers
TUNISIA
Mediterranean Sea
Alexandria
Cairo
ALGERIA
LIBYA
EGYPT
L. Nasser
Red Sea
Tropic of Cancer

MAURITANIA
MALI
NIGER
CHAD
SUDAN
ERITREA
DJIBOUTI
Gulf of Aden

CAPE
VERDE
SENEGAL
GAMBIA
GUINEA-
BISSAU
GUINEA
SIERRA
LEONE
LIBERIA
BURKINA
FASO
GHANA
CÔTE
D'IVOIRE
TOGO
BENIN
NIGERIA
Lagos
L. Chad
CENTRAL AFRICAN
REPUBLIC
CAMEROON
EQUATORIAL GUINEA
SÃO TOMÉ AND PRÍNCIPE
Equator
GABON
REP.
OF THE
CONGO DEM. REP.
OF THE CONGO
BURUNDI
RWANDA
UGANDA
KENYA
Nairobi
L. Turkana
L. Victoria
ETHIOPIA
SOMALIA
SEYCHELLES
Pemba I.
Zanzibar

ANGOLA
*ATLANTIC
OCEAN*
*St. Helena
(U.K.)*
TANZANIA
L. Tanganyika
ZAMBIA
L. Nyasa
MALAWI
COMOROS
ANGOLA
L. Kariba
ZIMBABWE
MOZAMBIQUE
Mozambique Channel
MADAGASCAR
*Réunion
(FRANCE)*
Tropic of Capricorn
NAMIBIA
BOTSWANA
Pretoria
Johannesburg
SWAZILAND
SOUTH
AFRICA
LESOTHO
Cape Town
INDIAN OCEAN

Land use
- Commercial agriculture
- Livestock raising
- Subsistence agriculture
- Nomadic herding
- Forestland
- Limited agriculture

Major resources
- Bauxite
- Coal
- Diamonds
- Fish
- Gold
- Iron ore
- Natural gas
- Oil
- Uranium
- Other minerals
- ● Manufacturing center

0 250 500 miles
0 250 500 kilometers

A1

The Geographic Grid

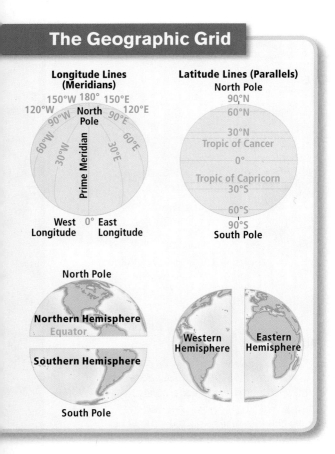

Longitude Lines (Meridians)

150°W 180° 150°E
120°W 120°E
90°W North 90°E
Pole
60°W 60°E
30°W 30°E
Prime Meridian

West 0° East
Longitude Longitude

Latitude Lines (Parallels)

North Pole
90°N
60°N
30°N
Tropic of Cancer
0°
Tropic of Capricorn
30°S
60°S
90°S
South Pole

North Pole

Northern Hemisphere
Equator
Southern Hemisphere

South Pole

Western Hemisphere **Eastern Hemisphere**

Longitude and Latitude Lines These lines appear together on a map and pinpoint the absolute locations of cities and other geographic features. You express these locations as coordinates of intersecting lines. These are measured in degrees.

Longitude Lines These imaginary lines run north and south; they are also known as meridians. They show distances in degrees east or west of the prime meridian. The prime meridian is a longitude line that runs from the North Pole to the South Pole through Greenwich, England. It marks 0° longitude.

Latitude Lines These imaginary lines run east to west around the globe; they are also known as parallels. They show distances in degrees north or south of the equator. The equator is a latitude line that circles Earth halfway between the North and South poles. It marks 0° latitude. The tropics of Cancer and Capricorn are parallels that form the boundaries of the tropics, a region that does not have a change of seasons.

Hemisphere The word *hemisphere* is a term for half the globe. The globe can be divided into northern and southern hemispheres (separated by the equator) or into eastern and western hemispheres. The United States is located in the northern and western hemispheres.

Scale What scale to use depends on how much detail is to be shown. If the area is small and many details are needed, a large scale is used. If the area is large and fewer details are needed, a small scale is used.

Large Scale: Washington, D.C.

Small Scale: Eastern United States

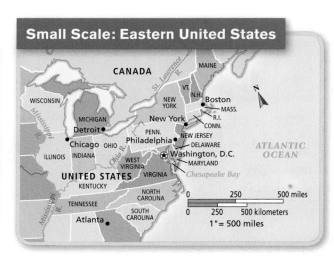

Projections A projection is a way of showing the curved surface of Earth on a flat map. Flat maps cannot show sizes, shapes, and directions with total accuracy. As a result, all projections distort some aspect of Earth's surface. Below are four projections.

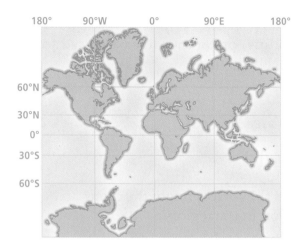

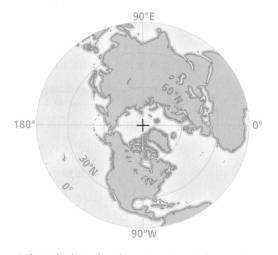

Mercator Projection The Mercator projection shows most of the continents as they look on a globe. However, the projection stretches out the lands near the North and South poles. The Mercator projection is used for navigation.

Azimuthal Projection An azimuthal projection shows Earth so that a straight line from the central point to any other point on the map corresponds to the shortest distance between the two points. Sizes and shapes of the continents are distorted.

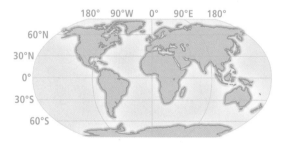

Homolosine Projection This projection shows landmasses' shapes and sizes accurately, but distances are not correct.

Robinson Projection For textbook maps, the Robinson projection is commonly used. It shows the entire Earth, with continents and oceans having nearly their true sizes and shapes. However, the land-masses near the poles appear flattened.

Map Practice

Use pages A1–A3 to help you answer these questions.

MAIN IDEA

1. What information is provided by the legend on page A1?

2. What do latitude and longitude lines show?

CRITICAL THINKING

3. Why do you think latitude and longitude are important to sailors?

4. How do the depictions of Antarctica in the Mercator and Robinson projections compare?

Different Types of Maps

Physical Maps Physical maps help you see the landforms and bodies of water in specific areas. By studying a physical map, you can learn the relative locations and characteristics of places in a region.

On a physical map, color, shading, or contour lines are used to show elevations or altitudes, also called relief.

THINK LIKE A GEOGRAPHER

- Where on Earth's surface is this area located?
- What is its relative location?
- What is the shape of the region?
- In which directions do the rivers flow? How might the directions of flow affect transportation in the region?
- Are there mountains or deserts? How might they affect the people living in the area?

Eurasia: Physical

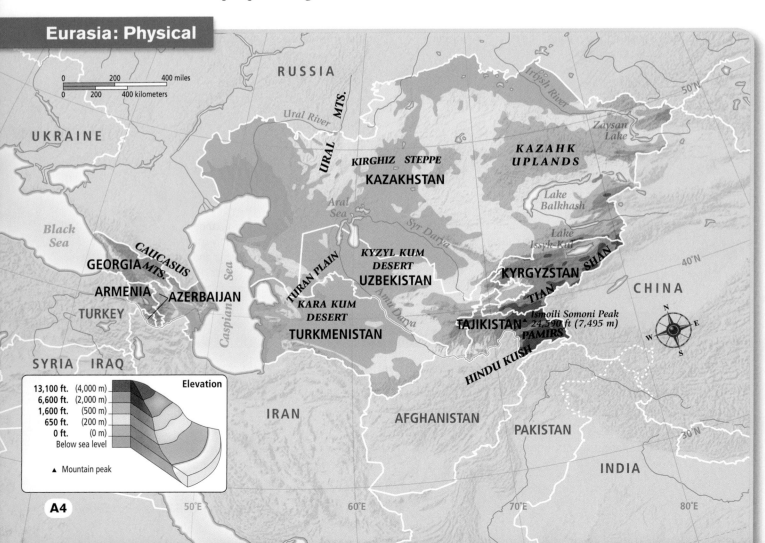

RUSSIA

UKRAINE

Ural River

URAL MTS.

Zaysan Lake

KIRGHIZ STEPPE

KAZAHK UPLANDS

KAZAKHSTAN

Aral Sea

Lake Balkhash

Syr Darya

Lake Issyk-Kul

Black Sea

CAUCASUS MTS.

GEORGIA

ARMENIA ⟶ AZERBAIJAN

TURKEY

Caspian Sea

TURAN PLAIN

KYZYL KUM DESERT

UZBEKISTAN

KARA KUM DESERT

Amu Darya

TURKMENISTAN

KYRGYZSTAN

TIAN SHAN

CHINA

Ismoili Somoni Peak ▲ 24,590 ft (7,495 m)

TAJIKISTAN

PAMIRS

HINDU KUSH

SYRIA   IRAQ

IRAN

AFGHANISTAN

PAKISTAN

INDIA

50°N
40°N
30°N

50°E   60°E   70°E   80°E

0   200   400 miles
0   200   400 kilometers

N E W S

Elevation

13,100 ft. (4,000 m)
6,600 ft. (2,000 m)
1,600 ft. (500 m)
650 ft. (200 m)
0 ft. (0 m)
Below sea level

▲ Mountain peak

Political Maps Political maps show features that humans have created on Earth's surface. Cities, states, provinces, territories, and countries are included on a political map.

- Where on Earth's surface is this area located?

- What is its relative location? How might a country's location affect its economy and its relationships with other countries?

- What is the shape and size of the country? How might its shape and size affect the people living in the country?

- Who are the region's, country's, state's, or city's neighbors?

- How populated does the area seem to be? How might that affect activities there?

Eurasia: Political

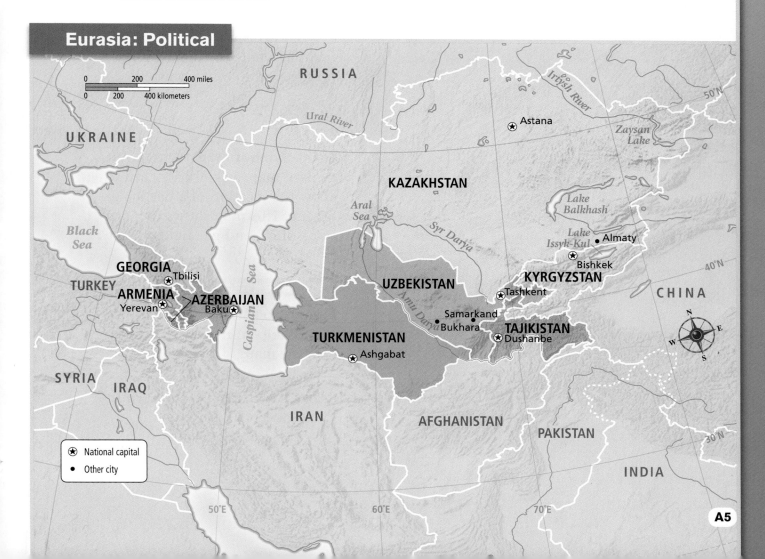

Thematic Maps Geographers also rely on thematic maps, which focus on specific topics. For example, in this textbook you will see thematic maps that show climates, types of vegetation, natural resources, population densities, and economic activities. Some thematic maps show historical trends; others focus on movements of people or ideas. Thematic maps may be presented in a variety of ways.

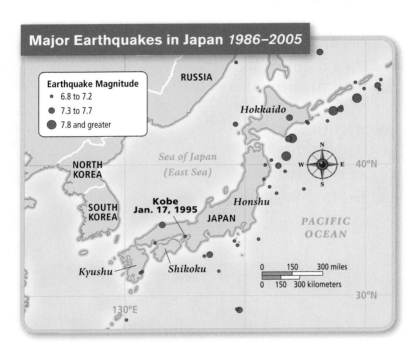

Major Earthquakes in Japan *1986–2005*

Earthquake Magnitude
- 6.8 to 7.2
- 7.3 to 7.7
- 7.8 and greater

RUSSIA

Hokkaido

Sea of Japan
(East Sea)

NORTH
KOREA

40°N

SOUTH
KOREA

Kobe
Jan. 17, 1995

Honshu

JAPAN

PACIFIC
OCEAN

Kyushu

Shikoku

0   150   300 miles
0   150   300 kilometers

130°E

30°N

Proportional Symbol Map On a proportional symbol map, the size of each symbol indicates the quantity of something at a specific location. The map shown here depicts the magnitude of earthquakes that occurred throughout Japan.

THINK LIKE A GEOGRAPHER

- What does the map title suggest about the theme of the map?
- What do the symbols tell you about where the largest magnitude earthquakes occurred?

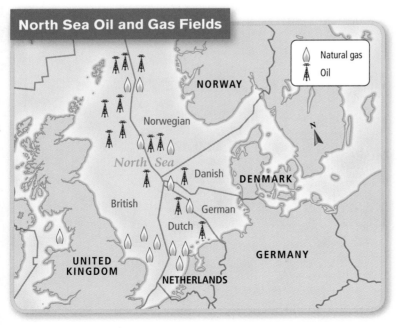

North Sea Oil and Gas Fields

Natural gas
Oil

NORWAY

Norwegian

North Sea

Danish

DENMARK

British

German

Dutch

UNITED
KINGDOM

GERMANY

NETHERLANDS

Point-Symbol Map On a point-symbol map, a symbol is used to show the location of a particular feature. This map shows the locations of oil and gas fields in the North Sea.

THINK LIKE A GEOGRAPHER

- How do the map title and legend help you know the theme of the map?
- How might the presence of oil and gas fields affect the countries located near them?

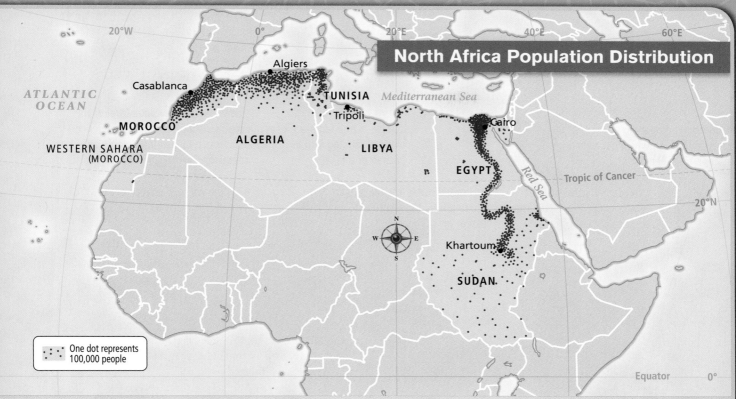

North Africa Population Distribution

One dot represents
100,000 people

Dot Maps These kinds of maps use dots to show how something is distributed in a certain area. This map shows how the population of North Africa is distributed.

THINK LIKE A GEOGRAPHER

- How do the title and legend of the map identify the data being presented?

- What does each dot on the map represent?

- How does this kind of map help you to see how densely populated different parts of a region are?

Map Practice

Use pages A4–A7 to help you answer these questions.

MAIN IDEA

1. Which desert is located in Turkmenistan?
2. Baku is the capital of which Eurasian republic?

CRITICAL THINKING

3. What country in North Africa is the least densely populated?
4. How are thematic maps an effective way of presenting information?

Geographic Dictionary

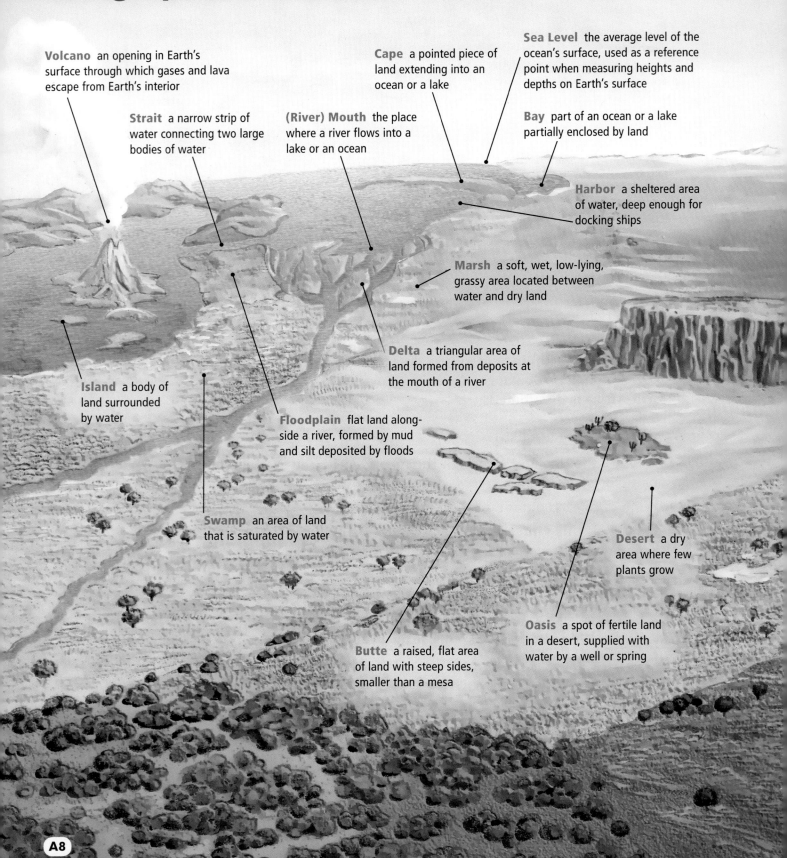

Volcano an opening in Earth's surface through which gases and lava escape from Earth's interior

Strait a narrow strip of water connecting two large bodies of water

(River) Mouth the place where a river flows into a lake or an ocean

Cape a pointed piece of land extending into an ocean or a lake

Sea Level the average level of the ocean's surface, used as a reference point when measuring heights and depths on Earth's surface

Bay part of an ocean or a lake partially enclosed by land

Harbor a sheltered area of water, deep enough for docking ships

Marsh a soft, wet, low-lying, grassy area located between water and dry land

Island a body of land surrounded by water

Delta a triangular area of land formed from deposits at the mouth of a river

Floodplain flat land alongside a river, formed by mud and silt deposited by floods

Swamp an area of land that is saturated by water

Desert a dry area where few plants grow

Butte a raised, flat area of land with steep sides, smaller than a mesa

Oasis a spot of fertile land in a desert, supplied with water by a well or spring

Mountain a natural elevation of Earth's surface with steep sides, higher than a hill

Glacier a large ice mass that moves slowly down a mountain or over land

Prairie a large, level area of grassland with few or no trees

Steppe a wide, treeless plain

Valley low land between hills or mountains

Mesa a wide, flat-topped mountain with steep sides, larger than a butte

Cataract a large, powerful waterfall

Plateau a broad, flat area of land higher than the surrounding land

Canyon a deep, narrow valley with steep sides

Cliff the steep, almost vertical edge of a hill, mountain, or plain

Graphs

Graphs are often used to show numbers in visual form. Bar graphs make it easy to compare numbers. Line graphs show changes over time. Pie graphs show the relationship among parts of a whole. Climographs show the monthly average temperature and precipitation in a place.

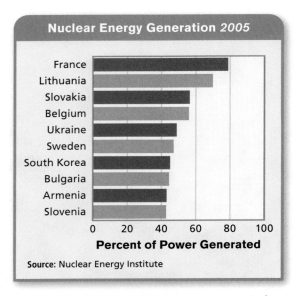

Bar Graph This bar graph compares ten countries' use of nuclear power to produce energy. The graph shows what percent of the energy each country used was from nuclear power.

Line Graph This line graph shows how the population of the Aztec and Inca changed between 1520 and 1620.

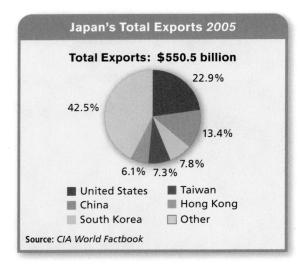

Pie Graph This pie graph shows how Japan's total exports are distributed. The graph shows what percentages of all the exports are sent to specific countries.

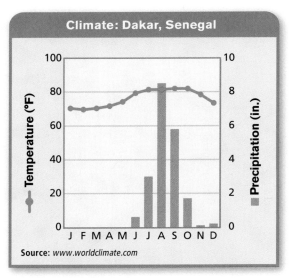

Climograph This climograph shows the climate of Dakar, Senegal. Bars represent the average monthly precipitation, and a line represents the average monthly temperature in the city.

Geography Standards

To help you study the world, geographers have set up 18 geography standards. These standards provide guidelines for what you will need to be informed about the people, places, and environments of Earth.

THE WORLD IN SPATIAL TERMS

1. How to use maps and other tools
2. How to use mental maps to organize information
3. How to analyze the spatial organization of people, places, and environments

PLACES AND REGIONS

4. The physical and human characteristics of places
5. How people create regions to interpret Earth
6. How culture and experience influence people's perceptions of places and regions

PHYSICAL SYSTEMS

7. The physical processes that shape Earth's surface
8. The distribution of ecosystems on Earth

HUMAN SYSTEMS

9. The characteristics, distribution, and migration of human populations
10. The complexity of Earth's cultural mosaics
11. The patterns and networks of economic interdependence on Earth
12. The patterns of human settlement
13. The forces of cooperation and conflict

ENVIRONMENT AND SOCIETY

14. How human actions modify the physical environment
15. How physical systems affect human systems
16. The distribution and meaning of resources

THE USES OF GEOGRAPHY

17. How to apply geography to interpret the past
18. How to apply geography to interpret the present and plan for the future

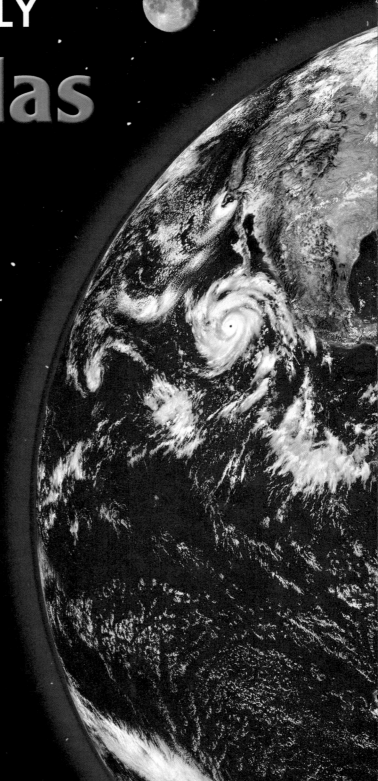

☼ RAND M̊NALLY
World Atlas

CONTENTS

Legend

Complete Legend for Physical and Political Maps

Water Features

ATLANTIC OCEAN — Ocean or sea

Lake

Salt lake

Seasonal lake

Mississippi — River

Niagara Falls — Waterfall

Ice pack

Land Features

Mt. Mitchell 6,684 ft. 2,037 m. △ — Mountain peak

Mt. McKinley 20,320 ft. 6,194 m. ▲ — Highest mountain peak

Great Basin — Physical feature (mountain range, desert, plateau, etc.)

Nantucket Island — Island

Cultural Features

———— International boundary

— — — State boundary

CANADA Country

KANSAS State

Population Centers

National capital	State capital	Town	Population
✪	✪	■	Over 1,000,000
✪	✪	▣	250,000 – 1,000,000
✪	✪	·	Under 250,000

Land Elevations and Ocean Depths

Land elevation

3,000 meters	9,840 feet
2,000 meters	6,560 feet
1,000 meters	3,280 feet
500 meters	1,640 feet
200 meters	656 feet
0 Sea level	0 Sea level

Water depth

0 Sea level	0 Sea level
200 meters	656 feet
2,000 meters	6,560 feet

RAND McNALLY

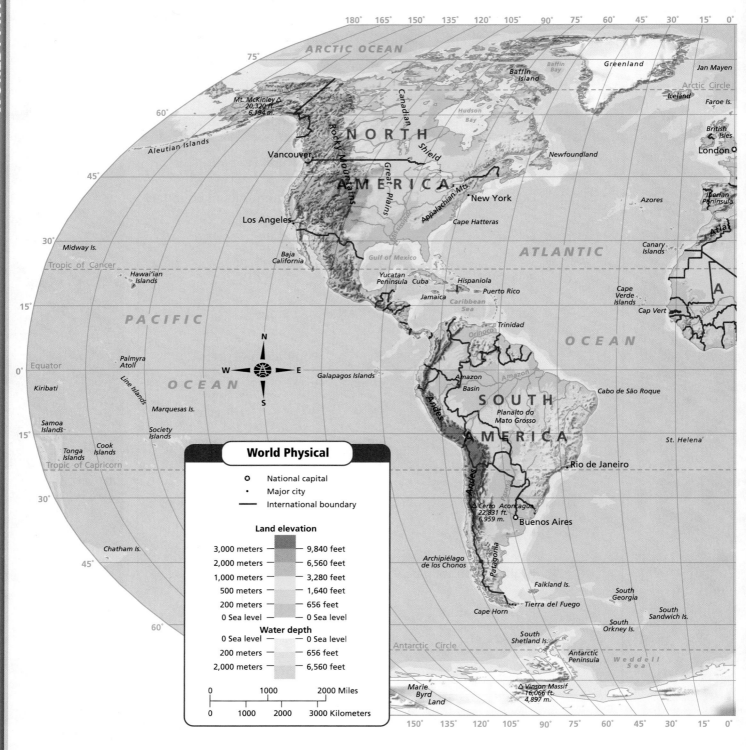

ARCTIC OCEAN

Baffin Bay

Greenland

Jan Mayen

Baffin Island

Arctic Circle

Iceland

Faroe Is.

Mt. McKinley △
20,320 ft.
6,194 m.

Hudson Bay

Canadian Shield

NORTH

British Isles

London ◉

Aleutian Islands

Vancouver

Rocky Mountains

Great Plains

AMERICA

Newfoundland

Azores

Iberian Peninsula

Los Angeles

St. Lawrence

Appalachian Mts.

New York

Cape Hatteras

Mississippi

ATLANTIC

Atlas

Midway Is.

Baja California

Gulf of Mexico

Canary Islands

Tropic of Cancer

Hawai'ian Islands

Yucatan Peninsula

Cuba

Hispaniola

Puerto Rico

Cape Verde Islands

A

PACIFIC

Jamaica

Caribbean Sea

Cap Vert

Palmyra Atoll

Orinoco

Trinidad

OCEAN

Equator

Line Islands

Kiribati

OCEAN

Galapagos Islands

Amazon

Amazon

Cabo de São Roque

Basin

SOUTH

Marquesas Is.

Andes

Planalto do Mato Grosso

Samoa Islands

Society Islands

AMERICA

St. Helena

Tonga Islands

Cook Islands

Tropic of Capricorn

Andes

Rio de Janeiro

World Physical

◉ National capital
• Major city
— International boundary

Chatham Is.

△ Cerro Aconcagua
22,831 ft.
6,959 m.

◉ Buenos Aires

Land elevation

3,000 meters	9,840 feet
2,000 meters	6,560 feet
1,000 meters	3,280 feet
500 meters	1,640 feet
200 meters	656 feet
0 Sea level	0 Sea level

Archipiélago de los Chonos

Patagonia

Falkland Is.

South Georgia

South Sandwich Is.

Water depth

0 Sea level	0 Sea level
200 meters	656 feet
2,000 meters	6,560 feet

Cape Horn

Tierra del Fuego

South Orkney Is.

South Shetland Is.

Antarctic Peninsula

Antarctic Circle

Weddell Sea

0 — 1000 — 2000 Miles

0 — 1000 — 2000 — 3000 Kilometers

Marie Byrd Land

△ Vinson Massif
16,066 ft.
4,897 m.

N
W ✦ E
S

180° 165° 150° 135° 120° 105° 90° 75° 60° 45° 30° 15° 0°

75°
60°
45°
30°
15°
0°
15°
30°
45°
60°

ARCTIC OCEAN

75°

Spitsbergen
Nordkapp
Franz Josef Land
Novaya Zemlya
Scandinavia
Siberia
60°
Bering Sea
North Sea
Moscow
Ural Mts.
Ob
Volga
Yenisey
Kamchatka Peninsula
Sakhalin
Sea of Okhotsk
45°
E U R O P E
Caucasus
A S I A
Aral Sea
Gora Elbrus 18,510 ft. 5,642 m.
Black Sea
Aral
Beijing
Gobi Desert
Hokkaidō
Honshū
Alps
Balkan Peninsula
Tigris
Zagros Mts.
Amur
Sea of Japan
Sardinia
Sicily
Crete
Cyprus
Mediterranean Sea
Plateau of Tibet
Himalayas
Kyūshū
East China Sea
30°
Mts.
Cairo
Sahara
Arabian Peninsula
Mt. Everest 29,028 ft. 8,848 m.
Taiwan
PACIFIC
Tropic of Cancer
A F R I C A
Nile
Red Sea
Mumbai (Bombay)
Deccan
Bay of Bengal
Hainan Dao
South China Sea
Luzon
Mariana Islands
Guam
Wake Island
15°
Sahel
Socotra
Arabian Sea
Lakshadweep
Sri Lanka
Malay Peninsula
Mindanao
Palau Islands
O C E A N
Caroline Islands
Marshall Islands
Gulf of Guinea
Ethiopian Plateau
Maldive Islands
Borneo
Celebes
Equator
0°
Congo Basin
Congo
Kilimanjaro 19,340 ft. 5,895 m.
Seychelles
Sumatra
Java
New Guinea
Solomon Islands
I N D I A N
Cocos Islands
15°
Madagascar
Mauritius
Reunion
Coral Sea
New Hebrides
New Caledonia
Fiji Is.
Kalahari Desert
O C E A N
Great Sandy Desert
A U S T R A L I A
Tropic of Capricorn
Johannesburg
Darling
Great Dividing Range
30°
Cape of Good Hope
Cape Leeuwin
Sydney
North Island
Aoraki (Mt. Cook) 12,316 ft. 3,754 m.
Tasmania
South Island
45°
Îles Kerguélen
S O U T H E R N   O C E A N
60°
Antarctic Circle
Queen Maud Land
Enderby Land
Wilkes Land
Victoria Land
75°
A N T A R C T I C A

© Rand McNally & Co.
Made in U.S.A.
N-MDG10000-A1- -1- -1

15° 30° 45° 60° 75° 90° 105° 120° 135° 150° 165° 180°

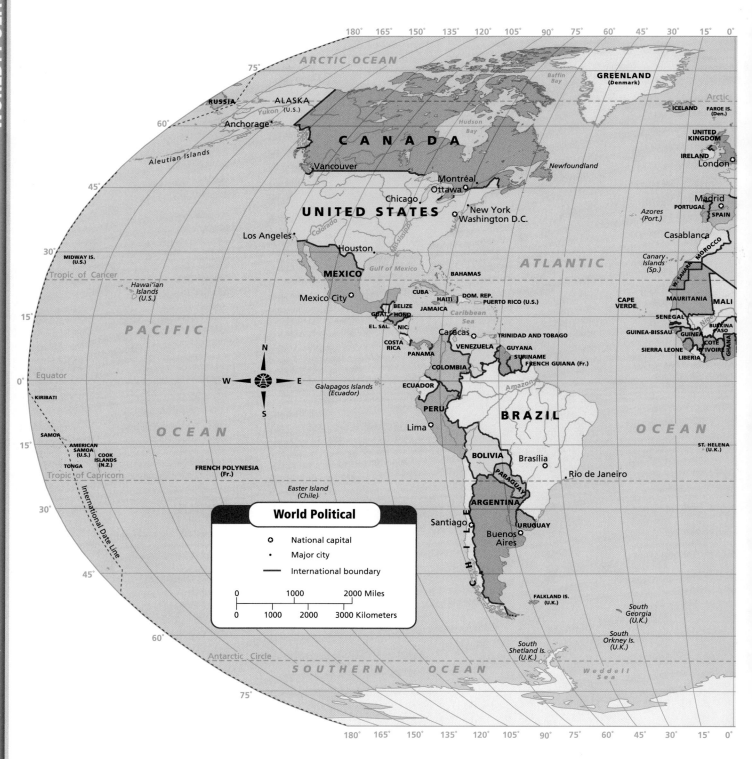

ARCTIC OCEAN

75°

RUSSIA
ALASKA (U.S.)
Yukon
Anchorage
60°
Aleutian Islands
45°

Baffin Bay

GREENLAND (Denmark)

Arctic
ICELAND   FAROE IS. (Den.)

Hudson Bay

UNITED KINGDOM

CANADA

IRELAND
London

Vancouver
Montréal
Ottawa
Chicago
UNITED STATES
New York
Washington D.C.

Newfoundland

Madrid
PORTUGAL   SPAIN

Azores (Port.)

30°

Los Angeles
Houston

Colorado

Mississippi

ATLANTIC

Casablanca
Canary Islands (Sp.)
W. SAHARA
MOROCCO

MIDWAY IS. (U.S.)
Tropic of Cancer
Hawai'ian Islands (U.S.)

MEXICO
Gulf of Mexico

BAHAMAS
CUBA
Mexico City
BELIZE
GUAT. HOND.
EL. SAL. NIC.
HAITI   DOM. REP.
PUERTO RICO (U.S.)
JAMAICA

CAPE VERDE
MAURITANIA   MALI
SENEGAL
GUINEA-BISSAU   GUINEA
SIERRA LEONE   CÔTE
LIBERIA   IVOIRE   GHANA
BURKINA FASO

15°

PACIFIC

Caribbean Sea
Caracas
TRINIDAD AND TOBAGO
VENEZUELA   GUYANA
COSTA RICA   SURINAME
PANAMA   FRENCH GUIANA (Fr.)
COLOMBIA

Niger

N
W   E
S

Equator   0°

KIRIBATI

Galapagos Islands (Ecuador)

ECUADOR

PERU
Lima

Amazon

BRAZIL

OCEAN

OCEAN

ST. HELENA (U.K.)

15°

SAMOA
AMERICAN SAMOA (U.S.)
TONGA   COOK ISLANDS (N.Z.)

FRENCH POLYNESIA (Fr.)

Tropic of Capricorn

BOLIVIA
Brasília

PARAGUAY

Rio de Janeiro

Easter Island (Chile)

30°

International Date Line

ARGENTINA
Santiago

World Political

⊙   National capital

•   Major city

—   International boundary

CHILE

URUGUAY
Buenos Aires

FALKLAND IS. (U.K.)

South Georgia (U.K.)

45°

0   1000   2000 Miles

0   1000   2000   3000 Kilometers

South Shetland Is. (U.K.)

South Orkney Is. (U.K.)

Weddell Sea

60°
Antarctic Circle

SOUTHERN   OCEAN

75°

180° 165° 150° 135° 120° 105° 90° 75° 60° 45° 30° 15° 0°

ARCTIC OCEAN

Franz Josef Land

Spitsbergen (Nor.)

Novaya Zemlya

Circle

NORWAY
FINLAND
SWEDEN
DEN.
EST.
LAT.
LITH.
BELARUS
NETH.
GERMANY
POLAND
FRANCE
LUX.
CZECH
SLVK.
AUS.
HUNG.
SLV.
CRO.
BOS.
SER.
ITALY
ALB.
ROM.
BUL.
GREECE
Rome

North Sea

Moscow

Volga

R U S S I A

Novosibirsk

Ob

Yenisey

Lena

Sea of Okhotsk

Bering Sea

International Date Line

MONGOLIA

KAZAKHSTAN

Beijing

C H I N A

NORTH KOREA
Sea of Japan
Seoul
SOUTH KOREA
JAPAN
Tōkyō

Black Sea
GEO.
ARM.
AZER.
TURKEY
UZBEKISTAN
KYRG.
TURKMENISTAN
TAJIK.
CYPRUS
SYRIA
LEB.
ISRAEL
IRAQ
JORDAN
KUWAIT
Tehrān
IRAN
AFGHANISTAN
PAKISTAN
NEPAL
BHU.
BNG.

Mediterranean Sea
Crete

Cairo

TUNISIA

ALGERIA

LIBYA
EGYPT
SAUDI ARABIA
QATAR
U.A.E.
OMAN
Karāchi
Mumbai (Bombay)
I N D I A
Kolkata (Calcutta)
MYANMAR
LAOS
Yangtze
Shanghai
TAIWAN
Hong Kong

PACIFIC

Tropic of Cancer

NORTHERN MARIANA ISLANDS (U.S.)
WAKE ISLAND (U.S.)

Red Sea
Nile
NIGER
CHAD
SUDAN
YEMEN
Arabian Sea
Ganges
Bay of Bengal
THAILAND
Bangkok
VIETNAM
CAMBODIA
South China Sea
PHILIPPINES
Manila
GUAM (U.S.)

ERITREA
DJIBOUTI
Addis Ababa
ETHIOPIA
SOMALIA
SRI LANKA
PALAU
FED. STATES OF MICRONESIA
MARSHALL ISLANDS

BENIN
NIGERIA
Lagos
CAMEROON
CENTRAL AFRICAN REPUBLIC
EQUATORIAL GUINEA
GABON
CONGO
DEM. REP. OF THE CONGO
UGANDA
RWANDA
BURUNDI
KENYA
TANZANIA
Congo
MALDIVES
SEYCHELLES
BRUNEI
MALAYSIA
SINGAPORE
Borneo
Sumatra
Java
Jakarta
INDONESIA
EAST TIMOR
New Guinea
PAPUA NEW GUINEA
SOLOMON ISLANDS

O C E A N

Equator

ANGOLA
ZAMBIA
MALAWI
ZIMBABWE
MOZAMBIQUE
NAMIBIA
BOTSWANA
COMOROS
MADAGASCAR
MAURITIUS
REUNION (Fr.)

I N D I A N

VANUATU
NEW CALEDONIA (Fr.)
FIJI
Coral Sea

Tropic of Capricorn

Johannesburg
SOUTH AFRICA
SWAZILAND
LESOTHO

O C E A N

Îles Kerguélen (Fr.)

A U S T R A L I A
Brisbane
Perth
Darling
Sydney
Auckland
Melbourne
NEW ZEALAND
Tasmania

S O U T H E R N   O C E A N

Antarctic Circle

A N T A R C T I C A

© Rand McNally & Co.
Made in U.S.A.
N-MDG10000-P1- -1-1-1

15° 30° 45° 60° 75° 90° 105° 120° 135° 150° 165° 180°

75°
60°
45°
30°
15°
0°
15°
30°
45°
60°
75°

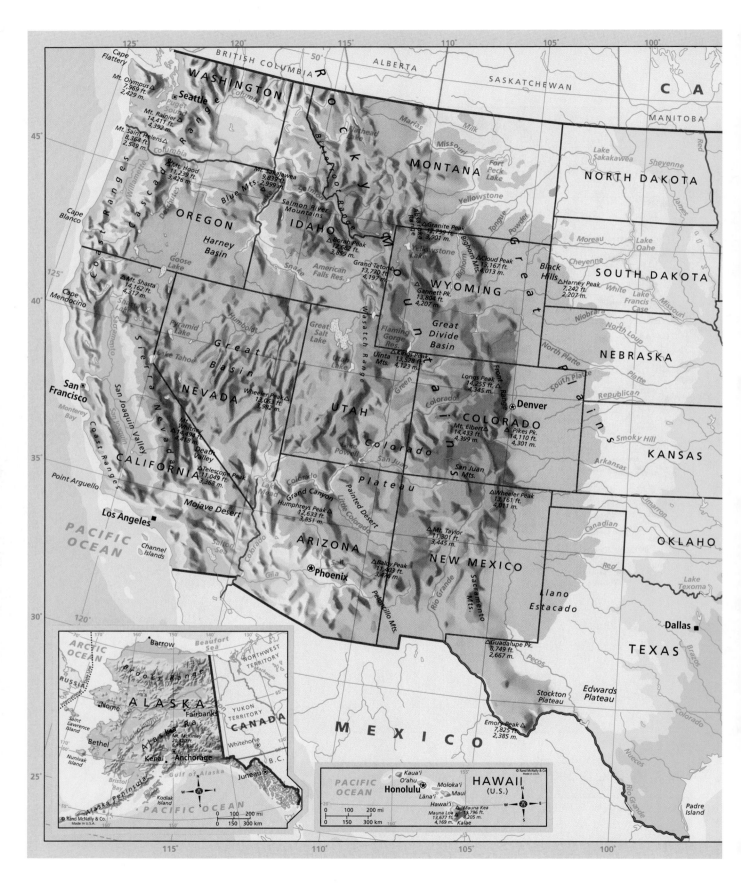

RAND McNALLY

A18

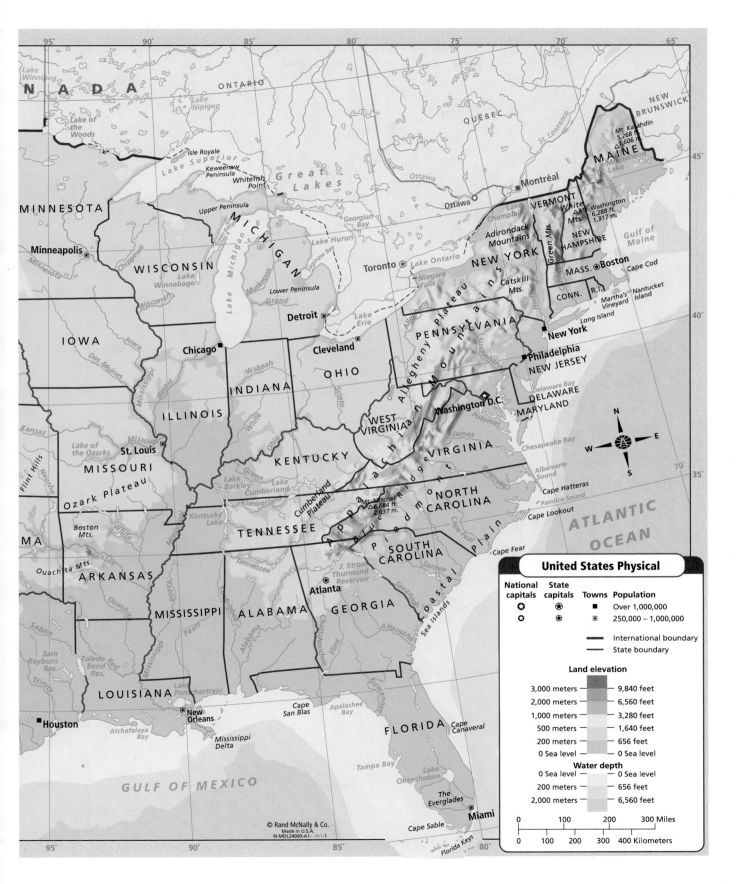

RAND McNALLY

United States Physical

National capitals	State capitals	Towns	Population
⊙	⊛	■	Over 1,000,000
⊙	⊛	▣	250,000 – 1,000,000

━━━ International boundary
─── State boundary

Land elevation

3,000 meters	9,840 feet
2,000 meters	6,560 feet
1,000 meters	3,280 feet
500 meters	1,640 feet
200 meters	656 feet
0 Sea level	0 Sea level

Water depth

0 Sea level	0 Sea level
200 meters	656 feet
2,000 meters	6,560 feet

0   100   200   300 Miles
0   100   200   300   400 Kilometers

© Rand McNally & Co.
Made in U.S.A.
N-MDL24000-A1- -1-1-1

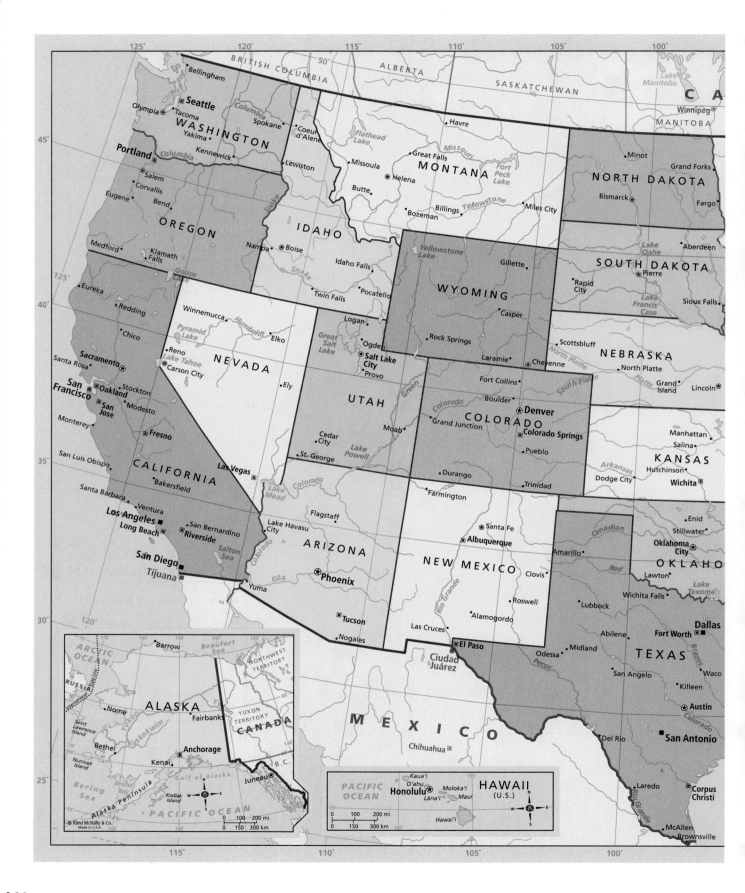

BRITISH COLUMBIA
ALBERTA
SASKATCHEWAN
Lake Manitoba
CA
Winnipeg
MANITOBA

Bellingham
Olympia
Tacoma
Seattle
Spokane
Coeur d'Alene
WASHINGTON
Yakima
Kennewick
Columbia

Portland
Salem
Corvallis
Eugene
Bend
OREGON
Medford
Klamath Falls
Goose Lake

Lewiston
IDAHO
Nampa
Boise
Idaho Falls
Twin Falls
Pocatello
Snake

Havre
Great Falls
Missoula
Helena
Butte
Bozeman
MONTANA
Billings
Missouri
Yellowstone
Fort Peck Lake
Miles City

Minot
Grand Forks
NORTH DAKOTA
Bismarck
Fargo

Aberdeen
SOUTH DAKOTA
Pierre
Rapid City
Lake Oahe
Sioux Falls
Lake Francis Case

Yellowstone Lake
WYOMING
Gillette
Casper
Rock Springs
Laramie
Cheyenne

Scottsbluff
NEBRASKA
North Platte
North Platte
Grand Island
Lincoln
South Platte

Eureka
Redding
Chico
Sacramento
Santa Rosa
San Francisco
Oakland
San Jose
Monterey
Stockton
Modesto
San Luis Obispo
CALIFORNIA
Fresno
Bakersfield
Santa Barbara
Ventura
Los Angeles
Long Beach
San Bernardino
Riverside
San Diego
Tijuana

Winnemucca
Pyramid Lake
Reno
Lake Tahoe
Carson City
NEVADA
Elko
Humboldt
Ely
Las Vegas

Logan
Great Salt Lake
Ogden
Salt Lake City
Provo
UTAH
Cedar City
St. George
Lake Powell
Moab
Green

Fort Collins
Boulder
Denver
Grand Junction
COLORADO
Colorado Springs
Pueblo
Durango
Trinidad
Colorado
Arkansas

KANSAS
Manhattan
Salina
Dodge City
Hutchinson
Wichita

Flagstaff
Lake Havasu City
ARIZONA
Phoenix
Tucson
Nogales
Yuma
Gila
Colorado
Lake Mead
Salton Sea

Farmington
Santa Fe
Albuquerque
NEW MEXICO
Clovis
Roswell
Las Cruces
Alamogordo
El Paso
Ciudad Juárez
Rio Grande
Canadian

Amarillo
Enid
Stillwater
Oklahoma City
OKLAHOMA
Lawton
Wichita Falls
Lake Texoma
Red

Lubbock
Abilene
Odessa
Midland
TEXAS
San Angelo
Dallas
Fort Worth
Waco
Killeen
Austin
Pecos
Brazos
Colorado

MEXICO
Chihuahua
Del Rio
San Antonio
Laredo
Corpus Christi
Rio Grande
McAllen
Brownsville

ARCTIC OCEAN
Barrow
Beaufort Sea
NORTHWEST TERRITORY
RUSSIA
Nome
Saint Lawrence Island
Nunivak Island
ALASKA
Fairbanks
YUKON TERRITORY
CANADA
Mackenzie
Bethel
Kuskokwim
Anchorage
Kenai
B.C.
Juneau
Bering Sea
Bristol Bay
Kodiak Island
Alaska Peninsula
Gulf of Alaska
PACIFIC OCEAN
Yukon
© Rand McNally & Co.
Made in U.S.A.
0 100 200 mi
0 150 300 km

PACIFIC OCEAN
Kaua'i
O'ahu
Honolulu
Moloka'i
Lāna'i
Maui
HAWAII (U.S.)
Hawai'i
0 100 200 mi
0 150 300 km

A20

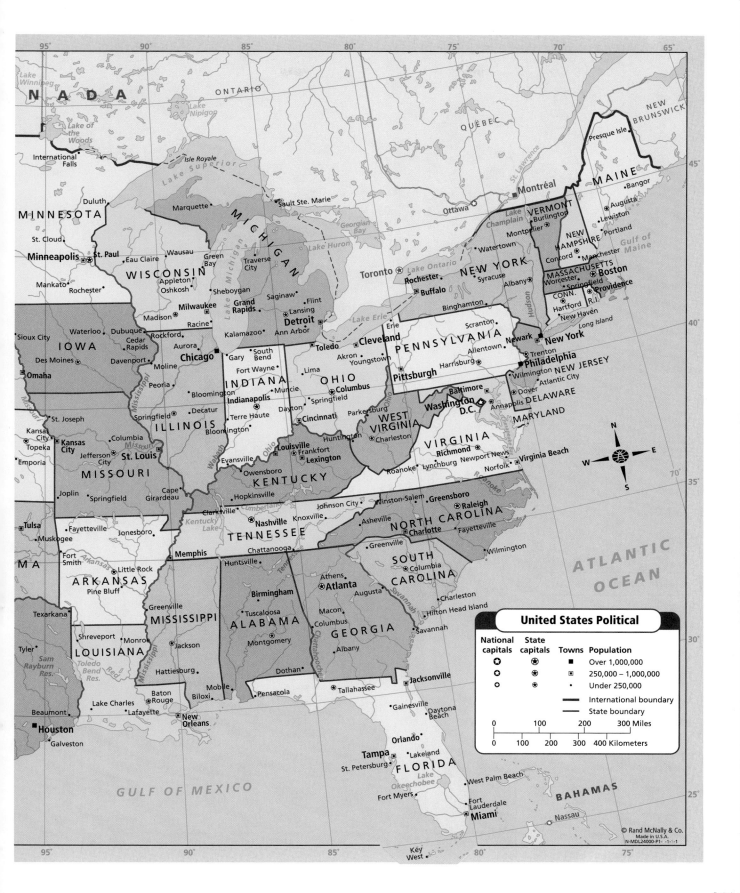

United States Political

National capitals	State capitals	Towns	Population
⊙	✪	■	Over 1,000,000
⊙	✪	▣	250,000 – 1,000,000
⊙	✪	•	Under 250,000

━━━ International boundary
─── State boundary

0   100   200   300 Miles

0   100   200   300   400 Kilometers

© Rand McNally & Co.
Made in U.S.A.
N-MDL24000-P1- -1-¹-1

RAND McNALLY

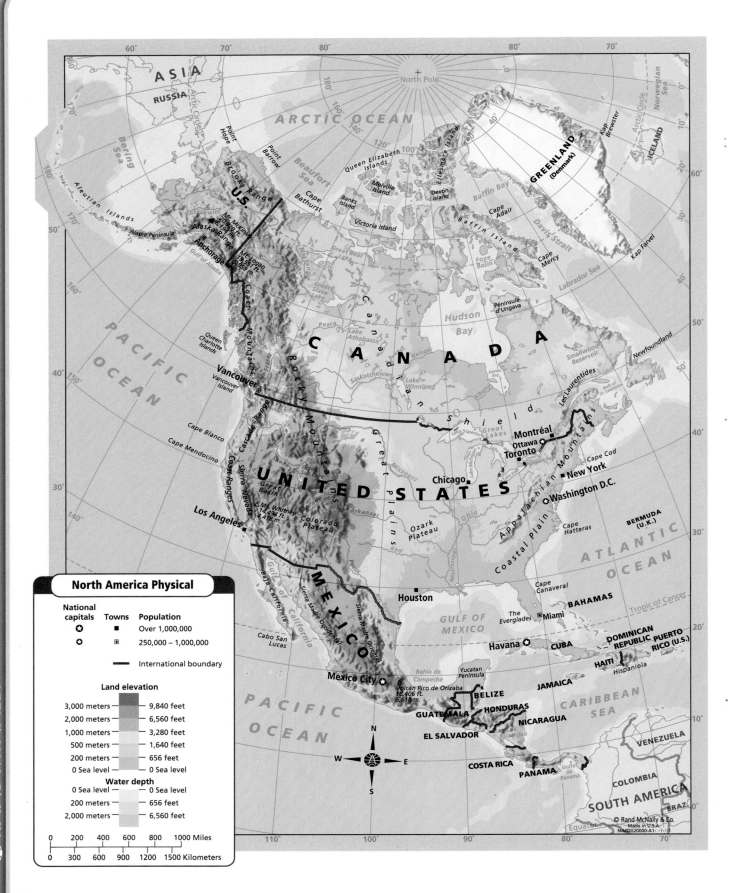

North America Physical

National capitals	Towns	Population
✪	▪	Over 1,000,000
✪	▣	250,000 – 1,000,000

—— International boundary

Land elevation

3,000 meters	9,840 feet
2,000 meters	6,560 feet
1,000 meters	3,280 feet
500 meters	1,640 feet
200 meters	656 feet
0 Sea level	0 Sea level

Water depth

0 Sea level	0 Sea level
200 meters	656 feet
2,000 meters	6,560 feet

0 200 400 600 800 1000 Miles

0 300 600 900 1200 1500 Kilometers

A22

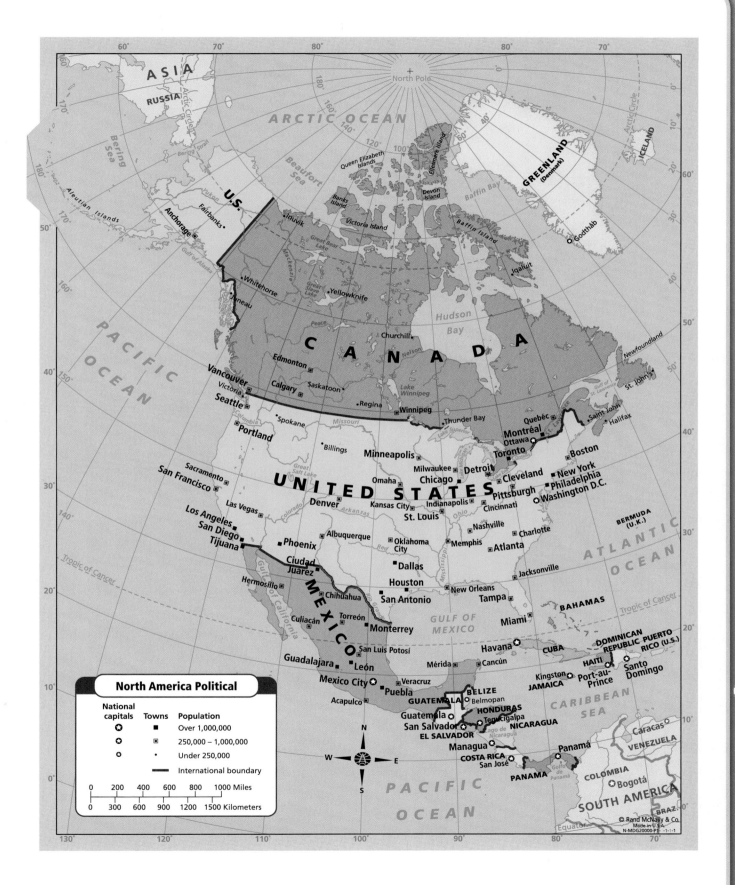

North America Political

National capitals | **Towns** | **Population**
- ⚙ | ■ | Over 1,000,000
- ⚙ | ▣ | 250,000 – 1,000,000
- ⚙ | • | Under 250,000
- —— International boundary

0 200 400 600 800 1000 Miles
0 300 600 900 1200 1500 Kilometers

RAND McNALLY

© Rand McNally & Co.
Made in U.S.A.
N-MDG20000-P1 -1-1-1

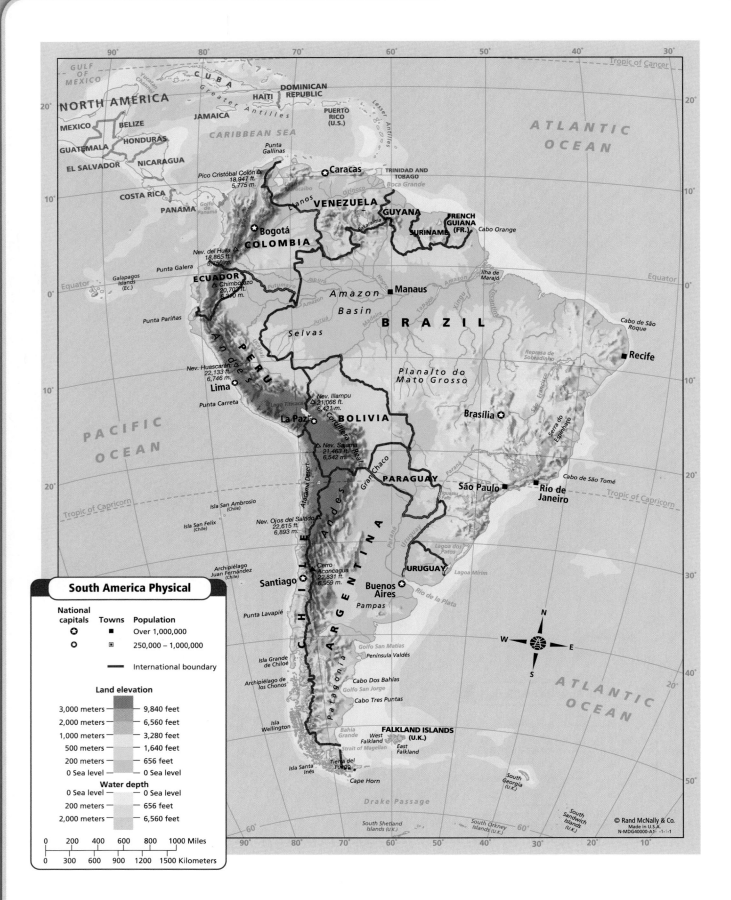

GULF OF MEXICO

NORTH AMERICA

CUBA

MEXICO
BELIZE
GUATEMALA
HONDURAS
EL SALVADOR
NICARAGUA
COSTA RICA
PANAMA
Golfo de Panamá

JAMAICA
HAITI
DOMINICAN REPUBLIC
PUERTO RICO (U.S.)

Greater Antilles
Lesser Antilles

CARIBBEAN SEA

TRINIDAD AND TOBAGO

ATLANTIC OCEAN

Tropic of Cancer

Punta Gallinas

Pico Cristóbal Colón △ 18,947 ft. 5,775 m.

Caracas

Boca Grande

Maracaibo
Llanos
Orinoco

VENEZUELA

GUYANA

SURINAME

FRENCH GUIANA (FR.)

Cabo Orange

Bogotá

COLOMBIA

Nev. del Huila △ 18,865 ft. 5,750 m.

Punta Galera

ECUADOR
△ Chimborazo 20,702 ft. 6,310 m.

Galapagos Islands (Ec.)

Equator

Putumayo
Japurá
Negro
Branco

Equator

Ilha de Marajó

Punta Pariñas

Juruá
Amazon
Madeira

Amazon Basin

Manaus

BRAZIL

Cabo de São Roque

Selvas

Tapajós
Xingu
Tocantins

Nev. Huascarán 22,133 ft. 6,746 m.

Andes
PERU

Lima

Punta Carreta

Lago Titicaca

Nev. Illampu △ 21,066 ft. 6,421 m.

Recife

Represa de Sobradinho

Planalto do Mato Grosso

São Francisco
Serra do Espinhaço

PACIFIC OCEAN

La Paz

Cordillera Real

BOLIVIA

Nev. Sajama △ 21,463 ft. 6,542 m.

Brasília ✪

Gran Chaco

Tropic of Capricorn

Isla San Ambrosio (Chile)

Isla San Félix (Chile)

Nev. Ojos del Salado 22,615 ft. 6,893 m.

Atacama Desert

PARAGUAY

Iguassu Falls
Paraná

São Paulo

Rio de Janeiro

Cabo de São Tomé

Tropic of Capricorn

Paraná
Uruguay

Lagoa dos Patos

Archipiélago Juan Fernández (Chile)

Cerro Aconcagua 22,831 ft. 6,959 m.

Santiago

CHILE
Andes
ARGENTINA

Buenos Aires ✪

Río de la Plata

URUGUAY

Lagoa Mirim

Pampas

Punta Lavapié

N
W   E
S

ATLANTIC OCEAN

Isla Grande de Chiloé

Golfo San Matías
Península Valdés

Archipiélago de los Chonos

Patagonia

Cabo Dos Bahías
Golfo San Jorge
Cabo Tres Puntas

Isla Wellington

Bahía Grande

FALKLAND ISLANDS (U.K.)
West Falkland
East Falkland

Strait of Magellan

Isla Santa Inés

Tierra del Fuego

South Georgia (U.K.)

Cape Horn

Drake Passage

South Shetland Islands (U.K.)

South Orkney Islands (U.K.)

South Sandwich Islands (U.K.)

© Rand McNally & Co.
Made in U.S.A.
N-MDG40000-A1- -1-!-1

South America Physical

National capitals	Towns	Population
✪	■	Over 1,000,000
✪	▪	250,000 – 1,000,000

—— International boundary

Land elevation

3,000 meters	9,840 feet
2,000 meters	6,560 feet
1,000 meters	3,280 feet
500 meters	1,640 feet
200 meters	656 feet
0 Sea level	0 Sea level

Water depth

0 Sea level	0 Sea level
200 meters	656 feet
2,000 meters	6,560 feet

0 200 400 600 800 1000 Miles
0 300 600 900 1200 1500 Kilometers

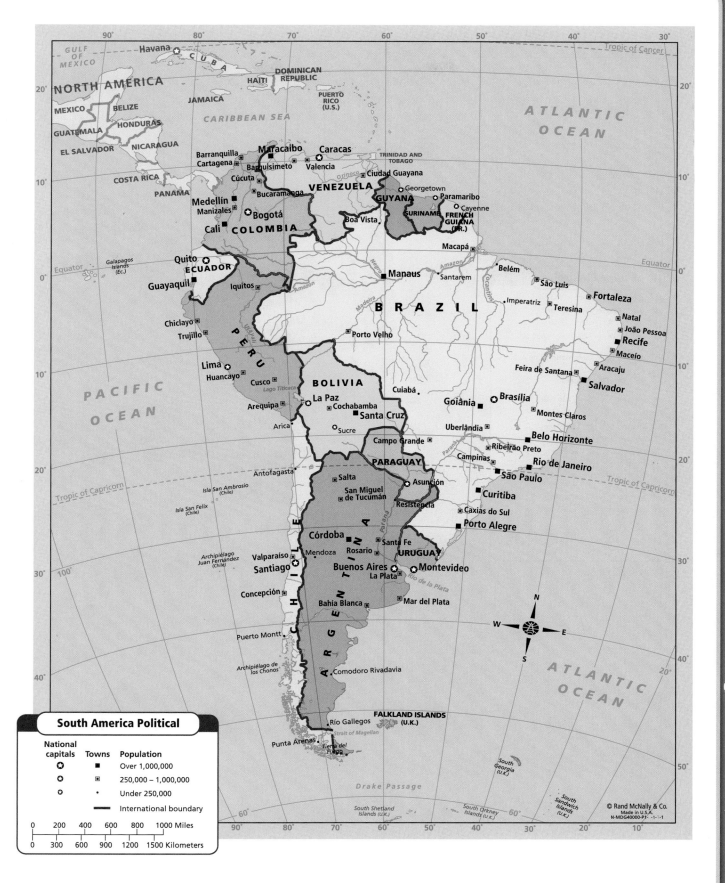

RAND M^cNALLY

South America Political

National capitals	Towns	Population
◎	■	Over 1,000,000
◉	▣	250,000 – 1,000,000
○	·	Under 250,000
	—	International boundary

0 200 400 600 800 1000 Miles
0 300 600 900 1200 1500 Kilometers

© Rand McNally & Co.
Made in U.S.A.
N-MDG40000-P1- -1-1-1

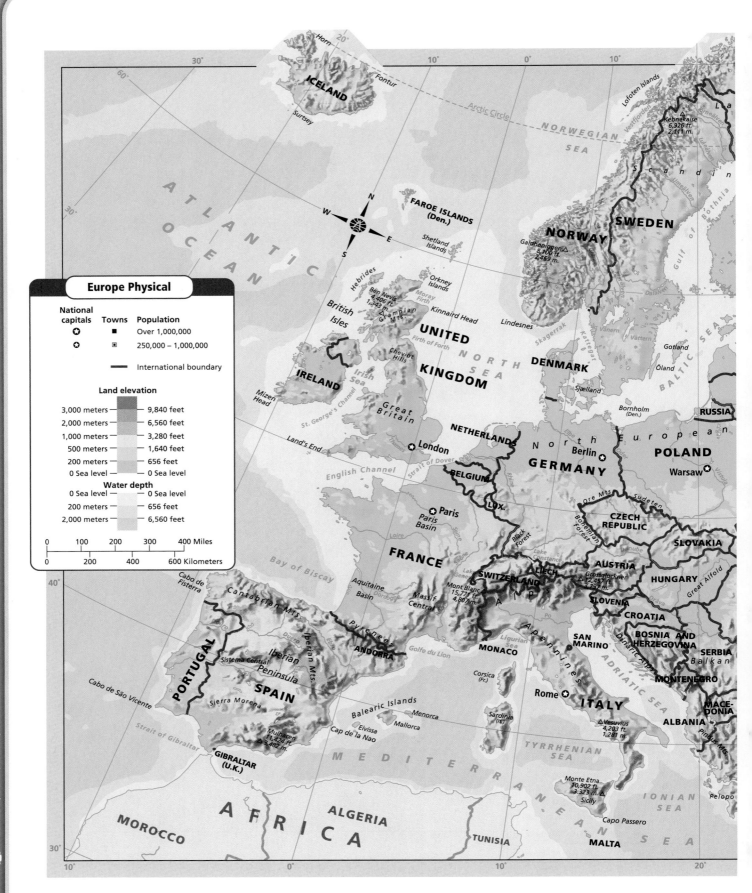

Europe Physical

National capitals
✪ Towns
◉ Population
■ Over 1,000,000
▣ 250,000 – 1,000,000
— International boundary

Land elevation

3,000 meters	9,840 feet
2,000 meters	6,560 feet
1,000 meters	3,280 feet
500 meters	1,640 feet
200 meters	656 feet
0 Sea level	0 Sea level

Water depth

0 Sea level	0 Sea level
200 meters	656 feet
2,000 meters	6,560 feet

0 100 200 300 400 Miles
0 200 400 600 Kilometers

ICELAND
Horn
Fontur
Surtsey

NORWEGIAN SEA

Lofoten Islands
Kebnekaise 6,926 ft. 2,111 m.

FAROE ISLANDS (Den.)
Shetland Islands

SWEDEN

NORWAY
Galdhøpiggen 8,100 ft. 2,469 m.

Gulf of Bothnia

ATLANTIC OCEAN

Hebrides
Orkney Islands
Moray Firth
Ben Nevis 4,406 ft. 1,343 m.
Grampian Mts.
Kinnaird Head
Lindesnes
Skagerrak
Kattegat
Vänern
Gotland
Vättern
Öland

British Isles
UNITED
Firth of Forth
Cheviot Hills
KINGDOM
NORTH SEA
DENMARK
Sjælland
BALTIC SEA

IRELAND
Irish Sea
Great Britain
Bornholm (Den.)
RUSSIA

Mizen Head
St. George's Channel
Land's End
NETHERLANDS
Elbe
North European
POLAND

London
Berlin
GERMANY
Warsaw
Vistula

English Channel
Strait of Dover
BELGIUM
Rhine
LUX.
CZECH REPUBLIC
Ore Mts.
Sudeten
SLOVAKIA

Paris
Paris Basin
Loire
Seine
Black Forest
Bohemian Forest
Danube
AUSTRIA
HUNGARY
Great Alföld

Bay of Biscay
FRANCE
Lake Constance
Lake Geneva
SWITZERLAND
LIECH.
Grossglockner 12,457 ft. 3,797 m.
A L P S
SLOVENIA
Drava

Cabo de Fisterra
Cantabrian Mts.
Aquitaine Basin
Dordogne
Massif Central
Mont Blanc 15,771 ft. 4,807 m.
Po
CROATIA

PORTUGAL
Iberian Peninsula
Pyrenees
ANDORRA
Golfe du Lion
MONACO
Ligurian Sea
Apennines
SAN MARINO
Dinaric Alps
BOSNIA AND HERZEGOVINA
SERBIA
Balkan

Sistema Central
Douro
Ebro
Iberian Mts.
Corsica (Fr.)
ADRIATIC SEA
MONTENEGRO

SPAIN
Sierra Morena
Balearic Islands
Menorca
Sardinia (It.)
Rome
ITALY
MACEDONIA

Cabo de São Vicente
Mulhacén 11,424 ft. 3,482 m.
Eivissa
Mallorca
Cap de la Nao
Vesuvius 4,203 ft. 1,281 m.
ALBANIA
Pindus Mts.

Strait of Gibraltar
GIBRALTAR (U.K.)
MEDITERRANEAN
TYRRHENIAN SEA
Monte Etna 10,902 ft. 3,323 m.
Sicily
IONIAN SEA
Pelopo

MOROCCO
AFRICA
ALGERIA
TUNISIA
Capo Passero
SEA
MALTA

N W E S

Arctic Circle

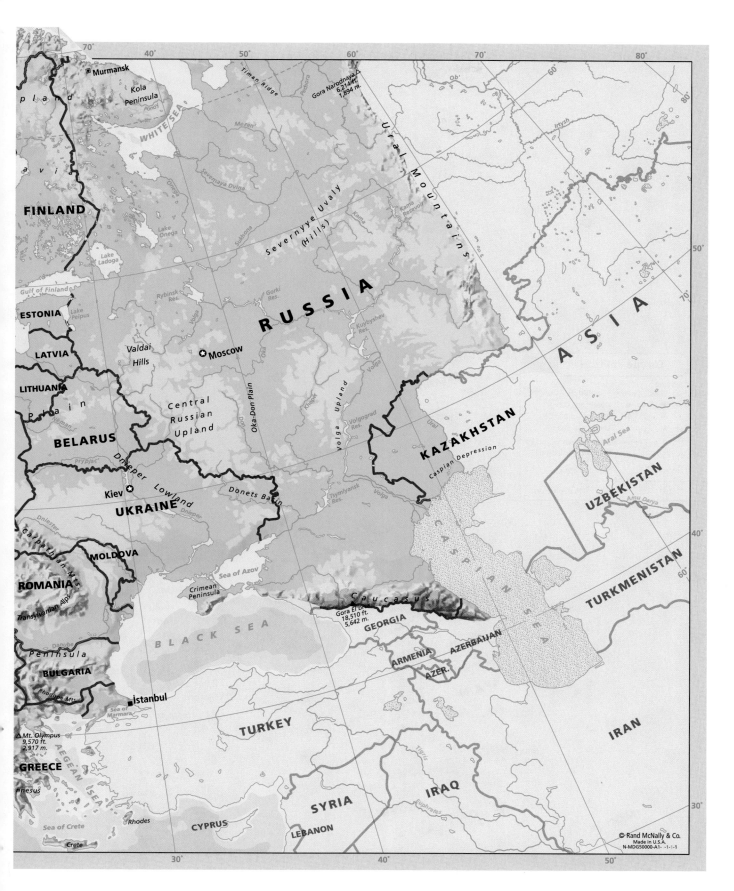

Murmansk

Kola
Peninsula

WHITE SEA

FINLAND

Lake
Onega

Lake
Ladoga

Gulf of Finland

ESTONIA

Lake
Peipus

LATVIA

Valdai
Hills

LITHUANIA

P l a i n

BELARUS

Central
Russian
Upland

Dnieper Lowland

Kiev

UKRAINE

Donets Basin

MOLDOVA

Carpathian Mts.

ROMANIA

Transylvanian Alps

Crimean
Peninsula

Danube

Peninsula

BULGARIA

Rhodope Mts.

İstanbul

△Mt. Olympus
9,570 ft.
2,917 m.

GREECE

Sea of
Marmara

AEGEAN SEA

nnesus

Rhodes

Sea of Crete

Crete

CYPRUS

Timan Ridge

Pechora

Mezen

Severnaya Dvina

Onega

Sukhona

Severnyye Uvaly
(Hills)

Rybinsk
Res.

Moscow

Volga

Oka

Oka-Don Plain

Khopr

Gora Narodnaya △
6,214 ft.
1,894 m.

Ob

Irtysh

R U S S I A

Ural Mountains

Kama

Kama
Reservoir

Gorki
Res.

Kuybyshev
Res.

Volga Upland

Volgograd
Res.

Ural

Tsymlyansk
Res.

Dnieper

Don

Volga

Sea of Azov

BLACK SEA

Gora El'brus
18,510 ft.
5,642 m.

C a u c a s u s

GEORGIA

ARMENIA

AZER.

AZERBAIJAN

TURKEY

Tigris

SYRIA

LEBANON

IRAQ

Euphrates

A S I A

KAZAKHSTAN

Caspian Depression

Caspian Depression

Aral Sea

UZBEKISTAN

Amu Darya

C A S P I A N   S E A

TURKMENISTAN

IRAN

70° 40° 50° 60° 70° 80°

80°

60°

50°

70°

40°

60°

40°

30°

30° 40° 50°

© Rand McNally & Co.
Made in U.S.A.
N-MDG50000-A1- -1-1-1

A27

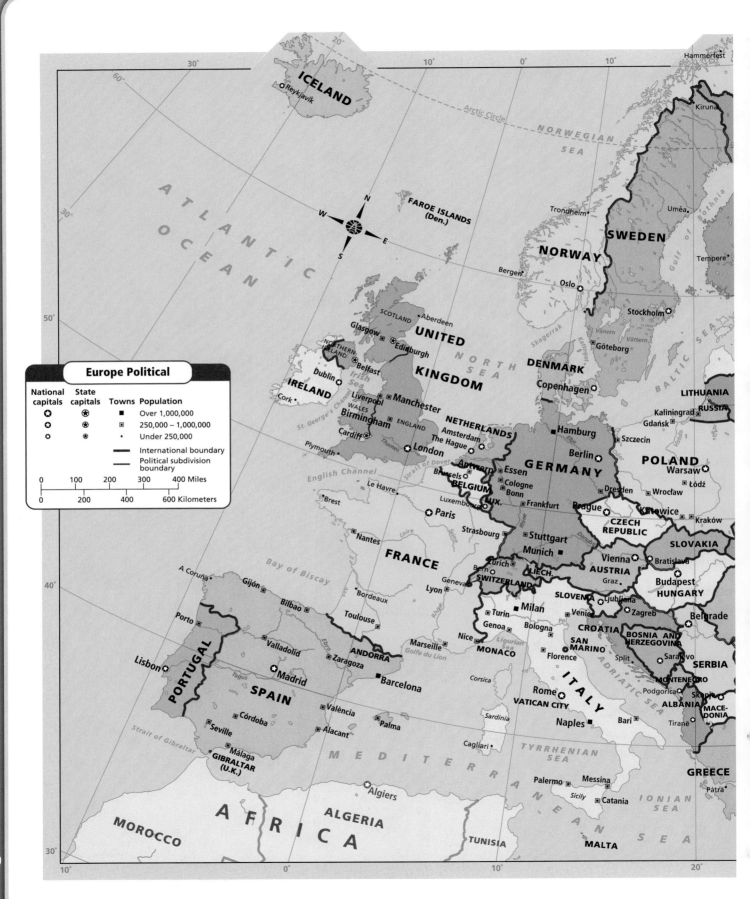

Europe Political

National capitals	State capitals	Towns	Population
✪	✪	■	Over 1,000,000
✪	✪	▣	250,000 – 1,000,000
✪	✪	•	Under 250,000

— International boundary
— Political subdivision boundary

0 100 200 300 400 Miles
0 200 400 600 Kilometers

ICELAND
Reykjavik

ATLANTIC OCEAN

FAROE ISLANDS (Den.)

NORWEGIAN SEA

Hammerfest
Kiruna

SWEDEN
Trondheim
Umeå
NORWAY
Bergen
Oslo
Tempere

Göteborg
Stockholm
Vänern
Vättern

Gulf of Bothnia

BALTIC SEA

DENMARK
Copenhagen
LITHUANIA
Kaliningrad
RUSSIA
Gdańsk

SCOTLAND
Aberdeen
Glasgow
Edinburgh
UNITED KINGDOM
NORTHERN IRELAND
Belfast
Dublin
IRELAND
Cork
Liverpool
Manchester
WALES
Birmingham
ENGLAND
Cardiff
Plymouth
London
NETHERLANDS
Amsterdam
The Hague
Hamburg
Szczecin
Berlin
POLAND
Warsaw
Łódź
GERMANY
Essen
Cologne
Bonn
Dresden
Wrocław
Katowice
Kraków
Frankfurt
Prague
CZECH REPUBLIC
SLOVAKIA
Antwerp
Brussels
BELGIUM
LUX.
Luxembourg

NORTH SEA
Irish Sea
St. George's Channel
English Channel
Strait of Dover
Brest
Le Havre
Paris
Nantes
Strasbourg
Stuttgart
Munich
Bern
Zürich
LIECH.
SWITZERLAND
Geneva
Lyon
Vienna
Bratislava
AUSTRIA
Graz
Budapest
HUNGARY
SLOVENIA
Ljubljana
Zagreb
Belgrade

FRANCE
Loire
Seine
Rhine
Danube
Bay of Biscay
A Coruña
Gijón
Bilbao
Bordeaux
Toulouse
ANDORRA
Turin
Milan
Venice
Genoa
Bologna
CROATIA
Nice
Marseille
Golfe du Lion
MONACO
SAN MARINO
Florence
Split
BOSNIA AND HERZEGOVINA
Sarajevo
SERBIA

Porto
Lisbon
PORTUGAL
Valladolid
Zaragoza
Madrid
SPAIN
Barcelona
València
Córdoba
Seville
Palma
Alacant
Málaga
GIBRALTAR (U.K.)
Strait of Gibraltar
Algiers

Tagus
Ebro

Corsica
Sardinia
ITALY
Rome
VATICAN CITY
Naples
Bari
Cagliari
TYRRHENIAN SEA
Ligurian Sea
ADRIATIC SEA
MONTENEGRO
Podgorica
Skopje
ALBANIA
MACEDONIA
Tirane

MEDITERRANEAN SEA
Palermo
Messina
Sicily
Catania
IONIAN SEA
GREECE
Pátra

MOROCCO
AFRICA
ALGERIA
TUNISIA
MALTA

Arctic Circle
60°
50°
40°
30°
30°
20°
10°
0°
10°
20°
Skagerrak
Kattegat
Elbe
Vistula
Po

RUSSIA

ASIA

Murmansk

WHITE SEA

Oulu

FINLAND

Arkhangel'sk

Ukhta

Pechora

Syktyvkar

Berezniki

Perm'

Petrozavodsk
Lake Onega

Kirov

Izhevsk

Naberezhnye Chelny

Ufa

Helsinki

Saint Petersburg

Cherepovets

Gorki Res.
Rybinsk Res.

Nizhniy Novgorod

Kazan'

Kuybyshev Res.

Tallinn

ESTONIA

Lake Ladoga

Gulf of Finland

Lake Peipus

Yaroslavl'

Ivanovo

Samara

Rīga

LATVIA

Tver'

Moscow

Oka

Ryazan'

Volga

Vilnius

Vicebsk

Tula

Penza

Saratov

Volgograd Res.

Minsk

Bryansk

Lipetsk

KAZAKHSTAN

BELARUS

Homel'

Don

Voronezh

Aral Sea

Chornobyl'

Kiev

Kharkiv

Volgograd

Ural

Atyraū

UZBEKISTAN

L'viv

UKRAINE

Dnieper

Luhans'k

Tsymlyansk Res.

Volga

Astrakhan'

Vinnytsia

Dnipro-petrovs'k

Donets'k

Rostov-na-Donu

Dniester

Kryvyi Rih

Zaporizhzhia

Mariupol'

TURKMENISTAN

MOLDOVA

Iași

Chișinău

Sea of Azov

Krasnodar

Stavropol'

CASPIAN SEA

Cluj-Napoca

Odesa

Vladikavkaz

Galați

Simferopol'

ROMANIA

Sevastopol'

BLACK SEA

GEORGIA

Tbilisi

Baku

Craiova

Bucharest

Constanța

ARMENIA

AZERBAIJAN

Danube

BULGARIA

Varna

Yerevan

AZER.

Sofia

Plovdiv

İstanbul

Thessaloníki

Sea of Marmara

Tehran

Ankara

TURKEY

IRAN

Athens

AEGEAN SEA

SYRIA

IRAQ

CYPRUS

Baghdad

LEBANON

Crete

RAND M?NALLY

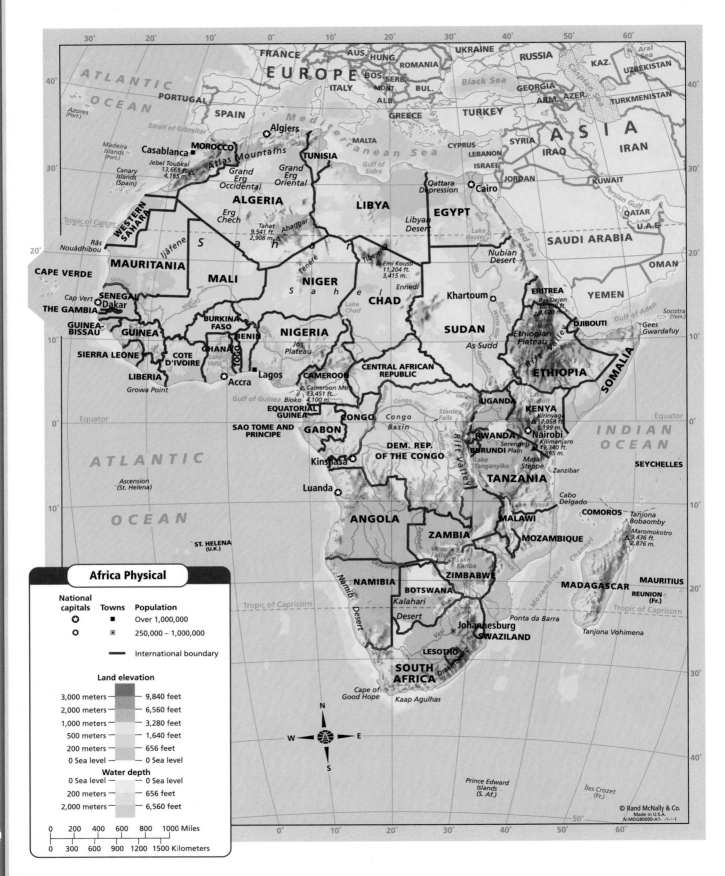

Africa Physical

National capitals   **Towns**   **Population**
- ✪   ■   Over 1,000,000
- ⊙   ▣   250,000 – 1,000,000
- ──   International boundary

Land elevation
3,000 meters	9,840 feet
2,000 meters	6,560 feet
1,000 meters	3,280 feet
500 meters	1,640 feet
200 meters	656 feet
0 Sea level	0 Sea level

Water depth
0 Sea level	0 Sea level
200 meters	656 feet
2,000 meters	6,560 feet

0   200   400   600   800   1000 Miles
0   300   600   900   1200   1500 Kilometers

RAND McNALLY

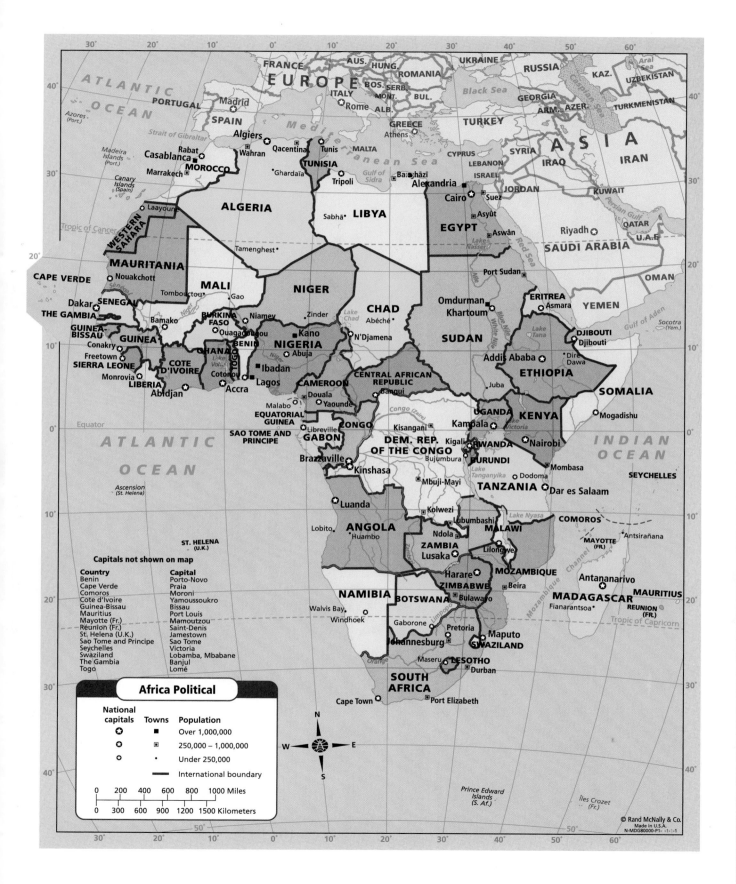

Africa Political

National capitals | **Towns** | **Population**
- ⊛ | ■ | Over 1,000,000
- ⊙ | ▣ | 250,000 – 1,000,000
- ⊙ | • | Under 250,000
- ▬▬▬ | | International boundary

0 200 400 600 800 1000 Miles
0 300 600 900 1200 1500 Kilometers

Capitals not shown on map

Country	Capital
Benin	Porto-Novo
Cape Verde	Praia
Comoros	Moroni
Cote d'Ivoire	Yamoussoukro
Guinea-Bissau	Bissau
Mauritius	Port Louis
Mayotte (Fr.)	Mamoutzou
Réunion (Fr.)	Saint-Denis
St. Helena (U.K.)	Jamestown
Sao Tome and Principe	Sao Tome
Seychelles	Victoria
Swaziland	Lobamba, Mbabane
The Gambia	Banjul
Togo	Lomé

N
W E
S

© Rand McNally & Co.
Made in U.S.A.
N-MDG80000-P1- -1-1-1

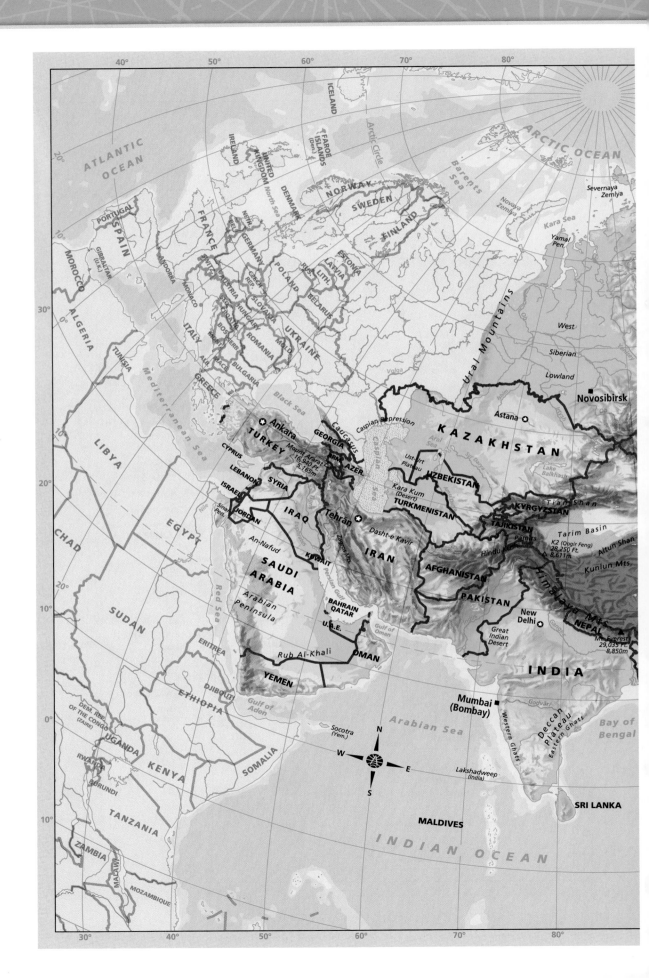

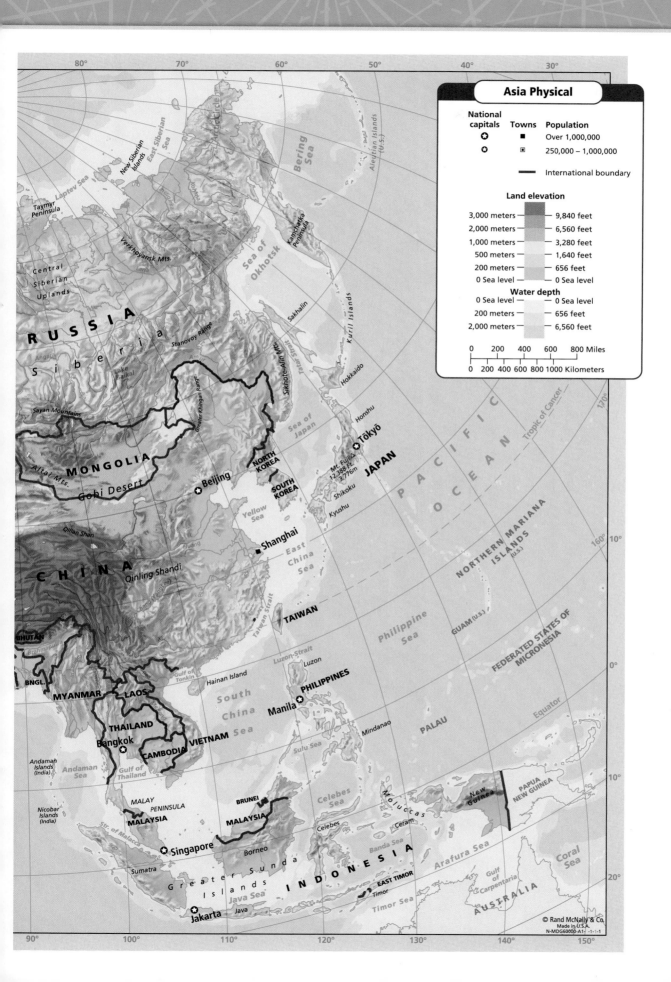

Asia Physical

National capitals	Towns	Population
✪	■	Over 1,000,000
✪	▣	250,000 – 1,000,000

———— International boundary

Land elevation

3,000 meters	9,840 feet
2,000 meters	6,560 feet
1,000 meters	3,280 feet
500 meters	1,640 feet
200 meters	656 feet
0 Sea level	0 Sea level

Water depth

0 Sea level	0 Sea level
200 meters	656 feet
2,000 meters	6,560 feet

0   200   400   600   800 Miles
0   200 400 600 800 1000 Kilometers

Taymyr Peninsula
Laptev Sea
New Siberian Islands
East Siberian Sea
Bering Sea
Kamchatka Peninsula
Aleutian Islands (U.S.)
Central Siberian Uplands
Verkhoyansk Mts.
Stanovoy Range
Sea of Okhotsk
Sakhalin
Sikhote-Alin Mts.
Tatar Strait
Kuril Islands
RUSSIA
Siberia
Angara
Lake Baikal
Sayan Mountains
Altai Mts.
MONGOLIA
Gobi Desert
Greater Khingan Range
Amur
Sea of Japan
Hokkaido
Honshu
Tōkyō
Mt. Fuji
12,388 ft.
3,776m
JAPAN
PACIFIC OCEAN
Tropic of Cancer
NORTH KOREA
SOUTH KOREA
Beijing
Shikoku
Kyushu
Yellow Sea
Qilian Shan
Huang
Qinling Shandi
CHINA
Shanghai
East China Sea
NORTHERN MARIANA ISLANDS (U.S.)
170°
160°
10°
TAIWAN
Taiwan Strait
GUAM (U.S.)
BHUTAN
Brahmaputra
BNGL.
MYANMAR
LAOS
Gulf of Tonkin
Hainan Island
Luzon-Strait
Luzon
Philippine Sea
FEDERATED STATES OF MICRONESIA
0°
PHILIPPINES
THAILAND
VIETNAM
Bangkok
CAMBODIA
South China Sea
Manila
Mindanao
PALAU
Equator
Andaman Islands (India)
Andaman Sea
Gulf of Thailand
Sulu Sea
10°
MALAY PENINSULA
Nicobar Islands (India)
BRUNEI
Celebes Sea
Moluccas
New Guinea
PAPUA NEW GUINEA
MALAYSIA
MALAYSIA
Str. of Malacca
Singapore
Celebes
Ceram
Banda Sea
Borneo
Greater Sunda Islands
INDONESIA
Arafura Sea
Gulf of Carpentaria
Coral Sea
10°
Sumatra
EAST TIMOR
Timor
AUSTRALIA
20°
Jakarta
Java
Java Sea
Timor Sea

© Rand McNally & Co.
Made in U.S.A.
N-MDG60000-A1- -1-1-1

80° 70° 60° 50° 40° 30°
90° 100° 110° 120° 130° 140° 150°

RAND M℠NALLY

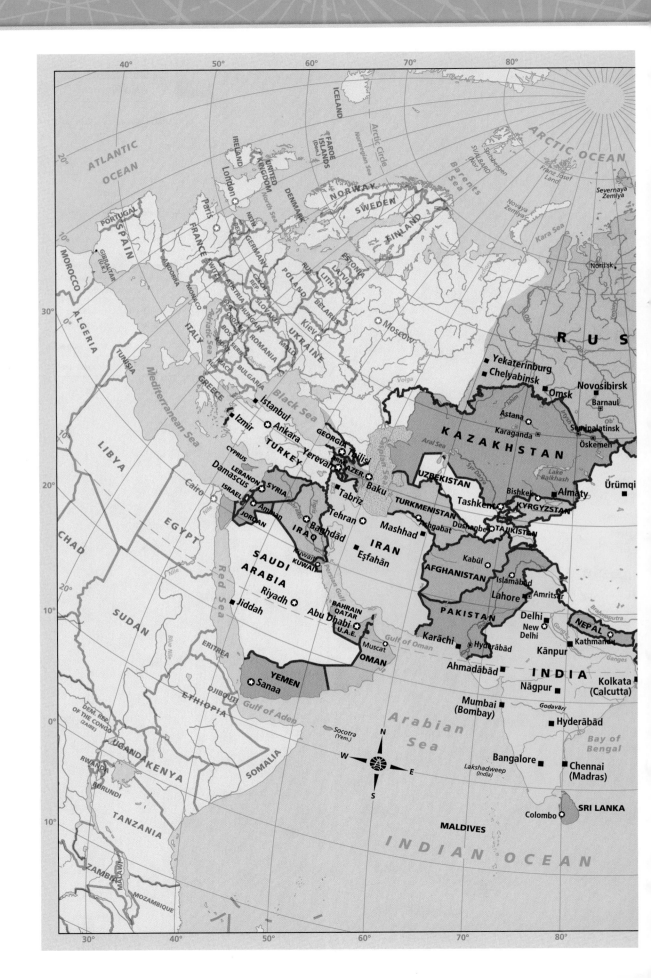

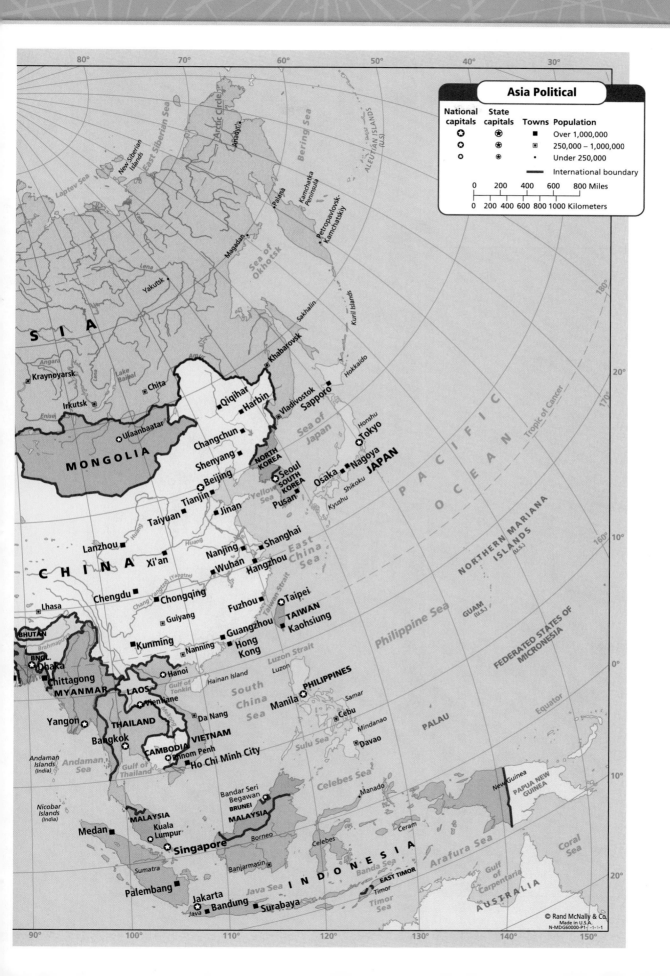

RAND M^cNALLY

Asia Political

National capitals	State capitals	Towns	Population
✪	✪	■	Over 1,000,000
✪	✪	◰	250,000 – 1,000,000
○	✶	·	Under 250,000
		———	International boundary

0 200 400 600 800 Miles

0 200 400 600 800 1000 Kilometers

80° 70° 60° 50° 40° 30°

Bering Sea

ALEUTIAN ISLANDS (U.S.)

Laptev Sea

New Siberian Islands

East Siberian Sea

Arctic Circle

Anadyr

Kamchatka Peninsula

Palana

Petropavlovsk-Kamchatskiy

Magadan

Sea of Okhotsk

Kamchatka

Sakhalin

Kuril Islands

A S I A

Angara

Lena

Lake Baikal

Yenisey

Enisei

Kraynoyarsk

Irkutsk

Chita

Yakutsk

Khabarovsk

Amur

Qiqihar Harbin

Vladivostok Sapporo

Hokkaido

20°

Sea of Japan

Ulaanbaatar

MONGOLIA

Changchun

Shenyang

NORTH KOREA

Honshu

Tokyo

Tropic of Cancer

180°

170°

Beijing

Tianjin

Jinan

Seoul

SOUTH KOREA

Pusan

Osaka Nagoya

JAPAN

Shikoku

Kyushu

Yellow Sea

Taiyuan

Lanzhou

Huang

Huang (Yangtze)

Xi'an

Nanjing

Shanghai

Wuhan

Hangzhou

East China Sea

NORTHERN MARIANA ISLANDS (U.S.)

10°

160°

C H I N A

Chengdu

Chang (Yangtze)

Chongqing

Fuzhou

Taipei

TAIWAN

Kaohsiung

Lhasa

Guiyang

GUAM (U.S.)

BHUTAN

Brahmaputra

Kunming

Nanning

Guangzhou

Hong Kong

Taiwan Strait

Philippine Sea

FEDERATED STATES OF MICRONESIA

0°

BNGL.

Dhaka

Chittagong

MYANMAR LAOS

Hanoi

Gulf of Tonkin

Hainan Island

Luzon Strait

Luzon

PHILIPPINES

Manila PHILIPPINES

Samar

Yangon

THAILAND

Vientiane

Da Nang

South China Sea

Cebu

PALAU

Bangkok

VIETNAM

CAMBODIA

Phnom Penh

Ho Chi Minh City

Mindanao

Davao

Andaman Islands (India)

Andaman Sea

Gulf of Thailand

Mekong

Sulu Sea

Celebes Sea

Manado

New Guinea

PAPUA NEW GUINEA

10°

140°

Nicobar Islands (India)

Bandar Seri Begawan

BRUNEI

MALAYSIA

MALAYSIA

Borneo

Ceram

Medan

Kuala Lumpur

Singapore

Celebes

Banda Sea

Arafura Sea

Gulf of Carpentaria

Coral Sea

Sumatra

Banjarmasin

I N D O N E S I A

AUSTRALIA

20°

Palembang

Jakarta

Bandung

Surabaya

Java

Java Sea

EAST TIMOR

Timor

Timor Sea

© Rand McNally & Co.
Made in U.S.A.
N-MDG60000-P1- -1-1-1

90° 100° 110° 120° 130° 140° 150°

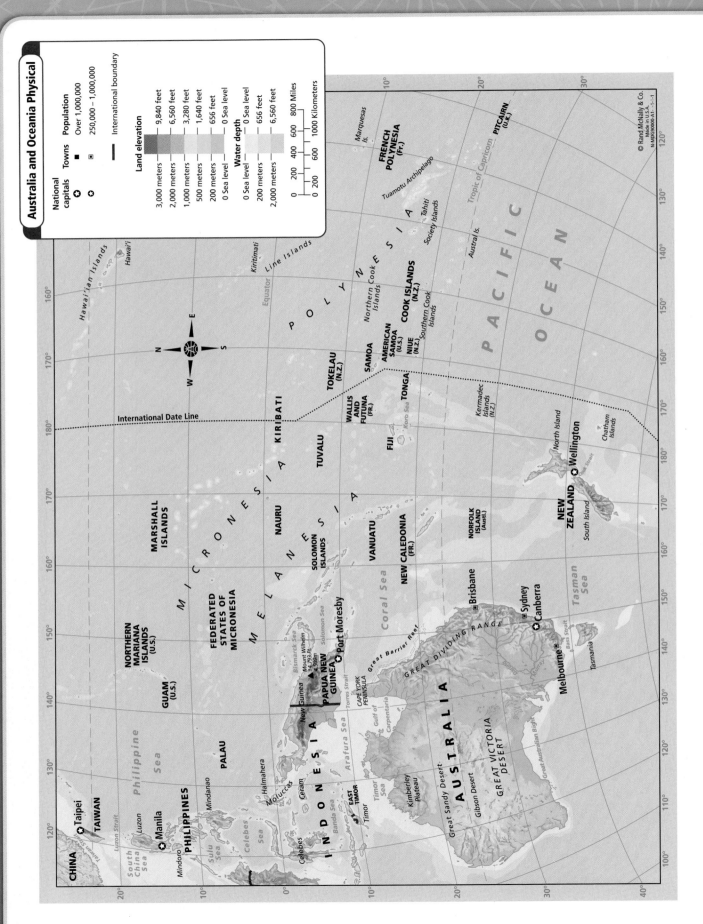

Australia and Oceania Physical

National capitals
⊕ Over 1,000,000
⊕ 250,000 – 1,000,000

Towns Population
■ Over 1,000,000
▣ 250,000 – 1,000,000

— International boundary

Land elevation
9,840 feet — 3,000 meters
6,560 feet — 2,000 meters
3,280 feet — 1,000 meters
1,640 feet — 500 meters
656 feet — 200 meters
0 Sea level — 0 Sea level

Water depth
0 Sea level — 0 Sea level
656 feet — 200 meters
6,560 feet — 2,000 meters

0   200   400   600   800 Miles
0   200   400   600   800   1000 Kilometers

© Rand McNally & Co.
Made in U.S.A.
N-MIG90000-A1-1-1-1

RAND M℃NALLY

CHINA ⊕ Taipei
TAIWAN
Luzon Strait
South China Sea
Mindoro Luzon
⊕ Manila
PHILIPPINES
Mindanao
Philippine Sea
Sulu Sea
Celebes Sea
Celebes
Halmahera
Moluccas
Ceram
Banda Sea
PALAU
INDONESIA
EAST TIMOR
Timor
Timor Sea
Arafura Sea

NORTHERN MARIANA ISLANDS (U.S.)
GUAM (U.S.)
FEDERATED STATES OF MICRONESIA
MICRONESIA
MARSHALL ISLANDS
NAURU
KIRIBATI
TUVALU
MELANESIA
PAPUA NEW GUINEA ⊕ Port Moresby
New Guinea
Mount Wilhelm 14,793 ft. 4,509m ▲
Bismarck Sea
Solomon Sea
SOLOMON ISLANDS
VANUATU
NEW CALEDONIA (FR.)
Coral Sea
FIJI
Koro Sea
TONGA
WALLIS AND FUTUNA (FR.)
TOKELAU (N.Z.)
SAMOA
AMERICAN SAMOA (U.S.)
NIUE (N.Z.)
COOK ISLANDS (N.Z.)
Northern Cook Islands
Southern Cook Islands
POLYNESIA
Line Islands
Kiritimati
Equator
Hawai'i
Hawai'ian Islands
Marquesas Is.
FRENCH POLYNESIA (Fr.)
Tuamotu Archipelago
Tahiti
Society Islands
Austral Is.
PITCAIRN (U.K.)
Tropic of Capricorn

PACIFIC OCEAN

International Date Line

Torres Strait
CAPE YORK PENINSULA
Gulf of Carpentaria
Great Barrier Reef
AUSTRALIA
Kimberley Plateau
Great Sandy Desert
Gibson Desert
GREAT VICTORIA DESERT
Great Australian Bight
GREAT DIVIDING RANGE
Murray
Darling
■ Brisbane
Sydney ■
⊕ Canberra
Melbourne ■
Bass Strait
Tasmania
Tasman Sea
NORFOLK ISLAND (Austl.)
Kermadec Islands (N.Z.)
NEW ZEALAND
North Island
Cook Strait
⊕ Wellington
South Island
Chatham Islands

North Pole

☆ National capital
● Town
— International boundary

0   200   400   600   800   1000 Miles
0   400   800   1200   1600 Kilometers

South Pole

0   200   400   600   800   1000 Miles
0   400   800   1200   1600 Kilometers

A37

UNIT 1

Introduction to World Geography

Why It Matters:

You live on a unique planet in the Sun's planetary system. It is the only planet capable of supporting a wide variety of life forms. As human beings we adapt and alter the environments on Earth.

Landsat satellite

CHAPTER 1 **Understanding the Earth and Its Peoples**

Fiery volcanic eruption

CHAPTER 2 **Earth's Interlocking Systems**

Indonesian rice fields

CHAPTER 3 **Human Geography**

Cave of Hands, Santa Cruz, Argentina

CHAPTER 4 **People and Culture**

Understanding the Earth and Its Peoples

 ESSENTIAL QUESTION

In what ways does geography help us understand our world?

CONNECT → Geography & History

Use the satellite image and the time line to answer the following questions.

1. The large continent in the center of the image is Africa. How would you describe the land?

2. Which of the events listed on the time line made this image possible?

Culture

◄ **c. A.D. 1st century**
Strabo describes the world known to the Greeks and Romans in his 17-volume *Geography*.

A.D. 1

Geography

c. A.D. 2nd century
Greek geographer Ptolemy writes his 8-volume *Geography* on mapmaking.

Geography

▲ **1100** Chinese begin using the magnetic compass.

Ⓑ

Ⓐ

Ⓐ
Amazon Rain Forest The Amazon rain forest in South America is the largest rain forest in the world.

Ⓑ
Sahara Desert The Sahara is the largest desert in the world.

History
1730 John Hadley creates the basic design for a sextant. ▼

History
1972 First Landsat satellite is launched.

Today

History
1960s Geographic Information Systems (GIS) development begins.

Geography
1983 The Global Positioning System (GPS) becomes operational. ▶

SECTION 1

Reading for Understanding

▶ Key Ideas

BEFORE YOU READ

Think about what you already know about the Earth's physical geography.

NOW YOU WILL LEARN

Geographers have specialized ways to view and interpret information about the world.

▶ Vocabulary

TERMS & NAMES

geography the study of people, places, and environments

environment the physical surroundings of a location

spatial where a place is located and its physical relationship to other places, people, or environments

location an exact position using latitude and longitude, or a description of a place in relation to places around it

place a geographical term that describes the physical and human characteristics of a location

region an area that has one or more common characteristics that unite or connect it with other areas

BACKGROUND VOCABULARY

three-dimensional an image in which there is a sense of depth and perspective

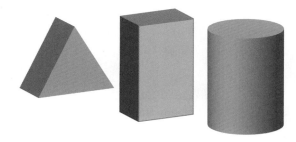

Visual Vocabulary Three-dimensional shapes

▶ Reading Strategy

Re-create the web diagram shown at right. As you read and respond to the **KEY QUESTIONS**, use the diagram to help you find main ideas about the themes and elements of geography.

 Skillbuilder Handbook, page R4

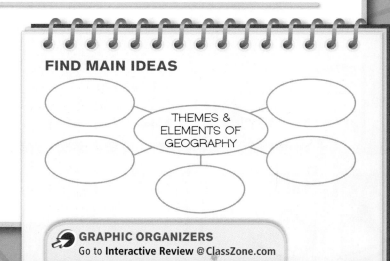

FIND MAIN IDEAS

THEMES & ELEMENTS OF GEOGRAPHY

GRAPHIC ORGANIZERS
Go to **Interactive Review** @ ClassZone.com

Themes and Elements of Geography

Connecting to Your World

Have you ever drawn a map to show someone how to get to your house? Or have you described your hometown to someone who doesn't live there? If you answered yes to these questions, you were doing what geographers do. Geographers try to answer the questions, "Where are things located?" and "Why are they there?" Basic questions like these form the framework for the subject called geography. **Geography** is the study of people, places, and environments. An **environment** is the physical surroundings of a location.

Ways of Thinking About Geography

▼ **KEY QUESTION** What are the themes and elements of geography?

Geographers study the world in **spatial** terms. This means they look at the space where a place is located and its physical relationship to other places, people, and environments. Geographers—and students of geography— use two different methods to organize geographic information: the five themes and the six essential elements of geography. The categories vary slightly, but the graphic on the next two pages will help you learn how to apply these ideas as you read this text.

Three-Dimensional Model This computer-generated model is used to study geographic conditions in the Los Angeles region.

5

The Five Themes of Geography

The world is a big place and studying it is a complicated task. You can make that job easier by learning five core themes of geography. These themes can help you answer geographic questions.

1 LOCATION

Where are things located?

Location means either an exact position using latitude or longitude, or a description of a place in relation to places around it.

Rio de Janeiro, Brazil

2 PLACE

What is a particular location like?

Place describes physical characteristics such as mountains or rivers, as well as human characteristics such as the people who live there.

Beijing, China

3 REGION

How are places similar or different?

Regions have physical or human characteristics that unite them and make them different from or similar to other regions.

Gobi Desert

4 MOVEMENT

How do people, goods, and ideas move from one location to another?

Movement of people, goods, and ideas changes places and regions and the people who live there.

Interstate Cloverleaf

5 HUMAN–ENVIRONMENT INTERACTION

How do people relate to the physical world?

Humans adapt to their environment and change elements of it.

Pacific Ocean Windsurfing

Six Essential Elements

Geographers use six key ideas or elements to help them understand people, places, and environments on the Earth.

1 **THE WORLD IN SPATIAL TERMS**

Geographers study the locations of places and distributions or patterns of features by using maps, data, and other geographic tools. Knowing about the world in spatial terms helps geographers understand physical and human patterns.

2 **PLACES AND REGIONS**

Geographers look for characteristics of places and then compare their similarities and differences.

Mount Everest

3 **PHYSICAL SYSTEMS**

Geographers study changes in the Earth's surface. Where and why people choose to live in certain locations may depend on Earth's surface conditions.

4 **HUMAN SYSTEMS**

Geographers study human settlement patterns and use of resources. This information helps explain human interactions and lifestyles.

5 **ENVIRONMENT AND SOCIETY**

Geographers study how people interact with the environment and how they use resources.

6 **THE USES OF GEOGRAPHY**

Geographers study patterns and processes in the world. This information helps people understand the past and plan for the future.

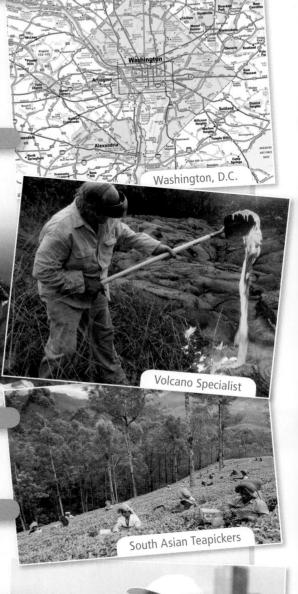

Washington, D.C.

Volcano Specialist

South Asian Teapickers

Surveyor

Understanding the Earth and Its Peoples **7**

Five Themes of Geography Now that you have seen the geographic themes and elements side by side, let's look more closely at an example of one of the themes and elements as it applies to a particular place.

The theme of human-environment interaction is a good place to get an idea of how a geographer thinks. For thousands of years, people have found it valuable to settle by rivers. A river can provide food, water, transportation, and other needs of daily life. However, rivers can flood, destroying homes and villages, and taking human life. So, humans began to alter their environment by building walls called levees to protect the land from floods. Sometimes they created dams to control the flow of water and to save some water for times when they needed it. A geographer who asks the questions "Where do people choose to live?" and "Why here?" will answer that the river provides many needs for a group of people. So, people will likely be found in areas that have rivers as a resource. As it turns out, we know that early civilizations such as those in Egypt, Southwest Asia, India, and China began in river valleys.

Six Essential Elements Using the six elements helps geographers make sense both of physical processes on the Earth and of human systems devised by the people who live there.

Let's look at the element of physical systems. Geographers want to know how these systems work to reshape the Earth's surface and what impact these changes have on plants, animals, and people. Volcanoes

CONNECT to Geography

Chicago The skyline of Chicago towers over the shore of Lake Michigan. One of the largest cities in the United States, Chicago has long been the economic and cultural center of the region.

CRITICAL THINKING
Find Main Ideas Look at the image of Chicago at right. Which of the five themes and six elements of geography do the captions reflect?

High-rise buildings maximize the use of valuable land.

Chicago is a major hub for Great Lakes water transportation and a main railroad headquarters.

Chicago is located in the upper Midwest of the United States.

are an example of a physical force that changes the shape of the Earth's surface and may have a dramatic effect on human populations. A volcanic eruption may kill people, plants, and animals living in the area. Flows of lava may change the landscape, burn forests or crops, and possibly alter the course of rivers. Islands in the Pacific Ocean have been created by volcanic eruptions, and still others have disappeared between the waves when they were blown apart by eruptions. Volcanoes can also trigger earthquakes. Geographers studying physical systems point out that many volcanoes take place in certain areas of the world. Studying this pattern of volcanic action helps explain where and why people live in certain locations.

Using the five themes of geography and the six essential elements will help you to think like a geographer. The themes and elements will help you to think about particular places and the physical processes and human activities that shaped those places in the past—and continue to do so. They will also enable you to look for patterns and connections in geographic information. You will be better able to answer the two main geographic questions, "Where are things located?" and "Why are they there?" You will learn about the tools used to record and analyze geographic information in the next section.

 FIND MAIN IDEAS Identify the five themes and six essential elements of geography.

Section ① Assessment

ONLINE QUIZ
For test practice, go to **Interactive Review** @ ClassZone.com

TERMS & NAMES

1. Explain the importance of
- geography
- environment
- spatial

USE YOUR READING NOTES

2. Find Main Ideas Use your completed web diagram to answer the following question:

What are the five themes of geography?

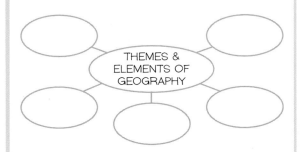

THEMES & ELEMENTS OF GEOGRAPHY

KEY IDEAS

3. What two questions do geographers try to answer?

4. How do geographers use the five themes?

5. What are the six elements that geographers use to look at the world?

CRITICAL THINKING

6. Summarize What does it mean to study the world in spatial terms?

7. Compare and Contrast How do you think the study of geography differs from that of history?

8. CONNECT to Today How does studying geography help you understand the world in which you live?

9. ART Make a Poster Create a poster that lists the five themes and six elements of geography. For each theme or element, include the definition and a photograph or drawing to illustrate it.

Reading for Understanding

▶ Key Ideas

BEFORE, YOU LEARNED

Geography is the study of Earth's physical features and the interaction of people with the environment and with each other.

NOW YOU WILL LEARN

Geographers use technological tools to help them understand both Earth's physical processes and the activities of people on Earth.

▶ Vocabulary

TERMS & NAMES

globe a model of the earth in the shape of a sphere

map a representation of a part of the Earth

cartographer (kahr•TAHG•ruh•fur) a geographer who creates maps

surveyor a person who measures the land

remote sensing obtaining information about a site by using an instrument that is not physically in contact with the site

Landsat a series of information-gathering satellites that orbit above Earth

Global Positioning System (GPS) a system that uses a network of earth-orbiting satellites to pinpoint location

Geographic Information Systems (GIS) a computer or Internet-based mapping technology

BACKGROUND VOCABULARY

database a collection of information that can be analyzed

debris (duh•BREE) the scattered remains of something broken or destroyed

▶ Reading Strategy

Re-create the web diagram shown at right. As you read and respond to the **KEY QUESTIONS**, use the diagram to summarize ideas about geographers' technological tools.

📖 **Skillbuilder Handbook, page R5**

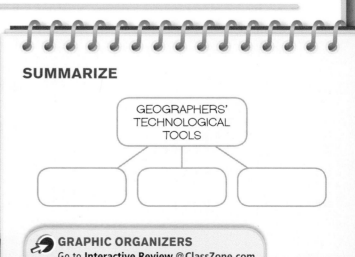

SUMMARIZE

GEOGRAPHERS' TECHNOLOGICAL TOOLS

🔁 **GRAPHIC ORGANIZERS**
Go to **Interactive Review** @ClassZone.com

Technology Tools for Geographers

Connecting to Your World

When you were a much younger student, you probably used paper and pencil to do your schoolwork. Now, when you have an assignment to complete, you most likely use a computer and the Internet. Today's geographers and other scientists use high-tech instruments and advanced computer software to create maps and databases. A **database** is a collection of information that can be analyzed. Geographers use these tools and their analysis to answer geographic questions.

Gerardus Mercator
A Flemish cartographer, Mercator developed a type of map still used today.

The Science of Mapmaking

🔻 **KEY QUESTION** How has technology changed mapmaking?

In their work, geographers use photographs, graphs, globes, and maps. A **globe** is a model of the Earth in the shape of a sphere. It shows the actual shape of the Earth. But you can only see half at any one time, and it is not easy to carry around. So, geographers use maps. A **map** is a representation of a part of the Earth. Maps can help geographers see patterns in the way human or physical processes occur. **Cartographers** (kahr•TAGH•ruh•furs) are geographers who create maps.

Animated GEOGRAPHY
Landsat Satellite
This satellite provides visible and infrared views of the Earth.

🔁 **Click here** to see how satellites gather data @ClassZone.com

Cartographers create maps from data collected in surveys. **Surveyors** are people who map and measure the land. They go out to a location and mark down the physical features they see, such as rivers, mountains, or towns. Today, cartographers use technologically advanced tools that provide a much more detailed and accurate picture of the world.

To create modern maps, geographers often use remote sensing equipment. **Remote sensing** means obtaining information about a site by using an instrument that is not physically in contact with the site. Generally, these instruments are cameras mounted on airplanes or Earth-orbiting satellites.

Satellites Two of the best-known satellites are Landsat and GOES. **Landsat** is actually a series of information-gathering satellites that orbit more than 100 miles above the Earth. Each has a variety of sensing devices to collect images and data. Each time a satellite makes an orbit, it gathers information from an area about 115 miles wide. Landsat can scan the entire Earth in 18 days.

GOES, or Geostationary Operational Environmental Satellite, is a weather satellite. This satellite flies in an orbit at the same speed as the

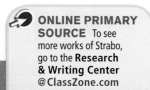

ONLINE PRIMARY SOURCE To see more works of Strabo, go to the **Research & Writing Center** @ ClassZone.com

ANALYZING Primary Sources

Strabo (c. 64 B.C.–A.D. 23) was a Greek who wrote books about geography and history. His 17-volume *Geography* is the main source for information about the world known to the ancient Greeks and Romans. Strabo drew the map below for his geography book.

Strabo

DOCUMENT–BASED QUESTION

Which two continents labeled on the map were known to the ancient Greeks and Romans?

Earth's rotation. In this way it remains "stationary" above a fixed area. It gathers images of conditions that are used to forecast the weather. In 2006, there were two GOES satellites. One provided images from the eastern United States and the other from the west. You see GOES images when you watch a TV weather forecast.

Global Positioning System The U.S. Department of Defense developed technology to help American military forces know exactly where they were. The **Global Positioning System (GPS)** employs a network of Earth-orbiting satellites to collect information about the location of a receiver. The satellites beam the receiver's exact position—latitude, longitude, elevation, and time—to Earth. This information is displayed on the receiver.

A GPS receiver can be small enough to fit in your hand. It has an electronic position locator that sends a beam from where you and the device are to an orbiting satellite. The satellite measures where the GPS device is and beams back your exact position.

GPS can be used from any point on the Earth and in any type of weather. You can use its data to help you figure out "Where am I?" and "Where am I going?" GPS data can be used to determine location, aid in navigating from place to place, create maps, and track the movement of people and things. Animal biologists, for example, use GPS devices to track animals and learn about their habits.

▲ **DRAW CONCLUSIONS** Explain how technology has changed mapmaking.

COMPARING ◄ Mapping Styles: Washington, D.C.

 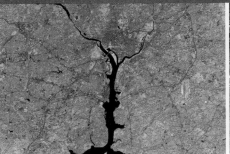 

Road Maps Road maps are created from information including aerial photographs, road surveys made with hand-held digitizers, and maps showing the positions of such features as lakes and mountains.

Satellite Images Satellite images are produced by equipment that records information in a digital format. The information is then converted to images that look like photographs.

Infrared Images Infrared images measure the radiation emitted by water bodies, vegetation, and buildings. In this type of image, the warm areas appear in light blue, areas with vegetation appear red, and water is black.

CRITICAL THINKING
Evaluate Which of these mapping styles would be the most valuable for determining where earthquake damage has occurred?

Geographic Information Systems

▼ **KEY QUESTION** How do Geographic Information Systems work?

A very technologically advanced tool geographers use is the **Geographic Information Systems (GIS)**. GIS is a computer-based mapping technology. The complete system is able to gather, store, analyze, and display spatial information about places. It combines information from a variety of sources into digital databases.

GIS can integrate geographic information, such as maps, aerial photographs, and satellite images. It can also include information such as population figures, economic statistics, or temperature readings. Someone using GIS selects the information needed to answer a geographic question. Then GIS combines layers of information to give the user a better understanding of how the data works together. It can display the information in different ways, such as on a map, design, chart, or graph. The diagram below shows how GIS works.

CONNECT ↘ Geography & Technology

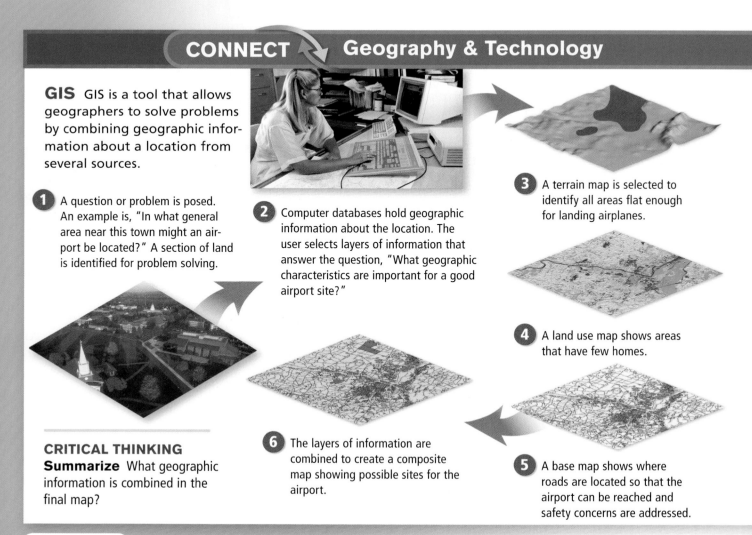

GIS GIS is a tool that allows geographers to solve problems by combining geographic information about a location from several sources.

1 A question or problem is posed. An example is, "In what general area near this town might an airport be located?" A section of land is identified for problem solving.

2 Computer databases hold geographic information about the location. The user selects layers of information that answer the question, "What geographic characteristics are important for a good airport site?"

3 A terrain map is selected to identify all areas flat enough for landing airplanes.

4 A land use map shows areas that have few homes.

5 A base map shows where roads are located so that the airport can be reached and safety concerns are addressed.

6 The layers of information are combined to create a composite map showing possible sites for the airport.

CRITICAL THINKING
Summarize What geographic information is combined in the final map?

GIS projects can range from simple, specific site questions to more complex global problems. For example, you could use GIS to determine the quickest and safest path to walk to your school. The federal government was able to use GIS to predict the location of **debris** (duh•BREE) from the space shuttle *Columbia*, which broke up upon reentry into the Earth's atmosphere in 2003. GIS can be used to plan for hurricane evacuations or to monitor the possible spread of avian flu. Urban planners use GIS to determine where to place a park or where to relocate a dangerous highway intersection. Private companies use GIS to decide where to drill for oil or even where to place a new fast-food restaurant.

GIS makes it possible for geographers to answer geographic questions quickly and accurately. They are better able to see relationships between data, to understand the past and present, and to predict future situations.

In the next section, you will learn about the many different kinds of jobs geographers perform.

 SUMMARIZE Explain how GIS works.

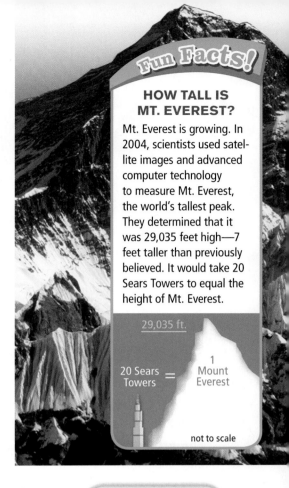

Fun Facts!

HOW TALL IS MT. EVEREST?

Mt. Everest is growing. In 2004, scientists used satellite images and advanced computer technology to measure Mt. Everest, the world's tallest peak. They determined that it was 29,035 feet high—7 feet taller than previously believed. It would take 20 Sears Towers to equal the height of Mt. Everest.

29,035 ft.

20 Sears Towers = 1 Mount Everest

not to scale

 **ONLINE QUIZ**
For test practice, go to
Interactive Review
@ ClassZone.com

Section 2 Assessment

TERMS & NAMES

1. Explain the importance of
- map
- cartographer
- Geographic Information Systems (GIS)

USE YOUR READING NOTES

2. Summarize Use your completed web diagram to answer the following question:

What are some geographers' tools besides maps and globes?

```
        GEOGRAPHERS'
        TECHNOLOGICAL
            TOOLS

   (    )  (    )  (    )
```

KEY IDEAS

3. What were two early means of showing the Earth's surface?

4. How did remote sensing change the way geographic data were obtained?

5. What are some ways GIS can be used?

CRITICAL THINKING

6. Make Inferences How were early geographers limited in gathering geographic information?

7. Draw Conclusions How does technology help geographers?

8. CONNECT to Today In what ways do you think that new geography technology might aid military forces in modern warfare?

9. TECHNOLOGY Make a Multimedia Presentation Use an Internet-based GIS to demonstrate the uses of this geographic tool. Give examples of the different tasks a GIS can do.

Reading for Understanding

▶ Key Ideas

BEFORE, YOU LEARNED

Geographers use technology to help them do their jobs of finding information about selected areas.

NOW YOU WILL LEARN

Geographers do many different kinds of jobs as they gather data and analyze and interpret it.

▶ Vocabulary

TERMS & NAMES

location analyst a person who studies an area to find the best location for a client

climatologist a geographer who studies climates

Visual Vocabulary Climatologist

urban planner a person who creates plans for developing and improving parts of a city

geomorphology (JEE•oh•mawr•FAHL•uh•jee) the study of how the shape of the Earth changes

REVIEW VOCABULARY

surveyor a person who maps and measures the land

Geographic Information Systems (GIS) a computer-based mapping technology

urban having to do with a city

▶ Reading Strategy

Re-create the web diagram shown at right. As you read and respond to the **KEY QUESTIONS**, use the web diagram to categorize details about careers in geography.

 Skillbuilder Handbook, page R7

CATEGORIZE

CAREERS

GRAPHIC ORGANIZERS
Go to **Interactive Review** @ClassZone.com

Careers in Geography

Connecting to Your World

"What are you going to be when you grow up?" is a question that you may have been asked. You may not even know there are a variety of geography-related jobs. The Association of American Geographers lists nearly 150 different geography jobs. So, if you are interested in people, places, and environments, consider a job in geography. Your work will not be limited to maps—it might range from analyzing data to planning projects, or making decisions about the environment.

Modern Cartographer
A cartographer works at updating a street map.

Processing Geographic Data

▼ **KEY QUESTION** What is a geographer's main activity?

A geographer's main activity is analyzing geographic information to answer geographic questions. Jobs processing geographic data begin, of course, with collecting the information. One on-the-ground job in data collection is that of a **surveyor**. Surveyors map and measure the land directly. They may mark boundaries, study the shape of the land, or even help find sewer and water systems beneath the Earth.

Surveyor A surveyor in Dhaka, Bangladesh, gathers data for a project.

High-tech information-gathering jobs include working with **Geographic Information Systems (GIS)** data. Some examples of these jobs include remote sensing specialists and GIS analysts. Take a look back at the GIS feature in Section 2 to get an idea of what a job using GIS would be like. Data analysis jobs require the ability to think critically, high-level computer skills, and a college education.

Once data have been processed, a geographer may study the information to use in planning projects such as a new urban area, a disaster evacuation plan, or the placement of a new highway. Planners can also help determine how to make a neighborhood a better place to live. These jobs, too, require good critical thinking, writing, and computer skills, as well as a college education. Planners are valuable to the success of a community.

▲ **FIND MAIN IDEAS** Explain the main job of a geographer.

Advising Businesses and Government

▼ **KEY QUESTION** How do geographers help businesses and government?

About half of jobs using geography are in business and government. All kinds of businesses use geographic information to help build and expand their operations. A **location analyst** studies an area to find the best location for a client. The client might be a large retail store chain that wants to know which location would be best for opening a new store. The location analyst can study GIS reports on such elements as transportation networks or population in an area and give the business owners the positive and negative points about a location being considered.

In 1967, the Mexican government was looking for a location to create a new international tourist resort. They used location analysts to find an area that had good beaches and was easy to reach from the United States. The result was Cancún, today one of the world's most desirable vacation sites.

Businesses connected with natural resources such as forests also rely on geographers. Geographers help them understand the relationship between their business and the environment where their business is located. **Climatologists** are geographers who study

CONNECT **Geography & Culture**

Cancún Then and Now

In 1967, Cancún was a small, swampy island on Mexico's Caribbean coast. It had white sand beaches, many birds and mangrove trees, but few people. After it was selected as a resort site, it was quickly transformed. Today, Cancún has more than 100 hotels and 500,000 permanent residents. Many work in the tourist industry that serves the millions of visitors who come each year from all over the world.

climates. They are used by businesses that need information about climate to conduct their operations. For example, coffee-growers in Brazil must have an idea if the weather during the next year will be helpful or harmful to their crop. To determine this, a climatologist might study the long-term climate data about the region to project future weather patterns.

City governments often use an **urban planner** to create plans for improving parts of the city. Planners may help locate and design residential or business areas, or parks and recreational spaces. They may find a location for an airport, mass transit routes, or sewer and water lines.

△ **FIND MAIN IDEAS** Explain how geographers help business and government.

Urban Planners Planners help city governments locate projects being built in a city. **What questions might a planner ask to help a city find the right location for a project?**

CONNECT to Your World

Geography Competitions

Across the United States and in foreign countries, students in grades four through eight compete in geography contests. Students are quizzed on all types of geography, including physical geography—such as locations of places and land and water features—and human geography.

Students compete in Washington, D.C., for the right to represent the United States in international competition for the world championship.

CRITICAL THINKING

Journal Entry Start a page in your journal with questions you could use in a geography contest at your school.

Physical and Human Geography

▼ **KEY QUESTION** What jobs are available related to physical and human geography?

Physical geographers are sometimes called earth scientists. Some study such topics as **geomorphology** (JEE•oh•mawr•FAHL•uh•jee), that is, the study of how the shape of the Earth changes. Others study weather and climate. Still others study water, the oceans, soils, or ecology. Jobs in these fields require special scientific training.

Some geographers study social, political, and economic issues as they relate to place or region. Human geographers are usually hired by government agencies to analyze a specific problem. These geographers work closely with political scientists, economists, and sociologists. Together, they provide possible solutions to problems from many different aspects of life in an area. And, of course, geographers teach the subject at all levels of education, from elementary schools to universities.

But no matter what geography jobs people might hold, they are always trying to answer the basic geographic questions: "Where are things located?" and "Why are they there?"

Surveying the Public
Human geographers ask residents about problems in the neighborhood. **Why would geographers ask residents questions about their neighborhood?**

▲ **SUMMARIZE** Name some physical and human geography jobs.

Section ❸ Assessment

ONLINE QUIZ
For test practice, go to
Interactive Review
@ ClassZone.com

TERMS & NAMES

1. Explain the importance of
- location analyst
- climatologist
- urban planner

USE YOUR READING NOTES

2. Categorize Use your completed web diagram to answer the following question:

In what ways could a business use the skills of a geographer?

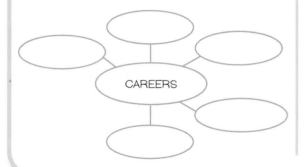

CAREERS

KEY IDEAS

3. What are three requirements for most careers in geography?

4. Who are the two major employers of geographers?

5. What questions do all types of geographers ask?

CRITICAL THINKING

6. Find Main Ideas How important are geographers to businesses?

7 Summarize How do you train for a geographer's job in business and government?

8. CONNECT to Today How do planners help governments with public projects?

9. WRITING Write a Job Description Select a specific job in the field of geography and research it on the Internet. Then write a description of the job's skill requirements and its responsibilities. If possible find a person doing that job and do an interview or have that person speak to the class.

Interactive ◀Review

Click here to complete these and other activities online @ ClassZone.com

CHAPTER SUMMARY

Key Idea 1
Geographers have specialized ways to view and interpret information about the world.

Key Idea 2
Geographers use technical tools to help them understand both the Earth's physical processes and the activities of people on Earth.

Key Idea 3
Geographers do many different kinds of jobs as they gather data and analyze and interpret it.

For **Review and Study Notes**, go to **Interactive Review** @ ClassZone.com

NAME GAME

Use the Terms & Names list to complete each sentence on paper or online.

1. I am a model of the Earth.
   _____ globe 🖑 _____

2. I am in orbit 100 miles above the Earth.
   _____

3. I am the study of people, places, and things. _____

4. I create plans for improving parts of a city.
   _____

5. I am an advanced technology tool used by geographers. _____

6. I am a representation of a part of the Earth.
   _____

7. I am a person who creates maps. _____

8. I am a group of places that have something in common. _____

9. I am a description of the physical and human characteristics of a location.
   _____

10. I am a person who maps and measures the land. _____

cartographer
climatologist
environment
Geographic Information Systems
geography
globe
Global Positioning System
Landsat
location analyst
map
spatial
surveyor
place
region
urban planner

Activities

Flip Cards

Use the online flip cards to quiz yourself on terms and names introduced in this chapter.

map

a representation of a part of the Earth

Crossword Puzzle

Complete an online crossword puzzle to test your knowledge of basic geographic terms.

ACROSS
1. a model of the Earth

VOCABULARY

Explain the significance of each of the following.

1. spatial
2. remote sensing
3. environment
4. database
5. geography

Explain how the terms and names in each group are related.

6. map, globe
7. map, cartographer
8. place, region
9. remote sensing, Landsat, Global Positioning System, Geographic Information System
10. cartographer, surveyor, climatologist, urban planner

KEY IDEAS

1 Themes and Elements of Geography

11. What are the three topics you study in geography?
12. Why is geography considered both science and social studies?
13. What is the difference between location and place?
14. What forces continually change Earth's surface?

2 Technology Tools for Geographers

15. What is remote sensing?
16. How do satellites aid in mapmaking?
17. What two basic geography questions does the Global Positioning System help you answer?
18. What is an example of a technologically advanced geographer's tool?

3 Careers in Geography

19. What is the main activity of a geographer's job?
20. What does a location analyst do?
21. What does an urban planner do?
22. What types of geography are included in physical geography?

CRITICAL THINKING

23. **Categorize** Create a table that lists the five themes of geography and shows two examples of geographic information that would be included in each theme's description.

FIVE THEMES	GEOGRAPHIC INFORMATION

24. **Find Main Ideas** How do people adapt to their physical world?
25. **Summarize** How does modern technology help geographers?
26. **Connect to Economics** What role do geographers play in business operations?
27. **Connect Geography & History** How does the study of geographic patterns help us to understand past events?
28. **Five Themes: Human-Environment Interaction** What can be learned about people by studying their interaction with the environment?

Answer the ESSENTIAL QUESTION

In what ways does geography help us understand our world?

Written Response Write a two- or three-paragraph response to the Essential Question. Be sure to consider the key ideas of each section as well as specific ideas about how geographers answer geographic questions. Use the rubric below to guide your thinking.

Response Rubric
A strong response will:
- discuss the two basic geographic questions
- identify and describe the five themes and six essential elements of geography

STANDARDS-BASED ASSESSMENT

POLITICAL MAP

Use the map to answer questions 1 and 2 on your paper.

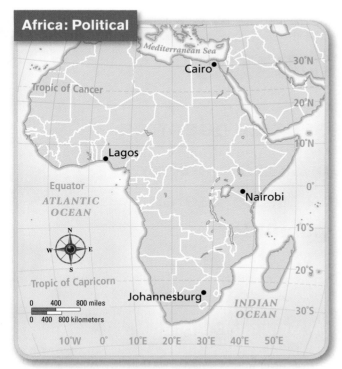

Africa: Political

1. Which of the cities shown on the map is located south of the Tropic of Capricorn?

A. Cairo
B. Johannesburg
C. Nairobi
D. Lagos

2. Which of the cities shown on the map is located at approximately 30° N and 31° E?

A. Cairo
B. Johannesburg
C. Nairobi
D. Lagos

CLIMATE GRAPH

Examine the climate graph below. Use the information in the graph to answer question 3 on your paper.

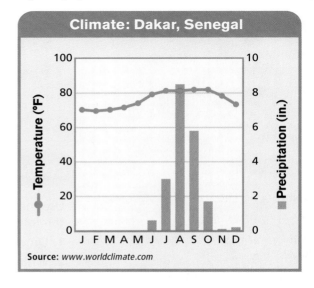

Climate: Dakar, Senegal

Source: www.worldclimate.com

3. In which months does Dakar get the most rainfall?

GeoActivity

1. INTERDISCIPLINARY ACTIVITY-TECHNOLOGY

With a small group, review new geographic technology. Choose one new tool to research further and create a museum-style display. Be sure your display shows the tool and how it works. Also, explain how the tool has changed the way geographic information is gathered.

2. WRITING FOR SOCIAL STUDIES

Imagine that you are an urban planner and have been asked to develop a plan for placement of a park in your city. Write one paragraph describing the location you chose and the reasons you selected it.

3. MENTAL MAPPING

Create an outline map of your neighborhood, city, or town and locate and label any of the following that are present in the area you map:

• physical features
• your home
• your school
• fire station
• hospital
• shopping area

CHAPTER
2

Earth's Interlocking Systems

ESSENTIAL QUESTION

How do Earth's physical systems make life on Earth possible?

CONNECT Geography & History

Use the map and the time line to answer the following questions.

1. On which plate does most of the United States sit?
2. Which event on the time line is supported by the evidence on this map?

1500

Geography
1883 Volcanic eruption destroys two-thirds of Krakatoa Island, Indonesia.

Geography
1620 English philosopher Francis Bacon suggests the continents were once a supercontinent. ▶

Animated GEOGRAPHY
Earth's Tectonic Plates

Click here to explore Earth and its systems @ ClassZone.com

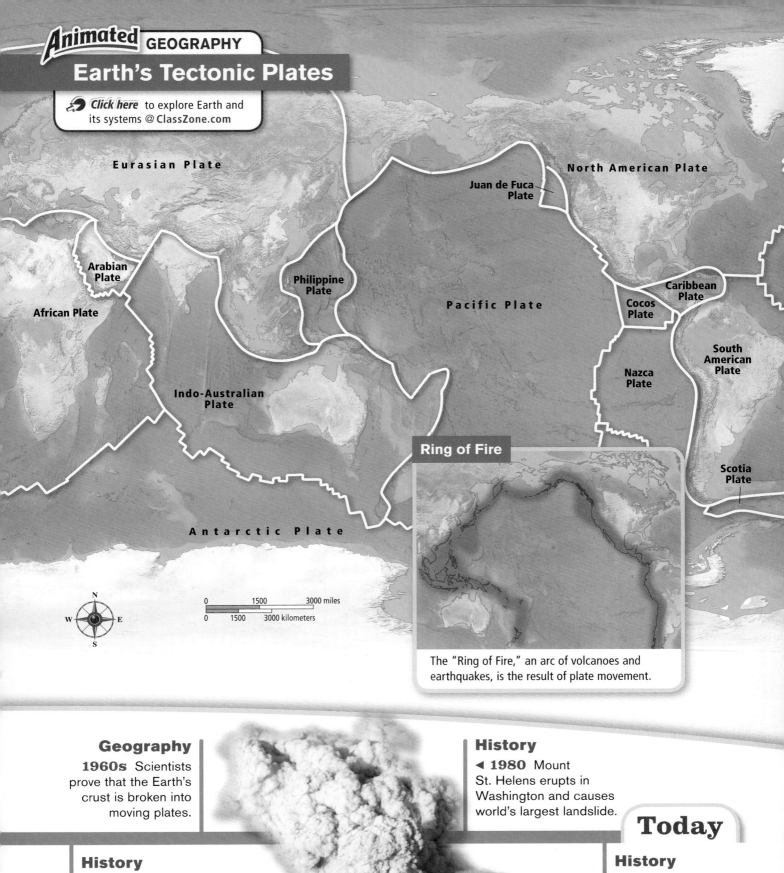

Eurasian Plate

North American Plate

Juan de Fuca Plate

Arabian Plate

Philippine Plate

African Plate

Pacific Plate

Caribbean Plate

Cocos Plate

South American Plate

Nazca Plate

Indo-Australian Plate

Scotia Plate

Antarctic Plate

Ring of Fire

The "Ring of Fire," an arc of volcanoes and earthquakes, is the result of plate movement.

N
W — E
S

0   1500   3000 miles
0   1500   3000 kilometers

Geography
1960s Scientists prove that the Earth's crust is broken into moving plates.

History
◄ **1980** Mount St. Helens erupts in Washington and causes world's largest landslide.

Today

History
1912 Continental drift theory proposed

History
2004 Indian Ocean earthquake and tsunami kill more than 280,000.

Reading for Understanding

▶ Key Ideas

BEFORE, YOU LEARNED

Geographers use technology to learn about physical processes on Earth.

NOW YOU WILL LEARN

The Earth is composed of many layers. Its surface continually changes because of the drifting of its plates.

▶ Vocabulary

TERMS & NAMES

magma molten rock

continent one of seven large landmasses on the Earth's surface

tectonic plate a large rigid section of the Earth's crust that is in constant motion

earthquake a sudden movement of the Earth's crust followed by a series of shocks

Ring of Fire a zone of volcanoes around the Pacific Ocean

volcano an opening in the Earth's crust from which molten rock, ash, and hot gases flow or are thrown out

weathering the gradual physical and chemical breakdown of rocks on the Earth's surface

erosion the wearing away and movement of weathered materials by water, wind, or ice

sediment pieces of rock in the form of sand, stone, or silt deposited by wind, water, or ice

glacier a large, slow-moving mass of ice

Visual Vocabulary glacier

▶ Reading Strategy

Re-create the chart shown at right. As you read and respond to the **KEY QUESTIONS**, use the chart to organize important details about the external and internal forces shaping the Earth.

 Skillbuilder Handbook, page R7

CATEGORIZE

INTERNAL FORCES	EXTERNAL FORCES
1.	1.
2.	2.
3.	3.
4.	4.

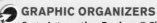 **GRAPHIC ORGANIZERS**
Go to **Interactive Review** @ ClassZone.com

Tectonic Plates The surface of the Earth is constantly moving and changing, even as you read this sentence. Geographers use technological tools to observe and measure forces deep inside the Earth and on the surface that reshape the Earth's crust.

Plate movement, earthquakes, and the activity of volcanoes are all internal forces that change the landscape. The Earth's crust is divided into a number of large rigid pieces called **tectonic plates**. These plates are shown on the map at the beginning of the chapter. The continents and oceans are located on these plates, which float on the magma of the Earth's mantle. Heated magma cools as it reaches the crust and then sinks downward. This process causes the magma to act like a conveyor belt under the plates. The plates move slowly against each other, at a rate of up to four inches a year. The plate movement can cause earthquakes and volcanic eruptions. There are four types of tectonic plate movements that are shown in the diagrams below. Each of the movements causes changes in the shape of Earth's crust.

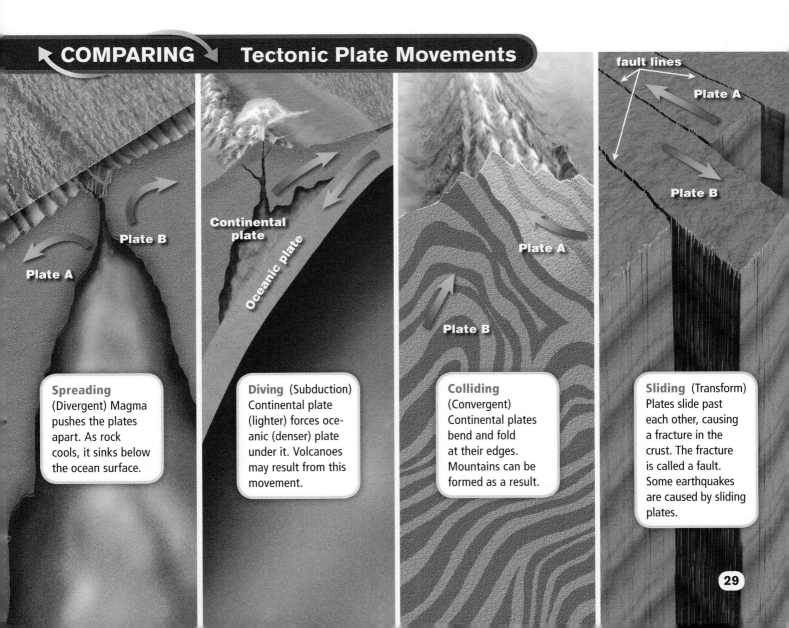

COMPARING ◄ Tectonic Plate Movements

fault lines

Plate A

Plate B

Plate B

Plate A

Continental plate

Oceanic plate

Plate A

Plate B

Spreading (Divergent) Magma pushes the plates apart. As rock cools, it sinks below the ocean surface.

Diving (Subduction) Continental plate (lighter) forces oceanic (denser) plate under it. Volcanoes may result from this movement.

Colliding (Convergent) Continental plates bend and fold at their edges. Mountains can be formed as a result.

Sliding (Transform) Plates slide past each other, causing a fracture in the crust. The fracture is called a fault. Some earthquakes are caused by sliding plates.

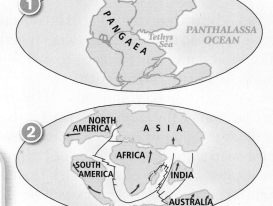

1 The world map at left shows the supercontinent of Pangaea about 200 million years ago as it begins to break apart.

2 This world map shows the Earth about 65 million years ago. Some of the modern-day continents are visible.

CONNECT Geography & History
Draw Conclusions Which continents were connected 65 million years ago?

Continental Drift If you look at the continents, they look like giant pieces of a jigsaw puzzle waiting to be fit together. Alfred Wegener, a German meteorologist, noticed this pattern. He believed that the continents were once part of a supercontinent called Pangaea (pan•JEE•uh). He suggested that Pangaea divided and drifted apart about 200 million years ago. It contained almost all of the landmasses on Earth and was surrounded by one vast ocean. When it began to break apart, its pieces slowly moved in different directions, and some formed the continents we now know. To this day, the continents continue to move.

▲ SUMMARIZE Explain how internal forces shape the Earth's surface.

Extreme Events

▼ KEY QUESTION How are earthquakes and volcanoes connected?

Two events caused by internal forces may dramatically reshape the Earth's surface—earthquakes and volcanic eruptions. Both can be deadly, and both have powerful effects on human life.

Earthquakes An **earthquake** is a sudden movement of the Earth's crust that is followed by a series of shocks. Huge rocks along a line where faults are located slide apart and break up, causing that area of the Earth's surface to shake. The stress in the rocks builds for years. Then, energy is swiftly released outward through the ground in vibrations called shock waves.

Earthquakes occur constantly. Some we may not feel, but scientific instruments record them. Some produce slight shock waves. Other earthquakes and their aftershocks cause major disasters. Buildings collapse, cities are destroyed, and thousands of lives may be lost. Fires, floods, landslides, and avalanches can also follow earthquakes.

Earthquakes may also be triggered by the explosive action of a volcano. Most of Earth's active volcanoes are located in a zone around the rim of the Pacific Ocean called the **Ring of Fire**. A number of tectonic plates meet in this zone, and many of the largest earthquakes in the world have occurred there.

One of the biggest earthquakes ever recorded took place near the coast of Indonesia in 2004. It occurred on the floor of the Indian Ocean where two tectonic plates meet. The quake produced a giant ocean wave called a tsunami (tsu•NAH•mee). Within hours, the tsunami had devastated the coasts of 12 countries in southern Asia and eastern Africa. Whole villages were swept away, and more than 280,000 people were killed.

Volcanoes A **volcano** is an opening in the Earth's crust from which molten rock, ash, and hot gases flow. Molten rock rises from the Earth's mantle and is stored in a chamber beneath the crust. Pressure builds and forces the molten rock, or lava, to erupt onto the Earth's surface, burning or burying anything it touches. The eruption may also throw large clouds of gases and ash into the atmosphere.

Some volcanoes erupt constantly. Others are inactive, but could erupt at some future time. The most destructive eruption in recorded history happened in 1883, when two-thirds of the Indonesian island of Krakatoa (KRAK•uh•TOH•uh) was blown apart. The most active volcano in the United States is Mount St. Helens in Washington. It blew its top off in 1980. Activity occurred again in 2005.

🔺 **UNDERSTAND CAUSES** Explain how earthquakes and volcanoes are connected.

CONNECT ➤ to Science

In a volcanic eruption, red-hot magma rises through cracks in the Earth's crust. Gases are released, causing a violent explosion of liquid rock, hot ash, and fiery gases into the air.

Kilauea, Hawaii

Activity
Make a Model of a Volcano
Materials
- small drink bottle (1/2 pint or 12 oz.)
- 1/4 cup of water
- a few drops of dishwashing detergent
- orange food coloring
- 1/4 cup vinegar
- 1 tablespoon baking soda
- a small square of tissue

1. Place the water, soap, food coloring, and vinegar in the bottle.

2. Wrap the baking soda in the tissue and drop the baking soda packet in the bottle. Watch the eruption.

External Forces Shaping the Earth

▼ **KEY QUESTION** What external forces shape the Earth?

External forces also reshape the Earth's surface. The two main external forces are weathering and erosion. **Weathering** is the gradual physical and chemical breakdown of rocks near or on the Earth's surface. **Erosion** is the wearing away and movement of weathered materials from one place to another by the action of water, wind, or ice. As you can see, weathering and erosion work together to shape the Earth.

Weathering Weathering occurs slowly, over many years or even centuries. The two types of weathering are mechanical weathering and chemical weathering. Mechanical weathering is a process in which rocks are broken down into smaller pieces by physical means. It takes place when ice, extremes of hot and cold, or even tree roots cause rocks to split apart. It also occurs when hard objects, such as other rocks or sand, scrape or rub against a rock, and pieces of the rock break off.

Chemical weathering is caused by chemical reactions between the minerals in the rock and elements in the air or water. This process changes the make-up of the rock itself. For example, most rocks contain iron. When iron comes in contact with water, it rusts, which helps to break down the rock. Water and elements in the air can cause other minerals in rocks to dissolve.

The Grand Canyon The Grand Canyon is located on the Colorado River in Arizona. It is an example of both weathering and erosion caused by wind and water.

UNITED STATES
Grand Canyon
ARIZONA
MEXICO

Erosion New landforms and new soil are formed by erosion. It occurs when materials loosened by weathering are moved by water, wind, or ice to new locations. Currents in streams and rivers pick up loose materials and deposit them downstream or carry them out to sea. These tiny pieces of rock, deposited by water, wind, or ice are called **sediment**. Sediment can be sand, stone, or finely ground particles called silt.

Wave action along coastlines carries rocks and sand from one place to another. Waves also pound boulders into smaller rocks. Wind erosion lifts particles from the Earth's surface and blows them great distances. The wind's actions can reshape rock surfaces. Arizona's Grand Canyon is a result of both wind and water erosion.

Another type of erosion is caused by glaciers. **Glaciers** are large, slow-moving masses of ice. They grind rocks and boulders underneath the ice and leave behind the rock when the ice melts. Parts of the central United States have been shaped by glacial erosion.

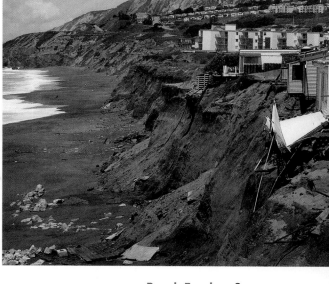

Beach Erosion Ocean waves and tides eroded this section of beach in California.

▲ **SYNTHESIZE** Explain how external forces shape the Earth's surface.

Section 1 Assessment

ONLINE QUIZ For test practice, go to **Interactive Review** @ ClassZone.com

TERMS & NAMES

1. Explain the importance of
- continent
- tectonic plate
- weathering
- erosion

USE YOUR READING NOTES

2. Categorize Use your completed chart to answer the following question:

Are external or internal forces responsible for volcanoes? Explain your answer.

INTERNAL FORCES	EXTERNAL FORCES
1.	1.
2.	2.
3.	3.
4.	4.

KEY IDEAS

3. What are the five layers that make up the Earth's interior and exterior?

4. How were the continents formed?

5. What are the two major external forces reshaping the Earth?

CRITICAL THINKING

6. Draw Conclusions How does the movement of wind, water, or ice reshape the Earth's surface?

7. Analyze Causes and Effects What is the relationship between plate movement, volcanoes, and earthquakes?

8. CONNECT to Today In which parts of the United States are external forces shaping the landscape?

9. ART Create a Puzzle Make a copy of a map of the world. Cut out the continents. Use the continents as puzzle pieces to form the continent of Pangaea. When you have finished putting the pieces together, draw an outline around the entire supercontinent.

Reading for Understanding

▶ Key Ideas

BEFORE, YOU LEARNED

Internal and external forces shape the surface of the Earth.

NOW YOU WILL LEARN

Interaction between landforms and bodies of water makes life on Earth possible.

▶ Vocabulary

TERMS & NAMES

drainage basin the area drained by a major river

ground water water found beneath the Earth's surface

hydrologic cycle the circulation of water between the Earth, the oceans, and the atmosphere

landform a feature on the Earth's surface formed by physical force

plateau a broad, flat area of land higher than the surrounding land

relief the difference in the elevation of a landform from its lowest point to its highest point

continental shelf the submerged land at the edge of a continent

BACKGROUND VOCABULARY

atmosphere the layer of gases that surround the Earth

Visual Vocabulary landform

▶ Reading Strategy

Re-create the web diagram shown at right. As you read and respond to the **KEY QUESTIONS**, use the diagram to organize important details about the Earth's landforms and bodies of water.

 See Skillbuilder Handbook, page R4

FIND MAIN IDEAS

WATER BODIES   LANDFORMS

🔁 **GRAPHIC ORGANIZERS**
Go to **Interactive Review** @ ClassZone.com

Bodies of Water and Landforms

Connecting to Your World

How important is water to your life and to life on Earth? Without enough usable water, there would be no life. The Earth is able to support plant and animal life because of its abundance of water. It appears to be the only planet in our solar system able to do so. The Earth is sometimes called the "blue planet" because bodies of water cover so much of its surface.

The Earth from Space

Bodies of Water

▼ **KEY QUESTION** What are the two types of water found on Earth?

Almost three-fourths of the surface of the Earth is covered by water. Most of the water—more than 97 percent of it—is salt water. This is the water in the oceans and seas. Only about 2.5 percent of the Earth's water is fresh water—that is, water containing little or no salt.

Fresh Water Most fresh water is locked in frozen form in ice caps or glaciers. Much of the rest is found in rivers, streams, and lakes.

Iguacu Falls This series of 275 falls is located between Brazil and Argentina.

BRAZIL
Iguacu Falls
ARGENTINA

The Great Salt Lake This huge lake in northern Utah covers about 1,700 square miles. It is a remnant, or remainder, of a huge ancient fresh water lake called Lake Bonneville. That lake existed around 14,000 years ago and was about ten times as large as the Great Salt Lake. As the climate became drier and warmer over the centuries, Lake Bonneville's waters began to evaporate. But the salt it contained did not. That's why the Great Salt Lake is one of the saltiest bodies of water in the world.

CRITICAL THINKING

Summarize How did freshwater Lake Bonneville become the Great Salt Lake?

Russia's Lake Baikal, for example, is the world's largest lake and contains 20 percent of all Earth's fresh water. Rivers and streams move water downhill to or from larger bodies of water. Smaller streams and rivers that flow into a major river are called tributaries. The region drained by a river and its tributaries is called a **drainage basin**. The Amazon River system in South America is the world's largest drainage basin.

Some fresh water, called **ground water**, is found beneath the Earth's surface. This water is held in the pores and cracks of rocks and can be pumped from the ground.

Salt Water The water in the Earth's oceans and seas is called salt water because it contains a small percentage of dissolved minerals and chemical compounds called salts. Actually, all of the oceans and seas are part of the same body of water, which is divided by the continents. Geographers gave names to the different areas of the oceans.

The Earth's oceans are the Pacific, Atlantic, Indian, and Arctic, and the Southern Ocean, which is the body of water around Antarctica. The Pacific Ocean is the largest and covers almost one-third of the Earth. A body of salt water that is completely or partly enclosed by land is called a sea. An example is the Mediterranean Sea. Oceans and seas are sources of food, energy, and minerals and are used for transportation and recreation. They also help to distribute Earth's heat.

▲ **COMPARE** Compare the two types of water on the Earth.

Hydrologic Cycle

The Earth's water is renewed by a never-ending process called the hydrologic cycle, or water cycle. The **hydrologic cycle** is the circulation of water between the Earth, the oceans, and the atmosphere. Approximately 119,000 cubic miles of water evaporates into the atmosphere each year. The **atmosphere** is the layer of gases that surround the Earth.

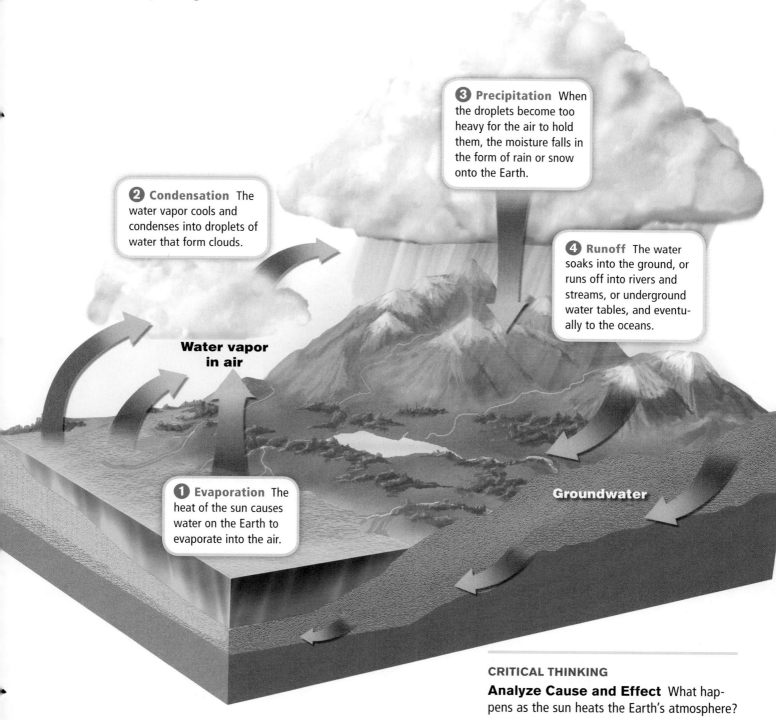

3 Precipitation When the droplets become too heavy for the air to hold them, the moisture falls in the form of rain or snow onto the Earth.

2 Condensation The water vapor cools and condenses into droplets of water that form clouds.

4 Runoff The water soaks into the ground, or runs off into rivers and streams, or underground water tables, and eventually to the oceans.

Water vapor in air

1 Evaporation The heat of the sun causes water on the Earth to evaporate into the air.

Groundwater

CRITICAL THINKING
Analyze Cause and Effect What happens as the sun heats the Earth's atmosphere?

Landforms

▼ **KEY QUESTION** How are landforms created?

Features on the Earth's surface formed by physical forces are called **landforms**. Landforms are produced by the internal and external forces that reshape the Earth. Internal forces push, move, and raise up parts of the Earth's crust. The result is the creation of new rock formations, such as mountains. External forces wear down these formations and transport the eroded materials to other locations. The eroded materials then become new landforms. These processes take a long time, but they are constantly at work. The location and size of landforms often affect where people choose to live.

Many of the same landforms found on dry land are also found under water. Those on the land are called continental landforms. Those on the sea floor are called oceanic landforms.

Continental Landforms The major continental landforms are mountains, hills, plains, and plateaus. A **plateau** is a broad area of land higher than the surrounding land. The same landforms are found on all of the continents. In fact, satellite photographs show a pattern on most continents: wide plains in the center and a narrow belt of mountains near the edge of the continent, where tectonic plates collide. For example, the landscape of the United States has the Rocky Mountains and coastal mountains in the west, the Appalachian Mountains in the east, and the Great Plains in the center.

The difference in the elevation of a landform from its lowest point to its highest point is called **relief**. Mountains show great relief compared to plains and plateaus. Many of the maps in this book have a relief indicator to show these differences in elevation.

Oceanic Landforms The landforms on the ocean floor are like an invisible landscape. Most cannot be seen from the surface of the water. But high mountains, vast plains, deep valleys, and coral reefs are present under the water's surface. Some are the result of the same tectonic forces that shape the continental landforms. The submerged

Monument Valley, Arizona In this photograph, you can see dramatic examples of relief between the floor of the valley and the tops of the landforms.

land at the edge of a continent is called the **continental shelf**. It slopes downward and then descends to the deep part of the ocean. On the deep ocean floor are volcanoes, mountain chains, plains, and trenches. These landforms are created by the movement of tectonic plates, the same forces as those on the continent.

Some of the oceanic landforms are pushed up above the water and become islands. Many islands, such as the Hawaiian Islands, are formed by volcanic action. Other islands are formed from coral reefs. However, all islands are subject to the same external forces that wear down landforms on the continent. These forces include the weathering and erosion caused by wind, water, and ice.

Indian Ocean Reef
A diver views plant and animal life on a coral reef.

 SUMMARIZE Explain how landforms are created.

Section ② Assessment

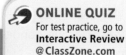 **ONLINE QUIZ**
For test practice, go to
Interactive Review
@ ClassZone.com

TERMS & NAMES

1. Explain the importance of
• hydrologic cycle
• landform
• relief
• continental shelf

USE YOUR READING NOTES

2. Find Main Ideas Use your completed web diagram to answer the following question:

How is it possible for the oceans to have landforms?

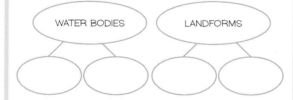

KEY IDEAS

3. How much water on the Earth's surface is fresh water?

4. What are the four components that keep the hydrologic cycle going?

5. What are the major continental landforms?

CRITICAL THINKING

6. Find Main Ideas Why are oceans important to life on Earth?

7. Compare and Contrast How are continental and oceanic landforms the same? different?

8. CONNECT to Today In what ways does water affect your daily life?

9. TECHNOLOGY Make a Multimedia Presentation Plan a slide show about the hydrologic cycle. Sketch each step in the cycle and explain what is happening.

▶ Key Ideas

BEFORE, YOU LEARNED

The Earth's surface is covered with both continental and oceanic landforms. The hydrologic cycle circulates the water.

NOW YOU WILL LEARN

The Earth's rotation and revolution influence weather, climate, and living conditions on Earth.

▶ Vocabulary

TERMS & NAMES

solstice the time during the year when the sun reaches the farthest northern or southern point in the sky

equinox one of the two times a year when the sun's rays are over the equator and days and night around the world are equal in length

weather the condition of the Earth's atmosphere at a given time and place

climate the typical weather conditions of a region over a long period of time

precipitation falling water droplets in the form of rain, snow, sleet, or hail

vegetation region an area that has similar plants

savanna a vegetation region with a mix of grassland and scattered trees

desert a region with plants specially adapted to dry conditions

Visual Vocabulary desert

▶ Reading Strategy

Re-create the diagram shown at right. As you read and respond to the **KEY QUESTONS**, use the diagram to help you summarize information about the world's climate and vegetation.

 See Skillbuilder Handbook, page R5

SUMMARIZE

CLIMATE

VEGETATION

GRAPHIC ORGANIZERS
Go to **Interactive Review** @ ClassZone.com

Climate and Vegetation

Connecting to Your World

Every moment in the day, weather and climate are a part of your life. They affect what clothes you wear and how you get to school. You might walk or ride your bike if it is not too cold or too wet. But if it's raining or snowing you may go in a car or by bus. Some school activities, like sports, depend on weather and climate, too. In fact, weather and climate affect plant and animal life and nearly every human activity.

Inupiat Woman
The harsh climate of the Arctic makes wearing a fur parka necessary.

The Earth's Rotation and Revolution

 KEY QUESTION How does Earth's revolution affect seasons?

The Earth rotates as it revolves around the sun. Rotation is the motion of the Earth as it spins on its axis once every 24 hours. Revolution is the motion of the Earth as it circles, or makes a year-long orbit, of the sun.

Earth's Movement The Earth is tilted at a 23.5° angle. The Earth's revolution around the sun affects patterns of Earth's weather and climate. The Earth's tilt stays the same as it revolves around the sun. As a result, different parts of the Earth get direct rays from the sun for more hours of the day at certain times of the year. This causes the changing seasons.

Midnight Sun in the Arctic Multiple exposures show the position of the sun over a 24-hour period in the Arctic summer.

ARCTIC OCEAN

ARCTIC CIRCLE

ALASKA

Earth's Revolution
The seasons are related to the Earth's tilt and revolution around the sun.

CRITICAL THINKING
Compare and Contrast Which part of the Earth's surface doesn't experience seasons?

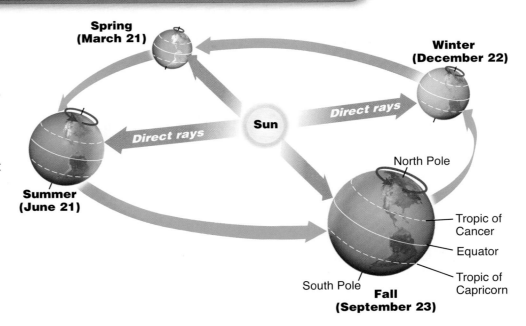

Spring (March 21)

Winter (December 22)

Direct rays

Sun

Direct rays

Summer (June 21)

North Pole

Tropic of Cancer

Equator

Tropic of Capricorn

South Pole

Fall (September 23)

Seasons The term **solstice** is used to describe the time during the year when the sun reaches the farthest northern or southern point in the sky. In the Northern Hemisphere, the summer solstice is the longest day of the year and begins summer. The winter solstice is the shortest day of the year and begins winter. These dates are reversed in the Southern Hemisphere. The beginning of spring and autumn start on the **equinox**. On these two days, the sun's rays are directly over the equator, and days and nights around the world are equal in length. The Earth's revolution brings the temperature and weather changes we call seasons to many parts of the Earth. But in some regions there is little change. The illustration above shows the position of the Earth at the start of the four seasons in the Northern Hemisphere.

▲ **SUMMARIZE** What causes seasons on Earth?

Weather and Climate

▼ **KEY QUESTION** What is the difference between weather and climate?

People often confuse weather and climate. **Weather** is the condition of the Earth's atmosphere at a given time and place. For example, today may be sunny and warm. **Climate** is the term for the typical weather conditions of a certain region over a long period of time.

Causes of Weather Several factors interact to cause weather at a particular location. They include solar energy, wind, landforms, bodies of water, water vapor, cloud cover, and elevation. The combination of all these factors varies from location to location, creating local weather conditions.

The most important weather factor is the amount of energy, in the form of heat from the sun, that a location receives. This is why, for example, the time of year influences the weather. In summer, much more solar energy is found in the atmosphere, and weather conditions change. Winds move the solar energy and moisture that air holds across the Earth. Also, land heats and cools more quickly than bodies of water do. So land located near a body of water has a different weather pattern from locations further inland.

Clouds and water vapor are connected to each other in weather patterns. Clouds hold water vapor in the atmosphere. Water vapor determines whether there will be **precipitation**, which is falling water droplets in the form of rain, snow, sleet, or hail.

Finally, as elevation above sea level rises, air becomes thinner and loses its ability to hold moisture, so it becomes cooler. The temperature drops by about 3.5°F for every 1,000-foot increase in elevation. So, you can find ice and snow on the tops of mountains even at the equator.

Causes of Climate There are many different climates around the world. A place's location on the Earth, especially its latitude, is important in determining climate. For example, climates are warmer near the equator and colder near the poles.

Wind and ocean currents help distribute the sun's heat from one part of the world to another. Ocean currents are like rivers flowing through the ocean. They move warm waters away from the equator and cold water from the poles. Air currents blowing over the ocean waters pick up heat and moisture and move them to other parts of the Earth.

▲ **COMPARE** Explain the difference between weather and climate.

Fun Facts!

IT'S RAINING FROGS!

Yes, it's true—there are recorded instances of frogs raining down on the Earth, most recently in Serbia in 2005. The most logical explanation is a strong wind that can suck light objects out of the water and later deposit them somewhere else.

In 1981, a city in southern Greece experienced a rain of frogs that landed in trees and in the streets. The species of frog was native to North Africa. That's one strong wind!

Climate and Vegetation Regions

▼ **KEY QUESTION** What are climate and vegetation regions?

To categorize climate regions, geographers divide the Earth into three general zones of latitude: tropical, middle, and high. These zones are found on both sides of the equator. Tropical latitudes are found between the equator and Tropic of Cancer and between the equator and the Tropic of Capricorn where it is usually hot. Middle latitudes extend from the tropic lines to the lines of the Arctic and Antarctic circles. High latitude refers to the cold areas around the North and South Poles.

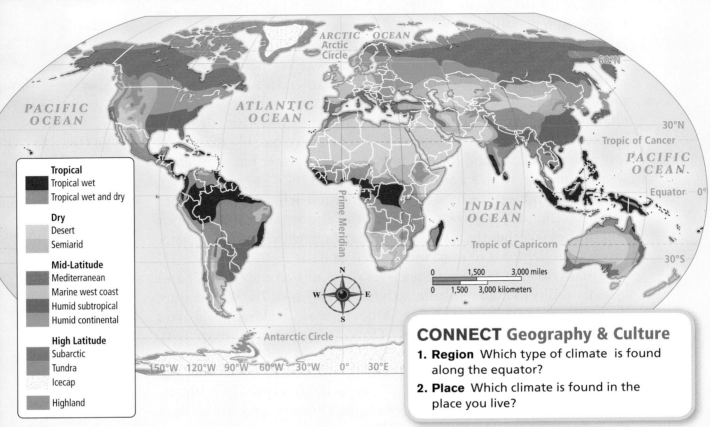

Tropical
- Tropical wet
- Tropical wet and dry

Dry
- Desert
- Semiarid

Mid-Latitude
- Mediterranean
- Marine west coast
- Humid subtropical
- Humid continental

High Latitude
- Subarctic
- Tundra
- Icecap

- Highland

CONNECT Geography & Culture

1. **Region** Which type of climate is found along the equator?
2. **Place** Which climate is found in the place you live?

	TYPES	CHARACTERISTICS	VEGETATION
TROPICAL	Tropical Wet	rainy all year round	broadleaf trees
	Tropical Wet and Dry	has a rainy season	grasslands and savanna
DRY	Desert	less than 10 inches of precipitation	specially adapted plants
	Semiarid	up to 20 inches of rain	grasslands called steppe
MID-LATITUDE	Mediterranean	wet winter	plants that have adapted to a dry season in the summer
	Marine West Coast	rainy year round	mixed forests of broadleaf and needleleaf trees or only needleleaf trees
	Humid Subtropical	long, hot, humid summers	
	Humid Continental	wide range of summer and winter temperatures	grasslands and savanna
HIGH LATITUDE	Subarctic	cold dry climate	specially adapted plants
	Tundra	permanent ice and snow	specially adapted plants
	Icecap	permanent ice and snow	none
HIGHLAND	Varies with latitude, elevation, and continental location		

Climate Regions As you can see on the map on the opposite page, the Earth has five general climate regions: tropical, mid-latitude, high latitude, dry, and highland. Tropical climates are always hot and can be rainy most of the year or only during one season. The middle latitudes have the greatest variety of climates, ranging from hot and humid to cool and fairly dry. Climates along the oceans are also included in this category. High latitude climates are cool to cold all year long. Dry climates can be found in every latitude region. Highland climates are based on the elevation of a particular place. So, for example, as you go up a mountain, the climate may change from warm to cooler to cold.

Vegetation Regions The term **vegetation region** refers to an area that has similar plants. A vegetation region is named for the types of trees, grasslands, and specially adapted plants found there. The four basic types of vegetation are: forest, savanna, grasslands, and desert. Forests can be cold, tropical, or temperate. **Savanna** is a mix of grasslands and trees. Grasslands can have short or tall grasses, depending on the amount of rain. Finally, a **desert**—which can be hot or cold—has plants specially adapted to very dry conditions.

 SUMMARIZE Identify the five main climate regions.

Section 3 Assessment

 ONLINE QUIZ
For test practice, go to **Interactive Review** @ ClassZone.com

TERMS & NAMES

1. Explain the importance of
- weather
- climate
- precipitation
- vegetation region

USE YOUR READING NOTES

2. Summarize Use your completed chart to answer the following question:

What are the basic causes of weather and which factor is the most important?

KEY IDEAS

3. What causes the changing seasons?

4. What are the causes of climate?

5. How are vegetation regions named?

CRITICAL THINKING

6. Analyze Causes and Effects Why are the seasons reversed in the Northern and Southern Hemispheres?

7. Draw Conclusions How does location affect climate and vegetation?

8. CONNECT to Today What weather conditions have caused problems in the United States recently?

9. WRITING Write a Description Determine what climate and vegetation region you live in. Then write a paragraph describing the climate features and types of vegetation.

Click here to enter the rain forest
@ ClassZone.com

AMAZON RAIN FOREST

The Amazon rain forest is one of the world's most important physical features. It acts as the "lungs of the planet" by producing oxygen, and is the home of millions of plants and animals.

Click here to learn more about this frog and the amazing diversity of plants and animals in the forest.

Click here to see Yanamamö village life in the rain forest and learn about how the Yanamamö interact with the forest.

Click here to see the methods scientists are using to study plants and animals in the rain forest.

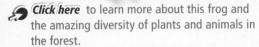

The Disappearing Amazon Rain Forest

Remaining Area of Rain Forest

89% 88% 86% 84% 81%

| 1980 | 1990 | 1995 | 2000 | 2005 |

Source: Brazilian National Institute of Space Research

GeoActivity

Plan a Scientific Study
With a small group, plan the scientific study of one of the plants or animals in the picture. Identify the subject you wish to study. Talk about what information you want to find. Then write questions that would help you track down that information.

Reading for Understanding

► Key Ideas

BEFORE, YOU LEARNED

Many different physical systems influence the way we live on Earth.

NOW YOU WILL LEARN

Human interference with physical systems can cause problems with the environment.

► Vocabulary

TERMS & NAMES

global warming an increase in the average temperature of the Earth's atmosphere

greenhouse effect the trapping of the sun's heat by gases in the Earth's atmosphere

greenhouse gas any gas in the atmosphere that contributes to the greenhouse effect

fossil fuels fuels such as coal, oil, and natural gas

desertification the process in which farmland becomes less productive because the land is degraded

sustainable using natural resources in a way that they exist for future generations

BACKGROUND VOCABULARY

carbon dioxide a gas composed of carbon and oxygen

emissions substances discharged into the air

degraded of lower quality

Visual Vocabulary desertification

► Reading Strategy

Re-create the chart shown at right. As you read and respond to the **KEY QUESTIONS**, use the chart to compare and contrast details about environmental challenges the world faces.

 Skillbuilder Handbook, page R9

COMPARE AND CONTRAST

GLOBAL WARMING	DESERTIFICATION

 GRAPHIC ORGANIZERS
Go to **Interactive Review** @ ClassZone.com

Environmental Challenges

Connecting to Your World

Have your parents or other adults ever told you that the climate seems to be changing? Maybe they said something like, "We never had hurricanes or tornados like these when I was a kid." They could be right—climates do change. Some changes take place naturally over many years, such as the build-up of ice during ice ages. But recently, scientists have noticed rapid climate changes that some believe is the result of human activity.

Global Warming

🔻 **KEY QUESTION** How are global warming and the greenhouse effect related?

Global warming and desertification are two possible threats to the environment. **Global warming** is an increase in the average temperature of the Earth's atmosphere. It refers to an increase large enough to cause changes in the Earth's overall climate. The Earth's average temperature has risen between 0.9 and 1.3°F since the late 1800s. Many scientists think that temperatures may rise another 2.5 to 10.4°F by the end of the century. Some scientists believe that this warming is part of the larger cycle of warm and cold periods in the Earth's history. Others suspect that it is caused by humans.

Dori, Burkina Faso Changes in the climate have caused drought in this region, leading to fewer crops.

AFRICA

BURKINA FASO

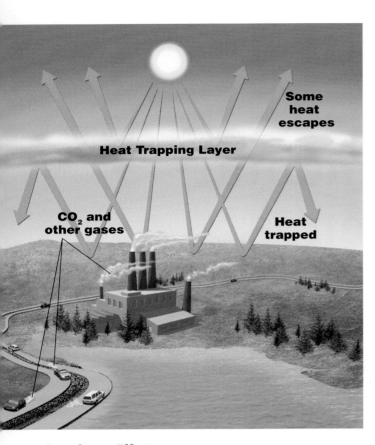

The Greenhouse Effect The trapping of the sun's heat by gases in the Earth's atmosphere is called the **greenhouse effect**. These gases act like the glass roof of a greenhouse. They let in solar energy, which heats up the planet, but they trap much of the heat that rises from the Earth's surface. So, the Earth becomes warmer. Some greenhouse effect is necessary. Without it, you would be living on a freezing cold planet. The temperature would be about zero degrees Fahenheit.

Any gas in the atmosphere that contributes to the greenhouse effect is called a **greenhouse gas**. Greenhouse gases include water vapor and **carbon dioxide**, a gas composed of carbon and oxygen. The burning of **fossil fuels**, such as coal, oil, and natural gas, has caused an increase in carbon dioxide in the atmosphere. As this gas builds in the atmosphere, the atmosphere becomes warmer and speeds up the heating effect.

Greenhouse Effect
Trapped gases and heat combine to change the Earth's temperature. **How do humans add to the greenhouse effect?**

The Impact on the Climate In theory, a more intense greenhouse effect could change the Earth's climate. Warmer temperatures could cause the ice caps and glaciers around the world to melt and sea levels to rise. Flooding could occur along coastal regions. Global land-use patterns would change. Some crops would no longer grow in certain areas. Some areas would become hotter and drier, with extreme heat waves, droughts, and more forest fires. These changes would alter the fragile relationships between living things and the environment.

Solutions Lowering the levels of greenhouse gases is a complex, worldwide goal. Some nations generate huge amounts of greenhouse gases. These gases affect not only those nations, but also the whole planet. So, humans need to take steps to reduce the levels of greenhouse gases. One solution might be to build more energy-efficient cars and factories. Another could be to use alternative energy sources such as energy produced by the sun, or the internal heat of the Earth.

In 1997, nations from around the world gathered at Kyoto, Japan, to discuss plans to reduce greenhouse gases. The result of their meeting was an agreement to cut emissions of carbon dioxide and other greenhouse gases. (**Emissions** are substances discharged into the air.) The agreement, called the Kyoto Protocol, went into effect in 2005.

🔺 **SUMMARIZE** Explain how global warming takes place.

Desertification

▼ **KEY QUESTION** What causes desertification?

Desertification is the process in which farmland becomes less productive because the land is **degraded**. The land becomes more desert-like, that is, dry and unproductive. Desertification is a serious problem because it turns arid and semiarid areas into nonproductive wasteland. Each year, about 25,000 square miles of land—an area the size of West Virginia—is degraded. This process is happening in many parts of the world, including Africa, China, and the American West.

Causes and Effects In desertification, natural vegetation is removed or destroyed, and soil is exposed to wind. Without shade from the sun, the moisture in the soil evaporates more quickly. The dry top layers of soil particles then blow away. The soil becomes less able to support plant life. The loss of moisture and plants may in itself cause more desertification. But destructive practices in arid and semiarid regions have speeded up the process. Some of these practices are

> **overgrazing** allowing animals to graze so much that plants are unable to grow back

> **cultivation of marginal land** planting crops on fragile soil

> **deforestation** cutting down trees and not replanting new trees

ONLINE PRIMARY SOURCE To read more of Wangari Maathai's writing, go to the **Research & Writing Center** @ClassZone.com

ANALYZING Primary Sources

Wangari Maathai (born 1940) won the 2004 Nobel Peace Prize for her work fighting deforestation in Africa. To combat desertification, she founded the Green Belt Movement, which has planted 30 million trees across Africa, including her native Kenya.

> [The Green Belt Movement] encourages women to create jobs, prevent soil loss, slow the process of desertification and [to] plant and to eat indigenous [local] food crops.
>
> Source: Speech to the 4th United Nations World Women's Conference, Beijing, China, 1995

DOCUMENT-BASED QUESTION
What is the goal of the Green Belt Movement?

CONNECT → Geography & Culture

Green Belt Movement

The Green Belt Movement, founded by Wangari Maathai in Kenya in 1977, is an example of a program of sustainable development. It started out as a jobs program to pay rural and urban women to plant trees. But it soon became a movement to improve the environment, slow deforestation, and halt desertification.

Solutions There are different solutions to the growing problem of desertification. Each depends on the underlying cause. Some simple solutions are to build sand fences that interrupt the wind, or to use straw mats to reduce evaporation so young plants can take root. Still another is to use solar ovens in place of open fires that require firewood. Planting tree fences and grass belts also reduces the spread of sandy areas. This practice is being used in China and Africa today.

Solutions like the ones above are examples of sustainable practices. **Sustainable** means that these practices use natural resources in such a way as to ensure that they exist for future generations. Sustainable practices work with the environment to protect the land, preserve wildlife, and repair the damage that has been done to it. The practices allow people to live a better life and ensure that resources will be available both now and in the future.

 DRAW CONCLUSIONS Explain what causes desertification.

Section 4 Assessment

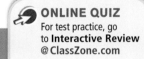
ONLINE QUIZ For test practice, go to **Interactive Review** @ ClassZone.com

TERMS & NAMES

1. Explain the importance of
- global warming
- greenhouse effect
- desertification
- sustainable

USE YOUR READING NOTES

2. Compare and Contrast Use your completed chart to answer the following question:

How does the greenhouse effect contribute to global warming?

GLOBAL WARMING	DESERTIFICATION

KEY IDEAS

3. Why is global warming a problem?

4. What are greenhouse gases?

5. What are three simple solutions to controlling desertification?

CRITICAL THINKING

6. Evaluate Which environmental problem, global warming or desertification, is a greater threat to the Earth? Why?

7. Summarize How does deforestation cause desertification?

8. CONNECT to Today What might happen if more gasoline-powered motor vehicles were used around the world?

9. MATH Make a Chart Use the Internet to find information about desertification. Then make a chart that shows locations and the percentage of land that has been degraded.

CHAPTER SUMMARY

Key Idea 1
The Earth is composed of many layers, and its surface continually changes because of the drifting of the continents.

Key Idea 2
Interaction between landforms and bodies of water makes life on Earth possible.

Key Idea 3
The Earth's rotation and revolution influence weather, climate, and living conditions on Earth.

Key Idea 4
Human interference with physical systems causes problems with the environment.

For **Review and Study Notes**, go to **Interactive Review** @ ClassZone.com

NAME GAME

Use the Terms & Names list to complete each sentence on paper or online.

1. I am the hot metal center of the Earth. _____core_____

2. I am a naturally formed feature on the Earth's surface. _____

3. I fall in the form of rain, snow, sleet, or hail. _____

4. I am an increase in the Earth's temperature. _____

5. I move weathered materials from one place to another. _____

6. I am the trapping of the sun's heat by gases in the atmosphere. _____

7. I am a large rigid piece of the Earth's crust that is in motion. _____

8. I am typical weather conditions over a period of time. _____

9. I circulate water between the Earth, oceans, and atmosphere. _____

10. I am plants that grow in a region. _____

climate
core
desertification
erosion
global warming
greenhouse effect
hydrologic cycle
landform
magma
precipitation
relief
sediment
tectonic plate
vegetation
weather

Activities

Flip Cards

Use the online flip cards to quiz yourself on terms and names introduced in this chapter.

magma

melted or liquid rock

Crossword Puzzle

Complete an online crossword puzzle to test your knowledge of Earth's physical systems.

ACROSS

1. a naturally formed feature on the Earth's surface

VOCABULARY

Explain the significance of each of the following.

1. tectonic plate
2. greenhouse effect
3. hydrologic cycle
4. global warming
5. desertification

Explain how the terms and names in each group are related.

6. magma, crust, and continent
7. weathering, erosion, and desertification
8. hydrologic cycle, precipitation, and atmosphere
9. greenhouse gas and global warming
10. vegetation and climate

KEY IDEAS

1 The Earth and Its Forces

11. What is the continental drift theory?
12. What are the four types of tectonic plate movements?
13. How do weathering and erosion reshape the Earth's surface?

2 Bodies of Water and Landforms

14. Why is the Earth sometimes called the "blue planet"?
15. What are the names of the world's five oceans?
16. What two general features do most continents have in common?

3 Climate and Vegetation

17. What are the two motions of the Earth in relation to the sun?
18. What are the four factors that influence climate?
19. What are the basic types of vegetation?

4 Environmental Challenges

20. What happens to the sun's heat in the greenhouse effect?
21. What are two alternative energy sources?
22. What are three areas of the world that have a serious problem with desertification?

CRITICAL THINKING

23. **Analyze Cause and Effect** Create a web diagram to show the effects of global warming. List at least five effects caused by a more intense greenhouse effect.

EFFECTS OF GLOBAL WARMING

24. **Summarize** Why are so many earthquakes and volcanoes found near the Ring of Fire?
25. **Draw Conclusions** Why is the surface of the Earth constantly changing?
26. **Connect to Economics** What are the economic costs of earthquakes or volcanoes?
27. **Five Themes: Human-Environment Interaction** What steps have been taken to control global warming?
28. **Connect Geography & Culture** Why might the location and size of landforms affect where people live?

Answer the ESSENTIAL QUESTION

How do Earth's physical systems make life on Earth possible?

Written Response Write a two- or three-paragraph response to the Essential Question. Be sure to consider the key ideas of each section as well as ways in which the systems interlock. Use the rubric below to guide your thinking.

Response Rubric
A strong response will:
- discuss how the hydrologic cycle makes human occupation of the Earth possible
- describe the causes of weather and climate
- explain how the above systems affect humans

✓ Test Practice

• Online Test Practice @ ClassZone.com
• Test-Taking Strategies and Practice
  at the front of this book

THEMATIC MAP

Use the map to answer questions 1 and 2 on your paper.

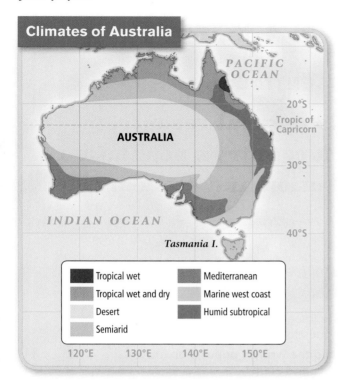

Climates of Australia

PACIFIC OCEAN

AUSTRALIA

20°S
Tropic of Capricorn

30°S

INDIAN OCEAN

40°S

Tasmania I.

- Tropical wet
- Tropical wet and dry
- Desert
- Semiarid
- Mediterranean
- Marine west coast
- Humid subtropical

120°E   130°E   140°E   150°E

1. Which climate takes up the largest portion of Australia?

A. Desert
B. Mediterranean
C. Semiarid
D. Tropical wet and dry

2. In which part of Australia would you find a tropical wet climate?

A. northwestern
B. northeastern
C. southwestern
D. southeastern

CHART

Study the chart below. Use the information in the chart to answer questions 3 and 4.

Deadliest Earthquakes 1975 to 2005		
Country	**Year**	**Deaths**
Indonesia	2004	283,106
China	1976	255,000
Pakistan	2005	80,361
Iran	1990	40,000
Iran	2003	26,200
Armenia	1988	25,000
Guatemala	1976	23,000
India	2001	20,230
Turkey	1999	17,119

Source: USGS Earthquake Hazards Program

3. Which country has experienced the greatest number of deadly earthquakes?

4. In what year did the single most deadly earthquake strike?

GeoActivity

1. INTERDISCIPLINARY ACTIVITY–SCIENCE

Select one of the Earth's major mountain chains and illustrate its creation on a poster. Be sure the poster shows the plates involved, the direction of the collision, and the name of the mountains that were formed.

2. WRITING FOR SOCIAL STUDIES

Review the illustration of the Earth's interior in Section 1. Write a one-paragraph description that would help a younger student understand the layers of the Earth's interior.

3. MENTAL MAPPING

Create an outline map of the world and label the following:

- the seven continents
- the five oceans

CHAPTER 3 Human Geography

1 GEOGRAPHY

The Geography of Population

2 CULTURE

Why People Move

3 ECONOMICS

Resources and Economics

4 GOVERNMENT

Why We Need Government

ESSENTIAL QUESTION

How do natural resources affect a country's population distribution and economy?

CONNECT ↻ **Geography & History**

Use the satellite image and the time line to answer the following questions.

1. How much did the world's population grow between 1 A.D. and 2000?

2. How different would this image have appeared when the population of the world hit one billion?

1000 B.C.

History
◀ **1000 B.C.** Bantu migrations in Africa

Geography
1 A.D. Total world population hits 300 million.

History
180 Roman Empire at its peak ▶

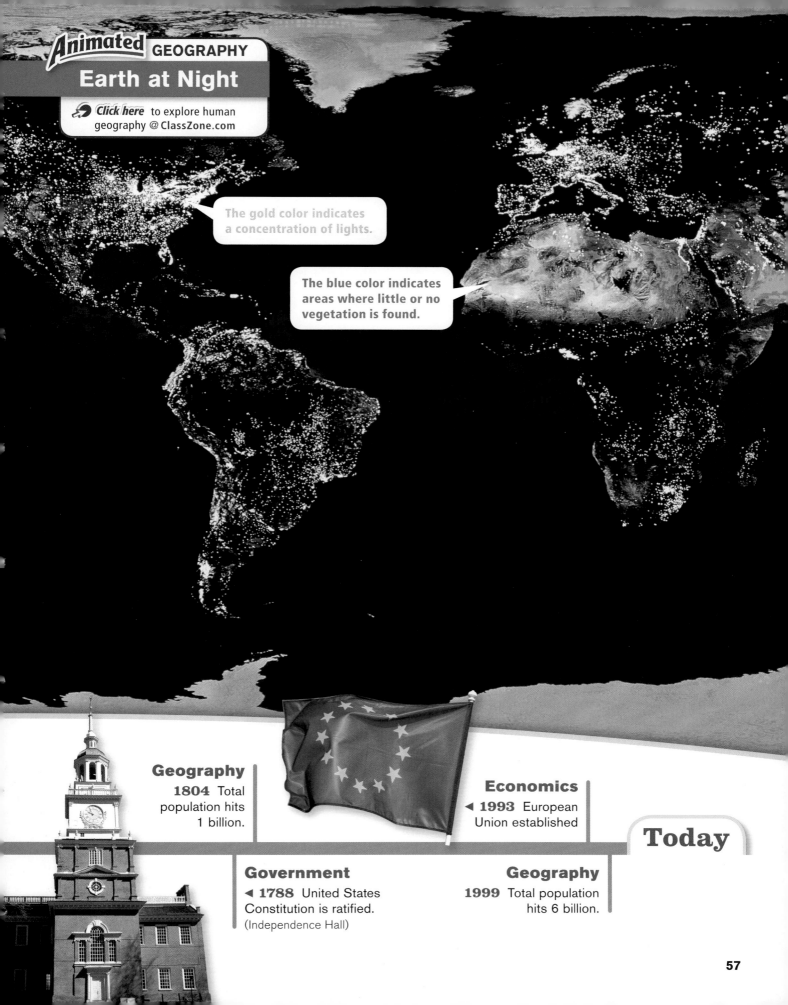

Animated GEOGRAPHY
Earth at Night

Click here to explore human geography @ ClassZone.com

The gold color indicates a concentration of lights.

The blue color indicates areas where little or no vegetation is found.

Geography
1804 Total population hits 1 billion.

Economics
◄ 1993 European Union established

Today

Government
◄ 1788 United States Constitution is ratified.
(Independence Hall)

Geography
1999 Total population hits 6 billion.

Reading for Understanding

▶ Key Ideas

BEFORE, YOU LEARNED

The interlocking physical systems of the Earth make life on the planet possible.

NOW YOU WILL LEARN

People are not equally distributed on the Earth's surface.

▶ Vocabulary

TERMS & NAMES

population the number of people who live in a specified area

birth rate the number of births per 1,000 people per year

death rate the number of deaths per 1,000 people per year

rate of natural increase the death rate subtracted from the birth rate

population density the average number of people who live in a certain area

urbanization the process of city development

demographer a geographer who studies the characteristics of human populations

BACKGROUND VOCABULARY

habitable lands lands suitable for human living

urban relating to, or located in, a city

rural relating to the country or farming

Visual Vocabulary Urbanization (Los Angeles, California)

▶ Reading Strategy

Re-create the web diagram shown at right. As you read and respond to the **KEY QUESTIONS**, use the diagram to help you identify important details to compare and contrast population growth, distribution, and density.

 See Skillbuilder Handbook, page R9

COMPARE AND CONTRAST

```
                POPULATION
           /        |         \
   Population   Population    Population
     Growth    Distribution    Density
```

 GRAPHIC ORGANIZERS
Go to **Interactive Review** @ClassZone.com

The Geography of Population

Connecting to Your World

Do you know how many people there are in the world? About 6.5 billion! In the time it takes you to read this paragraph, another 140 people will be born somewhere in the world. Where do the 6.5 billion people live? More than half of them live in Asia. In fact, over 2 billion are located in just two countries—China and India. The world's third most populous country is the United States, which has over 300 million people.

Population Growth

▼ **KEY QUESTION** What challenges does rapid population growth cause?

Geographers use the term **population** to mean the total number of people who live in a specified area. The population of the world today is more than 6 billion. It did not reach one billion until about 1804. Yet, over the last 200 years, the number has jumped by some 5 billion. What factors are responsible? The most important factors were increases in food production, discoveries in medical science, and improvements in sanitation. As a result, more babies survived and people lived longer, healthier lives.

Shanghai, China
China's largest city is home to more than 12 million people.

CHINA
Shanghai
East China Sea

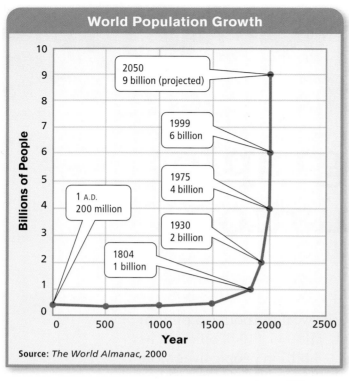

World Population Growth

Billions of People

10
9 — 2050 / 9 billion (projected)
8
7 — 1999 / 6 billion
6
5 — 1975 / 4 billion
4 — 1 A.D. / 200 million
3 — 1930 / 2 billion
2 — 1804 / 1 billion
1
0

0   500   1000   1500   2000   2500

Year

Source: *The World Almanac, 2000*

Measuring Growth Geographers measure population growth by figuring out how many people have been born and how many have died, how many have moved into and how many have moved out of a specific area. The **birth rate** measures the number of births per 1,000 people per year. The **death rate** measures the number of deaths per 1,000 people per year. To find out the **rate of natural increase**, the death rate is subtracted from the birth rate. This is the population growth that results from natural processes of birth and death.

Today, in most of Asia, Africa, and South America, the rate of natural increase is very high. Farming is a major way of life in these regions, and families need many children to help with the farm work. In most countries of Europe and North America, and also in Japan, the population growth rate is much lower. In these countries, most people live in cities and have few children, making their rate of natural increase much lower than in regions with a higher rural population.

Growth Challenges The expanding population creates serious challenges. The Earth's resources are limited and not evenly distributed throughout the world. In many countries, it is difficult just to provide the basic needs such as food, clean water, and housing. Many people move from rural areas to cities to make a better life for themselves and their families. If they cannot find housing, they often build houses on the outskirts of cities with whatever materials they can find. Some of these squatter settlements become very large, even as large as the city itself, but they often lack clean water, sewers, or paved roads.

▲ **SUMMARIZE** Explain the challenges of rapid population growth.

Rio de Janeiro, Brazil
These houses are part of squatter settlements on the outskirts of the main city.

BRAZIL

Rio de Janeiro

Population Distribution and Density

▼ **KEY QUESTION** What are the factors that influence where people choose to live?

As you read earlier, people are not distributed equally around the world. Where they choose to live is partly affected by climate, elevation, and resources such as fertile soil and fresh water. Today, the largest populations are found in what are called **habitable lands**.

Population Distribution Only a small portion of the Earth's surface is suitable for humans to settle. Almost 75 percent of the Earth's surface is water. In addition, between 35 and 40 percent of the Earth's land is too hot, too cold, too wet, or too dry for large-scale settlement. Most people live in the Northern Hemisphere, between 20° North and 60° North latitude. Fewer people live in the Southern Hemisphere because there is less land available. The edges of continents are more heavily populated than interior lands. Many people choose to live in coastal lands and in river valleys because these locations offer people opportunities to earn a living. About two-thirds of the world's population is found within 300 miles of ocean waters.

◀ COMPARING ▶ Urban Populations

More than 400 cities have populations of one million or more. Many cities in Africa and Asia, such as Lagos, Nigeria, and Mumbai, India, are expected to grow rapidly in the 21st century.

Mumbai, India

Top 7 Most Populous Cities	Population (in millions*)
Tokyo, Japan	34.45
Mexico City, Mexico	18.07
New York City, U.S.A.	17.85
São Paulo, Brazil	17.10
Mumbai, India	16.09
Kolkata, India	13.06
Shanghai, China	12.89

CRITICAL THINKING

Compare and Contrast What is the total population of the Indian cities listed? How does that compare with the population of Tokyo?

* Population shown is for an entire urban area, not just the city itself.

Source: *The World Almanac and Book of Facts, 2006*

CONNECT to Math

Population density is different from population distribution. Population distribution shows where people live. **Population density** shows on average how many people are living in a specific size area such as a square mile or square kilometer. The density number helps explain how crowded an area is.

To find the population density number, add up the total number of people living in an area and divide by the total amount of land they occupy. Some areas of Earth are very lightly populated and others are quite densely populated.

World Population Density

Calculating Population Density

Materials
• a calculator
• paper and pencil

1. Review the paragraph at left to see how population density is calculated.

2. Use the information below to calculate the population density for eight countries.

3. After you have completed your calculations, create a bar graph showing the population densities of the eight nations.

Country	Area (km²)	Population
Afghanistan	647,500	31,056,997
Brazil	8,511,965	188,078,227
Chad	1,284,000	9,944,200
Finland	338,145	5,231,372
France	547,030	60,876,136
Iraq	437,072	26,783,383
Thailand	514,000	64,631,595
United States	9,631,420	298,444,215

Source: *CIA World Factbook,* 2006

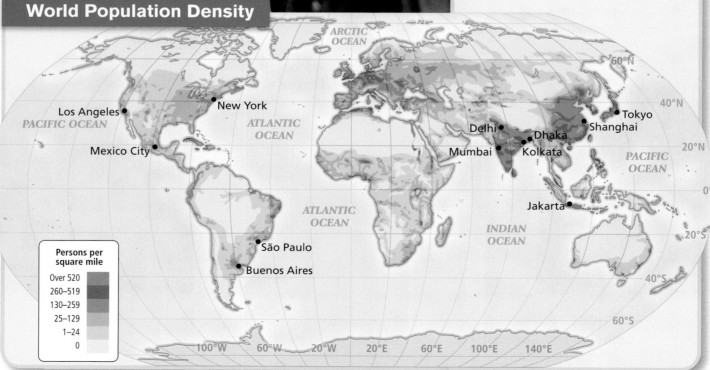

Persons per square mile

Over 520
260–519
130–259
25–129
1–24
0

Rural vs. Urban Today, about half the world's population lives in **urban** areas, such as cities and their suburbs. This is a big change from a hundred years ago. Then, most people lived in **rural** areas, on farms and in small villages. Only about 14 percent lived in cities. By 2030, population experts believe that 60 percent of all people will live in urban areas. This process of development from small settlements to large ones is called **urbanization**.

Population Density Geographers who study the characteristics of human populations are called **demographers**. They use population density to find out how heavily populated an area is. One of the most densely populated countries is Bangladesh in South Asia, with over 1,900 people per square mile. The average population density of the entire planet is 113 people per square mile.

Statistics can be deceiving because the number is an average. Some areas of a country might be lightly populated, while others are heavily populated. In the United States, the population density is about 80 people per square mile. However, New Jersey has 1,134 people per square mile and Alaska has only 1.1 people per square mile.

 UNDERSTAND CAUSES Identify the factors that influence where people choose to live.

Section 1 Assessment

ONLINE QUIZ
For test practice, go to
Interactive Review
@ ClassZone.com

TERMS & NAMES

1. Explain the importance of
- birth rate
- death rate
- population density
- urbanization

USE YOUR READING NOTES

2. Compare and Contrast Use your completed web diagram to answer the following question:

How is population density different from population distribution?

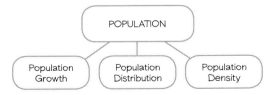

KEY IDEAS

3. What are three factors that have caused the world's population to grow so rapidly?

4. What is urbanization?

5. How is population density determined?

CRITICAL THINKING

6. Make Inferences Why are people unevenly distributed on the Earth's surface?

7. Compare and Contrast Why do some countries have much lower growth rates than others?

8. CONNECT to Today What do you think are the major problems that the world faces as the population continues to grow?

9. MATH **Create a Population Density Table** Use the Internet to find statistics for population and an average population density for each continent. Create a table and a bar chart showing these statistics. Continents should be listed in order from highest density to lowest density.

Population density is an average figure for a specific area. However, it does not account for the distribution of population in an area. Notice in these two examples how the pattern of population density varies even within a country.

Australia

Australia is ranked 54th in the world for total population, but 191st in population density. This is because Australia has a great deal of land but a small population. It has a lot of open space sometimes called the Outback, shown below. The heaviest population is found in the coastal cities.

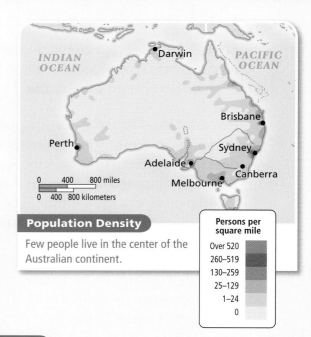

Population Density

Few people live in the center of the Australian continent.

Persons per square mile

Over 520
260–519
130–259
25–129
1–24
0

Work

Australia's wide open spaces makes cattle ranching one of the biggest businesses.

Transportation

A lone vehicle travels a dusty Outback road.

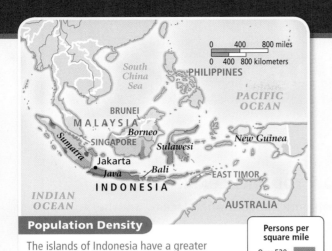

Population Density

The islands of Indonesia have a greater population density than Australia.

Persons per square mile	
Over 520	
260–519	
130–259	
25–129	
1–24	
0	

Transportation

Thousands of buses and cars are needed to move Jakarta's population.

Indonesia

Indonesia is ranked 4th in the world for total population, but 60th in population density. This is because two Indonesian islands, Bali and Java, and the capital, Jakarta, are heavily populated. Other parts of the island nation are not as densely populated. Jakarta is pictured below.

Work

Manufacturing takes place in the larger cities of Indonesia.

CRITICAL THINKING

1. **Compare and Contrast** How are the patterns of density different in the two countries?

2. **Draw Conclusions** In what ways do the images illustrate how density may affect ways of living in the two countries?

Reading for Understanding

▶ Key Ideas

BEFORE, YOU LEARNED

Population patterns differ by place and region and may change over time.

NOW YOU WILL LEARN

People move from one place to another to meet their needs.

▶ Vocabulary

TERMS & NAMES

migration the process of relocating to a new region

immigrant a person who leaves one area to settle in another

push factor a reason that causes people to leave an area

pull factor a reason that attracts people to another area

culture the shared attitudes, knowledge, and behaviors of a group

diversity having many different ways to think or to do something, or a variety of people

discrimination actions that might be hurtful to an individual or a group

BACKGROUND VOCABULARY

refugee a person who flees a place to find safety

persecution cruel treatment on the basis of religion, race, ethnic group, nationality, political views, gender, or class

Visual Vocabulary diversity

▶ Reading Strategy

Re-create the chart shown at right. As you read and respond to the **KEY QUESTIONS**, use the chart to compare and contrast important details about the reasons people move.

 See Skillbuilder Handbook, page R9

COMPARE AND CONTRAST

PUSH FACTORS	PULL FACTORS
1.	1.
2.	2.

 GRAPHIC ORGANIZERS
Go to **Interactive Review** @ ClassZone.com

Why People Move

Connecting to Your World

Have you ever moved from one part of the city or town where you live to another? Maybe you moved to be closer to your school or to where a parent works. It may be that one of your parents took a job in a different city. Perhaps your family had to move to a different climate for health reasons. Whatever the reason, moving to a new, unfamiliar area could change your life in many ways.

Moving Day About 112 million Americans relocate every year.

Causes of Migration

 KEY QUESTION Why do people move from place to place?

From earliest times, people have moved to new locations. This process of relocating to a new region is called **migration**. A person who leaves one country to settle in another is called an **immigrant**. Population geographers often talk about push-pull factors when they study migration. The **push factors** are the reasons that cause people to leave an area. **Pull factors** are the reasons that attract people to another area. For example, a group may decide to move to a better location after their crops fail for several years. The crop failure is the "push" factor, and the better location is the "pull" factor. Together, they give the group a reason for migrating. Generally, the causes of migration are environmental, economic, cultural, or political.

Ellis Island, New York Millions of people entered the United States here between 1892 and 1954.

Push Factors In early times, a change in environment was a major cause of migration. For example, climate changes thousands of years ago brought on an ice age. People in northern Europe moved south in order to survive. Sometimes, an environment is unable to support growing numbers of people. So some part of the group needs to move to a place that would better support them.

Political actions may push a person or group to migrate to a new area. **Refugees** might flee a place to find safety from war. For example, beginning in 2003, an ethnic war in the Darfur region of Sudan caused about 2 million people to flee to refugee camps. Governments can force people to relocate even if they do not want to go. Cruel treatment, or **persecution**, of a particular group could also cause people to leave. People have sometimes been persecuted for their religion, race, nationality, political views, or membership in an ethnic group.

Pull Factors The desire for land has pulled people to new regions for thousands of years. During the 1800s, millions immigrated to the United States in search of land to farm or ranch. Economic opportunities are still a major reason for migration. Today, people move to find a job or to get a better job.

Sometimes people move for cultural reasons. For example, they may want to return to an area they consider the homeland of their people. Another pull factor may be that the land or the region has religious significance. Israel is an example of both reasons. Jews from all over the world immigrate to Israel because they consider it their homeland, and because it also contains many Jewish holy sites.

▲ **SUMMARIZE** What are the push-pull factors of migration?

◄ COMPARING ► Migration Factors

PUSH FACTORS	PULL FACTORS
Environmental • lack of resources to support an entire group • change in climate or vegetation	**Economic** • availability of land • job opportunities
Political • escape from war or persecution • forced removal	**Cultural** • return to a homeland • desire to live near a holy site

CRITICAL THINKING

Make Inferences Which factor do you think is most often the cause of migration?

Where People Migrate

▼ **KEY QUESTION** What are the two kinds of migration?

Geographers identify two different types of migration. Internal migration occurs when people move within a country. Moving across a continent or even to another continent is called external migration.

Internal Migration Internal migration happens when people move from one place to another but stay within the same country. Someone who does this is called a migrant. If you move from Pennsylvania to California, you have moved a very long distance, but you have stayed within the United States, so you are an internal migrant. Two of the most common forms of internal migration are moving from rural areas or small towns to cities, and from cities to suburbs.

The world is becoming more urban. In many countries, more than 70 percent of the population lives in urban areas. Pull factors attract people to cities. If migrants can't find affordable housing in the city, they often build houses on the outskirts. This kind of growth on the outskirts of a city is sometimes called urban sprawl. In developed countries such as the United States, sprawl happens as new suburbs are built around the edges of a city.

External Migration Migration across parts of a continent may take place quickly, but sometimes it takes hundreds or even thousands of years. For example, Bantu-speaking people of Africa slowly spread across the southern half of the continent from 1000 B.C. to A.D. 1100. The push factor was environmental. The numbers of Bantu people were increasing, and they needed more land for farming and herding.

Migration also takes place from one continent to another continent. The countries of the Western Hemisphere as well as Australia and New Zealand, are filled with immigrants from Europe, Africa, and Asia.

▲ **COMPARE** Explain the difference between internal and external migration.

Kuba Mask The Kuba are a Bantu-speaking people.

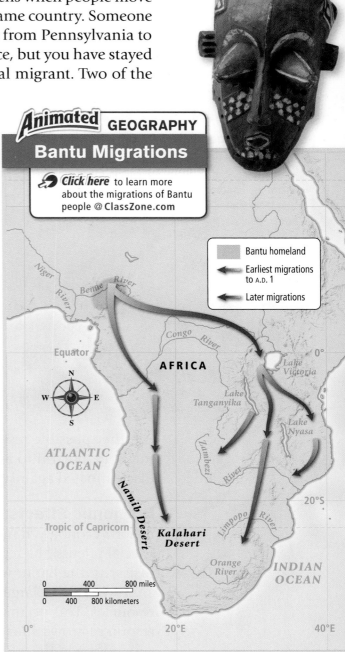

Animated GEOGRAPHY
Bantu Migrations

Click here to learn more about the migrations of Bantu people @ ClassZone.com

Bantu homeland
Earliest migrations to A.D. 1
Later migrations

CONNECT Geography & Culture
Movement Toward which body of water did the eastern branch of the early migrations move?

The Effects of Migration

▼ **KEY QUESTION** How does migration affect people and lands?

People bring the customs and traditions of their culture with them when they relocate. **Culture** is the shared attitudes, knowledge, and behaviors of a group. As a result of migration, the cultures of both the immigrants and the people living in an area may change. Migration also has economic and political effects, both positive and negative.

Cultural Effects When different groups in an area interact, they learn about each other—what they eat, wear, and believe. If people accept these different ideas and behaviors, it adds to the diversity of the group. **Diversity** means having many different ways to think about or to do something, or it may refer to a variety of people. Many people believe that having diversity in a group makes it stronger.

Earlier you learned about the Bantu-speaking people and how they spread across southern Africa. Wherever they settled, the Bantu brought their language and iron-making skills to the people in the region. Even if the Bantu moved on, their language and iron-working techniques remained. So migration changed the existing culture in several ways.

Migration does not always benefit the people who move. This is especially true if a group did not want to move. For example, refugees who flee war may be forced into overcrowded camps with little hope of returning home. Another possible result of migration is **discrimination**, actions that might be hurtful to an individual or group. For example, the group discriminated against may not be able to get jobs or housing.

CONNECT ⟳ Geography & Culture

Bantu Languages

The Bantu spread their languages when they migrated across Africa. Today, about 240 million Africans speak one of the hundreds of Bantu languages as their first language. Some 50 million of them in central and east Africa speak Swahili (swah•HEE•lee), also known as Kiswahili (KEY•swah•HEE•lee).

Economic Effects The arrival of a new group can help or hurt a region's economy. If more workers are needed or the new workers have special talents, the region's economy may be improved. This was the case with the Bantu who brought iron-making skills with them.

The arrival of large numbers of people sometimes strains a region's resources. This occurs when, for example, war refugees with limited resources crowd into refugee camps. The living conditions may be very poor and the additional numbers make life in the camps miserable. In 2005, many thousands of people fled their homes as warfare swept Sudan in Africa. The refugees found little shelter, water, or firewood in the camps. In fact, violence often broke out over the available water. Security and protection for the people in the camps can also become a problem. Governments may not be able to adequately provide for the refugees or may need to ask other nations to help care for the people.

Political Effects The policies of a country or region can be affected by the arrival of immigrants. Sometimes immigrants may be viewed as unwanted or dangerous. The government of a country might then support actions to remove the immigrants or allow them to be treated badly in hopes that they will leave. The immigrants may worry about their personal safety and ability to provide for themselves and their families.

In the best of times, the new immigrants make contributions to the country and are viewed as assets. For example, many immigrant groups brought valuable skills to the United States and were given the opportunity to become citizens.

Water Cans at a Refugee Camp Water is scarce in this African refugee camp. Each day people line up in hopes of getting a supply of water.

 DRAW CONCLUSIONS Identify positive and negative effects of migration.

Section ② Assessment

ONLINE QUIZ
For test practice, go to
Interactive Review
@ ClassZone.com

TERMS & NAMES
1. Explain the importance of
- migration
- push factor
- pull factor
- culture

USE YOUR READING NOTES
2. Compare and Contrast Use your completed chart to answer the following question:

Which factors do you think are more powerful in encouraging migration?

PUSH FACTORS	PULL FACTORS
1.	1.
2.	2.

KEY IDEAS
3. What has been a major push factor in migration since earliest times?

4. Which form of internal migration has affected most countries?

5. What are the three ways that migration affects people and lands?

CRITICAL THINKING
6. Analyze Causes and Effects How do push-pull factors work together?

7. Summarize How is a culture affected by migration?

8. CONNECT to Today What are the pull factors that would attract people to move to your community?

9. HISTORY Create a Push-Pull Poster Choose two immigrant groups that came to the United States at any time in its history. Create a poster with images to show where they came from, what pushed them from their homeland, and what pulled them to the United States.

Reading for Understanding

▶ Key Ideas

BEFORE, YOU LEARNED

Migration changes places and regions by introducing new people and cultures.

NOW YOU WILL LEARN

Economic activities in an area depend on the presence of natural resources.

▶ Vocabulary

TERMS & NAMES

natural resource something that is found in nature that is necessary or useful to humans

economy a system for producing and exchanging goods and services among a group of people

economic system a way people use resources to make and exchange goods

command economy an economic system in which the production of goods and services is decided by a central government

market economy an economic system in which the production of goods and services is decided by supply and the demand of consumers

Gross Domestic Product (GDP) the total value of all the goods and services produced in a country in a year

export a product or resource sold to another country

import a product or resource that comes into a country

specialization a focus on producing a limited number of a specific products

BACKGROUND VOCABULARY

raw material an unprocessed natural resource that will be converted to a finished product

▶ Reading Strategy

Re-create the chart shown at right. As you read and respond to the **KEY QUESTIONS**, use the chart to categorize important details about types of economic systems.

 Skillbuilder Handbook, page R7

CATEGORIZE

ECONOMIC SYSTEMS			
Traditional	Market	Command	Mixed
1.	1.	1.	1.
2.	2.	2.	2.
3.	3.	3.	3.

 GRAPHIC ORGANIZERS
Go to **Interactive Review** @ClassZone.com

Resources and Economics

Connecting to Your World

What natural resources are found in your area? A **natural resource** is something found in nature that is necessary or useful to humans. Forests, mineral deposits, and fresh water are examples of natural resources. Often, the presence of natural resources attracts people to a particular area. Think about how important natural resources are to your life, to your community, and to your country. How are they being used, and how long will they last?

Natural Resources

▼ **KEY QUESTION** What are the different types of natural resources?

Natural resources are essential for economic development, but resources are not equally distributed around the world. People learn to use the resources in their own areas to their best advantage. However, just because a natural resource is present does not mean it can or will be used. People in some countries may not have the technology to take the resource and turn it into usable products. For example, iron ore is useless until technology turns it into iron and steel products. Technology changes over time, making the value of resources change as well.

Copper Mine
This copper mine in Spain has been producing copper since Roman times.

SPAIN

Geographers divide natural resources into three main categories: renewable, non-renewable, and unlimited. Renewable resources are those that nature can replace, such as trees or plants. Unlimited resources are things such as sunlight and wind—these never run out and often are used to produce energy. Non-renewable resources can't be easily replaced, so when they are used up, there aren't additional resources. Minerals and fuels like coal and oil fall into this category.

▲ **CATEGORIZE** Identify three basic types of resources.

CONNECT ➤ Geography & Economics

Natural Resources The map below shows the location of some major non-renewable resources. When supplies of these resources are gone, countries relying on them for their economies will have to change their economic focus.

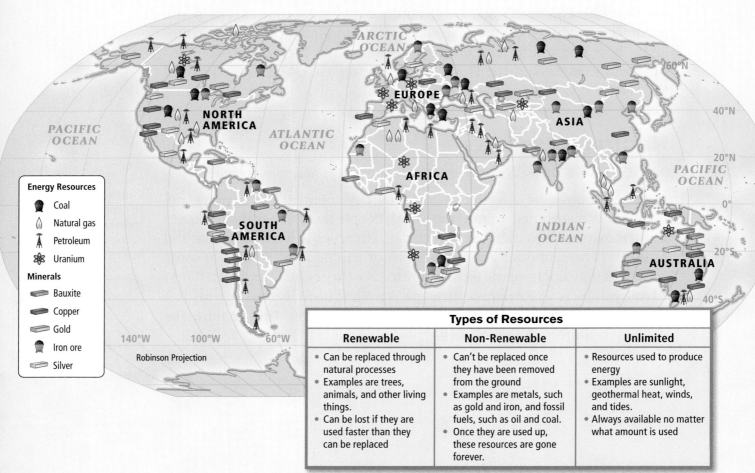

Energy Resources

- 🪨 Coal
- ⛽ Natural gas
- ⛏ Petroleum
- ⚛ Uranium

Minerals

- Bauxite
- Copper
- Gold
- Iron ore
- Silver

Robinson Projection

Types of Resources

Renewable	Non-Renewable	Unlimited
• Can be replaced through natural processes • Examples are trees, animals, and other living things. • Can be lost if they are used faster than they can be replaced	• Can't be replaced once they have been removed from the ground • Examples are metals, such as gold and iron, and fossil fuels, such as oil and coal. • Once they are used up, these resources are gone forever.	• Resources used to produce energy • Examples are sunlight, geothermal heat, winds, and tides. • Always available no matter what amount is used

CRITICAL THINKING

Draw Conclusions Which of the three categories of natural resources are likely to be most desirable?

Economic Systems

▼ **KEY QUESTION** What are the four basic economic systems?

An **economy** consists of the production and exchange of goods and services among a group of people. Economies exist at the local, regional, national, and international levels. **Economic systems** are different ways that people use resources to make and exchange goods and services.

Four basic economic systems are traditional, command, market, and mixed.

Traditional economy Goods and services are traded, but money is rarely exchanged. This process is called "barter" and is the oldest economic system. It is not used much today.

Command economy A **command economy** is one in which production of goods and services is decided by a central government. The government usually owns most of the resources and businesses that make the products or provide the services. This type of economy is also called a planned economy.

Food Market in Vietnam Supply and demand help determine which products will be sold. **How is this market different from most food markets in the United States?**

Market economy When the production of goods and services is determined by the supply and the demand of consumers it is called a **market economy**. It is also known as a demand economy, or capitalism. This is the type of economy found in the United States.

Mixed economy In this economy, a combination of command and market economies provides goods and services.

Economic activities are all the different ways that people make a living under these economic systems, including manufacturing, agriculture, fishing, and providing services. Some countries have a wide mix of economic activities while others may have only one or two main economic activities.

▲ **SUMMARIZE** Name the four basic types of economic systems.

Measuring Economic Development

▼ **KEY QUESTION** How is economic development measured?

To measure economic development, geographers may look at such figures as literacy, health information, life expectancy, or the value of a country's economy. One of the most important measures used is Gross Domestic Product (GDP). The **Gross Domestic Product (GDP)** measures the total value of all the goods and services produced in a country in a year. Countries are divided into two categories based on economic development: developing or developed nations.

Developing Nations These nations have low GDP and few economic activities. Many people raise food or animals to survive and have little or no machinery or advanced technology to do the work.

Developed Nations These nations have high GDP and many economic activities, especially business and information processing, and a lot of high-level technology. Food is grown on commercial farms, and most people work in offices and factories.

▲ **COMPARE** Identify information used to measure development.

COMPARING ◄ Economic Development

Geographers use many different measurements to look at the development level of a country's economy. Here is a comparison of some developing nations and some developed nations.

◄ *Brazilian coffee bean worker*

	Status	GDP	GDP/ Person In US Dollars*	Infant Mortality (1000 Live Births)	Life Expectancy (At Birth)	Literacy Rate (Percent)
Burkina Faso	developing	5.4 billion	1,300	91.4	48.9	26.6
India	developing	719.8 billion	3,400	54.6	64.7	59.5
Uruguay	developing	13.2 billion	9,600	11.6	76.3	98.0
Germany	developed	2.8 trillion	30,400	4.1	78.8	99.0
Japan	developed	4.9 trillion	31,500	3.2	81.3	99.0
United States	developed	12.5 trillion	42,000	6.4	77.9	99.0

* official exchange rate   **Source:** *CIA World Factbook, 2006*

CRITICAL THINKING

Compare and Contrast How can you tell Uruguay has developed more than Burkina Faso?

World Trade

▼ **KEY QUESTION** Why do countries trade with one another?

Early trade networks started because people who did not have certain resources, such as salt, wanted them. For trade to happen, nations usually have to give up some of their resources in exchange. Products or resources sold to other countries are called **exports**. Products or resources that come into a country are called **imports**. For example, U.S.-made mining equipment sold to Brazil is an export of the United States. Brazilian coffee sold to the United States is a U.S. import.

A country may choose to focus on producing only one or two products or resources and exclude other economic activities. This practice is called **specialization**. Countries specialize because it allows them to trade for products they can't produce themselves. For example, a country may sell cocoa beans or wheat or iron ore in exchange for machinery, or chemicals, or electronic goods. In general, developing nations specialize in **raw materials** or low-cost items, while developed nations sell high-level technology goods or services. This focus leads to interdependence between countries. When countries produce the same trade items, competition results.

▲ **FIND MAIN IDEAS** Explain why nations trade.

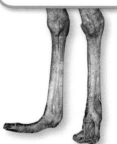

OSTRICH MEAT EXPORTS

Chile is known for its major exports of copper, fruit, and paper. But it has added a new export— ostrich meat—that is bringing in more than 17 billion dollars per year. This nontraditional export is bringing money and jobs to Chile.

Section ③ Assessment

ONLINE QUIZ
For test practice, go to
Interactive Review
@ ClassZone.com

TERMS & NAMES

1. Explain the importance of
- economic system
- Gross Domestic Product (GDP)
- export
- import

USE YOUR READING NOTES

2. Categorize Use your completed chart to answer the following question:

In which economic system are the production of goods and services determined by consumer demand?

ECONOMIC SYSTEMS			
Traditional	Market	Command	Mixed
1.	1.	1.	1.
2.	2.	2.	2.
3.	3.	3.	3.

KEY IDEAS

3. What is a natural resource?

4. What are the four basic economic systems?

5. What is the difference between an export and an import?

CRITICAL THINKING

6. Summarize How do geographers divide countries into developed and developing nations?

7. Compare and Contrast How are command and market economic systems different?

8. CONNECT to Today What natural resources are located in your area and how are they used?

9. TECHNOLOGY Create a Multimedia Presentation Use the Internet to study the imports and exports of the United States or another country. Plan a slide show about major exports and what countries buy them and major imports and what countries sell them.

Reading for Understanding

▶ Key Ideas

BEFORE, YOU LEARNED

People have different ways to use and trade the Earth's natural resources.

NOW YOU WILL LEARN

The world is divided into many political regions and organizations.

▶ Vocabulary

TERMS & NAMES

government an organization set up to make and enforce rules for a society

citizen a person who owes loyalty to a country and receives its protection

representative democracy a type of government in which citizens hold political power through elected representatives

monarchy a type of government in which a ruling family headed by a king or queen holds political power

oligarchy (AHL•ih•GAHR•kee) a type of government in which a small group of people holds power

dictatorship a type of government in which an individual holds complete political power

communism a type of government in which the Communist Party holds all political power and controls the economy

Visual Vocabulary monarchy (The queen of Denmark)

▶ Reading Strategy

Re-create the chart shown at right. As you read and respond to the **KEY QUESTIONS**, use the chart to categorize important details about types of government.

 See Skillbuilder Handbook, page R7

CATEGORIZE

	RULER	BASIS OF RULE
Democracy		
Monarchy		
Dictatorship		
Oligarchy		
Communism		

 GRAPHIC ORGANIZERS
Go to **Interactive Review** @ ClassZone.com

Why We Need Government

Connecting to Your World

You live in one of nearly 200 countries in the world. Some countries are tiny when compared to the United States; others are larger in physical size or in population. All countries have one thing in common—a government. A **government** is an organization set up to make and enforce rules for a group of people. It has authority over the land within its boundaries.

Passport An official document that allows a person to travel abroad.

Types of Government

▼ **KEY QUESTION** What types of government operate around the world?

Government is needed to provide security, make and enforce the laws, furnish the services that keep a country running, and protect the rights of citizens. A **citizen** is a person who owes loyalty to a country and receives its protection. The government also acts on behalf of the people in the country when it deals with other countries. As you have read, all countries have some type of government. The types differ mainly over how much power the people have. Some countries are ruled by a single person, others by a small group, and still others are ruled by many people.

U.S. Capitol Building This is the official seat of government for the country.

Washington, D.C.
UNITED STATES

79

COMPARING ▶ Governments

TYPES OF GOVERNMENT

DEMOCRACY
- Rule by citizens through elected officials
- Rule is based on citizenship.
- Majority rules

DICTATORSHIP
- Rule by a single individual
- Ruler controls military.
- Citizens have little power to change government.

OLIGARCHY
- Rule by a small group of citizens
- Rule is based on wealth or privilege.
- Ruling group controls military.

MONARCHY
- Rule by a king or queen
- Rule is hereditary.
- May share power through a constitution

COMMUNISM
- Rule by the Communist Party on behalf of the people
- Government owns all economic goods and services.
- Citizens have little power to change government.

CRITICAL THINKING

Evaluate In which type of government do citizens have the most power?

Generally, the type of government a country has falls into one of the following categories:

Representative Democracy Citizens hold political power and rule through elected representatives. In a **representative democracy**, such as the United States, representatives create laws for all the people. If the people object to the laws, they can work to change the laws or change the representatives through elections.

Monarchy In a **monarchy**, a ruling family headed by a king, queen, emperor, or sultan holds political power. Power may or may not be shared with citizens. Saudi Arabia is an example of a traditional monarchy, in which the monarch has complete power. The United Kingdom is a constitutional monarchy, in which the monarch's power is limited by a constitution.

Oligarchy A government where a small group of people holds power, usually because of their wealth, military strength, family connections, political influence, or privilege, is called an **oligarchy**. The military government of the country of Burma is an oligarchy.

Dictatorship In a **dictatorship**, an individual holds complete political power. North Korea is an example.

Communism In **communism**, all political power and control of the economy is held by the government, which is controlled by the Communist Party. The government controls all economic goods and services. Cuba is an example.

There are also different levels of government. The national government oversees the entire country. Countries often have smaller governmental units like state or provincial governments and local governments. Each of these political units deals with specific aspects of life at the state or local level.

▲ **DRAW CONCLUSIONS** What are the major types of government?

Being an Active Citizen

▼ **KEY QUESTION** What are your most important responsibilities as a citizen?

As a citizen in a democracy, you have important responsibilities. These responsibilities fall into two categories—personal and community. Personal responsibilities involve your personal behavior and relationships with others. They include taking care of yourself, helping your family, knowing right from wrong, and behaving in a respectful way. Community responsibilities involve the government and your community. They include obeying the law, voting, paying taxes, serving on a jury, and defending your country.

Being an informed citizen means you need to make yourself aware of the issues in an election and the positions held by the candidates running for office. You can also make elected officials aware of your concerns.

▲ **EVALUATE** Which responsibilities of a citizen apply to you?

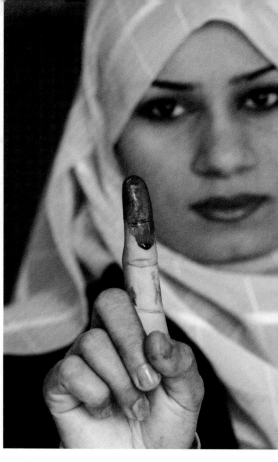

Iraqi Woman Voter This woman shows a purple finger, the sign she has voted. The 2005 election was the first free election in Iraq in 50 years. **How might having a democratic government change this woman's life?**

Responsibilities of a U.S. Citizen

As a young person, you can be a good citizen in a number of ways. Notice that some responsibilities are especially for people under 18, and some are specifically for those over 18. And all citizens have some responsibilities in common.

CRITICAL THINKING
Draw Conclusions
Which of the responsibilities shown are community responsibilities?

UNDER 18
- Attend and do well in school
- Take responsibility for one's behavior
- Help one's family

ALL AGES
- Obey rules and laws
- Be tolerant of others
- Pay taxes
- Volunteer for a cause
- Stay informed about issues

OVER 18
- Vote
- Serve on a jury
- Defend the country

United Nations Security Council This part of the UN deals with political situations that pose a threat to its members. **Why might a nation want to join an organization like the UN?**

International Organizations

 KEY QUESTION Why are international organizations formed?

Countries may join with other nations to form organizations to promote common goals. These organizations might have military, economic, or political goals. Sometimes, countries in a region will form an organization. One example, the Tsunami Warning System (TWS), is a group of 26 nations with coasts or territories on the Pacific Ocean. The TWS was organized to gather information about and send out warnings of these dangerous oceanic events. Other groups are organized to promote economic development, such as the Economic Community of West African States (ECOWAS).

The largest international organization in the world is the United Nations (UN). Nearly 200 countries belong to this organization. Its members work to improve political, cultural, educational, health, and economic conditions around the world.

▲ **SUMMARIZE** Explain why nations form international organizations.

Section 4 Assessment

ONLINE QUIZ
For test practice, go to **Interactive Review** @ ClassZone.com

TERMS & NAMES

1. Explain the importance of
- government
- citizen
- representative democracy
- dictatorship

USE YOUR READING NOTES

2. Compare and Contrast Use your completed chart to answer the following question:

In which form of government is power held by a small group of people?

	RULER	BASIS OF RULE
Democracy		
Monarchy		
Dictatorship		
Oligarchy		
Communism		

KEY IDEAS

3. What are the five types of government?

4. What civic responsibilities does a citizen have?

5. What is the main reason for creating a regional or international organization?

CRITICAL THINKING

6. Draw Conclusions Why do people form governments?

7. Make Inferences Why do local governments exist?

8. CONNECT to Today Identify the name of your state and local governments, and explain what each does.

9. WRITING Write a Web Log Entry Imagine that someone living under a different system of government has been critical of democracy on a web log. Write a response telling the reasons why you support your form of government.

Interactive Review

CHAPTER SUMMARY

Key Idea 1
People are not equally distributed on the Earth's surface.

Key Idea 2
People move from one place to another to meet their needs for certain resources.

Key Idea 3
Economic activities in an area depend on the presence of natural resources.

Key Idea 4
The world is divided into many political regions and organizations.

For **Review and Study Notes**, go to **Interactive Review @ ClassZone.com**

NAME GAME

Use the Terms & Names list to complete each sentence on paper or online.

1. I am the average number of people who live in a specific area.
   <u>**population density**</u>

2. I am something that is found in nature that is necessary or useful to humans. _____

3. I am the process of relocating to a new region.
   _____

4. I am an organization set up to make and enforce rules for society. _____

5. I am the growth in the number of people living in urban areas. _____

6. I am the way people use resources to make and exchange goods. _____

7. I am a reason that attracts people to another area. _____

8. I am a type of government in which citizens hold political power. _____

9. I am a product or resource sold to another country. _____

10. I am a person who owes loyalty to a country and receives its protection. _____

citizen
democracy
export
economic system
government
Gross Domestic Product
immigrant
import
migration
natural resource
population
population density
pull factor
push factor
urbanization

Activities

Flip Cards

Use the online flip cards to quiz yourself on the terms and names introduced in this chapter.

Monarchy

?

a type of government in which a ruling family headed by a king or queen holds political power

Crossword Puzzle

Complete an online crossword puzzle to test your knowledge of human geography.

ACROSS

1. something found in nature that is useful to humans

VOCABULARY

Explain the significance of each of the following.

1. urbanization
2. population density
3. economic system
4. Gross Domestic Product (GDP)

Explain how the terms and names in each group are related.

5. immigrant, push factor, and pull factor
6. democracy, dictatorship, and communism
7. government and citizen

KEY IDEAS

1 The Geography of Population

8. Where do most of the world's people live?
9. What are three factors that influence where people choose to live?
10. How does urbanization occur?

2 Why People Move

11. What are two main push factors and two main pull factors of migration?
12. How do internal and external migrations differ?
13. What are two cultural effects of migration?

3 Resources and Economics

14. What types of resources are renewable? Non-renewable?
15. In what ways is a mixed economy like both market and command economies?
16. What two categories do geographers use to refer to a country's level of economic development?

4 How Governments Work

17. What is a government?
18. What are three characteristics of a democracy?
19. What is the largest international organization in the world, and why was it formed?

CRITICAL THINKING

20. **Compare and Contrast** Create a table to compare and contrast who holds political power in the five systems of government.

TYPE OF GOVERNMENT	WHO HOLDS POWER

21. **Analyze Causes and Effects** How might migration affect population density?
22. **Compare and Contrast** What is the difference between a democracy and a dictatorship?
23. **Connect to Economics** Why do countries need to engage in trade?
24. **Connect Geography & History** Why have people needed to form governments?
25. **Five Themes: Movement** What might happen when a group of people brings their culture to a new area?

Answer the ESSENTIAL QUESTION

How do natural resources affect a country's population distribution and economy?

Written Response Write a two- or three-paragraph response to the Essential Question. Be sure to consider the key ideas of each section as well as specific ideas about population distribution and economics. Use the rubric below to guide your thinking.

Response Rubric
A strong response will:
- explain why natural resources influence population distribution
- discuss how natural resources impact an economy

THEMATIC MAP

Use the map to answer questions 1 and 2 on your paper.

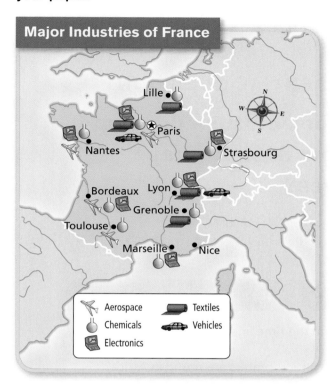

Major Industries of France

Lille

Paris

Nantes

Strasbourg

Bordeaux   Lyon

Grenoble

Toulouse

Marseille   Nice

✈ Aerospace	▬ Textiles
🜂 Chemicals	🚗 Vehicles
💻 Electronics	

1. Which of the industries shown on the map is not present at Lyon?

A. aerospace

B. chemicals

C. electronics

D. vehicles

2. In which part of France are the fewest industries located?

A. northern

B. central

C. eastern

D. southern

CHART

Use the information in the chart to briefly answer questions 3 and 4 on your paper.

Birth Rates		
Country	**Rank Out of 226**	**Birth Rate per 1000**
Niger	1	50.73
Tajikistan	49	32.65
Ecuador	90	22.29
Vietnam	131	16.86
United States	155	14.14
Italy	222	8.72

Source: *CIA World Factbook*, 2006

3. How does the birth rate of Niger compare with that of Italy?

4. How does the United States' rate compare with that of Vietnam?

GeoActivity

1. INTERDISCIPLINARY ACTIVITY–ECONOMICS

With a small group, come up with a list of 10 products that you use daily, such as a computer. Research these products to find out where they are produced. Create a slide show that displays the product and the country or countries that produce it.

2. WRITING FOR SOCIAL STUDIES

Reread the part of Section 1 that discusses population geography. Write a series of newspaper headlines that tell the story of the growth of the world's population. Arrange them in chronological order on a poster.

3. MENTAL MAPPING

Create an outline map of your state. Label the sites of the following:

• the state government

• your county government

• your community government

CHAPTER 4 People and Culture

1 CULTURE

What Is Culture?

2 CULTURE

How Does Culture Change?

 ESSENTIAL QUESTION

How does culture develop and how does it shape our lives?

CONNECT Geography & History

Use the map and the time line to answer the following questions.

1. Which early cultural centers are found in Africa?
2. One of the world's oldest religions developed in the Indus River valley. What is the religion?

Economics
8000 B.C.
Development of agriculture
(Early farm tools) ▶

9000 B.C.

Economics
9000 B.C.
Domestication of animals begins.

Culture
5000 B.C.
First cities develop.
(Home in early city) ▶

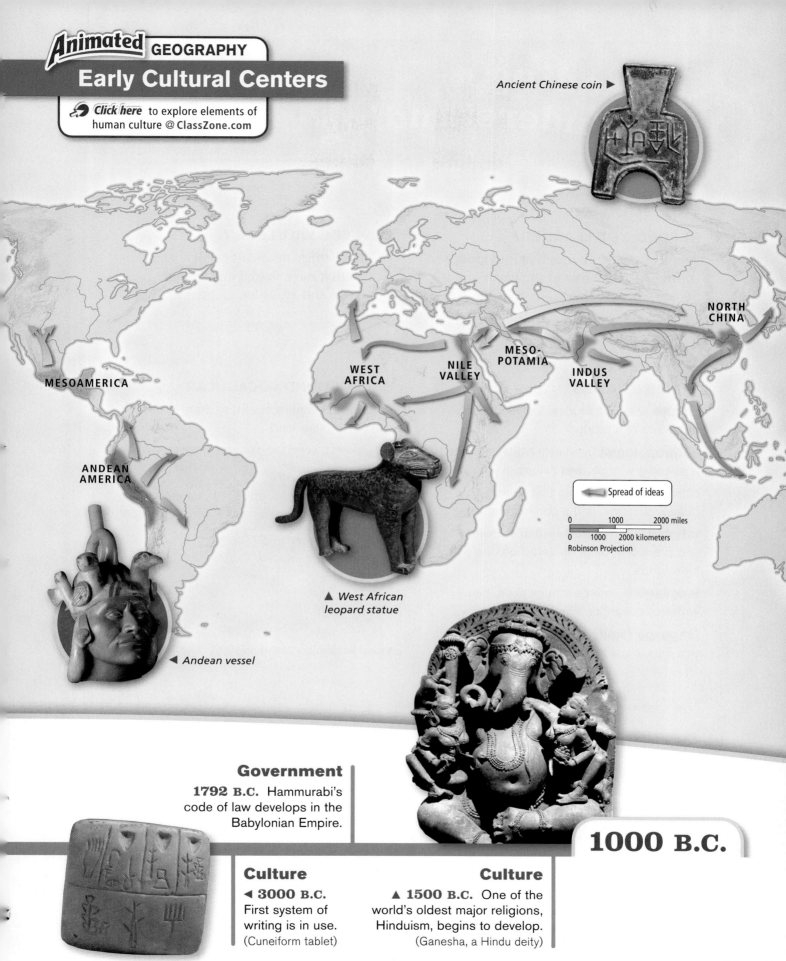

Animated GEOGRAPHY
Early Cultural Centers

🖱 Click here to explore elements of human culture @ ClassZone.com

Ancient Chinese coin ▶

NORTH CHINA

MESO-POTAMIA

NILE VALLEY

WEST AFRICA

INDUS VALLEY

MESOAMERICA

ANDEAN AMERICA

← Spread of ideas

0   1000   2000 miles
0   1000   2000 kilometers
Robinson Projection

▲ West African leopard statue

◀ Andean vessel

Government
1792 B.C. Hammurabi's code of law develops in the Babylonian Empire.

Culture
◀ **3000 B.C.** First system of writing is in use.
(Cuneiform tablet)

Culture
▲ **1500 B.C.** One of the world's oldest major religions, Hinduism, begins to develop.
(Ganesha, a Hindu deity)

1000 B.C.

Reading for Understanding

▶ Key Ideas

BEFORE, YOU LEARNED

People organize themselves into groups to control specific areas of the Earth and the people who live there.

NOW YOU WILL LEARN

Human beings are members of social groups that have shared and unique behaviors and attitudes.

▶ Vocabulary

TERMS & NAMES

culture shared attitudes, knowledge, and behaviors of a group

anthropologist (AN•thruh•PAHL•uh•jihst) a scientist who studies culture

ethnic group a people that shares a language, customs, and a common heritage

religion an organized system of beliefs and practices, often centered on one or more gods

language human communication, either written, spoken, or signed

language family a group of languages that have a common origin

BACKGROUND VOCABULARY

missionary a person sent to do religious work in another land

Visual Vocabulary anthropologist

▶ Reading Strategy

Re-create the web diagram shown at right. As you read and respond to the **KEY QUESTIONS**, use the diagram to find main ideas about culture.

 See Skillbuilder Handbook, page R4

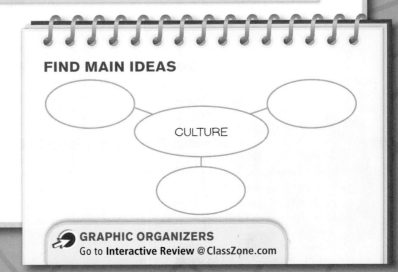

FIND MAIN IDEAS

CULTURE

🔗 **GRAPHIC ORGANIZERS**
Go to **Interactive Review** @ ClassZone.com

What Is Culture?

Connecting to Your World

How does your daily life compare to the lives of students in other parts of the world? Maybe you get up, have cereal for breakfast, and then walk to school. A young person your age in a rural area in Africa may have to work in the fields. When your school day ends, you may have sports or club activities before you go home. If you lived in China's crowded capital of Beijing, you might go home to your family's one-room apartment, where you would study or watch television.

Culture: A Way of Life

🔻 **KEY QUESTION** What is culture?

People meet their basic needs in many different ways. This is because each society has its own culture. **Culture** is the shared attitudes, knowledge, and behaviors of a group. It is the total way of life held in common by a specific group of people. Culture includes language, religion, art, and music. It also includes how a group of people live, what work they do, what food they eat, what beliefs they hold, and how they use the environment to meet their needs. Cultures also create social customs and technologies to solve problems. A culture unites people by helping them to understand their world and to relate to others in the group or those outside the group. Culture is passed from generation to generation.

Newspaper Rock, Utah For perhaps 2,000 years, native peoples and passersby have carved symbols into this sandstone rock.

Elements of Culture Scientists called **anthropologists** study culture. They have found that there are basic elements for all cultures. These include language, religion, certain foods and clothing, arts and crafts, technology, and government. Cultural elements also include a group's common practices, its shared understandings, and its social organization. The way a group uses these elements is what makes its culture unique, or one of a kind. Geographers study where different cultures are located and how they interact with their environment.

Every culture contains smaller social groups. The family is the smallest and most basic unit of a culture. Sometimes a culture includes ethnic groups. An **ethnic group** is a people that shares a language, customs, and a common heritage. Mexican Americans and Korean Americans are examples of ethnic groups that are part of the larger culture region that is the United States.

Learning Culture People are not born with cultural knowledge—they learn it from family, friends, and others. Generally, people learn culture in two ways: by observing others in their culture, and from direct teaching. Think about how you learned to speak. At first, you learned from listening to others and by imitating them. Later, when you went to school, you were directly taught the language, so that you could not only speak it, but write and read it too.

▲ **FIND MAIN IDEAS** Identify the elements of culture.

ANALYZING Primary Sources

Aimé Césaire (born 1913), a poet and political leader, was born in Martinique, a French island in the West Indies. He helped to found the Negritude movement. Its purpose was to glorify traditional African culture and identity.

> Culture is everything. Culture is the way we dress, the way we carry our heads, the way we walk, the way we tie our ties—it is not only the fact of writing books or building houses.

> Source: Aimé Césaire, speech to the World Congress of Black Writers and Artists, Paris, France, 1956

DOCUMENT-BASED QUESTION
What point is Césaire making about the role of culture in life?

To learn more about how culture is learned, go to the **Activity Center** @ ClassZone.com

How Culture Is Learned We learn about common practices, shared understandings, and social organization from direct teaching and from observing cultural practices. Family and friends, school, the media, the government, and religious institutions all help us learn our culture.

Family, Friends, and School Family and friends teach us social customs, values, religious and political beliefs, and the basics of living with others. At school, students learn about their culture and the cultures of others.

Media Media, such as television, the Internet, music, books, magazines, and newspapers, help communicate what is happening in our society and in the world around us.

Government Some of the most directed cultural learning comes from the government. It provides schools to instruct young people in the customs and traditions of their culture.

Religious Institutions Personal values and religious beliefs help people learn to live with others.

CONNECT to Your Life

Journal Entry Think about the culture in which you live. What objects might best represent parts of your culture? Record your ideas in your journal.

World Religions and Culture

▼ **KEY QUESTION** What role does religion have in a culture?

Because religion has such an influence on people's lives, it is an important element in most cultures. **Religion** is an organized system of beliefs and practices, often centered on one or more gods. Religion establishes beliefs and values. These beliefs and values guide people's behaviors toward each other and toward the environment.

Types of Religions There are thousands of religions in the world, but many religions have common elements. These elements may include specific behaviors to be practiced, important dates and rituals, holy books, and standards of proper behavior. Religions are often divided into three types—those with a belief in one god, those with a belief in more than one god, and those with a belief in divine forces in nature. The five major world religions are Buddhism, Christianity, Hinduism, Islam, and Judaism, as described in the chart below. You will learn more about them in other chapters of this book and in the World Religions handbook at the back of this text.

COMPARING World Religions

RELIGION	BASIC BELIEFS	TEACHER OR LEADER	FOLLOWERS
Buddhism	Followers can achieve enlightenment by understanding the Four Noble Truths and following the Eightfold Path.	Siddhartha Gautama, the Buddha	379 million
Christianity	There is only one God. Jesus is the Son of God. Jesus' death and resurrection made eternal life possible.	Jesus of Nazareth	2.1 billion
Hinduism	The soul never dies but is continually reborn until it becomes enlightened. Enlightenment comes after people free themselves from earthly desires.	no one leader	860 million
Islam	There is only one God. Persons achieve salvation by following the Five Pillars of Islam and living a just life.	Muhammad	1.3 billion
Judaism	There is only one God. According to believers, God loves and protects his people, but then holds them accountable for their sins.	Abraham	15.1 million

◄ *A Chinese-Buddhist Enlightened Being*

Spread of Religion Over the centuries, religions have spread from their points of origin to the rest of the world. All of the world's major religions began in Asia and moved to other continents. At first, religious beliefs were carried to different places by followers of the religion or traders. Later, **missionaries**, people sent to do religious work in other lands, spread their faiths. For example, Christianity began in Southwest Asia and was spread throughout the world by missionaries. Still later, immigrants brought their religious beliefs with them as they moved to other countries.

In some lands, traditional religions have been practiced for as long as people have lived in a culture group. In areas where there has been little immigration, most of the people have the same religion. In countries where there has been much immigration, several religions might be practiced. This is the case in the United States, where all the world's major religions and many others are practiced. In fact, the United States has more religious groups than any other country in the world, although the two largest groups are Protestant and Roman Catholic.

▲ SUMMARIZE Explain the role religion has in culture.

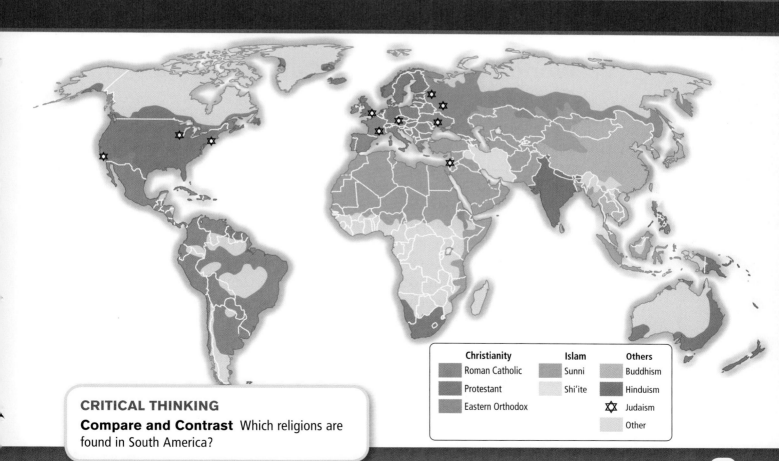

Christianity
Roman Catholic
Protestant
Eastern Orthodox

Islam
Sunni
Shi'ite

Others
Buddhism
Hinduism
✡ Judaism
Other

CRITICAL THINKING

Compare and Contrast Which religions are found in South America?

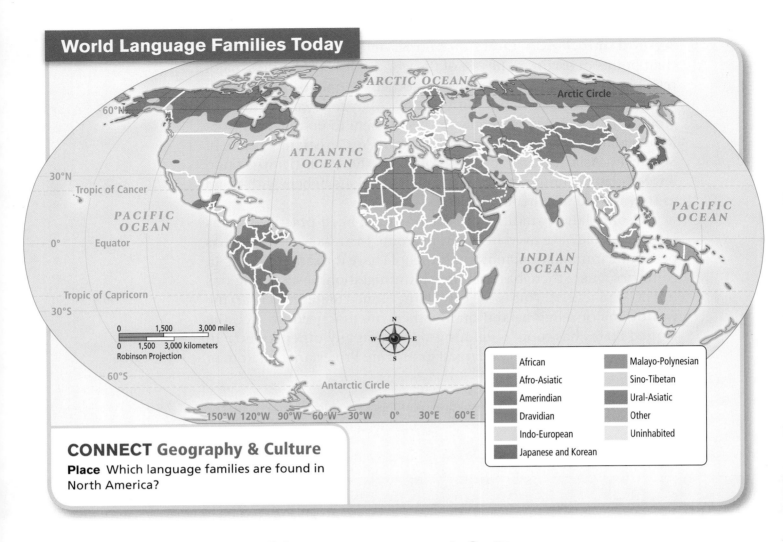

World Language Families Today

African
Afro-Asiatic
Amerindian
Dravidian
Indo-European
Japanese and Korean
Malayo-Polynesian
Sino-Tibetan
Ural-Asiatic
Other
Uninhabited

CONNECT Geography & Culture

Place Which language families are found in North America?

World Languages and Culture

▼ **KEY QUESTION** Why is language important?

Language is the way cultural values and traditions are passed from one generation to another. **Language** is human communication either written, spoken, or signed, such as American Sign Language. Your family and teachers use language to help you understand your world and how to live in it. Because language relates to all aspects of life, it helps a people to establish a cultural identity.

Sharing the same language is also important to a culture's sense of unity. Sometimes, if more than one language is spoken in an area, people don't feel connected to each other. In Canada, for example, both English and French are spoken. As a result, at times English- and French-speaking Canadians experience conflict.

Language Families Geographers believe that there are between 3,000 and 6,500 languages in the world today. India, for example, has 18 official languages, and more than 800 other languages are spoken there. Some of the world's languages are spoken by only a few thousand people. Other languages have millions of speakers. The language with the largest number of native speakers is Mandarin Chinese, spoken by an estimated 885 million people, mostly in China. English is the most widespread language in the world.

Scholars have arranged the world's languages into 11 main language families. A **language family** is a group of languages that have a common origin. English is in the Indo-European language family, the most widespread language family. An estimated one-half of the world's population speaks an Indo-European language.

Spread and Change of Language Geographers study how languages are distributed throughout the world as a way to learn more about cultures. Like religion and other elements of culture, language spreads in many ways. People bring their language and their culture with them when they move from place to place. Indo-European languages, such as English, Dutch, Portuguese, Spanish, and French, were carried to all parts of the world by European explorers and colonists.

Language not only spreads, it also changes. Language changes when people interact and borrow words from one another. Change also happens when people need new words to express new ideas or to represent new objects or activities, such as *weblog*, or *blog*.

Hello
Buon Giorno
Zdravstvui
Dzien Dobry Dia Dhuit
Namasté
Gei Sou

Fun Facts!

INDO–EUROPEAN LANGUAGES
All of the above greetings come to you from the same language family— Indo-European. These words are variations of *hello* in English, Italian, Russian, Polish, Hindi, Greek, and Irish. These seven languages are a part of more than 400 in this language family.

 FIND MAIN IDEAS Explain why language is important to culture.

Section ① Assessment

 ONLINE QUIZ
For test practice, go to **Interactive Review** @ ClassZone.com

TERMS & NAMES
1. Explain the importance of
- culture
- ethnic group
- religion
- language

USE YOUR READING NOTES
2. Summarize Use your completed chart to answer the following question:
Why is language important in a culture?

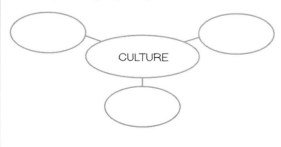

KEY IDEAS
3. What are the basic elements of culture?
4. What are the five major religions of the world?
5. How are the world's languages organized?

CRITICAL THINKING
6. Draw Conclusions Why is religion an important part of a group's culture?
7. Sequence Events How does culture pass from one generation to the next?
8. CONNECT to Today What are the most influential elements in the culture of the United States?
9. WRITING Write a Brief Description Choose a cultural group. Write a description that includes information on cultural elements, such as religion, language, government, technology, arts and crafts, and food and clothing.

Reading for Understanding

SECTION 2

▶ Key Ideas

BEFORE, YOU LEARNED

People belong to specific groups that share a common culture.

NOW YOU WILL LEARN

Cultures do not remain the same but change over time.

▶ Vocabulary

TERMS & NAMES

agricultural revolution the shift from gathering food to raising food

innovation something new that is introduced for the first time

technology people's application of knowledge, tools, and inventions to meet their needs

diffusion the spread of ideas, inventions, and patterns of behavior from one group to another

cultural hearth an area where a culture originated and spread to other areas

BACKGROUND VOCABULARY

domestication the raising and tending of a plant or animal to be of use to humans

nomad a person who has no set home but moves from place to place in search of food for animals

Visual Vocabulary nomad group

▶ Reading Strategy

Re-create the diagram at right. As you read and respond to the **KEY QUESTIONS**, use the diagram to analyze the causes and effects of cultural change.

 Skillbuilder Handbook, page R8

ANALYZE CAUSE AND EFFECT

Innovation	Diffusion
1._____	1._____
2._____	2._____

CULTURAL CHANGE

 GRAPHIC ORGANIZERS
Go to **Interactive Review** @ ClassZone.com

How Does Culture Change?

Connecting to Your World

Think about all the information and communication tools you have in your daily life. Did you include cell phones, mp3 players, DVDs, digital cameras, or laptop computers? When your parents were your age, none of these devices were available to them. These improvements in technology have changed the ways many people live their lives—and this change has taken place in only one generation. Cultural change happens much more rapidly now than it did in the past.

Zulu Girl, South Africa, with Cell Phone

Culture Change and Exchange

🔻 **KEY QUESTION** How does culture change?

Culture changes over time. The changes may be very slow or quite rapid. Some changes are simple, such as changes in clothing styles. Other changes are more complex, such as the agricultural revolution. In the **agricultural revolution**, which happened thousands of years ago, humans shifted from gathering food to raising food. Because the food source was more reliable, fewer people were needed for raising food, and ways of life changed. Two ways that culture changes are through innovation and diffusion.

Camels Go to Pasture Traditional ways are replaced by modern ones.

Innovation Something new that is introduced for the first time is called an **innovation**. New ideas, inventions, and patterns of behavior are types of innovations that change a culture. The computer is an example of an invention that changed cultures in the United States and around the world. Innovation may take place by accident, or it may be deliberate. The prehistoric control of fire was probably an accident, but it forever changed the way people lived. However, the use of existing resources and technology to solve an old or a new problem is a deliberate innovation. **Technology** refers to people's application of knowledge, tools, and inventions to meet their needs.

Some innovations can dramatically change the way people live. The domestication of wild plants thousands of years ago was such a change. **Domestication** means to raise or to tend plants or animals to be of use to humans. Dependence on agriculture resulted in more densely populated settlements.

Like most cultural changes, the agricultural revolution led to other changes. These settled societies needed to be organized differently from groups of **nomads**, who had no set home but moved from place to place to find food for their animals. This led to more innovations. For example, people needed to find ways to water crops in the field and to store the food once harvested. Look at the pictures below to see how different cultures used the resources and technology available to them to solve a storage problem. New or different tools were also needed to farm the land.

◄ COMPARING ◄ Storage Unit Innovations

Clay Pot Where clay was plentiful, clay pots served as storage units. **1. What would be the advantage of a clay pot for storage?**

Basket Woven grass or reeds created light, portable storage units. **2. Why would this material be used for storage?**

Leather Bag Hides made into bags made storage units easy to transport. **3. What would be a disadvantage of this type of storage?**

The Spread of Agriculture

The spread of agriculture is the most significant change in human history. Having available food year-round allowed people to settle and eventually to develop specialized labor and cities.

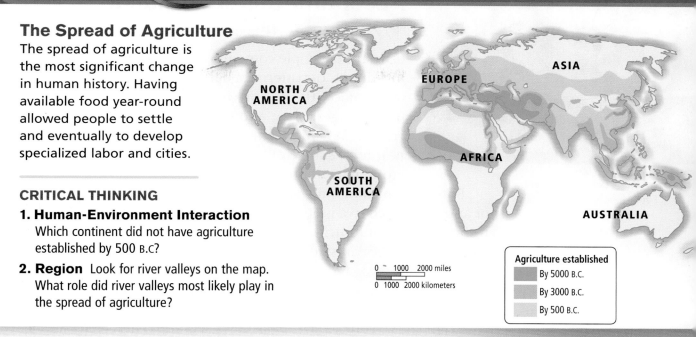

CRITICAL THINKING

1. **Human-Environment Interaction**
   Which continent did not have agriculture established by 500 B.C?

2. **Region** Look for river valleys on the map. What role did river valleys most likely play in the spread of agriculture?

0   1000   2000 miles
0 1000 2000 kilometers

Agriculture established
By 5000 B.C.
By 3000 B.C.
By 500 B.C.

Diffusion The spread of ideas, inventions, and patterns of behavior from one group to another is called **diffusion**. Whenever a group of people comes in contact with another group, diffusion is possible.

The spread of agriculture is an early example of diffusion. The spread of U.S. fast-food restaurants around the world is a modern example. In early times, traders often brought new ideas and inventions to other cultures. Written language, the use of coins, and religious beliefs all moved along ancient trade routes. Missionaries and invaders also carried cultural elements with them.

Geographers study diffusion to see patterns in the development of cultures across the Earth's surface. One pattern they have observed is diffusion from cultural hearths. A **cultural hearth** is an area with an advanced culture from which ideas or technology spread. The map above shows where early cultural hearths existed.

In the past, the spread of culture was usually slow because of geographic barriers. Large bodies of water, mountains, or deserts often made it difficult for people to interact with others. Sometimes political boundaries limited contact between peoples. In today's world, it's almost impossible to avoid some kind of interaction with other groups of people. Satellite television, the Internet, and other forms of mass communication speed new ideas, practices, and inventions around the globe.

▲ **FIND MAIN IDEAS** Identify the ways that culture changes.

Amish Transportation
Amish people choose not to drive automobiles, but use horse-drawn vehicles.

Accepting Cultural Change

▼ **KEY QUESTION** Is cultural change always accepted?

Over time, people come in contact with different ideas, inventions, or patterns of behavior. If a cultural exchange takes place, the culture begins to change. Sometimes this change is slow, and people just become used to the change. When the effects of cultural change— such as a new food source or a tool—are positive, the lives of the group may improve.

But sometimes an innovation is unacceptable, such as use of lands or animals sacred to a group. Sometimes a group may need to decide if the change would help or harm their society. For example, in the United States, the Amish choose not to drive cars, not to have electricity in their homes, and to send their children to private, one-room schoolhouses. They do this because they reject the impact of modern life on their way of life.

Change may sometimes be forced on a group. This often happens when a region is invaded. For example, Spanish conquerors pressed their culture on the native peoples of the Americas in the 1500s.

▲ **MAKE GENERALIZATIONS** Explain why some cultural changes might be rejected.

Section ② Assessment

ONLINE QUIZ
For test practice, go to
Interactive Review
@ ClassZone.com

TERMS & NAMES

1. Explain the importance of
- innovation
- technology
- diffusion
- cultural hearth

USE YOUR READING NOTES

2. Analyze Cause and Effect Use your completed web diagram to answer the following question:

What role do cultural hearths play in changing cultures?

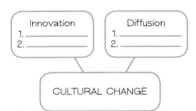

KEY IDEAS

3. What are two ways that bring about cultural change?

4. How does deliberate innovation take place?

5. What three groups helped to spread culture in earlier times?

CRITICAL THINKING

6. Make Inferences What are some reasons why a group may accept cultural change?

7. Draw Conclusions How has mass communication changed the way culture spreads?

8. CONNECT to Today How has the United States been affected by cultural exchange in recent times?

9. TECHNOLOGY Make a Multimedia Presentation Plan a power presentation slide show illustrating three inventions in transportation and three in communication that brought cultural change. Each slide should have a visual of the invention and a description of the change.

Interactive ⏪ Review

Click here to complete these and other activities online @ ClassZone.com

CHAPTER SUMMARY

Key Idea 1
Human beings are members of social groups that have shared and unique behaviors and attitudes.

Key Idea 2
Cultures do not remain the same but change over time.

For **Review and Study Notes**, go to **Interactive Review @ ClassZone.com**

NAME GAME

Use the Terms & Names list to complete each sentence on paper or online.

1. I am the spread of ideas, inventions, and patterns of behavior from one group to another. _____ **diffusion** _____

2. I am a scientist who studies culture. _____

3. I am a people that shares a language, customs, and a common heritage. _____

4. I am the methods, materials, or tools available to complete a task. _____

5. I am the total way of life held in common by a specific group of people. _____

6. I am something new that is introduced for the first time. _____

7. I am a group of languages that have a common origin. _____

8. I am an area where the transfer of elements of culture between two groups occurs. _____

9. I am human communication, either written, spoken, or signed. _____

10. I am an organized system of beliefs in a god or gods and a set of practices. _____

agricultural revolution
anthropologist
culture
cultural hearth
diffusion
domestication
ethnic group
innovation
language
language family
missionary
nomad
religion
technology

Activities

Flip Cards

Use the online flip cards to quiz yourself on terms and names introduced in this chapter.

anthropologist

? a scientist who studies culture

Crossword Puzzle

Complete an online crossword puzzle to test your knowledge of culture.

ACROSS
1. human communication, either written, spoken, or signed

VOCABULARY

Explain the significance of each of the following.

1. culture
2. ethnic group
3. religion
4. language
5. technology

Explain how the terms and names in each group are related.

6. culture, religion, and language
7. innovation, diffusion, and cultural hearth
8. domestication and agricultural revolution

KEY IDEAS

1 What Is Culture?

9. Why are there different cultures?
10. How do people learn about their culture?
11. What are two of the most important elements of culture?
12. What are the three types of religious beliefs?
13. Why is language important to a culture?
14. How does language change?

2 How Does Culture Change?

15. How does innovation change culture?
16. How does diffusion change culture?
17. What is a cultural hearth?
18. Why was culture change a slow process in earlier times?
19. Why might a people accept a cultural change?
20. In what way is cultural change forced upon a people?

CRITICAL THINKING

21. **Categorize** Create a table to list the factors that have helped or limited cultural change over the years.

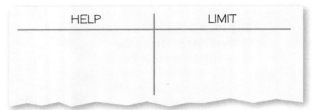

HELP	LIMIT

22. **Make Generalizations** What makes each culture unique?
23. **Make Inferences** Why are families important in a culture?
24. **Connect to Economics** Why was the agricultural revolution such a dramatic cultural change?
25. **Five Themes: Movement** How have aspects of culture been spread throughout history?
26. **Connect Geography & Culture** How important is culture to a person's sense of identity?

Answer the ESSENTIAL QUESTION

How does culture develop, and how does it shape our lives?

Written Response Write a two- or three-paragraph response to the Essential Question. Be sure to consider the key ideas of each section and the fact that all human beings are a part of a culture.

Response Rubric
A strong response will:
• explain the nature of culture and its elements
• discuss how culture shapes the lives of individuals

✓ Test Practice

• Online Test Practice @ ClassZone.com
• Test-Taking Strategies and Practice
  at the front of this book

THEMATIC MAP

Use the map and your knowledge of geography to answer questions 1 and 2 on your paper.

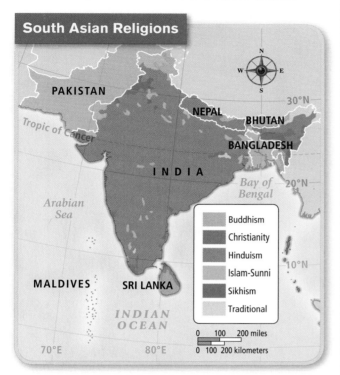

South Asian Religions

Legend:
- Buddhism
- Christianity
- Hinduism
- Islam-Sunni
- Sikhism
- Traditional

0   100   200 miles
0   100   200 kilometers

1. Which of the following countries has a large Buddhist population?

  A. India
  B. Sri Lanka
  C. Bangladesh
  D. Nepal

2. Which of the following countries has a large population of Muslims?

  A. Bhutan
  B. Sri Lanka
  C. Bangladesh
  D. India

CHART

Study the chart below. Use the information in the chart to answer questions 3 and 4.

Languages of Europe	
Country	**Languages Spoken**
Austria	German, Slovene, Croatian, Hungarian
Belgium	Flemish, French, German
France	French
Germany	German
Netherlands	Dutch, Frisian
Switzerland	German, French, Italian, Romansch

Source: *Infoplease database 2006*

3. In which countries is a single language spoken?

4. If you only spoke German, in which countries would you need a translator?

GeoActivity

1. INTERDISCIPLINARY ACTIVITY-MATHEMATICS

With a small group, research world religions on the Internet. Use a computer program to create a database and a graph showing the three countries with the largest number of members for each of the major religions, and the total population of those countries.

2. WRITING FOR SOCIAL STUDIES

Reread the paragraphs on the elements of culture. Then write a paragraph describing the culture of your community. Discuss such elements as religion, language, government, and economic activities.

3. MENTAL MAPPING

Create a map of your town or neighborhood showing schools and places of worship. Be sure to include

- elementary, middle, and high schools, public and private
- any places of worship

UNIT 2

The United States and Canada

Why It Matters:

The United States and Canada are two of the largest countries in the world. Because both nations have vast land areas, abundant resources, and well-educated populations, they have become two of the wealthiest countries in the world.

Statue of Liberty in New York

CHAPTER 5 **The United States**

Chateau Frontenac in Quebec

CHAPTER 6 **Canada**

◄ **Meet Kirima**

In this unit, you will meet Kirima, a middle-school girl from Nunavut, Canada. Learn more about her on **Worldster @ ClassZone.com**

The United States and Canada

The United States and Canada occupy the central and northern four-fifths of the continent of North America. The two countries are bound together not only by physical geography and cultural heritage but also by strong economic and political ties. As you study the maps, notice geographic patterns and specific details about the region. Answer the questions on each map in your notebook.

As you study the graphs on this page, compare the landmass, population, rivers, and mountains of Canada with those of the United States (and in a few cases other regions). Then jot down the answers to the following questions in your notebook.

Comparing Data

1. How does Canada compare in size to the United States?

2. Approximately how many times larger is the population of the United States than that of Canada?

3. Which U.S. rivers are more than twice as long as the Mackenzie River in Canada?

4. What is the difference in height between the tallest peak in the United States and the tallest peak in Canada?

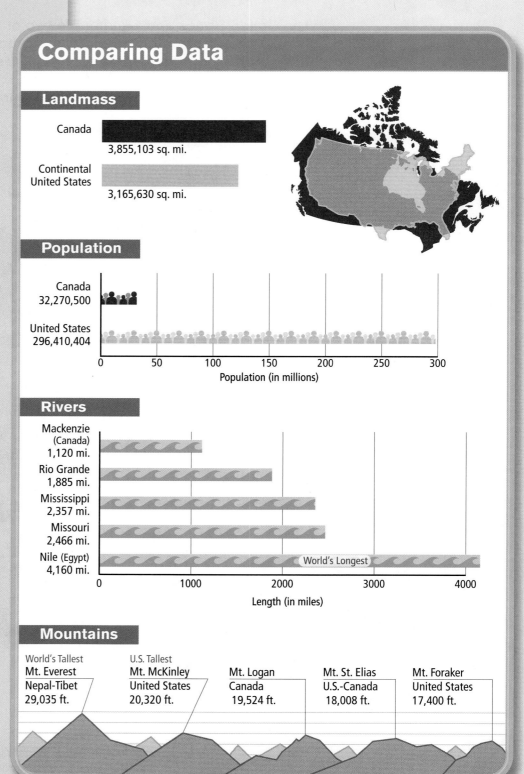

Comparing Data

Landmass

Canada
3,855,103 sq. mi.

Continental United States
3,165,630 sq. mi.

Population

Canada
32,270,500

United States
296,410,404

Population (in millions)
0   50   100   150   200   250   300

Rivers

Mackenzie (Canada) 1,120 mi.
Rio Grande 1,885 mi.
Mississippi 2,357 mi.
Missouri 2,466 mi.
Nile (Egypt) 4,160 mi. — World's Longest

Length (in miles)
0   1000   2000   3000   4000

Mountains

World's Tallest	U.S. Tallest			
Mt. Everest Nepal-Tibet 29,035 ft.	Mt. McKinley United States 20,320 ft.	Mt. Logan Canada 19,524 ft.	Mt. St. Elias U.S.-Canada 18,008 ft.	Mt. Foraker United States 17,400 ft.

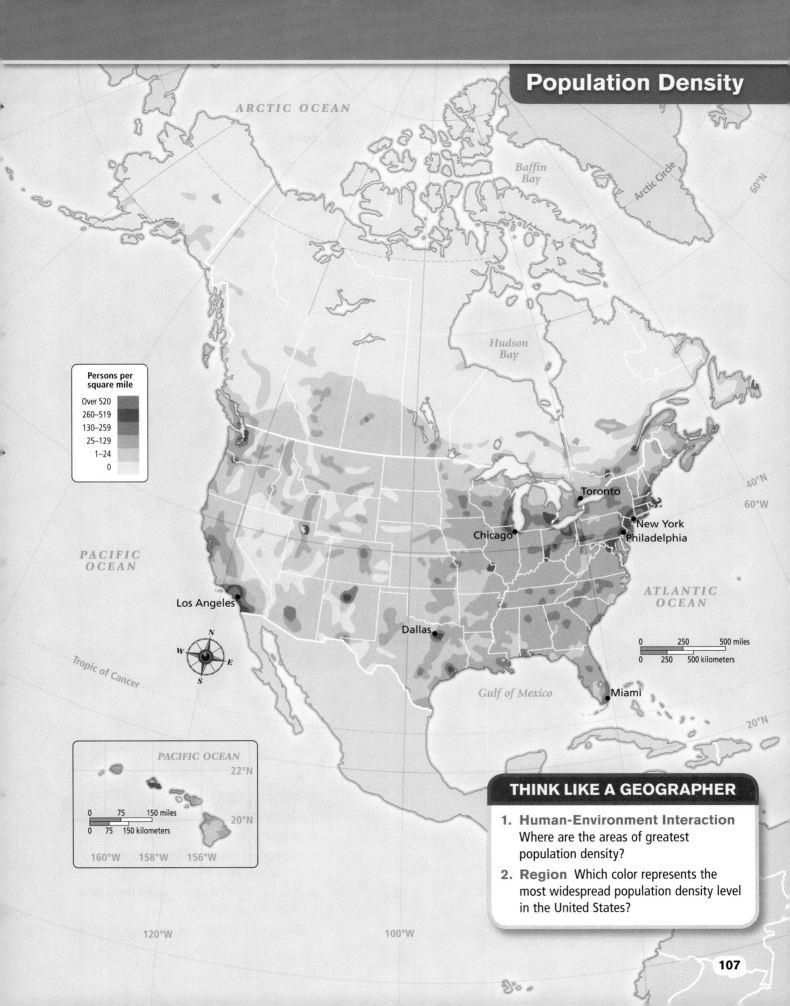

Population Density

ARCTIC OCEAN

Baffin
Bay

Arctic Circle

60°N

Hudson
Bay

**Persons per
square mile**

Over 520
260–519
130–259
25–129
1–24
0

Toronto

40°N

60°W

Chicago

New York
Philadelphia

PACIFIC
OCEAN

ATLANTIC
OCEAN

Los Angeles

| 0 | 250 | 500 miles |

| 0 | 250 | 500 kilometers |

N
W   E
S

Dallas

Tropic of Cancer

Gulf of Mexico

Miami

20°N

PACIFIC OCEAN

22°N

| 0 | 75 | 150 miles |

| 0 | 75 | 150 kilometers |

20°N

160°W   158°W   156°W

THINK LIKE A GEOGRAPHER

1. **Human-Environment Interaction**
   Where are the areas of greatest
   population density?

2. **Region** Which color represents the
   most widespread population density level
   in the United States?

120°W   100°W

Climate

ARCTIC OCEAN

ALASKA (U.S.)

Baffin Bay

Arctic Circle

60°N

40°W

CANADA

Hudson Bay

UNITED STATES

40°N

60°W

ATLANTIC OCEAN

PACIFIC OCEAN

Tropic of Cancer

N
W   E
S

Gulf of Mexico

20°N

Tropical
Tropical wet
Tropical wet and dry

Dry
Desert
Semiarid

Mid-Latitude
Mediterranean
Marine west coast
Humid subtropical
Humid continental

High Latitude
Subarctic
Tundra
Icecap
Highland

| 0 | 250 | 500 miles |
| 0 | 250 | 500 kilometers |

PACIFIC OCEAN

HAWAII
(U.S.)

22°N

20°N

| 0 | 75 | 150 miles |
| 0 | 75 | 150 kilometers |

160°W   158°W   156°W

120°W   100°W

THINK LIKE A GEOGRAPHER

1. **Region** Why might most of the population of Canada be clustered along the border with the United States?

2. **Place** What climate is found throughout most of Canada?

Economic Activity

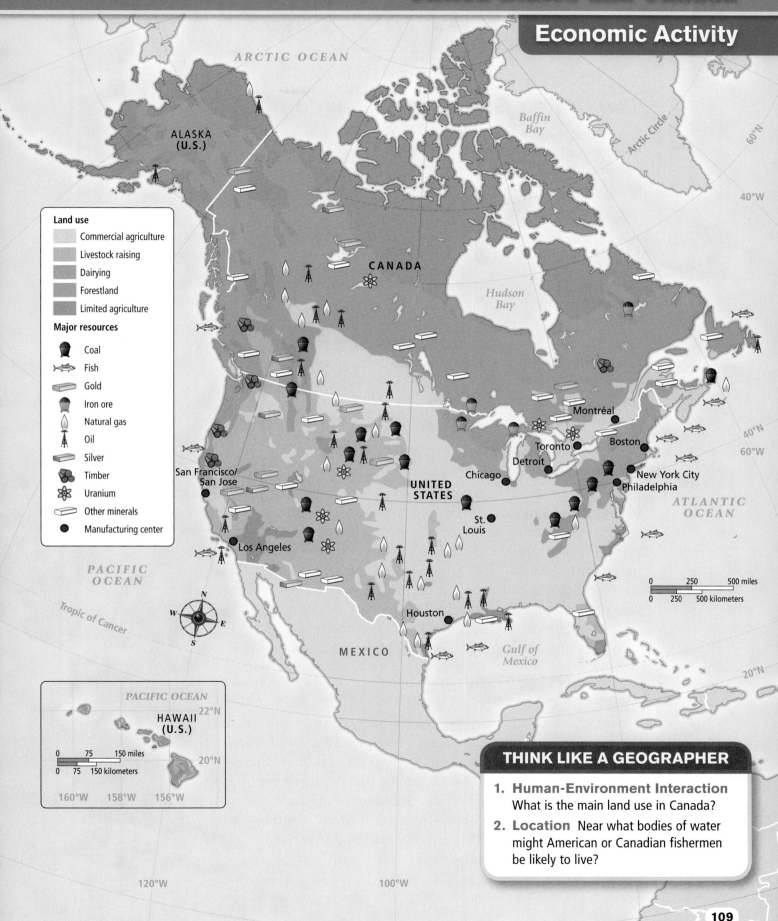

Land use

- Commercial agriculture
- Livestock raising
- Dairying
- Forestland
- Limited agriculture

Major resources

- Coal
- Fish
- Gold
- Iron ore
- Natural gas
- Oil
- Silver
- Timber
- Uranium
- Other minerals
- Manufacturing center

ARCTIC OCEAN

ALASKA (U.S.)

Baffin Bay

Arctic Circle

60°N

40°W

CANADA

Hudson Bay

Montréal

Toronto

Boston

Detroit

New York City
Philadelphia

40°N

60°W

San Francisco/
San Jose

Chicago

UNITED
STATES

St. Louis

ATLANTIC OCEAN

Los Angeles

PACIFIC OCEAN

Tropic of Cancer

Houston

MEXICO

Gulf of Mexico

20°N

0   250   500 miles
0   250   500 kilometers

PACIFIC OCEAN

HAWAII (U.S.)

22°N

20°N

0   75   150 miles
0   75   150 kilometers

160°W   158°W   156°W

120°W   100°W

THINK LIKE A GEOGRAPHER

1. **Human-Environment Interaction** What is the main land use in Canada?

2. **Location** Near what bodies of water might American or Canadian fishermen be likely to live?

The United States and Canada

The United States and Canada occupy the central and northern four-fifths of the continent of North America. The chapters in this unit provide information about the geography, history, culture, government, and economics of the United States and Canada.

GEOGRAPHY

The United States and Canada extend from the Atlantic to the Pacific oceans and north to the Arctic ocean. The United States also reaches to the Gulf of Mexico. In total area, each country ranks among the largest in the world—Canada ranks second and the United States is fourth. In addition to their huge landmass, both countries are rich in natural resources.

HISTORY

Both the United States and Canada have been settled by immigrants from all over the world, beginning with the first settlers who probably migrated from Asia after the last Ice Age. The geographic richness of North America's resources has attracted immigrants from around the world and has enabled both the United States and Canada to develop into global economic powers. This continuing immigration is a recurring theme in the history of both countries; so is the constant migration of people within each country.

CULTURE

As you know, culture involves the following factors: food and shelter, religion, language, education, and political and social organization. In Canada, there are two official languages—English and French—because France played an important early role in the history and development of the country. In the United States, English is the predominant language. Both countries have highly diverse populations that have come from around the world to live within their borders.

Samuel de Champlain
Champlain founded Quebec, the first permanent French settlement in North America.

GOVERNMENT

Both Canada and the United States are representative democracies. In such a system of government, citizens hold political power through elected representatives. Canada and the United States are also federal republics. In a federal republic, power is divided between the national government and various state, territorial, or provincial governments. The personal freedoms guaranteed by the Canadian and U.S. governments have drawn millions to their shores.

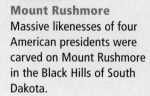

Mount Rushmore Massive likenesses of four American presidents were carved on Mount Rushmore in the Black Hills of South Dakota.

ECONOMICS

The United States and Canada both have market economies. This is an economy in which the production of goods and services is determined by the demand from consumers. This kind of economy is also called a demand economy, or capitalism. Migration across the continent, combined with industrialization and urbanization, stimulated economic development in the United States and Canada. The economies of these two nations have been transformed by technology and by the movement toward globalization.

Toronto People skate outdoors in Toronto, one of Canada's booming economic centers.

Country Almanac

UNIT 2 ATLAS

Click here to compare the most recent data on countries @ ClassZone.com

Unit Writing Project

News Broadcast

As you read this unit, think of an issue to present in a television news broadcast. You might choose an issue like immigration, poverty, or outsourcing of jobs. Pretend you are a TV news reporter and gather information as you read each chapter.

Think About:

- how you will organize your script
- five things to be sure to tell the viewer: who, what, where, when, and why

United States

The United States is made up of 50 states, the District of Columbia, and 4 territories. Alaska, Hawaii, and the territories are separated from the 48 mainland states.

United States

GEOGRAPHY
Capital: Washington, D.C.
Total Area: 3,718,711 sq. mi.
Population: 296,410,404

ECONOMY
Imports: cars; oil; televisions; clothes
Exports: food; computers; machinery

CULTURE
Language: No official language
Religion: Christian 85%; Jewish 2%; Muslim 2%

District of Columbia

Total Area: 68 sq. mi.
Population: 550,521

Alabama

Capital: Montgomery
Total Area: 52,419 sq. mi.
Population: 4,557,808

Alaska

Capital: Juneau
Total Area: 663,267 sq. mi.
Population: 663,661

Arizona

Capital: Phoenix
Total Area: 113,998 sq. mi.
Population: 5,939,292

Arkansas

Capital: Little Rock
Total Area: 53,179 sq. mi.
Population: 2,779,154

California

Capital: Sacramento
Total Area: 163,696 sq. mi.
Population: 36,132,147

Colorado

Capital: Denver
Total Area: 104,094 sq. mi.
Population: 4,665,177

Connecticut

Capital: Hartford
Total Area: 5,543 sq. mi.
Population: 3,510,297

Delaware

Capital: Dover
Total Area: 2,489 sq. mi.
Population: 843,524

Florida

Capital: Tallahassee
Total Area: 65,755 sq. mi.
Population: 17,789,864

Georgia

Capital: Atlanta
Total Area: 59,425 sq. mi.
Population: 9,072,576

Hawaii

Capital: Honolulu
Total Area: 10,931 sq. mi.
Population: 1,275,194

Idaho

Capital: Boise
Total Area: 83,570 sq. mi.
Population: 1,429,096

Illinois

Capital: Springfield
Total Area: 57,914 sq. mi.
Population: 12,763,371

Indiana

Capital: Indianapolis
Total Area: 36,418 sq. mi.
Population: 6,271,973

Corn Harvest A combine harvests corn in Indiana.

Iowa

Capital: Des Moines
Total Area: 56,272 sq. mi.
Population: 2,966,334

Kansas

Capital: Topeka
Total Area: 82,277 sq. mi.
Population: 2,744,687

Kentucky

Capital: Frankfort
Total Area: 40,409 sq. mi.
Population: 4,173,405

Louisiana

Capital: Baton Rouge
Total Area: 51,840 sq. mi.
Population: 4,523,628

Maine

Capital: Augusta
Total Area: 35,385 sq. mi.
Population: 1,321,505

Maryland

Capital: Annapolis
Total Area: 12,407 sq. mi.
Population: 5,600,388

Massachusetts

Capital: Boston
Total Area: 10,555 sq. mi.
Population: 6,398,743

Michigan

Capital: Lansing
Total Area: 96,716 sq. mi.
Population: 10,120,860

Gray Wolf A gray wolf lopes through the snow in Minnesota.

Minnesota

Capital: St. Paul
Total Area: 86,939 sq. mi.
Population: 5,132,799

Mississippi

Capital: Jackson
Total Area: 48,430 sq. mi.
Population: 2,921,088

Lizard A mountain short-horned lizard near Santa Fe, New Mexico

Missouri

Capital: Jefferson City
Total Area: 69,704 sq. mi.
Population: 5,800,310

Montana

Capital: Helena
Total Area: 147,042 sq. mi.
Population: 935,670

Nebraska

Capital: Lincoln
Total Area: 77,354 sq. mi.
Population: 1,758,787

Nevada

Capital: Carson City
Total Area: 110,561 sq. mi.
Population: 2,414,807

New Hampshire

Capital: Concord
Total Area: 9,350 sq. mi.
Population: 1,309,940

New Jersey

Capital: Trenton
Total Area: 8,721 sq. mi.
Population: 8,717,925

New Mexico

Capital: Santa Fe
Total Area: 121,590 sq. mi.
Population: 1,928,384

New York

Capital: Albany
Total Area: 54,556 sq. mi.
Population: 19,254,630

North Carolina

Capital: Raleigh
Total Area: 53,819 sq. mi.
Population: 8,683,242

North Dakota

Capital: Bismarck
Total Area: 70,700 sq. mi.
Population: 636,677

Ohio

Capital: Columbus
Total Area: 44,825 sq. mi.
Population: 11,464,042

Heron A heron takes flight.

Oklahoma

Capital: Oklahoma City
Total Area: 69,898 sq. mi.
Population: 3,547,884

Oregon

Capital: Salem
Total Area: 98,381 sq. mi.
Population: 3,641,056

Pennsylvania

Capital: Harrisburg
Total Area: 46,055 sq. mi.
Population: 12,429,616

Rhode Island

Capital: Providence
Total Area: 1,545 sq. mi.
Population: 1,076,189

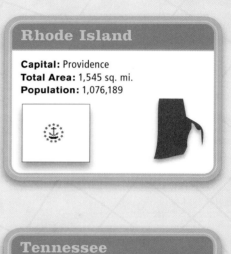

South Carolina

Capital: Columbia
Total Area: 32,020 sq. mi.
Population: 4,255,083

South Dakota

Capital: Pierre
Total Area: 77,117 sq. mi.
Population: 775,933

Tennessee

Capital: Nashville
Total Area: 42,143 sq. mi.
Population: 5,962,959

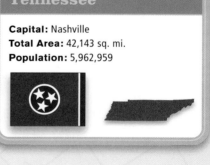

Texas

Capital: Austin
Total Area: 268,581 sq. mi.
Population: 22,859,968

Utah

Capital: Salt Lake City
Total Area: 84,899 sq. mi.
Population: 2,469,585

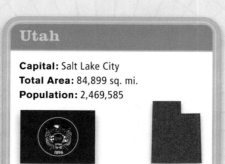

Vermont

Capital: Montpelier
Total Area: 9,614 sq. mi.
Population: 623,050

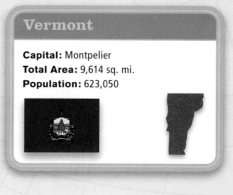

Virginia

Capital: Richmond
Total Area: 42,774 sq. mi.
Population: 7,567,465

Washington

Capital: Olympia
Total Area: 71,300 sq. mi.
Population: 6,287,759

West Virginia

Capital: Charleston
Total Area: 24,230 sq. mi.
Population: 1,816,856

Wisconsin

Capital: Madison
Total Area: 65,498 sq. mi.
Population: 5,536,201

Wyoming

Capital: Cheyenne
Total Area: 97,814 sq. mi.
Population: 509,294

Rocky Mountain Bighorn Sheep Bighorn sheep are found in many Rocky Mountain states, including Wyoming.

U.S. Territories

American Samoa

Capital: Pago Pago
Total Area: 84 sq. mi.
Population: 62,700 (2004)

Guam

Capital: Agana
Total Area: 209 sq. mi.
Population: 165,000 (2004)

U.S. Virgin Islands

Capital: Charlotte Amalie
Total Area: 136 sq. mi.
Population: 109,000 (2004)

Puerto Rico

Capital: San Juan
Total Area: 3,515 sq. mi.
Population: 3,895,000 (2004)

Country Almanac

Click here to compare the most recent data on countries @ ClassZone.com

Puffins Atlantic puffins on Machias Seal Island in Canada

Canada

Canada is made up of 10 provinces and 3 territories. The 3 territories are sparsely populated but make up about 41 percent of the country's landmass.

Canada

GEOGRAPHY
Capital: Ottawa
Total Area: 3,855,103 sq. mi.
Population: 32,270,500

ECONOMY
Imports: machinery; chemicals; oil
Exports: food; natural gas; wood

CULTURE
Language: English; French
Religion: Christian 77%; Muslim 2%; Jewish 1%

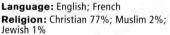

Alberta

Capital: Edmonton
Total Area: 255,541 sq. mi.
Population: 3,256,800

British Columbia

Capital: Victoria
Total Area: 364,764 sq. mi.
Population: 4,254,500

Manitoba

Capital: Winnipeg
Total Area: 250,116 sq. mi.
Population: 1,177,600

New Brunswick

Capital: Fredericton
Total Area: 28,150 sq. mi.
Population: 752,000

Newfoundland and Labrador

Capital: St. John's
Total Area: 156,453 sq. mi.
Population: 516,000

Northwest Territories

Capital: Yellowknife
Total Area: 519,734 sq. mi.
Population: 43,000

Nova Scotia

Capital: Halifax
Total Area: 21,345 sq. mi.
Population: 937,900

Nunavut

Capital: Iqaluit
Total Area: 808,185 sq. mi.
Population: 30,000

Ontario

Capital: Toronto
Total Area: 415,598 sq. mi.
Population: 12,541,400

Prince Edward Island

Capital: Charlottetown
Total Area: 2,185 sq. mi.
Population: 138,100

Quebec

Capital: Quebec City
Total Area: 595,391 sq. mi.
Population: 7,598,100

Saskatchewan

Capital: Regina
Total Area: 251,366 sq. mi.
Population: 994,100

Yukon Territory

Capital: Whitehorse
Total Area: 186,272 sq. mi.
Population: 31,000

Polar Bear A polar bear in a field of tundra fireweed near Hudson Bay

The United States

 ESSENTIAL QUESTION

How did a developing nation grow into a world power?

CONNECT Geography & History

Use the map and the time line to answer the following questions.

1. Which of the Great Lakes is located entirely within the United States?
2. In what year did Hurricane Katrina occur and how did the location of New Orleans contribute to the damage caused by it?

History
1565 Pedro Menéndes de Avilés founds the city of St. Augustine in Florida for Spain. ▶

1492

Government
1787 The Constitution of the United States is written in Philadelphia.

History
1775 American Revolution begins with the battles of Lexington and Concord. ▶

Animated GEOGRAPHY
Present-Day United States

Click here to explore the United States @ ClassZone.com

National capital ⊛
State capital ★
Other city •

0   200   400 miles
0   200   400 kilometers

CANADA

Seattle
Olympia ★
WASHINGTON
Portland
★ Salem
OREGON
Helena ★
MONTANA
NORTH DAKOTA
Bismarck ★
SOUTH DAKOTA
Pierre ★
MINNESOTA
St. Paul ★
WISC.
Madison ★
Lake Superior
L. Huron
MICH.
Lansing ★
L. Ontario
L. Erie
Buffalo
MAINE
Augusta ★
VT
Montpelier ★ N.H.
Concord ★
N.Y.
Albany ★
MA.
Boston ★
R.I.
Hartford ★ Providence ★
CT.
IDAHO
Boise ★
WYOMING
Cheyenne ★
NEVADA
Carson City ★
Sacramento ★
San Francisco
CALIFORNIA
Las Vegas •
Los Angeles •
Salt Lake City ★
UTAH
Denver ★
COLORADO
NEBRASKA
Lincoln ★
KANSAS
Topeka ★
IOWA
Des Moines ★
Chicago
ILL.
Springfield ★
St. Louis •
MISSOURI
Jefferson City ★
OHIO
Columbus ★
Indianapolis ★
IND.
Detroit •
PENN.
Harrisburg ★
Philadelphia •
Ohio River
KENTUCKY
Frankfort ★
W.V.
Charleston ★
VA.
Richmond ★
Trenton ★
New York
N.J.
Dover ★ DEL.
Washington, ⊛ Annapolis ★
D.C. MD.
UNITED STATES
ARIZONA
Phoenix ★
Tucson •
NEW MEXICO
Santa Fe ★
OKLAHOMA
Oklahoma City ★
Little Rock ★
ARK.
TENN.
Nashville ★
N.C.
Raleigh ★
S.C.
Columbia ★
Missouri River
TEXAS
Austin ★
Houston •
Dallas •
LA.
Baton Rouge ★
New Orleans •
MISS.
Jackson ★
ALA.
Montgomery ★
Atlanta ★
GEORGIA
Tallahassee ★
FLORIDA
Miami •
Rio Grande
MEXICO
Gulf of Mexico
ATLANTIC OCEAN
PACIFIC OCEAN

ALASKA
Yukon River
Arctic Circle
CANADA
Anchorage •
Juneau ★
Bering Sea
0   200   400 mi
0   200 400 km

PACIFIC OCEAN
HAWAII
Honolulu ★
0   100 mi
0   100 km

N W E S

Culture
1965 Martin Luther King Jr., leads voting rights march in Selma, Alabama. ▶

Geography
◀ **1804** Lewis and Clark begin expedition to explore Louisiana Purchase.

LEWIS AND CLARK EXPEDITION 1954
1804
UNITED STATES POSTAGE 3¢

Today

Geography
2005 Hurricane Katrina destroys much of New Orleans.

Reading for Understanding

▶ Key Ideas

BEFORE, YOU LEARNED

Our planet has a great variety of landforms and bodies of water, as well as great variety in its climate and vegetation.

NOW YOU WILL LEARN

The physical geography of the United States varies greatly from coast to coast.

▶ Vocabulary

TERMS & NAMES

Appalachian (AP•uh•LAY•chee•uhn)
Mountains a mountain chain in the eastern United States, running parallel to the Atlantic Ocean

Great Lakes five lakes forming the largest group of freshwater lakes in the world

Mississippi River the largest river and chief waterway of the United States

Great Plains a vast grassland in central North America

Gulf of Mexico an arm of the Atlantic Ocean that lies south of the United States

Piedmont (PEED•MAHNT) a hilly, upland region between the Appalachian Mountains and the coastal plain of the South

Everglades huge wetlands of southern Florida

Rocky Mountains a mountain range that extends about 3,000 miles from New Mexico to Alaska

Continental Divide a high ridge line in the Rocky Mountains that divides east-flowing from west-flowing rivers

Mt. McKinley (also called Denali) the tallest mountain of North America, located in Alaska

Grand Canyon a deep gorge cut through northern Arizona by the Colorado River

REVIEW

continent one of seven large landmasses on the surface of the earth

▶ Reading Strategy

Re-create the chart that is shown at right. As you read and respond to the **KEY QUESTIONS**, use the chart to organize important details about the physical geography of the United States.

 Skillbuilder Handbook, page R7

CATEGORIZE

	LANDFORMS	CLIMATE	VEGETATION
Northeast			
Midwest			
South			
West			

 **GRAPHIC ORGANIZERS**
Go to **Interactive Review** @ ClassZone.com

SECTION
1
GEOGRAPHY

From Coast to Coast

Connecting to Your World

What outdoor activities do you enjoy? Sports such as surfing and scuba diving are popular in Hawaii. Many people go skiing and snowboarding in the snowy mountains of Colorado. The United States is a large country with nearly every type of landscape and climate. One thing that helps to define the major U.S. regions is the type of activities common to the area.

Surfing and Skiing
These are two activities that can be enjoyed in the varied U.S. landscapes.

Northeast

🔻 **KEY QUESTION** What are the geographic advantages and disadvantages of the Northeast?

The United States stretches across the North American **continent**, or large landmass. The country can be divided into four regions: Northeast, Midwest, South, and West. The features that set the regions apart are their landforms, climates, plants, animals, and ways of life. The Northeast includes the New England states of Maine, New Hampshire, Vermont, Massachusetts, Rhode Island, and Connecticut, as well as New York, Pennsylvania, and New Jersey.

Appalachian Mountains These mountains extend for almost 2,000 miles in the eastern United States and Canada.

APPALACHIAN MTS.
ATLANTIC OCEAN

Landforms, Climate, and Vegetation The two most important physical features of the Northeast are the Atlantic Ocean Ⓐ (shown on the map on the next page) and the **Appalachian** (AP•uh•LAY•chee•uhn) **Mountains** Ⓑ. The Atlantic coastline, which forms the region's eastern border, has deep-water harbors that support trade. The Appalachians are a mountain chain that runs parallel to the Atlantic Coast.

In much of the Northeast, especially in New England, the terrain is too hilly and rocky to make good farmland. Most of the region lacks mineral wealth, but Pennsylvania has coal and iron ore deposits.

Summers are warm and humid. Winters are cold and snowy, with the most snow falling in the northernmost states. Despite the effects of the logging industry, forests still stretch over much of the region.

Life in the Northeast The Northeast was one of the first areas of North America to be heavily settled by Europeans. Because of the area's rocky land and good harbors, fishing and shipping became more profitable than farming. Textile mills built in the Northeast in Lowell, Massachusetts, were among the first U.S. factories.

The Northeast is still the most densely populated and industrialized region of the United States. The coast is crowded with cities. Shipping and manufacturing are major parts of the economy, but service industries also play a large part. New York City, the largest city in the country, is a world center of finance, trade, and culture.

🔺 **COMPARE AND CONTRAST** Describe the geographic advantages and disadvantages of the Northeast.

Midwest

🔻 **KEY QUESTION** What are the most important features of the Midwest's geography?

The central and northern part of North America has one of the largest areas of lowlands on the planet. Those plains make up most of the Midwest. The region stretches from Ohio west to the Dakotas and from Canada south to the Ohio River, Missouri, and Kansas.

Mississippi River
Minneapolis, Minnesota is located on the Mississippi River. **Why might important cities be located along a major river?**

Minneapolis
Mississippi River
Gulf of Mexico

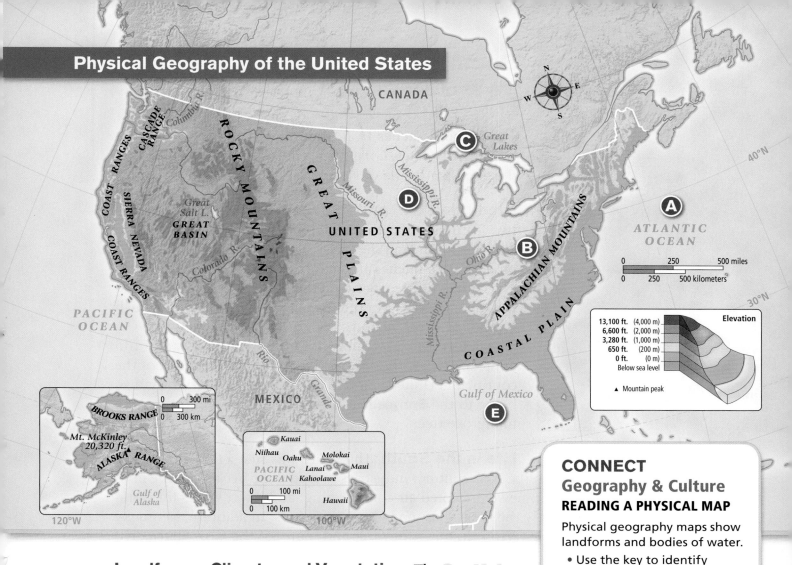

Physical Geography of the United States

CANADA

COAST RANGES

CASCADE RANGE

Columbia R.

ROCKY MOUNTAINS

SIERRA NEVADA

COAST RANGES

Great Salt L.

GREAT BASIN

Colorado R.

Rio Grande

GREAT PLAINS

Missouri R.

Mississippi R.

UNITED STATES

Ohio R.

Mississippi R.

APPALACHIAN MOUNTAINS

COASTAL PLAIN

MEXICO

Gulf of Mexico Ⓔ

PACIFIC OCEAN

ATLANTIC OCEAN Ⓐ

Ⓒ *Great Lakes*

Ⓓ

Ⓑ

40°N

30°N

120°W

100°W

| 0 | 250 | 500 miles |
| 0 | 250 | 500 kilometers |

Elevation

13,100 ft. (4,000 m)
6,600 ft. (2,000 m)
3,280 ft. (1,000 m)
650 ft. (200 m)
0 ft. (0 m)
Below sea level

▲ Mountain peak

BROOKS RANGE

Mt. McKinley 20,320 ft.

ALASKA RANGE

Gulf of Alaska

| 0 | 300 mi |
| 0 | 300 km |

Kauai
Niihau *Oahu* *Molokai*
Lanai *Maui*
PACIFIC OCEAN *Kahoolawe*
Hawaii

| 0 | 100 mi |
| 0 | 100 km |

Landforms, Climate, and Vegetation The **Great Lakes** Ⓒ make up the world's largest group of freshwater lakes. Four of the lakes—Ontario, Erie, Huron, and Superior—form part of the U.S.-Canada border. The **Mississippi River** Ⓓ is the largest river and most important trade waterway in the United States. West of the Mississippi lies the vast, mostly treeless **Great Plains**. Its native plants are prairie grasses and wildflowers. Huge herds of bison once roamed the plains. The Midwest has a harsh climate, with hot summers and cold winters.

Life in the Midwest The Midwest is the major farming region of the United States, with corn, wheat, and dairy among its important products. The Midwest also contains major manufacturing areas, such as Detroit, Michigan, home of the automobile industry. The Midwest's largest city is Chicago, a port and transportation hub along Lake Michigan. The St. Lawrence Seaway connects Chicago to the Atlantic, and canals and rivers connect the city to the **Gulf of Mexico** Ⓔ.

▲ **EVALUATE** Describe geographic features of the Midwest.

CONNECT
Geography & Culture
READING A PHYSICAL MAP

Physical geography maps show landforms and bodies of water.

• Use the key to identify elevation.
• Use the scale to estimate distance.

1. **Movement** What landform might have restricted movement westward from the east coast?

2. **Location** Which rivers flow into the Pacific Ocean?

South

▼ **KEY QUESTION** What is the climate of most of the South?

The South stretches from the Atlantic Ocean to Texas; it contains 16 states. On a map, its most noticeable feature is the giant peninsula of Florida.

Landforms, Climate, and Vegetation The South shares two features with other regions. The Appalachians extend into the South, and the Mississippi River runs through it. A broad plain stretches along the coasts of the Atlantic Ocean and Gulf of Mexico. Between the Atlantic Coastal Plain and the Appalachians lies the **Piedmont** (PEED•MAHNT), which is a hilly, upland region.

Most of the South has hot, rainy summers and mild winters. The southern tip of Florida is the only part of the continental United States to lie in the tropics. Florida is also home to the **Everglades**, a wetland filled with grasses and mangrove trees.

Everglades National Park A cluster of dwarf cypresses grows in this park in Florida. **What wildlife might thrive in a subtropical wetland such as the Everglades?**

Life in the South The South was first a farming region. Then in the 20th century, industries moved there because of the mild climate, newly invented air conditioning, and lower wages for workers. Now the South has many booming cities. In addition, Kentucky and West Virginia mine for coal, and many of the Gulf States drill for oil. Deadly hurricanes sometimes hit places on the South's long coastline. In 2005, Hurricane Katrina struck the Gulf Coast, including New Orleans, Louisiana. Most of the city was flooded. Rebuilding New Orleans is a challenge that will take years to complete.

▲ **FIND MAIN IDEAS** Describe the climate of the South.

West

▼ **KEY QUESTION** What are the climates found in the West?

A huge region of dramatic scenery, the West includes all the states from the Great Plains to the Pacific, plus Alaska and Hawaii.

Landforms, Climate, and Vegetation The West's most visible feature is the **Rocky Mountains**, which extend 3,000 miles from Alaska to New Mexico. The **Continental Divide**, a high ridge line that separates the east-flowing and west-flowing rivers of the continent, runs through the mountains. The tallest mountain in North America is **Mt. McKinley** (also called Denali) in Alaska.

The West has varied climates, plants, and animals. Much of the region has an arid or desert climate, but the Northwest coast is rainy. Hawaii has a tropical climate; most of Alaska is cold. Cacti such as the many-armed saguaro (suh•GWAHR•oh) grow in the deserts, while the redwoods, tallest of all trees, grow along the Pacific coast. Wildlife includes snakes, lizards, wild cats, wolves, and the massive grizzly bear.

Life in the West Ranching, mining, and logging are important industries in the region. Parts of California and Hawaii are devoted to agriculture, while oil drilling is a major industry in Alaska. Recently, high-tech industries have clustered in California and Washington.

Some areas, such as southern California, are very urban, but most Western states are sparsely populated. The West has many national parks to preserve its landscapes. One is at the **Grand Canyon**, a deep, colorful gorge that the Colorado River cut through northern Arizona over many millions of years.

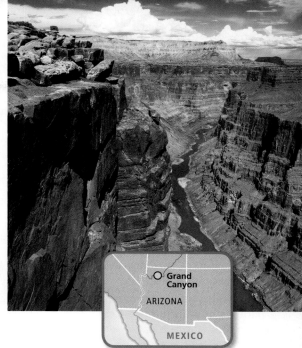

The Grand Canyon The Grand Canyon in Arizona was created by erosion caused by the Colorado River.

▲ **SUMMARIZE** Describe the climates of the West.

ONLINE QUIZ For test practice, go to **Interactive Review** @ ClassZone.com

Section 1 Assessment

TERMS & NAMES

1. Explain the importance of
- Great Lakes
- Mississippi River
- Great Plains
- Rocky Mountains

USE YOUR READING NOTES

2. Categorize Use your completed chart to answer the following question:

Which of the four regions have mountains? Name the mountains found in each region.

	LANDFORMS	CLIMATE	VEGETATION
Northeast			
Midwest			
South			
West			

KEY IDEAS

3. How did the geography of the Northeast affect its economic development?

4. In what way does the Mississippi River provide an economic link between the Midwest and South?

5. Why are there many national parks in the West?

CRITICAL THINKING

6. Draw Conclusions Why is the Northeast coast so crowded with cities?

7. Analyze Causes Why is the South in more danger from hurricanes than the Midwest or the Northeast?

8. CONNECT to Today In 2005, the U.S. government debated whether to allow companies to drill for oil in a part of Alaska that had been protected for wildlife. What arguments might be made for banning or allowing drilling?

9. SCIENCE Create a Poster Learn about the Grand Canyon in an encyclopedia or educational Web site. Then create a poster explaining how it was formed.

The United States is divided into four main regions. They are distinguished from one another by their landforms, bodies of water, climates, and economies.

WEST

The West has a great variety of scenery (see Wyoming's Grand Tetons below), climate, and economic activities.

Landforms: Rocky Mountains
Bodies of Water: Pacific Ocean
Climate: varied—arid; rainy and mild; cold; tropical
Economy: ranching, mining, logging, farming, high-tech industries

Bears are found throughout the West.

Bald eagles thrive in the Alaskan wilderness

Alaska

Hawaii

MIDWEST

The **Midwest** has extremes in weather and ways of life, ranging from farming (see Kansas alfalfa farm below) to manufacturing.

Landforms: Great Plains
Bodies of Water: Great Lakes, Mississippi River
Climate: hot summers, cold winters
Economy: farming, manufacturing, transportation, trade

Prairie dogs are common on the Great Plains.

NORTHEAST

The **Northeast** was the first area of North America to be heavily settled by Europeans. It is still the most densely populated region.

Landforms: Appalachian Mountains and Coastal Plain
Bodies of Water: Atlantic Ocean (see Maine lighthouse on Atlantic coast above)
Climate: warm, humid summers; cold, snowy winters
Economy: trade, manufacturing, service industries

Seagulls are common along the Atlantic coast.

SOUTH

The **South** has attracted industries and people in part because of the warm climate.

Landforms: Appalachian Mountains, Everglades (see above)
Bodies of Water: Gulf of Mexico, Mississippi River, Atlantic Ocean
Climate: hot rainy summers and mild winters
Economy: farming, manufacturing, coal mining, oil drilling

Alligators thrive in the Everglades.

CRITICAL THINKING

1. **Compare and Contrast** Which region does not have mountains as one of its basic landforms?

2. **Compare and Contrast** In which region does farming not play a major role in the economy?

Reading for Understanding

▶ Key Ideas

BEFORE, YOU LEARNED

The United States spans the North American continent from the Atlantic to the Pacific oceans.

NOW YOU WILL LEARN

Native Americans and peoples from other continents all came together to build a nation.

▶ Vocabulary

TERMS & NAMES

land bridge dry land that appeared between Asia and Alaska during the Ice Age

immigrant a person who moves to one country from another

colony a group of people who settle a distant land but are ruled by their homeland

Constitution the document that is the basis for the U.S. government

Louisiana Purchase the action by which President Thomas Jefferson bought the Louisiana Territory from France

Lewis and Clark Expedition a journey made by Lewis and Clark to explore the Louisiana Terrritory

manifest destiny the idea that the United States should own all the land between, and even beyond, the Atlantic and Pacific oceans

Civil War (1861–1865) a conflict between North and South over the issues of states' rights and slavery

transcontinental railroad a railroad that crosses a continent

Great Depression a period of severe economic decline from 1929 into the early 1940s

Dust Bowl a region of the Great Plains that suffered drought and suffocating dust storms

▶ Reading Strategy

Re-create the diagram shown at right. As you read and respond to the **KEY QUESTIONS**, use the outer ovals to note important details.

Skillbuilder Handbook, page R4

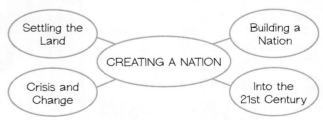

FIND MAIN IDEAS

- Settling the Land
- Building a Nation
- CREATING A NATION
- Crisis and Change
- Into the 21st Century

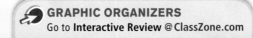

GRAPHIC ORGANIZERS
Go to **Interactive Review** @ ClassZone.com

Creating a Nation

Connecting to Your World

What do you think of when someone mentions U.S. history? Do you picture Native Americans hunting bison? Maybe you think of Pilgrims landing in New England or of the Liberty Bell. No matter what image comes to mind, it is probably connected in some way to geography. The ways that people chose to live on the land, the movement of people, and the interaction of cultures all have played a crucial role in shaping the past.

Settling the Land

🔻 **KEY QUESTION** Who were the first groups to settle the land that became the United States?

The history of the United States involves many different cultures, including Native Americans, Europeans, Asians, and Africans. Sometimes various groups such as Native Americans and European settlers fought, but more often, they learned from each other and helped to create a new, American culture. For example, the music of African slaves blended with that of Irish and Scottish settlers to form a new American music. The history of the United States is also the story of how a developing nation on the Atlantic coast grew to span a continent.

The Liberty Bell
The Liberty Bell was rung to announce the first public reading of the Declaration of Independence in Philadelphia on July 8, 1776.

Bison Hunt Huge herds of bison once roamed the Great Plains.

Native Americans Scientists believe that the first inhabitants of North America came from Asia. According to one theory, the Ice Age glaciers held so much frozen water that ocean levels fell. The drop in sea level uncovered a **land bridge**, a stretch of dry land between Asia and Alaska. Many thousands of years ago, Asians hunting for food crossed into North America. Other people dispute the land bridge theory. Some scientists believe that people came from Asia on boats.

No matter how humans arrived, people eventually spread to all parts of the Americas. Those who settled North America are split into two main groups: the Inuit, who live in the far north, and Native Americans, who are divided into many smaller groups. By the year 1500, hundreds of cultural groups lived in North America. They spoke different languages. Some lived by hunting and fishing, while others farmed. Most lived in close-knit societies organized by clans.

The First Colonies In the 1500s, Europeans began to come to North America. This began a pattern of immigrants coming to the United States from around the world. An **immigrant** is a person who moves to one country from another. Some Europeans came looking for gold or land. Others came to find religious freedom. Many Africans were brought to the colonies by force to work as slaves.

Over time, Europeans started many American colonies. A **colony** is a group of people who settle a distant land but are ruled by their homeland. The Spanish founded St. Augustine, Florida, one of the oldest U.S. settlements. They also built missions in the Southwest. English settlements include Jamestown, Virginia, and Plymouth Colony in Massachusetts. The French colony, New France, included eastern Canada and lands near the Great Lakes and Mississippi River.

▲ **SUMMARIZE** Describe the first groups that settled the United States.

Building a Nation

▼ **KEY QUESTION** How did the United States gain new territory?

In 1763, Great Britain defeated France in the French and Indian War and took over New France. To pay off the war debt, Britain's rulers imposed new taxes on the American colonists.

Thomas Jefferson (1743–1826) was the third president of the United States. He was proud of having written the Declaration of Independence. Here is the most famous quotation from it.

> We hold these truths to be self-evident [obvious], that all men are created equal, that they are endowed [provided] by their Creator with certain unalienable [not able to be taken away] Rights, that among these are Life, Liberty and the pursuit of Happiness.

Source: *The Declaration of Independence,* by Thomas Jefferson

DOCUMENT–BASED QUESTION

Why might it be more accurate to say that people have a right to pursue happiness instead of the right to be happy?

Benjamin Franklin reads Jefferson's Declaration. ▶

ONLINE PRIMARY SOURCE To read more of Thomas Jefferson's writing, go to the **Research & Writing Center** @ ClassZone.com

Britain also passed laws to control the colonies. The colonists objected to the new laws because they had no representatives in the British lawmaking body to speak for their interests and concerns.

The Revolution and Constitution In 1775, the Revolutionary War began, and in 1776, the colonies proclaimed their freedom in the Declaration of Independence, written by Thomas Jefferson. By 1783, the United States had won the war against Great Britain and become a new nation.

Americans feared abuses of power, so they set up a weak national government. But leaders soon realized that the government was too weak to run the country well. In 1787, leaders from 12 states met to create a new government. They wrote the **Constitution** of the United States, the document that is the basis for the U.S. government.

The Constitution set up a federal government—a union of states with a central authority—divided into three equal branches.

1. The legislative branch, Congress, makes the laws. It consists of two houses—the Senate and the House of Representatives.

2. The executive branch is led by the president, the head of the government. George Washington, who won the 1788 presidential election, was the first president of the United States.

3. The judicial branch settles disputes about laws and includes all the courts in the country, including the Supreme Court.

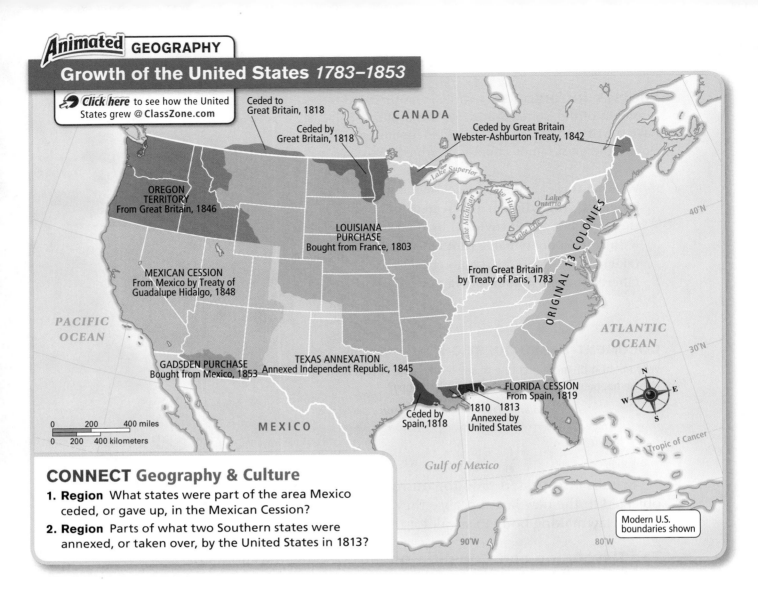

Growth of the United States *1783–1853*

Click here to see how the United States grew @ ClassZone.com

Ceded to Great Britain, 1818

Ceded by Great Britain, 1818

CANADA

Ceded by Great Britain Webster-Ashburton Treaty, 1842

Lake Superior

Lake Michigan

Lake Huron

Lake Ontario

Lake Erie

40°N

OREGON TERRITORY From Great Britain, 1846

LOUISIANA PURCHASE Bought from France, 1803

ORIGINAL 13 COLONIES

MEXICAN CESSION From Mexico by Treaty of Guadalupe Hidalgo, 1848

From Great Britain by Treaty of Paris, 1783

PACIFIC OCEAN

ATLANTIC OCEAN

30°N

GADSDEN PURCHASE Bought from Mexico, 1853

TEXAS ANNEXATION Annexed Independent Republic, 1845

FLORIDA CESSION From Spain, 1819

1810 1813 Annexed by United States

Ceded by Spain, 1818

MEXICO

N E W S

0   200   400 miles
0   200   400 kilometers

Gulf of Mexico

Tropic of Cancer

Modern U.S. boundaries shown

90°W

80°W

CONNECT Geography & Culture

1. **Region** What states were part of the area Mexico ceded, or gave up, in the Mexican Cession?

2. **Region** Parts of what two Southern states were annexed, or taken over, by the United States in 1813?

The Nation Grows Even before the war, Americans had begun to move west to new lands. After the war, the United States gained all of Britain's territory south of Canada and west to the Mississippi. In 1803, President Thomas Jefferson bought Louisiana, a large territory between the Mississippi River and the Rocky Mountains, from France. The **Louisiana Purchase** doubled the size of the United States. Jefferson sent Meriwether Lewis and William Clark to explore the region. The **Lewis and Clark Expedition** gained valuable knowledge of the West.

During the 1800s, many Americans believed in **manifest destiny**, the idea that the United States should own all the land between, and even some beyond, the oceans. The United States gained that territory piece by piece. Texas declared itself free from Mexico in 1836 and became a state in 1845. Then the United States and Mexico fought the Mexican War (1846–1848). The United States gained a huge region stretching from Texas west to the Pacific and north to Oregon.

▲ **FIND MAIN IDEAS** Describe how the United States acquired new territory.

Crisis and Change

 KEY QUESTION How did regional differences help to cause and end the Civil War?

The Northeast became the first manufacturing region. In contrast, large farms called plantations were common in the South. Plantations needed a lot of workers, and the South became a region that relied on African slave labor.

Growing Pains and Civil War From the nation's beginning, some Americans wanted to end slavery. In time, the country split into opposing sides: Northern free states and Southern slave states. The South came to believe that states had the right to reject federal laws and even to secede, or withdraw, from the Union.

In 1860, Abraham Lincoln, a Northerner who hated slavery, was elected president. In response, 11 Southern states seceded from the Union, forming the Confederate States of America. Fighting broke out over secession, and the **Civil War** began in 1861.

At first, the South won more battles. But the North had a larger population and factories to make the supplies the army needed, and so the North defeated the South in 1865. After the war, North and South were reunited.

Expansion In 1867, the U.S. government purchased Alaska from Russia. In 1898, the United States won the Spanish-American War and gained Puerto Rico, Guam, and the Philippines.

The economy also grew, especially in the Northeast. Immigrants poured into U.S. cities. A larger population needed more food, clothing, and housing. Factories replaced hand manufacturing with machines that made goods more quickly. In 1869, workers completed the first **transcontinental railroad** that crossed the continent from coast to coast. The United States continued to build railroads, making it easier to ship goods to market.

HISTORY MAKERS

Abraham Lincoln (1809–1865)

Born in a log cabin, Abraham Lincoln was a self-educated man. When he ran for president in 1860, his critics said he lacked experience. They mocked his rough appearance. Yet Lincoln became president and led the nation through its worst crisis.

During the Civil War, he helped plan the North's war strategy. His Gettysburg Address inspired the nation. Above all, he never forgot his main goal—to save the union. Lincoln achieved that goal but paid a terrible price. Days after the war ended, a Southerner killed him.

ONLINE BIOGRAPHY
For more on the life of Abraham Lincoln, go to the **Research & Writing Center @ ClassZone.com**

▲ **COMPARE AND CONTRAST** Explain how regional differences helped to cause and end the Civil War.

The Dust Bowl

During World War I, farmers plowed up the Great Plains to plant crops. When drought hit in the 1930s, crops died. Wind storms blew away the soil, which no longer had the deep roots of prairie plants to hold it. Dust damaged farms across a 25,000-square-mile region called the Dust Bowl. Dust clouds are shown rolling in over Lamar, Colorado, in 1934.

Into the 21st Century

▼ **KEY QUESTION** What changes did the United States experience during the 1900s?

During much of the 1700s and 1800s, Americans were more concerned with challenges that their own country faced than with events around the world. During the 1900s, however, the U.S. role in the world changed.

Turmoil and Change When World War I started in Europe in 1914, most Americans wanted to stay out of the fighting. Then Germany sank a number of ships, killing U.S. civilians. The United States joined the war in 1917 and help the Allies to win it.

After the war, the 1920s seemed to be an era of wealth and progress. For example, the affordable automobile was built and more people than ever owned stocks. But problems lurked behind the good times. In 1929, stock prices plunged, and many people lost their money. That began the **Great Depression**, a period of severe economic decline (1929–early 1940s) in the United States. Businesses failed, and millions were out of work. Life was hard in the **Dust Bowl**, a large area in the Great Plains that suffered drought and dust storms.

By the late 1930s, war was again raging in Europe and Asia, and again the United States wanted to avoid fighting. Then in 1941, Japan attacked Pearl Harbor, Hawaii, and the United States went to war. The fighting lasted for four more years until the war ended in 1945.

Fun Facts!

SEABISCUIT

During the dark days of the Depression, the story of Seabiscuit (at far right) lifted people's spirits. He was an unlikely looking race horse who managed to defeat some of the great racing champions of the day, such as War Admiral. Seabiscuit stood for the underdog overcoming adversity.

Nation and World U.S. life was transformed in the 20th century. The civil rights and women's liberation movements brought more equality. Rapid technological change was spurred by space exploration, including the moon flights and the space shuttle program.

After World War II, the United States became a world leader. For decades, it competed with the Communist Soviet Union to be the strongest political and military power. When the Soviet Union fell apart in 1991, the United States was the richest and most powerful nation in the world.

In the 21st century, the United States confronted the danger of terrorism, which is the use of violence for political purposes. On September 11, 2001, terrorists flew airplanes into the World Trade Center in New York City and into the Pentagon. Approximately 3,000 people died. The U.S. government responded by launching a war against terrorism.

The United States also tries to be a leader in helping people. For example, when a deadly tsunami struck South Asia in December 2004, Americans gave more than $1 billion to relief efforts. Americans also serve in agencies that improve life in developing countries.

Moon Landing Apollo 15 moon base, established between July 30 and August 7, 1971

▲ **FIND MAIN IDEAS** Describe U.S. changes during the 1900s.

Section 2 Assessment

ONLINE QUIZ
For test practice, go to **Interactive Review** @ ClassZone.com

TERMS & NAMES

1. Explain the importance of
- land bridge
- Louisiana Purchase
- manifest destiny
- Dust Bowl

USE YOUR READING NOTES

2. Find Main Ideas Use your completed diagram to answer the following question:

How did the U.S. role in the world change during the 1900s?

KEY IDEAS

3. Which three events added the largest amounts of land to the United States?

4. How did physical geography make human suffering during the Great Depression worse?

5. In what ways is the United States a world leader?

CRITICAL THINKING

6. Compare How was the U.S. response to the September 11 attacks similar to its response to the Pearl Harbor attack?

7. Evaluate Review the physical geography you studied in Section 1. What do you think was the biggest obstacle to building the transcontinental railroad?

8. CONNECT to Today Does technology make it more or less likely that the United States will return to its old policy of not taking part in world affairs? Explain.

9. WRITING Write a Personal Response Find one of Lincoln's Civil War speeches. Write a paragraph analyzing why that speech inspired people.

SECTION 3 — Reading for Understanding

▶ Key Ideas

BEFORE, YOU LEARNED

From the nation's beginnings until the present time, people from many countries have moved to the United States.

NOW YOU WILL LEARN

The United States is one of the most diverse nations in the world, and it has a rich culture blended from many world cultures.

▶ Vocabulary

TERMS & NAMES

public education schooling that is paid for by the government

literacy the ability to read and write

cultural blending something new created from combining the elements of two or more cultures

jazz a type of music that developed from a blending of African rhythms, American band music, and the musical styles of African Americans and Europeans

blues a type of music with lyrics that express sorrow, usually about problems in love or the hardships of life

BACKGROUND VOCABULARY

official language a language that by law must be used for government, business, and education

REVIEW

culture the behavior patterns, arts, and beliefs of a group of people

Visual Vocabulary Jazz in New Orleans

▶ Reading Strategy

Re-create the chart shown at right. As you read and respond to the **KEY QUESTIONS**, use the chart to organize important details about the diverse culture of the United States.

 Skillbuilder Handbook, page R7

CATEGORIZE

RELIGION	LANGUAGE	ETHNICITY	ARTS & CULTURE
1.	1.	1.	1.
2.	2.	2.	2.
3.	3.	3.	3.

GRAPHIC ORGANIZERS
Go to **Interactive Review** @ ClassZone.com

SECTION

3

CULTURE

A Diverse Culture

Connecting to Your World

Think about some of the most popular foods in the United States. Many of them are versions of food that came from another country. Many recreational activities, too, came from overseas. Martial arts developed in East Asia, yoga originated in India, skiing first began in Norway, and baseball grew out of an English game. The **cultures**—behavior, arts, beliefs—of countless immigrants have made American culture what it is today.

Cultural Diversity

▼ **KEY QUESTION** What are some ways that immigrants have made U.S. culture more diverse?

People have come to the United States from all over the world. As you learned in Section 2, the earliest colonists were Spanish, English, and French. In addition, hundreds of thousands of Africans were brought to America as slaves. In the mid 1800s, millions of Northern Europeans came, mainly from Ireland, Germany, and the United Kingdom. After 1900, immigrants came largely from Italy, as well as from Russia and other Eastern European countries. In recent years, most immigrants have come from Mexico, other Latin American nations, and Asia.

Martial Arts Students practice karate, a Japanese martial art.

New York City A crowd strolls in the middle of Fifth Avenue in New York during a street festival.

Diversity and Shared Beliefs Because the United States has accepted high numbers of immigrants for most of its history, U.S. society is quite diverse. Even so, most people who come to the United States have two things in common. First, they believe in the idea that anyone from any background can have a happy, successful life. Many immigrants come to the United States hoping to make life better for themselves and their children.

Second, most immigrants believe in the value of education. The United States offers free public education through high school. **Public education** is schooling for which the government pays. As a result, the United States has a high rate of **literacy**, or the ability to read and write. About 99 percent of all Americans are literate.

Language and Religion Although English is spoken by almost everyone, the United States does not have an **official language**—one that by law must be used for government, business, and education. Because of the large number of people from Latin America, Spanish is the second most common language.

The way immigrants learn English often follows a pattern. Some adult immigrants struggle with English. The children of those immigrants, however, usually speak two languages—English and the language of their parents. Finally, the children of the next generation use English as their first language.

Diversity is also seen in the variety of religions practiced in the United States. A majority of Americans identify themselves as Christian, with 52 percent being Protestant and 24 percent being Catholic. The remaining Americans are Jews, Mormons, Muslims, and people who practice other religions or no religion.

Cultural Blending Music, language, and food all provide examples of the coming together of the behavior patterns, arts, and beliefs of people from different cultures. In music, traditions from Africa and Europe have blended to create a new American music. The same blending has occurred with food. Different ingredients and recipes from Latin America, Africa, Asia, and Europe have come together to create American cuisine. When elements from two or more cultures combine into something new, it is called **cultural blending**.

American English is one of the best examples of cultural blending. Americans use many words that come from other languages. For example, the terms *kindergarten*, *frankfurter*, and *sauerbraten* come from German. Enslaved Africans brought many terms with them. Some of these evolved into words we use every day, such as *banana* and *cola*. *Rodeo* and *canyon* are examples of words that come from Spanish. Many place names are of Native American origin. For example, the name *Mississippi* means "big river."

Fun Facts!

LEETSPEAK
Have you heard of "133t5p34k" or "leet-speak"? Leetspeak is a kind of made-up written dialect. It comes from the word *elite*, which means a special, privileged group.

Leet began as part of the underground culture centered around text messaging on the Internet. It involves making changes to standard written text. So, for example, the term "leet" itself is often written "1337" or "133t."

ETHNICITY

These maps show the distribution of certain ethnic minorities. African Americans, for example, make up about 12 percent of the total U.S. population but in the Southeast they are more heavily concentrated and make up a higher percentage of the population. Hispanic Americans now make up about 13 percent and Asian Americans about 4 percent of the total U.S. population.

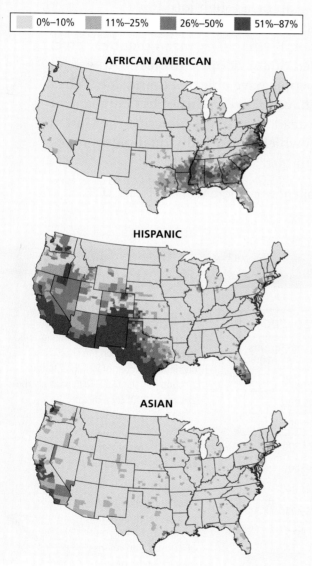

0%–10%	11%–25%	26%–50%	51%–87%

AFRICAN AMERICAN

HISPANIC

ASIAN

LANGUAGES

The chart below shows the most common languages spoken in U.S. households.

Rank	Language
1	English
2	Spanish
3	Chinese
4	French
5	German
6	Tagalog
7	Vietnamese
8	Italian
9	Korean
10	Russian

Source: U.S. Census Bureau (2000)

RELIGIONS

The pie graph below shows the religious preferences of Americans. Christians make up over three-quarters of the population.

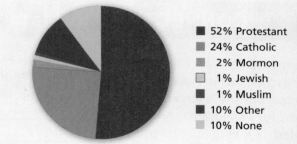

- 52% Protestant
- 24% Catholic
- 2% Mormon
- 1% Jewish
- 1% Muslim
- 10% Other
- 10% None

Source: *CIA World Factbook* (2002)

CRITICAL THINKING

1. **Categorize** What percentage of the population is Christian?

2. **Make Inferences** Why might Hispanics be so heavily concentrated in the West and Southwest?

Challenges of Diversity Immigrants have added much richness to American culture. But living in such a diverse country also has its difficulties. For example, immigrants tend to settle in cities where they can find other people from their homeland. As a result, some cities end up with high percentages of immigrants, many of whom don't speak English. These people face limited employment options and are more likely to live in poverty.

Diversity also affects education. Most immigrant children learn to speak and read English, but that learning doesn't happen overnight. In some places, such as California, teachers have classes in which students speak several different languages. Teaching such a group English—or any other subject—can be a tough job.

Finally, diversity sometimes leads to debate. Many people say that the United States is a melting pot. By that, they mean that over time, people who come to the United States adopt a uniform American culture. In recent times, some people have objected to that idea. They believe that a person does not have to give up his or her language or customs to be an American. Instead, they like to describe the United States as a quilt or a mosaic, in which many individual pieces make up the whole but still remain unique.

▲ **MAKE INFERENCES** Explain how immigrants have made U.S. culture more diverse.

CONNECT to Math

From 1892 to 1924, Ellis Island (shown below) in New York harbor was the main entry point for immigrants. An estimated 17 million immigrants passed through its facilities. After immigration services moved to New York City, Ellis Island served as a detention center for both aliens and deportees.

U.S. Immigration *1820–2004*

Country of Origin	Number of Immigrants (to the nearest thousand)
Germany	7,238,000
Mexico	6,849,000
Italy	5,446,000
United Kingdom	5,337,000
Ireland	4,788,000
Other	40,211,000
Total	69,869,000

Sources: Office of Immigration Statistics, Department of Homeland Security

Activity

Make a Pie Graph

1. Calculate the percentage of immigrants from each country on the chart. First divide the number of immigrants from a country by the total. Then multiply the answer by 100. For example:

   $7,238,000 \div 69,869,000 = .104$

   $.104 \times 100 = 10.4$ percent

   That is the percentage of immigrants who came from Germany.

2. Draw a circle on a piece of paper. Draw a wedge on the circle that represents 10.4 percent of its total. Add wedges for each of the other countries and for Other.

3. Color each wedge a different color. Label the wedges with the country names. Add the numbers beneath the names.

The Arts and Popular Culture

▼ **KEY QUESTION** How has cultural blending affected U.S. arts?

Cultural diversity has had a huge impact on American arts. This impact can clearly be seen in literature and music.

Literature Many writers have produced novels about immigrants and their children. For example, Amy Tan wrote *The Joy Luck Club* about Chinese mothers and their Chinese-American daughters. Much American literature deals with American history or American experiences. For example, *The Great Gatsby* by F. Scott Fitzgerald portrays a man chasing the American dream during the 1920s.

Jazz, Blues, Country, and Rock American music has also been affected by cultural blending. One example of this is jazz. **Jazz** is a type of music that African Americans developed from a blending of African rhythms, American band music, and the musical styles of African Americans and Europeans. Another distinctive type of music related to jazz is the blues. **Blues** features lyrics that express sorrow, usually about problems in love or the hardships of life.

Two other types of American music developed from the blending of different styles. Country music grew out of folk music, the blues, and religious music. Great artists of country music include Hank Williams and Patsy Cline. Rock music evolved from elements of the blues, country music, and American popular songs. Chuck Berry and Elvis Presley were important names in the early history of rock music.

CONNECT ↻ Geography & Culture

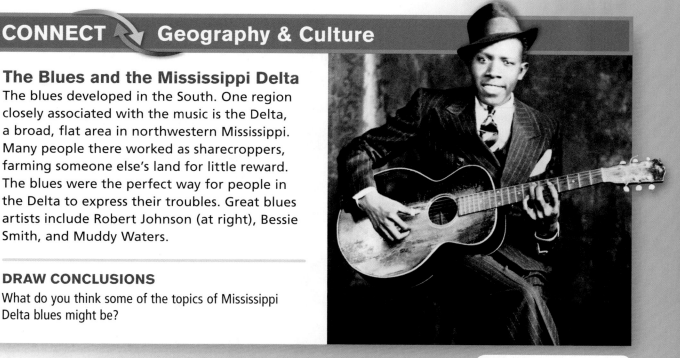

The Blues and the Mississippi Delta
The blues developed in the South. One region closely associated with the music is the Delta, a broad, flat area in northwestern Mississippi. Many people there worked as sharecroppers, farming someone else's land for little reward. The blues were the perfect way for people in the Delta to express their troubles. Great blues artists include Robert Johnson (at right), Bessie Smith, and Muddy Waters.

DRAW CONCLUSIONS
What do you think some of the topics of Mississippi Delta blues might be?

Today's American Music Scene Chances are that you and your friends listen to a wide range of music without even realizing it. Some of the most popular songs on the radio today echo the earlier blues and rock of your parents' generation, or even classical music. And there's a growing internationalism, with music from all parts of the world showing up in the CD racks. One of the most popular musical trends is hip-hop.

Hip-hop music developed in the South Bronx section of New York City in the 1970s. One technique involved in hip-hop is rapping, a form of chanted street poetry set to rhythmic music. Another technique is sampling, in which an existing song provides an underlying rhythm or melody and other sounds are superimposed over it—such as music made by scratching on a turntable or "beatboxing," creating beats and sound effects using the mouth. By the 1990s, hip-hop was a regular on the music charts and had begun to spread world-wide.

However, the biggest story in American music today has nothing to do with the kinds of music people are listening to—it's all about how we are listening. Access to music of all kinds and in huge numbers is higher than ever, thanks to the Internet. Online music services offer databases of inexpensive downloadable music from all genres with a click of the mouse. And all those songs can now be loaded right onto a player that easily fits into the palm of your hand. There's no predicting what the next change in music technology will be, but the evidence is clear: more people will be "wired" to a broad range of music that increases every day.

Play Ball Fans cheer during a Seattle Mariners baseball game at Safeco Field in Seattle.

Sports, Entertainment, and Leisure Americans are avid sports fans. Many people take part in team sports and individual activities such as in-line skating or golf. In addition, millions follow team sports such as baseball, basketball, and football—both at stadiums and on television. In fact, the national football championship, the Super Bowl, is one of the most highly watched television programs each year.

Americans spend a lot of time on leisure activities and entertainment. Leisure is time that is free from work or other duties. One reason Americans have so much leisure time is that the United States is a prosperous nation. Perhaps the two most popular forms of entertainment are movies and television. A film or TV program can have an audience of millions. These two forms of entertainment have created experiences that the majority of Americans share. They help to unify the culture.

Other common pastimes in the United States include a wide variety of hobbies. Some of the most popular are playing computer games, camping, raising pets, gardening, and collecting things such as baseball cards, stamps, or autographs.

Finally, many Americans use part of their free time to improve their society. For example, some people cook meals at shelters for homeless people. Others volunteer to pick up litter along highways. Often, people find that helping others not only makes them feel better about themselves, but it makes their communities better too.

Skateboarding An 11-year-old boy skateboards in New York City.

ANALYZE CAUSES AND EFFECTS Explain how cultural blending has affected the arts in the United States.

Section 3 Assessment

ONLINE QUIZ
For test practice, go to
Interactive Review
@ ClassZone.com

TERMS & NAMES

1. Explain the importance of
- public education
- literacy
- cultural blending
- jazz

USE YOUR READING NOTES

2. Categorize Use your completed chart to answer the following question:

What are some elements and examples of the diversity that makes up the culture of the United States?

RELIGION	LANGUAGE	ETHNICITY	ARTS & CULTURE
1.	1.	1.	1.
2.	2.	2.	2.
3.	3.	3.	3.

KEY IDEAS

3. Why do people come to the United States?

4. In what way is American English an example of cultural blending?

5. How has the physical geography of the United States affected its literature?

CRITICAL THINKING

6. Draw Conclusions How does public education help immigrants adapt to living in the United States?

7. Analyze Effects How did the development of the blues lead to additional cultural blending in music?

8. CONNECT to Today Do you think that the United States today is more like a melting pot or a mosaic? Use evidence to support your answer.

9. TECHNOLOGY **Plan a Web Page** Look for more examples of cultural blending in U.S. culture. Plan a Web page that would explain what cultural blending is and give examples from categories such as food, fashion, literature, music, and recreational activities.

Reading for Understanding

▶ Key Ideas

BEFORE, YOU LEARNED

The United States is a country of great diversity that continues to draw immigrants from around the world.

NOW YOU WILL LEARN

The United States purchases goods from and sells goods to many countries around the world.

▶ Vocabulary

TERMS & NAMES

amendment a written change to the U.S. Constitution that must go through an approval process

representative democracy a type of government in which citizens hold political power through elected representatives

republic another term for representative democracy

federal system a government system in which powers are divided between the national and state governments

free enterprise an economic system in which businesses are free to operate without much government involvement

market economy an economic system in which the production of goods and services is decided by supply and the demand of consumers

Interstate Highway System a network of more than 45,000 miles of roads that links every major U.S. city

global economy economy in which buying and selling occurs across national borders

multinational corporation a company that operates in more than one country

REVIEW

import to bring something from one country into another

export to send something from one country to another

▶ Reading Strategy

Re-create the chart shown at right. As you read and respond to the **KEY QUESTIONS**, use the chart to note the main ideas about the government and economy of the United States.

 Skillbuilder Handbook, page R7

CATEGORIZE

GOVERNMENT	ECONOMY
1.	1.
2.	2.
3.	3.

 GRAPHIC ORGANIZERS
Go to **Interactive Review** @ ClassZone.com

Democracy and Free Enterprise

Connecting to Your World

Have you ever had an election in your classroom? The candidate gives a speech and asks you and your classmates for their support and their votes. At national political conventions you may have seen on television, music is played, and balloons are dropped from the ceiling. People wave signs and cheer. Why do people become so excited? They hope that they have just chosen the person who will be elected the nation's next leader. In the United States, citizens play a role in selecting their own government. Not all countries recognize the people's right to choose their leaders.

The U.S. Government

▼ **KEY QUESTION** What are the three branches of the U.S. government?

As Section 2 explained, the U.S. government is based on a written constitution. This document has changed since it was first written in 1787. Changes are added through **amendments**, written additions that must go through an approval process. There have been 27 amendments.

Political Action
A crowd waves American flags at a political convention. **What issues are most important to you and your classmates?**

COMPARING Branches of the U.S. Government

LEGISLATIVE	EXECUTIVE	JUDICIAL
• U.S. Congress creates, abolishes, and changes laws	• President either signs laws or vetoes [rejects] them	• U.S. Supreme Court interprets laws
• approves appointments and treaties	• enforces laws	• overturns laws that conflict with the Constitution
• imposes taxes	• appoints judges and other officials	• hears certain cases involving federal law or treaties
• declares war	• commands the military forces	• reviews cases on appeal
• impeaches and tries officials for misconduct	• directs foreign and national security affairs	

CRITICAL THINKING

Draw Conclusions What is the main way in which the president acts as a check on the Congress?

A Federal Republic The U.S. government is a **representative democracy**. A democracy is a government in which the people govern. The United States is much too large for every citizen to take part in making laws and policies, so U.S. citizens elect officials to represent them. Another term for a representative democracy is a **republic**.

The Constitution also created a **federal system** in which power is divided between the national and state governments. As you learned in Section 2, the national government is further divided into three branches: legislative, executive, and judicial.

Checks and Balances Recall that Americans fought for independence because they believed that Britain had ruled them unfairly. As a result, they tried to prevent future abuses of power. They wrote a Constitution that gives each branch of government the ability to act as a check, or limit, upon the other two. Those limits keep power in balance by spreading it across the branches. That's why people say our government is a system of checks and balances.

For example, Congress makes the laws, but the president must sign them before they go into effect. And the Supreme Court has the power to say that a law is not valid. These are just some of the ways that the branches of government act as checks on each other.

▲ **CATEGORIZE** Describe the three branches of the U.S. government.

The U.S. Economy

▼ **KEY QUESTION** Who controls the U.S. economy?

The U.S. economy is based on **free enterprise**—businesses are free to operate without much government involvement. Individuals and companies own most of the resources, equipment, and factories.

A Market Economy The United States has a **market economy**, in which individuals and businesses can make their own choices about what to buy and sell. The freedom people have to try to make money has enriched the country as a whole. The U.S. economy produces goods and services worth more than the output of any other country.

Service industries—businesses that provide services, not products—account for 78 percent of the money earned by the U.S. economy. Service industries include banks, insurance companies, hotels, restaurants, and repair shops. Manufacturing accounts for 21 percent and agriculture accounts for 1 percent.

Agriculture and Industry of the United States

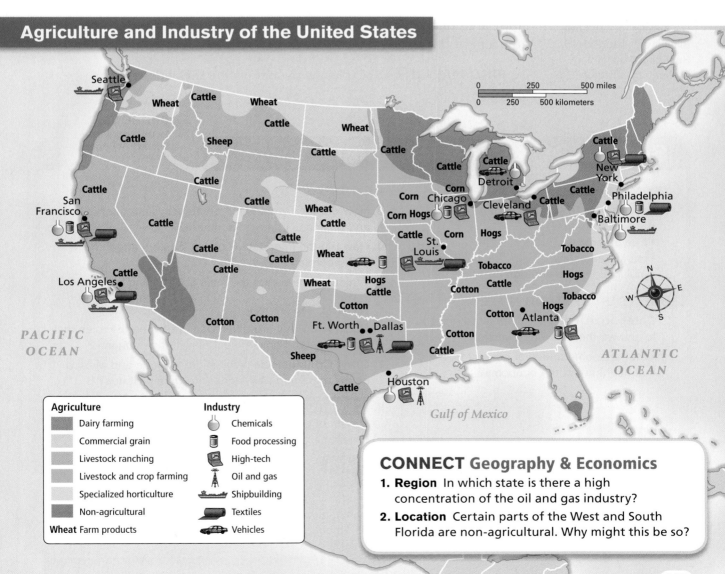

Agriculture
- Dairy farming
- Commercial grain
- Livestock ranching
- Livestock and crop farming
- Specialized horticulture
- Non-agricultural

Wheat Farm products

Industry
- Chemicals
- Food processing
- High-tech
- Oil and gas
- Shipbuilding
- Textiles
- Vehicles

CONNECT Geography & Economics
1. **Region** In which state is there a high concentration of the oil and gas industry?
2. **Location** Certain parts of the West and South Florida are non-agricultural. Why might this be so?

The U.S. government does not run the economy, but it plays an important role. It promotes safety, fights unfair business actions, and builds structures to help economic growth. For example, the government paid to construct the **Interstate Highway System**, a network of more than 45,000 miles of roads that links major U.S. cities. The highways improved the transport of goods and people.

Globalization and a Changing Economy One of the biggest changes in recent times is the rise of a **global economy**, in which much buying and selling occurs across international borders. Technologies such as the Internet have linked businesses around the world.

The United States trades with many other countries. It **imports** goods such as automobiles, clothing, and petroleum. It **exports** goods such as airplanes, computers, and plastics. Canada, Mexico, Japan, and China are among the biggest U.S. trading partners.

The creation of **multinational corporations**, or companies that operate in more than one country, has added to the global economy. Such corporations often locate factories in countries where resources or labor are cheap. Many multinational corporations have their headquarters in the United States.

Highway System The Los Angeles freeways help to unify a widespread city. **How might a highway system link a region?**

 FIND MAIN IDEAS Explain who controls the U.S. economy.

ONLINE QUIZ For test practice, go to **Interactive Review** @ ClassZone.com

Section 4 Assessment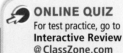

TERMS & NAMES

1. Explain the importance of
  • federal system
  • free enterprise
  • market economy
  • multinational corporation

USE YOUR READING NOTES

2. Categorize Use your completed chart to answer the following question:

What are some duties of government that might affect the economy?

GOVERNMENT	ECONOMY
1.	1.
2.	2.
3.	3.

KEY IDEAS

3. How did the Constitution create a system of checks and balances in the government?

4. How did the Interstate Highway System affect the U.S. economy?

5. Which countries are the main U.S. trading partners?

CRITICAL THINKING

6. Contrast What are differences between the roles that individuals and government play in the economy?

7. Draw Conclusions Why might Canada and Mexico be major trading partners of the United States?

8. CONNECT to Today How do you think that the growth of multinational corporations might affect the government's role in the economy?

9. MATH Create a Pie Graph Look back through this section to learn what percentage of the U.S. economy is service industries, what percentage is manufacturing, and what percentage is agriculture. Use those percentages to create a pie graph.

Click here to complete these and other activities online @ ClassZone.com

CHAPTER SUMMARY

Key Idea 1
The physical geography of the United States varies greatly from coast to coast.

Key Idea 2
Native Americans and peoples from other continents all came together to build a nation.

Key Idea 3
The United States is one of the most diverse nations in the world, and it has a rich culture blended from many world cultures.

Key Idea 4
The United States purchases goods from and sells goods to many countries around the world.

For **Review and Study Notes**, go to **Interactive Review** @ ClassZone.com

NAME GAME

Use the Terms & Names list to complete each sentence on paper or online.

1. I am a swampy region located in southern Florida. __Everglades__

2. I am vast grassland in north-central North America. _____

3. I am a mountain chain that runs from Alaska to New Mexico. _____

4. I am a mountain chain that runs parallel to the Atlantic coast from the Northeast to the South. _____

5. I cut through a plateau in Arizona. _____

6. Most of me lies on the U.S.–Canada border, although one part of me lies entirely inside the United States. _____

7. I run along the high ridge line of the Rocky Mountains. _____

8. I am located in Alaska. _____

9. I lie to the south of the United States. _____

10. I stretch across the United States and link every major city. _____

Appalachian Mountains
continental divide
Dust Bowl
Everglades
Grand Canyon
Great Lakes
Great Plains
Gulf of Mexico
Interstate Highway System
land bridge
Mississippi River
Mt. McKinley
Piedmont
Rocky Mountains

Activities

GeoGame

Use this online map to show what you know about the physical geography of the United States. Drag and drop each place name to its location on the map.

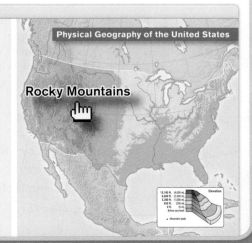

Geo GAME

Appalachian Mountains

Great Lakes

Great Plains

Mississippi River

Rocky Mountains

To play the complete game, go to **Interactive Review** @ ClassZone.com

Crossword Puzzle

Complete the online crossword puzzle to test your knowledge of how the United States became a nation.

ACROSS
1. president during the Civil War

VOCABULARY

Explain the significance of each of the following.

1. Lewis and Clark Expedition
2. Great Lakes
3. Civil War
4. Great Depression
5. literacy
6. cultural blending
7. republic
8. free enterprise

Explain how the first term in each group relates to the terms that follow.

9. immigrant: land bridge, colony
10. Constitution: amendment, federal system

KEY IDEAS

1 From Coast to Coast

11. What are three major geographic features that run from north to south?
12. What is the nation's largest agricultural region, and what are its main crops?
13. Which region has the most mountainous terrain?

2 Creating a Nation

14. How did the French and Indian War help lead to the Revolutionary War?
15. What was the purpose of Lewis and Clark's journey?
16. Which neighboring country lost large amounts of land to the United States?

3 A Diverse Culture

17. Which immigrant groups came to the United States in large numbers during the mid-1800s?
18. How have African Americans contributed to culture?
19. Why might some immigrants object to the concept of the United States as a melting pot?

4 Democracy and Free Enterprise

20. Why is the U.S. government considered a representative democracy?
21. What is a federal system?
22. What economic change was spurred by technology?

CRITICAL THINKING

23. **Compare and Contrast** Create a table to compare and contrast the transcontinental railroad and the Interstate Highway System.

RAILROAD	HIGHWAY SYSTEM

24. **Distinguish Fact from Opinion** The Declaration of Independence lists several complaints about the British king, including "imposing Taxes on us without our Consent." Is that complaint fact or opinion? Explain.

25. **Draw Conclusions** When you consider the part farming plays in the overall economy, do you think most Americans live in urban or rural areas? Why?

26. **Five Themes: Location** In 1941, Japan bombed the U.S. naval base at Pearl Harbor, Hawaii. Why would the Japanese view Pearl Harbor as a big military threat?

27. **Connect Geography & Culture** The number of Spanish speakers is growing. How might U.S. culture change as a result?

Answer the ESSENTIAL QUESTION

How did a developing nation grow into a world power?

Written Response Write a two paragraph response to the Essential Question. Be sure to consider the key ideas of each section as well as specific ideas about how the United States grew. Use the rubric below to guide your thinking.

Response Rubric
A strong response will:
- explain the steps by which U.S. territory grew
- discuss the influences that created U.S. diversity
- analyze the elements of the U.S. economy

Test Practice

• Online Test Practice @ ClassZone.com
• Test-Taking Strategies and Practice
  at the front of this book

ELEVATION GRAPH

Use the elevation graph to answer questions 1 and 2 on your paper about the elevation of the western United States at 38° north latitude.

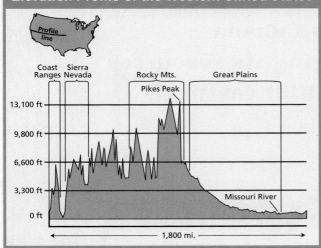

Elevation Profile of the Western United States

Coast Ranges | Sierra Nevada | Rocky Mts. | Great Plains
Pikes Peak
13,100 ft
9,800 ft
6,600 ft
3,300 ft
0 ft
Missouri River
1,800 mi.

1. Which of the following has the highest general elevation?

A. Coast Ranges
B. Sierra Nevada
C. Rocky Mountains
D. Great Plains

2. Which has the lowest elevation?

A. between Sierra Nevada and Rocky Mountains
B. between Rocky Mountains and Great Plains
C. between Coast Ranges and Sierra Nevada
D. in the Coast Ranges

ANALYZING PRIMARY SOURCES

Examine the Great Seal of the United States shown below. Use the seal to answer questions 3 and 4 on your own paper.

3. Why might the motto *E Pluribus Unum* (one from many) be on the Great Seal of the United States?

4. Why might the eagle on the seal clutch an olive branch in one claw and arrows in the other claw?

GeoActivity

1. INTERDISCIPLINARY ACTIVITY–MUSIC

Working in a small group, find three or four examples of jazz that you like. Concentrate on instrumental music, not songs with lyrics. In a group discussion, compare and contrast the pieces. Then play the music and present your findings in class.

2. WRITING FOR SOCIAL STUDIES

Research to find out more about the American bison—including how large it is, how long it lives, what it eats, what its habits are, and where it still can be found. Create a booklet about the bison to teach younger students about this American animal.

3. MENTAL MAPPING

Create an outline map of the United States and label the following:

• Appalachian Mountains
• Rocky Mountains
• Atlantic Ocean
• Pacific Ocean
• Gulf of Mexico
• Mississippi River
• Great Lakes
• Great Plains

CHAPTER 6

Canada

ESSENTIAL QUESTION

How is Canada managing its resources in the 21st century?

1
GEOGRAPHY

Mountains, Prairies, and Coastlands

2
HISTORY

First Peoples to a Modern Nation

3
CULTURE

A Nation of Immigrants

4
GOVERNMENT & ECONOMICS

Rich Resources in a Vast Land

CONNECT **Geography & History**

Use the map and the time line to answer the following questions.

1. When was the city of Quebec founded?
2. On what body of water are both Quebec and Montreal located?

Geography
1608 Samuel de Champlain founds Quebec City. ▶

1600

Geography
1791 Great Britain creates Upper and Lower Canada.

Culture
1763 Great Britain takes over New France, causing Canada to have two major languages. ▶

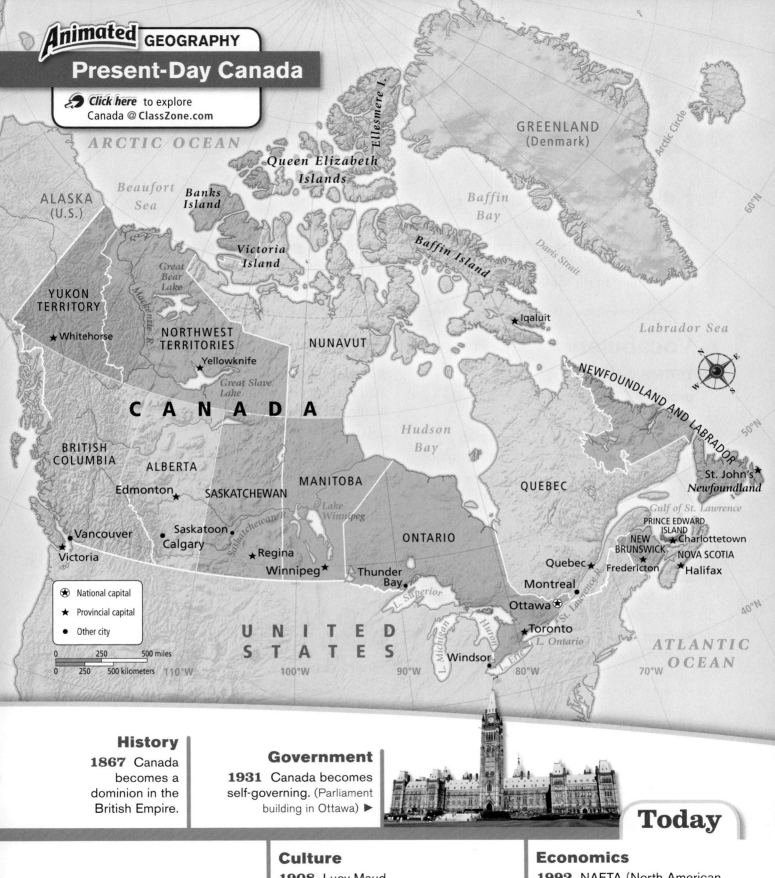

ARCTIC OCEAN

ALASKA
(U.S.)

Beaufort Sea

Banks Island

Victoria Island

Great Bear Lake

YUKON TERRITORY

★ Whitehorse

NORTHWEST TERRITORIES

★ Yellowknife

Great Slave Lake

Queen Elizabeth Islands

Ellesmere I.

GREENLAND
(Denmark)

Arctic Circle

60°N

Baffin Bay

Davis Strait

Baffin Island

NUNAVUT

• Iqaluit

Labrador Sea

C A N A D A

Hudson Bay

50°N

BRITISH COLUMBIA

ALBERTA

• Edmonton ★

• Vancouver

★ Victoria

SASKATCHEWAN

• Saskatoon
• Calgary

★ Regina

Saskatchewan R.

MANITOBA

Lake Winnipeg

Winnipeg ★

ONTARIO

Thunder Bay •

L. Superior

L. Michigan

L. Huron

NEWFOUNDLAND AND LABRADOR

St. John's
Newfoundland

QUEBEC

Gulf of St. Lawrence

PRINCE EDWARD ISLAND

NEW BRUNSWICK

Quebec ★
Fredericton ★

★ Charlottetown

NOVA SCOTIA
★ Halifax

Montreal •

Ottawa ☆
St. Lawrence R.

★ Toronto

L. Ontario

L. Erie

Windsor •

40°N

ATLANTIC OCEAN

U N I T E D
S T A T E S

National capital ⊛
Provincial capital ★
Other city •

0   250   500 miles
0   250   500 kilometers

110°W   100°W   90°W   80°W   70°W

History
1867 Canada becomes a dominion in the British Empire.

Government
1931 Canada becomes self-governing. (Parliament building in Ottawa) ▶

Today

Culture
1908 Lucy Maud Montgomery publishes *Anne of Green Gables*.

Economics
1992 NAFTA (North American Free Trade Agreement) unites Canada, the United States, and Mexico in a free-trade zone.

155

Reading for Understanding

▶ Key Ideas

BEFORE, YOU LEARNED

The United States has a great number of landforms and bodies of water, as well as great variety in its climate and vegetation.

NOW YOU WILL LEARN

The physical geography of Canada shares many landforms and bodies of water with the United States.

▶ Vocabulary

TERMS & NAMES

province a Canadian political unit, similar to a U.S. state

territory a Canadian political unit that doesn't have enough people to be a province

Canadian Shield a horseshoe-shaped, rocky plateau that covers much of eastern central Canada

Hudson Bay a large inland sea to the north of the province of Ontario

St. Lawrence Seaway a waterway made up of the St. Lawrence River, the Great Lakes, and several canals

hydroelectric having to do with electricity created by water-powered engines

Nunavut (NOO•nuh•VOOT) a territory created in 1999 from the eastern part of the Northwest Territories and home to many Inuit

REVIEW

Great Lakes five lakes forming the largest group of freshwater lakes in the world

tundra a cold, dry climate and vegetation adapted to the climate in the Arctic Circle

Visual Vocabulary tundra

▶ Reading Strategy

Re-create the chart that is shown at right. As you read and respond to the **KEY QUESTIONS**, use the chart to organize important details about the physical geography of Canada.

 Skillbuilder Handbook, page R7

CATEGORIZE

	LANDFORMS & WATER	CLIMATE	RESOURCES
Atlantic Provinces			
Core Provinces			
Prairie Provinces			
British Columbia & Territories			

 GRAPHIC ORGANIZERS
Go to **Interactive Review** @ClassZone.com

Mountains, Prairies, and Coastlands

Connecting to Your World

The United States has long coastlines on its eastern and western borders. It also has vast plains in the center and towering mountains in the west. What you may not know is that Canada, located north of the United States, shares many of the same geographic features. In this section, you will learn more about the landscape of Canada, the second largest country in the world. You will also learn how its northern location affects its climate.

Landforms and Bodies of Water

🔻 **KEY QUESTION** What are the four regions of Canada?

You have learned that the United States can be divided into four regions, and that each region contains many states. Canada can also be divided into regions. It has political units called **provinces**, which are similar to states. It also has **territories**, political units that don't have enough people to become provinces. Canada's 13 provinces and territories are often divided into four geographic regions: the Atlantic Provinces, the Core Provinces, the Prairie Provinces, and British Columbia and Territories.

Niagara Falls
Niagara Falls forms a natural boundary between Canada and the United States.

CANADA

Lake Ontario

Niagara Falls○

Lake Erie

U.S.

Atlantic Provinces This region includes Newfoundland, Nova Scotia, New Brunswick, and Prince Edward Island. (See map opposite.) The Appalachian Mountains **A** extend into the region. In most places, the soil is poor for farming. Because the Atlantic coast has good harbors, the Atlantic Provinces became a region of seafarers instead.

The western edge of the region lies on the **Canadian Shield B**, a horseshoe-shaped plateau that covers much of east-central Canada. During the Ice Age, glaciers scraped the soil from the shield, leaving exposed rock. Much of the Canadian Shield is too barren to settle.

Core Provinces Bodies of water border the Core Provinces of Quebec and Ontario. **Hudson Bay C** is a large inland sea to the north, and the St. Lawrence River **D** and **Great Lakes** lie to the south. That river, those lakes, and several canals form the **St. Lawrence Seaway**, a waterway linking the Atlantic Ocean to the heart of North America.

Quebec and Ontario are the most densely populated provinces, even though most of their lands lie on the barren Canadian Shield. People have crowded into a narrow region of fertile land along the Great Lakes and St. Lawrence River. Many rivers flow from the Canadian Shield into this area. Canadians have built **hydroelectric** plants on the rivers, to create electricity from water-powered engines.

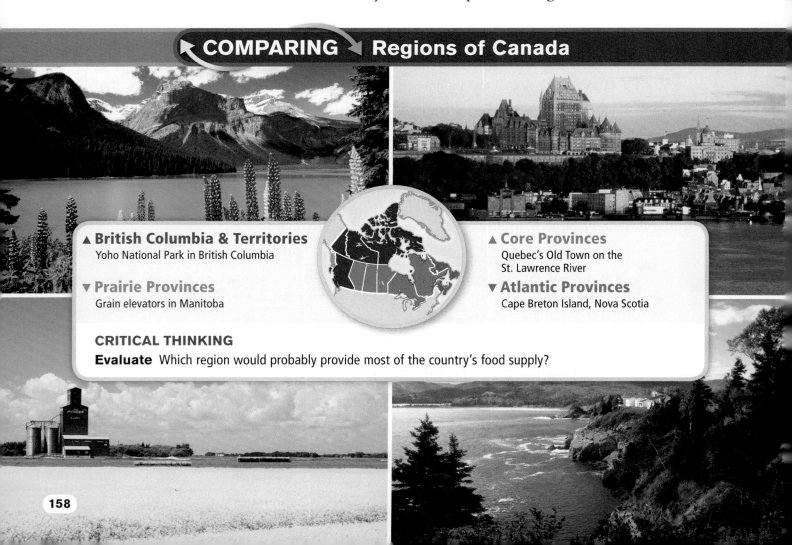

COMPARING ▶ Regions of Canada

▲ **British Columbia & Territories**
Yoho National Park in British Columbia

▼ **Prairie Provinces**
Grain elevators in Manitoba

▲ **Core Provinces**
Quebec's Old Town on the St. Lawrence River

▼ **Atlantic Provinces**
Cape Breton Island, Nova Scotia

CRITICAL THINKING
Evaluate Which region would probably provide most of the country's food supply?

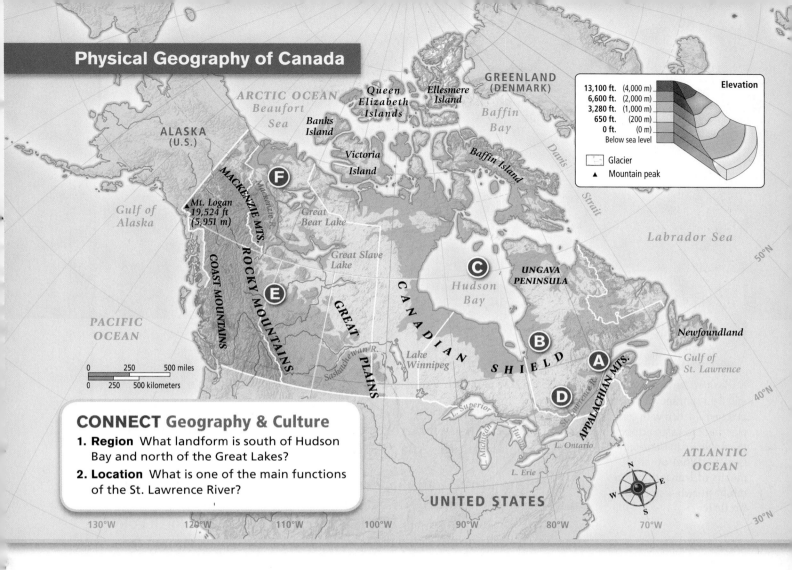

Physical Geography of Canada

Elevation
- 13,100 ft. (4,000 m)
- 6,600 ft. (2,000 m)
- 3,280 ft. (1,000 m)
- 650 ft. (200 m)
- 0 ft. (0 m)
- Below sea level

Glacier
▲ Mountain peak

GREENLAND (DENMARK)

ARCTIC OCEAN
Beaufort Sea
Queen Elizabeth Islands
Ellesmere Island
Banks Island
Baffin Bay
Baffin Island
Davis Strait
Labrador Sea

ALASKA (U.S.)
Victoria Island
Great Bear Lake
Great Slave Lake

Gulf of Alaska
▲ Mt. Logan 19,524 ft (5,951 m)
Mackenzie R.
MACKENZIE MTS.
COAST MOUNTAINS
ROCKY MOUNTAINS

F
E

PACIFIC OCEAN

GREAT PLAINS
Saskatchewan R.
Lake Winnipeg

C A N A D I A N   S H I E L D

Hudson Bay

UNGAVA PENINSULA

C

B

A
D
St. Lawrence R.
APPALACHIAN MTS.

Newfoundland
Gulf of St. Lawrence

L. Superior
L. Michigan
L. Huron
L. Ontario
L. Erie

ATLANTIC OCEAN

UNITED STATES

50°N
40°N
30°N

130°W 120°W 110°W 100°W 90°W 80°W 70°W

0 250 500 miles
0 250 500 kilometers

CONNECT Geography & Culture

1. **Region** What landform is south of Hudson Bay and north of the Great Lakes?
2. **Location** What is one of the main functions of the St. Lawrence River?

Prairie Provinces The Great Plains, which you studied in an earlier chapter, extend northward into the Prairie Provinces—Manitoba, Saskatchewan (sa•SKACH•uh•WAHN), and Alberta. To the west, this region is bordered by the Canadian Rockies **E**. The Prairie Provinces are mostly flat grasslands and are one of Canada's major farming regions. Evergreen forests are found in the north.

British Columbia and Territories British Columbia is bounded by the Pacific Ocean to the west and the Canadian Rockies to the east. British Columbia has a scenic coast and jagged coastal mountains.

Canada's three territories are the Yukon, the Northwest Territories, and **Nunavut** (NOO•nuh•VOOT), created in 1999 from the eastern part of the Northwest Territories. Nunavut is home to many native peoples. It has a rocky mainland and thousands of Arctic Islands.

The Northwest Territories contain two of Canada's largest lakes, the Great Bear and Great Slave lakes. The Mackenzie River **F**, Canada's longest, runs from the Great Slave Lake to the Arctic Ocean.

▲ **SUMMARIZE** Name the four regions of Canada.

Midnight Sun Under the midnight sun, snowmobiles pull sleds loaded with supplies back to camp across the Arctic ice in Nunavut, Canada. **What other means of transportation might people use on the Arctic ice?**

Climates of Canada

▼ **KEY QUESTION** What are some influences on Canada's climates?

Think of the coldest states that you know of within the United States. Canada is located even farther north than those states—so far north that it reaches into the Arctic Circle.

A Northern Land Canadians think of themselves as a people of the far north, but in reality the northernmost lands are thinly populated. Since the northern part of Canada lies much closer to the North Pole than to the equator, its climate is very cold. Some places remain frozen all year, and most of the region is **tundra**, flat treeless land near the Arctic Circle. Also, places that are far from the equator have a great variation in the hours of sunlight they receive during the year. Winter days are very short, and the long period of darkness increases the cold. Because life in the far north is so harsh, about 90 percent of all Canadians live within about 200 miles of the U.S. border.

Mild and Harsh Climates Bodies of water also influence Canada's climate. The Atlantic and Pacific oceans have a moderating effect on the coasts; winters are warmer and summers cooler there. Similarly, the Great Lakes make the climates of southern Ontario and Quebec milder. In contrast, the Prairie Provinces, located far from the oceans, have very cold winters and warm to hot summers.

The oceans and lakes make nearby lands humid, while the Prairie Provinces are drier. Mountains also play a role in causing this difference. Winds blowing in from the Pacific pass over the coastal mountains. As they rise, they drop moisture, causing high rainfalls in parts of British Columbia. The lands east of the mountains are arid.

▲ **FIND MAIN IDEAS** Describe influences on Canada's climate.

Resources of the Regions

▼ **KEY QUESTION** What are the main resources of each region?

Canada has many natural resources, which have helped it to develop a strong economy. Each region has its own distinct set of resources.

- The Atlantic Provinces have an abundance of timber and mineral wealth, especially coal. The Gulf of St. Lawrence and coastal waters supply plentiful stocks of seafood for export.

- The Core Provinces have a flat fertile plain in the south, plus a mild, humid climate that is good for farming. The St. Lawrence Seaway is a resource that aids transportation and economic growth. Other rivers are used to create hydroelectric power.

- The fertile plains of the southern Prairie Provinces are used to raise grain. Oil and natural gas are found in the region, especially in Alberta.

- British Columbia has forests, minerals, hydroelectric power, ocean fishing, and some fertile lands and valleys. The territories also have resources, such as oil, natural gas, and lead, that have not been developed because they are located far from markets.

▲ **CATEGORIZE** Describe the resources of each of Canada's regions.

Fun Facts!

BEARS ON ICE!
Churchill, Manitoba, is called the polar bear capital of the world. Polar bears live on sea ice and hunt seals. But in the southwestern Hudson Bay, the ice pack melts in summer, forcing the bears onto land. Every year in late fall, polar bears gather near Churchill waiting for the bay to freeze so they can return to the ice.

Section 1 Assessment

ONLINE QUIZ
For test practice, go to
Interactive Review
@ ClassZone.com

TERMS & NAMES

1. Explain the importance of
- province
- territory
- Hudson Bay
- Nunavut

USE YOUR READING NOTES

2. Categorize Use your completed chart to answer the following question:

What mountain chain separates the Prairie Provinces and British Columbia?

	LANDFORMS & WATER	CLIMATE	RESOURCES
Atlantic Provinces			
Core Provinces			
Prairie Provinces			
British Columbia & Territories			

KEY IDEAS

3. Which two regions are the biggest farming areas of Canada?

4. Which two regions have ocean fishing as a major part of their economies?

5. Why haven't Canadians developed the mineral resources of the territories?

CRITICAL THINKING

6. Analyze Effects Give one economic advantage and one disadvantage of the Canadian Shield.

7. Contrast How is the climate of the center of the country different from the climates of the coasts?

8. **CONNECT to Today** What technologies might make it possible to use the mineral wealth of the territories?

9. **SCIENCE** Sketch a Map Learn about the Ice Age glaciers in an encyclopedia, a science book, or an educational Web site. Then sketch a map showing which parts of North America were covered by glaciers.

Click here to enter the St. Lawrence Seaway @ ClassZone.com

SHIPS INTO THE HEARTLAND

The St. Lawrence Seaway connects the Great Lakes to the Atlantic Ocean by way of the St. Lawrence River and a system of canals and locks. The seaway enables ships to sail into the heart of the continent. It was completed in the 1950s as a joint project of the United States and Canada.

Click here to see how ships are raised and lowered 600 feet by a series of locks.

A A seaway lock is a watertight chamber with gates at either end that allows a ship to be lifted or lowered from one level to another. Here the lock gates open to allow a ship to enter.

B When all gates are shut, water is let into the lock through a sluice (small channel) to raise or lower the water level.

C Once the water in the chamber is level with the canal ahead, the second gate opens and the ship moves on.

Click here to see how millions of tons of goods are shipped on the seaway each year. Most of the freight, consisting of bulk cargo such as grains and minerals, travels from North America to Europe.

Route of the St. Lawrence Seaway

MINN.
• Duluth
Lake Superior
WISCONSIN
Lake Michigan
Lake Huron
U.S.
MICHIGAN
• Chicago
ILLINOIS   IND.   Detroit
OHIO   Lake Erie
• Cleveland
CANADA
QUEBEC
• Quebec
St. Lawrence River
St. Lawrence Seaway
ONTARIO   • Montreal   MAINE
• Toronto
St. Lawrence
Lake Ontario   VT.
• Buffalo   N.H.
N.Y.
PENN.   MASS.
ATLANTIC OCEAN
N

0   100   200 miles
0   100   200 kilometers

GeoActivity

Build a Lock Use a cardboard shoebox to make a lock. If you have two or more shoeboxes, you might show ships moving in two directions. Use small plastic boats and trucks to show how the boats move in the seaway. Cargo trucks and other vehicles might be positioned along the docks.

Reading for Understanding

▶ Key Ideas

BEFORE, YOU LEARNED

Canada spans the continent, from the Atlantic to the Pacific oceans, and from the U.S. border to the Arctic Ocean.

NOW YOU WILL LEARN

Canada's diversity is the result of regional differences and events in Canada's history.

▶ Vocabulary

TERMS & NAMES

bilingual using or able to use two languages equally

First Nations organized cultural groups of Canada's native peoples

Inuit (IHN•yoo•iht) the native peoples who inhabit the Arctic region of North America

Seven Years' War a conflict (1756–1763) between Britain and France that was fought in North America, Europe, and India

dominion in the British Empire, a nation that is allowed to govern its domestic affairs

William Lyon Mackenzie King Canadian prime minister who led his country to independence

Commonwealth of Nations an association including the United Kingdom and many of its former colonies

separatist a person who wants a region to break away from the nation it is a part of

BACKGROUND VOCABULARY

Loyalist a person who supported Great Britain during the American Revolutionary War

Visual Vocabulary bilingual

▶ Reading Strategy

Re-create the web diagram shown at right. As you read and respond to the **KEY QUESTIONS**, use the outer ovals to note important details about Canada's history.

 Skillbuilder Handbook, page R4

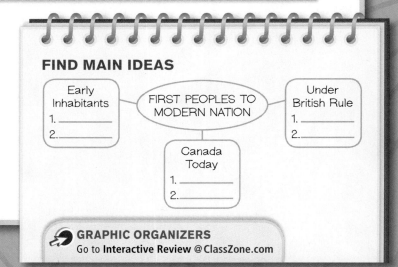

FIND MAIN IDEAS

Early Inhabitants
1. _____
2. _____

FIRST PEOPLES TO MODERN NATION

Under British Rule
1. _____
2. _____

Canada Today
1. _____
2. _____

GRAPHIC ORGANIZERS
Go to **Interactive Review** @ClassZone.com

First Peoples to a Modern Nation

Connecting to Your World

Marie is a student at a *polyvalente*, a secondary school in Quebec City. Most of her classes are taught in French, but she has one course in English conversation. Last year, Marie traveled as an exchange student to Manitoba. Unlike Quebec, most people in Manitoba conduct their daily business in English. Marie wants to become fluent in both languages to work in government. Canada is a **bilingual** country with two official languages—English and French.

Marie A young participant in Quebec City's *Fétes de la Nouvelle France* (Festival of New France) parade

Early Inhabitants and First Explorers

KEY QUESTION Which European countries started colonies in Canada?

Earlier, you learned that many scientists believe that the first inhabitants of North America came from Asia by crossing over on a land bridge. A second theory suggests that some people journeyed to North America by boat. Over time, humans spread throughout the Americas. The people in different regions developed separate cultural groups whose ways of life were adapted to the places where they lived.

Quebec City
Samuel de Champlain, an early explorer, founded Quebec City, shown below.

QUEBEC

Quebec City

U.S.

The Earliest Settlers In Canada, the organized cultural groups of native peoples are called **First Nations**. In the east lived the Algonquian (al•GAHNG•kwee•uhn) peoples, who hunted, and the Iroquois (IHR•uh•KWOY), who hunted and farmed. On the plains, the main groups were the Blackfoot, Cree, Ojibwa, and Sioux (soo). Most lived by hunting bison. The mild Pacific coast was heavily populated. Some groups were the Haida, Kwakiutl (KWAH•kee•OOT•uhl), and Salish. The frosty Arctic lands were inhabited by the **Inuit** (IHN•yoo•iht), who survived by hunting polar bears, whales, and seals.

First Colonies In 1497, the explorer John Cabot landed on the coast of Newfoundland and claimed it for England. In 1534, the French explorer Jacques Cartier (kahr•TYAY) arrived at the mouth of the St. Lawrence. He claimed the nearby lands for France.

Many of the French who came to Canada were single men who wanted to grow rich by trading for furs. Some British who came to Canada also wanted furs. The British Hudson's Bay Company set up many trading posts. But almost all the British who moved to North America came as colonists with families. Britain and France were bitter rivals for lands and wealth. The two nations fought several wars during the late 1600s and 1700s.

▲ **SUMMARIZE** Describe which countries started colonies in Canada.

CONNECT to History

A number of different European explorers contributed to knowledge of the lands that later became Canada.

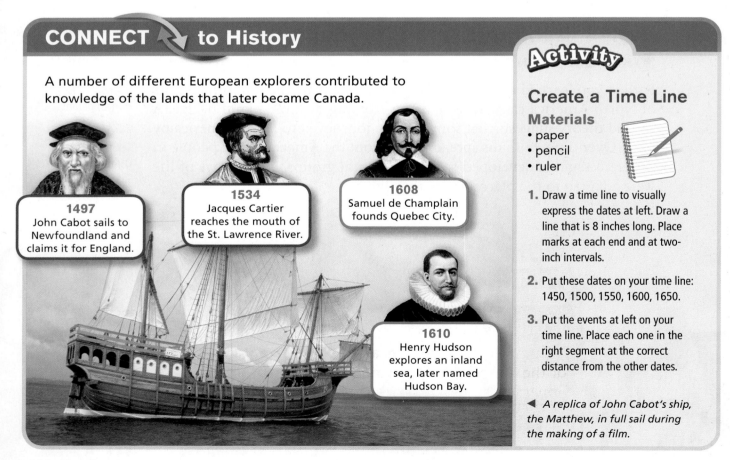

1497
John Cabot sails to Newfoundland and claims it for England.

1534
Jacques Cartier reaches the mouth of the St. Lawrence River.

1608
Samuel de Champlain founds Quebec City.

1610
Henry Hudson explores an inland sea, later named Hudson Bay.

Activity

Create a Time Line

Materials
- paper
- pencil
- ruler

1. Draw a time line to visually express the dates at left. Draw a line that is 8 inches long. Place marks at each end and at two-inch intervals.

2. Put these dates on your time line: 1450, 1500, 1550, 1600, 1650.

3. Put the events at left on your time line. Place each one in the right segment at the correct distance from the other dates.

◄ *A replica of John Cabot's ship, the Matthew, in full sail during the making of a film.*

Under British Rule

▼ **KEY QUESTION** What steps did Canada take to gain independence?

In 1754, fighting again broke out between the British and French in North America. The war, which spread to Europe and India, is called the **Seven Years' War** because it lasted from 1756 to 1763 in Europe. (In the United States, it is called the French and Indian War.) Britain won and took French lands, including the colony of Quebec.

Upper and Lower Canada Right after the war, French-speakers in Quebec outnumbered the English-speakers, but the population of English-speakers grew. After the American Revolution (1775–1783), thousands of **Loyalists**, people who had supported the British, moved to Canada. French-speakers and English-speakers mistrusted each other. So in 1791, the British divided Quebec into English-speaking Upper Canada (Ontario) and French-speaking Lower Canada (Quebec).

Canada Achieves Self-Government
In the 1800s, Canada underwent many changes. Explorers pushed west looking for new places to find furs. Canadians increased their trade with the United States.

In 1867, Canada became a **dominion**, a nation in the British Empire that is self-governing. The British monarch remained Canada's head of state, and the legislature was modeled on the British Parliament.

During the late 1800s, Canada continued to grow. In 1885, a transcontinental railroad was finished. European immigrants moved to Canadian cities and the wide-open plains. The economy boomed.

Canadians began to question their role in the British Empire. After World War I, Canadian leaders such as Prime Minister **William Lyon Mackenzie King** sought independence. This was granted in 1931. Canada joined the **Commonwealth of Nations**, an association of the United Kingdom and many of its former colonies.

HISTORY MAKERS

William Lyon Mackenzie King
(1874–1950)

Mackenzie King (top left) served as prime minister of Canada longer than anyone else. Perhaps his greatest accomplishment was leading Canada to independence. He also kept his country together during World War II by uniting French-speaking and English-speaking Canadians despite their opposing views. In the picture above, political leaders gather for the Quebec Conference in August, 1943. From the left: Mackenzie King, U.S. President Franklin D. Roosevelt, British Prime Minister Winston Churchill, and the Earl of Athlone (Governor General of Canada).

 ONLINE BIOGRAPHY
For more on the life of Mackenzie King, go to the **Research & Writing Center @ ClassZone.com**

▲ **FIND MAIN IDEAS** Explain how Canada gained independence.

Canada Today

▼ **KEY QUESTION** Which minority groups in Canada wanted to gain more self-rule?

One major political issue was resolved when Canada became independent, but the country has faced other ongoing concerns since then. Two of those issues have involved responding to minority groups within Canada and dealing with the United States.

Tensions over Quebec and Nunavut During the 1960s, some French Canadians campaigned against what they regarded as discrimination. A group of **separatists**—people who want a region to break away from a country it is a part of—wanted Quebec to break away from Canada. In response, the national government passed a law that required services to be offered in French and English in areas where 10 percent of the people speak French or English. The separatists continued to seek independence. The people of Quebec voted on the issue of separating in 1995, but the proposal was defeated.

The French-speakers were not the only Canadians to want more self-rule. The Inuit of the far north had a similar desire. But instead of seeking separation from Canada, the Inuit wanted self-rule within the country. They negotiated with the government to gain a separate Inuit territory as part of Canada, and Nunavut was created in 1999.

ONLINE PRIMARY SOURCE To learn more about the Canadian Multiculturalism Act of 1988, go to the **Research & Writing Center** @ ClassZone.com

---

ANALYZING Primary Sources

The Canadian Multiculturalism Act (1988) set forth the government's intention to help all members of Canadian society preserve their unique cultures.

> It is hereby declared to be the policy of the Government of Canada to . . . recognize and promote the understanding that multiculturalism reflects the cultural and racial diversity of Canadian society and acknowledges the freedom of all members of Canadian society to preserve [save], enhance [develop], and share their cultural heritage.
>
> Source: *The Canadian Multiculturalism Act of 1988*

DOCUMENT–BASED QUESTION

What aspects of cultural heritage do you think this act might apply to?

Mural painted by children for Canada Day ▶

Relations with the United States At times, tensions exist between Canada and the United States. For example, the two countries have some differences in their views of how best to fight terrorism. Global warming and trade are two other issues on which Canada and the United States occasionally have different opinions and follow divergent paths.

In spite of such disagreements, Canada and the United States have a good relationship. Their 5,525-mile border is the longest unprotected border in the world, although guards do check papers and inspect vehicles.

The U.S. and Canadian economies are closely linked. The two countries have signed agreements to promote trade with each other, such as the 1989 Free Trade Agreement and the 1994 North American Free Trade Agreement (NAFTA). From 1989 to 2004, U.S. exports to Canada more than doubled, and imports from Canada tripled.

CONNECT ➤ **Geography & History**

Environmental Partners
Canada and the United States work as partners to fight pollution. One area at risk is the heavily industrialized Great Lakes region. Air pollution was causing acid rain, which kills trees and fish. In 1991, the two nations signed an agreement to improve air quality. Since then, the gases that cause acid rain have been reduced by about a third.

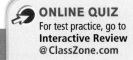

🔺 **SUMMARIZE** Explain which minorities in Canada wanted self-rule.

Section ❷ Assessment

🧲 **ONLINE QUIZ**
For test practice, go to
Interactive Review
@ ClassZone.com

TERMS & NAMES

1. Explain the importance of
- bilingual
- Inuit
- dominion
- separatist

USE YOUR READING NOTES

2. Find Main Ideas Use your completed diagram to answer the following question:

How has Canada accommodated the diversity of its population?

KEY IDEAS

3. How did the rivalry between Britain and France affect Canadian history?

4. What did dominion status mean for Canada?

5. What is unique about the U.S.-Canada border?

CRITICAL THINKING

6. Analyze Causes How did Canada's history cause it to become a bilingual country?

7. Contrast What was the main difference between the goals of the Quebec separatists and the Inuit?

8. CONNECT to Today How do you think the terrorist attacks of September 11, 2001, have affected the number of border guards and inspections on the U.S.-Canada border? Explain.

9. WRITING **Create a Venn Diagram** Make a Venn diagram showing how Canadian history and United States history are alike and different. Then write a paragraph summarizing the main ideas.

Reading for Understanding

▶ Key Ideas

BEFORE, YOU LEARNED

Canada has a history that begins about the same time as that of the United States, and like the United States, Canada is a nation of immigrants.

NOW YOU WILL LEARN

Because Canada is a nation of immigrants, it has a diverse population and a variety of cultures shaped by many influences.

▶ Vocabulary

TERMS & NAMES

Royal Canadian Mounted Police an organization of officers who were responsible for law enforcement in the Canadian West

Inuktitut the language of the Inuit

lacrosse a team sport invented by Native Americans

BACKGROUND VOCABULARY

igloo a house made of snow

Visual Vocabulary igloo

Visual Vocabulary lacrosse

▶ Reading Strategy

Re-create the chart that is shown at right. As you read and respond to the **KEY QUESTIONS**, use the chart to organize information about the diverse culture of Canada.

 Skillbuilder Handbook, page R7

CATEGORIZE

LANGUAGE	RELIGION	ETHNICITY	ARTS & CULTURE
1.	1.	1.	1.
2.	2.	2.	2.
3.	3.	3.	3.
4.	4.	4.	4.

 GRAPHIC ORGANIZERS
Go to **Interactive Review** @ ClassZone.com

A Nation of Immigrants

Connecting to Your World

Have you ever got caught up in the gunfights and horse chases of a television western? Like the United States, Canada also has a rugged western region that was settled later than the East. However, the settling of Canada's West was more peaceful than that of the U.S. West. A group of officers known as the **Royal Canadian Mounted Police** (RCMP) provided law enforcement in the Canadian West. Famous for their bright red uniforms, the Mounties have become a symbol of Canada around the world.

Mounted Police
A constable in the RCMP wears the ceremonial red uniform.

A Diverse Population

▼ **KEY QUESTION** Where have immigrants to Canada come from?

One of the first jobs assigned to the Mounties was to keep peace between the First Nations and the settlers who moved into the Canadian West. Today, Canada is still seeking ways to prevent conflicts between cultural groups. In general, the government works to protect the diversity of Canadian society.

Nunavut An Inuit with his dog team stands outside his igloo in Nunavut near Hudson Bay.

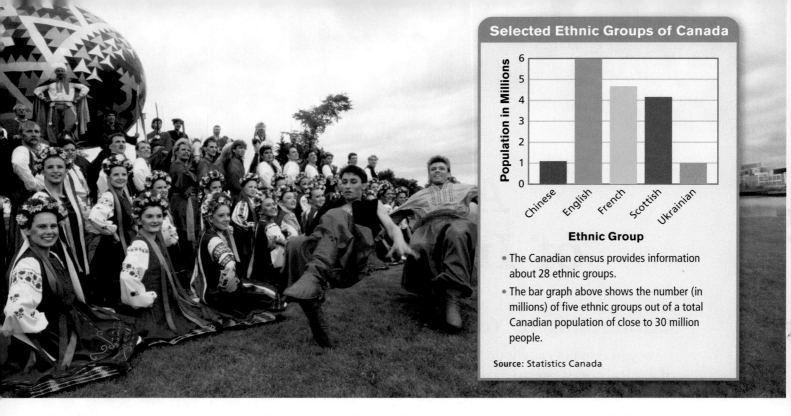

Selected Ethnic Groups of Canada

- The Canadian census provides information about 28 ethnic groups.
- The bar graph above shows the number (in millions) of five ethnic groups out of a total Canadian population of close to 30 million people.

Source: Statistics Canada

Ukrainian Dancers
Dancers perform at the Pysanka Festival in Vegreville, Alberta. A pysanka is a decorated Ukrainian Easter egg.
Why might people of British and French origins together make up more than one-third of the Canadian population?

Canada has been diverse from its beginning. The first inhabitants of Canada were different native groups, such as the Cree, the Ojibwa, and the Inuit. The first Europeans to arrive were the Norse, and then the English and French. In the 1800s and 1900s, people from a number of other countries moved to Canada—including people from Scotland, Ireland, Germany, Italy, China, Ukraine, Norway, and Sweden.

Because of its history, Canada is a bilingual country with two official languages. About 59 percent of the people speak English as a first language, and about 23 percent speak French. About 18 percent, mostly immigrants, speak other languages. Some Canadians speak native languages such as **Inuktitut**, the language of the Inuit.

About 43 percent of Canadians are Roman Catholic, and about 23 percent are Protestant. Many French Canadians are Catholic, as are many Italian, Ukrainian, and Irish immigrants. Many people of English descent are Protestant. About 2 percent of Canadians are Muslim.

▲ **SUMMARIZE** Describe where immigrants to Canada have come from.

Life in Canada

▼ **KEY QUESTION** What are three distinct ways of life in Canada?

Ethnic groups aren't spread evenly across Canada. French Canadians are concentrated in the province of Quebec. Ukrainians tended to settle in the Prairie Provinces, where the land is similar to the plains of Ukraine. Many Chinese immigrants live on the Pacific coast.

Where People Live As Section 1 explained, about 90 percent of all Canadians live near the southern border. One of the most densely populated regions of Canada is the area near the St. Lawrence River and the Great Lakes. Port cities are also densely populated.

More than 75 percent of Canadians live in cities. In general, cities are more modern and offer more jobs and cultural opportunities. Rural areas tend to have more traditional ways of life based on farming. But in recent times, technologies such as satellite dishes have been bringing modern life to the rural areas of Canada.

In Canada, a third way of life exists—Arctic life. For centuries, people in the Arctic region followed traditional ways. They lived in tents or **igloos**, traveled by dog sled, hunted and fished, and made clothes from animal skins. Many Inuit still hunt and fish, but they live in wooden houses and wear modern clothing designed for cold weather.

Arctic Life and the Snowmobile

Traditionally, the Inuit traveled by dogsled. Now, most Inuit families use snowmobiles instead. This new method of transportation is one of the changes allowing them to find wage-paying jobs. Dogs can be fed with meat caught by the Inuit themselves. Snowmobiles need gasoline that must be bought.

A Distinct Identity Canada has more land than the United States, but it has only about 10 percent as many people. As a result, Canadians sometimes fear that they will be overwhelmed by U.S. culture and customs. In fact, during the 1950s, the government issued a report warning that U.S. film, radio, and magazines were invading Canadian culture. The government legislated percentages of television and radio programming that had to have Canadian content.

To fight U.S. cultural dominance, Canadians have worked to develop their national identity. Many are proud of being a northern people and of having such a beautiful country. And as you are about to read, Canada has made distinctive contributions to the arts.

Toronto, Canada The Toronto skyline gleams at night.

▲ **COMPARE** Describe three distinct ways of life in Canada.

To learn more about Kirima and her world, go to the **Activity Center** @ ClassZone.com

Hi! My name is Kirima. I am a 13-year-old girl, and I live in the community of Taloyoak in Nunavut. My school has 240 students. We have a modern school with two computer labs, a science lab, and a gymnasium. But we are also proud of our traditional ways. A display about Inuit life is the very first thing that visitors to our school see. Let me tell you about my day.

In Inuktitut, Kirima's name looks like this:

PnL

9:30 A.M. I have a computer literacy class in the morning. Computer skills are very important, because e-mail and the Internet help link my community to southern Canada.

12:00 P.M. One day a week, one class is invited to stay at school for lunch instead of going home. Today is my class's turn, and we eat caribou stew. I love caribou meat, even though it is stringy and gets caught in my teeth.

3:45 P.M. Some of the kids from my class are playing street hockey; they play right in the middle of the road because there are so few cars! My friends and I prefer to jump up and down on a trampoline made of a stretched animal skin.

7:30 P.M. After dinner, my grandmother gives me a sewing or knitting lesson. Inuit women are able to sew seams so tightly that our clothes are waterproof. Even though my family buys many of our clothes at the store, Grandmother says it is important to learn traditional skills.

CONNECT to Your Life

Journal Entry Think about the skills that you have learned. Which of them are modern and which are traditional? How is your life similar to Kirima's life? Record your ideas in your journal.

Arts and Popular Culture

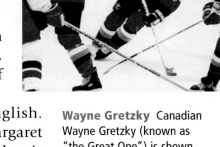

▼ **KEY QUESTION** How have Canadians won worldwide fame?

Education is an aspect of Canadian life that varies from region to region. Each province runs its own school system. Overall, Canada has well-educated people and a high literacy rate of 97 percent.

Canadian literature is written in both French and English. Several Canadian novelists, such as Michael Ondaatje and Margaret Atwood, are read around the world. A popular children's author is Lucy Maud Montgomery, who wrote *Anne of Green Gables*. The city of Stratford, Ontario, holds a yearly theater festival showcasing the plays of William Shakespeare.

Wayne Gretzky Canadian Wayne Gretzky (known as "the Great One") is shown at center competing in the 1998 Winter Olympics.

Because of Canada's cold climate, winter sports are common. Ice hockey is one of Canada's most popular sports, and Canadian hockey teams have won many international competitions. Wayne Gretzky, possibly the greatest hockey player of all time, is Canadian. **Lacrosse**, a team sport invented by Native Americans, is widely played in Canada. In fact, Canada has made ice hockey its official winter sport and lacrosse its official summer sport.

▲ **FIND MAIN IDEAS** Describe some areas in which Canadians have won worldwide fame.

Section ③ Assessment

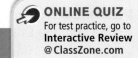
ONLINE QUIZ
For test practice, go to
Interactive Review
@ ClassZone.com

TERMS & NAMES
1. Explain the importance of
- Royal Canadian Mounted Police
- Inuktitut
- lacrosse

USE YOUR READING NOTES
2. Categorize Use your completed chart to answer the following question:

What are some elements and examples of the diversity that makes up the culture of Canada?

LANGUAGE	RELIGION	ETHNICITY	ARTS & CULTURE
1.	1.	1.	1.
2.	2.	2.	2.
3.	3.	3.	3.
4.	4.	4.	4.

KEY IDEAS
3. What languages are spoken in Canada?

4. What way of life is found in Canada but not in many other countries?

5. How has Canada's geography influenced its sports?

CRITICAL THINKING
6. Make Inferences Why do many Canadian performers pursue their careers in the United States?

7. Summarize What are some examples of Canada's contributions to literature?

8. CONNECT to Today You learned in Chapter 5 that many of today's immigrants to the United States come from Spanish-speaking countries. How would you explain the fact that Canada doesn't have a large number of Spanish-speaking immigrants?

9. WORLD LANGUAGES Create a Travel Dictionary Think of 20 words that travelers should know. Then use a French-English dictionary to create a French dictionary for travelers to Quebec.

Reading for Understanding

▶ Key Ideas

BEFORE, YOU LEARNED

Although Canada is a land of great diversity, it has a small population for such a large geographical area.

NOW YOU WILL LEARN

Canada has a vast wealth of resources and an educated population to support its government and economy.

▶ Vocabulary

TERMS & NAMES

constitution the set of laws and principles that defines the nature of a government

constitutional monarchy a government in which the powers of the king or queen are limited by the constitution

Parliament the legislature of Canada, named after the British Parliament

prime minister the head of the Canadian government

cabinet system a system of government that links the executive and legislative branches by choosing the prime minister and major department heads from the legislature

REVIEW

federal system a government system in which powers are divided between the national and state or provincial governments

free enterprise an economic system in which businesses are free to operate without much government interference

▶ Reading Strategy

Re-create the chart that is shown at right. As you read and respond to the **KEY QUESTIONS**, use the chart to note the main ideas about the government and economy of Canada.

 Skillbuilder Handbook, page R4

FIND MAIN IDEAS

GOVERNMENT	ECONOMY
1.	1.
2.	2.
3.	3.
4.	4.

 GRAPHIC ORGANIZERS
Go to **Interactive Review** @ ClassZone.com

Rich Resources in a Vast Land

Connecting to Your World

Have you ever seen the feature-length cartoons *Snow White* or *Alice in Wonderland*? *Snow White* features an evil, jealous queen. In *Alice*, the Queen of Hearts starts shouting "Off with her head" every time Alice upsets her. Many old stories portray kings and queens as having total power; they make the laws and punish anyone who disagrees with them. But some modern-day kings and queens have much less power than a president or other head of government. One of those is the monarch of Canada.

The Government of Canada

▼ **KEY QUESTION** What is the structure of Canada's government?

Canada's monarch is the reigning king or queen of Great Britain. But under the law, the monarch really has no power. He or she is just a symbol of Canada's past ties to Britain. Because the **constitution** limits the powers of the ruler, Canada's government is called a **constitutional monarchy**.

Changing of the Guard This ceremony takes place on the lawn of Parliament Hill in Ottawa, Ontario, Canada.

CANADA
ONTARIO
Ottawa★
U.S.

Parliament and Government Canada's government is also a representative democracy, but its government is quite different from that of the United States. The legislative body of Canada is called the **Parliament**. Like the U.S. Congress, the Canadian Parliament has two houses—the Senate and the House of Commons. Canada's citizens vote for members of the House of Commons. Senators are appointed.

The head of the executive branch is the **prime minister**. The prime minister is chosen because he or she is the leader of the dominant political party in the House of Commons (the legislative branch). The heads of the government departments also come from Parliament. They form a group of official advisers to the prime minister called a cabinet; this is called a **cabinet system** of government.

Queen Elizabeth II The Queen accepts flowers while on tour in the province of Saskatchewan. **Why might the Queen be popular in Canada?**

Federalism The nation of Canada is divided into smaller political units called provinces and territories. As in the United States, power is divided between the national government and the governments of the provinces and territories. A government that divides power in this way is called a **federal system**.

Originally, Canada's national government had much more power than the governments of the provinces. The provincial governments have control over issues such as health care, education, and the use of resources. These issues have become vital to modern life, so the provincial governments have become more important.

▲ **FIND MAIN IDEAS** Describe the structure of Canada's form of government.

The Economy of Canada

▼ **KEY QUESTION** What is Canada's biggest economic advantage?

Canada's economy is both similar to and different from the U.S. economy. One major similarity is that both economies are based on **free enterprise**, an economic system in which businesses are free to operate without much government interference. One difference is that the Canadian government plays a larger role in the economy (for example, in health care) than the U.S. government does.

What Canada Produces Canada has an abundance of natural resources such as forests, minerals, and land. This wealth of resources is Canada's biggest economic advantage. A second advantage that Canada has is a well-educated population. Some of the Canadian economy's main industries are listed on the next page.

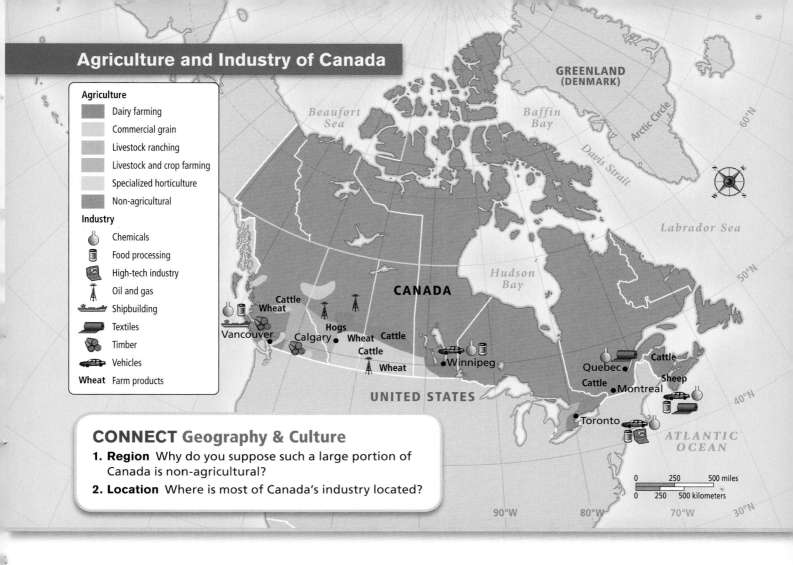

Agriculture and Industry of Canada

Agriculture
- Dairy farming
- Commercial grain
- Livestock ranching
- Livestock and crop farming
- Specialized horticulture
- Non-agricultural

Industry
- Chemicals
- Food processing
- High-tech industry
- Oil and gas
- Shipbuilding
- Textiles
- Timber
- Vehicles

Wheat Farm products

GREENLAND (DENMARK)

Beaufort Sea

Baffin Bay

Arctic Circle

Davis Strait

Labrador Sea

CANADA

Hudson Bay

Cattle
Wheat
Vancouver
Calgary
Hogs
Wheat
Cattle
Cattle
Wheat
Winnipeg
Quebec
Cattle
Cattle
Montreal
Toronto
Cattle
Sheep

UNITED STATES

ATLANTIC OCEAN

CONNECT Geography & Culture

1. Region Why do you suppose such a large portion of Canada is non-agricultural?

2. Location Where is most of Canada's industry located?

0   250   500 miles
0   250   500 kilometers

Agriculture, Forestry, and Fishing About two percent of Canadians work in agriculture, but Canada produces a great quantity of food. Wheat, beef, dairy products, and hogs are some of the main products. Forestry products include lumber, plywood, and paper. Fishing yields salmon, crab, and lobster.

Mining and Energy Canada is a major producer of uranium, zinc, nickel, copper, iron ore, coal, gold, and silver. It also produces oil and natural gas, as well as hydroelectricity.

Manufacturing About 14 percent of Canadians work in manufacturing, and five percent work in construction. One of the main industries is the processing of minerals and resources such as trees. Processing minerals involves removing useful metal from ore. Trees are processed into logs, boards, and wood pulp.

Service Industries About 75 percent of all Canadians work in service industries. These include government, education, health care, retail stores, hotels, restaurants, and banking.

Oil Pump Oil being pumped from the ground near Calgary, Alberta, Canada.

Canada's Role in the World Economy Historically, the economy of Canada has always relied on trade. The fur trade between Canada's native peoples and European fishermen was just the start of what would become a key Canadian industry.

Today, Canada is a major participant in international trade. Because Canada has such a wealth of natural resources, it has always relied on exporting those materials to other nations. In recent decades, Canada has also begun to export manufactured goods such as automobiles and machinery.

Many Canadian industries, especially those that process minerals and wood products, are partially owned by people in other countries. Most of those foreign owners are from the United States.

As you might guess, Canada's biggest trading partner is the United States, which is its closest neighbor and which has a much larger population. The United States buys up to 85 percent of Canada's exports. Most of the products that Canada imports come from the United States. Trade between the two countries has boomed because of NAFTA (North American Free Trade Agreement), signed in 1992. Japan is Canada's second largest trading partner. However, Canada has developed a growing trade relationship with China in recent years.

▲ **FIND MAIN IDEA** Explain Canada's biggest economic advantage.

 Section 4 Assessment

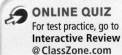 **ONLINE QUIZ**
For test practice, go to
Interactive Review
@ ClassZone.com

TERMS & NAMES

1. **Explain the importance of**
   • constitutional monarchy
   • Parliament
   • prime minister
   • cabinet system

USE YOUR READING NOTES

2. **Find Main Ideas** Use your completed chart to answer the following question:

   What are some examples of Canada's government structure and economic advantages?

GOVERNMENT	ECONOMY
1.	1.
2.	2.
3.	3.
4.	4.

KEY IDEAS

3. What role does the British monarch play in the Canadian government?

4. How is the prime minister chosen?

5. How has the Canadian economy changed recently?

CRITICAL THINKING

6. **Draw Conclusions** Why do you suppose that Canadian industries process resources before exporting them instead of exporting raw materials?

7. **Evaluate** Is Canada's government a good example of a representative democracy? Explain.

8. **CONNECT to Today** In 2010, Vancouver, British Columbia, will host the winter Olympics. Which part of the economy will benefit the most from that?

9. **TECHNOLOGY Plan a Web Page** Imagine that you work for the Canadian government, and your job is to encourage foreign industries to move to Canada. Plan a Web page that shows Canada's advantages.

Interactive ← Review

CHAPTER SUMMARY

Key Idea 1
The physical geography of Canada varies greatly among its 13 provinces and territories, which has resulted in different ways of life.

Key Idea 2
The history of Canada reflects the diversity of its regions and its population.

Key Idea 3
Because Canada is a nation of immigrants, it has a diverse population and a culture that is shaped by many influences.

Key Idea 4
Canada has a vast wealth of resources and an educated population to support its government and economy.

For **Review and Study Notes**, go to **Interactive Review** @ ClassZone.com

NAME GAME

Use the Terms & Names list to complete each sentence on paper or online.

1. I am a team sport invented by Native Americans. _____lacrosse_____

2. I am an organized cultural group of Canada's native people. _____

3. I am a Canadian political unit, similar to a U.S. state. _____

4. I am a government in which the powers of the king or queen are limited by law. _____

5. I am a territory that is home to many Inuit people. _____

6. I am a type of government that chooses the prime minister and major department heads from the legislature. _____

7. I am a large inland sea in northern Canada. _____

8. I am a waterway linking the Atlantic Ocean to inland North America. _____

9. I am a nation in the British Empire that is allowed to govern its domestic affairs. _____

10. I am the legislature of Canada, named after a similar institution in Britain. _____

cabinet system
Commonwealth of Nations
constitutional monarchy
dominion
First Nations
Hudson Bay
Inuktitut
lacrosse
Nunavut
Parliament
province
Royal Canadian Mounted Police
separatist
Seven Years' War
St. Lawrence Seaway

Activities

Flip Cards

Use the online flip cards to quiz yourself on the terms and names introduced in this chapter.

Royal Canadian Mounted Police

? An organization of officers responsible for law enforcement in the Canadian West

Crossword Puzzle

Complete an online puzzle to test your knowledge of Canada's path from its first peoples to a modern nation.

ACROSS
1. city founded by Samuel de Champlain in 1608

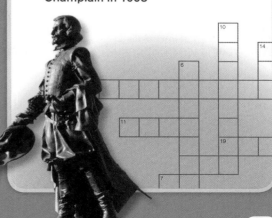

VOCABULARY

Explain the significance of each of the following.

1. province
2. territory
3. Canadian Shield
4. Hudson Bay
5. St. Lawrence Seaway
6. bilingual
7. First Nation

Explain how the terms in each group are related.

8. dominion, Commonwealth of Nations, constitutional monarchy
9. Nunavut, Inuit, Inuktitut

KEY IDEAS

1 Mountains, Prairies, and Coastlands

10. Where are the major mountains and plains of Canada located?
11. What is the economic significance of the St. Lawrence Seaway?
12. What is tundra?

2 First Peoples to a Modern Nation

13. How did the American Revolution affect Canada?
14. Why did Great Britain divide Quebec into Upper Canada and Lower Canada?
15. What was the most important accomplishment of William Lyon Mackenzie Smith?

3 A Nation of Immigrants

16. How has life in the Arctic changed recently?
17. What is an important annual event in Canadian theater?
18. What is the most popular sport in Canada?

4 Rich Resources in a Vast Land

19. How is the executive branch of the Canadian government linked to the legislative branch?
20. What are two economic advantages that Canada has?
21. How does Canada help the United States meet its energy needs?

CRITICAL THINKING

22. **Sequence Events** Create a chart like the one below on your own paper. Fill in the events that led to Canadian independence in the proper order.

23. **Make Predictions** What problems do you think Quebec might face if it did become a separate nation from Canada?
24. **Analyze Effects** Do you think it will be easier or harder for the Inuit to preserve their traditional culture in the future? Explain.
25. **Five Themes: Region** Why do you think the United States is Canada's main trading partner?
26. **Connect Geography & History** How might Canada be different if France had won the Seven Years' War?
27. **Connect Geography & Culture** Canada has tried to build its population by encouraging immigration. What effect will this have on the cultural makeup of Canada and on Canada's multiculturalism?

Answer the
ESSENTIAL QUESTION

How is Canada managing its resources in the 21st century?

Written Response Write a two- or three-paragraph response to the Essential Question. Be sure to consider the key ideas of each section. Use the rubric to guide your thinking.

Response Rubric
A strong response will:
- explain the structure of Canada's government
- discuss the way Canada uses its resources
- analyze the role of minority groups in Canada

PIE GRAPHS

Use the pie graphs to answer question 1 on your paper.

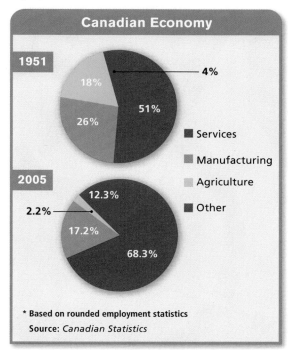

Canadian Economy

1951
- 4%
- 18%
- 51%
- 26%

■ Services
■ Manufacturing
■ Agriculture
■ Other

2005
- 12.3%
- 2.2%
- 17.2%
- 68.3%

* Based on rounded employment statistics
Source: Canadian Statistics

1. Which sector showed the greatest increase in growth from 1951 to 2005?

A. services
B. manufacturing
C. agriculture
D. other

CHART

Examine the chart below. Use the information and your knowledge of Canada to answer questions 2 and 3 on your paper.

Comparing the Canadian and U.S. Governments		
Aspects of Government	**CANADA**	**UNITED STATES**
Type	Constitutional Monarchy (limited power)	Constitutional Republic (limited power)
Head of State	Monarch	President
Head of Government	Prime Minister	President
Legislature	Parliament	Congress
System	Federal (central and provinces)	Federal (central and states)

2. What is one difference in the federal systems of the United States and Canada?

3. Who is the head of state and the head of government in Canada?

GeoActivity

1. INTERDISCIPLINARY ACTIVITY–SCIENCE

With a partner, use library books, encyclopedias, or Internet sites to learn more about the tundra and what grows there. Find out more about the climate of Arctic lands. Create an illustrated poster showing what tundra looks like and what plants grow upon it. Include a bar graph of average monthly temperature.

2. WRITING FOR SOCIAL STUDIES

Unit Writing Project Revisit the television news broadcast that you developed to showcase an important issue. What other important issues would you like to present in a broadcast? Choose an issue and write a script that tells the viewer five things: who, what, where, when, and why.

3. MENTAL MAPPING

Create an outline map of Canada and label the following:

• Appalachian Mountains
• Canadian Rockies
• St. Lawrence River
• Mackenzie River
• Hudson Bay
• Great Lakes
• Great Slave Lake

UNIT 3

Latin America

Why It Matters:

Latin America is a region of many countries. The region spans a large area north and south of the equator. The region faces political and economic challenges. How it meets these challenges will have an impact on other parts of the world.

The Andes Mountains, Chile

CHAPTER 7
Latin America
Physical Geography & History

Paseo de la Reforma, Mexico City

CHAPTER 8 **Mexico**

Marketplace in Guatemala

CHAPTER 9
Middle America and Spanish-Speaking South America

Amazon River

CHAPTER 10 **Brazil**

The region of Latin America stretches from Mexico to the tip of South America. As you study the maps, notice geographic patterns and specific details about the region. Answer the GeoActivity questions on each map in your notebook.

As you study the graphs on this page, compare the landmass, population, rivers, and mountains of Latin America with those of the United States. Then jot down the answers to the following questions in your notebook.

Comparing Data

1. Compare the population of Latin America with that of the United States. How many more people live in Latin America than in the United States?

2. The discharge rate of a river measures how much water moves through a certain location in a certain amount of time. The rate in this graph is measured in cubic feet per second. How much greater is the discharge rate of the Amazon River than that of the Mississippi River?

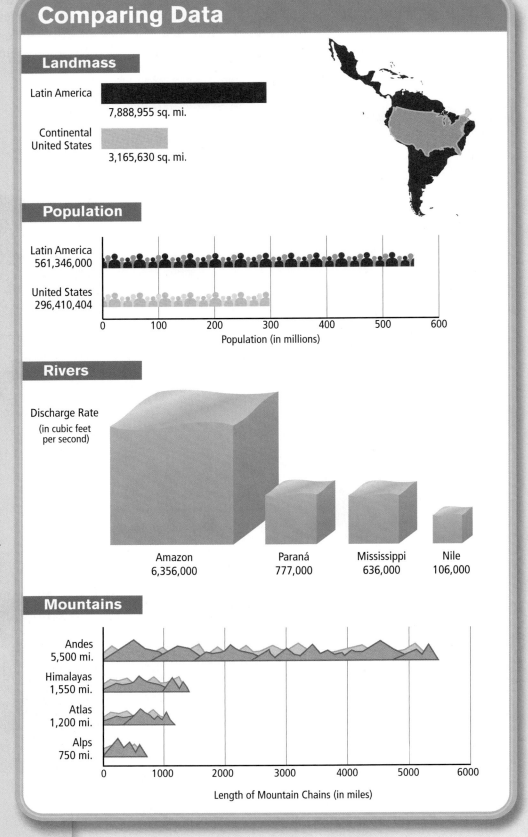

Comparing Data

Landmass

Latin America
7,888,955 sq. mi.

Continental United States
3,165,630 sq. mi.

Population

Latin America
561,346,000

United States
296,410,404

Population (in millions)
0   100   200   300   400   500   600

Rivers

Discharge Rate
(in cubic feet per second)

Amazon
6,356,000

Paraná
777,000

Mississippi
636,000

Nile
106,000

Mountains

Andes
5,500 mi.

Himalayas
1,550 mi.

Atlas
1,200 mi.

Alps
750 mi.

Length of Mountain Chains (in miles)
0   1000   2000   3000   4000   5000   6000

Population Density

Gulf of Mexico

Tropic of Cancer

20°N

ATLANTIC OCEAN

Caribbean Sea

PACIFIC OCEAN

• Mexico City

• Caracas

Equator

0°

Persons per square mile

- Over 520
- 260–519
- 130–259
- 25–129
- 1–24
- 0

N
W   E
S

Belo Horizonte •

Tropic of Capricorn

20°S

São Paulo •   • Rio de Janeiro

Santiago •

Buenos Aires •

ATLANTIC OCEAN

40°S

THINK LIKE A GEOGRAPHER

1. **Place** Where is the population of Mexico most dense?

2. **Region** Where do most people live in Latin America?

0   500   1,000 miles
0   500   1,000 kilometers

120°W   100°W   80°W   60°W   40°W

Gulf of
Mexico

MEXICO

BAHAMAS

Tropic of Cancer

20°N

CUBA

DOMINICAN
REPUBLIC

BELIZE

JAMAICA

HAITI

HONDURAS

Caribbean Sea

ATLANTIC
OCEAN

GUATEMALA

EL SALVADOR

NICARAGUA

COSTA RICA

PANAMA

GUYANA

SURINAME

VENEZUELA

FRENCH
GUIANA

PACIFIC
OCEAN

COLOMBIA

ECUADOR

Equator

0°

PERU

BRAZIL

Tropical
Tropical wet
Tropical wet and dry

Dry
Desert
Semiarid

Mid-Latitude
Mediterranean
Marine west coast
Humid subtropical
Highland

N
W   E
S

BOLIVIA

PARAGUAY

Tropic of Capricorn

20°S

CHILE

ARGENTINA

URUGUAY

ATLANTIC
OCEAN

40°S

THINK LIKE A GEOGRAPHER

1. **Place** What is the climate of the
   southernmost tip of South America?

2. **Region** In what parts of Latin America
   can you find a highland climate?

0   500   1,000 miles
0   500   1,000 kilometers

100°W   80°W   60°W   40°W   20°W

Monterrey
MEXICO
Mexico City
Gulf of Mexico
BAHAMAS
DOMINICAN REPUBLIC
CUBA
BELIZE
JAMAICA
HONDURAS
HAITI
GUATEMALA
EL SALVADOR
NICARAGUA
COSTA RICA
PANAMA
Caribbean Sea
Tropic of Cancer
20°N
ATLANTIC OCEAN
PACIFIC OCEAN
Caracas
VENEZUELA
COLOMBIA
GUYANA
SURINAME
FRENCH GUIANA
ECUADOR
PERU
BRAZIL
Equator
0°
BOLIVIA
Belo Horizonte
PARAGUAY
Rio de Janeiro
São Paulo
Tropic of Capricorn
20°S
CHILE
ARGENTINA
Santiago
Buenos Aires
URUGUAY
ATLANTIC OCEAN
40°S

Land use

- Commercial agriculture
- Livestock raising
- Subsistence agriculture
- Forestland
- Limited agriculture

Major resources

- Bauxite
- Copper
- Fish
- Gold
- Iron ore
- Natural gas
- Oil
- Silver
- Timber
- Tin
- Other minerals
- Manufacturing center

N
W   E
S

0   500   1,000 miles
0   500   1,000 kilometers

THINK LIKE A GEOGRAPHER

1. **Place** What do the colors on the economic activity map represent?

2. **Human-Environment Interaction** What are the main economic activities of Mexico?

120°W   100°W   80°W   60°W   40°W

Latin America

Latin America is a far-reaching region of many countries. The region spans a great distance both north and south of the equator. Latin America is diverse in its land, climate, and people.

GEOGRAPHY

Mountain ranges and highlands make up a large part of Latin America. The Andes Mountains, along the western coast of South America, are the largest and the longest mountain range above sea level in the world. Volcanoes, some of them active, extend through parts of Mexico, Central America, and South America. Large plateaus and vast plains provide lands for grazing and farming.

Latin America's climate is as varied as its landscape. The climate ranges from dry deserts to hot, tropical regions to cold highlands. Vegetation in Latin America varies based on the climate.

HISTORY

The Maya, Aztec, and Inca developed advanced civilizations in Latin America before the arrival of the Spanish in the 15th century. They built complex cities and structures and changed their environment to meet their needs.

After the voyages of Columbus, Spanish *conquistadors* destroyed these civilizations. Spain and Portugal set up colonies in the region and controlled most of it for the next 300 years. By the early 1800s, most Latin American countries had gained their independence.

Machu Picchu
This ancient Inca city is located near present-day Cuzco, Peru.

CULTURE

Latin American culture today is a blend of several cultures—Indian, European, African, Asian, and people of mixed ancestry. This blend is evident in the music, art, foods, and languages of the region. The majority of Latin Americans speak Spanish, but others speak Portuguese, French, English, and Dutch. Some Indian groups continue to speak their traditional languages.

GOVERNMENT

As colonies, Latin Americans had little or no say in how they were governed. This inexperience made it difficult to establish stable governments after gaining independence. As a result, the governments of many Latin American countries came under the rule of wealthy landowners or military dictators. By the 1980s, widespread protests against these governments occurred in several countries. Today more Latin American countries have democratic governments.

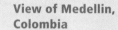

View of Medellin, Colombia

ECONOMICS

Since the 1800s, many Latin American countries have depended on one or two products for export, particularly agricultural products, and have imported most of their manufactured goods. Recently, however, many Latin American countries began to develop other industries. Some Latin American countries have become major exporters of manufactured goods. Latin American countries have also established organizations to promote trade among countries in the region.

Country Almanac

Click here to compare the most recent data on countries @ ClassZone.com

Unit Writing Project

As you read this unit, choose a country or an area of Latin America that interests you. Imagine that you are on a week's vacation there. Write a daily journal entry describing what you've seen and learned about the area and your reactions to it.

Think About:

- an area that you find interesting
- what you learned about the area that makes it interesting to you

Latin America

The Almanac provides information about the geography, economy, and culture of the countries of Latin America.

Antigua and Barbuda

GEOGRAPHY
Capital: St. John's
Total Area: 171 sq. mi.
Population: 68,722
ECONOMY
Imports: machinery; agricultural products
Exports: petroleum products
CULTURE
Language: English
Religion: Anglican 32%; Moravian 12%; Catholic 11%

Argentina

GEOGRAPHY
Capital: Buenos Aires
Total Area: 1,068,302 sq. mi.
Population: 38,747,000
ECONOMY
Imports: chemicals; machinery
Exports: food and livestock
CULTURE
Language: Spanish
Religion: Catholic 80%; Protestant 5%

Bahamas

GEOGRAPHY
Capital: Nassau
Total Area: 5,382 sq. mi.
Population: 323,000
ECONOMY
Imports: machinery; food products
Exports: crustaceans and mollusks
CULTURE
Language: English
Religion: Baptist 18%; Catholic 17%; Anglican 11%

Barbados

GEOGRAPHY
Capital: Bridgetown
Total Area: 166 sq. mi.
Population: 270,000
ECONOMY
Imports: capital goods; food
Exports: food; sugar and molasses; rum
CULTURE
Language: English
Religion: Anglican 26%; Pentecostal 11%

Belize

GEOGRAPHY
Capital: Belmopan
Total Area: 8,867 sq. mi.
Population: 270,000
ECONOMY
Imports: machinery; mineral fuels; food
Exports: seafood; sugar; bananas
CULTURE
Language: English
Religion: Catholic 50%; Protestant 32%; nonreligious 9%

Bolivia

GEOGRAPHY
Capital: Sucre
Total Area: 424,164 sq. mi.
Population: 9,182,000
ECONOMY
Imports: machinery; chemicals; food
Exports: soybean products; natural gas
CULTURE
Language: Spanish; Aymara; Quechua
Religion: Catholic 89%; Protestant 9%

Brazil

GEOGRAPHY
Capital: Brasília
Total Area: 3,286,488 sq. mi.
Population: 186,405,000
ECONOMY
Imports: machinery; chemicals
Exports: meat; sugar; coffee; soybeans
CULTURE
Language: Portuguese
Religion: Catholic 72%; Protestant 23%

Chile

GEOGRAPHY
Capital: Santiago
Total Area: 292,260 sq. mi.
Population: 16,295,000
ECONOMY
Imports: machinery; metals; copper
Exports: copper; food products; fruit
CULTURE
Language: Spanish
Religion: Catholic 70%; Protestant 15%

Colombia

GEOGRAPHY
Capital: Bogotá
Total Area: 439,736 sq. mi.
Population: 45,600,000

ECONOMY
Imports: capital goods; consumer goods
Exports: petroleum; chemicals; coal; food; machinery; coffee

CULTURE
Language: Spanish
Religion: Catholic 92%

Costa Rica

GEOGRAPHY
Capital: San José
Total Area: 19,730 sq. mi.
Population: 4,327,000

ECONOMY
Imports: general merchandise
Exports: bananas; coffee; tropical fruit

CULTURE
Language: Spanish
Religion: Catholic 86%; Protestant 9%; other Christian 2%

Cuba

GEOGRAPHY
Capital: Havana
Total Area: 42,803 sq. mi.
Population: 11,269,000

ECONOMY
Imports: food and livestock; cereals
Exports: raw sugar; nickel; seafood; medicines

CULTURE
Language: Spanish
Religion: Catholic 39%

Dominica

GEOGRAPHY
Capital: Roseau
Total Area: 291 sq. mi.
Population: 69,029

ECONOMY
Imports: food; machinery
Exports: coconut-based soaps; cosmetics

CULTURE
Language: English
Religion: Catholic 70%; six largest Protestant groups 17%

Dominican Republic

GEOGRAPHY
Capital: Santo Domingo
Total Area: 18,815 sq. mi.
Population: 8,895,000

ECONOMY
Imports: refined petroleum; food
Exports: ferronickel; ships' stores; raw sugar; cocoa

CULTURE
Language: Spanish
Religion: Catholic 82%; Protestant 6%

Ecuador

GEOGRAPHY
Capital: Quito
Total Area: 109,483 sq. mi.
Population: 13,228,000

ECONOMY
Imports: chemicals; food and live animals
Exports: fish and crustaceans; cut flowers

CULTURE
Language: Spanish; Quechua; Shuar
Religion: Catholic 94%; Protestant 2%

El Salvador

GEOGRAPHY
Capital: San Salvador
Total Area: 8,124 sq. mi.
Population: 6,881,000

ECONOMY
Imports: machinery; chemicals and chemical products; food; petroleum
Exports: clothing; coffee; paper; yarn

CULTURE
Language: Spanish
Religion: Catholic 78%; Protestant 17%

Grenada

GEOGRAPHY
Capital: St. George's
Total Area: 133 sq. mi.
Population: 89,502

ECONOMY
Imports: machinery; food; chemicals
Exports: electronic components; nutmeg; fish; paper products; cocoa beans

CULTURE
Language: English
Religion: Catholic 58%; Protestant 38%

Guatemala

GEOGRAPHY
Capital: Guatemala City
Total Area: 42,043 sq. mi.
Population: 12,599,000

ECONOMY
Imports: machinery; chemicals; crude and refined petroleum; road vehicles
Exports: coffee; sugar; bananas; spices

CULTURE
Language: Spanish
Religion: Catholic 76%; Protestant 22%

Rio de Janeiro Located on Brazil's southeast coast, Rio de Janeiro is Brazil's second-largest city.

Guyana

GEOGRAPHY
Capital: Georgetown
Total Area: 83,000 sq. mi.
Population: 751,000

ECONOMY
Imports: consumer goods; fuels
Exports: gold; sugar; shrimp; rice; timber

CULTURE
Language: English
Religion: Hindu 34%; Protestant 28%; Catholic 12%; Muslim 9%

Jamaica

GEOGRAPHY
Capital: Kingston
Total Area: 4,244 sq. mi.
Population: 2,651,000

ECONOMY
Imports: consumer goods; petroleum
Exports: alumina; bauxite; clothing; sugar; coffee; rum

CULTURE
Language: English
Religion: Protestant 61%; Catholic 3%

Panama

GEOGRAPHY
Capital: Panama City
Total Area: 30,193 sq. mi.
Population: 3,232,000

ECONOMY
Imports: mineral fuels; petroleum; machinery; transport equipment
Exports: bananas; seafoods

CULTURE
Language: Spanish
Religion: Catholic 82%; Christian 13%

Haiti

GEOGRAPHY
Capital: Port-au-Prince
Total Area: 10,714 sq. mi.
Population: 8,528,000

ECONOMY
Imports: food and livestock; machinery
Exports: clothing; mangoes; cacao; essential oils; leather goods

CULTURE
Language: Haitian Creole; French
Religion: Catholic 69%; Protestant 24%

Mexico

GEOGRAPHY
Capital: Mexico City
Total Area: 761,606 sq. mi.
Population: 107,029,000

ECONOMY
Imports: electronics; clothing; rubber and plastic products
Exports: road vehicles; machinery; textiles

CULTURE
Language: Spanish
Religion: Catholic 90%; Protestant 4%;

Honduras

GEOGRAPHY
Capital: Tegucigalpa
Total Area: 43,278 sq. mi.
Population: 7,205,000

ECONOMY
Imports: food and livestock; machinery
Exports: shrimp; coffee; palm oil

CULTURE
Language: Spanish
Religion: Catholic 87%; Protestant 10%

Nicaragua

GEOGRAPHY
Capital: Managua
Total Area: 49,998 sq. mi.
Population: 5,487,000

ECONOMY
Imports: consumer goods; fuels
Exports: food products; coffee

CULTURE
Language: Spanish
Religion: Catholic 85%; Protestant 12%

Paraguay

GEOGRAPHY
Capital: Asunción
Total Area: 157,047 sq. mi.
Population: 6,158,000

ECONOMY
Imports: machinery; chemicals; food
Exports: soybean products; meats

CULTURE
Language: Spanish; Guaraní
Religion: Catholic 90%; Protestant 5%

Green Crested Basilisk This lizard is one of many species of animals found in the rain forests of Latin America.

Peru

GEOGRAPHY
Capital: Lima
Total Area: 496,226 sq. mi.
Population: 27,968,000

ECONOMY
Imports: machinery; chemicals and chemical products; petroleum; food
Exports: gold; animal feed; copper

CULTURE
Language: Spanish; Quechua; Aymara
Religion: Catholic 96%

St. Kitts and Nevis

GEOGRAPHY
Capital: Basseterre
Total Area: 101 sq. mi.
Population: 38,958

ECONOMY
Imports: machinery; food; metals
Exports: raw sugar; telecommunications equipment

CULTURE
Language: English
Religion: Protestant 85%; Catholic 7%

St. Lucia

GEOGRAPHY
Capital: Castries
Total Area: 238 sq. mi.
Population: 161,000

ECONOMY
Imports: food; machinery; manufactured goods
Exports: bananas; beer and ale; clothing

CULTURE
Language: English
Religion: Catholic 69%; Protestant 22%

St. Vincent and the Grenadines

GEOGRAPHY
Capital: Kingstown
Total Area: 150 sq. mi.
Population: 119,000

ECONOMY
Imports: food products; machinery
Exports: bananas; packaged flour; packaged rice; eddoes and dasheens

CULTURE
Language: English
Religion: Protestant 58%; Catholic 11%

Suriname

GEOGRAPHY
Capital: Paramaribo
Total Area: 63,039 sq. mi.
Population: 449,000

ECONOMY
Imports: machinery; food; road vehicles
Exports: alumina; gold; petroleum; rice

CULTURE
Language: Dutch
Religion: Christian 50%; Hindu 18%; Muslim 14%

Trinidad and Tobago

GEOGRAPHY
Capital: Port of Spain
Total Area: 1,980 sq. mi.
Population: 1,305,000

ECONOMY
Imports: petroleum; industrial machinery
Exports: floating docks; iron and steel

CULTURE
Language: English
Religion: six largest Protestant bodies 30%; Catholic 29%; Hindu 24%

Uruguay

GEOGRAPHY
Capital: Montevideo
Total Area: 68,039 sq. mi.
Population: 3,463,000

ECONOMY
Imports: chemicals; food and tobacco
Exports: leather goods; beef

CULTURE
Language: Spanish
Religion: Catholic 78%; atheist 6%

Venezuela

GEOGRAPHY
Capital: Caracas
Total Area: 352,144 sq. mi.
Population: 26,749,000

ECONOMY
Imports: machinery; chemicals; vehicles
Exports: petroleum products; aluminum

CULTURE
Language: Spanish; 31 indigenous Indian Languages
Religion: Catholic 90%; Protestant 2%

Caribbean Islands The islands of the Caribbean are among the world's most popular tourist destinations.

CHAPTER 7

Latin America

Physical Geography and History

1 GEOGRAPHY

Physical Geography of Mexico, Central America, and the Caribbean

2 GEOGRAPHY

Physical Geography of South America

3 HISTORY

Ancient Civilizations

4 HISTORY

From Colonization to Independence

 ESSENTIAL QUESTION

How have Latin America's geography and resources helped shape its history?

CONNECT → Geography & History

Use the map and the time line to answer the following questions.

1. What is the largest country in Latin America?
2. What country is named after Simón Bolívar, one of the leaders for South American independence?

Culture

◄ **1200 B.C.** Olmec build the first known civilization in southeastern Mexico.

1200 B.C.

History

A.D. 900 Classic period of Mayan civilization ends.

Geography

1200s Inca settle in Cuzco Valley.

Geography

1325 Aztecs establish their capital city, Tenochtitlán. ►

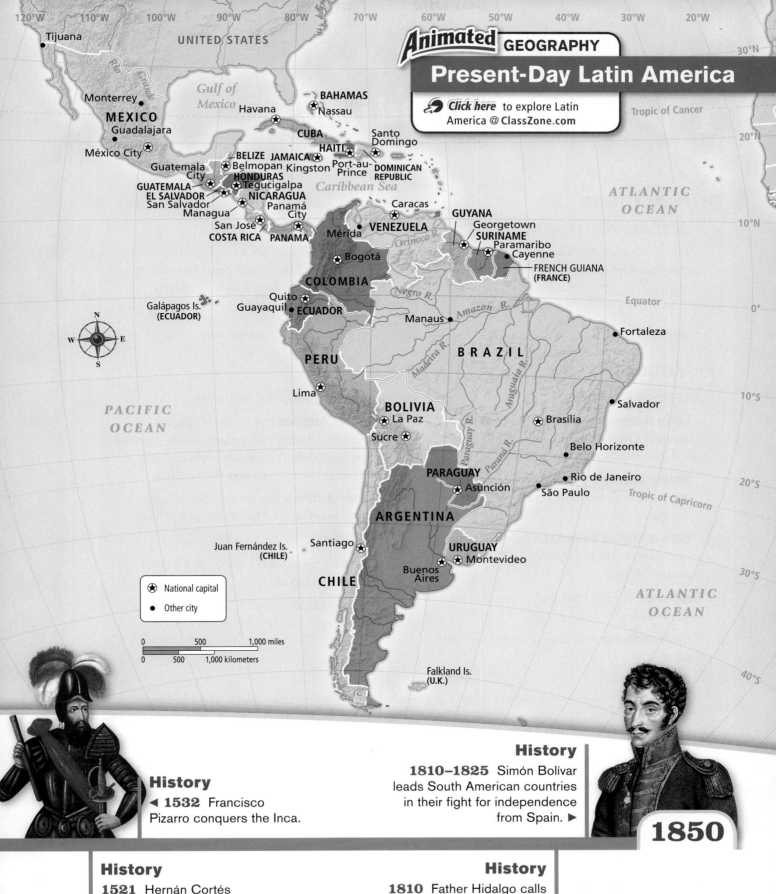

120°W 110°W 100°W 90°W 80°W 70°W 60°W 50°W 40°W 30°W 20°W

30°N

20°N

Tropic of Cancer

Tijuana

UNITED STATES

Gulf of Mexico

Monterrey

MEXICO
Guadalajara
México City

BAHAMAS
Havana
Nassau
CUBA
Santo Domingo
BELIZE JAMAICA HAITI
Belmopan Kingston Port-au- DOMINICAN
Guatemala Prince REPUBLIC
City
HONDURAS Caribbean Sea
GUATEMALA Tegucigalpa
EL SALVADOR NICARAGUA
San Salvador Panamá
Managua City
San José PANAMA
COSTA RICA

ATLANTIC OCEAN

10°N

Caracas
GUYANA
VENEZUELA Georgetown
Mérida SURINAME
Orinoco R. Paramaribo
Bogotá Cayenne
FRENCH GUIANA
(FRANCE)

COLOMBIA

Galápagos Is.
(ECUADOR)

Quito Negro R.
Guayaquil ECUADOR
Manaus Amazon R.

Equator 0°

Fortaleza

PERU

Madeira R.

B R A Z I L

10°S

N
W E
S

Lima

PACIFIC OCEAN

BOLIVIA
La Paz
Sucre

Araguaia R.

Paraguay R.

Salvador

Brasília

Belo Horizonte

PARAGUAY
Asunción

Paraná R.

Rio de Janeiro
São Paulo

Tropic of Capricorn

20°S

Juan Fernández Is.
(CHILE)

Santiago

ARGENTINA

URUGUAY
Montevideo

30°S

CHILE

Buenos Aires

ATLANTIC OCEAN

★ National capital
• Other city

0   500   1,000 miles
0 500 1,000 kilometers

Falkland Is.
(U.K.)

40°S

Reading for Understanding

▶ Key Ideas

BEFORE, YOU LEARNED

The United States and Canada share many cultural and geographic similarities.

NOW YOU WILL LEARN

The geography of Mexico, Central America, and the Caribbean Islands, south of the United States, contains mountains, highlands, and plains.

▶ Vocabulary

TERMS & NAMES

Latin America the region that includes Mexico, Central America, the Caribbean Islands, and South America

Sierra Madre Occidental mountain range that runs from north to south down the western part of Mexico

Sierra Madre Oriental mountain range that runs from north to south down the eastern part of Mexico

isthmus strip of land that connects two landmasses

highlands mountainous and hilly sections of a country

archipelago a chain of islands

Greater Antilles the northern largest Caribbean islands that include Cuba, Jamaica, Hispaniola (which includes Haiti and the Dominican Republic), and Puerto Rico

Lesser Antilles the smaller Caribbean islands southeast of the Greater Antilles

REVIEW

plateau a broad, flat area of land higher than the surrounding land

tectonic plate a large rigid section of the Earth's crust that is in constant motion

▶ Reading Strategy

Re-create the chart shown at right. As you read and respond to the **KEY QUESTIONS**, use the chart to organize details about the geography of Mexico, Central America, and the Caribbean Islands.

 See Skillbuilder Handbook, page R7

CATEGORIZE

LANDFORMS	INFLUENCES ON CLIMATE	VEGETATION
1.	1.	1.
2.	2.	2.
3.	3.	3.

 GRAPHIC ORGANIZERS
Go to **Interactive Review** @ ClassZone.com

Physical Geography of Mexico, Central America, and the Caribbean

Connecting to Your World

What would you do if the ground started to open up as you were walking? That is what happened to a Mexican farmer in February 1943. The farmer watched in amazement as the ground rumbled and split open while he worked. Within 24 hours, a small smoking cone had appeared. The cone was the beginning of the volcano Paricutín (pah•REE•koo•TEEN).

Volcanoes are just one feature of Latin America's geography. Let's take a look at some other geographic features.

Mountains and Islands

🔻 **KEY QUESTION** How is the geography of Mexico, Central America, and the Caribbean Islands alike?

The region of **Latin America** includes Mexico, Central America, the Caribbean Islands, which together make up Middle America, and South America. The Spanish and Portuguese colonized much of the region. Their languages derived from Latin, so they called the region *Latin America*. In this section, you will learn about the geography of Middle America.

Montserrat This Caribbean volcano lay dormant for 500 years, then erupted from 1995 through 1997.

Montserrat

Mexico Mexico's landforms include mountains, **plateaus**, and plains. You can see these on the map opposite. Two major mountain ranges are the **Sierra Madre Occidental** Ⓐ, located in western Mexico, and the **Sierra Madre Oriental** Ⓑ, located in eastern Mexico. Mexico sits on three large **tectonic plates**, and the movement of these plates causes earthquakes and volcanic activity.

Between the two mountain ranges lies the vast Mexican Plateau, making up about 40 percent of Mexico's land regions. Most of Mexico's people live in this area. The plateau rises about 4,000 feet above sea level in the northern part to about 8,000 feet in the southern part. Several volcanoes frame the southern edge of the plateau. East and west of the plateau, along the Gulf of Mexico and the Pacific Ocean, lie the coastal plains.

Mexico has few major rivers. Most of the rivers are not deep enough or wide enough for large boats to move through. Mexico's largest river is the Rio Grande, which is the northern border with Texas.

Sea Turtles These hawksbill sea turtles are swimming over reefs in the Caribbean Sea off the coast of the Cayman Islands.

Central America South of Mexico are the countries of Central America. Central America is an **isthmus**, a strip of land that connects two large landmasses. It connects the North and South American continents.

Highlands, the hilly sections of a country, make up most of Central America. Like Mexico, Central America lies at the edge of tectonic plates, so earthquakes occur often. A string of volcanoes, some of which are active, lines the Pacific Coast. Plains lie along both the Pacific and Caribbean coasts.

The Caribbean Islands East of Central America lie the Caribbean Islands. The islands are made up of three main parts. The Bahamas are an **archipelago**, a chain of nearly 700 islands. The **Greater Antilles** Ⓒ include the largest islands of Cuba, Jamaica, Hispaniola (which includes Haiti and the Dominican Republic), and Puerto Rico. The **Lesser Antilles** Ⓓ include the remaining smaller islands. Many of the Caribbean Islands are actually the exposed tops of underwater mountains. Mountains and highlands make up the interior of most Caribbean Islands, and plains circle the highlands.

▲ **COMPARE AND CONTRAST** Describe how the geography of Mexico, Central America, and the Caribbean Islands is alike.

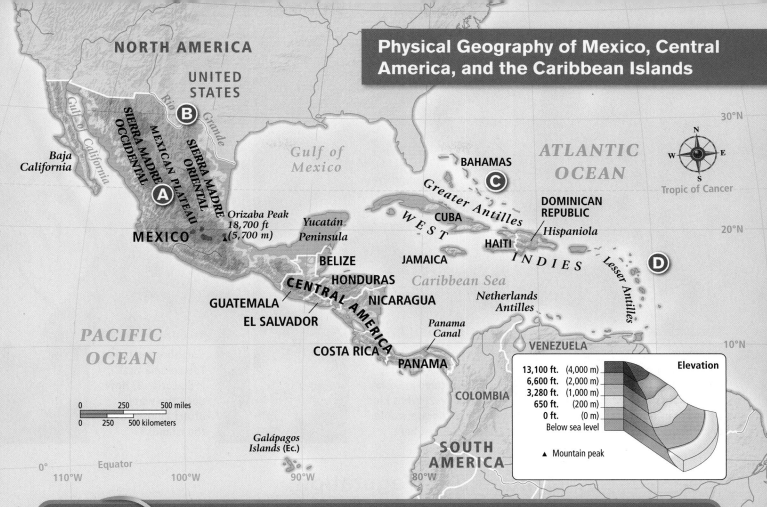

Physical Geography of Mexico, Central America, and the Caribbean Islands

NORTH AMERICA

UNITED STATES

Baja California

Gulf of California

SIERRA MADRE OCCIDENTAL

MEXICAN PLATEAU

SIERRA MADRE ORIENTAL

B

Rio Grande

Gulf of Mexico

A

MEXICO

Orizaba Peak 18,700 ft (5,700 m)

Yucatán Peninsula

BELIZE

GUATEMALA

EL SALVADOR

HONDURAS

CENTRAL AMERICA

COSTA RICA

NICARAGUA

PANAMA

Panama Canal

PACIFIC OCEAN

BAHAMAS

C

CUBA

JAMAICA

HAITI

Greater Antilles

DOMINICAN REPUBLIC

Hispaniola

WEST INDIES

Lesser Antilles

D

Caribbean Sea

Netherlands Antilles

ATLANTIC OCEAN

Tropic of Cancer

30°N

20°N

10°N

VENEZUELA

COLOMBIA

SOUTH AMERICA

Galápagos Islands (Ec.)

Equator

0°

110°W   100°W   90°W   80°W

0   250   500 miles
0   250   500 kilometers

Elevation

13,100 ft.   (4,000 m)
6,600 ft.   (2,000 m)
3,280 ft.   (1,000 m)
650 ft.   (200 m)
0 ft.   (0 m)
Below sea level

▲ Mountain peak

CONNECT Geography & Economics

Panama Canal The Panama Canal was built by cutting through the Central American land bridge, which connected the Atlantic and Pacific oceans. Before the canal was opened in 1914, a ship bringing copper from Peru to Florida had to sail south around South America and then north. Using the canal shortened the distance and time.

- - - Route before canal (almost 14,000 mi.)

——— Route after canal (roughly 4,000 mi.)

UNITED STATES
FLORIDA
Panama Canal
PERU
SOUTH AMERICA

CRITICAL THINKING

1. **Movement** By how many miles did the canal shorten a ship's journey?

2. **Make Inferences** Why was Panama a good choice for building a canal?

201

Desert Barrel cacti grow in Mexico's deserts. **1. How are these plants able to thrive in this dry climate?**

Rain Forest La Fortuna Waterfall is located in Costa Rica. **2. What kind of climate would you find here?**

Caribbean Islands This volcanic peak is in St. Lucia. **3. How does the water affect climate in the islands?**

Climate and Vegetation

▼ **KEY QUESTION** What is a major influence on the climate of the Caribbean Islands?

Latin America stretches across more than one-half of the Western Hemisphere. It has a wide variety of climates and vegetation.

Mexico About half of Mexico lies south of the tropic of Cancer. The temperatures in this part of Mexico are generally warm and constant year-round, with abundant rainfall. Tropical rain forests thrive here.

A greater variation in temperatures exists in places located north of the tropic of Cancer. The driest areas are in the deserts of northwestern Mexico, as well as in the northern part of the Mexican Plateau. Desert shrubs grow in this climate. In Mexico's mountains and highlands, average temperatures vary with increases in elevation. The vegetation here consists mostly of coniferous and deciduous forests.

Central America All of Central America is located in the tropical zone, so temperatures are generally warm year-round. The plains along the Caribbean coast receive the greatest amount of precipitation. The climate is perfect for the lush rain forests that grow there.

As in Mexico, places at higher elevations in Central America experience cooler average temperatures than those at lower elevations. Winds that blow inland from the warm Caribbean Sea bring heavy rains on the eastern side of the mountains. Places on the westward side and in the interior highlands receive the least amount of precipitation. Forests of oak and pine grow at higher elevations, while desert shrubs grow in the drier areas on the Pacific side.

The Caribbean Islands Winds play a big role in the climate of the Caribbean Islands. The waters in the Caribbean Sea stay warm most of the year and heat the air over them. Warm winds blow across the islands, keeping the temperatures warm and constant year-round. The Lesser Antilles are divided into islands that face the wind and those that are protected from the wind. Those protected from the wind receive less rain than those facing the wind.

As in Mexico and Central America, elevation influences climate in the islands' mountains. The islands' climates allow diverse vegetation, including rain forests, deciduous forests, and desert shrubs, to grow there.

 SUMMARIZE Describe the major influence on the climate of the Caribbean Islands.

Tree Frog A red-eyed tree frog, a unique animal found in Costa Rica's rain forest, hops a ride on a caiman, an alligator-like reptile.

Section ① Assessment

 **ONLINE QUIZ**
For test practice, go to **Interactive Review** @ ClassZone.com

TERMS & NAMES

1. Explain the importance of
- isthmus
- archipelago
- Greater Antilles
- Lesser Antilles

USE YOUR READING NOTES

2. Categorize Use your completed chart to answer the following question:

How does climate influence the location of rain forests in Central America?

LANDFORMS	INFLUENCES ON CLIMATE	VEGETATION
1.	1.	1.
2.	2.	2.
3.	3.	3.

KEY IDEAS

3. How did Latin America get its name?

4. Where do most people in Mexico live?

5. What affects climate in the mountains and highlands of Mexico and Central America?

CRITICAL THINKING

6. Analyze Causes and Effects How did the Panama Canal help trade in Latin America?

7. Make Generalizations What generalization can you make about climate in Mexico, Central America, and the Caribbean Islands?

8. **CONNECT to Today** In 1999, the United States gave control of the Panama Canal to Panama. How do you think the country of Panama will benefit from the canal?

9. **WRITING** **Create a Poster** Choose a country in Central America or one of the Caribbean Islands and prepare a captioned poster for a geography fair. Include information about the country's land, climate, and vegetation.

SECTION 2

Reading for Understanding

▶ Key Ideas

BEFORE, YOU LEARNED

The physical geography of much of Mexico, Central America, and the Caribbean Islands consists of mountains and highlands.

NOW YOU WILL LEARN

The physical geography of South America consists of a wide variety of landforms and climates.

▶ Vocabulary

TERMS & NAMES

Andes Mountains a mountain range located on South America's west coast and extending the full length of the continent

altiplano a high plateau

llanos (YAH•nohs) grasslands of western Venezuela and northeastern Colombia

Pampas grassy plains in south-central South America

Amazon River South America's longest river (about 4,000 miles, or 6,400 kilometers) and the second-longest river in the world

REVIEW

highlands mountainous or hilly sections of a country

rain forest a broadleaf tree region in a tropical climate

Visual Vocabulary *altiplano*

▶ Reading Strategy

Re-create the diagram shown at right. As you read and respond to the **KEY QUESTIONS**, use the diagram to summarize each of the main parts of Section 2.

 See Skillbuilder Handbook, page R5

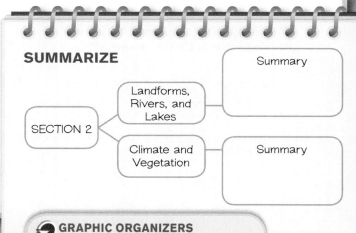

SUMMARIZE

SECTION 2 → Landforms, Rivers, and Lakes → Summary

SECTION 2 → Climate and Vegetation → Summary

🔁 **GRAPHIC ORGANIZERS**
Go to **Interactive Review** @ ClassZone.com

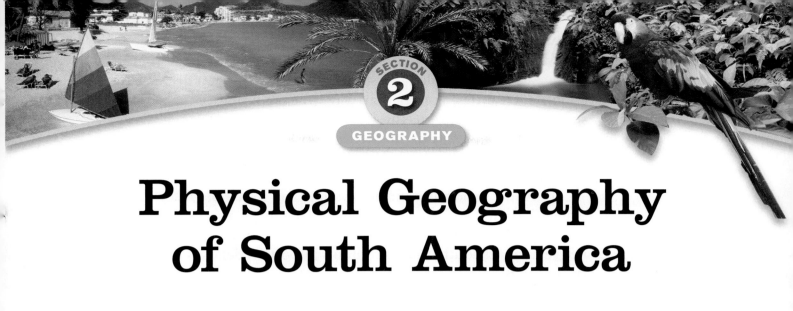

Physical Geography of South America

Connecting to Your World

Look carefully at a map of South America, and you will see many physical features similar to those that define North America, particularly the United States. Just as the Rocky Mountains rise in western North America, the Andes Mountains stretch the entire length of western South America. Great river systems drain both continents, and large plains are central to both North and South America. Of course, as you will soon learn, there are important differences as well.

Landforms, Rivers, and Lakes

▼ KEY QUESTION What are the main features of South America's landscape?

South America has nearly every type of physical feature, including mountains, grasslands, plains, and **highlands**. The continent has few large lakes but is drained by five major river systems, including the Amazon River, one of the largest rivers in the world.

Patagonia Deserts, plateaus, and highlands make up this area.

PATAGONIA

The Andes As the map on the opposite page shows, the **Andes Mountains** Ⓐ stretch along western South America for a distance of about 5,500 miles. Longer than any other mountain range above sea level, the Andes are the world's second-highest range. Only the Himalayas in Asia are higher. The tallest Andean peak, Mount Aconcagua, is the Western Hemisphere's tallest mountain. People living in the Andes grow crops on terraces cut into the mountains.

The Andes region also includes valleys and the *altiplano*, or "high plateau," shared by Peru and Bolivia. Made up of a series of basins between mountains, the *altiplano* is one of the world's highest inhabited regions. Its southern half contains important deposits of copper, silver, tungsten, and tin.

Plains and Highlands The Central Plains extend eastward from the Andes and cover about three-fifths of South America. The *llanos*, Gran Chaco, Amazon rain forest, and Pampas make up the Central Plains. The **llanos** (YAH•nohs) are wide grasslands that stretch across northeastern Colombia and western Venezuela. There, cattle ranches and small farms are common.

A tropical **rain forest** in the Amazon Basin Ⓑ covers about 40 percent of Brazil. The Gran Chaco is a largely uninhabited area consisting of subtropical grasslands and low forests. Nearly half of this region is located in Argentina. The remainder extends into Paraguay and Bolivia. Just south of the Gran Chaco lies a large grassy plain called the **Pampas**, Argentina's most populated area.

The Eastern Highlands are two separate regions. The Guiana Highlands Ⓒ to the north of the Amazon Basin consist of tropical forests and grasslands. The Brazilian Highlands Ⓓ to the south cover about one-fourth of South America and consist mostly of hills and plateaus.

Fun Facts!

ANGEL FALLS

Angel Falls in the Guiana Highlands of southeastern Venezuela, the world's tallest waterfall, drops 3,212 feet. The waterfall was named for Jimmy Angel, an American pilot who spotted it from his airplane in 1935.

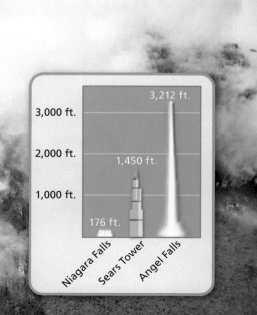

3,000 ft.

3,212 ft.

2,000 ft.

1,450 ft.

1,000 ft.

176 ft.

Niagara Falls   Sears Tower   Angel Falls

Physical Geography of South America

Caribbean Sea

Netherlands Antilles

CENTRAL AMERICA

VENEZUELA

ATLANTIC OCEAN

Orinoco River

Llanos

COLOMBIA

GUYANA

GUIANA HIGHLANDS

SURINAME

FRENCH GUIANA

ECUADOR

Negro River

Amazon River

AMAZON

PERU

Amazon River

Madeira River

BASIN

SOUTH AMERICA

B R A Z I L

ANDES

Araguaia River

Lake Titicaca

Mato Grosso Plateau

BRAZILIAN HIGHLANDS

Altiplano

BOLIVIA

Gran Chaco

PERU

Atacama Desert

PARAGUAY

ANDES

PACIFIC OCEAN

Paraná River

Paraguay River

ATLANTIC OCEAN

Tropic of Capricorn

Mount Aconcagua 22,834 ft (6,960 m)

Uruguay River

Pampas

URUGUAY

CHILE

Río de la Plata

ARGENTINA

Patagonia

Falkland Islands

Tierra del Fuego
Cape Horn

Drake Passage

Equator   0°

10°S

20°S

30°S

50°S

90°W   80°W   70°W   60°W   50°W   40°W   30°W   20°W

N W E S

Elevation

13,100 ft.	(4,000 m)
6,600 ft.	(2,000 m)
3,280 ft.	(500 m)
650 ft.	(200 m)
0 ft.	(0 m)

Below sea level

▲ Mountain peak

0   250   500 miles
0   250   500 kilometers

CONNECT Geography & History

READING A PHYSICAL MAP

Use the key in this physical map to identify the elevations of Patagonia and the Amazon Basin.

1. **Place** What two oceans border South America?

2. **Region** Where are large areas of highlands found in South America?

207

Rivers and Lakes South America has five large river systems. The largest is the Amazon river system, which carries about one-fifth of the Earth's river water. The **Amazon River** flows from the Andes to the Atlantic Ocean and is about 4,000 miles long. The river and its tributaries drain much of Brazil and Peru, as well as parts of Colombia, Ecuador, Bolivia, and Venezuela. South America's other river systems are the Rio de la Plata, the Magdalena-Cauca, the Orinoco, and the São Francisco.

South America has few large natural lakes. The largest, Lake Maracaibo in northwestern Venezuela, covers an area of more than 5,000 square miles. About two-thirds of Venezuela's total petroleum output comes from the Lake Maracaibo region. Lake Titicaca is the second largest lake in South America. Located in the altiplano at an elevation of 12,500 feet, Lake Titicaca is the world's highest navigable lake.

▲ **SUMMARIZE** List the main geographic features of South America.

Lake Maracaibo A girl uses a pole to move her boat between houses on Lake Maracaibo. **How have people living on Lake Maracaibo adapted to their environment?**

Climate and Vegetation

▼ **KEY QUESTION** What kinds of vegetation are found in the tropical and desert climates of South America?

South America has a wide range of climates—from the steamy rain forest of the Amazon Basin to the icy cold of the upper Andes. Because climate largely determines the vegetation of a region, South America has a great variety of plant life as well.

Mountain Climates The climate of the Andes Mountains changes with elevation. For example, near the equator, the climate at the lowest elevations is tropical. However, if you were to climb midway up the mountains, you would most likely find a more temperate, or mild, climate. At an elevation of more than 15,000 feet, you would encounter extremely low temperatures and icy winds. The only vegetation would be a sparse assortment of mosses, lichens, and dwarf shrubs. Climate zones at various elevations in the Andes are compared on the opposite page.

COMPARING ◄ Mountain Climate Zones

(A) Guanaco (a kind of llama) in the Chilean Andes

(B) Potato fields in Peru

(A) Tierra Helada (Frozen Land)
- Above 10,000 feet
- Livestock: llamas, sheep

(C) Tierra Templada (Temperate Land)
- 3,000–6,000 feet
- Crops: corn, cotton, coffee, citrus fruits

(B) Tierra Fría (Cold Land)
- 6,000–10,000 feet
- Crops: wheat, apples, potatoes, barley

(D) Tierra Caliente (Hot Land)
- Sea level–3,000 feet
- Crops: bananas, cacao, sugar cane, rice

CRITICAL THINKING
Draw Conclusions What zones are most productive for growing crops?

(C) Corn fields in Ecuador

(D) Sugar cane fields in Colombia

Tropical Rain Forests Much of South America lies in the low latitudes, which are tropical. There, the Amazon rain forest covers more than 2 million square miles. Located primarily in Brazil, the rain forest is bounded to the north by the Guiana Highlands, to the south by Brazil's central plateau, to the west by the Andes, and to the east by the Atlantic Ocean. The rain forest climate is hot and wet. Although the average temperature remains a fairly constant 80°F, high humidity makes it seem hotter. Rain falls throughout the year, for a yearly average of between 50 to 175 inches.

The Amazon rain forest has the world's richest collection of life forms. In fact, many of its insects, birds, and plants have yet to be named. Wildlife includes jaguars, monkeys, and manatees. Plant life is abundant. The rain forest's many varieties of trees include rosewood, Brazil nut, rubber, mahogany, and cedar.

Grasslands Located in Venezuela and Colombia, the *llanos* cover an area of about 220,000 square miles. They extend north and west to the Andes and south to the Amazon Basin. The *llanos* have a warm climate, and their rainfall averages between 45 and 180 inches.

The Pampas cover an area of about 295,000 square miles in central Argentina, and they extend into Uruguay. The grasslands are good for raising cattle, and the rich soil produces a variety of crops, particularly soybeans and wheat. In addition to being an important agricultural area, the Pampas are also home to most of Argentina's cities.

The *Llanos* Cattle graze on the *llanos* in Venezuela. **Why is this area a good place to raise cattle?**

Deserts Desert climates occur along much of Peru's coast, as well as in northern Chile's Atacama Desert and southern Argentina's Patagonian desert. Desert climates are dry, and temperatures may be hot or cold. The desert in southern Patagonia is an example of a cold desert, with temperatures averaging only about 44°F.

The Atacama Desert is warmer, with summer temperatures averaging in the mid-60s°F. Although an ocean current from the Antarctic mixes with warm air to produce clouds and fog in the Atacama Desert, there is little rain. In fact, in the center of the Atacama, no rainfall has ever been recorded. There, nothing grows. Yet in the desert's fog zones, cacti, ferns, and many other types of vegetation grow.

 CATEGORIZE Identify the kinds of vegetation found in South America's tropical and desert climates.

Jujuy Desert The Jujuy Desert is located in northwestern Argentina.

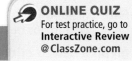
ONLINE QUIZ
For test practice, go to
Interactive Review
@ ClassZone.com

Section 2 Assessment

TERMS & NAMES

1. Explain the importance of
- *altiplano*
- *llanos*
- Pampas
- Amazon River

USE YOUR READING NOTES

2. Summarize Use your completed chart to answer the following question:

How is Lake Maracaibo important to South America?

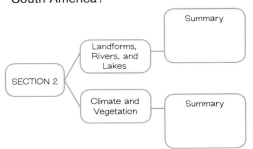

KEY IDEAS

3. What are the main river systems of South America?

4. Where are the Guiana and Brazilian Highlands located?

5. What relationship exists between elevation and climates of the Andes?

CRITICAL THINKING

6. Compare and Contrast How are the four main regions of the Central Plains different from one another?

7. Analyze Causes and Effects Why is a variety of plant life able to grow in the Atacama Desert?

8. CONNECT to Today The Amazon rain forest is a popular destination for tourists today. What features do you think attract tourists to this area?

9. ART **Create a Mural** Draw a panoramic mural of the geographic features of South America. Include the continent's landforms and waterways.

SECTION 3

Reading for Understanding

▶ Key Ideas

BEFORE, YOU LEARNED

Latin America contains a wide variety of landforms, climates, and vegetation.

NOW YOU WILL LEARN

People adapted to these challenging geographic and climatic conditions and developed great civilizations.

▶ Vocabulary

TERMS & NAMES

Olmec an early civilization along the Gulf Coast of what is now southern Mexico

Maya an early civilization located in what is now the Yucatán Peninsula, Guatemala, and northern Belize

cultural hearth the heartland, or place of origin, of a major culture

glyph a carved or engraved symbol that stands for a syllable or a word

empire a political system in which people or lands are controlled by one ruler

Aztec an early civilization in the Valley of Mexico

chinampas artificial islands used for farming

Inca an early civilization in the Andes Mountains of Peru

REVIEW

culture the shared attitudes, knowledge, and behaviors of a group

BACKGROUND VOCABULARY

jaguar a large cat mainly found in Central and South America

Visual Vocabulary glyph

▶ Reading Strategy

Re-create the Venn diagram shown at right. As you read and respond to the **KEY QUESTIONS**, use the diagram to show how the Aztec and Inca empires were alike and different.

 Skillbuilder Handbook, page R9

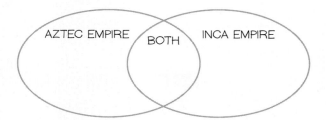

COMPARE AND CONTRAST

AZTEC EMPIRE   BOTH   INCA EMPIRE

 GRAPHIC ORGANIZERS
Go to **Interactive Review** @ClassZone.com

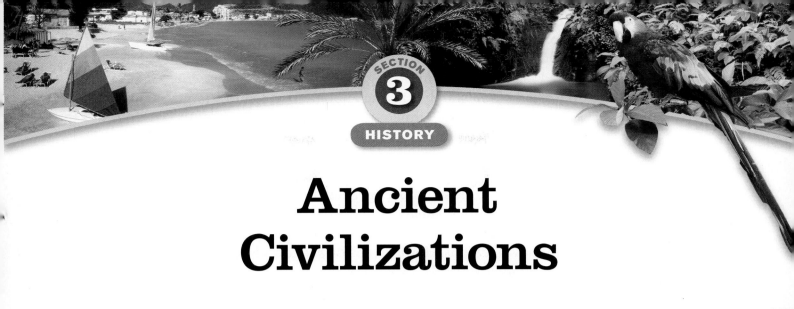

Ancient Civilizations

Connecting to Your World

How do you think the stone head pictured here was made? An ancient civilization in Latin America carved these heads about 3,000 years ago. What do you think of when you hear the word *pyramid*? Most likely, you think of the pyramids built about 4,500 years ago by the ancient Egyptians. Did you know that ancient civilizations in Latin America, such as the Maya, constructed these huge structures too? As you read this section, you will find out more about the Maya and other early civilizations that thrived in what is now Latin America.

Olmec Head The Olmec carved these large heads from a stone called basalt.

The Olmec and the Maya

▼ **KEY QUESTION** How were the Olmec and Mayan civilizations alike?

The first known civilization to develop in Latin America were the **Olmec**. They lived along the Gulf Coast of what is now southern Mexico about 3,200 years ago. Another civilization, the **Maya**, developed in the high-lands and flatlands of what is now the Yucatán Peninsula, Guatemala, and northern Belize. Archaeological evidence shows that these two cultures built well-laid-out cities and complex civilizations. They were farmers, artists, and architects.

The Tikal Pyramid The Maya built this pyramid in the rain forest of what is now Guatemala.

Tikal ○ GUATEMALA

The Olmec, a Cultural Hearth The Olmec were traders and skilled farmers. As farming began to thrive, the Olmec could count on a steady food supply. Having enough food led to a larger population and allowed the Olmec to focus on tasks other than farming. An adequate food supply also led to the growth of cities.

Olmec cities included plazas, housing areas, and ceremonial centers. Their oldest known city is San Lorenzo. The Olmec are known for their huge stone sculptures of heads. Some sculptures show a half-human, half-animal **jaguar**, the Olmec's chief god.

The Olmec began to abandon their cities beginning around 600 B.C. for unknown reasons. However, historians consider the Olmec civilization a **cultural hearth**, the place of origin of a major **culture**. The Olmec culture shaped other cultures in the region, particularly the Maya.

CONNECT History to Today

A Recent Maya Discovery

In 2005, archaeologists working in Guatemala at the site of an ancient Mayan city made an exciting discovery—a stone monument with the carving of a woman's face. The carving dates back to around the A.D. 500s, making it the earliest known likeness of a woman that the Maya carved in stone. This is significant because it suggests that women had important leadership roles in Mayan society early on in Mayan history.

An archaeology student wraps the Mayan stone monument to take for further study.

The Maya, Masters of the City The Maya lived in villages in southern Mexico and northern Central America as early as 1500 B.C. At the height of their civilization, around A.D. 250, the Maya built impressive cities with stone temples, pyramids, plazas, palaces, and ball courts. They were farmers and traders. Corn, beans, and squash were important crops. The Maya also traded salt, chocolate, and cotton with other cultures.

The Maya were advanced in their knowledge of science and technology. They created a 365-day calendar by watching the stars. The calendar identified events throughout the year, such as planting times and holidays. The Maya used a mathematical system based on the number 20 and were the first people to use the zero. They also developed **glyph** writing, carved symbols that stood for a syllable or a word.

In about A.D. 900, the Maya started abandoning their cities, like the Olmec had done earlier. The reasons remain unclear. However, descendants of the Maya still live in the region today.

▲ **COMPARE AND CONTRAST**
Explain how the Olmec and Mayan civilizations were alike and different.

Stone Carving
The drawing (right) helps to more clearly see what is carved in part of the stone monument.

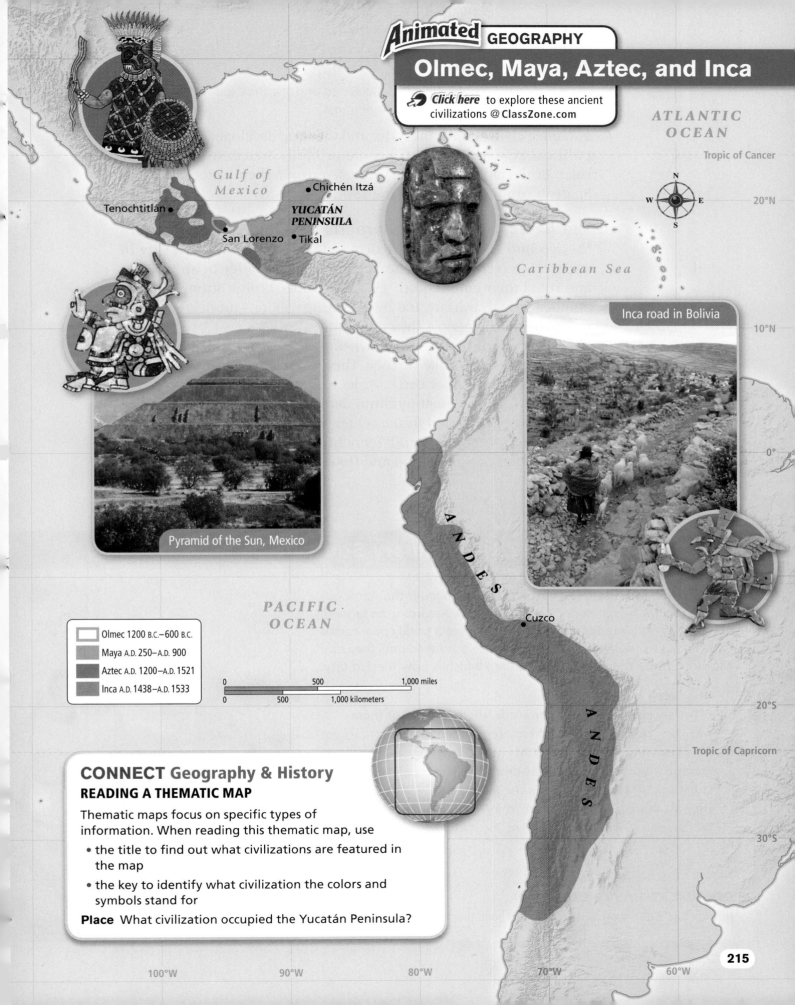

ATLANTIC OCEAN

Tropic of Cancer

20°N

Gulf of Mexico

• Chichén Itzá

Tenochtitlán •

YUCATÁN PENINSULA

San Lorenzo • • Tikal

Caribbean Sea

10°N

Inca road in Bolivia

0°

Pyramid of the Sun, Mexico

A N D E S

PACIFIC OCEAN

• Cuzco

20°S

Olmec 1200 B.C.–600 B.C.

Maya A.D. 250–A.D. 900

Aztec A.D. 1200–A.D. 1521

Inca A.D. 1438–A.D. 1533

0   500   1,000 miles

0   500   1,000 kilometers

A N D E S

Tropic of Capricorn

30°S

CONNECT Geography & History
READING A THEMATIC MAP

Thematic maps focus on specific types of information. When reading this thematic map, use

- the title to find out what civilizations are featured in the map
- the key to identify what civilization the colors and symbols stand for

Place What civilization occupied the Yucatán Peninsula?

100°W   90°W   80°W   70°W   60°W

The Aztec and the Inca

KEY QUESTION How did the Aztec and the Inca use their environments to develop their empires?

Two great civilizations, the Aztec and the Inca, developed vast **empires**, political systems in which people or lands are controlled by one ruler. Both civilizations were very powerful in their regions until the Spanish conquered them in the 1500s.

The Aztec, a Military Culture The **Aztec** moved from northern Mexico into the Valley of Mexico and what is now Mexico City in about the A.D. 1300s. They took control of the valley in about 1428 and ruled their empire until 1521. The Aztec built a strong military empire through warfare and by collecting tribute—money, goods, or crops—from the people they defeated.

The Aztec built Tenochtitlán (teh•NOHCH•tee•TLAHN), their capital city, on an island in Lake Texcoco. The city included houses and causeways, or roads made of earth. At its height, the population reached around 300,000. A great pyramid dedicated to Huitzilopochtli, the sun and war god, stood in the center of the city. The Aztec used the watery environment around Tenochtitlán to create *chinampas*, or island gardens, to grow food and flowers.

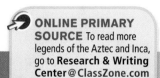

ONLINE PRIMARY SOURCE To read more legends of the Aztec and Inca, go to **Research & Writing Center** @ ClassZone.com

ANALYZING Primary Sources

The Eagle on the Prickly Pear Why would the Aztec build a city in the middle of a swampy lake? According to legend, one of their gods predicted that they would see a prickly pear cactus with an eagle sitting on top of it. The Aztec wandered until they saw this sign. There they built Tenochtitlán, which is now Mexico City.

> [A]s they passed through the reeds, there in front of them was the prickly pear with the eagle perched on top, . . . his claws punching holes in his prey. When he saw the Mexicans in the distance, he bowed to them. . . . The . . . spirit said, 'Mexicans, this is the place.' And with that they all wept. 'We are favored,' they said. 'We are blessed. We have seen where our city will be. Now let us go rest.'
>
> Source: *The Eagle on the Prickly Pear*, retold by John Bierhorst

DOCUMENT-BASED QUESTION
How did the Aztec know where to stop to build their capital city?

Inca, Mountain Empire The **Inca** lived in the Andes Mountains in what is now Peru. They controlled a large empire from the early 1400s until 1533. The empire centered around Cuzco (KOOZ•koh), the Inca's mountain capital city. By 1500, the empire extended about 2,500 miles along the west coast of South America. The Inca built complex cities such as Machu Picchu. To farm the steep land, they cut terraces into the mountainsides, where they grew corn and potatoes. They built aqueducts, or canals, to irrigate the land. On higher areas, the Inca grazed llamas.

The Inca adapted to difficult conditions. They built 14,000 miles of roads on which runners carried messages. To keep records, they used *quipus* (KEE•poos), counting tools of knotted cords. Today's descendants of the Inca, the Quechua (KEHCH•wuh), make up about 45 percent of Peru's population. They still use terraces and aqueducts, raise corn and potatoes, and graze llamas.

 SYNTHESIZE Describe how the Inca changed their environment to develop an empire.

Machu Picchu Flowers grow on the slopes of Machu Picchu today.

Section ❸ Assessment

 **ONLINE QUIZ**
For test practice, go to
Interactive Review
@ ClassZone.com

TERMS & NAMES

1. Explain the importance of
- Olmec
- Maya
- Aztec
- Inca

USE YOUR READING NOTES

2. Compare and Contrast Use your completed Venn diagram to answer the following question:

How were the ways the Aztec and Inca modified their environments similar?

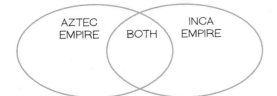

KEY IDEAS

3. What are the earliest known civilizations in what is now southern Mexico?

4. How did the Aztec build their large empire?

5. How were the Inca able to communicate throughout their large empire?

CRITICAL THINKING

6. Compare and Contrast How was the decline of the Mayan and Olmec civilizations different from the decline of the Aztec and Inca civilizations?

7. Identify Problems and Solutions What problems might an empire have in ruling millions of people?

8. CONNECT to Today Each year, around 300,000 people visit Machu Picchu. What problems do you think this presents for this archaeological site? Explain.

9. WRITING **Write a Newspaper Article** Imagine that you are a reporter visiting a city in one of the early Latin American civilizations. Write a short article that describes the city's architecture.

Click here to enter the *chinampas* @ ClassZone.com

ISLAND GARDENS

Much of the land around Tenochtitlán, where the Aztec settled, was swampy, posing a challenge for farming. The Aztec were resourceful at adapting to their environment. They built *chinampas*, human-made islands created for planting. The rich soil allowed the Aztec to grow crops and flowers.

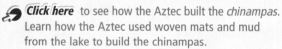 **Click here** to see how the Aztec built the *chinampas*. Learn how the Aztec used woven mats and mud from the lake to build the chinampas.

Click here to see how the Aztec lived on the *chinampas*. Learn where they lived, what they wore, and what they ate.

Click here to see how *chinampas* are used today and the problems they face.

Tenochtitlán

MEXICO
O
Tenochtitlán

Valley
of
Mexico

Lake
Texcoco

Tenochtitlán

— Causeways
▬ Chinampas

GeoActivity

Make a Model Work with a partner to create a small model of a *chinampa*. Apply what you have learned about how the Aztec built *chinampas* to make a model using materials similar to those the Aztec used.

219

Reading for Understanding

▶ Key Ideas

BEFORE, YOU LEARNED

Powerful civilizations arose in Latin America but eventually fell.

NOW YOU WILL LEARN

Life was hard, as the people of Latin America struggled to gain their independence.

▶ Vocabulary

TERMS & NAMES

Columbian Exchange the movement of plants and animals between Latin America and Europe after Columbus' voyage to the Americas in A.D. 1492

conquistador (kahn•KWIHS•tuh•DAWR) Spanish word for "conqueror"

colony overseas territory ruled by a nation

mestizo (mehs•TEE•zoh) person with mixed European and Indian ancestry

Father Hidalgo father of Mexican independence

Simón Bolívar leader for independence in northern South America

José de San Martín leader for independence in southern South America

REVIEW

empire a political system in which people or lands are controlled by one ruler

Visual Vocabulary *conquistador*

▶ Reading Strategy

Re-create the time line shown at right. As you read and respond to the **KEY QUESTIONS**, use the time line to show the events that led to independence in Mexico and countries in South America.

 See Skillbuilder Handbook, page R6

SEQUENCE EVENTS

```
┌──────┐   ┌──────┐   ┌──────┐   ┌──────┐
│      │   │      │   │      │   │      │
└──────┘   └──────┘   └──────┘   └──────┘
    ↓          ↓          ↓          ↓
```

A.D. 1521   A.D. 1826

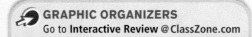

🔁 **GRAPHIC ORGANIZERS**
Go to **Interactive Review @ ClassZone.com**

SECTION
4
HISTORY

From Colonization to Independence

Connecting to Your World

If you had lived in Europe before Christopher Columbus arrived in the Americas, you would have never enjoyed chocolate, corn, turkey, peppers, potatoes, or tomatoes. And if you had lived in the Americas, you would never have eaten oranges, bananas, beef, or pork. After the Spanish came to America, plants and animals were exchanged, or traded, between America and Europe. This came to be known as the **Columbian Exchange**.

Conquered Lands

▼ **KEY QUESTION** How did Spanish rule affect life in Latin America?

After Columbus arrived in 1492, life for the Indians changed dramatically. In 1521, a Spanish ***conquistador*** (kahn•KWIHS•tuh•DAWR), or conqueror, Hernán Cortés, defeated the Aztec. And in 1533 Francisco Pizarro, another Spanish *conquistador*, defeated the Inca.

The Exchange
The graphic shows the goods and diseases transferred between the two hemispheres. **What vegetables did Europeans bring to the Americas?**

Columbian Exchange

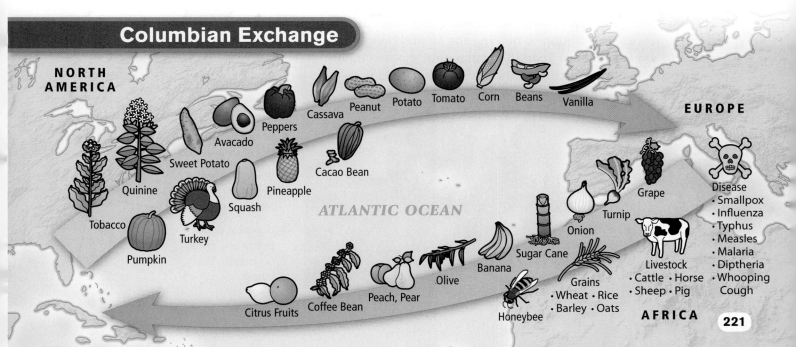

NORTH AMERICA

EUROPE

ATLANTIC OCEAN

Cassava · Peanut · Potato · Tomato · Corn · Beans · Vanilla

Peppers · Avacado · Sweet Potato · Pineapple · Cacao Bean

Quinine · Turkey · Squash

Tobacco · Pumpkin

Grape · Turnip · Onion · Livestock · Disease

Sugar Cane · Banana · Grains

Citrus Fruits · Coffee Bean · Peach, Pear · Olive · Honeybee

· Wheat · Rice · Barley · Oats

Livestock
· Cattle · Horse
· Sheep · Pig

Disease
· Smallpox
· Influenza
· Typhus
· Measles
· Malaria
· Diptheria
· Whooping Cough

AFRICA

221

Colonial Rule By the mid-1500s, the Spanish had set up **colonies**, or overseas territories ruled by a nation, in various parts of Latin America. Spain's goal was to take advantage of the resources and vast lands in its new **empire**.

To rule the empire, Spain set up a class society. At the top were the *peninsulares* (peh•neen•soo•LAHR•ehs), people born in Spain. They held the high government positions. Below them were the *criollos* (kree•OH•lohs), Spaniards born in Latin America. They were often wealthy, but could not hold high government offices. These two groups controlled land, wealth, and power in the colonies.

Below the *criollos* were the **mestizos** (mehs•TEE•zohs), people of Spanish and Indian ancestry. They had little power. Finally, African enslaved persons and Indians were at the bottom and had no power.

Colonial Economy One of Spain's main purposes in creating colonies was to make Spain wealthy. To do so, Spain set up a system known as *encomienda* (ehn•koh•mee•EHN•duh). Under this system, Indians mined, ranched, and farmed for Spanish landlords. The Indians lived in poverty and hardship, essentially enslaved.

Spain, however, grew wealthy. The Spanish established huge ranches to raise cattle and sheep and large plantations to grow sugar cane, coffee, and cacao in various parts of Latin America. Spain made huge profits from the gold and silver extracted from Mexican mines.

▲ **SYNTHESIZE** Explain how life changed for people in Latin America under Spanish rule.

CONNECT to Language Arts

The time during which Spain ruled its colonies in Latin America is often referred to as the region's *colonial period*. If you visited Latin America today, you would see many examples of Spanish influence. In addition to hearing the Spanish language, you would see examples of Spanish architectural styles in buildings that the Spanish constructed throughout their colonies, such as the church and fort pictured below.

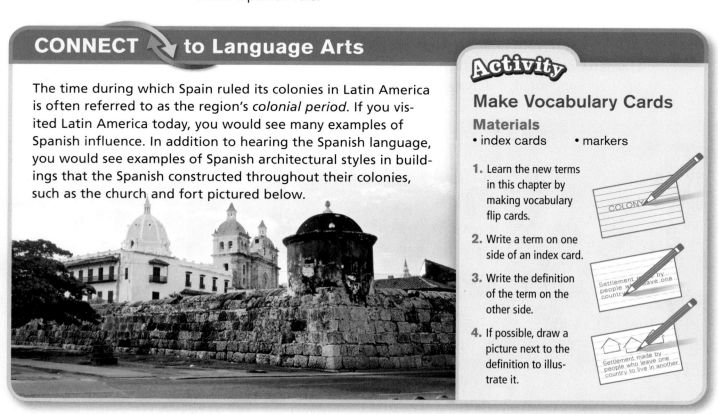

Activity

Make Vocabulary Cards

Materials
- index cards
- markers

1. Learn the new terms in this chapter by making vocabulary flip cards.

2. Write a term on one side of an index card.

3. Write the definition of the term on the other side.

4. If possible, draw a picture next to the definition to illustrate it.

Independence from the Spanish

▼ **KEY QUESTION** What events led to independence in Mexico and South America?

In the 1800s, Spain began paying less attention to its Latin American colonies because it was fighting a war in Europe against Napoleon. Various groups in Latin America saw a chance to gain their freedom. The *criollos* and *mestizos* began to organize an independence movement. They called upon the Indians and enslaved persons to join their rebellion. By 1826, all of Latin America, except Cuba and Puerto Rico, became independent.

Mexico's Path to Independence In the late 1700s and early 1800s, freedom was in the air. The people of Mexico had heard about the American Revolution of 1776 and the French Revolution of 1789. The rights of all people were being talked about around the world. Many people in Mexico became excited by these ideas. They wanted their independence from Spain.

The first step toward independence happened in 1810 in a small village in north central Mexico. **Father Hidalgo**, a priest in the village, called on the people to rebel against Spain. The rebellion failed, however, and Father Hidalgo was captured and executed by the Spanish.

A new leader took Father Hidalgo's place. José María Morelos y Pavón also organized an army to fight the Spanish. He and other revolutionaries declared Mexico's independence in 1813. However, the Spanish defeated Morelos, and he was executed in 1815.

In 1821, the revolutionaries made a plan to win the support of all the groups in Mexico. The plan guaranteed independence, freedom of religion, and equality. Spain then declared Mexico independent with the Treaty of Cordoba in August 1821.

Mexico's struggle for independence lasted 11 years. But Mexico still had hard times ahead. You will learn more about Mexico's struggle toward democracy in the next chapter.

HISTORY MAKERS

Father Miguel Hidalgo
1753–1811

Father Hidalgo, a priest in the village of Dolores, sympathized with the Indians and *mestizos* and joined a secret society to work for Mexican independence. On September 16, 1810, Father Hidalgo rang the church bell in Dolores and urged his parishioners to fight for freedom. Thousands joined his army, but with clubs and farm tools as weapons, they were no match against the Spanish soldiers.

Today, Father Hidalgo is known as the father of Mexican independence. To honor him, Mexican Independence Day is celebrated on September 16.

 ONLINE BIOGRAPHY
For more on the life of Father Hidalgo, go to the
Research & Writing Center @ ClassZone.com

Independence for South America Just as they did in Mexico, the American and French revolutions had inspired dreams of freedom among people throughout South America. Beginning in 1810, two leaders led the fight for independence from Spain.

Simón Bolívar, a Venezuelan general, led the fight in the northern part of South America. To honor his efforts, South Americans call him "the Liberator." **José de San Martín**, an Argentine general, led the fight for independence in the southern part of South America. By 1825, nearly all of South America was free from Spanish rule.

Brazil, a Portuguese colony, also gained independence at this time. When Brazilians demanded independence in 1822, Dom Pedro, the son of the Portuguese king, declared Brazil independent and made himself emperor. You will read more about Brazil in a later chapter.

 SUMMARIZE Discuss the events that led to independence in Mexico and South America.

CONNECT History & Economics

Coffee

Coffee was first grown in Africa. European colonists brought coffee trees, like those shown in the illustration below, to the Americas in the Columbian Exchange. Brazil and Colombia, along with the rest of Latin America, produce two-thirds of the world's coffee.

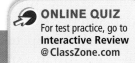 **ONLINE QUIZ**
For test practice, go to
Interactive Review
@ ClassZone.com

Section 4 Assessment

TERMS & NAMES

1. **Explain the importance of**
   - Columbian Exchange
   - *conquistador*
   - colony
   - *mestizo*

USE YOUR READING NOTES

2. **Sequence Events** Use your time line to answer the following question:

   How long was much of Latin America under Spanish rule?

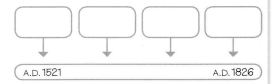

A.D. 1521   A.D. 1826

KEY IDEAS

3. Why were the *mestizos* important in Mexico's fight for independence?

4. Who was Father Hidalgo and why was he important?

5. How did most of South America gain its independence?

CRITICAL THINKING

6. **Analyze Causes and Effects** Why did Mexicans decide to fight for independence from Spain?

7. **Evaluate** What geographical challenges did South Americans have in their fight for independence?

8. **CONNECT to Today** What problems from the colonial days might still affect people in Latin America today?

9. **TECHNOLOGY** **Write a Biography** Use the Internet to find more information about one of the leaders for independence in Latin America discussed in this section. Then use a word processor to write a brief biography of that individual.

Interactive ◄Review

Click here to complete these and other activities online @ ClassZone.com

CHAPTER SUMMARY

Key Idea 1
The geography of Mexico, Central America, and the Caribbean Islands contains mountains, highlands, and plains.

Key Idea 2
The physical geography of South America consists of a wide variety of landforms and climates.

Key Idea 3
People adapted to these challenging geographic and climatic conditions and developed great civilizations.

Key Idea 4
Life under the conquerors was hard, as the people of Latin America struggled to gain their independence.

For **Review and Study Notes**, go to **Interactive Review** @ ClassZone.com

NAME GAME

Use the Terms & Names list to complete each sentence on paper or online.

1. I am built to make farming on mountainsides easier. _____terrace_____

2. I am the civilization that built a vast empire in Peru. _____

3. I am a large plain in Argentina. _____

4. I am the civilization that is considered the cultural hearth of southern Mexico. _____

5. I am the father of Mexican independence.
   _____

6. I am a large region that includes Mexico, Central and South America, and the Caribbean Islands.
   _____

7. I allowed plants, animals, and ideas to be traded between Europe and the Americas.
   _____

8. I am the large islands in the Caribbean Sea.
   _____

9. I am a landform on which the Panama Canal is located. _____

10. I am the place on which the Aztec grew food and flowers. _____

chinampas
Columbian Exchange
Father Hidalgo
Greater Antilles
Inca
isthmus
Latin America
Lesser Antilles
Olmec
Pampas
Simón Bolívar
terrace

Activities

GeoGame

Use this online map to show what you know about present-day Latin America. Click and drag each place name to its location on the map.

To play the complete game, go to **Interactive Review** @ ClassZone.com

Crossword Puzzle

Complete an online crossword puzzle to test your knowledge of the geography and history of Latin America.

ACROSS
1. Mayan writing—a carved symbol that stands for a syllable or word

VOCABULARY

Explain the significance of each of the following.

1. Latin America
2. isthmus
3. Andes Mountains
4. Pampas
5. Amazon River
6. Aztec
7. Inca
8. *chinampas*
9. *mestizo*
10. Simón Bolívar

Explain how the terms and names in each group are related.

11. Olmec, Maya, and Aztec
12. Pampas, Andes Mountains, and Amazon River

KEY IDEAS

1 Physical Geography of Mexico, Central America, and the Caribbean

13. Why are Mexico, Central and South America, and the Caribbean Islands called Latin America?
14. What are two mountain ranges in Mexico?
15. Why is Central America's climate warm year-round?

2 Physical Geography of South America

16. Where is the world's largest tropical rain forest?
17. What is the largest river system in South America?
18. What affects climate in the Andes Mountains?

3 Ancient Civilizations

19. Where was the Mayan civilization located?
20. What features did Tenochtitlán have?
21. How did the Inca keep records?

4 From Colonization to Independence

22. Who defeated the Aztec and Inca empires?
23. Who were the *mestizos* and why are they important?
24. How did most South American countries become independent?

CRITICAL THINKING

25. **Compare and Contrast** Create a table to compare and contrast the landforms, farming methods, and building methods in the Aztec and Inca empires.

AZTEC	INCA

26. **Analyze Causes and Effects** How did the lives of Indians change after the Spanish conquered them?
27. **Identify Problems and Solutions** How might the Spanish have prevented rebellion?
28. **Connect to Economics** How did the *encomienda* system prevent the Mexican economy from being open to all people?
29. **Five Themes: Human-Environment Interaction** How did the Aztec and Inca use technology to change the environment?
30. **Make Inferences** What problems did Latin Americans likely face after independence?

Answer the ESSENTIAL QUESTION

How have Latin America's geography and resources helped shape its history?

Written response Write a two- or three-paragraph response to the Essential Question. Be sure to consider the key ideas of each section as well as specific details about how geography affected ancient civilizations. Use the rubric to guide your thinking.

Response Rubric
A strong response will:
- discuss the geographic features in one region
- summarize how the geography affected the history of the region's people

STANDARDS-BASED ASSESSMENT

SECONDARY SOURCE

Use context clues in the paragraph below to answer questions 1 and 2.

> The full knowledge of the Maya calendar must have been guarded . . . by the ruling elite, since it was undoubtedly a source of great power. . . . One might assume, however, that even the poorest farmer had some knowledge of the basic system, by which to guide his family's daily life.
>
> Source: *The Ancient Maya*, by Robert J. Sharer

1. What is the most likely reason that the ruling elite guarded knowledge of the calendar?

A. They did not want the farmers to be confused.

B. They wanted to stop other people from stealing the calendar.

C. They believed the knowledge gave them power over others.

D. They didn't want others to use the knowledge against them.

2. What statement does the paragraph support?

A. The Maya did not know about the calendar.

B. Most Maya had some knowledge of the calendar.

C. Most Maya did not care about the calendar.

D. The ruling elite wanted everyone to know about the calendar.

LINE GRAPH

Use the line graph below to answer questions 3 and 4 on your paper.

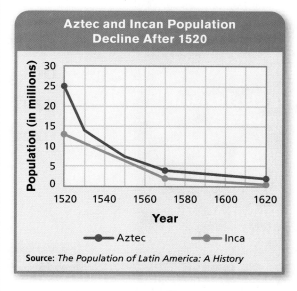

Source: *The Population of Latin America: A History*

3. Between what years did the Aztec population show the sharpest decline?

4. What was the Inca population in 1520? In 1620?

GeoActivity

1. INTERDISCIPLINARY ACTIVITY–DRAMA

With a small group, find another legend from the ancient civilizations of Latin America, such as the Aztec legend about the volcano Popocatépetl. Create a skit of the legend to present to the class.

2. WRITING FOR SOCIAL STUDIES

Reread the part of Section 2 about Tenochtitlán. Imagine that you are visiting the city. Write a letter to a friend telling about your visit. Describe the features of the city and give your impression of it.

3. MENTAL MAPPING

Create an outline map of Latin America and label the following:

• Mexico
• Mexico City
• Central America
• Panama Canal
• Greater Antilles
• Lesser Antilles
• South America
• Amazon River

Mexico

 ESSENTIAL QUESTION

How does Mexico reflect both ancient traditions and the challenges of the modern world?

1 HISTORY & GOVERNMENT

A Struggle Toward Democracy

2 CULTURE

A Blend of Traditions

3 GOVERNMENT & ECONOMICS

Creating a New Economy

CONNECT Geography & History

Use the map and the time line to answer the following questions.

1. What Mexican states are located on a peninsula on the Pacific Coast?
2. What was one result of the Mexican Revolution?

History
◄ **1864** Napoleon appoints Maximilian as Emperor of Mexico. (Maximilian)

Economics
1917 New constitution redistributes land more equally among the people.

1848

Geography
1848 Mexico signs treaty of Guadalupe Hidalgo and loses territory to the United States.

History
◄ **1910** Mexican Revolution begins.

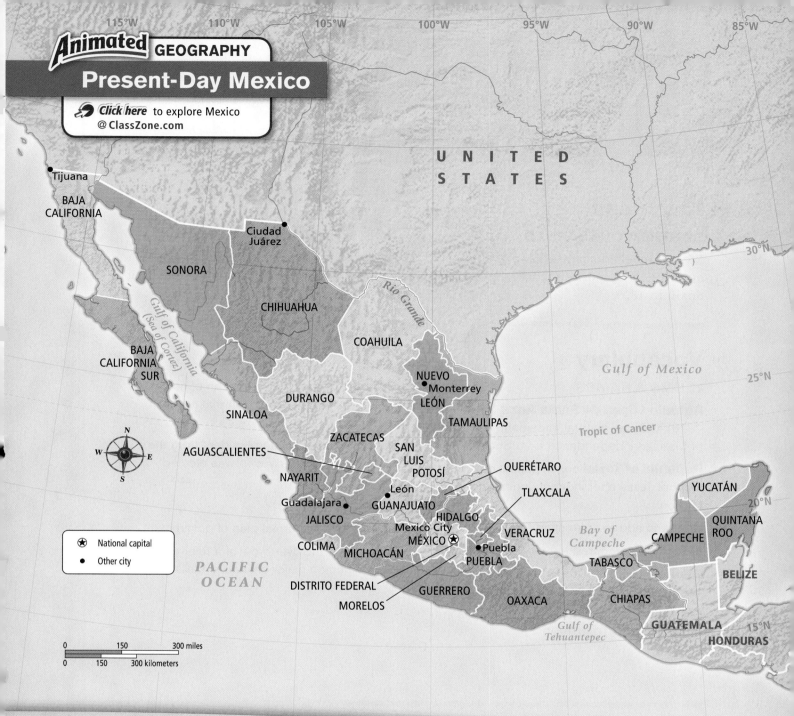

Animated GEOGRAPHY
Present-Day Mexico

Click here to explore Mexico
@ ClassZone.com

UNITED STATES

115°W 110°W 105°W 100°W 95°W 90°W 85°W

Tijuana
BAJA CALIFORNIA

Ciudad Juárez

SONORA

CHIHUAHUA

Rio Grande

COAHUILA

Gulf of California (Sea of Cortez)

BAJA CALIFORNIA SUR

30°N

Gulf of Mexico

NUEVO LEÓN
Monterrey

25°N

DURANGO

SINALOA

TAMAULIPAS

Tropic of Cancer

ZACATECAS

SAN LUIS POTOSÍ

AGUASCALIENTES

QUERÉTARO

TLAXCALA

NAYARIT

León

YUCATÁN

Guadalajara
GUANAJUATO

HIDALGO

JALISCO

Mexico City
MÉXICO ⊛

VERACRUZ

Bay of Campeche

QUINTANA ROO

COLIMA

Puebla

CAMPECHE

MICHOACÁN

PUEBLA

TABASCO

BELIZE

DISTRITO FEDERAL

GUERRERO

OAXACA

CHIAPAS

MORELOS

GUATEMALA

PACIFIC OCEAN

20°N

15°N

Gulf of Tehuantepec

HONDURAS

N W E S

★ National capital
• Other city

0   150   300 miles
0   150   300 kilometers

Government

▲ **1929** The Institutional Revolutionary Party (Partido Revolucionario Institucional, or PRI) comes to power.

Culture

1990 Octavio Paz wins Nobel Prize for Literature.

Economics

1992 Mexico signs the North American Free Trade Agreement (NAFTA).

Today

Government

◄ **2000** Vicente Fox is elected president of Mexico.

229

Reading for Understanding

▶ Key Ideas

BEFORE, YOU LEARNED

Mexico rebelled against colonial rule and gained its independence from Spain in 1821.

NOW YOU WILL LEARN

Mexico had to overcome many obstacles as the country moved toward establishing a democracy.

▶ Vocabulary

TERMS & NAMES

Antonio López de Santa Anna (1794–1876) Mexican general, president, and leader of Mexican independence from Spain

Republic of Texas constitutional government of Texas after independence from Mexico

annex to add to an existing territory

cession surrendered territory

Benito Juárez (1806–1872) Indian who became president and a Mexican national hero

Mexican Revolution a fight for reforms in Mexico from 1910 to 1920

Constitution of 1917 Mexican constitution written during the revolution that is still in effect today

Vicente Fox Mexican president from the National Action Party who was elected in 2000

REVIEW

constitution a formal plan of government

revolution the overthrow of a ruler or government; a major change in ideas

▶ Reading Strategy

Re-create the chart shown at right. As you read and respond to the **KEY QUESTIONS**, look for the effects of the causes that are listed.

 See Skillbuilder Handbook, page R8

ANALYZE CAUSES AND EFFECTS

CAUSES	EFFECTS
Mexico and the United States could not agree on the border of Texas.	
Benito Juárez instituted a new constitution in 1857.	
Huge gap existed between rich and poor; most Mexicans did not own land.	
The Constitution of 1917 was created.	

 GRAPHIC ORGANIZERS
Go to **Interactive Review** @ ClassZone.com

A Struggle Toward Democracy

Connecting to Your World

Think what an important part George Washington played in the U.S. fight for independence from Britain. In Mexican history, General **Antonio López de Santa Anna** played a key role in Mexico's fight for independence from Spain. He served as both a soldier and a president. As president, however, Santa Anna was not able to establish a secure government. Several factors made it difficult for the Mexican people to create a stable government.

War and Reform

▼ **KEY QUESTION** What challenges did Mexico have in establishing a stable government?

During Spanish rule, Mexicans had little control over their lives. Spain made many decisions for Mexico. As a result, after gaining independence in 1821, Mexico had trouble establishing a stable government. The Mexican people had no experience in governing themselves, and the nation had a weak economy. Invasion by foreign countries also prevented Mexico from establishing a strong government.

Santa Anna

Reform Demands
Protests, pictured in this mural by David Siquieros, led to the Mexican Revolution.

The Mexican War Until 1848, Mexican territory included what is now the southwestern part of the United States. In the early 1800s, few Mexicans lived there. To increase the population, Mexico encouraged settlers from the United States to move to Texas. To get land, the settlers had to follow Mexican law and pay a small fee.

Soon, the American settlers wanted more independence. When the Mexican government refused to grant independence, Texans revolted and broke away from Mexico. Santa Anna and his troops won early victories against the Texans, including the Battle of the Alamo in San Antonio, but eventually they were defeated at the Battle of San Jacinto in 1836. That same year, Santa Anna signed a treaty granting Texas independence, and the **Republic of Texas** was established.

Mexico faced another problem when the United States **annexed**, or added, Texas in 1845. The United States and Mexico could not agree on the southern boundary of Texas. By 1846, the dispute led to a war that lasted two years. Then in 1848, Mexico and the United States signed the Treaty of Guadalupe Hidalgo. As a result of this treaty, Mexico's surrendered territory, or **cession**, included the northern half of what was once Mexico.

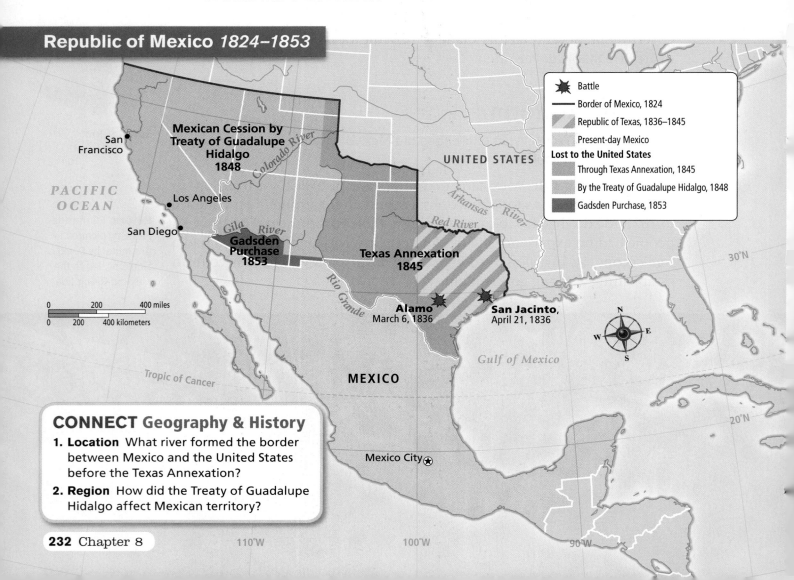

Republic of Mexico *1824–1853*

Legend:
- ✦ Battle
- ▬ Border of Mexico, 1824
- Republic of Texas, 1836–1845
- Present-day Mexico
- **Lost to the United States**
- Through Texas Annexation, 1845
- By the Treaty of Guadalupe Hidalgo, 1848
- Gadsden Purchase, 1853

Mexican Cession by Treaty of Guadalupe Hidalgo 1848

Gadsden Purchase 1853

Texas Annexation 1845

Alamo March 6, 1836

San Jacinto, April 21, 1836

San Francisco
Los Angeles
San Diego
PACIFIC OCEAN
UNITED STATES
Colorado River
Gila River
Arkansas River
Red River
Rio Grande
30°N
Gulf of Mexico
Tropic of Cancer
MEXICO
20°N
Mexico City
110°W 100°W 90°W

0   200   400 miles
0   200   400 kilometers

CONNECT Geography & History

1. **Location** What river formed the border between Mexico and the United States before the Texas Annexation?

2. **Region** How did the Treaty of Guadalupe Hidalgo affect Mexican territory?

Fight for Reforms The Mexican War drained Mexico's economy and left the government in disorder. After the war, two groups within the country, the liberals and conservatives, struggled for power.

Conservatives consisted of Mexico's rich landowners and military leaders. The liberals generally consisted of the nation's poor, landless people. A liberal leader, **Benito Juárez**, greatly influenced Mexican politics at this time. He led a reform movement that resulted in a new **constitution** in 1857. Among other things, the constitution guaranteed freedom of speech and called for a federal system of government. But it did not make Catholicism the official religion, as many church officials wanted. Juárez and other reformers fought against the opponents of the constitution. This struggle left Mexico weak and open to foreign invasion.

France, Spain, and Britain sent forces to Mexico in 1861. France captured Mexico City in 1863 and named Maximilian, a European nobleman, as emperor of Mexico. His rule ended when the Mexican people overthrew and executed him. Juárez, who had been elected president in 1861, returned to that office until his death in 1872.

 ANALYZE CAUSES AND EFFECTS Explain why establishing a stable government was difficult in Mexico.

HISTORY MAKERS

Benito Juárez 1806–1872

Benito Juárez, an Indian, was born in Oaxaca (wuh•HAH•kuh), where he received a law degree in 1831. Politics became Juárez's life, and he served in many capacities, including governor of Oaxaca and president of Mexico. His work for fairness and equality made Juárez a hero in the eyes of many Mexican people.

ONLINE BIOGRAPHY
For more on the life of Benito Juárez, go to the **Research & Writing Center @ ClassZone.com**

Revolution and Constitutional Change

▼ **KEY QUESTION** Why was the election of President Vicente Fox significant?

After Juárez's death, the reform movement weakened. Juárez's successors were more interested in developing the economy than in reform. They believed in government controlled by a small group.

In 1876, General Porfirio Díaz became dictator. Unlike Juárez, he gave land, power, or favors to anyone who supported him. Those who did not support him were shut out of power. By 1910, the gap between the rich and poor had grown huge. Just one percent of landowners controlled more than 90 percent of the land. Most Mexicans owned no land at all. This gap set the stage for the Mexican Revolution.

The Mexican Revolution By 1910, Mexicans from various walks of life were protesting Díaz's rule and calling for reforms. Farmers wanted land, and workers wanted fair wages and better working conditions.

CONNECT Geography & History

Pancho Villa: Knowing the Land

Pancho Villa's knowledge of northern Mexico's geography helped him to avoid being captured by the U.S. army. In 1916, Villa, angry over U.S. involvement in the Mexican Revolution, led an attack in Columbus, New Mexico, in which 18 U.S. citizens were killed. The United States sent soldiers to capture Villa, but Villa's knowledge of the land and his popularity helped him elude the U.S. army.

The **Mexican Revolution** began when Francisco Madero, a wealthy rancher, called for a **revolution** to defeat Díaz. Leaders arose in different parts of Mexico and gathered their own armies. Emiliano Zapata led an army in southern Mexico and fought for land ownership for poor farmers. Pancho Villa led forces in northern Mexico. He became popular for his policy of stealing from the rich to give to the poor. Madero became president, but was soon overthrown. The fighting among the various Mexican groups for control of the government continued, turning the Revolution into a civil war. By the time it was over in 1920, more than one million Mexicans had been killed.

New Constitution The **Constitution of 1917** was adopted during the revolution to meet the demands of Mexico's various groups and regions. Land reform was the central issue. Eventually, the government redistributed nearly half of Mexico's farmland to poor people. Millions of acres of farmland were divided into *ejidos* (eh•HEE•thaws), community farms owned by villagers. The constitution also brought about changes regarding workers' rights and the relationship of the government and the Church. The Constitution of 1917 is still in effect in Mexico today.

LAND
- Breakup of large estates
- Restriction on foreign land ownership
- Government control of resources like oil

RELIGION
- State takeover of Church land

STATE PROPERTY

Reforms of the Mexican Constitution of 1917

LABOR
STRIKE! STRIKE!
- Workers' minimum wage
- Workers' right to strike
- Workers' labor unions

SOCIAL ISSUES
- Equal pay for equal work
- Limited legal rights for women (spending money and bringing lawsuits)

Democratic Rule In the 1920s, one political party came to power by making peace among the various armies. Today it is called the Institutional Revolutionary Party (Partido Revolucionario Institucional, or PRI). The party controlled the government from 1929 until 2000. It helped introduce elements of democracy and stability to Mexico. But the party often blocked opposition to its policies and was accused of corruption.

In 2000, **Vicente Fox**, a member of the National Action Party (Partido Acción Nacional, or PAN), was elected president. His election signaled Mexico's move toward a multiparty democracy. In 2006, Felipe Calderon, also a member of PAN, won the presidential election. Today, besides PRI and PAN, there are at least five other political parties in Mexico.

Today, Mexico is a democracy organized much like the U.S. government. Mexico is a federal republic made up of 31 states and a federal district. Mexico also has three branches of government. But the Mexican president has more control than the U.S. president.

Campaign Rally Supporters take part in an election rally for PAN in June 2000.

 MAKE INFERENCES Explain the significance of the election of Vicente Fox as Mexico's president.

Section 1 Assessment

ONLINE QUIZ
For test practice, go to
Interactive Review
@ ClassZone.com

TERMS & NAMES

1. Explain the importance of
- Antonio López de Santa Anna
- Benito Juárez
- Constitution of 1917
- Vicente Fox

USE YOUR READING NOTES

2. Analyze Causes and Effects Use your completed chart to answer the following question:

What effect did the Constitution of 1857 have on Mexico?

CAUSES	EFFECTS
Mexico and the United States could not agree on the border of Texas.	
Benito Juárez instituted a new constitution in 1857.	
Huge gap existed between rich and poor; most Mexicans did not own land.	
The Constitution of 1917 is created.	

KEY IDEAS

3. What dispute led to war between Mexico and the United States?

4. Why was the Mexican Revolution fought among different groups?

5. How did the Constitution of 1917 help farmers?

CRITICAL THINKING

6. Analyze Points of View Before 1910, how did different groups in Mexico view the need for reform?

7. Make Inferences Why do you think that Benito Juárez's background might have led him to support reform in Mexico?

8. CONNECT to Today How might having more than one political party benefit Mexico today?

9. TECHNOLOGY Use the Internet Find out more about a political leader mentioned in this lesson by using the Internet. Then prepare a bulleted list of the top five most interesting facts about the person.

Reading for Understanding

▶ Key Ideas

BEFORE, YOU LEARNED

Mexico's history reflects the impact of ancient civilizations, colonial powers, and the modern world.

NOW YOU WILL LEARN

These three influences affect the culture and daily lives of the Mexican people.

▶ Vocabulary

TERMS & NAMES

Plaza of the Three Cultures plaza in Mexico City that shows parts of Aztec, Spanish, and modern influences in Mexico

colonia a neighborhood in Mexico

squatter person who settles on unoccupied land without having legal claim to it

mural a wall painting

Diego Rivera famous muralist who painted the history of Mexico on the walls of the National Palace

fiesta a holiday celebrated with parades, games, and food

Day of the Dead holiday to remember loved ones who have died

REVIEW

urban having to do with a city

rural having to do with the countryside

push factor a reason that causes people to leave an area

Visual Vocabulary fiesta

▶ Reading Strategy

Re-create the chart shown at right. As you read and respond to the **KEY QUESTIONS**, use the chart to summarize each of the main sections of Section 2.

 See Skillbuilder Handbook, page R5

SUMMARIZE

SECTION	SUMMARY
People and Lifestyle	
Mexico's Great Murals	
Celebrations and Sports	

GRAPHIC ORGANIZERS
Go to **Interactive Review** @ ClassZone.com

A Blend of Traditions

Connecting to Your World

When you look around your community, do you see the influences of different cultures? Are there places that date back many years and places that are modern? Mexico today reflects a blend of different cultures, both traditional and modern. The **Plaza of the Three Cultures** in Mexico City displays this blend. The plaza contains the ruins of an Aztec city, a Spanish colonial church, and modern government buildings. Other parts of life in Mexico also reflect these influences.

People and Lifestyle

🔻 **KEY QUESTION** How do urban and rural life in Mexico differ?

Mexico today is a living blend of Indian, Spanish, and modern influences. The majority of Mexican people are *mestizos*. Almost all Mexicans speak Spanish, the nation's official language. Many Mexican Indians also speak their Indian languages, such as Maya and Náhuatl. Most Mexicans are Roman Catholics, but some belong to other religions.

The Plaza of the Three Cultures This plaza in Mexico City reflects the influences of the Aztec, Spanish, and modern cultures.

Spanish colonial cathedral

Modern-day apartments

Ruins of Aztec temple

237

City and Country Life Today, over three-fourths of Mexico's people live in **urban** areas. More than 22 million people live in and around Mexico City, making it one of the largest cities in the world. Mexican cities include high-rise office buildings and modern apartment buildings, as well as older houses built in the Spanish colonial style.

The cities' neighborhoods are called **colonias**. Wealthy people generally live in prosperous neighborhoods, away from the city center. Poorer people live closer to the center of the city, sometimes in neighborhoods with unpaved streets and no running water. Some people work in factories or as street vendors, but many are unemployed.

In contrast to city life, people in Mexico's **rural** areas live in villages or on farms, near their fields. Homes are small, often having only one room and a dirt floor. Rural areas have few health-care services, roads, and schools. The Mexican government is working to improve the public services in rural areas.

The poor conditions in the rural areas are the **push factors** that cause people to move to cities. But once there, they become **squatters**, people who settle on unoccupied land without having legal claim to it. Over time, these areas develop into new *colonias*. Some rural Mexicans migrate to other countries, including the United States.

◀ COMPARING ▶ Urban and Rural Life

URBAN
- Densely populated; about 75% of the population
- Primary schools, secondary schools, and universities
- Major source of energy is electricity
- Clothes similar to those worn in the United States; bought in stores

RURAL
- Less densely populated; about 25% of the population
- Primary schools; almost no secondary schools; no universities
- Major source of energy is firewood
- Clothes often traditional; sometimes homemade

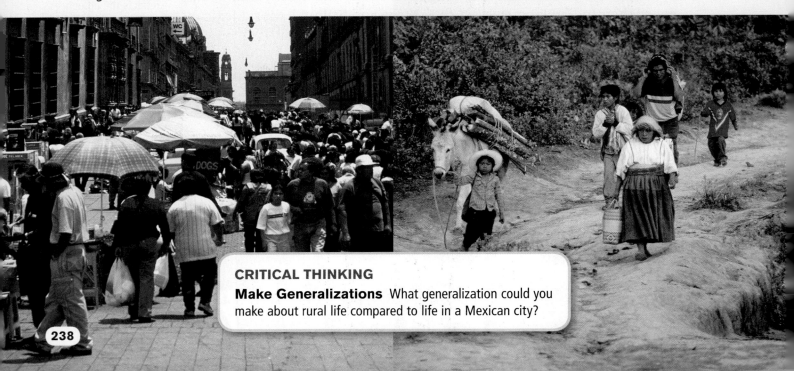

CRITICAL THINKING
Make Generalizations What generalization could you make about rural life compared to life in a Mexican city?

Family Life Family life is important in Mexico. In some families, several generations of family members may live together. Older members of the family are honored. Children are taught to respect adults.

The social life of many Mexicans centers on the family. Families gather together to celebrate birthdays and other kinds of holidays.

Mexican children are required to attend school for nine years—six years of primary school and three years of middle school. Some continue their education in a three-year high school and then a university. In some rural areas, students attend classes in one-room schools. They often travel to nearby towns to go to middle school or high school.

▲ **COMPARE AND CONTRAST** Describe the differences between urban and rural life in Mexico.

Mexico's Great Murals

▼ **KEY QUESTION** What common subjects do Mexican artists and writers focus on in their works?

Creating art has a long history in Mexico. The Olmec carved sculptures. The Aztec wrote music and poetry. The Maya created paintings in their pyramids and the Spanish in their colonial churches. Mexican art today blends these influences.

After the Mexican Revolution, Mexican art experienced a great awakening. Just as ancient artists had created paintings on their pyramids, Mexican artists created **murals**, or wall paintings, that often depicted scenes from Mexico's history. Many important painters portrayed such scenes on murals in Mexico's public buildings. The most famous Mexican muralists are José Orozco, David Siquieros, and **Diego Rivera**. Frida Kahlo, another important Mexican painter, is known for paintings that show her personal feelings about events in her life.

Self-portrait with Monkey Frida Kahlo is known for her self-portraits. Monkeys and other animals roamed the gardens around her home and were often included in her artwork.

Mexican writers have often written about Mexico's social and political problems. Octavio Paz, Carlos Fuentes, and Laura Esquivel are three well-known Mexican writers. Paz won the 1990 Nobel Prize for Literature; he was the first Mexican to win this award. Fuentes writes novels about Mexican history. In one popular novel, Esquivel described life for rural Mexican women during the Mexican Revolution.

▲ **SUMMARIZE** Describe the subjects that Mexican artists and writers focus on in their works.

Celebrations and Sports

▼ **KEY QUESTION** What kinds of holidays do Mexicans celebrate?

Mexicans celebrate many holidays and events with a fiesta. A **fiesta** is a celebration with fireworks, parades, music, dancing, and foods. At some fiestas, children enjoy themselves by trying to break open a piñata. A piñata is a decorated container filled with candy and toys, usually hung from the ceiling. Children are blindfolded and given a stick to break open the piñata and gather its treats. Fiestas bring people together to have fun.

Celebrations Mexicans celebrate Mexico's Independence Day on September 16. Mexicans also celebrate *Cinco de Mayo* (May 5), which is the day in 1862 when the Mexican army defeated the French.

Mexicans celebrate religious holidays such as Easter with church services and processions. They celebrate the **Day of the Dead** on November 1 and 2 to honor family members who have died.

La Quinceañera is a celebration of a Mexican girl's 15th birthday. The girl dresses in a full-length gown. She first takes part in church services with family and friends. After church, everyone goes to a reception where a huge fiesta takes place.

Fun Facts!

PIÑATAS

Piñatas are part of many Mexican fiestas. But where did piñatas come from? Some historians believe Marco Polo brought them from China to Italy in the 1200s. The Spanish brought them to Spain and then introduced them to Mexico.

CONNECT ➤ History & Culture

Day of the Dead This holiday has its roots in an ancient Aztec celebration, in which people remembered dead ancestors. Today, particularly in rural areas, relatives celebrate the Day of the Dead by gathering in cemeteries to decorate family graves with candles and flowers and to share stories about loved ones who have died.

CRITICAL THINKING

Make Inferences How does this holiday show the importance of family to Mexican people?

Sports The number one sport in Mexico is *fútbol*, or soccer. Mexicans enjoy playing it and watching it. Fans cheer on their favorite teams in stadiums located in several Mexican cities. Aztec Stadium in Mexico City holds 114,000 fans! Mexicans also enjoy playing baseball and watching their professional baseball teams.

Many Mexicans enjoy bullfighting, a sport brought to Mexico by the Spanish. The number of bullfights has decreased in recent years because some people have led campaigns to ban them. However, people still attend bullfights in the bullrings found in many Mexican cities.

A sport growing in popularity in Mexico is jai alai, a fast-paced ball game played in a three-walled court. The equipment includes a hard rubber ball and wicker-basket scoops, which players use to catch and throw the ball.

 FIND MAIN IDEAS Identify the kinds of holidays that Mexican people celebrate today.

Soccer in Aztec Stadium Fans watch as a player from the Mexican team (left) battles for the ball in a game with a player from Argentina.

Section 2 Assessment

ONLINE QUIZ For test practice, go to **Interactive Review** @ClassZone.com

TERMS & NAMES

1. Explain the importance of
- Plaza of the Three Cultures
- *colonia*
- mural
- fiesta

USE YOUR READING NOTES

2. Summarize Use your completed chart to answer the following question:

What are some ways Mexicans spend their leisure time?

SECTION	SUMMARY
People and Lifestyle	
Mexico's Great Murals	
Celebrations and Sports	

KEY IDEAS

3. What two cultures have influenced modern Mexico?

4. Where do most Mexican people live today?

5. What is the subject of many Mexican murals?

CRITICAL THINKING

6. Draw Conclusions Why do many people in Mexico's rural areas move to cities?

7. Form and Support Opinions What problems of urban and rural life do you think are most important for Mexico to address?

8. CONNECT to Today Some people have led campaigns to ban bullfighting. What kinds of campaigns does your area have on behalf of animals?

9. ART Create a Mural Panel Work with a group to research an important event in the history of your community. Decide what aspect of the event you want to illustrate. Then create a mural panel to depict the scene you have chosen.

Mexican culture is a blend of both Indian and Spanish traditions. The influences of both cultures are evident in Mexico today.

Indian Traditions

Before the Spanish conquest in 1521, Mexico's Indian groups had well-established, unique cultures. Indian groups created cities with huge structures. They held celebrations, such as festivals to remember those who died. Crops such as corn, chilies, and tomatoes contributed to their flavorful diet.

Food

Tortillas, a popular Mexican food made from corn, date back to the ancient Aztecs.

Clothing

These girls wear handmade, colorful dresses.

▲ *Ruins of Mayan temple at Palenque, Mexico*

Festivals

Mexican children of Indian ancestry dressed in traditional clothing participate in a local festival.

Spanish Traditions

The Spanish conquest brought European customs and traditions to the region. The Spanish built their traditional square cities that surrounded plazas and included government buildings and churches. They honored their dead on All Saints' Day and All Souls' Day in November. They introduced foods such as oranges, wheat, beef, pork, sugar cane, coffee, and onions to the Mexican diet.

Food
Mexican sweet breads are made from wheat, which the Spaniards brought to Mexico.

Clothing
These dancers are dressed in traditional Spanish clothing from the colonial period.

Festivals
Mexican children participate in a procession celebrating Easter, a Roman Catholic holiday.

▲ *Spanish colonial church in Taxco, Mexico*

CRITICAL THINKING

1. **Evaluate** Why are Mexican traditions today a blend of Native American and Spanish traditions?

2. **Compare and Contrast** Based on the large photos, how do Native American and Spanish architecture compare?

Reading for Understanding

▶ Key Ideas

BEFORE, YOU LEARNED

The Mexican government has become more democratic with the elimination of the one-party system.

NOW YOU WILL LEARN

Mexico faces new challenges as the country takes steps to modernize its economy.

▶ Vocabulary

TERMS & NAMES

maquiladora factory in which materials are imported and assembled into products for export

global economy economy in which buying and selling occurs across national borders

North American Free Trade Agreement (NAFTA) agreement that reduced trade barriers among Mexico, Canada, and the United States

REVIEW

immigration process of coming to another country to live

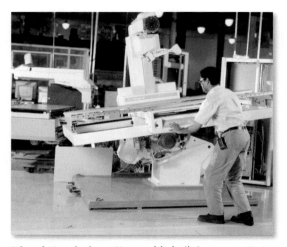

Visual Vocabulary X-ray table built in a *maquiladora*

▶ Reading Strategy

Re-create the web diagram shown at right. As you read and respond to the **KEY QUESTIONS**, find supporting details for each main idea in Section 3.

 See Skillbuilder Handbook, page R4

FIND MAIN IDEAS

Increases its industries

BUILDING A MODERN ECONOMY

GRAPHIC ORGANIZERS
Go to **Interactive Review** @ ClassZone.com

Creating a New Economy

Connecting to Your World

Do you add tomatoes to a salad or to your favorite kind of sandwich? Chances are that the tomatoes you eat were grown in Mexico. Tomatoes make up the largest percentage of vegetables that Mexico exports to the United States. Agriculture is an important part of Mexico's economy. In this section, you will learn how Mexico has expanded its economy.

Building a Modern Economy

▼ **KEY QUESTION** How has Mexico created a strong modern economy?

Vicente Fox's election as president in 2000 changed Mexico from a one-party system to a multiparty democracy. With a stable government, Mexico is working to improve the quality of life for its people. It has been modernizing its industry and economy by cooperating with other North American countries.

Animated GEOGRAPHY

Mexican Industry
Workers perform their jobs on a floating oil-rig platform off the Mexican coast in the Gulf of Mexico.

➔ *Click here* for an interactive map of Mexican industry @ ClassZone.com

Vicente Fox promised as president to improve education, jobs, and opportunities in Mexico. For his official portrait, Fox posed with Mexican people from all walks of life to show, as the caption indicates, that "We are all Mexico." Read what Fox had to say in his inaugural speech.

> It is time we recognized that everything cannot be solved by the State [government]. . . . Quality education, employment and regional development are the levers to remove, once and for all, the signs of poverty.
>
> Source: Vicente Fox's inaugural speech

Vicente Fox

TODOS SOMOS MÉXICO

DOCUMENT-BASED QUESTION
What does Fox think is the best way to reduce poverty?

ONLINE PRIMARY SOURCE To read more works of Vicente Fox, go to the **Research & Writing Center** @ ClassZone.com

Industrialization Traditionally, Mexico's economy depended upon agriculture and mining. But since the 1940s, Mexico has become more industrialized. Mexico continues to be one of the world's major producers of silver. Its most profitable industry is oil production. Today, Mexico is tied with China as the world's fifth largest producer of crude petroleum.

Other industries have also become important to Mexico's economy. In recent years, many factories have been located along Mexico's border with the United States. These factories are called *maquiladoras*. A ***maquiladora*** is a factory that assembles imported materials into finished goods that are exported. Jeans, appliances, car engines, and computers are some of the products manufactured in this way.

Global Economy In 1992, Mexico took a stronger role in the **global economy**, in which nations cooperate to trade goods and services. It signed the **North American Free Trade Agreement (NAFTA)** with the United States and Canada. NAFTA created rules about trade in North America. The agreement made it easier for the three countries to transport goods and services across their borders.

▲ **DRAW CONCLUSIONS** Discuss the steps Mexico has taken to build its economy.

Facing New Challenges

▼ **KEY QUESTION** What are some problems Mexico must solve in order to continue to develop a stronger economy?

Mexico faces two major challenges in continuing to develop a strong economy. It has to reduce pollution, and it has to create more jobs in order to improve conditions for its people and to slow migration to other countries.

Pollution Like other large international cities, Mexico City has had to deal with increased air pollution, brought on in large part by industrialization. Mexico City sits in a valley, almost completely surrounded by mountains. The mountains help produce a layer of warm air above the city. This layer keeps gases from car exhaust and thousands of industries from blowing away. These gases react with sunlight to form smog, a thick brown haze, over the city. The smog causes health problems for many people.

Recently, the Mexican government has taken steps to deal with the pollution problem. It has urged automobile manufacturers to produce cars that use cleaner fuels and helped companies develop smog controls. It has also encouraged public transportation.

CONNECT to Science

Like many modern cities, Mexico City became industrialized in the last 50 years. While developing a modern economy helps a country, the increase in industries often causes pollution problems. Many other cities have experienced situations similar to Mexico City's.

Mexico City Smog blankets the city.

Activity

Create a Pollution Hot Spot Map

Materials
• newspapers and magazines
• large blank world map
• markers

1. Find information about pollution problems in other parts of the world.

2. Locate and label the places on the world map. Include Mexico City on the map.

3. Choose one of the locations and find out what is being done to reduce pollution there.

4. Present your map and findings to the class.

Providing Jobs These men are working on a large-scale construction project. **How might such projects help develop Mexico's economy?**

Creation of Jobs The movement of people from rural to urban areas and across international borders presents a second challenge to Mexico's economy. Many Mexicans from rural areas move to cities for jobs. There, they often live in poor conditions, with no jobs or low-wage jobs.

Many Mexicans move to the United States for economic opportunities. Some risk the dangerous border crossing to the United States and enter the country illegally. Many earn money to help their families back home. Once in the United States, immigrants often work long hours at low-paying jobs, sometimes at more than one job.

As the Mexican economy creates more and better-paying jobs, the problem of illegal **immigration** may improve. In the meantime, Mexico and the United States continue to cooperate to strengthen security on their border and to find ways to resolve the immigration problems.

 IDENTIFY PROBLEMS AND SOLUTIONS
Identify the challenges Mexico faces in developing its economy.

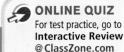 **ONLINE QUIZ**
For test practice, go to **Interactive Review** @ ClassZone.com

Section ❸ Assessment

TERMS & NAMES
1. Explain the importance of
- *maquiladora*
- NAFTA
- global economy
- immigration

USE YOUR READING NOTES
2. Find Main Ideas Use your completed chart to answer the following question:

What steps has Mexico taken to build a modern economy?

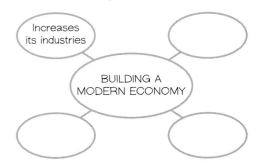

KEY IDEAS
3. What was Mexico's traditional economy based on until the 1940s?

4. What are Mexico's most important industries?

5. What are two challenges Mexico faces today?

CRITICAL THINKING
6. Evaluate What are the advantages and disadvantages of Mexico's membership in NAFTA?

7. Analyze Causes and Effects How did the growth of urban areas and industrialization contribute to Mexico's pollution problems?

8. **CONNECT to Today** Why is creating jobs important for Mexico today?

9. **WRITING** **Prepare a Report** Choose one of Mexico's major industries. Find out how many people are employed in the industry, its major locations, and how much money the industry brings to Mexico's economy. Prepare an illustrated report of your findings.

Click here to complete these and other activities online @ ClassZone.com

CHAPTER SUMMARY

Key Idea 1
Mexico overcame many obstacles as the country moved toward establishing a democracy.

Key Idea 2
Three cultures blended to create the heritage and daily life of the Mexican people.

Key Idea 3
Mexico continues to face challenges as it tries to modernize its economy.

For **Review and Study Notes**, go to **Interactive Review** @ ClassZone.com

NAME GAME

Use the Terms & Names list to complete each sentence on paper or online.

1. I am the place that became independent from Mexico in 1837. **Republic of Texas**

2. I am the place where the cultural sources of modern Mexico can be seen. _____

3. I am a document that brought reforms to Mexico and is still in effect in Mexico today.
   _____

4. I am the president who broke Mexican one-party rule. _____

5. I am a neighborhood or suburb of a Mexican city. _____

6. I am an agreement made between North American countries. _____

7. I am a person who lives on land that is not my own. _____

8. I am a tax on imported goods. _____

9. I am a Mexican writer who won the Nobel Prize for Literature. _____

10. I am a famous Mexican mural painter.
    _____

colonia
Constitution of 1917
Vicente Fox
Benito Juárez
maquiladora
NAFTA
Octavio Paz
Plaza of the Three Cultures
Republic of Texas
Diego Rivera
squatter
tariff

Activities

Flip Cards

Use the online flip cards to quiz yourself on the terms and names introduced in this chapter.

Benito Juárez

Mexican president and reformer who helped write the Constitution of 1857

Crossword Puzzle

Complete an online crossword puzzle to test your knowledge of the history and culture of Mexico.

ACROSS
1. a holiday celebrated with parades, games, and food

VOCABULARY

Explain the significance of each of the following.

1. Republic of Texas
2. annex
3. Plaza of the Three Cultures
4. *colonia*
5. squatter
6. mural
7. Diego Rivera
8. fiesta
9. Day of the Dead
10. immigration

Explain how the terms and names in each group are related.

11. Mexican Revolution and Constitution of 1917
12. Antonio López de Santa Anna, Benito Juárez, and Vicente Fox
13. *maquiladoras*, global economy, and NAFTA

KEY IDEAS

1 A Struggle Toward Democracy

14. Why was it difficult for Mexicans to rule themselves after independence?
15. What contributions did Benito Juárez make to Mexico?
16. How and why did the Mexican Revolution happen?
17. Why was the 2000 presidential election in Mexico significant?

2 A Blend of Traditions

18. What are three influences on Mexican culture today?
19. What conditions led Mexican people to move from rural to urban areas?
20. Why is Mexican mural painting a continuation of ancient Mexican tradition?
21. What do Mexicans celebrate on *Cinco de Mayo*?

3 Creating a New Economy

22. Why is oil important to Mexico's economy?
23. What steps did Mexico take to modernize its economy?
24. What factors contribute to air pollution in Mexico City?
25. Why do many Mexicans migrate to the United States?

CRITICAL THINKING

26. **Analyze Causes and Effects** Complete a cause and effect diagram to explain the effects of Mexico's conflicts with Texas and the United States in the 1800s.

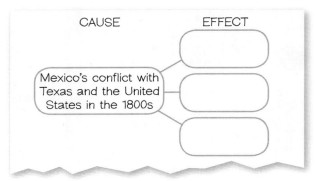

CAUSE   EFFECT

Mexico's conflict with Texas and the United States in the 1800s

27. **Make Inferences** How do Mexico's holidays and arts show the influence of Mexico's history?
28. **Draw Conclusions** How did Mexico's frequent changes in leaders before the Mexican Revolution affect the country?
29. **Connect History & Art** Why did so many Mexican artists and writers paint and write about Mexico's past?
30. **Five Themes: Location** How does Mexico City's location contribute to the problem of smog in the city?

Answer the ESSENTIAL QUESTION

How does Mexico reflect both ancient traditions and the demands of the modern world?

Written Response Write a two- or three-paragraph response to the Essential Question. Be sure to include a discussion of Mexican life, government, and economy. Use the rubric below to guide your thinking.

Response Rubric

A strong response will:

- describe how Mexican life reflects both ancient and modern traditions
- discuss the challenges Mexico faced in creating a democratic government and a modern economy

STANDARDS-BASED ASSESSMENT

THEMATIC MAP

Use the map and your knowledge of Mexico to answer questions 1 and 2.

Selected Products of Mexico

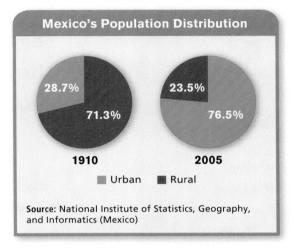

Legend:
- Coffee
- Cotton
- Corn
- Fish
- Natural gas
- Petroleum
- Silver
- Wheat

Gulf of Mexico

PACIFIC OCEAN

1. In what region of Mexico is petroleum produced?

A. along the Pacific coast
B. along the U.S. border
C. along the coast of the Gulf of Mexico
D. along the interior of the country

2. In what part of Mexico is cotton grown?

A. in the southern part
B. in the northern part
C. only on the western coast
D. only on the eastern coast

CIRCLE GRAPH

Examine the graph below. Use the information in the graph to answer questions 3 and 4.

Mexico's Population Distribution

1910: 28.7% / 71.3%
2005: 23.5% / 76.5%

Legend: Urban | Rural

Source: National Institute of Statistics, Geography, and Informatics (Mexico)

3. What percentage of Mexico's population was urban in 1910? in 2005?

4. What does this tell you about changes that have taken place in Mexican society?

GeoActivity

1. INTERDISCIPLINARY ACTIVITY–SCIENCE

Find out about the habitat of the monarch butterfly in Mexico. Research the butterfly's migration pattern and life cycle. Find out what the Mexican government has done to protect these butterflies. Present your findings in an illustrated and captioned poster.

2. WRITING FOR SOCIAL STUDIES

Create a guide for visitors to Mexico City. Use the Internet to learn about places to visit, such as museums, and cultural institutions, such as the ballet. Write a description of each of these places, and include illustrations.

3. MENTAL MAPPING

Create an outline map of Mexico and label the following:

- Mexico City
- Rio Grande
- Sierra Madre Occidental
- Sierra Madre Oriental
- Gulf of Mexico
- Pacific Ocean

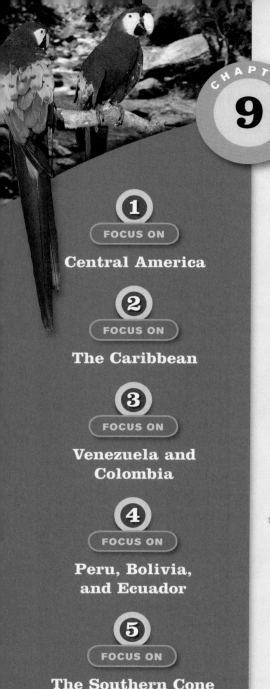

CHAPTER 9

Middle America and Spanish-Speaking South America

① **FOCUS ON**

Central America

② **FOCUS ON**

The Caribbean

③ **FOCUS ON**

Venezuela and Colombia

④ **FOCUS ON**

Peru, Bolivia, and Ecuador

⑤ **FOCUS ON**

The Southern Cone

ESSENTIAL QUESTION

How are the countries of this region working to strengthen their governments and economies?

CONNECT **Geography & History**

Use the map and the time line to answer the following questions.

1. What country connects Central and South America?
2. Who led the Cuban independence movement?

History

1804 Haiti is the first Caribbean Island to become independent. (Present-day Haitian flag) ▶

1800

History

1821 Central American countries gain independence from Spain.

History

1902 Cuba gains independence.

History

◀ **1895** José Martí leads Cuban revolution against Spanish rule.

MEXICO

Gulf of Mexico

ATLANTIC OCEAN

Havana

BAHAMAS

Tropic of Cancer

Greater Antilles

CUBA

DOMINICAN REPUBLIC

Santo Domingo

HAITI

WEST

BELIZE

Belmopan

JAMAICA

Kingston

Port-au-Prince

INDIES

Lesser Antilles

Guatemala City

HONDURAS

Tegucigalpa

GUATEMALA

EL SALVADOR

San Salvador

NICARAGUA

Managua

San José

COSTA RICA

Panamá City

PANAMA

Caribbean Sea

Caracas

VENEZUELA

GUYANA

Georgetown

SURINAME

Paramaribo

FRENCH GUIANA (France)

Bogotá

COLOMBIA

Galápagos Is. (Ecuador)

Quito

ECUADOR

Equator 0°

PERU

PACIFIC OCEAN

Lima

B R A Z I L

BOLIVIA

La Paz

Sucre

ATLANTIC OCEAN

Tropic of Capricorn

PARAGUAY

Asunción

20°S

Juan Fernández Is. (Chile)

Santiago

ARGENTINA

URUGUAY

Buenos Aires

Montevideo

CHILE

★ National capital

0	500	1,000 miles
0	500	1,000 kilometers

40°S

Falkland Is. (U.K.)

South Georgia (U.K.)

Culture

1911 Archaeologist Hiram Bingham locates the site of Machu Picchu.
(Incan watchtower) ▼

Government

1959 Fidel Castro overthrows government of Fulgencio Batista.
(Fulgencio Batista) ▶

Culture

1992 Rigoberta Menchú wins the Nobel Peace Prize.

Today

History

1952 Puerto Rico becomes a U.S. commonwealth.

History

1990s Many Central American countries develop democracies.

253

Reading for Understanding

▶ Key Ideas

BEFORE, YOU LEARNED

Mexico faces many challenges as it modernizes its economy.

NOW YOU WILL LEARN

Central American countries also face challenges as they develop democratic governments and improve their economies.

▶ Vocabulary

TERMS & NAMES

ecotourism travel to a natural habitat in a way that does not damage the habitat

dictator a person with complete control over a country's government

subsistence farming a kind of farming in which farmers grow only enough to feed their families

Central America Free Trade Agreement (CAFTA) trade agreement to promote trade between the United States and countries of Central America

service industry an industry that provides services rather than objects

artisan a worker skilled in making products or art with his or her hands

REVIEW

maquiladora factory in which materials are imported and assembled into products for export

North American Free Trade Agreement (NAFTA) agreement that reduced trade barriers among Mexico, Canada, and the United States

mestizo person with mixed European and Indian ancestry

▶ Reading Strategy

Re-create the web diagram shown at right. As you read and respond to the **KEY QUESTIONS**, use the diagram to outline the major aspects of Central America's government, economy, and culture.

 See Skillbuilder Handbook, page R7

CATEGORIZE

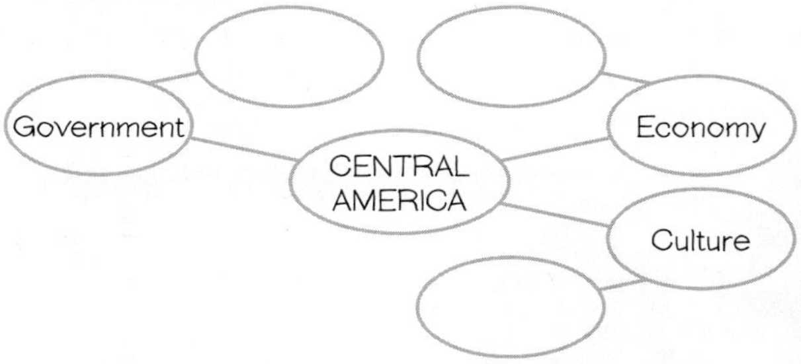

Government — CENTRAL AMERICA — Economy — Culture

GRAPHIC ORGANIZERS
Go to **Interactive Review** @ClassZone.com

Central America

Connecting to Your World

What is the most exotic animal you have ever seen? If you were to visit the rain forest in Costa Rica's Corcovado National Park, you would see many exotic animals, such as macaws, coatis, and anteaters. People's interest in visiting this and other natural habitats has led some countries in Central America to promote **ecotourism**, or travel to natural habitats in a way that does not damage the habitat. Ecotourism is just one way that Central American countries are expanding their economies.

Government and Economy

▼ **KEY QUESTION** What steps have Central American countries taken to improve their economies?

Central America today faces major challenges. In most countries, a wide gap exists between the small number of wealthy people and the large number of poor people. A large percentage of the population is unemployed. In many areas, people lack basic services, such as running water and electricity. In recent years, Central American countries have been working to improve their economies and to develop democratic governments.

Keel-billed Toucan
This bird makes its home in the treetops of the rain forests.

Ecotourism The people shown here are standing on a bridge, looking down over a rain forest in Costa Rica.

COSTA
RICA

Path Toward Democracy Since gaining independence from Spain in 1821, most Central American countries have struggled to develop democratic governments. As in Mexico, the wealthy in Central America controlled most aspects of government. Most of the population remained poor, with no say in how they were governed.

Costa Rica is the only country in the region that has been a democracy since the early 1900s. Nearly all the other Central American countries have been under the rule of **dictators**, or leaders with complete control over their governments. Starting in the 1950s, civil wars fought for equal rights led to years of suffering in countries such as Guatemala, El Salvador, and Nicaragua (NIHK•uh•RAH•gwuh). Since the 1990s, however, many Central American nations have developed democracies in which more people participate in government.

Developing the Economy During the colonial period, Spain set up large plantations that focused on growing one kind of crop. Today, agriculture is the main economic activity in Central America. Large plantations still produce crops, mainly bananas, sugar cane, and coffee, for export. Cattle are raised on large ranches in the drier western parts of Central America. But most agriculture consists of **subsistence farming**, in which poor farmers grow a variety of crops, such as corn and vegetables, on small plots to feed their own families.

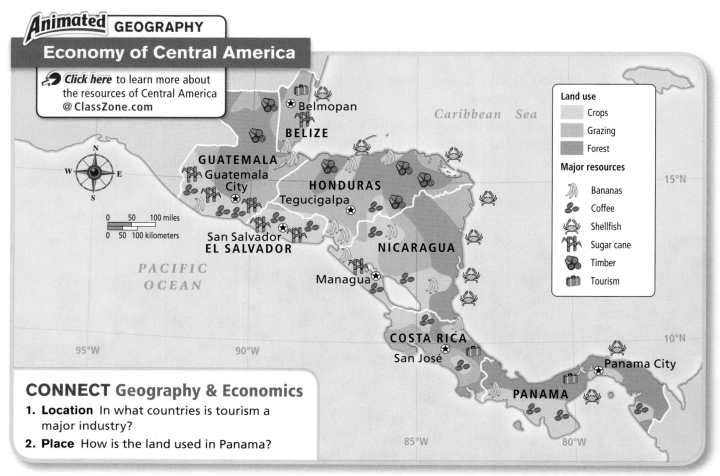

Animated GEOGRAPHY

Economy of Central America

Click here to learn more about the resources of Central America @ ClassZone.com

Land use
- Crops
- Grazing
- Forest

Major resources
- Bananas
- Coffee
- Shellfish
- Sugar cane
- Timber
- Tourism

Caribbean Sea

Belmopan
BELIZE
GUATEMALA
Guatemala City
HONDURAS
Tegucigalpa
San Salvador
EL SALVADOR
NICARAGUA
Managua
PACIFIC OCEAN
COSTA RICA
San José
PANAMA
Panama City

0 50 100 miles
0 50 100 kilometers

15°N
10°N
95°W
90°W
85°W
80°W

CONNECT Geography & Economics

1. **Location** In what countries is tourism a major industry?
2. **Place** How is the land used in Panama?

In the late 1800s, the sugar industry in the Caribbean islands was in trouble. Places in other parts of the world that raised sugar cane charged lower prices for their sugar. As a result, the sugar trade in the Caribbean islands declined.

The Caribbean nations found they had to diversify their economies. They began to raise other crops, such as bananas, pineapples, and citrus fruits. They also developed industries such as fishing, mining, and chemical plants. **Tourism**, which provides services for travelers, has become a very important industry. Residents of the islands are able to find jobs in the hotels, restaurants, and resorts on the islands. They also work as guides on sailing trips, snorkeling, and other activities for tourists.

Several Caribbean nations today are members of the **Caribbean Community and Common Market (CARICOM)**, a trade organization similar to NAFTA and **CAFTA**. The purpose of the organization is to coordinate economic and trade relations among the member nations.

▲ **DRAW CONCLUSIONS** Explain what Caribbean nations have done to develop their economies.

Two Different Governments

▼ **KEY QUESTION** How are the Puerto Rican and Cuban governments different?

Most Caribbean nations have at some time been under the rule of **dictators**. Today, most nations have democratically elected governments. Two islands, however, Cuba and Puerto Rico, have developed two distinctly different forms of government.

Cuba Spain controlled Cuba until the United States defeated Spain in the Spanish-American War in 1898. The United States military occupied the island until Cuba became an independent country in 1902. However, U.S. influence continued until 1959, when rebel forces led by Fidel Castro overthrew an unpopular dictator. By 1961, Castro had established communism in Cuba, with close ties to the Soviet Union. **Communism** is a type of government in which the Communist Party holds all political power and controls the economy. Castro's government

HISTORY MAKERS

Fidel Castro born 1926

Castro was the son of a wealthy farmer. As a boy, he worked in his father's sugar cane fields. He attended private schools and received a law degree from the University of Havana in 1950. There he also developed an interest in politics. As a lawyer, Castro worked on behalf of poor people. In 1953, he unsuccessfully tried to overthrow Cuba's dictator, Batista. After succeeding in 1959, Castro himself has ruled as a dictator for more than 40 years.

ONLINE BIOGRAPHY
For more on the life of Fidel Castro, go to the **Research & Writing Center @ ClassZone.com**

	PUERTO RICO	CUBA
Political Status	U.S. commonwealth	Independent country
Type of Government	Democracy	Communist state
Head of Government	Governor	President
Voting Age	18	16
Number of Political Parties	2	1
Political Divisions	Divided into 78 municipalities	Divided into 14 provinces
Relationship to U.S.	Non-voting commissioner in the U.S. House of Representatives	None

CRITICAL THINKING

Evaluate How does a two-party system help make a government more democratic?

improved health care and education for the Cuban people. However, Castro has ruled Cuba as a dictator and has denied Cubans many rights and freedoms.

Puerto Rico Like Cuba, Puerto Rico was a Spanish colony until 1898, when it became a U.S. territory. Puerto Rico, however, was never independent. In 1952, Puerto Rican voters approved a constitution that made Puerto Rico a commonwealth of the United States. As a **commonwealth**, Puerto Rico is self-governing but is still a part of the United States. Although Puerto Ricans are U.S. citizens, they cannot vote for the U.S. president.

▲ **COMPARE AND CONTRAST** Describe the similarities and differences between the governments of Cuba and Puerto Rico.

People and Culture

▼ **KEY QUESTION** Why has African culture been a major influence on Caribbean life?

The cultures of the Caribbean islands reflect Indian, African, and European influences. Because the region was the center of the slave trade, African influences have left a mark on many aspects of

Caribbean life. People in the islands speak a variety of languages. Spanish is the official language in Cuba, French in Haiti, and English in Jamaica.

Music in the Caribbean also reflects a blend of cultures. Calypso music began in Trinidad. It combines styles from Africa, Spain, and the Caribbean. Steel drums and guitars accompany calypso songs. Reggae developed in Jamaica in the 1960s. It blends African music, Caribbean music, and U.S. music to make its own unique style. Caribbean music includes many guitar-like instruments that have been created in the region, such as the Puerto Rican *cuatro* and the Cuban *tres*.

Most people in the Caribbean live in urban areas, where they hope to find jobs in the tourist industry. People celebrate festivals, such as Carnival. Artisans create folk art, such as oil drum art and papier-mâché sculptures. Popular sports are football, known as soccer in the United States, and baseball.

 EVALUATE Explain why African culture has been a major influence on life in the Caribbean.

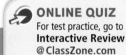

STEEL DRUMS

The steel drum was first made in Trinidad from the end and part of the sides of a 55-gallon steel oil barrel. The surface was hammered in certain ways to produce various tones. The steel drum is one of the few acoustic musical instruments created in the 20th century.

Section 2 Assessment

ONLINE QUIZ
For test practice, go to **Interactive Review** @ ClassZone.com

TERMS & NAMES

1. Explain the importance of
- Taino
- dependency
- tourism
- commonwealth

USE YOUR READING NOTES

2. Summarize Use your completed chart to answer the following question:

Why did the Caribbean islands diversify their economies?

ECONOMY	GOVERNMENT	CULTURE
1.	1.	1.
2.	2.	2.
3.	3.	3.

KEY IDEAS

3. What was the main economic activity in the Caribbean islands during colonial times?

4. How did Fidel Castro come to power in Cuba?

5. Why do people in the Caribbean Islands speak a variety of languages?

CRITICAL THINKING

6. Compare and Contrast How is Cuba's government different from the U.S. government?

7. Draw Conclusions Why do most people in the Caribbean islands live in urban areas?

8. CONNECT to Today In recent years Puerto Ricans have debated the issue of becoming a state of the United States. Why might people support or oppose Puerto Rican statehood?

9. WRITING Write a Country Profile Choose one Caribbean island and prepare a country profile for its Web site. Include its location, the kind of government and economy it has, and tourist attractions.

Reading for Understanding

▶ Key Ideas

BEFORE, YOU LEARNED

Many Caribbean nations are working together to increase trade.

NOW YOU WILL LEARN

Venezuela's economy depends heavily on petroleum, while Colombia's economy depends more on agricultural products.

▶ Vocabulary

TERMS & NAMES

federal republic form of government in which power is divided between a national government and state governments

Caracas capital city of Venezuela

joropo (huh•ROH•poh) Venezuelan national folk dance

Bogotá capital city of Colombia

Gabriel García Márquez Colombian author and Nobel Prize winner

Fernando Botero Colombian artist known for portraits of people with exaggerated forms

REVIEW

Simón Bolívar (boh•LEE•vahr) leader for independence in northern South America

dictator person with complete control over a country's government

llanos (YAH•nohs) grasslands of South America's Central Plains

BACKGROUND VOCABULARY

mosaic a picture made by placing small, colored pieces of tile or glass on a surface

▶ Reading Strategy

Re-create the cluster diagram shown at right for Venezuela and Colombia. As you read and respond to the **KEY QUESTIONS**, use the diagram to record details about the two countries' government, economy, and people.

 Skillbuilder Handbook, page R4

FIND MAIN IDEAS

```
           VENEZUELA
      ┌────────┼────────┐
 Government  Economy   People

 1._____   1._____   1._____
 2._____   2._____   2._____
```

GRAPHIC ORGANIZERS
Go to **Interactive Review** @ ClassZone.com

Venezuela and Colombia

Connecting to Your World

Many civilizations have created beautiful mosaic art. A **mosaic** involves placing small, colored pieces of stone, tile, or glass next to each other on a surface to make a picture or design. The countries of South America form a kind of mosaic of their own, a cultural mosaic. People from different cultural groups live near each other but keep their own cultural identities. *Mestizos*, Indians, and people of African ancestry form part of the cultural mosaic in Venezuela and Colombia.

Cultural Mosaic
South Americans today reflect a blend of cultures.

Venezuela

▼ **KEY QUESTION** What are the main economic activities of Venezuela?

Venezuela and Colombia are located in the northern and northwestern part of South America. Both countries border the Caribbean Sea, and Colombia also borders the Pacific Ocean. In both countries, most people live in urban areas. While Venezuela and Colombia share similar histories, their governments and economies have developed differently.

Caracas, Venezuela

267

Simón Bolívar (1783–1830) is known as the liberator of South America. But his dream of uniting South America into one nation failed. In a letter, he explained what kind of government he thought would be best for South America.

> Events . . . have proved that institutions which are wholly representative are not suited to our . . . customs, and present knowledge. . . . As long as our countrymen do not acquire the abilities and political virtues that distinguish our brothers of the north [the United States], . . . popular systems, far from working to our advantage, will, I greatly fear, bring about our downfall.
>
> Source: Jamaican Letter

Simón Bolívar

DOCUMENT-BASED QUESTION

What "abilities" would be needed to set up a representative system?

History and Government Venezuela became part of Spain's empire in the early 1500s. When Spanish explorers saw Indian villages built on stilts on Lake Maracaibo, they named the area "Venezuela" after Venice, an Italian city built on water. By the 1700s, Venezuela was a colony, and most residents had little control over their lives.

Led by the Venezuelan **Simón Bolívar**, Venezuela became the first colony to declare independence from Spain in 1811 and to win it in 1821. After independence, the country went through years of civil war and **dictators**. Although establishing a democracy was not easy, Venezuela's leaders have been democratically elected since 1958.

Today, Venezuela is a **federal republic**, a government in which power is divided between a national government and state governments. The national government consists of a president, a congress, and a supreme court. Venezuela has 22 states and a Federal District. Each state and the Federal District have a governor and a congress.

Economy Venezuela's economy today is dependent on oil production. Its oil fields are located in the Maracaibo Basin, the location of Lake Maracaibo (South America's largest lake), and on the eastern plains. Venezuela is one of the world's leading oil producers. About 75 percent of the nation's exports are oil exports, especially to the United States and Canada. But, like the Caribbean countries with one-crop economies, Venezuela's dependence on one product sometimes results in economic instability, as oil prices rise and fall.

About ten percent of Venezuela's workers are farmers. More than half of them cultivate small farms, where they raise enough food and animals to support their families. Larger farms and ranches supply most of Venezuela's commercial products. Large farms grow bananas, coffee, corn, oranges, and rice. Large cattle ranches are an important part of the economy of Venezuela's **llanos** (YAH•nohs).

People and Culture Like the majority of Central Americans, most Venezuelans are *mestizos*. Other Venezuelans are Indians or people of European or African ancestry. Because Venezuela is a former Spanish colony, the official language is Spanish, and most Venezuelans are Roman Catholics.

Most Venezuelans live in cities, such as the capital city, **Caracas**. Many city dwellers live comfortably in houses and apartment buildings and work as professionals such as doctors, government workers, and lawyers. However, as in many parts of Latin America, the gap between the rich and the poor continues to be large. Many poor people from rural areas travel to cities in search of jobs. They live as squatters in crowded settlements outside the cities. To encourage people to stay in rural areas, Venezuela's government has paved roads, created health and education services, and provided electrical service in many rural areas.

Venezuelans enjoy sports, music, and dancing. Football (soccer) and baseball are among the most popular sports. Rodeos are popular, especially in cattle-raising regions in the llanos. The plains also inspired the *joropo* (huh•ROH•poh), Venezuela's national folk dance. While Venezuelans love to dance to Caribbean salsa, meringue, and calypso, they change each dance to make it truly Venezuelan.

Baseball Fans Venezuelans cheer on their baseball team as it plays Italy in the 2006 World Baseball Classic.

▲ **CATEGORIZE** Describe the economic activities of Venezuela.

COLOMBIA

Colombia

▼ **KEY QUESTION** What are the characteristics of Colombia's population?

Colombia was named after Christopher Columbus. It is second in population and fourth in size among South American countries. The Andes Mountains stretch across western Colombia. Hot lowlands are located along the coasts of the Caribbean Sea and the Pacific Ocean, and plains are found in the eastern part of the country.

History and Government Like Venezuela, Colombia was a Spanish colony until 1819, when Simón Bolívar gained Colombia's independence. Periods of violence and civil war followed. Colombians could not agree on what kind of government to establish. Some people wanted a strong central government, and others supported strong regional governments. Political violence and civil war continue to threaten the nation today.

Today, Colombia is a republic. The national government is made up of a legislative, executive, and judicial branch. A president, elected to a four-year term, heads the executive branch. Colombia is divided into 32 departments and the district of **Bogotá**, the nation's capital. Each department has an elected legislature and governor.

CONNECT Geography & Economics

Coffee

Coffee was brought to Colombia in 1808. Colombia today is the world's second-leading coffee producer. Its land and climate are perfect for growing a certain type of coffee—Arabica. This coffee grows best in rainy regions near the equator, at elevations between 3,600 and 6,300 feet. One coffee tree produces only enough beans to make one pound of coffee a year!

Economy Unlike Venezuela, Colombia's economy relies on agricultural products. Coffee is Colombia's leading legal export. Large plantations produce bananas, corn, cotton, and sugar. Colombian ranches raise cattle for meat and for leather goods. Stopping the illegal cocaine trade has been a major economic challenge for Colombia. Over the past 30 years, Colombia has supported the cut-flower industry as an alternative to growing cocaine-producing coca plants. It has become the second-largest exporter of cut flowers in the world.

Manufacturing and service industries have become increasingly important to Colombia's economy. Manufactured goods include clothing, chemicals, and processed foods. Service industries employ about 45 percent of Colombian workers.

Colombia produces large amounts of coal and petroleum. Emeralds from Colombian mines account for more than 90 percent of the world's supply.

People and Culture Spanish is Colombia's official language, and most Colombians are Roman Catholics. Most people are *mestizos*. About 70 percent of Colombia's people live in the highland valley basins in western Colombia. Colombia's capital and largest city, Bogotá, is located in a basin in the Andes Mountains.

Most Colombians live in urban areas. People who work in the business, service, and government industries in the cities live quite comfortably. Since the mid-1900s, rural Colombians have moved to cities in search of a better life. However, their lack of education and skills make it difficult to find jobs. They sometimes end up living in poverty in squatter settlements that circle the cities.

Colombia has produced famous writers and artists. **Gabriel García Márquez**, a Nobel Prize winner, writes about Colombian life using a mixture of realism and fantasy. **Fernando Botero** is an artist known for portraits that show people in exaggerated forms.

Bogotá Colombia's capital city lies more than 8,000 feet above sea level and is home to nearly seven million people.

SUMMARIZE Describe the characteristics of Colombia's population.

Section 3 Assessment

ONLINE QUIZ
For test practice, go to
Interactive Review
@ ClassZone.com

TERMS & NAMES

1. Explain the importance of
- federal republic
- Caracas
- *joropo*
- Bogotá

USE YOUR READING NOTES

2. Find Main Ideas Use your completed diagram to answer the following question:

What kind of government do Venezuela and Colombia have today?

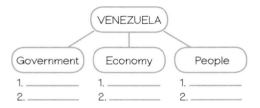

VENEZUELA

Government — Economy — People

1. _____   1. _____   1. _____
2. _____   2. _____   2. _____

KEY IDEAS

3. What are Venezuela's main products and crops?

4. What three geographic regions are found in Colombia?

5. What industries are important to Colombia's economy?

CRITICAL THINKING

6. Identify Problems and Solutions How has the Venezuelan government attempted to curb the movement of people from rural to urban areas?

7. Compare and Contrast How are the histories of Venezuela and Colombia similar?

8. CONNECT to Today Much of Venezuela's income comes from oil production. How can that be both positive and negative for its economy?

9. WRITING Write a Marketing Campaign Ad Choose a product from Venezuela or Colombia, such as oil or cut flowers, and write an ad to convince other countries to buy this product.

Reading for Understanding

▶ Key Ideas

BEFORE, YOU LEARNED

The cultures of Venezuela and Colombia have been greatly influenced by their Spanish colonial heritage.

NOW YOU WILL LEARN

Indians and *mestizos* make up a large part of the population of Peru, Bolivia, and Ecuador.

▶ Vocabulary

TERMS & NAMES

llama a South American mammal related to the camel

alpaca a South American mammal related to the llama

selva Spanish name for the eastern Peruvian regions that contain rain forests

indigenous native to a region

landlocked surrounded by land with no access to a sea

quinoa a kind of weed from the Andean region that produces a small grain

REVIEW

altiplano the high plateau region of Bolivia

BACKGROUND VOCABULARY

edible fit for eating

Visual Vocabulary landlocked

▶ Reading Strategy

Re-create the chart shown at right. As you read and respond to the **KEY QUESTIONS**, use the chart to categorize details about Peru, Bolivia, and Ecuador.

 Skillbuilder Handbook, page R7

CATEGORIZE

	PERU	BOLIVIA	ECUADOR
Government			
Economy			
People			

 GRAPHIC ORGANIZERS
Go to **Interactive Review** @ ClassZone.com

SECTION 4

FOCUS ON

Peru, Bolivia, and Ecuador

Peruvian Girl and Baby Alpaca

Connecting to Your World

How would you adapt to living in a mountain region, where it was cold much of the time? For hundreds of years, Indians have lived in the Andes Mountains, where they developed innovative ways to deal with their harsh environment. They raised **llamas** and **alpacas**, small camel-like animals, on the mountainsides. The Inca used the freezing nighttime temperatures and the strong daytime sunlight to preserve and store potatoes and meat by freezing and drying them. Today, people in the Andes Mountains continue to adapt to their environment.

PERU

Peru

▼ KEY QUESTION What products are made in Peru's coastal regions?

The Andes Mountains are located in Bolivia, Ecuador, and Peru. Peru is South America's third largest country. It has three land regions—the coast along the Pacific Ocean, the Andes Mountains, and the **selva**, an area of rain forests in eastern Peru.

Adapting to the Mountains Farmers in Bolivia plant crops on mountain terraces, such as these.

History and Government Between about 1200 and the early 1500s, Peru was home to the Inca civilization. The empire in the Andes Mountains extended from present-day Colombia to Argentina. In 1533, the Spanish conquered the Inca and ruled Peru for 300 years.

Since gaining independence in 1821, Peru has suffered military takeovers, dictatorships, and wars with neighboring countries and revolutionary groups. Today, Peru is a democratic republic. In 2001, Peruvians elected Alejandro Toledo, the first Indian president.

Economy Peru's rugged geography and scarce farmland have made it difficult for the country to create a strong economy. About one-third of the people are farmers. Coffee, potatoes, and grains are grown on highland terraces. Sugar cane, cotton, and asparagus are grown in coastal valleys. Peru is one of the world's leading producers of asparagus.

Peru is a leading producer of copper, lead, silver, and zinc, which are mined in the Peruvian mountains. It also has a profitable fishing industry. Factories that process metals, fish, and sugar cane have been built along Peru's coast. Peru also exports petroleum.

Peruvian Weaver This woman weaves colorful yarns with a hand loom. **What do you think she will do with the products she creates?**

People and Culture *Mestizos* and **indigenous** people, or people native to a region, make up most of Peru's population. About ten percent are of European, African, or Asian ancestry. Spanish and Quechua (KEHCH•wuh) are Peru's official languages. About 75 percent of Peruvians speak Spanish, and about 25 percent speak Quechua or another Indian language.

Most Peruvians live in cities. While the middle and upper classes live in houses and apartment buildings, the poor live in slums or squatter settlements. Peru's government has tried to develop these settlements by providing running water and sewer systems.

Peruvians create beautiful sculpture, pottery, and textiles. Music and dancing are popular throughout Peru. As elsewhere in Latin America, football (soccer) is the most popular sport.

🔺 **CATEGORIZE** Identify the kinds of products that are produced in Peru's coastal regions.

The Lake Dwellers The Uros, descendants of an ancient people, live on floating islands on Lake Titicaca. Titicaca, the world's highest lake, is on the border of Peru and Bolivia. They use a kind of reed, or wetland grass, called *totora* (toh•TOH•rah) to make floating mats. They use the mats to create islands in the lake. The Uros also make reed boats and houses. They even have a floating soccer field!

CRITICAL THINKING
Make Inferences How might the Uros have contributed to making Lake Titicaca a popular tourist spot?

Bolivia and Ecuador

🔻 **KEY QUESTION** How are Bolivia's and Ecuador's geographies, histories, and economies alike?

Bolivia is a **landlocked** country, surrounded entirely by land with no access to a sea. The country has two capital cities—Sucre, which is the official capital, and La Paz, which is the administrative capital. Ecuador is one of South America's smallest countries. Large plains are located in northern and eastern Bolivia and on Ecuador's Pacific coastal plain. The Andes Mountains circle a high plateau in western Bolivia and run through the center of Ecuador.

Evo Morales An Aymara, Morales was elected president of Bolivia by a large margin in December 2005. He took office in January 2006.

History and Government Both Bolivia and Ecuador were colonized by the Spanish and achieved independence in the 1800s. Bolivia was named for Simón Bolívar. *Ecuador* is the Spanish word for "equator," which crosses the country.

Both Bolivia and Ecuador struggled to develop democracies. Each country has had several constitutions that provided for free elections. But dictators and military leaders often took control.

Today, both Bolivia and Ecuador are democratic republics. Both governments include a national legislature, a supreme court, and an elected president. In 2005, Bolivians elected Evo Morales as president, the first indigenous person to be elected to that office in Bolivia.

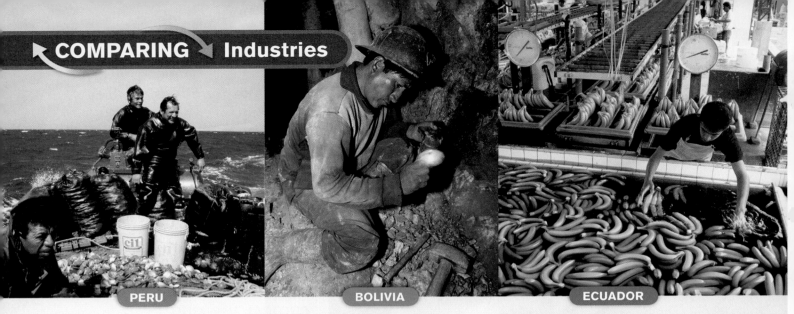

COMPARING Industries

PERU

- **Major industries:** mineral production, steel, petroleum refining, fishing (Above: fishing crew harvesting shellfish off the coast of Peru)
- **Major agricultural products:** coffee, cotton, sugar cane, asparagus
- **Major trading partner:** United States

BOLIVIA

- **Major industries:** mining, petroleum, food and beverages (Above: miner underground in Bolivian silver mine)
- **Major agricultural products:** soybeans, coffee, cotton, corn, potatoes
- **Major trading partner:** Brazil

ECUADOR

- **Major industries:** petroleum, food processing, textiles, wood products
- **Major agricultural products:** bananas, coffee, cacao, balsa wood, shrimp (Above: Ecuadorian workers in a banana-processing plant)
- **Major trading partner:** United States

CRITICAL THINKING

Compare and Contrast What agricultural products do Peru, Bolivia, and Ecuador have in common?

Economy Bolivia and Ecuador both have natural resources that have not been fully developed. Bolivia has many minerals and fertile soil. Ecuador's farm and timberland on the coast and in the eastern lowlands still need development. Both nations are working to develop their resources and help improve their economies.

One of Bolivia's leading exports is natural gas. Bolivia is also a leading producer of tin, but only a small percentage of the nation's workers are employed in this industry. About half of Bolivia's workers are farmers. Potatoes, wheat, and **quinoa**, a kind of weed that produces a small **edible** grain, are grown on the **altiplano**, the high plateau region of Bolivia, just east of the Andes Mountains. Bananas, beans, cacao, coffee, soybeans, and corn are also important agricultural products.

Ecuador's major export is petroleum. Gold is also an important mineral product. Most manufacturing in Ecuador takes place in Guayaquil (gwy•uh•KEEL), the nation's largest city, and in Quito, the capital. Ecuador's major manufacturing products include cement, processed foods, and textiles. Ecuador is the world's major supplier of balsa wood, used to make model airplanes. Like Bolivians, most Ecuadorians are farmers. They grow bananas, cacao, coffee, and sugar cane on the country's coastal plain.

People and Culture Spanish and the Indian languages Quechua and Aymara are Bolivia's three official languages. Most Bolivians practice subsistence farming. They have traditionally raised llamas to transport goods and alpacas to provide food, clothing, and fertilizer. In fact, Bolivia has more llamas than any other place in the world!

Most Ecuadorians are Indians or *mestizos*. Many Indians live in the Andes, speak Indian languages, and wear traditional clothes.

As they have for thousands of years, indigenous people in Bolivia today create jewelry, rugs, and shawls. Ecuadorian artists carve objects using the tagua plant. The tagua nut resembles ivory, which is a material that comes from elephant tusks. The tagua nut is used to make buttons and works of art. No animals are harmed to create tagua art.

Countries in the Andes Mountains are famous for panpipe music. Aymara and Quechua peoples play these flute-type instruments combined with drums and guitar-like instruments to create unique regional music.

 COMPARE AND CONTRAST Compare the geographies, histories, and economies of Bolivia and Ecuador.

Playing a Panpipe Peruvian musicians play panpipes, like the one this girl is playing.

Section 4 Assessment

ONLINE QUIZ
For test practice, go to
Interactive Review
@ ClassZone.com

TERMS & NAMES

1. Explain the importance of
- llama
- selva
- landlocked
- quinoa

USE YOUR READING NOTES

2. Categorize Use your chart to answer the following question:

How are Bolivia and Ecuador working to improve their economies?

	PERU	BOLIVIA	ECUADOR
Government			
Economy			
People			

KEY IDEAS

3. What kind of government do Peru, Ecuador, and Bolivia have?

4. How are most people in Peru, Ecuador, and Bolivia employed?

5. What groups of people make up a large percentage of the population of all three countries?

CRITICAL THINKING

6. Analyze Causes and Effects How do you think being a landlocked nation affects Bolivia's economy?

7. Make Inferences Why do you think that so many Indian communities have been able to keep their traditional customs and ways of life?

8. CONNECT to Today Why is it important for Bolivia and Ecuador to fully develop their natural resources?

9. WRITING Create a Picture Essay Choose an indigenous group in Peru, Bolivia, or Ecuador. Research their customs and ways of life. Create a captioned picture essay to present the information.

Tropical and mountain climates are both found in Middle America and Spanish-speaking South America. Each climate supports its own unique vegetation and animal life.

Tropical

The climate in tropical regions is hot year-round, with abundant rainfall. This climate produces the thick, green rain forests and the many exotic plants and animals that live in them. Farmers plant crops, such as sugar cane and bananas, that thrive in the tropical conditions.

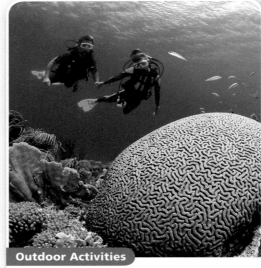

Outdoor Activities
Scuba divers explore the coral reefs off the coast of Bonaire, one of the Caribbean islands.

Nevis Peak and Botanical Gardens on the Caribbean island of Nevis ▼

Agriculture
A farmer harvests sugar cane on the island nation of Barbados.

Wildlife
Sloths, such as this one hanging upside down from a branch, live in the tropical forests of Central America and South America and spend most of their lives in trees.

Ice climbers make their way up Huayna Potosi, a mountain in Bolivia popular among mountain climbers.

Mountain

Unlike the fairly constant climate of the tropical areas, the highland climate of the Andes Mountains varies with changes in elevation. Temperatures range from warm in the lower elevations to freezing in the highest elevations. Farming is difficult in this climate, but several crops, such as potatoes, barley, and wheat, grow well there. Various species of plants and animals have adapted to the mountain conditions.

Sacsayhuamán, an ancient Inca fortress, overlooks the city of Cuzco, Peru. ▼

Agriculture

These Ecuadorian farmers are harvesting barley.

Wildlife

The spectacled bear makes its home in the Andes Mountains. It gets its name from the markings around its eyes.

CRITICAL THINKING

1. **Compare and Contrast** What differences can be seen between tropical and mountain climate regions?

2. **Form an Opinion** Which climate region is more appealing to you? Why?

Reading for Understanding

▶ Key Ideas

BEFORE, YOU LEARNED

Geography has influenced the economies and people's ways of life in Peru, Bolivia, and Ecuador.

NOW YOU WILL LEARN

Geography has also influenced the economies of the nations in the Southern Cone.

▶ Vocabulary

TERMS & NAMES

gaucho Argentinian cowboy

Southern Cone South American nations located in the cone-shaped southernmost part of South America

estancia (eh•STAHN•syah) large farm or ranch in Argentina

Mercosur association of several South American countries to promote trade among the countries

REVIEW

José de San Martín leader for independence in southern South America

gross domestic product (GDP) the total value of all the goods and services produced in a country in a year

Pampas grassy plains in south-central South America

landlocked surrounded by land with no access to sea

Visual Vocabulary
Southern Cone

▶ Reading Strategy

Re-create the web diagram shown at right for each country in the section. As you read and respond to the **KEY QUESTIONS**, use the diagram to organize details about the nation's history and government, economy, and population.

 Skillbuilder Handbook, page R4

FIND MAIN IDEAS

History and Government

Economy

Population

GRAPHIC ORGANIZERS
Go to **Interactive Review** @ ClassZone.com

The Southern Cone

Connecting to Your World

Cowboys played an important role in cattle ranching in the American West in the 1800s. In Argentina, **gauchos**, or cowboys, also play an important role in cattle ranching. As in the United States, the life and culture of gauchos is the subject of many Argentinian stories and movies. But the gaucho is just one aspect of the culture of Argentina and its neighbors.

Argentinian gaucho

Argentina and Chile

CHILE ARGENTINA

🔻 **KEY QUESTION** How do Argentina's plains and Chile's mountains affect their economies?

Together with Paraguay and Uruguay, Argentina and Chile form part of South America's **Southern Cone**, the cone-shaped southernmost area of South America. The largest of the four countries is Argentina, a country of plains, plateaus, mountains, forests, and a long coastline. The Andes Mountains make up much of Chile, the world's longest and narrowest country. Argentina is bordered by Paraguay on the north and Uruguay on the east.

Patagonia Sheep farmers round up their sheep. **How would you describe the land on which this sheep ranch is located?**

Michelle Bachelet
Michelle Bachelet won more than 53 percent of the votes. She promised to bring more jobs to Chile and to work for social justice.

History and Government The Spanish who first arrived in Argentina expected to find gold and silver. In fact, *Argentina* comes from the Latin word *argentum*, which means "silver." *Chile* likely comes from the Native American word meaning "where the land ends." In the 1500s, the Spanish came looking for gold and silver in both regions. Later, **José de San Martín** of Argentina helped both countries gain independence from Spain by 1818.

Like other South American nations, Argentina was controlled by dictators into the 20th century. Chile's government, on the other hand, was more stable. Presidents were often elected because they promised social reforms. In 1973, however, General Augusto Pinochet took control of Chile's government and ruled as a military dictator until 1990. Today, Argentina and Chile are republics. In 2006, Chile elected its first female president, Michelle Bachelet.

Economy In both Argentina and Chile, service industries make up most of the nations' **gross domestic product (GDP)** and employ more than half of the nations' workers. Most of Argentina's manufacturing occurs in factories in and around Buenos Aires. The **Pampas** and Patagonia are important to Argentina's agriculture. Beef cattle and grain and fruits, such as wheat and grapes, are raised on large ranches and farms, called *estancias* (eh•STAHN-syahs), on the Pampas. Thousands of sheep graze in Patagonia. Petroleum from Patagonia is Argentina's main mineral. Fishing along Argentina's long coastline is also an important part of Argentina's economy.

CONNECT to Math

The GDP is an important indicator of the strength of a nation's economy. A strong GDP indicates a healthy economy and usually influences a nation's stock market in a positive way.

Stock market in Buenos Aires, Argentina

Activity

Make a GDP Bar Graph

Materials
- Gross domestic product figures for Argentina, Chile, Paraguay, and Uruguay
- Graph paper

1. Research the latest GDP figures for Argentina, Chile, Paraguay, and Uruguay.

2. Make a graph. Label the horizontal axis "Country." Label the vertical axis "GDP in U.S. billions of dollars." Label the axis by 100s, starting from 0.

3. Draw a bar for each country to represent the GDP figure for that country.

Because only about three percent of Chile's land can be farmed, Chile developed copper mining in its mountains and fishing industries along its coast. Today, Chile is the world's leading copper producer. Both Argentina and Chile are part of **Mercosur**, an association of several South American countries, to promote trade among the countries.

People and Culture Argentina and Chile have large urban populations, particularly in the major cities of Buenos Aires and Santiago. Like other South American cities, these cities are surrounded by squatter settlements.

About 85 percent of Argentina's population is of European ancestry. Although gauchos still work on Argentina's ranches today, they are also celebrated, much like American cowboys, in Argentinian poetry, literature, painting, and music. The tango, a dance that combines European and African influences, is Argentina's national dance.

Chile's population, unlike Argentina's, is mostly *mestizo.* Many Chileans have left difficult conditions in rural areas for opportunities in the cities. Chile has produced many famous writers, such as poets Gabriela Mistral and Pablo Neruda. Chileans spend their leisure time going to the movies and playing and watching football (soccer), the most popular sport.

Dancing the Tango The tango involves alternating long, slow steps with quick, short steps.

▲ **DRAW CONCLUSIONS** Explain how geography affects parts of Argentina's and Chile's economies.

Paraguay and Uruguay

▼ **KEY QUESTION** How is the population of Paraguay different from Uruguay's?

Paraguay is a small **landlocked** country of rivers, hills, and forests. Hilly grasslands cover much of Uruguay, located southeast of Paraguay. Both countries won independence from the Spanish, experienced political turmoil, and today are constitutional republics.

Paraguay Most people in Paraguay work in service industries and in agriculture. Cattle raising and most farming take place in eastern Paraguay, where the richest soil is found. Forests cover much of eastern Paraguay, and wood products are important industries. Paraguay is a founding member of Mercosur.

Mestizos make up most of Paraguay's population, and the Guaraní (GWAH•ruh•NEE) are the nation's largest indigenous group. The Guaraní influence is reflected in Paraguay's arts, particularly in music and handicrafts. The Guaraní are especially known for nanduti lace, which incorporates a lace-making technique introduced by the Spanish.

Montevideo The Plaza Independencia is located in the center of Montevideo in Uruguay. **What other culture makes use of plazas in its cities?**

Uruguay More than 60 percent of Uruguay's people work in service industries. Uruguay's plains and grasslands are perfect for raising cattle and sheep. Meat, hides, and wools are the nation's biggest exports. Like other Southern Cone nations, Uruguay is a member of Mercosur.

Most of Uruguay's people are of Spanish and Italian ancestry. Most people live in cities, half in Montevideo, the capital city. Unlike many other South American nations, Uruguay's culture is influenced more by European traditions than by native ones. Gaucho folklore has inspired Uruguay's music and art and Montevideo's Gaucho Museum.

 COMPARE AND CONTRAST Compare the populations of Paraguay and Uruguay.

Section 5 Assessment

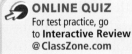 **ONLINE QUIZ**
For test practice, go to **Interactive Review** @ ClassZone.com

TERMS & NAMES

1. Explain the importance of
- gaucho
- Southern Cone
- *estancia*
- Mercosur

USE YOUR READING NOTES

2. Find Main Ideas Use your completed diagram to answer the following question:

What products account for most of Uruguay's exports?

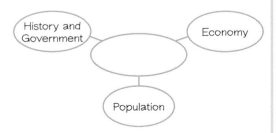

KEY IDEAS

3. How are the histories of the Southern Cone nations alike?

4. What industry employs a majority of the people in Argentina and Chile?

5. Why does most farming and cattle ranching occur in eastern Paraguay?

CRITICAL THINKING

6. Make Inferences Why have Southern Cone nations become members of Mercosur?

7. Draw Conclusions How might Argentina's geography and size contribute to its strong economy?

8. CONNECT to Today In 2006, Chileans elected their first female president. What do you think this says about women's role in Chilean politics?

9. MATH Create a Pie Graph Choose one of the Southern Cone nations and research its major exports. Make a pie graph to present the information.

Interactive ◀ Review

Click here to complete these and other activities online @ ClassZone.com

CHAPTER SUMMARY

Key Idea 1
Central American countries face challenges as they improve their economies.

Key Idea 2
Europe and Africa have influenced Caribbean cultures.

Key Idea 3
Venezuela's economy depends heavily on petroleum, while Colombia's economy depends more on agricultural products.

Key Idea 4
Indians and *mestizos* make up a large part of Peru, Bolivia, and Ecuador.

Key Idea 5
Geography has influenced the economies of Southern Cone nations.

For **Review and Study Notes**, go to **Interactive Review** @ ClassZone.com

NAME GAME

Use the Terms & Names list to complete each sentence on paper or online.

1. I am a place that is ruled by or closely connected with another country. __**dependency**__

2. I describe the countries in the southern part of South America. _____

3. I describe the countries of Bolivia and Paraguay.
_____

4. I am the national folk dance of Venezuela.
_____

5. I am a measure of a country's economy. _____

6. I am a trade agreement made between Central American countries._____

7. I am an important animal in the Andes Mountains. _____

8. I am a kind of grassy plain. _____

9. I draw tourists to a natural habitat without harming the environment. _____

10. I am a large farm in Argentina. _____

CAFTA
commonwealth
dependency
ecotourism
estancia
gaucho
gross domestic product, or GDP
joropo
landlocked
llama
llanos
Southern Cone

Activities

GeoGame

Use this online map to show what you know about the geography of Middle America and Spanish-Speaking South America. Drag and drop each place name to its location on the map.

Geo GAME

Bogotá

Caracas

Cuba

Panama

Andes Mountains

Present-Day Middle America and Spanish-Speaking South America

Caracas

To play the complete game, go to **Interactive Review** @ ClassZone.com

Crossword Puzzle

Complete an online crossword puzzle to test your knowledge of the region's history, culture, government, and economics.

ACROSS
1. a small camel-like animal, related to the llama

VOCABULARY

Explain the significance of each of the following.

1. ecotourism
2. one-crop economy
3. Taino
4. commonwealth
5. landlocked

Explain how the terms in each group are related.

6. CAFTA and Mercosur
7. dictator and communism
8. Pampas, gaucho, and *estancia*

KEY IDEAS

1 Central America

9. What is Central America's main economic activity?
10. What group of people makes up most of Central America's population?

2 The Caribbean

11. Why did the Spanish bring enslaved Africans to the Caribbean islands?
12. What kind of government does Puerto Rico have?

3 Venezuela and Colombia

13. What product is the most important to the economy of Venezuela?
14. What is Colombia's leading export?

4 Peru, Bolivia, and Ecuador

15. What are three economic activities in Peru?
16. What are the major mineral exports of Bolivia and Ecuador?

5 Argentina and Chile

17. What economic activity provides most of Argentina's and Chile's gross domestic product?
18. In what parts of Argentina does farming and ranching take place?
19. Where do most people in Uruguay live?

CRITICAL THINKING

20. **Compare and Contrast** Create a chart to compare the industries and major products of Venezuela, Peru, and Argentina.

COUNTRY	MAJOR INDUSTRIES/PRODUCTS
Venezuela	
Peru	
Argentina	

21. **Evaluate** What challenges do Central American countries face today?
22. **Identify Problems and Solutions** What have Central American and Caribbean nations done to help solve the problem of one-crop economies?
23. **Five Themes: Movement** How has the settlement of Caribbean nations affected the culture of those nations?
24. **Connect to History** What conditions created during the Spanish conquest of South America made it difficult for nations there to form stable governments?

Answer the ESSENTIAL QUESTION

How are the countries of this region working to strengthen their governments and economies?

Written response Write a two- or three- paragraph response to the Essential Question. Be sure to consider the key ideas of each section. Use the rubric below to guide your thinking.

Response Rubric
A strong response will:

- discuss ways in which the countries have strengthened their governments
- explain how the nations have strengthened their economies

THEMATIC MAP

Use the map to answer questions 1 and 2.

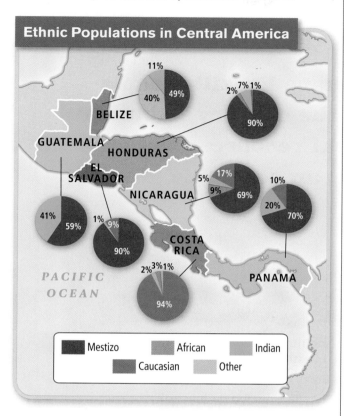

Ethnic Populations in Central America

BELIZE
GUATEMALA
HONDURAS
EL SALVADOR
NICARAGUA
COSTA RICA
PANAMA

PACIFIC OCEAN

Legend:
- Mestizo
- Caucasian
- African
- Other
- Indian

1. What percentage of Guatemalans are *mestizo*?

A. about 59 percent
B. about 33 percent
C. about 3 percent
D. about 1 percent

2. Which of the following countries has the largest percentage of *mestizos*?

A. Belize
B. Panama
C. El Salvador
D. Guatemala

TABLE

Use the table below to answer questions 3 and 4 on your paper.

Literacy and Life Expectancy in Selected Countries		
	Literacy Rate	**Life Expectancy**
Haiti	53 percent	53 years
Costa Rica	96 percent	77 years
Ecuador	93 percent	76 years
Argentina	97 percent	76 years

Source: *The World Factbook*, 2006

3. Which country has the lowest life expectancy?

4. What conclusion can you draw about the relationship between literacy rates and life expectancy?

GeoActivity

1. INTERDISCIPLINARY ACTIVITY–SCIENCE

Use the library or visit a zoo to find out about an animal that makes its home in the region, such as the Andean condor, spectacled bear, tapir, or toucan. Find out how the animal adapts to its environment. Present the information in an illustrated, captioned poster.

2. WRITING FOR SOCIAL STUDIES

Write an ad that encourages people to visit one of the countries discussed in the chapter. Your ad should focus on the landforms, people, and cultural features that visitors to the country would find interesting.

3. MENTAL MAPPING

Create an outline map of South America and label the following:

- Southern Cone nations
- llanos
- altiplano
- Pampas
- Andes Mountains
- coastal plains
- equator

Brazil

 ESSENTIAL QUESTION

How have Brazil's people used the country's abundant natural resources to make Brazil an economic giant?

① HISTORY & GOVERNMENT

From Portuguese Colony to Modern Giant

② CULTURE

A Multicultural Society

③ ECONOMICS

Developing an Abundant Land

CONNECT ⟳ **Geography & History**

Use the map and the time line to answer the following questions.

1. When was Brazil claimed by Portugal?

2. How far is Brasília from Rio de Janeiro?

Geography
◄ **1494** Spain and Portugal sign the Treaty of Tordesillas.

1494

History
1500 Pedro Álvares Cabral claims Brazil for Portugal. ►

History
1822 Brazil declares independence from Portugal.

History
1888 Brazil abolishes slavery.

Present-Day Brazil

Click here to explore Brazil
@ ClassZone.com

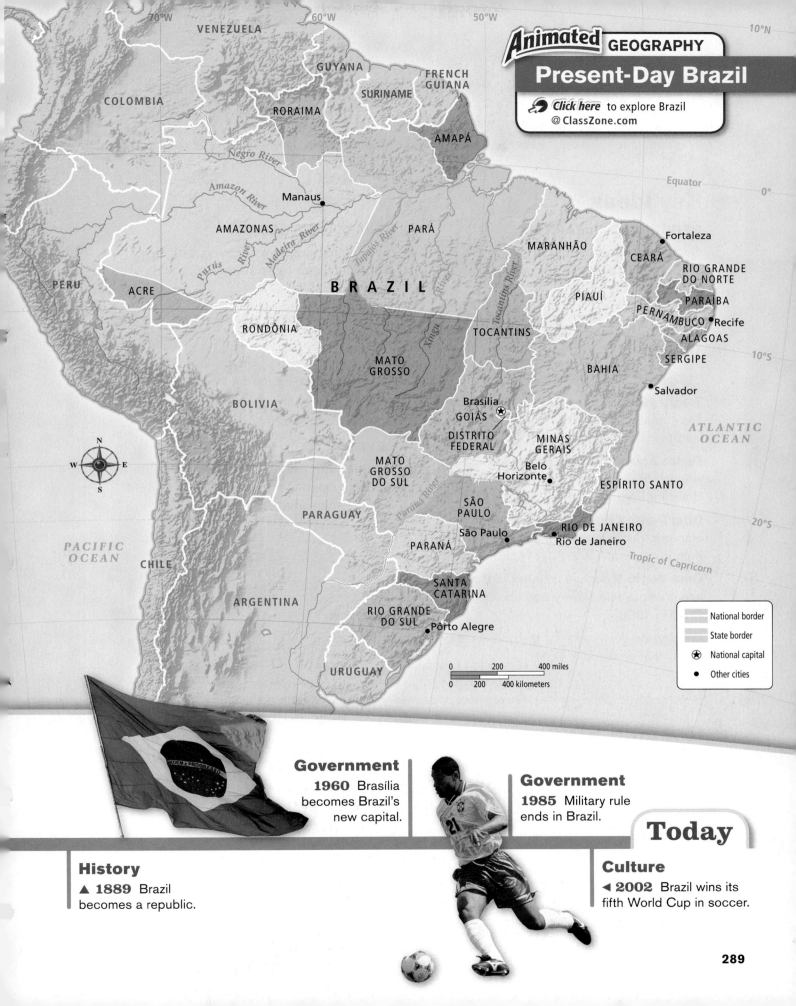

VENEZUELA

GUYANA

SURINAME

FRENCH GUIANA

COLOMBIA

RORAIMA

AMAPÁ

Negro River

Manaus

AMAZONAS

PARÁ

MARANHÃO

Fortaleza

CEARÁ

Amazon River

Madeira River

Purús River

B R A Z I L

RIO GRANDE DO NORTE

PIAUÍ

PARAÍBA

PERNAMBUCO

Recife

PERU

ACRE

RONDÔNIA

Xingu River

Tapajos River

Tocantins River

TOCANTINS

ALAGOAS

SERGIPE

MATO GROSSO

BAHIA

Salvador

BOLIVIA

Brasília

GOIÁS

DISTRITO FEDERAL

MINAS GERAIS

Belo Horizonte

ATLANTIC OCEAN

MATO GROSSO DO SUL

PARAGUAY

Parana River

SÃO PAULO

São Paulo

ESPÍRITO SANTO

RIO DE JANEIRO

Rio de Janeiro

PARANÁ

Tropic of Capricorn

PACIFIC OCEAN

CHILE

ARGENTINA

SANTA CATARINA

RIO GRANDE DO SUL

Pôrto Alegre

URUGUAY

Equator

10°N

0°

10°S

20°S

70°W   60°W   50°W

	National border
	State border
★	National capital
•	Other cities

0   200   400 miles
0   200   400 kilometers

Government
1960 Brasília becomes Brazil's new capital.

Government
1985 Military rule ends in Brazil.

Today

History
▲ **1889** Brazil becomes a republic.

Culture
◀ **2002** Brazil wins its fifth World Cup in soccer.

Reading for Understanding

▶ Key Ideas

BEFORE, YOU LEARNED

Geography plays an important role in the economic activities of the countries of the Southern Cone.

NOW YOU WILL LEARN

Brazil's government is dealing with the problems resulting from urbanization.

▶ Vocabulary

TERMS & NAMES

Treaty of Tordesillas (TAWR•day•SEEL•yahs) 1494 treaty that gave Portugal control over land that is now part of Brazil

Pedro Álvares Cabral Portuguese explorer who in 1500 claimed land that is now part of Brazil for Portugal

Dom Pedro I Brazil's first Portuguese emperor; declared Brazil's independence from Portugal in 1822

Dom Pedro II second emperor of Brazil, under whose rule slavery was abolished in Brazil in 1888

favelas Brazilian name for the poor neighborhoods that surround the cities

Rio de Janeiro (REE•oh day zhuh•NAYR•OH) Brazil's capital city from 1763 to 1960

Brasília Brazil's current capital city

REVIEW

urbanization growth in the number of people living in urban areas

Visual Vocabulary
Dom Pedro I

▶ Reading Strategy

Re-create the time line shown at right. As you read and respond to the **KEY QUESTIONS**, use the time line to show the major events in Brazil's history and the development of a democratic government.

 See Skillbuilder Handbook, page R6

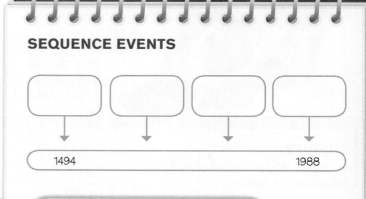

SEQUENCE EVENTS

1494   1988

GRAPHIC ORGANIZERS
Go to **Interactive Review** @ClassZone.com

From Portuguese Colony to Modern Giant

Connecting to Your World

What does the Statue of Liberty represent to you? For many people, it represents the United States, symbolizes freedom, and welcomes those who arrive at the nation's shores. In Brazil, a similar symbol is the statue of Christ the Redeemer, which welcomes people to Rio de Janeiro, Brazil's second largest city. Like the Statue of Liberty, it is one of the world's best-known and most-visited monuments.

Portuguese Build a Colony

▼ **KEY QUESTION** What helped to make Brazil a profitable colony for Portugal?

After Columbus' expeditions, Portugal feared that if Columbus had found a route to Asia, Spain might claim lands that Portugal had already claimed. So in 1494, both countries signed the **Treaty of Tordesillas** (TAWR•day•SEEL•yahs), which drew an imaginary line from north to south around the world. Spain could claim all lands west of the line, and Portugal those east of the line. This gave Portugal control of the land in what is now eastern Brazil. The treaty line is illustrated on the map on the next page.

Rio de Janeiro The statue of Christ the Redeemer overlooks Rio de Janeiro and Guanabara Bay. Sugarloaf Mountain is seen in the distance.

BRAZIL

Rio de Janeiro

Treaty of Tordesillas, 1494

EUROPE

PORTUGAL SPAIN

AFRICA

SOUTH
AMERICA

Portuguese

Spanish

| 0 | 1,500 | 3,000 miles |

| 0 | 1,500 | 3,000 kilometers |

CONNECT Geography & History

Region In 1494, which country claimed most of the lands in North and South America?

The Colony Expands In 1500, **Pedro Álvares Cabral** landed on the coast of what is now eastern Brazil and claimed the land for Portugal. Like the Spanish in South America, the Portuguese came to find gold and silver. When they found neither, Portuguese colonists cleared out large areas of the land to establish sugar cane plantations. The huge demand for sugar made it an important export and a source of wealth for Portugal.

The Portuguese later developed tobacco and cotton plantations and cattle ranches for meat and hides. They forced the indigenous people to work on the plantations and ranches. Many died from disease and overwork, and others fled into the rain forest. African slaves were brought in to replace them.

The discovery of gold in the late 1600s and diamonds in the early 1700s west of present-day Rio de Janeiro attracted many people farther inland. Coffee plants were introduced in Brazil in 1727, and by the mid-1800s coffee had become Brazil's chief export.

Independence to Republic Portugal controlled Brazil from 1500 to 1822. In 1807, the French ruler, Napoleon, invaded Portugal. As a result, Prince John, the Portuguese ruler, fled to Brazil and established a monarchy there.

In 1821, Prince John returned to Portugal, leaving his son, Pedro, in charge of the colony. Pedro and other officials declared Brazil's independence from Portugal in 1822, and Pedro became **Dom Pedro I**, Brazil's first emperor. Unpopular with the people, he returned to Portugal in 1831, and his son became Emperor **Dom Pedro II**.

Under Dom Pedro II's rule, Brazil started to become industrialized. Railroads and telegraph lines improved transportation and communication. Pedro II worked to end slavery, which was abolished in 1888. This angered wealthy plantation owners, who forced Pedro II to give up the throne. Brazil became a constitutional republic in 1889.

🔺 **FIND MAIN IDEA** Explain what made Brazil a profitable Portuguese colony.

Dom Pedro II

	UNITED STATES	**BRAZIL**
Type of Government	federal republic	federal republic
Branches of Government	legislative, executive, judicial	legislative, executive, judicial
Election of President	elected directly by the people and the electoral college	elected directly by the people; must win 50 percent plus one votes
Voting	voters must be at least 18 years old; voting is a choice	voters must be at least 16 years old; voting is mandatory for citizens ages 18 to 70

CRITICAL THINKING
1. **Compare** How are the Brazilian and U.S. governments alike?
2. **Contrast** How are elections different in the two countries?

Challenges of a Modern Nation

▼ **KEY QUESTION** What challenges does the government of Brazil face today?

After adopting a constitution in 1891 that was based on the U.S. constitution, Brazil struggled to establish a democratic government. Dictators and military leaders ruled the nation until 1985. Today's government faces the problem of **urbanization** and the wide gap between the nation's rich and poor.

Establishing a Democratic Government After military rule ended, Brazilians voted for a president for the first time since 1960. Today, Brazil is ruled by the constitution established in 1988.

Brazil's federal government includes an executive branch led by a president, a two-house legislature, and a court system. The country is divided into 26 states and a federal district in Brasília. Since Brazil has many political parties with different viewpoints, elected officials have to work with all the parties in order to rule effectively.

Urbanization During the last half of the 20th century, millions of people from rural areas moved to Brazil's cities in search of jobs. Brazil's urban population more than doubled between 1950 and 2000. Several of Brazil's cities are among the largest cities in the world in population. All but two of Brazil's heavily populated cities are located near Brazil's eastern coast.

São Paulo

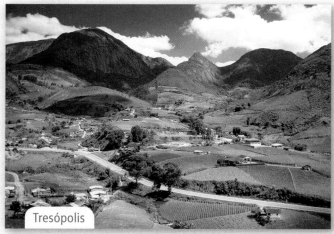

Tresópolis

Urban and Rural Populations *1950–2000*

1950 Total Population: 53,975,000

36%
64%

1975 Total Population: 108,124,000

38.8%
61.2%

2000 Total Population: 173,858,000

18.9%
81.1%

■ Urban ☐ Rural

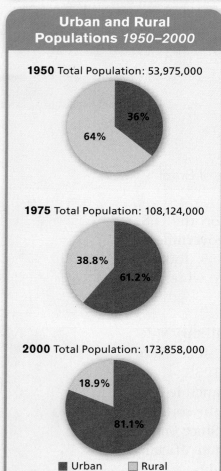

Population Density of Brazilian States

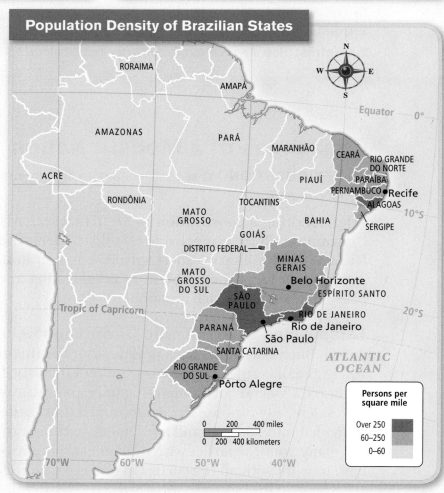

RORAIMA
AMAPÁ
Equator 0°
AMAZONAS
PARÁ
MARANHÃO
CEARÁ
RIO GRANDE DO NORTE
ACRE
PIAUÍ
PARAÍBA
PERNAMBUCO ● Recife
RONDÔNIA
TOCANTINS
ALAGOAS
10°S
MATO GROSSO
BAHIA
SERGIPE
GOIÁS
DISTRITO FEDERAL
MINAS GERAIS
MATO GROSSO DO SUL
Belo Horizonte
ESPÍRITO SANTO
SÃO PAULO
Tropic of Capricorn
RIO DE JANEIRO
20°S
PARANÁ
Rio de Janeiro
São Paulo
SANTA CATARINA
ATLANTIC OCEAN
RIO GRANDE DO SUL
Pôrto Alegre

0 200 400 miles
0 200 400 kilometers

Persons per square mile
Over 250
60–250
0–60

70°W 60°W 50°W 40°W

Source: Population Division of the Department of Economic and Social Affairs of the United Nations Secretariat, *World Population Prospects: The 2004 Revision* and *World Urbanization Prospects: The 2003 Revision*

CRITICAL THINKING

1. Draw Conclusions What is the population density in most of Brazil?

2. Evaluate About how many people lived in urban areas in Brazil in 2000?

Many poor Brazilians who moved from rural areas work at low-income jobs or are unemployed. Most live in neighborhoods called *favelas*, located on the outskirts of cities. In 1960 the Brazilian government moved the capital city from **Rio de Janeiro** (REE•oh day zhuh•NAYR•oh) to **Brasília**, about 600 miles inland. The Brazilian government has encouraged people to move inland, even offering land to people who are willing to move to the nation's interior.

Favela This *favela* is located outside of Rio de Janeiro. **Why might it be located there?**

Bridging the Gap Between Rich and Poor Today, Brazil has one of the largest economies in the world. However, one of the major challenges facing Brazil is how to bridge the large gap between the rich and poor. A small number of Brazilians live comfortably or in luxury, but most Brazilians are poor. Brazil has one of the most uneven distributions of land in the world. Two percent of landowners own most of the land, while more than half of Brazil's farmers work on less than three percent of the land. To help narrow the income gap, Brazil will have to create more jobs for the nation's poor.

 SUMMARIZE Discuss some of the challenges facing Brazil today.

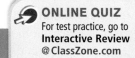

ONLINE QUIZ
For test practice, go to
Interactive Review
@ ClassZone.com

Section 1 Assessment

TERMS & NAMES

1. Explain the importance of
- Pedro Álvares Cabral
- *favela*
- Rio de Janeiro
- Brasília

USE YOUR READING NOTES

2. Sequence Events Use your time line to answer the following question:

How long after becoming a republic did military rule end in Brazil?

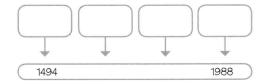

1494   1988

KEY IDEAS

3. What European nation developed Brazil as its colony?

4. Where do most people in Brazil live today?

5. Why did the Brazilian government offer land to people to move to the nation's interior?

CRITICAL THINKING

6. Make Inferences How has uneven land distribution contributed to poverty in Brazil?

7. Analyze Causes and Effects Why has urbanization resulted in the creation of *favelas* in Brazil's cities?

8. CONNECT to Today What is one action Brazil's government hopes to take to narrow the income gap between its rich and poor?

9. WRITING Write a Newspaper Article Research information about Brazil's government. Find out who is the current president, how the legislative branch is organized, and the term of office for both. Present your findings in the form of a newspaper article.

Reading for Understanding

▶ Key Ideas

BEFORE, YOU LEARNED

Brazil's government is dealing with problems resulting from urbanization.

NOW YOU WILL LEARN

Several cultures have influenced Brazil's unique culture.

▶ Vocabulary

TERMS & NAMES

Candomblé (kahn•duhm•BLEH) African religious practices that are mixed with Roman Catholic beliefs to produce a unique belief

quilombos (kih•LOHM•buhs) communities created by escaped African slaves

samba (SAM•buh) music and dance, with roots in African rhythms; the most famous form of Brazilian music worldwide

cuíca (kwee•kuh) a friction drum used in the samba

bossa nova (BAHS•uh NOH•vuh) a jazz version of the samba

capoeira (KAP•oh•AY•ruh) a Brazilian dance combined with martial arts

REVIEW

immigrant a person who leaves one area to settle in another

mural a wall painting

Visual Vocabulary *capoeira*

▶ Reading Strategy

Re-create the chart shown at right. As you read and respond to the **KEY QUESTIONS**, use the chart to organize important details about Brazil's people and culture.

 See Skillbuilder Handbook, page R7

CATEGORIZE

ART AND ARCHITECTURE	MUSIC	ENTERTAINMENT
1.	1.	1.
2.	2.	2.
3.	3.	3.

 GRAPHIC ORGANIZERS
Go to **Interactive Review** @ ClassZone.com

A Multicultural Society

Connecting to Your World

Think about some of the foods you eat. Think about the music that you and your family enjoy. Chances are that many of the foods you enjoy and the music you listen to have their roots in a variety of cultures. If you visited Brazil, you would see how a variety of cultures has also influenced the foods, music, and other aspects of Brazilian culture today.

A Blend of Many Cultures

▼ **KEY QUESTION** What cultures have most influenced Brazil?

Brazilian culture includes European, African, Asian, and Indian influences. Portuguese is the official language. Most Brazilians are Roman Catholic. At the same time, Brazilians of African ancestry mix ***Candomblé*** (kahn•duhm•BLEH), West African religious practices, with Catholicism to create a unique Brazilian blend.

Brazilian Diversity
These Brazilian girls are getting ready to participate in Carnival in Rio de Janeiro.

Daniel Munduruku is a Munduruku Indian. He has written several books about his culture. Here he describes learning the ancient myths of his people.

When I was a . . . boy, my grandfather would . . . tell the stories that explained the origins of our people and the vision of the universe. . . . Now . . . I realize that those ancient myths say what cannot be said. They are pure poetry, and through them I see how an identity can be created in the oral tradition.

Source: *Tales of the Amazon, How the Munduruku Indians Live*

CRITICAL THINKING

Summarize How is storytelling important in the Munduruku culture?

Native Brazilians Up to 6 million Indians lived in Brazil before the Portuguese arrived. Tens of thousands died from diseases brought by the European colonists. Today, only about 700,000 Indians live in Brazil, mostly in the Amazon rain forest. They make up less than one percent of Brazil's population. The Tupi and Guarani make up the largest groups. Other tribes, such as the Yanomami and Bororo, still follow traditional ways of hunting and farming.

The Brazilian government has set up reservations to protect these cultures. But even isolated groups now have contact with outsiders, such as miners, loggers, and researchers, who move into the area to study native cultures. This increased contact threatens the groups' traditional ways of life, arts, crafts, and languages.

Yanomami Woman A Yanomami woman poses with her child. **How might being photographed threaten the Yanomami's traditional way of life?**

Africans Today, most Brazilians with African ancestry live in the nation's northern and coastal regions and make up about 6 percent of the population. The Portuguese brought Africans to Brazil between the 1500s and 1800s to work on the sugar plantations. In fact, of all the slaves brought to North and South America, more than a third were brought to Brazil.

Some of these slaves escaped to freedom in Brazil's inland northern region, where they established communities that were similar to their African homes. They called the settlements **quilombos** (kih•LOHM•buhs), an African word for "housing." By the end of the 1600s, as many as 25,000 Africans may have lived in these communities. *Quilombos* can still be found in parts of Brazil today, particularly in the northern part, where people continue their traditional way of life. Today most Brazilians of African ancestry live in the northeastern state of Bahia. Its capital, Salvador, was the center of the Portuguese empire, sugar industry, and slave trade.

African influences are evident in various parts of Brazilian culture. African slaves created Brazil's national food, *feijoada* (fayh•zhoo•AH•duh), a bean stew. African rhythms play an important role in Brazilian music. Brazil's art and literature also reflect an African influence.

Europeans and Asians In the 1700s, Europeans viewed Brazil as a place to acquire wealth. With the discovery of gold and diamonds, many immigrated to Brazil to make their fortunes. After Brazil declared its independence, many Europeans, including Italians, Spanish, Portuguese, and Germans, came to work in Brazil, mostly in the coffee industry. Today, people of European ancestry make up about half of Brazil's population. Most live in the southern part of the country.

Japanese **immigrants** first began arriving in Brazil in the early 1900s. Most came to work on coffee or tea farms. More Japanese arrived after World War II. Today Brazil has the largest Japanese population outside of Japan, with most making their homes in the state of São Paulo. In recent years, Asians from China and Korea have also immigrated to Brazil.

▲ **EVALUATE** Explain how Brazil's culture is a blend of several cultures.

CONNECT History & Culture

African Influence on Brazilian Food

Since most slaves brought to Brazil arrived from West Africa, West African cooking has had a strong influence on Brazilian food. Palm oil, called *dendê*, and chili peppers, called *malagueta*, are basic West African cooking ingredients. Today, Bahian cooks make *moqueca*, a popular stew. It is made with seafood, coconut, garlic, onion, parsley, *malagueta*, and *dendê*.

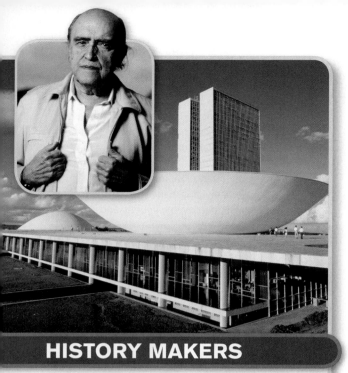

Arts and Entertainment

▼ **KEY QUESTION** What are some ways Brazilians enjoy holidays and leisure time?

Brazil's art, literature, music, and celebrations reflect the nation's blend of cultural traditions. Brazil's Carnival, in particular, highlights Brazil's cultural diversity.

Architecture and Art Brazil's earliest art included the crafts made by Brazil's Indian groups. Their work included such items as pottery, baskets, and jewelry. Native American groups today continue to make these handicrafts, many of which are sold to tourists in Brazilian markets.

António Francisco Lisboa, known as Aleijadinho, is a well known sculptor of the colonial period. He created religious sculptures for many churches in the mid- to late 1700s. Today, Mario Cravo Junior is an important sculptor who creates statues made with concrete.

Cândido Portinari is a famous Brazilian painter and muralist. His six largest **murals** are found in New York's United Nations building and in Washington's Library of Congress. Much of his art reflects rural life and social concerns.

Brazil is the home of Oscar Niemeyer, one of the world's most famous architects. He is best known for designing several buildings in Brasília, Brazil's capital. Niemeyer has also designed a variety of buildings in several countries throughout the world, including France, Ghana, Israel, and Lebanon. More recently, Niemeyer created a unique design for an art museum near the city of Rio de Janeiro.

Music and Dance Brazilian music is a blend of African, European, and Indian cultures. Brazilians enjoy dancing to the **samba** (SAM•buh), the most famous form of Brazilian music. The samba developed in the early 1900s and has its roots in African rhythms. The samba has many forms, but the most popular is the street samba danced during the celebrations of Carnival, a Brazilian holiday. The drum plays a major role in Brazilian music. Brazilian drums come in many shapes and sizes, each producing its own sound and rhythm. Drummers play the surdo, a bass drum, and the **cuíca** (kwee•kuh), a friction drum, to create samba rhythms.

Worldster

A Day in Pedro's Life

To learn more about Pedro and his world, go to the **Activity Center** @ ClassZone.com

This is how to say "Hello, my name is Pedro" in Portuguese:

"Oi, meu nome é Pedro."

Hi! My name is Pedro. I am 13 years old and live in São Paulo, the largest city in Brazil and the third largest city in the world in population. I attend a public school, a short walk from my apartment. Many of my friends live in the same apartment building, so there's always someone to do things with. Let me tell you about my day.

6 A.M. My family and I have breakfast before my parents go to work and my sister and I go to school. Today we're having cereal and papaya.

7 A.M.–noon My school day begins early. Because of overcrowded schools, many students go to school in two shifts. I like having the morning shift. My school year runs from March to December.

1 P.M. My family and I get together for the main meal of the day. Today I'm looking forward to *feijoada*, which is a dish made with black beans and beef.

6 P.M. After I finish my homework and have a small snack, I'm off to the local park to play soccer. Next to playing the game, my favorite thing to do is to watch our city's professional team play soccer.

CONNECT to Your Life

Journal Entry Think about your typical daily schedule. How are the meals you eat and the time you eat the same as and different from Pedro's? Record your ideas in your journal.

The *cuíca* and other percussion instruments create the energetic sounds of the samba during Carnival celebrations (shown below). The *cuíca* is an African friction drum made by attaching a stick to the center of a drum skin. The drummer holds the drum in one hand and puts the other arm inside the drum. The sound is made by rubbing the stick with a wet piece of cloth or leather. When the stick is rubbed, the drum skin vibrates, producing a distinctive sound.

▲ *The inside of a cuíca*

Make a *Cuíca*

Materials
• plastic cup or strong food container
• nail
• waxed dental floss

1. With a nail, make two holes, about an inch apart , in the bottom of the cup or container.

2. Push a three-foot piece of dental floss through both holes and make sure the two ends of the floss are the same length.

3. Tie the two ends into a knot as close to the hole inside the cup as possible so the string doesn't slip out.

4. Hold the cup in one hand and slide your fingers along the string with the other to make your own *cuíca* music.

Another popular form of Brazilian music and dance is the **bossa nova** (BAHS•uh NOH•vuh). It mixes the samba beat with the sounds of jazz. Brazilian jazz musicians popularized the bossa nova in the rest of the world. Brazilian samba-reggae is a popular form of music based on African drum traditions. **Capoeira** (kap•oh•AY•ruh) combines dance and the martial arts. It developed in Brazil from African origins. During Portuguese rule, the Portuguese forbade the African slaves to fight. So the Africans created fight dances, which developed into *capoeira*.

Festivals Brazilians are known for Carnival, celebrated every year for four days before the beginning of the Christian season of Lent. The holiday combines a Roman Catholic festival with African celebrations and includes parades and street parties. The world's most famous Carnival takes place in Rio de Janeiro. Thousands of spectators line the streets to watch costumed people ride elaborately decorated floats. In clubs and other places, thousands of dancers, who have been practicing for months, participate in samba dance competitions.

Recreation Brazil's thousands of miles of coastline provide extensive sandy beaches. On weekends, thousands of Brazilian families flock to the beaches to swim and enjoy picnics. Copacabana Beach in Rio de Janeiro attracts millions of tourists every year.

Brazil's most famous sport is football (soccer). It is played everywhere—in cities, beaches, and rural areas. People of all ages play it for fun. Professional football teams draw huge crowds of enthusiastic fans in football stadiums in many Brazilian cities. Maracana Stadium in Rio de Janeiro, one of the world's largest stadiums, holds more than 150,000 people. Brazil's teams have produced some of the world's top football players, such as Pelé and Ronaldo. Brazil's national football team has won 5 of the 17 World Cups ever awarded, the most for any football team. The World Cup is a trophy awarded to a nation's football team for winning the world championship.

Beach in Recife, Brazil
Children enjoy playing in the waters of Boa Viagem beach, a popular beach in Recife.

▲ **SUMMARIZE** Describe the ways Brazilians enjoy holidays and their leisure time.

Section 2 Assessment

🧲 **ONLINE QUIZ**
For test practice, go to **Interactive Review** @ClassZone.com

TERMS & NAMES

1. Explain the importance of
- *Candomblé*
- *quilombos*
- *cuíca*
- *capoeira*

USE YOUR READING NOTES

2. Categorize Use your completed chart to answer the following question.

What contributions has Oscar Niemeyer made to Brazilian culture?

ART AND ARCHITECTURE	MUSIC	ENTERTAINMENT
1.	1.	1.
2.	2.	2.
3.	3.	3.

KEY IDEAS

3. What four cultures have contributed to modern Brazilian culture?

4. Where do most Brazilians of African ancestry live?

5. What type of music and dance is identified worldwide as Brazilian?

CRITICAL THINKING

6. Make Inferences Why are the traditional ways of life of some Indian groups in Brazil threatened?

7. Draw Conclusions How have Africans contributed to Brazilian culture?

8. CONNECT to Today Why do you think the Brazilian government has set up reservations to protect traditional Indian cultures?

9. ART Make a Collage Create a collage that illustrates ways people enjoy themselves in Brazil. Use the information in the section as well as in other sources. Then make a collage that features the various sources of entertainment in Brazil.

Reading for Understanding

▶ Key Ideas

BEFORE, YOU LEARNED

The culture of Brazil today is a blend of many cultures.

NOW YOU WILL LEARN

An abundance of natural resources helps make Brazil a major industrial nation.

▶ Vocabulary

TERMS & NAMES

hydroelectricity electric power generated by water

ethanol (EHTH•uh•NAWL) a liquid made by using a chemical process to convert sugar cane to a kind of alcohol that can be used for fuel

deforestation the cutting and clearing away of trees

boycott to stop buying and using products from certain sources as a way of protest

REVIEW

economy a system for producing and exchanging goods and services among a group of people

export a product or resource sold to another country

rain forest a broadleaf-tree region in a tropical climate

global warming an increase in the average temperature of the Earth's atmosphere

BACKGROUND VOCABULARY

mechanized equipped with machinery

self-sufficient able to provide for one's own needs without outside help

▶ Reading Strategy

Re-create the web diagram shown at right. As you read and respond to the **KEY QUESTIONS**, use the diagram to organize main ideas and details about Brazil's economy.

 See Skillbuilder Handbook, page R4

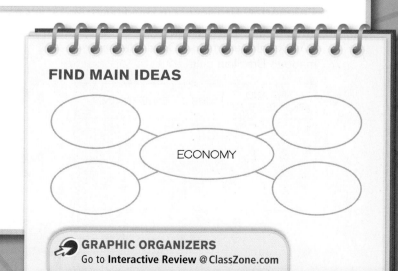

FIND MAIN IDEAS

ECONOMY

GRAPHIC ORGANIZERS
Go to **Interactive Review** @ ClassZone.com

Developing an Abundant Land

Connecting to Your World

In the early 1900s, Henry Ford invented a way to manufacture cars that would make them affordable for most people. His invention sparked the U.S. automobile industry and made the United States a major producer of automobiles. Today Brazil has become a leading maker of automobiles in the world and one of the most industrialized countries in South America.

Creating an Economic Giant

▼ **KEY QUESTION** What factors have helped Brazil become an important industrial nation?

Brazil's **economy** is the largest in South America and one of the largest in the world. Brazil's climate makes it possible for the nation to grow a wide range of crops. The abundance of natural resources, used to develop a variety of industries and manufactured goods, has helped to make Brazil a growing economic power. **Hydroelectricity**, or electric power generated by water, is provided by power plants along the Amazon River and many other rivers flowing through Brazil. Hydroelectricity supplies most of the energy needed to run these industries.

Itaipu Dam The dam, built on the Paraná River, provides about 25 percent of Brazil's power.

Agriculture About one-fifth of Brazil's workers are employed in agriculture. Most farming and livestock grazing takes place in the southern and southeastern parts of Brazil, which have the nation's best soil and climate for agriculture. Farms and ranches in this part of Brazil are generally large and **mechanized**. Farms in the northern part of Brazil, however, are smaller and generally depend on manual labor to produce crops.

Brazil is one of the world's leading exporters of agricultural products, second only to the United States. Brazil is the world's largest producer of sugar cane and coffee. It is a major producer of soybeans (the nation's primary farm **export**), oranges, wheat, corn, and beef, as well as a world leader in the raising of cattle, hogs, and poultry.

Industries Brazil is rich in minerals, and a major producer of the world's gold and diamonds. Brazil has large deposits of iron, manganese, and bauxite, which are important raw materials used in manufacturing. Most large manufacturing plants are located in Brazil's southeastern section. In recent years, Brazil has invested in high-tech equipment to run its manufacturing industries, which employ about 10 percent of its workers. Brazil has one of the largest steel plants in Latin America and is a world leader in automobile production.

CONNECT ➤ Geography & Economics

Deforestation More than half of the Amazon rain forest is located in Brazil. As Brazil's economy developed, many people moved to the Amazon region to develop its resources. Several economic activities have contributed to deforestation, including:

- logging by the timber industry to export woods such as mahogany
- clearing the forests for raising crops and livestock and for housing
- mining minerals for export and as raw materials

CRITICAL THINKING

Make Inferences How might the opportunity to make money contribute to deforestation?

Slash-and-Burn Agriculture Trees in the Amazon rain forest are burned to clear the land for farming and ranching.

Service industries employ about half of Brazil's workers. Many Brazilians work for government agencies, hotels and restaurants, and stores.

Brazil is leading the way in becoming energy **self-sufficient**. Hydroelectric power from Brazil's major rivers provide most of the nation's energy needs. In fact, Brazil expects to become energy-independent in the near future.

▲ **ANALYZE CAUSES AND EFFECTS** Explain why Brazil has become an important industrial nation.

Preserving the Rain Forest

▼ **KEY QUESTION** Why is preserving the rain forest important?

The Amazon **rain forest**, the world's largest rain forest, covers one-third of South America. In the past, rain forests covered about 14 percent of the Earth's surface. Today, because of **deforestation**, the cutting down and clearing away of trees, rain forests cover only 6 percent of the Earth's surface.

Sloth The sloth makes its home in the treetops of the rain forest. **How might deforestation affect this animal?**

Logging in the Rain Forest Although today logging in the Amazon rain forest is controlled by the Brazilian government, illegal logging continues.

Endangering Ways of Life Deforestation threatens the homes and ways of life of some of the people who live in the rain forests.

Why Save It? You read earlier in this book that the rain forest is an important resource. Rain forests help to regulate the world's climate by absorbing carbon dioxide and producing oxygen. As trees are cut down, less carbon dioxide is absorbed, which contributes to **global warming**. Rain forests are home to millions of species of plants and animals, more than half of the world's species. Many medicines are made from rain-forest plants. Destroying rain forests endangers the traditional ways of life of some of the people who live there.

Preserving the Brazilian Rain Forest These children are planting trees to reverse the effects of deforestation.

What Is Being Done? Many governments, groups, and individuals are working to preserve the rain forests. Recently, Brazil's government presented plans to declare about 193,000 square miles of the Amazon rain forest a protected area. Some groups raise money to buy land to create large rain forest reserves. Some organize protests against plans that might result in deforestation. Others organize boycotts of products that destroy the forests. To **boycott** is to stop buying or using certain products as a form of protest. Still others work to educate people about the importance of rain forests to the world.

 SUMMARIZE Explain why preserving rain forests is important.

Section 3 Assessment

ONLINE QUIZ
For test practice, go to
Interactive Review
@ ClassZone.com

TERMS & NAMES

1. **Explain the importance of**
   • hydroelectricity
   • ethanol
   • deforestation
   • boycott

USE YOUR READING NOTES

2. **Find Main Ideas** Use your web diagram to answer the following question:

   What industry employs half of Brazilian workers?

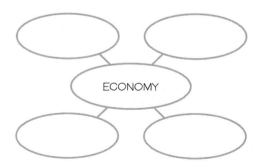

ECONOMY

KEY IDEAS

3. What is Brazil's major export crop?

4. Where does most farming take place in Brazil?

5. How is Brazil becoming energy self-sufficient?

CRITICAL THINKING

6. **Analyze Causes and Effects** What effect has rain-forest deforestation had on the world's climate?

7. **Identify Problems and Solutions** What do you think is the best solution for curbing the deforestation of rain forests?

8. **CONNECT to Today** Brazil is becoming energy-independent. What effect might that have on Brazil's economy?

9. **LANGUAGE ARTS** **Write a Slogan** Imagine that you are working for an organization dedicated to preserving the rain forest. Write a slogan for the organization to use to educate people about the reasons that preserving rain forests is important.

Click here to complete these and other activities online @ ClassZone.com

CHAPTER SUMMARY

Key Idea 1
Brazil's government is dealing with the problems resulting from urbanization.

Key Idea 2
Several cultures have influenced Brazil's unique culture.

Key Idea 3
An abundance of natural resources helps make Brazil a major industrial nation.

For **Review and Study Notes**, go to **Interactive Review @ ClassZone.com**

NAME GAME

Use the Terms & Names list to complete each sentence on paper or online.

1. I am the capital of Brazil. __Brasília__ 🖑

2. I am a community created by escaped African slaves. _____

3. I am the first emperor of Brazil.
   _____

4. I am a government official who helped abolish slavery in Brazil. _____

5. I am the city famous for Carnival.
   _____

6. I am the music of Brazil that is best known worldwide. _____

7. I am a neighborhood located in areas surrounding big cities.
   _____

8. I am a cleaner, renewable fuel for cars.
   _____

9. I am a religious practice brought from Africa to Brazil. _____

10. I destroy millions of acres of forest.
    _____

Brasília
Candomblé
capoeira
cuíca
deforestation
Dom Pedro I
Dom Pedro II
ethanol
favela
quilombo
Rio de Janeiro
samba

Activities

Flip Cards

Use the online flip cards to quiz yourself on the terms and names introduced in this chapter.

Pedro Álvares Cabral

? Portuguese explorer who claimed Brazil for Portugal

Crossword Puzzle

Complete an online puzzle to test your knowledge of Brazil's history, economy, and culture.

ACROSS
1. friction drum used in the samba

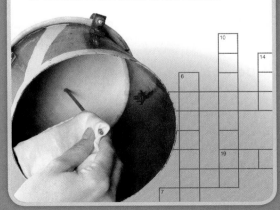

VOCABULARY

Explain the significance of each of the following.

1. Treaty of Tordesillas
2. Pedro Álvares Cabral
3. Dom Pedro I
4. Dom Pedro II
5. Brasília
6. Rio de Janeiro
7. hydroelectricity
8. ethanol
9. deforestation
10. boycott

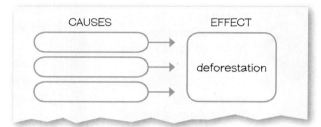

Explain how the terms and names in each group are related.

11. *Candomblé, cuíca,* and *quilombos*
12. samba and *capoeira*

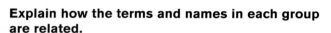

KEY IDEAS

1 From Portuguese Colony to Modern Giant

13. What explorer claimed Brazil for Portugal?
14. How did Brazil become independent?
15. What is Brazil's biggest economic challenge?
16. How has Brazil's urban population changed in the last half of the 20th century?

2 A Multicultural Society

17. What Portuguese influences are seen in Brazil today?
18. Where does the largest Japanese population live in Brazil today?
19. How have Africans influenced Brazilian culture?
20. Why is Carnival considered a blend of European and African traditions?

3 Developing an Abundant Land

21. How has having an abundance of natural resources benefited Brazil?
22. Why does most farming and ranching in Brazil take place in the southern and southeastern parts?
23. What provides most of Brazil's energy needs?
24. What actions are people taking today to help preserve the rain forest?

CRITICAL THINKING

25. **Analyze Causes and Effects** Create a diagram to explain the causes of deforestation of the Amazon rain forest.

CAUSES	EFFECT
⟶	
⟶	deforestation
⟶	

26. **Evaluate** How did the introduction of coffee plants in Brazil affect its economy?
27. **Summarize** What did Brazil's government do to try to relieve overcrowding in its cities?
28. **Five Themes: Human-Environment Interaction** How might deforestation affect the Indians of the Amazon rain forest?
29. **Connect to Economics** Why is narrowing the income gap important for Brazil's government to address?
30. **Connect Geography & History** What historical events have contributed to Brazil's cultural diversity?

Answer the ESSENTIAL QUESTION

How have Brazil's people used the country's abundant natural resources to make Brazil an economic giant?

Written response Write a two- or three-paragraph response to the Essential Question. Be sure to consider the key ideas of each section. Use the rubric below to guide your thinking.

Response Rubric
A strong response will:
- include how Brazil's natural resources have contributed to the growth of industries
- explain how Brazilian Indians, Africans, and European and Asian immigrants have helped make Brazil an economic power

PRIMARY SOURCE

Use the primary source below to answer questions 1 and 2.

It is not just those who depend directly on the tropical forests who suffer from deforestation, but the entire population of tropical forest countries. The forests assist in the regulation of local climate patterns, protecting watersheds, preventing floods, guaranteeing and controlling huge flows of life-giving water. Strip away the forests and there is, first, too much water . . . and then too little.

Source: Charles, Prince of Wales, from a speech given on February 6, 1990

1. What observation does the passage support?

A. Deforestation hurts no one.
B. Deforestation prevents flooding.
C. Rain forests help to prevent floods.
D. Rain forests affect only a few people.

2. What is the best title for this passage?

A. Prince Charles Helps the Rain Forests
B. Where Are the Rain Forests?
C. Deforestation—Is It Serious?
D. The Rain Forest and Water Supply

LINE GRAPH

Use the graph below to answer questions 3 and 4.

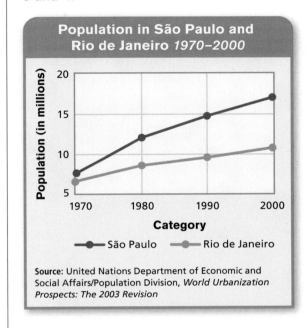

Population in São Paulo and Rio de Janeiro 1970–2000

Source: United Nations Department of Economic and Social Affairs/Population Division, *World Urbanization Prospects: The 2003 Revision*

3. What was the population of Rio de Janeiro in 2000?

4. Between what years did São Paulo's population increase the most?

GeoActivity

1. INTERDISCIPLINARY ACTIVITY–SCIENCE

Research the four layers of a tropical rain forest. Find out the differences in the four layers, the kinds of plants that grow there, and the kinds of animals that live in each layer. Include a diagram to illustrate the four layers.

2. WRITING FOR SOCIAL STUDIES

Unit Writing Project Decide on the place from your journal that you found most interesting, and find more information about it. Then write an article for a travel magazine describing the place and giving reasons for people to visit it.

3. MENTAL MAPPING

Create an outline map of Brazil and label the following:

• Bahia
• Salvador
• São Paulo
• Brasília
• Rio de Janeiro
• The Amazon River

UNIT 4

Europe

Why It Matters:

In the past, Europeans used the oceans and seas to make voyages for trade and to build empires. Their culture spread around the world. Today, Europeans still play a large part in world affairs.

The Alps

CHAPTER 11 **Europe:** Physical Geography and History

Notre Dame Cathedral

CHAPTER 12 Western Europe

London Street Scene

CHAPTER 13 United Kingdom

Prague, Czech Republic

CHAPTER 14 Eastern Europe

Europe

Europe occupies the western portion of the Eurasian landmass. Many people view the Ural Mountains as the eastern border of Europe, which means that Europe includes part of Russia. However, for historic and cultural reasons, Russia and the Eurasian republics are not considered in this unit.

As you study the graphs on this page, compare the landmass, population, rivers, and mountains of Europe with those of the United States and the world. Then jot down the answers to the following questions in your notebook.

Comparing Data

1. How does Europe compare in size to the United States?

2. Is Europe's population bigger or smaller than that of the United States? Given what you know about Europe's size, do you think that makes Europe more or less densely populated than the United States?

3. How does the Danube River compare to the Mississippi River in the United States?

4. What is the tallest peak in Europe? Is it taller or shorter than Mt. McKinley, the tallest mountain in the United States?

Comparing Data

Landmass

Europe — 2,276,109 sq. mi.

Continental United States — 3,165,630 sq. mi.

Population

Europe 584,413,424

United States 296,410,404

Population (in millions): 0, 100, 200, 300, 400, 500, 600

Rivers

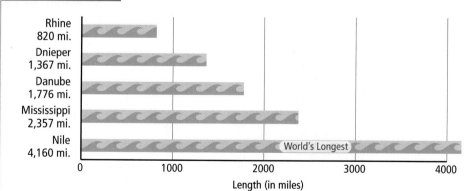

Rhine 820 mi.
Dnieper 1,367 mi.
Danube 1,776 mi.
Mississippi 2,357 mi.
Nile 4,160 mi. — World's Longest

Length (in miles): 0, 1000, 2000, 3000, 4000

Mountains

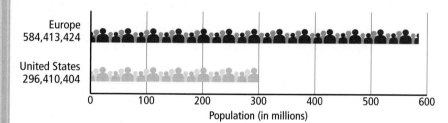

World's Tallest
Mt. Everest
Nepal-Tibet
29,035 ft.

U.S. Tallest
Mt. McKinley
United States
20,320 ft.

Mont Blanc
France-Italy
15,771 ft.

Monte Rosa
Switzerland-Italy
15,203 ft.

Dom
Switzerland
14,913 ft.

Population Density

Persons per square mile

- Over 520
- 260–519
- 130–259
- 25–129
- 1–24
- 0

Arctic Circle

Norwegian Sea

North Sea

Baltic Sea

ATLANTIC OCEAN

Bay of Biscay

Mediterranean Sea

Adriatic Sea

Black Sea

Oslo
Stockholm
Helsinki
Manchester
London
Amsterdam
Brussels
Berlin
Warsaw
Leipzig
Kiev
Paris
Milan
Budapest
Belgrade
Bucharest
Lisbon
Madrid
Rome
Naples
Athens

60°N
50°N
40°N
30°N
0°
10°E
20°E

0   125   250 miles
0   125   250 kilometers

THINK LIKE A GEOGRAPHER

1. **Place** Where on the continent is the population density highest?

2. **Region** Which is less densely populated, far northern or far southern Europe?

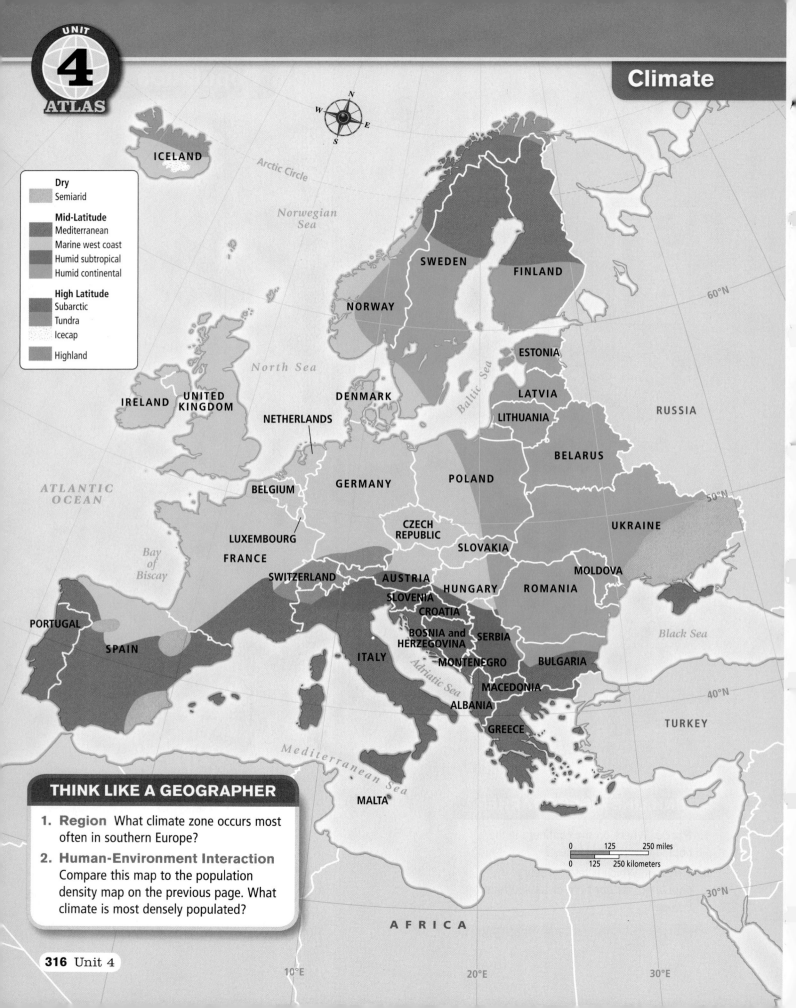

Dry
Semiarid

Mid-Latitude
Mediterranean
Marine west coast
Humid subtropical
Humid continental

High Latitude
Subarctic
Tundra
Icecap

Highland

ICELAND

Arctic Circle

Norwegian
Sea

SWEDEN

FINLAND

60°N

NORWAY

ESTONIA

North Sea

Baltic Sea

LATVIA

RUSSIA

IRELAND
UNITED
KINGDOM

DENMARK

LITHUANIA

NETHERLANDS

BELARUS

ATLANTIC
OCEAN

BELGIUM

GERMANY

POLAND

50°N

CZECH
REPUBLIC

UKRAINE

LUXEMBOURG

SLOVAKIA

Bay
of
Biscay

FRANCE

MOLDOVA

SWITZERLAND

AUSTRIA

HUNGARY

ROMANIA

SLOVENIA

CROATIA

PORTUGAL

BOSNIA and
HERZEGOVINA

SERBIA

Black Sea

SPAIN

MONTENEGRO

BULGARIA

ITALY

Adriatic Sea

MACEDONIA

40°N

ALBANIA

TURKEY

GREECE

Mediterranean Sea

MALTA

THINK LIKE A GEOGRAPHER

1. **Region** What climate zone occurs most
often in southern Europe?

2. **Human-Environment Interaction**
Compare this map to the population
density map on the previous page. What
climate is most densely populated?

0   125   250 miles
0   125   250 kilometers

AFRICA

30°N

10°E

20°E

30°E

ICELAND

Arctic Circle

Norwegian Sea

SWEDEN

FINLAND

NORWAY

North Sea

Stockholm

ESTONIA

LATVIA

LITHUANIA

RUSSIA

DENMARK

IRELAND

UNITED KINGDOM

Birmingham

NETHERLANDS

Amsterdam/Rotterdam

London

BELGIUM

GERMANY

Essen

POLAND

BELARUS

ATLANTIC OCEAN

Paris

LUXEMBOURG

FRANCE

Munich

CZECH REPUBLIC

Katowice

UKRAINE

Donetsk

50°N

Bay of Biscay

SWITZERLAND

AUSTRIA

SLOVAKIA

MOLDOVA

Milan

SLOVENIA

HUNGARY

ROMANIA

PORTUGAL

SPAIN

Marseille

CROATIA

Black Sea

Barcelona

ITALY

BOSNIA and HERZEGOVINA

MONTENEGRO

SERBIA

BULGARIA

Adriatic Sea

MACEDONIA

40°N

ALBANIA

TURKEY

GREECE

Mediterranean Sea

MALTA

Land use
- Commercial agriculture
- Dairying
- Livestock raising
- Nomadic herding
- Forestland
- Limited agriculture

Major resources
- Bauxite
- Coal
- Fish
- Iron ore
- Natural gas
- Oil
- Other minerals
- Timber
- Uranium
- Manufacturing center

0   125   250 miles
0   125   250 kilometers

THINK LIKE A GEOGRAPHER

1. **Human-Environment Interaction** What activity is the majority of the land in Europe used for?

2. **Region** Which sea is the source of many of Europe's energy resources? What countries are most likely to benefit from these resources?

AFRICA

0°   10°E   20°E   30°E

30°N

Regional Overview

UNIT 4 ATLAS

Europe

Europe is the world's second smallest continent in area, but one of the largest in population. The population is diverse, with many different cultures developing on the small landmass. The chapters in this unit provide more information about the geography, history, culture, government, and economics of Europe.

GEOGRAPHY

Europe extends from the Arctic Ocean in the north to the Mediterranean Sea in the south. Geographically, the European continent stretches from the Atlantic Ocean all the way to the Ural Mountains in Russia, but in this unit, we will mark Europe's western border where Russia begins.

HISTORY

For centuries, different groups of people settled, lived in, and fought over the lands of Europe. Though some regions are still troubled by conflict, Europe is more unified than ever before.

CULTURE

Since the time of the ancient Greeks and Romans, Europe's culture has had a global influence. European ideas about politics, science, art, philosophy, and religion have spread around the world.

GOVERNMENT

The governments of Europe come in all shapes and sizes. Some are democracies. Other nations have monarchs who govern alongside a parliament chosen by the people.

ECONOMICS

Europe has many natural resources and abundant farmland that strengthen its economies. Many European countries are also highly industrialized. The European Union has worked to continue Europe's role as an economic power.

Leaning Tower of Pisa Construction started on this Italian monument in 1173. It began to tilt when only three of its eight stories were completed.

Country Almanac

 Click here to compare the most recent data on countries @ ClassZone.com

Unit Writing Project

Imagine that your class is planning a trip to Europe. Choose a country from this unit that you would like to visit. Write a persuasive speech to convince your classmates to pick your country for their trip.

Think About:

- specific sites you would visit
- the people you would meet
- how it differs from your home

Europe

Europe is made up of 43 different countries.

Albania

GEOGRAPHY
Capital: Tiranë
Total Area: 11,100 sq. mi.
Population: 3,130,000
ECONOMY
Imports: food; machinery; minerals; clothing
Exports: clothing; metals
CULTURE
Language: Albanian
Religion: Muslim 39%; Catholic 17%

Andorra

GEOGRAPHY
Capital: Andorra la Vella
Total Area: 181 sq. mi.
Population: 70,549
ECONOMY
Imports: food; tobacco; machinery
Exports: motor vehicles; photo equipment
CULTURE
Language: Catalan
Religion: Catholic 89%; nonreligious 5%

Austria

GEOGRAPHY
Capital: Vienna
Total Area: 32,382 sq. mi.
Population: 8,189,000
ECONOMY
Imports: machinery; vehicles; chemicals
Exports: transportation equipment; steel
CULTURE
Language: German
Religion: Catholic 75%; nonreligious 9%; Protestant 5%

Belgium

GEOGRAPHY
Capital: Brussels
Total Area: 11,787 sq. mi.
Population: 10,419,000
ECONOMY
Imports: machinery; medicine; food
Exports: machinery; vehicles; medicine
CULTURE
Language: Dutch; French; German
Religion: Catholic 88%; Muslim 3%

Belarus

GEOGRAPHY
Capital: Minsk
Total Area: 80,155 sq. mi.
Population: 9,755,000
ECONOMY
Imports: petroleum; chemicals; food
Exports: food; petroleum; road vehicles
CULTURE
Language: Belarusian; Russian
Religion: Belarusian Orthodox 32%; Catholic 18%

Bosnia and Herzegovina

GEOGRAPHY
Capital: Sarajevo
Total Area: 19,741 sq. mi.
Population: 3,907,000
ECONOMY
Imports: machinery; chemicals; fuels
Exports: metals; clothing; wood products
CULTURE
Language: Bosnian
Religion: Sunni Muslim 43%; Serbian Orthodox 30%; Catholic 18%

Bulgaria

GEOGRAPHY
Capital: Sofia
Total Area: 42,823 sq. mi.
Population: 7,726,000
ECONOMY
Imports: textiles; crude petroleum; plastics
Exports: clothing; metals; mineral fuels
CULTURE
Language: Bulgarian
Religion: Bulgarian Orthodox 72%; Sunni Muslim 12%

Croatia

GEOGRAPHY
Capital: Zagreb
Total Area: 21,831 sq. mi.
Population: 4,551,000
ECONOMY
Imports: machinery; metals; petroleum
Exports: chemicals; clothing; petroleum
CULTURE
Language: Croatian
Religion: Catholic 89%; Eastern Orthodox 6%; Sunni Muslim 2%

Czech Republic

GEOGRAPHY
Capital: Prague
Total Area: 30,450 sq. mi.
Population: 10,220,000

ECONOMY
Imports: machinery; chemicals; vehicles
Exports: computers; vehicles; metals

CULTURE
Language: Czech
Religion: Catholic 40%; nonreligious 32%; Protestant 3%

Denmark

GEOGRAPHY
Capital: Copenhagen
Total Area: 16,639 sq. mi.
Population: 5,431,000

ECONOMY
Imports: machinery; food; tobacco
Exports: agricultural products; swine

CULTURE
Language: Danish
Religion: Evangelical Lutheran 86%; Muslim 2%

Estonia

GEOGRAPHY
Capital: Tallinn
Total Area: 17,462 sq. mi.
Population: 1,330,000

ECONOMY
Imports: textiles; food
Exports: wood; textiles; paper

CULTURE
Language: Estonian
Religion: Orthodox 20%; Evangelical Lutheran 14%

Finland

GEOGRAPHY
Capital: Helsinki
Total Area: 130,559 sq. mi.
Population: 5,249,000

ECONOMY
Imports: machinery; mineral fuels; vehicles
Exports: paper products; wood products

CULTURE
Language: Finnish; Swedish
Religion: Evangelical Lutheran 85%; nonreligious 13%

France

GEOGRAPHY
Capital: Paris
Total Area: 211,209 sq. mi.
Population: 60,496,000

ECONOMY
Imports: machinery; chemicals; food
Exports: aircraft; perfumes; cosmetics

CULTURE
Language: French
Religion: Catholic 82%; Muslim 7%; Protestant 4%

Germany

GEOGRAPHY
Capital: Berlin
Total Area: 137,847 sq. mi.
Population: 82,689,000

ECONOMY
Imports: televisions; computers; food
Exports: televisions; medical instruments

CULTURE
Language: German
Religion: Protestant 36%; Catholic 34%; nonreligious 17%

Greece

GEOGRAPHY
Capital: Athens
Total Area: 50,942 sq. mi.
Population: 11,120,000

ECONOMY
Imports: chemicals; petroleum; ships
Exports: fruits and nuts; aluminum

CULTURE
Language: Greek
Religion: Eastern Orthodox 94%; Muslim 1%

Hungary

GEOGRAPHY
Capital: Budapest
Total Area: 35,919 sq. mi.
Population: 10,098,000

ECONOMY
Imports: machinery; vehicles
Exports: telecommunications equipment

CULTURE
Language: Hungarian
Religion: Catholic 58%; Reformed 18%; nonreligious 19%

Tour de France Each year, about 200 riders compete in this famous bicycle race.

Iceland

GEOGRAPHY
Capital: Reykjavik
Total Area: 39,769 sq. mi.
Population: 295,000

ECONOMY
Imports: machinery; food; clothing
Exports: fish; aluminum; medicines

CULTURE
Language: Icelandic
Religion: Evangelical Lutheran 87%; Catholic 2%

Ireland

GEOGRAPHY
Capital: Dublin
Total Area: 27,135 sq. mi.
Population: 4,148,000

ECONOMY
Imports: computers; electronics; food
Exports: computers; recording devices

CULTURE
Language: Irish; English
Religion: Catholic 88%; Church of Ireland (Anglican) 3%

Italy

GEOGRAPHY
Capital: Rome
Total Area: 116,306 sq. mi.
Population: 58,093,000

ECONOMY
Imports: machinery; chemicals; iron; steel
Exports: chemicals; textile yarn and fabrics; food

CULTURE
Language: Italian
Religion: Catholic 80%; nonreligious 13%

Latvia

GEOGRAPHY
Capital: Riga
Total Area: 24,938 sq. mi.
Population: 2,307,000

ECONOMY
Imports: machinery; chemicals; vehicles
Exports: wood; metals; textiles

CULTURE
Language: Latvian
Religion: Catholic 15%; Lutheran 15%; Orthodox 8%

Liechtenstein

GEOGRAPHY
Capital: Vaduz
Total Area: 62 sq. mi.
Population: 33,717

ECONOMY
Imports: machinery; glass and ceramics
Exports: precision tools; food products

CULTURE
Language: German
Religion: Catholic 80%; Protestant 8%; Muslim 3%

Lithuania

GEOGRAPHY
Capital: Vilnius
Total Area: 25,174 sq. mi.
Population: 3,431,000

ECONOMY
Imports: chemicals; clothing
Exports: mineral fuels; clothing; food

CULTURE
Language: Lithuanian
Religion: Catholic 79%; nonreligious 10%; Orthodox 5%

Luxembourg

GEOGRAPHY
Capital: Luxembourg
Total Area: 998 sq. mi.
Population: 465,000

ECONOMY
Imports: machinery; metals; chemicals
Exports: metals; transport equipment; food

CULTURE
Language: Luxemburgian; French
Religion: Catholic 91%; Protestant 2%

Macedonia

GEOGRAPHY
Capital: Skopje
Total Area: 9,781 sq. mi.
Population: 2,034,000

ECONOMY
Imports: mineral fuels; food; live animals
Exports: clothing; iron; tobacco; beverages

CULTURE
Language: Macedonian; Albanian
Religion: Orthodox 59%; Sunni Muslim 28%

Malta

GEOGRAPHY
Capital: Valletta
Total Area: 122 sq. mi.
Population: 402,000

ECONOMY
Imports: electronics; petroleum; food
Exports: clothing; children's toys and games

CULTURE
Language: Maltese; English
Religion: Catholic 95%

Republic of Moldova

GEOGRAPHY
Capital: Chişinău
Total Area: 13,067 sq. mi.
Population: 4,206,000

ECONOMY
Imports: minerals; chemicals; textiles
Exports: food; textiles

CULTURE
Language: Romanian
Religion: Orthodox 46%; Muslim 6%; Catholic 2%; Protestant 2%

Monaco

GEOGRAPHY
Capital: Monaco
Total Area: 1 square mile
Population: 32,409

ECONOMY
Imports: perfumes; clothing; publishing
Exports: plastic products; glass; paper

CULTURE
Language: French
Religion: Catholic 89%; Jewish 2%

Montenegro

GEOGRAPHY
Capital: Podgorica
Total Area: 5,415 sq. mi.
Population: 630,548

ECONOMY
Imports: no information available
Exports: no information available

CULTURE
Language: Serbian
Religion: Orthodox, Muslim, Catholic

Netherlands

GEOGRAPHY
Capital: Amsterdam
Total Area: 16,033 sq. mi.
Population: 16,299,000

ECONOMY
Imports: computers; chemicals; food
Exports: chemicals; food; mineral fuels

CULTURE
Language: Dutch
Religion: nonreligious 43%; Catholic 31%; Reformed 14%

Norway

GEOGRAPHY
Capital: Oslo
Total Area: 125,182 sq. mi.
Population: 4,620,000

ECONOMY
Imports: road vehicles; ships; metals
Exports: crude petroleum; metals; fish

CULTURE
Language: Norwegian
Religion: Church of Norway 86%; Muslim 2%, Catholic 1%

Poland

GEOGRAPHY
Capital: Warsaw
Total Area: 120,728 sq. mi.
Population: 38,530,000

ECONOMY
Imports: machinery; textiles
Exports: food; furniture; ships

CULTURE
Language: Polish
Religion: Catholic 91%; Polish Orthodox 1%

Portugal

GEOGRAPHY
Capital: Lisbon
Total Area: 35,672 sq. mi.
Population: 10,495,000

ECONOMY
Imports: telecommunications equipment
Exports: road vehicles; clothing; fabrics

CULTURE
Language: Portuguese
Religion: Catholic 87%; nonreligious 7%

Romania

GEOGRAPHY
Capital: Bucharest
Total Area: 91,699 sq. mi.
Population: 21,711,000

ECONOMY
Imports: fabrics; chemicals; petroleum
Exports: clothing; iron and steel

CULTURE
Language: Romanian
Religion: Romanian Orthodox 87%; Protestant 6%; Catholic 5%

San Marino

GEOGRAPHY
Capital: San Marino
Total Area: 24 sq. mi.
Population: 28,880

ECONOMY
Imports: electricity; gold
Exports: postage stamps; leather goods; ceramics; wine

CULTURE
Language: Italian
Religion: Catholic 89%

Serbia

GEOGRAPHY
Capital: Belgrade
Total Area: 34,116 sq. mi.
Population: 9,396,400

ECONOMY
Imports: machinery; mineral fuels
Exports: food & live animals; machinery

CULTURE
Language: Serbian
Religion: Serbian Orthodox 63%; Muslim 19%; nonreligious 13%

Slovakia

GEOGRAPHY
Capital: Bratislava
Total Area: 18,859 sq. mi.
Population: 5,401,000

ECONOMY
Imports: machinery; fuels
Exports: road vehicles; machinery; metals

CULTURE
Language: Slovak
Religion: Catholic 69%; Slovak Evangelical 7%

Slovenia

GEOGRAPHY
Capital: Ljubljana
Total Area: 7,827 sq. mi.
Population: 1,967,000

ECONOMY
Imports: machinery; vehicles; fuels
Exports: medicines and pharmaceuticals; furniture

CULTURE
Language: Slovene
Religion: Catholic 84%; nonreligious 8%

Spain

GEOGRAPHY
Capital: Madrid
Total Area: 194,897 sq. mi.
Population: 43,064,000

ECONOMY
Imports: vehicles; chemicals; petroleum
Exports: fruits and vegetables; chemicals

CULTURE
Language: Castilian Spanish; Euskera (Basque); Catalan; Galician
Religion: Catholic 92%

Sweden

GEOGRAPHY
Capital: Stockholm
Total Area: 173,732 sq. mi.
Population: 9,041,000

ECONOMY
Imports: machinery; chemicals; vehicles
Exports: vehicles; electronics; medicines

CULTURE
Language: Swedish
Religion: Church of Sweden 87%; Muslim 2%; Catholic 2%

Switzerland

GEOGRAPHY
Capital: Bern
Total Area: 15,942 sq. mi.
Population: 7,252,000

ECONOMY
Imports: machinery; vehicles; food
Exports: precision instruments, watches

CULTURE
Language: French; German; Italian
Religion: Catholic 42%; Protestant 35%; Muslim 4%; Orthodox 2%

Ukraine

GEOGRAPHY
Capital: Kiev
Total Area: 233,090 sq. mi.
Population: 46,481,000

ECONOMY
Imports: natural gas; chemicals; food
Exports: metals; wood; food

CULTURE
Language: Ukrainian
Religion: Ukrainian Orthodox 29%; Catholic 7%; Protestant 4%

United Kingdom

GEOGRAPHY
Capital: London
Total Area: 94,526 sq. mi.
Population: 59,668,000

ECONOMY
Imports: radios; televisions; aircraft
Exports: computers; aircraft; petroleum

CULTURE
Language: English
Religion: Anglican 29%; nonreligious 16%; Catholic 11%

Vatican City

GEOGRAPHY
Capital: Vatican City
Total Area: 0.2 sq. mi.
Population: 921

ECONOMY
Imports: no information available
Exports: no information available

CULTURE
Language: Italian; Latin
Religion: Catholic

Majorca, Spain

CHAPTER 11

Europe:
Physical Geography and History

1 GEOGRAPHY
Europe's Dramatic Landscape

2 HISTORY
Classical Greece and Rome

3 HISTORY
The Middle Ages and Renaissance

4 HISTORY
Modern European History

 ESSENTIAL QUESTION

What changes have taken place in Europe since ancient times?

CONNECT Geography & History

Use the map and the time line to answer the following questions.

1. What countries share borders with France?
2. The European Union's headquarters are in the capital of Belgium. What city is that?

2000 B.C.

History
◀ **27 B.C.** Augustus forms the Roman Empire, which lasts until A.D. **476.** (Coin showing Augustus)

Geography
A.D. 79 Eruption of Mount Vesuvius destroys Roman city of Pompeii.

History
400s Beginning of the Middle Ages ▶

20°W

0°

20°E

ARCTIC OCEAN

Arctic Circle

N
W E
S

60°N

ICELAND
Reykjavík

Faroe Islands (Den.)

Shetland Islands (U.K.)

Norwegian Sea

SWEDEN

FINLAND

RUSSIA

Helsinki ★

0   200   400 miles
0   200   400 kilometers

ATLANTIC OCEAN

NORWAY

Oslo ★

Gulf of Bothnia

Stockholm ★

Gulf of Finland

Tallinn ★
ESTONIA

Dublin ★

North Sea

LATVIA
Riga ★

ALB.	Albania
B.& HER.	Bosnia and Herzegovina
LEICH.	Leichtenstein
LUX.	Luxembourg
MAC.	Macedonia
MONT.	Montenegro
SLOV.	Slovenia
SWITZ.	Switzerland

IRELAND

UNITED KINGDOM

DENMARK
Copenhagen ★

Baltic Sea

LITHUANIA
Vilnius

Minsk ★

British Isles

NETHERLANDS
Amsterdam ★

London ★

Berlin ★

POLAND

BELARUS

Channel Islands (U.K.)

English Channel

Brussels ★

GERMANY

Warsaw ★

Kiev ★

BELGIUM

LUX.

Prague ★
CZECH REPUBLIC

Paris ★

Vienna ★
AUSTRIA ★
LIECH.

SLOVAKIA
Bratislava ★

UKRAINE

MOLDOVA
Chișinău ★

FRANCE

Bern ★
SWITZ.

Budapest ★
HUNGARY

Bay of Biscay

SLOV.
Ljubljana ★
Zagreb ★
CROATIA

ROMANIA

SAN MARINO

MONACO

Bucharest ★

Black Sea

PORTUGAL

ANDORRA
Corsica (Fr.)

B. & HER.
Sarajevo ★

Belgrade ★
SERBIA

Madrid ★

ITALY

Adriatic Sea

MONT.

Sofia ★
BULGARIA

Lisbon ★

VATICAN CITY
Rome ★

Podgorica ★
Tiranë ★

Skopje ★
MAC.

SPAIN

Balearic Islands (Sp.)

Sardinia (It.)

ALB.

50°N

40°N

ASIA

Strait of Gibraltar

GIBRALTAR (U.K.)

Tyrrhenian Sea

Ionian Sea

Aegean Sea

GREECE

Athens ★

AFRICA

Mediterranean Sea

Sicily (It.)

MALTA

Crete (Gr.)

Cyprus

★ National capital

Culture
c. 1300 The Renaissance begins in Italy.

Government
1799 Napoleon seizes power in France following the French Revolution. ▶

Economics
▲ **1992** Treaty forming the European Union is signed.

Today

325

Reading for Understanding

▶ Key Ideas

BEFORE, YOU LEARNED

The Earth's surface is covered with a variety of landforms, produced by internal and external forces.

NOW YOU WILL LEARN

Europe, too, has landforms ranging from mountains to plains. Its climate is influenced by its nearness to the ocean.

▶ Vocabulary

TERMS & NAMES

peninsula a body of land nearly surrounded by water

Alps Europe's tallest mountain range, stretching across southern Europe

Northern European Plain vast area of flat or gently rolling land from France to Russia

North Atlantic Drift warm ocean current that helps keep Europe's climate mild

fossil fuels sources of energy from ancient plant and animal remains

renewable energy sources sources of energy able to be replaced through ongoing natural processes

hydroelectric power electricity made by water-powered engines

BACKGROUND VOCABULARY

seafaring using the sea for transportation

Visual Vocabulary The Alps

▶ Reading Strategy

Re-create the chart shown at right. As you read and respond to the **KEY QUESTIONS**, use the chart to organize important details about the physical geography of Europe.

 See Skillbuilder Handbook, page R7

CATEGORIZE

PENINSULAS	MOUNTAINS	RIVERS
1.	1.	1.
2.	2.	2.
3.	3.	3.

 GRAPHIC ORGANIZERS
Go to **Interactive Review** @ ClassZone.com

Europe's Dramatic Landscape

Connecting to Your World

What comes to mind when you think of Europe? Snowcapped mountains on travel posters? Medieval castles next to winding rivers that you've seen in jigsaw puzzles? Or perhaps you've watched the Winter Olympics on television and seen skiers speeding down steep mountain slopes. Each of these images tells us something about Europe's physical geography. High mountain ranges, oceans, long broad rivers, and fertile plains are all a part of it. Let's see how they fit together.

Alcazar Castle Europe is famous for its castles, like this one in Segovia, Spain.

Peninsula of Peninsulas

▼ **KEY QUESTION** Why is Europe called a peninsula of peninsulas?

A quick look at a map of Europe explains why it is called the "peninsula of peninsulas." A **peninsula** is a piece of land nearly surrounded by water. The entire continent of Europe is a peninsula with smaller peninsulas jutting out from it. Because of these peninsulas, most places in Europe are no more than 300 miles from an ocean or sea. Its nearness to these bodies of water has influenced Europe in many ways. The ocean modifies Europe's climate. Many Europeans use the ocean for both business and pleasure.

Opatija, Croatia This town is located on the Istria Peninsula in southern Europe.

Opatija

ISTRIA PENINSULA

Europe's Coastline Europe's peninsulas extend off the continent in all directions, as the map on the opposite page shows. Far to the north, the Scandinavian Peninsula Ⓐ juts out into the North Sea. Spain and Portugal occupy the Iberian Peninsula Ⓑ, which extends into the Mediterranean Sea in southern Europe. The Italian and Balkan Peninsulas also stretch into the Mediterranean Sea.

Europe's many bays and peninsulas give it a long, uneven coastline, dotted with islands and stretching almost 24,000 miles. Europe has more coastline than Africa, a much larger continent. Long ago, Europe's nearness to the sea and its many natural harbors encouraged **seafaring**, or the use of the sea for transportation. Europeans fished, traded, and in time set out to explore other parts of the world.

Mountains Mountains are another key landform in Europe. They affect climate, travel, and culture. The **Alps** Ⓒ, Europe's tallest mountain range, stretch across eight countries in southern Europe. The Pyrenees Ⓓ once formed a natural barrier between France and Spain. Europe also has smaller mountain ranges, such as the Apennines.

Europe's mountain ranges separated the groups of people who settled the land thousands of years ago. This is one reason different cultures developed in Europe. Mountain ranges also contain natural resources, such as timber, which influence where people settle.

Mountains surround the **Northern European Plain** Ⓔ, a vast area of flat or gently rolling land from France to Russia. Parts of the plain have fertile soil, making them Europe's major farming areas. Other parts are rich with coal. Industrial centers developed near the coal deposits. These variations have made settlement across the plain uneven.

▲ **SUMMARIZE** Explain why Europe is called a peninsula of peninsulas.

CONNECT Geography & Economics

Seafaring Economies

Europe's vast coastline boosted its economy by encouraging exploration, fishing, and trade. Europe provides over half of the world's international shipping. Countries with large fleets, such as Great Britain, ship goods around the world. To do so, they use ports on rivers like the Thames in London, shown here.

Renewable Energy As an alternative to fossil fuels, many European nations are trying to find renewable sources of energy. **Renewable energy sources** can be replaced through ongoing natural processes, such as sunshine, wind, and flowing water. These types of energy sources are also sustainable, meaning that they can be utilized without being used up.

Hydroelectric power is a renewable energy source that uses water-powered engines to make electricity. Austria generates energy by damming Alpine rivers. Coastal countries such as Ireland and Portugal are developing technology to harness wave energy. Germany, Spain, and Denmark lead the pack in producing electricity from wind energy. Other nations, including the Netherlands, generate heat and electricity by collecting solar energy from the sun. Italy and Iceland tap geothermal energy by drilling into naturally hot groundwater. These alternative energy sources have many benefits. They are sustainable. They reduce pollution. They mean that European nations can rely less on importing energy from other countries.

European Renewable Energy Sources

In 2001, 15 European countries used renewable energy sources to supply 15.2 percent of the energy they consumed. This pie graph shows how much energy came from each source.

1.6% 9.7%
8.8%
79.9%

- ■ Hydroelectric
- ■ Wind
- ■ Geothermal
- ■ Other

Source: European Commission, *Electricity from Renewable Energy Sources,* 2004

 DRAW CONCLUSIONS Explain why energy resources are important to Europe's growth.

Section 1 Assessment

 **ONLINE QUIZ**
For test practice, go to
Interactive Review
@ ClassZone.com

TERMS & NAMES

1. Explain the importance of
- Alps
- Northern European Plain
- North Atlantic Drift
- fossil fuels

USE YOUR READING NOTES

2. Categorize Use your completed chart to answer the following question:

What are the major mountain ranges of Europe?

PENINSULAS	MOUNTAINS	RIVERS
1.	1.	1.
2.	2.	2.
3.	3.	3.

KEY IDEAS

3. Why is the Northern European Plain important to Europe's economy?

4. How does the North Atlantic Drift affect the climate of Europe?

5. What are Europe's most important mineral resources?

CRITICAL THINKING

6. Draw Conclusions Why might mountains be both an asset and a disadvantage?

7. Make Inferences Why are coal and iron important to industrializing nations?

8. CONNECT to Today Why is Europe's network of rivers still important to its economy?

9. WRITING Write a Report Choose one of Europe's major rivers to write a report about. List the countries the river runs through. Include some major cities you might see if you sailed along the river. Finally, explain one way the river is important to Europe's economy.

Reading for Understanding

▶ Key Ideas

BEFORE, YOU LEARNED

Europe has diverse landforms. Its climate and vegetation vary by latitude and distance from the ocean.

NOW YOU WILL LEARN

Ancient Greek and Roman achievements in government, art and architecture, engineering, and law continue to influence Europe and the world today.

▶ Vocabulary

TERMS & NAMES

democracy a government in which the citizens make political decisions, either directly or through elected representatives

Peloponnesus (PEHL•uh•puh•NEE•suhs) the peninsula in southern Greece where Sparta was located

city-state a political unit made up of a city and its surrounding lands

tyrant someone who takes power illegally

oligarchy (AHL•ih•GAHR•kee) a government ruled by a few powerful individuals

republic a government in which citizens elect representatives to rule in their name

patrician (puh•TRIHSH•uhn) a wealthy landowner who held a high government position in ancient Rome

plebeian (plih•BEE•uhn) a commoner who was allowed to vote but not to hold government office in ancient Rome

BACKGROUND VOCABULARY

isolate to cut off or set apart from a group

REVIEW

monarchy a type of government in which a ruling family headed by a king or queen holds political power

▶ Reading Strategy

Re-create the chart shown at right. As you read and respond to the **KEY QUESTIONS**, use the chart to help you compare and contrast the governments of ancient Greece, the Roman Republic, and the Roman Empire.

 See Skillbuilder Handbook, page R9

COMPARE AND CONTRAST

GOVERNMENT	WHO RULED	HOW CHOSEN	WHO PARTICIPATED
Greek Democracy			
Roman Republic			
Roman Empire			

 GRAPHIC ORGANIZERS
Go to **Interactive Review** @ClassZone.com

Classical Greece and Rome

Connecting to Your World

Have you ever been to the nation's capital, Washington, D.C.? It is the center of the U.S. government. The United States is a **democracy**, a government in which citizens make political decisions. You are about to learn about ancient Greece, the place where modern democracy began. Ideas about what democracy should be have changed over time. Democratic government in Greece stands as a remarkable first step.

Lincoln Memorial Some buildings in Washington, D.C., reflect ancient Greek architecture.

History of Ancient Greece

▼ **KEY QUESTION** How did ancient Greek culture spread?

Between 5000 and 3000 B.C., groups of people began settling on the **Peloponnesus** (PEHL•uh•puh•NEE•suhs), a mountainous peninsula in southern Europe. Almost 2,000 small islands surrounded the peninsula. Villages were **isolated**, or cut off, from each other. The rugged terrain and remote islands made it difficult to unite the villages under one government. In time, people had settled throughout what is now Greece.

The Acropolis This part of Athens held important buildings constructed in the second half of the fifth century B.C.

GREECE
Athens
Sparta

Rise of City-States: Athens and Sparta Eventually, Greek towns and cities became **city-states**, political units made up of a city and surrounding villages. Most people were farmers and herders, but where land was rocky and soil was poor, people made their living from the sea. They fished, sailed, and traded with other city-states.

Greek city-states shared a common culture and language, but each had unique features. They chose different forms of government. At first, many were monarchies, ruled by kings. Others were ruled by tyrants. In Greece, a **tyrant** was someone who took power illegally.

Athens and Sparta, the largest Greek city-states, had different governments. Sparta was an **oligarchy** (AHL•ih•GAHR•kee), a system ruled by a few powerful individuals. Two kings governed the state, making all major decisions with the help of a few officials. Sparta was a military state. Its large slave class farmed the land, freeing male citizens to serve in the army. Spartan boys began receiving military training at age seven. After decades of military service, they became citizens at 30. They faced losing their citizenship if they did not fight bravely.

At first, kings also governed Athens. Then, at the end of the sixth century B.C., Athens became a limited democracy. All citizens had the right to take part in the government and decide on laws. However, only free adult males were citizens. Women, slaves, and foreigners were not. Athens became a center of Greek culture. It attracted the finest scholars, artists, and philosophers from all over the Mediterranean.

ANALYZING Primary Sources

Pericles (495–429 B.C.) was an Athenian statesman and general. His "Funeral Oration" honors those who died in the Peloponnesian War and praises democracy. Pericles saw participation in government as a civic duty. Greek citizens often discussed politics in an agora, or marketplace, like the one shown at left.

> An Athenian citizen does not neglect public affairs when attending to his private business. . . . We consider a man who takes no interest in the state not as harmless, but as useless.
>
> Source: Thucydides, from *The Peloponnesian War*

DOCUMENT–BASED QUESTION
Why was an interest in politics considered a public duty?

Pericles ▲

Wars and Conquest In the early fifth century B.C., the rulers of Persia, the region in southwestern Asia that is now Iran, tried to conquer Greece. Led by Sparta and Athens, the Greeks resisted. Conflict between the Greeks and Persians lasted on and off for many years. The Greeks defeated the Persians, keeping Greek culture alive.

Decades later, Athens and Sparta fought each other in the Peloponnesian War. Sparta won the war, becoming the dominant power in Greece. Weakened by their internal conflict, the city-states paid little attention to neighboring Macedonia, a kingdom north of Greece that was preparing to attack.

In 338 B.C., King Philip II of Macedonia used his well-trained army to seize control of Greece. After Philip's death, his son Alexander took control. A brilliant military planner, Alexander conquered vast new territories and became known as Alexander the Great. His empire extended into North Africa, the Middle East, and Asia. As his empire expanded, Greek culture spread. When Alexander died, three of his generals divided his territory among themselves, ending one of the great empires of the ancient world.

▲ **EVALUATE** Explain the differences between Athens and Sparta.

History of Ancient Rome

▼ **KEY QUESTION** How were the governments of the Roman Republic and the Roman Empire different?

While Athens was creating a democracy, the people of Rome, located west of Greece on the Italian Peninsula, were also making changes to their government. They overthrew the foreign kings that ruled them and set up a **monarchy** of their own. Then, in 509 B.C., the Romans rejected rule by kings and created a new form of government.

From Republic to Empire The Romans set up a **republic**, a form of government in which citizens elect representatives to rule in their name. It was not a democracy. All male citizens could vote, but only **patricians** (puh•TRISH•uhnz), members of rich and powerful families, could hold the highest government offices. Farmers, merchants, and craftspeople made up the class known as **plebeians** (plih•BEE•uhnz). Over time, the plebeians gained more political power.

HISTORY MAKERS

Alexander 356–323 B.C.

One important effect of Alexander's conquest was the spread of Greek culture to other parts of the world. When Alexander was young, the great Greek thinker Aristotle was his teacher. Alexander came to know and admire Greek culture. His many conquests enabled him to spread Greek language, ideas, and beliefs far beyond the Greek peninsula. Greek culture influenced life throughout his vast empire.

🔎 **ONLINE BIOGRAPHY**
For more on the life of Alexander the Great, go to the **Research & Writing Center @ ClassZone.com**

Over centuries the Roman Republic grew, until it controlled the entire Italian Peninsula. As they conquered, the Romans offered citizenship to many groups, a policy that strengthened the republic. After almost 500 years, however, the republic began to fall apart. By 27 B.C., military leaders were fighting civil wars. Worn down by the conflict and seeking order at the cost of liberty, the Romans allowed Octavian—later known as Augustus—to take over the government. The republic became an empire, united under a supreme leader.

Augustus and later emperors greatly expanded the empire, as the map below shows. Palestine, a Jewish kingdom on the eastern edge of the Mediterranean, came under Roman control. It was here that Jesus was born and Christianity began. The new religion quickly spread across the empire, becoming its official religion in A.D. 380.

The Empire Falls Apart By the third century A.D., the Roman Empire faced serious problems, which you can see in the chart below. To make the empire easier to govern, it was divided it into two halves. Constantinople became the capital of the eastern empire. Rome remained the capital of the western part. Germanic tribes who lived outside of Rome's borders began pushing into Roman territory. In A.D. 476, the Western Roman Empire fell. The Eastern Roman Empire lasted about 1,000 years more.

▲ COMPARE AND CONTRAST Explain how the governments of the Roman Republic and the Roman Empire were different.

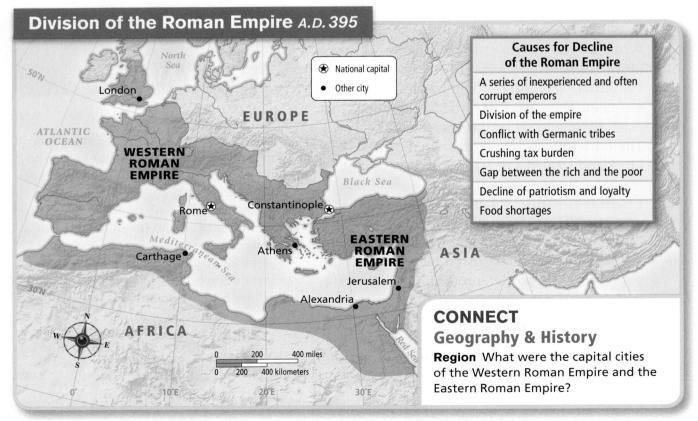

Division of the Roman Empire A.D. 395

★ National capital
● Other city

North Sea
50°N
London
EUROPE
ATLANTIC OCEAN
WESTERN ROMAN EMPIRE
Black Sea
Rome ★
Constantinople ★
Mediterranean Sea
Athens
EASTERN ROMAN EMPIRE
ASIA
Carthage ●
Jerusalem ●
30°N
Alexandria ●
AFRICA
Red Sea
0°   10°E   20°E   30°E

0   200   400 miles
0   200   400 kilometers

Causes for Decline of the Roman Empire

A series of inexperienced and often corrupt emperors
Division of the empire
Conflict with Germanic tribes
Crushing tax burden
Gap between the rich and the poor
Decline of patriotism and loyalty
Food shortages

CONNECT
Geography & History
Region What were the capital cities of the Western Roman Empire and the Eastern Roman Empire?

Classical Culture

 KEY QUESTION What accomplishments of ancient Greece and Rome still influence modern life?

The ancient Greeks and Romans left a powerful legacy. The Greeks excelled as artists, writers, and philosophers. Their ideas led to developments in theater, science, and government that still influence life today. Perhaps the greatest legacy of the Greeks is democracy. Greek society was one of the first to give people a voice in government. Democracy is a goal for many countries.

The Romans adopted many aspects of Greek culture, but they also had many practical skills of their own. Roman engineers designed and built roads, aqueducts, and public buildings such as the Colosseum. Their system of roads helped expand trade networks and spread culture, including Christianity. The Romans invented the idea of the republic and created a written code of law, the Law of the Twelve Tables. These ideas later shaped legal systems throughout Europe and the Americas.

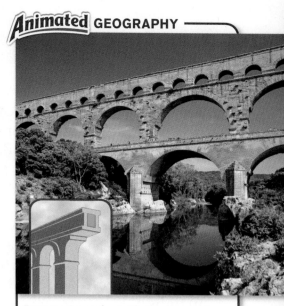

Animated GEOGRAPHY

Roman Aqueduct Their advances in engineering allowed the Romans to build aqueducts, like this one in France, which carried fresh water from distant sources into cities and towns.

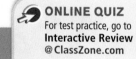 **Click here** to see how aqueducts work
@ ClassZone.com

▲ **SUMMARIZE** Describe the achievements of ancient Greece and Rome that continue to influence modern life.

Section 2 Assessment

ONLINE QUIZ
For test practice, go to
Interactive Review
@ ClassZone.com

TERMS & NAMES

1. Explain the importance of
- democracy
- oligarchy
- patrician
- plebeian

USE YOUR READING NOTES

2. Compare and Contrast Use your completed chart to answer the following question:

Who participated in elections in the Roman Republic?

GOVERNMENT	WHO RULED	HOW CHOSEN	WHO PARTICIPATED
Greek Democracy			
Roman Republic			
Roman Empire			

KEY IDEAS

3. Why were the waters surrounding the Greek peninsulas an important resource for ancient Greece?

4. How did Alexander help spread Greek culture to foreign lands?

5. What role did patricians and plebeians play in the early Roman Republic?

CRITICAL THINKING

6. Compare and Contrast What are some differences between the achievements of the ancient Greek and Roman civilizations?

7. Analyze Causes Which of the causes of the fall of the Western Roman Empire do you think was most significant? Why?

8. CONNECT to Today How was the original Roman Republic similar to the U.S. government today?

9. WRITING Rewrite a Myth Pick a myth from Greek or Roman literature. Rewrite it as a poem or short story set in the present.

The cultures of ancient Greece and Rome shaped the people who came after them. The influence of both cultures can still be seen today.

Greece

The Greeks developed new ideas about architecture and the gods. They created a new art form—the Greek drama. Other cultures, including ancient Rome, picked up many of these ideas. We can still see ancient Greece in ruins like the Acropolis, shown below, and reflected in our own culture.

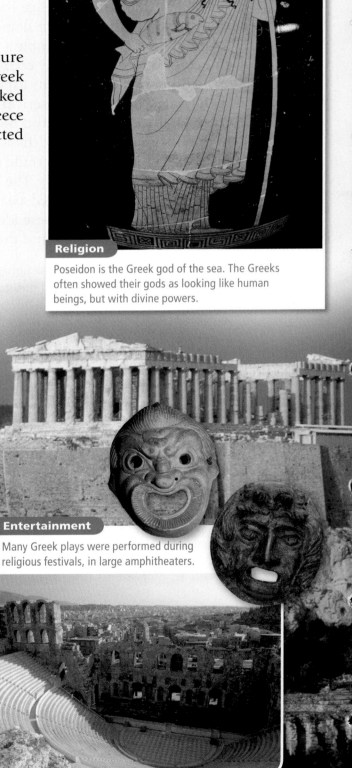

Religion

Poseidon is the Greek god of the sea. The Greeks often showed their gods as looking like human beings, but with divine powers.

Daily Life

Greek pottery provides a good record of daily life. This pot shows women collecting water from a public fountain.

Entertainment

Many Greek plays were performed during religious festivals, in large amphitheaters.

Rome

Roman culture was based on values of strength and loyalty. The Romans picked up some Greek ideas about the gods and architecture. They transformed these ideas into styles that were uniquely Roman, as seen in the Forum, shown below.

Religion

The Romans called the god of the sea Neptune. Roman depictions of their gods and goddesses frequently seem more realistic and three-dimensional than those of the Greeks.

Daily Life

Agriculture and trade formed the basis of the Roman economy. Shops occupied the ground story of many ancient buildings.

Entertainment

Chariot races, which took place in oval arenas called circuses, drew huge crowds.

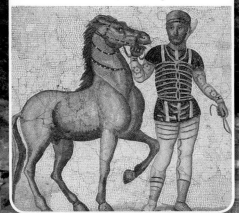

CRITICAL THINKING

1. **Compare and Contrast** What do their forms of entertainment suggest about the differences between Greek and Roman culture?

2. **Make Inferences** Why might these cultures have saved their classical buildings?

Reading for Understanding

▶ Key Ideas

BEFORE, YOU LEARNED

Ancient Greek and Roman achievements continue to influence our world today.

NOW YOU WILL LEARN

Feudalism provided stability after the fall of the Roman Empire. The Renaissance marked a rebirth of creativity in Europe.

▶ Vocabulary

TERMS & NAMES

Middle Ages the period between the fall of the Roman Empire and the modern era, from about A.D. 476 to 1453

medieval from the Middle Ages

feudalism a political system in which lords gave land to vassals in exchange for services

lord a powerful landowner

vassal a less wealthy noble who paid taxes to and served a lord in exchange for land

knight a vassal trained in combat who fought on behalf of lords

serf a person who lived and worked on the manor of a lord or vassal

manor a noble's house and the villages on his land where the peasants lived

Renaissance (REHN•ih•SAHNS) a rebirth of creativity, literature, and learning in Europe from about 1300 to 1600

patron a wealthy or powerful person who provides money, support, and encouragement to an artist or a cause

secular worldly or not related to religion

perspective a technique used by artists to give the appearance of depth and distance

Reformation a movement in the 1500s to change practices in the Catholic Church

Protestant a member of a Christian Church founded on the principles of the Reformation

▶ Reading Strategy

Re-create the cause-and-effect diagram shown at right. As you read and respond to the **KEY QUESTIONS**, use the diagram to help you find the effect of the events listed in the first ovals in each pair.

 See Skillbuilder Handbook, page R8

ANALYZE CAUSE AND EFFECT

Fall of the Roman Empire

↓

The Plague and the Crusades

↓

Challenges to the Church

↓

GRAPHIC ORGANIZERS
Go to **Interactive Review** @ ClassZone.com

The Middle Ages and Renaissance

Connecting to Your World

Sometimes it can be difficult to imagine life without the ideas and technology that exist today. The pace of change seems to increase with every passing decade. Even 25 years ago, cell phones were just being invented. Now they are everywhere. At the beginning of the period in European history you are about to study, new ideas and inventions traveled much more slowly than they do today. Yet change did take place. In time, new ideas and discoveries challenged many Europeans' accepted beliefs about how the world worked and their place in it.

The Middle Ages

▼ **KEY QUESTION** Why did feudalism develop in Europe?

Historians call the period of history between the fall of the Roman Empire and the beginning of the modern era the **Middle Ages**. It is also called the **medieval** period, from the Latin words for "Middle Ages." The collapse of the Western Roman Empire made many people fearful and uncertain. Europeans no longer had a strong central government, an army to protect them, or a common culture and belief system to unite them. Many advances of the ancient world were lost.

Cell phones Many people today use cell phones.

Bayeux Tapestry This textile shows feudal knights during the Norman Conquest of England from 1064 to 1066.

Medieval Society The Germanic tribes in western Europe were quite different from the Romans. They had no tradition of central government. At first, many small kingdoms replaced the Roman Empire. Roads and water systems were not kept up. Trade declined. As their economies slowed, western European towns shrank. Residents abandoned them, heading to the countryside to become farmers. Literacy—and with it the educated middle class—all but disappeared.

During the early Middle Ages, invaders such as the Huns, Moors, and Vikings threatened Europe. Constant conflict and warfare plagued the region. In the 700s, a ruler named Charlemagne (SHAHR•luh•MAYN) brought much of France and Germany under his control. Charlemagne was a strong military leader. He worked with the pope, the leader of the Roman Catholic Church, to strengthen the church and his own empire. Pope Leo III crowned him emperor in 800. However, Charlemagne died in 814. In 843, his three grandsons divided his empire among themselves. Europe again became a disorderly group of small kingdoms.

Faced with such disorder, Europeans turned to a political system called **feudalism**, which would remain in place from about the 9th to the 14th century. Feudalism created a new social structure in Europe. The king ruled at the top of society. Nobles, church officials, knights, and peasants had their places below the king.

Feudalism depended on an agreement between two groups of nobles—lords and vassals.

- **Lords**, or powerful landowners, gave some of their land to less-wealthy nobles called vassals.

- **Vassals** pledged to serve their lords. They paid taxes to the lords in exchange for their plots of land, called fiefs (feefs).

- Some vassals were warriors known as **knights**, who began combat training as young boys. Knights fought on behalf of their lords.

- The feudal structure also included peasants. Most were **serfs**, who lived and worked on a noble's land. Serfs received housing and protection in return.

This political system kept Europe divided into many small kingdoms and estates, with little trade between them. As a result, the nobles' lands became the center of most economic activity. The main part of a noble's land was called a **manor**. Often the manor was a fortified house, surrounded by farmland worked by serfs. Manors supplied much of what their residents needed. Towns grew less important, as townspeople left to work on manors.

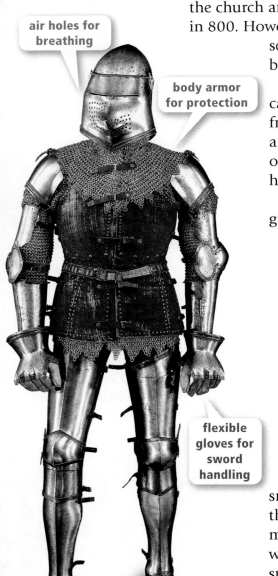

European Knight Knights often wore a suit of armor to protect themselves in battle. These suits made it difficult to move quickly—the average suit weighed 65 pounds! **What might the advantages and disadvantages of armor be?**

air holes for breathing

body armor for protection

flexible gloves for sword handling

The Role of the Church The Roman Catholic Church was one institution that survived the fall of Rome. After the division of the Roman Empire, Christianity split into several different churches. The Roman Catholic Church developed in the Western Roman Empire. Many of the Germanic tribes that invaded Rome converted to Christianity. The religion spread slowly across Europe. The church became the main source of education during the Middle Ages. Church officials built universities where nobles could go and study.

Eventually, the territory once controlled by Charlemagne became the Holy Roman Empire. It was a loose confederation of states associated with the Catholic Church, rather than a unified empire with a strong central government. Even so, the Holy Roman Empire helped to bring Europe back together after the divisions of the Middle Ages.

▲ **ANALYZE CAUSES** Explain how events in Europe contributed to the rise of feudalism.

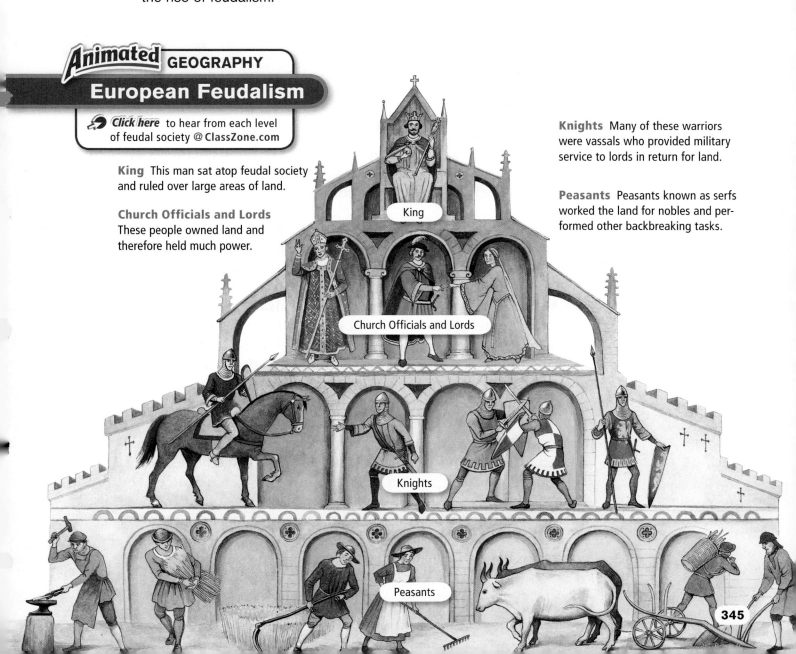

Animated GEOGRAPHY

European Feudalism

Click here to hear from each level of feudal society @ ClassZone.com

King This man sat atop feudal society and ruled over large areas of land.

Church Officials and Lords These people owned land and therefore held much power.

Knights Many of these warriors were vassals who provided military service to lords in return for land.

Peasants Peasants known as serfs worked the land for nobles and performed other backbreaking tasks.

King

Church Officials and Lords

Knights

Peasants

Feudal castles were designed for defense against enemy attacks. Many included the following defensive features:

- Moats **A**, filled with water, prevented attackers from getting too close.
- Watchtowers **B** allowed guards to fire on approaching enemies from a protected position.
- Thick stone walls **C** kept enemies out of the castle's inner courtyard.

Design a Castle Floor Plan

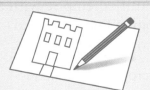

Materials
- paper
- pencil
- ruler

1. Be sure your castle has these features: walls, windows, and moat.

2. Research and add one other defensive feature to your castle.

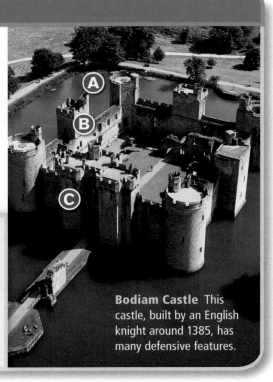

Bodiam Castle This castle, built by an English knight around 1385, has many defensive features.

The Renaissance

▼ **KEY QUESTION** How did the Renaissance change Europe?

Peace and stability were returning to Europe. Merchants again felt safe traveling on the roads. Trade began again. Towns grew. Travel spread new ideas, which set the stage for change.

Forces of Change At the end of the 11th century, thousands of western European Christians took part in the Crusades, a series of military expeditions to take back the Holy Land, Palestine, from the Muslims. The Crusades led to centuries of mistrust between Christians and Muslims and imposed economic burdens on many Europeans. However, they resulted in economic growth, increasing trade between towns on the Mediterranean Sea and in the Middle East.

The importance of towns increased during the Crusades, when towns were needed to supply armies. As towns grew into cities and serfs left manors to find better work, feudal lords lost power. In the 1300s, the deadly plague, known as the Black Death, swept through Europe. About one-third of Europe's population died. The high death rate led to a labor shortage, which further weakened feudal ties.

All these forces helped bring about the Renaissance. The **Renaissance** (REHN•ih•SAHNS) was a 300-year period of renewed interest in learning and art from about 1300 to 1600. The rediscovery of ancient Greek and Roman knowledge influenced the Renaissance. Europeans developed new ideas about art, science, and humanity.

The Rebirth of Europe The Renaissance began in the city-states of the Italian Peninsula. Increased trade between Italian towns and the Middle East after the Crusades had made many Italian merchants and bankers wealthy. They used their new wealth to build and furnish beautiful palaces. Some became **patrons** of the arts, supporting painters and writers. They showed their pride in their city by hiring architects to build churches, public fountains, and sculptures. City-states like Florence, Rome, and Venice competed to display the talents of Italy's finest artists, such as Michelangelo and Leonardo da Vinci.

Renaissance art reflected the beliefs of the period. Many scholars began to study humanity, prompting a new interest in the individual and in **secular**, or worldly, concerns. Many Renaissance paintings still had religious themes, but others depicted contemporary people instead of biblical figures. Painters also found new ways to create more lifelike portraits and realistic landscapes. The technique known as **perspective** gave objects in a painting the appearance of depth and distance. The Renaissance also produced notable writers. Many wrote in their national languages, rather than Latin, which was the practice before the Renaissance. For example, the poet Dante wrote his finest works in Italian.

Mona Lisa Leonardo da Vinci's *Mona Lisa* is one of the most famous paintings of the Renaissance.

Click here to see more works by Renaissance artists @ ClassZone.com

COMPARING ➤ Medieval and Renaissance Art

MEDIEVAL

Madonna Enthroned by Duccio di Buoninsegna

- Created art with religious themes, especially scenes from the Bible
- Created flat, two-dimensional art

RENAISSANCE

Peasant Wedding by Pieter Brueghel

- Created art about secular as well as religious themes, with more emphasis on the individual and daily life
- Created lifelike, realistic sculptures and paintings

CRITICAL THINKING

Form and Support Opinions Which artistic style seems more lifelike? Why?

The Printing Press The invention of the printing press had a huge impact on European society. Johann Gutenberg, a German, created a machine that pressed movable type against paper. Until then, Europeans copied books slowly by hand. The printing press allowed 500 times as many books to be printed in the same amount of time. The first book printed on Gutenberg's press was a Bible. Ideas spread as books became cheap enough for many to buy.

CRITICAL THINKING

Draw Conclusions How did the printing press help ideas spread during the Renaissance?

The Renaissance Spreads In the late 1400s, the Renaissance began to spread north from Italy to France, England, Germany, and Flanders, a region that today is part of Belgium. The Hundred Years' War, a series of battles between France and England, ended in 1453. With the conflict over, cities and trade routes expanded. A wealthy merchant class developed. Like the Italian merchants, they eagerly sponsored artists and writers. So did the monarchs of these countries, who viewed artistic achievements as a source of national pride.

Unlike the Italian artists, many northern European artists chose to paint scenes of everyday life. Pieter Brueghel the Elder, an artist from Flanders, painted peasants dancing and feasting. His paintings included many details of daily life. Authors such as William Shakespeare examined human nature. Many of Shakespeare's plays, including *Hamlet* and *Romeo and Juliet*, are still performed today. Scholars also made scientific advances, learning more about the human body and the minerals that make up the Earth's surface.

The scholars in northern Europe were also more interested in studying Christianity than ancient Greek and Roman art. Their studies led them to call for reforms to existing religious practices. They criticized the Catholic Church for caring more about wealth and power than about spiritual matters. Renaissance knowledge and ideas like these spread across Europe, aided by the printing press. People began to examine and question the institutions around them.

▲ **FIND MAIN IDEAS** Explain how the ideas of the Renaissance changed Europe.

The Reformation

▼ **KEY QUESTION** What concerns led Martin Luther and others to break with the Catholic Church?

During the 14th and 15th centuries, criticisms of the Catholic Church grew more intense. In the 1500s, these concerns set the stage for the **Reformation**, a movement to change church practices. Martin Luther, a German monk, led this movement. In 1517, Luther wrote his Ninety-Five Theses, a list of statements of belief. He attacked practices he saw as corrupt. Luther posted his theses on a church door in Wittenberg, Germany. His supporters sent copies throughout Europe.

Luther's ideas spread quickly. Many northern countries broke with the Catholic Church. Other reformers in Switzerland, Scotland, and England created their own **Protestant** sects, the name given to Christians who protested against the Catholic Church. The Catholic Church tried to slow the expansion of Protestantism. They began their own Catholic Reformation. Luther was excommunicated, or cast out of the Catholic Church. Church leaders sent missionaries overseas in an effort to spread Catholic ideas around the world.

Martin Luther Luther nails his Ninety-Five Theses to the church door in Wittenberg.

▲ **SUMMARIZE** Explain what concerns led Martin Luther and others to break with the Catholic Church.

Section 3 Assessment

> ⟳ **ONLINE QUIZ**
> For test practice, go to
> **Interactive Review**
> @ ClassZone.com

TERMS & NAMES

1. Explain the importance of
- Middle Ages
- feudalism
- Renaissance
- Reformation

USE YOUR READING NOTES

2. Analyze Cause and Effect Use your completed diagram to answer the following question:

How did the plague help bring about the Renaissance?

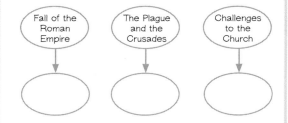

KEY IDEAS

3. In what ways did the Crusades contribute to the start of the Renaissance?

4. Where did the Renaissance begin?

5. What was Martin Luther's role in the Reformation?

CRITICAL THINKING

6. Compare and Contrast What were the main differences between the Italian Renaissance and the Renaissance in northern Europe?

7. Draw Conclusions What did the leaders of the Catholic Church hope to achieve with the Catholic Reformation?

8. CONNECT to Today How is the Internet similar to the printing press? How are they different?

9. WRITING **Prepare an Art Lecture** Choose a painting by a Renaissance artist. Visit an art museum or library to do research. Prepare a short talk for the class on the artist and the significance of the painting. Show the class a picture of the artwork.

▶ Key Ideas

BEFORE, YOU LEARNED

Feudalism and religion provided stability during the Middle Ages. The Renaissance marked a rebirth of creativity in Europe.

NOW YOU WILL LEARN

Revolutions in science, politics, and industry transformed Western Europe. After two world wars, European nations found new ways to cooperate.

▶ Vocabulary

TERMS & NAMES

Scientific Revolution a major change in European thinking in the mid-1500s that led to the questioning of old theories

Enlightenment a philosophical movement in the 1600s and 1700s that was characterized by the use of reason and scientific methods

French Revolution a conflict in France between 1789 and 1799 that ended the monarchy and led to changes in the way France was governed

nationalism pride in and loyalty to one's nation

Industrial Revolution the shift that began in Britain in the 1760s from making goods by hand to making them by machine

imperialism the practice of one country controlling the government and economy of another country or terrritory

Holocaust the systematic murder of Jews and other minorities by the Nazis during World War II

European Union (EU) an organization of European nations whose members cooperate on economic, social, and political issues

▶ Reading Strategy

Re-create the time line shown at right. As you read and respond to the **KEY QUESTIONS**, use the time line to help you place the events of modern European history in order.

See Skillbuilder Handbook, page R6

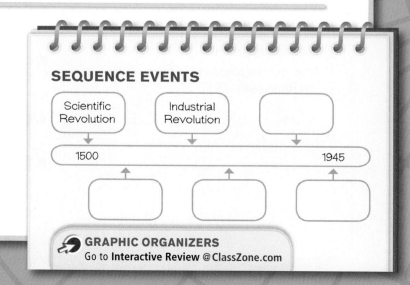

SEQUENCE EVENTS

Scientific Revolution →

Industrial Revolution →

 →

1500 ←←← 1945

GRAPHIC ORGANIZERS
Go to **Interactive Review** @ ClassZone.com

Modern European History

Connecting to Your World

How would you feel if you learned that what you knew about the world was wrong? Today, students aren't likely to disagree when a teacher describes how planets revolve around the sun. In the 1600s, when the Italian astronomer Galileo Galilei observed the sky through his telescope, he was looking for proof of this theory. Some things that seem obvious to us now weren't accepted as fact until a few hundred years ago. In this section, you will learn how new ideas changed Europeans' views of the world.

New Ideas Produce Change

🔻 **KEY QUESTION** How did Enlightenment ideas affect the struggle for independence in many European countries?

In the 1500s and 1600s, scientists such as Galileo examined accepted scientific ideas using reason and careful observation. Knowledge grew rapidly in astronomy, anatomy, and other fields. These discoveries were part of the **Scientific Revolution**, which caused scientists to re-examine old theories.

   In the 1600s, European philosophers began to question traditional beliefs and accepted ideas. They argued that reason could be used to study both human behavior and the natural world. Because of the influence of these ideas, this era is known as the **Enlightenment**, or the Age of Reason.

Telescope Galileo built his first telescope in 1609.

Accademia del Cimento This scientific academy was founded by students of Galileo in 1657.

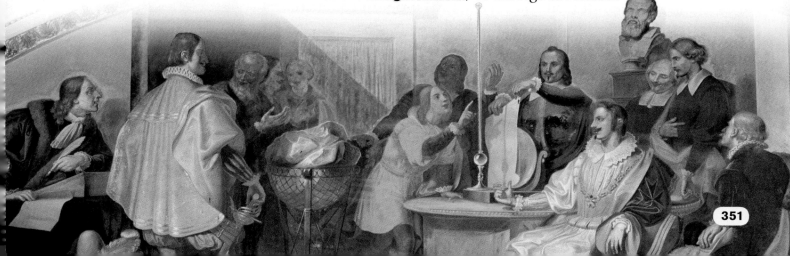

The Guillotine

Before the French Revolution, only nobles had the privilege of execution by beheading. Commoners faced hanging or more gruesome methods. In 1792, Dr. Joseph-Ignace Guillotin proposed a law requiring a machine to carry out executions. The guillotine, with its weighted blade that severed a victim's neck in one cut, was thought to be more humane and democratic than previous methods.

Enlightenment and Revolution

The Enlightenment thinker John Locke argued that people had the rights to life, liberty, and property. The government's job was to protect these rights. When it failed to do so, people had the right to rebel. In 1789, Enlightenment ideas inspired French citizens to challenge the monarchy and the privileges of the wealthiest classes. Their protests led to the **French Revolution**. Radical revolutionary leaders took control of the government. They beheaded the king and abolished the monarchy.

Napoleon Seizes Power

During the French Revolution, Napoleon Bonaparte distinguished himself as a brilliant leader of the French army. In 1799, Napoleon seized control of France. His goal was to create and rule a great empire. His army rapidly conquered most of Europe.

However, his hopes of a long-lasting empire ended after a poorly planned attack on Russia killed many of his soldiers. In 1815, Napoleon faced his final defeat against allied European troops at the Battle of Waterloo.

Nationalism Sweeps Europe

The French Revolution helped spread **nationalism**, pride and loyalty to one's nation. Many Europeans began to see themselves as citizens of a nation, not subjects of a king. Alarmed by the French Revolution, Europe's leaders sought to stop the spread of democracy. They put kings back on their thrones, but ideas of democracy and nationalism were too powerful to fade quickly. Many European countries revolted against their rulers. By the 1870s, the smaller states that made up Italy and Germany had become unified nations. Much of western Europe had achieved self-government, inspired by the spirit of nationalism.

Napoleon's Coronation
Napoleon crowned himself emperor of France in an elaborate ceremony at Paris's Notre Dame Cathedral in 1804. **Why do you think Napoleon staged such an elaborate ceremony?**

▲ **SUMMARIZE** Explain how Enlightenment ideals contributed to European revolutions.

Europe's Expanding Power

▼ **KEY QUESTION** How did the Industrial Revolution change Europe?

In the 1700s, new methods of making goods started a peaceful revolution. Industrialization led European nations to build empires.

Industrial Revolution Many of the inventions of the Scientific Revolution changed the way Europeans worked. New machines produced goods more quickly with fewer workers. The change became known as the **Industrial Revolution**. Factories were built near rivers, so that they could be powered by water. By the 1760s, steam powered the machines, and factories appeared in cities. People moved to cities from the countryside, in search of work. The Industrial Revolution began in Great Britain and spread to other European countries.

Imperialism The newly industrial nations of Europe needed raw materials and new markets for their products. Major European nations looked to Asia and Africa for valuable natural resources. Many nations made **imperialism** their foreign policy, seeking to control smaller, weaker countries politically and economically. European nations claimed overseas colonies without considering how their policies might affect the lives of the people living in these places.

▲ **UNDERSTAND EFFECTS** Explain how the Industrial Revolution changed Europe.

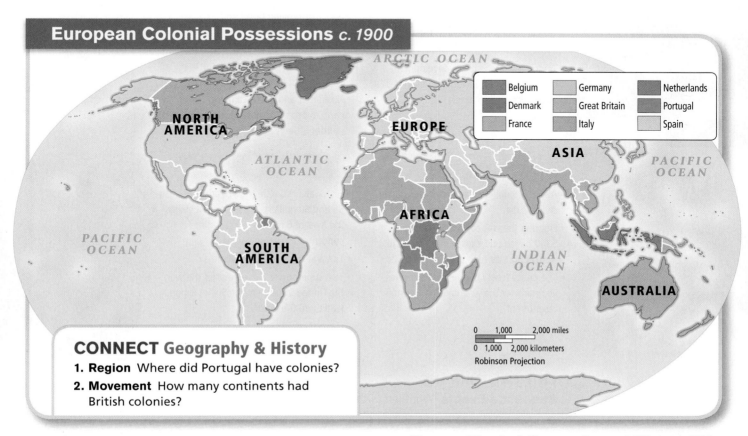

European Colonial Possessions c. 1900

Belgium | Germany | Netherlands
Denmark | Great Britain | Portugal
France | Italy | Spain

0   1,000   2,000 miles
0   1,000   2,000 kilometers
Robinson Projection

CONNECT Geography & History

1. **Region** Where did Portugal have colonies?
2. **Movement** How many continents had British colonies?

Europe in Conflict During the 20th century, tensions between European nations led to two devastating wars, World War I (1914–1918) and World War II (1939–1945). These wars left much of Europe in ruins.

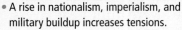

WORLD WAR I	WORLD WAR II
1914–1918	1939–1945

Why

WORLD WAR I
- A rise in nationalism, imperialism, and military buildup increases tensions.
- European nations form mutual protection alliances.
- The assassination of Archduke Franz Ferdinand, shown at left, forces allied nations into war.

WORLD WAR II
- A global economic depression worsens conditions in Europe.
- Adolf Hitler, leader of the Nazi Party, at right, gains control of Germany in 1933 and promises to expand German territory.
- Under Hitler's leadership, Germany invades Poland in 1939.

Who

Central Powers vs. Allies
- Central Powers: Germany, Austria-Hungary, and Turkey
- Allies: Russia, France, the United Kingdom, and the United States (in 1917)

Axis Powers vs. Allies
- Axis Powers: Germany, Italy, and Japan
- Allies: The United Kingdom, France, the Soviet Union, and the United States (in 1941)

How

WORLD WAR I
- Machine guns make it difficult for forces to advance.
- Soldiers on both sides fight from defensive trenches.
- Trench warfare leads to development of new weapons, including poison gas and tanks, shown at left.

WORLD WAR II
- The German strategy of *blitzkrieg* uses fast-moving tanks and airplanes followed by ground troops to overwhelm enemies.
- Airplanes like this one allow the war to be fought over great distances.
- Nazi labor and death camps carry out the **Holocaust**, the mass murder of Jews and others.

Outcomes

WORLD WAR I
- About 8.5 million soldiers and 13 million civilians die.
- Fighting the war costs Europe over $330 billion and causes mass physical destruction, as seen in France at left.
- The peace treaty blames and punishes Germany for the war, causing German resentment.

WORLD WAR II
- Historians estimate total deaths between 35 and 60 million. The Holocaust claims the lives of 6 million Jews. (right: concentration camp survivors)
- The war costs over $1 trillion.
- Two superpowers emerge after the war, the United States and the Soviet Union, leading to the Cold War.

CRITICAL THINKING

Sequence Events What led to the start of Europe's two world wars?

Uniting After War

▼ **KEY QUESTION** How did the two world wars encourage European nations to work together?

After World War II, Europe was devastated. European nations had been at war with each other for several years. Two goals emerged in the war's aftermath: to rebuild Europe's shattered nations and their economies and to work together to prevent future wars.

Creating a European Union In 1952, Belgium, France, Italy, Luxembourg, the Netherlands, and West Germany formed the European Coal and Steel Community (ECSC). Its six members agreed to combine their iron, steel, and coal industries. Their success with these commodities led them to drop trade barriers on others.

In 1967, they created the European Community (EC). Members worked to find ways to move goods, workers, and money more easily across their borders. Trade increased, and more countries wanted to join. In 1973, the EC began to admit other nations, paving the way for the European Union.

By 1992, 12 Western European nations belonged to the EC. That year, all of them signed the Maastricht (MAH-strikt) Treaty. The treaty formed the **European Union (EU)**, an organization of European nations whose members cooperate on economic, social, and political issues. By 2004, the EU had expanded to include Eastern European nations, bringing the total number of members to 25 countries. Candidate nations continue to apply.

How Does the EU Work? The goal of the European Union is to bring the people and countries of Europe closer together. Citizens of EU nations have European citizenship. They can travel freely throughout the EU. They can live and work anywhere in the union. They can vote in elections in the country they live in, even if they are citizens elsewhere.

The European Union member nations also work together on political and social matters such as immigration, law enforcement, and the environment. For instance, the EU sponsors many of Europe's efforts toward finding cleaner, sustainable sources of energy, which you read about earlier in the chapter. The EU also tries to protect the diverse cultures and traditions of its member nations. It funds cultural programs, including education in the languages of other EU nations.

Members of the European Union

Date	Country
By 1952 (ECSC)	Belgium
	France
	Italy
	Luxembourg
	Netherlands
	West Germany
By 1973 (EC)	Denmark
	Ireland
	United Kingdom
By 1995	Greece
	Portugal
	Spain
	East Germany*
	Austria
	Finland
	Sweden
By 2004	Cyprus
	Czech Republic
	Estonia
	Hungary
	Latvia
	Lithuania
	Malta
	Poland
	Slovakia
	Slovenia
By 2007 or 2008	Bulgaria
	Romania

*East Germany joined through German reunification and not as a separate state.

The Euro

The front sides of euro coins have the same image, showing the value of the coin. The backs of the coins have a national image chosen by the country that issued the coin. This is one small way that countries are able to belong to the European Union and share a common currency, but maintain their own cultural heritages.

Euro Front   **Spain**   **Germany**

Netherlands   **France**   **Belgium**

Economic Unity One major area of EU cooperation is its economic policy. The EU is a single market, which means that its members can trade goods freely, without paying taxes on those goods. Many EU members also use the same currency, called the euro. In 1999, 11 EU nations adopted the euro. This decision made it easier for members to trade with each other.

As a single economic unit, the EU is powerful, more than any member nation on its own. However, the EU is weak in other ways. The countries that belong to the union remain independent. The EU does not yet have a constitution. Its leaders make decisions but have little authority to enforce them. So far, the member nations have cooperated on most issues, and the EU has been successful. However, keeping such a large organization unified could be challenging, especially as new countries join.

 SUMMARIZE Explain how two wars encouraged European nations to work together.

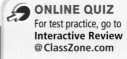 **ONLINE QUIZ**
For test practice, go to **Interactive Review @ ClassZone.com**

Section 4 Assessment

TERMS & NAMES

1. Explain the importance of
- Enlightenment
- nationalism
- imperialism
- European Union

USE YOUR READING NOTES

2. Sequence Events Use your completed time line to answer the following question:

Which event occurred between the Scientific Revolution and the French Revolution?

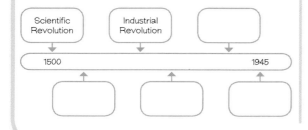

KEY IDEAS

3. How did Enlightenment ideas influence the French Revolution?

4. How did the Industrial Revolution affect imperialism?

5. What steps did the EU and its predecessors take to bring the nations of Europe closer together?

CRITICAL THINKING

6. Analyze Cause and Effect How did the Industrial Revolution change where people lived?

7. Compare and Contrast In what ways were World War I and World War II similar?

8. CONNECT to Today Why might Eastern European nations want to join the European Union?

9. WRITING Write a Speech Imagine that you have been asked to speak to EU members about why you think the nations of Europe should or should not form a "United States of Europe." Write a brief speech expressing your opinion.

Interactive Review

Click here to complete these and other activities online @ ClassZone.com

CHAPTER SUMMARY

Key Idea 1
Europe has diverse landforms ranging from mountains to plains. Its climate is influenced by its nearness to the ocean.

Key Idea 2
The achievements of the ancient Greeks and Romans continue to influence our modern world.

Key Idea 3
Feudalism provided stability after the fall of the Roman Empire. The Renaissance marked a rebirth of creativity.

Key Idea 4
Revolutions in science, politics, and industry transformed Europe. After two world wars, European nations found new ways to cooperate.

For **Review and Study Notes**, go to **Interactive Review @ ClassZone.com**

NAME GAME

Use the Terms & Names list to complete each sentence on paper or online.

1. I am Europe's tallest mountain range. ___Alps___
2. I am the vast area of flat or gently rolling land from France to Russia. _____
3. I make the climate in much of Europe warmer than it would be otherwise. _____
4. I am the form of government that originated in the Greek city-state of Athens. _____
5. I am the form of government that Rome had before it became an empire. _____
6. I am the medieval political system that gave nobles, peasants, and serfs protection in exchange for service. _____
7. I am a time of rebirth in creativity and the arts in Europe. _____
8. I am the religious protest and reform movement that split the Church in the 1500s._____
9. I am a time of great interest in using reason to understand and improve society. _____
10. I am an organization made up of European nations that works together to solve common problems. _____

Alps
city-state
democracy
Enlightenment
European Union
feudalism
French Revolution
imperialism
Industrial Revolution
North Atlantic Drift
Northern European Plain
Peloponnesus
Reformation
Renaissance
republic

Activities

GeoGame

Use this online map to reinforce your understanding of Europe's physical geography. Drag and drop each place name in the list to its location on the map.

Geo GAME

The Pyrenees

Danube River

Greece

Iberian Peninsula

France

To play the complete game, go to **Interactive Review @ ClassZone.com**

Crossword Puzzle

Complete an online crossword puzzle to test your knowledge of Europe's geography and history.

ACROSS
1. vassal trained in combat who fought on behalf of lords

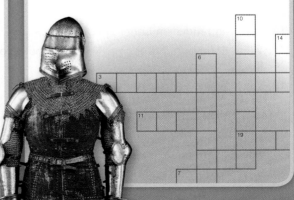

VOCABULARY

Explain the significance of each of the following.

1. fossil fuels
2. republic
3. manor
4. Renaissance
5. Holocaust
6. European Union

Choose the best answer from each pair.

7. This influences Europe's mild climate. (Northern European Plain/North Atlantic Drift)
8. This group of people could hold government office in ancient Rome. (patrician/plebeian)
9. This group of people pledged service to wealthy landowners in exchange for land under the feudal structure. (lords/vassals)
10. This is a feeling of pride for and loyalty to one's nation. (nationalism/imperialism)

KEY IDEAS

1 Europe's Dramatic Landscape

11. How does the North Atlantic Drift affect the climate of Europe?
12. How do Europe's waterways affect its economy?
13. Why is the Northern European Plain a valuable resource?

2 Classical Greece and Rome

14. Why is Athens considered the birthplace of modern democracy?
15. What did the Romans give conquered peoples?

3 The Middle Ages and Renaissance

16. How did feudalism benefit lords?
17. What contributed to the growth of towns before the Renaissance?
18. Why did the Renaissance begin in Italy?

4 Modern European History

19. How did the Industrial Revolution change the way goods were made?
20. Why were many European leaders upset by the French Revolution?

CRITICAL THINKING

21. **Form and Support Opinions** Create a graphic organizer like the one below. Include three factors that influence the mild climate of Europe.

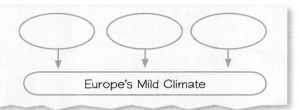

Europe's Mild Climate

22. **Connect Geography & History** What effect have Europe's peninsulas had on its development?
23. **Five Themes: Place** How did Athens and Sparta differ in their views of citizens?
24. **Connect Geography & Culture** How did feudalism affect trade and daily life in medieval Europe?
25. **Analyze Causes and Effects** How are the Renaissance and the Reformation related to each other?
26. **Make Inferences** How did the World War I peace agreement contribute to the start of World War II?

Answer the ESSENTIAL QUESTION

What changes have taken place in Europe since ancient times?

Written Response Write a two- or three-paragraph response to the Essential Question. Consider the key ideas of each section as well as specific ideas about how Europe has changed. Use the rubric below to guide you.

Response Rubric
A strong response will:
• identify elements of ancient society and politics
• discuss three major historical events that occurred after the fall of the Roman Empire
• explain how each of those events changed European society and politics

STANDARDS-BASED ASSESSMENT

Test Practice
- Online Test Practice @ ClassZone.com
- Test-Taking Strategies and Practice at the front of this book

PHYSICAL MAP

Use the map to provide short answers to questions 1 and 2 on your paper.

European Peninsulas

1. **Which of the peninsulas is located farthest north?**

2. **Which of the peninsulas has a coastline on the Black Sea?**

PRIMARY SOURCE

The following excerpt is from Pericles's "Funeral Oration." Use context clues within the quotation to answer questions 3 and 4 on your paper.

> Our constitution is named a democracy, because it is in the hands not of the few but of the many. But our laws secure equal justice for all in their private disputes, and our public opinion welcomes and honors talent in every branch of achievement, not as a matter of privilege but on grounds of excellence alone.
>
> Source: Thucydides, from *The Peloponnesian War*

3. **According to Pericles, what made Athens a democracy?**

   A. It had laws that protect only the elite.

   B. It granted privileges to the rich.

   C. It was governed by a small group of leaders.

   D. It was governed by the many.

4. **Whom did the laws of Athens protect?**

   A. everyone

   B. government officials

   C. privileged citizens

   D. peasants

GeoActivity

1. INTERDISCIPLINARY ACTIVITY–HISTORY

With a small group, learn more about the events of the French Revolution. Create a political cartoon about one of these events such as the rioting by the poor, or Napoleon's takeover of government. Your cartoon should show a clear point of view.

2. WRITING FOR SOCIAL STUDIES

Reread the part of Section 4 on the growth of nationalism in Western Europe. Imagine that you live in a European monarchy in the mid-1800s. Write a letter to a friend telling why you believe in independence for your country.

3. MENTAL MAPPING

Create an outline map of France and label the following:

- Rhone River
- Pyrenees
- Massif Central
- Seine River
- English Channel
- Atlantic Ocean

CHAPTER

12 Western Europe

1
FOCUS ON

Greece and Italy

2
FOCUS ON

Spain and Portugal

3
FOCUS ON

France and the Benelux Countries

4
FOCUS ON

Germany and the Alpine Countries

5
FOCUS ON

The Nordic Countries

 ESSENTIAL QUESTION

What geographic and cultural characteristics define the subregions of Western Europe?

CONNECT ⤵ **Geography & History**

Use the map and the time line to answer the following questions.

1. How many Western European nations have territory that extends east of 20° E longitude?
2. What country is Berlin the capital of, and when did the city reunite?

476

Geography

1418 Prince Henry of Portugal begins sponsoring expeditions of exploration.

History

▲ **476** Beginning of the Byzantine Empire (Empress Theodora)

Culture

1880 Bastille Day is set aside as a French national holiday. ▶

ICELAND
★ Reykjavík

Arctic Circle

Norwegian Sea

Faroe Islands (Den.)

Shetland Islands (U.K.)

★ National capital

FINLAND

SWEDEN

NORWAY

Helsinki ★

Oslo ★   ★ Stockholm

Gulf of Bothnia

Gulf of Finland

ESTONIA

RUSSIA

LATVIA

LITHUANIA

RUSSIA

BELARUS

North Sea

SCOTLAND

NOTHERN IRELAND

ATLANTIC OCEAN

Dublin ★

IRELAND

UNITED KINGDOM

WALES   ENGLAND

British Isles

London ★

English Channel

Channel Islands (U.K.)

DENMARK
Copenhagen ★

NETHERLANDS
★ Amsterdam

Brussels ★

BELGIUM

Elbe R.

Berlin ★

GERMANY

Rhine R.

LUXEMBOURG

POLAND

CZECH REPUBLIC

SLOVAKIA

UKRAINE

MOLDOVA

Seine R.

Paris ★

FRANCE

Loire R.

Bay of Biscay

Rhône R.

Bern ★

SWITZERLAND

LIECHTENSTEIN

Danube R.

Vienna ★

AUSTRIA

HUNGARY

SLOV.

CROATIA

ROMANIA

Black Sea

Po R.

SAN MARINO

MONACO

ANDORRA

Corsica (Fr.)

ITALY
★ Rome

VATICAN CITY

BOSNIA & HERZ.

SERBIA

MONT.

MAC.

ALB.

BULGARIA

Adriatic Sea

PORTUGAL

Madrid ★

Ebro River

Tagus River

Lisbon ★

SPAIN

Balearic Islands (Sp.)

Sardinia (It.)

Tyrrhenian Sea

Ionian Sea

Aegean Sea

GREECE

★ Athens

TURKEY

Strait of Gibraltar

GIBRALTAR (U.K.)

MOROCCO

ALGERIA

TUNISIA

Sicily (It.)

Mediterranean Sea

MALTA

Crete (Gr.)

0   200   400 miles
0   200   400 kilometers

Geography

1989 Berlin reunites after the opening of the Berlin Wall. ▶

Government

1920 The Nazi Party forms in Germany.

Government

2006 Finland's first female president, Tarja Halonen, is elected to a second term. ▶

Today

Reading for Understanding

▶ Key Ideas

BEFORE, YOU LEARNED

Ancient Greece began as many independent city-states with different ways of life. Ancient Rome began as a republic and expanded into a vast empire.

NOW YOU WILL LEARN

For many centuries, Greece and Italy were collections of small states. Fueled by nationalism, each struggled to gain independence and unite as a nation.

▶ Vocabulary

TERMS & NAMES

Byzantine Empire the eastern half of the Roman Empire that survived for a thousand years after the fall of Rome

fascism (FASH•IHZ•uhm) a political philosophy that promotes blind loyalty to the state and a strong central government controlled by a powerful dictator

Romance language any of the languages that developed from the Roman language, Latin, such as Spanish, Portuguese, French, Italian, and Romanian

Vatican the official residence of the pope in Vatican City, and the political and religious center of the Roman Catholic Church

coalition an alliance or partnership, often a temporary one

BACKGROUND VOCABULARY

compulsory required

REVIEW

nationalism pride in and loyalty to one's nation

European Union (EU) an organization of European nations whose members cooperate on economic, social, and political issues

▶ Reading Strategy

Re-create the chart shown at right. As you read and respond to the **KEY QUESTIONS**, use the chart to help you summarize what you learn about Greece and Italy.

 Skillbuilder Handbook, page R5

SUMMARIZE

	GREECE	ITALY
History		
Language		
Government		
Economy		

 GRAPHIC ORGANIZERS
Go to **Interactive Review** @ ClassZone.com

Greece and Italy

Connecting to Your World

It's not surprising that Greece and Italy are popular tourist destinations. Stretching across southern peninsulas in the Mediterranean Sea, both countries have mild climates and warm, sunny weather much of the year. In both places, visitors can see the magnificent treasures of the distant past. While both countries were once part of the Roman Empire, after it divided, these nations developed different cultures. In the 1800s, both Greece and Italy fought for independence and tried to preserve their ancient heritage as they became modern nations.

Greece

▼ **KEY QUESTION** How has Greece's government changed since the Byzantine Empire?

As you learned in Chapter 11, ancient Greece began as a series of independent city-states. Eventually, it became part of the Roman Empire. When the Roman Empire divided, Greece was in the eastern half, called the **Byzantine Empire**. Most of the Byzantine Empire's inhabitants spoke Greek, not Latin, and followed the eastern traditions of Christianity. By 1453, the Byzantines had been conquered by the Islamic Ottoman Turks. Before declaring their independence in 1829, Greeks had lived under foreign rule for over 2,000 years.

Greek Pottery
Tourists come to Greece to see artifacts like this fifth century B.C. pot.

Byzantine Ruins in Greece

BYZANTINE EMPIRE

Mediterranean Sea

History When the Byzantine Empire fell, Greece became part of the Ottoman Empire for approximately 400 years. By the late 1700s, desire for independence was growing. **Nationalism** increased as more Greeks learned about their past. Interest and pride in Greece's history as a center of culture and democracy grew.

In 1829, after a long struggle, Greece broke free from Ottoman rule. Its leaders made the nation a monarchy. Then, in 1967, Greek military officers seized control of the government. When the military government collapsed, voters decided not to return to a monarchy. Since 1975, Greece has been a parliamentary democracy.

Culture Most Greeks share the same ethnic background, language, and religion. They speak Greek and belong to the Greek Orthodox Church, a form of Christianity. Every major town has a patron saint, and townspeople celebrate their saint with an annual festival. Easter is also an important religious holiday in Greece.

About two-thirds of Greeks live in cities. Many live in Athens, Greece's capital. Cities have both older sections with narrow streets and newer areas with high-rise apartments and shopping centers. Many cities have a coffee house, or *kafeneio*, where friends meet.

Government and Economics Greece is a parliamentary democracy. The president's job is mostly ceremonial. The country is governed by the prime minister, the cabinet, and the parliament. Voting in Greece is **compulsory**, or required. Failing to vote is against the law.

Greece has fewer high-tech industries and service jobs than many countries in Western Europe. Although it is a member of the **European Union (EU)**, its economy lags behind other nations. Agriculture makes up a greater percentage of its economy than wealthier nations. Because of Greece's position on the Mediterranean Sea, tourism, shipping, and fishing remain important.

▲ **SEQUENCE EVENTS** Explain the changes to Greece's government since the Byzantine Empire.

Greek Orthodox Church This church, with its typical whitewashed walls and blue domes, is located in Oia on the island of Santorini.

The percentage of a nation's labor force employed in agriculture is a good indication of that country's economic development. Take a look at how Greece compares to these other Western European countries.

	GDP (Per Capita*)	Agriculture	Industry	Services
		(Percentage Employed in Selected Sectors)		
Denmark	$34,600	3	21	76
France	$29,900	4	24	72
Spain	$25,500	5	30	65
Greece	$22,200	12	20	68
Portugal	$19,300	10	30	60

*GDP: Gross Domestic Product
Source: *CIA World Factbook, 2006*

CRITICAL THINKING
Compare and Contrast How do Greece's GDP per capita and agricultural employment compare to the other countries listed in the chart?

Italy

🔻 **KEY QUESTION** What changes has Italian society experienced in recent years?

After the Western Roman Empire fell in the late 400s, the Italian peninsula split into many small kingdoms and city-states. Sometimes they were independent. At other times, France, Austria, and Spain ruled over them.

Benito Mussolini
Fascist dictator Mussolini took control of Italy in the early 1920s.

History In 1796, France conquered much of the Italian Peninsula. French rule led to new laws, better roads, and a common currency. Italians saw the benefits of unity and began to work toward independence. In 1861, Italian patriots such as Giuseppe Garibaldi and Camillo Cavour succeeded in unifying Italy.

In the early 1920s, Benito Mussolini took control of the Italian government. He promoted **fascism** (FASH•IHZ•uhm), a political system based on fierce nationalism and a strong central government led by a dictator. Mussolini gained support by promising a return to a powerful Roman Empire. During World War II, Italy fought with Germany against the Allies. After Italian forces suffered major defeats, Mussolini was forced out and killed as he tried to escape Italy. In 1946, Italians replaced the monarchy with democracy.

Culture Like Greece, modern Italy has been influenced by traditions. The official language is Italian, a Romance language. **Romance languages** come from Latin and are spoken in places that used to be part of the Roman Empire. Take a look at the map below to see where other Romance languages are spoken.

Most Italians are Roman Catholics. For many centuries, Catholic Church leaders and the Italian government were closely allied. The political and religious center of the Church, the **Vatican**, is located in Italy. Although it lies within the city of Rome, it is an independent country, the smallest such country in the world.

In recent years, Italy has become more diverse as immigrants have come from nearby Morocco and Tunisia in North Africa and Albania on the Balkan Peninsula. Much of Italy has changed from a rural, agricultural nation to a modern, urban society. However, life differs between northern and southern Italy. Northern Italy is richer, with more people employed in manufacturing than in the south, where more people work in agriculture.

Italian food changes depending on the region of the country, from pasta with tomato sauce in the south to a dish made of rice called *risotto* in the north. Sports are also important to Italian culture. Many Italians enjoy watching race car driving, cycling, and soccer.

Languages of Western Europe

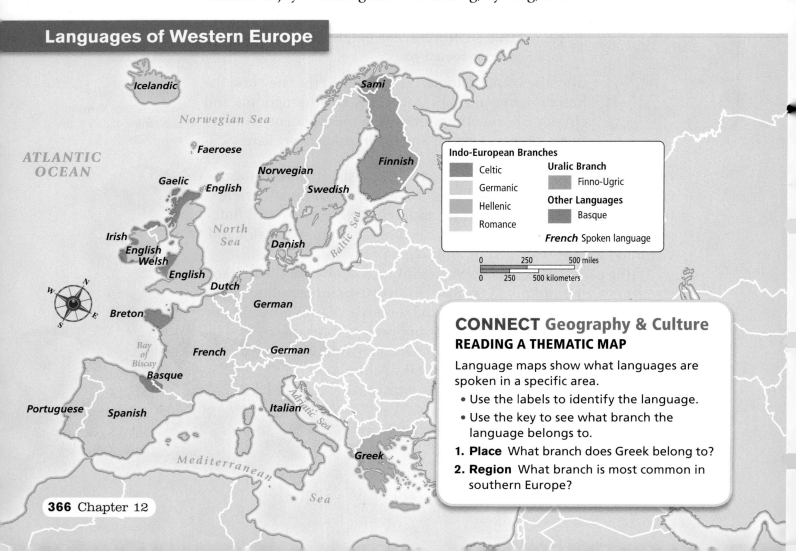

Indo-European Branches

Celtic
Germanic
Hellenic
Romance

Uralic Branch
Finno-Ugric

Other Languages
Basque

French Spoken language

0   250   500 miles
0   250   500 kilometers

CONNECT Geography & Culture
READING A THEMATIC MAP

Language maps show what languages are spoken in a specific area.
- Use the labels to identify the language.
- Use the key to see what branch the language belongs to.

1. **Place** What branch does Greek belong to?
2. **Region** What branch is most common in southern Europe?

Government and Economics Italy is a parliamentary democracy. Voters elect three-fourths of parliament members. The rest are assigned by a complex system designed to make sure each of Italy's many political parties is represented in the government. A prime minister heads the government. Usually this leader comes from the party that wins the most votes in the election. Because Italy has so many parties, leaders often have to form coalition governments. A **coalition** is an alliance or partnership, which is often temporary. Members of several parties agree to work together. If parties withdraw from a coalition, leaders have to form a new one. As a result, Italy has had many changes in government.

Once a mainly agricultural country, Italy is now a prosperous industrial nation. Only five percent of the population has a farm-related job. European Union membership has helped Italy grow, opening new markets for its products, which include fashionable clothing, shoes, and cars. Milan, in northern Italy, is world-famous for its fashion shows. However, economic growth for the country has been uneven. The north has many of Italy's factories, while the south remains largely farmland. Italy continues to look for ways to bring greater prosperity to the southern region.

Runway Model
A model walks the runway at a Milan fashion show.

▲ **SUMMARIZE** Describe the changes that Italian society has experienced in recent years.

Section ① Assessment

🔄 **ONLINE QUIZ**
For test practice, go to **Interactive Review** @ ClassZone.com

TERMS & NAMES

1. Explain the importance of
- Byzantine Empire
- fascism
- Vatican
- coalition

USE YOUR READING NOTES

2. Summarize Use your completed chart to answer the following question:

How is Greece's economy different from Italy's economy?

	GREECE	ITALY
History		
Language		
Government		
Economy		

KEY IDEAS

3. In what ways did Greek culture develop differently from Italian culture after the division of the Roman Empire?

4. Why are so many Italians members of the Catholic Church?

5. How has Italy's economy changed over time?

CRITICAL THINKING

6. Analyze Cause and Effect How did the Byzantine Empire influence Greek culture?

7. Make Inferences What are the disadvantages for Italy of having had so many coalition governments?

8. CONNECT to Today Why would it be an advantage for Italy to make sure that southern Italy is as prosperous as northern Italy?

9. MATH Create a Bar Graph Look at the chart on Western European economies in this section. Create a bar graph showing the percentage of workers employed in agriculture in each country.

COMPARING Regions of Italy

Italy can be roughly divided into three regions: northern, central, and southern. While northern and southern Italy share aspects of Italian culture, they are also different.

Northern Italy

The craggy Alps of northern Italy are dotted with villages, such as St. Magdalena, shown below. Tourists often come to hike or ski in the mountains. The northern region is also highly industrialized, however, with major metropolitan areas such as Milan and Turin. Many of Italy's cities with populations of 100,000 or greater are in the north.

Recreation

Like these hikers, many people enjoy the rugged trails winding through the Italian Alps.

Work

Northern Italy has more factories than farms defining the region's major cities. Workers at this factory in Bologna manufacture Ducati motorcycles.

Southern Italy

Southern Italy also has mountains, but it benefits more from the coastline along the Mediterranean and Adriatic seas than does northern Italy. Many of the tourists visiting southern Italy come to relax on sandy beaches in towns such as Minori, shown below.

The south is also much less industrialized than the north. Southern Italy has fewer big cities and more people are employed in agriculture, such as growing and harvesting grapes and olives.

Recreation
Sunbathers lounge on the beach in Sorrento, enjoying its warm Mediterranean climate.

Work
These men are gathering olives to make olive oil in an orchard in Bisceglie. It is located in the southern region of Puglia, where the arid climate is particularly suited to growing olives.

CRITICAL THINKING

1. **Compare and Contrast** What geographic features are characteristic of each region?

2. **Make Inferences** Which region do you think is wealthier and why?

Reading for Understanding

▶ Key Ideas

BEFORE, YOU LEARNED

After the division and fall of the Roman Empire, Greece and Italy developed into different nations.

NOW YOU WILL LEARN

Like Greece and Italy, Spain and Portugal were ruled by foreigners. After gaining independence, both developed overseas empires to fuel their economies.

▶ Vocabulary

TERMS & NAMES

Moors the group of Muslims from North Africa who conquered Spain in the eighth century

Reconquista the successful effort by the Spanish to drive the Moors out of Spain

Christopher Columbus Italian navigator and explorer who sailed for Spain and explored the Caribbean and the coast of Central and South America

Basque (bask) an ethnic group living in the western Pyrenees and along the Bay of Biscay in Spain and France; also the name of their language

BACKGROUND VOCABULARY

separatist a person who wants a region to break away from the nation it is a part of

Visual Vocabulary Christopher Columbus reaches the New World.

▶ Reading Strategy

Re-create the Venn diagram shown at right. As you read and respond to the **KEY QUESTIONS**, use the diagram to help you compare and contrast Spain and Portugal.

 Skillbuilder Handbook, page R9

COMPARE AND CONTRAST

SPAIN   BOTH   PORTUGAL

GRAPHIC ORGANIZERS
Go to **Interactive Review** @ ClassZone.com

Spain and Portugal

Connecting to Your World

Without ever visiting Spain, most Americans know more about Spanish culture than they think. For over 300 years, Spain had an empire in what is today Mexico and the southwestern United States. In places where Spain once ruled, the impact of Spanish culture is easy to see. Many southwestern cities have Spanish names and buildings influenced by Spanish architecture. Throughout the United States, many people speak Spanish and eat Spanish food. Spanish culture itself was the product of influences from many other cultures.

Spanish Food
Spanish food—including small appetizers called *tapas*, such as this squid dish—has become popular in the United States.

Spain

🔻 **KEY QUESTION** What regional differences affect Spain's culture?

For centuries, Spain was part of the Roman Empire. When the empire fell, a Germanic tribe conquered the peninsula and established a Christian kingdom. It lasted until the early A.D. 700s, when the **Moors**, Muslim peoples from North Africa, took control of southern Spain. Spain's Moorish rulers brought a more advanced culture to medieval Europe. Muslim scholars made new discoveries in medicine, mathematics, and other fields. They remained there for almost eight centuries, when groups of Christians still living in northern Spain succeeded in driving them out of the region.

The Alhambra
Located in Granada, Spain, the Alhambra was a Moorish palace and fortress.

SPAIN
• Granada

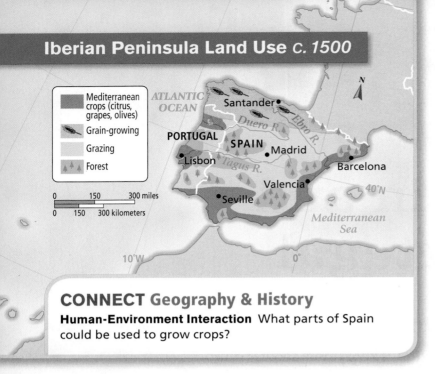

Iberian Peninsula Land Use c. 1500

Mediterranean crops (citrus, grapes, olives)

Grain-growing

Grazing

Forest

0   150   300 miles
0   150   300 kilometers

ATLANTIC OCEAN

Santander

Duero R.

PORTUGAL

SPAIN

Lisbon

Tagus R.

Madrid

Barcelona

Valencia

Seville

Ebro R.

40°N

Mediterranean Sea

10°W   0°

N

CONNECT Geography & History

Human-Environment Interaction What parts of Spain could be used to grow crops?

History In the 1000s, Christians in northern Spain began the **Reconquista**, the effort to drive the Moors out of Spain. It lasted until the 1400s, when King Ferdinand and Queen Isabella conquered the last Muslim kingdom. Once unified under its Catholic monarchs, Spain began to look beyond its territory, which was poor in resources and farmland. Spain turned to the sea, and sponsored **Christopher Columbus's** first voyage to the Americas in 1492. By the 1500s, Spain's conquests in the Americas had made it rich. Its colonies provided Spain with resources it lacked. For a time, Spain was the world's greatest power. By the 1800s, Spain's power had faded, and its colonies declared independence.

Spain remained neutral during World War I. In the 1930s, the Spanish fought a civil war over whether the country should be a monarchy or a republic. During the struggle, Francisco Franco of Spain's fascist party won control of the government. He ruled as a dictator for almost 40 years.

Culture The Spanish share many cultural traits. Until a few decades ago, however, most people identified more with the region they lived in than the country. Spain has many regional languages, such as Catalan and Valencian, which emphasize cultural differences. The Roman Catholic Church was the biggest common tie. Almost all Spaniards are Catholic.

In the 1950s and 1960s, Spain's economy developed quickly and changed the way many people lived. Many people left farms to take manufacturing jobs in cities. Today, most of Spain's people live in cities or towns. Their homes are apartments rather than houses. Even in rural areas, better farming methods and labor-saving machinery have made life easier.

Flamenco Flamenco, a traditional Spanish dance, consists of men and women in elaborate costumes performing intricate steps and gestures. **How do dances like the flamenco preserve Spanish culture?**

The Running of the Bulls Every July, tourists come to Pamplona in northern Spain for the Fiesta de San Fermín. The main attraction is the daily stampede of a half-dozen bulls through the city's narrow streets to the bullfighting ring. Runners sprint ahead, trying to avoid getting slashed by sharp horns. According to legend, the run may have started in the 1200s as a way to move the bulls through town to be sold at market.

CRITICAL THINKING

Make Inferences Why might some people object to the Running of the Bulls?

While the shift to an urban society threatened some Spanish traditions, many Spaniards still enjoy taking part in the old customs. *Paella* (pah•AY•yah), a flavorful dish of seafood, meat, and vegetables mixed with yellow rice, remains a popular choice. Spaniards like soccer, but bullfighting remains Spain's most famous traditional sport. Audiences also enjoy watching Spanish dances, such as the flamenco.

Government and Economics After Franco's death in 1975, Spain became a parliamentary monarchy. This change allowed the people to have a voice in their government. King Juan Carlos I has ruled the country alongside elected officials since the monarchy was formed.

Today, Spain's leaders face demands by some in the **Basque** (bask) ethnic group to create a separate Basque nation. The Basque people live in the Pyrenees Mountains. They have lived in Spain longer than any other group and have kept a distinct language and customs. Some Basque **separatist** groups have tried violence to further their cause.

For centuries, Spain's economy depended heavily on fishing and farming. It lagged behind most of Western Europe in industrial growth. After World War II, Spain's economy grew more rapidly. Factories began turning out cars and steel, and tourism increased. In the 1980s, Spain joined the EU. Membership boosted the economy by promoting trade and by making financial aid from the EU available.

▲ **EVALUATE** Explain some of the regional differences that exist within Spanish culture.

Portugal

PORTUGAL
SPAIN

▼ **KEY QUESTION** How did Portugal's location contribute to its role as a leader in the Age of Exploration?

Portugal shares the Iberian Peninsula with Spain, but occupies a much smaller area. It is located on Europe's western coastline along the Atlantic Ocean. Despite its small size, its location and keen interest in exploration helped it build an empire.

HISTORY MAKERS

Prince Henry 1349–1460

Historians call Prince Henry "the Navigator" because he made major contributions to maritime exploration. He wasn't a sailor, and he rarely traveled far from his homeland of Portugal. During his lifetime, he sponsored more than 50 voyages of exploration. His dedication to exploration eventually led Portugal to discover valuable trade routes to Asia. These voyages greatly advanced European knowledge of the world. Prince Henry's efforts helped make Portugal a major sea power and put the nation on the path to empire.

ONLINE BIOGRAPHY
For more on the life of Prince Henry, go to the
Research & Writing Center @ ClassZone.com

History For many centuries, the region that is now Portugal was, like Spain, under Muslim rule. In 1143, Portugal became an independent kingdom. Because of its coastal location, the Portuguese became skilled sailors, navigators, and shipbuilders. In the 1400s and 1500s, Portugal played a key role in Europe's Age of Exploration. Prince Henry of Portugal sponsored many expeditions. Portuguese explorers helped their country build an empire.

For a time, overseas colonies brought prosperity. Portugal profited from the spice trade with Asia and the gold, diamonds, and other resources taken from its African and South American colonies. By the 1800s, however, Portugal had lost its position as a world power to larger European nations. In 1822, Brazil, Portugal's richest colony, declared independence.

In 1908, revolutionaries overthrew Portugal's king and made the country a republic, but political unrest continued. In 1926, military leaders seized control. Dictators ruled until 1976, when Portugal became a parliamentary democracy in a peaceful revolution.

Culture The official language of Portugal is Portuguese. Like Spanish, Portuguese is a Romance language. Most Portuguese are Roman Catholics. Especially in rural areas, Catholic priests play a key role in political and social life. Traditional Catholic celebrations are important. Unlike much of Western Europe, Portugal today is still a largely rural country with many small farming and fishing villages. Just under half of its citizens live in rural areas. Although Portugal remains a rural country, its cities are growing. Each year, many people move from the countryside in search of jobs in the cities.

France and the Benelux Countries

Connecting to Your World

Can you imagine spending three weeks riding your bike from Chicago to Los Angeles? Every July, about 200 riders in the Tour de France bicycle race cover that distance and more in one of the world's most watched sporting events. The course of the race runs through much of France and some of the surrounding countries. Riders cover terrain from the mountainous roads of the Alps to the cobbled streets of Paris. The race is a great source of national pride for the French people.

Tour de France
Cyclists race down a curvy mountain road in western France.

France

▼ **KEY QUESTION** How has its colonial empire changed the population of France?

France is the largest country in Western Europe. Its landscape ranges from the peaks of the Alps and the beaches on the Mediterranean Sea to cities such as Paris and fishing villages along the Atlantic Ocean. For much of its history, kings ruled this territory. Then, in 1789, the French were inspired to fight for their independence. Since then, France has gone back and forth many times between monarchy and democracy.

Arc de Triomphe
This monument in Paris celebrates military victories.

•Paris

FRANCE

History In 1792, French revolutionaries decided to make France a democracy. Soon after, Napoleon Bonaparte seized power and ruled as emperor until his defeat in 1815. France then returned briefly to a monarchy. In 1848, a second, less violent revolt occurred that led to another democracy. Voters chose Louis Napoleon Bonaparte, a nephew of Napoleon, as president of the new government, but like his famous uncle, he declared himself emperor. After his armies suffered major defeats, he was forced to step down, and France once again became a republic. Political instability and frequent changes in government continued. Then, in 1958, French voters agreed to a new constitution that gave their president greater power.

Despite its many changes in government, France became a powerful nation. Like other major powers, it developed a colonial empire in Africa and Asia that boosted its economy. In the 1900s, however, many battles of World War I and World War II were fought on French soil. These conflicts devastated France. Millions died, and the destruction of factories, farms, and cities shattered the French economy. In the 1960s and 1970s, the French colonies overseas gained their independence, another blow to the French economy. It has since recovered, as a result of hard work and access to natural resources.

CONNECT to History

Bastille Day is celebrated each year on July 14. It marks the beginning of the French Revolution. On July 14, 1789, an angry mob took control of the Bastille, a French prison. On August 4, 1789, frightened French nobles allowed the common people a greater role in government. In June 1791, fearing for his life, King Louis XVI tried to escape from France. He was imprisoned in August 1792. In January 1793, revolutionaries beheaded the king. Three constitutions were adopted during the revolution, one in 1791, one in 1793, and the last in 1795. In October 1799, Napoleon Bonaparte seized power, ending the revolution.

Bastille Day parade in Paris

Activity

Make an Illustrated Time Line

Materials
- markers
- butcher paper

1. To create a French Revolution time line, pick beginning and end dates.

2. Draw a line and divide it into segments. Leave room to illustrate each event.

3. Choose three or four events to show on the time line.

4. Use markers to create drawings and write short captions describing each event.

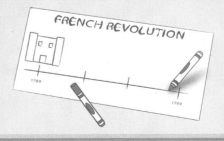

Culture Most French citizens have a very strong cultural identity, and take pride in French culture, history, and language. In recent decades, France has become more diverse. People have emigrated from its former colonies in North Africa and Asia. Many Muslims now live in this primarily Roman Catholic nation.

France, like much of Western Europe, is highly urbanized and densely settled. Three out of four people live in cities. Because space is scarce, apartments are more common than houses. People often walk or ride public transportation. In fact, many cities limit car use and parking on city streets.

French culture has had a global influence. French painters such as Claude Monet and Pierre-Auguste Renoir influenced the popular Impressionist style of painting in the late 1800s. French chefs are well-known for creating culinary masterpieces. Chefs in restaurants around the world try to master French techniques. Each year on July 14, the French celebrate their nation and its culture on Bastille Day. Fireworks displays and parades commemorate French independence.

Government and Economics Today, France is a parliamentary democracy with power concentrated at the national level. Its government spreads power across executive, legislative, and judicial branches, like the United States. In France, however, the executive branch includes a president and a prime minister. France's president serves a five-year term and oversees foreign affairs. He or she appoints a prime minister to take care of the daily operation of the government.

After the devastation of World War II, France worked hard to modernize its economy. Now, its economy is one of the world's strongest. Although a small percentage of French workers are farmers, France is Europe's largest exporter of farm produce. This is because of the fertile soil of the **Northern European Plain** that covers much of France, as well as modern farming methods. France, an EU member, is a major producer of cars, high-speed trains, and airplanes.

Tourism is a key industry. France has been the world's top tourist destination for several years running. Many people travel to France to visit its museums, castles, and cathedrals. Visitors also wait in long lines to go to the top of the most famous landmark in Paris, the Eiffel Tower.

ANALYZE EFFECTS Explain how France's colonial empire has changed its population.

THE EIFFEL TOWER

Height: 1,063 feet

Weight: 10,100 tons

Date Completed: March 31, 1889

Elevators: Seven elevators travel over 64,000 miles each year, equal to more than two and a half times around the Earth.

Materials: The tower is made of iron, and is painted about every 5 years with 50 to 60 tons of paint to keep it from rusting.

Composition: It consists of 18,038 pieces, joined together by 2.5 million rivets.

NETHERLANDS

BELGIUM

LUXEMBOURG

The Benelux Countries

▼ **KEY QUESTION** How has belonging to an economic union helped the Benelux countries?

The Netherlands, Belgium, and Luxembourg belong to an economic union known as the **Benelux** (BEHN•uh•LUHKS) countries. The name was created by combining the first few letters of each country's name. The Benelux nations are alike in many ways. All are constitutional monarchies. All are highly urbanized with well-developed economies. All belong to the EU and depend on trade with larger neighbors.

The Netherlands Following centuries of foreign rule, the Dutch declared their independence from Spain in 1581. Spain finally recognized the Netherlands as an independent nation in 1648. The 1600s were an era of prosperity and achievement for the Dutch. They became a great sea power with colonies in Southeast Asia and the Americas. Dutch is the official language of the Netherlands. Many people also speak English, German, or French. Most Dutch are Christians, though many Muslim immigrants have come from former Dutch colonies in Indonesia and Suriname.

The Netherlands is very densely populated. Because nearly half of its land is below sea level, living space is scarce. The Dutch have used dikes, dams, canals, and pumping systems to reclaim land that is below sea level. The drained lands, called **polders** (POHL•durz), have rich soil and are often used for farming. The Dutch also build factories and towns on them. Forty percent of the land in the Netherlands is from polders.

The Netherlands is also highly urbanized. Because of the shortage of land, Dutch rural areas are close to cities. Bicycles are very common, both for recreation and as a means of transportation in crowded cities.

Belgium and Luxembourg For many years, Belgium was part of the Netherlands. It gained its independence in 1830. Belgium's central location has been both an advantage and a disadvantage. It has enabled Belgium to prosper through trade with its neighbors. But it also made Belgium a battleground during the two world wars, which caused great destruction and loss of life.

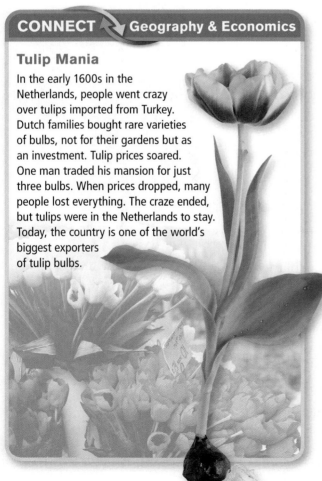

CONNECT Geography & Economics

Tulip Mania

In the early 1600s in the Netherlands, people went crazy over tulips imported from Turkey. Dutch families bought rare varieties of bulbs, not for their gardens but as an investment. Tulip prices soared. One man traded his mansion for just three bulbs. When prices dropped, many people lost everything. The craze ended, but tulips were in the Netherlands to stay. Today, the country is one of the world's biggest exporters of tulip bulbs.

At one time, cultural differences between Dutch-speaking Flemings in the north and French-speaking Walloons in the south caused serious tensions. In recent years, the government has eased tensions by giving both ethnic groups greater **autonomy**. Now, the Belgian constitution recognizes separate cultural communities based on language, as well as separate economic regions for the two groups.

Luxembourg is one of the smallest countries in Europe. In 1890, it broke away from the Netherlands to become a **duchy**, a state ruled by a duke or duchess. The country has three official languages: French, used in government; German, used in newspapers; and Luxembourgish, used for everyday matters. Many of its people are **multilingual**, or able to speak several languages. This has made Luxembourg attractive to foreign companies looking for new locations. At one time, steel was Luxembourg's most important product. Today, its economy is more diversified, with banking and other financial services making up a key segment of its economy.

Antwerp, Belgium
The cafés in this square in the heart of Antwerp's historic district are typical of Europe's outdoor cafés.

▲ **MAKE INFERENCES** Explain how belonging to an economic union has helped the Benelux countries.

Section 3 Assessment

🔗 **ONLINE QUIZ**
For test practice, go to
Interactive Review
@ ClassZone.com

TERMS & NAMES

1. Explain the importance of
- Benelux
- polders
- duchy
- multilingual

USE YOUR READING NOTES

2. Find Main Ideas Use your completed web diagram to answer the following question:

How are France and the Benelux countries similar?

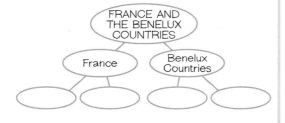

FRANCE AND THE BENELUX COUNTRIES

France

Benelux Countries

KEY IDEAS

3. What are France's leading industrial products and services?

4. How have the people of the Netherlands used technology to reshape their environment?

5. What cultural differences have caused problems within Belgium?

CRITICAL THINKING

6. Make Inferences How has France's location been beneficial for its economy?

7. Analyze Effects How do the Benelux countries benefit from their nearness to Germany and France?

8. CONNECT to Today Why might France object to trade barriers on farm produce?

9. WRITING Create an Advertisement You have been asked by a French travel agency to make a list of the top five reasons to visit France. Create an advertisement explaining why France is an interesting and fun place to visit.

Reading for Understanding

▶ Key Ideas

BEFORE, YOU LEARNED

France prospered as a result of natural resources. The Benelux countries have benefited from their economic union.

NOW YOU WILL LEARN

Germany's central location helped it to dominate neighboring lands. Germany and the Alpine countries are linked in many ways.

▶ Vocabulary

TERMS & NAMES

Prussia the most powerful German state in the Holy Roman Empire

Adolf Hitler German head of state from 1933 to 1945

Berlin Wall a wall built by East Germany's Communist government to close off East Berlin from West Berlin

Alpine having to do with the Alps mountain range

neutrality a policy of not taking part in war

BACKGROUND VOCABULARY

reunify to bring something that has been separated back together

REVIEW

Holocaust the systematic murder of Jews and other minorities by the Nazis during World War II

market economy an economic system in which the production of goods and services is decided by supply and the demand of consumers

▶ Reading Strategy

Re-create the time line shown at right. As you read and respond to the **KEY QUESTIONS**, use the time line to help you sequence the events that have shaped Germany and the Alpine countries.

 See Skillbuilder Handbook, page R6

SEQUENCE EVENTS

```
┌──────┐  ┌──────┐  ┌──────┐  ┌──────┐
│      │  │      │  │      │  │      │
└──────┘  └──────┘  └──────┘  └──────┘
    │         │         │         │
    ▼         ▼         ▼         ▼
┌──────────────────────────────────────┐
│ 1648                            2005   │
└──────────────────────────────────────┘
```

GRAPHIC ORGANIZERS
Go to **Interactive Review** @ ClassZone.com

Germany and the Alpine Countries

Connecting to Your World

Germany has had a big influence on the United States, and for good reason. In 1990, more Americans reported that their ancestors came from Germany than from any other country. It's no wonder that Americans enjoy eating hot dogs, or frankfurters—a sausage named after Frankfurt, Germany. American children go to kindergarten, a type of school borrowed from Germany. And in December, many Americans decorate trees for the holidays, a German tradition.

Germany

🔽 **KEY QUESTION** How was Germany reshaped after World War II?

German traditions are part of Germany's strong national identity. For a long time, military strength was another aspect of Germany's identity. Germany is a large country centrally located on the European continent. It is well-positioned to dominate other nations and has conquered surrounding lands several times.

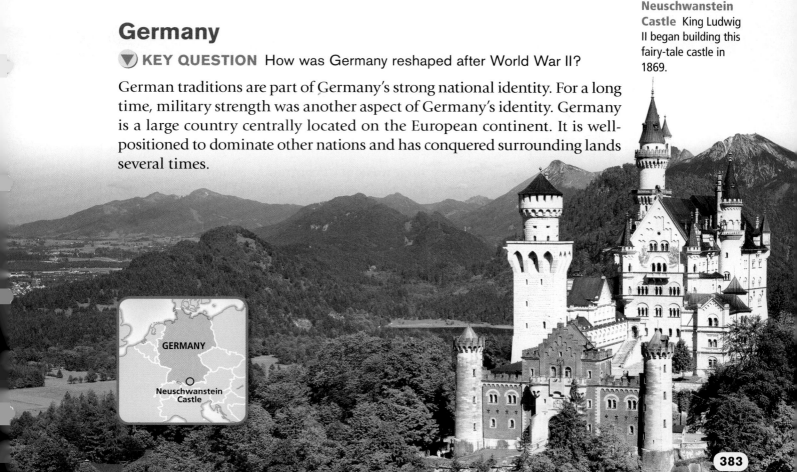

Neuschwanstein Castle King Ludwig II began building this fairy-tale castle in 1869.

GERMANY

Neuschwanstein Castle

History Like Italy, Germany was once a collection of small states instead of a united nation. **Prussia** was the most powerful German state. In 1871, Prussia unified the German states into one nation. Germany was a military power until its defeat in World War I, which weakened its economy and reduced its territory.

Many Germans, frustrated by the poor economy, began to support the fascist Nazi Party. The Nazis promised to make Germany the world power it had once been. In 1933, **Adolf Hitler**, the party's leader, became Germany's head of state. Hitler began a movement to gain more territory for Germany that eventually led to World War II. The war devastated Germany and much of Europe. The Nazis also carried out the **Holocaust**, the systematic murder of millions of Jews and other ethnic minorities.

The Allies defeated the Germans and divided Germany into four zones. The United States, France, and Britain merged their zones into the democratic West Germany. The Soviet Union's zone became East Germany, a Communist country. Berlin, located in East Germany, was divided into east and west sides. In 1961, the East German government built the **Berlin Wall** to formally divide the city in two. East Germany's government fell in 1989, and the Berlin Wall came down. In 1990, Germany decided to **reunify**, ending the east-west division.

ONLINE PRIMARY SOURCE To read more eyewitness accounts, go to the **Research & Writing Center** @ClassZone.com

ANALYZING Primary Sources

Andreas Ramos traveled from Denmark to Germany in 1989. He was one of the five million people in Berlin to witness the fall of the Berlin Wall. Afterwards, he wrote the following.

> Everything was out of control. . . . There were fireworks, kites, flags and flags and flags, dogs, children. The wall was finally breaking. . . .
> I saw an indescribable joy in people's faces. It was the end of the government telling people what not to do, it was the end of the Wall, the war, the East, the West.

Source: Andreas Ramos, *A Personal Account of The Fall of the Berlin Wall*

DOCUMENT-BASED QUESTION
What do you think Ramos meant by "it was the end . . . of the East, the West"?

Culture Germany has the largest population in Western Europe. German is the official language, though different forms of the language are spoken. Catholics and Protestants each account for about one-third of Germany's population. About four percent are Muslims.

Today, approximately 90 percent of Germany's population lives in cities and their surrounding suburbs. Cities offer greater employment opportunities and more varied entertainment. German culture has a strong musical tradition. Some great classical composers, including Bach, Beethoven, and Brahms, were German. Richard Wagner wrote spectacular operas based on German myths. With teenagers, American music is popular. Many German pop stars sing in English.

Government and Economics Germany is a federal republic—a union of states similar to that of the United States. Germany's president acts as the country's formal chief of state, mainly performing ceremonial duties. The chancellor heads the government. The German people elect the president, but the chancellor is selected by parliament. In 2005, Angela Merkel became Germany's first female chancellor.

Germany has had to overcome some serious economic problems. At the time of reunification, East German industries were outdated. Almost half of East Germany's workers were unemployed. In 1990, East Germany adopted West Germany's currency and **market economy**. The German economy continues to adjust and is getting stronger.

▲ **EVALUATE** Explain how World War II reshaped Germany.

Angela Merkel Germany's first female chancellor

CONNECT ⟲ Government & Culture

The Reichstag When East and West Germany reunited in 1990, they chose Berlin as their capital. In 1999, the German legislature began meeting in Berlin's renovated Reichstag building (shown at right). The building's prominent glass dome contains a ramp leading to an observation platform. It is a symbol of the people being able to raise themselves above their leaders, who meet in the chamber below.

CRITICAL THINKING

Make Inferences What else could the Reichstag building symbolize about Germany and its government?

LIECHTENSTEIN
AUSTRIA
SWITZERLAND

The Alpine Countries

▼ **KEY QUESTION** How has Austrian history been tied to war?

Austria, Switzerland, and Liechtenstein are **Alpine** countries, named for the Alps Mountains common to all three. The Alpine countries have historic and cultural ties to Germany. All three, like Germany, once were part of the Holy Roman Empire. All three share a common border with Germany. They also share the German language.

Austria Austria was once a powerful nation. In 1804, Austria became an empire. For a time, it was the leader of the German states. But in 1866, Austria lost a war with Prussia. The next year, it joined a dual monarchy with Hungary. The two countries cooperated in foreign affairs but had separate governments. Then, Austria fought on the losing side in World War I. Following its defeat, Austria separated from Hungary. After World War II, the nation adopted a policy of **neutrality**, meaning that it does not participate in military conflicts.

Almost all Austrians speak German, and the majority are Roman Catholics. Although most Austrians live in cities or towns, they still manage to enjoy the outdoors. Austria, about three-fourths of which is covered by mountains, is a nation of skiers. The Austrian Alps offer nearly perfect conditions for this winter sport. In the summer, the scenic beauty of the Alps attracts many hikers and backpackers.

After World War II, Austria became a federal republic with both a president and a chancellor. Austria belongs to the European Union. One of its major industries is iron and steel production. Tourism also plays a major role in Austria's economy. Many people visit the mountainous country to ski, hike, and admire the scenery.

Skiing Like the other Alpine countries, many tourists visit Austria to ski its many slopes. Tourism is a billion-euro industry for Austria. **What are the economic disadvantages of a seasonal industry?**

Switzerland and Liechtenstein Switzerland and Liechtenstein are small countries that share a border. They were once part of the Holy Roman Empire. Switzerland became independent in 1648, and Liechtenstein in 1866. Both are officially neutral.

German, French, and Italian are Switzerland's official languages. Liechtenstein's official language is German. Switzerland has a mix of Catholics and Protestants, while most Liechtensteiners are Catholic. Switzerland is famous for the high-quality chocolate and watches it produces. Liechtenstein is known for its postage stamps, which are prized by collectors all over the world. Both countries are popular tourist destinations because of their beautiful Alpine landscapes. Both have reputations as centers of international finance. Tiny Liechtenstein uses Swiss money.

Switzerland is a federal republic, like Austria and Germany. The Swiss government is very democratic. The Swiss can vote to change laws passed by their legislature. Liechtenstein is a constitutional monarchy ruled by a prince. It also has a prime minister and parliament.

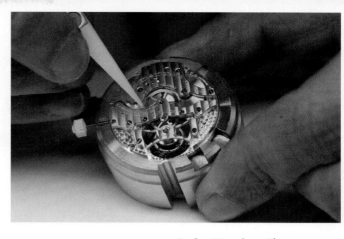

Swiss Watches The intricate works of many Swiss watches are still made and repaired by hand.

 SUMMARIZE Explain how Austrian history has been tied to war.

Section 4 Assessment

ONLINE QUIZ
For test practice, go to **Interactive Review** @ ClassZone.com

TERMS & NAMES

1. Explain the importance of
- Adolf Hitler
- Berlin Wall
- Alpine
- neutrality

USE YOUR READING NOTES

2. Sequence Events Use your completed time line to answer the following question:

What significant event occurred in Germany in 1961?

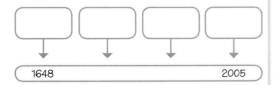

1648   2005

KEY IDEAS

3. What role has geographic location played in Germany's rise to power?

4. How did Prussia's actions strengthen the German states?

5. What do the Alpine countries have in common?

CRITICAL THINKING

6. Make Inferences What did the fall of the Berlin Wall symbolize for Germany?

7. Draw Conclusions How have the Alps helped shape the cultures and economies of the Alpine countries?

8. CONNECT to Today Why would it be important for the Alpine countries to maintain good relations with Germany?

9. TECHNOLOGY Prepare an Oral Presentation Choose one of Germany's many famous musicians—Bach, Beethoven, or Brahms—and do research to create a short biography of his life. Choose one of his songs to play during your presentation.

Reading for Understanding

▶ Key Ideas

BEFORE, YOU LEARNED

Germany and the Alpine countries share common borders and a common language. They are linked in many ways.

NOW YOU WILL LEARN

The Nordic countries have histories and cultures that are closely intertwined.

▶ Vocabulary

TERMS & NAMES

Vikings a seafaring Scandinavian people who raided northern and western Europe from the 9th to the 11th century

Sami people of northern Scandinavia who traditionally herd reindeer; also the name of their language

ombudsman an official who investigates citizens' complaints against the government

welfare state a social system in which the government provides for many of its citizens' needs

BACKGROUND VOCABULARY

Nordic relating to Scandinavia

REVIEW

hydroelectric power electricity made by water-powered engines

Visual Vocabulary Sami with a reindeer

▶ Reading Strategy

Re-create the chart shown at right. As you read and respond to the **KEY QUESTIONS**, use the chart to help you organize important details about the Nordic countries.

 See Skillbuilder Handbook, page R7

CATEGORIZE

	Language	Government	Economy
Sweden			
Norway			
Finland			
Denmark			
Iceland			

 GRAPHIC ORGANIZERS
Go to **Interactive Review** @ ClassZone.com

The Nordic Countries

Connecting to Your World

Who were the first Europeans to reach North America? Many think that Columbus and his crew were the first to do so. In fact, Leif Ericson, a Viking, was probably the first. According to an ancient account from Greenland, Ericson hoped to find a forested land glimpsed by an Icelandic trader and sailor. Ericson and his men sailed west from Greenland. They landed and spent the winter on the North American continent, at a place Ericson called Vinland.

Leif Ericson

Sweden and Norway

▼ **KEY QUESTION** Why do Sweden and Norway have so much in common?

Five nations in northernmost Europe make up the **Nordic**, or Scandinavian, countries: Sweden, Norway, Finland, Denmark, and Iceland. These lands were first settled thousands of years ago. Sweden and Norway share the same landmass, the Scandinavian Peninsula. Their histories are intertwined. Sweden and Norway were both influenced by the **Vikings**, seafaring Scandinavians who raided Europe from the 9th to the 11th century.

Viking Ship
This Viking longship was recovered from a farm in Slagen, Norway, in 1904.

History The Vikings were some of the world's best sailors and shipbuilders. They also were pirates and fierce warriors. During the three centuries that the Vikings lived in Scandinavia, they invaded much of Europe, as you can see from the map here.

The Viking Invasions of Western Europe 820–941

CONNECT Geography & History

1. **Region** Where was the Viking homeland?
2. **Movement** What was the southernmost city reached by the Vikings?

In the late 1000s, the Vikings converted to Christianity and settled down. Sweden and Norway became monarchies. Finland became part of Sweden in 1323. In 1397, Denmark's Queen Margaret formed a union with Sweden and Norway, which lasted until Sweden withdrew in 1523. Sweden had become a great power, often battling Denmark, Russia, and Poland for territory. In 1700, those three countries attacked Sweden. Sweden's king, Charles XII, fell in battle in 1718, bringing Sweden's domination to an end. In 1809, Sweden lost control of Finland to Russia.

Norway came under Sweden's control in 1814. In 1905, Sweden recognized Norway's independence. During the two world wars, Sweden and Norway remained neutral. However, during World War II, Norway was invaded and occupied by the Germans.

Culture Although Swedes and Norwegians speak different languages, Swedish and Norwegian are similar. As a result, speakers of the two languages often are able to communicate with each other. In both countries, Lutheranism is the official state religion. However, Swedes and Norwegians have the freedom to practice different religions.

In Sweden, Finns make up the largest immigrant population, while immigrants in Norway come from many nations. In the northern regions of Sweden and Norway, there is a large minority population of **Sami**, whose traditional way of life involves caring for herds of reindeer. Their native language is also called Sami.

Because of their climates, Sweden and Norway are less densely populated than other European countries. Most people live in the countries' southern and central regions. About 80 percent of Swedes and 75 percent of Norwegians live in urban areas. Many people in both countries own vacation homes. Swedes and Norwegians enjoy outdoor sports year round. Skiing and ice skating are both popular.

Worldster

A Day in Ulrika's Life

To learn more about Ulrika and her world, go to the **Activity Center** @ ClassZone.com

To introduce herself, Ulrika says:

"Hello, mitt namn är Ulrika."

Hi! My name is Ulrika. I am 14 years old and live in Uppsala, a city of 180,000 people. Uppsala is about 50 miles north of Stockholm, Sweden's capital. I like to read and play computer games. On the weekends, I leave the city with some of my friends to take horseback-riding lessons. Riding is really popular here. Of course, like you, I go to school. Here's what my day is usually like.

School At my school, all of our books and school supplies are free—even paper! We also get a free lunch every day. This year, one of my favorite classes is metal working. I'm making a modern sculpture for our yard.

Break Time We have a lot of breaks during the day. Usually, we go outside and play soccer, field hockey, or another game or sport. It's great to be able to go outdoors.

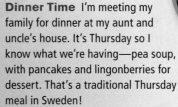

After School Today I'll be spending two hours at the hospital. No, I'm not sick! This is part of going to school here. In the eighth grade, we get to learn about different kinds of jobs. I want to be a doctor, so I work one afternoon a week at the hospital as an aide.

Dinner Time I'm meeting my family for dinner at my aunt and uncle's house. It's Thursday so I know what we're having—pea soup, with pancakes and lingonberries for dessert. That's a traditional Thursday meal in Sweden!

CONNECT to Your Life

Journal Entry Do you know what kind of job you want when you're older? Would volunteering like Ulrika does help you decide? Record your thoughts in your journal.

Government and Economics Sweden and Norway are constitutional monarchies. Although both have monarchs, their prime ministers and cabinets hold most of the executive power. Both Sweden and Norway appoint ombudsmen to protect their citizens. An **ombudsman** investigates complaints against the government and makes sure that governmental power is not abused.

Sweden and Norway are welfare states. **Welfare states** use taxes to provide a wide range of services to their citizens. Families with children under age 16 are given money to care for them. Workers receive good retirement and unemployment plans.

Sweden has a highly industrialized economy. It also has a reputation for modern design, which has spread to other countries through two major Swedish companies, household goods store IKEA and clothing store H&M. Norway took longer to develop manufacturing because it did not have enough energy resources to power factories.

Scandinavian Design
Scandinavian design, known for its use of simple forms, has become popular in the United States.

By 1900, Norway was able to use hydroelectric power from its rivers. Today, Norway also has access to North Sea oil. Sweden joined the European Union in 1995, but Norway's citizens voted not to join.

▼ **DRAW CONCLUSIONS** Explain why Sweden and Norway share so many similarities.

Finland

▼ **KEY QUESTION** How did Finland's neighbors affect its history?

Finland's location between Sweden and Russia has played a major role in Finland's history. Both countries have influenced its culture.

History and Culture In 1155, Finland became part of Sweden. It remained under Swedish control until 1809, when Russia conquered Finland. In 1917, Finland gained its independence from Russia. During World War II, Finland had to fight off two invasions by the Soviet Union.

Because of its history, Finland's culture is strongly influenced by Sweden. Finland's two official languages are Finnish and Swedish. Most people in Finland are Finnish. Swedes make up the largest minority group. Small groups of Sami also live in Finland.

About three out of five Finns live in urban areas. Still, many of them find opportunities to enjoy outdoor recreation. With snow on the ground for almost half the year, sports like cross-country skiing and ice hockey are especially popular. Northern Finland even has reindeer races!

Fun Facts!

REINDEER RACING
What do you do when you've got snow on the ground and a herd of reindeer? If you're in Finland, you race! Each year, the Sami in northern Finland hold a championship reindeer race. Drivers on skis wearing aerodynamic outfits and helmets are harnessed to reindeer. They compete in races against the clock and against other jockeys.

Government and Economics Finland is a democratic republic. A president and prime minister share executive power. Voters elect the president, who appoints the prime minister. In 2000, Finland elected its first female president, Tarja Halonen. Finland is a welfare state.

Finland's forests are its most plentiful natural resource. Forests cover almost two-thirds of the land, more than in any other European country. Paper and other forest products make up 30 percent of Finland's exports. Finland also produces mobile phones and other high-tech items. In 1995, Finland joined the European Union.

▼ **SUMMARIZE** Explain how Finland's neighbors affected its history.

Denmark and Iceland

▼ **KEY QUESTION** How are Denmark and Iceland similar?

Denmark occupies the Jutland Peninsula and over 400 small islands surrounding the peninsula. The nation also includes Greenland and the Faroe Islands. Denmark is a small country, but it has played a large role in Scandinavian history. Iceland is an island nation just south of the Arctic Circle. It was ruled by Denmark for over 500 years.

History Viking raids on other countries shaped Denmark's early history. Denmark's power expanded during the late 1100s and early 1200s. For a time, Denmark controlled Sweden, Norway, and Iceland. Sweden withdrew from the union in 1523. Denmark continued to rule Norway until 1814. Iceland gained its independence in 1944.

Culture Most Danes have Danish ancestry, though some are descended from Germans. Icelanders are mainly of Norwegian or Celtic descent. Over 90 percent of Iceland's population lives in urban areas, as do most Danes. The Evangelical Lutheran Church is the official religion of both countries. Danish is spoken in Denmark, and Icelandic in Iceland.

Nyhavn Harbor These colorful old sailors' quarters in Copenhagen, Denmark, have been converted to cafés and dance clubs.

Government and Economics Denmark is a constitutional monarchy. The Danish monarch has mainly ceremonial duties. The prime minister serves as the head of government. Like other Scandinavian nations, Denmark and Iceland have welfare systems that provide for many of their citizens' needs. Iceland is a republic. Its people elect a president, who serves a four-year term and has limited powers. The prime minister and cabinet perform most executive functions.

Despite lacking natural resources, Denmark has a strong, modern economy. The cost of living in Iceland is high because so many goods have to be imported to the small island nation. Denmark belongs to the EU but has not adopted the euro. Iceland is not an EU member.

 COMPARE AND CONTRAST Explain how Denmark and Iceland are similar to each other.

Section 5 Assessment

 **ONLINE QUIZ** For test practice, go to **Interactive Review** @ ClassZone.com

TERMS & NAMES

1. Explain the importance of
• Vikings
• Sami
• ombudsman
• welfare state

USE YOUR READING NOTES

2. Categorize Use your completed chart to answer the following question:

Which of the Nordic countries are welfare states?

	Language	Government	Economy
Sweden			
Norway			
Finland			
Denmark			
Iceland			

KEY IDEAS

3. What cultural characteristics do Sweden and Norway share?

4. How has Finland's location affected its history?

5. Why is Iceland's cost of living so high?

CRITICAL THINKING

6. Make Inferences How has the climate of the Scandinavian countries helped define their cultures?

7. Summarize What benefits do welfare states offer their citizens?

8. **CONNECT to Today** How do you think having ombudsmen would change the U.S. government?

9. **WRITING** **Write a Speech** Use appropriate sources to research and prepare a speech explaining three advantages and disadvantages of welfare states like those in Scandinavia. Then explain why you would or would not like to live in a country with that kind of economy.

CHAPTER SUMMARY

Key Idea 1
Greece and Italy began as collections of small states that gained independence.

Key Idea 2
Both Spain and Portugal were ruled by foreigners and developed colonial empires.

Key Idea 3
France and the Benelux nations have prospered.

Key Idea 4
Germany and the Alpine countries are linked in many ways.

Key Idea 5
The Nordic countries have histories and cultures that are closely intertwined.

For **Review and Study Notes**, go to **Interactive Review** @ ClassZone.com

NAME GAME

Use the Terms & Names list to complete each sentence on paper or online.

1. I was a barrier that divided a city in half.
   _____**Berlin Wall**_____
2. I investigate complaints against the government.
   _____
3. I was the eastern half of the Roman Empire after the fall of Rome. _____
4. I am a political system based on a strong central government led by a dictator. _____
5. I am one of a group of people living in Sweden's far north. _____
6. I am an ethnic group living in the northern Pyrenees. _____
7. I am the official home of the Pope.
   _____
8. I was Germany's leader during World War II.
   _____
9. I am an economic union formed by three western European nations. _____
10. I was a powerful German state in the Holy Roman Empire. _____

Adolf Hitler
Basque
Benelux
Berlin Wall
Byzantine Empire
Christopher Columbus
coalition
fascism
Moors
ombudsman
Prussia
Reconquista
Sami
Vatican
Vikings

Activities

GeoGame

Use this online map to reinforce your understanding of the countries and cities of Western Europe. Drag and drop each place name in the list to its location on the map.

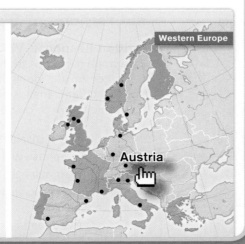

Geo GAME

Greece
Spain
Paris
Berlin
Austria

Western Europe

Austria

To play the complete game, go to **Interactive Review** @ClassZone.com

Crossword Puzzle

Complete an online crossword puzzle to test your knowledge of Western Europe.

ACROSS
1. seafaring Scandinavians who raided Europe from the 9th to 11th century

VOCABULARY

Explain the significance of each of the following.

1. Byzantine Empire
2. Romance language
3. coalition
4. Christopher Columbus
5. Benelux
6. Berlin Wall
7. neutrality

Explain how the terms and names in each group are related.

8. Moors, Reconquista
9. Basque, Sami
10. Adolf Hitler, Holocaust
11. ombudsman, welfare state

KEY IDEAS

1 Greece and Italy

12. How has Greece's geography defined some of its major economic activities?
13. Why has the Catholic Church had such a strong impact on Italian culture?

2 Spain and Portugal

14. What was the Reconquista?
15. How has Portugal improved its economy?

3 France and the Benelux Countries

16. How is the French government similar to and different from the U.S. government?
17. How are the three Benelux countries alike?

4 Germany and the Alpine Countries

18. How did World War II affect Germany's economy?
19. What geographical characteristic most clearly defines the Alpine countries?

5 The Nordic Countries

20. Why did Norway's manufacturing sector lag behind other Scandinavian countries?
21. Who were the Vikings?

CRITICAL THINKING

22. **Compare and Contrast** Create a table to compare and contrast the geography, work, and recreation of northern and southern Italy.

NORTHERN ITALY	SOUTHERN ITALY

23. **Analyze Causes and Effects** Why did Spain begin exploring the world by sea?
24. **Connect Geography & History** What geographical factor helped Portugal to establish an empire despite its small size?
25. **Compare** How do France's experiences with its eastern neighbor Germany compare to Finland's experiences with Russia?
26. **Connect Geography & Economics** How has the presence of offshore oil contributed to Norway's economy?
27. **Five Themes: Location** How has Scandinavia's northern location helped shape its culture?

Answer the ESSENTIAL QUESTION

What geographic and cultural characteristics define the subregions of Western Europe?

Written Response Write a two- or three-paragraph response to the Essential Question. Consider the key ideas of each section and the specific characteristics of each subregion. Use the rubric below to guide your thinking.

Response Rubric
A strong response will:
- identify each subregion
- explain how geographic characteristics define each subregion
- compare and contrast cultural characteristics within each subregion

✔ **Test Practice**

• Online Test Practice @ ClassZone.com
• Test-Taking Strategies and Practice at the front of this book

THEMATIC MAP

Use the map and your knowledge of Europe to answer questions 1 and 2 on your paper.

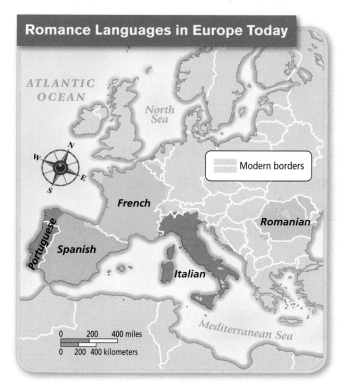

Romance Languages in Europe Today

ATLANTIC OCEAN

North Sea

Modern borders

French

Romanian

Portuguese

Spanish

Italian

Mediterranean Sea

0   200   400 miles
0   200 400 kilometers

1. The Romance languages are concentrated in which part of Europe?

A. north
B. east
C. southwest
D. southeast

2. Which statement best describes the pattern of Romance languages?

A. They are not spoken along the Mediterranean Sea.
B. They are found in the former Roman Empire.
C. They are dying out.
D. They are spoken only in northern Europe.

BAR GRAPH

Use the information in the graph below to answer questions 3 and 4 on your paper.

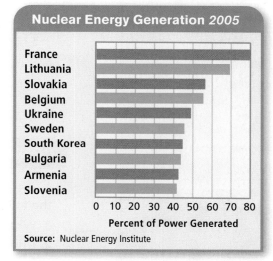

Nuclear Energy Generation 2005

France
Lithuania
Slovakia
Belgium
Ukraine
Sweden
South Korea
Bulgaria
Armenia
Slovenia

0 10 20 30 40 50 60 70 80
Percent of Power Generated

Source: Nuclear Energy Institute

3. How many countries get more of their energy from nuclear power than France?

4. How many of the top ten nuclear energy producers are in Western Europe?

GeoActivity

1. INTERDISCIPLINARY ACTIVITY–HISTORY

With a small group, research Viking ships and create a poster about them. Be sure your poster shows how the ship was built, what materials were used, and when and where the Vikings traveled.

2. WRITING FOR SOCIAL STUDIES

Reread the part of Section 5 that describes Ulrika's day. Then write a letter to Ulrika about how you spend a typical day. Use interesting details to describe your activities and point out how your day differs from Ulrika's day.

3. MENTAL MAPPING

Create an outline map of Scandinavia and label the following:

• Denmark
• Finland
• Norway
• Iceland
• Sweden
• Greenland
• Faroe Islands

United Kingdom

1 **HISTORY**

Building a British Empire

2 **CULTURE**

From Shakespeare to J.K. Rowling

3 **GOVERNMENT & ECONOMICS**

Parliament and Free Enterprise

 ESSENTIAL QUESTION

How did being an island nation influence the development of the United Kingdom?

CONNECT ➤ **Geography & History**

Use the map and the time line to answer the following questions.

1. What is the capital of the United Kingdom?
2. Under what body of water would a railroad tunnel between England and France run?

8000 B.C.

Geography
◄ **8000 B.C.** People begin settling the British Isles.
(rock formation in Cornwall)

Government
1689 Parliament passes the English Bill of Rights.

Government
◄ **1215** King John signs the Magna Carta.

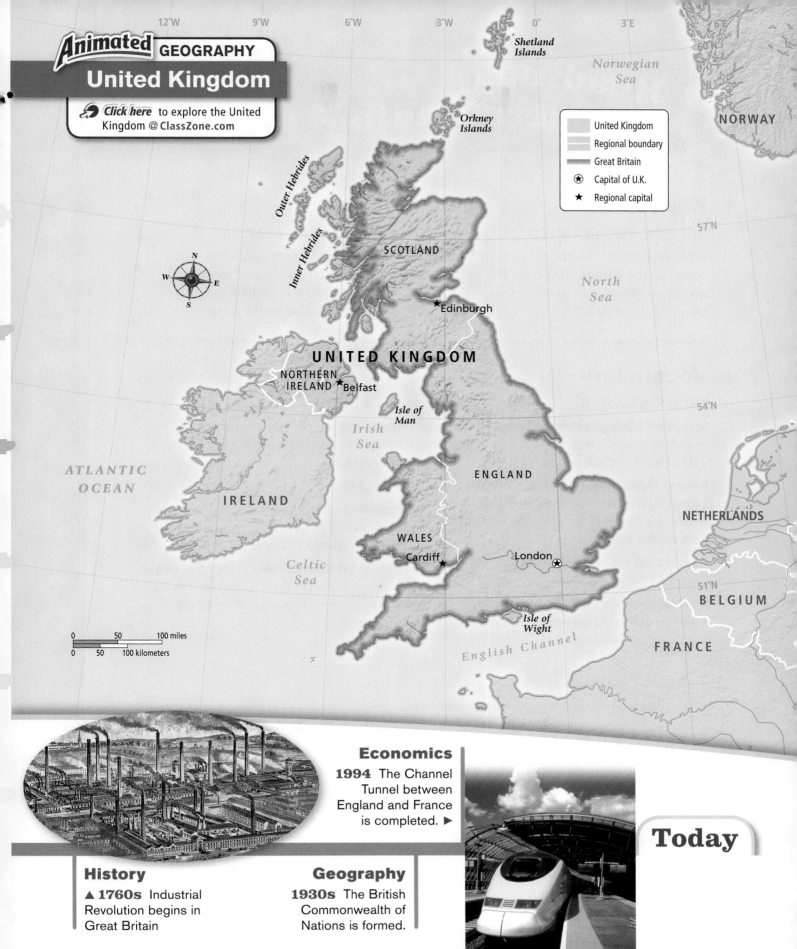

Shetland
Islands

*Norwegian
Sea*

NORWAY

Orkney
Islands

	United Kingdom
	Regional boundary
	Great Britain
⊛	Capital of U.K.
★	Regional capital

Outer Hebrides

57°N

SCOTLAND

Inner Hebrides

★ Edinburgh

*North
Sea*

UNITED KINGDOM

NORTHERN
IRELAND ★ Belfast

*Isle of
Man*

54°N

*Irish
Sea*

ATLANTIC
OCEAN

IRELAND

ENGLAND

NETHERLANDS

WALES
Cardiff ★

London ⊛

*Celtic
Sea*

51°N

BELGIUM

*Isle of
Wight*

English Channel

FRANCE

0 50 100 miles
0 50 100 kilometers

Economics

1994 The Channel Tunnel between England and France is completed. ▶

Today

History

▲ **1760s** Industrial Revolution begins in Great Britain

Geography

1930s The British Commonwealth of Nations is formed.

Reading for Understanding

▶ Key Ideas

BEFORE, YOU LEARNED

Western Europe's industrial growth began in the United Kingdom. Its inventors caused a revolution that changed the world.

NOW YOU WILL LEARN

Many developments, including the Industrial Revolution and a colonial empire, helped the United Kingdom grow into a major world power.

▶ Vocabulary

TERMS & NAMES

representative government a system of government with a legislature that is at least partly elected by the people

Magna Carta a charter, or document, signed by England's King John in 1215 that limited the power of the monarch and guaranteed nobles basic rights

Parliament the national legislature of the United Kingdom

Commonwealth of Nations an association made up of the United Kingdom and many former British colonies

BACKGROUND VOCABULARY

mainland the primary landmass of a continent or territory rather than its islands or peninsulas

REVIEW

imperialism the policy where one country controls the government and economy of another country or territory

Industrial Revolution the shift that began in Great Britain in the 1760s from making goods by hand to making them by machine

▶ Reading Strategy

Re-create the chart shown at right. As you read and respond to the **KEY QUESTIONS**, use the chart to help you identify the solutions to problems faced by the United Kingdom.

 Skillbuilder Handbook, page R10

IDENTIFY PROBLEMS AND SOLUTIONS

PROBLEMS	SOLUTIONS
Divided Territory	
Monarchy Too Powerful	
Need for Resources	

 GRAPHIC ORGANIZERS
Go to **Interactive Review** @ ClassZone.com

Building a British Empire

Connecting to Your World

When someone asks you what country you live in, do you say America, the United States, or the U.S.? Our country has many names. So does the United Kingdom. Few use its official name, the United Kingdom of Great Britain and Northern Ireland. Some say the United Kingdom. Some call it Great Britain, the name of the island shared by England, Scotland, and Wales. Others just use Britain. Its different names reflect its history.

Patriotic Teen An American teenager displays one of her country's names.

Creating a United Kingdom

🔻 **KEY QUESTION** What aspects of culture did Britain's settlers influence?

Different groups settled the British Isles over time. The Celts, the Romans, Germanic tribes called the Angles and the Saxons, and the Normans from France all inhabited the region. Each contributed to British culture. They shaped its language, government, and customs. By the late 1200s, English kings wanted to bring the British Isles under their control. They conquered Wales and much of Ireland. In 1707, England, Wales, and Scotland united as the Kingdom of Great Britain. Ireland became part of the union in 1801, creating the United Kingdom of Great Britain and Ireland. Ireland split into two parts in 1949, and Northern Ireland stayed in the union.

Stonehenge Early settlers of the British Isles built Stonehenge between about 3100 and 1500 B.C.

WALES   ENGLAND
○ Stonehenge

Although the United Kingdom is a small island group, it has had an influence on world affairs far greater than its size would suggest. At the height of its power, its colonies spanned the globe. As it became a world leader, the United Kingdom's location set it apart from nations on the European **mainland**, allowing it to create a unique identity.

▲ **SUMMARIZE** Explain the aspects of culture that Britain's early settlers influenced.

Influencing the Modern Age

▼ **KEY QUESTION** How did British governmental and economic ideas influence the rest of the world?

British ideas and customs have had a lasting influence on the way people around the world live. The British policy of **imperialism** helped spread new developments, such as representative government and the Industrial Revolution, which still affect political and economic life.

Representative Government In 1215, the kingdom took steps toward **representative government**, a system in which the legislature is at least partly elected by the people. British nobles forced King John to sign the **Magna Carta**. This document outlined nobles' rights and limited the king's powers. British kings gradually acknowledged that they needed the people's support to govern. A group of representatives called **Parliament** was established. Some call King Edward's 1295 Parliament a "model parliament" because it was more representative of British society than earlier versions. Today, several other European governments, such as Greece and Hungary, also have parliaments.

In 1689, the English Bill of Rights strengthened the rights of citizens. This document outlined the relationship between the monarchy and Parliament. In doing so, it limited the power of the monarch and guaranteed basic freedoms to English citizens. It became a model for other nations, including the United States. Many countries have been influenced by British advances in representative government.

Houses of Parliament
This building in London, finished in 1860, contains the chambers where the United Kindom's Parliament meets. **How might the building's exterior show that an important group meets inside?**

English Bill of Rights In 1689, Parliament passed the English Bill of Rights. They presented the document to King William III and Queen Mary, who agreed to uphold it.

> That the . . . suspending of laws, or the execution of laws, by regal authority, without consent of parliament, is illegal . . .
>
> That election of members of parliament ought to be free . . .
>
> And that for redress [remedy] of all grievances, and for the amending, strengthening, and preserving of the laws, parliaments ought to be held frequently.
>
> Source: English Bill of Rights

DOCUMENT–BASED QUESTION

How did the English Bill of Rights protect English citizens?

▲ *King William III and Queen Mary with the English Bill of Rights*

The British Empire In the 1500s, Britain joined other European nations in the race to claim overseas colonies in order to gain resources and expand trade networks. By the 1800s, Great Britain used its strong navy to control a prosperous empire. At its height, the empire covered one-fourth of the globe. British colonies included Canada, Australia, New Zealand, Singapore, India, and Pakistan, as well as parts of Africa and the Caribbean. They provided raw materials needed for industrialization and markets for British goods. As British control spread, so did its language and culture.

Commonwealth of Nations This World War II poster shows soldiers from several Commonwealth nations, including India, South Africa, New Zealand, Canada, and Australia.

In the 1920s, several British colonies controlled their internal affairs, but also wanted to manage their foreign policy and defense. In response, the United Kingdom created the **Commonwealth of Nations**, an association of countries that had been part of the British empire. Original members included Australia, Canada, and South Africa. Members of the Commonwealth were independent, but agreed to cooperate in trade and political matters. The British empire still controlled many other territories.

THE BRITISH COMMONWEALTH OF NATIONS

TOGETHER

The Industrial Revolution The **Industrial Revolution** that you read about earlier began in Great Britain in the 1760s. The country's geographic advantages helped make it the world's first industrial nation. Early on, rivers provided power to fuel machines. Rivers and harbors on the Atlantic Ocean offered ways to transport raw materials from British colonies to factories and finished goods to overseas markets. The nation also had ample supplies of coal and iron ore.

By the 1800s, the United Kingdom had become the world's leading industrial power. Although Britain tried to keep its new technology to itself, other nations sought to industrialize. British knowledge spread first to nearby Belgium and France, then to much of the world.

▲ **ANALYZE EFFECTS** Explain how British governmental and economic ideas influenced the world.

HISTORY MAKERS

Winston Churchill 1874–1965

A brilliant speaker and enemy of Nazi Germany, Prime Minister Winston Churchill led the United Kingdom during World War II. His stirring speeches on the radio and in the British Parliament rallied the British people. As the British prepared for an expected invasion by Germany, Churchill urged them to show courage and make this "their finest hour." His confidence that democratic government would in the end win out over dictatorships inspired the United Kingdom and its allies to work hard for victory.

ONLINE BIOGRAPHY
For more on the life of Winston Churchill, go to the
Research & Writing Center @ ClassZone.com

Britain in Today's World

▼ **KEY QUESTION** How has Great Britain's position in world politics changed?

At the beginning of the 1900s, Great Britain was a major world power. Its leaders governed a prosperous nation and a vast empire. Today, the United Kingdom is no longer the world's richest or most powerful nation. However, it remains a respected world leader.

Fighting Two World Wars The United Kingdom played a major role in two world wars. As you learned earlier, it served as a leader of the Allies in both struggles. The British people showed great courage. During World War II, civilians faced massive German air raids on their cities. British and Commonwealth soldiers fought bravely in Europe, North Africa, and Asia. In stirring radio addresses, Prime Minister Winston Churchill inspired confidence as the British people faced the threat of a German invasion.

The two wars had a devastating effect on the United Kingdom's economy. Bombs had destroyed large parts of London and other cities. When the war ended, Britain had huge debts. All the industry that had been devoted to the war effort had to be converted back to manufacturing consumer goods. It took the British economy years to recover fully.

The End of the Empire In the postwar period, many British colonies in Africa and Asia began demanding independence. Great Britain was struggling to recover from the war. Its leaders lacked the time or resources to maintain its colonies. Between 1947 and 1980, about 40 British colonies became independent. Almost all of them joined the Commonwealth of Nations.

Today, the United Kingdom works closely with its former colonies and with other European nations. Its ties to Commonwealth nations have strengthened its role in world affairs. The United Kingdom is also a member of the European Union. However, some British citizens think that their country should be less involved with the rest of Europe, which is a source of tension for the government.

The Struggle for Independence

Colonial Independence This time line shows when some of Great Britain's many colonies achieved their independence from the empire.

India	Ghana		Kenya		The Bahamas	
1947	**1957**	**1962**	**1963**	**1965**	**1973**	**1981**
Pakistan		Jamaica		Singapore		Belize

 EVALUATE Explain how Britain's role in world politics has changed.

Section ① Assessment

🔄 **ONLINE QUIZ**
For test practice, go to
Interactive Review
@ ClassZone.com

TERMS & NAMES

1. **Explain the importance of**
   - Magna Carta
   - Parliament
   - Commonwealth of Nations

USE YOUR READING NOTES

2. **Identify Problems and Solutions**
   Use your completed chart to answer the following question:

   How did the United Kingdom meet its needs for more natural resources?

PROBLEMS	SOLUTIONS
Divided Territory	
Monarchy Too Powerful	
Need for Resources	

KEY IDEAS

3. How did the creation of Parliament change the British monarchy?

4. What were the effects of Industrial Revolution on the way the British lived?

5. What benefits did the Commonwealth of Nations have for British colonies?

CRITICAL THINKING

6. **Analyze Causes and Effects** Why did the United Kingdom have to give up its colonial empire?

7. **Make Inferences** How did the British overcome the disadvantages of being an island nation?

8. **CONNECT to Today** Why might the United Kingdom want to maintain ties with former colonies?

9. **ART Design a Memorial** Research the experiences of British soldiers or civilians during World War II. Create a design for a war memorial honoring their part in the war.

Victorian London

🖱 **Click here** to enter Victorian London
@ ClassZone.com

LONDON AROUND 1890

London grew rapidly during the 19th century. By 1901, over 6.5 million people lived there. All these people required services, such as transportation and law enforcement. Rapid growth also affected London society as different social classes interacted.

🖱 **Click here** to experience what daily life in Victorian London would have been like. Learn more about the different social classes that shared the city, such as the upper-class residents shown above. See some of the public services needed to keep the city running, including electricity and the London Underground.

🖱 **Click here** to learn more about the economic activities that might have taken place in this important commercial center. Connected to the world by the Thames River, the city attracted all types of businesses, from street stalls to major factories.

Growth of London

0 2.5 5 miles
0 2.5 5 kilometers

Thames River

London, 1700
Growth to 1800
Growth to 1900
Greater London, 2007

N

GeoActivity

A Victorian Talk Show
Break into groups of four. One person will pretend to be someone from this London street who is appearing on a talk show. The rest of the group will interview him or her. Choose the best question and answer from your group and share it with the class.

SECTION 2

Reading for Understanding

▶ Key Ideas

BEFORE, YOU LEARNED

Great Britain became an industrial leader with a worldwide empire. Today, it no longer has a great empire, but it remains a respected European power.

NOW YOU WILL LEARN

Britain's history as an industrial and colonial power has shaped its culture. Britain's increasingly diverse population continues to enrich its cultural life.

▶ Vocabulary

TERMS & NAMES

Briton a British person

Gaelic any of the Celtic family of languages spoken in Ireland or Scotland

multicultural relating to or including many different cultures

Church of England the official church of England headed by the Archbishop of Canterbury

William Shakespeare an English playwright and poet during the late 16th and early 17th centuries

REVIEW

immigrant a person who leaves one area to settle in another

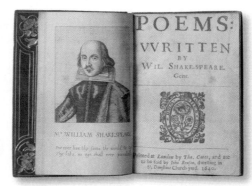

Visual Vocabulary William Shakespeare

▶ Reading Strategy

Re-create the web diagram shown at right. As you read and respond to the **KEY QUESTIONS**, use the diagram to help you find main ideas about British culture.

 Skillbuilder Handbook, page R4

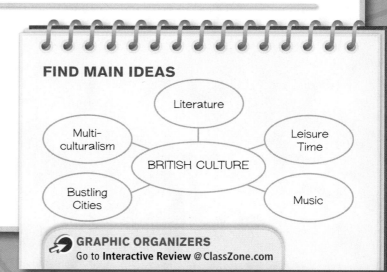

FIND MAIN IDEAS

Literature

Multi-culturalism

Leisure Time

BRITISH CULTURE

Bustling Cities

Music

GRAPHIC ORGANIZERS
Go to **Interactive Review** @ClassZone.com

From Shakespeare to J.K. Rowling

Connecting to Your World

Have you ever read a Harry Potter book? One day in 1990, an idea for a book popped into the head of J.K. Rowling, a British author. She wanted to write about a young boy named Harry who could do magic. Today, millions of people around the world know about this boy. Rowling's Harry Potter books have made publishing history, selling out at bookstores hours after they are put on the shelves. Rowling is just one part of Great Britain's rich cultural heritage.

Harry Potter Fans Like these boys, many fans dress up as their favorite Harry Potter characters.

Life in the United Kingdom

▼ **KEY QUESTION** What influences have made British culture more diverse in recent years?

Before World War II, most British people shared the same ethnicity and religious beliefs. Today, people of many different faiths and customs make their home in the United Kingdom. Many of them have immigrated from the former colonies of the British empire. The influence of these newcomers can be seen throughout Britain. Although some changes have caused tensions, the mix of old and new traditions is making many British cities lively places to live.

Tower Bridge The Tower Bridge, built in 1894, spans the Thames River near London's modern City Hall, the round building at right.

Bustling Cities For many centuries, Great Britain was a largely rural country. The Industrial Revolution sparked urban growth. Today, nine out of ten **Britons**, or British people, live in cities. London, the capital of the United Kingdom, is by far the largest city, with over 7 million residents. While London is the biggest, the nation has several other major cities. The map below shows the location of Britain's largest cities by population, most of which fall within industrial areas.

By the 1800s, London was already a busy city. Today, it is a multi-level city with a subway system below ground and skyscrapers above. It is a global center of culture and commerce. It also has many tourist attractions that draw millions of visitors each year.

Edinburgh People stroll down a street in Edinburgh, Scotland, during a festival.

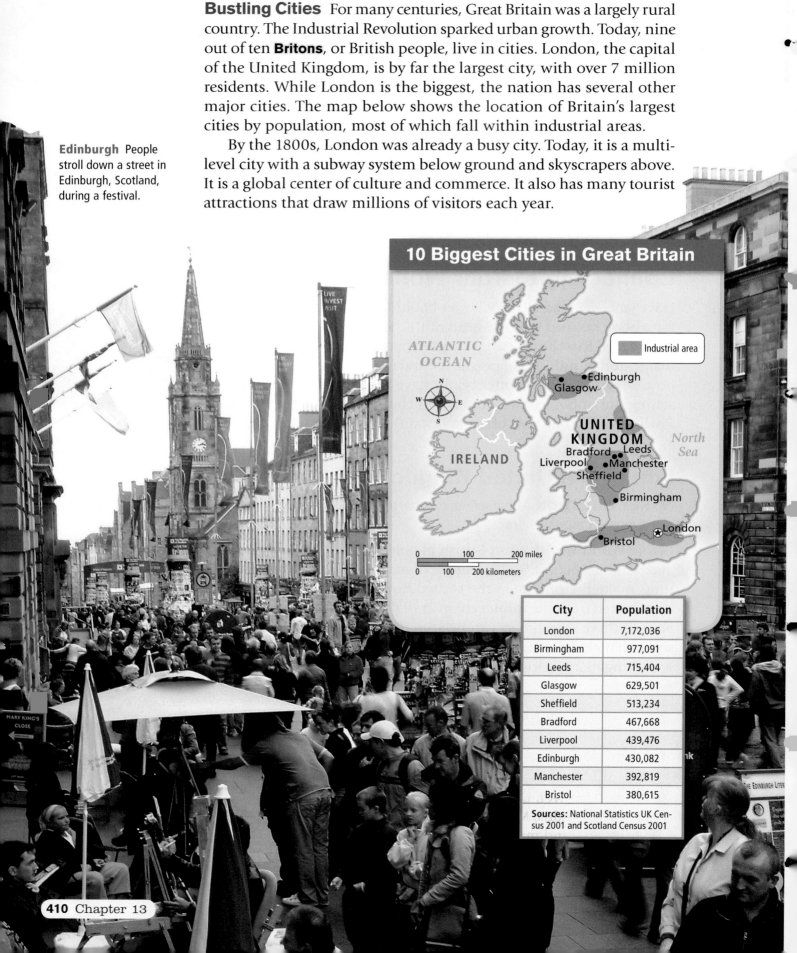

10 Biggest Cities in Great Britain

City	Population
London	7,172,036
Birmingham	977,091
Leeds	715,404
Glasgow	629,501
Sheffield	513,234
Bradford	467,668
Liverpool	439,476
Edinburgh	430,082
Manchester	392,819
Bristol	380,615

Sources: National Statistics UK Census 2001 and Scotland Census 2001

CONNECT → to Language Arts

Would you know what to do if someone told you to go find a bobby? If you were British, you would know to look for a police officer, like those shown below. Although British English and American English are similar, some of the words used by Britons are very different—and some can be difficult to translate.

Activity

Translate British to American English

Materials
- flipcards
- pencil
- dictionary

1. Write each of the words listed below on one side of a flipcard: *biscuit, bloke, boot, chemist, jumper, lift, lorry, mate, petrol,* and *zebra crossing.*

2. Think about what each word might mean. Write your guess next to each one.

3. Look up each word in the dictionary. Look for the definition identified as British. Write the definition on the other side of each flipcard.

Multiculturalism Each region in the United Kingdom—England, Scotland, Wales, and Northern Ireland—has its own customs. English is Great Britain's official language. In Scotland and Ireland, however, some speak **Gaelic**, the language brought to the British Isles by the Celtic people. In Wales, about one-fifth of the population speaks Welsh, another Celtic language.

Over the years, the United Kingdom has welcomed **immigrants** from around the world. After World War II, the nation saw an increase in immigration from former colonies in South Asia, Africa, and the Caribbean. Today, about one in ten people in Britain is an immigrant. These newcomers have added variety to British culture and influenced tastes in food and music. They have made the United Kingdom one of the most **multicultural** countries in the world, meaning that it includes many cultures. This has also caused tensions, however, as diverse customs and viewpoints occasionally clash.

Immigration has also had an impact on religion in the United Kingdom. Many Britons belong to the **Church of England**. As the nation's official church, it combines both Catholic and Protestant traditions. In Northern Ireland, about two-fifths of the population are Roman Catholics. However, Great Britain also has many religious minorities, such as Hindus, Muslims, and Sikhs. Their faiths are reflected in the temples and mosques found in many British cities.

🔺 **EVALUATE** Explain why British culture has become more diverse.

Fun Facts!

CHICKEN TIKKA MASALA

At one time fish and chips was England's favorite dish, but no more. Now Britons prefer an Indian-influenced dish called chicken tikka masala. The dish is an Indian meal called chicken tikka, to which the Britons have added a masala sauce to satisfy their love of gravy. The new creation is a true combination of British and Indian culture.

A Rich Cultural Heritage

▼ **KEY QUESTION** What cultural achievements is Britain known for?

Many of the United Kingdom's most treasured exports don't come from factories. Literature, music, and popular culture make up a rich cultural heritage. With its history as an imperial power, the nation has been exporting its culture around the world for centuries.

Literature Many consider English playwright and poet **William Shakespeare** the finest writer of all time. His plays have entertained audiences for over 400 years. In 1997, a replica of the Globe Theatre—where Shakespeare's plays were originally performed—opened in London, introducing a new generation of Britons to his work.

Many talented authors followed Shakespeare. Jane Austen wrote about British life in the late 1700s and early 1800s in such books as *Pride and Prejudice*. In books such as *Oliver Twist* and *A Christmas Carol*, Charles Dickens explored Britain's social problems. Modern British authors have written many stories for young people. C. S. Lewis crafted fantastic tales in the *Chronicles of Narnia*. J. R. R. Tolkien created the magical world of the *Lord of the Rings* series. Most recently, J. K. Rowling's young wizard Harry Potter has charmed readers of all ages.

Leisure Time Many Britons are sports fans. Soccer, known as football in Europe, is the nation's favorite sport. The modern form of the game played worldwide is thought to have originated in England.

COMPARING ▸ Sports

European Football Ten players on each team try to kick a round ball into a goal defended by one player. **1. How do the balls used differ?**

American Football Teams of 11 heavily padded players carry or throw an oval ball across a goal line. **2. Which version uses more padding?**

Two other games invented in Britain have become popular in its former colonies. Cricket is played with a bat and a ball. Teams from the United Kingdom and other Commonwealth nations such as India and Pakistan often compete in international games. Rugby, a sport like football, is popular in Australia and South Africa.

The United Kingdom has also produced some well-known films and television shows that have been exported around the world. One British reality television program, *Pop Idol*, allowed viewers to vote for their favorite singers each week. The show was an instant success. Versions of it spread to over 30 countries, including the United States.

Music In the 1960s, the United States faced an unusual kind of invasion, not by soldiers but by music. American teenagers went crazy for British rock 'n' roll. Mobs of screaming fans greeted "British Invasion" bands like the Beatles and the Rolling Stones wherever they performed. Since then, many other British bands, such as Coldplay, have gained popularity with Americans.

Playing Cricket Some Pakistani Muslim boys use a traffic cone to play cricket on a London street.

▲ **SUMMARIZE** Describe British cultural achievements that have had a global impact.

Section ❷ Assessment

 **ONLINE QUIZ**
For test practice, go to **Interactive Review** @ ClassZone.com

TERMS & NAMES

1. Explain the importance of
- Briton
- Gaelic
- multicultural
- Church of England

USE YOUR READING NOTES

2. Find Main Ideas Use your completed web diagram to answer the following question:

What British authors have written books for young people?

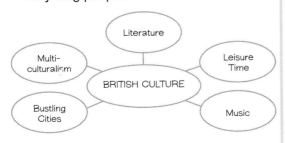

KEY IDEAS

3. In addition to English, what other languages are spoken in the United Kingdom?

4. How have immigrants changed British culture?

5. What early writer helped make the United Kingdom well known for its literary achievements?

CRITICAL THINKING

6. Draw Conclusions How did British sports become popular in countries like India and Australia?

7. Form and Support Opinions What are the advantages of having a diverse British population?

8. CONNECT to Today What challenges might the United Kingdom face if the diversity of its population continues to grow?

9. WRITING Create a Brochure In 2012, London will host the Summer Olympic Games. Use a word processor to create a brochure telling Americans why they should come to London for the 2012 Olympics. Find a picture to illustrate your brochure.

United Kingdom **413**

Reading for Understanding

▶ Key Ideas

BEFORE, YOU LEARNED

British culture is changing as the population becomes more diverse.

NOW YOU WILL LEARN

The United Kingdom's government is a constitutional monarchy. Its economy is strong and adapts to global changes.

▶ Vocabulary

TERMS & NAMES

constitutional monarchy a government in which the powers of the king or queen are limited by a constitution

unwritten constitution a framework for government that is not a single written document but includes many different laws, court decisions, and political customs

devolution the process of shifting some power from national to regional government

Good Friday Agreement an agreement between Northern Ireland's unionists and nationalists that set up a new government

wind farm a power plant that uses windmills to generate electricity

Channel Tunnel the underwater railroad tunnel between France and England under the English Channel

Visual Vocabulary wind farm

▶ Reading Strategy

Re-create the web diagram shown at right. As you read and respond to the **KEY QUESTIONS**, use the web diagram to help you summarize information about the government and economy of the United Kingdom.

 Skillbuilder Handbook, page R5

SUMMARIZE

```
        GOVERNMENT          ECONOMY
       /        \          /        \
   [    ]     [    ]    [    ]     [    ]
```

⚡ **GRAPHIC ORGANIZERS**
Go to **Interactive Review** @ClassZone.com

Parliament and Free Enterprise

Connecting to Your World

Most Americans know that the United Kingdom has a monarch, Queen Elizabeth II. You may have seen pictures of her, her son Prince Charles, or her grandsons Prince William and Prince Harry. While most Americans have heard of Queen Elizabeth II, many aren't sure exactly what role she plays in British political life. Does she help govern Britain? Does she control the nation's foreign policy or manage its economy? Keep reading to learn more about how the British government works and how monarchs and elected leaders fit into it.

Queen and Parliament

🔻 **KEY QUESTION** How are the regions of the United Kingdom governed?

The British sovereign, or monarch, serves as an important symbol of the British nation, but not as the leader of the government. Elected leaders govern the country. The sovereign is not above the law, and he or she rules and acts with Parliament's approval. The king or queen performs mostly ceremonial duties, which can include attending formal dinners or appointing ambassadors to other countries.

The Royal Family Queen Elizabeth II (above) with her grandsons, William and Harry. The queen uses this gold coach (below) for special occasions, such as a parade celebrating her reign.

Constitutional Monarchy The United Kingdom is a **constitutional monarchy**, in which the monarch's power is limited by a constitution. Unlike most countries, it has an **unwritten constitution** made up of laws, court decisions, and political customs. Parliament, the United Kingdom's legislature, can change it as needed.

Parliament is made up of two houses and the sovereign. Members of the House of Lords are mostly appointed. This house has little real power. The House of Commons, the key lawmaking body, consists of elected officials. Usually, the leader of the party with the most seats in the House of Commons becomes prime minister. The prime minister heads the executive branch of the government. He or she governs with the support of the Cabinet. Tony Blair served as prime minister until 2007, when he was replaced by Gordon Brown.

Regional Governments All four regions of the United Kingdom— England, Wales, Scotland, and Northern Ireland—are represented in Parliament. In the late 1990s, Parliament shifted some power from the national level to regional governments, a process called **devolution**. Scotland and Wales set up parliaments. They took over their domestic affairs, while Parliament kept charge of foreign policy and defense.

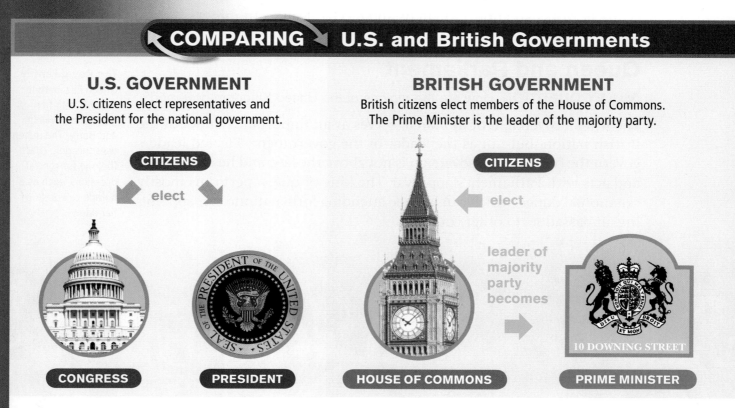

COMPARING U.S. and British Governments

U.S. GOVERNMENT
U.S. citizens elect representatives and the President for the national government.

CITIZENS

elect

CONGRESS   PRESIDENT

BRITISH GOVERNMENT
British citizens elect members of the House of Commons. The Prime Minister is the leader of the majority party.

CITIZENS

elect

leader of majority party becomes

10 DOWNING STREET

HOUSE OF COMMONS   PRIME MINISTER

CRITICAL THINKING

Compare and Contrast Where do citizens more directly choose their leader?

Establishing a government in Northern Ireland has been more difficult. The English first expanded into Ireland in the 1100s. The Irish, who had their own culture, bitterly resented the English. In 1949, the southern part of Ireland became the Republic of Ireland. Since the 1920s, Northern Ireland has been divided by conflict between two groups. The nationalists, who are mostly Catholic, believe Northern Ireland should unite with the Republic of Ireland. The unionists, mainly Protestants, want to stay part of the United Kingdom. In 1998, both sides signed the **Good Friday Agreement**, which set up a new government. In 2002, however, renewed violence led to the government's shutdown. Recent efforts toward self-government have failed, but violence between the two sides has decreased and talks continue.

▲ **SUMMARIZE** Explain how the United Kingdom governs its regions.

The British Economy

▼ **KEY QUESTION** How has the United Kingdom's economy changed?

Today, the United Kingdom is a densely populated urban nation. Cities cover most areas that were once farmland. The country also lost its empire, which had boosted its economy. These changes have forced it to adapt.

A Powerful Economy For decades, manufacturing formed the basis of Great Britain's economy. It was fueled by natural resources such as iron ore, coal, and oil deposits in the North Sea. As these resources are depleted, British scientists have begun looking for sustainable energy sources, including wind energy. The map at right shows Britain's development of **wind farms**, power plants that use windmills to generate electricity.

At one time, Great Britain was known for its textile and steel industries. While it remains a leader in the production of textiles, chemicals, and motor vehicles, it has fewer manufacturing jobs than before. Over three-fourths of Britain's labor force now works in service industries. The nation is a world leader in insurance and financial services. London's banks and stock exchange have made it one of Europe's leading business centers.

Wind Farms in Britain

- Operational farms
- Farms under construction

North Sea

ATLANTIC OCEAN

SCOTLAND
28 operational
14 under construction

NORTHERN IRELAND
10 operational
1 under construction

ENGLAND
47 operational
9 under construction

UNITED KINGDOM

IRELAND

WALES
21 operational
3 under construction

0   100   200 miles
0   100   200 kilometers
Source: British Wind Energy Association

CONNECT Geography & Economics

1. **Human-Environment Interaction** Are more wind farms located inland or near the coast?
2. **Region** Which of the four regions has the most wind farms under construction?

The Channel Tunnel Trains like this one, operated by a company called Eurotunnel, shuttle passengers and freight through the Channel Tunnel. In June 2006, the 100 millionth passenger traveled on the train.

Participating in the Global Economy Winston Churchill once said of Great Britain, "We are with Europe but not of it." In some ways the nation still stands apart. In 2002, most European Union members agreed to replace their own currency with the euro. Britain chose to continue using its national currency, the pound.

In most other ways, however, the United Kingdom is now closely tied to Europe through participation in the European Union and trade with industrial and developing nations. The nation has a trillion-dollar economy. Because of its prosperity, it can trade with other countries. It has goods and services that other nations want. Most of the United Kingdom's trade is with other EU members.

Technology has also drawn the United Kingdom closer to its neighbors in Europe. In 1994, British and French workers completed construction of the 31-mile undersea **Channel Tunnel**. The tunnel links Britain to France by train. Every day, an average of 45,000 people make the 35-minute journey to the European mainland.

 ANALYZE EFFECTS Explain how the United Kingdom's economy has changed.

Section ③ Assessment

ONLINE QUIZ
For test practice, go to
Interactive Review
@ ClassZone.com

TERMS & NAMES

1. Explain the importance of
- constitutional monarchy
- unwritten constitution
- Good Friday Agreement
- Channel Tunnel

USE YOUR READING NOTES

2. Summarize Use your completed web diagram to answer the following question:

What decision did the United Kingdom make that kept its economy separate from the rest of the European Union?

KEY IDEAS

3. Why is the United Kingdom said to have an unwritten constitution?

4. What are the roles of the monarch, prime minister, and Parliament within the British government?

5. What are the United Kingdom's most important service industries?

CRITICAL THINKING

6. Compare and Contrast How are the British Parliament and the U.S. Congress alike and different?

7. Analyze Causes and Effects Why might a long history of conflict make it hard for Northern Ireland to set up a workable government?

8. **CONNECT to Today** How might London's growing cultural diversity help it expand its global financial and business services?

9. **WRITING** **Write a Report** Choose a major British industry to research. Write a paragraph explaining why it is important to the United Kingdom's economy.

Interactive ⟨⟩ Review

Click here to complete these and other activities online @ ClassZone.com

CHAPTER SUMMARY

Key Idea 1
Many developments, including the Industrial Revolution and a colonial empire, helped the United Kingdom grow into a major world power.

Key Idea 2
Britain's long history as an industrial and colonial power has shaped its culture. Britain's increasingly diverse population continues to enrich its cultural life.

Key Idea 3
The United Kingdom's government is a constitutional monarchy. Its economy is strong and adapts to global changes.

For **Review and Study Notes**, go to **Interactive Review** @ ClassZone.com

NAME GAME

Use the Terms & Names list to complete each sentence on paper or online.

1. I am a famous English playwright.
   William Shakespeare 🖱

2. I connect Britain with France by rail.
   _____

3. I am the United Kingdom's official church.
   _____

4. I am a British person. _____

5. I am a government in which the powers of the king and queen are limited by a constitution.
   _____

6. I am a document written in 1215 that limited the power of the English monarch. _____

7. I am the language spoken by some people in Scotland and Ireland along with English.
   _____

8. I am the process of shifting power from national to regional government. _____

9. I am the legislative branch of the British government. _____

10. I am the organization made up of former British colonies. _____

Briton
Channel Tunnel
Church of England
Commonwealth of Nations
constitutional monarchy
devolution
Gaelic
Good Friday Agreement
imperialism
Magna Carta
multicultural
Parliament
unwritten constitution
William Shakespeare

Activities

GeoGame

Use this online map to reinforce your understanding of the United Kingdom. Drag and drop each place name in the list to its location on the map.

Geo GAME

London
Edinburgh
Wales
Scotland
England

To play the complete game, go to **Interactive Review** @ ClassZone.com

United Kingdom

Wales 🖱

Crossword Puzzle

Complete an online crossword puzzle to test your knowledge of the United Kingdom.

ACROSS
1. a power plant that uses windmills to generate electricity

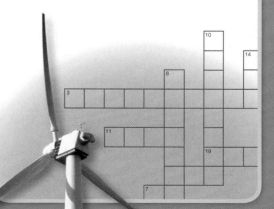

VOCABULARY

Explain the significance of each of the following.

1. Parliament
2. multicultural
3. Church of England
4. William Shakespeare
5. unwritten constitution
6. Good Friday Agreement

Match the item on the left with its description on the right.

7. Magna Carta   **A.** spoken in Scotland and Ireland
8. Gaelic   **B.** limited the power of the monarchy
9. Briton   **C.** connects Britain to France underwater
10. devolution   **D.** a British person
11. Channel Tunnel   **E.** shifting power from national to regional government

KEY IDEAS

1 Building a British Empire

12. What four regions make up the United Kingdom?
13. How did Great Britain benefit from its empire?
14. What geographic factors led to the start of the Industrial Revolution in Great Britain?
15. Why did Great Britain's standing as a world power change after World War II?

2 From Shakespeare to Harry Potter

16. What is Great Britain's largest city?
17. What languages are spoken in Wales, Ireland, and Scotland besides English?
18. How did Shakespeare contribute to British culture?
19. In what areas has British culture influenced popular culture in the United States in recent decades?

3 Parliament and Free Enterprise

20. What has the United Kingdom done to give more self-government to the regions of Scotland, Wales, and Northern Ireland?
21. Which part of the United Kingdom's economy is expanding, and which has become smaller?
22. How does the United Kingdom participate in the global economy?

CRITICAL THINKING

23. **Draw Conclusions** Create a diagram and include two factors that led to British industrial growth.

British Industrial Growth

24. **Five Themes: Movement** How did the Industrial Revolution contribute to the urbanization of the United Kingdom?
25. **Connect Geography & Culture** How do sports keep Great Britain tied to its former colonies?
26. **Compare and Contrast** How does the selection of the British prime minister differ from that of the U.S. president?
27. **Connect to Economics** What effect might a decline in North Sea oil have on the United Kingdom's economy?
28. **Draw Conclusions** How is Britain's role in the global economy different today from its role during the height of the British Empire?

Answer the
ESSENTIAL QUESTION

How did being an island nation influence the development of the United Kingdom?

Written Response Write a two- or three-paragraph response to the Essential Question. Be sure to consider the key ideas of each section as well as specific ideas about the United Kingdom. Use the rubric below to guide your thinking.

Response Rubric
A strong response will:
- discuss how Britain's location, waterways, and natural resources influenced its development
- explain why Britain needed to look beyond its island home for resources and how it met this need through empire building and trade

✔ **Test Practice**

• Online Test Practice @ ClassZone.com
• Test-Taking Strategies and Practice at the front of this book

THEMATIC MAP

Use the map below to answer questions 1 and 2 on your paper.

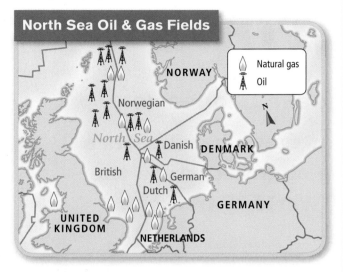

North Sea Oil & Gas Fields

Natural gas
Oil

NORWAY

Norwegian

North Sea

Danish DENMARK

British

German

Dutch

GERMANY

UNITED KINGDOM

NETHERLANDS

1. **The map above shows sectors of natural gas and oil fields in the North Sea. Which sector has the fewest oil fields?**

   A. Norwegian Sector
   B. German Sector
   C. British Sector
   D. Dutch Sector

2. **How many oil fields are shown in the British Sector of the North Sea?**

   A. four   **C.** nine
   B. seven   **D.** ten

LINE GRAPH

Examine the graph below. Use the graph to answer questions 3 and 4 on your paper.

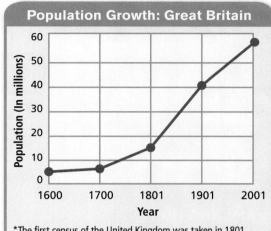

Population Growth: Great Britain

Population (In millions)

60
50
40
30
20
10
0

1600   1700   1801   1901   2001
Year

*The first census of the United Kingdom was taken in 1801. Population figures for 1600 and 1700 are estimates. Figures include Ireland, except for 2001.

Sources: GenDocs, "Population of Great Britain & Ireland 1570–1931" and National Statistics UK Census 2001

3. **When did Great Britain experience the greatest population growth?**

   A. 1600s   **C.** 1800s
   B. 1700s   **D.** 1900s

4. **What was the British population in 1901?**

   A. 416,000   **C.** 16.3 million
   B. 4.8 million   **D.** 41.6 million

GeoActivity

1. INTERDISCIPLINARY ACTIVITY–LANGUAGE ARTS

Review the section on British literature. Pick one writer in this section. Find a short excerpt from one of his or her works to read aloud to the class. Introduce your choice and provide some information about the writer.

2. WRITING FOR SOCIAL STUDIES

Reread the part of Section 2 on British culture. Pick three things described in this section and write a paragraph on each explaining how they are similar to and different from your own culture.

3. MENTAL MAPPING

Create an outline map of the United Kingdom and label the following:

• England
• Scotland
• Wales
• Northern Ireland

• London
• English Channel
• Atlantic Ocean

CHAPTER 14

Eastern Europe

1 FOCUS ON

Poland, Ukraine, and the Baltic States

2 FOCUS ON

Hungary and the Czech Republic

3 FOCUS ON

The Balkans

ESSENTIAL QUESTION

In what ways has Eastern Europe changed since the end of World War II?

CONNECT Geography & History

Use the map and the time line to answer the following questions.

1. What four Eastern European countries border the Baltic Sea?
2. What city in the Ukraine still carries the name of an early Slavic state?

Government
◄ **970** Magyar leaders establish a stable kingdom in Hungary. (Magyar artifact)

800

Geography
800s Kievan Rus, the first eastern Slavic state, is established.

History
1918 Yugoslavia is formed at the end of World War I. (King Peter I) ►

Animated GEOGRAPHY
Present-Day Eastern Europe

Click here to explore Eastern Europe @ ClassZone.com

NORWAY

SWEDEN

FINLAND

RUSSIA

DENMARK

Baltic Sea

⊛ Tallinn
ESTONIA

⊛ Riga
LATVIA

LITHUANIA

RUSSIA

Vilnius ⊛

⊛ Minsk

BELARUS

NETHERLANDS

BELGIUM

GERMANY

LUXEMBOURG

POLAND
Warsaw ⊛
Łódź •

Chernobyl •

Kiev ⊛

Kharkiv •

Prague ⊛
CZECH REPUBLIC

Kraków •

Oder River

Vistula River

UKRAINE

Dniester River

Dnieper River

Dnipropetrovsk •

Donetsk •

50°N

SLOVAKIA
⊛ Bratislava

AUSTRIA

⊛ Budapest
HUNGARY

MOLDOVA
Chişinău ⊛

Odessa •

SWITZERLAND

SLOVENIA
Ljubljana ⊛
Zagreb •
CROATIA

ROMANIA

Bucharest ⊛

Danube River

BOSNIA AND HERZEGOVINA
Sarajevo ⊛

⊛ Belgrade
SERBIA

Black Sea

ITALY

Adriatic Sea

MONTENEGRO
Podgorica •

⊛ Skopje
MACEDONIA

Tiranë ⊛

BULGARIA
Sofia •

ALBANIA

GREECE

Aegean Sea

TURKEY

40°N

⊛	National capital
•	Other city

0   200   400 miles
0   200   400 kilometers

History

1940s Communists gain power in Eastern Europe. (Josip Broz Tito) ▼

Economics

2004 The first Eastern European nations—the Czech Republic, Hungary, Poland, Slovenia, and the Baltic states—join the EU.

Geography

1986 Chernobyl nuclear disaster in Ukraine ▶

Today

DANGER
НЕБЕЗПЕКА

423

Reading for Understanding

▶ Key Ideas

BEFORE, YOU LEARNED

European nations experienced many changes after World War II.

NOW YOU WILL LEARN

Poland, Ukraine, and the Baltic States faced many challenges after shaking off Communist rule.

▶ Vocabulary

TERMS & NAMES

Baltic States Latvia, Lithuania, and Estonia, three countries that border the Baltic Sea

Lech Walesa (lehk wah•LEHN•suh) Polish leader who cofounded Solidarity and served as president of Poland from 1990 to 1995

Solidarity Poland's first independent labor union, cofounded by Lech Walesa

Russification the effort to make countries occupied by the Soviet Union more Russian by replacing local languages and customs

bread basket an abundant grain-producing region

deport to expel from a country

BACKGROUND VOCABULARY

brain drain the loss of skilled workers who move in search of better opportunities

REVIEW

communism a type of government in which the Communist Party holds all political power and controls the economy

command economy an economic system in which the production of goods and services is decided by a central government

market economy an economic system in which the production of goods and services is decided by the supply of goods and the demand of consumers

▶ Reading Strategy

Re-create the chart shown at right. As you read and respond to the **KEY QUESTIONS**, use the chart to help you categorize information about the Eastern European nations in this chapter.

 Skillbuilder Handbook, page R7

CATEGORIZE

	LANGUAGE	GOVERNMENT	ECONOMY
Poland			
Ukraine			
Latvia			
Lithuania			
Estonia			

 GRAPHIC ORGANIZERS
Go to **Interactive Review** @ ClassZone.com

Poland, Ukraine, and the Baltic States

Connecting to Your World

After the American Revolution, Americans quickly learned that building a strong independent nation was not easy. It took time to create a stable government and prosperous economy. In this section, you will read about Poland, Ukraine, and the three **Baltic States**, Latvia, Lithuania, and Estonia. Along with the rest of Eastern Europe, they gained independence from **communism** in the 1990s. Like the United States, they faced difficult choices. Many countries found the new freedom challenging.

Poland

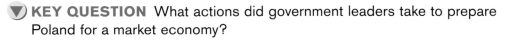

▼ **KEY QUESTION** What actions did government leaders take to prepare Poland for a market economy?

Poland's name comes from the Slavic word *Polanie*, which means plain or field. The Northern European Plain covers much of Poland. Its flat, fertile land began attracting Slavic settlers as early as 2000 B.C. During the Middle Ages, Poland ruled an empire that covered much of central and eastern Europe. By the late 18th century, however, Poland was conquered by its neighbors. It did not regain its independence until after World War I.

Polish Countryside
Freshly plowed fields cover these gently rolling hills in the Roztocze region of southeast Poland.

POLAND
Roztocze

History During World War II, both Germany and the Soviet Union, a union of Communist republics led by Russia, invaded Poland. At the end of the war, Soviet troops drove the Germans out of Poland and supported Communists in gaining control of the government. By the 1950s, Communist rule was firmly established in Poland and throughout Eastern Europe. Communist leaders took over the economy and limited the rights of citizens.

During the 1970s, Poland faced food shortages and rising prices. As economic conditions worsened, people questioned Communist rule. In 1980, thousands of Polish workers went on strike, led by **Lech Walesa** (lehk wah•LEHN•suh). They demanded better pay, greater political freedom, and recognition of **Solidarity**, the nation's first independent labor union. Communist leaders saw public support for Solidarity growing. In 1989, they reached an agreement with Solidarity that led to government reform. Poland held its first free elections. The new government lifted many restrictions on Polish citizens.

Culture Before World War II, Poland was a diverse nation, with Germans, Jews, Ukrainians, and other ethnic groups. However, the war caused many groups to migrate and shifted Poland's borders. Almost all of the 3 million Jews living in Poland were killed during the Holocaust. Today, most people in Poland are Poles. Their ancestors belonged to the Slavic tribes that settled in Poland long ago. Polish, a Slavic language, is spoken throughout the country.

Catholic Mourners
People gather in Pilsudski Square in Warsaw, Poland, to mourn the death of Pope John Paul II.

Most Poles are Roman Catholics, which unites the Polish people. During Communist rule, when religious practice was restricted, many continued to practice the Catholic faith. In 1978, Cardinal Karol Wojtyla (voy•TIH•wah) became the world's first Polish pope, Pope John Paul II. He made Catholic Poles very proud. In visits to Poland, he encouraged efforts to gain greater freedom.

Poland has a rich cultural tradition, with a strong emphasis on education. Many outstanding scientists, such as Nicolaus Copernicus and Marie Curie, were Polish. Like other nations, Poland has to work hard to preserve its folk culture in the face of mass media and urbanization.

Government and Economics In 1990, Lech Walesa became Poland's first president. He helped Poland shift to democracy. In 1997, Poland adopted a new constitution to reflect its democratic government. Today, Poland is a republic. Voters elect the nation's president and legislature. The prime minister runs the government.

In the 1990s, Poland's leaders enacted a series of economic reforms to pave the way from a **command economy** to a **market economy**. Polish leaders sold government-owned industries to private companies. They shut down many old and inefficient factories and invited foreign companies to invest in Poland. Today, the country's major industries include production of coal, iron, steel, and machinery. Poland also has a large shipbuilding industry. Poland joined the European Union in 2004. Membership gave it new markets for such farm products as potatoes and rye and for manufactured goods.

Although Poland's transition to a market economy was more successful than that of many Eastern European nations, it still faces many economic challenges. High unemployment remains a serious problem. Factory closings have left many workers without jobs. Lack of good jobs for skilled workers has caused a serious **brain drain**, as many of Poland's bright young people leave the country in search of better job opportunities in Western Europe or the United States.

▲ **SUMMARIZE** Explain how Poland became a market economy.

ONLINE PRIMARY SOURCE To read the rest of Walesa's speech, go to the **Research & Writing Center** @ ClassZone.com

ANALYZING Primary Sources

Lech Walesa (born 1943) led the struggle to form Solidarity. His peaceful resistance helped end Communist rule in Poland.

> We respect the dignity and the rights of every man and every nation. The path to a brighter future of the world leads through honest reconciliation [resolution] of the conflicting interests and not through hatred and bloodshed.

Source: Lech Walesa, Nobel Peace Prize acceptance speech, 1983

DOCUMENT–BASED QUESTION

How does Walesa suggest conflicts among nations should be settled?

UKRAINE

Ukraine

▼ **KEY QUESTION** How did Soviet control affect the economy and culture of Ukraine?

For Ukraine, once a part of the Soviet Union, independence has not been easy. Nearby Russia still plays a part in its political and economic life. Ukraine faces many challenges as it seeks ties with the West while maintaining good relations with Russia.

History In the 800s, the town of Kiev in Ukraine was the center of the first eastern Slavic state, Kievan Rus. After 400 years as a powerful state, invading nomads conquered the territory. Ukraine came under foreign rule for centuries. By the late 1700s, it was part of the Russian Empire. In 1922, Ukraine became one of the first Soviet republics.

Soviet policies caused great hardships for the nation. In the 1930s, the Soviets took land from Ukrainian farmers to form huge, government-run farms called collectives. They required almost all crops to be sent to cities to feed the workers there. Millions of farm families starved. On April 26, 1986, the world's worst nuclear power accident occurred in Ukraine at the Chernobyl power plant. Radiation from Chernobyl has affected an estimated 7 million people in and around Ukraine.

Ukrainians had been protesting Soviet rule since the 1960s. When the Soviet Union collapsed in 1991, Ukraine finally gained its independence and began to rebuild.

CONNECT to Science

The Chernobyl explosion put large amounts of radiation into the atmosphere. The chart below shows the radiation released by a form of radioactive iodine during the week after the accident. The petabecquerel, or PBq, is a measure of radioactivity. For reference, a household smoke detector, which is very safe, emits 0.00000000003 PBq of radiation.

Date of Release	Amount (in PBq)
April 26	704
April 27	204
April 28	150
April 29	102
April 30	69
May 1	62
May 2	102

Source: Nuclear Energy Agency, "Chernobyl: Assessment of Radiological and Health Impacts"

◀ *radiation inspectors*

Activity

Make a Line Graph

Materials
• Graph paper
• Markers

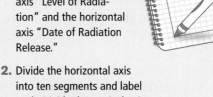

1. Draw two lines for your graph. Label the vertical axis "Level of Radiation" and the horizontal axis "Date of Radiation Release."

2. Divide the horizontal axis into ten segments and label each. Divide the vertical axis into units of 100. Put a dot on the graph that represents the radiation measured for each date. Connect the dots. Title your line graph.

Culture About three-fourths of Ukraine's population is ethnic Ukrainian. Russians are the largest ethnic minority, at about one-fifth of the population. Under Soviet rule, the government imposed a **Russification** policy on the country. The Russian language replaced Ukrainian in schools, newspapers, and the government. After decades of speaking Russian, many Ukrainians knew it better than their native language. In 1991, Ukrainian became the official language, but Russian is still widely spoken.

About two-thirds of Ukrainians live in Kiev and other cities. Western Ukraine is heavily rural. Most people in rural areas live in large villages. They are employed in farming or in making small handicrafts, such as the traditional decorated eggs known as *pysanky*.

Government and Economics In 1990, Ukraine held its first free, multiparty election. Today, Ukraine is a democracy with a president, prime minister, and legislature. Ukrainians are committed to free elections. In 2004, tens of thousands of them took part in the Orange Revolution, a peaceful protest against fraud in the presidential election.

Ukrainians remain divided on plans for reform. Some favor closer ties to Russia. Others hope for EU membership and trade with Western Europe. Ukraine maintains good relations with Russia, whom it depends on for oil and natural gas. Ukraine belongs to the Commonwealth of Independent States (CIS), a group of former Soviet republics that cooperate on political and economic matters.

Ukraine is rich in natural resources and fertile soil. Most heavy industries are in eastern Ukraine near the nation's coal deposits. Ukraine's rich soil has made it the **bread basket**, or major grain-producing region, of Europe. However, Ukraine has lagged behind many former Communist countries in converting to private ownership. Many farms and factories also lack modern equipment.

▲ **ANALYZE EFFECTS**
Identify how Soviet control affected Ukraine's economy and culture.

CONNECT ⤷ History & Culture

Pysanky

Beautifully decorated Easter eggs known as *pysanky* are among the most famous Ukrainian crafts. The word *pysanky* means "written egg." Artists create intricate and colorful designs by drawing patterns on the eggs with wax and then dipping them in different-colored dyes. The wax prevents parts of the egg from picking up color. Many of the images and colors on the egg have special meaning. Designs are often passed down within a family for generations. The eggs are given as gifts during the Easter holiday.

Ukrainian Farm
Farmers harvest wheat on a collective farm near Lvov, Ukraine. **How does equipment affect farm production?**

ESTONIA
LATVIA
LITHUANIA

The Baltic States

🔻 **KEY QUESTION** How are the Baltic States alike and different from each other?

The Baltic States—Estonia, Latvia, and Lithuania—share a coastline on the Baltic Sea. They also share the challenge of becoming part of prosperous, modern Europe.

Striving for Independence The Baltic States have a long history of foreign rule. At different times, Danes, Swedes, Poles, and Germans have controlled them. By the late 1700s, they belonged to the vast Russian Empire. They remained a part of it until it ended in 1918. In 1940, the Soviet Union occupied the Baltic States and forced them to join it. In all three countries, the Soviets decided to **deport**, or expel, the thousands of people who resisted their rule. The Soviets brought in Russian workers to replace them. In 1990, the Baltic States became the first Soviet republics to declare independence. The Soviet Union formally recognized their claims in September 1991.

Culture Although they share a common history, each Baltic state has its own language and customs. In Lithuania, most people speak Lithuanian and are Roman Catholics. The people of Latvia speak Latvian, while Estonians speak Estonian, a language related to Finnish. Most Estonians and Latvians are Lutheran Protestants.

Throughout the Baltic States, the Soviet policy of Russification brought population changes. For instance, before Soviet rule, Latvians made up three-fourths of that country's population. Now they make up just over half. In each country, Russians are the largest minority. During the Soviet era, many people left farms and villages to work in urban factories. Today, two-thirds of the people in the Baltic States live in cities. The people of Latvia, Lithuania, and Estonia have had to work to preserve their own languages, customs, and traditions.

Song Festival These girls are dressed up to participate in the All-Estonian Song Festival, held every five years in the capital city of Tallinn.

Government and Economics The Baltic States are republics with an elected president and legislature. A prime minister heads the government and carries out government operations.

The Baltic States are now successful market economies. Most industries and farms are privately owned. In 2004 all became EU members. Germany has become a key trade partner, while trade with Russia is decreasing. Estonia's major industries are electronics, wood products, and textiles. Latvia's factories make vehicles, farm machinery, and fertilizers. Lithuania produces machine tools, appliances, and electric motors.

During decades of Communist rule, government leaders ignored many serious environmental problems. Old and faulty wastewater-treatment plants, leaking sewers, and fertilizer, oil, and chemical run-off from factories and farms have polluted the Baltic Sea. All Baltic countries are now involved in the cleanup.

Independence Rally
Many Eastern European nations held rallies to protest Communist rule, such as this one in Kaunas in southern Lithuania in 1989.

 COMPARE AND CONTRAST Explain how the Baltic States are similar to and different from each other.

Section ❶ Assessment

 ONLINE QUIZ
For test practice, go to
Interactive Review
@ClassZone.com

TERMS & NAMES

1. Explain the importance of
• Baltic States
• Solidarity
• Russification
• deport

USE YOUR READING NOTES

2. Categorize Use your completed chart to answer the following question:

What kind of government does Poland have?

	LANGUAGE	GOVERNMENT	ECONOMY
Poland			
Ukraine			
Latvia			
Lithuania			
Estonia			

KEY IDEAS

3. What were the goals of Solidarity in Poland?

4. How did the Soviet Union carry out its Russification policy in the Ukraine?

5. What environmental issue do the Baltic States face today?

CRITICAL THINKING

6. Form and Support Opinions Why do many Eastern European countries want to join the European Union?

7. Analyze Causes and Effects Why are many people in the Baltic States concerned about each country's national identity?

8. CONNECT to Today Why might Polish leaders want to encourage young people to stay in Poland?

9. ART **Give a Presentation** Do research to learn more about one of the folk arts of the countries in this section. Give a short presentation on where and how this craft is made, how it is used, and any customs associated with it. Show pictures of the craft.

Reading for Understanding

SECTION 2

▶ Key Ideas

BEFORE, YOU LEARNED

Independence brought political and economic changes and new challenges for Poland, Ukraine, and the Baltic States.

NOW YOU WILL LEARN

After decades of Communist rule, Hungary and the Czech Republic made economic and political reforms.

▶ Vocabulary

TERMS & NAMES

Magyar an ethnic Hungarian person or the Hungarian language

Czechoslovakia (CHEHK•uh•sluh•VAH•kee•uh) former country in Eastern Europe that existed from 1918 until 1993, when it split into the Czech Republic and Slovakia

Velvet Revolution the peaceful protest by the Czech people that led to the smooth end of communism in Czechoslovakia

BACKGROUND VOCABULARY

strategic relating to a plan of action designed to achieve a specific goal

standard of living an economic measure relating to the quality and amount of goods available to a group of people and how those goods are distributed across the group

eclectic made up of parts from a variety of sources

Visual Vocabulary Velvet Revolution

▶ Reading Strategy

Re-create the Venn diagram shown at right. As you read and respond to the **KEY QUESTIONS**, use the diagram to help you compare and contrast Hungary and the Czech Republic.

 Skillbuilder Handbook, page R9

COMPARE AND CONTRAST

HUNGARY   BOTH   CZECH REPUBLIC

GRAPHIC ORGANIZERS
Go to **Interactive Review** @ClassZone.com

Hungary and the Czech Republic

Connecting to Your World

Have you ever played chess or checkers? In these games, the player who controls the middle of the board can have a **strategic** advantage. That player can move in many different directions. Hungary sits right between the eastern and western regions of Europe and shares borders with seven other countries. It can choose which neighbors to befriend. Unlike good chess players, however, Hungary did not always have a choice about which way it moved.

Hungary

▼ **KEY QUESTION** How is Hungary's location an advantage in rebuilding its economy?

Hungary's central location attracted many groups. Hungary's earliest settlers were the **Magyar**, or ethnic Hungarian, people. In the late tenth century, Magyar leaders created a stable and prosperous kingdom. Then, in 1526, the Ottoman Turks and Austria conquered and divided Hungary's territory. Eventually, Austria drove out the Ottomans and took over. Hungary fought for independence from Austria's harsh rule.

Playing Chess A boy learns to play chess from his father.

Budapest The Széchenyi Chain Bridge was the first to cross the Danube River in Budapest.

•Budapest

HUNGARY

433

History By 1867, Austria had been weakened by many costly wars, and it was forced to share power with Hungary. Together they ruled an empire known as Austria-Hungary. During World War I, Austria-Hungary fought on the losing side. After its defeat, its territory was divided up. Hungary was independent but lost much of its land.

During World War II, Soviet troops invaded Hungary. They were followed by Communist Party agents, who wanted to make sure the Communists gained control of the government. Many Hungarians opposed Communist rule. They resented the loss of their freedom. In 1956, thousands of protesters flooded the streets of Budapest, the nation's capital, demanding that Soviet troops leave. The Soviet Union responded by sending more troops and tanks to crush the uprising. Thousands of protesters died in the fighting.

In later decades, Communist Party officials gave Hungarians greater economic freedom, allowing some private ownership of business. In 1989, as the Soviet government began to fall apart, the Hungarian government agreed to allow other political parties. A year later, Hungarian reformers removed the Communists from power in the country's first free elections.

Culture Most Hungarians are Magyars, descendants of Hungary's early settlers. Hungarians speak Hungarian, also called Magyar, a language related to Finnish and Estonian. As you can see from the map at right, Hungarian is different from the languages spoken in surrounding countries. About two-thirds of Hungarians are Roman Catholics. One-fourth are Protestants. Other ethnic groups include Croats, Roma (also called Gypsies), Romanians, and Slovaks.

During the Communist era, many Hungarians moved from farms to cities. Everyday life changed as a result. In cities today, modern influences like blue jeans and pop music clash with traditional dress and folk songs. Budapest is a good example of Hungary's mix of old and new. It is actually two cities divided by the Danube River. Medieval Buda sits on the western bank and Pest, which underwent a surge of development in the 18th century, sits on the eastern bank.

Traditional and Modern (left) Teenagers perform at a Hungarian folk dance. (right) The crowd enjoys the show at the Sziget Music Festival in Budapest.

434

Languages of Eastern Europe

North Sea

Baltic Sea

Estonian

Latvian

Lithuanian

Belarusian

Polish

Czech

Slovak

Ukrainian

Hungarian

Moldovan

Slovene

Romanian

Serbo-Croatian

Adriatic Sea

Bulgarian

Albanian   Macedonian

Indo-European Branches
- Baltic
- Slavic
- Romance
- Illyrian

Uralic Branch
- Finno-Ugric

Polish Spoken language

CONNECT Geography & Culture

1. **Place** What language branch does Albanian belong to?
2. **Region** Which branch is most common in Eastern Europe?

Government and Economics Hungary is a parliamentary democracy. Voters elect the members of parliament, called the National Assembly, to serve four-year terms. The National Assembly elects the president and the prime minister. The president—who serves a five-year term—is the commander in chief of the armed forces, but has little power. The prime minister is the head of government.

Before World War II, most Hungarians were farmers living in rural villages. Under Communist rule, officials worked hard to expand industry. As industry increased, many Hungarians moved to cities to work in government-run factories. By the 1990s, employment in agriculture decreased from over half to one-eighth of the population.

In the decades after the failed Hungarian revolt in 1956, the government began to allow some private businesses to operate. After the Communists lost the 1990 elections, Hungary's new leaders lifted many government controls on business and sold most remaining state-owned businesses and farms. The country moved rapidly toward a market economy. Today, it has one of the highest **standards of living** in Eastern Europe. Hungary joined the EU in 2004. The nation's central location and the Danube River help boost trade. EU members Germany, Austria, France, and Italy are its main trade partners.

🔺 **FIND MAIN IDEAS** Explain how Hungary's location is helpful in rebuilding its economy.

CZECH REPUBLIC SLOVAKIA

The Czech Republic

KEY QUESTION How did freedom from Communist rule change the Czech Republic?

Like Hungary, the Czech Republic was once part of Austria-Hungary. It also spent many decades controlled by a Communist government. Today, it is one of the most prosperous countries in Eastern Europe.

History In the 900s, Slavic peoples established the kingdom of Bohemia alongside two other regions, Moravia and Slovakia. The Czech regions of Bohemia and Moravia maintained close ties throughout their histories. Both became part of the Austrian empire in 1526. Slovakia, a region of Slovaks, became part of Hungary. In 1918, after Austria-Hungary's defeat in World War I, Europe's leaders made the lands that had been Bohemia, Moravia, and Slovakia into the nation of **Czechoslovakia** (CHEHK•uh•sluh•VAH•kee•uh). Czechs and Slovaks were thrown together within the new borders.

Czechoslovakia lasted only a few decades as an independent nation. In 1948, Communists took over the country. In 1968, the Soviet Union crushed efforts by Czech Communist leaders to give citizens greater freedom. Fearing their own people might demand more freedom, the Soviets sent troops and tanks to end protests.

In 1989, thousands of protesters filled the streets of Prague calling for an end to Communist rule. Massive protests convinced Communist leaders to resign. The end of Communist rule took place so smoothly, that this protest became known as the **Velvet Revolution**. In 1990, voters elected protest leader Václav Havel president. Three years later, Czech and Slovak leaders agreed to divide the country into the Czech Republic and Slovakia. Some call this friendly split the "Velvet Divorce."

Culture Most people in the Czech Republic are Czechs. They speak Czech, a Slavic language. The country has many smaller ethnic groups including Slovaks, Germans, Roma (Gypsies), Hungarians, and Poles. Before World War II, Czechoslovakia had a large Jewish population. Almost all the nation's Jews were killed during the Holocaust. Roman Catholics are the largest religious group in the Czech Republic.

HISTORY MAKERS

Václav Havel (born 1936)

Václav Havel's (VAHT-slahv HAH-vuhl) admirers call him a hero for his role in leading the Velvet Revolution. During Czechoslovakia's years of Communist rule, the country's leaders called him a danger to society. A well-known playwright, he spent several years in prison for openly opposing Communist rule. After the end of communism, grateful citizens chose Havel as Czechoslovakia's first president. He later served as the first president of the new Czech Republic.

 ONLINE BIOGRAPHY
For more on the life of Václav Havel, go to the
Research & Writing Center @ ClassZone.com

The Czech Republic has a tradition of fine art. Composer Antonín Dvořák (DVAWR•zhahk) wrote music inspired by the Czech landscape and folk music. Famous Czech writers include Franz Kafka and Milan Kundera, whose books explore the human condition. For centuries, Czech artists have crafted beautiful glassware. Glittering Czech crystal chandeliers hang in opera houses, palaces, and mansions around the world today.

Prague Residents and tourists alike use the Charles Bridge to cross the Vltava River and get around Prague.

The culture of the Czech Republic is a vibrant mix of old and new. Prague is the nation's capital and largest city. In the 1300s, it became a center of art and learning in Europe. The city has many beautiful Renaissance buildings. It is known as the "City of a Hundred Spires" because of the churches that dot its streets. Contemporary influences are making their marks on Prague. Young people dance to modern pop music in clubs that have opened in basements in the historic sections of town. Each year, millions of tourists add to the **eclectic** atmosphere of the Czech Republic.

CONNECT → Geography & Culture

The Dancing House Prague is known for its architecture. A popular stop on any tour of Prague is the Rasin Building, nicknamed the Dancing House. Although it is made of concrete, steel, and glass, it seems to swirl and twist, like a couple dancing.

Not everyone is a fan of the building, built by American architect Frank Gehry and Czech architect Vlado Milunic in 1996. Some feel it clashes with the older historic buildings that surround it. However, supporters find it lively and exciting, a symbol of the new Czech Republic.

CRITICAL THINKING

Make Inferences Why might some Prague residents want the city to build more new buildings like the Dancing House?

To learn more about Radek and his world, go to the **Activity Center** @ ClassZone.com

Hello! My name is Radek. I am 14 years old and live in Brno in the southeastern part of the Czech Republic. With almost 400,000 people, it is the second largest city after Prague. We live in a small apartment. On weekends, I like to read, listen to music, or watch television. Sometimes my family takes the train to Prague. Here's my day.

To introduce himself, Radek says:

"Dobrý den. Jmenuju se Radek."

7 A.M. My sister and I eat breakfast with our parents. They both have to go to work and we go to school. I have rye bread or a roll with butter and jam and a glass of milk. Sometimes we have slices of cheese or salami, too.

8 A.M.–4 P.M. I have to work hard at school, especially in my English class. Everyone has to take courses in at least one foreign language. My school has many after-school activities. I joined the gymnastics club. I'm looking forward to our first competition!

6 P.M. In the evening, my family eats dinner. Sometimes, my grandmother comes over and helps my mother make roast duck with *knedlíky*, or potato dumplings, and cabbage. It's one of my favorite meals.

7 P.M. Today is my name day. In the Czech Republic, each day of the year has a different name assigned to it. It's traditional to celebrate your birthday and your name day. Some of my friends and I are going out for ice cream sundaes to celebrate.

CONNECT to Your Life

Journal Entry Think about your own birthday. How do you celebrate it? Do you have other special occasions, like Radek, that you celebrate with your family? Record your ideas in your journal.

Government and Economics The Czech Republic is a parliamentary democracy. Voters elect members of parliament. The parliament elects the president, who serves as the head of state. The president appoints a prime minister to oversee the daily operations of government.

Before Communist rule, the Czech economy was diverse and balanced. Under communism, however, the government shifted the economy toward heavy industry. After Communist control ended, the country's new leaders had to regain the balance that it once had. This has led to some unemployment as factory jobs decline.

On the whole, however, the Czech Republic's transition from a command to a market economy has been a smooth one. Most farms and factories have been sold to private owners. The Czech Republic joined the EU in 2004. Foreign investment and exports of Czech products, especially to Germany, have helped the economy continue growing. It has been among the most successful economies of the former Communist nations in Eastern Europe.

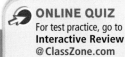
Škoda Auto This Czech company has been manufacturing cars for over 100 years. When Communist rule ended, the industry privatized and Volkswagen took over the company.

 SUMMARIZE Explain how the Czech Republic changed after gaining freedom from Communist rule.

ONLINE QUIZ
For test practice, go to
Interactive Review
@ ClassZone.com

Section 2 Assessment

TERMS & NAMES

1. Explain the importance of
- Magyar
- Czechoslovakia
- Velvet Revolution

USE YOUR READING NOTES

2. Compare and Contrast Use your completed chart to answer the following question:

How did Hungary's fight for independence differ from the Czech Republic's and how were they similar?

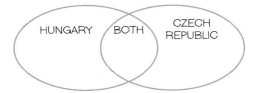

HUNGARY   BOTH   CZECH REPUBLIC

KEY IDEAS

3. What ethnic group do many Hungarians belong to?

4. How was Czechoslovakia formed?

5. How did the Velvet Revolution change Czechoslovakia?

CRITICAL THINKING

6. Analyze Causes and Effects How do you think the failure of the 1956 Hungarian revolt affected other Eastern European nations?

7. Find Main Ideas How did Václav Havel influence Czechoslovakia?

8. CONNECT to Today Why do you think the Czech Republic recently built new expressways and rail links to Germany?

9. WRITING Express an Opinion The young people who led the Hungarian revolt in 1956 were called freedom fighters by some and lawbreakers and traitors by others. Write a paragraph telling how you think they should be remembered.

Reading for Understanding

▶ Key Ideas

BEFORE, YOU LEARNED

The Czech Republic and Slovakia became independent countries without conflict or bloodshed.

NOW YOU WILL LEARN

In the 1990s the breakup of Yugoslavia was violent. Ethnic divisions and economic and political issues led to war.

▶ Vocabulary

TERMS & NAMES

Yugoslavia a country on the Balkan Peninsula from 1918 to 1991

Josip Broz Tito the Communist leader of Yugoslavia from 1953 to 1980

ethnic cleansing removing an ethnic or religious group from an area by force or the mass killing of members of such a group

Kosovo a self-governing province within Serbia

Slobodan Milosevic president of Serbia from 1989 to 1997 and of Yugoslavia from 1997 to 2000; a key figure in the ethnic conflicts in the Balkans in the 1990s

BACKGROUND VOCABULARY

Bosniac an ethnic Muslim from Bosnia and Herzegovina

refugee a person who flees a place to find safety

Visual Vocabulary Josip Broz Tito

▶ Reading Strategy

Re-create the web diagram shown at right. As you read and respond to the **KEY QUESTIONS**, use the diagram to help you find main ideas about the Balkans.

 Skillbuilder Handbook, page R4

FIND MAIN IDEAS

Creation of Yugoslavia

Yugoslavia Falls Apart

THE BALKANS

Cultural Differences

Government and Economics

GRAPHIC ORGANIZERS
Go to **Interactive Review** @ ClassZone.com

The Balkans

Connecting to Your World

At the opening ceremonies of the Olympic Games, athletes from around the globe proudly display their national flags as they march around a packed stadium. The games demonstrate that people of different religions, languages, and beliefs can come together without conflict. In 1984, the Winter Olympic Games took place in Sarajevo, a city in what was then Yugoslavia on the Balkan Peninsula. In the 1990s, wars caused by ethnic conflict destroyed much of the city, including the Olympic facilities. Sarajevo has been rebuilt, but memories of the violence that destroyed it remain.

Sarajevo The flame is lit (above) at the 1984 Winter Olympics opening ceremonies. This Muslim cemetery (below) is in Sarajevo.

History and Culture

▼ **KEY QUESTION** What caused the breakup of Yugoslavia?

In the 500s, various groups of Slavic peoples settled the Balkan Peninsula. Centuries of foreign rule created differences in the religion, language, and customs of these Slavic groups. When these groups joined together in one nation in the 20th century, their ethnic differences became a time bomb waiting to explode.

BOSNIA AND
HERZEGOVINA •Sarajevo

441

Creation of Yugoslavia After World War I, Slavic groups formed a country on the Balkan Peninsula called the Kingdom of Croats, Serbs, and Slovenes. It was renamed **Yugoslavia** in 1929. When World War II ended, **Josip Broz Tito** took over Yugoslavia. It became a Communist state consisting of six republics: Bosnia-Herzegovina, Croatia, Macedonia, Montenegro, Serbia, and Slovenia. Within each republic, the majority of people belonged to the same ethnic group. Tito's tight control brought political stability and helped unite Yugoslavia.

Yugoslavia Falls Apart After Tito died in 1980, Yugoslavia faced many economic and political problems. The other republics felt Serbia was trying to take control. In 1991, Slovenia, Macedonia, Croatia, and Bosnia-Herzegovina each declared independence. War broke out in Bosnia, as Serbs clashed with **Bosniacs** and Croats. Serbian troops occupied parts of Bosnia, using force to drive all non-Serbs out. This tactic, known as **ethnic cleansing**, left thousands dead or homeless. A 1995 peace plan gave most of Bosnia to the Bosniacs and Croats and the rest to the Bosnian Serbs. In 1998, rebels in the Serbian province of **Kosovo** began fighting for independence. Violence between Serb forces and the Albanian majority in Kosovo lasted until late 1999. In 2002, Serbian leader **Slobodan Milosevic** was tried for war crimes related to ethnic cleansing in Bosnia and Kosovo. He died in prison before his trial ended. By 2003, Yugoslavia no longer existed.

Cultural Differences Five new nations resulted from the breakup of Yugoslavia: Bosnia and Herzegovina, Croatia, Macedonia, Serbia and Montenegro, and Slovenia. As the map on the next page suggests, most of the former Yugoslav republics are dominated by one ethnic group. Most Balkan peoples speak Slavic languages. The biggest difference among ethnic groups is in religion. These countries have had to find ways to accept their differences. They have also had to work to return their cities to the cultural centers they once were.

▲ **ANALYZE CAUSES** Explain why Yugoslavia collapsed.

Dubrovnik, Croatia
Dubrovnik is known for its terra cotta roofs, some of which were damaged in the ethnic conflict in the 1990s and needed to be repaired.

Similarities and Differences Yugoslavia brought many ethnic groups together in one nation. In the 1990s, differences in language, religion, and culture overwhelmed similarities, until the region erupted in conflict. Today, these groups must find ways to live together.

A Slovenia Most residents of Slovenia are Slovenes. They speak Slovenian and are mostly Roman Catholic. Slovenia has much in common with its Western European neighbors.

B Montenegro Following the breakup of Yugoslavia, Montenegro and Serbia were joined as one country. Montenegro declared independence in 2006. Montenegrins speak Serbo-Croatian. Most of them are Orthodox Christians.

C Serbia Serbia includes a mix of ethnic groups. Like Croats, Serbs speak Serbo-Croatian, but they use the Cyrillic alphabet. They are mostly Orthodox Christians. The province of Kosovo has a large Albanian population. They speak Albanian—which is not related to any surrounding language—and are mostly Muslim.

F Croatia The majority population in Croatia is Croat. They speak a language called Serbo-Croatian, which is written in the Roman alphabet. Most are Roman Catholics.

E Bosnia and Herzegovina This republic is one of the most ethnically diverse of the former Yugoslav republics. It is made up of Croats, Bosniacs, and Serbs. Bosniacs are Muslims, and they speak Serbo-Croatian.

D Macedonia For the most part, Macedonians and Albanians live here. Macedonians speak Macedonian and are mostly Orthodox Christians.

Legend:
- Albanian
- Croat
- Hungarian
- Macedonian
- Montenegrin
- Muslim
- Serb
- Slovene
- No clear majority
- —— Former Yugoslavia, 1992
- Current Border

Source: CIA Reference Map Series, 1993, 1995; Yugoslavian Census of 1991

CRITICAL THINKING

1. **Make Inferences** Given the distribution of ethnic groups, which region do you think experienced the most conflict?

2. **Compare and Contrast** What are the main differences between Serbs, Croats, and Bosniacs?

Government and Economics

 KEY QUESTION What governmental and economic problems do many former Yugoslav republics face?

Today, the remaining ethnic tensions have made it difficult for the former Yugoslav republics to form stable governments. One concern is protecting the rights of all ethnic groups to prevent future conflicts. In Bosnia and Herzegovina, the people elect the legislature and a three-member presidency—one Bosniac, one Croat, and one Serb—to represent the country's ethnic majorities. Serbia and Montenegro are two republics that formed one country in 2003. In 2006, however, a majority of Montenegrins voted to become an independent nation.

Wartime destruction and the movement of **refugees** between nations have forced the Balkan countries to rebuild their economies. Market economies have been slow to develop. Macedonia and Bosnia and Herzegovina are the poorest. Like Serbia, they suffer from high unemployment. Slovenia is the most prosperous nation, as a result of stable government and less involvement in the 1990s conflict. It is the only EU member. Croatia was another wealthy republic. Today, it is slowly recovering from billions of dollars worth of war damage.

Ljubljana, Slovenia
Visitors enjoy the sights on this street in Slovenia's capital. **Why is tourism important to the former Yugoslav republics' economies?**

 ANALYZE EFFECTS Explain the governmental and economic problems faced by the former Yugoslav republics.

Section ❸ Assessment

TERMS & NAMES

1. Explain the importance of
- Yugoslavia
- Josip Broz Tito
- ethnic cleansing
- Kosovo

USE YOUR READING NOTES

2. Find Main Ideas Use your completed chart to answer the following question:

How did Tito's death affect Yugoslavia?

Creation of Yugoslavia

Cultural Differences

THE BALKANS

Yugoslavia Falls Apart

Government and Economics

KEY IDEAS

3. What kind of economic system did Yugoslavia have under Tito?

4. Why did much of the ethnic fighting occur in Bosnia and Kosovo?

5. What economic problem is shared by many of the former Yugoslav republics?

CRITICAL THINKING

6. Analyze Causes and Effects How did ethnic diversity make it harder to unite Yugoslavia?

7. Identify Problems and Solutions How might Balkan nations protect the rights of all ethnic groups equally in order to prevent future conflicts?

8. CONNECT to Today What might be the benefits of EU membership for Slovenia?

9. GOVERNMENT Draft a Bill of Rights Draft a Bill of Rights for the ethnic groups living in the Balkans. List ten rights these groups should have. Consider the rights of ethnic minorities in these countries.

Interactive ⟵Review

CHAPTER SUMMARY

Key Idea 1
Poland, Ukraine, and the Baltic states faced challenges after shaking off Communist rule.

Key Idea 2
After decades of Communist rule, Hungary and the Czech Republic made economic and political reforms.

Key Idea 3
In the 1990s the breakup of Yugoslavia was violent. Ethnic divisions and economic and political issues led to war.

For **Review and Study Notes**, go to **Interactive Review** @ ClassZone.com

NAME GAME

Use the Terms & Names list to complete each sentence on paper or online.

1. I am a self-governing province within Serbia and Montenegro. _____Kosovo_____

2. I am the Communist leader who kept Yugoslavia from splitting apart for over 40 years. _____

3. I am a region where grain production thrives. _____

4. I am the policy practiced by the Soviet Union in an effort to make occupied countries more Russian._____

5. I am another name for the countries of Latvia, Lithuania, and Estonia. _____

6. I am another term for ethnic Hungarians. _____

7. I mean to expel someone from a country. _____

8. I am the leader who helped start Poland's first independent trade union. _____

9. I am the Serbian leader who was charged with war crimes. _____

10. I am the Balkan country that split into six nations._____

Baltic States
bread basket
crossroads
Czechoslovakia
deport
ethnic cleansing
Josip Broz Tito
Kosovo
Lech Walesa
Magyar
Russification
Slobodan Milosevic
Solidarity
Václav Havel
Yugoslavia

Activities

GeoGame

Use this online map to reinforce your understanding of Eastern Europe. Drag and drop each place name in the list to its location on the map.

GeoGAME

Poland
Kiev
Budapest
Czech Republic
Ukraine

Present-Day Eastern Europe

Ukraine

National capital

To play the complete game, go to **Interactive Review** @ClassZone.com

Crossword Puzzle

Complete an online crossword puzzle to test your knowledge of Eastern Europe.

ACROSS
1. Communist leader of Yugoslavia from 1953 to 1980

VOCABULARY

Explain the significance of each of the following.

1. Lech Walesa
2. bread basket
3. Magyar
4. Velvet Revolution
5. ethnic cleansing
6. Kosovo

Explain how the terms and names in each group are related.

7. Baltic States and Russification
8. Yugoslavia and Czechoslovakia
9. Josip Broz Tito and Slobodan Milosevic

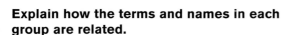

KEY IDEAS

1 Poland, Ukraine, and the Baltic States

10. Which Eastern European countries were part of the Soviet Union before it collapsed?
11. What effect did Solidarity have on Polish resistance to Communist rule in the 1980s?
12. How did the ownership of farms and factories in Poland, Ukraine, and the Baltic States change after the collapse of communism?
13. How did the Soviet policy of Russification affect Ukraine and the Baltic States?

2 Hungary and the Czech Republic

14. Why did the 1956 Hungarian revolt fail?
15. How has industrial growth affected where people in Hungary and the Czech Republic live?
16. What is the Czech Republic's capital and largest city?
17. How was the Czech Republic able to move peacefully from Communist rule to democratic government?

3 The Balkans

18. How did Yugoslavia change during Tito's rule?
19. What led to the violence in Kosovo?
20. In what way are many of the languages spoken in the Balkans similar?
21. What helped Slovenia make a smooth transition to a market economy?

CRITICAL THINKING

22. **Compare and Contrast** How have Poland, Hungary, and the Czech Republic changed from command to market economies?

COMMAND ECONOMY	MARKET ECONOMY

23. **Form and Support Opinions** Why have many former Communist countries wanted closer ties with Western Europe?
24. **Compare and Contrast** How were the roles of Lech Walesa and Václav Havel in their nations' history similar?
25. **Connect Geography & Government** What effect did the collapse of Communist governments have on Eastern Europe?
26. **Connect Geography & History** How do the new governments of the former Yugoslav republics reflect their recent history?
27. **Five Themes: Place** How were the breakups of Czechoslovakia and Yugoslavia different?

Answer the ESSENTIAL QUESTION

In what ways has Eastern Europe changed since the end of World War II?

Written Response Write a two- or three-paragraph response to the Essential Question. Consider the key ideas of each section as well as specific ideas about Eastern Europe. Use the rubric below to guide your thinking.

Response Rubric
A strong response will:
- discuss changes in government and civil rights
- discuss changes in economies
- discuss the impact of Communist rule on language and national identity

HISTORICAL MAP

Use the map to answer questions 1 and 2 on your paper.

Division of Poland *1795*

SWEDEN

Baltic Sea

0 100 200 miles
0 100 200 kilometers

Gdansk

P R U S S I A
Warsaw•

R U S S I A

•Kiev

A U S T R I A

HUNGARY

OTTOMAN EMPIRE

OTTOMAN EMPIRE

Legend:
- To Russia
- To Prussia
- To Austria
- Poland before partition, 1772

1. What three countries divided Poland among them?

A. Russia, Prussia, and Austria
B. Sweden, Prussia, and Hungary
C. Sweden, Russia, and Prussia
D. Russia, Hungary, and the Ottoman Empire

2. Which country gained the majority of Polish territory?

A. Austria   C. Prussia
B. Russia   D. Sweden

BAR GRAPH

Examine the graph below. Use the graph to answer questions 3 and 4 on your paper.

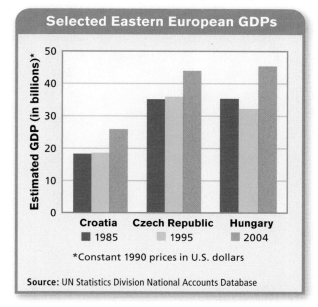

Selected Eastern European GDPs

Estimated GDP (in billions)*

Croatia   Czech Republic   Hungary
■ 1985   ■ 1995   ■ 2004

*Constant 1990 prices in U.S. dollars

Source: UN Statistics Division National Accounts Database

3. Which country's GDP dropped between 1985 and 1995?

4. During which time period did all three nations see the biggest increase in GDP?

GeoActivity

1. INTERDISCIPLINARY ACTIVITY–MATHEMATICS

With a small group, pick a country in this section. Find information on the religious makeup of the country, the percentage of people who live in urban and rural areas, and the percentage of people who can read. Use the information to create three pie graphs.

2. WRITING FOR SOCIAL STUDIES

Unit Writing Project Review your presentation about the European country you want to visit. Write a journal entry that describes how you spent your favorite day there, after your class decided to make the trip.

3. MENTAL MAPPING

Create an outline map of Eastern Europe and label the following:

- Hungary
- Poland
- Czech Republic
- Ukraine
- Latvia
- Lithuania
- Estonia
- Prague
- Chernobyl

UNIT 5

Russia and the Eurasian Republics

Why It Matters:

Since gaining their independence, Russia and the Eurasian republics have worked to stabilize their governments and economies. Achieving these goals will help ensure peace in the region and strengthen Russia's position as a world leader.

Moscow's Red Square

CHAPTER 15 Russia

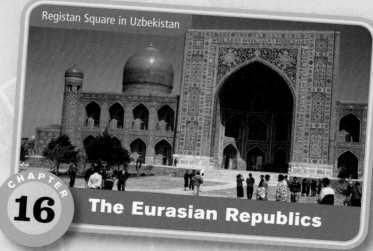

Registan Square in Uzbekistan

CHAPTER 16 The Eurasian Republics

◄ Meet Zuhura

In this unit, you will meet Zuhura, a middle-school girl from Uzbekistan. Learn more about her on **Worldster** @ClassZone.com

Russia and the Eurasian Republics

Russia and the Eurasian republics span two continents. The part of the region that lies to the west of the Ural Mountains is part of Europe. The part of the region that lies to the east of the Urals is part of Asia. As you study the maps, notice geographic patterns and specific details about the region. Answer the questions on each map in your notebook.

As you study the graphs on this page, compare the landmass, population, and lakes of Russia and the Eurasian republics with those of the United States. Then jot down the answers to the following questions in your notebook.

Comparing Data

1. Compare the landmass and population of Russia and the Eurasian republics with those of the United States. Based on these data, which region do you think has a higher population density? Why?

2. How much deeper is Lake Baikal than the deepest lake in the United States?

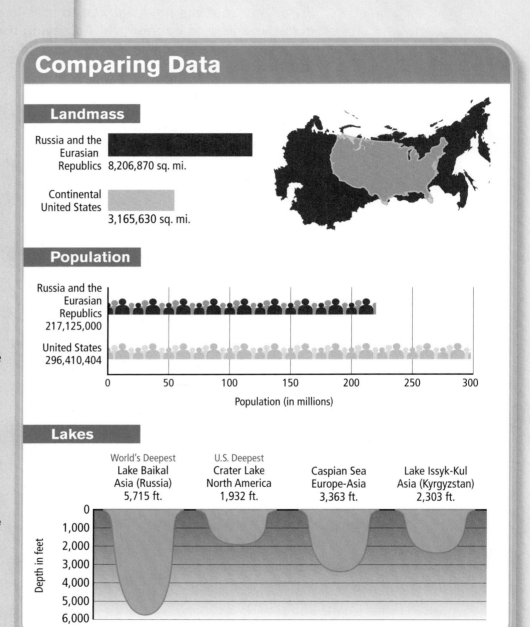

Comparing Data

Landmass

Russia and the Eurasian Republics 8,206,870 sq. mi.

Continental United States 3,165,630 sq. mi.

Population

Russia and the Eurasian Republics 217,125,000

United States 296,410,404

Population (in millions)
0   50   100   150   200   250   300

Lakes

| World's Deepest | U.S. Deepest | | |
| Lake Baikal Asia (Russia) 5,715 ft. | Crater Lake North America 1,932 ft. | Caspian Sea Europe-Asia 3,363 ft. | Lake Issyk-Kul Asia (Kyrgyzstan) 2,303 ft. |

Depth in feet
0
1,000
2,000
3,000
4,000
5,000
6,000

ICELAND

GREENLAND

ARCTIC OCEAN

Bering Sea

180°

NORWAY

SWEDEN

FINLAND

80°N

60°N

Baltic Sea

ESTONIA

RUSSIA

LATVIA

LITHUANIA

• St. Petersburg

• Novgorod

BELARUS

NORTHERN

☆ Moscow

EUROPEAN

UKRAINE

PLAIN

Black Sea

Volga R.

Mt. Elbrus 18,510 ft. (5,642 m)

CAUCASUS MTS.

GEORGIA

☆ Tbilisi

☆ Yerevan

AZERBAIJAN

ARMENIA

☆ Baku

Caspian Sea

TURKMENISTAN

Ashgabat ☆

IRAN

AFGHANISTAN

PAKISTAN

OMAN

URAL MOUNTAINS

Ob R.

WEST

RUSSIA

SIBERIAN

PLAIN

Omsk

Astana ☆

KAZAKHSTAN

Aral Sea

Lake Balkhash

UZBEKISTAN

Tashkent

Bishkek

☆ KYRGYZSTAN

Dushanbe ☆ TAJIKISTAN

Novosibirsk

TIAN SHAN

PAMIRS

INDIA

NEPAL

BHUTAN

BANGLADESH

SIBERIA

CENTRAL

SIBERIAN

PLATEAU

Yenisey R.

Lena R.

Lena R.

• Yakutsk

KAMCHATKA PENINSULA

160°E

Sea of Okhotsk

140°E

Irkutsk •

Lake Baikal

Amur R.

MONGOLIA

Vladivostok •

40°N

Sea of Japan (East Sea)

NORTH KOREA

SOUTH KOREA

JAPAN

PACIFIC OCEAN

CHINA

Tropic of Cancer

TAIWAN

20°N

MYANMAR

LAOS

THAILAND

Arctic Circle

N W S E

Elevation

13,100 ft.	(4,000 m)
6,600 ft.	(2,000 m)
3,280 ft.	(1,000 m)
650 ft.	(200 m)
0 ft.	(0 m)
Below sea level	

▲ Mountain peak

0   500   1,000 miles

0   500   1,000 kilometers

THINK LIKE A GEOGRAPHER

1. **Location** On which landform is Russia's capital located?

2. **Place** How would you describe much of the elevation in Tajikistan?

60°E   80°E   100°E

451

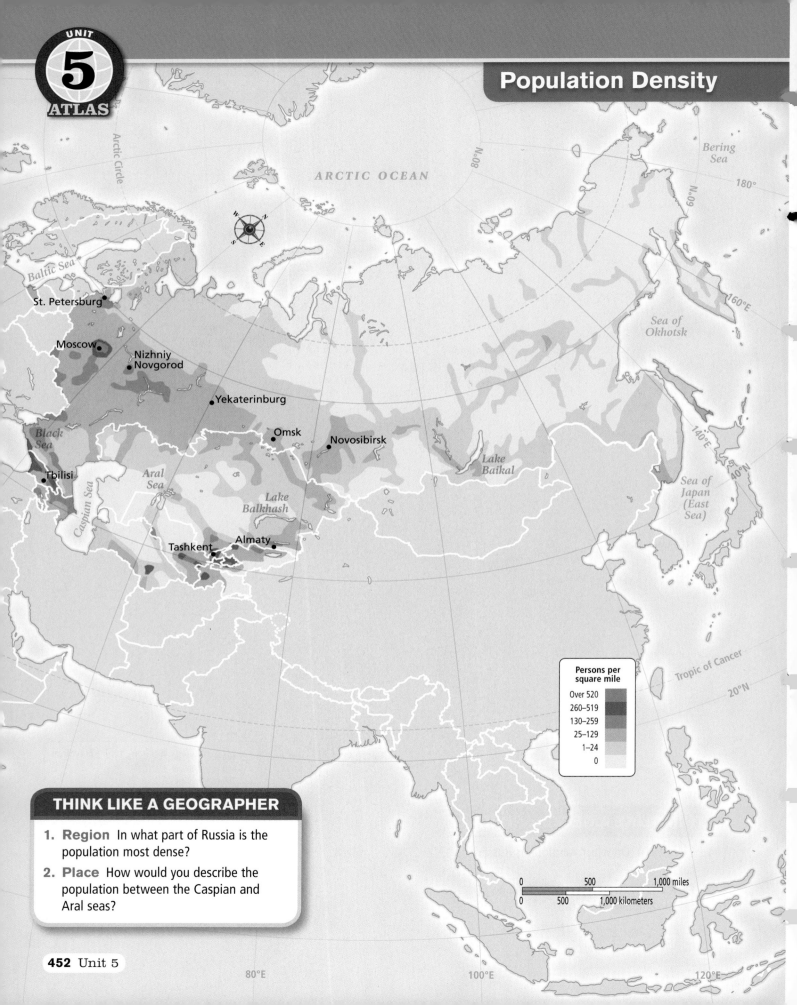

Population Density

ARCTIC OCEAN

Bering Sea

80°N

180°

60°N

Baltic Sea

St. Petersburg

Moscow

Nizhniy Novgorod

Yekaterinburg

Omsk

Novosibirsk

Sea of Okhotsk

160°E

140°E

40°N

Black Sea

Tbilisi

Aral Sea

Caspian Sea

Lake Balkhash

Lake Baikal

Sea of Japan (East Sea)

Tashkent

Almaty

Arctic Circle

Tropic of Cancer

20°N

Persons per square mile

Over 520	
260–519	
130–259	
25–129	
1–24	
0	

0   500   1,000 miles

0   500   1,000 kilometers

THINK LIKE A GEOGRAPHER

1. **Region** In what part of Russia is the population most dense?

2. **Place** How would you describe the population between the Caspian and Aral seas?

80°E   100°E   120°E

Climate

ICELAND
GREENLAND
ARCTIC OCEAN
Bering Sea
NORWAY
SWEDEN
FINLAND
Baltic Sea
RUSSIA
ESTONIA
LATVIA
LITHUANIA
BELARUS
UKRAINE
RUSSIA
Sea of Okhotsk
Black Sea
GEORGIA
ARMENIA
AZERBAIJAN
Caspian Sea
Aral Sea
KAZAKHSTAN
Lake Balkhash
Lake Baikal
UZBEKISTAN
TURKMENISTAN
KYRGYZSTAN
TAJIKISTAN
IRAN
AFGHANISTAN
PAKISTAN
MONGOLIA
CHINA
NORTH KOREA
SOUTH KOREA
Sea of Japan (East Sea)
JAPAN
BHUTAN
NEPAL
BANGLADESH
INDIA
MYANMAR
LAOS
THAILAND
SRI LANKA
Tropic of Cancer
TAIWAN
PHILIPPINES

Arctic Circle
80°N
60°N
180°
160°E
140°E
40°N
20°N
60°E
80°E
100°E

Dry
Desert
Semiarid

Mid-Latitude
Mediterranean
Humid subtropical
Humid continental

High Latitude
Subarctic
Tundra

Highland

0   500   1,000 miles
0   500   1,000 kilometers

THINK LIKE A GEOGRAPHER

1. **Place** What is the climate of the area that is closest to the Arctic Ocean?

2. **Region** What area has a desert climate?

GREENLAND

ARCTIC OCEAN

Bering Sea

NORWAY

SWEDEN

FINLAND

Baltic Sea

RUSSIA ESTONIA
LATVIA
LITHUANIA

St. Petersburg

BELARUS

Moscow

UKRAINE

Black Sea

Perm

Yekaterinburg

RUSSIA

Sea of Okhotsk

Novosibirsk

Krasnoyarsk

GEORGIA

Aral Sea

KAZAKHSTAN

Lake Baikal

Sea of Japan (East Sea)

ARMENIA
AZERBAIJAN

Caspian Sea

Lake Balkhash

UZBEKISTAN

NORTH KOREA

JAPAN

TURKMENISTAN

SOUTH KOREA

MONGOLIA

IRAN

KYRGYZSTAN

TAJIKISTAN

AFGHANISTAN

CHINA

PAKISTAN

BHUTAN

NEPAL

TAIWAN

Tropic of Cancer

BANGLADESH

INDIA

MYANMAR LAOS

PHILIPPINES

THAILAND VIETNAM

SRI LANKA

Land use

- Commercial agriculture
- Livestock raising
- Nomadic herding
- Forestland
- Limited agriculture

Major resources

- Bauxite
- Coal
- Diamonds
- Gold
- Iron ore
- Natural gas
- Oil
- Other minerals
- Manufacturing center

0   500   1,000 miles
0   500   1,000 kilometers

THINK LIKE A GEOGRAPHER

1. **Human-Environment Interaction** Where in Russia is most of the land used for commercial agriculture?

2. **Region** Around what body of water is oil a major resource?

Regional Overview

Russia and the Eurasian Republics

Russia and the Eurasian republics span two continents: Europe and Asia. Both continents have had a significant influence on the regions' histories and cultures.

GEOGRAPHY

Both Russia and the Eurasian republics contain rugged areas, with towering mountains, wide deserts, and vast plains. The climates in these regions range from the frigid weather in Siberia to more mild temperatures in Georgia.

Frozen Water A group of boys plays hockey on Lake Baikal.

HISTORY

Many groups have influenced Russia and the Eurasian republics. Throughout their histories, the regions have often been divided between holding onto Eastern, or Asian, traditions and adopting more modern ideas from the West, or Europe.

CULTURE

The blend of East and West is reflected in the culture of both regions. More than 100 ethnic groups from both Asia and Europe live in Russia and the Eurasian republics.

GOVERNMENT

When the Soviet Union dissolved in 1991, Russia and 14 other republics formed. Since then, Russia and the Eurasian republics have struggled to establish democratic governments.

ECONOMICS

Russia's economy has boomed as a result of its abundant energy resources. The countries of the Eurasian republics also have vast supplies of oil and coal. However, these countries are only beginning to benefit economically from their natural resources.

Country Almanac

Click here to compare the most recent data on countries @ ClassZone.com

Unit Writing Project

Travel Itinerary

As you read this unit, pick a country or region that interests you. Then imagine that you are planning a trip to this place. Write an itinerary for a week-long stay.

Think About:

- the clothes you should bring
- what specific sites you would like to visit
- what foods you would like to eat
- the questions you would like to ask the people who live there

Russia and the Eurasian Republics

The country cards on these pages contain information about Russia and the Eurasian republics. As you study the land area of Russia, consider that the country is bigger than the continents of Europe and Antarctica combined.

Russian Federation

GEOGRAPHY

Capital: Moscow
Total Area: 6,592,772 sq. mi.
Population: 143,202,000

ECONOMY

Imports: food; chemicals; cars
Exports: fuels; metals; chemicals

CULTURE

Language: Russian
Religion: Christian 57%; Muslim 8%; nonreligious 27%; atheist 5%

Russian Bear The brown bear of Eurasia is sometimes considered the symbol of Russia.

Armenia

GEOGRAPHY
Capital: Yerevan
Total Area: 11,506 sq. mi.
Population: 3,016,000

ECONOMY
Imports: mineral fuels; rough diamonds
Exports: alcohol; cut diamonds

CULTURE
Language: Armenian
Religion: Armenian Apostolic 65%

Azerbaijan

GEOGRAPHY
Capital: Baku
Total Area: 33,436 sq. mi.
Population: 8,411,000

ECONOMY
Imports: natural gas; iron and steel
Exports: petroleum; food

CULTURE
Language: Azerbaijani
Religion: Muslim 93%; Russian
Orthodox 1%; Armenian Apostolic 1%

Georgia

GEOGRAPHY
Capital: Tbilisi
Total Area: 26,911 sq. mi.
Population: 4,474,000

ECONOMY
Imports: food; mineral fuels
Exports: aircraft; food; mineral fuels

CULTURE
Language: Georgian
Religion: Christian 46%;
Sunni Muslim 11%

Kazakhstan

GEOGRAPHY
Capital: Astana
Total Area: 1,049,155 sq. mi.
Population: 14,825,000

ECONOMY
Imports: mineral fuels; chemicals
Exports: petroleum; metals; food

CULTURE
Language: Kazakh
Religion: Muslim 47%; Russian
Orthodox 8%; Protestant 2%

Kyrgyzstan

GEOGRAPHY
Capital: Bishkek
Total Area: 76,641 sq. mi.
Population: 5,264,000

ECONOMY
Imports: petroleum; food; chemicals
Exports: metals; electricity; tobacco

CULTURE
Language: Kyrgyz; Russian
Religion: Muslim 75%; Christian 7%

Tajikistan

GEOGRAPHY
Capital: Dushanbe
Total Area: 55,251 sq. mi.
Population: 6,507,000

ECONOMY
Imports: natural gas; grain and flour
Exports: aluminum; electricity

CULTURE
Language: Tajik
Religion: Sunni Muslim 80%; Shi'a
Muslim 5%; Russian Orthodox 2%

Turkmenistan

GEOGRAPHY
Capital: Ashgabat
Total Area: 188,456 sq. mi.
Population: 4,833,000

ECONOMY
Imports: chemicals; food
Exports: natural gas; fabrics; raw cotton

CULTURE
Language: Turkmen
Religion: Muslim 87%; Russian
Orthodox 2%

Uzbekistan

GEOGRAPHY
Capital: Tashkent
Total Area: 172,742 sq. mi.
Population: 26,593,000

ECONOMY
Imports: food; metalworking products
Exports: cotton fiber; food; gold; metals

CULTURE
Language: Uzbek
Religion: Muslim 76%; nonreligious 18%

Ural Mountains The Urals extend from the Arctic Ocean to the Caspian Sea and contain a wealth of mineral resources.

CHAPTER 15 Russia

 ESSENTIAL QUESTION

How is Russia preserving its Eastern culture while adapting to Western influences?

1

GEOGRAPHY

Sweeping Across Eurasia

2
HISTORY

Governing a Vast Land

3
CULTURE

Blending Europe and Asia

4

GOVERNMENT & ECONOMICS

The Struggle for Reform

CONNECT **Geography & History**

Use the map and the time line to answer the following questions.

1. What is the capital of Russia today?

2. What was the capital in 1703?

Culture
◄ **988** Orthodox Christianity becomes the official religion of Russia.

Geography
1703 St. Petersburg is founded and becomes Russia's capital.
(Palace of Catherine the Great) ▼

950

History
1237 Mongols conquer Russian lands.

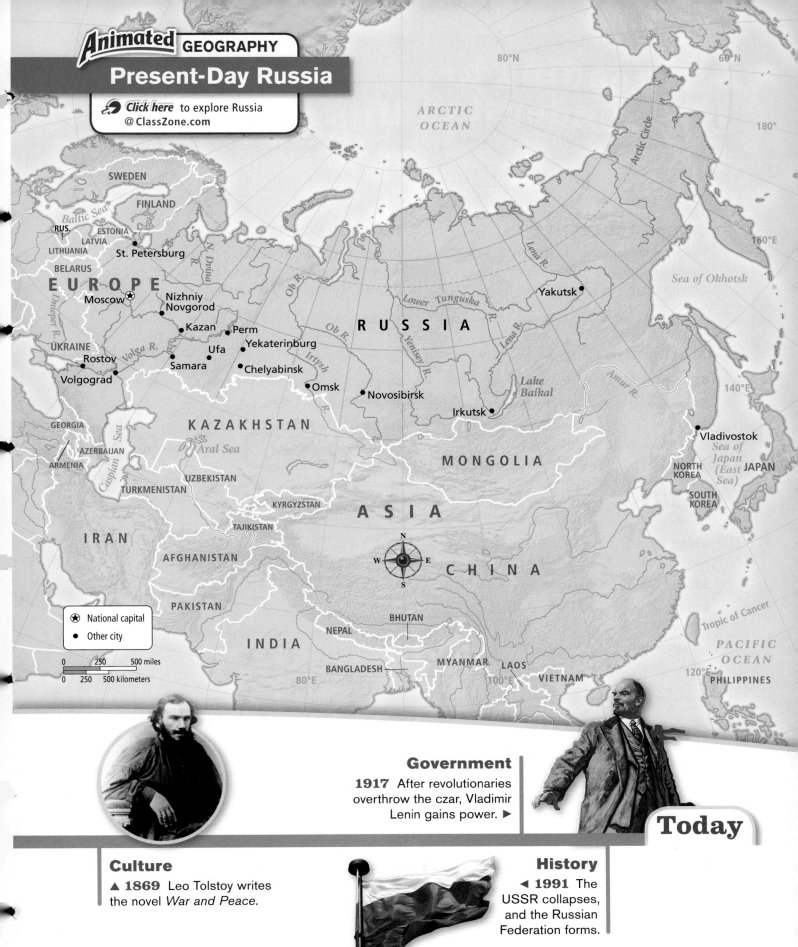

80°N   60°N

ARCTIC OCEAN

Arctic Circle   180°

160°E

SWEDEN

FINLAND

Baltic Sea

RUS.

ESTONIA
LATVIA
LITHUANIA

BELARUS

N. Dvina R.

Sea of Okhotsk

EUROPE

St. Petersburg

Moscow ⊛

Nizhniy Novgorod

Kazan   Perm

Ufa   Yekaterinburg

Dnieper R.

UKRAINE

Rostov

Volgograd

Volga R.

Samara

Chelyabinsk

Omsk

Ob R.

Ob R.

Irtysh R.

Lower Tunguska R.

RUSSIA

Yenisey R.

Lena R.

Lena R.

Yakutsk

140°E

GEORGIA

AZERBAIJAN

ARMENIA

Caspian Sea

Aral Sea

KAZAKHSTAN

Novosibirsk

Irkutsk

Lake Baikal

Amur R.

MONGOLIA

Vladivostok

Sea of Japan (East Sea)

JAPAN

NORTH KOREA

SOUTH KOREA

UZBEKISTAN

TURKMENISTAN

KYRGYZSTAN

TAJIKISTAN

IRAN

AFGHANISTAN

ASIA

N
W   E
S

CHINA

PAKISTAN

BHUTAN

NEPAL

Tropic of Cancer

PACIFIC OCEAN

120°E

⊛ National capital
• Other city

0   250   500 miles
0   250   500 kilometers

INDIA

BANGLADESH

80°E

MYANMAR

LAOS

100°E

VIETNAM

PHILIPPINES

Culture
▲ **1869** Leo Tolstoy writes the novel *War and Peace.*

Government
1917 After revolutionaries overthrow the czar, Vladimir Lenin gains power. ▶

Today

History
◀ **1991** The USSR collapses, and the Russian Federation forms.

459

Reading for Understanding

▶ Key Ideas

BEFORE, YOU LEARNED

The smaller nations of Eastern Europe have been greatly influenced by their overpowering neighbor, Russia.

NOW YOU WILL LEARN

Russia is a vast country that contains a variety of landforms, climates, vegetation regions, and natural resources.

▶ Vocabulary

TERMS & NAMES

Eurasia a term used to refer to a single continent made up of Europe and Asia

Ural Mountains a north–south mountain range that forms the border between European and Asian Russia

Caspian Sea a large body of water bordering Russia to the south

Volga River the longest river in Europe, flowing through European Russia

Siberia a huge region in Asian Russia

tundra a treeless plain around the Arctic Ocean; in Russia, located in the far north

taiga (TY•guh) a vast forest in Russia that lies south of the tundra

steppe a grassy plain; in Russia, this area lies south of the taiga

BACKGROUND VOCABULARY

permafrost ground that is frozen throughout the year

EUROPE

URAL MTS.

ASIA

Visual Vocabulary Eurasia

▶ Reading Strategy

Re-create the chart shown at right. As you read and respond to the **KEY QUESTIONS**, use the chart to organize important details about the physical geography of Russia.

 Skillbuilder Handbook, page R7

CATEGORIZE

GEOGRAPHIC FEATURES	EUROPEAN RUSSIA	ASIAN RUSSIA
Climate		
Plants and Animals		
Agriculture		
Resources		

 GRAPHIC ORGANIZERS
Go to **Interactive Review** @ ClassZone.com

Sweeping Across Eurasia

Connecting to Your World

Russia is huge. It is the largest country in the world and spans 11 time zones. However, many parts of the country have few people. In fact, even though Russia is nearly twice the size of the United States, it has less than half as many people. Like the United States, Russia contains a variety of landforms, including vast forests, snow-capped mountains, and wind-swept plains. But, because of its location, the climate is much colder. The size, geography, and climate of Russia have a major impact on its people.

Crossing Two Continents

▼ **KEY QUESTION** How are western and eastern Russia similar and different?

Does Russia lie on one continent or on two? Some geographers recognize the Ural Mountains as a dividing line between Europe and Asia. Since Russia crosses the Urals, these geographers claim that the country lies in both Europe and Asia. Others view Europe and Asia as a single continent called **Eurasia**. These geographers divide Russia into western and eastern regions. This book shares that view. In this chapter, the two regions are referred to as European (or western) Russia and Asian (or eastern) Russia.

Lake Baikal This very deep lake in eastern Russia holds over 20 percent of Earth's fresh water. **What can you tell about the physical geography of the area from this picture?**

RUSSIA
Lake Baikal

CHINA

461

WESTERN RUSSIA EASTERN RUSSIA *URAL MOUNTAINS*

European, or Western, Russia Study the map on the opposite page. Note that the borders of European Russia are formed by the Arctic Ocean and Baltic Sea to the north, the **Ural Mountains** Ⓐ to the east, and the Caucasus Mountains, the Black Sea, and the **Caspian Sea** Ⓑ to the south. To the west lie the European countries of Finland, Estonia, Latvia, Belarus, and Ukraine. Most of European Russia consists of a very flat expanse of land called the Northern European Plain Ⓒ. This plain contains rich farmland but does not provide any natural barriers to the west. As a result, the landform offers no protection from invaders.

Many rivers flow through European Russia, including the **Volga** Ⓓ, Europe's longest. Several canals and overland routes connect these rivers and form a transport system that carries two-thirds of Russia's waterway traffic. Another important body of water in western Russia is the Black Sea. It contains the country's busiest port.

Asian, or Eastern, Russia By far the largest part of Russia lies to the east of the Urals in Asian Russia. This region is bordered by the Urals to the west, the Arctic Ocean to the north, the Pacific Ocean to the east, and a series of mountain ranges to the south.

Most of Asian Russia is made up of a huge expanse of land called **Siberia** Ⓔ. Siberia contains the largest flat region in the world. Other parts of Siberia are not at all flat. Southeastern Siberia has mountain ranges with some of the world's highest peaks. Kamchatka Peninsula Ⓕ, in the far eastern part of Russia, has about 20 active volcanoes.

Asian Russia has several major rivers, including the Lena and the Yenisey rivers. Some of these rivers are frozen for much of the year and so limit transportation. Thousands of lakes are also found in Asian Russia. One of these, Lake Baikal Ⓖ, is the deepest in the world at 5,715 feet.

🔺 **COMPARE AND CONTRAST** Explain how western and eastern Russia are similar and different.

FRESHWATER SEALS

Lake Baikal is home to the world's only freshwater seal—the nerpa. Nerpas are very graceful and can remain underwater for nearly 70 minutes. Scientists don't know how the seals ended up in a lake in the middle of Asia. But in Lake Baikal, the seals have found an ideal habitat with plenty of food.

Physical Geography of Russia

ARCTIC OCEAN

PACIFIC OCEAN

F KAMCHATKA PENINSULA

Kuril Islands

FINLAND

RUSSIA

C

NORTHERN

EUROPEAN

PLAIN

UKRAINE

Baltic Sea

N. Dvina R.

CENTRAL SIBERIAN PLATEAU

S I B E R I A

E

Lower Tunguska R.

Yenisey R.

Ob R.

URAL MTS.

WEST
R U S S I A
SIBERIAN

Volga R.

D

STEPPE PLAIN

A

Black Sea

Mt. Elbrus
18,510 ft
(5,642 m)
TURKEY

CAUCASUS MTS.

Caspian Sea

B

KAZAKHSTAN

Irtysh R.

ALTAI SHAN

Amur R.

G

Lake Baikal

Sea of Japan (East Sea)

JAPAN

MONGOLIA
100°E

CHINA

60°E

80°E

120°E

40°N

60°N

180°

160°E

0 250 500 miles
0 250 500 kilometers

Elevation	
13,100 ft.	(4,000 m)
6,600 ft.	(2,000 m)
3,280 ft.	(1,000 m)
650 ft.	(200 m)
0 ft.	(0 m)
Below sea level	

▲ Mountain peak

D Volga River, Western Russia

F Kamchatka, Eastern Russia

CONNECT Geography & Culture
READING A PHYSICAL MAP

Locate the Ural Mountains on the map above. This mountain range separates European Russia to the west from Asian Russia to the east. As you study these two regions,

- contrast their respective sizes
- compare their landforms and elevation
- consider how these features affect population

1. **Region** How do the landforms in Asian Russia differ from those in European Russia?
2. **Human-Environment Interaction** Which region do you think is more heavily populated? Why?

Climate, Vegetation, and Resources

▼ **KEY QUESTION** What types of natural resources are found in Russia?

Although Russia has many climates, it is mainly a cold-weather country. One Siberian town has recorded temperatures as low as –96°F. Such cold can burst tires and crack steel.

Extreme Climate All of Siberia has frigid weather during the winter. Temperatures remain so low in some areas that they are covered by a layer of permanently frozen ground called **permafrost**. However, the region can also have temperatures of nearly 100°F during the summer. These extreme temperature ranges are caused by two factors: Russia's northern latitude and its distance from any ocean. Much of the country lies many miles away from the oceans, which help moderate temperatures.

The climate is milder in European Russia. As a result, this region is more densely populated. However, even here the climate can be challenging. For example, the area around Moscow has snow on the ground for about five months of the year.

CONNECT to Math

Siberian winters are very cold. As you can see in the photo below, boiling water tossed into the region's wintry air can explode into a shower of ice crystals. Find out just how cold the winter is in Siberia. Follow the steps shown here to calculate the average temperature for each season in the Siberian town of Yakutsk.

Activity
Calculate Averages

1. Study the graph below.

2. Add the temperatures for the months in each season. For winter, you would add together: 18 + 40 + 45 + 33 + 8. Place a negative sign before the sum of these numbers.

3. Divide by the number of months in each season. For winter, you would divide by 5. Place the negative sign before the result. This is the average winter temperature in Yakutsk.

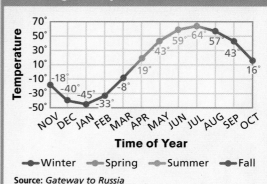

Average Temperatures in Yakutsk

Source: *Gateway to Russia*

COMPARING Vegetation

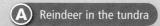

A **Tundra** The **tundra** in far northern Russia is a flat, treeless plain with long, harsh winters and short summers.

C **Steppe** The **steppe** is the grassland plain that stretches south of the taiga. Rich, fertile soil covers much of the steppe.

B **Taiga** The **taiga** (TY•guh) is a vast forest that lies south of the tundra. It is the largest forestland in the world.

D **Semidesert & Mountain** This area in the far southwest of Russia has dry lowlands around the Caspian Sea and rich vegetation near the Caucasus Mountains.

CRITICAL THINKING
Evaluate Which region probably provides the best farmland?

C Steppe in south-central Siberia

D Wildflowers in the central Caucasus Mountains

Varied Wildlife A wide variety of wildlife survives in Russia's four vegetation regions.

- Although few people live in the tundra, it is home to many animals, including reindeer, Arctic foxes, and snowy owls.

- The taiga also has a small human population. Bears, deer, and wolves thrive in the region because there are so few people.

- The animals in the steppe region are largely grazing animals. These include cattle, antelope, and wild horses.

- Only animals that can survive very dry conditions live in Russia's semidesert region. Lizards, snakes, rodents, and camels adapt well to this environment.

Snowy Owl The snowy owl lives in the tundra for about half of the year. Although the birds are excellent fliers, they nest on the ground.

Abundant Natural Resources Russia has some of the largest reserves of natural gas, oil, and coal in the world. Despite this, the vast majority of these riches remains untouched. Many of Russia's resources are located in remote areas of northern Siberia. The geography and climate in these areas make it difficult to remove and transport the resources. However, Russia is able to take better advantage of other resources. These include iron ore in the south and west, as well as gold, diamonds, copper, and lumber in both the east and the west.

▲ **SUMMARIZE** Describe Russia's natural resources.

Animated GEOGRAPHY

Russia's Natural Resources

⟶ *Click here* to see an interactive map of Russia's natural resources and vegetation @ ClassZone.com

Copper Foundry A Russian worker in western Siberia pours melted copper into molds.

Timber Industry Russia's taiga region holds one-fifth of the world's timber resources.

Oil Field This pump is extracting oil from an area in western Siberia that produces about six percent of the world's oil.

Human-Environment Interaction

▼ **KEY QUESTION** What has caused some of the environmental problems in Russia?

As you have learned, Russia has some of the world's most abundant natural resources. Unfortunately, the process of extracting and developing some of these resources has created many environmental problems. Mining operations, in particular, have caused great damage. The mining sites have polluted the air in surrounding areas and contaminated nearby rivers. Industries that extract oil and gas have also added to the air and water pollution. In addition, overcutting trees in the taiga has caused problems. The loss of much of this forestland has endangered many plant and animal species.

Russia has taken steps to clean up its environment and prevent further damage. For example, the country has begun to enforce stricter rules on oil industries. The government has also discussed spending more money on solving environmental problems. Like other modern nations, Russia will have to balance its need for economic growth with its responsibility to protect the environment.

▲ **ANALYZE CAUSES** Detail what has caused some of Russia's environmental problems.

 Section **1** **Assessment**

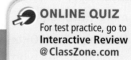 **ONLINE QUIZ**
For test practice, go to
Interactive Review
@ ClassZone.com

TERMS & NAMES

1. Explain the importance of
- Ural Mountains
- Siberia
- tundra
- steppe

USE YOUR READING NOTES

2. Categorize Use your completed chart to answer the following question:

Why do more people live in European Russia than in Asian Russia?

GEOGRAPHIC FEATURES	EUROPEAN RUSSIA	ASIAN RUSSIA
Climate		
Plants and Animals		
Agriculture		
Resources		

KEY IDEAS

3. How do the rivers of European Russia provide the region with a transportation network?

4. Why does Siberia have extremely cold weather?

5. Why have many of Russia's natural resources remained untouched?

CRITICAL THINKING

6. Draw Conclusions Do you think many people live on the Kamchatka Peninsula? Why or why not?

7. Analyze Causes and Effects Why do you think that only plants with short roots grow in the tundra?

8. CONNECT to Today In 2006, Russia held a contest to develop a technology to turn coal-processing waste into usable energy. What impact might such a technology have on Russia's pollution problems?

9. WRITING Make a Poster Design and write a poster on the animal and plant life found in one of the four vegetation regions of Russia. Include pictures and captions.

Reading for Understanding

▶ Key Ideas

BEFORE, YOU LEARNED

Russia sprawls across Eurasia, a landmass that includes both Europe and Asia.

NOW YOU WILL LEARN

The sometimes conflicting influences of the East and West have helped shape Russian history.

▶ Vocabulary

TERMS & NAMES

czar (zahr) title for the rulers of Russia from the mid-1500s to the early 1900s

serf a peasant who is bound to the land

Peter the Great a czar who ruled Russia from 1682 to 1725 and tried to make Russia more European

Bolsheviks (BOHL•shuh•VIHKS) a group of revolutionaries who took control of the Russian government in 1917

communism a government and economic system in which nearly all political power and means of production are held by the government in the name of the people

Union of Soviet Socialist Republics (USSR), or **Soviet Union** a new nation with a Communist government created by the Bolsheviks in 1922; dissolved in 1991

Joseph Stalin a cruel 20th-century dictator who had millions of his political enemies executed

totalitarian (toh•TAL•ih•TAIR•ee•uhn) a government that controls public and private life

Cold War a conflict between the United States and the Soviet Union after World War II that never developed into open warfare

Mikhail Gorbachev (GAWR•buh•CHAWF) Soviet leader from 1985 to 1991 who increased freedoms for the Russian people

▶ Reading Strategy

Re-create the chart shown at right. As you read and respond to the **KEY QUESTIONS**, use the chart to help you analyze causes and effects in Russia's history.

 See Skillbuilder Handbook, page R8

ANALYZE CAUSES AND EFFECTS

CAUSES	EFFECTS
Rise of the czars	
Russian expansion	
Communist revolution	
Collapse of Soviet Union	

GRAPHIC ORGANIZERS
Go to **Interactive Review** @ ClassZone.com

Governing a Vast Land

Connecting to Your World

Think about a country that started out being settled by a few groups of people. Gradually the country expanded until it covered a vast area. As this happened, more and more ethnic groups influenced this country's culture. Sound familiar? If you guessed that the country is the United States, you're right. However, Russia has followed a similar pattern. Russia was settled mainly by the Slavs, people of eastern Europe. But as Russia expanded, it was strongly influenced by groups from both the East and the West.

The Rise of an Empire

▼ **KEY QUESTION** How did the Russian Empire develop?

By the 800s, Slavic groups established many settlements in what is now called European Russia. In the 900s, the region came under the control of the Varangians. These people, also called Rus, were most likely Vikings from Scandinavia. The name "Russia" is taken from this group. Eventually, civil war weakened the Rus. In the 1200s, they fell to invaders from Mongolia, a region to the southeast.

Kremlin During the 1100s, the Rus began to develop a fortified town, or Kremlin. The walled fortress complex stands today in Moscow.

MOSCOW
Kremlin

Moscow's Princes Gain Power The Mongols allowed the grand prince of Moscow to collect taxes and keep a portion of them. This money, along with wealth gained through trade, helped Moscow to grow in power. At the same time, Mongol control weakened. Led by Ivan III, the Moscow state broke away from the Mongols in 1480.

Ivan IV became the grand prince of Moscow and, in 1547, the first ruler to be officially called **czar** (zahr). The word *czar* comes from "caesar," the title used for Roman emperors. Ivan IV came to be known as Ivan the Terrible because he was a harsh and suspicious ruler. He murdered hundreds of aristocrats and even killed his eldest son.

Ivan IV and the other czars who came after him passed several laws that bound peasants to the land. These peasants were called **serfs**. Serfdom formed the basis of the Russian economy until the late 1800s. Because of their poverty, harsh working conditions, and the strict controls on their lives, the serfs resented the czars' authority.

HISTORY MAKERS

Peter the Great 1672–1725

As a child, Peter had a lot of energy and curiosity. He would often organize his friends into an army and then play at war. As an adult, Peter still showed many of his childhood qualities. A dynamic ruler, he built up the navy and army. His enthusiasm for Western ways was extreme. He insisted that nobles shave off their beards, wear European fashions, and study the sciences. Those who opposed these changes were often punished.

 ONLINE BIOGRAPHY
For more on the life of Peter the Great, go to the **Research & Writing Center @ ClassZone.com**

Peter the Great After Ivan IV's death, Russia suffered under a series of weak rulers. Then in 1682, two half-brothers, Peter I (later known as **Peter the Great**) and Ivan, ruled together. Peter assumed full power when Ivan died in 1696.

The new czar was strongly influenced by the West and worked hard to modernize Russia. Peter believed that a more modern Russia would be better able to compete with Europe militarily and economically. As a result, he introduced European-style customs, factories, and schools in Russia. Peter even moved Russia's capital west from Moscow to an area on the Gulf of Finland. Architects modeled the new capital, called St. Petersburg, after European cities. Its construction cost huge amounts of money and the lives of about 30,000 workers.

Peter also reorganized Russia's government. He replaced inefficient administrative departments with a system of well-organized units. Each one had authority in a certain area, such as finances or justice.

In spite of Peter's efforts, many Russians remained suspicious of western Europeans. They considered western Europeans outsiders. Religious differences widened the gap. The Russians had adopted the Eastern Orthodox branch of Christianity, while western Europeans were mostly Catholics or Protestants.

Russia Expands After Peter's death in 1725, several rivals struggled to gain the throne. Eventually, in 1762, Empress Catherine II (known as Catherine the Great) came to power.

Catherine acquired the northern shore of the Black Sea and the Crimea through a series of wars with the Ottoman Empire. By gaining access to the Black Sea, Russia secured a warm-water port, one in which the water does not freeze in winter. As a result, the port could be used all year for trade. Also, through political deals, Russia obtained much of Poland and its territory.

Like Peter, Catherine admired European culture. She supported the arts, such as ballet and Italian opera. She also tried to pass legal reforms but did little to improve the life of the Russian serfs. In fact, when discontented serfs rebelled in 1773 and 1774, Catherine brutally crushed the revolt. She then tightened control over the serfs.

Catherine the Great died in 1796. Succeeding czars continued to expand Russia's territory. The empire also survived an invasion by the French emperor Napoleon I in 1812. By the late 1800s, Russia controlled land across Central Asia to the Pacific. To connect this vast expanse, Russia started to build the Trans-Siberian Railroad. Completed in 1916, it extended nearly 6,000 miles and greatly helped develop Siberia. You will learn more about this railroad in Animated Geography at the end of this section.

▲ **SUMMARIZE** Explain how the Russian Empire developed.

CONNECT ➤ History & Geography

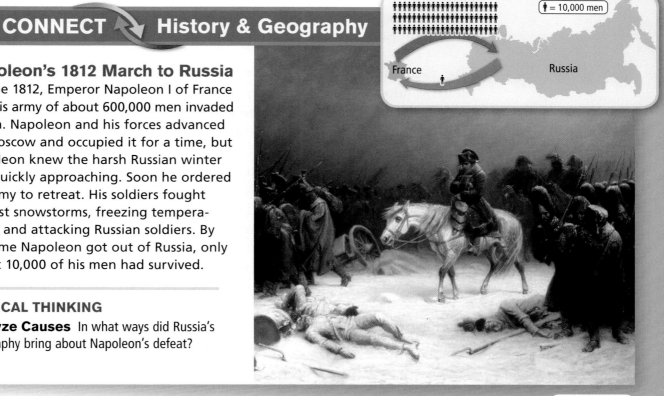

Napoleon's 1812 March to Russia

In June 1812, Emperor Napoleon I of France and his army of about 600,000 men invaded Russia. Napoleon and his forces advanced on Moscow and occupied it for a time, but Napoleon knew the harsh Russian winter was quickly approaching. Soon he ordered his army to retreat. His soldiers fought against snowstorms, freezing temperatures, and attacking Russian soldiers. By the time Napoleon got out of Russia, only about 10,000 of his men had survived.

CRITICAL THINKING

Analyze Causes In what ways did Russia's geography bring about Napoleon's defeat?

$\dagger$ = 10,000 men

France   Russia

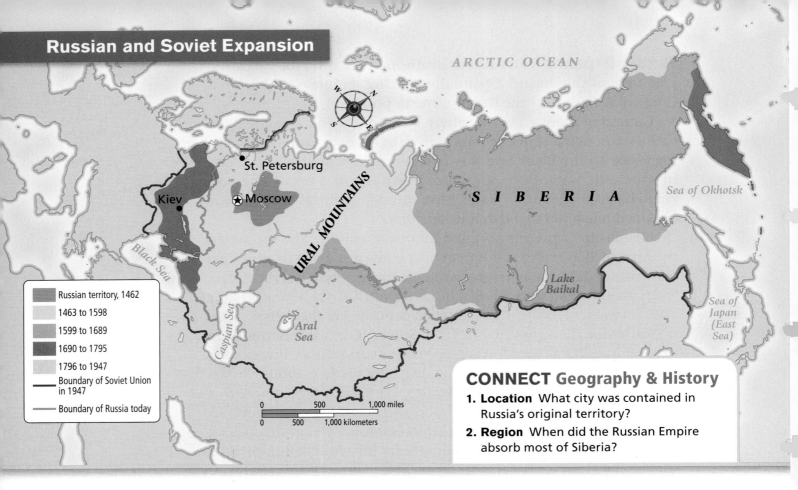

ARCTIC OCEAN

St. Petersburg

Kiev

Moscow

S I B E R I A

Sea of Okhotsk

URAL MOUNTAINS

Black Sea

Caspian Sea

Aral Sea

Lake Baikal

Sea of Japan (East Sea)

Russian territory, 1462
1463 to 1598
1599 to 1689
1690 to 1795
1796 to 1947
Boundary of Soviet Union in 1947
Boundary of Russia today

0   500   1,000 miles
0   500   1,000 kilometers

CONNECT Geography & History

1. **Location** What city was contained in Russia's original territory?

2. **Region** When did the Russian Empire absorb most of Siberia?

Revolution Brings Communism

▼ **KEY QUESTION** Why did the Soviet Union rise and fall?

In the 1800s, the czars continued their harsh rule. A few reforms, such as freeing the serfs, were carried out. Many people, though, did not think that these reforms went far enough.

The Bolshevik Revolution Then, in 1917, the Bolshevik (BOHL•shuh•VIHK) Party overthrew czar Nicholas II, and Vladimir Lenin came to power. The **Bolsheviks** believed that all political power and means of production should be held by the government in the name of the people. This type of system is called **communism**.

In 1922, the Bolsheviks created a new Communist nation called the **Union of the Soviet Socialist Republics (USSR)**, or **Soviet Union**. By 1929, **Joseph Stalin** had become dictator. Stalin was a cruel ruler who had millions of his political enemies executed. As dictator, Stalin also set up a **totalitarian** (toh•TAL•ih•TAIR•ee•uhn) government. This form of government controls every aspect of public and private life. Stalin controlled all newspapers, film, radio, and other sources of information. He also censored writers, composers, and other artists who did not glorify his achievements. Stalin's control even extended to education and religion. He built a police state to enforce his power.

Superpower and Collapse The Soviet Union joined the Allies during World War II and gained control of many countries in Eastern Europe during and after the war. Before long, deep distrust developed between the Soviet Union and the West. The United States and the Soviet Union each began to produce more and more powerful nuclear weapons. However, open warfare between the two never broke out. This conflict is called the **Cold War**. The buildup of military weapons during the Cold War drained money from the Soviet Union. As a result, food and other basic items were in short supply. Soviet citizens had to wait in line for hours to buy ordinary items.

In 1985, Soviet leader **Mikhail Gorbachev** (GAWR•buh•CHAWF) tried to revive the nation's economy by reducing government control. He also began allowing more freedom of expression and a free flow of information. However, Gorbachev's policy of openness had an unexpected result. It allowed Soviet citizens the right to complain about economic problems. They also began to call for more freedom.

The efforts to reform the Soviet Union led to its breakup. In 1991, the Soviet Union collapsed, and the Cold War ended. Russia continues to be a world leader. But, as you will learn in Section 4, Russia is still struggling to overcome many problems.

Mikhail Gorbachev
Gorbachev brought about great change, but he did not want to end communism.

🔺 **ANALYZE CAUSES AND EFFECTS** Tell why the Soviet Union rose and fell.

Section ❷ Assessment

ONLINE QUIZ
For test practice, go to
Interactive Review
@ ClassZone.com

TERMS & NAMES

1. Explain the importance of
- czar
- Bolsheviks
- totalitarian
- Cold War

USE YOUR READING NOTES

2. Analyze Causes and Effects Use your completed chart to answer the following question:

What effect do you think the Cold War had on Western people and on the people of the Soviet Union?

CAUSES	EFFECTS
Rise of the czars	
Russian expansion	
Communist revolution	
Collapse of Soviet Union	

KEY IDEAS

3. Why was the Moscow state able to break away from Mongol rule?

4. What were the major accomplishments of Catherine the Great?

5. What caused the Cold War?

CRITICAL THINKING

6. Make Inferences Why do you think Peter the Great wanted to westernize Russia?

7. Compare and Contrast How were the collapses of czarist Russia and of the Soviet Union similar and different?

8. CONNECT to Today The Trans-Siberian Railroad continues to be a popular means of transportation today. Why do you think the railroad is still important?

9. HISTORY **Prepare an Oral Report** In your report, contrast western Europe and Eastern-influenced Russia during the time of Peter the Great. Include information on government, economy, and culture.

Animated GEOGRAPHY
The Trans-Siberian Railroad

Click here to to explore the
Trans-Siberian Railroad @ ClassZone.com

CONNECTING EAST AND WEST

In the 1800s, Siberia was Russia's frontier. The region had plentiful natural resources, but these remained largely untapped—until 1891. That's when construction on the Trans-Siberian Railroad began, and the process of linking East and West got under way.

Click here to see how the railroad helped small villages develop into large cities.

Click here to learn how the workers lived, laid tracks, and blasted through the ice.

O'322

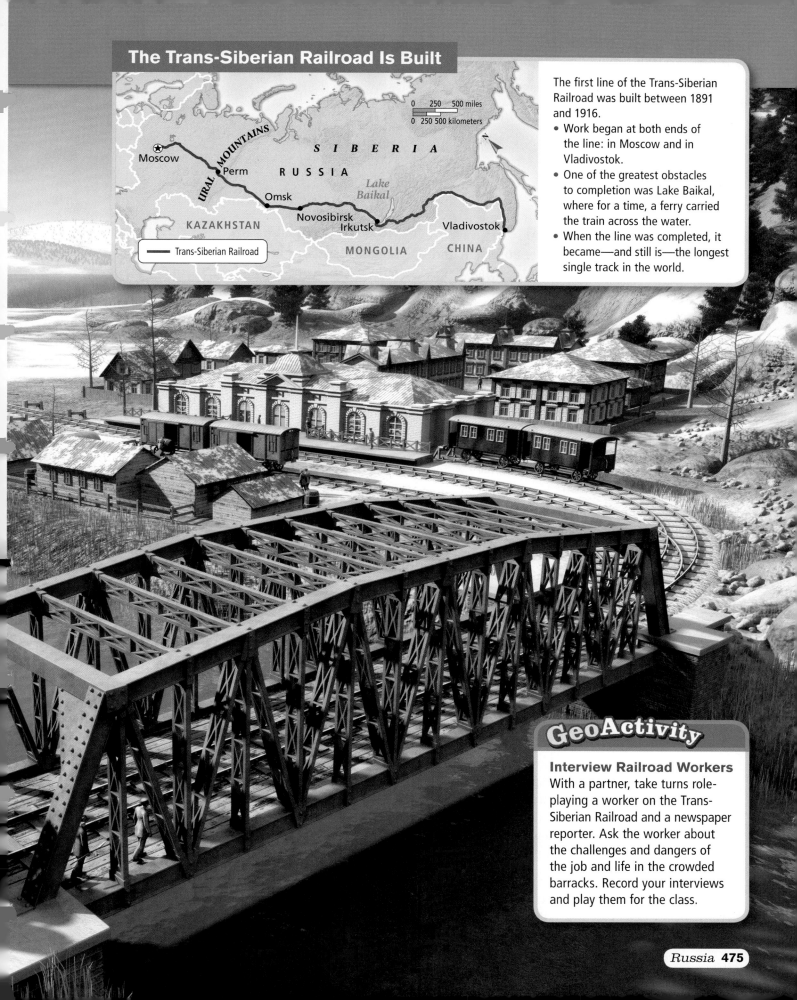

The Trans-Siberian Railroad Is Built

Map labels: Moscow, Perm, URAL MOUNTAINS, SIBERIA, RUSSIA, Omsk, Novosibirsk, Irkutsk, Lake Baikal, Vladivostok, KAZAKHSTAN, MONGOLIA, CHINA

0 250 500 miles
0 250 500 kilometers

— Trans-Siberian Railroad

The first line of the Trans-Siberian Railroad was built between 1891 and 1916.

- Work began at both ends of the line: in Moscow and in Vladivostok.
- One of the greatest obstacles to completion was Lake Baikal, where for a time, a ferry carried the train across the water.
- When the line was completed, it became—and still is—the longest single track in the world.

GeoActivity

Interview Railroad Workers
With a partner, take turns role-playing a worker on the Trans-Siberian Railroad and a newspaper reporter. Ask the worker about the challenges and dangers of the job and life in the crowded barracks. Record your interviews and play them for the class.

Reading for Understanding

▶ Key Ideas

BEFORE, YOU LEARNED

Russia has struggled to unite European and Asian influences throughout its history.

NOW YOU WILL LEARN

The influences of Europe and Asia are reflected in the people and culture of Russia.

▶ Vocabulary

TERMS & NAMES

Cyrillic (suh•RIHL•ihk) **alphabet** the official writing system of Russia

icon religious image used by Orthodox Christians in their worship

Leo Tolstoy (TOHL•stoy) a 19th-century writer who is one of Russia's greatest novelists

propaganda information that deliberately tries to influence opinion

BACKGROUND VOCABULARY

Orthodox Christianity the Eastern branch of Christianity that spread to Russia in the 900s and became the state religion

Islam a religion based on the teachings of the prophet Muhammad

Buddhism a religion that began in India and that is based on the teachings of Siddhartha Gautama

Judaism a religion based on the Hebrew Scriptures, whose followers are called Jews

REVIEW

ethnic group a group of people who share language, customs, and a common heritage

Visual Vocabulary dual-language sign depicting the Cyrillic alphabet

▶ Reading Strategy

Re-create the diagram shown at right. As you read and respond to the **KEY QUESTIONS**, use the diagram to record main ideas about Russian culture. Use a new diagram for each aspect of Russian culture you learn about.

 Skillbuilder Handbook, page R4

FIND MAIN IDEAS

RUSSIAN CULTURE

GRAPHIC ORGANIZERS
Go to **Interactive Review** @ ClassZone.com

Blending Europe and Asia

Connecting to Your World

The United States is made up of **ethnic groups** from all over the world. Their influence has shaped our country. You can see this in many big cities. There, you will find signs and advertisements in many different languages, including Spanish, Korean, and Arabic. Another country that has been strongly influenced by ethnic groups is Russia. In fact, the immense territory of Russia contains more than a hundred different ethnic groups. Most of these groups come from Europe and Asia and have made many cultural contributions.

The Russian People

▼ KEY QUESTION What elements shape the daily lives of the Russian people?

Most Russians live in western, or European, Russia. The rugged terrain and harsh climate in eastern Russia have kept populations low in that part of the country. Eighty percent of Russia's people are ethnic Russians, who are descended from the Slavs. Other ethnic groups include the Tatars, Ukrainians, Belarusians, and Chechens (CHECH•uhnz).

Ethnic Russians
Russian women relax in front of Kazan Cathedral in St. Petersburg. Ethnic Russians form one of the largest ethnic groups in the world, with over 160 million people worldwide.

City and Country Life About three-fourths of Russia's people live in cities. The two largest cities are Moscow and St. Petersburg. Red Square in Moscow is the most famous city square in Russia. It was built in the late 1400s and served as a meeting place for the Russian people. The name of the square comes from an old Russian word for "beautiful," which today also means "red." You can see some of Red Square's most famous buildings on the opposite page.

During World War II, many of the buildings in Russia's urban areas were destroyed. After the war, Russia had housing shortages. The Soviet government tried to solve this shortage by building huge high-rises. Many people still live in these dwellings.

In the country, more people live in single-family homes. However, in remote areas, some homes lack plumbing, running water, gas, and electric power. The quality of health care and education is lower in rural areas than in cities. As a result, many people from rural areas have moved to the cities in search of jobs.

Religion By far the most common religion in Russia is **Orthodox Christianity**. During the 900s, missionaries brought this religion to Russia, and with it, the **Cyrillic** (suh•RIHL•ihk) **alphabet**. This alphabet was soon adopted and used to write the Russian language. Around 988, Vladimir I made Orthodox Christianity the state religion.

Before long, Russian Orthodox churches were constructed in the Byzantine style. These churches have distinctive onion-shaped domes. St. Basil's Cathedral in Moscow's Red Square, shown on the opposite page, is a famous example of Russia's Byzantine church style. The churches also usually contain religious paintings called **icons**. Icons are often painted according to strict rules set up by the church authorities and frequently depict God, Jesus, angels, or saints.

Orthodox Christmas Russian girls light candles inside a church near Moscow during a midnight Christmas service. Orthodox Christians celebrate Christmas on January 7.

Moscow's Red Square

Red Square lies just outside the Kremlin's eastern wall. For over 500 years, the huge square (over 500,000 square feet) has served as a meeting place for the Russian people. Over the centuries, they have gathered there to celebrate festivals, hear announcements from the czar, and witness parades of Soviet military might. Today, Red Square is a popular spot for both Russians and tourists. The images here show some of the square's most legendary sites.

GUM Department Store Moscow's "State Department Store" is actually a huge mall that contains over 150 stores.

Lenin's Mausoleum Lenin's body—or at least a wax copy— lies in state in this red and black pyramid.

St. Basil's Cathedral St. Basil's was built in the 1550s to celebrate military victories over the Mongols.

Islam, **Buddhism**, **Judaism**, and other forms of Christianity are also practiced. In fact, over 15 percent of the population practices Islam. However, many Jews left Russia for the United States and Israel because they were persecuted for practicing their religion.

Food Russians generally eat a hearty diet that uses a lot of root vegetables, such as beets, carrots, onions, and potatoes. These vegetables grow well in the cool Russian climate. They are also warm and filling foods for the cold Russian winters.

Traditional Russian dishes are eaten throughout the world. They include thin pancakes, served with smoked salmon and sour cream, called *blinis* (BLEE•neez), and beet soup called *borscht* (bawrsht). Tea is a traditional beverage, which Russians enjoy piping hot and strong.

Sports Not surprisingly, winter sports, such as hockey, ice skating, and skiing, are popular in Russia. However, the most popular sport is soccer. Tennis has also soared in popularity. In fact, in 2006, five of the top 15 women tennis players in the world were Russian, including tennis star Maria Sharapova. Russian athletes also compete seriously in the Olympics.

▲ **FIND MAIN IDEAS** Identify some of the elements that shape the daily lives of the Russian people.

CONNECT ↷ History & Culture

Russia and the Olympics During the Soviet era, Russian Olympic athletes were supported by the government. The athletes excelled in ice skating, ice hockey, and gymnastics. Today, the old Soviet system of supporting athletes no longer exists. Nonetheless, between the time of the Soviet breakup and 2006, Russia has won four Olympic gold medals in men's figure skating and four in pairs skating. The Russians who won the 2006 Olympic gold medal in pairs figure skating are shown here.

Gold medalists Tatiana Totmianina and Maxim Marinin ▼

CRITICAL THINKING

Make Inferences What can you infer about the dedication of the Russian athletes who compete in the Olympics?

Cultural Heritage

▼ **KEY QUESTION** Who are some of the great Russian writers, artists, and composers of the 1800s and 1900s?

As you have learned, rulers such as Peter the Great and Catherine the Great encouraged the Russian people to adopt European customs. As a result, European culture gradually influenced Russian culture. Eventually, Russian literature and music that blended European and traditional styles began to emerge during the early 1800s. Soon Russia began to produce important works of literature, music, and art that are still highly regarded today.

Literature **Leo Tolstoy** (TOHL•stoy) is one of Russia's greatest novelists. In novels such as *War and Peace* (1869), Tolstoy showed deep concern for moral issues and for the welfare of the Russian people. In fact, the writer influenced Indian leader Mohandas Gandhi and his nonviolent independence movement. In turn, Gandhi inspired the nonviolent activism of civil rights leader Martin Luther King Jr.

Russia also boasted one of the best playwrights of the early 1900s. Anton Chekhov (CHEHK•awf) wrote insightful plays, including *The Three Sisters* (1901) and *The Cherry Orchard* (1904). Later in the century, Alexander Solzhenitsyn (SOHL•zhuh•NEET•sihn) described life in a Soviet labor camp under Stalin's rule in his short novel, *One Day in the Life of Ivan Denisovich* (1962). This novel led the Soviet Union to increase censorship.

ANALYZING Primary Sources

Alexander Solzhenitsyn (born 1918) is a Russian novelist who was arrested in 1945 for criticizing Stalin and spent eight years in prisons and labor camps like the one shown here. In this essay, Solzhenitsyn writes about what freedom means to him.

> This, I believe, is the single most precious freedom that prison takes away from us: the freedom to breathe freely, as I now can. No food on earth . . . is sweeter to me than this air steeped in the fragrance of flowers, of moisture and freshness.

Source: "Freedom to Breathe," essay by Alexander Solzhenitsyn

DOCUMENT–BASED QUESTION
What do you think Solzhenitsyn means by "the freedom to breathe freely"?

Marc Chagall In this 1925 painting called *Peasant Life*, Chagall uses vivid colors to celebrate rural Jewish life.

Art Russian painting was slower to adopt European influences than was Russian literature. However, around 1911, Wassily Kandinsky (kan•DIHN•skee) became one of the first artists to paint in the abstract style. Abstract painting does not represent objects using realistic forms. Instead, Kandinsky used bold colors and shapes. Around the same time, Jewish artist Marc Chagall (shuh•GAHL) created imaginative paintings in which the figures often seem to float in the air.

Music and Dance Russian music flowered during the 1800s. Using traditional Russian melodies, Peter Ilich Tchaikovsky (chy•KAWF•skee) wrote many great works, including the ballet *Swan Lake* (1877). Igor Stravinsky introduced modern forms of musical expression with his bold compositions, including the ballet *Rite of Spring* (1913).

You may have noticed that both Tchaikovsky and Stravinsky wrote ballets. That is because dance, especially ballet, had become very popular in Russia. In fact, by the mid-1800s, Russia boasted two world-class ballet companies: the Bolshoi (BOHL•shoy) Ballet and a company that came to be known as the Kirov (KEE•RAWF).

▲ **SUMMARIZE** Explain what Russian writers, artists, and composers of the 1800s and 1900s contributed to Russian culture.

Bolshoi Ballet *Bolshoi* is Russian for "grand." The company first performed *Swan Lake* in 1877. **Why do you think the Bolshoi is popular outside of Russia?**

Soviet Arts

▼ KEY QUESTION What purpose did Soviet propaganda serve?

The establishment of the Soviet government in the early 1920s led to the censorship of literature in Russia. The Soviet era, though, did produce some strong works of art in other media. For instance, the films of Sergei Eisenstein, such as *Battleship Potemkin* (1925), influenced the art of filmmaking.

The Soviets also used the arts for propaganda. **Propaganda** is information that deliberately tries to influence opinion. Much of Soviet propaganda was conveyed through posters. Artists were required to create posters that supported and glorified the Communist Party and its programs. These posters were mass-produced and placed in very visible areas. They were constant reminders of Communist policy and guides for proper thought. Under Stalin's rule, the Communist Party outlawed artists who did not promote Communist ideals.

Soviet Poster This 1930s poster shows Soviet citizens waving a flag with Stalin's image and looking toward a bright future. **What feelings do you think posters like this one were meant to inspire in Soviet citizens?**

▲ **RECOGNIZE BIAS AND PROPAGANDA** Discuss the purpose of propaganda and how the Soviets used it.

Section ❸ Assessment

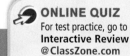 **ONLINE QUIZ**
For test practice, go to **Interactive Review** @ ClassZone.com

TERMS & NAMES

1. Explain the importance of
- Cyrillic alphabet
- Leo Tolstoy
- icon
- ethnic group

USE YOUR READING NOTES

2. Find Main Ideas Use your completed diagram to answer the following question:

How do Russian people blend Western and Eastern cultures?

RUSSIAN CULTURE

KEY IDEAS

3. What are some of the distinctive features of Russian Orthodox churches?

4. Why are winter sports so popular in Russia?

5. What impact did the Soviet era have on the arts?

CRITICAL THINKING

6. Make Inferences Why do you think Russia has developed so many great tennis players?

7. Compare and Contrast How does life in the country compare with city life in Russia?

8. CONNECT to Today Fast food and soft drinks are popular in Russia today. What does this fact suggest about Western influence in Russia?

9. TECHNOLOGY Present a Slide Show Use pictures to present a slide show about Russian culture. Listen to music by Tchaikovsky and Stravinsky and select your favorite piece. Play the piece as you present your slide show.

COMPARING ▶ Traditional and Modern Russia

Throughout its history, Russia has adopted cultural influences from the West. That cultural exchange continues today. But even as Russia changes, it maintains its character. As these pictures show, the country mixes Western styles with a definite Russian flavor.

Traditional Russia

For hundreds of years, Russians have retreated to their country houses, or dachas, to work in their vegetable gardens. They might also boil water for their tea in a samovar or listen to music played on a balalaika (BAL•uh•LY•kuh). Who knows? The house might even be decorated with nesting Matryoshka (MA•tree•OHSH•kuh) dolls.

Matryoshka Dolls

Traditional dolls nestle one inside the other and depict a round-faced peasant girl.

Beverages

Since the mid-1700s, beautifully decorated samovars have been used in Russia to prepare tea.

◀ *A traditional dacha in western Russia*

Music

This triangular folk guitar comes in many sizes, including the bass balalaika shown here.

Modern Russia

Many people in Russian cities live in high-rise apartment buildings built during the Soviet era. Further Western influence can be seen in the vending machines and music clubs that dot the cities. Even some traditional Matryoshka dolls now have a Western twist.

Matryoshka Dolls

Today, Matryoshka dolls can depict anyone, including George W. Bush and Vladimir Putin.

Soviet-style apartment blocks in a suburb of Moscow ▼

Beverages

Russians enjoy American-style soft drinks, but the machines dispense the soda into real glasses.

Music

Russian rock musicians often play unusual instruments, such as the cello seen here, in addition to electric guitars and drums.

CRITICAL THINKING

1. **Compare and Contrast** What different lifestyles do the dacha and apartment building suggest?

2. **Draw Conclusions** Which pictures best represent a blend of traditional and modern Russia?

Reading for Understanding

▶ Key Ideas

BEFORE, YOU LEARNED

The Communist government in Russia controlled the country's economy for most of the 20th century.

NOW YOU WILL LEARN

Russia is on its way to establishing a market economy but has struggled to change its government.

▶ Vocabulary

TERMS & NAMES

Vladimir Putin (POOT•ihn) president of Russia who increased executive power in the 2000s

Chechnya (CHEHCH•nee•uh) a largely Islamic republic in southwestern Russia that continues to fight for its independence

command economy an economic system in which the production of goods and services is controlled by a central government

market economy an economic system in which the production of goods and services is decided by the supply and demand of consumers

privatization (pry•vuh•tih•ZAY•shuhn) the process of selling government-owned businesses to private individuals

Boris Yeltsin (YEHLT•sihn) president who abruptly transformed the Russian economy after the Soviet Union collapsed

shock therapy term applied to Yeltsin's economic plan, which called for an abrupt shift from a command economy to a market economy

▶ Reading Strategy

Re-create the chart shown at right. As you read and respond to the **KEY QUESTIONS**, use the chart to identify the problems the Russian government faced after the collapse of the Soviet Union and the solutions they came up with.

 Skillbuilder Handbook, page R10

IDENTIFY PROBLEMS AND SOLUTIONS

PROBLEMS	SOLUTIONS
Establishing a new government	
Responding to internal troubles	
Changing the economy	

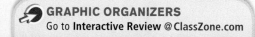

GRAPHIC ORGANIZERS
Go to **Interactive Review** @ ClassZone.com

The Struggle for Reform

Connecting to Your World

Freedom of speech. Freedom of the press. Freedom of religion. These are some of the freedoms we enjoy under a democracy. You probably take them for granted. But the Russian people are still trying to gain many of these freedoms. Since the breakup of the Soviet Union, Russia has worked to establish a new form of government. But internal conflicts and violence have threatened to tear the country apart. In addition, Russia has abruptly changed its economic system. In the midst of these problems and changes, democratic reform has proved difficult to achieve.

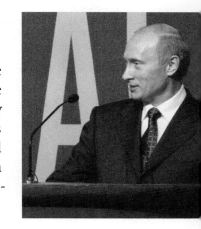

Vladimir Putin Putin worked for 15 years in the KGB, the Soviet Union's intelligence agency, before he entered politics.

A New Government

▼ **KEY QUESTION** Why did Russian democratic reform slow at the beginning of the 21st century?

After the breakup of the Soviet Union in 1991, Russians introduced many democratic reforms to their government. They set up several political parties, elected a president, and reorganized the structure of the government. However, while Russia has taken some steps forward, the country has also taken some steps back. In the early part of the 21st century, the government reversed some earlier reforms and seized more control.

Pro-Putin Rally Young people demonstrate their support for Putin in a rally in 2002. The word on the banner means "Russia."

487

U.S. GOVERNMENT

U.S. citizens elect the president, but the Constitution imposes a series of checks and balances on the president.

appoints federal judges

can declare executive acts unconstitutional

PRESIDENT

can veto acts of Congress

can override veto

can refuse to confirm judicial appointments

SUPREME COURT

CONGRESS

can declare acts of Congress unconstitutional

RUSSIAN GOVERNMENT

Russian citizens directly elect the president, but the Russian Constitution gives the president a great deal of power.

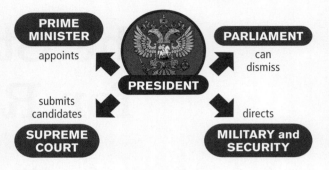

PRIME MINISTER

appoints

PRESIDENT

PARLIAMENT

can dismiss

submits candidates

SUPREME COURT

directs

MILITARY and SECURITY

CRITICAL THINKING

Compare and Contrast What are some similarities and differences between the powers of the president of Russia and those of the president of the United States?

Presidential Power The structure of the Russian government has much in common with that of the U.S. government. For example, the legislative branch of each government consists of two sections. Also, both governments' legislatures propose laws that they then submit to the president. However, the powers of the presidents differ. As you can see from the graphic above, the Russian president has more power than the U.S. president. By the early 2000s, President **Vladimir Putin** (POOT•ihn) of Russia had steadily begun to increase those powers.

When he became president, Putin made many changes to Russia's political system. He decreased the power of rival political parties and greatly increased the power of his own. He also took powers away from elected representatives and restricted the freedom of Russia's newspapers and other media. Today, some fear that Russia may return to the one-party system that ruled the Soviet Union.

Internal Troubles The Russian government restricted freedom, in part, in response to the rise in lawlessness and organized crime that occurred after 1991. The sudden social, political, and economic changes that followed independence encouraged this lawlessness. To combat crime in their country, many Russians have been willing to sacrifice their own liberty for order and the rule of law.

The Russian government also reversed some of its earlier reforms in reaction to terrorism and war with Chechnya. **Chechnya** (CHEHCH•nee•uh) is a largely Islamic region in southwestern Russia. When the people of Chechnya demanded their independence in 1991, Russia refused. Russia invaded the region in 1994 and again in 1999. Militants from Chechnya have also committed many acts of violence. The struggle between Russia and Chechnya continues today.

▲ **ANALYZE EFFECTS** Explain why Russia's democratic reforms have slowed.

Building a Market Economy

▼ **KEY QUESTION** What led to Russia's economic boom?

Although Russia has struggled to establish a democratic government, the country has had greater success reforming its economy. Russia is changing from a **command economy**, which is controlled by the government, to a **market economy**. This is an economic system in which private individuals own most of the businesses and operate them with little government control. The process of selling government-owned businesses to private individuals is called **privatization**.

Making the Transition Privatization has not been easy, however. When the Soviet Union broke apart, the economy was in a state of confusion. Encouraged by Western economists, Russian president **Boris Yeltsin** (YEHLT•sihn) adopted a plan to establish a market economy that involved **shock therapy**. This plan called for abrupt, widespread privatization. Many workers, though, were unwilling to privatize industries and farms. Soon industrial production fell, prices rose, businesses closed, and thousands of people lost work. Some critics of Yeltsin's plan complained that Russia got a lot of "shock" but no "therapy." In time, however, the economy began to prosper.

Moscow Mall Russia's new prosperity can be seen in this Western-style shopping mall. **How does this mall compare with those in your town?**

CONNECT ▸ History & Economics

From Bust to Boom

The graph shown here measures Russia's economic growth. As you can see, the economy has experienced many ups and downs since the breakup of the Soviet Union. But, overall, Yeltsin's shock therapy plan and the country's move toward a market economy have been a success.

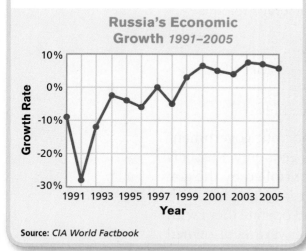

Russia's Economic Growth *1991–2005*

Source: *CIA World Factbook*

An Economic Boom Economic prosperity was not easy to achieve, though. In 1998, the country's money lost value, and the Russian stock market crashed. Economic hardships caused a steep rise in homelessness and a decline in life expectancy. But by 2001, Russia's economy showed steady growth and began to boom. The boom was largely due to Russian exports of oil.

As a result of the surging economy, salaries rose, unemployment decreased, and the Russian people could afford to buy goods. A growing middle class began to emerge. Unfortunately, not everyone has been able to take part in Russia's economic success. Many Russians are still unemployed or underpaid. But Russia has come a long way in a short amount of time.

 SEQUENCE EVENTS Identify the series of events that led to Russia's economic boom.

Section 4 Assessment

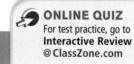 **ONLINE QUIZ**
For test practice, go to
Interactive Review
@ ClassZone.com

TERMS & NAMES

1. Explain the importance of
- shock therapy
- market economy
- command economy
- privatization

USE YOUR READING NOTES

2. Identify Problems and Solutions

Use your completed problem-solution chart to answer the following question:

How successful was Boris Yeltsin's shock therapy plan?

PROBLEMS	SOLUTIONS
Establishing a new government	
Responding to internal troubles	
Changing the economy	

KEY IDEAS

3. How did President Putin increase the powers of the Russian president?

4. How did Russia begin the shift from a command economy to a market economy?

5. How have the Russian people benefited from their country's economic boom?

CRITICAL THINKING

6. Make Inferences Why might Russians be willing to accept a very powerful president?

7. Evaluate What connection can you draw between Russia's physical geography and its economic boom?

8. CONNECT to Today What appears to be the most positive development in today's Russia?

9. MATH Create Graphs Use the Internet and your library to look up data on the unemployment rates for several years in the Soviet Union and in Russia. Then create a graph for each. Write a summary that compares and contrasts the graphs.

Interactive ⟨⟩ Review

CHAPTER SUMMARY

Key Idea 1
Russia is a vast country that contains a variety of land-forms, climates, vegetation regions, and natural resources.

Key Idea 2
The sometimes conflicting influences of the East and West have helped shape Russian history.

Key Idea 3
The influences of Europe and Asia are reflected in the people and culture of Russia.

Key Idea 4
Russia is on its way to establishing a market economy but has struggled to change its government.

For **Review and Study Notes**, go to **Interactive Review @ ClassZone.com**

NAME GAME

Use the Terms & Names list to complete each sentence on paper or online.

1. I separate European Russia from Asian Russia.
   _____Ural Mountains_____

2. I am a large body of water bordering Russia to the south. _____

3. I am the longest river in Europe. _____

4. I am a vast forest that lies south of the tundra in Russia. _____

5. I am a peasant who is bound to the land. _____

6. I am the title for the ruler of Russia from the mid-1500s to the early 1900s. _____

7. I am a type of government that controls every aspect of public and private life. _____

8. I am the official writing system of Russia.
   _____

9. I am an economic system in which the production of goods and services is controlled by a central government. _____

10. I am the process in which government-owned businesses are sold to private individuals.
    _____

Caspian Sea
command economy
Cyrillic alphabet
czar
Eurasia
icon
market economy
privatization
serf
Slav
steppe
taiga
totalitarian
Ural Mountains
Volga River

Activities

GeoGame

Use this online map to show what you know about Russia's location, geographic features, and important places. Drag and drop each place name to its location on the map.

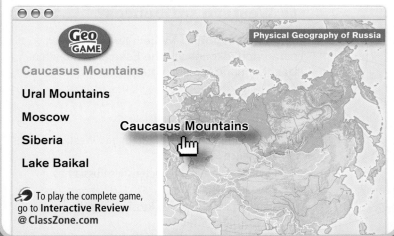

Geo GAME

Caucasus Mountains

Ural Mountains

Moscow

Siberia

Lake Baikal

To play the complete game, go to **Interactive Review @ ClassZone.com**

Physical Geography of Russia

Caucasus Mountains

Crossword Puzzle

Complete an online crossword puzzle to test your knowledge of Russia.

ACROSS
1. czar who tried to make Russia more European

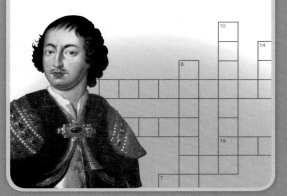

491

VOCABULARY

Explain the significance of each of the following.

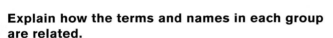

1. Eurasia
2. Ural Mountains
3. czar
4. serf
5. Bolsheviks
6. Joseph Stalin
7. totalitarian
8. Cyrillic alphabet
9. icon
10. command economy

Explain how the terms and names in each group are related.

11. tundra, taiga, and steppe
12. market economy and privatization

KEY IDEAS

1 Sweeping Across Eurasia

13. Why has the Northern European Plain in Russia been both a blessing and a curse?
14. Why are many of the main rivers in Siberia hardly ever used for transportation?
15. Why do few people live on the tundra?

2 Governing a Vast Land

16. How did the serf system arise in Russia?
17. How did Peter the Great attempt to make Russia's government run efficiently?
18. What was the Cold War?

3 Blending Europe and Asia

19. What are icons and how are they used?
20. What winter sports are popular in Russia?
21. Who did Leo Tolstoy inspire?

4 The Struggle for Reform

22. What are some of the Russian president's powers?
23. What was the purpose of President Boris Yeltsin's shock therapy plan?
24. What helped bring about Russia's economic boom?

CRITICAL THINKING

25. **Compare and Contrast** Create a chart to compare and contrast the landforms, climate, and natural resources of European Russia and Asian Russia.

EUROPEAN RUSSIA	ASIAN RUSSIA

26. **Analyze Causes** What led to the overthrow of the czar in 1917?
27. **Draw Conclusions** How did the censorship of Solzhenitsyn reflect totalitarianism?
28. **Connect to Economics** How did privatization change Russia?
29. **Connect History & Culture** How do Peter the Great's efforts to westernize Russia affect the country's culture today?
30. **Five Themes: Movement** How did the Trans-Siberian Railroad help unite western and eastern Russia?

Answer the ESSENTIAL QUESTION

How is Russia preserving its Eastern culture while adapting to Western influences?

Written Response Write a two- or three-paragraph response to the Essential Question. Use the rubric below to guide your thinking.

Response Rubric
A strong response will:
- discuss the history of Eastern and Western influence in Russia
- identify Western characteristics Russia has adopted
- explain ways in which Russia maintains its Eastern flavor today

THEMATIC MAP

Use the map to answer questions 1 and 2 on your paper.

Vegetation Regions of Russia

ARCTIC OCEAN

Black Sea

Caspian Sea

- Tundra
- Taiga
- Steppe
- Semidesert

0   500   1,000 miles
0 500 1,000 kilometers

1. Which vegetation region covers most of Russia?

A. tundra
B. taiga
C. steppe
D. semidesert

2. Which region is closest to the Arctic Ocean?

A. tundra
B. taiga
C. steppe
D. semidesert

LINE GRAPH

Examine the graph below. Use the information in the graph to answer questions 3 and 4.

Russian Male Life Expectancy

Age

75
70
65
60
55
50

1970 1980 1990 2000 2010 2020

Year

Source: U.N. World Population Division

3. What was the life expectancy in 1990?

A. about 60
B. about 65
C. about 63
D. about 67

4. When did the life expectancy of Russian men decline the most?

A. between 1985 and 1990
B. between 1990 and 1995
C. between 1995 and 2000
D. between 2000 and 2005

GeoActivity

1. INTERDISCIPLINARY ACTIVITY–ECONOMICS

With a small group, prepare a short speech that President Boris Yeltsin might have given to the Russian people about his shock therapy plan. In the speech, explain the long-term benefits of the plan, but also warn the people about the short-term harm it may cause.

2. WRITING FOR SOCIAL STUDIES

Recall what you have learned about censorship under a totalitarian government. Do you think government should ever have the power to control what citizens say or create? Examine the conflicting viewpoints and then explain your position.

3. MENTAL MAPPING

Create a physical map of Russia and label the following:

- Volga River
- Ural Mountains
- Black Sea
- Caspian Sea
- Siberia
- Arctic Ocean
- Lake Baikal
- Kamchatka Peninsula

CHAPTER 16 The Eurasian Republics

1 GEOGRAPHY

Center of a Landmass

2 HISTORY & CULTURE

Historic Crossroads

3 GOVERNMENT & ECONOMICS

The Challenge of Independence

 ESSENTIAL QUESTION

How can the Eurasian republics meet the challenges of independence?

CONNECT Geography & History

Use the map and the time line to answer the following questions.

1. When did the Mongols conquer Central Asia?
2. What body of water lies between Azerbaijan and Turkmenistan?

Culture

◄ **600s** Arabs spread Islam to Transcaucasia and Central Asia. (Muslim prayer rug)

600

Culture

700s Turkish peoples migrate to Central Asia.

History

1200s Mongols conquer Central Asia and stabilize trade along Silk Roads. (Mongol conqueror Timur the Lame) ►

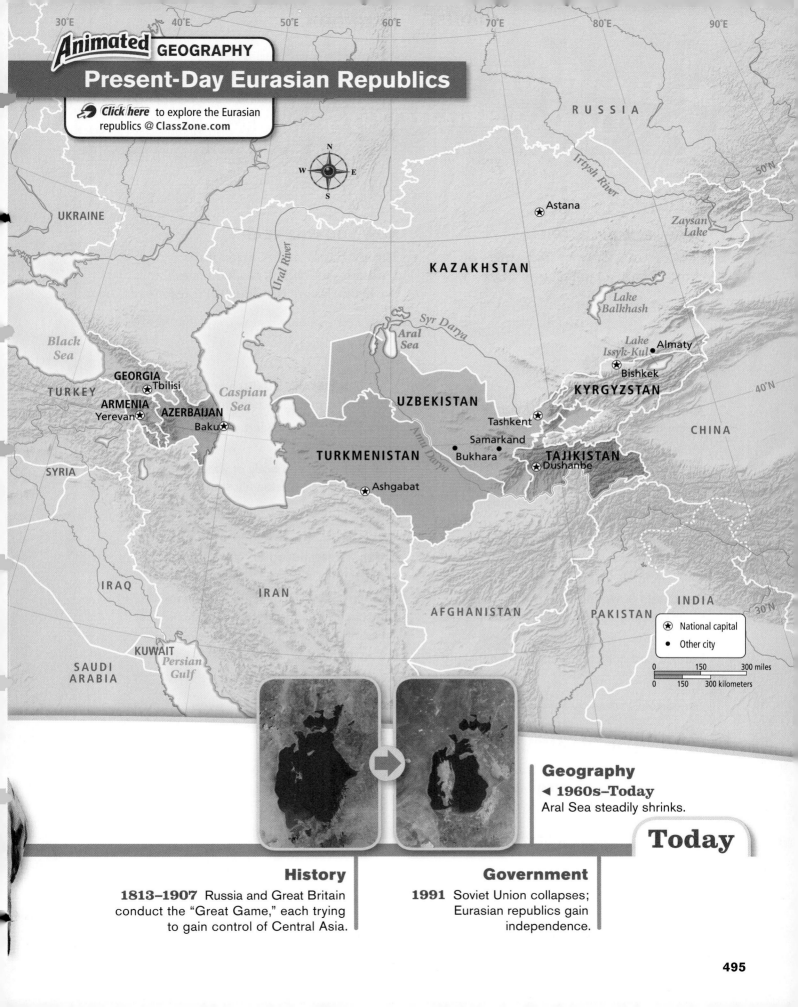

Present-Day Eurasian Republics

Click here to explore the Eurasian republics @ ClassZone.com

RUSSIA

★ Astana

KAZAKHSTAN

Irtysh River

Zaysan Lake

Lake Balkhash

Ural River

UKRAINE

Black Sea

Caspian Sea

Syr Darya

Aral Sea

Lake Issyk-Kul • Almaty

GEORGIA ★ Tbilisi

ARMENIA
Yerevan ★ **AZERBAIJAN**
Baku ★

TURKEY

UZBEKISTAN

★ Bishkek

KYRGYZSTAN

Tashkent ★

Samarkand •
Bukhara • **TAJIKISTAN**
★ Dushanbe

CHINA

TURKMENISTAN

Amu Darya

★ Ashgabat

SYRIA

IRAQ

IRAN

AFGHANISTAN

PAKISTAN

INDIA

KUWAIT
Persian Gulf

SAUDI ARABIA

★ National capital
• Other city

0   150   300 miles
0   150   300 kilometers

Geography
◄ **1960s–Today**
Aral Sea steadily shrinks.

Today

History
1813–1907 Russia and Great Britain conduct the "Great Game," each trying to gain control of Central Asia.

Government
1991 Soviet Union collapses; Eurasian republics gain independence.

Reading for Understanding

▶ Key Ideas

BEFORE, YOU LEARNED

Russia's vast geography and variety of climates form a land of great diversity.

NOW YOU WILL LEARN

The geography and climate of the Eurasian republics pose challenges, but the countries are rich in natural resources.

▶ Vocabulary

TERMS & NAMES

Transcaucasia (TRANS•kaw•KAY•zhuh) a region between the Black and Caspian seas that contains the republics of Armenia, Azerbaijan (AZ•uhr•by•JAHN), and Georgia

Central Asia a region that contains the republics of Kazakhstan (KAH•zahk•STAN), Kyrgyzstan (KEER•gee•STAN), Tajikistan (tah•JIHK•ih•STAN), Turkmenistan (TURK•mehn•ih•STAN), and Uzbekistan (uz•BEHK•ih•STAN)

Caucasus (KAW•kuh•suhs) **Mountains** a mountain range that runs between the Black Sea and the Caspian Sea

landlocked completely surrounded by land

Tian Shan (TYAHN SHAHN) a mountain range that runs across Kyrgyzstan and Tajikistan

Kara Kum a huge desert that covers most of Turkmenistan

Aral Sea an inland body of water in Central Asia that has been steadily shrinking

Lake Balkhash a lake in eastern Kazakhstan

REVIEW

Eurasia a term used to refer to a single continent that is made up of Europe and Asia

Caspian Sea a sea situated between Transcaucasia and Central Asia; the largest inland body of water in the world

▶ Reading Strategy

Re-create the Venn diagram shown at right. As you read and respond to the **KEY QUESTIONS**, use the diagram to compare and contrast the landforms, climates, and resources of Transcaucasia and Central Asia.

 See Skillbuilder Handbook, page R9

COMPARE AND CONTRAST

TRANSCAUCASIA — BOTH — CENTRAL ASIA

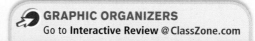

GRAPHIC ORGANIZERS
Go to **Interactive Review** @ ClassZone.com

Center of a Landmass

Connecting to Your World

You have already learned that the Soviet Union was a Communist country that consisted of Russia and the surrounding republics. Remember that some geographers place this enormous nation in a region they call **Eurasia**, a landmass made up of both Europe and Asia. When the Soviet Union broke apart in 1991, 15 independent republics were formed. Three of these republics are located between the Black and Caspian seas in a region called Transcaucasia. Five more independent republics lie in Central Asia, a region east of the Caspian Sea.

Landforms and Bodies of Water

▼ **KEY QUESTION** What are the major landforms and bodies of water in Transcaucasia and Central Asia?

Transcaucasia consists of the republics of Armenia, Azerbaijan, and Georgia. **Central Asia** contains the republics of Kazakhstan, Kyrgyzstan, Tajikistan, Turkmenistan, and Uzbekistan. Both regions are very mountainous and boast some of the largest lakes in the world.

Tian Shan The Tian Shan, which is Chinese for "Heavenly Mountains," stretch for nearly 1,500 miles.

TIAN SHAN

Transcaucasia As you can see on the map on the opposite page, Transcaucasia is bounded by Turkey and Iran to the south. The **Caucasus Mountains**  rise in the north and form the border between Russia and Transcaucasia. These mountains lie between two bodies of water. The Black Sea borders Georgia on the west. The **Caspian Sea** Ⓑ, which is actually a saltwater lake, borders Azerbaijan on the east. It is the largest inland body of water in the world.

Armenia lies between Georgia and Azerbaijan. In fact, Armenia is **landlocked**, or completely surrounded by land. The country contains fertile volcanic soil on a southern plateau. Fertile coastal plains lie in Georgia on the Black Sea and along the Caspian Sea in Azerbaijan.

Central Asia This region is bordered by Russia to the north, the Caspian Sea to the west, a series of mountain ranges to the south, and China to the east. Mountains dominate Kyrgyzstan and Tajikistan. Most of this rugged terrain is part of the Alay and **Tian Shan** Ⓒ mountain ranges. The towering Tian Shan range contains some of the largest alpine glaciers in the world. An even higher mountain range, called the Pamirs, is located in southeastern Tajikistan.

Kazakhstan has a variety of landforms. The mountainous terrain in the east lowers to a large steppe in the north and a desert in the south. Then the land lowers even more toward the Caspian Sea, where it sinks to about 433 feet below sea level. The huge desert of **Kara Kum** Ⓓ covers most of Turkmenistan. Another vast desert, the Kyzyl Kum, occupies much of Uzbekistan.

The two most important rivers of Central Asia, the Syr Darya and the Amu Darya, flow into the **Aral Sea** Ⓔ. *Darya* means "river." Much of the water from these rivers is used for irrigation. You will learn about the impact of this irrigation on the Aral Sea later in this section. **Lake Balkhash** Ⓕ is situated in eastern Kazakhstan. It is unusual because the lake is composed of fresh water in its western half and salt water in its eastern half.

Kara Kum The few people who live in this desert are mainly sheep and camel herders. **Why do you think the Kara Kum is sparsely populated?**

🔺 **CATEGORIZE** Describe the major landforms and bodies of water in Transcaucasia and Central Asia.

Physical Geography of the Eurasian Republics

Cotton farmers in Uzbekistan

LATVIA

BELARUS

UKRAINE

RUSSIA

URAL MOUNTAINS

Ural River

Black Sea

Ⓐ

GEORGIA

CAUCASUS MTS.

ARMENIA

TURKEY

AZERBAIJAN

Ⓑ

Caspian Sea

KIRGHIZ STEPPE

KAZAKHSTAN

Aral Sea

Ⓔ

Syr Darya

TURAN PLAIN

KYZYL KUM DESERT

UZBEKISTAN

KARA KUM DESERT

Ⓓ

TURKMENISTAN

Amu Darya

KAZAHK UPLANDS

Ⓕ

Zaysan Lake

Lake Balkhash

Lake Issyk-Kul

KYRGYZSTAN

TIAN SHAN

Ⓒ

TAJIKISTAN

Ismoili Somoni Peak 24,590 ft (7,495 m)

PAMIRS

HINDU KUSH

Irtysh River

50°N

40°N

CHINA

IRAQ

IRAN

AFGHANISTAN

PAKISTAN

N
W   E
S

0	200	400 miles
0	200	400 kilometers

Elevation

13,100 ft. (4,000 m)
6,600 ft. (2,000 m)
3,280 ft. (1,000 m)
650 ft. (200 m)
0 ft. (0 m)
Below sea level

▲ Mountain peak

CONNECT Geography & Culture
READING A PHYSICAL MAP

As you study the map,
- identify and locate the republics in Transcaucasia and Central Asia
- note which republics in each region are landlocked
- compare elevation across the two regions

1. **Region** Which two republics in Central Asia appear to be as mountainous as those in Transcaucasia?

2. **Human-Environment Interaction** What impact might this mountainous terrain have on the people there?

50°E   60°E   70°E   *The Eurasian Republics* **499**

Transcaucasia
Visitors enjoy a day on Georgia's Black Sea coast. **1. How does this image reflect the area's climate?**

Central Asia
Kyrgyzstan averages less than 20 inches of rain a year. **2. How might this climate affect vegetation?**

Climate

▲ **KEY QUESTION** How do the climates in Transcaucasia and Central Asia differ?

Climate in the two regions ranges from the subtropical areas of Transcaucasia to the semiarid and desert climates of Central Asia. The high elevations of the mountains and distance from the sea have a big impact on climate in both regions.

Transcaucasia In the lowlands of Azerbaijan, winters are mild and summers are hot. In the mountainous areas of Armenia, on the other hand, temperatures are colder, and snow in the winter can be heavy. Georgia has a milder climate than either Armenia or Azerbaijan. The Caucasus Mountains protect the coastal areas from too much rain. In addition, moist air from the Black Sea moderates Georgia's climate.

Central Asia Like Armenia, the nations of Central Asia are land-locked. They are many miles from the moderating influence of the world's oceans. As a result, Central Asia has a much harsher climate than Transcaucasia, with extreme high and low temperatures. Southern and southeastern mountain ranges block any moist air and contribute to the semiarid and desert climates of the region.

▼ **COMPARE AND CONTRAST** Compare the climates of Transcaucasia and Central Asia.

Resources

▼ **KEY QUESTION** What resources are abundant in Transcaucasia and Central Asia?

Both Transcaucasia and Central Asia are rich in natural resources. The regions have huge reserves of coal and metals, but oil and natural gas are especially plentiful. In fact, the petroleum deposits around and under the Caspian Sea are among the world's largest. The development of the oil resources in both regions should help the young nations thrive.

Transcaucasia Most of the oil in Transcaucasia lies in Azerbaijan. In fact, the country's name means "land of flames." The name refers to fires that erupted from the rocks and the rivers leading to the Caspian Sea. The fires were the result of underground oil and gas deposits.

The Transcaucasian republics also have fertile farmland. In the rich soil along the coastal plain of Georgia, farmers grow grapes, citrus fruit, and tea. In the highlands of Armenia, farm products include peaches, apricots, walnuts, and wheat. Because of the lack of precipitation, many of the farms in Azerbaijan require irrigation.

Central Asia Much of the oil in Central Asia can be found in Kazakhstan and Turkmenistan. Nations all over the world are interested in buying this oil, which may eventually bring great wealth to the region. In addition, rich deposits of highly valued energy resources, such as coal and natural gas, are plentiful. Mines also provide valuable minerals, including gold, copper, and lead.

Unlike Transcaucasia, Central Asia has little fertile soil, and many areas do not receive much rain. For that reason, water often has to be brought in to irrigate crops. Cotton is an important crop for all of the Central Asian republics. Other crops include grain, fruits, and vegetables.

CONNECT **Geography & Economics**

Oil and the Caspian Sea

For years, the five countries that border the Caspian Sea have argued over rights to the oil-rich area. In 2003, Azerbaijan, Kazakhstan, and Russia agreed to a division of the sea and its resources. However, Iran and Turkmenistan did not agree to the plan. Nonetheless, progress has been made in extracting the oil. In 2005, a pipeline was built to pump oil from Azerbaijan to Turkey. In this photograph, a mosque in the Azerbaijan capital of Baku overlooks oil derricks in the Caspian.

▲ **SUMMARIZE** Identify the resources that are abundant in Transcaucasia and Central Asia.

Human-Environment Interaction

▼ **KEY QUESTION** What has led to some of the environmental problems in Central Asia?

For decades the Soviet Union attempted to overcome its geographic limits by trying to increase its farmable land. The government also took advantage of some of its vast, uninhabited areas by carrying out experimental projects in them. Unfortunately, these projects sometimes had unintended negative results, particularly in Central Asia.

Aral Sea In the 1960s, the Soviet Union began using river water from the Syr Darya and Amu Darya for an irrigation project. This project was part of a plan to convert areas of Central Asian desert into thriving cotton farms. Indeed, the production of cotton soon soared. However, since the Aral Sea received most of its water from the two rivers, the irrigation caused the sea to drastically shrink. The sea even split into two, the small Aral and the large Aral. Recent efforts have helped raise the level of the small Aral. As a result, fish, jobs, and people have begun to return to the area. But the Soviet plan caused one of Earth's greatest environmental disasters.

CONNECT to Science

By the end of the 20th century, irrigation and evaporation had caused the Aral Sea to shrink about 75 percent. The retreating waters left behind dry beds filled with salt, fertilizers, and pesticides. These chemicals had washed into the sea from the cotton farms. Windstorms then blew the chemicals into the surrounding area. As a result, the rates of cancer and other diseases greatly increased in the nearby population.

Disappearing Sea A camel stands before an abandoned ship on what was once the floor of the Aral Sea.

Activity

Conduct an Evaporation Experiment

Materials
- 2 tablespoons of salt
- measuring cup of water
- spoon
- shallow bowl

1. Place salt into the measuring cup.

2. Fill the cup with warm water and stir to dissolve the salt.

3. Pour the mixture into the bowl and place near a window.

4. Check the bowl every day for a week. Note what evaporates and what remains behind.

Nuclear Testing Other Soviet programs have caused problems in Central Asia. As you may recall, the Soviet Union and the United States engaged in a weapons race during the Cold War. Between 1949 and 1990, the Soviet government used part of the vast steppes in northern Kazakhstan to test their nuclear weapons. Unfortunately, radiation from this testing poisoned the soil, food, and water over about a 7,000-square-mile area. The radiation caused dramatic increases in the rates of leukemia, birth defects, and mental illness in the area.

Recently, the nations of Central Asia have taken steps to avoid more environmental problems. For example, Kazakhstan has started to develop more light industry to prevent an over-dependence on heavy industries. This measure should help decrease the region's air and water pollution problems.

Nuclear Blast The Soviets conducted about 715 nuclear tests. In this picture, a test site is destroyed in Kazakhstan in 2000.

 ANALYZE CAUSES Explain what led to some of the environmental problems in Central Asia.

Section ① Assessment

ONLINE QUIZ
For test practice, go to
Interactive Review
@ ClassZone.com

TERMS & NAMES

1. **Explain the importance of**
   • Transcaucasia
   • Central Asia
   • Kara Kum
   • Aral Sea

USE YOUR READING NOTES

2. **Compare and Contrast** Use your completed Venn diagram to answer the following question:

   What element of their physical geography offers great promise for the futures of both Transcaucasia and Central Asia?

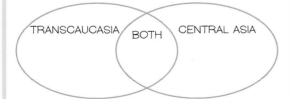

KEY IDEAS

3. What types of landforms are found in Kazakhstan?

4. Why does Central Asia have a harsh climate?

5. What areas of Transcaucasia have rich soil?

CRITICAL THINKING

6. **Make Inferences** Which region do you think is more densely populated, Transcaucasia or Central Asia? Explain your answer.

7. **Compare and Contrast** How are the landforms and bodies of water of Georgia and Armenia similar and different?

8. **CONNECT to Today** What lessons can be learned today from the Aral Sea environmental disaster?

9. **WRITING** **Prepare an Environmental Report** Do further research about the causes and effects of pollution in Central Asia. Also find out about possible solutions for these problems. Then write an environmental report that summarizes your research.

Reading for Understanding

▶ Key Ideas

BEFORE, YOU LEARNED

The Eurasian republics are largely mountainous and desert regions with harsh climates.

NOW YOU WILL LEARN

The geographic location of the Eurasian republics has attracted many different cultures, ideas, and conquerors.

▶ Vocabulary

TERMS & NAMES

nomad member of a group who makes a living by herding animals and moving from place to place as the seasons change

Islam a religion that is based on the teachings of the prophet Muhammad

Muslim a follower of Islam

Silk Roads major trade routes that ran from China to the rest of East Asia, through Central Asia, and into Europe

Russification the process of making a culture more Russian

yurt a portable, tentlike structure used by the nomads of Central Asia

REVIEW

ethnic group a group of people who share language, customs, and a common heritage

Visual Vocabulary Russification

▶ Reading Strategy

Re-create the web diagram shown at right. As you read and respond to the **KEY QUESTIONS**, use the diagram to record main ideas about the history and culture of the Eurasian republics. Add ovals as needed.

 See Skillbuilder Handbook, page R4

FIND MAIN IDEAS

Influenced by many ethnic groups

HISTORY AND CULTURE IN EURASIAN REPUBLICS

 GRAPHIC ORGANIZERS
Go to **Interactive Review** @ ClassZone.com

Historic Crossroads

Connecting to Your World

Imagine that you had to move every few months. In the summer, you might live in New England. Then in the fall, you would move to the Midwest. Finally, in the winter, you would go to the Southwest. In the spring, you would start the cycle all over again. This way of life probably sounds very different from your own, but it is similar to the way thousands of nomads live. **Nomads** are people who make a living by herding animals and moving from place to place as the seasons change. The people who first lived in Transcaucasia and Central Asia led a nomadic way of life.

Regions of Exchange

▼ **KEY QUESTION** How have various groups of people and trade influenced Transcaucasia and Central Asia?

For centuries, many groups of people moved through Transcaucasia and Central Asia. Some of them settled in these regions and had a major influence on culture. Three main reasons for this movement were military conquest, migration, and trade.

Nomadic Man This man's weather-beaten face reflects a life lived largely out of doors.

Nomadic Home Nomads live in yurts, portable tents that usually consist of several layers of felt stretched around a wooden frame.

Migrations, Invasions, and Trade Three groups that had a major impact on the cultures of Transcaucasia and Central Asia were the Arabs, the Turks, and the Mongols.

In the 600s, Arabs moved into Transcaucasia in great numbers and introduced Islam. **Islam** is a religion based on the teachings of the prophet Muhammad. The followers of Islam are called **Muslims**. During the 1000s, tribes from Turkey moved into the region. Eventually, Transcaucasia became part of the Ottoman Empire, which ruled the area until World War I. In addition, Mongols raided Georgian lands from the 1200s to the early 1400s.

Central Asia followed a similar pattern of migration and invasion. Arabs spread Islam to parts of Central Asia. Turkish peoples began to migrate into Central Asia during the 700s. In the 1200s, the Mongols conquered the region.

The Mongol Empire brought stability to Central Asia. This stability encouraged trade in the region. A network of major trade routes, called the **Silk Roads**, flourished. They ran from China to the rest of East Asia, through Central Asia, and into Europe. Cities, such as Samarkand in present-day Uzbekistan and Merv in present-day Turkmenistan, sprang up along the Silk Roads. Central Asian nomads helped stimulate trade by traveling along the routes and exchanging livestock for food and manufactured products. Goods traded included jade, gold, horses, wool, and, of course, silk. Religions, including Islam, and inventions, such as the compass and gunpowder, also spread along these routes.

The Silk Roads

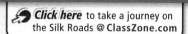 **Click here** to take a journey on the Silk Roads @ ClassZone.com

Travel along the demanding terrain of the Silk Roads was difficult and often dangerous. Traders avoided the harsh Taklimakan Desert as much as possible. Temperatures in the desert often reach 120°F in the summer. Even caravans that traveled along the edge of the desert often dealt with fierce sandstorms.

After the Taklimakan, caravans had to cross the steep Pamir Mountains. Caravans that traveled on southern routes had to cross over the Himalayas on narrow passes that dropped off into deep ravines.

CONNECT Geography & History

Human-Environment Interaction What do the difficulties along the Silk Roads suggest about the traders who traveled them?

Geographic Challenges A camel train winds through the Taklimakan Desert under the hot sun.

Ethnic Groups The movement of the Arabs, Turks, and Mongols into Transcaucasia and Central Asia had a major impact on the ethnic makeup of these regions. For example, in Central Asia, many people are descended from Turkish and Mongol tribes. The Silk Roads also brought many different ethnic groups to the regions. Remember that an **ethnic group** is made up of people who share a common heritage.

As a result of this migration and trade, people belonging to many different ethnic groups live in the Eurasian republics today. The pie graphs at right show the ethnic distributions in Transcaucasia and Central Asia. Most of the people practice Islam or Orthodox Christianity.

In Transcaucasia, Armenian, Azerbaijani, and Georgian are the most common languages. Russian and various languages related to Turkish are commonly spoken in Central Asia.

Like people in other parts of the world, those in Transcaucasia and Central Asia do not always get along. Allegiance to their ethnic group is often of greater importance than loyalty to their country. For instance, in Georgia, the Ossetians continue to fight for their independence from the republic. In Central Asia, the Kyrgyz and the Uzbeks have had conflicts over territorial claims.

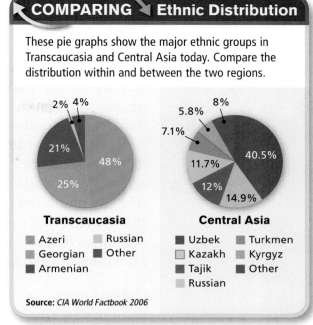

COMPARING ► Ethnic Distribution

These pie graphs show the major ethnic groups in Transcaucasia and Central Asia today. Compare the distribution within and between the two regions.

Transcaucasia
- 48%
- 25%
- 21%
- 4%
- 2%

Legend:
- Azeri
- Georgian
- Armenian
- Russian
- Other

Central Asia
- 40.5%
- 14.9%
- 12%
- 11.7%
- 7.1%
- 5.8%
- 8%

Legend:
- Uzbek
- Kazakh
- Tajik
- Russian
- Turkmen
- Kyrgyz
- Other

Source: *CIA World Factbook 2006*

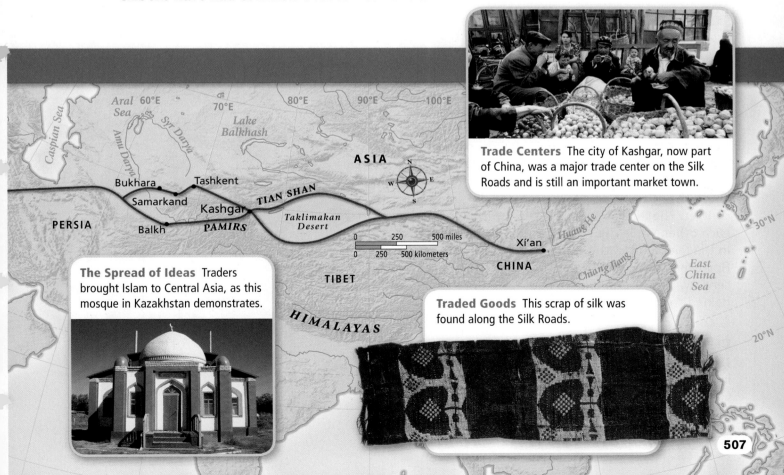

Trade Centers The city of Kashgar, now part of China, was a major trade center on the Silk Roads and is still an important market town.

The Spread of Ideas Traders brought Islam to Central Asia, as this mosque in Kazakhstan demonstrates.

Traded Goods This scrap of silk was found along the Silk Roads.

Soviet Control In 1922, Russia joined with three other territories to form the Soviet Union. These territories came to include Transcaucasia, Central Asia, and the western republics—Belarus, Moldova, Ukraine, and the Baltic republics. The Soviets then divided their land into 15 republics. When they divided the land, however, they often ignored traditional boundaries. This policy created deep resentment.

As the Soviets developed their republics, they tried to make them more Russian. For example, they forced a large number of Russians to move to Kazakhstan to work on farms and in cities. They also strongly promoted the Russian language and the use of the Cyrillic alphabet in all of their republics. Traditional ethnic ways of life were discouraged. This process of making other cultures more Russian is called **Russification**.

Independence When the Soviet Union collapsed in 1991, the republics in Transcaucasia and Central Asia gained their independence. Since then, they have begun to move toward market economies. However, widespread poverty and ethnic disputes are still common. As a result, many people have migrated from the former Soviet republics into Russia, seeking better conditions.

🔺 **EVALUATE** Explain how trade and various groups of people have influenced Transcaucasia and Central Asia.

CONNECT Geography & History

The Great Game From about 1813 to 1907, the Russian Empire and Great Britain competed for control of Central Asia. The Russian Empire wanted to use the region to invade India, a British colony. Battles between the two empires took place in the Kingdom of Afghanistan. Their struggle came to be called the "Great Game." The cartoon illustrates the conflict. The Russian bear and the British lion stare at each other, while the ruler of Afghanistan is caught in the middle. Great Britain managed to protect India. However, by the end of the 19th century, the Russian Empire had gained control of Central Asia.

CRITICAL THINKING

Draw Conclusions What lasting impact did the Great Game have on Central Asia in the 20th century?

PUNCH, OR THE LONDON CHARIVARI.—November 30, 1878.

"SAVE ME FROM MY FRIENDS!"

RUSSIAN EMPIRE

KINGDOM OF AFGHANISTAN

BRITISH INDIA

◀ *The empires in 1900*

People and Traditions

🔻 **KEY QUESTION** What are some of the characteristics of life in Transcaucasia and Central Asia?

Many of the people of the Eurasian republics follow the same traditions as their ancestors. Most people in Central Asia live in rural areas, where they farm or herd livestock. In Transcaucasia, on the other hand, more than half the people live in urban areas. These people often work in offices or factories.

Family Life In both Transcaucasia and Central Asia, family life is very important. In many countries, extended families live together. These families include parents, grandparents, aunts, and uncles.

In the cities of Armenia and Azerbaijan, many families live in large apartment buildings. One- or two-story houses and apartment buildings are common in the cities of Georgia. Apartment buildings are also common in the cities of Central Asia.

In rural areas of Central Asia, however, nomads often live in a dwelling called a yurt. A **yurt** is a portable, tentlike structure covered with hides or textiles. Inside, yurts are lined with decorative rugs. When nomads search for good pasture for their livestock, they carry their yurts with them on horseback or in wagons.

In the Eurasian republics, families observe many ethnic and religious holidays. In Central Asia, the Muslim spring holiday of Noruz is widely celebrated. Orthodox Easter is a popular Christian holiday in Armenia and Georgia. Since gaining independence, the people of the Eurasian republics value the freedom to celebrate their ethnic and religious holidays. Under Soviet rule, these holidays were often banned.

Kazakh Picnic Many generations gather to enjoy a feast that includes meat dumplings, rice with roasted garlic, and bread. **What does the picture suggest about family life in Kazakhstan?**

To learn more about Zuhura and her world, go to the **Activity Center** @ ClassZone.com

Hi! My name is Zuhura. I am 14 years old and live in a rural town in Uzbekistan. School and doing chores are an important part of my life. But I also have fun with my friends. I enjoy watching Bollywood movies, which are films made in India. In fact, I have covered my school notebook with stickers of Bollywood movie stars. This is what my day is like.

This is how to say "My name is Zuhura" in Uzbek:

"Mening ismim Zuhura."

6:30–7:30 A.M. I wake up and eat a breakfast of tea and bread with jam. Then I feed the chickens and milk the family cow. When I'm done, I head off to school with my brothers and sisters.

8 A.M.–2:30 P.M. School has seven 45-minute periods. Our school doesn't have heat. In the winter, it gets really cold. So we keep our coats on while we sit at our desks.

3 P.M. When I get home, I eat a snack of bread and tea and then help clean house and wash clothes by hand. Later, we all help my mother prepare dinner. Only then do I have time to spend with my friends.

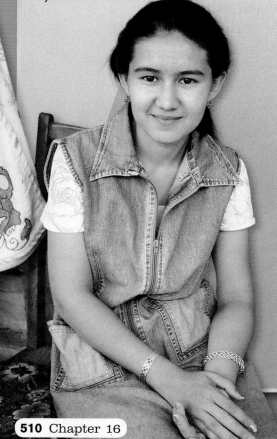

8 P.M. We're having my favorite meal tonight: soup made of broth, carrots, potatoes, and meat. In the winter, we eat a lot of cabbage soup, which I don't like as well. After dinner, I do homework and watch TV.

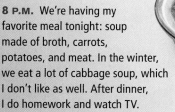

CONNECT to Your Life

Journal Entry In your journal, write a schedule detailing your typical school day. Then compare your schedule with Zuhura's. How are the two schedules similar and how are they different?

Traditions People in the Eurasian republics eat a variety of foods. Many of the dishes in Central Asia and Transcaucasia use meat and milk products. This diet is part of the heritage of the nomadic life. Traditional foods of Kyrgyzstan include lamb, noodles with broth and mutton, and vegetable soup. In Kazakhstan, the people drink *kumiss*, which is made from horse's milk. In Transcaucasia, Georgians and Armenians enjoy shish kabob. In Azerbaijan, pilaf (a rice dish) and grilled goat and lamb are popular. Pilaf is also a popular dish in Central Asia.

Traditional arts thrive in Transcaucasia and Central Asia. For hundreds of years, Armenian artisans have constructed beautiful stone churches with many domes. The craftspeople of Turkmenistan, Uzbekistan, and Azerbaijan are known for weaving decorative rugs and tapestries.

HORSEBACK SPORTS

Many of Central Asia's sports involve horses. These include *kokpar*, a type of polo, and horseback wrestling. In Kazakhstan, riders still practice the ancient art of eagle hunting, as shown above. These traditional sports reflect the importance of horses and riding in the region's culture.

 FIND MAIN IDEAS Identify some of the characteristics of life in Transcaucasia and Central Asia.

Section 2 Assessment

ONLINE QUIZ For test practice, go to **Interactive Review** @ ClassZone.com

TERMS & NAMES

1. Explain the importance of
- nomad
- Silk Roads
- Russification
- yurt

USE YOUR READING NOTES

2. Find Main Ideas Use your completed diagram to answer the following question:

Why does traditional ethnic culture play such a large role in the lives of the people of the Eurasian republics?

KEY IDEAS

3. What three groups had major impacts on the cultures of Transcaucasia and Central Asia?

4. How did the Soviet Union attempt to make its republics more Russian?

5. How do the dishes of the Eurasian republics reflect the region's nomadic heritage?

CRITICAL THINKING

6. Make Inferences Why did the Soviet Union ignore traditional boundaries when setting up its republics?

7. Compare and Contrast How do the dwellings of urban people and nomads in Central Asia compare?

8. CONNECT to Today After living under Soviet rule, why do you think the people in the Eurasian republics today value the freedom to celebrate their holidays?

9. ART Design a Rug Research rug making in Turkmenistan, Uzbekistan, and Azerbaijan. Draw a picture illustrating one of the rug designs. Then write a brief summary explaining what the design represents.

Reading for Understanding

▶ Key Ideas

BEFORE, YOU LEARNED

The Eurasian republics gained their independence after many years under the control of the Soviet Union.

NOW YOU WILL LEARN

The republics are working to overcome internal problems and establish democratic governments and market economies.

▶ Vocabulary

TERMS & NAMES

Rose Revolution a peaceful uprising in Georgia that helped force a corrupt president to resign

Nagorno-Karabakh (nuh•GAWR•noh KAHR•uh•BAHK) a province in Azerbaijan that Armenians believe should be a part of their country

foreign investment money put into a business by people from another country

one-crop economy an economy that relies on one crop for much of its earnings

REVIEW

Joseph Stalin Soviet Union dictator who was born in Georgia

command economy an economic system in which the production of goods and services is controlled by a central government

market economy an economic system in which the production of goods and services is decided by the supply and demand of consumers

privatize to sell government-owned businesses to private individuals

▶ Reading Strategy

Re-create the problem-solution chart shown at right. As you read and respond to the **KEY QUESTIONS**, use the chart to identify some of the solutions the Eurasian republics have come up with to settle their problems.

 See Skillbuilder Handbook, page R10

IDENTIFY PROBLEMS AND SOLUTIONS

PROBLEMS	SOLUTIONS
Establishing democracies	
Changing their economies	
Developing their resources	

GRAPHIC ORGANIZERS
Go to **Interactive Review** @ ClassZone.com

The Challenge of Independence

Connecting to Your World

Imagine that you are one of the founders of a new country. What challenges will you face? Well, to begin with, you will have to form a new government and economic system. Suppose you want to establish a democracy. What will you do if your people have no previous experience with democratic rule? How will you make democracy work? This is one of the challenges faced by the people of the Eurasian republics today.

Mixed Success with Democracy

▼ **KEY QUESTION** What obstacles have the Eurasian republics faced in their efforts to establish democracies?

For centuries, the peoples of Transcaucasia and Central Asia have sought independence. In the 800s, for example, Armenia established an independent kingdom that lasted for more than one hundred years. In the early 1900s, many Eurasian groups fought for independence—first from czarist Russia and then from the Soviet Union. The republics did not gain their independence until 1991, when the Soviet Union collapsed.

Elected Presidents Many of the presidents of former Soviet republics pose before their countries' flags in 2004.

Overcoming the Soviet Past The Eurasian republics had little experience with democracy. Under Soviet dictators such as **Joseph Stalin**, the Communist Party had controlled all aspects of the government. As a result, most of the politicians in the Eurasian republics were Communists. After independence, these officials often remained in office and ran the governments. In addition, Russia has continued to try to exert its influence over the Eurasian republics.

Many times, the Eurasian republics have taken on the appearance of democracies. Kyrgyzstan, for instance, adopted a parliament and allowed a free press. But in reality, the people had little voice in the government. Throughout the Eurasian republics, in fact, most people have very little political power.

Recently, however, some progress has been made. For example, in 2003, Mikhail Saakashvili (SAH•kahsh•VEE•lee) led a campaign against government corruption under Georgia's president and forced him to resign. Saakashvili himself became president. This peaceful uprising is known as the **Rose Revolution**.

Dealing with Conflicts As you know, the Soviet Union paid little attention to traditional boundaries when setting up the republics. For example, the Soviet government created a province named **Nagorno-Karabakh**, in which 76 percent of the people were Armenians, but placed it within the borders of Azerbaijan. After Armenia and Azerbaijan gained their independence, Nagorno-Karabakh remained in Azerbaijan. Fighting between Armenia and Azerbaijan over this territory soon began. A cease-fire was declared in 1994, but the dispute remains unresolved.

In Georgia, two ethnic groups—the Ossetians and the Abkhazians (ab•KAY•zhuhnz)—believe they should each have independent states. Both of these groups have fought with the Georgians over this issue, which also remains unresolved.

During the 1990s in Tajikistan, former Communist officials fought anti-Communists and Islamic groups for control of the country. This civil war killed thousands of people. Eventually, a peace agreement was reached.

▲ **IDENTIFY PROBLEMS** Identify the obstacles the Eurasian republics have faced in their efforts to establish democracies.

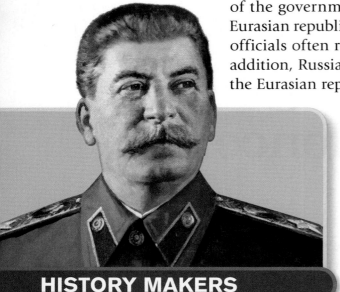

HISTORY MAKERS

Joseph Stalin 1879–1953

Joseph Stalin was born in a small town near Tbilisi, Georgia. He spent most of his childhood in this region. However, after he became dictator of the Soviet Union in 1929, he did not show a preference for Georgia. Indeed, he believed that it would be better off under Soviet rule. Stalin even enforced the same economic policy with Georgia that he put into effect in other Soviet republics. This policy required Georgia to change from a farm-based to an industry-based society.

ONLINE BIOGRAPHY
For more on the life of Joseph Stalin, go to the
Research & Writing Center @ ClassZone.com

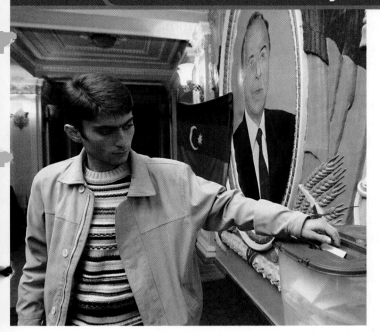

Heydar Aliyev (1923?–2003) served as president of Azerbaijan for the last ten years of his life. His son became president when he died. The image here shows an Azeri man casting his ballot in a parliamentary election under a portrait of Heydar Aliyev. In the following speech, Aliyev talks about the difficulties of establishing a democracy.

> Some people think we should be able to establish democracy in a short time, but that's impossible. Azerbaijan is a young nation and democracy is a new concept. . . . Democracy is not an apple you buy at the market and bring back home.
>
> Source: Heydar Aliyev, Speech at Georgetown University, July 30, 1997

DOCUMENT–BASED QUESTION

What does Aliyev suggest about the process of establishing a democracy?

Changing to a Market Economy

▼ **KEY QUESTION** What steps have the Eurasian republics taken toward developing their economies?

The Eurasian republics have many highly desired resources, including oil, natural gas, and coal. To take greater advantage of these resources, the Eurasian republics are attempting to develop market economies.

Controlling the Economy How does a country change from a command economy to a market economy? As you may recall, a **command economy** is one in which the government controls all businesses. In a **market economy**, private individuals own most of the businesses. To develop this type of economy, many Eurasian republics have started to **privatize** their businesses, or sell government-owned businesses to private individuals.

In addition, most of them have aggressively tried to obtain **foreign investments**. That means that they have encouraged people from other countries to put money into their businesses. Unfortunately, some republics are held back by being one-crop economies. A country with a **one-crop economy** relies on one crop for much of its earnings. The economy of Uzbekistan, for example, relies heavily on the country's production of cotton.

Energy Resources Drive the Future The people of the Eurasian republics believe that developing their resources will greatly benefit their economies. As a result, Azerbaijan has worked for several years with many countries to build a $4 billion pipeline from Baku to Turkey's Mediterranean coast. In 2006, one million barrels of oil a day began to pump through it. Georgia also benefits from the pipeline because it extends through that republic. The pipeline has brought Georgia many job opportunities and much foreign investment. In addition, Kazakhstan reached an agreement with China in 2005 that involves building an oil pipeline from the Caspian Sea eastward into China.

Tajikistan is also attempting to develop its natural resources. The republic has a great potential for water power. As a result, it is planning to build several huge dams to increase its production of electricity. If completed, these dams would be the largest in the world.

Azerbaijan Pipeline The president of Turkey has called the 1,100-mile oil pipeline "the Silk Road of the 21st century." **How will the pipeline encourage trade in the region?**

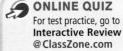 **EVALUATE** Describe the steps that the Eurasian republics have taken toward developing their economies.

ONLINE QUIZ
For test practice, go to **Interactive Review** @ ClassZone.com

Section 3 Assessment

TERMS & NAMES

1. Explain the importance of
- Rose Revolution
- Nagorno-Karabakh
- foreign investment
- one-crop economy

USE YOUR READING NOTES

2. Identify Problems and Solutions
Use your completed chart to answer the following question:

Why was the Rose Revolution a good step toward establishing a democracy in Georgia?

PROBLEMS	SOLUTIONS
Establishing democracies	
Changing their economies	
Developing their resources	

KEY IDEAS

3. How did the Nagorno-Karabakh conflict develop?

4. Why have many of the Eurasian republics pursued foreign investment?

5. How has the Azerbaijan pipeline benefited Georgia?

CRITICAL THINKING

6. Make Inferences Why might Uzbekistan's reliance on cotton production hold back its economy?

7. Form and Support Opinions Do you think there are any drawbacks to obtaining foreign investments? Explain your answer.

8. CONNECT to Today In 2006, Azerbaijan began to pump one million barrels of oil a day through its pipeline. What effect do you think this pipeline will have on Azerbaijan's economy?

9. TECHNOLOGY Create a Multimedia Presentation Show how an oil pipeline works. Include a diagram showing where it starts and where it ends, and illustrations of the machinery used.

Interactive ← Review

Click here to complete these and other activities online @ ClassZone.com

CHAPTER SUMMARY

Key Idea 1
The geography and climate of the Eurasian republics pose challenges, but the countries are rich in natural resources.

Key Idea 2
The geographic location of the Eurasian republics has attracted many different cultures, ideas, and conquerors.

Key Idea 3
The republics are working to overcome internal problems and establish democratic governments and market economies.

For **Review and Study Notes**, go to **Interactive Review @ ClassZone.com**

NAME GAME

Use the Terms & Names list to complete each sentence on paper or online.

1. I describe a country that is completely surrounded by land. **landlocked**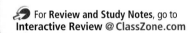

2. I contain some of the largest alpine glaciers in the world. _____

3. I have been steadily shrinking as a result of irrigation. _____

4. I make my living by moving from place to place. _____

5. I am a huge desert that covers much of Turkmenistan. _____

6. I am a peaceful uprising that took place in Georgia. _____

7. I am the process of making a culture more Russian. _____

8. I am a portable, tentlike dwelling. _____

9. I am an area that Azerbaijan and Armenia have fought over. _____

10. I am money put into businesses in other countries. _____

Aral Sea
Caucasus Mountains
foreign investment
Islam
Kara Kum
Lake Balkhash
landlocked
Muslim
Nagorno-Karabakh
nomad
Rose Revolution
Russification
Silk Roads
Tian Shan
yurt

Activities

Flip Cards

Use the online flip cards to quiz yourself on the terms and names introduced in this chapter.

Tian Shan

?

mountain range that runs across Kyrgyzstan and Tajikistan

Crossword Puzzle

Complete an online crossword puzzle to test your knowledge of the Eurasian republics.

ACROSS
1. major trading routes in Central Asia

517

VOCABULARY

Explain the significance of each of the following.

1. Transcaucasia
2. Central Asia
3. Caucasus Mountains
4. Aral Sea
5. nomad
6. Islam
7. Silk Roads
8. Russification
9. Rose Revolution
10. foreign investment

Explain how the terms and names in each group are related.

11. Transcaucasia, Central Asia, and Russification
12. Rose Revolution and Nagorno-Karabakh

KEY IDEAS

1 Center of a Landmass

13. What bodies of water border Transcaucasia?
14. How do mountains affect Georgia's precipitation?
15. What deserts lie in Turkmenistan and Uzbekistan?
16. What effect did Soviet policies have on Central Asia?

2 Historic Crossroads

17. How did the Mongol Empire affect trade in Central Asia?
18. What was exchanged on the Silk Roads?
19. How did the Soviets create resentment among ethnic groups in the Eurasian republics?
20. What are the craftspeople of Turkmenistan, Uzbekistan, and Azerbaijan known for?

3 The Challenge of Independence

21. Why did many Communists continue to run the governments in the Eurasian republics after 1991?
22. What conflicts have arisen in Georgia?
23. How have the Eurasian republics attempted to change from command economies to market economies?
24. Which countries are working to market their natural resources?

CRITICAL THINKING

25. **Analyze Causes and Effects** Create a cause-and-effect chart to identify some of the policies of the Soviet Union and their impact on the Eurasian republics.

CAUSES	EFFECTS

26. **Identify Problems** What do you think are the biggest problems facing the Eurasian republics today?
27. **Make Inferences** Why do you think the Soviet Union promoted Russification?
28. **Evaluate** What aspects of Central Asian culture reflect its nomadic heritage?
29. **Connect Geography & Economics** How have geographic factors helped and hindered the republics' economies?
30. **Five Themes: Location** How did the location of Central Asia promote trade in the region?

Answer the
ESSENTIAL QUESTION

How can the Eurasian republics meet the challenges of independence?

Written Response Write a two- or three-paragraph response to the Essential Question. Be sure to consider specific ideas about the challenges the Eurasian republics face. Use the rubric below to guide your thinking.

Response Rubric
A strong response will:
• identify the resources of the Eurasian republics
• discuss the problems confronting the republics
• explain the steps the republics have taken to modernize their governments and economies

STANDARDS-BASED ASSESSMENT

THEMATIC MAP

Use the map to answer questions 1 and 2 on your paper.

Industries in the Eurasian Republics

KAZAKHSTAN

Aral Sea

GEORGIA

Caspian Sea

ARMENIA AZERBAIJAN

UZBEKISTAN

KYRGYZSTAN

TURKMENISTAN

TAJIKISTAN

🍶	Chemicals	⚙️	Machinery
🪣	Coal	🛢️	Oil and gas
🥫	Food processing	📜	Textiles

1. Which republic contains the only coal industry in the two regions?

- **A.** Kazakhstan
- **B.** Azerbaijan
- **C.** Turkmenistan
- **D.** Uzbekistan

2. Where is most of the oil and gas produced?

- **A.** in Kazakhstan
- **B.** in Turkmenistan
- **C.** around the Caspian Sea
- **D.** around the Aral Sea

PHOTOGRAPH

Examine the photograph below showing the inside of a yurt. Use the photograph to write brief answers for questions 3 and 4 on your paper.

3. What might the carpets in this yurt be used for?

4. Why is it important that the yurt and all of its furnishings be lightweight?

GeoActivity

1. INTERDISCIPLINARY ACTIVITY–SCIENCE

With a small group, review the information you read on the Aral Sea in Section 1. Then research further to learn about the evaporation of the sea. Present your findings on a poster. Include pictures and information on the effects of the evaporation.

2. WRITING FOR SOCIAL STUDIES

Unit Writing Project Review the itinerary you created for a week-long stay in a country in this unit. Add a hike along the old Silk Roads to your travel plans. Write a journal entry about your experiences and the people you meet there.

3. MENTAL MAPPING

Create an outline map of Transcaucasia and Central Asia and label the following:

- Tian Shan
- Kara Kum
- Kyzyl Kum
- Caspian Sea
- Aral Sea
- Lake Balkhash
- Syr Darya
- Amu Darya

UNIT 6

Africa

Why It Matters:

Human life began millions of years ago in Africa. It is the second-largest continent in the world, and its resources could lead to great growth throughout the continent.

Mt. Kilimanjaro

CHAPTER 17
Africa: Physical Geography and Early History

Great Sphinx, Egypt

CHAPTER 18
Egypt and North Africa

Marketplace on the Niger River

CHAPTER 19
West Africa

Village in the Democratic Republic of Congo

CHAPTER 20
East, Central, and Southern Africa

Africa is the world's second-largest continent in terms of both landmass and population. The equator runs across the middle of the continent. The vast Sahara Desert dominates Africa's northern half. As you study the maps, notice geographic patterns and details about the region. Answer the questions on each map in your notebook.

As you study the graphs on this page, compare the landmass, population, rivers, and deserts of Africa with those of the United States. Then jot down the answers to the following questions in your notebook.

Comparing Data

1. Compare Africa's landmass to that of the United States. About how much larger is Africa than the United States?

2. Of the rivers listed, which two are closest in length?

Comparing Data

Landmass

Africa
11,618,197 sq. mi.

Continental United States
3,165,630 sq. mi.

Population

Africa
903,243,544

United States
296,410,404

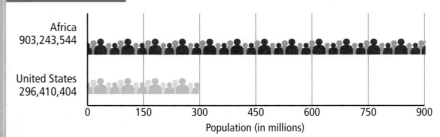

| 0 | 150 | 300 | 450 | 600 | 750 | 900 |

Population (in millions)

Rivers

Niger
2,600 mi.

Congo
2,900 mi.

Zambezi
2,200 mi.

Mississippi
2,357 mi.

Nile
4,160 mi.   World's Longest

| 0 | 1000 | 2000 | 3000 | 4000 |

Length (in miles)

Deserts

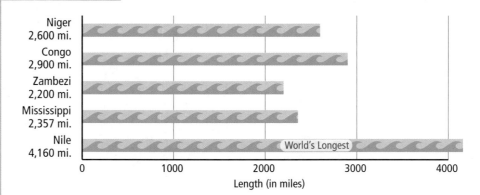

World's Largest
Sahara
Africa
3,500,000 sq. mi.

U.S. Largest
Mojave
United States
25,000 sq. mi.

Namib
Africa
102,248 sq. mi.

Kalahari
Africa
about 100,000 sq. mi.

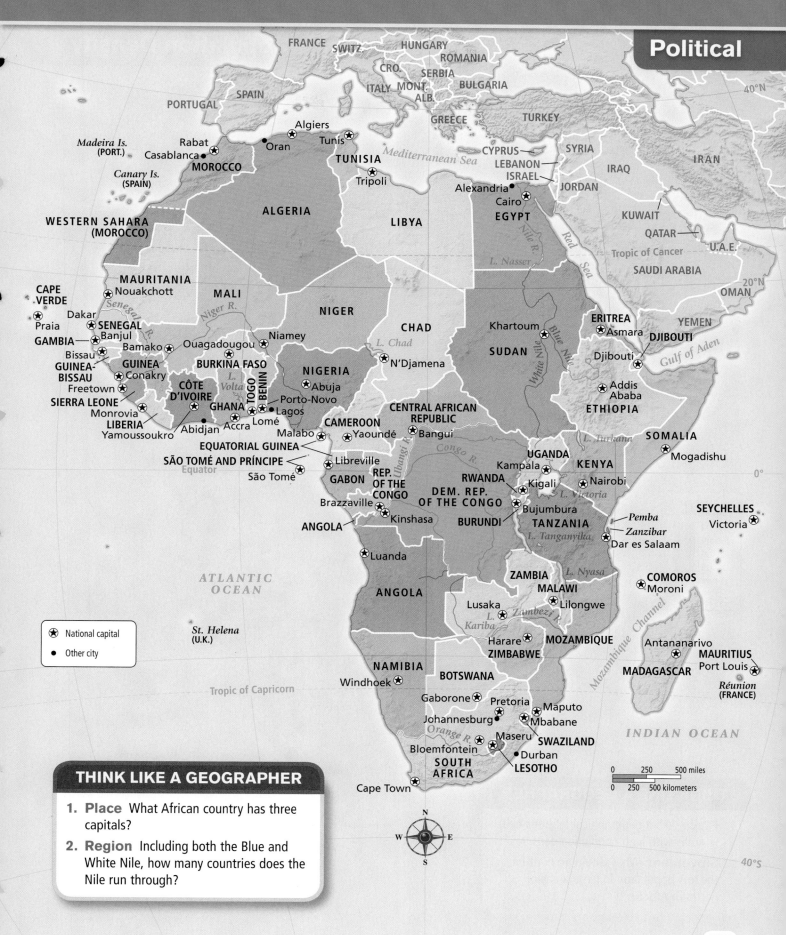

FRANCE
SWITZ.
HUNGARY
ROMANIA
CRO.
SERBIA
ITALY MONT.
ALB. BULGARIA
SPAIN
PORTUGAL
GREECE TURKEY
CYPRUS SYRIA IRAN
*Algiers LEBANON
Rabat Oran *Tunis Mediterranean Sea ISRAEL IRAQ
Madeira Is. Casablanca TUNISIA Alexandria JORDAN
(PORT.) MOROCCO Tripoli Cairo KUWAIT
Canary Is. EGYPT QATAR
(SPAIN) U.A.E.
Tropic of Cancer
WESTERN SAHARA SAUDI ARABIA OMAN
(MOROCCO) ALGERIA LIBYA 20°N
Nile R.
MAURITANIA L. Nasser YEMEN
CAPE *Nouakchott MALI Khartoum ERITREA
VERDE NIGER *Asmara DJIBOUTI
Praia Dakar Senegal R. Niger R. CHAD SUDAN Djibouti
SENEGAL Niamey L. Chad White Nile Blue Nile Gulf of Aden
GAMBIA Banjul Bamako Ouagadougou *N'Djamena Addis
Bissau BURKINA FASO NIGERIA Ababa
GUINEA- GUINEA Conakry L. TOGO Abuja CENTRAL AFRICAN ETHIOPIA
BISSAU CÔTE Volta BENIN Porto-Novo REPUBLIC L. Turkana
Freetown D'IVOIRE GHANA Lagos CAMEROON Bangui SOMALIA
SIERRA LEONE Abidjan Accra Lomé Yaoundé UGANDA Mogadishu
Monrovia Malabo Kampala KENYA
LIBERIA EQUATORIAL GUINEA Congo R. RWANDA Nairobi
Yamoussoukro Libreville Kigali L. Victoria 0°
SÃO TOMÉ AND PRÍNCIPE GABON REP. DEM. REP. BURUNDI SEYCHELLES
Equator São Tomé OF THE OF THE Bujumbura Victoria
CONGO CONGO Pemba
Brazzaville Kinshasa TANZANIA Zanzibar
ANGOLA Dar es Salaam
ATLANTIC L. Tanganyika
OCEAN Luanda
ZAMBIA L. Nyasa COMOROS
ANGOLA MALAWI Moroni
Lusaka Lilongwe
L.
Kariba Zambezi R. Antananarivo
Harare MOZAMBIQUE MAURITIUS
ZIMBABWE MADAGASCAR Port Louis
St. Helena NAMIBIA Réunion
(U.K.) BOTSWANA (FRANCE)
National capital Windhoek Pretoria Maputo
Other city Gaborone Mbabane
Johannesburg SWAZILAND INDIAN OCEAN
Orange R. Maseru
Tropic of Capricorn Bloemfontein Durban
SOUTH LESOTHO 0 250 500 miles
AFRICA 0 250 500 kilometers
Cape Town

THINK LIKE A GEOGRAPHER

1. **Place** What African country has three capitals?

2. **Region** Including both the Blue and White Nile, how many countries does the Nile run through?

N
W E
S

Population Density

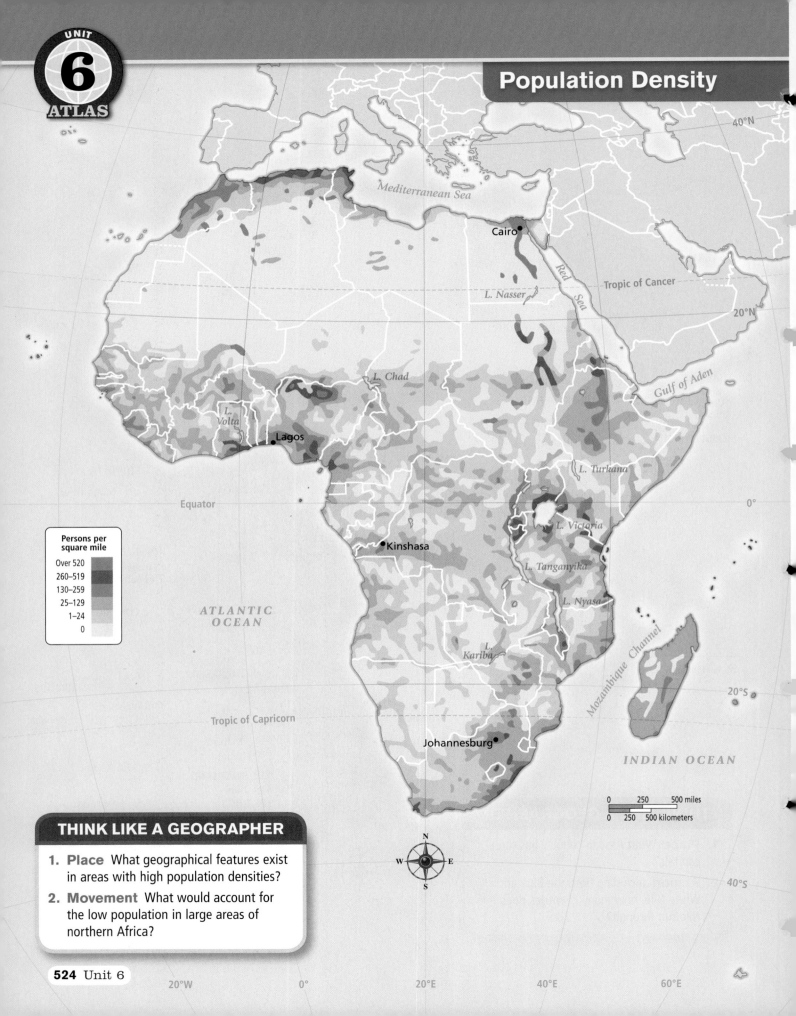

40°N

Mediterranean Sea

Cairo

L. Nasser

Tropic of Cancer

20°N

Red Sea

Gulf of Aden

L. Chad

L.
Volta

Lagos

L. Turkana

Equator

0°

Kinshasa

L. Victoria

L. Tanganyika

L. Nyasa

ATLANTIC
OCEAN

L.
Kariba

Mozambique Channel

20°S

Tropic of Capricorn

Johannesburg

INDIAN OCEAN

**Persons per
square mile**

Over 520
260–519
130–259
25–129
1–24
0

0   250   500 miles
0   250   500 kilometers

N
W   E
S

THINK LIKE A GEOGRAPHER

1. **Place** What geographical features exist in areas with high population densities?

2. **Movement** What would account for the low population in large areas of northern Africa?

20°W   0°   20°E   40°E   60°E

Economic Activity

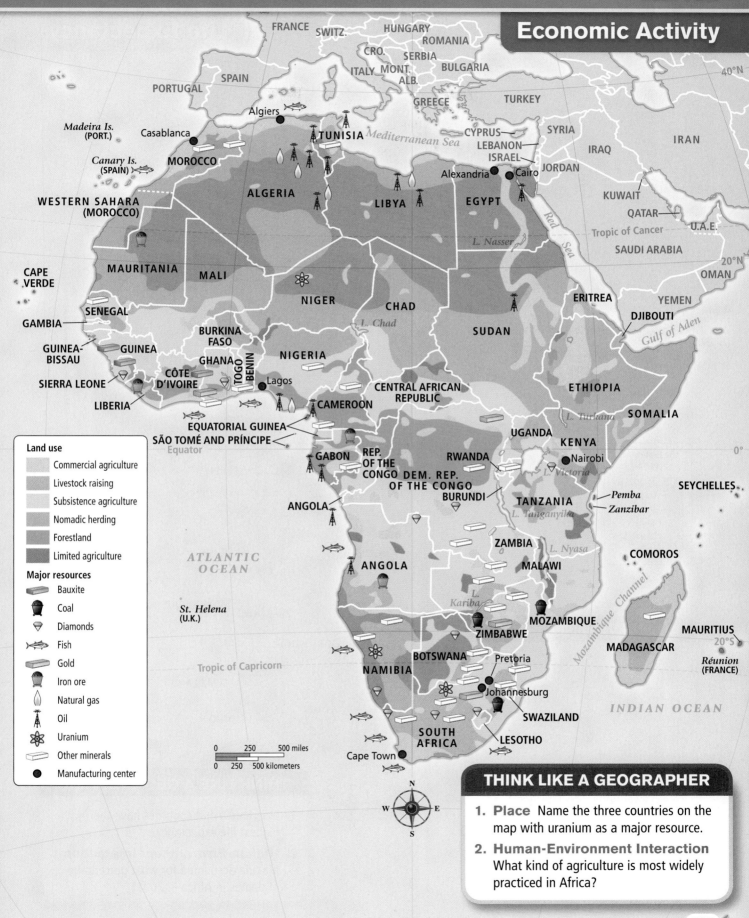

FRANCE SWITZ. HUNGARY
ROMANIA
CRO. SERBIA
ITALY MONT. BULGARIA
ALB.
SPAIN GREECE TURKEY
PORTUGAL
Madeira Is. (PORT.)
Algiers
Casablanca CYPRUS SYRIA
TUNISIA LEBANON IRAN
Mediterranean Sea ISRAEL IRAQ
Canary Is. (SPAIN) Alexandria Cairo JORDAN
MOROCCO KUWAIT
ALGERIA LIBYA EGYPT QATAR U.A.E.
WESTERN SAHARA (MOROCCO) Tropic of Cancer
L. Nasser SAUDI ARABIA OMAN
CAPE VERDE MAURITANIA MALI NIGER CHAD ERITREA YEMEN
DJIBOUTI
SENEGAL L. Chad SUDAN Gulf of Aden
GAMBIA BURKINA FASO
GUINEA-BISSAU GUINEA NIGERIA ETHIOPIA
GHANA SOMALIA
SIERRA LEONE CÔTE D'IVOIRE TOGO BENIN CENTRAL AFRICAN REPUBLIC L. Turkana
LIBERIA Lagos CAMEROON UGANDA KENYA
EQUATORIAL GUINEA Nairobi
SÃO TOMÉ AND PRÍNCIPE RWANDA
Equator GABON REP. OF THE CONGO DEM. REP. OF THE CONGO BURUNDI L. Victoria SEYCHELLES
ANGOLA TANZANIA Pemba
Zanzibar
L. Tanganyika
ATLANTIC OCEAN ANGOLA ZAMBIA L. Nyasa COMOROS
MALAWI
St. Helena (U.K.) L. Kariba MOZAMBIQUE MAURITIUS
ZIMBABWE MADAGASCAR
Tropic of Capricorn BOTSWANA Pretoria Réunion (FRANCE)
NAMIBIA Johannesburg INDIAN OCEAN
SWAZILAND
SOUTH AFRICA LESOTHO
Cape Town

Land use
- Commercial agriculture
- Livestock raising
- Subsistence agriculture
- Nomadic herding
- Forestland
- Limited agriculture

Major resources
- Bauxite
- Coal
- Diamonds
- Fish
- Gold
- Iron ore
- Natural gas
- Oil
- Uranium
- Other minerals
- ● Manufacturing center

0   250   500 miles
0   250   500 kilometers

N
W   E
S

THINK LIKE A GEOGRAPHER

1. **Place** Name the three countries on the map with uranium as a major resource.

2. **Human-Environment Interaction** What kind of agriculture is most widely practiced in Africa?

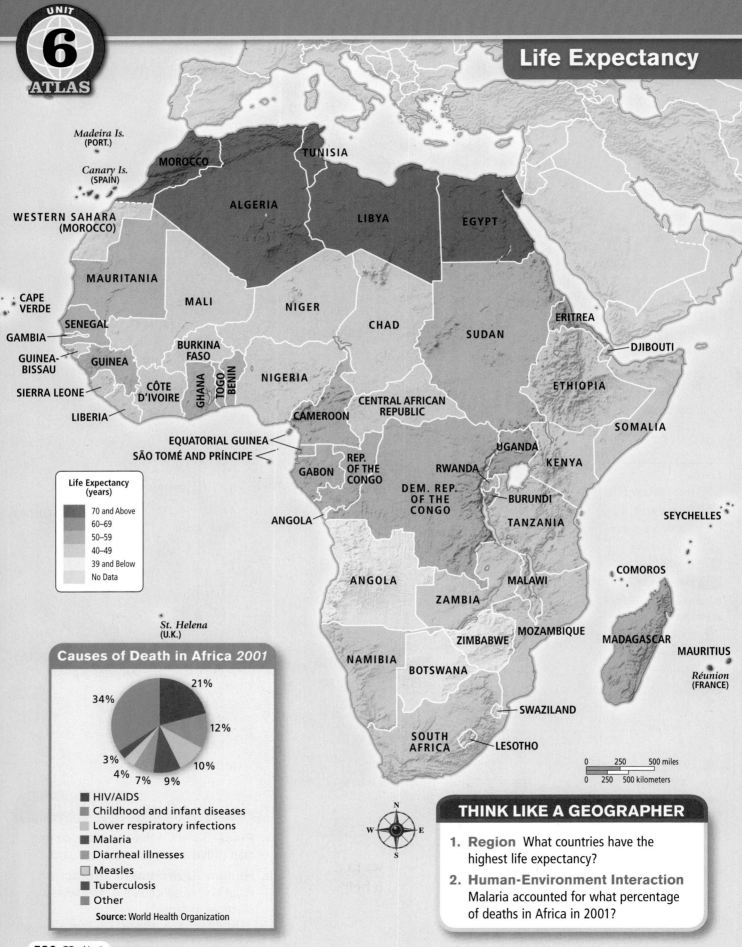

Madeira Is.
(PORT.)

MOROCCO

Canary Is.
(SPAIN)

TUNISIA

WESTERN SAHARA
(MOROCCO)

ALGERIA

LIBYA

EGYPT

MAURITANIA

CAPE
VERDE

MALI

NIGER

CHAD

SUDAN

ERITREA

SENEGAL

GAMBIA

DJIBOUTI

GUINEA-
BISSAU

GUINEA

BURKINA
FASO

ETHIOPIA

SIERRA LEONE

CÔTE
D'IVOIRE

GHANA

TOGO

BENIN

NIGERIA

CENTRAL AFRICAN
REPUBLIC

SOMALIA

LIBERIA

CAMEROON

EQUATORIAL GUINEA

SÃO TOMÉ AND PRÍNCIPE

GABON

REP.
OF THE
CONGO

UGANDA

RWANDA

KENYA

ANGOLA

DEM. REP.
OF THE
CONGO

BURUNDI

SEYCHELLES

TANZANIA

**Life Expectancy
(years)**

70 and Above
60–69
50–59
40–49
39 and Below
No Data

ANGOLA

MALAWI

ZAMBIA

COMOROS

St. Helena
(U.K.)

MOZAMBIQUE

MADAGASCAR

MAURITIUS

ZIMBABWE

Réunion
(FRANCE)

Causes of Death in Africa *2001*

NAMIBIA

BOTSWANA

21%

34%

12%

SWAZILAND

3%

10%

SOUTH
AFRICA

LESOTHO

4%

7%

9%

0   250   500 miles

0   250   500 kilometers

■ HIV/AIDS
■ Childhood and infant diseases
■ Lower respiratory infections
■ Malaria
■ Diarrheal illnesses
□ Measles
■ Tuberculosis
■ Other

Source: World Health Organization

THINK LIKE A GEOGRAPHER

1. **Region** What countries have the highest life expectancy?

2. **Human-Environment Interaction** Malaria accounted for what percentage of deaths in Africa in 2001?

Regional Overview

Africa

The four chapters in this unit provide information on the geography, history, culture, government, and economics of selected African countries.

GEOGRAPHY

Savanna covers much of Africa, with rain forests located on the equator. The vast Sahara dominates northern Africa. The world's longest river, the Nile, flows through the northeast.

HISTORY

Great empires arose in Africa, including Egypt, Aksum, and Songhai. In the 18th and 19th centuries, European nations divided up most of Africa, creating colonies to enrich their own countries. African colonies began winning independence after World War II, but colonial history still affects Africa.

Nelson Mandela Nelson Mandela won South Africa's first multiracial election.

CULTURE

Africa is home to hundreds of ethnic groups and more than 1,000 languages. Major religions in Africa include Islam, Christianity, and traditional local faiths. Soccer is popular throughout the continent. Western and African cultures have affected each other, particularly in art and music.

GOVERNMENT

When African nations won independence, many kept the European colonial borders, leading some traditional ethnic enemies to clash. Some nations with young democracies are learning to share power among different groups.

ECONOMICS

Africa has potential for great wealth. But years of instability have made it hard for some countries to improve their economies. Other nations are working to help African economies, lending aid and trying to erase debt.

Country Almanac

🖱 *Click here* to compare the most recent data on countries @ ClassZone.com

Unit Writing Project

Music Review

Research and listen to some of the music from a region mentioned in this unit. Write a review of a CD or song. Learn what you can about the artist, and styles or instruments unique to the region.

Think About:

- how African musical styles or instruments influence music you regularly listen to
- how American or European music influenced African music

Africa

The country cards on these pages present information about the 53 nations in Africa.

Algeria

GEOGRAPHY
Capital: Algiers
Total Area: 919,595 sq. mi.
Population: 32,854,000

ECONOMY
Imports: industrial equipment; food; consumer goods
Exports: petroleum; natural gas

CULTURE
Language: Arabic; Tamazight
Religion: Sunni Muslim 99%

Angola

GEOGRAPHY
Capital: Luanda
Total Area: 481,354 sq. mi.
Population: 15,941,000

ECONOMY
Imports: consumer and capital goods
Exports: petroleum; diamonds; coffee

CULTURE
Language: Portuguese
Religion: Catholic 62%; Protestant 15%; traditional beliefs 5%

Benin

GEOGRAPHY
Capital: Porto-Novo
Total Area: 43,483 sq. mi.
Population: 8,439,000

ECONOMY
Imports: food; petroleum
Exports: cotton yarn

CULTURE
Language: French
Religion: traditional beliefs 35%; Catholic 26%; Muslim 21%

Botswana

GEOGRAPHY
Capital: Gaborone
Total Area: 231,804 sq. mi.
Population: 1,765,000

ECONOMY
Imports: machinery; food; tobacco; wood
Exports: diamonds; textiles; meat

CULTURE
Language: English; Tswana
Religion: traditional beliefs 39%; African Christian 31%; Protestant 11%

Burkina Faso

GEOGRAPHY
Capital: Ouagadougou
Total Area: 105,869 sq. mi.
Population: 13,228,000

ECONOMY
Imports: petroleum; food
Exports: cotton; shea nuts; gold

CULTURE
Language: French
Religion: Muslim 49%; traditional beliefs 34%; Christian 17%

Burundi

GEOGRAPHY
Capital: Bujumbura
Total Area: 10,745 sq. mi.
Population: 7,548,000

ECONOMY
Imports: consumer and capital goods
Exports: coffee; tea

CULTURE
Language: Rundi; French
Religion: Catholic 57%; Protestant 20%; traditional beliefs 7%

Cameroon

GEOGRAPHY
Capital: Yaoundé
Total Area: 183,568 sq. mi.
Population: 16,322,000

ECONOMY
Imports: minerals; industrial equipment
Exports: petroleum; lumber; cocoa beans

CULTURE
Language: French; English
Religion: Christian 47%; traditional beliefs 24%; Muslim 21%

Cape Verde

GEOGRAPHY
Capital: Praia
Total Area: 1,557 sq. mi.
Population: 507,000

ECONOMY
Imports: food; machinery; metals
Exports: shoes; clothing; fish

CULTURE
Language: Portuguese
Religion: Catholic 91%; Muslim 3%

Yellow-billed hornbill
found in southern Africa

Central African Republic

GEOGRAPHY
Capital: Bangui
Total Area: 240,535 sq. mi.
Population: 4,038,000

ECONOMY
Imports: road vehicles; raw cotton; food
Exports: wood; diamonds; cotton; coffee

CULTURE
Language: French; Sango
Religion: Catholic 18%; Muslim 16%; Protestant 14%; other Christian 35%

Chad

GEOGRAPHY
Capital: N'Djamena
Total Area: 495,755 sq. mi.
Population: 9,749,000

ECONOMY
Imports: petroleum
Exports: cattle, sheep, and goats; cotton

CULTURE
Language: Arabic; French
Religion: Muslim 54%; Catholic 20%; Protestant 14%

Comoros

GEOGRAPHY
Capital: Moroni
Total Area: 838 sq. mi.
Population: 798,000

ECONOMY
Imports: rice; meat and fish; vehicles
Exports: vanilla; cloves; ylang-ylang

CULTURE
Language: Comorian; Arabic; French
Religion: Sunni Muslim 98%

Democratic Republic of Congo

GEOGRAPHY
Capital: Kinshasa
Total Area: 905,568 sq. mi.
Population: 57,549,000

ECONOMY
Imports: petroleum products
Exports: diamonds; cobalt; copper; gold

CULTURE
Language: French; English
Religion: Catholic 41%; Protestant 32%

Republic of Congo

GEOGRAPHY
Capital: Brazzaville
Total Area: 132,047 sq. mi.
Population: 3,999,000

ECONOMY
Imports: petroleum products
Exports: wood; sugar

CULTURE
Language: French; Lingala; Monokutuba
Religion: Catholic 49%; Protestant 17%; African Christian 13%

Côte d'Ivoire

GEOGRAPHY
Capital: Yamoussoukro
Total Area: 124,503 sq. mi.
Population: 18,154,000

ECONOMY
Imports: petroleum; food products
Exports: cocoa beans; wood; coffee beans

CULTURE
Language: French
Religion: Muslim 39%; Christian 30%; nonreligious 17%; animist 12%

Djibouti

GEOGRAPHY
Capital: Djibouti
Total Area: 8,880 sq. mi.
Population: 793,000

ECONOMY
Imports: food; transport equipment
Exports: hides and skins; leather

CULTURE
Language: Arabic; French
Religion: Sunni Muslim 97%; Christian 3%

Egypt

GEOGRAPHY
Capital: Cairo
Total Area: 386,662 sq. mi.
Population: 74,033,000

ECONOMY
Imports: machinery; food; iron and steel
Exports: petroleum; food; raw cotton

CULTURE
Language: Arabic
Religion: Muslim 84%; Christian 15%

Equatorial Guinea

GEOGRAPHY
Capital: Malabo
Total Area: 10,831 sq. mi.
Population: 504,000

ECONOMY
Imports: petroleum products; machinery
Exports: methanol; wood; cocoa beans

CULTURE
Language: Spanish; French
Religion: Catholic 80%; Muslim 4%; African Christian 4%

 Eritrea

GEOGRAPHY
Capital: Asmara
Total Area: 46,842 sq. mi.
Population: 4,401,000

ECONOMY
Imports: live animals; cereals; iron
Exports: raw sugar; vegetables and fruits; fish; sesame seeds

CULTURE
Language: Afar; Arabic; Tigre; Kunama
Religion: Christian 51%; Muslim 45%

 Ethiopia

GEOGRAPHY
Capital: Addis Ababa
Total Area: 435,186 sq. mi.
Population: 77,431,000

ECONOMY
Imports: machinery; road vehicles; iron
Exports: coffee; leather; sesame seeds

CULTURE
Language: Amharic
Religion: Ethiopian Orthodox 50%; Muslim 33%; Protestant 10%

 **Gabon**

GEOGRAPHY
Capital: Libreville
Total Area: 103,347 sq. mi.
Population: 1,384,000

ECONOMY
Imports: petroleum products
Exports: wood; manganese

CULTURE
Language: French
Religion: Catholic 57%; Protestant 18%; Muslim 3%

 The Gambia

GEOGRAPHY
Capital: Banjul
Total Area: 4,363 sq. mi.
Population: 1,517,000

ECONOMY
Imports: food; machinery; petroleum
Exports: peanuts; fruits and vegetables

CULTURE
Language: English
Religion: Muslim 95%; Christian 4%

 Ghana

GEOGRAPHY
Capital: Accra
Total Area: 92,456 sq. mi.
Population: 22,113,000

ECONOMY
Imports: petroleum; machinery; food
Exports: gold; cocoa beans; aluminum

CULTURE
Language: English
Religion: traditional beliefs 24%; Muslim 20%; Protestant 17%; African Christian 14%

 Guinea

GEOGRAPHY
Capital: Conakry
Total Area: 94,926 sq. mi.
Population: 9,402,000

ECONOMY
Imports: refined petroleum; food
Exports: bauxite; gold; diamonds; fish

CULTURE
Language: French
Religion: Muslim 85%; Christian 10%

 Guinea-Bissau

GEOGRAPHY
Capital: Bissau
Total Area: 13,946 sq. mi.
Population: 1,586,000

ECONOMY
Imports: food; transport equipment
Exports: cashews; cotton; logs

CULTURE
Language: Portuguese
Religion: traditional beliefs 45%; Muslim 40%; Christian 13%

 Kenya

GEOGRAPHY
Capital: Nairobi
Total Area: 224,962 sq. mi.
Population: 34,256,000

ECONOMY
Imports: petroleum; machinery; chemicals
Exports: horticultural products; coffee

CULTURE
Language: Swahili; English
Religion: Catholic 22%; African Christian 21%; Protestant 20%

 Lesotho

GEOGRAPHY
Capital: Maseru
Total Area: 11,720 sq. mi.
Population: 1,795,000

ECONOMY
Imports: food products; commodities
Exports: clothing; machinery

CULTURE
Language: Sotho; English
Religion: Catholic 38%; Protestant 13%; African Christian 12%

Liberia

GEOGRAPHY
Capital: Monrovia
Total Area: 43,000 sq. mi.
Population: 3,283,000

ECONOMY
Imports: food and live animals; petroleum
Exports: logs and timber; rubber

CULTURE
Language: English
Religion: traditional beliefs 63%; Muslim 16%; Protestant 14%

Libya

GEOGRAPHY
Capital: Tripoli
Total Area: 679,362 sq. mi.
Population: 5,853,000

ECONOMY
Imports: machinery; food; road vehicles
Exports: crude and refined petroleum; natural gas

CULTURE
Language: Arabic
Religion: Sunni Muslim 96%

Madagascar

GEOGRAPHY
Capital: Antananarivo
Total Area: 226,657 sq. mi.
Population: 18,606,000

ECONOMY
Imports: petroleum; machinery
Exports: textiles; vanilla; cloves; shellfish

CULTURE
Language: Malagasy; French
Religion: traditional beliefs 48%; Protestant 23%; Catholic 20%

Malawi

GEOGRAPHY
Capital: Lilongwe
Total Area: 45,745 sq. mi.
Population: 12,884,000

ECONOMY
Imports: food; machinery; chemicals
Exports: tobacco; sugar; tea; clothing

CULTURE
Language: Chichewa
Religion: Protestant 39%; Catholic 25%; Muslim 15%

Mali

GEOGRAPHY
Capital: Bamako
Total Area: 478,767 sq. mi.
Population: 13,518,000

ECONOMY
Imports: machinery; petroleum products
Exports: gold; raw cotton; live animals

CULTURE
Language: French
Religion: Muslim 82%; traditional beliefs 16%

Mauritania

GEOGRAPHY
Capital: Nouakchott
Total Area: 397,955 sq. mi.
Population: 3,069,000

ECONOMY
Imports: food products; vehicles
Exports: iron ore; fish

CULTURE
Language: Arabic; Fulani; Soninke; Wolof
Religion: Sunni Muslim 99%

Mauritius

GEOGRAPHY
Capital: Port Louis
Total Area: 788 sq. mi.
Population: 1,245,000

ECONOMY
Imports: fabrics; yarn; food; live animals
Exports: sugar; fabric; ships' stores

CULTURE
Language: English
Religion: Hindu 50%; Christian 32%; Muslim 17%

Morocco

GEOGRAPHY
Capital: Rabat
Total Area: 172,414 sq. mi.
Population: 31,478,000

ECONOMY
Imports: food; tobacco; cotton fabric
Exports: knitwear; phosphoric acid

CULTURE
Language: Arabic
Religion: Muslim 98%

Mozambique

GEOGRAPHY
Capital: Maputo
Total Area: 309,496 sq. mi.
Population: 19,792,000

ECONOMY
Imports: machinery; refined petroleum
Exports: aluminum; electricity; cotton

CULTURE
Language: Portuguese
Religion: traditional beliefs 50%; Catholic 16%; Muslim 11%

Meerkats Meerkats, like this family in South Africa, live in groups of between 3 and 25.

Namibia

GEOGRAPHY
Capital: Windhoek
Total Area: 318,696 sq. mi.
Population: 2,031,000

ECONOMY
Imports: food; machinery; metals
Exports: diamonds; metals; fish; meat

CULTURE
Language: English
Religion: Protestant 48%; Catholic 18%; African Christian 11%

Niger

GEOGRAPHY
Capital: Niamey
Total Area: 489,191 sq. mi.
Population: 13,957,000

ECONOMY
Imports: food; capital goods
Exports: uranium; cattle; onions; cowpeas

CULTURE
Language: French
Religion: Sunni Muslim 91%

Nigeria

GEOGRAPHY
Capital: Abuja
Total Area: 356,669 sq. mi.
Population: 131,530,000

ECONOMY
Imports: machinery; chemicals; food
Exports: crude petroleum

CULTURE
Language: English
Religion: Muslim 44%; independent Christian 15%; African indigenous 10%

Rwanda

GEOGRAPHY
Capital: Kigali
Total Area: 10,169 sq. mi.
Population: 9,038,000

ECONOMY
Imports: capital goods; food
Exports: niobium and tantalum; tea; coffee

CULTURE
Language: Rwanda; French; English
Religion: Catholic 51%; Protestant 29%; traditional beliefs 9%

São Tomé and Príncipe

GEOGRAPHY
Capital: São Tomé
Total Area: 386 sq. mi.
Population: 157,000

ECONOMY
Imports: investment goods; agricultural products; petroleum
Exports: cocoa beans; copra; coffee

CULTURE
Language: Portuguese
Religion: Catholic 90%

Senegal

GEOGRAPHY
Capital: Dakar
Total Area: 75,749 sq. mi.
Population: 11,658,000

ECONOMY
Imports: food and live animals
Exports: petroleum; fresh crustaceans

CULTURE
Language: French
Religion: Muslim 88%; traditional beliefs 6%; Christian 6%

Seychelles

GEOGRAPHY
Capital: Victoria
Total Area: 176 sq. mi.
Population: 81,188

ECONOMY
Imports: food; mineral fuels; machinery
Exports: canned tuna; fresh and frozen fish; petroleum

CULTURE
Language: Creole; English; French
Religion: Catholic 90%; Anglican 7%

Sierra Leone

GEOGRAPHY
Capital: Freetown
Total Area: 27,699 sq. mi.
Population: 5,525,000

ECONOMY
Imports: food and live animals; fuels
Exports: diamonds; cacao; rutile

CULTURE
Language: English
Religion: Sunni Muslim 46%; traditional beliefs 40%; Christian 11%

Somalia

GEOGRAPHY
Capital: Mogadishu
Total Area: 246,201 sq. mi.
Population: 8,228,000

ECONOMY
Imports: raw sugar; cereals
Exports: goats; sheep; bovines; camels

CULTURE
Language: Somali; Arabic
Religion: Sunni Muslim 99%

South Africa

GEOGRAPHY
Capital: Pretoria/Cape Town/Bloemfontein
Total Area: 471,011 sq. mi.
Population: 47,432,000

ECONOMY
Imports: machinery; petroleum; chemicals
Exports: diamonds; gold; iron and steel

CULTURE
Language: Afrikaans; English; Xhosa; Zulu
Religion: independent churches 39%; Protestant 32%; traditional beliefs 8%

Sudan

GEOGRAPHY
Capital: Khartoum
Total Area: 967,499 sq. mi.
Population: 36,233,000

ECONOMY
Imports: machinery; food; chemicals
Exports: petroleum; sesame seeds; gold

CULTURE
Language: Arabic; English
Religion: Sunni Muslim 70%; traditional beliefs 12%; Catholic 8%

Swaziland

GEOGRAPHY
Capital: Mbabane
Total Area: 6,704 sq. mi.
Population: 1,032,000

ECONOMY
Imports: food; machinery; chemicals
Exports: soft drink concentrates; sugar

CULTURE
Language: Swati; English
Religion: African indigenous Christian 46%; Protestant 15%

Tanzania

GEOGRAPHY
Capital: Dodoma
Total Area: 364,900 sq. mi.
Population: 36,766,356

ECONOMY
Imports: food; machinery
Exports: gold; diamonds; gemstones; cashews; coffee; tea

CULTURE
Language: Swahili; English
Religion: Christian 47%; Muslim 32%

Togo

GEOGRAPHY
Capital: Lomé
Total Area: 21,925 sq. mi.
Population: 6,145,000

ECONOMY
Imports: food; petroleum; cement
Exports: cement; phosphates; cotton

CULTURE
Language: French
Religion: traditional beliefs 38%; Catholic 24%; Muslim 19%

Tunisia

GEOGRAPHY
Capital: Tunis
Total Area: 63,170 sq. mi.
Population: 10,102,000

ECONOMY
Imports: fabric; food; machinery
Exports: clothing; knitwear; phosphates

CULTURE
Language: Arabic
Religion: Sunni Muslim 99%

Uganda

GEOGRAPHY
Capital: Kampala
Total Area: 91,136 sq. mi.
Population: 28,816,000

ECONOMY
Imports: machinery; food
Exports: fish products; tea; cereal; cotton

CULTURE
Language: English
Religion: Catholic 33%; Protestant 33%; traditional beliefs 18%; Muslim 16%

Zambia

GEOGRAPHY
Capital: Lusaka
Total Area: 290,586 sq. mi.
Population: 11,668,000

ECONOMY
Imports: machinery; printed matter; cereals
Exports: refined copper; base metals; food

CULTURE
Language: English
Religion: traditional beliefs 27%; Protestant 23%; Catholic 17%

Zimbabwe

GEOGRAPHY
Capital: Harare
Total Area: 150,804 sq. mi.
Population: 13,010,000

ECONOMY
Imports: machinery; chemicals; food
Exports: tobacco; ferroalloys; cotton lint

CULTURE
Language: English
Religion: animist 41%; Protestant 24%; African indigenous Christian 14%

Hippopotamuses Once common across the continent, hippos are now found mostly in East and Central Africa.

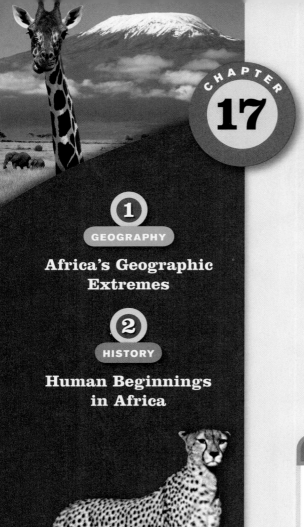

Africa
Physical Geography and Early History

1 GEOGRAPHY

Africa's Geographic Extremes

2 HISTORY

Human Beginnings in Africa

 ESSENTIAL QUESTION

How do humans interact with the extreme African environment?

CONNECT Geography & History

Use the map and the time line to answer the following questions.

1. The highest mountain in Africa is closest to what coast?

2. From what locations might it have been easiest for *Homo erectus* to migrate out of Africa?

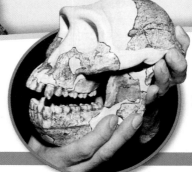

History
6–7 Million Years Ago
First hominids appear. ▶

8,000,000 B.C.

History
1.8 Million Years Ago
Homo erectus begins to migrate out of Africa.

Culture
2.5 Million Years Ago
Hominids develop first tools, beginning the Stone Age. ▶

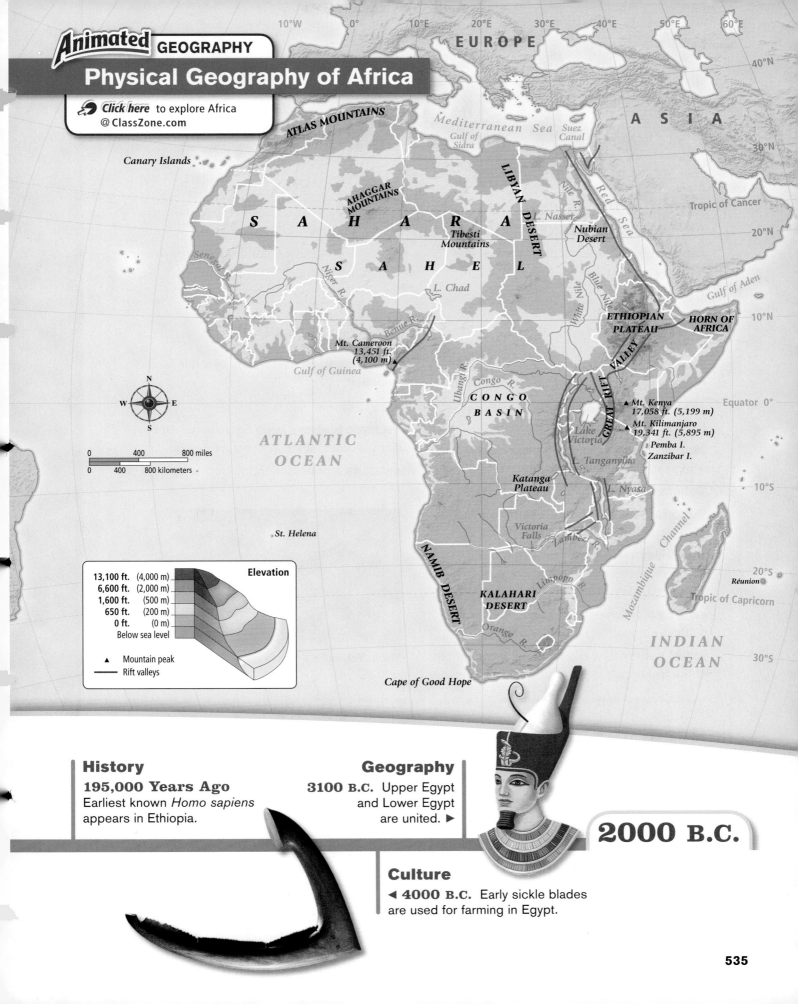

10°W 0° 10°E 20°E 30°E 40°E 50°E 60°E

EUROPE

40°N

ATLAS MOUNTAINS

A S I A

Mediterranean Sea

Suez Canal

30°N

Gulf of Sidra

Canary Islands

Tropic of Cancer

AHAGGAR MOUNTAINS

S A H A R A

LIBYAN DESERT

L. Nasser

20°N

Nubian Desert

Tibesti Mountains

Senegal R.

S A H E L

Nile R.

Red Sea

Niger R.

L. Chad

White Nile

Blue Nile

Gulf of Aden

10°N

Benue R.

ETHIOPIAN PLATEAU

HORN OF AFRICA

Mt. Cameroon
13,451 ft.
(4,100 m)▲

Ubangi R.

Congo R.

Gulf of Guinea

C O N G O B A S I N

GREAT RIFT VALLEY

▲ Mt. Kenya
17,058 ft. (5,199 m)

Equator 0°

▲ Mt. Kilimanjaro
19,341 ft. (5,895 m)

Lake Victoria

Pemba I.

Zanzibar I.

ATLANTIC OCEAN

L. Tanganyika

Katanga Plateau

L. Nyasa

10°S

St. Helena

Victoria Falls

Zambezi R.

Mozambique Channel

NAMIB DESERT

Limpopo R.

20°S

Réunion

KALAHARI DESERT

Tropic of Capricorn

Orange R.

INDIAN OCEAN

30°S

Cape of Good Hope

Elevation

13,100 ft.	(4,000 m)
6,600 ft.	(2,000 m)
1,600 ft.	(500 m)
650 ft.	(200 m)
0 ft.	(0 m)
Below sea level	

▲ Mountain peak
— Rift valleys

Scale:
0   400   800 miles
0   400   800 kilometers

History
195,000 Years Ago
Earliest known *Homo sapiens* appears in Ethiopia.

Geography
3100 B.C. Upper Egypt and Lower Egypt are united. ▶

2000 B.C.

Culture
◄ **4000 B.C.** Early sickle blades are used for farming in Egypt.

SECTION 1

Reading for Understanding

▶ Key Ideas

BEFORE, YOU LEARNED

Landforms in the Earth's tropical zones have warm climates.

NOW YOU WILL LEARN

Africa, the world's second largest continent, lies almost entirely in the tropics.

▶ Vocabulary

TERMS & NAMES

basin a region drained by a river system

escarpment a steep slope separating two flat areas of different heights

Mount Kilimanjaro the highest mountain in Africa, in northeast Tanzania (TAN•zuh•NEE•uh)

Sahara the world's largest desert

Victoria Falls a 355-foot waterfall on the Zambezi River in South Central Africa

Nile River the longest river in the world, which empties into the Mediterranean Sea in northeast Egypt

canopy the highest layer in a forest, formed by the treetops

Sahel (suh•HAYL) a semiarid region just south of the Sahara

desertification the change of fertile land to desert

REVIEW

tectonic plates a large rigid section of the Earth's crust that is in constant motion

savanna a grassland in the tropics or subtropics

Visual Vocabulary Sahara

▶ Reading Strategy

Re-create the chart shown at right. As you read and respond to the **KEY QUESTIONS**, use the chart to summarize information about the physical geography of Africa.

 Skillbuilder Handbook, page R5

SUMMARIZE

	AFRICA'S CLIMATE	AFRICA'S VEGETATION
Along Equator		
Tropical Zones		
Outside Tropics		

 GRAPHIC ORGANIZERS
Go to **Interactive Review** @ClassZone.com

Africa's Geographic Extremes

Connecting to Your World

Africa, the world's second largest continent, is a land of geographic extremes. Parts of the vast Sahara may not see a drop of rain for years. In contrast, areas in Africa's rain forest region may receive more than five feet of rain a year. On Africa's savanna, herds of zebras, gazelles, and elephants graze, hunted by lions and leopards. They are just a few of Africa's thousands of animal and plant species.

The Plateau Continent

▼ **KEY QUESTION** What are some of Africa's geographic features?

Most of Africa is a plateau, a high and flat landform. The African plateau overlooks a thin strip of coastline. Several places on the plateau contain bowl-shaped areas called **basins**. The Niger River flows through the Niger Basin, the Sudan River flows through the Sudan Basin, and the Congo River flows through the Congo Basin. In the Chad Basin in West Central Africa, water collected to form Africa's fourth largest lake, Lake Chad.

Lion Most African lions, like this one in Kenya, now live in protected wildlife reserves.

Africa's Serengeti Wildebeests and zebras graze on the Serengeti Plain in Tanzania.

KENYA

Lake
Victoria

Serengeti
Plain

TANZANIA

Distinctive Landforms Slow, dramatic forces shaped Africa. Erosion gradually molded southern Africa's **Great Escarpment**, a slope separating the high plateau of the interior from the narrow eastern coast.

Earlier you learned that **tectonic plates** move inside the earth. In eastern Africa, sections of the African Plate are slowly pulling apart. This change, called divergence, opened the Great Rift, a series of valleys running 4,000 miles down most of the continent. Long, deep lakes formed in the Great Rift, including Lake Nyasa and Lake Tanganyika. However, Lake Victoria, Africa's largest lake, lies in a shallow basin between two rift valleys. The Earth's plates pushing together produced Africa's volcanic mountains. These include Mount Kenya, Mount Cameroon, and Africa's highest mountain, **Mount Kilimanjaro**.

The **Sahara**, the world's largest desert, stretches across North Africa. Sahara is the Arabic word for "desert." Its total area is roughly equal to that of the continental United States. Other African deserts include the Kalahari and Namib, both located in southern Africa.

Congo River This satellite photo shows Kinshasa and Brazzaville, two capital cities on opposite banks of the Congo River. The city areas are the lighter areas in the photo. **What might the dark green areas represent?**

Rivers of Africa Most of Africa's rivers have rapids and waterfalls, making them hard to navigate. The Congo River winds through Central Africa. Many tributaries feed into the Congo, making the Congo river system the largest in Africa. While much of the upper Congo is navigable, 32 high waterfalls dot the river near its mouth. People who live near **Victoria Falls**, a 355-foot waterfall on southern Africa's Zambezi River, call it Mosi-oa-Tunya (MOH•see•oh•ah•TOON•yah), "the smoke that thunders," because of its roaring mist.

Congo River from Space

REP. OF THE CONGO
Brazzaville
DEM. REP. OF THE CONGO
Kinshasa
Congo R.

Brazzaville

Kinshasa

Congo River

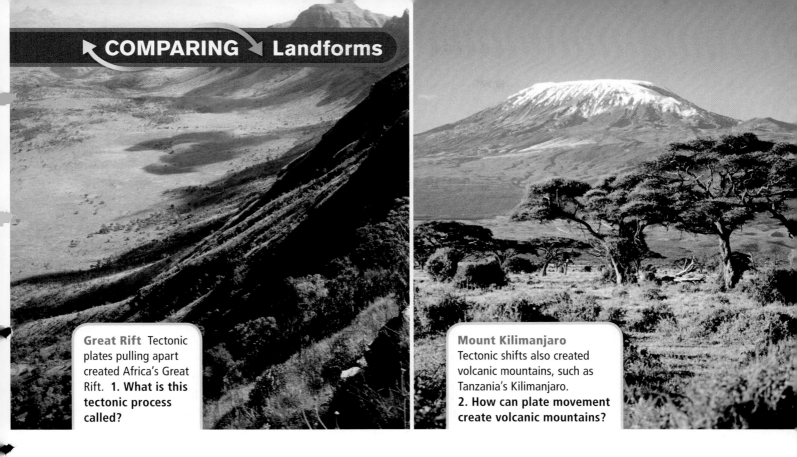

Great Rift Tectonic plates pulling apart created Africa's Great Rift. **1. What is this tectonic process called?**

Mount Kilimanjaro Tectonic shifts also created volcanic mountains, such as Tanzania's Kilimanjaro. **2. How can plate movement create volcanic mountains?**

The world's longest river, the **Nile**, flows north through northeast Africa for more than 4,000 miles. For thousands of years, people have depended on the Nile's annual floods to enrich their soil for farming. But for most of that time, no one knew where the river began. The ancient Greek geographer Ptolemy guessed the Nile's source was in a snowy area he called the "Mountains of the Moon." In the 1870s explorers found that Lake Victoria was the main source of the Nile.

▲ **SUMMARIZE** Describe the key geographic features in Africa.

Climate, Plants, and Animals

▼ **KEY QUESTION** How does Africa's location shape its climate?

The Equator divides the Earth into two hemispheres, and also runs right through Africa's midpoint. Turn the page to see climate and vegetation maps of Africa.

A Warm Continent Along the Equator, the climate is tropical wetland. Bands of tropical wet and dry climate border these wetlands. Next come strips of semiarid climate, and then deserts. In the southeast part of the continent lies a small area of humid subtropical and marine west coast climates. Areas of higher elevation have a highland climate, with rainy winters, dry summers, and typically cooler temperatures than tropical and semiarid climates.

Africa's vegetation mirrors the climate, with rain forests **A** (on the map, opposite) along the Equator. Areas of grasslands and woodlands, called **savannas** **B**, are in the wet, dry, and semiarid regions. Scattered shrubs and some grasses grow in the desert **C**. The plants most able to survive in the desert have long root systems that can reach underground water sources. Mediterranean vegetation grows along Africa's northern coast and southern tip. In those areas, native plants include shrubs, small trees, and grasses.

Animal and Plant Life Ferns and mosses make up the rain forest's ground floor, below a middle story of trees and palms. The top layer, towering to about 150 feet, is called the **canopy**. There, leaf-filled branches sprout dazzling orchids. The canopy is also home to fruit-eating parrots and pigeons, seed-eating beetles, and gorillas and chimpanzees.

Grazing animals feed on the grasses and trees of the savanna. Bordering both the savanna and the Sahara Desert is a semiarid region called the **Sahel** (suh•HAYL), from the Arabic word for "shore." But **desertification**, a process in which fertile land becomes desert, is turning the Sahel into the Sahara. The illustrations below show how human activity is speeding desertification.

▲ **DRAW CONCLUSIONS** Describe how Africa's location affects its vegetation.

CONNECT Geography & Science

Desertification Climate change expanded the Sahara in ancient times. Today, human activity is speeding up the process.

1. The Sahel receives very little rainfall. The vegetation lives in a fragile state.

2. Farming, overgrazing by livestock, and the collection of wood for fuel can erode and expose soil.

3. Vegetation gradually disappears. The remaining plants do not cover the soil as well as the grass did.

4. With less vegetation covering the fertile topsoil, the soil eventually dries up and blows away.

CRITICAL THINKING

Draw Conclusions What impact might desertification have on people living in the affected areas?

Vegetation Regions of Africa

Click here to see regions of Africa
@ ClassZone.com

Legend:
- Tropical rain forest
- Tropical grassland
- Desert and dry shrub
- Temperate grassland
- Mediterranean shrub

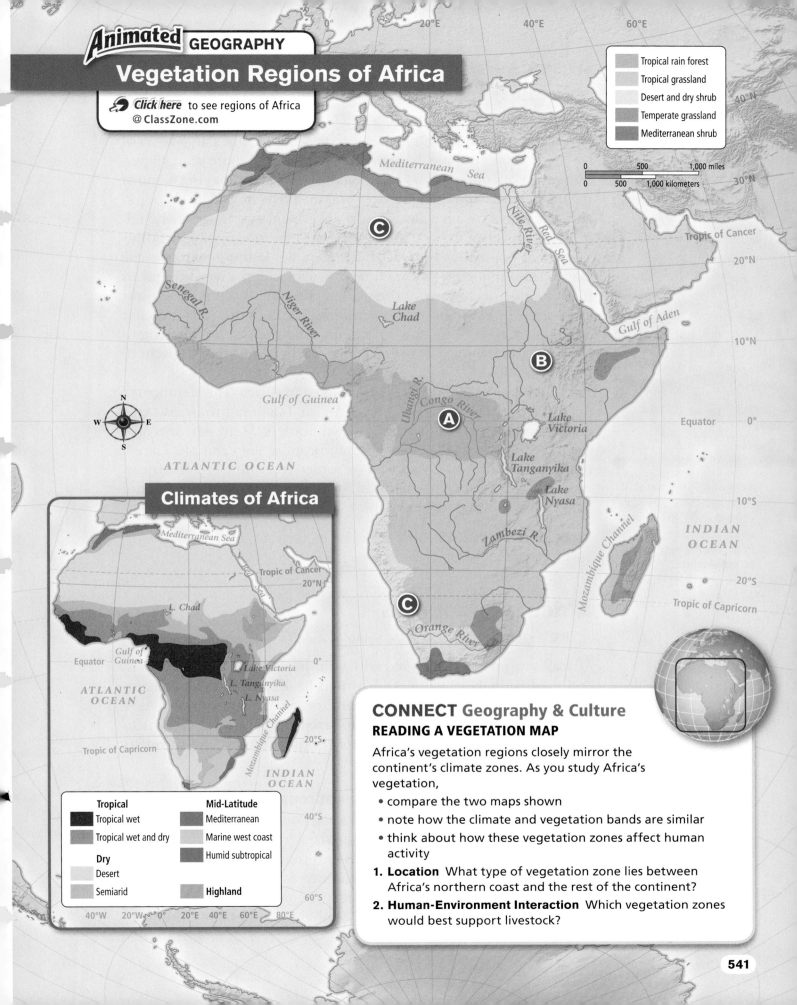

Mediterranean Sea

Senegal R.

Niger River

Lake Chad

Nile River

Red Sea

Gulf of Aden

Tropic of Cancer

Gulf of Guinea

Ubangi R.

Congo River

Lake Victoria

Lake Tanganyika

Lake Nyasa

Zambezi R.

Mozambique Channel

Equator

ATLANTIC OCEAN

INDIAN OCEAN

Orange River

Tropic of Capricorn

0   500   1,000 miles
0   500   1,000 kilometers

Climates of Africa

Mediterranean Sea

Red Sea

Tropic of Cancer

L. Chad

Equator

Gulf of Guinea

Lake Victoria

L. Tanganyika

L. Nyasa

ATLANTIC OCEAN

Mozambique Channel

INDIAN OCEAN

Tropic of Capricorn

Legend:

Tropical
- Tropical wet
- Tropical wet and dry

Dry
- Desert
- Semiarid

Mid-Latitude
- Mediterranean
- Marine west coast
- Humid subtropical

Highland

CONNECT Geography & Culture

READING A VEGETATION MAP

Africa's vegetation regions closely mirror the continent's climate zones. As you study Africa's vegetation,

- compare the two maps shown
- note how the climate and vegetation bands are similar
- think about how these vegetation zones affect human activity

1. **Location** What type of vegetation zone lies between Africa's northern coast and the rest of the continent?

2. **Human-Environment Interaction** Which vegetation zones would best support livestock?

Africa's Population

▼ **KEY QUESTION** What challenges does Africa's growing population face?

Schoolgirl in Ghana
Although school is free for children under 16 in Ghana, nearly 25 percent of children in the country have never attended school.

Population distribution in Africa varies dramatically. Large areas of the Sahara, for example, have no people at all. But more than 95 percent of Egypt's population live along the Nile Valley, making it one of the most densely populated places on Earth. The most densely populated areas in Africa are along rivers, lakes, and coastlines. Although most Africans live in rural areas, African cities are growing steadily.

Africa's population is the second-largest, but fastest-growing, in the world. This rapid growth sometimes causes problems. Most countries have few doctors to care for the sick. In addition, the United Nations estimates that about 40 million children south of the Sahara do not attend primary school. African nations and the UN are working to improve education by training more teachers and making school more affordable.

More than 1,500 languages are spoken in Africa. The Democratic Republic of the Congo, in Central Africa, has more than 200 languages and dialects just within its own borders. Many Africans also use a second language to ease communication. For example, French is a language commonly spoken in some West and Central African countries. The language remains in Africa from the years when France held colonies in the region.

▲ **FIND MAIN IDEAS** Describe some of the challenges for Africa's growing population.

Africa's Resources

▼ **KEY QUESTION** What are some of Africa's natural resources?

Africa's savannas once teemed with wildlife. But hunters and poachers killed animals for game, and farmers have turned grassland habitats into farmland. To halt this decline, many African countries have established national parks. There, protected animals live in their natural habitats, tourists can take pictures of the animals, and scientists can study their behavior.

Energy and Other Mineral Resources Oil is one of Africa's most valuable resources. Oil-producing countries include Algeria, Kenya, Libya, Egypt, Angola, and Nigeria. Africa also produces about 40 percent of the world's diamonds and more than half of its gold. South Africa has abundant gold, diamonds, and platinum. Other diamond-producing countries include Ghana and Namibia. Zambia produces copper and cobalt, while Zimbabwe mines chromium.

Are Resources Enough? Even the richest mineral resources do not guarantee economic success. For example, the oil that enriches Nigeria has also led to conflicts between ethnic groups over who profits from the resources. Oil production also brings natural gas deposits to the surface, which are often burned off. This "gas flaring" wastes an energy source and harms the environment. Oil companies are now looking for ways to better use natural gas resources. In Angola, rebel groups have mined diamonds, possibly using slave labor, and have sold them to fund civil wars. The United Nations and other groups are working to keep these "conflict diamonds" off the world market.

Drying Food These Nigerian women are using the heat from gas flares to dry food on round trays. However, the flaring releases pollutants into the air.

African countries that export farm crops usually concentrate on one or two crops, a practice put in place during Africa's colonial era. For example, Ethiopia and Uganda export coffee, while Chad exports cotton. But, as with oil wealth, relying on any single crop puts a country at risk when prices fall or resources run out. Many countries are working to make their economies more diverse.

 SUMMARIZE Identify some of Africa's key resources.

Section 1 Assessment

ONLINE QUIZ
For test practice, go to
Interactive Review
@ ClassZone.com

TERMS & NAMES

1. Explain the importance of
- basin
- savanna
- Sahel
- desertification

USE YOUR READING NOTES

2. Summarize Use your completed chart to answer the following question:

How does Africa's vegetation reflect the climate it grows in?

	AFRICA'S CLIMATE	AFRICA'S VEGETATION
Along Equator		
Tropical Zones		
Outside Tropics		

KEY IDEAS

3. The Nile is the world's longest river, but the Congo river system is Africa's longest. How is this difference possible?

4. What process formed the Great Escarpment?

5. What have been some of the problems associated with Africa's oil resources?

CRITICAL THINKING

6. Analyze Causes and Effects How have plate tectonics shaped Africa's landscape?

7. Identify Problems and Solutions Why is it risky for a country to depend on a single resource?

8. CONNECT to Today How might increasing oil consumption in the United States affect African oil-exporting countries?

9. ART Tourism Brochure Create a brochure for an African national park. Include information on the animals and habitats people will see, and explain how the park will protect those animals and habitats.

Reading for Understanding

▶ Key Ideas

BEFORE, YOU LEARNED

Africa is home to thousands of plant and animal species, and has a wealth of natural resources.

NOW YOU WILL LEARN

Human life first emerged on this warm continent.

▶ Vocabulary

TERMS & NAMES

hominid a human primate; an early human

bipedal walking on two feet

Stone Age the earliest period of human culture, in which people used stone tools

animism the belief that spirits exist in animals, plants, natural forces, and ancestors

griot (gree•OH) a West African storyteller

stateless societies groups that have no single authority, but make decisions based on compromise

lineage descent from an ancestor

REVIEW

fossil remains of early life preserved in the ground

culture the shared attitudes, knowledge, and behaviors of a group

BACKGROUND VOCABULARY

ancestor an early relative

domesticate to adapt or train plants or animals for human use

patrilineal descent from father to father

▶ Reading Strategy

Re-create the web diagram shown at right. As you read and respond to the **KEY QUESTIONS**, use the diagram to record the main ideas about African societies.

 Skillbuilder Handbook, page R4

FIND MAIN IDEAS

Values
1._____
2._____

AFRICAN SOCIETIES

Stateless Societies
1._____
2._____

Lineage
1._____
2._____

🔄 **GRAPHIC ORGANIZERS**
Go to **Interactive Review** @ ClassZone.com

Human Beginnings in Africa

Connecting to Your World

Have you ever made an exciting discovery? Perhaps you found a treasure on the street or learned something that made you decide to become a drummer, dancer, hockey player, or scientist.

If you're really lucky, you may make a find that changes the way people think. Anthropologist Donald Johanson had that kind of luck in Ethiopia in 1974 when he and his assistants took a new route back to their vehicle. They stumbled on the bones of a **fossil**, which they named Lucy after a popular song. Lucy was an early human, called a **hominid**. She lived about 3.2 million years ago.

Lucy This early human is the most-studied fossil to date.

Human Ancestors

▼ **KEY QUESTION** What were some of the important hominid finds in Africa?

Lucy, an adult female, probably stood about three and a half feet tall and weighed a little over 60 pounds. She and other hominids were **bipedal**, meaning they walked on two feet. If early hominids used tools, the tools have since disappeared. The first tools that scientists have found—stones to cut meat—date back a mere 2.5 million years.

Animated GEOGRAPHY

Archaeological Dig in East Africa
Scientists continue to look to Africa for clues about early human development.

Click here to see fossils found in East Africa @ ClassZone.com

Chad Skull A reconstruction of the 6.5-million-year-old skull found in Chad in 2001

Important Discoveries Older hominids have been found since Lucy's discovery. Scientists unearthed a six- to seven-million-year-old skull in Chad in 2001. It resembles both a human skull and an ape skull. Scientists wonder whether this and other finds could be early human **ancestors**. Other important discoveries include:

Australopithecines (aw•STRAY•loh•PIHTH•uh•seenz) Like Lucy, these hominids first walked upright in eastern, southern, and central Africa about 4 million years ago.

Homo habilis (HOH•moh–HAB•uh•luhs) Tool-using hominids appeared between 1.5 and 2 million years ago in Africa. In 1960, Mary and Louis Leakey found the skull of a creature they named *Homo habilis*, or "handy man," near chipped pebble tools.

Homo erectus (HOH•moh–ih•REHK•tus) In 1984, scientists found the skeleton of "Turkana Boy" in Kenya. This pre-teen lived about 1.6 million years ago. *Homo erectus* fossils have also been discovered in Asia. They were the first hominids to leave Africa.

Homo sapiens (HOH•moh–SAY•pee•EHNZ) People identical to modern humans first appeared about 150,000 years ago.

Stone Age The **Stone Age**, during which hominids first began using stone tools, began 2.5 million years ago. During this important period, people also learned how to control fire and use language.

 SUMMARIZE Describe the key hominid finds in Africa.

ONLINE PRIMARY SOURCE To read accounts of important discoveries, go to the **Research & Writing Center** @ClassZone.com

ANALYZING Primary Sources

Oldest human footprints Mary Leakey and the footprints she discovered in 1978

Mary Leakey (1913–1996), as a young girl, was determined to study the Stone Age. Her most famous discovery was a set of hominid footprints, preserved in dried lava in Tanzania. In a 1978 letter, she wrote:

> We have found magnificent hominid footprints this year, in a dual trail 23 metres [75 feet] long! (confidential) It is a most important find and demonstrates that 3½ m.y. [million years] ago the fully bipedal, striding gait had been completely developed.
>
> Mary Leakey, letter to paleontologist Dick Hooijer

DOCUMENT–BASED QUESTION:
Why were these footprints so important?

The Stone Age in Africa is divided into two periods. The Paleolithic period lasted from 2.5 million years ago to 8000 B.C. During this period, hominids hunted and gathered food. Early humans also chopped meat with sharpened stone tools. Later, they tamed fire, used harpoons and needles, and developed language. The Neolithic period lasted from 8000 B.C. to 3500 B.C. People living at this time polished stone tools and made pottery. They began to grow crops, **domesticate** animals, and live in villages. Around 3500 B.C. they developed writing.

Hand axes These stone tools from the Paleolithic period were found in Tanzania.

Create a Time Line

Materials
- paper
- pencil
- ruler

| Hunter/Gatherers | Stone Tools | Language | | Grow Crops | Domesticate Animals | Develop Writing |

PALEOLITHIC   NEOLITHIC

2.5 million years ago   8000 B.C.   3500 B.C.

1. Reread this chapter and add the dates for the sequence of hominid discoveries in Africa.

2. Look for specific dates in the text. Make sure to match the correct events and dates.

Characteristics of African Societies

▼ **KEY QUESTION** What is the nature of an extended family in African society?

In the previous section, you learned that hundreds of separate languages may be spoken in a single African country. Still, many African **cultures** share certain traits.

Beliefs and Values A typical African family probably wouldn't fit around your dinner table. The extended family of Africa consists of as many as five generations of relatives and spouses who all obey a single leader. This large family works together, protects its members from outsiders, and cares for its weakest members.

Today many Africans are Muslims or Christians. But Africans may also practice traditional religions. Traditional African religions maintain that an all-powerful God created everything. They also believe that spirits exist in animals, plants, natural forces, and ancestors, an idea called **animism**.

One generation of Africans passes information to the next by telling stories. West Africans call their storytellers **griots** (gree•OHZ). You need a good memory to be a griot because some of the best stories about ancestors and other heroes go on for hours or even days. Griots usually accompany their stories with music. Today many popular griots perform on television and record their stories on CDs.

Elders in African Societies
Elders often fill teaching roles, like this Masai elder in Kenya.

Stateless Societies Traditional African cultures didn't organize themselves into states, with one person at the top. Instead they formed stateless societies. In a **stateless society**, two or more equal groups would cooperate.

The extended families that made up these groups were based on lineage. **Lineage** means descent from one parent back several generations to a single ancestor. For example, your own **patrilineal** descent goes back from your father, to his father, and so on.

In traditional African stateless societies, lineages with equal power would share authority. If members clashed, elders from the warring lineage groups would meet to make peace.

To create relationships with people in other lineages, a stateless society uses a system of age sets. Your age set would be the boys or girls born around the same time as you. If you were a boy in the Nandi tribe of Kenya, for example, you would go through military training with your age set. The warrior set, responsible for fighting and governing the tribe, would stay in power for about 15 years. Then it would become a set of elders, and the next younger age set would move up.

 FIND MAIN IDEAS Describe the structure of an African extended family.

ONLINE QUIZ
For test practice, go to
Interactive Review
@ ClassZone.com

Section 2 Assessment

TERMS & NAMES

1. Explain the importance of
- hominid
- animism
- stateless societies
- lineage

USE YOUR READING NOTES

2. Find Main Ideas Use your completed diagram to answer the following question:

What are the roles of elders in traditional African societies?

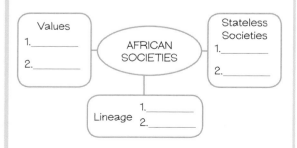

Values
1._____
2._____

AFRICAN SOCIETIES

Stateless Societies
1._____
2._____

Lineage
1._____
2._____

KEY IDEAS

3. Who is Lucy, and how old is she?

4. Which was the first human to leave Africa?

5. How would warring lineage groups make peace?

CRITICAL THINKING

6. Summarize What major human advances took place during the Stone Age?

7. Compare and Contrast What similarities do African cultures share?

8. CONNECT to Today What systems of age sets exist in the United States?

9. MATH Draw a Scale Time Line Find a way to demonstrate how long ago Lucy lived. You might start by making a scale with 100 years equal to 1 inch. How many inches, feet, or yards would it take to show 1,000 or 1 million years? How about 3.5 million years?

CHAPTER SUMMARY

Key Idea 1
Africa, the world's second largest continent, lies almost entirely in the tropics.

Key Idea 2
Human life first emerged on this warm continent.

For **Review and Study Notes**, go to **Interactive Review** @ ClassZone.com

NAME GAME

Use the Terms & Names list to complete each sentence on paper or online.

1. I am the longest river in the world. _____
   _____ **Nile River** 🖱 _____

2. I am a process that changes grasslands and semi-arid regions into deserts. _____

3. I am a landform some Africans call Mosi-oa-Tunya, "the smoke that thunders."
   _____

4. I am the top layer of the rain forest.
   _____

5. I am Africa's grasslands, where antelopes, giraffes, and elephants graze. _____

6. We are the slowly shifting blocks that make up the Earth's surface layer. _____

7. I can tell stories that last for many hours or even days. _____

8. I am the belief that trees, animals, and ancestors have living spirits. _____

9. We do not have a single leader, but resolve problems by having our elders meet and talk until they agree. _____

10. I am the earliest period of human history.
    _____

animism

canopy

desertification

griot

hominid

Mount Kilimanjaro

Nile River

Sahel

savanna

stateless societies

Stone Age

tectonic plates

Victoria Falls

Activities

Flip Cards

Use the online flip cards to quiz yourself on the terms and names introduced in this chapter.

Hominid

? an early human ancestor

Crossword Puzzle

Complete an online crossword puzzle to test your knowledge of Africa's geography and early history.

ACROSS
1. the world's largest desert

VOCABULARY

Explain the significance of each of the following.

1. Mount Kilimanjaro
2. Nile River
3. savanna
4. Sahel
5. desertification
6. hominid
7. bipedal
8. animism
9. stateless societies
10. lineage

Explain how the terms and names in each group are related.

11. Sahel, desertification, savanna
12. stateless societies, culture, lineage

KEY IDEAS

1 **Africa's Geographic Extremes**

13. What geographic process formed Africa's Great Rift Valley?
14. What makes many African rivers hard to navigate?
15. How do many Africans communicate with people who don't speak their language?
16. What minerals make South Africa a wealthy country?

2 **Human Beginnings in Africa**

17. Why was Lucy such an important discovery?
18. What does a griot do?
19. How are African extended families structured?
20. How do stateless societies create relationships between people of different lineages?

Goliath Beetle

CRITICAL THINKING

21. **Analyze Causes and Effects** Create a table to show some of the effects of human settlement on rain forests and grasslands.

CAUSES	EFFECTS
cut down rain forests for farmland	
cut trees for firewood and use grass for grazing	

22. **Summarize** What events led to the formation of game parks in Africa?
23. **Compare and Contrast** How are traditional African religions similar to and different from Christianity and Islam?
24. **Five Themes: Movement** How might family members moving to a city affect a traditional extended family structure?
25. **Connect Geography & Science** Why can't scientists say for sure whether *Australopithecines* like Lucy used tools?

Answer the ESSENTIAL QUESTION

How do humans interact with the extreme African environment?

Written Response Write a two- or three-paragraph response to the Essential Question. Be sure to consider the key ideas of each section. Use the rubric below to guide your thinking.

Response Rubric
A strong response will:
- describe Africa's landforms, climate, and vegetation
- explain how climate and terrain have influenced African population density
- identify the resources available in Africa

STANDARDS-BASED ASSESSMENT

Test Practice

- Online Test Practice @ ClassZone.com
- Test-Taking Strategies and Practice
  at the front of this book

LINE GRAPH

Use the line graph and your knowledge of Africa to answer questions 1 and 2.

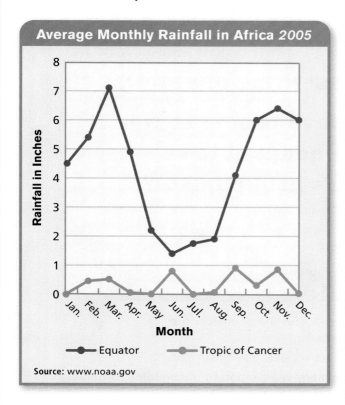

Average Monthly Rainfall in Africa 2005

Source: www.noaa.gov

1. When is the "dry season" along the Equator?

A. September through December
B. January through March
C. March through May
D. June through August

2. In what month did the most rain fall along the Tropic of Cancer?

A. March
B. June
C. September
D. November

ELEVATION PROFILE

Use the elevation profile at the Equator to answer questions 3 and 4 on your own paper.

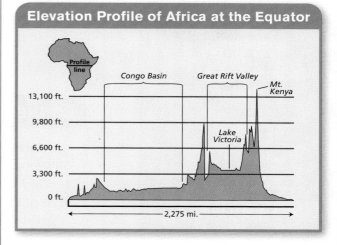

Elevation Profile of Africa at the Equator

3. At what elevation is Mount Kenya?

4. Based on this elevation profile, why might Africa be called the "plateau continent"?

GeoActivity

1. INTERDISCIPLINARY ACTIVITY–SCIENCE

With a small group, choose one of Africa's native animals to research. Find out where the animal lives, what it eats, whether it has predators, and if its habitat has been threatened by hunting or farming. Present your findings to the class.

2. WRITING FOR SOCIAL STUDIES

Reread the description of griots in Section 2. Write a story, poem, or rap about one of your ancestors or an American folk hero. Memorize your story and present it to your class without using notes.

3. MENTAL MAPPING

Create an outline map of Africa and label the following:

- Lake Victoria
- Lake Chad
- Nile River
- Great Rift
- Great Escarpment
- Sahara Desert
- Sahel

Africa: Physical Geography and Early History **551**

Egypt and North Africa

①
HISTORY

Ancient Egypt: Pyramids and Pharaohs

②
FOCUS ON

Modern Egypt and Sudan

③
FOCUS ON

Other Nations of North Africa

ESSENTIAL QUESTION

How have people in North Africa adapted to the region's arid climate?

CONNECT ◆ **Geography & History**

Use the map and time line to answer the following questions.

1. Which country receives the most rainfall?
2. About how many years separate the building of the Great Pyramid and Suez Canal?

3100 B.C.

Culture
◀ **2600 B.C.–2500 B.C.**
Great Pyramid built

History
3100 B.C. Upper and Lower Egypt united

History
1516 Selim I rules the Ottoman Empire at the time of Egypt's conquest. ▶

History
A.D. 642 Muslim invaders spread Islam to North Africa.

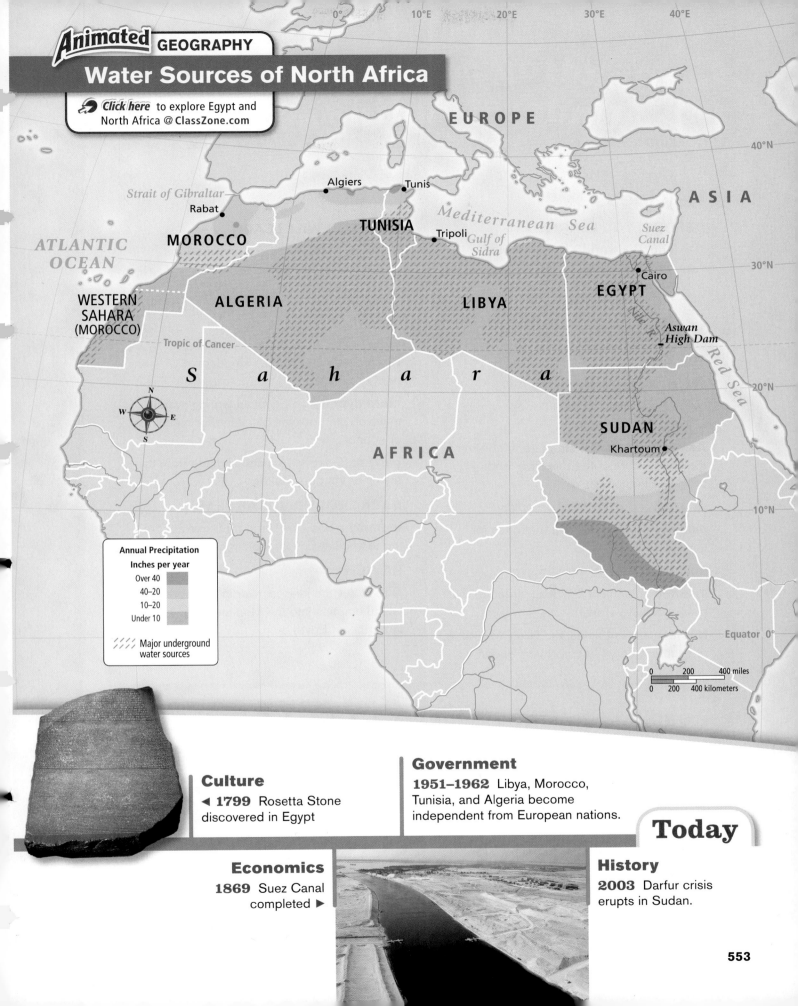

EUROPE

ASIA

Mediterranean Sea

Strait of Gibraltar

Algiers
Tunis
Rabat
TUNISIA
Tripoli
Gulf of Sidra
Suez Canal

MOROCCO

ATLANTIC OCEAN

ALGERIA
LIBYA
EGYPT
Cairo

WESTERN SAHARA (MOROCCO)

Tropic of Cancer

Aswan High Dam

Nile

Red Sea

S a h a r a

N
W   E
S

SUDAN
Khartoum

AFRICA

Equator 0°

40°N
30°N
20°N
10°N

0° 10°E 20°E 30°E 40°E

Annual Precipitation

Inches per year

Over 40
40–20
10–20
Under 10

/// Major underground water sources

0   200   400 miles
0   200   400 kilometers

Culture

◀ **1799** Rosetta Stone discovered in Egypt

Government

1951–1962 Libya, Morocco, Tunisia, and Algeria become independent from European nations.

Today

Economics

1869 Suez Canal completed ▶

History

2003 Darfur crisis erupts in Sudan.

553

Reading for Understanding

▶ Key Ideas

BEFORE, YOU LEARNED

The Nile, the world's longest river, runs through Egypt.

NOW YOU WILL LEARN

The Nile made the great civilizations of ancient Egypt possible.

▶ Vocabulary

TERMS & NAMES

silt fertile soil deposited by a river

delta the triangle-shaped deposit of rich soil at a river's mouth

Aswan High Dam a structure to control the floodwaters of the Nile River and provide electricity

cataract a high waterfall or rapids

dynasty a family or group that rules for several generations

pharaoh a ruler of ancient Egypt

pyramid an ancient Egyptian structure, built over or around a tomb

Nubia in ancient times, the Nile River valley of southern Egypt and northern Sudan

Kush an ancient Nubian kingdom in northern Sudan

hieroglyphics an Egyptian writing system in which picture symbols stand for meanings or sounds

papyrus a paperlike material made from the stems of the papyrus reed

BACKGROUND VOCABULARY

mummy a body prepared for burial according to ancient Egyptian practice

REVIEW

Nile River the longest river in the world, which empties into the Mediterranean Sea in northeast Egypt

▶ Reading Strategy

Re-create the chart shown at right. As you read and respond to the **KEY QUESTIONS**, use the chart to analyze causes and effects related to the Nile River's annual floods.

 See Skillbuilder Handbook, page R8

ANALYZE CAUSE AND EFFECT

CAUSE	EFFECT
1.	1.
2.	2.
3.	3.

 GRAPHIC ORGANIZERS
Go to **Interactive Review** @ClassZone.com

Ancient Egypt: Pyramids and Pharaohs

Connecting to Your World

In 1993, the Mississippi River overflowed after heavy rains. Levees broke, submerging farms, towns, and roads under the muddy water. About 50 people died, and thousands more had to leave their homes. The Mississippi River flood of 1993 was a disaster. But in ancient Egypt, annual river floods were seen as a good thing.

Egypt's Lifeline

▼ **KEY QUESTION** Why is the Nile called Egypt's lifeline?

Egypt, in Africa's northeast corner, receives little rainfall. As a result, the country has relied on the **Nile River** for its economy. Each year, the Nile flooded due to upstream rain, depositing rich black soil called **silt** along its banks. The silt at the river's mouth formed a triangular shape, called a **delta**. Most of Egypt's population clustered in the Nile's river valley and delta. The Nile's yearly floods made these regions so fertile that ancient Egyptians called their country Kemet, or the Black Land.

Animated GEOGRAPHY
The Nile Valley
The world's longest river creates a ribbon of fertile soil, cutting through the desert.

Click here to take a journey down the ancient Nile @ ClassZone.com

Desert

Fertile soil irrigated by the Nile

Nile River

Aswan High Dam

The Aswan High Dam contains the Nile floodwaters in a reservoir called Lake Nasser. In addition to increasing irrigated land, the dam provides electricity for factories and farm villages. But with little silt reaching the Nile's mouth and flood plain, farmers must now use costly chemical fertilizers, and the Nile delta is actually decreasing in size.

Aswan High Dam

Lake Nasser

The Nile Then and Now In ancient Egypt, the Nile Valley provided various grasses and reeds used for huts, sandals, baskets, simple boats, and other products. Ancient Egyptians also dug canals to irrigate their fields and channel the Nile's water. Each June, floods would leave behind silt in a narrow strip along the flood plain and at the delta. Today the **Aswan High Dam** controls the Nile's flooding and provides year-round irrigation. Since the Aswan High Dam opened in 1970, Egypt has doubled its agricultural production.

△ **FIND MAIN IDEAS** Describe how the Nile has acted as Egypt's lifeline.

History of Ancient Egypt

▽ **KEY QUESTION** What other civilizations competed with ancient Egypt for power?

Ancient Egypt, one of the world's first great civilizations, arose along the banks of the Nile. For centuries, geography kept Egypt isolated. Six **cataracts**, or high waterfalls and rapids, make the Nile hard to navigate in the south. Deserts surround the Nile in the west and east, and the Mediterranean Sea borders Egypt to the north. People created farming villages along the Nile by about 4000 B.C. Eventually these villages became two kingdoms, Upper Egypt in the south and Lower Egypt at the Nile delta.

Uniting Upper and Lower Egypt Tradition says that around 3100 B.C., King Menes of Upper Egypt conquered Lower Egypt, uniting the two kingdoms. Modern historians believe King Menes may have been a legend, and that it probably took several rulers to join the kingdoms. King Menes is said to have founded the first Egyptian **dynasty**, or series of rulers from one family. These rulers came to be known as **pharaohs**, from the Egyptian words for "great house."

Old, Middle, and New Kingdoms Historians divide ancient Egyptian history into three periods. During the Old Kingdom, a strong central government supervised the construction of gigantic tombs called **pyramids**. Farmers and laborers built these structures when the Nile's floodwaters covered their fields. During the Middle Kingdom, Egypt conquered its southern neighbor, **Nubia**. Nubia provided Egypt with slaves, soldiers, and gold. Instead of pyramids, Middle Kingdom pharaohs built tombs in the desert sands. During the New Kingdom, Egypt became the strongest power in the world. A powerful pharaoh named Queen Hatshepsut led armies, sent off trade expeditions, and built splendid temples. Egypt's power peaked under the 66-year reign of Ramses II. He regained Asian territories that earlier pharaohs had lost. Statues of Ramses II still stand all over Egypt.

Conquest by Foreigners After Ramses' death in 1213 B.C., Egypt began to decline. Eventually, it fell to foreign invaders, including the **Kush** kingdom of Nubia. After an Assyrian invasion ended Kushite rule of Egypt, the Kush civilization withdrew south. In 332 B.C., Alexander the Great of Macedonia conquered Egypt. After Alexander's death, one of his generals, Ptolemy (TAHL•uh•mee), became king of Egypt, starting a dynasty that lasted nearly 300 years. One of the last Ptolemies, Queen Cleopatra, married the co-ruler of Rome, Mark Antony. Antony and Cleopatra's attempt to seize power from Antony's co-ruler failed in 31 B.C. The next year, Egypt became a Roman territory.

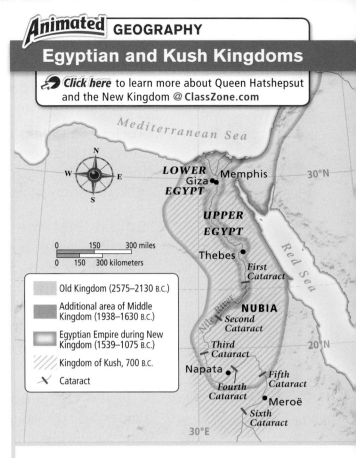

Animated GEOGRAPHY

Egyptian and Kush Kingdoms

Click here to learn more about Queen Hatshepsut and the New Kingdom @ ClassZone.com

Mediterranean Sea

N W E S

LOWER EGYPT
Giza • Memphis
30°N

UPPER EGYPT
Thebes •
First Cataract

Red Sea

0   150   300 miles
0   150   300 kilometers

Old Kingdom (2575–2130 B.C.)

Additional area of Middle Kingdom (1938–1630 B.C.)

Egyptian Empire during New Kingdom (1539–1075 B.C.)

Kingdom of Kush, 700 B.C.

Cataract

NUBIA
Nile River
Second Cataract

Third Cataract
20°N

Napata •
Fourth Cataract
Fifth Cataract

Meroë
Sixth Cataract
30°E

CONNECT Geography & History

Movement Which kingdom extended farthest north?

▲ **SUMMARIZE** List the civilizations that interacted with ancient Egypt.

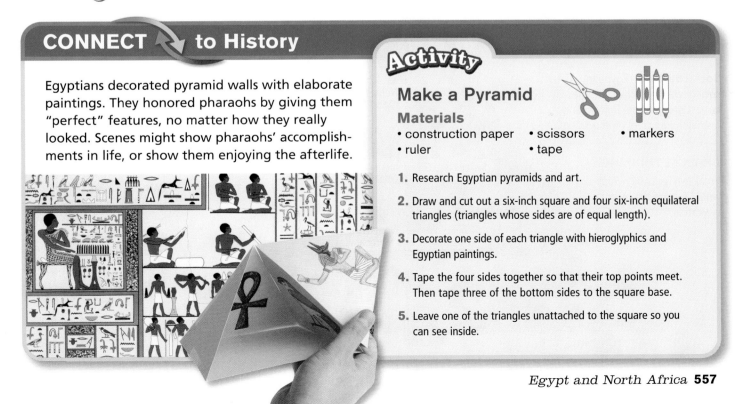

CONNECT to History

Egyptians decorated pyramid walls with elaborate paintings. They honored pharaohs by giving them "perfect" features, no matter how they really looked. Scenes might show pharaohs' accomplishments in life, or show them enjoying the afterlife.

Activity

Make a Pyramid

Materials
• construction paper   • scissors   • markers
• ruler   • tape

1. Research Egyptian pyramids and art.

2. Draw and cut out a six-inch square and four six-inch equilateral triangles (triangles whose sides are of equal length).

3. Decorate one side of each triangle with hieroglyphics and Egyptian paintings.

4. Tape the four sides together so that their top points meet. Then tape three of the bottom sides to the square base.

5. Leave one of the triangles unattached to the square so you can see inside.

Culture of Ancient Egypt

▼ **KEY QUESTION** What were some of the accomplishments of ancient Egyptian culture?

Ancient Egyptians built great cities, where architects, doctors, artisans, and engineers worked. They also invented a form of paper. But their most lasting achievement is probably the pyramids. These giant structures served as both monuments and tombs for the pharaohs.

Social Systems Ancient Egyptian social classes formed a kind of pyramid, as shown below. At the top was the pharoah, then a small upper class. Skilled or educated workers made up the middle classes. The largest groups, farmers, laborers and slaves, were at the pyramid's base.

Most boys followed their fathers' occupations, and girls usually became wives and mothers. Women could own, buy, sell, and inherit property, and divorce their husbands.

Egypt's Gods and the Afterlife Egyptians worshiped several deities, and considered their pharaohs to be earthly versions of them. One New Kingdom pharaoh, Akhenaton, promoted the worship of only one deity, the sun god Aton. When Akhenaton died, the new king, Tutankhamen, brought back worship of the old gods.

Tutankhamen "King Tut" was nine years old when he became pharaoh, and he ruled with the help of advisors.

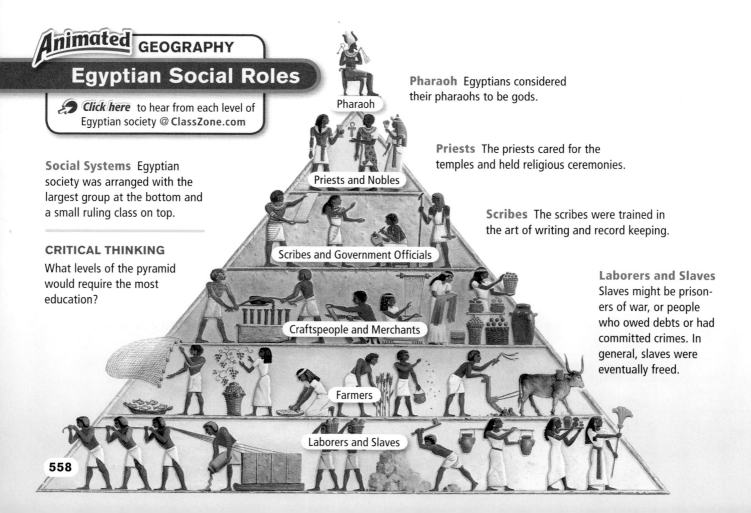

Animated GEOGRAPHY

Egyptian Social Roles

Click here to hear from each level of Egyptian society @ ClassZone.com

Social Systems Egyptian society was arranged with the largest group at the bottom and a small ruling class on top.

CRITICAL THINKING
What levels of the pyramid would require the most education?

Pharaoh Egyptians considered their pharaohs to be gods.

Pharaoh

Priests The priests cared for the temples and held religious ceremonies.

Priests and Nobles

Scribes The scribes were trained in the art of writing and record keeping.

Scribes and Government Officials

Laborers and Slaves Slaves might be prisoners of war, or people who owed debts or had committed crimes. In general, slaves were eventually freed.

Craftspeople and Merchants

Farmers

Laborers and Slaves

Egyptians believed in an afterlife that resembled life on Earth. To preserve a person's body for the next life, they embalmed and dried it, and wrapped it in linen bandages, making a **mummy**. Egyptians also mummified pets, such as cats and monkeys. They packed their family members' tombs with items they thought they would need in the afterlife: clothes, food, makeup, and jewelry. Egyptian rulers had the fanciest tombs of all. The pharaohs' burial chambers were full of items such as sparkling gold treasures and statues of servants to care for them in the afterlife.

Ancient Egyptian Contributions Ancient Egypt made advances in language, science, and mathematics. Egyptians invented a form of picture writing called **hieroglyphics** which was used in temples, tombs, and on monuments. A different script was used on scrolls of **papyrus**, a paperlike material made from papyrus grass. The Egyptian calendar was based on the Nile farming cycle of flooding, planting, and harvesting. Doctors in ancient Egypt understood that a person's pulse was connected to the heart, and knew how to set broken bones. Egyptians used geometry to set land borders and design buildings.

Hieroglyphics The word hieroglyphics comes from the Greek word for "sacred carving." **Why might the Greeks have called hieroglyphics "sacred"?**

 SUMMARIZE Name some of the advancements of ancient Egypt.

ONLINE QUIZ
For test practice, go to **Interactive Review** @ ClassZone.com

Section 1 Assessment

TERMS & NAMES

1. Explain the importance of
- Nile River
- delta
- Kush
- hieroglyphics

USE YOUR READING NOTES

2. Analyze Cause and Effect Use your completed chart to answer the following question:

What were the results of the Nile's annual floods?

CAUSE	EFFECT
1.	1.
2.	2.
3.	3.

KEY IDEAS

3. Why did ancient Egyptians cluster around the valley and delta of the Nile River?

4. What three periods make up ancient Egyptian history?

5. What was the largest social class in ancient Egypt?

CRITICAL THINKING

6. Summarize What are some positive and negative effects of the Aswan High Dam?

7. Evaluate What rights did women have in ancient Egypt?

8. CONNECT to Today What are the risks and benefits of living near a great river?

9. SCIENCE Create a Multimedia Presentation Using the library or Internet, research mummification and create a slide show to demonstrate the process. Show all the steps from removal of organs and embalming to drying and wrapping.

The Great Pyramid

Click here to enter the Great Pyramid @ ClassZone.com

PYRAMIDS

The Great Pyramid of Khufu is Egypt's largest pyramid, originally standing 481 feet high. For more than 4,000 years it stood as the world's tallest building.

Click here to visit the pyramids of Egypt today. Learn about the rulers of ancient Egypt and their belief in the afterlife.

Click here to see how a pyramid was built. Learn about the materials and methods and the people who built them.

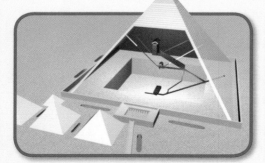

Click here to explore the passageways and chambers of the Great Pyramid's interior.

Plan a Pyramid Split into groups of three and plan a pyramid for a newly crowned pharaoh. Consider how to keep the burial chamber safe from thieves and what sort of facilities the workers will need.

Reading for Understanding

▶ Key Ideas

BEFORE, YOU LEARNED

Ancient Egyptians built a great civilization, but were conquered by foreign powers.

NOW YOU WILL LEARN

A blending of cultures has made Egypt a leader for North Africa, as well as for Southwest Asia.

▶ Vocabulary

TERMS & NAMES

Rosetta Stone an ancient Egyptian stone that provided a key to decipher hieroglyphics

Islam a religion believing in one god, called Allah, and his prophet on Earth, Muhammad

Muslim a follower of Islam

Suez Canal a waterway linking the Red Sea with the Mediterranean Sea

protectorate a weaker country or area controlled by a stronger country

Anwar el-Sadat president of Egypt from 1970 to 1981

Camp David Accords peace treaty between Egypt and Israel, signed in 1979

Sudan a country of northeast Africa, located south of Egypt

BACKGROUND VOCABULARY

modernize to accept modern ways or ideas

Visual Vocabulary Suez Canal

▶ Reading Strategy

Re-create the time line shown at right. As you read and respond to the **KEY QUESTIONS**, use the time line to order important events in Egypt and Sudan.

 See Skillbuilder Handbook, page R6

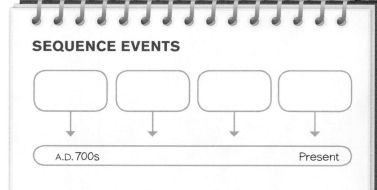

SEQUENCE EVENTS

A.D. 700s   Present

GRAPHIC ORGANIZERS
Go to **Interactive Review** @ ClassZone.com

Modern Egypt and Sudan

Connecting to Your World

Have you ever created a secret code? Typically, one set of letters stands for letters you already know. Hieroglyphics were like a mysterious code until the 1799 discovery of a carved stone called the **Rosetta Stone**. It contained the same text in ancient Greek, Egyptian script, and hieroglyphics. Since scholars knew the first two scripts, they were able to crack the code of hieroglyphics. But no one in the world today knows how ancient Egyptian was spoken.

From Ancient to Modern Times

▼ **KEY QUESTION** What foreign powers ruled Egypt?

The Arabic language became the dominant language in Egypt and North Africa because of a culture shift in the 600s and 700s. Around that time, Arabs from Southwest Asia introduced a new religion called Islam.

Rosetta Stone
This discovery was the key to decoding Egyptian hieroglyphics.

Temple of Luxor A white mosque stands amid the ruins of this ancient temple.

563

Influence of Islam **Islam** is the belief in one god, called Allah, and his prophet on Earth, Muhammad. Followers of Islam are called **Muslims**. (You will learn more about the spread of Islam in the next unit.) Arab Muslims invaded Egypt in A.D. 639. Afterward, Egyptians began to speak Arabic, and many adopted the Muslim faith. Islamic empires ruled Egypt for more than 1,000 years. The Ottoman Empire took control in 1517, but other groups contended for power.

During Napoleon Bonaparte's rule, France briefly occupied Egypt, beginning in 1798. The Ottomans regained control in 1801 under a military leader, Muhammad Ali. He tried to **modernize** Egypt. Though Muhammad Ali's efforts failed, his son Said (sa•EED) made a more lasting change. Under Said's reign, in 1859, workers began to dig the **Suez Canal**, a waterway linking the Red Sea with the Mediterranean. The canal continues to be a key trade route for Egypt, Europe, and Southwest Asia.

Becoming Independent The valuable trade route created by the Suez Canal led more foreign powers to try to control Egypt. Britain invaded Egypt in 1882. During World War I, Britain declared Egypt a **protectorate**, or country controlled by a stronger nation.

After the war, Egyptians began to call for independence. Britain granted independence in 1922, but kept troops in Egypt to guard the Suez Canal. During World War II, Egypt and other Arab nations formed the Arab League, which opposed the formation of Israel in 1948. Egypt lost four wars with Israel between 1948 and 1973. In 1977, Egyptian President **Anwar el-Sadat** traveled to Israel. In 1979, Egypt and Israel signed the **Camp David Accords**, the first peace treaty between Israel and an Arab state. The Arab League expelled Egypt for signing the treaty, but readmitted Egypt in 1989.

Egypt remains a leader in North Africa and the Arab world. Its capital, Cairo, is Africa's biggest city. In Africa, only Nigeria has more people. Although Egypt is not a big oil producer, Saudi Arabia is the only Middle Eastern country with a stronger economy.

🔺 **SEQUENCE EVENTS** Identify the foreign powers that ruled Egypt.

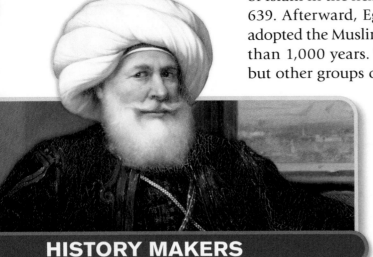

HISTORY MAKERS

Muhammad Ali Pasha 1769–1849

As an officer in the Ottoman army, Muhammad Ali helped rid Egypt of French invaders. In 1805, he became Egypt's governor, or Pasha. During his 44-year reign, he attempted to transform Egypt into a modern country. Muhammad Ali brought European advisors and teachers to Egypt and sent Egyptians to study in Europe. He also tried to bring industry to this agricultural land. Muhammad Ali's descendants ruled under British control, but his family held power in Egypt until 1953.

ONLINE BIOGRAPHY
For more on the life of Muhammad Ali Pasha, go to the
Research & Writing Center @ ClassZone.com

Life in Egypt Today

▼ **KEY QUESTION** How do most Egyptians live?

Egyptian city life is hectic and noisy. Huge slums adjoin wealthy residential areas, and the streets teem with traffic and overcrowded streetcars. People might wear Western clothes or traditional Egyptian clothing: a shirt and pants for men and a long, colorful flowing gown for women. Culturally, most Egyptians consider themselves Arabs and practice Islam.

More than half of Egyptians live in the countryside. Most villagers tend small farms on land often owned by wealthier landowners. Electric power is common in rural areas. Poor city dwellers and villagers alike eat a diet of bread, beans, and vegetable stew. Sweetened coffee or tea are popular drinks.

National Government Egypt's president serves a six-year term and may be re-elected indefinitely. The powerful president also leads the armed forces, appoints a prime minister and cabinet, and even appoints some members of the parliament. In 2005, Egypt allowed multiple candidates to run for president. Previously, parliament had selected single candidates for citizens to vote on.

Economic Structure and Activities Despite its role as a regional leader, Egypt is still a developing nation, struggling with unemployment and with how to feed its growing population. Agriculture employs more than one-third of Egyptian workers, but accounts for only one-sixth of the economy.

Cairo The Nile winds through Egypt's capital city. **If you are traveling south along the Nile, are you headed upstream or downstream?**

Service industries, such as banking, education, and trade, employ half of Egypt's workers and account for more than half of the economy. Thanks to Egypt's high-grade cotton, textile production provides one-third of the economy. In this socialist country, the government owns most major industries. But change is under way. To stimulate Egypt's economy, the government tries to attract foreign investment in Egypt's energy and tourism industries. Tourists, lured by ancient temples and pyramids, provide the largest share of Egypt's foreign funds.

▲ **SUMMARIZE** Describe daily life in Egypt.

Sudan: Egypt's Neighbor

SUDAN

▼ **KEY QUESTION** What cultural differences are behind the conflicts in Sudan?

You already learned that ancient Egypt controlled Nubia, or northern Sudan. After ancient Egypt lost control, Nubia's Kush kingdom endured until its collapse around A.D. 350. Modern **Sudan**, Egypt's southern neighbor, is Africa's largest nation in area. Part of Sudan extends into central Africa, with its savannas and rain forests. Northern Sudan is covered by desert.

Culture: Regional Differences Most people who live in the northern two-thirds of Sudan speak Arabic, the country's official language, and follow Islam. In the southern third of Sudan, various African groups practice traditional animist religions. A few are Christians.

Most Sudanese people live on subsistence farms or herd animals in the desert. Three out of ten Sudanese live in cities and towns. Sudan's main urban center—the area surrounding the capital, Khartoum—is home to more than six million people. Near the capital, two million more Sudanese live in refugee camps, displaced by civil wars.

Modern History of Sudan In the 1800s, Sudan again came under Egyptian control. But in 1881, a Sudanese Muslim teacher led a four-year revolt, overturning Egyptian rule. In 1898, Britain and Egypt joined forces to conquer Sudan. Britain ruled Sudan until 1956.

Between independence and 1998, military governments ruled Sudan. Conflicts between Sudan's Arab Muslim north and non-Muslim,

CONNECT History & Culture

Lost Boys of Sudan

The Lost Boys were orphans of Sudan's civil war. These children and young adults banded together to make a harrowing journey from Sudan to Ethiopia, back to Sudan, and then to refugee camps in Kenya. In 2001, the United States took in 3,600 Lost Boys across the country, primarily in Texas, Michigan, and Arizona. Now mostly adults, many Lost Boys work one or two jobs while attending high school or college classes.

Modern North Africa As the Ottoman Empire weakened in the 1800s and 1900s, European countries seized land in North Africa. France invaded Algeria in 1830, and France and Spain each had zones of control in Morocco. Until the end of World War II, Italy controlled Libya. You'll learn more about European control of Africa in the next two chapters.

After World War II, independence movements strengthened in North Africa. Morocco won independence from France in 1956, and Spain also gave up most claims on Moroccan territory. Algeria won independence in 1962, after a bloody eight-year struggle with France. Since independence, many Algerians and Moroccans have immigrated to Europe for work. Today five million Muslims, mostly from Morocco and Algeria, live in France.

Maghrib Geography North Africa's main features are

- the Sahara, the world's largest desert
- the **Atlas Mountains**, a chain of several mountain ranges stretching from Morocco to Tunisia
- the coastal area, where most North Africans live

The Atlas Mountains dominate Morocco, and make up much of Algeria's coastline. The coastal and mountain regions of the Maghrib have rainy winters and hot, dry summers. Mountain rainfall forms rivers flowing to the coast and desert, but many desert rivers dry out during the hot summer months.

The Sahara is not all sand. While about a quarter of the desert is sandy, rocks and gravel cover much of the land. Some Saharan areas receive less than two inches of rain a year, but underground water sources also exist. About 2.5 million people live in the Sahara, traveling as nomadic herders or gathering at oasis towns.

Daily Life and Culture Centuries of intermarriage between Arabs and Berbers have made the two groups look indistinguishable. Almost all North Africans are Muslim. While most North Africans speak a dialect of Arabic, many people also speak French, Spanish, English, or Berber. North African writers often publish in French or Arabic.

Algiers Algeria's modern-day capital was once a base for the Barbary pirates.

MOROCCO
• Marrakech

Souk Colorful goods line the streets in this market in Marrakech, Morocco.

Between 1960 and 1990, the percentage of city dwellers in North Africa jumped from less than one-third to about one-half of the population. Urban living quarters include small attached houses, large apartment buildings, and slum towns near larger cities. In the countryside, large extended families may still share one all-purpose room. At an open-air market, called a **souk** (sook), people buy and sell produce or handicrafts, and visit with friends. They may also share a plate of couscous, a wheat dish, covered with a tagine, or stew.

In the countryside, Moroccan men and women wear traditional Berber clothing, such as a **jellaba**, or robe with full sleeves, or a hooded cloak called a burnoose. Men also wear a turban, a skullcap, or a red Moroccan hat called a fez. In cities, people often combine traditional and Western clothing. Mosques are popular North African gathering places. So are movie theaters and soccer stadiums.

Most North African countries offer free elementary and at least some secondary education. Girls are more likely to stay at home instead of working or going to school, especially in rural areas. Tunisia leads the region in improving opportunities for women, including better schooling and jobs, and divorce reform. In Libya, only about one in ten women work outside the home.

▲ **SUMMARIZE** Identify the cultures that have most influenced North Africa.

Government and Economics

▼ **KEY QUESTION** What product is most important to North Africa?

Because of occupation and colonization, Europe and Southwest Asia influenced culture across North Africa. But despite a shared cultural history, each North African country has developed its own government and economy. Algeria, Libya, and Morocco are good examples.

Algeria Algeria has an elected president, a prime minister the president appoints, and a Council of Ministers the prime minister selects. Voters elect one house of the legislature, with the other house partly elected from local assemblies and partly appointed by the president. Algeria became a multi-party state in 1989.

Algeria's government controls its major industries, including natural gas and petroleum production. To export its natural gas, Algeria built two pipelines running under the Mediterranean Sea to Spain and Sicily. Other industries include construction materials, steel, and textiles. These industries and small-scale farming, which occupies about one out of five Algerians, don't provide enough jobs. Hundreds of thousands of Algerians have emigrated to find work in developed countries such as France.

Libya In 1969, Colonel Muammar Gaddafi (guh•DAH•fee) led a military revolt that overthrew the country's monarchy. Gaddafi still heads Libya, though he holds no official title. Opposition groups exist, but only one political party is legal. In this **dictatorship**, or rule by an unelected, absolute leader, the government also controls television and the press. Local groups elect members of a General People's Congress.

Most Libyans live in overcrowded cities, lured by the discovery of petroleum in 1959. The government controls most economic activity. Although almost one in five Libyans are farmers, just about one percent of the land is farmable. Libya exports its oil, but the oil industry employs few workers.

Libya's strained relationship with the United States broke after Libyan terrorists blew up a U.S. airplane in 1988. In 2003, these relations improved when Libya compensated the victims' families and gave up its pursuit of nuclear weapons. The United States and United Nations agreed to end economic sanctions against Libya.

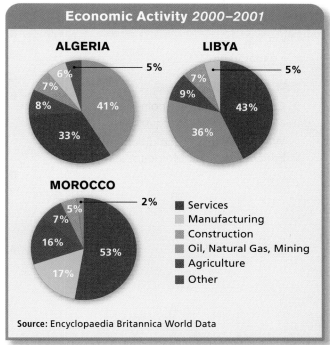

Economic Activity 2000–2001

ALGERIA: 5%, 6%, 7%, 8%, 41%, 33%
LIBYA: 5%, 7%, 9%, 43%, 36%
MOROCCO: 2%, 5%, 7%, 16%, 53%, 17%

■ Services
■ Manufacturing
■ Construction
■ Oil, Natural Gas, Mining
■ Agriculture
■ Other

Source: Encyclopaedia Britannica World Data

Berbers Morocco has the largest Berber population. Here, they sell goods in an open market.

Morocco A king heads Morocco's constitutional monarchy. His extensive powers include commanding the armed forces, issuing laws, and controlling government agencies. He also appoints a prime minister and cabinet of other ministers. The largest parties support the king, though smaller opposition parties also exist. Voters elect one house of the legislature. Local and professional groups choose the other house.

Morocco's mining, communications, and some manufacturing industries are publicly owned. But most of its businesses and farms have private owners. This country's developing economy mostly depends on mining and agriculture. Farming and fishing employ about four out of ten Moroccan workers. Morocco exports most of the phosphate rock used for fertilizer. The country also produces wheat, barley, wine, citrus fruits, olive oil, sheep, and goats, while its factories turn out textiles, leather goods, fertilizers, and petroleum products. Tourism, one of Morocco's main industries, brings nearly two million visitors each year, mostly from Europe.

 FIND MAIN IDEAS Describe the important product or products in North African economies.

Section 3 Assessment

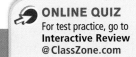 **ONLINE QUIZ** For test practice, go to **Interactive Review** @ ClassZone.com

TERMS & NAMES

1. Explain the importance of
- Berbers
- Carthage
- Punic Wars
- dictatorship

USE YOUR READING NOTES

2. Compare Use your completed chart to answer the following question.

What are some of the differences between Algeria, Morocco, and Libya?

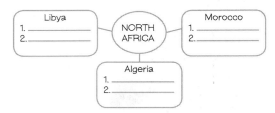

KEY IDEAS

3. Which people first settled in North Africa?

4. What percentage of North Africans live in cities?

5. How does Arab Muslim culture affect life in North Africa?

CRITICAL THINKING

6. Find Main Ideas What ties do North African countries still have with Europe?

7. Compare and Contrast How does Libya's government compare with Algeria's?

8. CONNECT to Today In 2006, France had Europe's largest Muslim community, about five million North Africans. What problems might Muslim North Africans face in Europe?

9. HISTORY Research a Report Research a report on the Barbary Pirates. Include information on European and American attempts to stop piracy out of North Africa.

Interactive ◄ Review

Click here to complete these and other activities online @ ClassZone.com

CHAPTER SUMMARY

Key Idea 1
The Nile made possible the great civilizations of ancient Egypt.

Key Idea 2
A blending of cultures has made Egypt a leader for North Africa as well as for Southwest Asia.

Key Idea 3
The Ottomans and Islam also influenced North African nations, as did Europeans and colonizing powers.

For **Review and Study Notes**, go to **Interactive Review** @ ClassZone.com

NAME GAME

Use the Terms & Names list to complete each sentence on paper or online.

1. I am the rich land at the mouth of a river.
   _____ delta 🖑

2. I am the tomb of a pharaoh. _____

3. I am one of the six waterfalls along the Nile.
   _____

4. Ancient Egypt conquered my empire; later I conquered Egypt. _____

5. I helped scholars translate the hieroglyphics of ancient Egypt. _____

6. I signed the Camp David Accords, a peace treaty with Israel. _____

7. I am Africa's largest country. _____

8. I am the Arab name for a region that means "west." _____

9. I was an ancient city-state in North Africa.
   _____

10. I am a system of absolute rule by one unelected person. _____

Berber
Carthage
cataract
delta
dictatorship
dynasty
Kush
Maghrib
Nubia
papyrus
pyramid
Rosetta Stone
Anwar el-Sadat
Sudan
Suez Canal

Activities

GeoGame

Use this online map to reinforce your understanding of North African geography. Drag and drop each place name in the list to its location on the map.

Geo GAME

Egypt

Sudan

Cairo

Khartoum

Libya

Present-Day North Africa

Libya 🖑

To play the complete game, go to **Interactive Review** @ ClassZone.com

Crossword Puzzle

Complete an online crossword puzzle to test your knowledge of North Africa.

ACROSS

1. a traditional Berber garment; a robe with full sleeves

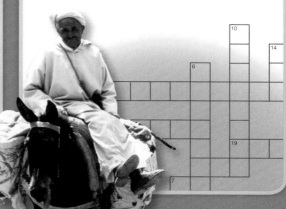

575

VOCABULARY

Explain the significance of each of the following.

1. dynasty
2. Aswan High Dam
3. Anwar el-Sadat
4. Maghrib
5. Berbers
6. Islam
7. Atlas Mountains

Explain how the terms and names in each group are related.

8. dynasty, pharaoh, and pyramid
9. Sudan, Nubia, and Kush

KEY IDEAS

① Ancient Egypt: Pyramids and Pharaohs

10. Why were the yearly floods so important to Egyptian farmers?
11. What powers invaded and subdued ancient Egypt?
12. How did ancient Egyptians honor their pharaohs?
13. What do you think was ancient Egypt's greatest accomplishment?

② Modern Egypt and Sudan

14. Which powerful empires clashed over control of Egypt between 1517 and 1922?
15. Who founded the dynasty that ruled modern Egypt?
16. Why is modern Egypt considered a leader in the region?
17. Which groups have been fighting in the Darfur region of Sudan?

③ Other Nations of North Africa

18. When did most North African countries win their independence from European colonizing powers?
19. What are some of Morocco's major products?
20. Why hasn't Libya's oil wealth brought its people out of poverty?
21. What hopeful developments improved the United States' relationship with Libya in 2003?

CRITICAL THINKING

22. **Analyze Cause and Effect** Create a table to assess the causes, intended effects, and unintended effects of the move of North Africans to cities.

CAUSES	INTENDED EFFECTS	UNINTENDED EFFECTS
move of North Africans to cities		

23. **Summarize** Summarize the history of Egypt's connection to Britain.
24. **Evaluate** What push-pull factor has led North Africans to immigrate to Europe?
25. **Five Themes: Place** What body of water was created by the Aswan High Dam?
26. **Connect Geography & History** Why did North Africa's history differ from that of the rest of Africa?

Answer the ESSENTIAL QUESTION

How have people in North Africa adapted to the region's arid climate?

Written Response Write a two- or three-paragraph response to the Essential Question. Be sure to consider the key ideas of each section. Use the rubric below to guide your thinking.

Response Rubric
A strong response will:
- describe North Africa as primarily desert
- discuss the yearly flooding of the Nile
- explain how the Aswan High Dam and Suez Canal contributed to the economy of Egypt
- mention the trans-Mediterranean trade between North Africa and Europe

STANDARDS-BASED ASSESSMENT

 **Test Practice**
• Online Test Practice @ ClassZone.com
• Test-Taking Strategies and Practice
  at the front of this book

POPULATION MAP

Use the map and your knowledge of Africa to answer questions 1 and 2 on your paper.

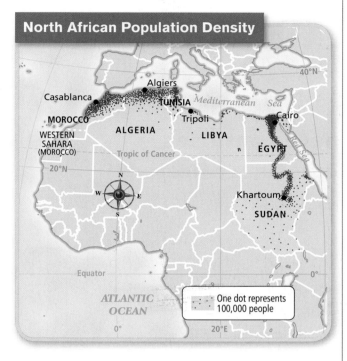

North African Population Density

One dot represents 100,000 people

1. What geographic feature explains the winding band of heavy population in the east?

2. Why are there fewer people scattered throughout northern Sudan than in the south?

BAR GRAPH

Examine the graph below. Use the information in the graph to answer questions 3 and 4 on your paper.

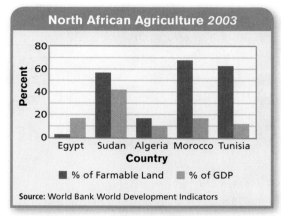

North African Agriculture 2003

■ % of Farmable Land   ■ % of GDP

Source: World Bank World Development Indicators

3. Agriculture is most important to which country's economy?

A. Egypt
B. Sudan
C. Morocco
D. Tunisia

4. Which country uses the smallest percentage of its land for agriculture?

A. Algeria
B. Sudan
C. Morocco
D. Egypt

GeoActivity

1. INTERDISCIPLINARY ACTIVITY–SCIENCE

In addition to weakening the soil and increasing erosion, the Aswan High Dam has also caused the increase of a disease caused by tiny worms that breed in snails discharged into the Nile and its canals. With a small group, research other environmental effects of the Aswan High Dam.

2. WRITING FOR SOCIAL STUDIES

Reread the description of the packing of an Egyptian tomb in this section. Compile a list of the things you would put in such a tomb for a famous person, a favorite pet, or someone you know. Explain why you would include each of these things.

3. MENTAL MAPPING

Create an outline map of North Africa and label the following:

• Aswan High Dam
• Mediterranean Sea
• Sahara
• Egypt
• Sudan
• Tunisia
• Morocco
• Algeria
• Libya
• Maghrib

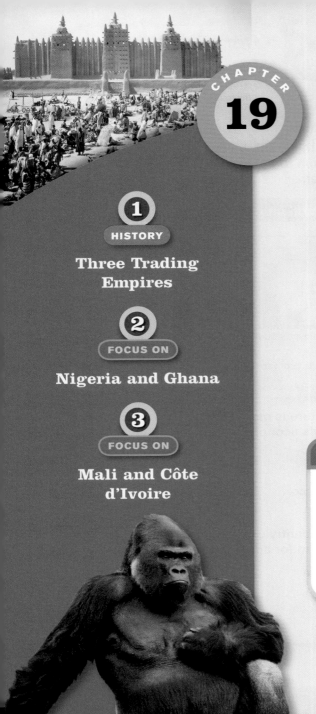

CHAPTER 19

West Africa

1 HISTORY
Three Trading Empires

2 FOCUS ON
Nigeria and Ghana

3 FOCUS ON
Mali and Côte d'Ivoire

 ESSENTIAL QUESTION

How have centuries of colonialism affected West Africa?

CONNECT Geography & History

Use the map and the time line to answer the following questions.

1. What two European powers held the most land in Africa?

2. How did colonial boundaries appear to compare to traditional African ethnic boundaries?

History
c. 700 Ghana empire founded by Soninke people.

History
c. 1300 Songhai empire begins to rise.

History
c. 1500 The Songhai empire reaches its peak.

A.D. 700

Geography
1300s Mali empire at its peak; Timbuktu, Mali's largest city, becomes center for trade and scholarship. ▶

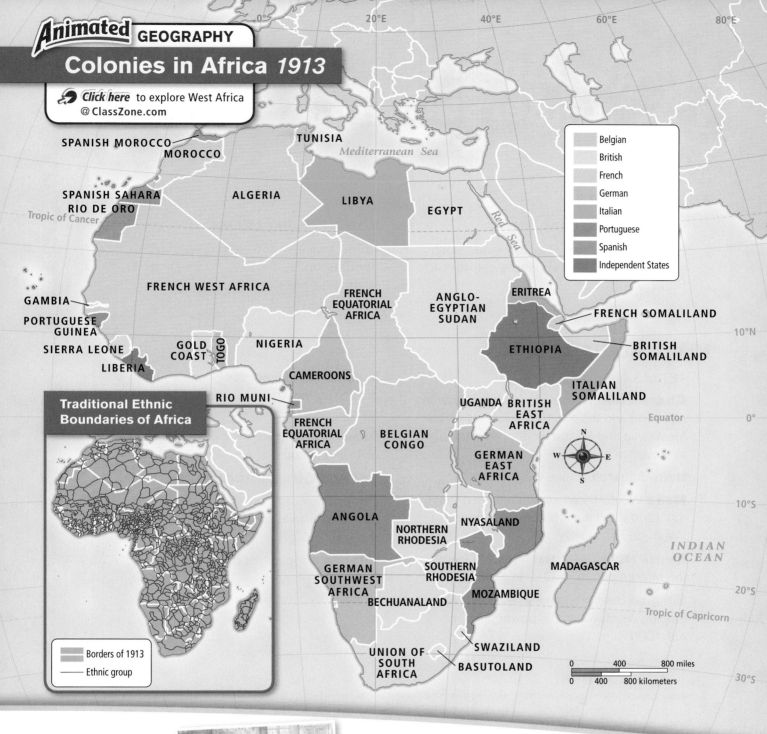

Click here to explore West Africa @ ClassZone.com

SPANISH MOROCCO
MOROCCO
TUNISIA
Mediterranean Sea

SPANISH SAHARA
RIO DE ORO
Tropic of Cancer
ALGERIA
LIBYA
EGYPT
Red Sea

	Belgian
	British
	French
	German
	Italian
	Portuguese
	Spanish
	Independent States

FRENCH WEST AFRICA
FRENCH EQUATORIAL AFRICA
ANGLO-EGYPTIAN SUDAN
ERITREA
FRENCH SOMALILAND
10°N

GAMBIA
PORTUGUESE GUINEA
SIERRA LEONE
LIBERIA
GOLD COAST
TOGO
NIGERIA
CAMEROONS
ETHIOPIA
BRITISH SOMALILAND
ITALIAN SOMALILAND

RIO MUNI
FRENCH EQUATORIAL AFRICA
BELGIAN CONGO
UGANDA BRITISH EAST AFRICA
Equator 0°

Traditional Ethnic Boundaries of Africa

GERMAN EAST AFRICA
N W E S

ANGOLA
NORTHERN RHODESIA
NYASALAND
MADAGASCAR
10°S
INDIAN OCEAN

GERMAN SOUTHWEST AFRICA
SOUTHERN RHODESIA
BECHUANALAND
MOZAMBIQUE
Tropic of Capricorn
20°S

| | Borders of 1913 |
| —— | Ethnic group |

UNION OF SOUTH AFRICA
SWAZILAND
BASUTOLAND

| 0 | 400 | 800 miles |
| 0 | 400 | 800 kilometers |

30°S

History
1591 Moroccan invaders destroy Songhai.

Government
1957 Modern Ghana wins independence from Great Britain, beginning a continent-wide independence movement.

Today

Government
▲ **1884–1885** The Berlin Conference divides Africa among European nations.

History
◄ **2005** Signed agreement ends fighting in Côte d'Ivoire.

Reading for Understanding

▶ Key Ideas

BEFORE, YOU LEARNED

Europeans traveled to other lands, such as the Americas, establishing colonies to build wealth.

NOW YOU WILL LEARN

Colonizers also traveled to West Africa, dividing up land once held by great trading empires.

▶ Vocabulary

TERMS & NAMES

Ghana a West African kingdom between the A.D. 700s and the A.D. 1000s in what is now Mauritania and Mali; a modern country in West Africa

trans-Saharan across the Sahara

Mali a West African empire between the A.D. 1200s and the A.D. 1500s; a modern West African country

Mansa Musa (MAHN•sah moo•SAH) leader of the Mali empire from 1312 to about 1337

Songhai (sawng•hy) an ancient West African empire, which was most powerful about A.D. 1500

imperialism the practice of one country controlling the government and economy of another country or territory

Pan-Africanism a movement calling for the unity of all people of African descent

BACKGROUND VOCABULARY

camel a humped mammal used in the desert as a pack animal and provider of meat, milk, and wool

self-rule independent government

▶ Reading Strategy

Re-create the diagram shown at right. As you read and respond to the **KEY QUESTIONS**, use the diagram to organize important details about West Africa.

 Skillbuilder Handbook, page R4

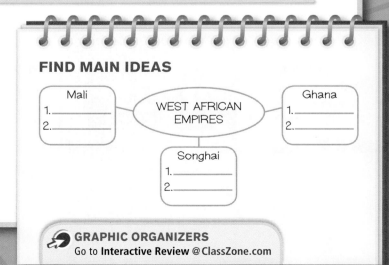

FIND MAIN IDEAS

Mali
1. _____
2. _____

WEST AFRICAN EMPIRES

Ghana
1. _____
2. _____

Songhai
1. _____
2. _____

GRAPHIC ORGANIZERS
Go to **Interactive Review** @ ClassZone.com

Three Trading Empires

Connecting to Your World

What makes a country strong? Is it the size of a nation or population? The United States' strength results partly from its size, population, and military power, but also from trade. Trade helps a nation build wealth, which makes it strong. Trade with other peoples allowed early West African cultures to build empires in Africa.

Three Trading Empires

▼ **KEY QUESTION** How did West African trading empires become wealthy?

Crossing the Sahara was always difficult, but it became easier around 2,000 years ago. That's when southwest Asian traders introduced camels to the region. **Camels** are perfectly adapted to the desert. Their feet can navigate soft sand, and they can survive without food or water for weeks. For centuries, camel caravans crossed the Sahara along established trade routes. These routes gave rise to three great empires.

Camel Caravan
Nomadic Tuareg people lead their camels across the Sahara.

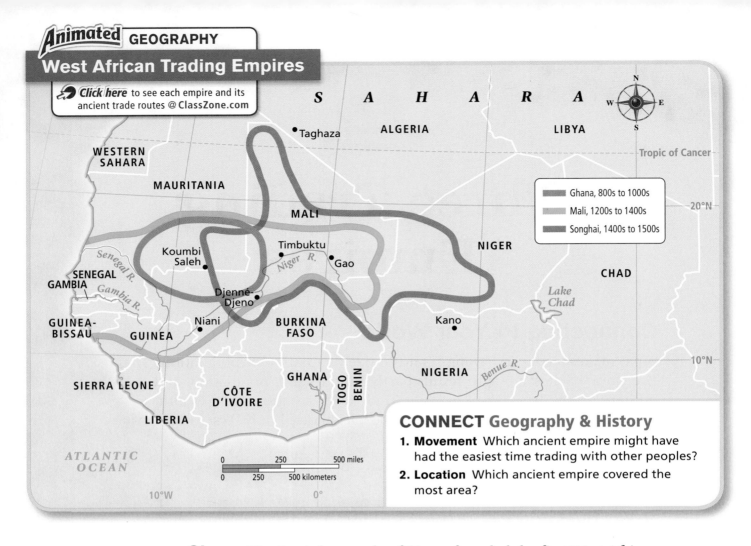

Animated GEOGRAPHY

West African Trading Empires

Click here to see each empire and its ancient trade routes @ ClassZone.com

SAHARA

WESTERN SAHARA

Taghaza

ALGERIA

LIBYA

Tropic of Cancer

MAURITANIA

MALI

20°N

Koumbi Saleh

Timbuktu

Gao

NIGER

CHAD

Senegal R.

SENEGAL

GAMBIA

Gambia R.

Djenné-Djeno

Niger R.

Lake Chad

GUINEA-BISSAU

Niani

BURKINA FASO

Kano

GUINEA

SIERRA LEONE

CÔTE D'IVOIRE

GHANA

TOGO BENIN

NIGERIA

Benue R.

10°N

LIBERIA

ATLANTIC OCEAN

Legend:
- Ghana, 800s to 1000s
- Mali, 1200s to 1400s
- Songhai, 1400s to 1500s

0   250   500 miles
0   250   500 kilometers

10°W   0°

CONNECT Geography & History

1. **Movement** Which ancient empire might have had the easiest time trading with other peoples?
2. **Location** Which ancient empire covered the most area?

Ghana The Soninke people of **Ghana** founded the first West African empire around A.D. 700. Ancient Ghana began as a trading center for grains, cattle, and metals. Camel caravans from the Arabic world arrived at Ghana's markets, introducing Islam to the region and establishing a **trans-Saharan** trade. *Trans-Sahara* means "across the Sahara." Caravans brought books, salt, cloth, and tools from Arabia to Ghana, and carried back slaves, ivory, and gold. Taxing the gold trade enriched Ghana's rulers. In 1076, Moroccan Berbers conquered Ghana's major city. More defeats followed, and Ghana collapsed around 1200.

Mali As Ghana declined, several small states competed to control the empire. Between 1235 and 1240, a king named Sundiata conquered the other states to found a new empire east of Ghana. This empire, **Mali**, thrived because it controlled a large new gold field at the center of the trans-Saharan trade.

Sundiata's great-nephew **Mansa Musa** (MAHN•sah moo•SAH) ruled Mali from 1312 to about 1337, spreading Islam throughout the empire. Mosques, courts, and schools in Timbuktu, the capital of Mali's trading empire, made the city a major center of Muslim learning. After 1400, Mali gave way to a stronger empire.

Songhai The **Songhai** empire developed from large towns near the present-day border between Mali and Niger. Songhai's strength came from its control of the trans-Saharan trade. Sunni Ali, a great military leader, ruled Songhai from 1464 to 1492. In 1493, Askia Muhammad became king, eventually enlarging Songhai to its greatest extent. Askia, known as Askia the Great, promoted the spread of both Islam and trade. The last of West Africa's three great empires declined after Moroccan fighters defeated Songhai in 1591.

▲ **SUMMARIZE** Describe how the three empires of West Africa gained wealth.

European Imperialism

▼ **KEY QUESTION** Why did Europeans come to Africa?

In the 1500s, Portuguese traders made their way to Africa. Soon Holland and other European powers also vied for the rich trade in slaves, gold, and ivory.

The Slave Trade Shortly after the Portuguese arrived in West Africa, they started enslaving Africans and shipping them to Europe. Before this time, African powers had sent some slaves to Asia and Europe. But the Atlantic slave trade exceeded anything that had come earlier. Scholars say it was history's single largest forced movement of people. African merchants and rulers sold enslaved Africans to Europeans, who sent the slaves to the Americas. The slave trade devastated Africa. Between the late 1400s and the middle 1800s, 10 to 12 million enslaved persons came to the Americas. Slave raiding and warfare emptied towns and villages, destroying ancient patterns of culture, work, and trade.

Europeans Carve Up Africa Even after the slave trade ended, Europeans continued to raid Africa for cheap labor, natural resources, and markets. European **imperialism**, or control of weaker nations, grew with the European industrialization of the late 19th century. Railroads, steamships, and the repeating rifle helped Europeans control much of Africa. In the 1880s, European powers carved Africa into a colonial map for European convenience. The new colonial boundaries ignored traditional ethnic boundaries. In many cases, this grouped long-standing enemies together in colonies.

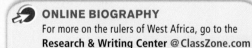

HISTORY MAKERS

Askia Muhammad 1441?–1538

Askia (AS•kee•uh) Muhammad, shown here in an artist's rendering, ruled the West African Songhai empire at its most powerful. He became king by overthrowing the son of Sunni Ali, an earlier ruler. Askia enlarged Songhai by seizing big chunks of Mali. He also conquered several states ruled by the Hausa people, and colonized Berber towns. In 1528, Askia Muhammad's son took power.

ONLINE BIOGRAPHY
For more on the rulers of West Africa, go to the **Research & Writing Center @ ClassZone.com**

Impact of Imperialism By 1914, only Liberia, founded by former U.S. slaves, and Ethiopia were free of European control. Africans resisted colonization, but superior weapons helped Europeans hold power. Different colonial powers had different styles of control, as shown in the chart below. The British ruled indirectly, letting Africans take over some parts of government. France refused to share any power, considering its colonies part of a global French nation.

The scars of imperialism still mark Africa. Colonizers discouraged industrial development, keeping colonies dependent. Wars of conquest and resistance cost many lives. So did the brutal demands of plantation work. Colonial boundaries remained after independence and still cut across ethnic lines.

▲ **ANALYZE POINTS OF VIEW** Describe why Europeans wanted to colonize Africa.

African Colonies Gain Independence

▼ **KEY QUESTION** How did African colonies win independence?

In the early 1900s, some colonies sent African students overseas to universities. These well-educated Africans began to dream of freedom for their own people. They joined with former slaves and descendents of slaves in the Americas in calling for freedom and unity for all people of African descent. Their movement became known as **Pan-Africanism**. African soldiers fought alongside Allied forces in World War I and World War II. After the wars, Africans began to demand independence for their own countries. Some Europeans also

◄ COMPARING ► Forms of Colonial Rule

	INDIRECT RULE of African Colonies	**DIRECT RULE** of African Colonies
Methods	• Local governments used • Limited self-rule • Goal: to develop future leaders • Government based on European styles, but may have local influences	• Foreign officials brought in to rule • No self-rule • Goal: to get colonies to adopt European culture • Government based only on European styles
Examples	British colonies such as Nigeria	French colonies such as French West Africa

CRITICAL THINKING

Draw Conclusions Which form of rule do you think would be the best long-term method, and why?

began to question whether it was right to maintain colonies. Britain's indirect control of its colonies helped prepare African leaders for eventual **self-rule**. More tightly controlled colonial governments left newly independent nations to struggle on their own.

Methods of Attaining Independence The first West African colony to win independence was the Gold Coast. In 1957, it peacefully separated from Great Britain and reclaimed the ancient name of Ghana. Nigeria won independence in 1960. Independence for some other West African countries came only after years of guerrilla warfare. For example, war erupted in the Portuguese colony of Guinea-Bissau in the early 1960s. The conflict dragged on until 1974. By the end of 1975, Portugal had given up the last of its African claims.

Independence Guinea-Bissau citizens celebrate the end of Portuguese colonization in 1974.

 COMPARE Describe the paths different colonies took toward independence.

Section 1 Assessment

ONLINE QUIZ
For test practice, go to
Interactive Review
@ ClassZone.com

TERMS & NAMES

1. Explain the importance of
- Ghana
- Mansa Musa
- Songhai
- Pan-Africanism

USE YOUR READING NOTES

2. Find Main Ideas Use your completed diagram to answer the following question:

What did the ancient West African empires have in common?

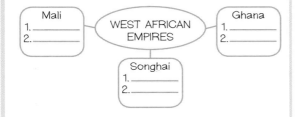

KEY IDEAS

3. What were the names of West Africa's great empires?

4. How did industrialization promote European imperialism in Africa?

5. How did West African countries win independence from their colonizers?

CRITICAL THINKING

6. Evaluate How did World Wars I and II lead some Europeans to question colonialism?

7. Make Inferences Why do you think the modern nation of Ghana chose the name of an ancient empire in a different location?

8. CONNECT to Today In 1994 in Rwanda, 800,000 people were killed in ethnic fighting. How has Africa's colonial past promoted such conflicts?

9. TECHNOLOGY Create a Multimedia Presentation Create a slide show about historical Timbuktu. Focus on Timbuktu's history as a prominent center of trade and Islamic learning.

Reading for Understanding

▶ Key Ideas

BEFORE, YOU LEARNED

Colonizers traveled to West Africa, dividing up land once held by great trading empires.

NOW YOU WILL LEARN

Nigeria and Ghana have struggled to maintain stable governments and productive economies.

▶ Vocabulary

TERMS & NAMES

Hausa (HOW•suh) a people of northern Nigeria and southern Niger

Yoruba (YAWR•uh•buh) a people of south-western Nigeria, parts of Benin, and Togo

Igbo (IHG•bo) a people of southeastern Nigeria

coup (koo) military takeover

Biafra (bee•AF•ruh) a largely Igbo region of Nigeria that declared its independence in 1967, but surrendered after losing a civil war in 1970

Kwame Nkrumah (KWAHM•eh uhn•KROO•muh) modern Ghana's first president

Kente cloth a brightly colored, woven cloth made by the Ashanti and Ewe peoples

BACKGROUND VOCABULARY

stability durability; resistance to change

subsistence farming farming that produces just enough to feed the farmer's family

Ashanti (uh•SHAN•tee) a people of Ghana

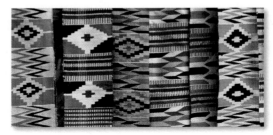

Visual Vocabulary kente cloth

▶ Reading Strategy

Re-create the chart shown at right. As you read and respond to the **KEY QUESTIONS**, use the chart to summarize information about Nigeria and Ghana.

 Skillbuilder Handbook, page R5

SUMMARIZE

NIGERIA	GHANA
1.	1.
2.	2.
3.	3.
4.	4.

 GRAPHIC ORGANIZERS
Go to **Interactive Review @ ClassZone.com**

Nigeria and Ghana

Connecting to Your World

How does your family make important decisions, such as where to take a vacation or whether to move to a new apartment? In some families, a parent or both parents make the decisions. Some families seek out the advice of an older relative. However your family makes decisions, you're probably used to your own system. Like your family, West African societies had their own familiar ways of ruling themselves and solving conflicts. But when a familiar system disappears, things get confusing.

NIGERIA

Nigeria

🔻 **KEY QUESTION** How have Nigeria's main ethnic groups gotten along since independence?

When European powers colonized Africa, they didn't recognize the systems of governing the Africans used. Instead, they imposed European-style centralized governments to replace African stateless systems. Most ruling officials were Europeans. When African nations gained freedom in the mid-1900s, few Africans knew how to run a European-style government. As a result, many African governments lacked **stability**.

River Port The Niger River remains an important West African transportation route. **Why might the Niger River be important to international trade?**

History Since Independence In Section 1, you learned that colonial powers drew Africa's borders without considering the culture or history of African peoples. Nigeria is just one of the African countries where conflict has grown from cultural divisions.

The three largest groups in Nigeria are the **Hausa**, who live in the north; the **Yoruba**, who live in the southwest; and the **Igbo** (IHG•bo), who live in the east. After independence in 1960, Nigeria's major ethnic groups clashed. The Igbo and other southern groups resented the Hausa's greater political power.

Ethnic conflict between the groups fueled an Igbo-led **coup**, or military takeover, in 1966. In 1967, the Igbo broke away from Nigeria to create their own state, called **Biafra**. A three-year civil war followed, causing many deaths from fighting and starvation. Biafra surrendered and rejoined Nigeria in 1970. Military leaders ruled Nigeria from 1966 to 1979, and again from 1983 until 1999. A new constitution and democratic elections restored a civilian government in 1999. But ethnic and religious tensions still simmer.

Nigerian Culture and Daily Life More than 250 ethnic groups, who speak many different languages, live in Nigeria, whose official language is English. Nigeria's 132 million people make it Africa's most populous nation, and one of the world's largest. About half of Nigerians are Muslim, while 40 percent are Christian. Many people also practice traditional animist religions or mix them with Islam or Christianity.

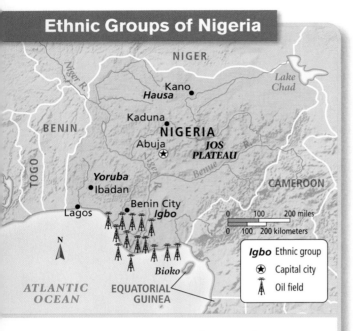

Ethnic Groups of Nigeria

Igbo Ethnic group
★ Capital city
⚒ Oil field

CONNECT Geography & History

Place Abuja, Nigeria's capital, was a planned city. Why might Nigeria want its capital in the center of the country?

At least two-thirds of Nigerians survive on less than one dollar a day. Most are poor farmers who live in grass, mud, or wood homes in clusters called compounds. In rural areas, people wear long, loose robes. Wealthy city dwellers live in modern houses or apartments and often wear Western clothes. Poor Nigerians, who have flooded the cities since the 1960s, often crowd into slums.

Nigerian authors Chinua Achebe (CHIHN•wah ah•CHAY•bay) and Wole Soyinka (WOH•lay shaw•YING•kuh) wrote their most famous works in English. In 1986, Soyinka became the first African to win the Nobel Prize for Literature. Nigerian music pulses with drums, xylophones, and string and wind instruments. The Yoruba are famous for their wood carvings. Nigerian art, especially sculptures, have inspired Western artists.

Ken Saro-Wiwa was a Nigerian activist fighting for the rights of his Ogoni people. He and eight others were arrested and hanged in 1995 by Nigeria's military government. Many around the world believed Saro-Wiwa was convicted on false charges. Shortly before his death, Saro-Wiwa smuggled writings out of prison.

> It is also very important that we have chosen the path of non-violent struggle. Our opponents are given to violence and we cannot meet them on their turf, even if we wanted to. Non-violent struggle offers weak people the strength which they otherwise would not have. The spirit becomes important, and no gun can silence that.
>
> Source: Ken Saro-Wiwa, *A Month and a Day: A Detention Diary*

DOCUMENT–BASED QUESTION
What does "we cannot meet them on their turf" mean?

 ONLINE PRIMARY SOURCE To read more of Saro-Wiwa's works, go to the **Research & Writing Center** @ClassZone.com

Government and Economics An elected president and vice president head Nigeria's government. They're assisted by an appointed cabinet and a two-house National Assembly.

Nigerians depend largely on agriculture for their livelihood. Two out of three Nigerian workers are farmers, who produce much of the world's cocoa, peanuts, and rubber. But most of Nigeria's farmers practice **subsistence farming**. Their food crops include maize, beans, and other vegetables and fruits. While manufacturing industries are developing, mining and petroleum produce the majority of the nation's wealth. In addition to producing coal, gold, iron ore, and natural gas, Nigeria is also one of the world's biggest oil exporters. Oil has contributed to Nigeria's wealth—and to its problems. In the 1970s, oil profits funded government programs to improve the standard of living. But relying too heavily on oil exports slowed development of Nigeria's other industries. Oil spills have also polluted certain areas, ruining farmland and poisoning fish.

▼ **SUMMARIZE** Summarize Nigeria's ethnic conflicts since independence.

Elections A new Nigerian constitution and free elections in 1999 ended nearly 30 years of military rule.

GHANA

Ghana

🔻 **KEY QUESTION** What are the key points of Ghana's art and culture?

When Portuguese sailors landed on the west coast of Africa in 1471, they named this gold-rich coastal territory the Gold Coast. In 1957, the Gold Coast was the first African state to win independence. The new republic's leaders chose the name Ghana to recall the greatness of the ancient empire, even though no part of ancient Ghana was located within the modern country.

History Since Independence During the late 1940s and early 1950s, the British who controlled Ghana began to encourage educated Africans to participate in governing. **Kwame Nkrumah** (KWAHM•eh uhn•KROO•muh), a Ghanaian who had served as prime minister under British rule, became Ghana's first president in 1960. Nkrumah tried to boost living conditions, build factories, and expand education. Corruption and a failing economy triggered a coup in 1966.

A series of military leaders revolved through Ghana's capital, Accra. One of these soldiers, Jerry Rawlings, headed Ghana's government between 1979 and 2001. Ghana's new constitution, accepted in 1992, turned Ghana into a multiparty democracy.

Ghana's Culture and Daily Life Like Nigerians, most Ghanaians speak African languages and study Ghana's official language, English, in school. **Ashanti**, or Akan, members outnumber Ghana's 100 other groups, such as the Ewe, Ga, and Moshi-Dagomba. Many Ghanaians

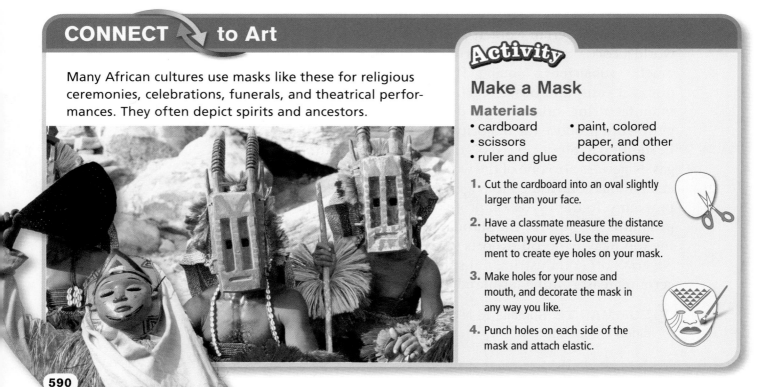

CONNECT to Art

Many African cultures use masks like these for religious ceremonies, celebrations, funerals, and theatrical performances. They often depict spirits and ancestors.

Activity

Make a Mask
Materials
- cardboard
- scissors
- ruler and glue
- paint, colored paper, and other decorations

1. Cut the cardboard into an oval slightly larger than your face.

2. Have a classmate measure the distance between your eyes. Use the measurement to create eye holes on your mask.

3. Make holes for your nose and mouth, and decorate the mask in any way you like.

4. Punch holes on each side of the mask and attach elastic.

wear Western-style clothing. For special social and religious occasions, Ashanti and Ewe craftspeople weave **Kente cloth**, a brightly colored ceremonial cloth made into wraps, skirts, and blouses. More than six out of ten Ghanaians are Christian, just over 20 percent follow traditional African religions, and 16 percent are Muslim.

Marketplaces are central meeting places in Ghana. At a market, you might find carvings and copies of Ashanti stools. In Ashanti culture, the head of each lineage group has a stool to symbolize his power.

Government and Economics Ghana's democratic government includes a president, cabinet, and an elected parliament. Compared to Nigeria, whose economy rises or falls with the price of oil, Ghana boasts several exports. In addition to its biggest export, cocoa, Ghana also supplies the world with diamonds, gold, manganese, and timber. But as in Nigeria, most Ghanaians work as subsistence farmers.

Ghana's Arts Wearing Kente cloth, a Ghanaian boy holds an Ashanti stool.

 FIND MAIN IDEAS Describe major points of Ghana's art.

Section 2 Assessment

ONLINE QUIZ
For test practice, go to
Interactive Review
@ ClassZone.com

TERMS & NAMES

1. Explain the importance of
- Igbo
- subsistence
- Kwame Nkrumah
- Kente cloth

USE YOUR READING NOTES

2. Summarize Use your completed chart to answer the following question:

What are some of Nigeria and Ghana's main products?

NIGERIA	GHANA
1.	1.
2.	2.
3.	3.
4.	4.

KEY IDEAS

3. How do most Nigerians and Ghanaians support themselves?

4. What religions predominate in Nigeria and Ghana?

5. What does an Ashanti stool symbolize?

CRITICAL THINKING

6. Categorize What kind of governments do Nigeria and Ghana have today?

7. Draw Conclusions Why do you think Nigeria has struggled for so long to keep a stable government?

8. CONNECT to Today Nigeria is the fifth-largest supplier of oil to the United States. What problems could an unstable Nigerian government pose to the United States?

9. SCIENCE Draw a Flow Chart Research cocoa production in Ghana. Construct a flow chart to show how cocoa beans are harvested, processed, and turned into chocolate for cocoa and candy.

While most West African countries have some sort of coastline, the Sahara still dominates countries such as Mauritania, Mali, and Niger.

Desert Life

Desert settlements, like this one in Mali, form near water sources. Mud-brick structures can provide insulation from the desert heat. Still, many African desert-dwellers live nomadically, moving from place to place.

Desert village near Mopti, Mali ▼

Work
Cattle herders move their livestock from one place to another.

Transportation
For centuries, camels have been the traditional means of crossing the Sahara.

Traditional mud-brick houses ▶

Coastal Life

West African coastal villages, like this one in Côte d'Ivoire, rely heavily on fishing for food. Commercial fishing further out to sea can jeopardize fish stocks. Countries such as Mauritania are banning some foreign fishing boats from fishing off their coasts.

Fishing village near Fresco, Côte d'Ivoire ▼

Work

A fisherman casts a net in Ghana.

Transportation

Fishing boat in Ghana

◄ *Coastal housing*

CRITICAL THINKING

1. **Compare and Contrast** How do people in these regions adapt their living arrangements to their surroundings?

2. **Make Inferences** Why would cattle herders need to move from place to place?

Reading for Understanding

▶ Key Ideas

BEFORE, YOU LEARNED

Nigeria and Ghana have struggled to maintain stable governments and productive economies.

NOW YOU WILL LEARN

Mali and Côte d'Ivoire are developing countries with lively cultural traditions.

▶ Vocabulary

TERMS & NAMES

federation colonies, states, or countries that have joined together

inflation a price increase or a fall in the purchasing power of money

infrastructure basic services a community needs, such as roads, railroads, water and power lines, schools, and post offices

millet a grain raised in West Africa, often made into porridge

BACKGROUND VOCABULARY

rig to influence or fix the results of an election

REVIEW

drought a long period of little or no rainfall

famine a severe food shortage

Visual Vocabulary millet

▶ Reading Strategy

Re-create the Venn diagram shown at right. As you read and respond to the **KEY QUESTIONS**, use the diagram to compare and contrast information about Mali and Côte d'Ivoire.

 Skillbuilder Handbook, page R9

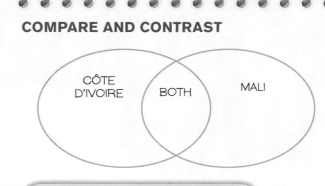

COMPARE AND CONTRAST

CÔTE D'IVOIRE   BOTH   MALI

GRAPHIC ORGANIZERS
Go to **Interactive Review** @ClassZone.com

Mali and Côte d'Ivoire

Connecting to Your World

Have you ever worked hard on something, only to feel like you got none of the benefit or credit? Mali produces more gold than any other African country except South Africa and Ghana. But despite Mali's natural wealth, local mining communities keep little of the wealth that their mines produce.

Panning for Gold
Gold helped build the West African trading empires and is a key resource in modern Mali.

MALI

Mali

▼ **KEY QUESTION** What does Mali's economy rely on?

Mali, located where three powerful African empires once reigned, remains one of the world's poorest countries. Nearly two-thirds of Mali's people live in poverty. Residents of Mali cluster in the basin of the Niger River because most of the country is located within the Sahara.

After overcoming fierce resistance from Africans, France seized a huge territory in West Africa in 1895. This territory included present-day Mali, then called French Sudan. French Sudan joined the Federation of West Africa in 1904. A **federation** is a group of colonies or states with a single government. In 1958, French Sudan won the right to govern itself within the larger French community. In 1960, the Republic of Mali gained full independence from France.

Mud-Brick Mosque
Rebuilt in 1907, the mud-brick Great Mosque dominates the ancient trading town of Djenné.

595

History Since Independence This young country has faced many difficulties. During the 1960s, Mali was left in debt as the result of worldwide inflation. **Inflation** means that costs rise and the value of money falls. In the 1970s and 1980s, rainfall shortages caused regional **droughts**. Thousands starved or died of malnutrition from the resulting **famines**. Mali lived under one-party rule or military dictatorship until 1992. That year, Mali adopted a constitution allowing a multiparty system and a democratically elected government.

Animated GEOGRAPHY

Modern Griots Part musician, part storyteller, part historian, griots play a key role in West African culture.

Click here to learn more about and see griots today @ ClassZone.com

Mali's Daily Life and Culture Most Malians are Muslims. The others follow traditional African religions or Christianity. French, the official language, is taught in schools, but most people speak African languages. Only a small percentage of Mali's school-age children attend schools, so fewer than half of the country's adults can read and write. Mali also has few doctors to treat many cases of malaria and waterborne illnesses. Buildings in Mali range from modern structures to buildings made of sun-dried mud bricks. The Great Mosque of Djenné, shown on the previous page, is an example of mud-brick architecture.

Despite its poverty, Mali's blend of Muslim cultures in the north and black African cultures in the south produces a rich cultural stew. Griots, or Jelis, as they are called in Mali's Bambara language, are important parts of Mali's culture. A famous musician is Salif Keita, a descendant of ancient Mali's founder, Sundiata. Mali's Malinka and Songhai peoples specialize in music and dancing, while the Bambara and Voltaic groups make fine masks, statues, and stools.

Economy Mali faces many challenges. Since it has no coast, it must rely on roads and ports leading to neighboring countries. Most Malians are livestock herders, fishers, or subsistence farmers, but less than four percent of Mali's land is fertile. The inland delta of the Niger River is an important source of fish. Farmers grow millet, rice, and sorghum for their families, or export cotton, peanuts, or sugar cane. However, the country suffers periodic droughts.

Mali has few factories, and the country's **infrastructure**—basic services such as roads and schools—remains undeveloped. Only about ten percent of Mali's roads are paved. Mali has important mineral resources, including gold, salt, and limestone. Gold is its most important mineral export. There are also large deposits of iron, bauxite, and uranium, but they are not significantly mined yet.

▲ **CATEGORIZE** Describe Mali's economy.

To learn more about Ali and his world, go to the **Activity Center** @ ClassZone.com

Hi! My name is Ali. I'm 12 years old and live in Mali's capital city of Bamako. My city has almost 1.5 million people. My big brother and I share one room, and my parents share our second room with my younger sister. Five other families live in my compound.

To introduce himself, Ali might say:

"Salut! Je m'appelle Ali."

7 A.M. It's still dark when I hear my mom cooking outside. For breakfast, we usually eat porridge. Sometimes, we also have beans and coffee. We eat together right outside our rooms.

8 A.M.–12 noon My seventh-grade class has 85 students—lots more boys than girls. I share a desk and a reading book with two other students. We also learn science, math, and French.

2 P.M.–6 P.M. I go to work. I'm an apprentice auto mechanic. I spend about four hours there every afternoon, doing whatever small jobs I'm given. I get paid only a little money, but I'm learning things I can use to make money later.

6 P.M.–8 P.M. Before dinner, I ride bikes or play soccer with my friends. We eat around eight o'clock. Our usual dinner is rice served with fish or meat sauce. Chocolate for dessert is a special treat.

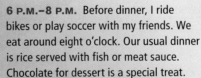

CONNECT to Your Life

Journal Entry Think about your school and outside activities. What sort of things are you learning? How are they similar to what Ali is learning? Record your ideas in your journal.

Our Lady of Peace This cathedral in Côte d'Ivoire's capital is the world's largest Christian church.

Côte d'Ivoire

KEY QUESTION How has Côte d'Ivoire's economy suffered in recent years?

Côte d'Ivoire (KOHT dee•vwahr) lies west of Ghana and east of Liberia on Africa's west coast. Like Mali, its northern neighbor, Côte d'Ivoire was once part of French West Africa. In the early 1700s, the French established coastal trading posts in present-day Côte d'Ivoire, exchanging European goods for ivory and slaves. Later, French colonizers forced West Africans to build roads and railroads, and to toil on cocoa, coffee, and logging plantations. These thriving plantations made Côte d'Ivoire West Africa's wealthiest French colony. The colony won independence from France in 1960, 14 years after the French ended forced labor.

History Since Independence Félix Houphouët-Boigny (OOF•WAY BWAH•nyuh), an African doctor, led the independence movement of French West African colonies. He became Côte d'Ivoire's first president in 1960, and held office until he died in 1993. After Houphouët-Boigny's death, political instability hurt Côte d'Ivoire's economy. The military took over the government in 1999. In 2000, a **rigged**, or fixed, election caused mass protest, leading to a three-year civil war. In 2003, a power-sharing government came to office, but occasional violence continued. In 2005, South Africa hosted talks between the Ivoirian government and rebel leaders. Although the war formally ended, rebels still control the northern half of the country.

Government President Houphouët-Boigny spent millions transforming his hometown, Yamoussoukro (YAH•moo•SOO•kroh), into Côte d'Ivoire's capital. But most business still takes place in Abidjan, the nation's largest city. Under Côte d'Ivoire's constitution, the president is elected by popular vote for a five-year term. He appoints a prime minister, who governs with the aid of a one-house National Assembly. Until 1990, Côte d'Ivoire had a single-party government.

Economics Two out of three Ivoirians are farmers, and the country is one of the world's biggest exporters of coffee, cocoa, and palm oil. But Côte d'Ivoire's dependence on a few products means the economy rises or falls with shifting worldwide prices. Continuing warfare threatens profits too. Côte d'Ivoire has offshore oil reserves, which may feed this developing nation's growth. The country's infrastructure is well-developed, with more than 4,000 miles of paved roads, cell phone access, and some Internet availability. Abidjan's seaport is one of the most modern in West Africa.

World Cup Côte d'Ivoire's national soccer team earned its first World Cup trip in 2006.

Ivoirian Culture and Daily Life Our Lady of Peace, the world's largest Christian church, dominates the skyline of Côte d'Ivoire's capital. But Christians in the southern regions of the country are outnumbered by Muslims and people following traditional African religions, especially in rural regions and the north. Most Ivoirians belong to the Akan, Kru, Mandes, or Voltaic peoples. Soccer is popular in Côte d'Ivoire. The Elephants, Côte d'Ivoire's national team, surprised the world by qualifying for their first-ever World Cup in 2006. About 25 percent of the population are immigrants, mostly from poorer neighboring countries. French is the country's official language, but most people speak ethnic languages or a common tongue, Dioula. Côte d'Ivoire's literacy rate—over 50 percent—is among the highest in West Africa.

Nearly half of Ivoirians live in cities, and many urban areas have French and Southwest Asian communities. However, the recent civil war led many Europeans to leave the country. There is a large divide in the cities between the poor and wealthier people. Crime has risen because of recent fighting. Côte d'Ivoire had more than 215,000 homeless children in 2004, including 50,000 in Abidjan.

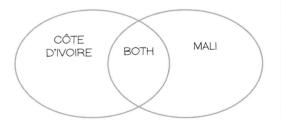
Mask Festival Yacouba people celebrate the Festival of Ignames, or yams.

Villagers live with extended families in compounds. The compounds are usually dried clay structures with thatched or metal roofs. Ethnic groups govern their villages in different ways; some with councils of elders, some with single chiefs. Trading, herding, and farming are the main activities. Important crops in the region are yams, root vegetables similar to sweet potatoes; and **millet**, a grain often made into porridge.

Ivoirian arts include music, storytelling by griots, and mask-making. The Dan people use masks to symbolize a chief's authority. The popular Festival of Masks is held in Côte d'Ivoire's forest region each November. Other mask ceremonies celebrate harvests. Alpha Blondy, a world-famous Ivoirian musician, blends African and Caribbean sounds in a style called "Afro-reggae." Zouglou is a musical style originating in Abidjan. Sung in French slang and local languages, it is similar to American hip-hop.

 SEQUENCE EVENTS Explain what led to Côte d'Ivoire's economic struggles.

Section ❸ Assessment

🔄 **ONLINE QUIZ**
For test practice, go to
Interactive Review
@ ClassZone.com

TERMS & NAMES

1. Explain the importance of
- inflation
- infrastructure
- drought
- famine

USE YOUR READING NOTES

2. Draw Conclusions Use your completed diagram to answer the following question:

Why is Côte d'Ivoire's economy more successful than Mali's?

CÔTE D'IVOIRE   BOTH   MALI

KEY IDEAS

3. In what year did both Mali and Côte d'Ivoire win their independence from France?

4. What are Mali's main exports?

5. What natural resource may improve Côte d'Ivoire's economy?

CRITICAL THINKING

6. Compare and Contrast How did Mali's taking the name of an ancient empire differ from Ghana's?

7. Analyze Cause and Effect What happened to spark Côte d'Ivoire's civil war?

8. CONNECT to Today Tensions remain high between Côte d'Ivoire's government and opposition leaders. What do you think might happen if French and West African peacekeeping troops leave the country?

9. ART **Draw a Mask** Research Bambara masks on the Internet. Copy a picture of your favorite mask and label it to describe its key elements and their symbolic meanings.

Interactive ⟲ Review

Click here to complete these and other activities online @ ClassZone.com

CHAPTER SUMMARY

Key Idea 1
Colonizers traveled to West Africa, dividing up land once held by great trading empires.

Key Idea 2
Nigeria and Ghana have struggled to maintain stable governments and productive economies.

Key Idea 3
Mali and Côte d'Ivoire have a wealth of natural resources, but are two of Africa's poorest countries.

For **Review and Study Notes**, go to **Interactive Review** @ ClassZone.com

NAME GAME

Use the Terms & Names list to complete each sentence on paper or online.

1. I am an ancient empire as well as a modern country that used to be known as the Gold Coast. _____Ghana_____

2. I led the Mali Empire in the 14th century. _____

3. I am perfectly equipped for desert travel. _____

4. I am an ancient empire, whose main city was Timbuktu, as well as a modern West African country._____

5. I am a region of Nigeria that broke away in a civil war in 1967. _____

6. I was modern Ghana's first president. _____

7. I am used by the Ashanti people to make clothing for religious ceremonies. _____

8. I am a nation's roads, bridges, schools, and post offices. _____

9. I am rising prices or a fall in the value of money.

10. I am a collection of states, colonies, or countries. _____

Biafra
camel
federation
Ghana
Igbo
imperialism
inflation
infrastructure
Kente cloth
Mali
Mansa Musa
Kwame Nkrumah
Songhai
subsistence
trans-Saharan
Yoruba

Activities

GeoGame

Use this map to reinforce your knowledge of West African geography. Drag and drop each name in the list to its location on the map.

Geo GAME

Ghana
Mali
Côte d'Ivoire
Bamako
Abuja

West Africa

Abuja

To play the complete game, go to **Interactive Review** @ ClassZone.com

Crossword Puzzle

Complete an online crossword puzzle to test your knowledge of the region.

ACROSS
1. a woven ceremonial fabric from Ghana

VOCABULARY

Explain the significance of each of the following.

1. Songhai
2. federation
3. infrastructure
4. imperialism
5. Ghana
6. Kente cloth
7. coup
8. Kwame Nkrumah

Explain how the terms and names in each group are related.

9. trans-Saharan, Ghana, and Mali
10. coup, Igbo, and Biafra

KEY IDEAS

1 Three Trading Empires

11. Why is Askia Muhammad known as Askia the Great?
12. Which European countries first explored Africa?
13. Which West African country remained free in the era of European imperialism?
14. What effect did World War II have on the African struggle for independence?

2 Nigeria and Ghana

15. What is the official language of Nigeria and Ghana?
16. Which African nation is the continent's most populous country?
17. What Nigerian art form inspired Western painters?
18. Why did the Gold Coast choose the ancient name of Ghana?

3 Mali and Côte d'Ivoire

19. What difficulties has Mali faced since independence?
20. In what year did Mali get its first democratic government?
21. What made Côte d'Ivoire the wealthiest colony in French West Africa?
22. What are Côte d'Ivoire's main exports?

CRITICAL THINKING

23. **Compare and Contrast** Create a chart to compare and contrast Ghana and Mali. Show their dates of independence, major products or industries, and chief challenges.

	GHANA	MALI
challenges		

24. **Make Predictions** What factors could affect Côte d'Ivoire's economy in the future?
25. **Connect to Economics** Which West African country would you predict will have the greatest economic success in the coming years? Why?
26. **Five Themes: Region** In Nigeria and Côte d'Ivoire, why does Islam dominate in northern regions, while Christianity and African religions prevail in the south or along the coast?
27. **Connect Geography & Culture** What makes Mali a cultural crossroads?

Answer the ESSENTIAL QUESTION

How have centuries of colonialism affected West Africa?

Written Response Write a two- or three-paragraph response to the Essential Question. Be sure to consider the key ideas of each section. Use the rubric below to guide your thinking.

Response Rubric
A strong response will:
- summarize colonialism in West Africa
- note colonialism's lingering effects on industry, ethnic conflict, and government corruption
- explain how concentration on a single crop or resource benefited colonizers, not Africans

BAR GRAPH

Use the bar graph and your knowledge of geography to answer questions 1 and 2.

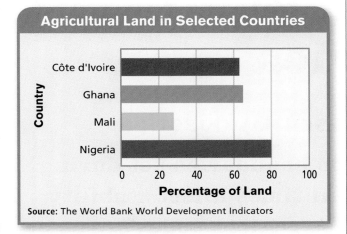

Agricultural Land in Selected Countries

Source: The World Bank World Development Indicators

1. Which nation has the highest percentage of agricultural land?

A. Côte d'Ivoire
B. Ghana
C. Mali
D. Nigeria

2. Why might Mali have such a low percentage of agricultural land?

A. because Mali is landlocked
B. because Mali's economy is more focused on industry
C. because the northern part of Mali is in the Sahara
D. because Mali has no rivers for irrigation

PRIMARY SOURCE

Nigerian author Chinua Achebe gained fame for *Things Fall Apart*, his novel about Nigeria under colonial rule. In this passage, he discusses why his book is read worldwide. Use the passage to answer questions 3 and 4.

> I knew I had a story, but how it fit into the story of the world—I really had no sense of that. Its meaning for my Igbo people was clear to me, but I didn't know how other people elsewhere would respond to it. Did it have any meaning or resonance for them? I realized it did when . . . the whole class of a girls' college in South Korea wrote to me and each one expressed an opinion about the book. And then I learned something, which was that they had a history that was similar to the story of *Things Fall Apart*—the history of colonization.

Source: Chinua Achebe, interview in *Atlantic Monthly*, August 2, 2000

3. Why might people from other countries relate to Achebe's novel?

4. What can you infer about Achebe's reaction to the book's success?

GeoActivity

1. INTERDISCIPLINARY ACTIVITY–SCIENCE

With a small group, research malaria and the waterborne illnesses that plague much of West Africa. Make a brief oral presentation to your class, describing preventive measures.

2. WRITING FOR SOCIAL STUDIES

Research the beginnings of Pan-Africanism. Write a short essay on how the movement for freedom in Africa was related to the struggle for African-American civil rights.

3. MENTAL MAPPING

Create an outline map of West Africa and label the following:

• Atlantic Ocean
• Ghana
• Accra
• Nigeria
• Abuja
• Lagos
• Côte d'Ivoire
• Yamoussoukro
• Mali
• Bamako

20 East, Central, and Southern Africa

ESSENTIAL QUESTION

How do boundaries set during colonial times affect stability in these regions today?

1 FOCUS ON
Ethiopia

2 FOCUS ON
Kenya

3 FOCUS ON
Democratic Republic of the Congo

4 FOCUS ON
South Africa

5 FOCUS ON
Zimbabwe, Botswana, and Angola

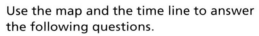

CONNECT Geography & History

Use the map and the time line to answer the following questions.

1. What nation is surrounded completely by the country of South Africa?

2. What sea route would Portuguese explorers have had to take to reach Kenya's coast in 1498?

Geography
1000 Great Zimbabwe is built. ▶

A.D. 50

History
50 Aksum begins to emerge. (Obelisk of Aksum) ▶

Culture
330 King Ezana establishes Christianity as Aksum's state religion.

Geography
1498 Vasco da Gama of Portugal reaches Kenya's coast.

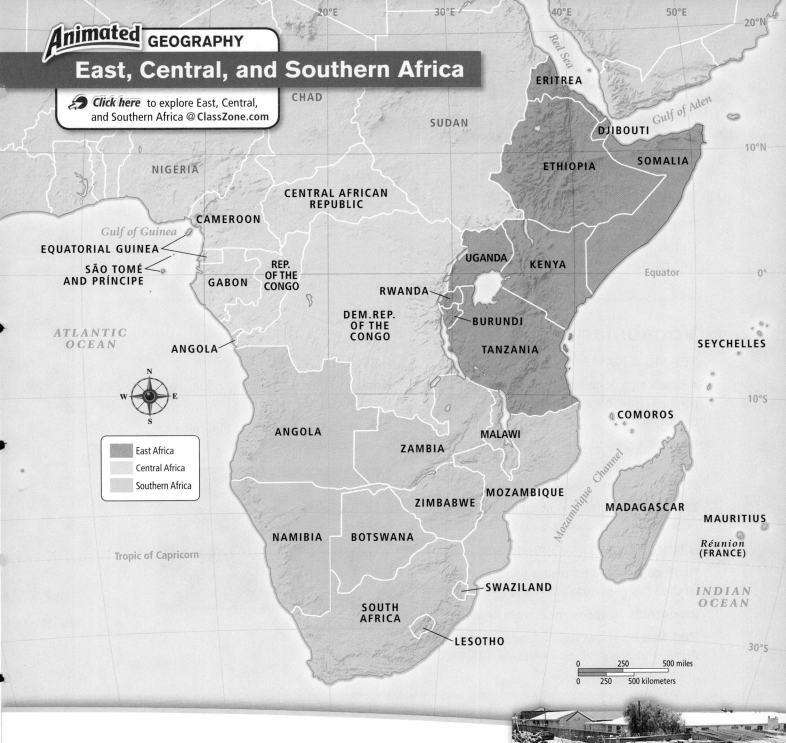

Animated GEOGRAPHY

East, Central, and Southern Africa

Click here to explore East, Central, and Southern Africa @ ClassZone.com

CHAD

SUDAN

ERITREA

DJIBOUTI

ETHIOPIA

SOMALIA

Gulf of Aden

Red Sea

NIGERIA

CENTRAL AFRICAN REPUBLIC

CAMEROON

Gulf of Guinea

EQUATORIAL GUINEA

SÃO TOMÉ AND PRÍNCIPE

GABON

REP. OF THE CONGO

DEM. REP. OF THE CONGO

UGANDA

KENYA

RWANDA

BURUNDI

TANZANIA

ANGOLA

ATLANTIC OCEAN

Equator

SEYCHELLES

ANGOLA

ZAMBIA

MALAWI

COMOROS

MOZAMBIQUE

MADAGASCAR

MAURITIUS

Réunion (FRANCE)

Mozambique Channel

ZIMBABWE

NAMIBIA

BOTSWANA

SWAZILAND

SOUTH AFRICA

LESOTHO

INDIAN OCEAN

Tropic of Capricorn

N W E S

	East Africa
	Central Africa
	Southern Africa

0   250   500 miles
0   250   500 kilometers

History
1908 Belgium takes control of Congo Free State.

History
1963 Kenya wins independence. (Jomo Kenyatta) ▶

Government
1994 South Africa holds its first free, democratic election. ▶

Today

Government
2006 Angola and Congo (Kinshasa) hold long-awaited national elections.

Reading for Understanding

▶ Key Ideas

BEFORE, YOU LEARNED

Colonial powers took over many regions in Africa.

NOW YOU WILL LEARN

Ethiopia remained an independent nation throughout most of its history.

▶ Vocabulary

TERMS & NAMES

Aksum an empire that controlled much of northern Ethiopia from the first to the eighth century A.D.

obelisk a pillar-shaped stone monument

Haile Selassie (HY•lee suh•LAS•ee) emperor of Ethiopia from 1930 to 1974

Eritrea a former region of Ethiopia that became an independent country in 1993

BACKGROUND VOCABULARY

Horn of Africa a horn-shaped extension of land on the east coast of Africa

modernize to accept new ways or ideas

Red Sea a narrow sea that divides northeast Africa from the Arabian Peninsula

REVIEW

Kush an ancient Nubian kingdom in northern Sudan

dynasty a family or group that rules for several generations

Visual Vocabulary Red Sea

▶ Reading Strategy

Re-create the web diagram shown at right. As you read and respond to the **KEY QUESTIONS**, use the diagram to organize important ideas about Ethiopia.

 Skillbuilder Handbook, page R4

FIND MAIN IDEAS

History — Culture — ETHIOPIA — Government — Economy

GRAPHIC ORGANIZERS
Go to **Interactive Review** @ ClassZone.com

Ethiopia

Connecting to Your World

Hundreds of workers took more than six years to create 60-foot carvings of four presidents at Mount Rushmore, South Dakota. Ethiopia's mountains contain an even more amazing monument. Eight hundred years ago, using nothing but hand tools, workers carved 11 Christian churches out of solid rock.

Rock Church One of 11 churches carved out of solid rock in Lalibela, Ethiopia.

A History of Independence

▼ **KEY QUESTION** How did ancient Aksum's location make it a powerful trading empire?

Ethiopia is one of the longest-settled regions in the world. **Aksum**, the first major state to develop in Ethiopia, became important about A.D. 100. This kingdom achieved its greatest strength between the 300s and 600s.

Ancient Aksum Aksum was located near the **Horn of Africa** and expanded into parts of southwest Arabia. This major trade center exported spices, ivory, ebony, animal skins, and tortoiseshell. Trading partners included Arabia, India, and perhaps China. Aksumites built more than 100 carved stone pillars, called **obelisks**, in their capital. Some stood as monuments over rulers' tombs.

A Rugged Country Ethiopia's landforms include rift valleys and highlands.

ETHIOPIA
Rift Valley

607

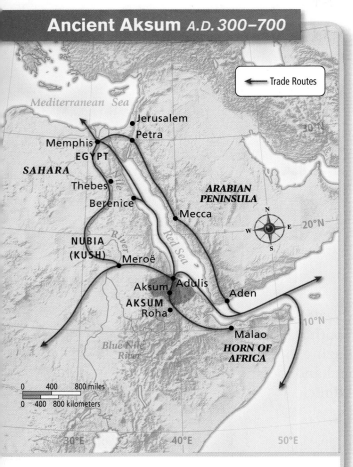

Ancient Aksum A.D. 300–700

← Trade Routes

Mediterranean Sea
Jerusalem
Petra
Memphis
EGYPT
SAHARA
Thebes
Berenice
Mecca
ARABIAN PENINSULA
NUBIA (KUSH)
Meroë
Aksum Adulis
AKSUM
Roha
Aden
Malao
HORN OF AFRICA
Blue Nile River
Red Sea
River

0 400 800 miles
0 400 800 kilometers

30°E   40°E   50°E
30°N
20°N
10°N

CONNECT Geography & History

1. **Movement** Aksum had trade access to what areas outside of Africa?
2. **Location** Traveling by land, what was Aksum's closest trading partner?

During the 300s, Aksum's King Ezana conquered **Kush** and made Christianity Aksum's state religion. But Muslim conquests in North Africa in the 600s hurt Aksum's trading power by taking over sea routes. The kingdom shifted to the south and moved its capital to Roha, the city that would become Lalibela. As Aksum declined, a new **dynasty**, the Zagwe, rose beginning in 1137. During the Zagwe reign, workers created 11 Christian churches from the rock at Lalibela.

Remaining Independent The Zagwe dynasty lasted less than 100 years, replaced by a line of emperors said to descend from the biblical King Solomon. These emperors had the backing of the Ethiopian Christian church and built a national identity. Menelik II became emperor of Ethiopia in 1889 and defeated Italy's 1896 invasion attempt.

Ethiopia's next important leader, **Haile Selassie**, took power in 1930. Haile Selassie's attempts to **modernize** Ethiopia included ending legal slavery and giving the country its first constitution. Ethiopia briefly fell to Italy during World War II but regained independence afterwards. In the later years of Haile Selassie's rule, Ethiopia fought a civil war in a region called **Eritrea**, along the **Red Sea**. In 1974, a coup removed Haile Selassie from power.

Recent Ethiopian History Ethiopia has suffered many setbacks in recent years. The coup that removed Haile Selassie brought a brutal military dictator named Mengistu to power. The state took control of land, industry, and banking. Mengistu waged war with neighboring Somalia and continued the conflict with Eritrea. The Mengistu government also badly mishandled a famine in 1984. A rebel group defeated Mengistu in 1991 and agreed to Eritrea's independence. But fighting along this tense border continued during 2005. More droughts in the 1990s and early 2000s resulted in millions of deaths. Ethiopia adopted a new constitution in 1994 and held multiparty elections the following year. But in November 2005, election violence led to scores of shootings.

▲ **DRAW CONCLUSIONS** Describe how location helped Aksum dominate trade.

Government and Economics

▼ **KEY QUESTION** What problems have hurt Ethiopia's economy?

Ethiopia is the oldest independent country in Africa, and one of the oldest in the world. Yet its first multiparty elections weren't held until 1995. The party that won in 1995 repeated its victories in 2000 and 2005. But some Ethiopians believed the 2005 election was dishonest, and they disputed the results in violent protests.

Structure of the Government and Economy Ethiopia has many political parties. The party with the most members in the legislature chooses the prime minister, who runs the executive branch and chooses the cabinet ministers. Ethiopia's legislature has two houses. The members of one house are elected directly by the voters, while representatives of the other house of the legislature are selected by state councils.

Despite its fertile soil and plentiful highland rainfall, Ethiopia remains poor. It has suffered from bad government; conflicts, such as the wars with Eritrea; natural disasters, including droughts; and limited use of its resources. The government owns all the land. A few farmers grow cash crops, but most Ethiopians are subsistence farmers. Overgrazing and deforestation have eroded the soil, destroying productive land while leaving fertile ground uncultivated. This landlocked country has no commercial fishing, and little mining and industry. Political instability has discouraged foreign investment in Ethiopia's economy. Most of the roads are unpaved, and only one railroad operates.

Like many other developing countries, Ethiopia has inadequate educational and health systems. Since schooling isn't required, the country's literacy rate hovers at just about 40 percent. Malaria, typhoid, and other diseases pose serious health risks.

What the Economy Produces Ethiopia's factories produce textiles, cement, food products, and shoes for domestic use. The country's top export is coffee. Other exports include animal skins and hides, oilseed, and sugarcane.

Like coffee, the cereal product teff is native to Ethiopia. Teff is the world's smallest grain. Its name comes from the Amharic word for "lost." Teff is well adapted to Ethiopia's highland soil, high in nutrients, and easily digested by people who can't eat wheat and other grains. Sorghum, another major grain product, is favored for its ability to grow in very dry conditions.

▲ **ANALYZE CAUSES** Identify causes of Ethiopia's economic troubles.

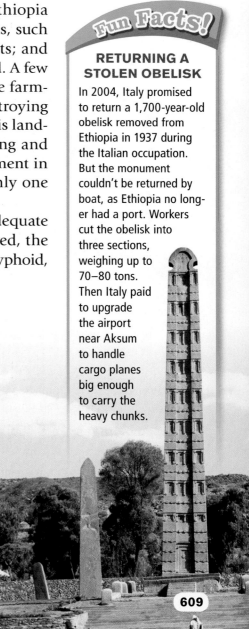

Fun Facts!

RETURNING A STOLEN OBELISK
In 2004, Italy promised to return a 1,700-year-old obelisk removed from Ethiopia in 1937 during the Italian occupation. But the monument couldn't be returned by boat, as Ethiopia no longer had a port. Workers cut the obelisk into three sections, weighing up to 70–80 tons. Then Italy paid to upgrade the airport near Aksum to handle cargo planes big enough to carry the heavy chunks.

Ethiopian Culture and Life

▼ **KEY QUESTION** What effects has religion had on Ethiopian culture?

When ancient Aksum moved south, its Christian population was separated from other Christian states. This led Ethiopian Orthodox Christianity to develop apart from other types of Christianity. For one thing, Ethiopian Orthodox Christians observe the Jewish laws of diet. They also pray in their ancient language of Ge'ez (gee•EHZ).

Daily Life Most Ethiopians live in rural areas, where they farm or herd cattle, goats, or sheep. Using wooden plows and oxen, subsistence farmers depend on rain to grow their cereal crops, such as teff, corn, wheat, or sorghum. Herders, like the Borana in the arid south, often must migrate to find water for their animals.

Ethiopian city dwellers live in Western-style houses, work in tall office buildings, and wear Western clothing. In rural regions, some people live in round mud and wood houses with thatched or tin roofs, while others live in rectangular stone houses. Many adults wear a white cotton cloth called a *shamma* over their shirts or dresses.

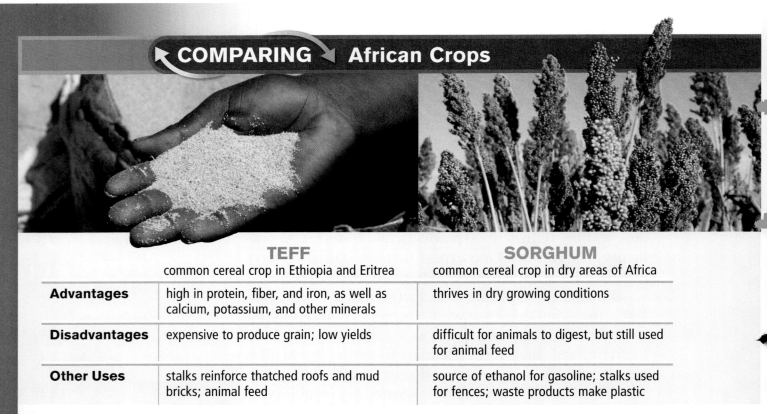

COMPARING ► African Crops

	TEFF common cereal crop in Ethiopia and Eritrea	**SORGHUM** common cereal crop in dry areas of Africa
Advantages	high in protein, fiber, and iron, as well as calcium, potassium, and other minerals	thrives in dry growing conditions
Disadvantages	expensive to produce grain; low yields	difficult for animals to digest, but still used for animal feed
Other Uses	stalks reinforce thatched roofs and mud bricks; animal feed	source of ethanol for gasoline; stalks used for fences; waste products make plastic

CRITICAL THINKING

1. **Evaluate** Which grain would you grow for animal feed, and why?

2. **Make Inferences** Which grain might be useful in reducing dependence on oil, and why?

Ethiopians eat spicy meat or vegetable stews called *wat*, scooped up by hand with *injera* (ihn•JEER•uh), a flat sour bread made from fermented teff. Soccer and volleyball are popular sports. A game called *genna*, which resembles field hockey, is traditionally played at Christmas.

Cultural Traits Until 1974, Christianity was the official religion of the country's rulers, and it inspired much of Ethiopia's art and literature. In today's Ethiopia, however, Muslims slightly outnumber Christians. About nine out of ten Ethiopians are Muslim or Christian, while the rest follow traditional African religions.

Ethiopians of all faiths place a high value on moral behavior, hospitality, politeness, respect for elders, and the pursuit of wisdom. Some of Ethiopia's hundred languages are related to Arabic and Hebrew. Others are African.

Injera A woman pours injera batter onto a hot griddle. **How does injera appear to differ from sandwich bread?**

The Arts Traditional Ethiopian arts include obelisks, the rock churches of Lalibela, church walls covered with paintings called frescoes, and lavishly illustrated Bibles. Modern artists and musicians continue to draw on their Ethiopian Orthodox faith for artistic inspiration. Today's Ethiopian writers write in modern Ethiopian languages, including Amharic.

▲ **SUMMARIZE** Explain how religion has influenced Ethiopian culture.

Section 1 Assessment

ONLINE QUIZ
For test practice, go to
Interactive Review
@ ClassZone.com

TERMS & NAMES

1. Explain the importance of
- Aksum
- Horn of Africa
- Haile Selassie
- Red Sea

USE YOUR READING NOTES

2. Find Main Ideas Use your completed diagram to answer the following question:

What is Ethiopia's main export?

KEY IDEAS

3. What major accomplishment occurred during the Zagwe dynasty?

4. What features differentiate Ethiopian Orthodox Christianity from other Christian sects?

5. Why is there little commercial fishing in Ethiopia?

CRITICAL THINKING

6. Make Inferences Why do you think Menelik II is a national hero in Ethiopia?

7. Identify Solutions What changes could improve conditions in Ethiopia? Explain your answer.

8. CONNECT to Today In 2006, Ethiopia announced that its economy had grown due to a shift away from its concentration on agriculture. How could diversifying Ethiopia's products improve its economy?

9. WRITING Create a Menu Design a menu for an Ethiopian restaurant, including simple illustrations. Research the Ethiopian dishes *injera* and *wat*, so that you can describe their ingredients.

Reading for Understanding

SECTION **2**

▶ Key Ideas

BEFORE, YOU LEARNED

West African kingdoms built vast trading empires.

NOW YOU WILL LEARN

Trade was also important in East Africa, particularly in what is now Kenya.

▶ Vocabulary

TERMS & NAMES

safari an overland expedition for exploring, hunting, or photography

monsoon a seasonal wind bringing heavy rainfall

Swahili an African language, commonly spoken in East Africa

Mau Mau a Kenyan independence movement that began in the 1940s

Jomo Kenyatta independent Kenya's first president

BACKGROUND VOCABULARY

porridge a soft food made by boiling cereal grain in milk or water

Visual Vocabulary safari

▶ Reading Strategy

Re-create the chart shown at right. As you read and respond to the **KEY QUESTIONS**, use the chart to make inferences about Kenya's government, history, and culture.

 Skillbuilder Handbook, page R11

MAKE INFERENCES

FACTS	INFERENCES
1.	1.
2.	2.
3.	3.
4.	4.

 GRAPHIC ORGANIZERS
Go to **Interactive Review** @ClassZone.com

SECTION

2

FOCUS ON

Kenya

Connecting to Your World

One hundred years ago, Europeans and Americans traveled to Africa on hunting or exploring expeditions called **safaris**. This year, thousands of people will go on safari to Kenya's Masai Mara, famous for lions, or Amboseli National Reserve, noted for elephants. But the only shooting tourists will do is with their cameras. Safaris bring Kenya millions of tourist dollars each year.

History of a Trading Region

▼ **KEY QUESTION** How did the Swahili language develop?

The ancient kingdom of Aksum controlled trade to Arabia. After the 600s, that trade fell into the hands of Muslim invaders. Now you'll learn how Muslim trading cities spread down the East African coast, affecting inland African populations.

Inland Villages, Coastal Cities Earlier you learned that the Bantu-speaking people of Africa migrated across the southern part of the continent between 1000 B.C. and A.D. 1100. Bantu speakers, seeking land for their farms and herds, eventually reached Africa's east coast. Their iron-working skills helped them produce farming tools.

Elephants Elephants graze at Amboseli National Reserve.

Mombasa Arches representing elephant tusks welcome visitors to Kenya's main port city.

KENYA

Mombasa

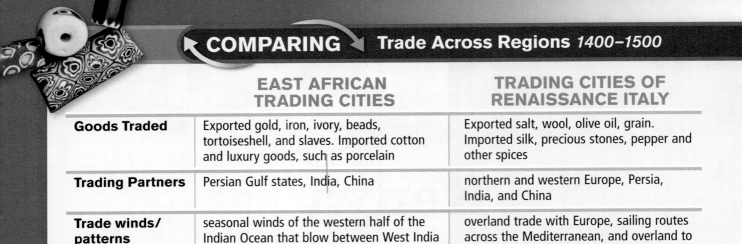

COMPARING Trade Across Regions *1400–1500*

	EAST AFRICAN TRADING CITIES	TRADING CITIES OF RENAISSANCE ITALY
Goods Traded	Exported gold, iron, ivory, beads, tortoiseshell, and slaves. Imported cotton and luxury goods, such as porcelain	Exported salt, wool, olive oil, grain. Imported silk, precious stones, pepper and other spices
Trading Partners	Persian Gulf states, India, China	northern and western Europe, Persia, India, and China
Trade winds/ patterns enabling trade	seasonal winds of the western half of the Indian Ocean that blow between West India and East Africa	overland trade with Europe, sailing routes across the Mediterranean, and overland to the Far East along the Silk Roads

CRITICAL THINKING

1. Analyze Effects Why did East African trading cities depend on trade winds?

2. Make Inferences How did merchants become wealthy?

Along this same coast, traders from Arabia had established several dozen thriving trading cities by the 1400s, including Mombasa and Malindi in today's Kenya. **Monsoons**, seasonal rain-bearing winds, propelled Arab trade ships to India. These ships carried gold, leopard skins, beads, copper, and ivory, brought to the coast by inland African traders. Other than trade, the inland villagers—farmers and herders who practiced African religions—had little to do with the Muslim city dwellers. But their trade contacts produced one important cultural effect. By the 1400s, most townspeople spoke a blend of Bantu and Arabic, an ancestor of today's African language **Swahili**.

European Domination By the early 1500s, Portugal controlled the wealthy East African cities. The Portuguese traded small numbers of slaves. In the late 1800s, Europe began the scramble for African colonies you learned about in the last chapter. After Germany and Britain divided East Africa, the territory that would become Kenya was called British East Africa. The British encouraged Europeans to settle in British East Africa and establish huge farms.

Independence and Afterward During the 1940s, East Africans began uniting to oppose British rule. Britain's refusal to consider their demands triggered a revolution in 1952. A resistance group called the **Mau Mau** led this revolt. The British imprisoned thousands of rebels, including **Jomo Kenyatta**, a Kenyan political leader. Kenyatta spent seven years in prison, despite denying Mau Mau involvement.

By the late 1950s, Britain agreed to national elections. Kenya won independence in 1963, and the following year Jomo Kenyatta became the nation's first president. Kenyatta's attempts to modernize Kenya included expanding educational opportunities and limiting property ownership to Kenyans. Kenyatta died in 1978 and was succeeded by his vice president, Daniel Moi, who led until 2002. For most of its recent history, Kenya has been a one-party state, despite a 1991 amendment establishing a multiparty system. In 2002, the head of a multi-ethnic party won a peaceful democratic presidential election.

▲ **SUMMARIZE** Describe how East African trade created Swahili.

Life in Kenya

▼ **KEY QUESTION** What interests do many Kenyans share?

Since independence, the Kenyan government has tried to promote national pride. That's difficult in a country where some 40 ethnic groups struggle to get along and no single culture dominates.

Daily Life and Activities Kenya's largest ethnic group is the Kikuyu, followed by the Luhya (LOO•yah), Kalenjin (KAL•uhn•jihn), Luo, and Kamba. Most groups have their own language, but many Kenyans also know Swahili and English, the country's official languages. At least two-thirds of Kenyans are Christian. About 10 percent follow traditional African religions. Another 10 percent are Muslim, living mostly along the coast.

Kenyan Runners
Catherine Ndereba celebrates her marathon victory at the 2003 world track and field championships.
What is Ndereba holding behind herself?

One of Kenya's most famous writers, Ngugi wa Thiong'o, wrote novels in English and in his native Kikuyu. Most Kenyans enjoy dancing and dance performances and follow their favorite soccer teams. Several Kenyan runners have won Olympic medals for track and field. Kenyan runners also regularly win the yearly Boston Marathon.

About three out of four Kenyans live in rural areas. A farming family typically occupies a small house with a thatched roof, mud walls, and dirt floors. A few Kenyans, like the Masai, are nomadic herders. Every day, most Kenyans eat maize, or corn, which they grind and cook as **porridge**, then mix with other vegetables to make a stew.

▲ **SUMMARIZE** Identify the common interests of many Kenyans.

Jomo Kenyatta (1894–1978) headed the Kenya African Union (K.A.U.), a pro-liberty party, before Kenya's independence. The British said that the K.A.U. was responsible for the Mau Mau rebellion, and they arrested Kenyatta after this speech:

> K.A.U. is you and you are the K.A.U. If we unite now, each and every one of us, and each tribe to another, we will cause the implementation in this country of that which the European calls democracy. True democracy has no colour distinction. It does not choose between black and white. We are here in this tremendous gathering under the K.A.U. flag to find which road leads us from darkness into democracy. In order to find it we Africans must first achieve the right to elect our own representatives.

Source: Jomo Kenyatta, speech at the Kenya African Union Meeting, July 26, 1952

DOCUMENT-BASED QUESTION
What right did Kenyatta say was the first step to democracy?

Jomo Kenyatta used a traditional flywhisk, or flyswatter, as a presidential symbol. ▶

ONLINE PRIMARY SOURCE To see more of Jomo Kenyatta's works, go to the **Research & Writing Center** @ClassZone.com

Government and Economy

▼ **KEY QUESTION** How has Kenya's government changed since independence?

Kenya's national motto is "Harambee," the Swahili word for cooperation. But pulling together this ethnically diverse developing country continues to pose a challenge. Both Kenya's government and its economy have been plagued by corruption.

Regional assemblies had many powers after independence. Changes since then have given much more power to the president. For example, the president heads the military. In addition, the president's cabinet, chosen from the National Assembly, helps pass laws the president favors. The president and the National Assembly are popularly elected for five-year terms. The Kenyan constitution guarantees many freedoms, but the president can jail people who threaten public security.

Private citizens own most of Kenya's land and businesses, but the government keeps partial ownership of some businesses and regulates others. In the past, government regulators have taken bribes.

Kenya's new government is trying to root out corruption to promote the country's economic growth.

Kenya's economy is based on agriculture. Four out of ten Kenyans were unemployed in 2000, and half its people live in poor conditions. Kenya's subsistence farmers use traditional tools to grow enough maize to feed their families. But some large farms turn out Kenya's main cash crops, coffee and tea, and food processing is a growing industry.

Coffee and tea are Kenya's top moneymakers, but tourism is a key industry. Half a million tourists visit Kenya's national parks and game reserves each year. Tourism pumps $200 million into the economy annually. Some Kenyans resist tourism, saying this industry exploits resources to benefit relatively few Kenyans and recalls Kenya's colonial past. But other Kenyans feel that tourism is a good replacement for subsistence farming in a dry country with unpredictable rain.

 SUMMARIZE Describe how Kenya's government has changed since independence.

Economic Activities of Kenya *2004*

- ■ Services, Government — 49%
- Agriculture, Fishing — 26%
- Tourism — 12%
- ■ Manufacturing — 11%
- Mining, Forestry — 2%

Source: Central Bank of Kenya Statistical Bulletin

"Say cheetah" A photographer gets a close-up view of a cheetah at Masai Mara National Reserve.

 ONLINE QUIZ
For test practice, go to **Interactive Review** @ ClassZone.com

Section 2 Assessment

TERMS & NAMES

1. Explain the importance of
- Safari
- Swahili
- Mau Mau
- Jomo Kenyatta

USE YOUR READING NOTES

2. Make Inferences Use your completed diagram to answer the following question:

Why did Kenya's one-party system offer only limited democracy?

FACTS	INFERENCES
1.	1.
2.	2.
3.	3.
4.	4.

KEY IDEAS

3. What European country colonized Kenya in the late 1800s?

4. How did President Kenyatta try to modernize Kenya?

5. What are Kenya's key industries?

CRITICAL THINKING

6. Make Predictions Could a multi-ethnic party end Kenya's history of corrupt government? Explain.

7. Evaluate Do you think tourism is a good idea or a bad idea for Kenya's economy? Explain.

8. CONNECT to Today Kenyan Nobel Prize winner Wangari Maathai said, "Protecting the global environment is directly related to securing peace." What do you think she meant by this statement?

9. TECHNOLOGY Make a Mini-Dictionary Use the Internet to research 20 Swahili words and phrases for a mini-dictionary of useful terms for a safari. List the word or phrase, its English meaning, and its origin.

Reading for Understanding

▶ Key Ideas

BEFORE, YOU LEARNED

As some African nations won political freedom from colonial powers, they fell under dictatorships or military rule.

NOW YOU WILL LEARN

The Democratic Republic of the Congo is still struggling with setting up a true democracy.

▶ Vocabulary

TERMS & NAMES

Congo River Africa's second-longest river

Pygmy a member of a people with an average height of less than five feet

hunter-gatherer a person who hunts animals and gathers plants for food

Kongo a member of a people living along the lower Congo River; a Bantu-speaking kingdom of the Congo River region arising in the 1300s

Leopold II King of Belgium, who was forced to give up his private ownership of the Congo Free State

Mobutu Sese Seko dictator of the Democratic Republic of the Congo from 1965 to 1997

Zaire name of the Democratic Republic of the Congo between 1971 and 1997

BACKGROUND VOCABULARY

quota a target amount for production

▶ Reading Strategy

Re-create the diagram shown at right. As you read and respond to the **KEY QUESTIONS**, use the diagram to help you make generalizations about the Democratic Republic of the Congo.

 Skillbuilder Handbook, page R12

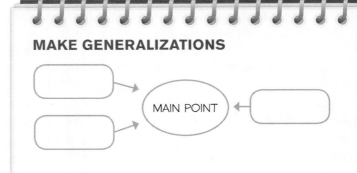

MAKE GENERALIZATIONS

MAIN POINT

GRAPHIC ORGANIZERS
Go to **Interactive Review** @ClassZone.com

Democratic Republic of the Congo

Connecting to Your World

Have you ever known two classmates with the same first name? To avoid confusion, did people add last names or initials when talking about them? Two African countries, both called Congo, lie along the Congo River. The capital of the Democratic Republic of the Congo is Kinshasa; the Republic of the Congo's capital is Brazzaville. In this section you'll learn about the larger of the two, the Democratic Republic of the Congo, also called Congo (Kinshasa).

A River Culture

🔻 **KEY QUESTION** What groups have controlled what is now Congo?

The **Congo River**, the continent's second-longest, rises near the country's southeast corner and flows in a giant counterclockwise circle before draining into the Atlantic Ocean. The river's name comes from the Kongo kingdom that arose here in the 1300s. This mighty river flows through Congo (Kinshasa), and along the border with Congo (Brazzaville). Four deep lakes, including Lake Tanganyika, line Congo's eastern border.

Congo River The Congo and its tributaries form Africa's largest river system.

619

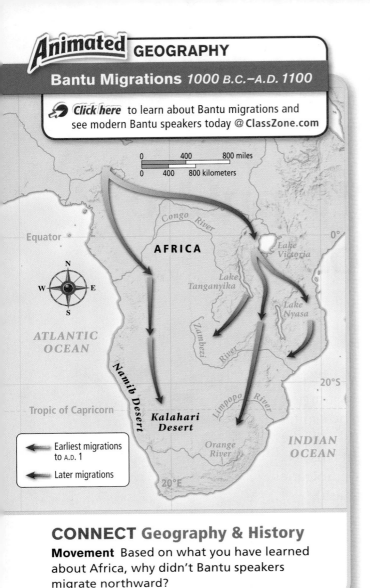

CONNECT Geography & History

Movement Based on what you have learned about Africa, why didn't Bantu speakers migrate northward?

Early History Congo's earliest inhabitants were **Pygmies**, very short people who still live as hunter-gatherers. **Hunter-gatherers** hunt animals and collect wild food instead of practicing agriculture and herding. The Bantu migrations brought Bantu-speaking peoples into the region between the 900s and 1300s. They established several important kingdoms, including Luba, Lunda, and **Kongo**. The Kongo kingdom ruled the coast. Kongo traded with Portugal, and members of the Kongo royal family became Catholic. But Portugal came to view Kongo as a source for slaves.

Belgian Control European enslavement of Kongo's people continued through the 1800s. In 1885, Belgium's King **Leopold II** convinced other European leaders to let him rule his own personal colony, to be called the Congo Free State. Instead of telling the truth—that he wanted to get richer—Leopold promised to bring Christianity and progress to Africa and end slavery. After forcing Africans to build a railroad, the king's agents cruelly punished those who failed to produce their **quota** of rubber. Protests from the United States and Britain led the Belgian government to take control of the Congo Free State in 1908, slightly improving living conditions.

Independence and Afterward When Belgian Congo suddenly won independence in 1960, its leaders were unprepared to govern. During the 1960s, Congolese troops rebelled against their Belgian officers, leaving behind a dangerous, undisciplined army. The inexperienced government couldn't unify the country, and several of Congo's provinces left or threatened to secede. A coup in 1965 gave Joseph Mobutu the presidency. President Mobutu tried to reduce ethnic divisions and instill pride in the country's heritage. He changed his own name to **Mobutu Sese Seko** and the country's name to **Zaire**. But Mobutu was a corrupt dictator who made himself rich at his country's expense. He was overthrown in 1997. The new leader, Laurent Kabila, renamed the country the Democratic Republic of the Congo. Kabila's 2001 assassination left his son Joseph in power.

🔺 **SEQUENCE EVENTS** Name the powers who controlled the Congo region from its earliest history to 1960.

Culture and Life in Congo

▼ KEY QUESTION What are Congo's four national languages?

As in many other African nations created by colonial powers, ethnic conflicts have plagued Congo (Kinshasa). Central Africa's largest country is home to more than 200 different languages.

A Land of Diversity Most of today's Congolese people descend from Bantu speakers who migrated to Congo centuries ago. Of the country's many local languages, almost all belong to the Bantu group and are closely related. French, the country's official language, is used in government and taught in school. Many Congolese also speak Swahili or another of the country's national languages, Kikongo, Lingala, or Tshiluba.

About four out of five Congolese are Christians. Most of these are Roman Catholic. Ten percent of Congolese are Muslims, and a similar number follow African religions.

Daily Life More than a dozen cities in Congo have at least 100,000 people. Kinshasa's population has grown to more than six million since independence. Still, most of Congo's 62.5 million people live in villages containing a few dozen to a few hundred people. These villagers live in mud brick or dried mud-and-stick houses with thatched roofs. A wealthy family might install a metal roof.

Congolese Music Boys from the Bodjaba tribe play a Mokoto drum.

Following independence, many Congolese businessmen traded Western-style dress for a national outfit of pants and a collarless jacket worn without shirt or tie. Women typically wear long, one-piece cotton dresses or a long skirt and blouse. Most Congolese meals feature porridge made of corn, rice, or cassava meal, topped with a spicy sauce. People who can afford meat or fish add it to the porridge. But many poor Congolese suffer malnutrition from a lack of protein.

Congolese Arts Centuries ago, enslaved Africans brought their musical styles to the Caribbean. Modern Congolese music takes those Afro-Caribbean rhythms and mixes them with African sounds. *Soukous*, a popular guitar-based musical style, developed in Kinshasa. The name comes from the French word *secouer*, or "to shake."

African Textiles Woven textiles play important roles in many African cultures. A design may symbolize a culture's myths, or say something about the social status of the person wearing it.

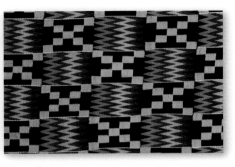

Adinkra cloth originated with West Africa's Ashanti and Gyaman peoples. Patterns and symbols are stamped onto the cloth using dyes.

Kuba cloth comes from the Congo region. Weavers make the basic cloth from a palm fiber called raffia, then designs are sewn into it.

Kente cloth, also made by the Ashanti people, uses colored threads in the weaving process. Only royalty could wear certain kente patterns.

CRITICAL THINKING
Compare and Contrast What are some of the differences in the way these textiles are created?

Congolese art styles differ from region to region. In the southwest, the Kongo people make statues studded with stones and nails. The Kuba people craft statues of their royal leaders. Luba artists make small statues of mothers. Mangbetu sculptors of the north specialize in long, stylized heads.

▲ **SUMMARIZE** Explain how the Congolese communicate when more than 200 languages are spoken in the country.

Economics and Government

▼ **KEY QUESTION** What social effects have resulted from Congo's long dictatorship and frequent wars?

Congo's rich deposits of copper, industrial diamonds, and petroleum make it a potentially strong economy. But decades of dictatorship and wars have hurt the country. Ongoing violence has scared off investors, reduced production, driven up the debt, and killed millions.

Despite Congo's resources, most Congolese live as subsistence farmers. Their chief food crops include bananas, cassava, corn, rice, and peanuts, which Africans call "groundnuts." A few farmers also grow cash crops of cocoa, coffee, cotton, and tea. But years of war and government neglect have damaged the country's few paved roads and made some railroads unusable. As a result, Congolese farmers continue to transport their goods on the Congo River. Fertile soil along the riverbanks remains largely unused for large-scale agriculture.

The country's chief economic activity is diamond mining. Congo also has petroleum reserves off the country's small coastline, as well as cadmium, cobalt, gold, manganese, iron ore, and copper. There's more potential wealth in Congo's forests, which cover more than half the country. Its rushing rivers teem with fish and could provide half of Africa's electric power needs.

Congo's current government consists of a president, four vice presidents, and a 300-member assembly appointed by the president. In 2006 Congolese voters held the first general elections under a new constitution. The future will show whether Congo's new government will be strong enough to overcome continuing regional unrest.

New Constitution
A woman in Kinshasa celebrates the Democratic Republic of the Congo's new constitution in 2006.

▲ **UNDERSTAND EFFECTS** Describe how dictatorship and civil war have hurt Congo.

Section ③ Assessment

 **ONLINE QUIZ**
For test practice, go to
Interactive Review
@ ClassZone.com

TERMS & NAMES

1. Explain the importance of
- Kongo
- Leopold II
- Mobutu Sese Seko
- Zaire

USE YOUR READING NOTES

2. Make Generalizations Use your completed graphic organizer to answer the following question:

How could Congo's resources help its economy?

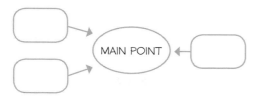

MAIN POINT

KEY IDEAS

3. Who were Kongo's earliest inhabitants?

4. Where do most Congolese live?

5. What is Congo's main product?

CRITICAL THINKING

6. Make Inferences Why might Congolese business people have rejected Western dress shortly after independence?

7. Summarize Why is the Congo River so important to the Congolese people?

8. CONNECT to Today In 2006, the Congolese elected a new government. What steps might the new leadership take to improve the Democratic Republic of the Congo's economy?

9. GEOGRAPHY Map Congo's Resources Sketch a map of Congo (Kinshasa). Label your map with the country's major regional resources, using a symbol for each resource that you explain in a key.

Reading for Understanding

▶ Key Ideas

BEFORE, YOU LEARNED

When power in a nation changes hands, there are often violent conflicts.

NOW YOU WILL LEARN

South Africa made a successful change from a minority-rule nation to a majority-rule government but still faces many challenges.

▶ Vocabulary

TERMS & NAMES

Boer a Dutch colonist or descendant in South Africa

Cape Colony South African land settled by Dutch colonists called Boers in the 1600s and 1700s

Afrikaner a South African of European ancestry who speaks a language called Afrikaans

apartheid (uh•PAHRT•hyt) the official policy of racial segregation practiced in South Africa

African National Congress (ANC) South African political party opposing apartheid

sanction a penalty or pressure applied to a country for not obeying an order or law

Nelson Mandela South Africa's first African president

BACKGROUND VOCABULARY

Commonwealth of Nations an association of British colonies

segregation the policy of separating people of different races

▶ Reading Strategy

Re-create the time line shown at right. As you read and respond to the **KEY QUESTIONS**, use the time line to order events related to South Africa.

 Skillbuilder Handbook, page R6

SEQUENCE EVENTS

1652   PRESENT

🔄 **GRAPHIC ORGANIZERS**
Go to **Interactive Review** @ ClassZone.com

South Africa

Connecting to Your World

In the presidential election of 2004, just over half the eligible adults in the United States cast ballots. In contrast, in the South African elections of 1994, almost 90 percent of eligible voters came to the polls. Millions of people stood in long lines, patiently awaiting their turn to vote. Some had to wait for a day or more, but they didn't mind. The 1994 election in South Africa was the first time most South Africans had ever been allowed to vote.

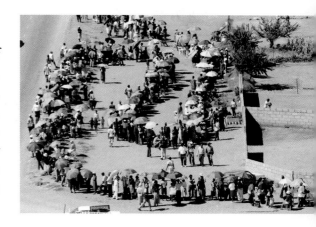

Voting Lines South Africans wait to vote in the 1994 election.

Competition for the Land

▼ **KEY QUESTION** What forms of external and internal protest helped bring an end to South Africa's minority rule?

The San, hunter-gatherers who lived in small bands, were the earliest modern human beings to populate the area. Around A.D. 100, a related group called the Khoikhoi (KOY•koy) migrated from the north. Today these groups are called the Khoisan. The great Bantu migration later brought Bantu speakers from the north. These peoples included the Zulu, the Xhosa (KOH•sah), the Sotho, and the Tswana. They herded cattle, raised grain, made iron tools and weapons, and traded with other peoples.

Johannesburg The Hillbrow Tower dominates the skyline of South Africa's largest metropolitan area.

SOUTH AFRICA

Johannesburg

Colonizers Clash European settlers working for the Dutch East India Company landed in South Africa in 1652. In 1657 the company let some workers start their own farms. These farmers became known as **Boers**. By the end of the 1700s, the Boer population had expanded into a large section of land called the **Cape Colony**.

This European intrusion shattered the Khoikhoi and San. Many died of diseases, such as smallpox. The survivors fought the colonists or became their slaves and servants. Gradually the Boers' Dutch language changed, blending with San, Khoikhoi, and other languages into a new language called Afrikaans. By 1770, white Afrikaans speakers, called **Afrikaners**, began to spread beyond the Cape Colony.

British settlers began arriving in 1820, after Britain won control of the Cape Colony. The British clashed with the Boers, defeating them in 1902. Five years earlier, Britain had defeated the last independent Zulu kingdom in South Africa. The Union of South Africa, which was established in 1910, joined the British **Commonwealth of Nations** in 1931.

HISTORY MAKERS

Nelson Mandela (born 1918)

Nelson Mandela, head of the African National Congress, spent almost 30 years in prison for resisting apartheid. In 1993, three years after his release from prison, Mandela accepted the Nobel Peace Prize on behalf of all South Africans who had sacrificed so much for freedom. In 1994, Mandela won South Africa's first free democratic election, and he served as the country's president until 1998.

ONLINE BIOGRAPHY
For more on the life of Nelson Mandela, go to the
Research & Writing Center @ ClassZone.com

Apartheid and Its Overthrow Afrikaners and English-speaking whites controlled South African politics, excluding the black majority from power. Some Afrikaners wanted to make Afrikaans a national language and to enforce stricter **segregation**, or separation, between blacks and whites. After World War II, the Afrikaner National Party put into place a harsh program of **apartheid** (uh•PART•hyt), which made segregation a law. The new laws classified South Africans by race and separated the groups into their own schools and neighborhoods.

In South Africa, many groups opposed apartheid, including the **African National Congress (ANC)**, a black political party. Internal protests took the form of boycotts, strikes, marches, and occasional violence. The United States and other countries applied **sanctions**, or economic pressure, on South Africa, refusing to trade with the country. South Africa left the Commonwealth of Nations. It was banned from competing in the Olympics for nearly 30 years. In 1990 and 1991, the South African government repealed all its apartheid laws. The country's first free multiracial election in 1994 awarded the presidency to ANC leader **Nelson Mandela**. In 1996, South Africa adopted a new constitution guaranteeing basic freedoms to all its citizens.

▲ **COMPARE** Compare the internal and external protests that helped end apartheid.

South African Life and Culture

▼ **KEY QUESTION** How are South Africans adjusting to life after apartheid?

The effects of apartheid linger in today's South Africa. Whites still have higher-paying jobs and enjoy a better standard of living than other groups. The government wants to correct these inequalities, but it takes time.

Cultural Characteristics Black Africans make up about 79 percent of South Africa's population. Ten percent of the population is white, about 9 percent are mixed race, and 2 percent are Asian. Four out of five South Africans are Christians. Many black South Africans belong to African independent churches that mix Christian and African beliefs. Before apartheid ended, English and Afrikaans were the country's only official languages. Today nine African languages also have official status, including Zulu, Xhosa, Sepedi, and Setswana. More than half of black South Africans and about 90 percent of whites live in urban areas.

Ladysmith Black Mambazo This popular ten-member group takes its name from a Zulu village called Ladysmith. "Mambazo" is a Zulu word for "axe."

Varied Ways of Life Many white South Africans live in roomy single-family suburban homes. English and Afrikaans speakers have recently begun to mix, moving into each other's neighborhoods. While there is a growing black urban middle class, many blacks still live in poor, segregated areas far from city centers, or in shelters. In rural areas, some blacks work as subsistence farmers on small farms, or on larger white-owned farms that raise cash crops.

South African artists excel in dance, painting, music, and writing. This country's wealth of languages has produced a rich literature in English, Zulu, Sotho, and Afrikaans. The vocal group Ladysmith Black Mambazo introduced the world to South African harmony singing, performed in an African humming style. Another popular South African group, the African Jazz Pioneers, performed for President Mandela.

▲ **IDENTIFY CAUSES** Describe how life has changed in South Africa since the end of apartheid.

Government and Economics

▼ **KEY QUESTION** How is South Africa's national government like and unlike that of the United States?

While creating its new constitution, South Africa gave its citizens a large role in the decision-making process. Local leaders met with the public and gathered ideas on how the new government should work. South Africa's constitution, adopted in 1996, includes a Bill of Rights which guarantees rights of religious freedom, security, health care, property, education, and self-expression.

Like the United States, South Africa has three branches of government: executive, judicial, and a two-house legislative branch. However, the legislative branch operates in a British parliamentary style. The lower house of parliament, the National Assembly, chooses the president from among its members. The National Council of Provinces, or upper house, protects regional interests such as ethnic traditions. Also, South Africa has a separate capital for each branch of government. The parliament meets in Cape Town. The executive branch is based in Pretoria, while South Africa's highest court, the Constitutional Court, meets in Bloemfontein.

South Africa enjoys Africa's most advanced economy and turns out one-fourth of the goods and services produced by the entire continent. Having many different economic activities keeps the country's economy strong and protects against a fall in demand for any one product.

CONNECT to Economics

A country's economic activities can tell you about its level of development. Instead of a GDP based heavily on agriculture, developed economies have more industry and service jobs. In South Africa's developed economy, less than 3 percent of GDP comes from agriculture, 30 percent from industries such as manufacturing, and over 67 percent from service industries.

Activity

Make a Pie Graph

Materials
- paper
- colored pens
- protractor
- compass
- scratch paper or calculator

1. Research the economic activities of an African country. Look for data given as a percentage of the country's GDP.

2. Convert the percentages into decimals, then multiply each decimal by 360. This gives you the angles of each "slice" of your pie chart.

3. Use a compass and protractor to draw a large circle and angles within the circle.

4. Label each slice of the pie chart, then give your chart a title.

South Africa's strong industries include mining, agriculture, fishing, and manufacturing. South Africa supplies one-third of the world's gold and produces coal, copper, diamonds, iron, and other minerals. South Africa's farms grow most of the country's food, and export fruits, corn, potatoes, sugar, wheat, and wool. Rich coastal waters produce fish and shellfish for export, while South African factories turn out chemicals, clothing and textiles, steel, machinery, motor vehicles, and processed foods. South Africa's trade is helped by the continent's best-developed infrastructure.

Unfortunately, black poverty and unemployment remain as effects of apartheid. Blacks are moving into better-paying jobs, but whites still occupy the most powerful roles.

Mineral Resources of South Africa

- Coal
- Copper
- Diamonds
- Gold
- Iron
- Phosphates
- Uranium

ATLANTIC OCEAN

Pretoria
Johannesburg
SWAZILAND
Kimberley
LESOTHO
Durban
Cape Town
Port Elizabeth
INDIAN OCEAN

CONNECT Geography & History

Location Which resource would require the most transportation infrastructure, and why?

 COMPARE AND CONTRAST Describe the similarities between the United States government and South Africa's.

Section 4 Assessment

ONLINE QUIZ
For test practice, go to **Interactive Review** @ ClassZone.com

TERMS & NAMES

1. Explain the importance of
- Boer
- Afrikaner
- apartheid
- Nelson Mandela

USE YOUR READING NOTES

2. Sequence Events Use your completed graphic organizer to answer the following question:

For how long were there European colonies in what is now South Africa?

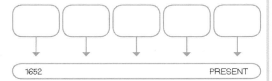

1652 — PRESENT

KEY IDEAS

3. Which two European countries colonized South Africa?

4. What are three of South Africa's official languages?

5. What are some of South Africa's leading industries?

CRITICAL THINKING

6. Make Inferences What makes Afrikaans an African language?

7. Draw Conclusions How do you think trade sanctions pressured South Africa to end apartheid?

8. **CONNECT to Today** South Africa's coastal waters produce tons of fish and seafood each year. But overfishing has severely reduced fish stocks. What can South Africa do to protect the fishing industry in the future?

9. **LANGUAGE ARTS** **Give a Speech** Research the writings and speeches of Nelson Mandela. Memorize a paragraph from a speech that you especially like and deliver it to your class. Explain the circumstances of the speech in a brief introduction.

Reading for Understanding

▶ Key Ideas

BEFORE, YOU LEARNED

A common problem after colonialism is how to distribute a nation's wealth.

NOW YOU WILL LEARN

Zimbabwe, Botswana, and Angola have all taken different paths since the end of colonialism.

▶ Vocabulary

TERMS & NAMES

Great Zimbabwe an empire built by the Shona people

Rhodesia the colonial name for the countries that are today Zambia and Zimbabwe

land reform dividing up large plots of land to distribute land more evenly

Kalahari a desert in southern Africa

Bechuanaland colonial name for Botswana

Marxist a person who supports the philosophy behind communism, including government ownership of the land and the means of production

BACKGROUND VOCABULARY

guerrilla a member of an irregular army that operates in small bands

Visual Vocabulary Great Zimbabwe

▶ Reading Strategy

Re-create the web diagram shown at right. As you read and respond to the **KEY QUESTIONS**, use the diagram to compare and contrast Zimbabwe, Botswana, and Angola's exports

 Skillbuilder Handbook, page R9

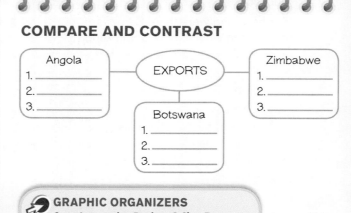

COMPARE AND CONTRAST

Angola
1. _____
2. _____
3. _____

EXPORTS

Zimbabwe
1. _____
2. _____
3. _____

Botswana
1. _____
2. _____
3. _____

GRAPHIC ORGANIZERS
Go to **Interactive Review** @ClassZone.com

Zimbabwe, Botswana, and Angola

Connecting to Your World

Do you know someone who gets a big allowance but always runs short of money? Sometimes people who have less money realize that they need to plan more carefully. Indeed, careful planning can help someone with less money end up with more. You'll learn from studying about Zimbabwe, Botswana, and Angola—three countries in Southern Africa—that having abundant resources doesn't always lead to wealth.

Zimbabwe

▼ **KEY QUESTION** How has Robert Mugabe stayed in power?

Zimbabwe, a nation to the north of South Africa, is situated on a high plateau. Although it lies in the tropics, Zimbabwe's elevation gives it a temperate climate. Almost all of Zimbabwe's people are black Africans, and most belong to the Shona people. Since the late 1800s, Zimbabwe's political history has been troubled and violent.

Victoria Falls
Africa's widest waterfall is twice as deep and wide as Niagara Falls on the U.S.–Canadian border.

Precolonial History By about A.D. 1000, the Shona people had built **Great Zimbabwe**, which means "house of stone." This great city's ruins include an 800-foot-long wall and a 30-foot-high tower. The precisely cut stones nestle together without mud or mortar. Great Zimbabwe declined around 1500. The large population around it had probably used up the area's fertile land and clean water. Smaller Shona trading empires succeeded Great Zimbabwe.

British Rule The British South Africa Company, owned by Cecil Rhodes, built a railroad in what is now Zimbabwe in the 1890s. The new railroad encouraged British settlement. Settlers named the territory **Rhodesia** and defeated Africans who resisted colonization. In 1964, the northern part of Rhodesia broke off to form the independent nations of Malawi and Zambia. White Rhodesians defiantly refused to share power with blacks, despite worldwide sanctions. Through the 1970s, small groups of Africans engaged in **guerrilla** warfare, launching surprise attacks. A peace settlement in 1979 established Rhodesia's independence. The country was renamed Zimbabwe the following year. Since independence, Robert Mugabe has ruled the country as a dictator. He has kept power by jailing opponents and rigging elections. In the early 2000s, Mugabe ordered **land reform**, granting white-owned farms to black farmers. In the resulting chaos, food production dipped, and many whites fled the country.

CONNECT to History

Great Zimbabwe The largest remaining section of Great Zimbabwe is called the Great Enclosure. Its maximum diameter is about the length of a football field, and its walls are about 36 feet high.

1 Scholars believe kings and queens lived in the Great Enclosure, while farmers and workers lived outside.

2 A passage between the outer and inner walls leads to a 30-foot cone-shaped tower. Historians speculate that it may have had religious purposes.

CRITICAL THINKING

Draw Conclusions Scholars think the Great Enclosure's walls were not built for defense. Why do you think this is the case?

Life and Culture English is the official language in Zimbabwe. Most people also speak Chishona or another tribal language called isiNdebele (ee•see•UHN•duh•BEHL•ay). Most of Zimbabwe's people are subsistence farmers. Most people follow traditional African religions or combine them with Christianity.

Government and Economics In Zimbabwe, the president is elected to a six-year term. Opponents and observers accused President Mugabe of manipulating the 2002 elections. The legislature consists of a 150-member House of Assembly and a 66-member Senate.

Most of Zimbabwe's income comes from large farms, which export beef, cotton, sugar, and tobacco. But Mugabe's land reform schemes threw many farmers out of work. In addition, the country's inflation rate has skyrocketed. Before Zimbabwe fixed its exchange rate in 2006, one U.S. dollar was worth 250,000 Zimbabwe dollars.

▲ **SUMMARIZE** Describe Robert Mugabe's rule since independence.

Botswana

▼ **KEY QUESTION** How has Botswana been a success?

Botswana, located to the west and south of Zimbabwe and north of South Africa, is also landlocked. Its main river is the Okavango, which forms a swampy inland delta in the northeast. Much of Botswana lies in the **Kalahari** Desert, and surrounding regions are dry. Despite these disadvantages, Botswana is a success. For the past 40 years, this poor nation has maintained peace, economic growth, and a democratic government.

History Like South Africa and Zimbabwe, Botswana was first settled by the San. The Tswana, a Bantu-speaking people, migrated into this region between A.D. 1 and A.D. 1000. By the 1700s, several stone-walled villages and large towns had developed. During the 1800s, the Tswana sought British aid in their struggles with rival African groups. Britain brought the area under its protection in the late 1880s, naming it **Bechuanaland**. Britain governed Bechuanaland until the 1960s, refusing South Africa's attempts to take over. But Britain did little to develop the colony. In fact, Bechuanaland's capital was actually in Mafeking, South Africa, for nearly 70 years.

Okavango Delta Most of the swampy Okavango cannot be navigated. **Why might a swampy river be hard to navigate?**

The country won independence peacefully in 1966, taking the name Botswana, a modern spelling of Bechuana. Seretse Khama, a former chief of the Ngwato people, was elected president. The new nation had a difficult road ahead of it. Bechuanaland had been poor; most people lived by raising cattle or by migrating to South Africa for work. Botswana relied on Britain for financial support for its first five years. The discovery of diamonds soon afterward gave Botswana the funds to improve its infrastructure and build other industries.

HISTORY MAKERS

Seretse Khama 1921–1980

While studying overseas, Seretse Khama married Ruth Williams, a white British woman, in 1948. The idea of an interracial couple ruling in Bechuanaland upset South Africa, which had recently set up its apartheid laws. Britain exiled the Khamas from the colony in 1950.

The Khamas returned to Bechuanaland in 1956, after Seretse gave up his title of chief. Seretse Khama became active in national politics in 1961 and was elected Botswana's first president five years later.

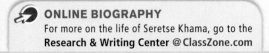

ONLINE BIOGRAPHY
For more on the life of Seretse Khama, go to the
Research & Writing Center @ ClassZone.com

Life and Culture English is the official language in Botswana. Most people also speak Setswana. Since the 1980s, novels have been published in this African language. More than half of Botswana's population lives in cities. People in Botswana adopted Christianity and Western dress in the late 1800s.

Zimbabwe, Botswana, and South Africa share a common problem with many other African countries: a serious disease called HIV or AIDS. One in four adults in Zimbabwe and almost two in five adults in Botswana are affected. HIV/AIDS has been a medical and social tragedy because it strikes young adults, strains medical budgets in poor countries, and orphans many children. Botswana's model program to deal with this disease includes providing HIV/AIDS therapy to all its sick citizens.

Government and Economics Seretse Khama held office until his death in 1980, when he was replaced by his vice-president. Although Botswana has a multiparty system, Khama's Botswana Democratic Party (BDP) has won every national election since independence.

Botswana's republic has a popularly elected legislative body called the National Assembly, which selects the president. A House of Chiefs, made up of leaders from eight major tribes, advises the government on ethnic matters. Between the late 1960s and the 1990s, when the AIDS epidemic hit, Botswana enjoyed rapid economic growth. Mining and raising livestock are this country's main industries. In addition to beef, Botswana exports diamonds, copper, nickel, hides and skins, and textiles. It must import food.

🔺 **DRAW CONCLUSIONS** Describe how Botswana has succeeded since independence.

ANGOLA

Angola

▲ **KEY QUESTION** Why has Angola had only one election since 1992?

Angola offers a stark contrast to Botswana. Angola has greater natural wealth, and it enjoyed prosperity in colonial times. But a quarter-century of conflict has destroyed much of its economy.

History Portugal colonized Angola in the 1500s, sending enslaved Africans to work on its colony in Brazil. Angolans began to demand independence in the 1950s. After three rebel groups finally won Angola's independence in 1975, civil war erupted among them. One group received aid from Cuba and the Soviet Union. These communist countries hoped that Angola would follow **Marxist** ideas, such as government ownership of the land and central economic planning. The winning rebel group, the MPLA, formed a Marxist government in Angola, but the other groups joined forces to continue fighting. Angola's government gradually cut its Marxist ties and allowed multiparty elections in 1992. Still, fighting between the MPLA and the main rebel group, UNITA, continued despite the signing of several peace agreements. The death of UNITA's leader in 2002 finally ended 27 years of civil war.

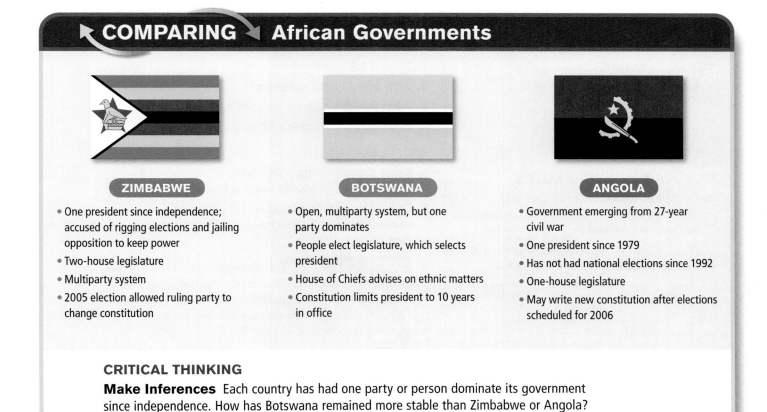

COMPARING ▶ African Governments

ZIMBABWE

- One president since independence; accused of rigging elections and jailing opposition to keep power
- Two-house legislature
- Multiparty system
- 2005 election allowed ruling party to change constitution

BOTSWANA

- Open, multiparty system, but one party dominates
- People elect legislature, which selects president
- House of Chiefs advises on ethnic matters
- Constitution limits president to 10 years in office

ANGOLA

- Government emerging from 27-year civil war
- One president since 1979
- Has not had national elections since 1992
- One-house legislature
- May write new constitution after elections scheduled for 2006

CRITICAL THINKING

Make Inferences Each country has had one party or person dominate its government since independence. How has Botswana remained more stable than Zimbabwe or Angola?

Angolan Art Called *O Pensador*, or "The Thinker," this image has become a national symbol in Angola.

Angolan Culture Forty native languages are spoken in Angola, with Portuguese serving as an official language. After the government dropped its anti-religious Marxist doctrines, Christianity gained popularity. Now about nine out of ten Angolans are Christians. Like other Bantu-speaking Africans, Angolans share a rich culture in music and art. A Chokwe sculpture of a person apparently deep in thought has been widely reproduced. But decades of warfare have ruined many fine collections of traditional art, and MPLA censorship during the civil war years kept a literary tradition from growing.

Government and Economics If Angola's next national election for president and National Assembly proceeds as planned in 2006, it will be the country's first election since 1992. Angola's lengthy war destroyed the diversified, prosperous economy it enjoyed during colonial times. Currently, one in two Angolans practice subsistence farming, and the country imports half its food. Oil production currently accounts for 90 percent of its exports. Only Nigeria produces more oil south of the Sahara. Angola's other rich natural resources include gold, diamonds, forests, and fish. But benefiting from these resources will require a long period of peace and good government.

▲ **SUMMARIZE** Describe what has caused Angola's instability since independence.

ONLINE QUIZ For test practice, go to **Interactive Review** @ ClassZone.com

Section 5 Assessment

TERMS & NAMES

1. Explain the importance of
- Great Zimbabwe
- Rhodesia
- land reform
- Kalahari

USE YOUR READING NOTES

2. Compare and Contrast Use your completed graphic organizer to answer the following question:

What export is important to Angola, but less so to Zimbabwe and Botswana?

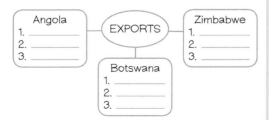

Angola
1. _____
2. _____
3. _____

EXPORTS

Zimbabwe
1. _____
2. _____
3. _____

Botswana
1. _____
2. _____
3. _____

KEY IDEAS

3. Who built Great Zimbabwe?

4. What was Botswana's colonial name?

5. Who fought in Angola's lengthy civil war?

CRITICAL THINKING

6. Draw Conclusions What were some negative effects of Mugabe's land reform?

7. Compare and Contrast What geographic advantage does Angola have that Botswana and Zimbabwe lack?

8. CONNECT to Today In Botswana, soldiers prevent poachers from killing elephants on game preserves. Today the elephant population in Botswana exceeds 120,000. What are some benefits and risks of a growing elephant population?

9. MATH **Make a Graph** Research Angola's oil imports over the past several decades. Graph the recent rise in production, and include predicted future production.

Click here to complete these and other activities online @ ClassZone.com

CHAPTER SUMMARY

Key Idea 1
Ethiopia remained independent throughout most of its history.

Key Idea 2
Trade was important in East Africa, particularly in what is now Kenya.

Key Idea 3
The Democratic Republic of the Congo is still struggling with setting up a true democracy.

Key Idea 4
South Africa made a successful change to a majority-rule government.

Key Idea 5
Zimbabwe, Botswana, and Angola have all taken different paths since the end of colonialism.

For **Review and Study Notes**, go to **Interactive Review** @ ClassZone.com

NAME GAME

Use the Terms & Names list to complete each sentence on paper or online.

1. I was the legal separation of races in South Africa. _____**apartheid**_____

2. I am an extension of land on Africa's east coast, across the Gulf of Aden from the Arabian peninsula. _____

3. I am a language spoken by many East Africans. _____

4. I was independent Kenya's first president. _____

5. I was the name of the Democratic Republic of the Congo from 1971 to 1997. _____

6. I get my food by stalking animals and collecting roots, berries, and nuts. _____

7. I am a Dutch farmer who settled in South Africa. _____

8. I was South Africa's first democratically elected president. _____

9. I am a desert in southern Africa. _____

10. I am a member of an irregular army that fights in small bands. _____

Aksum
apartheid
Boer
guerrilla
Eritrea
Haile Selassie
Horn of Africa
hunter-gatherer
Jomo Kenyatta
Kalahari
Mau Mau
Nelson Mandela
Swahili
Zaire

Activities

GeoGame

Use this online map to show what you know about East, Central, and Southern Africa. Drag and drop each place name to its location on the map.

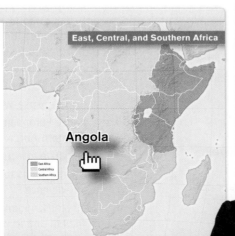

To play the complete game, go to **Interactive Review** @ClassZone.com

Crossword Puzzle

Complete an online crossword puzzle to test your knowledge of African regions.

ACROSS
1. ruler of Congo (Kinshasa) from 1965 to 1997

VOCABULARY

Explain the significance of each of the following.

1. Haile Selassie
2. Swahili
3. Leopold II
4. Afrikaner
5. apartheid
6. Great Zimbabwe
7. Bechuanaland

Explain how the terms and names in each group are related.

8. Ezana, Aksum, and Horn of Africa
9. Pygmy, hunter-gatherer, and Kongo

KEY IDEAS

1 Ethiopia

10. What values do most Ethiopians share?
11. What natural advantages does Ethiopia have?

2 Kenya

12. What languages do Kenyans from different ethnic groups speak to each other?
13. What cash crops are most important to Kenya's economy?

3 The Democratic Republic of the Congo

14. Who enslaved the people of Congo?
15. What art forms do the Congolese specialize in?

4 South Africa

16. Who were South Africa's earliest human inhabitants?
17. Why do whites still hold most of the highest positions in business in South Africa?

5 Zimbabwe, Botswana, and Angola

18. What factors probably caused the decline of Great Zimbabwe?
19. When was Angola's last election before its planned election in 2006?

CRITICAL THINKING

20. **Categorize** Fill in this chart, categorizing these languages of East, Central, and Southern Africa: Portuguese, Swahili, English, Amharic, Dutch, Kikuyu, Kikongo, Zulu, French, Setswana, Afrikaans.

COLONIAL LANGUAGES	CONTEMPORARY AFRICAN LANGUAGES	ORIGINAL AFRICAN LANGUAGES

21. **Five Themes: Region** How have corruption and violence interfered with economic growth in countries like Kenya, Zimbabwe, Angola, and Congo (Kinshasa)?
22. **Evaluate** Why might it be difficult for South Africa to guarantee the rights in its Bill of Rights?
23. **Connect to Economics** Which southern African country would probably be most affected by a drop in world oil prices? Explain.

Answer the ESSENTIAL QUESTION

How do boundaries set during colonial times affect stability in these regions today?

Written Response Write a two- or three-paragraph response to the Essential Question. Be sure to consider the key ideas of each section. Use the rubric below to guide your thinking.

Response Rubric
A strong response will:
- summarize European colonialism in East, Central, and Southern Africa
- note negative effects of colonialism
- discuss transitions to independent rule that led to years of violence
- include a description of South Africa's apartheid government and its overthrow

✓ **Test Practice**

• Online Test Practice @ ClassZone.com
• Test-Taking Strategies and Practice at the front of this book

THEMATIC MAP

Use the map to answer questions 1 and 2.

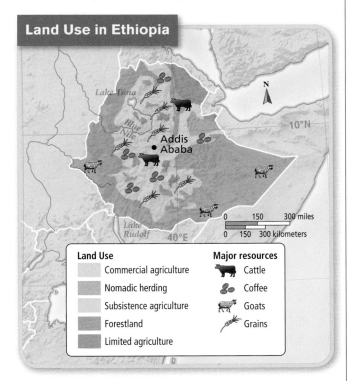

Land Use in Ethiopia

Land Use
- Commercial agriculture
- Nomadic herding
- Subsistence agriculture
- Forestland
- Limited agriculture

Major resources
- Cattle
- Coffee
- Goats
- Grains

1. Where are most goats raised?

A. in commercial agriculture areas
B. in nomadic herding areas
C. in subsistence agriculture areas
D. in forest areas

2. Which major resource is most common in commercial agricultural areas?

A. cattle
B. coffee
C. goats
D. grains

PRIMARY SOURCE

Use the editorial cartoon and your knowledge of Africa to answer questions 3 and 4.

Source: Patrick Chappatte, *International Herald-Tribune*

3. What country does the flag on the polling station represent?

4. What does the cartoon imply about the man on the poster, Robert Mugabe?

GeoActivity

1. INTERDISCIPLINARY ACTIVITY–SCIENCE

The introduction of modern farming techniques in developing Asian and Latin American countries has been called the "Green Revolution" and has helped feed millions of people. Research the difficulties involved and the progress made in bringing the Green Revolution to Africa.

2. WRITING FOR SOCIAL STUDIES

Unit Writing Project Find a protest song in the African music you studied to complete the Unit Writing Project. Research the issue the song addressed and how the song dealt with the issue.

3. MENTAL MAPPING

Create an outline map of East, Central, and Southern Africa and label the following:

- Ethiopia
- Eritrea
- Kenya
- Lake Victoria
- Zimbabwe
- Congo (Kinshasa)
- Angola
- Botswana
- Kalahari Desert
- South Africa

UNIT 7

Southwest Asia and South Asia

Why It Matters:

Southwest Asia is the home of oil rich lands, vast deserts, and difficult political problems. South Asia is a region of ancient cultures, spectacular landforms, and rapidly growing populations.

Arabian Desert

CHAPTER 21 Southwest Asia and South Asia

Dome of the Rock in Jerusalem

CHAPTER 22 Southwest Asia

Taj Mahal in Agra

CHAPTER 23 India

Marketplace in Bangladesh

CHAPTER 24 South Asian Neighbors

Southwest Asia and South Asia

Southwest Asia and South Asia span a large area of an enormous continent. As you study the maps, notice geographic patterns and specific details about the region. Complete the GeoActivity with each map.

As you study the graphics and data on this page, compare the landmass, population, rivers, and deserts of Southwest and South Asia with those of the United States and, in a few cases, other regions. Then jot down answers to the following questions in your notebook.

Comparing Data

1. Which has the larger land-mass—the continental United States or Southwest and South Asia?

2. Approximately how many times larger is the combined population of Southwest and South Asia than that of the United States?

3. How much longer is the Nile than the longest rivers in South Asia?

4. How much larger than the Mojave Desert is the Rub al-Khali?

Comparing Data

Landmass

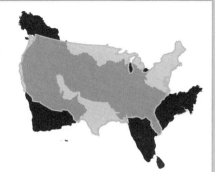

Southwest Asia and South Asia	4,298,900 sq. mi.
Continental United States	3,165,630 sq. mi.

Population

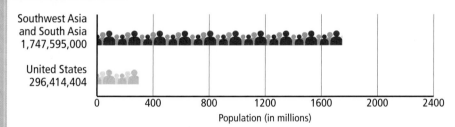

Southwest Asia and South Asia
1,747,595,000

United States
296,414,404

Population (in millions): 0   400   800   1200   1600   2000   2400

Rivers

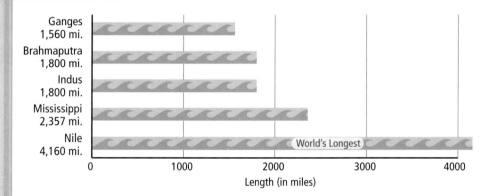

Ganges 1,560 mi.
Brahmaputra 1,800 mi.
Indus 1,800 mi.
Mississippi 2,357 mi.
Nile 4,160 mi. — World's Longest

Length (in miles): 0   1000   2000   3000   4000

Deserts

World's Largest Sahara Africa 3,500,000 sq. mi.	U.S. Largest Mojave United States 25,000 sq. mi.	Rub al-Khali Arabian Peninsula 250,000 sq. mi.	An-Nafud Arabian Peninsula 25,000 sq. mi.	Negev Israel 4,700 sq. mi.

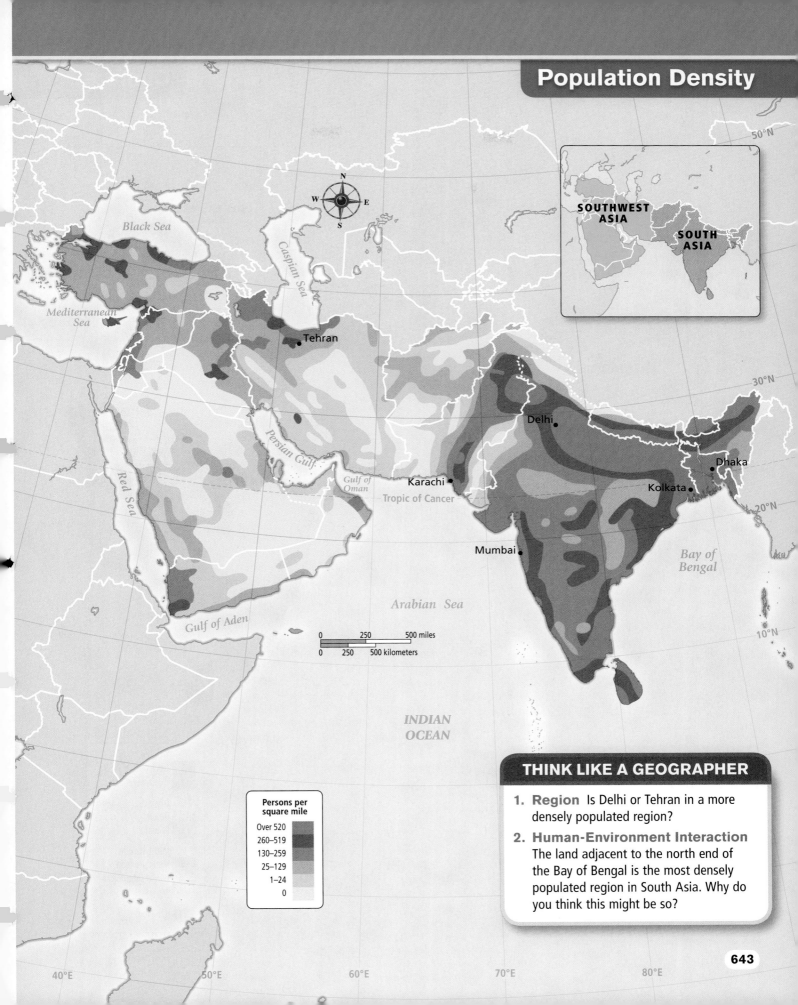

Population Density

SOUTHWEST ASIA

SOUTH ASIA

Black Sea

Mediterranean Sea

Caspian Sea

Tehran

Red Sea

Persian Gulf

Gulf of Oman

Karachi

Tropic of Cancer

Delhi

Dhaka

Kolkata

Mumbai

Bay of Bengal

Gulf of Aden

Arabian Sea

INDIAN OCEAN

0   250   500 miles
0   250   500 kilometers

50°N

30°N

20°N

10°N

40°E   50°E   60°E   70°E   80°E

Persons per square mile

Over 520
260–519
130–259
25–129
1–24
0

THINK LIKE A GEOGRAPHER

1. **Region** Is Delhi or Tehran in a more densely populated region?

2. **Human-Environment Interaction** The land adjacent to the north end of the Bay of Bengal is the most densely populated region in South Asia. Why do you think this might be so?

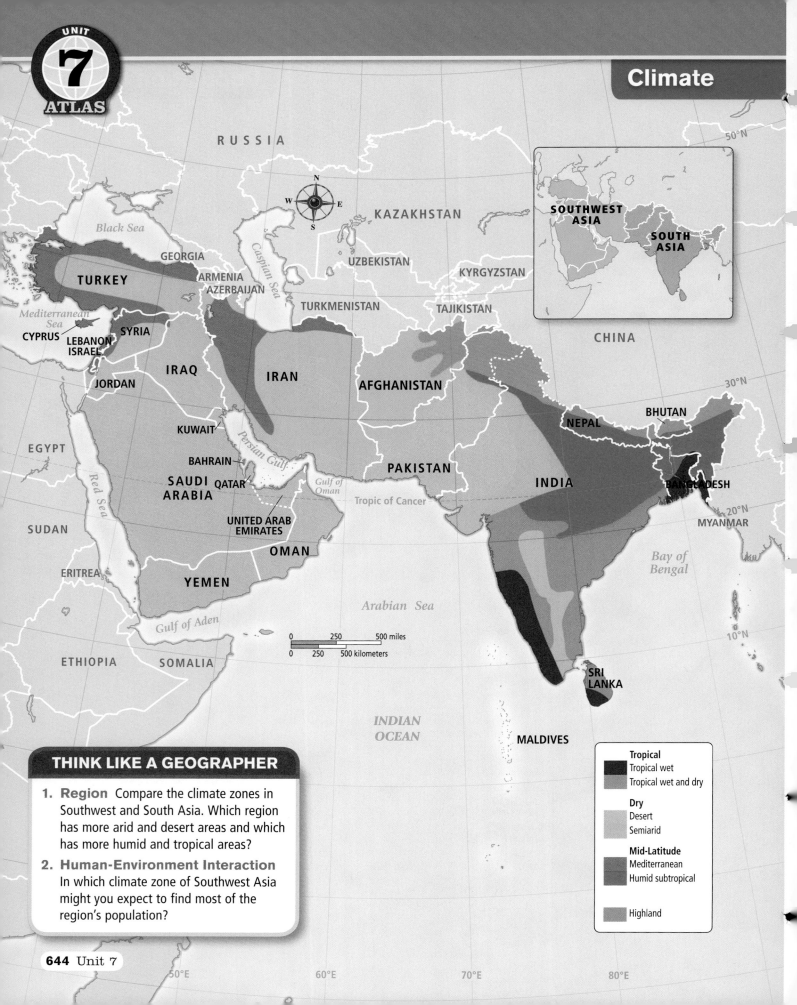

RUSSIA

KAZAKHSTAN

UZBEKISTAN

KYRGYZSTAN

Black Sea

GEORGIA

TURKEY

ARMENIA
AZERBAIJAN

Caspian Sea

TURKMENISTAN

TAJIKISTAN

CHINA

Mediterranean
Sea

CYPRUS
LEBANON
ISRAEL

SYRIA

IRAQ

IRAN

AFGHANISTAN

JORDAN

30°N

NEPAL

BHUTAN

EGYPT

KUWAIT

Persian Gulf

BAHRAIN

SAUDI
ARABIA

QATAR

Gulf of
Oman

PAKISTAN

INDIA

BANGLADESH

Red Sea

SUDAN

UNITED ARAB
EMIRATES

Tropic of Cancer

20°N

MYANMAR

OMAN

Bay of
Bengal

ERITREA

YEMEN

Arabian Sea

10°N

Gulf of Aden

0   250   500 miles

SRI
LANKA

0 250 500 kilometers

ETHIOPIA

SOMALIA

INDIAN
OCEAN

MALDIVES

SOUTHWEST
ASIA

SOUTH
ASIA

THINK LIKE A GEOGRAPHER

1. **Region** Compare the climate zones in Southwest and South Asia. Which region has more arid and desert areas and which has more humid and tropical areas?

2. **Human-Environment Interaction** In which climate zone of Southwest Asia might you expect to find most of the region's population?

Tropical
Tropical wet
Tropical wet and dry

Dry
Desert
Semiarid

Mid-Latitude
Mediterranean
Humid subtropical

Highland

50°E   60°E   70°E   80°E

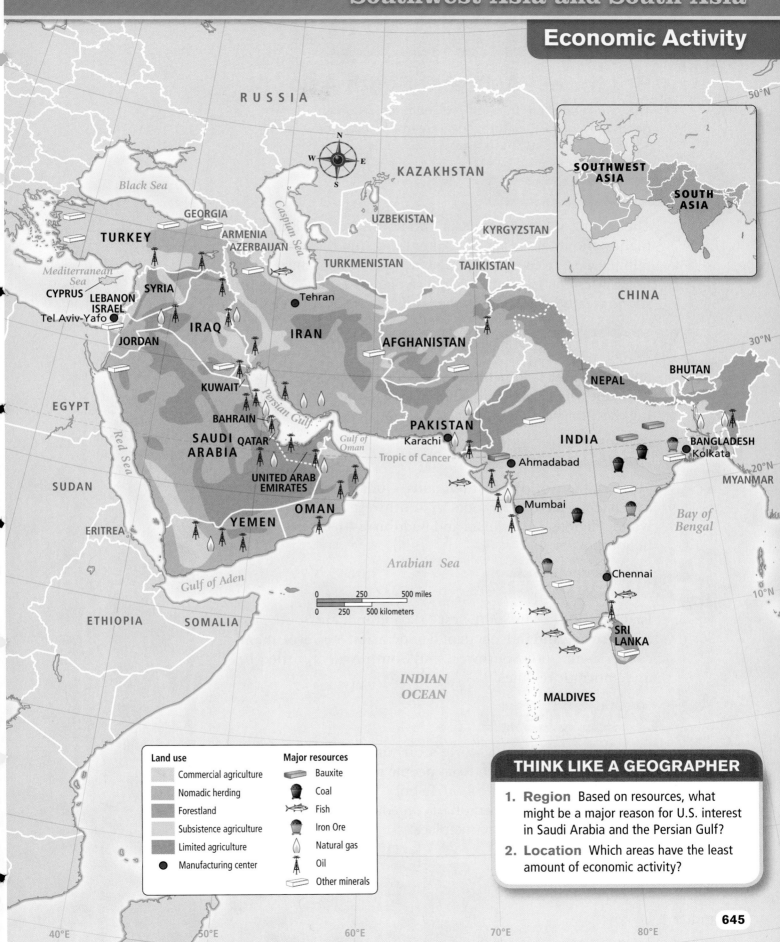

RUSSIA

KAZAKHSTAN

SOUTHWEST ASIA

SOUTH ASIA

Black Sea

GEORGIA

TURKEY

ARMENIA
AZERBAIJAN

Caspian Sea

UZBEKISTAN

KYRGYZSTAN

TURKMENISTAN

TAJIKISTAN

CHINA

Mediterranean Sea

CYPRUS

SYRIA

Tehran

IRAN

AFGHANISTAN

NEPAL

BHUTAN

LEBANON
ISRAEL

Tel Aviv-Yafo

IRAQ

JORDAN

EGYPT

KUWAIT

Persian Gulf

BAHRAIN

PAKISTAN

Karachi

INDIA

BANGLADESH

Kolkata

SAUDI
ARABIA

QATAR

Gulf of Oman

Tropic of Cancer

Ahmadabad

MYANMAR

UNITED ARAB
EMIRATES

Red Sea

SUDAN

YEMEN

OMAN

Mumbai

Bay of Bengal

ERITREA

Gulf of Aden

Arabian Sea

Chennai

ETHIOPIA

SOMALIA

SRI
LANKA

250   500 miles

0   250   500 kilometers

INDIAN OCEAN

MALDIVES

Land use

- Commercial agriculture
- Nomadic herding
- Forestland
- Subsistence agriculture
- Limited agriculture
- ● Manufacturing center

Major resources

- Bauxite
- Coal
- Fish
- Iron Ore
- Natural gas
- Oil
- Other minerals

THINK LIKE A GEOGRAPHER

1. **Region** Based on resources, what might be a major reason for U.S. interest in Saudi Arabia and the Persian Gulf?

2. **Location** Which areas have the least amount of economic activity?

Regional Overview

Southwest Asia and South Asia

The four chapters in this unit provide information about the geography, history, culture, government, and economics of Southwest Asia and South Asia.

GEOGRAPHY

The region of Southwest Asia and South Asia includes the highest mountain range, the Himalayas, and highest mountain, Everest, in the world. It also includes one of the world's largest deserts, the Rub al-Khali in Saudi Arabia. The monsoons greatly affect the weather and climate of South Asia.

HISTORY

Southwest Asia is sometimes called the cradle of civilization. A number of ancient civilizations arose in the region, including the Sumerian, Babylonian, Assyrian, and Hebrew.

Flower Market
An Indian farmer sells marigolds for use at Hindu temples to honor deities.

CULTURE

Three of the world's great religions—Judaism, Christianity, and Islam—have their roots in Southwest Asia. Two other world religions—Hinduism and Buddhism—have their roots in South Asia.

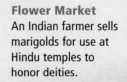

GOVERNMENT

Israel and Turkey in Southwest Asia and India in South Asia are all strong and independent democracies. However, many countries in both Southwest and South Asia are ruled by undemocratic regimes.

ECONOMICS

About one-half of the world's oil reserves are found in Southwest Asia. In South Asia, people rely heavily on farming and fishing to provide food. In both Southwest and South Asia there is a growing emphasis on education as the key to compete in the global marketplace.

Country Almanac

🔁 *Click here* to compare the most recent data on countries @ ClassZone.com

Unit Writing Project

Lobbying Plan

As you read this unit, choose an important cause that you would like to lobby for—that is, convince local, state, or federal government officials to support. Pretend you are a lobbyist and create a written plan for your cause.

Think About:

- which leaders to contact
- a detailed plan of action that you would like them to support

Southwest Asia and South Asia

The Almanac provides information about the geography, economy, and culture of the countries of Southwest Asia and South Asia.

Afghanistan

GEOGRAPHY
Capital: Kabul
Total Area: 250,001 sq. mi.
Population: 29,863,000

ECONOMY
Imports: machinery; medicine; clothing
Exports: rugs, dried fruit

CULTURE
Language: Dari; Pashto
Religion: Sunni Muslim 89%; Shiite Muslim 9%

Bahrain

GEOGRAPHY
Capital: Manama
Total Area: 257 sq. mi.
Population: 727,000

ECONOMY
Imports: machinery; food; petroleum
Exports: aluminum; clothing; petroleum

CULTURE
Language: Arabic
Religion: Sunni Muslim 41%; Shiite Muslim 41%; Christian 11%; Hindu 6%

Bangladesh

GEOGRAPHY
Capital: Dhaka
Total Area: 55,599 sq. mi.
Population: 141,822,000

ECONOMY
Imports: textiles; cotton; rice and wheat
Exports: clothing; frozen fish; knitwear

CULTURE
Language: Bengali
Religion: Muslim 86%; Hindu 12%

Bhutan

GEOGRAPHY
Capital: Thimphu
Total Area: 18,147 sq. mi.
Population: 2,163,000

ECONOMY
Imports: computers; cars; food; petroleum
Exports: electricity; cement

CULTURE
Language: Dzongkha
Religion: Buddhist 74%; Hindu 21%

Cyprus

GEOGRAPHY
Capital: Nicosia
Total Area: 3,571 sq. mi.
Population: 835,000

ECONOMY
Imports: mineral fuels; consumer goods
Exports: pharmaceuticals; clothing

CULTURE
Language: Greek; Turkish
Religion: Greek Orthodox 95%; Catholic 2%; Muslim 1%

India

GEOGRAPHY
Capital: New Delhi
Total Area: 1,269,346 sq. mi.
Population: 1,103,371,000

ECONOMY
Imports: petroleum; gold and silver
Exports: jewelry; chemicals; food; cotton

CULTURE
Language: Hindi, English
Religion: Hindu 74%; Sunni Muslim 9%; Christian 6%; Shiite Muslim 3%

Iran

GEOGRAPHY
Capital: Tehran
Total Area: 636,296 sq. mi.
Population: 69,515,000

ECONOMY
Imports: machinery; cars; chemicals; food
Exports: petroleum; carpets; nuts

CULTURE
Language: Farsi
Religion: Shiite Muslim 90%; Sunni Muslim 6%; Zoroastrian 3%

 Iraq

GEOGRAPHY
Capital: Baghdad
Total Area: 168,754 sq. mi.
Population: 28,807,000

ECONOMY
Imports: consumer goods
Exports: petroleum; food

CULTURE
Language: Arabic; Kurdish
Religion: Shiite Muslim 62%; Sunni Muslim 34%; Christian 3%

 Israel

GEOGRAPHY
Capital: Jerusalem
Total Area: 8,019 sq. mi.
Population: 6,725,000

ECONOMY
Imports: machinery; diamonds; chemicals
Exports: diamonds; chemicals; electronics

CULTURE
Language: Hebrew; Arabic
Religion: Jewish 76%; Muslim 16%; Christian 2%

 Jordan

GEOGRAPHY
Capital: Amman
Total Area: 35,637 sq. mi.
Population: 5,703,000

ECONOMY
Imports: food; machinery; petroleum
Exports: clothing; chemicals; potash

CULTURE
Language: Arabic
Religion: Sunni Muslim 94%; Christian 4%

 Kuwait

GEOGRAPHY
Capital: Kuwait
Total Area: 6,880 sq. mi.
Population: 2,687,000

ECONOMY
Imports: machinery; food; chemicals
Exports: petroleum; ethylene

CULTURE
Language: Arabic
Religion: Muslim 85%

Lebanon

GEOGRAPHY
Capital: Beirut
Total Area: 4,015 sq. mi.
Population: 3,577,000

ECONOMY
Imports: machinery; food; chemicals
Exports: jewelry; machinery; chemicals

CULTURE
Language: Arabic
Religion: Christian 38%; Shiite Muslim 34%; Sunni Muslim 21%; Druze 7%

 Maldives

GEOGRAPHY
Capital: Male
Total Area: 116 sq. mi.
Population: 329,000

ECONOMY
Imports: food; oil; constuction goods
Exports: clothing; tropical fish; jet fuel

CULTURE
Language: Divehi
Religion: Sunni Muslim 100%

 Nepal

GEOGRAPHY
Capital: Kathmandu
Total Area: 54,363 sq. mi.
Population: 27,133,000

ECONOMY
Imports: machinery; fabrics; fuels
Exports: clothing; carpets; shawls

CULTURE
Language: Nepali
Religion: Hindu 81%; Buddhist 11%; Muslim 4%; Kirat 4%

 Oman

GEOGRAPHY
Capital: Muscat
Total Area: 82,031 sq. mi.
Population: 2,567,000

ECONOMY
Imports: machinery; cars; food; chemicals
Exports: petroleum; natural gas

CULTURE
Language: Arabic
Religion: Ibadiyah Muslim 75%; Hindu 6%; Christian 5%; Buddhist 1%

Pakistan

GEOGRAPHY
Capital: Islamabad
Total Area: 310,403 sq. mi.
Population: 157,935,000

ECONOMY
Imports: machinery; petroleum; chemicals
Exports: textiles; leather; rice; carpets

CULTURE
Language: Urdu
Religion: Sunni Muslim 79%; Shiite Muslim 17%; Christian 3%; Hindu 1%

Qatar

GEOGRAPHY
Capital: Doha
Total Area: 4,416 sq. mi.
Population: 813,000

ECONOMY
Imports: machinery; cars; food; chemicals
Exports: natural gas; petroleum; iron; steel

CULTURE
Language: Arabic
Religion: Muslim 83%; Christian 10%; Hindu 3%

Saudi Arabia

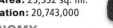

GEOGRAPHY
Capital: Riyadh
Total Area: 756,985 sq. mi.
Population: 24,573,000

ECONOMY
Imports: cars; machinery; food; chemicals
Exports: petroleum; chemicals

CULTURE
Language: Arabic
Religion: Sunni Muslim 84%; Shiite Muslim 10%; Christian 4%

Sri Lanka

GEOGRAPHY
Capital: Colombo
Total Area: 25,332 sq. mi.
Population: 20,743,000

ECONOMY
Imports: textiles; petroleum; food
Exports: clothing; tea; precious stones

CULTURE
Language: Sinhala, Tamil
Religion: Buddhist 77%; Muslim 9%; Hindu 8%; Christian 7%

Syria

GEOGRAPHY
Capital: Damascus
Total Area: 71,498 sq. mi.
Population: 19,043,000

ECONOMY
Imports: food; chemicals; machinery; iron
Exports: petroleum; cotton; vegetables

CULTURE
Language: Arabic
Religion: Sunni Muslim 74%; Shiite Muslim 12%; Christian 6%; Druze 3%

Turkey

GEOGRAPHY
Capital: Ankara
Total Area: 301,384 sq. mi.
Population: 73,193,000

ECONOMY
Imports: chemicals; machinery; petroleum
Exports: textiles; cars; machinery; iron

CULTURE
Language: Turkish
Religion: Sunni Muslim 67%; Shiite Muslim 30%; Christian 1%

United Arab Emirates
the Burj Al Arab Hotel in Dubai in the United Arab Emirates

United Arab Emirates

GEOGRAPHY
Capital: Abu Dhabi
Total Area: 32,000 sq. mi.
Population: 4,496,000

ECONOMY
Imports: machinery; food; textiles
Exports: petroleum; natural gas; gold

CULTURE
Language: Arabic
Religion: Sunni Muslim 80%; Shiite Muslim 16%

Yemen

GEOGRAPHY
Capital: San'a
Total Area: 203,850 sq. mi.
Population: 20,975,000

ECONOMY
Imports: food; machinery; petroleum
Exports: petroleum; fish; fruits

CULTURE
Language: Arabic
Religion: Sunni Muslim 60%; Shiite Muslim 40%

Southwest Asia and South Asia

Physical Geography and History

1

GEOGRAPHY

Physical Geography of Southwest Asia

2

GEOGRAPHY

Physical Geography of South Asia

3

HISTORY

River Valley Civilizations

 ESSENTIAL QUESTION

How have physical geography and history interacted in Southwest and South Asia?

CONNECT ↘ **Geography & History**

Use the map and the time line to answer the following questions.

1. When did cities appear in the Indus River valley?

2. In ancient times, people of the Indus Valley traded with people on the Tigris and Euphrates rivers. What water route would they take between the regions?

3000 B.C.

Culture

◀ **c. 3000 B.C.** Cotton cloth is woven in South Asia (and is still being woven today, as the photo shows).

Culture

c. 2400 B.C. Sumerians use the cuneiform writing system. ▼

Geography

c. 2500 B.C. Cities develop in the Indus River valley of South Asia.

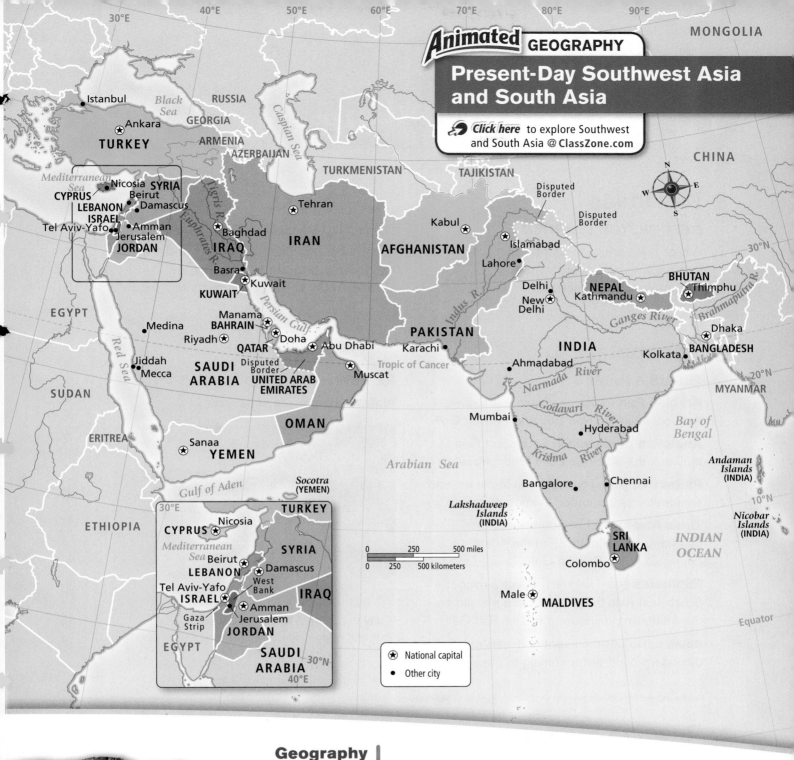

MONGOLIA

Istanbul

Black Sea

RUSSIA

GEORGIA

Ankara

TURKEY

ARMENIA

AZERBAIJAN

Caspian Sea

TURKMENISTAN

TAJIKISTAN

CHINA

Mediterranean Sea

Nicosia SYRIA

CYPRUS   Beirut

LEBANON   Damascus

ISRAEL

Tel Aviv-Yafo   Amman

Jerusalem   JORDAN

Tehran

Tigris R.

Baghdad

IRAQ

Euphrates R.

Basra

Kuwait

KUWAIT

IRAN

Kabul

AFGHANISTAN

Islamabad

Lahore

Disputed Border

Disputed Border

30°N

EGYPT

Medina

Manama

BAHRAIN

Riyadh   Doha

QATAR

Disputed Border

SAUDI ARABIA

Persian Gulf

Abu Dhabi

UNITED ARAB EMIRATES

Muscat

Red Sea

Jiddah

Mecca

Indus R.

PAKISTAN

Karachi

Delhi

New Delhi

NEPAL

Kathmandu

Ganges River

BHUTAN

Thimphu

Brahmaputra R.

INDIA

Dhaka

BANGLADESH

Kolkata

Ahmadabad

Tropic of Cancer

Narmada River

20°N

MYANMAR

OMAN

SUDAN

ERITREA

Sanaa

YEMEN

Godavari River

Mumbai

Hyderabad

Krishna River

Bangalore

Chennai

Arabian Sea

Bay of Bengal

Andaman Islands (INDIA)

ETHIOPIA

Gulf of Aden

Socotra (YEMEN)

30°E

Lakshadweep Islands (INDIA)

Nicobar Islands (INDIA)

10°N

Nicosia

CYPRUS

TURKEY

Mediterranean Sea

Beirut

LEBANON

Tel Aviv-Yafo

ISRAEL

Damascus

SYRIA

West Bank

IRAQ

Amman

Jerusalem

Gaza Strip

JORDAN

EGYPT

SAUDI ARABIA

30°N

40°E

SRI LANKA

Colombo

INDIAN OCEAN

Male

MALDIVES

Equator

	250	500 miles
0	250	500 kilometers

⊛ National capital

• Other city

Geography

c. 1900 B.C. The Sarasvati River of South Asia disappears, perhaps because of earthquakes.

1500 B.C.

History

▲ c. 2200 B.C. Ziggurats are first built in Sumerian cities.

Government

◄ c. 1750 B.C. Hammurabi of Babylon compiles a law code.

651

Reading for Understanding

▶ Key Ideas

BEFORE, YOU LEARNED

Africa has variety in its physical geography, including savannas, mountains, and deserts.

NOW YOU WILL LEARN

Southwest Asia has vast deserts and extensive mountain ranges that are similar to those in certain parts of Africa.

▶ Vocabulary

TERMS & NAMES

Arabian Peninsula peninsula of Southwest Asia between the Red Sea and Persian Gulf

Anatolian peninsula in Southwest Asia between the Black Sea and Mediterranean

Plateau of Iran a high plateau in central and eastern Iran, surrounded by mountains

Tigris River a river of Southwest Asia that flows from a plateau on the Anatolian peninsula to the Persian Gulf

Euphrates (yoo•FRAY•teez) **River** a river of Southwest Asia that flows from a plateau on the Anatolian peninsula to the Persian Gulf

oasis fertile or green spot in desert created by underground water coming to the surface

REVIEW

plateau a high area of flat land

Visual Vocabulary Women carry water from an oasis near Khimsar, Rajasthan, India.

▶ Reading Strategy

Re-create the diagram shown at right. As you read and respond to the **KEY QUESTIONS**, use the outer ovals to note important details about the region's physical features, water shortage, and earthquake threats.

 See Skillbuilder Handbook, page R4

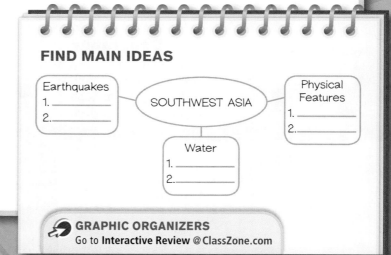

FIND MAIN IDEAS

Earthquakes
1. _____
2. _____

SOUTHWEST ASIA

Physical Features
1. _____
2. _____

Water
1. _____
2. _____

GRAPHIC ORGANIZERS
Go to **Interactive Review** @ ClassZone.com

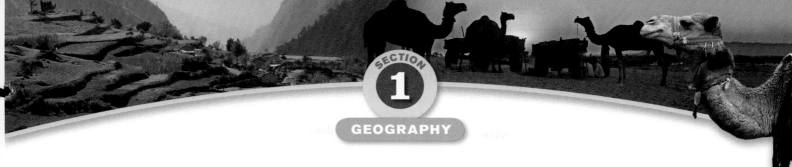

Physical Geography of Southwest Asia

Connecting to Your World

Have you ever seen pictures of the moon's surface? Many of NASA's moon photographs show plains of powdery grey dust with mountains looming in the background. The moon is a very dry place with no water or plants. Although Earth has water, did you know that some regions on Earth look almost as desolate? Southwest Asia has harsh deserts and tall mountains. Yet Southwest Asia also has livable areas, small watered regions where millions of people live.

Physical Features

▼ **KEY QUESTION** What are the three subregions of Southwest Asia?

Perhaps you have heard the name *Middle East* on the news. That term is often used for the region of Southwest Asia. If you look at the map in this section, you will see that Southwest Asia is located where three continents—Africa, Asia, and Europe—meet. As a result, it has historically been a crossroads, a place where roads meet and a place through which many travelers journey.

Mt. Damavand
Snow-capped Mount Damavand is located in Iran.

Rub al-Khali
Deserts such as the Rub al-Khali cover most of the Arabian Peninsula.

SAUDI ARABIA

Rub al-Khali

Peninsulas and Plateaus Southwest Asia can be divided into three subregions, which are listed below. (See map on opposite page.)

1. The **Arabian Peninsula**  is bordered by the Red Sea, Arabian Sea, and Persian Gulf. A peninsula is a piece of land linked to a larger landmass but nearly surrounded by water. Deserts cover most of the Arabian Peninsula. The Rub al-Khali is the largest.

2. The **Anatolian peninsula** Ⓑ, or Anatolia (also called Asia Minor), is home to most of Turkey. This peninsula is bounded by the Black Sea to the north and the Mediterranean to the south.

3. Extending east from Anatolia is the **Plateau of Iran** Ⓒ. A **plateau** is a high area of uplifted, then eroded land. The Persian Gulf lies to the southwest and the Caspian Sea to the north.

Deserts, Mountains, and Rivers Southwest Asia is an arid region with many deserts. The dry climate is partially caused by the terrain. For example, mountains lining the Mediterranean and Black Sea coasts of Anatolia prevent rain from reaching inland areas.

Mountains also affect the climate of the Plateau of Iran. The Elburz Mountains stop moist winds blowing from the Caspian Sea, and the Zagros Mountains block winds from the Persian Gulf.

Rivers are the major freshwater sources in the region. The **Tigris River** and the **Euphrates River** both flow from the Anatolian peninsula to the Persian Gulf. The land between these rivers is a farming region. To the southwest, the Jordan River borders parts of Syria, Jordan, the West Bank, and Israel. The river flows into a lake that is called the Dead Sea because it is so salty that almost nothing can live in it.

▲ **SUMMARIZE** Identify the three subregions of Southwest Asia.

Providing Water

▼ **KEY QUESTION** What methods have people used to provide water to arid Southwest Asia?

Living in an arid region can be challenging because people need water for drinking, bathing, and farming. Most people in Southwest Asia are crowded into coastal areas that receive rain or places with sources of water, such as river valleys and oases. An **oasis** is a fertile or green spot in the desert where underground water comes to the surface.

Ancient Techniques Residents of Southwest Asia have found ways to get the water they need to live in dryer areas. About 2,500 years ago, the people living in what is now Iran developed a technology called the qanat (KA•naht). A qanat Ⓓ, a type of underground water supply system, is illustrated on the next page.

Fun Facts!

THE DEAD SEA
The Dead Sea is a land-locked salt lake, so salty that almost nothing can live in the water. It is so salty that you cannot sink. Salt concentration in the Dead Sea is around 31.5 percent, about nine times higher than in the world's oceans. The evaporation rate of the water is more than 55 inches per year. This keeps the water very salty.

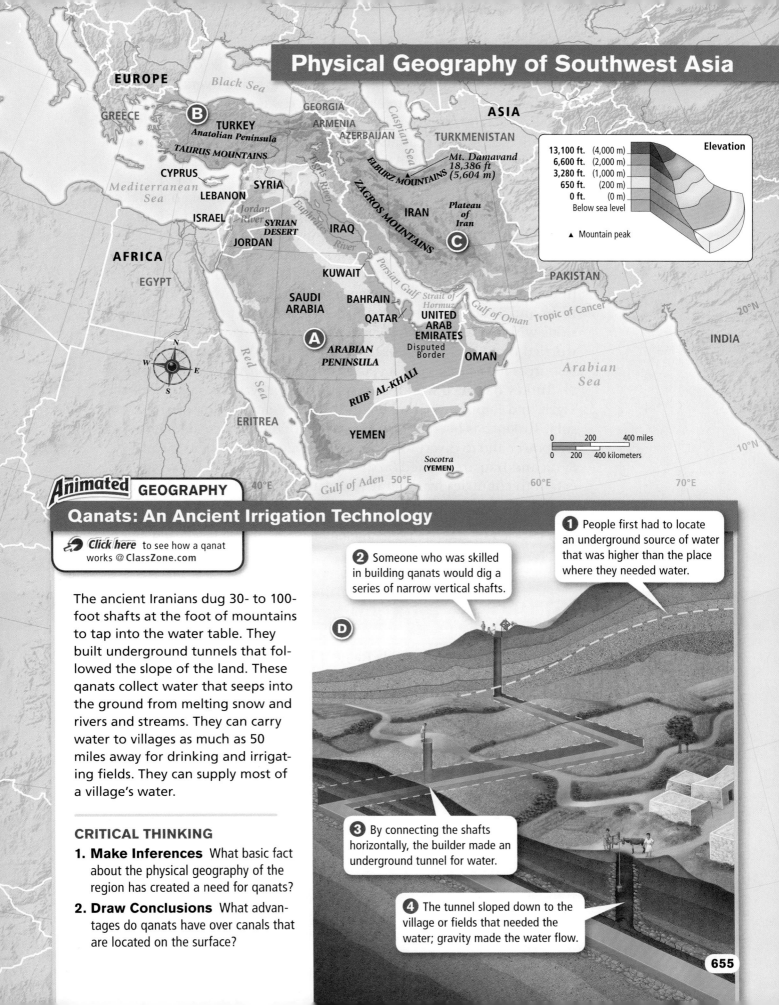

Physical Geography of Southwest Asia

Elevation

13,100 ft.	(4,000 m)
6,600 ft.	(2,000 m)
3,280 ft.	(1,000 m)
650 ft.	(200 m)
0 ft.	(0 m)
Below sea level	

▲ Mountain peak

Mt. Damavand 18,386 ft (5,604 m)

EUROPE
Black Sea
GREECE
GEORGIA
ASIA
TURKEY
Anatolian Peninsula
ARMENIA
AZERBAIJAN
Caspian Sea
TURKMENISTAN
TAURUS MOUNTAINS
CYPRUS
ELBURZ MOUNTAINS
Mediterranean Sea
SYRIA
LEBANON
Jordan River
ISRAEL
SYRIAN DESERT
JORDAN
IRAQ
ZAGROS MOUNTAINS
IRAN
Plateau of Iran
Tigris River
Euphrates River
AFRICA
EGYPT
KUWAIT
Persian Gulf
SAUDI ARABIA
BAHRAIN
QATAR
UNITED ARAB EMIRATES
Strait of Hormuz
Gulf of Oman
Tropic of Cancer
PAKISTAN
INDIA
20°N
ARABIAN PENINSULA
Disputed Border
OMAN
Arabian Sea
Red Sea
RUB' AL-KHALI
ERITREA
YEMEN
Socotra (YEMEN)
Gulf of Aden
40°E
50°E
60°E
70°E
10°N

0   200   400 miles
0   200   400 kilometers

Animated GEOGRAPHY

Qanats: An Ancient Irrigation Technology

Click here to see how a qanat works @ ClassZone.com

The ancient Iranians dug 30- to 100-foot shafts at the foot of mountains to tap into the water table. They built underground tunnels that followed the slope of the land. These qanats collect water that seeps into the ground from melting snow and rivers and streams. They can carry water to villages as much as 50 miles away for drinking and irrigating fields. They can supply most of a village's water.

CRITICAL THINKING

1. **Make Inferences** What basic fact about the physical geography of the region has created a need for qanats?

2. **Draw Conclusions** What advantages do qanats have over canals that are located on the surface?

1 People first had to locate an underground source of water that was higher than the place where they needed water.

2 Someone who was skilled in building qanats would dig a series of narrow vertical shafts.

3 By connecting the shafts horizontally, the builder made an underground tunnel for water.

4 The tunnel sloped down to the village or fields that needed the water; gravity made the water flow.

In ancient times, the knowledge of how to make qanats spread from Iran to many other places. People living along rivers such as the Tigris and the Euphrates relied on surface water to grow their crops. They irrigated by building large canals to carry water from the river to their villages. Smaller canals carried water to the fields. In some arid regions such as Iran and Afghanistan, people still use qanats.

Modern Techniques Many nations in Southwest Asia have taken on huge projects to bring water to dry areas. Such water projects can make it possible to live on and farm previously unusable land. But sometimes the projects cause tension and even conflict.

In the 1950s, Israel began to build a giant system of canals, pipelines, and tunnels. Its purpose was to carry water from the Jordan River and Sea of Galilee to the Negev Desert. The project caused tensions with Syria and Jordan, who share those two water sources and worried that Israel would use too much water. Water and oil are two resources in the region that cause competition over scarce supplies.

Turkey has been working on its own large water project. Both the Tigris and Euphrates rivers begin in Turkey on the Anatolian peninsula. Turkey has been building a system of dams to create hydroelectric power and to divert water from the rivers to some of its farmlands. Syria and Iraq are located farther down the Tigris and Euphrates rivers. Both countries fear that if Turkey uses too much water for irrigation, they won't receive enough to meet their needs.

▲ **FIND MAIN IDEAS** Describe the methods people have used to provide water in Southwest Asia.

CONNECT to Math

One definition of a desert is a region that receives less than 10 inches of precipitation a year. By that definition, many cities of Southwest Asia are built in deserts. One such city is Damascus, Syria, which receives approximately seven inches of rain a year (see chart). One way to learn more details about the climate of a place is to create a graph in which the bars show average monthly rainfall.

Average Monthly Rainfall
(Damascus, Syria)

Month	Rainfall (inches)
January	1.5
February	1.3
March	0.9
April	0.5
May	0.2
June	0.0
July	0.0
August	0.0
September	0.0
October	0.4
November	1.0
December	1.7

Source: www.worldclimate.com

Activity

Make a Rainfall Graph

Materials

- graph paper
- ruler
- pencil
- colored pencils

1. On a piece of paper, draw the horizontal axis and the vertical axis. On the vertical axis, place 20 marks, evenly spaced. Mark them 0.1, 0.2, 0.3, 0.4, etc., on up to 2.0.

2. Below the horizontal axis, write the names of all 12 months. You may abbreviate them. Space them evenly.

3. For each month, draw a bar whose height indicates the average amount of rainfall. Color all of the bars the same color.

The Threat of Earthquakes

 KEY QUESTION Why does Southwest Asia have many earthquakes?

Southwest Asia has long been a crossroads where people meet, but it is also a place where several of the great plates that make up Earth's crust meet in a kind of continental collision zone. As a result, Southwest Asia is prone to deadly earthquakes. In August 1999, a major earthquake hit Izmit, Turkey. More than 17,000 people were killed, many of them crushed when buildings collapsed on them. Thousands more lost their homes. In December 2003, the city of Bam, Iran, experienced an earthquake that killed about 26,000 people. Sometimes, faulty building construction, rather than the strength of the earthquakes, causes many of these deaths.

Earthquake Damage People walk past rubble from collapsed buildings in western Turkey after the 1999 earthquake.

SUMMARIZE Explain why Southwest Asia has many earthquakes.

Section 1 Assessment

ONLINE QUIZ
For test practice, go to
Interactive Review
@ ClassZone.com

TERMS & NAMES

1. Explain the importance of
- Arabian Peninsula
- Plateau of Iran
- Euphrates River
- oasis

USE YOUR READING NOTES

2. Find Main Ideas Use your completed chart to answer the following question:

What are some possible solutions to the problems caused by living in such an arid region?

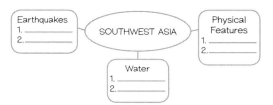

KEY IDEAS

3. How do the mountains of Southwest Asia affect its climate?

4. How did people in ancient times move water from the Tigris and Euphrates rivers to their crops?

5. What might be done to limit earthquake damage in the region?

CRITICAL THINKING

6. Make Inferences When two countries rely on the same river, what issues might arise?

7. Compare and Contrast How is a qanat different from a surface irrigation system?

8. **CONNECT to Today** What might be some problems with building dams in a region prone to earthquakes?

9. **SCIENCE** **Create an Informative Poster** Working with a partner, research in the library or on the Internet to learn about the Richter scale, which is used to measure earthquakes. Then create a poster listing how much damage happens at each level on the scale.

Reading for Understanding

▶ Key Ideas

BEFORE, YOU LEARNED

The physical geography of Southwest Asia is made up of deserts and mountains, and the region is mostly arid.

NOW YOU WILL LEARN

The physical geography of South Asia is made up of mountains, plateaus, and plains, and there are wet and dry seasons.

▶ Vocabulary

TERMS & NAMES

subcontinent a large landmass that is part of a continent but is considered a separate region

Himalayas (HIHM•uh•LAY•uhz) the highest mountains in the world, which stretch along northern India, separating it from the rest of Asia

Mount Everest the world's tallest mountain, located in the Himalayas

Deccan (DEHK•uhn) **Plateau** a high area of land at the center of the Indian subcontinent

Indus River a river in South Asia that flows from the Himalayas to the Arabian Sea

Ganges (GAN•JEEZ) **River** a river of South Asia that flows southeast from the Himalayas to the Bay of Bengal

monsoon a seasonal wind system that produces a wet or dry period in a region

cyclone a violent storm with fierce winds that rotate in a circular pattern like a hurricane

tsunami (tsu•NAH•mee) a series of giant, destructive ocean waves caused by underwater earthquakes, volcanoes, or landslides

BACKGROUND VOCABULARY

famine a severe shortage of food that causes widespread hunger

▶ Reading Strategy

Re-create the chart shown at right. As you read and respond to the **KEY QUESTIONS**, use the chart to compare and contrast the physical geography of South Asia with that of Southwest Asia.

 See Skillbuilder Handbook, page R9

COMPARE AND CONTRAST

	SOUTH ASIA	SOUTHWEST ASIA
Physical Features		
Climate		

 **GRAPHIC ORGANIZERS**
Go to **Interactive Review** @ClassZone.com

Physical Geography of South Asia

Connecting to Your World

In many places, just five inches of rain can cause floods. In Mumbai (also known as Bombay), India, 37 inches of rain fell on July 26, 2005. Streets flooded and landslides buried neighborhoods. India has a climate with separate dry and wet seasons, but even during the wet season, 37 inches of rain in one day is rare.

Mumbai, India Man buying vegetables from a street vendor during the 2005 monsoon

Physical Features of the Peninsula

▼ **KEY QUESTION** What are the three main rivers of the Indian subcontinent?

Millions of years ago, a huge supercontinent, Pangaea, broke apart into separate continents. Scientists believe that when that happened, India became a separate landmass. Over time, it inched north until it hit Asia. The collision pushed up high mountains where the two landmasses met. Those mountains form the northern boundary of the kite-shaped Indian subcontinent. A **subcontinent** is a large landmass that is part of a continent, yet is considered a separate region or entity.

Indian Subcontinent Scientists predict that as the two tectonic plates that formed the Himalayas continue to push against each other, India will become one huge mountain range.

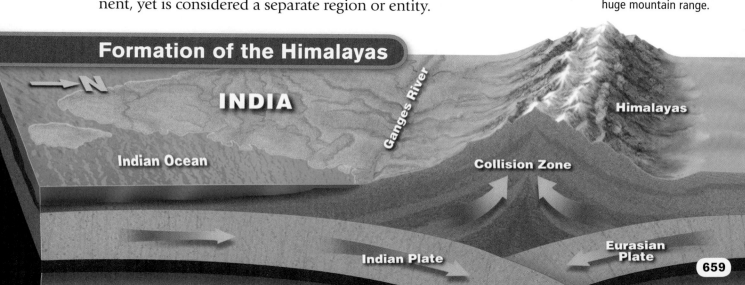

Formation of the Himalayas

N

INDIA

Ganges River

Himalayas

Indian Ocean

Collision Zone

Indian Plate

Eurasian Plate

Mountains and Plateaus The mountains of South Asia include the Hindu Kush in the northwest. The **Himalayas** (HIHM•uh•LAY•uhz) extend east of the Hindu Kush. **Mount Everest** Ⓐ, the world's tallest peak, is located in the Himalayas. (See map on opposite page.)

Mountains called the Western Ghats and Eastern Ghats run along India's two coastlines, which form a "V" in the south. Between them stretches an area of high land called the **Deccan Plateau** Ⓑ. It is a largely arid region. One of the world's largest deserts, the Thar Desert, lies northwest of the Deccan.

Bodies of Water and Islands The Arabian Sea borders India's west coast and the Bay of Bengal borders the east. Both are part of the Indian Ocean, which lies to the south. Several rivers water the subcontinent. In the west, the **Indus River** Ⓒ runs from the Himalayas to the Arabian Sea. The **Ganges** (GAN•JEEZ) **River** Ⓓ—one of the largest, most important rivers of India—flows from the Himalayas to the Bay of Bengal. The Brahmaputra (BRAH•muh•POO•truh) River Ⓔ also starts in the Himalayas, but it joins the Ganges before reaching the bay. Together, the rivers have deposited silt and created an immense fertile delta in what is now Bangladesh (BAHN•gluh•DEHSH).

◀ COMPARING ▶ River Systems

Indus River, Stakna Ldakh, India

Ganges River, Varanasi, India

	INDUS RIVER	GANGES RIVER
Source	the Himalayas	the Himalayas
Route	mostly south through Pakistan	mostly southeast through India
Length	1,800 miles	1,560 miles
Destination	Arabian Sea	Bay of Bengal

CRITICAL THINKING

Compare *What do the two rivers have in common?*

Physical Geography of South Asia

TURKMENISTAN

TAJIKISTAN

CHINA

HINDU KUSH

KARAKORAM RANGE

Khyber Pass

Disputed border

Disputed border

AFGHANISTAN

H I M A L A Y A S

PAKISTAN

Indus River

C

Thar Desert

Mt. Everest
29,035 ft.
(8,850 m.)

NEPAL

A

BHUTAN

INDO-GANGETIC PLAIN

D

Ganges River

Brahmaputra River

E

Tropic of Cancer

BANGLADESH

MYANMAR

Narmada River

Ganges Delta

INDIA

THAILAND

Godavari River

Arabian Sea

B

DECCAN PLATEAU

GHATS

Bay of Bengal

Krishna River

WESTERN GHATS

EASTERN

N
W   E
S

INDIAN OCEAN

SRI LANKA

Elevation

13,100 ft. (4,000 m)
6,600 ft. (2,000 m)
1,600 ft. (500 m)
650 ft. (200 m)
0 ft. (0 m)
Below sea level

▲ Mountain peak

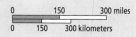

0   150   300 miles
0   150   300 kilometers

MALDIVES

CONNECT
Geography & Culture
READING A PHYSICAL MAP

Physical geography maps show landforms and bodies of water. When reading a physical map, use

• the scale to estimate distance across India at its widest point

• the legend to identify elevation of regions and major mountain peaks in the Himalayas

1. **Location** Into what body of water does the Indus River flow?

2. **Movement** What barriers restrict movement into the Indian subcontinent?

0° Equator

40°N

30°N

20°N

10°N

Two island nations lie off India's coast. To the southeast is Sri Lanka, a tropical island with some mountains. To the southwest is a group of islands called the Maldives, flung over 500 miles of ocean. The Maldives are made of reefs, ridges of coral formed on the slopes of undersea volcanoes. They barely rise above the water's surface.

▲ **SUMMARIZE** List the three main rivers of the Indian subcontinent.

Extreme Weather and Natural Disasters

▼ **KEY QUESTION** What are some natural disasters in South Asia?

Floods are common in South Asia. Even though the climate has wet and dry seasons, no one can predict yearly rainfall. The variable rainfall sometimes causes problems.

Monsoons India's climate is affected by monsoons. A **monsoon** is a seasonal wind system that produces wet and dry seasons. In India, winter winds blow from the northeast and cross vast stretches of land and high mountains before reaching India. As a result, the winter monsoon is dry. Summer winds blow from the southwest and cross the Indian Ocean, so they pick up moisture and bring rain.

If the summer monsoon brings too much rain, floods occur. But that is not the only danger. A drought can result if the monsoon has failed to bring normal levels of moisture. Drought can lead to **famine**, a severe shortage of food that causes widespread hunger.

ANALYZING Primary Sources

Associated Press Newspapers cover disasters as they are happening. This story tells of monsoon flooding in India.

August 16, 2002 Monsoon rains have sent India's Brahmaputra River surging from its channel, swallowing up villages, drowning hundreds of people and leaving millions homeless. . . . Annual monsoon flooding has wreaked havoc across South Asia, killing more than 900 people in India, Bangladesh, and Nepal since June and displacing or trapping about 25 million more.

Source: *The Associated Press*

DOCUMENT–BASED QUESTION
Why might rain in the Himalayas contribute to flooding in Bangladesh?

Another kind of weather that causes hardship and destruction is a **cyclone**, a violent storm with fierce, rotating winds, similar to a hurricane. Cyclones can form in the ocean and then blow ashore. In 1970, a severe cyclone hit Bangladesh, and about 300,000 people were killed.

Natural Disasters India became part of Asia when one great landmass collided with another. Those two plates of Earth's crust are still pushing against each other, which makes South Asia prone to earthquakes. In October 2005, an earthquake that measured 7.6 on the Richter scale rocked Kashmir. Many buildings collapsed or were buried by landslides. About 75,000 people died.

Earthquakes in the ocean floor can lift part of Earth's crust, shifting a huge amount of seawater. The result is a **tsunami**, a series of giant ocean waves that wash over coastal areas. In December 2004, a powerful undersea earthquake occurred in the Indian Ocean near Indonesia. This triggered a tsunami that raced west across the ocean and caused damage in 12 nations, including a number in South Asia. The waves left destroyed villages, ruined fields, and dead bodies. An estimated 300,000 people died.

2004 Tsunami Aerial photo shows damage caused by the 2004 tsunami to a seaside town in Sri Lanka.

▲ **CATEGORIZE** List some natural disasters in South Asia.

Section ❷ Assessment

ONLINE QUIZ
For test practice, go to **Interactive Review** @ ClassZone.com

TERMS & NAMES

1. **Explain the importance of**
   - Himalayas
   - Ganges River
   - cyclone
   - tsunami

USE YOUR READING NOTES

2. **Compare and Contrast** Use your completed chart to answer the following question:

   What are some of the differences between South and Southwest Asia in terms of physical features and climate?

	SOUTH ASIA	SOUTHWEST ASIA
Physical Features		
Climate		

KEY IDEAS

3. Why is India considered a subcontinent?

4. Why is the winter monsoon dry and the summer monsoon wet?

5. Why is South Asia so prone to earthquakes?

CRITICAL THINKING

6. **Make Inferences** How might farmers in a monsoon climate plan their work around the seasons?

7. **Evaluate** What might be some advantages and disadvantages of living in Bangladesh?

8. **CONNECT to Today** Many scientists claim that the global climate is getting warmer and polar icecaps might melt, raising the level of the oceans. Predict how that might affect the Maldives and Bangladesh.

9. **WRITING** **Write an Appeal** Review the descriptions of the disasters in this section. Choose one disaster, and imagine that you work for a relief agency such as UNICEF. Write an appeal or advertisement asking for aid for the victims.

LIVING WITH EXTREME WEATHER

Monsoons shape the lives of people in South Asia. If the summer monsoons bring the right amount of rain, then crops grow and there is a good harvest. If monsoons bring too much rain, then crops are flooded and the harvest is spoiled. The illustration at right shows both positive (near right) and negative (far right) effects of summer monsoons.

Click here to see how Asia benefits from summer monsoons. Learn how monsoons provide relief from months of scorching heat. Rain helps crops to grow (as shown above in a rice field), nourishes the rain forest, and produces floodwaters that deposit sediment to replenish the soil. **A**

Click here to witness the harmful effects of summer monsoons. See how too much monsoon rain causes floods that ruin crops and lives. **B**

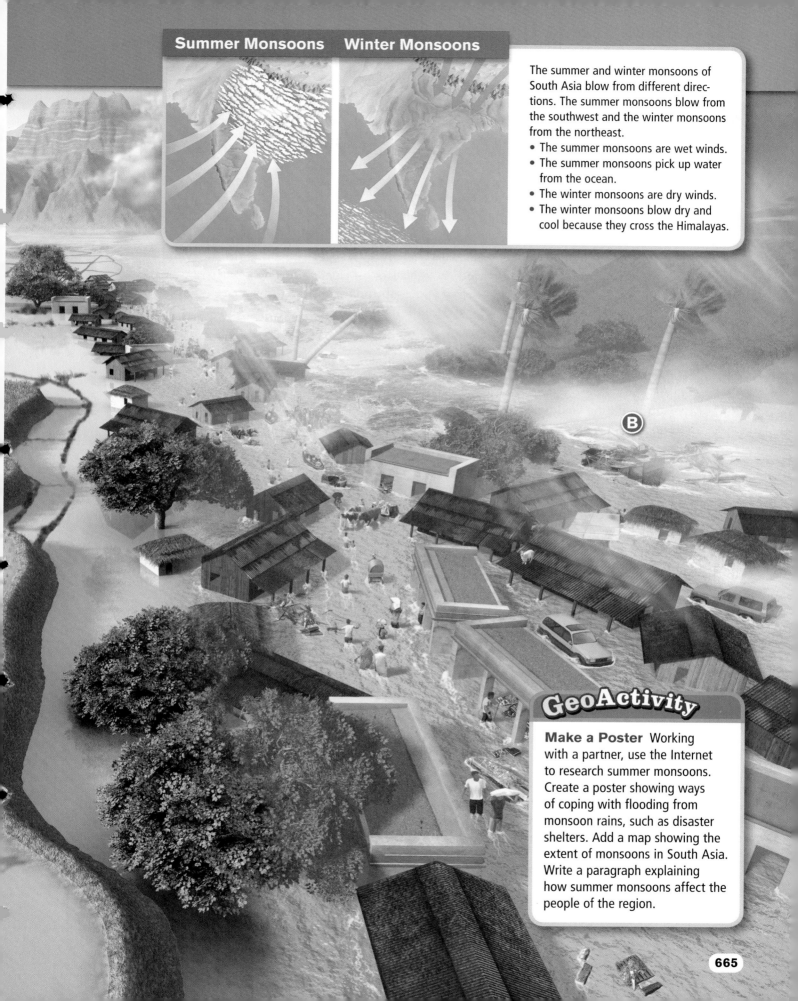

Summer Monsoons **Winter Monsoons**

The summer and winter monsoons of South Asia blow from different directions. The summer monsoons blow from the southwest and the winter monsoons from the northeast.

- The summer monsoons are wet winds.
- The summer monsoons pick up water from the ocean.
- The winter monsoons are dry winds.
- The winter monsoons blow dry and cool because they cross the Himalayas.

Ⓑ

GeoActivity

Make a Poster Working with a partner, use the Internet to research summer monsoons. Create a poster showing ways of coping with flooding from monsoon rains, such as disaster shelters. Add a map showing the extent of monsoons in South Asia. Write a paragraph explaining how summer monsoons affect the people of the region.

Reading for Understanding

▶ Key Ideas

BEFORE, YOU LEARNED

The physical geography of both Southwest Asia and South Asia is rich and varied.

NOW YOU WILL LEARN

In both regions, civilizations developed first in river valleys where there was an abundant supply of water.

▶ Vocabulary

TERMS & NAMES

Mesopotamia the land between the Tigris and Euphrates rivers

silt the fine soil carried by rivers and deposited on nearby lands

civilization an advanced form of culture that developed in cities

Sumer a region of city-states in Mesopotamia that was home to the first civilization

city-state a political unit made up of a city and its surrounding lands

ziggurat a temple built atop a series of increasingly smaller platforms

polytheistic believing in many gods

cuneiform the first-known writing system, which used wedge-shaped symbols and was developed in Sumer

Fertile Crescent a region stretching from the Persian Gulf northwest up the Tigris and Euphrates rivers and west over to the Mediterranean Sea

Hammurabi's Code one of the world's first law codes, compiled by the ruler Hammurabi

Harappan civilization an ancient civilization that developed along the Indus River

BACKGROUND VOCABULARY

grid a network of horizontal and vertical lines that create squares or rectangles

▶ Reading Strategy

Re-create the chart shown at right. As you read and respond to the **KEY QUESTIONS**, use the chart to note the main achievements of the civilizations discussed in this section.

 See Skillbuilder Handbook, page R5

SUMMARIZE

SUMERIAN	HARAPPAN

🚀 **GRAPHIC ORGANIZERS**
Go to **Interactive Review** @ ClassZone.com

River Valley Civilizations

Connecting to Your World

How would you get to sporting events or to the mall if the wheel had never been invented? How would you keep track of important information if you had no way to write it down? Think about what life would be like if your home didn't have indoor toilets, or if you couldn't wear cotton T-shirts or jeans. The people of ancient river valley civilizations invented many things that we rely on every day, including the wheel, writing, indoor plumbing, and cotton cloth.

Wheel The two-wheeled chariot was invented by the Sumerians in Mesopotamia around 3000 B.C.

Mesopotamia and the Fertile Crescent

▼ **KEY QUESTION** What are the main characteristics of civilization?

In Section 1, you learned that the Tigris and the Euphrates rivers flow from Anatolia to the Persian Gulf. What you didn't learn is that the land between the two has its own name—**Mesopotamia**, which means "land between the rivers." In the spring, rain and melting snow in the Anatolian highlands fed the Tigris and Euphrates. As the swollen rivers rushed downhill, they picked up soil. When the rivers reached the flat region of Mesopotamia, they overflowed and spread over a wide area. The fine soil in the water, called **silt**, settled on the land. Silt is very fertile and makes good soil for farming.

Animated GEOGRAPHY

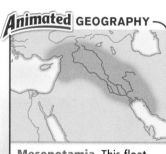

Mesopotamia This floating village is located in the marshes of southern Iraq near the eastern end of Mesopotamia.

Click here to learn more about Mesopotamia @ ClassZone.com

667

Civilization Arises The earliest humans lived by hunting animals and by gathering nuts, fruits, and seeds. Over time, they learned to save and plant some seeds to ensure they would have a food supply. That was the start of agriculture. When people began to irrigate their fields, their ability to grow crops improved and they had extra food.

Farming changed human life. Instead of wandering to find food, people settled in one place. In time, villages grew into cities. City dwellers had to figure out how to defend their city and how to do jobs such as building irrigation canals. To solve such problems, societies developed a more complex way of life. The advanced form of culture that arose in cities is called **civilization**. Civilization has five traits:

Advanced Cities Cities arose as places where farmers could store and trade their extra food.

Specialized Workers When a society has extra food, not everyone has to farm. Some can build houses or make pottery.

Complex Institutions A civilization has institutions such as an army, schools, a government, and a temple for worship.

Record Keeping People in cities needed to record information such as how much food they had stored. So civilizations developed record keeping, which involved writing.

Advanced Technology Early civilizations developed new technologies such as irrigation and bronze tools.

CONNECT → Geography & Culture

Cuneiform

For writing supplies, Sumerians used a material they had a lot of—tablets made of clay from the riverbeds. At first, Sumerians drew pictures that stood for words. Later, they used a sharpened reed to make wedge-shaped marks in soft clay. The marks were combined into symbols that became the writing system called cuneiform. When the clay dried, it hardened, making a permanent record.

Sumerian Civilization The first civilization of Mesopotamia arose in **Sumer**, which was a land of many city-states. A **city-state** was made up of a city and nearby farmlands.

Walls surrounded the cities of Sumer. Buildings were made of dried mud because few trees grew in Mesopotamia. In many Sumerian cities, one building towered over all the others. It was the **ziggurat**, a temple built on a series of increasingly smaller platforms that made the ziggurat peak like a mountain. The Sumerian people were **polytheistic**, which means they believed in many gods.

The Sumerians invented many things we still use today, including the wheel and the plow. The Sumerians also developed the first writing system, which is called **cuneiform**.

▲ **FIND MAIN IDEAS** Give the main characteristics of civilization.

City-States and Empires

▼ KEY QUESTION Who were two rulers of Mesopotamian empires?

The first rulers of city-states were priests, because people believed priests communicated with the gods. However, cities often came under attack because they stored extra food and wealth that outsiders wanted. In wartime, military leaders gained power. Eventually, those leaders became permanent rulers called kings, chosen with the approval of the priests.

The First Empire In 2334 B.C., a ruler named Sargon came to power. He conquered many cities and became the first king to rule all of Mesopotamia. His empire stretched from the Persian Gulf up the two great rivers and over to the Mediterranean Sea, a region called the **Fertile Crescent**. Sargon built a wealthy capital city called Akkad. During his grandson's rule, invaders broke up the empire.

Hammurabi About 500 years after Sargon, another great empire rose in Mesopotamia. A king of Babylon named Hammurabi conquered other city-states and built a vast and powerful empire. Because of his conquests, Hammurabi was the ruler of many peoples with different customs. He wanted a consistent way to govern his subjects, so he compiled a set of laws that applied to everyone under his rule. **Hammurabi's Code** was one of the earliest law codes in the world. His concept of justice—that punishment should fit the crime—has continued to evolve.

▲ **SUMMARIZE** Identify two rulers of Mesopotamian empires.

HISTORY MAKERS

Hammurabi (died about 1750 B.C.)

When Hammurabi became king, Babylon was a small state. Hammurabi led Babylon in conquering surrounding lands. One tactic he used was to dam main waterways to deprive his enemies of water.

During his reign, Hammurabi oversaw the creation of one of the world's oldest set of laws. He made Babylon so magnificent that for centuries after his death, it remained one of the most important cities of the ancient world.

 ONLINE BIOGRAPHY
For more on the life of Hammurabi, go to the **Research & Writing Center @ ClassZone.com**

Indus River Valley Civilization

▼ KEY QUESTION What were some of the accomplishments of the Harappan civilization?

An ancient civilization also developed on the Indus River in what is now Pakistan. As you know, monsoons cause South Asia to have a rainy season and a dry season. During the rainy season, the Indus River often flooded and deposited fertile silt on the land. Farming villages sprang up, and some gradually grew into cities.

Ruins of more than 100 settlements have been found spread across a vast area of South Asia. The two greatest cities of this civilization are called Mohenjo-Daro and Harappa, and the culture is called the **Harappan civilization**. It is also known as the Indus Valley civilization. The ruins of those cities show that the Harappan people had advanced technology and a system of measurement. The cities were laid out on a **grid** with straight streets that crossed at right angles. Houses had indoor plumbing, and there was a sewer system. The Harappan civilization used a system of weights and bricks that were a standard size. The Harappan people engaged in trade with Afghanistan, Persia, and Mesopotamia. The Harappans developed their own writing system to keep records. Around 2000 to 1500 B.C., the Harappan civilization declined, and people left the cities. No one knows why, but possible causes include earthquakes, a shift in the river's course, and attacking invaders. The Harappan people might simply have exceeded the environment's ability to support the population.

▲ **SUMMARIZE** Describe accomplishments of Harappan civilization.

Mohenjo-Daro Ruins of the ancient city of Mohenjo-Daro, located in present-day Pakistan

---

Section 3 Assessment

ONLINE QUIZ
For test practice, go to
Interactive Review
@ ClassZone.com

TERMS & NAMES
1. Explain the importance of
- Mesopotamia
- civilization
- Sumer
- Harappan civilization

USE YOUR READING NOTES
2. Summarize Use your completed chart to answer the following question:

What were some achievements of the civilizations mentioned in this section?

SUMERIAN	HARAPPAN

KEY IDEAS
3. What were examples of complex institutions in Sumer?

4. What was Sargon's important achievement?

5. What are some possible causes for the decline of the Harappan civilization?

CRITICAL THINKING
6. Make Inferences Which developed first, specialized workers or complex institutions? Explain.

7. Compare How were the Sumerian and Harappan civilizations similar?

8. CONNECT to Today In Southwest Asia, farmers dig up objects from ancient ruins and sell them. Do you think historic objects should be kept in museums or owned by individuals? Explain.

9. TECHNOLOGY Plan a Multimedia Presentation Choose either the Sumerian or Harappan civilization and use books, the Internet, or a field trip to a museum to learn more about it. Plan a multimedia presentation showing its art, geography, and technology.

Interactive ◀◀ Review

Click here to complete these and other activities online @ ClassZone.com

CHAPTER SUMMARY

Key Idea 1
Southwest Asia has vast deserts and extensive mountain ranges that are similar to those in certain parts of Africa.

Key Idea 2
The physical geography of South Asia is made up of mountains, plateaus, and fertile plains, and the climate has wet and dry seasons.

Key Idea 3
In both regions, civilizations developed first in river valleys where there was an abundant supply of water.

For **Review and Study Notes**, go to **Interactive Review @ ClassZone.com**

NAME GAME

Use the Terms & Names list to complete each sentence on paper or online.

1. I am a mountain range running between the Indian subcontinent and Asia. **Himalayas**
2. I am the region that lies between the Tigris and Euphrates rivers. _____
3. I am a landform covered mostly by desert. _____
4. I flow from the Himalayas to the Bay of Bengal. _____
5. I lie in the center of the Indian subcontinent. _____
6. I am home to most of Turkey in Asia. _____
7. I am the tallest of my kind in the world. _____
8. I flow from the Himalayas to the Arabian Sea. _____
9. I flow from Anatolia to the Persian Gulf not far from the Euphrates. _____
10. I stretch from the Persian Gulf up two rivers and over to the Mediterranean Sea. _____

Anatolian peninsula
Arabian Peninsula
Deccan Plateau
Euphrates River
Fertile Crescent
Ganges River
Himalayas
Indus River
Plateau of Iran
Mesopotamia
Mount Everest
Sumer
Tigris River

Activities

Flip Cards

Use the online flip cards to quiz yourself on the terms and names introduced in this chapter.

ziggurat

A temple built atop a series of increasingly smaller platforms

Crossword Puzzle

Complete an online crossword puzzle to test your knowledge of Southwest Asia and South Asia.

ACROSS
1. Sumerian writing system that used clay tablets

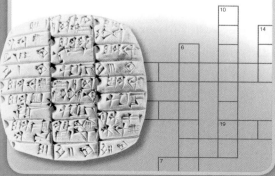

671

VOCABULARY

Explain the significance of each of the following.

1. Arabian Peninsula
2. Anatolian peninsula
3. Plateau of Iran
4. Tigris River
5. subcontinent
6. Indus River
7. monsoon
8. Mesopotamia
9. ziggurat
10. Fertile Crescent

Explain how the first term in each group relates to the terms that follow.

11. civilization: city-state, cuneiform, ziggurat
12. subcontinent: Himalayas, Deccan Plateau

KEY IDEAS

1 Physical Geography of Southwest Asia

13. Where are the three subregions of Southwest Asia located in relationship to each other?
14. What is a qanat, and how does it work?
15. What is the main climate on the Arabian Peninsula?
16. Why does Turkey's water project worry its neighbors?

2 Physical Geography of South Asia

17. How were the Himalayas formed?
18. How were the Maldives formed?
19. What happens when the summer monsoon brings either too much or too little rain?
20. What are the dangers associated with cyclones?

3 River Valley Civilizations

21. What is one positive result of having rivers that overflow their banks during spring floods?
22. How did humans change from hunting and gathering to farming?
23. How did the leadership of city-states in Sumer change from priests to kings?
24. What were Harappan cities like?

CRITICAL THINKING

25. **Compare and Contrast** Create a table to compare and contrast the physical geography of Southwest Asia and South Asia.

SOUTHWEST ASIA	SOUTH ASIA

26. **Draw Conclusions** How did Sumerian priests retain some power under kings?
27. **Compare** What do the Indus, Ganges, and Brahmaputra rivers all have in common?
28. **Connect to Language Arts** An ancient Sumerian proverb says, "Whoever has walked with truth generates life." What do you think that means?
29. **Five Themes: Human-Environment Interaction** Cities with the gridlike design of Harappan culture were found across South Asia. How might that have happened?

Answer the
ESSENTIAL QUESTION

How have physical geography and history interacted in Southwest and South Asia?

Written Response Write a two- or three-paragraph response to the Essential Question. Be sure to consider the key ideas of each section about the rise of civilization in the region. Use the rubric below to guide your thinking.

Response Rubric
A written response will
- discuss the physical geography of each region
- relate physical geography to Sumerian civilization
- relate the physical geography of South Asia to the Harappan civilization

BAR GRAPH

Use the bar graph and your knowledge of Southwest Asia to answer questions 1 and 2 on your paper.

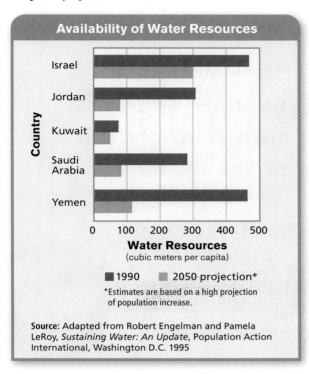

Availability of Water Resources

Country (y-axis): Israel, Jordan, Kuwait, Saudi Arabia, Yemen

Water Resources (cubic meters per capita) — x-axis: 0, 100, 200, 300, 400, 500

■ 1990   ▮ 2050 projection*

*Estimates are based on a high projection of population increase.

Source: Adapted from Robert Engelman and Pamela LeRoy, *Sustaining Water: An Update*, Population Action International, Washington D.C. 1995

1. Which country is projected to have the greatest supply of water by 2050?

A. Yemen
B. Israel
C. Kuwait
D. Jordan

2. Which country is projected to have the smallest supply of water by 2050?

A. Kuwait
B. Jordan
C. Saudi Arabia
D. Yemen

INFOGRAPHIC

Use this Indian farming calendar to answer questions 3 and 4 on your paper.

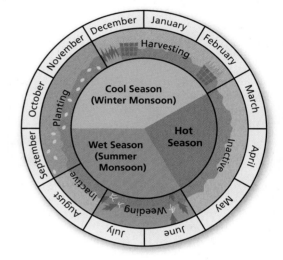

Cool Season (Winter Monsoon) — Harvesting, Planting
Wet Season (Summer Monsoon) — Weeding, Inactive
Hot Season — Inactive

Months: December, January, February, March, April, May, June, July, August, September, October, November

Source: India Country Studies

3. Which season is the most productive?

4. Which season is the least productive?

GeoActivity

1. INTERDISCIPLINARY ACTIVITY–ART

Working in a small group, find photographs of the statues and jewelry created by the ancient Sumerian and Harappan civilizations. Choose three from each region, and plan a multimedia presentation that will show and compare the art of the two regions.

2. WRITING FOR SOCIAL STUDIES

Research to learn what some of the laws in Hammurabi's code were. Write a review of those laws, quoting two or three examples and then explaining what you think their effect on society was and whether they were fair.

3. MENTAL MAPPING

Create an outline map of South Asia and label the following:

• Himalayas
• Deccan Plateau
• Indus River
• Ganges River
• Brahmaputra River
• Arabian Sea
• Bay of Bengal
• Indian Ocean
• Sri Lanka

CHAPTER

22 Southwest Asia

1
FOCUS ON

Saudi Arabia,
Iraq, and Iran

2
FOCUS ON

Israel and the
Palestinian
Territories

3
FOCUS ON

Turkey, Syria,
and Lebanon

 ESSENTIAL QUESTION

How might changes in
political culture affect the
stability of the region?

CONNECT → Geography & History

Use the map and the time line to answer
the following questions.

1. Which country in the region has the world's
largest oil reserves?

2. What body of water is surrounded by oil-producing
nations?

History
◄ c. 960s B.C.
Solomon, king of Israel,
builds a temple.

Culture
about 4 B.C. Jesus
of Nazareth is born.

1000 B.C.

Geography
c. 330 B.C. Alexander the Great
(at right) conquers Palestine. ►

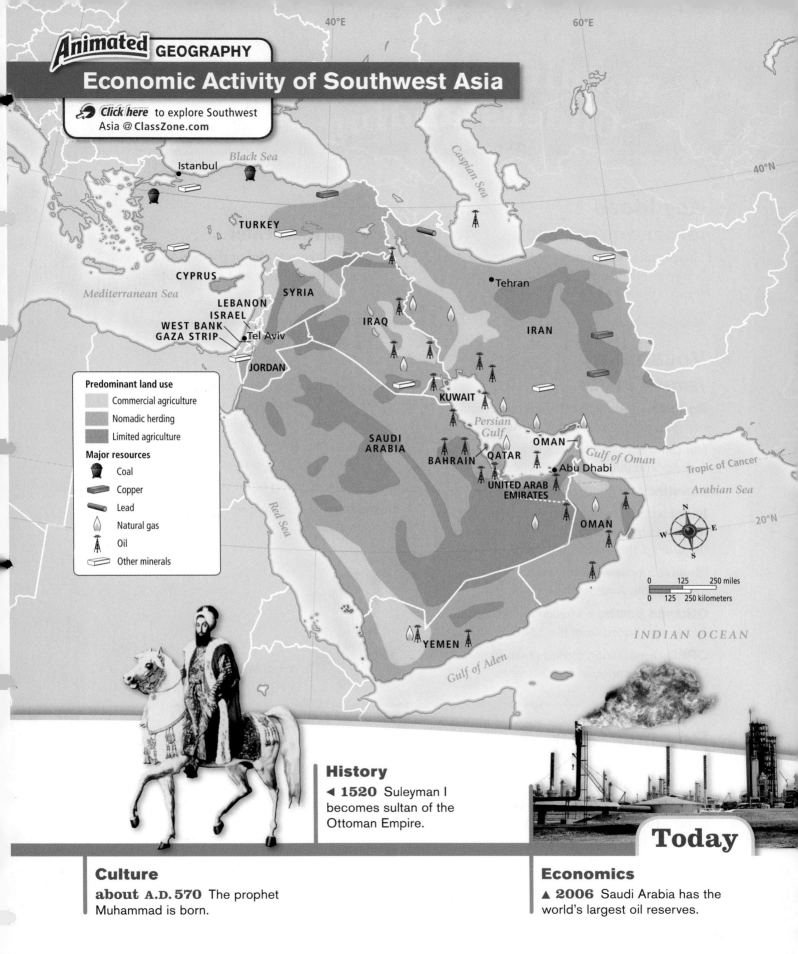

Black Sea

Istanbul

40°E

60°E

40°N

Caspian Sea

TURKEY

CYPRUS

Mediterranean Sea

SYRIA

LEBANON
ISRAEL
WEST BANK
GAZA STRIP
•Tel Aviv

JORDAN

IRAQ

•Tehran

IRAN

KUWAIT

Persian Gulf

SAUDI
ARABIA

BAHRAIN   QATAR

OMAN

Gulf of Oman

•Abu Dhabi

UNITED ARAB
EMIRATES

OMAN

Tropic of Cancer

Arabian Sea

20°N

Red Sea

YEMEN

Gulf of Aden

INDIAN OCEAN

Predominant land use

- Commercial agriculture
- Nomadic herding
- Limited agriculture

Major resources

- Coal
- Copper
- Lead
- Natural gas
- Oil
- Other minerals

N
W   E
S

0   125   250 miles
0   125   250 kilometers

History

◄ **1520** Suleyman I becomes sultan of the Ottoman Empire.

Culture

about A.D. 570 The prophet Muhammad is born.

Today

Economics

▲ **2006** Saudi Arabia has the world's largest oil reserves.

Reading for Understanding

▶ Key Ideas

BEFORE, YOU LEARNED

The physical geography of Southwest Asia is harsh, with mountains, deserts, and a severe climate.

NOW YOU WILL LEARN

The physical geography of the region has influenced the history and culture of many countries.

▶ Vocabulary

TERMS & NAMES

Bedouin an Arabic-speaking, traditionally nomadic people of Southwest Asia

Muhammad (also spelled Mohammed) the founder and major prophet of Islam

monotheism a belief in one god

Islam a monotheistic religion based on the teachings of Muhammad and the writings of the Qur'an, the Muslim holy book

Muslim a believer in the religion of Islam who accepts Allah as the only god

Ottoman Empire a Muslim empire based in Turkey that lasted from the 1300s to 1922

OPEC Organization of Petroleum Exporting Countries, founded in 1960

Kurd a member of an ethnic group that does not have its own country but whose homeland lies in parts of Turkey, Iraq, and Iran

Persia a historic region of Southwest Asia located mostly in what is now Iran

shah title for the king of Persia or Iran

theocracy a government run by religious leaders

Visual Vocabulary
Shah of Persia (Iran)

▶ Reading Strategy

Re-create the chart shown at right. As you read and respond to the **KEY QUESTIONS**, use the chart to note the main ideas about the region's history, government, culture, and economics.

 Skillbuilder Handbook, page R4

FIND MAIN IDEAS

	SAUDI ARABIA	IRAQ	IRAN
History			
Government			
Culture			
Economics			

 GRAPHIC ORGANIZERS
Go to **Interactive Review** @ClassZone.com

Saudi Arabia, Iraq, and Iran

Connecting to Your World

Have you ever heard people say that they can't wake up until they've had their morning cup of coffee? Drinking coffee is just one of many things that our culture gained from Southwest Asia. The people of Southwest Asia (along with people in Egypt) invented algebra, recorded many observations about the stars, and discovered medicines that we still use today. Southwest Asia was also the birthplace of three major religions—Judaism, Christianity, and Islam. You will learn about Islam in this section.

Saudi Arabia

▼ **KEY QUESTION** How did the Arabian Peninsula become a Muslim region?

Saudi Arabia occupies more than three-fourths of the Arabian Peninsula. As you learned earlier, deserts such as the Rub al-Khali cover most of the peninsula. Hardly anyone lives in the deserts; in fact, the name *Rub al-Khali* means "empty quarter." Lack of water is one of Saudi Arabia's biggest problems. No permanent rivers exist, and the country is using up its supplies of underground water.

Saudi Arabia Sand dunes are common in the deserts of the Arabian Peninsula, with an occasional water source such as the springs shown here. **How might scarcity of water affect settlement in the Arabian Peninsula?**

677

Fun Facts!

THE BEDOUIN

Since about 1950, many Bedouin have given up their nomadic life. They have taken up farming or moved to cities in search of health care, education, and jobs such as police officers and oil workers.

To maintain their identity, some Bedouin return to the desert each year to live in tents and renew their sense of roots.

History, Government, and Culture Among the early inhabitants of Saudi Arabia were **Bedouin** nomads who moved around to find grazing for their herds. However, many trade routes crossed Saudi Arabia, and over time towns grew up along those routes. At first, most people in the towns believed in many gods. In the 600s, the prophet **Muhammad** began to preach a belief in one god, called **monotheism**. Muhammad's teachings and the writings of the Qur'an (the Muslim holy book) became the religion of **Islam**. Most people in Arabia became **Muslims**, or followers of Islam. Mecca, Muhammad's birthplace, became the holiest city of Islam. Various Muslim empires rose and fell over the next thousand years.

In the early 1900s, the **Ottoman Empire**, a Muslim empire founded in Turkey in the 1300s, ruled Arabia. A young Arab in the Saudi clan, Ibn Sa'ud, led a fight for independence, and after he succeeded in 1932, he became the king of Saudi Arabia. His family still rules the country. The king controls the government. The laws are based on Islamic religious law.

Economics and Oil Saudi Arabia has more petroleum deposits than any other country, and oil production creates about half the nation's wealth. Service industries, manufacturing, construction, and utilities account for much of the rest.

Beginning in the late 1800s, oil companies searched all over the world for oil resources. In 1938, these companies found large oil fields in the Arabian Peninsula. In 1948, portions of what would become one of the world's largest oil fields were discovered at al-Ghawar, just on the eastern edge of the Rub al-Khali. This field contains approximately one-quarter of Saudi Arabia's oil reserves.

Arabian Peninsula Neighbors A number of very small countries share the peninsula with Saudi Arabia. To the east are several states on the Persian Gulf—Bahrain, Kuwait, Qatar, and United Arab Emirates. To the south, Oman and Yemen face the Indian Ocean. Each of these countries is a Muslim nation that relies on oil production.

The region grew in importance as the global demand for oil increased. Arabian Peninsula nations make almost all of their export money and a large share of GDP (Gross Domestic Product) from oil. Large increases in oil prices allow oil-producing nations to funnel money into the development of other parts of their economies.

In 1960, a group of oil-rich nations, including Saudi Arabia and Kuwait, established a cartel, or organization of independent groups, to coordinate policies on selling petroleum. The group is the Organization of Petroleum Exporting Countries, also known as **OPEC**. The purpose of OPEC is to influence worldwide oil supply and prices.

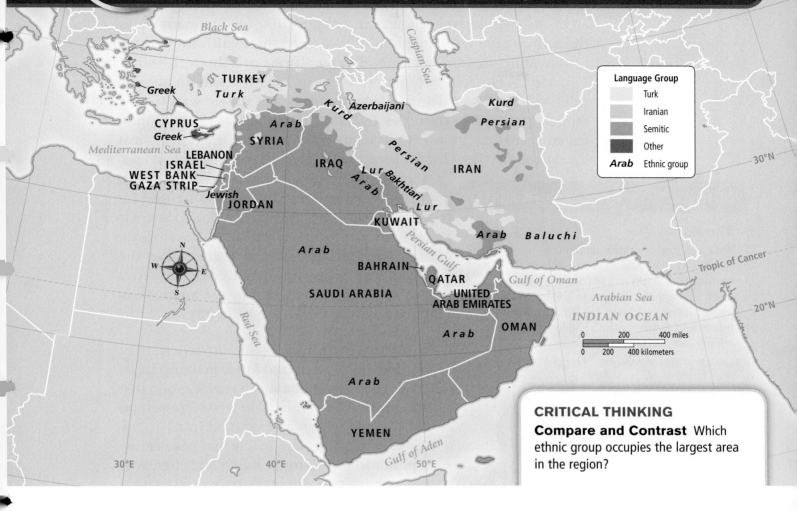

Language Group
- Turk
- Iranian
- Semitic
- Other
- *Arab* Ethnic group

CRITICAL THINKING
Compare and Contrast Which ethnic group occupies the largest area in the region?

They do this by adjusting production quotas, or supply of oil. OPEC is a powerful force in international trade. Other members include Qatar, the United Arab Emirates, Iran, Iraq, and countries outside the region such as Venezuela, Indonesia, Libya, and Algeria.

▲ **SUMMARIZE** Explain how the Arabian Peninsula became Muslim.

Iraq

▼ **KEY QUESTION** How effective a ruler was Saddam Hussein?

The region in Mesopotamia between the Tigris and Euphrates rivers is now part of the nation of Iraq, another Muslim country whose people speak Arabic. Islam spread to Mesopotamia during the 600s. After the rise and fall of a number of Muslim empires, the Ottoman Empire ruled the region at the start of the 1900s. But the Ottomans were on the losing side in World War I, so their empire ended. Great Britain took over Iraq temporarily.

Government and Economics Iraq became an independent monarchy in 1932. Iraq made much money by selling oil, but many Iraqis thought the government should have used the wealth to help the people more. In 1958, a group of army officers overthrew the king.

Saddam Hussein became president in 1979. He was an abusive ruler who imprisoned and killed opponents and started wars to take oil fields from other countries. By 2003, the United States and Britain feared that Hussein might use weapons of mass destruction against his neighbors. They led an invasion of Iraq and overthrew Hussein. They found no weapons of mass destruction, but Hussein was put on trial and hanged for crimes against his people. The United States is helping Iraq form a democratic government. Iraq has great petroleum reserves. But the recent war in Iraq has damaged its refineries and pipelines. The war damage and lack of trade have crippled Iraq's economy.

Culture Arabs make up about 75 percent of the Iraqi population, and Kurds make up about 20 percent. The **Kurds** are an ethnic group that does not have a country but whose homeland lies in parts of Turkey, Iraq, and Iran.

Most Iraqis are Muslim, but they practice two types of Islam—Sunni and Shi'a. Differences between the two, originally based on the issue of choosing leaders, have caused conflicts.

🔺 **SUMMARIZE** Describe Saddam Hussein.

CONNECT ➤ Geography & History

The Kurds

The Kurds lived as nomads for centuries, so they never founded a nation-state. Their home region includes lands that are legally part of Iraq, Iran, Turkey, and other nations that don't want to give up land to form a new nation of Kurdistan. The Kurdish refugees below fled Saddam Hussein's Iraq for safety in a refugee camp in Turkey.

Iran

🔻 **KEY QUESTION** What international conflicts has Iran been involved in since the 1979 revolution?

Iranians are a non-Arab people. Their ancestors were Aryans, who settled the Plateau of Iran in ancient times. That region had been called **Persia** throughout much of history. Today the country is called Iran, which means "land of the Aryans."

History, Government, and Economics The Persian Empire controlled Southwest Asia and Egypt during the 500s B.C. and was a great rival of ancient Greece. From the 300s B.C. onward, a series of foreign powers ruled Persia off and on, but Iranians regained control in the A.D. 1700s. In 1925, an army officer took over the government and became **shah**, or king. He and later his son ruled for 54 years.

They promoted reforms. Conservative Muslims believed the reforms violated Islamic law, so revolutionaries overthrew the shah in 1979. A religious leader became the ruler of Iran and established a **theocracy**, a government run by clergy according to religious law. U.S. support for the shah led the revolutionaries to hold a group of U.S. citizens hostage for nearly 15 months.

Like many nations of Southwest Asia, Iran has petroleum reserves and an economy that depends on oil. Yet it has severe economic problems. The revolution of 1979 caused many trained workers to flee Iran, creating a shortage of skilled labor. In the 1980s, Iraq and Iran fought an eight-year war that was in part about oil. Bombing during the war damaged refineries. In 1995, the United States accused Iran of helping terrorists and cut off trade.

Persian Rug Weavers Iranian girls work on a Persian rug.

Culture People around the world prize Persian rugs, which are woven in highly decorative and colorful patterns, often featuring flowers. Mosques, Muslim places of worship, show Persian architecture at its best. Onion-shaped domes and slender towers called minarets give the buildings a graceful beauty.

▲ **SUMMARIZE** Describe conflicts Iran has had since 1979.

Section ❶ Assessment

🔎 **ONLINE QUIZ** For test practice, go to **Interactive Review** @ ClassZone.com

TERMS & NAMES

1. Explain the importance of
- Muhammad
- Islam
- Kurd
- Persia

USE YOUR READING NOTES

2. Find Main Ideas Use your completed chart to answer the following question:

What valuable resource do all three countries discussed in this section possess, and why is it so valuable?

	SAUDI ARABIA	IRAQ	IRAN
History			
Government			
Culture			
Economics			

KEY IDEAS

3. Why does Saudi Arabia face a water problem?

4. Why did the United States and Britain lead an invasion of Iraq in 2003?

5. What type of government was set up in Iran in 1979?

CRITICAL THINKING

6. Analyze Causes Why did towns grow in the deserts of the Arabian Peninsula?

7. Compare and Contrast How is Iran different from Saudi Arabia and Iraq?

8. CONNECT to Today How might newspapers and schools help Iraq become a more democratic country? Explain.

9. LANGUAGE ARTS Give a News Broadcast Working with a partner, research in the library or on the Internet to learn more about the U.S.-Iran hostage crisis of 1979 to 1981. Use a word-processing program to create, format, and present a news broadcast on the topic.

Reading for Understanding

▶ Key Ideas

BEFORE, YOU LEARNED

Saudi Arabia, Iraq, and Iran are Muslim countries rich in oil resources with a history of nondemocratic governments.

NOW YOU WILL LEARN

Israel is a thriving democracy, and the Palestinian territories are trying to develop a representative government.

▶ Vocabulary

TERMS & NAMES

Holocaust the systematic killing of millions of Jews and other groups by the Nazis during World War II

Gaza Strip a narrow territory along the Mediterranean Sea

West Bank a region west of the Jordan River

Palestinian territories the West Bank and Gaza Strip combined

Palestine Liberation Organization (PLO) a political group that claims to represent all Palestinians and to be working toward gaining an independent Palestinian nation

Jerusalem (juh•ROO•suh•luhm) the current capital of Israel and an ancient city that is holy to Judaism, Christianity, and Islam

Judaism (JOO•day•IHZ•uhm) the monotheistic religion of the Jews, based on the writings of the Hebrew Bible

Christianity a monotheistic religion based on the life and teachings of Jesus of Nazareth and on the writings of the Christian Bible

kibbutz (kih•BUTS) a type of settlement in Israel in which the community shares all wealth and property

▶ Reading Strategy

Re-create the chart shown at right. As you read and respond to the **KEY QUESTIONS**, use the chart to record possible solutions to the problems that are listed.

 Skillbuilder Handbook, page R10

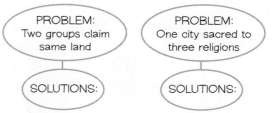

IDENTIFY PROBLEMS AND SOLUTIONS

PROBLEM: Two groups claim same land

PROBLEM: One city sacred to three religions

SOLUTIONS:

SOLUTIONS:

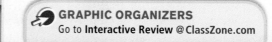
GRAPHIC ORGANIZERS
Go to **Interactive Review @ ClassZone.com**

Israel and the Palestinian Territories

Connecting to Your World

Have you ever seen a TV show in which two people who share a room have a fight and then draw a line down the middle of the floor? Usually, they argue about the fairest way to divide the room. Now, think about what happens when two different cultural groups want to establish a nation on the same land. That situation exists between the Israelis and the Palestinians.

Israeli Security Barrier The Israeli security barrier separates parts of Israel from the West Bank.

History and Government

🔻 **KEY QUESTION** What foreign rulers have controlled Palestine?

Today, the land between the Mediterranean Sea and Jordan River is divided between Israel and the Palestinian territories. But for much of the last 3,000 years, that land was considered a single region. During ancient times, it was called Canaan. A people called the Hebrews moved there from Mesopotamia and eventually became known as Israelites. About 1000 B.C., they set up a kingdom, which soon afterward split into two kingdoms, Israel and Judah.

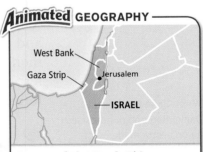

Animated GEOGRAPHY

West Bank
Gaza Strip
Jerusalem
ISRAEL

Dome of the Rock This Jerusalem mosque covers the site where Muslims believe that Muhammad rose into heaven. Jews believe it is the site where Abraham prepared to sacrifice his son Isaac.

🔁 **Click here** for more about the holy sites of Jerusalem @ ClassZone.com

Foreign Rule Beginning in the 700s B.C., a series of ancient empires ruled Canaan, including Alexander the Great in the 300s B.C. The last of these was Rome, which invaded in 63 B.C. The Romans renamed the region Palestine and called the people there Jews (after the name *Judah*). When the Jews staged uprisings, the Romans defeated them and drove them from Jerusalem. During the A.D. 600s, Muslim Arabs moved into the region. In 1099, Christian armies from Europe conquered Jerusalem. That began a series of wars known as the Crusades between Christians and Muslims to control the region. In the early 1500s, the Ottoman Empire conquered Palestine. After World War I, the League of Nations authorized Great Britain to govern Palestine.

A New Israel During World War II, Nazi Germany killed six million Jews in Europe in the **Holocaust**. Afterward, many people felt that the Jews should have their own country in Southwest Asia, site of their ancestral roots. The United Nations proposed dividing Palestine into two nations—Arab and Jewish—and the Jewish state of Israel was born in 1948. Its official language is Hebrew. The Arabs opposed a Jewish state in the region, so war broke out. Israel won the war, and many Palestinians fled to Arab countries as refugees.

The Palestinian Territories Arab-Israeli wars were also fought in 1956, 1967, and 1973, and each time Israel won. In the 1967 war, Israel took the **Gaza Strip**, a narrow territory on the Mediterranean coast, and the **West Bank**, a region west of the Jordan River. The two regions together make up the **Palestinian territories**. A political group called the **Palestine Liberation Organization (PLO)** began to fight to have a Palestinian state on those lands. The PLO and Israelis began to hold peace talks in the 1990s. Israel withdrew its troops from Gaza and much of the West Bank, and the Palestinians elected a government. Even so, the situation remains unstable, and issues need to be resolved. For example, the two sides disagree over who should control **Jerusalem**, which is sacred to Judaism, Christianity, and Islam.

West-East Orchestra Daniel Barenboim rehearses an orchestra made up of Israelis and Palestinians.

▲ **CATEGORIZE** Describe the rulers who have controlled Palestine.

684

Culture and Religion

▼ **KEY QUESTION** Why do three religions regard Jerusalem as holy?

Some people are working to help the two main groups in the region, Arabs and Jews, better understand each other. For example, Israeli conductor Daniel Barenboim and Palestinian-American author Edward Said started an orchestra for Israeli and Palestinian musicians.

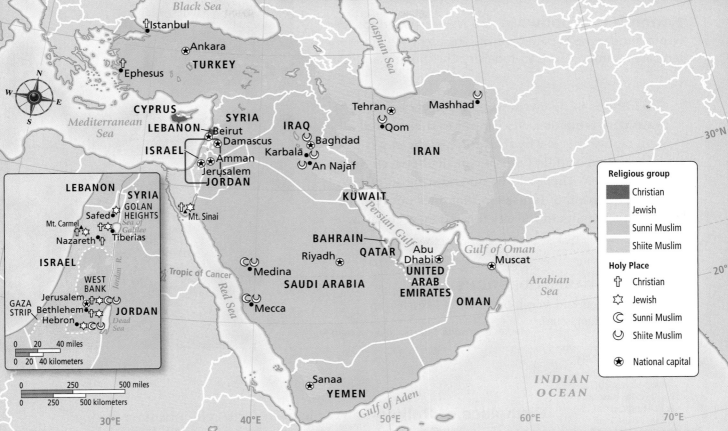

Religious Groups of Southwest Asia

Black Sea

Caspian Sea

☩Istanbul
★Ankara
TURKEY
✝Ephesus

Mediterranean Sea

CYPRUS

SYRIA
LEBANON
☪Beirut
★Damascus
ISRAEL
★Amman
Jerusalem
JORDAN

IRAQ
☪Baghdad
Karbala☪
☪An Najaf

Tehran☪
★Qom

Mashhad☪

IRAN

✝☆Mt. Sinai

Red Sea

KUWAIT

Persian Gulf

BAHRAIN
QATAR
Riyadh★
Abu Dhabi★
UNITED ARAB EMIRATES

Gulf of Oman
Muscat☪

SAUDI ARABIA
☪☪Medina
☪☪Mecca

OMAN

Arabian Sea

Tropic of Cancer

★Sanaa
YEMEN

Gulf of Aden

INDIAN OCEAN

30°N
20°N

30°E   40°E   50°E   60°E   70°E

N W E S

Religious group
	Christian
	Jewish
	Sunni Muslim
	Shiite Muslim

Holy Place
✝ Christian
☆ Jewish
☪ Sunni Muslim
☽ Shiite Muslim

★ National capital

Inset map:

LEBANON
SYRIA
GOLAN HEIGHTS
Safed☆
Mt. Carmel✝☆
Nazareth✝
Tiberias✝
Sea of Galilee

ISRAEL
Jordan R.

WEST BANK
Jerusalem✝☆☪☽
GAZA STRIP
Bethlehem✝☆☪☽
Hebron☆☪☽
JORDAN
Dead Sea

0   20   40 miles
0   20   40 kilometers

0   250   500 miles
0   250   500 kilometers

Islamic Mosque Dome of the Rock, Jerusalem

Jewish Synagogue Old Synagogue in Mazkeret Batyz, Israel

Christian Church Getsemani Church, Jerusalem

CONNECT Geography & Culture
READING A THEMATIC MAP

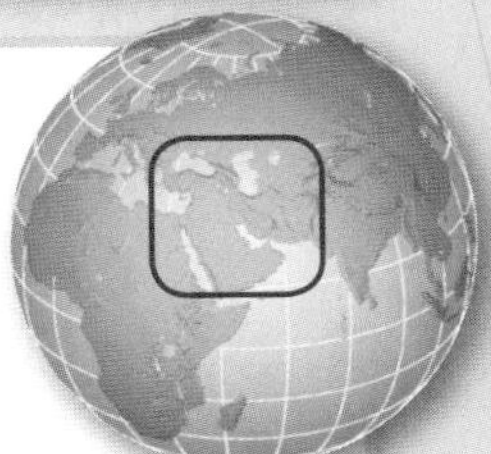

Thematic maps show specific types of information, such as population density or economic activity. This map shows the diversity and distribution of religious groups in Southwest Asia. When reading a thematic map, remember that

- qualitative maps use colors (as well as dots and lines) to help you see patterns related to a specific idea
- an inset map makes a small or congested area on a thematic map easier to see

1. Place Which places have holy sites for three major religions?

2. Location Why might the location of these places be a problem?

Kenneth L. Woodward is a *Newsweek* editor who wrote about who should control Jerusalem. He mentioned Jerusalem's importance to Judaism, Christianity, and Islam.

> For billions of believers who may never see it, Jerusalem remains a city central to their sacred geography. This is why the future of the city is not just another Middle Eastern conflict between Arabs and Jews. . . . There will be no enduring solution to the question of Jerusalem that does not respect the attachments to the city formed by each faith.
>
> Source: "A City That Echoes Eternity," by Kenneth L. Woodward

Market in Muslim Quarter of Jerusalem ▶

DOCUMENT-BASED QUESTIONS

According to Woodward, why is the future of Jerusalem an especially important issue?

ONLINE PRIMARY SOURCE For more writings on Jerusalem today, go to the **Research & Writing Center** @ ClassZone.com

Birthplace of Religions People from three religions have strong ties to the land that Israel occupies. It was the birthplace of two monotheistic religions, Judaism and Christianity. **Judaism**, the religion of the Jews, is based on the writings of the Hebrew Bible. This Bible includes Jewish law and historical and prophetic writings. It teaches that the Jews are descended from Abraham, who obeyed God's command to move from Mesopotamia to Canaan (later Palestine).

Christianity is based on the teachings of Jesus, who lived in Palestine under Roman rule. As a Jew, Jesus taught Jewish ideas. But he also taught ideas that some people found dangerous, so the Romans killed him. Christians believe he rose from the dead and ascended to heaven. Israel is special to Christians because Jesus taught there.

Jerusalem Jews and Muslims have their own reasons for regarding Jerusalem as holy. Jews hold it sacred because the ancient Jewish temple stood there. The temple was destroyed by Babylonian conquerors, rebuilt by Jews, and destroyed again by the Romans. Only one wall remains. One reason for conflict over Jerusalem is that a mosque now stands where the Jewish temple used to be. Muslims chose the site for a house of worship because they believe the prophet Muhammad was taken into heaven from that very spot.

▲ **FIND MAIN IDEAS** Explain why three religions regard Jerusalem as holy.

Israel Builds Its Economy

▼ **KEY QUESTION** What are the main economic activities in Israel?

Israel has few water resources and, unlike its Arab neighbors, hardly any petroleum. But from the start, it did have a highly trained workforce. These workers helped Israel to develop the most advanced economy in Southwest Asia.

First, Israel developed agriculture, using irrigation in dry areas. Today, many farms use drip irrigation, in which computers control the flow of water. Many Israelis moved onto a **kibbutz**, a settlement whose members share wealth and property. They receive housing and food in exchange for labor. The first kibbutzim were farms, although some have switched to manufacturing.

Farming is now a small part of the economy, which relies more on service industries and manufacturing. Israel's most important industries include the production of electronics and chemicals and the cutting of imported diamonds. Tourism also brings a lot of money to Israel, as people from many faiths visit the holy sites there.

Electronics A computer technician inspects hardware in Israel.

▲ **SUMMARIZE** Describe the main economic activities in Israel.

 Section **2** **Assessment**

ONLINE QUIZ
For test practice, go to **Interactive Review** @ ClassZone.com

TERMS & NAMES

1. Explain the importance of
- Palestinian territories
- Jerusalem
- Judaism
- Christianity

USE YOUR READING NOTES

2. Identify Problems and Solutions
Use your completed chart to answer the following question:

How might three religions share Jerusalem peacefully?

PROBLEM:
Two groups claim same land

SOLUTIONS:

PROBLEM:
One city sacred to three religions

SOLUTIONS:

KEY IDEAS

3. How did Palestine become an Arab region?

4. Why do some Jews regard Jerusalem as holy?

5. How has life on a kibbutz changed?

CRITICAL THINKING

6. Make Inferences Why do you think the Holocaust convinced many people that there needed to be a Jewish state?

7. Evaluate What do you think is the most serious challenge to Arab-Israeli peace?

8. **CONNECT to Today** As part of the peace process, in 2005 Israel forced Jewish settlers to withdraw from the Gaza Strip and parts of the West Bank. The Israeli economy improved. Why might that have happened?

9. **TECHNOLOGY** **Plan a Virtual Tour** With a partner, research Jerusalem and make a list of its holy places from three religions. Plan a Web page that offers a tour of the city. Decide on links to other Web sites, design your Web page, and write captions.

▶ Key Ideas

BEFORE, YOU LEARNED

Various countries in the region are struggling with how to preserve past legacies as they organize their societies to move into the future.

NOW YOU WILL LEARN

Turkey, Syria, and Lebanon are all struggling with similar issues of how to reconcile representative government with their traditions.

▶ Vocabulary

TERMS & NAMES

Istanbul the largest city of Turkey, formerly called Constantinople (capital of the Byzantine, or Eastern Roman, Empire) and originally called Byzantium in ancient times

European Union an organization of European nations whose members cooperate on economic, social, and political issues

Golan Heights a region that was formerly part of southwest Syria that Israel has occupied since the 1967 war

peacekeeping referring to military forces whose purpose is to prevent or end war

extended family the family unit that contains more relatives than just parents and children, including grandparents and other close family

Beirut capital of Lebanon and a center of banking and finance

REVIEW

Ottoman Empire a Muslim empire based in Turkey that lasted from the 1300s to 1922

Palestine Liberation Organization (PLO) a political group that claims to represent all Palestinians and to be working toward gaining an independent Palestinian nation

▶ Reading Strategy

Re-create the chart shown at right. As you read and respond to the **KEY QUESTIONS**, use the chart to organize important facts about Turkey, Syria, and Lebanon.

 Skillbuilder Handbook, page R7

CATEGORIZE

	TURKEY	SYRIA	LEBANON
History			
Culture			
Government			
Economics			

 GRAPHIC ORGANIZERS
Go to **Interactive Review** @ ClassZone.com

Turkey, Syria, and Lebanon

Connecting to Your World

Think about the other students who were in your class last year. Even if you come from very different backgrounds or families, you have something in common. You know what that teacher was like and what the classroom rules were. And you share some of the same memories. The countries of Turkey, Syria, and Lebanon have a similar link. Their people have very different ethnic heritages, but they were all part of the Ottoman Empire that you read about in Section 1.

Istanbul

Turkey

▼ **KEY QUESTION** What steps did Mustafa Kemal take to modernize Turkey?

The **Ottoman Empire** began in the 1300s when a group of Turkish people took over most of Anatolia and parts of the Balkan Peninsula in Europe. During the next two centuries, the empire expanded to include more of Europe and most of Southwest Asia and North Africa. But over time, the empire grew weak because of losses in wars and revolts within the empire. After being defeated in World War I, the empire came to an end. In its place, the much-smaller nation of Turkey was founded in 1923 on the Anatolian Peninsula.

Istanbul Shown is the Galata Bridge in Istanbul, Turkey. The western part of the city is in Europe and the eastern part is in Asia. **Why might Istanbul be a good location for trade?**

History, Government, and Culture The first president of the Turkish republic was Mustafa Kemal (known as Ataturk), who wanted to modernize Turkey. His government made reforms such as updating the Turkish alphabet, encouraging economic development, creating modern courts and schools, and giving women the right to vote.

The Ottoman capital was **Istanbul**, which had earlier been the capital of the Byzantine Empire. It has many notable religious and government buildings:

- The Hagia Sophia is a cathedral built in 537, which is famous for its large, beautiful dome. The building is now a museum.

- The Topkapi Palace is a complex of several buildings and gardens. It was the home of the Ottoman ruler, or sultan.

- The Suleiman Mosque is similar in design to the Hagia Sophia; the Blue Mosque has six minarets.

Economics After World War II, several European nations formed what is now called the **European Union (EU)**, a political and economic organization to promote trade and peace. Since 1959, Turkey has tried to join the EU, but it has not been accepted. One reason is that Turkey is very different from Europe in terms of history, culture, and religion. Because of economic and trade ties, discussion continues.

▲ **SUMMARIZE** Explain how Mustafa Kemal modernized Turkey.

CONNECT to History

Built astride the waterway that links the Mediterranean and Black seas, Istanbul stands in Europe and Asia. It was founded about 657 B.C. as Byzantium. In A.D. 330, the Roman emperor Constantine made the city his capital, and it was renamed Constantinople. When the Ottomans conquered the city in 1453, they began to call it Istanbul. In 1923, Turkey moved its capital from Istanbul to Ankara.

Activity

Make a Time Line

Materials
- paper
- pencil and eraser
- ruler

1. Draw a time line, starting with the date 1000 B.C. Add these dates: 500 B.C., A.D. 1, 500, 1500, 2000.

2. Find dates and events in this section to add to the time line.

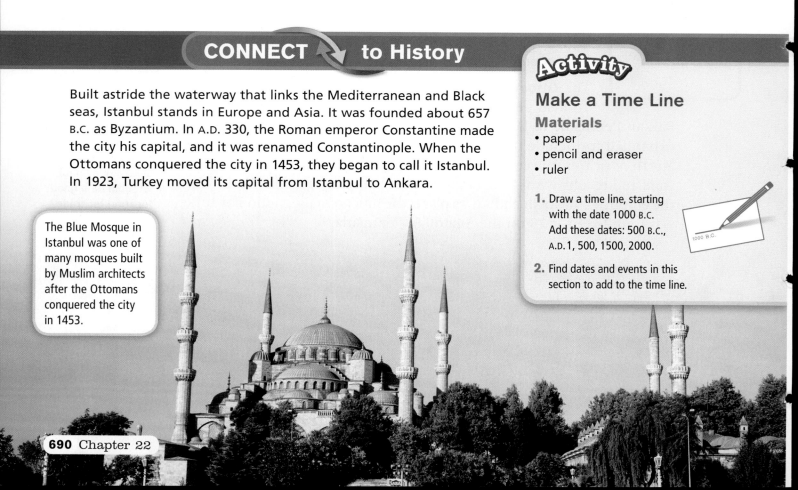

The Blue Mosque in Istanbul was one of many mosques built by Muslim architects after the Ottomans conquered the city in 1453.

Syria and Lebanon

▼ **KEY QUESTION** What is the major cultural difference between Syria and Lebanon?

Like much of Southwest Asia, Syria and Lebanon were ruled by a series of empires ending with the Ottomans. After World War I, the Ottoman Empire was forced to give up most of its territory. The League of Nations issued mandates (commissions) to Britain and France to administer former Ottoman lands. France controlled Syria and Lebanon until they gained independence—Lebanon in 1943 and Syria in 1946. Even though Lebanon and Syria share a border and a history, Syria is almost entirely Muslim, while Lebanon's population is about 60 percent Muslim and 40 percent Christian.

History and Government At independence, Syria became a republic headed by a president. It opposed having a Jewish state in Southwest Asia and took part in three of the Arab-Israeli wars. In 1967, Syria lost a region called the **Golan Heights** to Israel. Syria has demanded the return of the region and the creation of a Palestinian state.

Lebanon, which shares borders with Syria and Israel, is the only nation in the region to have a large number of Christians. When the country gained independence, Muslims and Christians agreed to share power. In the late 1960s, the **Palestine Liberation Organization (PLO)** began to conduct raids into Israel from bases in Jordan and later Lebanon. Lebanese Muslims supported those actions, but Lebanese Christians did not. Muslims demanded a larger role in government because their numbers had grown.

In 1975, civil war broke out between Muslims and Christians. Syria sent troops into Lebanon, while Israel invaded Lebanon to drive out the PLO. In 1978, the UN sent **peacekeeping** forces to Lebanon, but the war dragged on. During the 1990s, steps were taken to disarm various groups of fighters, and elections were held in 1998. In 2005, a Lebanese politician who opposed Syria's influence was killed. Many people blamed Syria, so Syria withdrew from Lebanon.

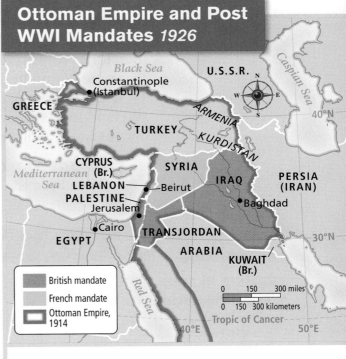

Ottoman Empire and Post WWI Mandates 1926

British mandate
French mandate
Ottoman Empire, 1914

CONNECT Geography & History

1. **Location** In 1926, with what countries did Syria share borders?
2. **Region** Which countries in the region were controlled by France and which by Britain?

Culture About half of all Syrians live in cities and half live in small villages. Many Syrians live in **extended families** composed of older parents and their sons' families. People in villages build houses of stone or sun-dried brick. People in cities live in modern housing and wear Western clothes.

More than 80 percent of Lebanon's people live in cities. During the 1975 civil war, bombs destroyed much of **Beirut**, the capital and financial center. The city was rebuilt, but warfare between Israel and the terrorist group Hezbollah that began in July 2006 inflicted heavy damage on the city.

Beirut This view of downtown Beirut shows the Mediterranean Sea.

Economics Both Syria and Lebanon have developing economies. Syria has petroleum deposits, but not as much as Saudi Arabia or Iraq. It has some fertile land, so agriculture is important; the main crops are cotton and wheat. Syria has little manufacturing. Until 1975, Lebanon's chief industries were the service industries of finance and banking. Warfare has greatly interfered with business, and these once-thriving industries are now struggling to recover.

▲ **COMPARE AND CONTRAST** Describe the main cultural difference between Syria and Lebanon.

Section ❸ Assessment

🔎 **ONLINE QUIZ**
For test practice, go to **Interactive Review** @ ClassZone.com

TERMS & NAMES

1. Explain the importance of
- Istanbul
- Golan Heights
- peacekeeping
- Beirut

USE YOUR READING NOTES

2. Categorize Use your completed chart to answer the following question:

How were Turkey, Syria, and Lebanon affected by World War I?

	TURKEY	SYRIA	LEBANON
History			
Culture			
Government			
Economics			

KEY IDEAS

3. What did Mustafa Kemal do to modernize Turkey?

4. How is Lebanon different from every other country in Southwest Asia?

5. What role did Syria play in the Lebanese civil war?

CRITICAL THINKING

6. Compare and Contrast How was the culture of the Ottoman rulers similar to and different from the cultures of the people they ruled in Southwest Asia?

7. Analyze Causes Why does tension continue between Syria and Israel?

8. **CONNECT to Today** What are some of the reasons that Turkey has not yet been accepted into the EU?

9. **WRITING** **Create a Tour Guide** Using the information in this section, write a paragraph describing Istanbul for tourists.

CHAPTER SUMMARY

Key Idea 1
The physical geography of Southwest Asia has influenced the history and culture of many countries.

Key Idea 2
Israel is a thriving democracy, and the Palestinian territories are trying to develop a representative government.

Key Idea 3
Turkey, Syria, and Lebanon are all struggling with similar issues of how to reconcile representative government with their traditions.

For **Review and Study Notes**, go to **Interactive Review** @ ClassZone.com

NAME GAME

Use the Terms & Names list to complete each sentence on paper or online.

1. I am an ancient city that is holy to three major religions. _____Jerusalem_____

2. I am the religion based on the teachings of Muhammad. _____

3. I am the religion that is based on the life and teachings of Jesus of Nazareth. _____

4. I am the religion that is based on the writings of the Hebrew Bible. _____

5. I am a member of an Arabic-speaking nomadic people. _____

6. I am a member of an ethnic group that lives in Southwest Asia but does not have its own country._____

7. I am the group of oil-producing countries that tries to coordinate its policies._____

8. I am a settlement in Israel in which the community shares all wealth and property.
_____

9. I am the largest city of Turkey and its former capital. _____

10. I used to be the title for the king of Iran. _____

Bedouin
Christianity
Islam
Istanbul
Gaza Strip
Jerusalem
Judaism
kibbutz
Kurd
monotheism
OPEC
Ottoman Empire
Palestinian territories
shah
West Bank

Activities

GeoGame

Use this online map to show what you know about the geography of Southwest Asia. Drag and drop each place name to its location on the map.

Geo GAME

Saudi Arabia

Israel

Turkey

Persian Gulf

Mediterranean Sea

Present-Day Southwest Asia

Turkey

To play the complete game, go to **Interactive Review** @ ClassZone.com

Crossword Puzzle

Complete an online puzzle to test your knowledge of Southwest Asia's history, culture, government, and economics.

ACROSS
1. member of Arabic-speaking nomadic people

VOCABULARY

Explain the significance of each of the following.

1. Islam
2. Istanbul
3. Jerusalem
4. Kurd
5. monotheism
6. OPEC
7. Ottoman Empire
8. Persia

Explain what the terms in each pair have in common.

9. Gaza Strip and West Bank
10. shah and theocracy

KEY IDEAS

1 Saudi Arabia, Iraq, and Iran

11. How did Arabia's geographic location lead to the growth of ancient cities?
12. What has prevented the Iraqi economy from benefiting from its oil fields?
13. Which two of the countries in this section fought a lengthy war, and why?
14. What type of relationship exists between Iran and the United States? Explain.

2 Israel and the Palestinian Territories

15. What historic event of the 20th century caused many people to support the idea of a Jewish state? Why?
16. Why is Palestine considered the birthplace of Christianity?
17. How is a kibbutz different from most other communities?
18. What obstacles remain to the Israeli-Palestinian peace process?

3 Turkey, Syria, and Lebanon

19. Why might the Turkish people honor Mustafa Kemal?
20. What damaged Lebanon's status as a financial center?
21. Why did Syria finally withdraw its troops from Lebanon?
22. What are the main economic activities in Syria?

CRITICAL THINKING

23. **Sequence Events** Create a time line showing the order in which nations of Southwest Asia gained independence.

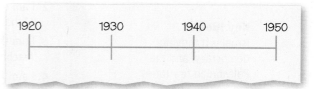

24. **Draw Conclusions** Which site in Jerusalem is most likely to cause conflict?
25. **Five Themes: Region** The economies of many Southwest Asian nations depend on oil, a resource that may run out. What might they do to prepare for the future?
26. **Connect to Science** Companies in Israel are developing technology to take salt out of seawater. Why would they want to do this?
27. **Connect Geography & History** How did the 2003 invasion of Iraq affect Iraq's most valuable natural resource and its economy?
28. **Connect Geography & Culture** What do the religions of Judaism, Christianity, and Islam have in common?

Answer the
ESSENTIAL QUESTION

How might changes in political culture affect the stability of the region?

Written Response Write a two- or three-paragraph response to the Essential Question. Be sure to consider the key ideas of each section as well as specific ideas about the forms of government each nation has. Use the rubric below to guide your thinking.

Response Rubric
A strong response will:
- examine which nations have representative governments
- examine which have authoritarian governments
- discuss the impact of war on politics in the region

☑ **Test Practice**

- **Online Test Practice** @ ClassZone.com
- **Test-Taking Strategies and Practice** at the front of this book

PIE GRAPH

Use this pie graph to answer questions 1 and 2 on your paper.

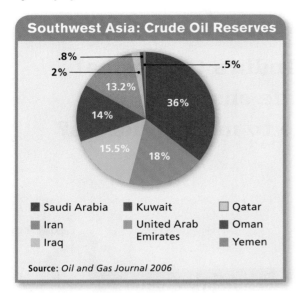

Southwest Asia: Crude Oil Reserves

.8%
2%
.5%
13.2%
36%
14%
15.5%
18%

■ Saudi Arabia   ■ Kuwait   ☐ Qatar
■ Iran   ■ United Arab Emirates   ■ Oman
☐ Iraq   ■ Yemen

Source: *Oil and Gas Journal 2006*

1. Which two countries have the second and third largest oil reserves in the region?

A. Iraq and Iran
B. Kuwait and Iran
C. Yemen and Oman
D. United Arab Emirates and Yemen

2. Which country has the largest oil reserves?

A. Iran
B. Iraq
C. Saudi Arabia
D. Kuwait

BAR GRAPH

Examine the bar graph below. Use the information in the graph to answer questions 3 and 4 on your paper.

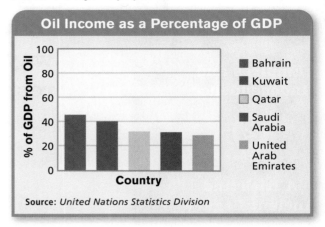

Oil Income as a Percentage of GDP

% of GDP from Oil

100
80
60
40
20
0

Country

■ Bahrain
■ Kuwait
☐ Qatar
■ Saudi Arabia
■ United Arab Emirates

Source: *United Nations Statistics Division*

3. In which country is oil income the largest percentage of gross domestic product (GDP)?

A. Bahrain
B. Kuwait
C. Qatar
D. Saudi Arabia

4. In which countries is oil income the smallest percentage of GDP?

A. Bahrain and Kuwait
B. Kuwait and Saudi Arabia
C. Qatar and Bahrain
D. Saudi Arabia and United Arab Emirates

GeoActivity

1. INTERDISCIPLINARY ACTIVITY–ART

Using books and the Internet, look at photographs of Persian rugs. Research to learn about traditional patterns and colors used in the rugs. Then using crayons, colored pencils, or felt-tip markers, design your own rug.

2. WRITING FOR SOCIAL STUDIES

Research to learn about Suleyman I, the greatest ruler of the Ottoman Empire. Find out about his military campaigns and government, and about Ottoman culture under his rule. Then write a "History Maker" about him.

3. MENTAL MAPPING

Create an outline map of Southwest Asia and label the following:

- Iran
- Iraq
- Israel
- Palestinian territories
- Lebanon
- Saudi Arabia
- Syria
- Turkey

CHAPTER 23 India

1 HISTORY
Empires and Independence

2 CULTURE
A Rich and Ancient Legacy

3 GOVERNMENT & ECONOMICS
The World's Largest Democracy

 ESSENTIAL QUESTION

How is India's traditional way of life changing in response to modern forces?

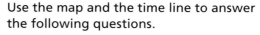

CONNECT Geography & History

Use the map and the time line to answer the following questions.

1. Which Indian cities have the greatest populations?

2. The Taj Mahal was built in Agra, halfway between Delhi and Kanpur. In what year was it built? What is the population density in that area?

Geography
c. 1500 B.C. According to theory, the Aryans migrate to India where they encounter the Dravidians.

1500 B.C.

History
273 B.C. Asoka becomes king of Mauryan empire and builds pillars inscribed with his laws. ▶

Culture
▲ c. A.D. 400s Ancient Sanskrit epic the *Mahabharata* reaches its present form.

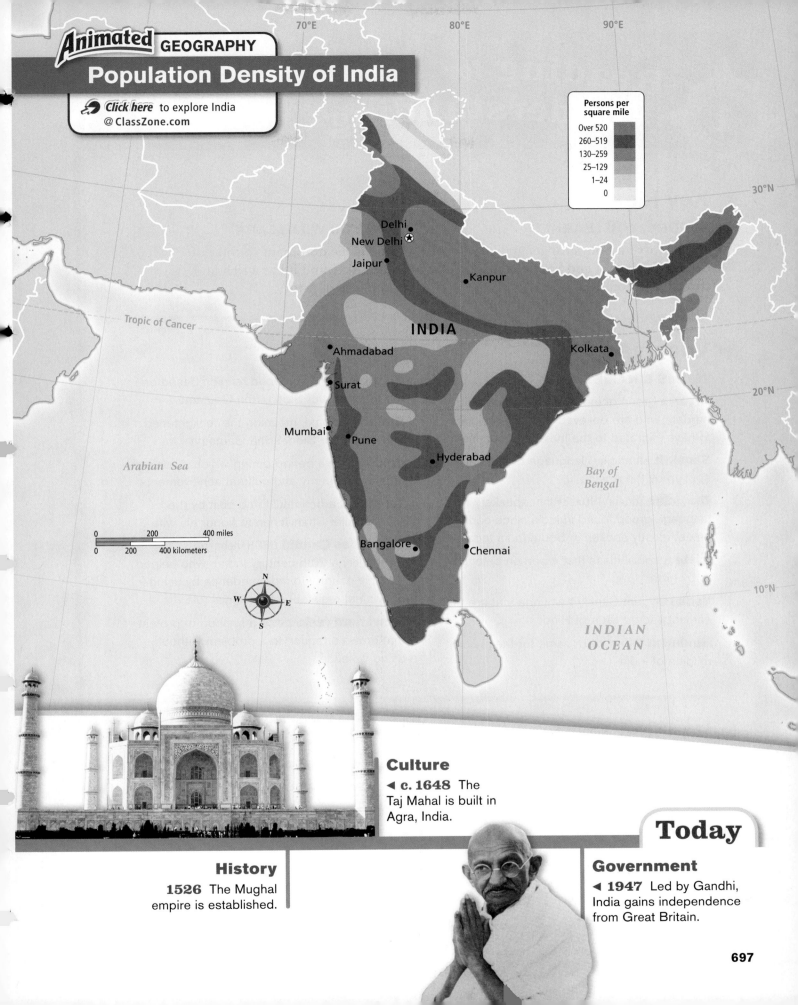

Population Density of India

Click here to explore India
@ ClassZone.com

Persons per square mile

- Over 520
- 260–519
- 130–259
- 25–129
- 1–24
- 0

70°E

80°E

90°E

30°N

Delhi

New Delhi ☆

Jaipur

Kanpur

INDIA

Tropic of Cancer

Ahmadabad

Kolkata

20°N

Surat

Mumbai

Pune

Hyderabad

Bay of Bengal

Arabian Sea

0   200   400 miles
0   200   400 kilometers

N
W   E
S

Bangalore

Chennai

10°N

INDIAN OCEAN

Culture

◄ **c. 1648** The Taj Mahal is built in Agra, India.

Today

History

1526 The Mughal empire is established.

Government

◄ **1947** Led by Gandhi, India gains independence from Great Britain.

Reading for Understanding

▶ Key Ideas

BEFORE, YOU LEARNED

The history and physical geography of Southwest Asia and South Asia are diverse and complex.

NOW YOU WILL LEARN

India is the dominant country of South Asia, and it has a rich and complicated history.

▶ Vocabulary

TERMS & NAMES

Aryan a group of Indo-European nomadic herders who are believed by many scholars to have migrated to the Indian subcontinent

Sanskrit an ancient language of India, first spoken by the Aryans

Dravidian (druh•VIHD•ee•uhn) speakers of a language group found in India since earliest times; mostly spoken in South India today

caste a social class that a person belongs to by birth

Vedas ancient Sanskrit writings that are the earliest sacred texts of Hinduism

Hinduism the modern name for the major religion of India

Buddhism a major world religion based on the teachings of Siddhartha Gautama

Buddha a name, meaning the "enlightened one," used for Siddhartha Gautama

golden age a period during which a society attains prosperity and cultural achievements

Taj Mahal a beautiful tomb built by the Mughal ruler Shah Jahan to honor his wife

Mohandas Gandhi (MOH•hehn•DAHS GAHN•dee) a 20th-century Indian who helped lead his country to independence by using nonviolent resistance to colonial rule

nonviolent resistance a method of protest that draws attention to a problem without using violence

▶ Reading Strategy

Re-create the chart that is shown at right. As you read and respond to the **KEY QUESTIONS**, use the chart to note the main ideas about India's long history.

 Skillbuilder Handbook, page R4

FIND MAIN IDEAS

EARLY SOCIETY	ANCIENT EMPIRES	BRITISH RULE	INDEPENDENCE
1.	1.	1.	1.
2.	2.	2.	2.
3.	3.	3.	3.

 GRAPHIC ORGANIZERS
Go to **Interactive Review** @ClassZone.com

Empires and Independence

Connecting to Your World

When you learned about U.S. history in the past, where did you start? Perhaps you began in 1492 with Columbus. The history of India begins further back in time. In fact, the Harappan civilization dates back to about 2500 B.C. So when you study Indian history, you are studying a time period of 4,500 years. During those years, many changes have occurred on the Indian subcontinent.

Early Societies

▼ **KEY QUESTION** Which two groups contributed to the development of a complex culture in India?

As you read in an earlier chapter, the Harappan civilization had many advanced cities with streets and sewers. After several centuries, the civilization went into decline and people left the cities. Scholars still don't know why. But many believe that another important event occurred shortly after the cities were abandoned. According to this theory, a group of people from the north or northwest came through a pass in the Hindu Kush Mountains onto the Indian subcontinent by about 1500 B.C.

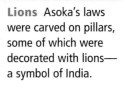

Lions Asoka's laws were carved on pillars, some of which were decorated with lions—a symbol of India.

Hindu Kush This mountain range in eastern Afghanistan and northern Pakistan borders India.

HINDU KUSH

First Inhabitants The group of people who are believed to have migrated to India was the **Aryans**. They spoke an Indo-European language called **Sanskrit**, and their way of life was very different from that of the **Dravidians** (druh•VIHD•ee•uhn), the people living in India when the Aryans arrived. The term Dravidian refers to the family of languages they spoke. The Aryans were nomadic herders. The Dravidians might have been descended from the urban Harappan civilization, although until the Harappan script is deciphered, the language of the Indus Valley remains a mystery. The Aryans taught the Dravidians their language and religion and the Dravidians taught the Aryans about city life. A new and complex culture arose in India.

The idea of the Aryan migration is still a theory because no one has found physical evidence of such a move. Historians formed the theory because of clues in ancient religious stories and also because they noticed patterns in the languages that people speak.

Social Structure In earliest times, Aryan society was organized into three classes: warriors, priests, and commoners. In time, a system developed that divided society into five groups based broadly on work or occupation. The first group was the Brahmans, which included priests and teachers. The second was the Ksatriya (kuh•SHAT•ree•uh), which included rulers, nobles, and warriors. The third group, the Vaisya (VY•shuh), included bankers, merchants, and farmers. The fourth group, the Sudra, was made of artisans and laborers. The fifth group, which came into being much later, was the Untouchables. They did the jobs that no one else wanted to do. When Europeans first came to India in the 1500s, they called the social classes of India **castes**, classes to which people belonged by birth.

Early Religion Today, people call the early religion of the Aryans Brahmanism, after the priests, or Brahmans. Most of what we know about this early religion comes from ancient Sanskrit sacred texts called the **Vedas**, which contain hymns and teachings. The Aryans worshiped nature deities, and the priests made sacrifices to them.

Over time, Brahmanism gradually became **Hinduism**, which is the major religion of India. One big change was that many people came to believe that only one spirit or supreme being governs the universe. That supreme being, God, has different powers, so Hindus worship God in different forms.

Vishnu Vishnu the preserver is an important Hindu deity. He is blue, the color of infinity for Hindus. ▶

▲ **CATEGORIZE** Describe the two groups that contributed to a complex culture in India.

Sanskrit Sanskrit has been used by the educated classes in India for thousands of years. It is important in the history of India because it is the language of the sacred texts. Sanskrit is part of a major group of languages called the Indo-European family. Languages from the same family often have similar words for basic things.

English	father	mother	two	three	mouse
Sanskrit	pitar	matar	dva	trayas	mooshak
Greek	patros	matros	duo	treis	mūs
Latin	pater	mater	duo	tres	mūs
Spanish	padre	madre	dos	tres	raton
German	vater	mutter	zwei	drei	maus

CRITICAL THINKING

Compare Which word do you think is most alike in all of these Indo-European languages?

Scroll of Sanskrit text with illustrations of Hindu stories ▶

The Empires of India

🔻 **KEY QUESTION** What were the three main empires to rule India?

Different powers controlled India during its long history. Of the various empires that ruled India, some were Indian and some were not.

The Mauryan Empire About 321 B.C., an Indian ruler named Chandragupta Maurya (CHUNH•druh•GUHP•tuh MAH•ur•yuh) built an empire that would control most of India. About 50 years later, his grandson Asoka became the ruler of the Mauryan empire. Asoka adopted a religion called **Buddhism**, based on the teachings of Siddhartha Gautama, also called the **Buddha**, or "enlightened one." Asoka gave up warfare and sent missionaries to spread Buddhism, but he also allowed non-Buddhists to practice their faiths.

Golden Age of the Guptas After Asoka died, the Mauryan empire began to decline. The last Mauryan emperor died in 185 B.C. The Gupta empire took over India in A.D. 320. Trade made the Gupta empire wealthy. Historians call the Gupta empire a **golden age**—a time of prosperity and cultural achievements. Indians developed the decimal system and zero. Kalidasa wrote plays that are great works of literature. Beautiful temples and cave paintings were created.

Ancient Empires of India

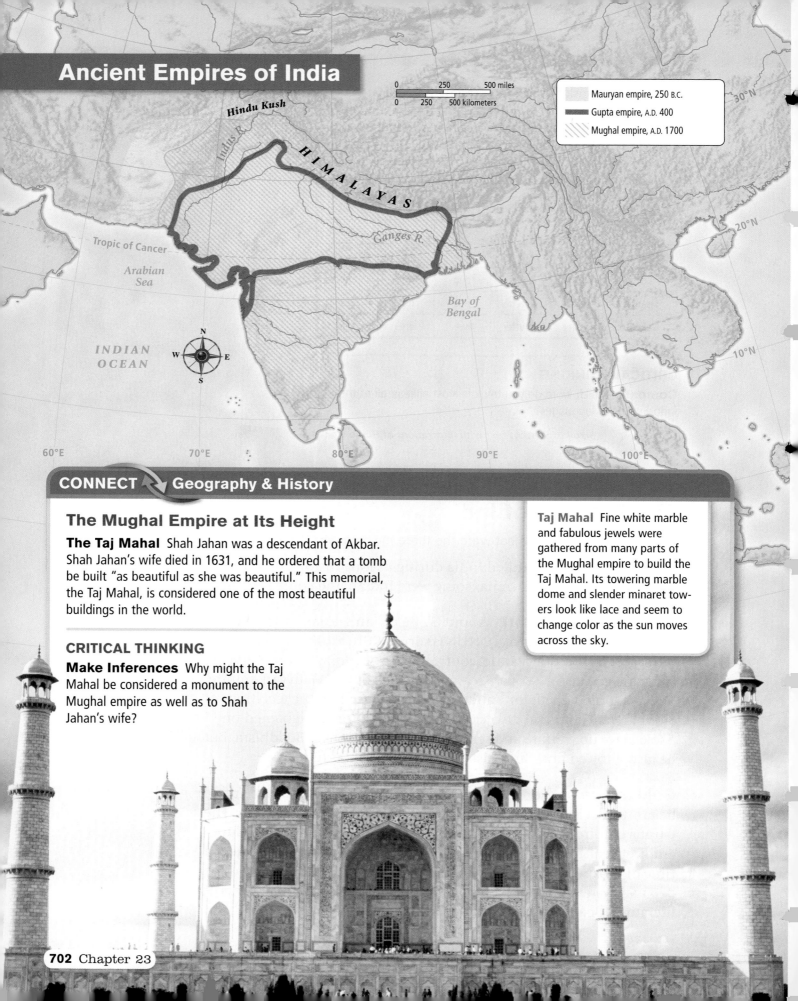

Scale: 0 — 250 — 500 miles / 0 — 250 — 500 kilometers

Legend:
- Mauryan empire, 250 B.C.
- Gupta empire, A.D. 400
- Mughal empire, A.D. 1700

Hindu Kush

Indus R.

HIMALAYAS

Tropic of Cancer

Ganges R.

Arabian Sea

Bay of Bengal

INDIAN OCEAN

60°E 70°E 80°E 90°E 100°E

10°N 20°N 30°N

CONNECT Geography & History

The Mughal Empire at Its Height

The Taj Mahal Shah Jahan was a descendant of Akbar. Shah Jahan's wife died in 1631, and he ordered that a tomb be built "as beautiful as she was beautiful." This memorial, the Taj Mahal, is considered one of the most beautiful buildings in the world.

CRITICAL THINKING

Make Inferences Why might the Taj Mahal be considered a monument to the Mughal empire as well as to Shah Jahan's wife?

Taj Mahal Fine white marble and fabulous jewels were gathered from many parts of the Mughal empire to build the Taj Mahal. Its towering marble dome and slender minaret towers look like lace and seem to change color as the sun moves across the sky.

Muslims and Mughals As you learned earlier, the religion of Islam began in Arabia during the 600s. Starting in the 700s, different groups of Muslims invaded India. The Muslims who came to India brought their beliefs with them, and some Indians converted to Islam. Over time, Muslims became a large minority group in India.

In 1526, a Muslim group from Central Asia called the Mughals made India part of their empire. The greatest ruler of this empire was Akbar, who ruled India fairly and gave many Hindus jobs in his government. A later Mughal ruler, Shah Jahan, is famous for having built the **Taj Mahal**, a beautiful memorial tomb for his wife. It is one of the most famous and most frequently visited buildings in the world.

▲ **SUMMARIZE** Describe the ancient empires that ruled India.

Independence

▼ **KEY QUESTION** What steps led to Indian independence?

During the 1600s, the Mughal emperor fought wars that weakened his empire. Meanwhile, traders from Portugal, the Netherlands, Great Britain, and France had set up trading posts on India's coasts. As the Mughal empire weakened, Europeans seized more power. Of these, the British took over the most Indian territory.

British Rule In 1858, Britain established direct rule over most of India. Britain allowed local princes to retain their thrones as long as they swore allegiance to the British throne. Britain imposed taxes, took over Indian lands, and passed laws that gave the British more rights than Indians. In addition, Britain used Indian crops and products to enrich the British Empire. Indian resentment against British rule grew.

Indian National Congress In 1885, the Indian National Congress was formed to gain equal status for Indians. Its members included people from all over India. The Congress became a nationalistic organization and adopted the goal of independence for India. By 1920, an Indian lawyer named **Mohandas Gandhi** became one of the Indian National Congress's best-known leaders for independence from Britain.

HISTORY MAKERS

Mohandas Gandhi (1869–1948)

Gandhi (pictured above with his grand-daughters) was born in India and studied law in England. His beliefs were influenced by Hinduism and his studies of Christianity and Islam. A few years after his return to India in 1915, Gandhi convinced the Indian National Congress to use nonviolent methods in the struggle for independence. Gandhi himself, the father of modern India, died violently when an assassin shot him. His methods and leadership influenced others such as Martin Luther King, Jr.

 ONLINE BIOGRAPHY
For more on the life of Mohandas Gandhi, go to the **Research & Writing Center @ ClassZone.com**

Mohandas Gandhi (1869–1948) was arrested by the British for his protests against colonial rule. In 1922, he was brought to trial for organizing opposition to the government. This excerpt comes from his testimony.

> I came reluctantly [unwillingly] to the conclusion that that British connection had made India more helpless than she ever was before, politically and economically. . . . The government established by law in British India is carried on for this exploitation [unfair treatment for gain] of the masses.
>
> Source: *India Emerges* by Steven Warshaw

DOCUMENT-BASED QUESTION

According to Gandhi, what did the British government do to the majority of Indians?

Gandhi leads a protest march ▶

ONLINE PRIMARY SOURCE To read more of Gandhi's writing, go to the **Research & Writing Center** @ ClassZone.com

Gandhi wanted the British to leave India, but he did not believe in fighting to make that happen. He urged Congress to practice **nonviolent resistance**, which meant that only peaceful methods would be used to force the British to give up their rule. Such methods included holding marches, refusing to buy British products, and refusing to pay taxes. Gandhi led many marches himself. His emphasis on nonviolence also included the teaching that Indians of all religions could live peacefully together.

Muslim League Many Muslim members of the Indian National Congress shared Gandhi's dream of a free India where Muslims and Hindus could live in harmony. But other Muslims within Congress feared that the Hindu majority would shut them out of government after India gained independence. These Indians created a second nationalistic group called the Muslim League. An important member of the Muslim League was Muhammad Ali Jinnah.

At first, the Muslim League's goal was to give Muslims a role in Indian government. Over time, however, they began to fear that Muslims would suffer discrimination under majority rule by the Hindus. The Muslim League began to demand that India be partitioned, or split, into two independent countries—one Hindu and the other Muslim.

Independence and Partition Talks between British and Indian leaders went on for decades. Finally, the British government granted India independence in 1947. Because of the disagreements between the Indian National Congress and the Muslim League, India was partitioned into two nations. The lands that had a Hindu majority became India. The lands that had a Muslim majority became Pakistan—which was made of two regions separated by over a thousand miles of Indian territory. West Pakistan lay on the northwest border of India, while East Pakistan (now Bangladesh) lay in the east.

Although there was a clear religious majority in most areas, both Hindus and Muslims lived in every part of India and Pakistan. After the partition, millions of Indian Muslims decided to move to Pakistan, and millions of Pakistani Hindus decided to move to India. This sudden migration of ten million people reawakened old angers, and about one million people were killed. Today, although conflicts continue, the two countries are learning to live and work together.

Partition Muslim refugees cram into coaches and climb onto the roof of a train leaving New Delhi, India, for Pakistan.

 FIND MAIN IDEAS Explain the steps that led to Indian independence.

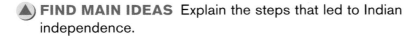

Section 1 Assessment

ONLINE QUIZ
For test practice, go to
Interactive Review
@ ClassZone.com

TERMS & NAMES

1. Explain the importance of
- Sanskrit
- Hinduism
- Buddhism
- nonviolent resistance

USE YOUR READING NOTES

2. Find Main Ideas Use your completed chart to answer the following question:

What are some of the elements that contributed to India's rich history?

EARLY SOCIETY	ANCIENT EMPIRES	BRITISH RULE	INDEPENDENCE
1.	1.	1.	1.
2.	2.	2.	2.
3.	3.	3.	3.

KEY IDEAS

3. What were the five major social classes that developed in ancient Indian society?

4. What cultural achievements occurred under the Guptas?

5. What two nationalistic groups worked for Indian independence, and what did they achieve?

CRITICAL THINKING

6. Contrast What is one major difference between Brahmanism and Hinduism?

7. Analyze Effects Which of Gandhi's goals were achieved, and which were not?

8. CONNECT to Today Recently, some cities changed their names to sound more Indian. For instance, the city that Europeans called Bombay was renamed Mumbai. Why do you think Indian cities did this?

9. WRITING Write an Editorial Choose a view held by members of the Indian National Congress, such as equal rights for Indians. Write an editorial expressing that viewpoint.

Reading for Understanding

▶ Key Ideas

BEFORE, YOU LEARNED

India has a diverse history to which many different peoples have contributed over thousands of years.

NOW YOU WILL LEARN

The culture of India is a blend of all of the many influences that have shaped its history.

▶ Vocabulary

TERMS & NAMES

Bhagavad-Gita one of the sacred writings of Hinduism

reincarnation the rebirth of a soul in another body

karma in Hinduism, the consequences of a person's actions in this life, which determines his or her fate in the next life

nirvana in Buddhism, a state of wisdom that breaks the cycle of reincarnation

REVIEW

Hinduism the modern name for the major religion of India, which developed from Brahmanism

Buddhism a major world religion based on the teachings of Siddhartha Gautama

Buddha a name, meaning the "enlightened one," used for Siddhartha Gautama

Visual Vocabulary Buddha statue from 10th-century Kashmir

▶ Reading Strategy

Re-create the web diagram shown at right. As you read and respond to the **KEY QUESTIONS**, use the diagram to organize important details about the culture of India.

 Skillbuilder Handbook, page R7

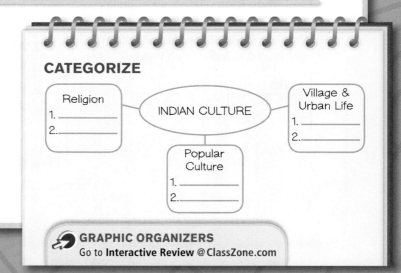

CATEGORIZE

Religion
1. _____
2. _____

INDIAN CULTURE

Village & Urban Life
1. _____
2. _____

Popular Culture
1. _____
2. _____

GRAPHIC ORGANIZERS
Go to **Interactive Review** @ ClassZone.com

A Rich and Ancient Legacy

Connecting to Your World

How many languages are spoken in your town or city? How many different ethnic groups live there? Because of the many groups that have migrated to India throughout its history, it has a larger diversity of languages than any other country in the world. More than 1,000 languages are spoken there. Many ethnic groups live in India. These groups have enriched Indian culture and have given it great variety. But even with all their differences, most Indians are linked by the strong ties of religion and daily life.

Shiva Shiva the destroyer is an important Hindu deity.

Birthplace of Many Religions

▼ KEY QUESTION Which religions originated in India?

The religions of Hinduism and Buddhism, which you first read about in Section 1, both originated in India. Today, about 80 percent of all Indians practice Hinduism. Buddhism has practically disappeared from the land of its birth, but it is widely practiced in other parts of Asia. Other religions, including Sikhism and Jainism, have also played an important role in the history and culture of India.

Ganges Bathers descend steps called ghats to reach the Ganges River at Varanasi. To Hindus, it is the holiest river in India.

Hinduism As you learned, **Hinduism** developed from Brahmanism. The Vedas are the oldest of Hinduism's holy writings, but Hindus also have other sacred texts, including the ***Bhagavad-Gita***, which discusses duty, the meaning of life, and devotion to God. Hindus believe that one supreme spirit is the only reality in the universe. All living things have a soul, which comes from that one spirit. Hinduism does not focus on physical life, but teaches that souls should seek union with God. Most Hindus believe in **reincarnation**, the idea that the soul is reborn into a new body. **Karma**, the consequences of a person's actions in this life, decides what will happen to the soul in the next life.

Buddhism The religion of **Buddhism** is based on the teachings of Siddhartha Gautama, who gave up being a prince to seek the meaning of life. He taught the Four Noble Truths. First, life is filled with suffering. Second, people suffer because they want worldly things. Third, people can stop suffering if they stop wanting. And fourth, they can stop wanting by following the Eightfold Path, which teaches right living. When people give up desire, they achieve **nirvana**, a state of wisdom that breaks the cycle of reincarnation. Many people adopted the teachings of Siddhartha Gautama, whom they called the **Buddha**, or "enlightened one." Buddhism spread throughout Asia, in part because of missionaries whom the Mauryan ruler Asoka sent out.

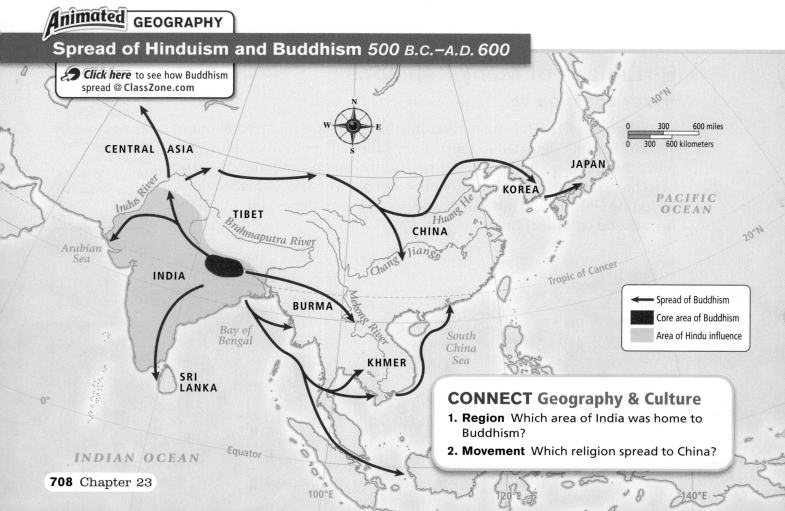

Animated GEOGRAPHY

Spread of Hinduism and Buddhism *500 B.C.–A.D. 600*

Click here to see how Buddhism spread @ ClassZone.com

Legend:
← Spread of Buddhism
■ Core area of Buddhism
▨ Area of Hindu influence

CONNECT Geography & Culture

1. **Region** Which area of India was home to Buddhism?
2. **Movement** Which religion spread to China?

Sikhism and Other Religions As you know, Islam arrived in India during the 700s. Today, about 13 percent of Indians are Muslims, and about 2 percent are Christians. Another 2 percent practice Sikhism, which originated in northern India. Sikhs believe in one god, in reincarnation, and in leading good, simple lives. Another religion that began in India is Jainism, which emphasizes the importance of doing no harm to other living beings.

▲ CATEGORIZE Describe which religions originated in India.

Village and Urban Life

▼ KEY QUESTION How are city life and village life different?

With more than one billion people, India is the second most populous country in the world after China. Six of the world's 100 largest cities are in India. Even so, more than 70 percent of Indians live in rural areas where life is largely unchanged.

Family Life Most Indians live in extended families, which include several generations together. When a woman marries, she moves in with her husband's family—his parents, his brothers and their wives, and any unmarried sisters. Even today, parents often choose their children's spouses, because marriage is viewed as a union of two families.

Village Life Village life varies a great deal across India. In some regions, people live in small one-story structures made of mud. In more prosperous villages, the houses might be made of brick. In rice-growing regions, houses are built on bamboo stilts above the flooded paddies. Many villages across India still have no electricity or running water.

The tradition of sons who learn their fathers' occupations remains strong in many villages. This keeps villages stable by making sure that all the necessary jobs continue to be done. But in recent decades, many young villagers have decided to move to cities, where they can earn more money and choose different ways of life.

Traditional Clothing: The Sari

The sari is a traditional Indian garment that is still commonly worn today.

Folding A sari is a single six- to nine-yard piece of cloth. A young Indian woman must learn to wrap, pleat, and drape the sari.

Fabric Saris are made from a variety of fabrics, including natural fibers such as cotton and silk, as well as synthetic fibers. Brides traditionally wear a red silk sari.

Use The sari can be used to cradle babies, lift hot cooking utensils, protect from the sun, preserve modesty, hold shopping purchases, wipe sweat, dust a table, and protect from smog.

Urban Life Because of that migration, India's cities have grown. With 18 million residents, Mumbai (Bombay) is the world's third largest city. Kolkata (Calcutta) has more than 14 million residents. In addition, Hyderabad, Chennai (Madras), and Bangalore all have more than five million people.

Rapid urban growth causes shortages of housing, transportation, and services. In addition, because there are not enough jobs for everyone in the growing cities, there is a high rate of poverty. Many new arrivals can find no place to live except slums, where people construct shacks of flimsy materials. Slums have no electricity or running water, and sewage runs in the open, spreading disease.

However, the government is dealing with population growth. (See Section 3.) Despite their problems, the cities are also centers of creativity and technological innovation. That is one of the reasons that young people in particular have been drawn to the cities.

▲ **COMPARE AND CONTRAST** Describe how city and village life differ.

COMPARING ⤵ Rural and Urban India

Itanagar, Arunachal Pradesh

Mumbai

	VILLAGES	CITIES
Population	5,000 or less	up to 18 million
Housing	mostly small houses	houses, apartments, shacks
Shopping	street markets and shops	street markets, shops, and stores
Jobs	mostly farming	manufacturing, services, high-tech
Production	hand tools, oxen-pulled plows	machines and technology, some hand tools

CRITICAL THINKING

1. **Compare** What aspect of life is most different in villages and cities?
2. **Draw Conclusions** Why do you think it is more common to have electricity in a city than in a village?

Popular Culture

▼ **KEY QUESTION** What are the major religious festivals of India?

Many groups have shaped India's culture, including the Dravidians and Aryans, the invading Muslims, and the British colonists. As a result, some of India's culture is very old and some is modern. For example, the *Bhagavad-Gita* and the epic poem the *Ramayana* were originally written in the ancient language of Sanskrit. Millions of people still read those poems today, but in modern translations.

Bollywood Movies are a very popular form of entertainment in India, which has the largest motion picture industry in the world. India's movie industry is often called Bollywood, a word that combines the names *Hollywood* and *Bombay* (the former name of Mumbai). About 5 million people work in Indian movies. India's cultural diversity is reflected in its films, which are produced in 52 different languages. Indian movies are often based on ancient myths and folk tales. Frequently, they feature love stories, crime dramas, and stories about social issues. One thing that sets Indian movies apart is that many films feature song-and-dance numbers.

Sports One positive way that British rule influenced Indian culture is in sports, especially cricket. The sport of cricket is played by teams of 11 on a field with wickets, which are made of three upright sticks and two horizontal ones. The game involves defending the wickets by batting away balls that are pitched at them. Players score runs by running between two wickets while the opponent chases down a batted ball. Cricket is the most popular sport in India. Athletes become celebrities, and people follow the matches. Other popular sports include soccer and field hockey.

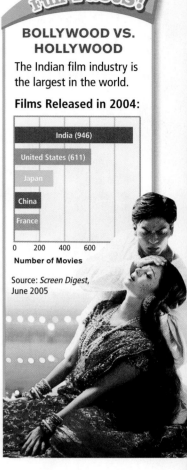

Fun Facts!

BOLLYWOOD VS. HOLLYWOOD

The Indian film industry is the largest in the world.

Films Released in 2004:

India (946)	
United States (611)	
Japan	
China	
France	

0   200   400   600
Number of Movies

Source: *Screen Digest*, June 2005

Film Stars Shahrukh Khan and Aishwarya Rai star in the Indian film *Devdas*.

Cricket Indian boys play cricket in the southern Indian city of Nagapattinam.

To learn more about Savita and her world, go to the **Activity Center** @ ClassZone.com

In Hindi, Savita's name looks like this:

सविता

Hi! My name is Savita. I am 12 years old, and I live in the town of Panna in north-central India. I have an 18-year-old sister and a 13-year-old brother. Let me tell you about my day.

9:30 A.M. I have a math test today, and I'm worried that I didn't study enough last night. My other classes are Hindi, English, science, geography, history, and art.

12:30 P.M. I go home for lunch. My mother cooks a vegetarian biryani, which is a rice dish. After I eat, I carry lunch to my father, who owns a snack shop near the bus station.

3:30 P.M. After school, my brother goes to the shop to give my father a break. I hurry home to see my older sister, who is bringing her baby for a visit. Then I go out to play soccer.

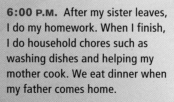

6:00 P.M. After my sister leaves, I do my homework. When I finish, I do household chores such as washing dishes and helping my mother cook. We eat dinner when my father comes home.

CONNECT to Your Life

Journal Entry What appeals to you about Savita's life? In your journal, describe those activities and ways of life.

Celebrations Many of the celebrations that take place throughout the year are religious festivals. Some of the most popular include:

- Dussehra, which celebrates the triumph of good over evil, is celebrated in different ways across India. In the north, people create likenesses of the evil king Ravana, stuff them with firecrackers, and explode them. In the east, the festival is called Durga Puja and involves worship of a deity named Durga.

- Diwali occurs only 20 days after Dussehra. Known as a festival of lights, it is celebrated by lighting oil lamps and setting off fireworks. During the festival, people worship Lakshmi, the deity of wealth. Because of its association with prosperity, the festival is very important to business people.

- Holi, which celebrates the end of winter, is a joyful festival. To express that joy, people throw colored water and powder on each other. They also exchange sweets. Originally a harvest festival, Holi also celebrates the triumph of good over evil.

Holi Hindus in India celebrate the joyous festival of Holi. People dance in the streets and shower each other with colored powder and dyed water.

 CATEGORIZE Describe the major religious festivals of India.

Section 2 Assessment

ONLINE QUIZ
For test practice, go to
Interactive Review
@ ClassZone.com

TERMS & NAMES
1. Explain the importance of
- *Bhagavad-Gita*
- reincarnation
- karma
- nirvana

USE YOUR READING NOTES
2. Categorize Use your completed chart to answer the following question:

How do Indian films blend both ancient and modern culture?

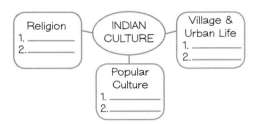

KEY IDEAS
3. Which religion was introduced to India from another region?

4. Why do many young villagers move to cities?

5. What does the festival of Dussehra celebrate?

CRITICAL THINKING
6. Draw Conclusions Which of Buddhism's teachings might have most appealed to people and helped the religion to spread throughout Asia?

7. Make Inferences Why do you think that Indian society regards marriage as the union of two families rather than two individuals?

8. CONNECT to Today If you were a government official in an Indian city, what would be the first service you would try to provide to the slum areas—electricity, running water, sewers, or something else? Explain.

9. TECHNOLOGY **Plan a Web Site** With a partner, learn more about Bollywood films. Design a Web site that would appeal to fans of those movies.

India is one of the oldest cultures in the world. It continues to observe many of its traditions in terms of beliefs, clothing, diet, and work. At the same time, it is rushing in the 21st century to embrace the modern world and improve the standard of living of its people.

Traditional India

Traditional India is a land of the Taj Mahal, Hindu temples, beautiful saris, and rickshaws careening down narrow village streets. Although much of the developing middle class is modernizing, millions continue to follow the traditional ways in clothing, food, work, and daily life.

Architecture

Carvings cover this Hindu temple in Chennai.

The village of Gulmarg, a former hill station to which the British retreated to escape the heat of the plains, sits on a hillside beneath the Himalayas. ▼

Transportation

Even in cities, tradition still plays a part, as shown by bicycle rickshaws in Varanasi.

Jobs

A potter throws pots on wheel in the village of Gunupur.

Modern India

Modern India is racing to become a center of high-tech jobs and widespread prosperity. India's growing middle class is increasingly willing to abandon the sari for jeans, the railway for jet flights across the country, and the farming village for high-tech centers such as Bangalore.

Architecture

The Mumbai Stock Exchange is an example of contemporary architecture in the city of Mumbai.

Transportation

Traffic jams the street in front of the Capitol movie theater in Mumbai.

Jobs

Call-center workers in Bangalore serve customers in the United States and Britain.

▲ *Aerial view of Mumbai, India*

CRITICAL THINKING

1. **Compare and Contrast** What differences can be seen in the kinds of jobs that are available in the city and in the village?

2. **Make Inferences** How would a person's life change in moving from village to city?

Reading for Understanding

▶ Key Ideas

BEFORE, YOU LEARNED

India's rich history and culture have contributed to its present diversity.

NOW YOU WILL LEARN

Out of India's diversity, a robust democracy has developed.

▶ Vocabulary

TERMS & NAMES

parliamentary relating to a government with the parliament form of legislature

prime minister the head of the cabinet and chief executive of government in a parliamentary system

Kashmir a region in the northwestern part of the Indian subcontinent; India and Pakistan dispute control of Kashmir

Green Revolution the use of special seeds, irrigation, fertilizers, and pesticides to pro-duce high crop yields and food production

cottage industry a small business in which the workers manufacture items in their homes

Bangalore Indian city that is home to many high-tech industries

BACKGROUND VOCABULARY

legislature the law-making body of a government

monarch a king or queen who rules a country or territory

Visual Vocabulary Kashmir: boats on Dal Lake

▶ Reading Strategy

Re-create the chart shown at right. As you read and respond to the **KEY QUESTIONS**, use the chart to note the main ideas about India's government and economy.

 Skillbuilder Handbook, page R4

FIND MAIN IDEAS

GOVERNMENT	ECONOMY	ISSUES AND TRENDS
1.	1.	1.
2.	2.	2.
3.	3.	3.
4.	4.	4.

 GRAPHIC ORGANIZERS
Go to **Interactive Review** @ClassZone.com

The World's Largest Democracy

Connecting to Your World

Imagine what the United States might be like if it had 20 political parties. It might be difficult for any party to win control of government. Countries with a large number of political parties sometimes use a **parliamentary** system. This is a system in which the party with the most seats in the **legislature**, or Parliament, selects the head of government. India has a parliamentary system with many political parties.

Indian Elections Government official shows voters how to use a voting machine.

A Giant Republic

▼ **KEY QUESTION** What are some of the challenges faced by the Indian government?

After India gained independence, its leaders decided that it should be a representative democracy. In fact, because India is the second most populous nation, it is the world's largest democracy. The structure of the national government is similar to that of Great Britain, except that India does not have a **monarch**. Like the United States, India has a federal system of government, which divides power between the central government and the states. India is divided into 28 states and 7 union territories.

New Delhi The Viceroy's House in New Delhi (now the Presidential Palace and Parliament), designed by Sir Edwin Lutyens

Government Structure The Parliament of India consists of two houses. The first is the Lok Sabha (LAWK SUHB•hah)—House of the People. The second is the Rajya Sabha (RAHJ•yuh SUHB•hah)—Council of the States. The people of India vote for the members of the Lok Sabha, who serve five–year terms. The state and territorial legislatures choose almost all the members of the Rajya Sabha.

Parliament is led by a president, who is chosen by the elected members of Parliament and the state and territorial legislatures. In India, the president is the head of state, which is a largely ceremonial position of limited power. The president's duties are to give his assent to all bills before they become law, to name the prime minister, and to appoint 12 members of the Rajya Sabha.

The head of government and most powerful person in India is the **prime minister**. Usually, the prime minister is the leader of the party with the most seats in Parliament. The prime minister heads a Council of Ministers, which oversees the daily work of government. The prime minister and council usually serve for five years. But if the prime minister loses the legislature's support, the president may dissolve the Lok Sabha and call for new elections. In that case, a new parliament is formed and a new prime minister chosen.

Indian Flag In the center of the flag of modern India is a Buddhist symbol—the wheel of dharma.

Government Challenges As you read in Section 1, when the British colony of India gained independence, it was divided into India and Pakistan. The partition triggered mass migrations of refugees and outbreaks of violence between Muslims and Hindus. Since then, India and Pakistan have worked to resolve problems such as the conflict over Kashmir and the expanding populations in both countries.

COMPARING U.S. and Indian Governments

	UNITED STATES	INDIA
Type	representative democracy	parliamentary democracy
Head of State	president	president (symbolic position)
Head of Government	president	prime minister
Legislature	two-house congress (both popularly elected)	two-house congress (only one popularly elected)
System	federal	federal

CRITICAL THINKING

Make Inferences How would you explain India's preference for a parliamentary system of government rather than a presidential system?

Kashmir An ongoing source of tension between the two nations is the region of **Kashmir** (KASH•meer) in the northwestern part of the subcontinent. The region is important because through it flows the Indus River, an important water source for both nations.

Kashmir was one of the princely states, which Britain had allowed to be ruled by a local prince. As such, it had the right to decide whether to join India or Pakistan. The ruler of Kashmir was Hindu, but most of the people were Muslims who wanted to join Pakistan. Some of those Muslims started an uprising, and Pakistani forces invaded Kashmir. The prince then announced Kashmir would join India, causing war to erupt between India and Pakistan. Eventually, the two countries divided Kashmir, but since then, fighting over the region has broken out several times.

The simmering tension between the two countries is a source of concern. During the late 1990s, India and Pakistan each tested nuclear weapons. Other nations worry that if a new war starts between India and Pakistan, they might resort to using those weapons.

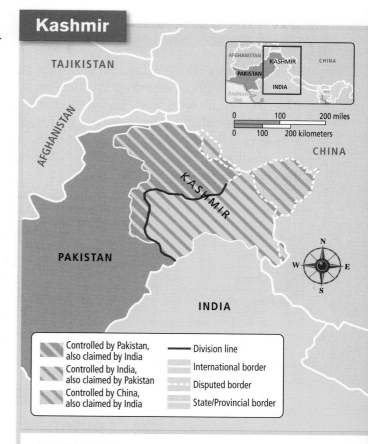

Kashmir

Legend:
- Controlled by Pakistan, also claimed by India
- Controlled by India, also claimed by Pakistan
- Controlled by China, also claimed by India
- Division line
- International border
- Disputed border
- State/Provincial border

CONNECT Geography & History
1. **Region** Which countries does Kashmir border?
2. **Location** Where was the division line drawn?

Population Explosion In 2005, India had 1.1 billion people. Experts estimate that by 2050, India will have 1.6 billion people, the world's largest population. Providing for all those people will be a challenge. They will need housing, food, water, jobs, health care, and government services.

The Indian government is taking several steps to deal with this challenge. First, it has run publicity campaigns to persuade people to have fewer children. Second, it has tried to improve women's lives by offering them more education and job opportunities. Finally, many experts believe that India must improve its education system. Many children drop out of school to work, so only about 60 percent of Indians can read and write. Education helps people to get better jobs, which enable them to afford better health care and housing. As families gain more wealth, they tend to have fewer children and their children tend to stay in school longer.

▲ **FIND MAIN IDEAS** Describe challenges faced by the Indian government.

Most countries take a census, or count, of their population. For example, the United States takes a census every 10 years. People who study population also use mathematical formulas to predict what the future population of a country might be. The table below gives statistics about the actual and predicted population for India, China, and the United States from 1950 to 2050.

Population of India, China, and the United States (in millions)						
Country	1950	1970	1990	2010*	2030*	2050*
India	357	554	849	1,183	1,449	1,592
China	554	830	1,155	1,354	1,446	1,392
United States	157	210	255	312	360	394

Sources: World Population Prospects   * Estimated Figures

Activity

Make a Line Graph

1. Draw the horizontal axis of your graph. Along that axis, make six marks at even intervals. Label them 1950, 1970, 1990, 2010, 2030, and 2050.

2. Draw the vertical axis of your graph. Along that axis, make 17 marks at even intervals. Label them 100, 200, and so on up to 1,700.

3. Choose a different colored pencil for each country. Using the color for India, place dots on the graph to mark the population for each year listed on the chart. Using your ruler, connect the dots with lines. Label the line "India." Then repeat for China and the United States.

A Booming Economy

▼ **KEY QUESTION** What resources does India have to help its economy?

Food for Peace Norman Borlaug won the Nobel Peace Prize for his work as an agricultural scientist in developing new seeds to feed the world's people. Here he stands with Pradeep Singa, a progressive Indian farmer, in a wheat field.

As you just read, creating jobs helps a country to slow population growth and reduce poverty. In recent years, India has succeeded in promoting economic growth, which in turn led to the creation of new jobs. One reason for the growth is that the government lessened its control of the economy and encouraged private ownership of companies. This decision caused foreign investment to increase, and the inflow of money helped business to boom.

Agriculture In spite of the growth of business, most people in India make their living from farming. About half of all the land in India is used for agriculture. Farms are generally small. The average size is five acres, with more than half of all farms less than three acres. Many farmers cannot afford machinery, so they use plows that are pulled by oxen. Some of the main crops of India are rice, wheat, oilseed, cotton, tea, sugar cane, and a fiber called jute. Most farm families struggle to survive on what they grow for themselves.

One solution being considered for this problem is land reform—a more balanced distribution of land among farmers than now exists. Around the year 2000, 5 percent of India's farm families owned nearly 25 percent of India's farmland. Because the large landowners have great political influence, land-reform proposals have never made much progress.

After a series of famines in the 1960s, scientists introduced new farming techniques. India underwent a **Green Revolution**, which was the introduction of seeds that yielded more crops per acre. This increased food production, especially of wheat and rice. In addition, better methods of farming, fertilizers, pesticides, and irrigation have helped farmers to grow more. Today, India produces enough crops to feed all its people.

Industry Although agriculture is the main economic activity in India, industry is also an important element. Cotton textiles are a major product of India. In the early 20th century, other industries began to develop.

India has a number of natural resources that can help its economy grow. It has iron ore and coal to make steel, and other minerals such as manganese, bauxite, and chromite. Besides steel, India manufactures cloth, chemicals, processed foods, transportation equipment, and cement. The map on this page shows where some of India's industries are located. The main industrial regions are centered around Kolkata in the east, Mumbai and Ahmadabad in the west, Chennai in the south, and Delhi in the north.

In addition, India has a very large number of **cottage industries**, businesses in which workers produce goods in their homes. Millions of craftspeople create textiles, brassware, jewelry, leather goods, matches, and incense in these industries.

In addition to manufacturing, India benefits from the mining industry. India exports some of its iron ore to other countries. Indian mines also produce precious metals and gemstones, such as silver, diamonds, and emeralds. India exports many cut diamonds to various parts of the world.

High Tech Perhaps the fastest growing industry in India is the information technology industry. During the period from 1991 to 2000, the computer software industry increased its earnings from $150 million to $5.7 billion. That is an increase of 38 times!

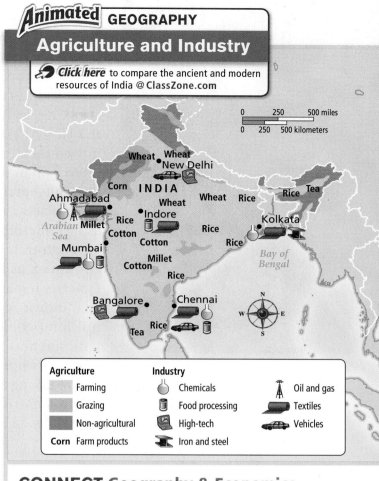

Animated GEOGRAPHY

Agriculture and Industry

Click here to compare the ancient and modern resources of India @ ClassZone.com

CONNECT Geography & Economics

Location Why might most of India's industrial cities be on the coasts?

One reason for the rapid growth of high-tech industries is that a large percentage of Indians speak English, which has become the international language of business. India has the second-largest number of English-speaking, technically skilled workers in the world (after the United States). In fact, some U.S. companies have moved their technical support departments to India and hired Indian workers to help customers over the phone. This outsourcing of American jobs to India, as well as to other places in the world, is an increasingly controversial aspect of global economic interdependence.

High-tech industries are spread across India in many cities such as Hyderabad, Mumbai, Kolkata, and Delhi. One city in particular, **Bangalore**, is home to many high-tech industries. Bangalore is a large city of more than 6 million people located in southern India. Many international and Indian high-tech businesses have offices there. It is home to over a thousand computer software companies that are taking advantage of India's low wages and highly skilled workers. To some observers, Bangalore represents the future of the Indian economy.

Software A chip designer looks through a microscope in Bangalore.

 SUMMARIZE Describe India's resources.

Section ❸ Assessment

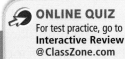 **ONLINE QUIZ**
For test practice, go to **Interactive Review** @ ClassZone.com

TERMS & NAMES

1. **Explain the importance of**
   • parliamentary
   • Kashmir
   • Green Revolution
   • Bangalore

USE YOUR READING NOTES

2. **Find Main Ideas** Use your completed chart to answer the following question:

   What challenges does India's expanding population present?

GOVERNMENT	ECONOMY	ISSUES AND TRENDS
1.	1.	1.
2.	2.	2.
3.	3.	3.
4.	4.	4.

KEY IDEAS

3. What happens if the Indian prime minister loses the support of the legislature?
4. Why is Pakistan so interested in controlling Kashmir?
5. How did the Green Revolution help Indian agriculture?

CRITICAL THINKING

6. **Compare and Contrast** In India, how do the positions of president and prime minister differ?

7. **Analyze Causes** Why do other countries consider the Kashmir conflict a global problem rather than just a South Asian problem?

8. **CONNECT to Today** What modern technologies have made it possible for U.S. high-tech companies to hire Indian workers to do their customer support?

9. **SCIENCE** **Prepare an Educational Poster** With a partner, research the Green Revolution. Prepare a poster that shows what crops scientists developed high-yielding seeds for and how much more they produced than regular seeds.

Interactive ←Review

Click here to complete these and other activities online @ ClassZone.com

CHAPTER SUMMARY

Key Idea 1
India is the dominant country of South Asia, and it has a rich and complicated history.

Key Idea 2
The culture of India is a blend of all of the many influences that have shaped its history.

Key Idea 3
Out of India's diversity, a robust democracy has developed.

For **Review and Study Notes**, go to **Interactive Review @ ClassZone.com**

NAME GAME

Use the Terms & Names list to complete each sentence on paper or online.

1. I am a region that India and Pakistan have fought over. _____ **Kashmir** _____

2. I am the state of wisdom that breaks the cycle of reincarnation. _____

3. I am the chief executive of government in a parliamentary system. _____

4. I am an ancient language of India. _____

5. I am one of the people living in India before the arrival of the Aryans. _____

6. I am a city in southern India that is home to many high-tech industries. _____

7. I am the sum of a person's actions, which determines his or her fate in the next life.

   _____

8. I am a small business in which the workers manufacture items in their homes. _____

9. I am a method of protest that draws attention to a problem without using violence. _____

10. I am the rebirth of the soul in another body.

   _____

Aryan
Bangalore
Buddhism
cottage industry
Dravidian
Hinduism
karma
Kashmir
nirvana
nonviolent resistance
parliamentary
prime minister
reincarnation
Sanskrit
Vedas

Activities

Flip Cards

Use the online flip cards to quiz yourself on the terms and names introduced in this chapter.

Taj Mahal

? Beautiful tomb erected by the Mughal emperor Shah Jahan

Crossword Puzzle

Complete an online puzzle to test your knowledge of India's path from early societies to a modern nation.

ACROSS
1. leader of Indian independence movement

VOCABULARY

Explain the significance of each of the following.

1. Buddhism
2. cottage industry
3. golden age
4. Green Revolution
5. Hinduism
6. Kashmir
7. Mohandas Gandhi
8. nonviolent resistance
9. parliamentary
10. prime minister

Explain how the terms in each group are related.

11. karma, reincarnation, and nirvana
12. Aryan, Sanskrit, and *Bhagavad-Gita*

KEY IDEAS

1 Empires and Independence

13. How were the Aryans and Dravidians different?
14. How did converting to Buddhism affect Asoka?
15. Why are Akbar and Shah Jahan famous Mughal rulers?
16. Why did partition lead to violence?

2 A Rich and Ancient Legacy

17. What religions are practiced in India?
18. According to the Buddha, how does a person stop suffering?
19. How is village life changing?
20. How are Indian movies different from most American movies?

3 The World's Largest Democracy

21. In what way does India have a federal system?
22. How are the members of the parliament chosen?
23. How is the Indian government trying to deal with the population explosion?
24. What are India's main crops?

CRITICAL THINKING

25. **Sequence Events** Create a time line showing the various empires and major powers that ruled India.

| 325 B.C. | A.D. 1150 | 1950 |

26. **Analyze Causes** Why do you think Indians objected to British rule?
27. **Compare and Contrast** How is Indian government similar to and different from British government?
28. **Connect to Economics** Having many English speakers gives India an economic advantage. Why do you think so many Indians speak English?
29. **Connect Geography & History** What geographic difficulty did the new nation of Pakistan face?
30. **Five Themes: Movement** More Dravidian-speaking people live in southern India than in the north. What might explain that pattern?

Answer the
ESSENTIAL QUESTION

How is India's traditional way of life changing in response to modern forces?

Written Response Write a two- or three-paragraph response to the Essential Question. Be sure to consider the key ideas of each section, as well as specific ideas about traditional ways of life and modern changes. Use the rubric below to guide your thinking.

Response Rubric
A strong response will:
- discuss traditional ways of life
- examine the modern forces for change
- give examples of how Indian culture blends the two

STANDARDS-BASED ASSESSMENT

THEMATIC MAP

Use the map and your knowledge of India to answer questions 1 and 2 on your paper.

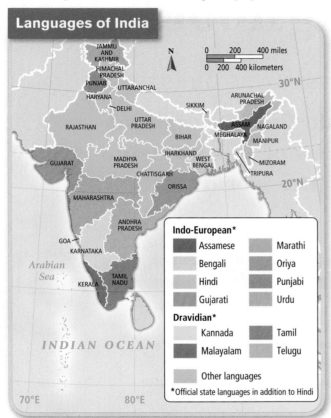

Languages of India

Indo-European*
- Assamese
- Bengali
- Hindi
- Gujarati
- Marathi
- Oriya
- Punjabi
- Urdu

Dravidian*
- Kannada
- Malayalam
- Tamil
- Telugu

Other languages

*Official state languages in addition to Hindi

1. In what states are the Dravidian languages mainly spoken?

2. What language would you hear spoken in the state of Rajasthan?

3. What language would you hear spoken in the state of Kerala?

PRIMARY SOURCE

Use the following quote from Gandhi to answer question 4 on your paper.

> I do not want my house to be walled in on all sides and my windows to be stuffed. I want the cultures of all lands to be blown about my house as freely as possible. But I refuse to be blown off my feet by any.
>
> Source: Mohandas Gandhi

4. Which of the following choices best restates Gandhi's opinion?

A. He believed that people of all nations should integrate, or mix, cultures.

B. He believed that it is dangerous for people to try to mix cultures.

C. He wanted to appreciate other cultures, yet he didn't want people of a foreign culture to rule him.

D. He wanted to keep elements of his culture in the privacy of his home, and not to display it in public.

GeoActivity

1. INTERDISCIPLINARY ACTIVITY—MATH

Using textbooks, encyclopedias, or the Internet, look up information about the decimal system—how it represents fractions and how numbers are written. Create a poster that illustrates this by converting fractions into decimals.

2. WRITING FOR SOCIAL STUDIES

Research to learn more about the life of Mohandas Gandhi. Focus especially on the methods he used to protest British rule. Then write a longer "History Maker" about him.

3. MENTAL MAPPING

Create an outline map of India and label the following:
- Mumbai
- Kolkata
- Hyderabad
- Chennai
- Bangalore
- New Delhi

CHAPTER 24 South Asian Neighbors

① **FOCUS ON**

Afghanistan, Pakistan, and Bangladesh

② **FOCUS ON**

Mountain Kingdoms and Island Nations

 ESSENTIAL QUESTION

How do the history and cultures of India's neighbors affect the world?

CONNECT Geography & History

Use the map and the time line to answer the following questions.

1. What countries separated East Pakistan (now Bangladesh) from Pakistan?

2. Which resource is common to Afghanistan, Pakistan, India, and Bangladesh?

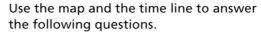

Geography

1947 The colony of India is partitioned, and Pakistan becomes an independent nation.

History

◄ **1979** The Soviet Union invades Afghanistan.

1945

Geography

1971 East Pakistan wins independence as the new nation of Bangladesh.

Culture

1983 Ethnic tension causes a Tamil rebel group to start civil war in Sri Lanka. ►

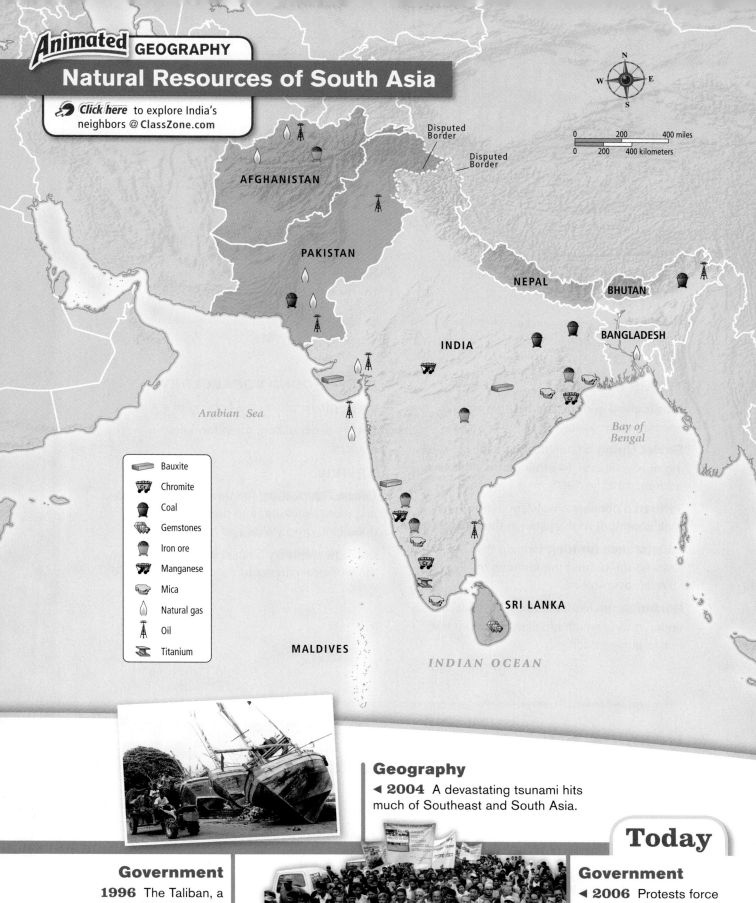

Disputed Border

Disputed Border

AFGHANISTAN

PAKISTAN

NEPAL

BHUTAN

BANGLADESH

INDIA

Arabian Sea

Bay of Bengal

SRI LANKA

MALDIVES

INDIAN OCEAN

	Bauxite
Cr	Chromite
	Coal
	Gemstones
	Iron ore
	Manganese
	Mica
	Natural gas
	Oil
	Titanium

0   200   400 miles
0   200   400 kilometers

Geography

◄ **2004** A devastating tsunami hits much of Southeast and South Asia.

Today

Government

1996 The Taliban, a conservative Muslim group, takes control of Afghanistan.

Government

◄ **2006** Protests force Nepal's king to restore parliamentary government.

Reading for Understanding

▶ Key Ideas

BEFORE, YOU LEARNED

India is the largest country of South Asia, with a huge population and many resources.

NOW YOU WILL LEARN

Other nations and cultures in the region besides India have managed to develop their own distinct identities.

▶ Vocabulary

TERMS & NAMES

landlocked surrounded by land with no access to the ocean

Soviet Union a Communist nation, consisting of Russia and 14 other states, that existed from 1922 to 1991

Taliban a conservative Islamic group that took control of Afghanistan in the mid-1990s

subsistence farming farming that produces just enough to feed the farmer's family with little left over to sell

Ramadan the ninth month of the Muslim calendar, during which Muslims fast from sunrise to sunset each day

BACKGROUND VOCABULARY

strategic helpful in the fighting of a war

fast to avoid eating, often for religious reasons

REVIEW

Green Revolution the use of special seeds, irrigation, fertilizers, and pesticides to produce high crop yields and food production

cottage industry a small business in which the workers manufacture items in their homes

▶ Reading Strategy

Re-create the chart shown at right. As you read and respond to the **KEY QUESTIONS**, use the chart to organize important details about the history, government, culture, and economies of three nations.

 Skillbuilder Handbook, page R7

CATEGORIZE

	AFGHANISTAN	PAKISTAN	BANGLADESH
History			
Government			
Culture			
Economics			

 GRAPHIC ORGANIZERS
Go to **Interactive Review** @ClassZone.com

1

FOCUS ON

Afghanistan, Pakistan, and Bangladesh

Connecting to Your World

India's South Asian neighbors have been in the news often. In some cases, they make headlines because of natural disasters, such as the 2005 earthquake in Pakistan. Political events have also put a spotlight on the region. In the fall of 2001, for example, the United States went to war in Afghanistan to fight the terrorists who planned the attacks of September 11, 2001.

AFGHANISTAN

Afghanistan

▼ **KEY QUESTION** Why have empires throughout history wanted to rule Afghanistan?

Afghanistan is a **landlocked** country with no access to the ocean. However, it has a **strategic** location where Southwest Asia, Central Asia, and South Asia meet. The mountain pass that allows people to cross the Hindu Kush lies on the Afghanistan-Pakistan border. Because of this, any empire that ruled India usually also tried to control Afghanistan to prevent invasions. Afghanistan's foreign rulers have included Persians, Greeks, and Mongols.

Afghanistan Farmland among the mountain valleys in Jabul Saraj, Afghanistan. **Why might mountain valleys be suitable for farming?**

History and Government During the 1800s, Russia and Great Britain fought over Afghanistan. Britain wanted to protect its colony in India; Russia wanted a warm-water port and was trying to extend its empire to the Indian Ocean. Britain won the conflict and took partial control of Afghanistan. The country did not win its independence from Britain until 1919.

In 1979, the **Soviet Union**, a Communist nation that included Russia, invaded Afghanistan. Many Afghans rejected Communist beliefs and fought the invaders with aid from the United States. By 1989, the Soviets had withdrawn. Local groups fought for power until the **Taliban**, a conservative Islamic group, took over Afghanistan.

The Taliban allowed al-Qaeda (ahl•KY•dah)—the group that carried out the terrorist attacks of September 11, 2001—to train in Afghanistan. In late 2001, the United States invaded the country, suppressed the Taliban, and bombed al-Qaeda's bases. The United States and other countries helped the Afghans form a government. In 2004, Hamid Karzai (hah•MEED KAHR•zy) was elected president.

ONLINE PRIMARY SOURCE To read the entire speech of Hamid Karzai, go to the **Research & Writing Center** @ ClassZone.com

ANALYZING Primary Sources

Hamid Karzai (born 1957) became the first elected president in Afghanistan's history in 2004. This quotation comes from the speech he gave when he was sworn into office.

> Our fight against terrorism is not yet over, even though we have succeeded to reduce this common enemy of humanity to a lesser threat in this country. . . . A decisive victory over terrorism requires serious and continued cooperation at regional and international levels.
>
> Three years ago, . . . international cooperation rid Afghanistan from the rule of terrorism. The same cooperation has led to the rebuilding of the Afghan state, and significant progress in restoring peace, stability, and security to our country.

Source: Inaugural Speech by President Hamid Karzai

DOCUMENT–BASED QUESTION
How do you think Karzai feels about the continued presence of the U.S. troops in his country?

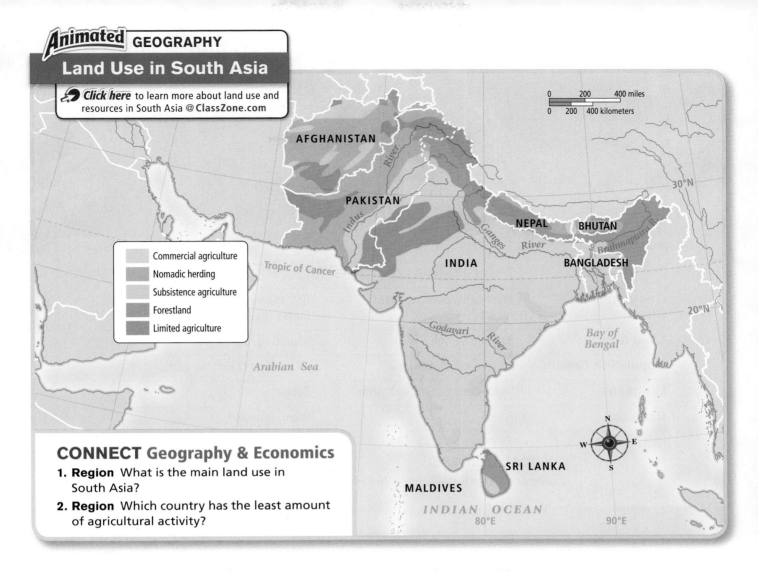

Animated GEOGRAPHY

Land Use in South Asia

Click here to learn more about land use and resources in South Asia @ ClassZone.com

Legend:
- Commercial agriculture
- Nomadic herding
- Subsistence agriculture
- Forestland
- Limited agriculture

Map labels: AFGHANISTAN, PAKISTAN, NEPAL, BHUTAN, INDIA, BANGLADESH, SRI LANKA, MALDIVES, Indus River, Ganges River, Brahmaputra R., Godavari River, Arabian Sea, Bay of Bengal, INDIAN OCEAN, Tropic of Cancer, 30°N, 20°N, 80°E, 90°E

Scale: 0 200 400 miles / 0 200 400 kilometers

CONNECT Geography & Economics

1. **Region** What is the main land use in South Asia?
2. **Region** Which country has the least amount of agricultural activity?

Economics and Culture Afghanistan is one of the world's poorest countries. About 85 percent of Afghans live by **subsistence farming**, which means they raise only enough food to feed their families. The long years of war severely damaged the economy and prevented the development of industry. Since the fall of the Taliban, foreign nations have sent aid to Afghanistan, and the economy is starting to grow.

Both Islam and history strongly influence Afghan culture. The Afghan people belong to many ethnic groups and speak several languages, but almost all share the Muslim faith. Many rural people live in homes made of mud bricks and dress in traditional clothing. Few people can read, so folk tales, folk songs, and dances are important art forms. A popular sport is competitive kite flying, in which contestants try to cut down each other's kites by using strings coated with ground glass. Another sport is *buzkashi*, which dates from Mongol times. In it, horsemen compete to grab an animal carcass and drag it across a goal line.

▲ **ANALYZE CAUSES** Explain why empires have wanted to rule Afghanistan.

Baltoro Glacier

Karnaphuli River

	PAKISTAN	BANGLADESH
Geography & Climate	mountains, plateau, plains, desert	flat, low-lying plain, humid climate, monsoons
Land Area	310,403 sq. mi.	55,600 sq. mi.
Population Density	166 million (535/sq. mi.)	147 million (2,644/sq. mi.)
Language	Urdu, Punjabi, Sindhi, Pashto	Bengali
Religion	Islam	Islam, Hinduism

CRITICAL THINKING

Compare What is the biggest similarity between Pakistan and Bangladesh?

PAKISTAN

BANGLADESH

Pakistan and Bangladesh

▼ **KEY QUESTION** Why did Bangladesh break away from Pakistan?

Pakistan and Bangladesh both have large populations. In 1947, they gained independence as one nation—Pakistan—that had two different regions separated by 1,000 miles of Indian territory.

Independence and Challenges Although they had the religion of Islam in common, West Pakistan and East Pakistan were very different in terms of culture, politics, and economics.

The capital of the country was located in West Pakistan, which controlled the government, army, and economy. The people of East Pakistan resented being ruled by people who were so far away and so different. In 1970, a cyclone and storm surge hit East Pakistan, killing more than 300,000 people. The survivors believed that West Pakistan delayed sending help. In 1971, a civil war broke out. East Pakistan won and became the parliamentary democracy of Bangladesh.

Pakistan has had several periods of military rule and has struggled to develop democracy. One problem facing the Pakistani government today is the threat of terrorist groups. Like Afghanistan, much of Pakistan is mountainous. Pakistani officials are trying to find members of al-Qaeda and the Taliban hiding in those mountains.

Culture and Developing Economies Islam has shaped the cultures of both Pakistan and Bangladesh. Men and women have little contact with each other outside their families, and many marriages are arranged. A major holiday is **Ramadan**, a month when Muslims **fast**, or avoid eating, each day from sunrise to sunset.

Because Pakistan has a dry climate, its farmers rely on irrigation from its rivers. Pakistan underwent a **Green Revolution** that improved yields. Wheat is the main farm product. Pakistan is trying to develop its natural gas reserves. Bangladesh's greatest resource is fertile soil from silt deposited by rivers. Bangladesh often has too much water, which floods fields. Rice is the main crop. Bangladesh has **cottage industries**, in which people weave cloth or make crafts at home.

Cottage Industry
A young girl makes matchboxes in Khulna, Bangladesh.

 SUMMARIZE Explain why Bangladesh broke away from Pakistan.

Section ❶ Assessment

ONLINE QUIZ
For test practice, go to **Interactive Review** @ ClassZone.com

TERMS & NAMES

1. Explain the importance of
- Taliban
- Ramadan

USE YOUR READING NOTES

2. Categorize Use your completed chart to answer the following question:

Although the countries of Afghanistan, Pakistan, and Bangladesh differ in many ways, what binds them together?

	AFGHANISTAN	PAKISTAN	BANGLADESH
History			
Government			
Culture			
Economics			

KEY IDEAS

3. Why did many Afghans rebel against Soviet rule?

4. How do Muslims observe the holiday of Ramadan?

5. How have Bangladesh's rivers both helped and harmed the country?

CRITICAL THINKING

6. Make Inferences Why is the United States trying to help build a democratic government in Afghanistan?

7. Identify Solutions How might West Pakistan have prevented civil war with East Pakistan?

8. **CONNECT to Today** Why do you think the Pakistani government might be willing to help the United States capture terrorists who are hiding in the mountains of Pakistan?

9. **WRITING** **Write an Analysis** Write a paragraph explaining the relationship between natural disasters and economic growth in Bangladesh.

COMPARING ⟩ Disaster Responses

Different parts of South Asia are vulnerable to different natural disasters. Pakistan and Afghanistan are prone to earthquakes. India and Bangladesh are prone to floods.

Earthquakes

The Indian subcontinent became part of Asia when two great landmasses collided with each other. The Indian-Australian Plate and the Eurasian Plate are still pushing against one another, which makes South Asia prone to earthquakes. In October 2005, an earthquake devastated Pakistan, killing approximately 75,000 people.

Aid

Pakistani paramilitary work at a collapsed building in Islamabad in 2005.

Aerial view shows collapsed buildings in the village of Bagh, Pakistan, after the October 2005 earthquake. ▼

Temporary Housing

Earthquake survivors live in a tent camp.

Destroyed Infrastructure

Earthquake survivors in 2005 cross a damaged bridge over the Neelum River.

Floods

There are two main causes of flooding in South Asia: monsoon rains and cyclones. During the monsoons, heavy rains can cause severe flooding. But the most extreme weather pattern of South Asia is the cyclone, a violent storm with fierce winds and heavy rain. Cyclones are most destructive in low-lying Bangladesh, where high waves can swamp large parts of the country. In 1970, a cyclone struck Bangladesh. The winds, rains, and floods claimed at least 300,000 lives in the 20th century's worst cyclone.

Aid
Bangladeshi policewoman pours drinking water for flood victims in August, 2004.

Temporary Housing
Bangladeshi flood victims take shelter along a highway.

Destroyed Infrastructure
Bangladeshis cross a railroad track damaged by floodwaters.

▲ *Aerial view of town of Brahmanbaria, Bangladesh, shows damage from 2004 floods.*

CRITICAL THINKING

1. **Make Inferences** What probably causes the most deaths in earthquakes and floods?

2. **Identify Problems and Solutions** What different methods might be used to deal with earthquakes and floods?

Reading for Understanding

▶ Key Ideas

BEFORE, YOU LEARNED

India's larger neighbors have developed their own distinct cultures and identities.

NOW YOU WILL LEARN

Some of India's smaller neighbors have also developed in distinctive and unique ways.

▶ Vocabulary

TERMS & NAMES

constitutional monarchy a government in which the powers of the king or queen are limited by the constitution

ecotourism travel to unique environments by people who take care to preserve them in their natural state

plantation agriculture the use of large farms to raise cash crops

REVIEW

subsistence farming agriculture that produces just enough to feed the farmer's family with little left over to sell

archipelago (AHR•kuh•PEHL•uh•GOH) group of islands

tsunami (tsu•NAH•mee) very large, destructive ocean waves caused by an underwater earthquake or volcanic eruption

Visual Vocabulary archipelago

▶ Reading Strategy

Re-create the diagram shown at right. As you read and respond to the **KEY QUESTIONS**, use the outer ovals to organize important details about the economies of the mountain kingdoms and island nations.

 Skillbuilder Handbook, page R7

CATEGORIZE

Nepal — Sri Lanka

ECONOMIES

Bhutan — Maldives

GRAPHIC ORGANIZERS
Go to **Interactive Review** @ClassZone.com

SECTION

2

FOCUS ON

Mountain Kingdoms and Island Nations

Connecting to Your World

Imagine seeing a travel poster that shows a village of small stone houses built in a high valley among jagged, snowy mountains. Now, imagine a poster of a low-lying island with palm trees, sandy beaches, and lagoons. These two images will help you to understand the different types of countries you will learn about in this section.

Island Nation A holiday resort in the Maldives

Nepal and Bhutan

▼ **KEY QUESTION** What are some of the main economic activities of the two countries?

Nepal and Bhutan are two landlocked kingdoms in the Himalayas. Because travel in the mountains is difficult, both countries are isolated. Few links to the outside world existed before the 1960s. However, Nepal and Bhutan have always been influenced by India and China.

Mountain Kingdom Village of Jharkot in Nepal

A number of the highest mountains in the world are found in the Himalayas within the borders of Nepal. At left, climbers trek through the snow on a path near Mount Everest in Nepal.

Highest Mountain Peaks in the Himalayas	
Cho-Yo	26,906 feet
Everest	29,029 feet
Kanchenjunga	28,169 feet
Lhotse	27,940 feet
Makalu	27,766 feet
Source: www.welcomenepal.com	

Activity
Make a Bar Graph

1. On a piece of notebook paper, rearrange the list of five mountains in order of height, with the tallest first.

2. Draw the horizontal axis of your graph. Along that axis, write the names of the five mountains from tallest to shortest.

3. Draw the vertical axis of your graph. Along that axis, mark intervals of 1,000 feet up to 30,000.

4. Choose a different colored pencil for each mountain. Make a bar to indicate height. Use the vertical axis to determine the correct height of the bar.

Government Nepal is a **constitutional monarchy**, in which a constitution limits the ruler's power. In recent years, Communist rebels have led uprisings against Nepal's government. In fighting the rebels, the king dissolved the government and began to rule alone. But early in 2006, protests forced him to restore democratic government.

Bhutan's monarchy has traditionally been a powerful one, with the monarch choosing the members of the legislature. However, in 2001, the king asked a commission to write a constitution, which was finished in 2005.

Developing Economies Both Nepal and Bhutan are poor countries that rely on agriculture. In each country, the southern region near the Indian border has fertile lowlands that are mostly used for **subsistence farming**. The main crops are rice and wheat. Nepal also produces herbs and spices, while Bhutan produces rice, corn, cattle, and yaks. Both countries export hydroelectricity, generated by their fast-flowing mountain rivers. India is their main trading partner. In addition, both of the kingdoms benefit from tourism. Every year, climbers go to Nepal to try to reach the top of Mount Everest and other tall peaks. Bhutan promotes **ecotourism**, which occurs when people travel to unique environments but take care to preserve them.

Culture and Religion Each of the mountain kingdoms has a mixed population. The official language of Nepal is Nepali, which half the people speak. But Nepal is also home to ethnic groups that speak other languages. The two largest groups of Bhutan are the Bhote and the Nepalese. The official language is Dzongkha (DZAHNG•kah).

Fun Facts!

THUNDER DRAGON

The flag of Bhutan features a dragon, and in the Bhutanese language, the country is called "Land of the Thunder Dragon." Traditionally, the Bhutanese have believed the sound of thunder echoing through the mountains is the voice of dragons roaring.

India has influenced the cultures of both countries, especially their religions. Nepal is officially a Hindu country, but it also has a Buddhist minority of about 10 percent. Siddhartha Gautama, founder of Buddhism, was born in Nepal, and many Nepalese Hindus combine Buddhist practices with their Hindu faith. Bhutan, on the other hand, is a mostly Buddhist country with a Hindu minority of 25 percent. Nepal has many Hindu temples and Buddhist shrines, while Bhutan has Buddhist monasteries.

MAKE GENERALIZATIONS Describe the main economic activities of Nepal and Bhutan.

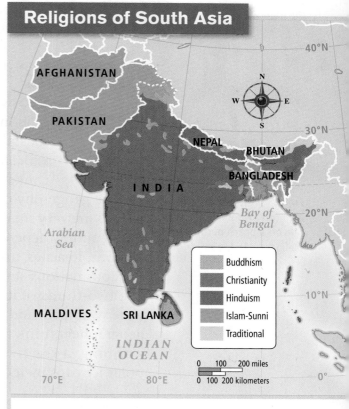

Religions of South Asia

	Buddhism
	Christianity
	Hinduism
	Islam-Sunni
	Traditional

CONNECT Geography & Culture

1. **Region** What other country besides India is mostly Hindu?
2. **Region** What is the predominant religion in Bhutan?

Sri Lanka and the Maldives

KEY QUESTION What do Sri Lanka and the Maldives have in common?

Two of India's neighbors are island nations that are physically quite different from each other. Sri Lanka (formerly Ceylon) has one main island just 20 miles off the southeast coast of India. The Maldives is an **archipelago** of about 1,200 small islands that stretch over a distance of about 500 miles.

History, Culture, and Government People from India settled Sri Lanka more than 2,000 years ago. The Sinhalese, whose ancestors came from northern India, make up 74 percent of the population. Most Sinhalese are Buddhist. The next largest group is the Tamils, who originally came from southern India and who are mostly Hindu.

Starting in the 1500s, Sri Lanka was controlled by Europeans—first the Portuguese, then the Dutch, then the British. Sri Lanka gained independence in 1948 and set up a parliamentary government. Ethnic conflict is a serious problem there. Because the Sinhalese run the government, the Tamils believe that they are denied opportunities. A group called the Liberation Tigers of Tamil Eelam is fighting for a separate Tamil state in northern and eastern Sri Lanka. Civil war began in 1983 and continued until a cease-fire was signed in 2002. Since then, violence has resumed.

Gone Fishing Stilt fishermen fish for sardines at high tide off a beach north of Weligama, Sri Lanka.

Most Maldivians are related culturally to the Sinhalese of Sri Lanka. However, the Maldivians are Muslim because traders brought Islam to the islands. In 1968, the country became an independent republic.

Economics of Plantations and Tourism The economy of Sri Lanka is based mainly on farming. The coastal areas have fertile plains that support **plantation agriculture**, or the growing of cash crops on estates. Sri Lanka is one of the world's leading producers of tea.

The geography of the Maldives affects its economy. Most of the islands are very small and rise no more than six feet above the ocean. The economy depends on fishing and tourism, as people visit for the lagoons, beaches, and warm climate.

Both nations suffered damage from the 2004 **tsunami**. Sri Lanka lost two-thirds of its fishing fleet and 99,000 homes. The Maldives were swamped, and property was destroyed. Tourism declined. Some geographers think that the Maldives may be in danger from global warming, a rise in world temperatures caused by pollution. If the polar ice caps melt, the oceans might rise and cover the Maldives.

 COMPARE AND CONTRAST Explain what Sri Lanka and the Maldives have in common.

 **ONLINE QUIZ**
For test practice, go to
Interactive Review
@ ClassZone.com

Section ② Assessment

TERMS & NAMES

1. Explain the importance of
- ecotourism
- archipelago
- plantation agriculture

USE YOUR READING NOTES

2. Categorize Use your completed chart to answer the following question:

What are the main economic activities of Nepal, Bhutan, Sri Lanka, and the Maldives?

KEY IDEAS

3. Why did the king of Nepal disband the government and then later restore it?

4. What caused the civil war in Sri Lanka?

5. Why did the Maldives suffer so much damage from the 2004 tsunami?

CRITICAL THINKING

6. Analyze Effects How do you think the tsunami affected Sri Lanka's economy? Explain.

7. Compare How are the political problems in Nepal and Sri Lanka similar?

8. CONNECT to Today What are some rules that you think visitors might have to follow in ecotourism?

9. TECHNOLOGY **Plan a Multimedia Presentation** Plan a presentation on the tsunami damage to Sri Lanka and the Maldives. Be sure to include photographs, graphs or charts, and quotations or interviews.

Interactive ◀Review

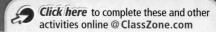 **Click here** to complete these and other activities online @ ClassZone.com

CHAPTER SUMMARY

Key Idea 1
Other nations and cultures in the region besides India have managed to develop their own distinct identities.

Key Idea 2
Some of India's smaller neighbors have also developed in distinctive and unique ways.

For **Review and Study Notes**, go to **Interactive Review** @ ClassZone.com

NAME GAME

Use the Terms & Names list to complete each sentence on paper or online.

1. I am a conservative Muslim group that ruled Afghanistan from the mid-1990s until 2002.
_____ **Taliban** 🖑 _____

2. I am a small business in which the workers manufacture items in their homes.
_____

3. I am a Muslim holiday in which people fast for a whole month. _____

4. I am a system of growing cash crops on large estates. _____

5. I am a Communist nation that existed from 1922 to 1991._____

6. I am a series of ocean waves caused by an undersea earthquake or eruption. _____

7. I am the practice of visiting a region while taking care to preserve its environment. _____

8. I am a group of islands._____

9. I produce just enough to feed a family with little left over to sell. _____

10. I refer to a region that has no access to the sea.
_____

archipelago
constitutional monarchy
cottage industry
ecotourism
Green Revolution
landlocked
plantation agriculture
Ramadan
Soviet Union
subsistence farming
Taliban
tsunami

Activities

GeoGame

Use this online map to show what you know about South Asia. Click and drag each place name to its location on the map.

○ ○ ○
Geo GAME

Present-Day South Asian Neighbors

Afghanistan

Bhutan

the Maldives

Arabian Sea

Bay of Bengal

Arabian Sea 🖑

To play the complete game, go to **Interactive Review** @ClassZone.com

Crossword Puzzle

Complete the online crossword puzzle to test your knowledge of the history and cultures of South Asia.

ACROSS
1. first elected president of Afghanistan

VOCABULARY

Explain the significance of each of the following.

1. subsistence farming
2. archipelago
3. ecotourism
4. constitutional monarchy
5. plantation agriculture
6. Ramadan
7. Taliban

Explain how the terms in each group differ.

8. plantation agriculture and subsistence farming
9. archipelago and landlocked

KEY IDEAS

1 Afghanistan, Pakistan, and Bangladesh

10. What cultural influence do Afghanistan, Pakistan, and Bangladesh share?
11. How has Afghanistan's location affected its history?
12. How has the U.S. war on terrorism affected Afghanistan and Pakistan?
13. What natural disasters are common in the region?
14. How does Pakistan meet its agricultural needs?

2 Mountain Kingdoms and Island Nations

15. Who are the rebels fighting the Nepalese government?
16. How has the king of Bhutan recently tried to change government?
17. What major influence has India had on Nepal and Bhutan?
18. What is the biggest economic difference between Sri Lanka and the Maldives?
19. What is the goal of the Liberation Tigers of Tamil Eelam?

CRITICAL THINKING

20. **Compare and Contrast** Create two Venn diagrams. Use one to compare and contrast Nepal and Bhutan. Use the other to compare and contrast Sri Lanka and the Maldives.

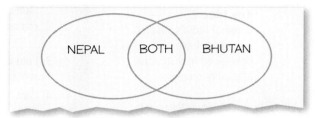

21. **Make Inferences** How was East Pakistan able to win independence from West Pakistan when the latter controlled the army?
22. **Compare and Contrast** How have the recent actions of the kings of Nepal and Bhutan differed?
23. **Connect to Economics** Would subsistence farming or plantation agriculture do more to develop a nation's economy?
24. **Five Themes: Region** What geographic reasons explain why India has been a strong influence on many countries?
25. **Connect Geography & Culture** What is the origin of the cultural differences between the Sinhalese and Tamil peoples?

Answer the ESSENTIAL QUESTION

How do the history and cultures of India's neighbors affect the world?

Written Response Write a three-paragraph response to the Essential Question. Be sure to give at least three examples of how countries in this region have affected recent world events. Use the rubric to guide your thinking.

Response Rubric
A strong response will:

- discuss natural disasters and their impacts
- examine political changes in the region
- analyze the region's role in war against terrorism

STANDARDS-BASED ASSESSMENT

✓ **Test Practice**

• Online Test Practice @ ClassZone.com
• Test-Taking Strategies and Practice
  at the front of this book

PHYSICAL MAP

Use the map to answer questions 1 and 2 on your paper.

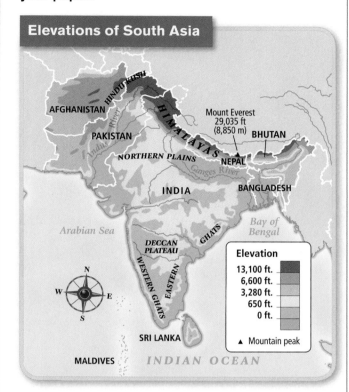

Elevations of South Asia

AFGHANISTAN

HINDU KUSH

HIMALAYAS

PAKISTAN

Indus River

NORTHERN PLAINS

Ganges River

NEPAL

BHUTAN

Mount Everest
29,035 ft
(8,850 m)

INDIA

BANGLADESH

Arabian Sea

Bay of Bengal

DECCAN PLATEAU

GHATS

WESTERN GHATS

EASTERN GHATS

Elevation
13,100 ft.
6,600 ft.
3,280 ft.
650 ft.
0 ft.

▲ Mountain peak

SRI LANKA

MALDIVES

INDIAN OCEAN

1. Which mountain range includes Mount Everest?

A. Hindu Kush
B. Western Ghats
C. Himalayas
D. Eastern Ghats

2. Which mainland country in South Asia has overall the lowest elevations?

A. Bangladesh
B. Afghanistan
C. Nepal
D. Bhutan

PIE GRAPHS

Examine the pie graphs below. Use the information in the graphs to answer questions 3 and 4 on your paper.

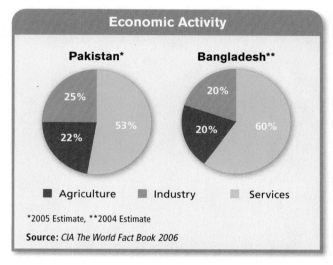

Economic Activity

Pakistan*

25%
53%
22%

Bangladesh**

20%
20%
60%

■ Agriculture   ■ Industry   ■ Services

*2005 Estimate, **2004 Estimate

Source: *CIA The World Fact Book 2006*

3. Which country is less industrialized?

4. Which economic sector in both countries employs the most people?

GeoActivity

1. INTERDISCIPLINARY ACTIVITY-SCIENCE

Using textbooks, encyclopedias, or the Internet, look up information about the possible causes of global warming and what might be done to prevent it. Create a poster that illustrates what individuals can do to deal with global warming.

2. WRITING FOR SOCIAL STUDIES

Unit Writing Project Revisit the plan of action that you developed as a lobbyist to support a cause. What other causes would you like to support? Develop a written plan of action for one or two of your favorite causes.

3. MENTAL MAPPING

Create an outline map of South Asia and label the following:

• Afghanistan
• Bangladesh
• Bhutan
• India
• the Maldives
• Nepal
• Pakistan
• Sri Lanka

UNIT 8

East Asia and Southeast Asia

Why It Matters:

East Asia is home to several countries that are important members of the world economy. The nations of Southeast Asia are working hard to strengthen their economies. In the coming decades, both regions are expected to have a strong voice in world affairs.

Forbidden City in Beijing

CHAPTER 25 China

Blend of old and new in Seoul, South Korea

CHAPTER 26 The Korean Peninsula

Floating Shinto gate near Hiroshima

CHAPTER 27 Japan

Mosque and Petronas Towers in Kuala Lumpur, Malaysia

CHAPTER 28 Southeast Asia

Use the Unit Atlas to learn about the geography of East Asia and Southeast Asia. As you study the maps in the atlas, notice geographic patterns and specific details about the two regions. Answer the questions on each map in your notebook.

As you study the graphs on this page, compare the landmass, population, rivers, and mountains of East Asia and Southeast Asia with those of the United States. Then jot down the answers to the following questions in your notebook.

Comparing Data

1. Compare the landmass and population of East Asia and Southeast Asia with those of the United States. Based on these data, which region do you think has a higher population density? Why?

2. What is the second longest river shown here? Which East Asian mountain is taller than Mount McKinley?

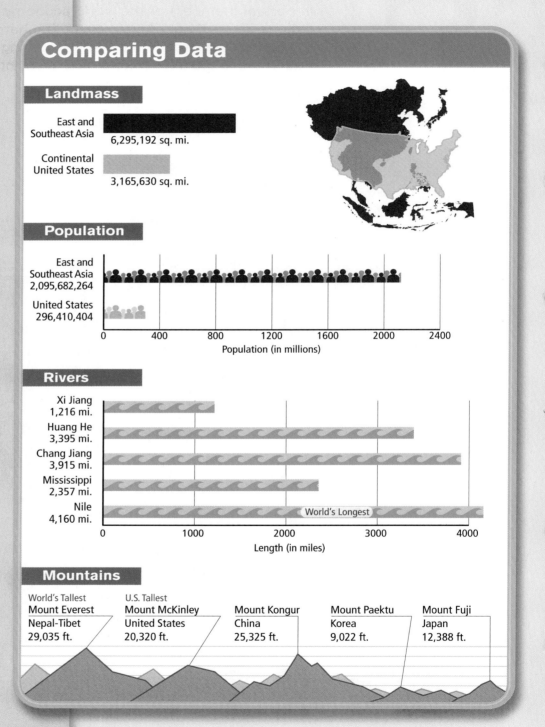

Comparing Data

Landmass

East and Southeast Asia
6,295,192 sq. mi.

Continental United States
3,165,630 sq. mi.

Population

East and Southeast Asia
2,095,682,264

United States
296,410,404

Population (in millions)
0   400   800   1200   1600   2000   2400

Rivers

Xi Jiang
1,216 mi.

Huang He
3,395 mi.

Chang Jiang
3,915 mi.

Mississippi
2,357 mi.

Nile
4,160 mi.
World's Longest

Length (in miles)
0   1000   2000   3000   4000

Mountains

World's Tallest
Mount Everest
Nepal-Tibet
29,035 ft.

U.S. Tallest
Mount McKinley
United States
20,320 ft.

Mount Kongur
China
25,325 ft.

Mount Paektu
Korea
9,022 ft.

Mount Fuji
Japan
12,388 ft.

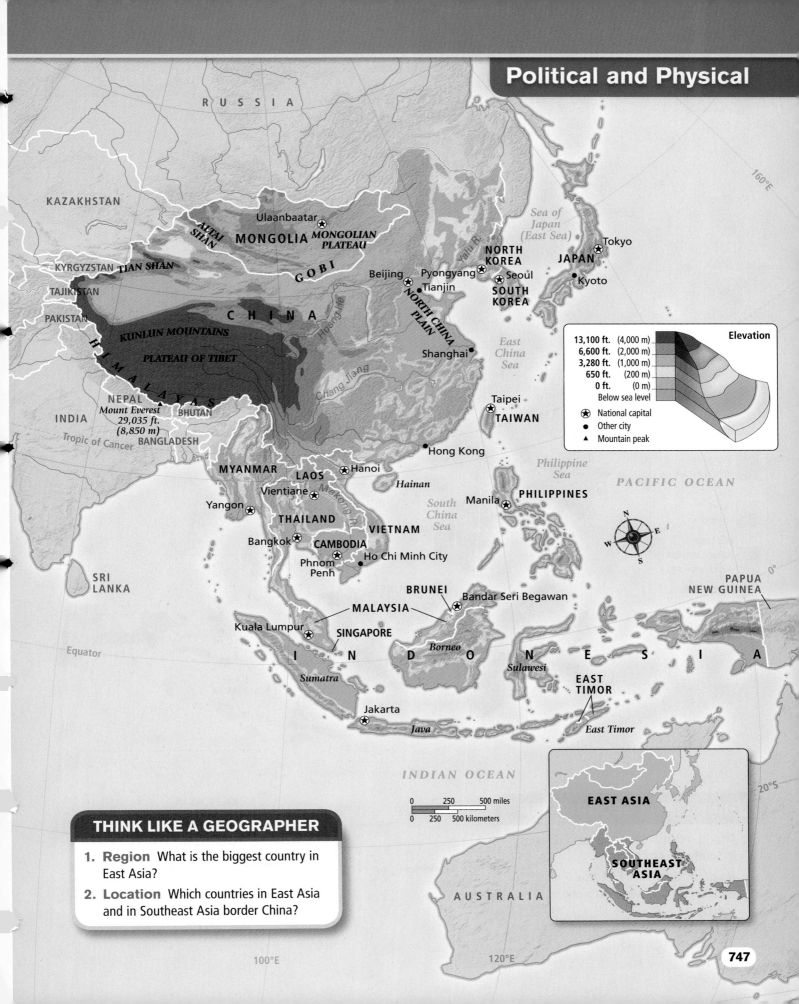

RUSSIA

KAZAKHSTAN

KYRGYZSTAN

TAJIKISTAN

PAKISTAN

ALTAI SHAN

TIAN SHAN

Ulaanbaatar ★

MONGOLIA **MONGOLIAN PLATEAU**

G O B I

C H I N A

KUNLUN MOUNTAINS

PLATEAU OF TIBET

H I M A L A Y A S

NEPAL

INDIA

Mount Everest 29,035 ft. (8,850 m)▲

Tropic of Cancer

BHUTAN

BANGLADESH

Huang He

Beijing ●

Tianjin ●

Chang Jiang

Shanghai ●

NORTH CHINA PLAIN

Yalu R.

Pyongyang ★

NORTH KOREA

Seoul ★

SOUTH KOREA

Sea of Japan (East Sea)

JAPAN

Tokyo ★

Kyoto ●

Tokyo

East China Sea

Taipei ★

TAIWAN

Elevation	
13,100 ft. (4,000 m)	
6,600 ft. (2,000 m)	
3,280 ft. (1,000 m)	
650 ft. (200 m)	
0 ft. (0 m)	
Below sea level	

★ National capital
● Other city
▲ Mountain peak

● Hong Kong

MYANMAR

LAOS

Hanoi ★

Vientiane ★

Yangon ★

THAILAND

Bangkok ★

CAMBODIA

Phnom Penh ★

Mekong R.

Hainan

VIETNAM

Ho Chi Minh City ●

South China Sea

Manila ★

PHILIPPINES

Philippine Sea

PACIFIC OCEAN

N
W ● E
S

SRI LANKA

Equator

BRUNEI

Bandar Seri Begawan ★

MALAYSIA

Kuala Lumpur ★

SINGAPORE

Sumatra

Borneo

I N D O N E S I A

Sulawesi

EAST TIMOR

East Timor

PAPUA NEW GUINEA

0°

20°S

Jakarta ★

Java

INDIAN OCEAN

| 0 | 250 | 500 miles |
| 0 | 250 | 500 kilometers |

AUSTRALIA

100°E

120°E

160°E

EAST ASIA

SOUTHEAST ASIA

THINK LIKE A GEOGRAPHER

1. **Region** What is the biggest country in East Asia?

2. **Location** Which countries in East Asia and in Southeast Asia border China?

747

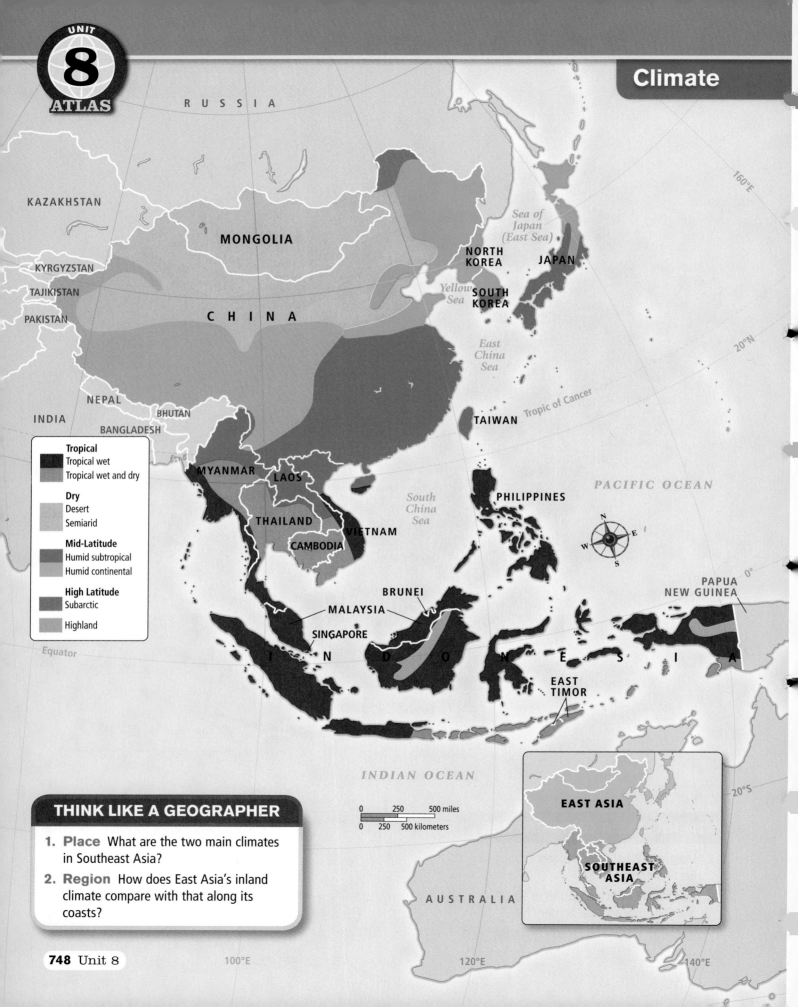

RUSSIA

KAZAKHSTAN

KYRGYZSTAN

TAJIKISTAN

PAKISTAN

MONGOLIA

C H I N A

NEPAL

BHUTAN

INDIA

BANGLADESH

MYANMAR

LAOS

THAILAND

VIETNAM

CAMBODIA

NORTH
KOREA

SOUTH
KOREA

Sea of
Japan
(East Sea)

JAPAN

Yellow
Sea

East
China
Sea

Tropic of Cancer

TAIWAN

South
China
Sea

PHILIPPINES

PACIFIC OCEAN

20°N

160°E

BRUNEI

MALAYSIA

SINGAPORE

I N D O N E S I A

EAST
TIMOR

Equator

0°

PAPUA
NEW GUINEA

INDIAN OCEAN

AUSTRALIA

Legend

Tropical
- Tropical wet
- Tropical wet and dry

Dry
- Desert
- Semiarid

Mid-Latitude
- Humid subtropical
- Humid continental

High Latitude
- Subarctic
- Highland

250   500 miles
250   500 kilometers

20°S

EAST ASIA

SOUTHEAST
ASIA

THINK LIKE A GEOGRAPHER

1. **Place** What are the two main climates in Southeast Asia?

2. **Region** How does East Asia's inland climate compare with that along its coasts?

100°E   120°E   140°E

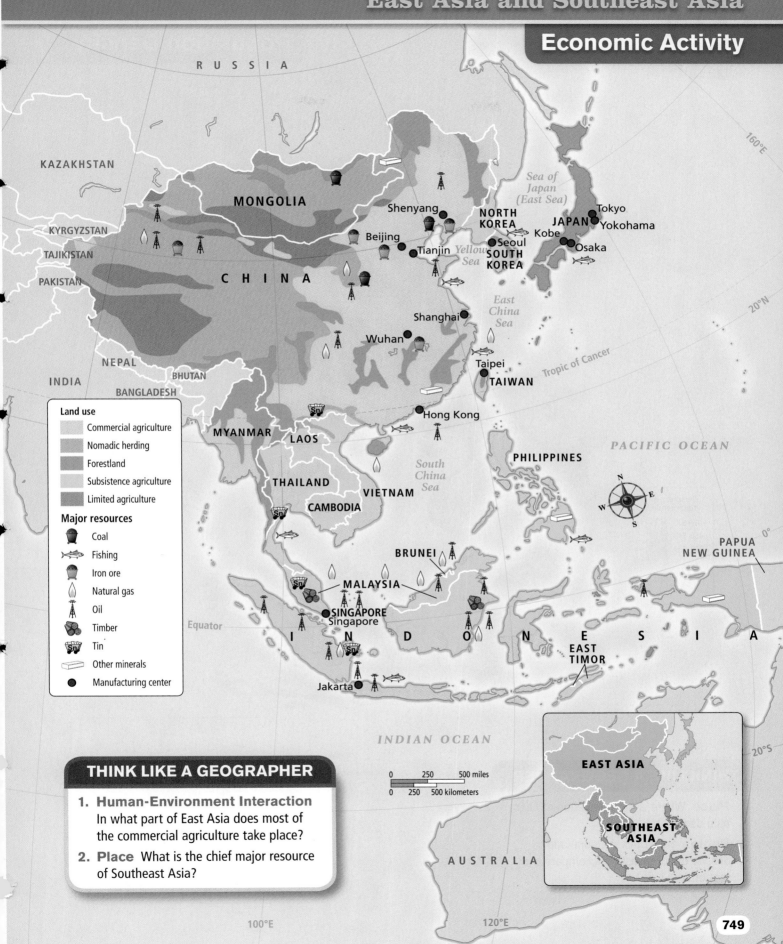

Economic Activity

RUSSIA

KAZAKHSTAN

KYRGYZSTAN

TAJIKISTAN

PAKISTAN

MONGOLIA

Shenyang

NORTH KOREA

Beijing
Tianjin
Yellow Sea

Sea of Japan (East Sea)

Tokyo
JAPAN
Yokohama
Kobe
Osaka

Seoul
SOUTH KOREA

CHINA

NEPAL
BHUTAN
BANGLADESH

INDIA

Shanghai

Wuhan

East China Sea

Taipei
TAIWAN

Tropic of Cancer

20°N

160°E

Land use
- Commercial agriculture
- Nomadic herding
- Forestland
- Subsistence agriculture
- Limited agriculture

Major resources
- Coal
- Fishing
- Iron ore
- Natural gas
- Oil
- Timber
- Tin
- Other minerals
- Manufacturing center

MYANMAR

LAOS

THAILAND

VIETNAM

CAMBODIA

Hong Kong

South China Sea

PHILIPPINES

PACIFIC OCEAN

BRUNEI

MALAYSIA

SINGAPORE
Singapore

I N D O N E S I A

Equator

EAST TIMOR

PAPUA NEW GUINEA

Jakarta

INDIAN OCEAN

20°S

0   250   500 miles
0   250   500 kilometers

EAST ASIA

SOUTHEAST ASIA

AUSTRALIA

THINK LIKE A GEOGRAPHER

1. **Human-Environment Interaction** In what part of East Asia does most of the commercial agriculture take place?

2. **Place** What is the chief major resource of Southeast Asia?

100°E

120°E

749

Population Density

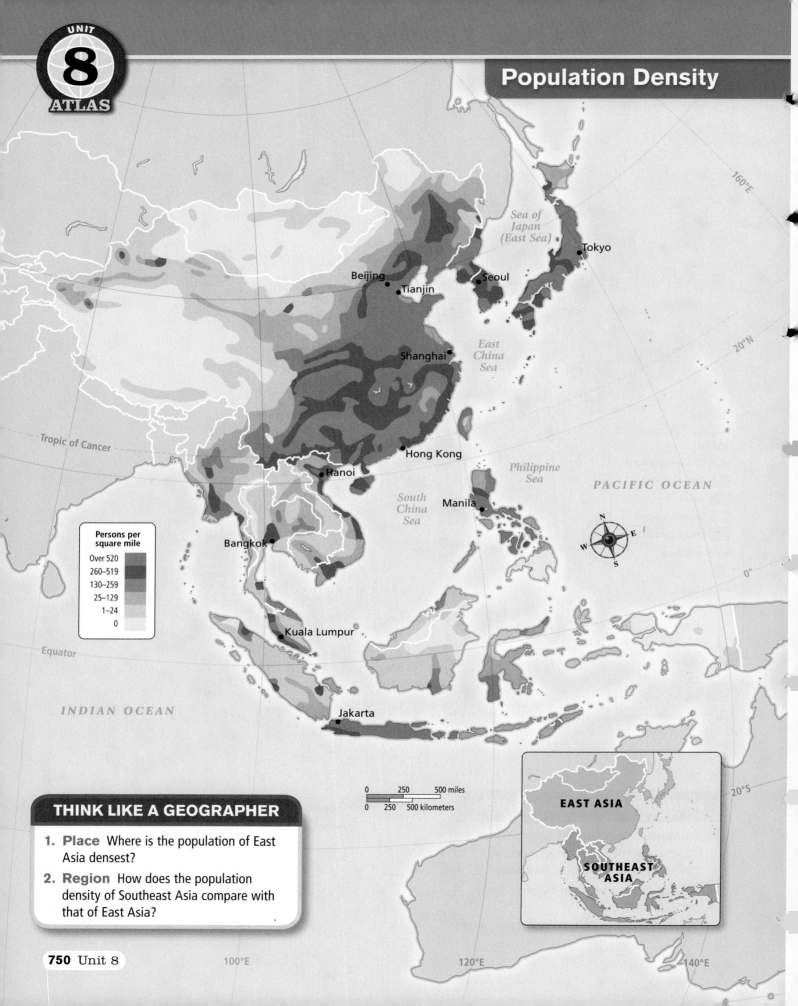

Sea of Japan (East Sea)

Tokyo

Beijing

Tianjin

Seoul

East China Sea

Shanghai

Tropic of Cancer

Hong Kong

Hanoi

Philippine Sea

PACIFIC OCEAN

South China Sea

Manila

Persons per square mile

Over 520

260–519

130–259

25–129

1–24

0

Bangkok

N
W   E
S

Kuala Lumpur

INDIAN OCEAN

Equator

Jakarta

0   250   500 miles
0   250   500 kilometers

160°E

20°N

0°

20°S

EAST ASIA

SOUTHEAST ASIA

THINK LIKE A GEOGRAPHER

1. **Place** Where is the population of East Asia densest?

2. **Region** How does the population density of Southeast Asia compare with that of East Asia?

100°E   120°E   140°E

Regional Overview

East Asia and Southeast Asia

The countries of East Asia and Southeast Asia are home to about one-third of all the people on Earth. Many of the countries share cultural traditions and a common historical past.

GEOGRAPHY

Both East Asia and Southeast Asia consist of a mainland and a number of important islands off their coasts. The regions are rugged, with many high mountain ranges. Volcanic eruptions and earthquakes frequently occur in these areas.

HISTORY

China has played a large role in both regions. In East Asia, China influenced the ancient civilizations of Japan and Korea. Many cultures had an impact on ancient Southeast Asia, including China and India. The region also changed when European colonists began to take control in the 1500s.

CULTURE

In spite of these historical influences, the countries of East Asia and Southeast Asia have retained their own character. In East Asia, countries such as China and Japan have distinct cultural traditions. Countries such as Indonesia in Southeast Asia are more culturally diverse.

GOVERNMENT

The two regions contain several different forms of government, including democracy, communism, and constitutional monarchy. Many of the countries have strong executive branches that enforce strict control over their people.

ECONOMICS

Most of the countries of East Asia have strong economies. The economies of Southeast Asia are not quite as powerful. Some are still developing, while others—including those in Singapore and Malaysia—are thriving.

Great Buddha The Great Buddha of Kamakura, Japan, is about 40 feet high and was cast in 1252. The statue was originally located inside a temple, which was washed away in a tsunami in the 1400s.

751

UNIT 8 ATLAS
Country Almanac

🖱 **Click here** to compare the most recent data on countries @ ClassZone.com

East Asia and Southeast Asia

As you study these cards, note that Southeast Asia contains one of the smallest countries in the word—Singapore—and East Asia contains one of the largest—China.

Unit Writing Project

Slide Show

Imagine that your family is considering a trip to a country in East Asia or Southeast Asia. Choose the country from this unit that you would most like to visit and prepare a slide show that will convince your family to go there.

Think About:

- how to convey the country's geography and climate
- what cultural and historical information to include
- what makes this place special

Brunei

GEOGRAPHY
Capital: Bandar Seri Begawan
Total Area: 2,228 sq. mi.
Population: 374,000
ECONOMY
Imports: machinery; food; chemicals
Exports: petroleum; natural gas
CULTURE
Language: Malay
Religion: Muslim 64%; traditional beliefs 11%; Buddhist 9%; Christian 8%

Cambodia

GEOGRAPHY
Capital: Phnom Penh
Total Area: 69,900 sq. mi.
Population: 14,071,000
ECONOMY
Imports: petroleum products; gold
Exports: clothing; rubber; timber
CULTURE
Language: Khmer
Religion: Buddhist 85%; Chinese folk-religionist 5%; traditional beliefs 4%

China

GEOGRAPHY
Capital: Beijing
Total Area: 3,705,407 sq. mi.
Population: 1,315,844,000
ECONOMY
Imports: machinery; petroleum; plastics
Exports: machinery; clothing; textiles
CULTURE
Language: Mandarin Chinese
Religion: nonreligious 42%; Chinese folk-religionist 29%; Buddhist 8%; atheist 8%

East Timor

GEOGRAPHY
Capital: Dili
Total Area: 5,794 sq. mi.
Population: 1,040,880
ECONOMY
Imports: food; construction materials
Exports: coffee; livestock; food; clothing
CULTURE
Language: Tetum; Portuguese
Religion: Catholic 87%; Protestant 5%; Muslim 3%; traditional beliefs 3%

Indonesia

GEOGRAPHY
Capital: Jakarta
Total Area: 741,100 sq. mi.
Population: 222,781,000
ECONOMY
Imports: machinery; petroleum; food
Exports: natural gas; petroleum
CULTURE
Language: Indonesian
Religion: Muslim 77%; Christian 13%; Hindu 3%; traditional beliefs 3%

Japan

GEOGRAPHY
Capital: Tokyo
Total Area: 145,883 sq. mi.
Population: 128,085,000
ECONOMY
Imports: machinery; petroleum; food
Exports: machinery; cars; metals
CULTURE
Language: Japanese
Religion: Shinto 93%; Buddhism 70% (many practice both); Christian 1%

Laos

GEOGRAPHY
Capital: Vientiane
Total Area: 91,429 sq. mi.
Population: 5,924,000
ECONOMY
Imports: mineral fuels; textiles
Exports: electricity; clothing; wood
CULTURE
Language: Lao
Religion: Buddhist 49%; traditional beliefs 42%; nonreligious 4%; Christian 2%

Malaysia

GEOGRAPHY
Capital: Kuala Lumpur
Total Area: 127,317 sq. mi.
Population: 25,347,000
ECONOMY
Imports: microcircuits; computers
Exports: transistors; computers
CULTURE
Language: Malay
Religion: Muslim 60%; Buddhist 19%; Christian 9%; Hindu 6%

Mongolia

GEOGRAPHY
Capital: Ulaanbaatar
Total Area: 603,909 sq. mi.
Population: 2,646,000

ECONOMY
Imports: machinery; food; fuels; textiles
Exports: copper concentrate; gold

CULTURE
Language: Khalkha Mongolian
Religion: Tantric Buddhist 96%; Muslim 4%

Myanmar

GEOGRAPHY

Capital: Yangon
Total Area: 261,970 sq. mi.
Population: 50,519,000

ECONOMY
Imports: machinery; chemicals; fuels; food
Exports: food; fuels; wood

CULTURE
Language: Burmese
Religion: Buddhist 73%; traditional beliefs 13%; Christian 8%; Muslim 2%; Hindu 2%

North Korea

GEOGRAPHY
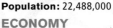
Capital: Pyongyang
Total Area: 46,541 sq. mi.
Population: 22,488,000

ECONOMY
Imports: food; machinery; fuels; textiles
Exports: animals; textiles; machinery

CULTURE
Language: Korean
Religion: nonreligious 56%; atheist 16%; Ch'ondogyo 13%; traditional beliefs 12%

Philippines

GEOGRAPHY

Capital: Manila
Total Area: 115,831 sq. mi.
Population: 83,054,000

ECONOMY
Imports: electronics; petroleum; chemicals
Exports: electronics; clothing; food

CULTURE
Language: Filipino; English
Religion: Catholic 81%; Protestant 7%; Muslim 5%; indigenous Christian 4%

Singapore

GEOGRAPHY
Capital: Singapore
Total Area: 267 sq. mi.
Population: 4,326,000

ECONOMY
Imports: electronics; petroleum; computers
Exports: electronics; computers; chemicals

CULTURE
Language: Chinese; Malay; Tamil; English
Religion: Buddhist 43%; Muslim 15%; Christian 15%; nonreligious 15%; Taoist 9%

South Korea

GEOGRAPHY
Capital: Seoul
Total Area: 38,023 sq. mi.
Population: 47,817,000

ECONOMY
Imports: electronics; petroleum
Exports: electronics; machinery; chemicals

CULTURE
Language: Korean
Religion: nonreligious 49%; Buddhist 23%; Protestant 20%; Catholic 7%

Taiwan

GEOGRAPHY
Capital: Taipei
Total Area: 13,892 sq. mi.
Population: 22,894,384

ECONOMY
Imports: machinery; minerals; chemicals
Exports: machinery; textiles; plastics

CULTURE
Language: Mandarin Chinese
Religion: Buddhist 22%; Taoism 21%; I-kuan Tao 4%; Protestant 2%

Thailand

GEOGRAPHY
Capital: Bangkok
Total Area: 198,457 sq. mi.
Population: 64,233,000

ECONOMY
Imports: machinery; chemicals; petroleum
Exports: food; electronics; chemicals

CULTURE
Language: Thai
Religion: Buddhist 94%; Muslim 5%; Christian 1%

Vietnam

GEOGRAPHY
Capital: Hanoi
Total Area: 127,244 sq. mi.
Population: 84,238,000

ECONOMY
Imports: machinery; petroleum; fertilizers
Exports: petroleum; clothing; fish

CULTURE
Language: Vietnamese
Religion: Buddhist 67%; Christian 9%; Cao Dai 4%; Hoa Hao 2%

Laos Towering limestone cliffs line the Nam Song River in Laos.

China

ESSENTIAL QUESTION

How is China's traditional way of life changing in response to global trends?

①
GEOGRAPHY

Land of Three Rivers

②
HISTORY

Middle Kingdom to Communist Power

③
CULTURE

Changing Chinese Culture

④
GOVERNMENT & ECONOMICS

A Rising Power

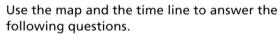

CONNECT ➤ **Geography & History**

Use the map and the time line to answer the following questions.

1. What is the capital of China?

2. On what river is the Three Gorges Dam?

Culture

479 B.C. Confucius, China's greatest teacher, dies. ▶

500 B.C.

Culture

A.D. 65 Buddhism begins to travel to China from India.

History

221 B.C. Shi Huangdi unifies China into an empire. ▶

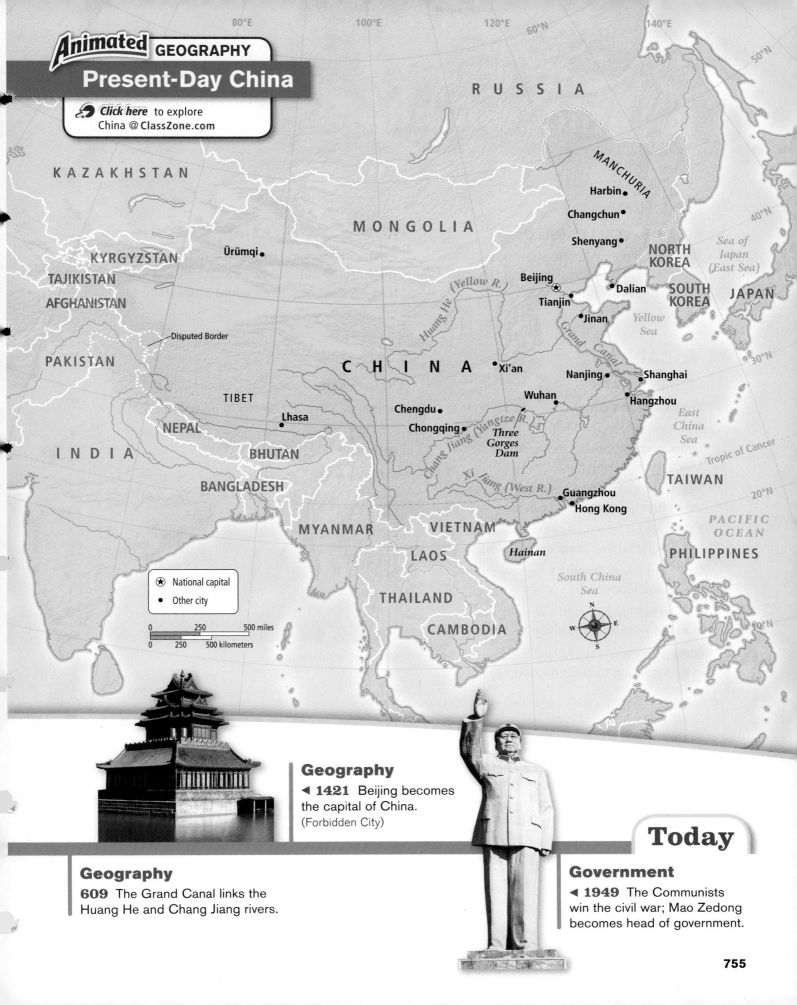

RUSSIA

KAZAKHSTAN

MONGOLIA

MANCHURIA

Harbin

Changchun

Shenyang

NORTH KOREA

Sea of Japan (East Sea)

JAPAN

KYRGYZSTAN

Ürümqi

TAJIKISTAN

AFGHANISTAN

Beijing

Dalian

SOUTH KOREA

Tianjin

Jinan

Yellow Sea

Huang He (Yellow R.)

Disputed Border

PAKISTAN

C H I N A

Xi'an

Nanjing

Shanghai

Wuhan

Hangzhou

TIBET

Chengdu

Lhasa

Chongqing

Chang Jiang (Yangtze R.)

Three Gorges Dam

East China Sea

NEPAL

BHUTAN

I N D I A

BANGLADESH

Xi Jiang (West R.)

Guangzhou

Hong Kong

Tropic of Cancer

TAIWAN

MYANMAR

VIETNAM

LAOS

Hainan

PACIFIC OCEAN

PHILIPPINES

South China Sea

THAILAND

CAMBODIA

★ National capital

• Other city

0   250   500 miles
0   250   500 kilometers

Geography
◄ **1421** Beijing becomes the capital of China.
(Forbidden City)

Today

Geography
609 The Grand Canal links the Huang He and Chang Jiang rivers.

Government
◄ **1949** The Communists win the civil war; Mao Zedong becomes head of government.

Reading for Understanding

▶ Key Ideas

BEFORE, YOU LEARNED

South Asia contains mountains, plateaus, and plains. Its wet and dry seasons can cause floods and drought.

NOW YOU WILL LEARN

China has varied landforms, ranging from high mountains to river valleys. It has diverse climates, plants, and animals.

▶ Vocabulary

TERMS & NAMES

Three Gorges Dam a barrier built on the Chang Jiang to control floods

hydroelectric power electricity made by water-powered engines

Himalayas (HIHM•uh•LAY•uhz) a mountain range that divides China from India

Taklimakan (TAH•kluh•muh•KAHN) **Desert** the second largest sand desert in the world

Gobi (GOH•bee) **Desert** a high desert in China and Mongolia

Huang He (hwahng huh) a river that flows from the Kunlun Mountains to the Yellow Sea

Chang Jiang (chahng jyahng) the longest river in Asia, flowing through eastern China

Xi (she) **Jiang** a river in southeast China

seismic (SYZ•mihk) having to do with earthquakes

REVIEW

plateau a high area of flat land

Visual Vocabulary plateau

▶ Reading Strategy

Re-create the chart shown at right. As you read and respond to the **KEY QUESTIONS**, use the chart to organize important details about the physical geography of China.

 See Skillbuilder Handbook, page R7

CATEGORIZE

	WESTERN CHINA	EASTERN CHINA
Geographic Features		
Climate		
Plants and Animals		
Types of Agriculture		
Natural Disasters		

 GRAPHIC ORGANIZERS
Go to **Interactive Review** @ ClassZone.com

Land of Three Rivers

Connecting to Your World

Much like the Mississippi in the United States, the Chang Jiang (chahng jyahng) River in eastern China has been both China's best friend and worst enemy. The fertile farmland and the transportation that the river provides help China feed its enormous population. But seasonal floods take a terrible toll on the million or so people who live near the river's banks. The **Three Gorges Dam** should prevent the floods. The dam will also generate **hydroelectric power**, electricity from water-powered engines. The dam was completed in 2006 but is not projected to begin operating until 2009.

China's Geographic Features

▼ **KEY QUESTION** What are the main geographic features of western China and eastern China?

Everything about the People's Republic of China is on a big scale. China is the third largest country in area and has a population of 1.3 billion—the largest in the world. Western China contains some of the world's harshest geographic features, while eastern China is one of the world's most densely populated places.

Animated GEOGRAPHY

Lake to be created by the dam — Three Gorges Dam

Chang Jiang (Yangtze R.)

Chongqing • Wuhan • Shanghai

CHINA

Three Gorges Dam Officials say the dam will relieve flooding on the Chang Jiang and produce more energy. Some people disagree. **What problems do you think the dam could cause?**

Click here to see more of the Three Gorges Dam project @ ClassZone.com

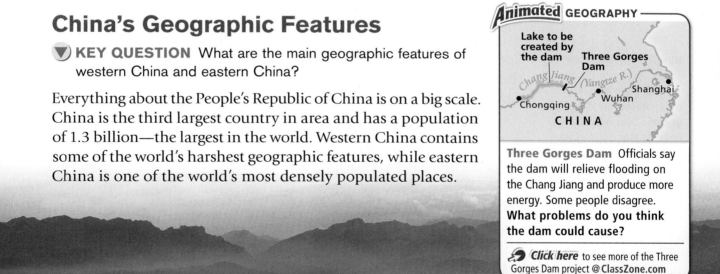

Western China One important fact about western China is that its rugged terrain acted as a barrier between China and other lands. As a result, Chinese culture developed with limited outside influences.

Western China is dotted with dramatic mountain ranges. The **Himalayas** (HIHM•uh•LAY•uhz), which separate China from India, contain the world's highest mountains. The Plateau of Tibet lies between the Himalayas and the Kunlun mountains. This **plateau,** or high area of flat land, is more than 13,000 feet above sea level and is called the "Roof of the World."

Two vast deserts stretch across northwestern China. The **Taklimakan** (TAH•kluh•muh•KAHN) **Desert** is the world's second largest sand desert. And the **Gobi** (GOH•bee) **Desert,** a high desert of China and Mongolia, is about five times the size of Colorado. With so much harsh landscape, western China has far fewer people than eastern China.

Eastern China An important feature of eastern China is its rivers. Three major rivers start in the highlands of western China and flow through eastern China. You can see all three on the map opposite:

1. The **Huang He** (hwahng huh) **Ⓐ**, or Yellow River, flows through northeast China. The river's floods deposit silt on the North China Plain, making it one of China's richest farming areas.

2. The **Chang Jiang Ⓑ**, or Yangtze River, is 3,915 miles long. It is the longest river in Asia and is a very busy waterway.

3. The **Xi** (she) **Jiang Ⓒ**, or West River, flows through southeast China. It is a major transportation route in southern China.

These rivers are critical to productive farming in eastern China. Spring floods deposit silt, a fertile soil good for growing crops, along the riverbanks. Because of the rich, flat river basins that result, most Chinese farmers live in eastern China's river valleys. The rivers also transport people and goods, connecting inland China with its coast.

▲ **SUMMARIZE** Describe the main geographic features of western China and eastern China.

Huang He (Yellow River) The Huang He carries fine dirt that gives it a yellowish color. **Based on the geographic features shown here, is the river most likely flowing through eastern or western China?**

Physical Geography of China

Click here to see geographic features of China @ ClassZone.com

KAZAKHSTAN

RUSSIA

MONGOLIA

MANCHURIA

ALTAI SHAN

KYRGYZSTAN

TIAN SHAN

TAJIKISTAN

PAMIRS Kongur Shan
25,325 ft.
(7,719 m)

TAKLIMAKAN DESERT

Disputed Border

PAKISTAN

KUNLUN SHAN

PLATEAU OF TIBET

HIMALAYAS

TIBET

NEPAL

INDIA

BHUTAN

BANGLADESH

MYANMAR

GOBI DESERT

CHINA

Huang He (Yellow R.)

Ⓐ QINLING SHANDI

Gongga Shan
24,790 ft.
(7,556 m)

Chang Jiang (Yangtze R.)

Ⓑ

Ⓒ Xi Jiang (West R.)

VIETNAM

LAOS

MANCHURIAN PLAIN

NORTH KOREA

SOUTH KOREA

Sea of Japan
(East Sea)

JAPAN

Yellow Sea

Grand Canal

NORTH CHINA PLAIN

East China Sea

Tropic of Cancer

TAIWAN

Hainan

South China Sea

PACIFIC OCEAN

PHILIPPINES

THAILAND

Equator

N
W   E
S

0   250   500 miles
0   250   500 kilometers

Elevation

13,100 ft.   (4,000 m)
6,600 ft.   (2,000 m)
3,280 ft.   (1,000 m)
650 ft.   (200 m)
0 ft.   (0 m)
Below sea level

▲ Mountain peak

CONNECT Geography & Culture
READING A PHYSICAL MAP

Locate China's three main rivers on the map. As you study the map,

- note the direction the rivers flow
- think about how the direction of flow might affect travel in China
- consider how areas of high and low elevation might affect local populations

1. **Location** Which of the three main rivers labeled on this map does not start in the Plateau of Tibet?

2. **Movement** Would it be easier for boats to travel from east to west along the rivers of China or from west to east? Explain.

90°E   100°E   110°E

China's Varied Climate and Resources

▼ **KEY QUESTION** How are the climate and resources of western and eastern China different?

Western and eastern China have very different climates and natural resources. Because of its climate differences, China also has a variety of plants and animals.

CONNECT ⮀ **Geography & History**

The Silk Roads

Trade moved along routes on the edges of the Taklimakan and Gobi deserts. Traders traveled the routes by camel caravans. Among other items, they carried silver, jade, medicines, foods, and animals. But they carried so much silk that the routes came to be called the Silk Roads.

Life in Western China You've learned that western China is thinly populated because it is mostly mountains and deserts. The highest mountains are cold year-round. At lower elevations, summers are cool but sunny. Animals such as wild sheep and mountain antelope roam the highlands. Forests grow at elevations of around 12,000 feet and provide a home for wildcats.

As you might guess, almost nothing survives in the Gobi and Taklimakan deserts. They get little rain and have very sparse vegetation. Temperatures dip below 0°F in winter and rise to higher than 120°F in summer.

Many highlanders are nomadic herders of horses and of grazing animals, such as yaks, sheep, and goats. Because vegetation is scarce—mostly mosses and short shrubs— grazing herds must keep moving to find new sources of food.

Western China's main resources are petroleum, natural gas, and lead. Pipelines carry both oil and natural gas to the east.

Life in Eastern China Eastern China has a milder climate than western China. Northeastern China has a climate like the Northeast and Midwest of the United States, with cold winters, warm summers, and enough rain for farming. Mixed and broadleaf forests provide homes for leopards, deer, and more than 265 kinds of birds. In contrast, southeastern China has mild winters and hot, rainy summers. The region has mixed forests of wild tea and citrus trees, oaks, cypresses, and pines. Alligators, giant salamanders, monkeys, and pangolins—scaly animals that look like anteaters—live inland.

Wherever rain falls in China, bamboo grows. Bamboo is important to Chinese culture. Its long, woody stems are used to make chopsticks, among other things. Bamboo is also a vital food for the giant panda, China's most treasured animal. The panda, an endangered species, spends about 12 hours a day eating—and it eats mainly bamboo.

Most of China's farmland is in eastern China. Many people think that all Chinese farmers grow rice, but in northern China they grow wheat, soybeans, and millet. These crops need less water than rice. Rice is grown in the rainy southeast, where the climate is so mild and the soil is so rich that farmers grow two or three crops a year.

Chinese farmers use traditional methods that are centuries old. They don't have the huge tractors or other large farm equipment that U.S. farmers use. The use of farm machinery, such as small hand-held tractors, has been on the rise since the 1990s, but China still relies on long hours of human labor in the fields.

Eastern China has abundant natural resources, such as tin and iron. In 2003, China produced about 35 percent of the world's coal, but at a deadly cost; 80 percent of all deaths in coal mines worldwide occur in China. The government is using clean coal technologies and modernizing equipment to improve safety.

▲ **COMPARE AND CONTRAST** Compare the climate and resources of western and eastern China.

COMPARING Western and Eastern China

	WESTERN	EASTERN
Population	thinly populated	heavily populated
Geographic Features	an arid climate and little usable farmland	important rivers, plentiful rain, rich farmland
Land Use	used mostly for grazing animals	used for agriculture
Resources	supplies of petroleum, natural gas, and lead	rich with coal and other resources

CRITICAL THINKING

1. **Analyze Effects** How is land use in each part of China affected by its geographic features?

2. **Make Inferences** Which part of China would most likely contribute more to the country's overall economy?

Flooded City Floods continue to plague China. In 2004, heavy rains caused flash floods along the Chang Jiang. The raging waters swamped cities and destroyed homes, roads, and power lines. **What special problems might occur when large cities experience floods?**

Natural Disasters in China

▼ **KEY QUESTION** How have floods and earthquakes affected China?

China has had its share of natural disasters. Severe floods and **seismic** (SYZ•mihk), or earthquake, activity often threaten Chinese lives.

Floods China's damaging floods have killed, injured, or displaced millions of people over the centuries. In fact, the Huang He has flooded so often that the Chinese call it "China's Sorrow."

One of the worst floods of recent times took place along the Chang Jiang in 1998. Heavy rains were one cause. Another cause was the cutting down of forests for farmland and urban growth. Without trees to hold the soil in place, the rainwater rushed into the river, causing it to rise. More than 3,000 people died in the resulting flood. Fourteen million people in four provinces lost homes, and railways and roads were destroyed. Deadly diseases such as cholera spread.

The Chinese government hopes the Three Gorges Dam will prevent future floods on the Chang Jiang. However, critics of the project raise tough issues:

- The dam will force more than 1 million people to leave their farms and homes. Hundreds of cities, towns, and villages will be under water.

- The lake will cover more than 1,000 important historical sites.

- The dam may create pollution and increase health risks because the river will no longer wash sewage away.

Will the benefits of the dam outweigh the risks? We won't know until the dam begins operating in 2009. Meanwhile, the Chinese people make the best of the ebb and flow of their powerful rivers.

Earthquakes Eastern and western China both experience earthquakes because many fault lines, or cracks in the earth's crust, cross the country. But earthquakes in eastern China carry a much higher death toll because the region is so heavily populated.

One example is a devastating earthquake that hit Tangshan (tahng•shahn), about 90 miles from the capital city of Beijing (bay•jing), in July 1976. The quake destroyed roads, canals, sewers, hospitals, factories, and homes. The quake hit at about 4:00 A.M., when people were sleeping. About 250,000 people died, and more than 500,000 were injured. A strong aftershock killed many people already trapped in the rubble.

More than 90 percent of the city's housing was lost. Survivors lived in tents with no electricity or clean water. Despite the hardships, the government began to rebuild the city right away. Today the Chinese call Tangshan the "Brave City of China."

Earthquake Detector In this ancient Chinese invention, an earthquake would cause a ball to fall from a dragon's mouth into a frog's mouth. The frog's position revealed the direction of the quake.

▲ **ANALYZE EFFECTS** Explain how floods and earthquakes have affected China.

Section 1 Assessment

ONLINE QUIZ
For test practice, go to
Interactive Review
@ ClassZone.com

TERMS & NAMES

1. Explain the importance of
- Three Gorges Dam
- Taklimakan Desert
- Huang He
- Chang Jiang

USE YOUR READING NOTES

2. Categorize Use your completed chart to answer the following question:

Which part of the country is more in danger of floods, the western part or the eastern part? Why?

	WESTERN CHINA	EASTERN CHINA
Geographic Features		
Climate		
Plants and Animals		
Types of Agriculture		
Natural Disasters		

KEY IDEAS

3. Why does the majority of Chinese people live in the eastern third of the country?

4. How did the 1998 flood affect people?

5. Why is it difficult for humans to live in the Taklimakan and Gobi deserts?

CRITICAL THINKING

6. Analyze Effects How does the silt carried by rivers both help farmers and create problems for them?

7. Make Inferences Why do you think Chinese civilization developed near the rivers?

8. ⬤ **CONNECT to Today** In 2002, China imported nearly half the oil it used. How do you think China's lack of oil affects its use of farm machinery?

9. ⬤ **WRITING** **Prepare a Travel Brochure** Choose a geographical area of China and prepare a brochure for tourists. Include pictures and describe the best places to see.

▶ Key Ideas

BEFORE, YOU LEARNED

China is one of the largest countries in the world, but much of its farmland lies only in the eastern part.

NOW YOU WILL LEARN

Throughout history, China's rulers have struggled with the problem of feeding so many people.

▶ Vocabulary

TERMS & NAMES

Shi Huangdi (shee hwahng•dee) the first emperor to unify much of China

emperor a ruler of an empire, which is a group of different territories or cultures led by a single all-powerful authority

dynasty (DY•nuh•stee) a line of rulers from the same family

North China Plain the fertile region between the Huang He and Chang Jiang rivers

Middle Kingdom an ancient Chinese name for China

dynastic (dy•NAS•tihk) **cycle** the pattern of the rise and fall of dynasties

Great Wall a huge and long wall built to keep nomads out of China

Confucianism (kuhn•FYOO•shuh•nihz•uhm) a belief system based on the teachings of Confucius, a Chinese scholar

scholar-official an educated person who worked in China's government

communism a government and economic system in which the government holds nearly all political power and the means of production in the name of the people

Mao Zedong (MOW dzuh•dahng) Communist leader of China from 1949 to 1976

▶ Reading Strategy

Re-create the problem-solution chart shown at right. As you read and respond to the **KEY QUESTIONS**, use the chart to explain how Chinese leaders tried to solve some of the problems they faced.

 See Skillbuilder Handbook, page R10

IDENTIFY PROBLEMS AND SOLUTIONS

PROBLEMS	SOLUTIONS
Gaining Power	
Keeping Order	
Feeding a Large Population	

GRAPHIC ORGANIZERS
Go to **Interactive Review** @ ClassZone.com

Middle Kingdom to Communist Power

Connecting to Your World

In democracies like the United States, people elect leaders, but that isn't the only way that rulers come to power. **Shi Huangdi** (shee hwahng•dee) became king of the state of Qin (chihn) when he was only 13 because he was the son of a king. Older people actually ran the government until 238 B.C., when Shi Huangdi became the sole ruler at the age of 21. He employed smart generals and advisers, who helped him conquer other Chinese kingdoms. By 221 B.C., Shi Huangdi became China's first **emperor**, or ruler of many states.

Shi Huangdi Shi Huangdi ruled as emperor from 221 to 210 B.C.

Emperors and Dynasties

🔻 **KEY QUESTION** What was the dynastic cycle?

Shi Huangdi ruled harshly. To keep control, he killed hundreds of people who criticized him. He took away the nobles' power and forced peasants to build roads, forts, and canals. Many died from overwork.

Historians divide Chinese history into dynasties. A **dynasty** (DY•nuh•stee) is a line of rulers from one family. Shi Huangdi began the Qin Dynasty, but Chinese history began long before Qin rule.

Terra Cotta Army Shi Huangdi had an army of 7,500 life-size terra cotta (clay) soldiers created to guard his tomb. **What do you think he wanted this army to convey about him?**

Early Culture A major Chinese civilization developed on the **North China Plain**, which lies between the Huang He and Chang Jiang. As you have learned, the rivers deposit silt, so the land is fertile. Chinese farming started there, and around 2000 B.C., cities began to grow.

Some traits of that early culture have been part of Chinese culture ever since. For example, the Chinese had invented a writing system by 1000 B.C. Those characters evolved into the ones that are still used today. Also, the ancient Chinese placed great value on the family. Respect for the family is still central to Chinese life.

Uniting and Ruling China Other dynasties ruled northern China before the Qin, but Shi Huangdi was the first ruler to unite the kingdoms into one empire. Wars between the separate kingdoms ended. In the peace that followed, farming and trade grew.

A united China could better protect itself from attacks. Nomads from the north often invaded China. The Chinese saw the nomads as uncivilized, and in contrast, thought their own culture was very advanced. In fact, the Chinese called their country the **Middle Kingdom** because they thought they were the center of the world.

The Chinese believed that their rulers needed the Mandate of Heaven, or the gods' approval. A dynasty had the mandate as long as it ruled well. When a dynasty ruled badly, it lost the mandate. The people then rebelled, and a new dynasty took power. This pattern, called the **dynastic** (dy•NAS•tihk) **cycle**, was repeated many times.

For example, after Shi Huangdi died, his son ruled badly. War broke out, and the Han Dynasty took power in 202 B.C. At first, the Han ruled well, and people believed they had the mandate. After 400 years, however, rebellions and other problems brought Han rule to an end.

Dynastic Cycle

Chinese Dragon The Chinese consider dragons to be powerful but helpful creatures that bring good luck. This dragon decorates the wall of a palace.

CRITICAL THINKING
Make Inferences Why do you suppose dragons came to symbolize the emperor?

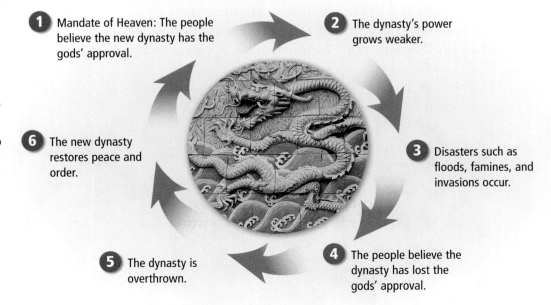

1. Mandate of Heaven: The people believe the new dynasty has the gods' approval.

2. The dynasty's power grows weaker.

3. Disasters such as floods, famines, and invasions occur.

4. The people believe the dynasty has lost the gods' approval.

5. The dynasty is overthrown.

6. The new dynasty restores peace and order.

The Great Wall China's history caused the Chinese to erect a unique structure. In ancient times when small kingdoms often fought each other, many of them built defensive walls. After Shi Huangdi united China, he decided to connect existing walls to stop invading nomads. Hundreds of thousands of peasants were forced to work on this **Great Wall**. Some later dynasties added to and rebuilt the wall. You will learn more about the Great Wall at the end of this section.

▲ **FIND MAIN IDEAS** Describe the dynastic cycle.

Scholars and Inventors

▼ **KEY QUESTION** How did scholars and inventions influence life in China?

China's rulers faced two difficult problems. First, they had to keep order in a huge country. Second, China had a large population to feed. Scholars and inventions helped Chinese emperors solve these two problems.

Confucius To help produce order, a teacher named Confucius (kuhn•FYOO•shuhs) created a code of behavior that was based on traditional values. Confucius taught that people must do what is right. However, he stressed different virtues for people in different social roles. For instance, rulers should be kind and set a good example. People who work in the government should be polite, honest, and fair. All subjects should be obedient and loyal to the ruler. Confucius also urged all men to get an education.

Starting with the Han Dynasty, China's rulers adopted Confucius' ideas. The rulers wanted well-trained people to help them run the country. They also wanted people who were virtuous and loyal. A state exam based on **Confucianism** (kuhn•FYOO•shuh•nihz•uhm), or the teachings of Confucius, was used to test men for government work. The exam was very difficult. It tested people's knowledge of history, law, and poetry as well as Confucianism. Most people failed the test. Those who passed became **scholar-officials**, or educated people who worked in the government. This orderly approach to choosing officials helped the Chinese emperors rule their large country.

HISTORY MAKERS

Confucius 551–479 B.C.

Confucius was the most important teacher in Chinese history. As a boy, he worked hard to learn all subjects. In his 30s, Confucius became a popular teacher. Later, he became a minor court official and tried to put his ideas about duty and social order into practice. Other officials resented Confucius' talk of virtue, so he did not keep his job for long. As a result, he felt like a failure. Little did he know that his ideas would guide rulers for centuries after his death.

🔎 **ONLINE BIOGRAPHY**
For more on the life of Confucius, go to the **Research & Writing Center @ ClassZone.com**

ANALYZING Primary Sources

Marco Polo (1254–1324) was an Italian merchant who lived in China for 17 years during the 1200s. Here is a description he wrote about one Chinese invention.

> [The emperor] has money made . . . out of the bark of trees. . . . [The money is] cut up into rectangles of various sizes, longer than they are broad [and worth different amounts]. . . . With this currency [money] he orders all payments to be made throughout every province and kingdom and region of his empire.

Source: *The Travels of Marco Polo*, translated by Ronald Latham

Marco Polo

DOCUMENT–BASED QUESTION
Why do you think paper money was adopted by other cultures?

ONLINE PRIMARY SOURCE To read more of Marco Polo's writing, go to the **Research & Writing Center** @ClassZone.com

Chinese Inventions
The Chinese people invented many things that solved problems or created prosperity. Some inventions helped the Chinese to feed their large population. The iron plow loosened soil to prepare it for planting crops. The horse collar enabled farmers to use horses to pull plows and carts. The wheelbarrow made it easier to move heavy loads. Water mills used the power of rivers to grind grain.

Some inventions aided government and education. For example, the invention of paper helped officials to keep records. More books became available after the invention of block printing—printing from large wooden blocks on which a whole page of information has been carved. Later, printing became easier with the invention of movable type—small blocks carved with a single character. The blocks can be rearranged to print new pages. The inventions of paper and printing allowed the Chinese to make records that exist to this day.

China and the World
Other cultures adopted some of China's inventions such as paper money, the compass, and gunpowder. For centuries, however, the Chinese kept the secret of how to make silk, a luxurious fabric, and porcelain, a hard white ceramic also called china. Silk and porcelain were rare and beautiful, so the Chinese could trade them in foreign lands to gain wealth.

In contrast, the Chinese had little interest in obtaining foreign goods or technology because they thought their culture was more advanced. For centuries, the Chinese engaged in trade but adopted few foreign ideas.

During the 1200s and 1300s, a foreign people called the Mongols ruled China and encouraged the trade of ideas. They also allowed merchants, such as Marco Polo, to come to China. In the early 1400s, the Ming Dynasty ruled China and sponsored great voyages of exploration to Arabia and Africa. These were led by an admiral named Zheng He (juhng huh).

After the 1430s, scholar-officials urged the emperor to cut off contact with foreigners. As a result, China turned inward and was not interested in developments in other lands. By the 1800s, the West had developed more advanced technology and weapons than China had.

▲ **ANALYZE EFFECTS** Discuss how scholars and inventions influenced life in China.

CONNECT to Science

Some time in the 1100s, sailors in China discovered how to make a magnetic compass. Earth is like a gigantic magnet. Lodestone, a magnetic rock, will point north if it is placed on a stick floating in water. After identifying where north is, sailors can find any other direction. So the invention of the compass greatly helped sailors and other travelers to plan their routes.

People in other countries also began to use the magnetic compass. This new technology helped to bring about an increase in trade. It also helped European explorers to go on voyages around the world.

Magnetic Compass
The Chinese characters around the rim of this compass give directions.

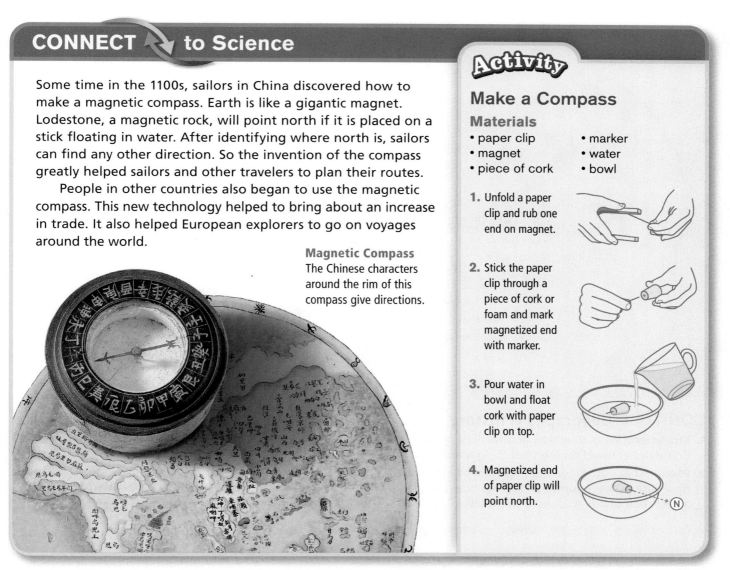

Activity

Make a Compass

Materials
- paper clip
- magnet
- piece of cork
- marker
- water
- bowl

1. Unfold a paper clip and rub one end on magnet.

2. Stick the paper clip through a piece of cork or foam and mark magnetized end with marker.

3. Pour water in bowl and float cork with paper clip on top.

4. Magnetized end of paper clip will point north.

The Rise of Communism

🔻 **KEY QUESTION** What impact did communism have on China?

A new dynasty called the Qing (chihng) took over China in 1644. During the 1800s, European nations wanted to trade with China. When the Qing rulers refused, the Europeans defeated China in a series of wars. The Europeans forced the Qing to open China and let them trade in several port cities. The United States and Japan were also given the right to trade in China.

China's population had grown rapidly, but food production did not increase at the same rate. People became angry about the widespread hunger and also about China's defeat at the hands of foreigners. As a result, many rebellions against the Qing took place.

In 1912, a group called the Nationalist Party defeated the Qing and set up a republic. The Nationalists then had to fight many warlords. By 1928, they had united China.

Communist Revolution In 1921, a group of students and others formed the Chinese Communist Party. **Communism** is a system in which the government holds nearly all political power and the means of production in the name of the people. The Communists wanted to take over China. They set up bases in the countryside and gave land to peasants, many of whom joined them.

By 1930, civil war had broken out between the Nationalists and Communists. In 1934, the Nationalist army surrounded the Communists. To escape, the Communists fled on the Long March, walking for 6,000 miles.

Japan invaded China in 1937. The Nationalists and Communists stopped fighting and worked together to fight Japan. After Japan was defeated at the end of World War II, the civil war began again. In 1949, the Communists won and formed the People's Republic of China. The Nationalists fled to Taiwan (TY•wahn), an island off of China's southeast coast.

The Long March 1934–1935

CONNECT Geography & History

1. **Movement** What direction or directions did the Communists travel during their Long March?
2. **Place** What advantage did they gain by moving to a new base in the mountains? Explain how this would affect their ability to defend themselves.

Chairman Mao In 1949, **Mao Zedong** (MOW dzuh•dahng) became chairman, or head, of China's Communist government. He seized farmland from large landholders and divided it among the peasants. The government also took over all industry and business. It even controlled the personal lives of the Chinese people.

In 1958, Mao started an economic plan called the Great Leap Forward. He believed in using the hard work of peasants instead of modern technology to increase food production. Thousands of peasants were sent to work on huge, government-owned farms. Mao's program failed to increase food production, so in 1961 it was stopped. The Great Leap Forward resulted in over 20 million deaths from starvation. Some leaders began to talk about reversing Mao's policies.

In 1966, Mao called for a Cultural Revolution to stop those plans. He urged millions of high school and college students to form groups called Red Guards. They attacked educated people and criticized leaders who wanted change. The Red Guards closed schools and factories. They caused so much chaos that Mao finally had to send the army to stop them. After Mao died in 1976, the leaders who wanted change took over China.

Mao Zedong For 27 years, Mao Zedong was the most powerful man in China. This portrait still hangs outside the old palace of the emperors. **Why do you think Mao's portrait hangs outside a palace?**

▲ **DRAW CONCLUSIONS** Explain the impact of communism on China.

Section 2 Assessment

🔗 **ONLINE QUIZ** For test practice, go to **Interactive Review** @ ClassZone.com

TERMS & NAMES

1. Explain the importance of
- Shi Huangdi
- dynastic cycle
- Confucianism
- Mao Zedong

USE YOUR READING NOTES

2. Identify Problems and Solutions
Use your completed problem-solution chart to answer the following question:

How successful was Mao Zedong at solving the two problems of keeping order and feeding people? Explain.

PROBLEMS	SOLUTIONS
Gaining Power	
Keeping Order	
Feeding a Large Population	

KEY IDEAS

3. Why did China's emperors think it was a good idea to employ scholar-officials who had studied Confucianism?

4. How did the iron plow and the horse collar help to feed China's large population?

5. How did the inventions of paper and block printing make record-keeping easier?

CRITICAL THINKING

6. Draw Conclusions How was the Mandate of Heaven connected to the dynastic cycle?

7. Analyze Effects In what ways did the Communists promote change, and in what ways did they oppose it?

8. CONNECT to Today Why do you think the Chinese people still honor Mao?

9. TECHNOLOGY Create a Multimedia Presentation Create a slide show about a group of inventions that changed farming, government, education, or trade. Show how the inventions work and explain why they made a difference.

Animated GEOGRAPHY
The Great Wall of China

🔊 **Click here** to enter the Great Wall of China @ ClassZone.com

DEFENDING CHINA

Many barriers protect China: mountains to the west and south, an ocean to the east. But in the north, nomads were able to invade China, so the Chinese built a barrier—the Great Wall—to try to stop them.

🔊 **Click here** to see the Great Wall as it snakes across mountains, plains, and deserts. Learn about the challenges of building and maintaining about 4,000 miles of walls.

🔊 **Click here** to see the weapons used in a Great Wall battle. Learn about watchtowers, lookout soldiers, and the signals used to warn of an attack.

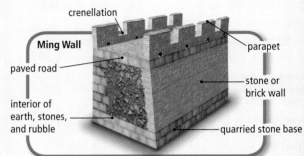

Ming Wall

crenellation
parapet
paved road
stone or brick wall
interior of earth, stones, and rubble
quarried stone base

🔊 **Click here** to see inside the Great Wall. The construction methods were so sound that the Wall has lasted for centuries.

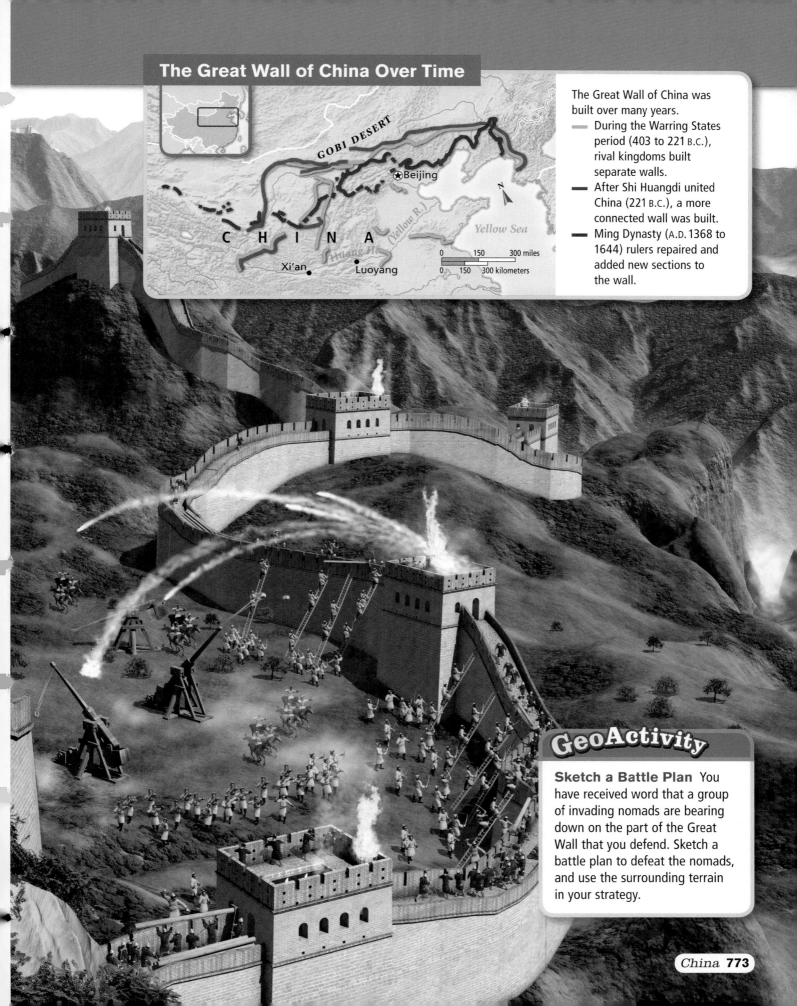

The Great Wall of China Over Time

GOBI DESERT

★Beijing

CHINA

(Yellow R.)

Huang He

Yellow Sea

Xi'an Luoyang

N

0   150   300 miles
0   150   300 kilometers

The Great Wall of China was built over many years.

— During the Warring States period (403 to 221 B.C.), rival kingdoms built separate walls.

— After Shi Huangdi united China (221 B.C.), a more connected wall was built.

— Ming Dynasty (A.D. 1368 to 1644) rulers repaired and added new sections to the wall.

GeoActivity

Sketch a Battle Plan You have received word that a group of invading nomads are bearing down on the part of the Great Wall that you defend. Sketch a battle plan to defeat the nomads, and use the surrounding terrain in your strategy.

Reading for Understanding

▶ Key Ideas

BEFORE, YOU LEARNED

China has a very long history. The people lived a traditional life during much of that history—until the Communist Revolution.

NOW YOU WILL LEARN

Some aspects of traditional life survive in China, while new ways of life have been developed.

▶ Vocabulary

TERMS & NAMES

Daoism (DOW•IHZ•uhm) a Chinese belief system based on the idea of natural order in the world

Dao (DOW) according to the belief system of Daoism, a force that guides the whole universe

Silk Roads trade routes used between China and Southwest Asia

Buddhism a religion that is based on the teaching of Siddhartha Gautama

Siddhartha Gautama (sihd•DAHR•tuh GAW•tuh•muh) the founder of Buddhism also known as the Buddha, or "enlightened one"

Buddha the founder of Buddhism who taught that people could end their suffering by stopping their desire for wordly goods

BACKGROUND VOCABULARY

ritual a set of regularly followed ceremonies

communal shared ownership of property

REVIEW

Confucianism a Chinese belief system based on the teachings of Confucius

▶ Reading Strategy

Re-create the web diagram shown at right. As you read and respond to the **KEY QUESTIONS**, use the outer ovals to record main ideas about changes in Chinese culture. Add ovals as needed.

 See Skillbuilder Handbook, page R4

FIND MAIN IDEAS

Influence of western nations

CHANGES IN CHINESE CULTURE

🔁 **GRAPHIC ORGANIZERS**
Go to **Interactive Review** @ ClassZone.com

Changing Chinese Culture

Connecting to Your World

Have you ever asked your grandparents what life was like when they were your age? Cultural change can happen at any place and time. For example, Mei (may) Ling's grandmother, who lives in the country, talks of the village school she attended. Mei Ling's parents moved to Shanghai in search of better jobs. As a result, Mei Ling attends a big urban school instead of a village school. The move from the farm to the city is just one type of change in China. In this section, you'll learn how traditional Chinese culture is affected by these changes.

Chinese Family Like Mei Ling, this Chinese girl has a strong relationship with her grandmother.

Traditional Chinese Culture

🔽 **KEY QUESTION** What are some aspects of traditional Chinese culture?

Chinese culture is thousands of years old. Though life has changed in modern China, traditional values—such as close family ties and respect for one's parents and ancestors—remain strong.

Martial Arts Chinese students practice traditional martial arts.

Family and Village Life In traditional Chinese culture, family was very important. Older men made all the major decisions for the family. Men were taught to perform **rituals** honoring their ancestors. Women were taught that it was their duty to marry, have children, and care for their husbands' parents. Children were expected to respect their parents and care for them in old age.

For thousands of years, most Chinese people were farmers. Each day the villagers would go out to the fields to work. Nearly all Chinese lived in small rural villages of about 200 people. Houses in the village were crowded closely together. Most had a courtyard where chickens and pigs wandered in search of food. Small vegetable gardens provided food for the family meals. The villagers shared a well and bought some goods at local markets.

Beliefs Three different belief systems—Confucianism, Daoism, and Buddhism—have influenced Chinese life. **Confucianism** is the belief system based on the teachings of Confucius, whom you learned about in Section 2. In Confucianism, the person who is older or has more power has a responsibility to be kind to others. The younger or less powerful person is expected to be respectful and obedient. Confucianism also teaches that people can help to better themselves through education.

The second Chinese belief system, **Daoism** (DOW•IHZ•uhm), is based on the ideas of a teacher named Laozi. He taught that the world has a natural order and that a force called the **Dao** (DOW), meaning "the Way," guides all things. Laozi taught that people should observe nature and use those observations to find a way to peace and harmony.

Confucius' Birthday Celebration Dancers in traditional costumes celebrate the birth of Confucius in 551 B.C. **Why do the Chinese still honor Confucius?**

CONFUCIANISM

- Social order and good government should be based on strong family relationships.
- Respect for parents and elders helps to create order in society.
- Education helps to improve both individuals and society.

DAOISM

- The natural order—or the relationship among all living things in the universe— matters more than the social order.
- A universal force called the Dao (meaning "the Way") guides all things.
- Humans should learn to live simply and in harmony with nature.

BUDDHISM

- People suffer because of emotional attachments and their desire for worldly goods.
- People can stop suffering and achieve peace (or nirvana) by not wanting.
- To achieve nirvana, people should follow the Eightfold Path: right views, goals, speech, actions, job, effort, concentration, and meditation.

CRITICAL THINKING

Compare and Contrast How are the three belief systems similar? How are they different?

Missionaries who traveled the **Silk Roads**, the trade routes used between China and Southwest Asia, brought **Buddhism** to China. Buddhism is a religion based on the teachings of **Siddhartha Gautama** (sihd•DAHR•tuh GAW•tuh•muh), also known as the **Buddha**, or "enlightened one." Buddha taught that people suffer because their minds are not at ease. This suffering comes from wanting life to be different. The Buddha said people could stop the suffering by accepting life as it is and following the Eightfold Path, detailed above.

Written Language The development of a written Chinese language allowed the government to communicate with people in all parts of the empire, no matter what language they spoke. Chinese characters do not represent sounds, as Western letters do. They represent ideas or words. People who spoke differently could still read each other's letters because they used the same characters to write.

The Arts Some of traditional China's greatest achievements in the arts were in bronze casting, jade carving, and dance. Bronze objects such as bells and containers featured geometric designs and were decorated with tigers, snakes, birds, and oxen. Jade was used to make jewelry, containers, and statues. There were two kinds of traditional Chinese dance: one based on proper behavior as taught by Confucius, and one based on Chinese warrior exercises, which we call martial arts.

SUMMARIZE Discuss some of the aspects of traditional Chinese culture.

Chinese Character This character stands for the Dao, which means "the way."

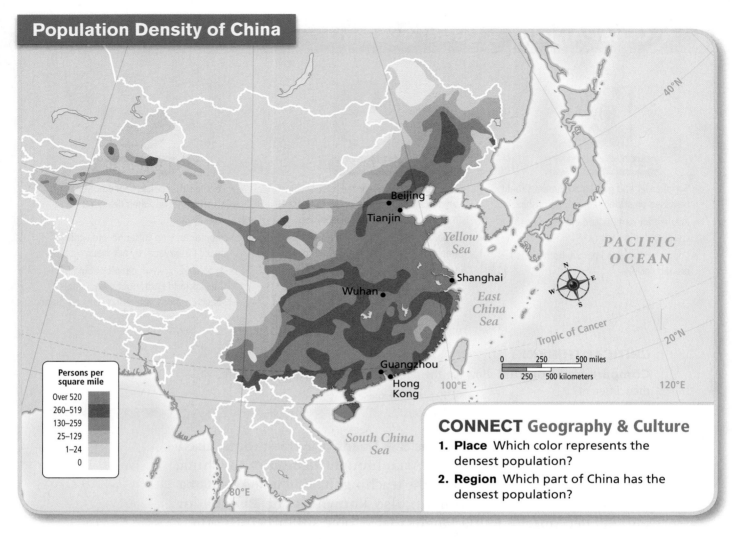

Beijing
Tianjin
Yellow Sea
PACIFIC OCEAN
Shanghai
Wuhan
East China Sea
Tropic of Cancer
20°N
Guangzhou
Hong Kong
100°E
120°E
South China Sea
80°E
40°N

0 250 500 miles
0 250 500 kilometers

Persons per square mile

Over 520
260–519
130–259
25–129
1–24
0

CONNECT Geography & Culture
1. **Place** Which color represents the densest population?
2. **Region** Which part of China has the densest population?

Changes in Chinese Life

▼ **KEY QUESTION** How did life change in China after the Communists took over?

The traditional Chinese way of life changed dramatically with the rise of communism. Family farms ceased to exist, and farms were reorganized into **communal** farms where ownership was shared. The farms were strictly controlled by the government. Every family had a registration booklet listing its members. Families needed the booklet to get food, medical services, housing, schooling, and jobs.

Moving to Cities As a part of the new way of life under the Communists, people had to get government permission to move. But little movement was allowed until after 1978, when economic reforms were made. These reforms brought new industry to the cities. As a result, workers were allowed to move from farms into towns or cities to fill jobs there. Workers also moved into cities on the east coast where the booming economy required many construction workers. Industry even began to emerge in rural areas.

Beijing China's capital is a crowded, rapidly modernizing city. Today, China has about 1.3 billion people, compared with about 298 million in the United States.

Population in China

1950

12.5%

87.5%

2005

40.5%

59.5%

■ Urban ■ Rural

Source: *China Statistical Yearbook 2004* and *Globalis*

CRITICAL THINKING
Compare and Contrast
By how much did the urban population increase between 1950 and 2005?

The shift in population to the cities was a major change in Chinese society. Today, about 60 percent of Chinese people live in rural areas, compared to almost 88 percent in 1950. Part of the reason for this spectacular urban growth is due to the expanded industrial sites in smaller towns, especially in eastern China. China has 34 cities with over a million people. In comparison, the United States has 9 cities of that size. China's two largest cities, Beijing and Shanghai, are huge. At the end of 2004, Beijing had 14.9 million residents and Shanghai, China's largest city, had 17.4 million. The population of these two cities is about equal to that of the state of California.

Jobs and Education After the economic reforms of 1978, China's new leaders set very high standards for education. Today, students are expected to study many hours; they have little time for extracurricular activities. The law calls for school attendance through ninth grade. More rural children now complete nine years of schooling. Students must then do well on national exams to be able to go on to trade school, high school, or college. However, education is not free. Parents must pay fees and buy textbooks.

Cities have more educational opportunities than rural areas. Many city teenagers go on to high school. However, in the past, only a very small percentage of students went to college. Today, China's goal is to have 20 percent of its students in college by 2010.

▲ **EVALUATE** Explain how life changed in China after the Communists took over.

A Day in Cheng's Life

To learn more about Cheng and his world, go to the **Activity Center** @ ClassZone.com

In Chinese, Cheng's name looks like this:

Hi! My name is Cheng. I am 14 years old and live in Yihuang, a rural town of about 20,000 in eastern China. Studying is very important to me. But I don't study all the time! On weekends, my friends and I play table tennis, basketball, or use the computers at the community center. Let me tell you about my day.

7 A.M. I have breakfast with my parents before they go to work and I leave for school. Today we're having eggs, peanuts, and steamed buns for breakfast.

8 A.M.–5:30 P.M. I have a long school day. We begin by saluting the flag and exercising. During the day, I have classes in Chinese, math, science, and history.

6 P.M. I'm meeting my parents and other family members at my grandparents' house for dinner. Tonight we're having one of my favorites, Four Happiness Pork along with rice and vegetables.

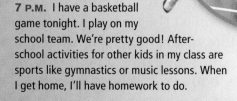

7 P.M. I have a basketball game tonight. I play on my school team. We're pretty good! After-school activities for other kids in my class are sports like gymnastics or music lessons. When I get home, I'll have homework to do.

CONNECT to Your Life

Journal Entry Think about your own daily schedule. What do you spend most of your day doing? How is your life different from Cheng's life? Record your ideas in your journal.

SECTION

4

GOVERNMENT & ECONOMICS

A Rising Power

Connecting to Your World

Take a look at the labels in your clothing or shoes, or on a small electronic device such as an inexpensive calculator. Many goods that Americans use every day are made in China. This is a big change from the days of Mao when most products produced in China stayed there. Chinese people had little contact with foreigners or their businesses. Today, China, a rising power in Asia and the world, welcomes foreigners and foreign companies.

A Strong Central Government

▼ **KEY QUESTION** Who controls China's central government?

For centuries, China has had a strong national government. It controlled **provinces**, state-like governmental units, and local areas. Today, the national government makes decisions that the provinces and local governments must carry out. The Chinese national law-making body is called the **National People's Congress**, or **NPC**. Local and provincial People's Congresses elect members of this body. However, in reality, the Communist Party sets the country's policies by selecting candidates for elections and controlling the NPC.

2008 Summer Olympics
When China hosts the Summer Olympics in 2008, thousands of foreigners will have an opportunity to see how much more modern China has become.

Shanghai Harbor Shanghai's harbor is one of the largest ports in the world.

785

Government and the Communist Party As you can see in the diagram below, the NPC chooses the president and the State Council, or cabinet. The president chooses a prime minister to run the government. The NPC also selects judges for the courts. However, every government office is watched over by Communist Party officials. They make sure the government follows the Party's plans.

Political Trends You learned that the government keeps tight control of people's lives. Beginning in April 1989, **demonstrations** against corruption and for more democratic freedoms took place at Beijing's **Tiananmen** (tyahn•ahn•mehn) **Square**. In early June, the government brutally cracked down on the demonstrators. But the event reflected increasing citizen pressure for reforms in China.

Today, people are a little freer to protest against government policies. But the government still limits many basic rights. Demonstrations are often broken up by force. Protestors are beaten or jailed if they continue to speak out against the government.

▲ **FIND MAIN IDEAS** Tell who controls China's central government.

COMPARING ◀ Chinese and U.S. Governments

CHINESE GOVERNMENT
Chinese citizens elect members of their local People's Congress. After that election they have no more input into government.

LOCAL PEOPLE'S CONGRESSES
↓ select ↓

NATIONAL PEOPLE'S CONGRESS
↓ select ↓ select ↓ select ↓

PRESIDENT   JUDICIARY
MILITARY COMMISSION   STATE COUNCIL

U.S. GOVERNMENT
U.S. citizens elect representatives and the President for the national government.

CITIZENS
↓ elect ↓

CONGRESS   PRESIDENT
approve ↓   ↓ appoint

SUPREME COURT

CRITICAL THINKING
1. **Compare and Contrast** How is the selection of a president in China different from the selection of a president in the United States?
2. **Evaluate** How does division of power in the U.S. government differ from China's?

Economic Reforms

▼ **KEY QUESTION** How did economic reforms bring Western influences to China?

Under Mao, China had a **command economy**. That means the central government owned all the land, materials, and factories. It decided what goods would be produced. However, in 1978, leader Deng Xiaoping (duhng show•pihng) began to allow elements of **free enterprise**. In this type of economy, people can own a business and sell their products for a profit. The government invited foreign companies to invest in big projects and build factories in China.

International Trade The **reforms**, or improvements, described above dramatically changed China's economy. Today, China makes more low-cost goods than any other country and is a big player in international trade. Most of China's trade is with the United States, Taiwan, and Japan. As you can see in the graph below, in 15 years China's exports and imports skyrocketed.

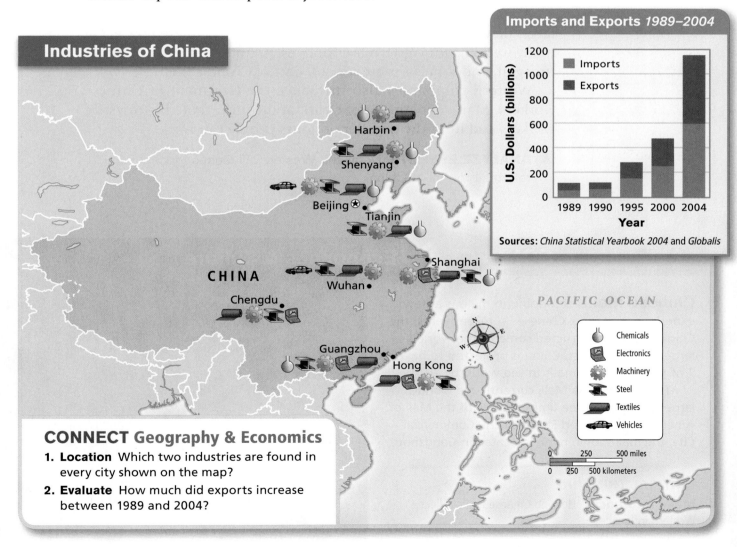

Industries of China

Imports and Exports *1989–2004*

Sources: *China Statistical Yearbook 2004* and *Globalis*

Chemicals
Electronics
Machinery
Steel
Textiles
Vehicles

CONNECT Geography & Economics

1. **Location** Which two industries are found in every city shown on the map?
2. **Evaluate** How much did exports increase between 1989 and 2004?

More Economic Opportunities The Chinese government still owns part of most large Chinese firms, but now there are also many privately owned Chinese companies. In a move to attract foreign businesses, Chinese cities give companies tax breaks. They have also built airports, hotels, malls, and public transportation. Many foreign companies build factories in China. Some sell their products in China, and others buy products made by Chinese companies. As a result, many new jobs have been created.

Now the government is starting to develop western China. It is building roads and railways to the area and drilling there for oil and natural gas. Foreign companies are opening offices, factories, and stores in western Chinese cities.

Western Influences Economic changes have brought more Chinese people into contact with Europeans and Americans. Some of these people are students, scientists, and business people who travel to the West. Others work with Westerners in China. As a result, these groups have become more comfortable with Western ideas.

American and European chains opened stores in China—some in large, new malls like the one shown below. The Chinese now eat at many well-known Western fast-food restaurants. Water parks, miniature golf, and ski resorts are now all part of Chinese life.

Western companies also influence the treatment of Chinese workers. Many demand safe, clean, and comfortable factories for workers and limit the number of hours people can work.

▲ **ANALYZE EFFECTS** Detail the Western influences that economic reforms brought to China.

CONNECT ⟳ Economics & Culture

Chinese Malls Shopping in malls is a new experience for most Chinese. In recent years, the Chinese have constructed some of the world's largest malls. In fact, China is projected to have 7 of the 10 largest malls in the world by 2010.

The South China Mall, currently the world's largest, is about three times the size of the Mall of America in the United States. Luchu Commercial City, the mall shown here, is located in Gangzhou.

CRITICAL THINKING

Make Inferences How do Chinese malls reflect Western influences?

Current Issues and Trends

▼ **KEY QUESTION** What challenges does China face in the 21st century?

With a population of over a billion, China needs to make sure its economy continues to grow. That growth is needed to supply enough jobs for its workers. The transportation and communication systems need to be expanded, and the country also needs to generate more electricity. As you learned in Section 1, the Three Gorges Dam will help produce more electricity. China has plans for 46 additional dams. However, this expansion does not come without problems. Huge projects like the dams or the creation of immense farms in western China often have negative effects on the environment.

Environment China faces serious air and water pollution problems. The country has 16 of the 20 most polluted cities in the world. China ranks behind only the United States in the creation of greenhouse gases. Because most industries use coal for fuel, China also creates large amounts of sulphur dioxide, a gas that contributes to acid rain. Agricultural projects in the northwestern regions of China have turned some farms into dust bowls. Each year, dust blowing out of China sweeps into Korea, Japan, and the United States.

Many rivers and lakes are polluted with wastes from manufacturing processes and raw sewage. Overall, about 700 million people only have contaminated water to use for drinking, cooking, and bathing. The Chinese government has begun to actively enforce environmental protection laws.

Expanding Freedoms In part, the Chinese government began to work on environmental issues as a result of pressure from groups within the country. Changes in China's government have made some environmental protests possible.

Though Chinese society is changing, concerns about basic personal freedoms remain. For example, many workers are forced to work long hours in unhealthy conditions. Some religious groups are not allowed to worship as they wish. As a result, newly formed civic organizations are looking for ways to gain democratic freedoms for the Chinese people.

Air Pollution Getting to work in Chinese cities often requires masks to filter out harmful pollution. Lung-related diseases are on the rise in polluted cities. **Why has pollution increased so much in Chinese cities?**

Chinese Space Program Two years after its first manned space flight, China put two more astronauts in space. They spent five days performing experiments and testing equipment. **What does having a space program tell you about the nation?**

Space Program As China develops, it has tried to show the world that it is a modern nation. Its space program, which China began in the 1950s, is one of those efforts. By 1970, it had sent a satellite into orbit. China's spacecraft are launched and returned to China's space center located in Inner Mongolia.

Only three nations in the world—China, the United States, and Russia—have a manned space program. In 2003, the spacecraft Shenzhou V (shen•joh five) carried a Chinese taikonaut, or astronaut, into space. The name of the spacecraft means "Divine Vessel." In 2005, millions of Chinese watched on television as two men were sent into space in Shenzhou VI. China's space program has a goal of reaching the moon with an unmanned probe by the year 2010. Eventually, China will launch a space station. The Chinese government hopes their space program will build Chinese pride and show the rest of the world how far China has advanced in science and technology.

▲ **CATEGORIZE** Discuss the challenges that China faces in the future.

Section 4 Assessment

ONLINE QUIZ
For test practice, go to **Interactive Review** @ ClassZone.com

TERMS & NAMES

1. Explain the importance of
- NPC
- Tiananmen Square
- command economy
- free enterprise

USE YOUR READING NOTES

2. Summarize Use your completed chart to answer the following question:

What economic challenges does China face?

GOVERNMENT	ECONOMY	ISSUES AND TRENDS

KEY IDEAS

3. What role does the Chinese Communist Party play in the government of China?

4. How has China's economy changed since the death of Mao?

5. Why are some Chinese concerned about basic personal freedoms?

CRITICAL THINKING

6. Synthesize In what way is the Communist Party more powerful than the Chinese government?

7. Draw Conclusions How might the presence of Western companies in China change working conditions?

8. **CONNECT to Today** How could environmental problems hold back the growth of China's economy?

9. **MATHEMATICS** **Create a Graph** Review the chart on exports and imports. Create a line graph with one line showing China's exports and one line showing its imports.

Interactive ◀◀Review

Click here to complete these and other activities online @ ClassZone.com

CHAPTER SUMMARY

Key Idea 1
China has varied landforms, ranging from high mountains to river valleys. It has diverse climates, plants, and animals.

Key Idea 2
Throughout history, China's rulers have struggled with the problem of feeding so many people.

Key Idea 3
Some aspects of traditional life survive in China, while new ways of life have been introduced.

Key Idea 4
Small changes in the Chinese government and big changes in the Chinese economy are taking place.

For **Review and Study Notes**, go to **Interactive Review** @ ClassZone.com

NAME GAME

Use the Terms & Names list to complete each sentence on paper or online.

1. I am also known as the Yellow River or "China's Sorrow." **Huang He** 🖐

2. I am China's longest river and the Three Gorges Dam was built to control my floods. _____

3. I am the highest mountain range in the world and divide China from India. _____

4. I am the emperor who united China. _____

5. I am the second-largest sand desert in the world. _____

6. I am a high desert that divides Mongolia and China. _____

7. I will provide hydroelectric power to parts of China. _____

8. I am the area where China's earliest civilization began. _____

9. I am the routes that brought traders and Buddhism to China. _____

10. I am the location of an important political demonstration for democratic rights. _____

Buddhism
Chang Jiang
Confucianism
Gobi Desert
Great Wall
Himalayas
Huang He
Mao Zedong
Middle Kingdom
North China Plain
Shi Huangdi
Silk Roads
Taklimakan Desert
Three Gorges Dam
Tiananmen Square

Activities

GeoGame

Use this online map to show what you know about China's location, geographic features, and important places. Drag and drop each place name to its location on the map.

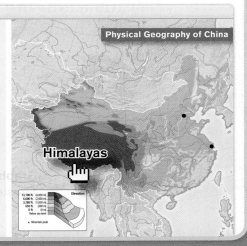

Geo GAME

Himalayas

North China Plain

South Korea

Beijing

Shanghai

To play the complete game, go to **Interactive Review** @ ClassZone.com

Crossword Puzzle

Complete an online crossword puzzle to test your knowledge of China's road to the present.

ACROSS
1. the first emperor to rule China

VOCABULARY

Explain the significance of each of the following.

1. Three Gorges Dam
2. Taklimakan Desert
3. Chang Jiang
4. Shi Huangdi
5. Confucianism
6. Mao Zedong
7. Daoism
8. Silk Roads
9. Buddhism
10. National People's Congress

Explain how the terms and names in each group are related.

11. Confucianism, Daoism, and Buddhism
12. Shi Huangdi and Mao Zedong

KEY IDEAS

1 Land of Three Rivers

13. How does China depend on its rivers?
14. What crops are grown in eastern China?
15. What natural disasters are most common in China?

2 Middle Kingdom to Communist Power

16. What was the Mandate of Heaven?
17. How did Confucius' teaching help produce order?
18. What was Mao Zedong's goal for China, and how did he try to accomplish it?

3 Changing Chinese Culture

19. What is the role of family in Chinese life?
20. Which of China's three belief systems had the greatest influence on Chinese society and government? Why?
21. Where do the majority of Chinese live?

4 A Rising Power

22. What is the role of the NPC in China's government?
23. What has China done to improve its economy?
24. Why are the Chinese concerned about their environment?

CRITICAL THINKING

25. **Compare and Contrast** Create a chart to compare and contrast the landforms and water, climate, and population density of eastern China and western China.

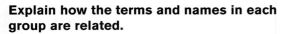

EASTERN CHINA	WESTERN CHINA

26. **Analyze Causes and Effects** How did China change after Shi Huangdi unified it?
27. **Draw Conclusions** What parts of Chinese culture have changed little since dynastic times?
28. **Connect to Economics** How has the right to own private businesses changed the economy in China?
29. **Five Themes: Human-Environment Interaction** Explain which natural barriers helped to shape Chinese civilization.
30. **Connect Geography & Economics** How will the presence of oil and natural gas in western China influence its economy?

Answer the
ESSENTIAL QUESTION

How is China's traditional way of life changing in response to global trends?

Written Response Write a two- or three-paragraph response to the Essential Question. Use the rubric below to guide your thinking.

Response Rubric
A strong response will:
• identify the characteristics of traditional life
• discuss the modern global trends affecting China
• explain ways in which the Chinese culture has adapted to the global trends

STANDARDS-BASED ASSESSMENT

THEMATIC MAP

Use the map to answer questions 1 and 2 on your paper.

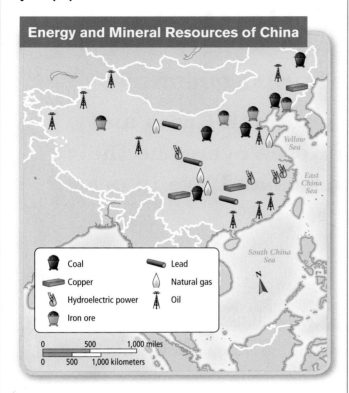

Energy and Mineral Resources of China

Yellow Sea

East China Sea

South China Sea

N

Coal
Copper
Hydroelectric power
Iron ore
Lead
Natural gas
Oil

0   500   1,000 miles
0   500   1,000 kilometers

1. Which source of energy is found throughout China?

A. coal
B. hydroelectric power
C. natural gas
D. oil

2. Where is most of China's hydroelectric power found?

A. in the far west
B. in the southeast
C. in central China
D. in the far north

LINE GRAPH

Examine the graph below. Use the information in the graph to write short answers for questions 3 and 4.

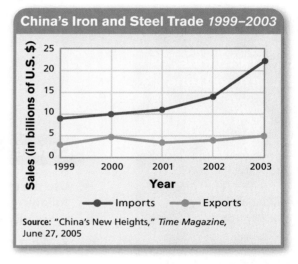

China's Iron and Steel Trade *1999–2003*

Sales (in billions of U.S. $)

25
20
15
10
5
0

1999   2000   2001   2002   2003

Year

— Imports   — Exports

Source: "China's New Heights," *Time Magazine,* June 27, 2005

3. What was the approximate value of China's exports in 2001?

4. Based on the graph, how would you describe China's iron and steel trade between 1999 and 2003?

GeoActivity

1. INTERDISCIPLINARY ACTIVITY–SCIENCE

With a small group, review the Chinese inventions discussed in Section 2. Choose one invention to research further and create a museum-style display. Be sure your display shows how the invention works, and explain how it changed life in China or elsewhere.

2. WRITING FOR SOCIAL STUDIES

Reread the part of Section 3 on Chen's day. Imagine that Chen is coming to visit your town or city. Write a tour schedule describing the places you would take Chen so that he would experience life the way you do.

3. MENTAL MAPPING

Create an outline map of China and label the following:

• Himalayas
• Huang He
• Chang Jiang
• Gobi Desert
• Taklimakan Desert
• East China Sea
• Yellow Sea
• Beijing

The Korean Peninsula

 ESSENTIAL QUESTION

How can North Korea and South Korea overcome their differences and live in peace?

CONNECT ➤ Geography & History

Use the map and the time line to answer the following questions.

1. Which countries are the Koreas' closest neighbors?
2. What major religion spread to the Korean Peninsula from China?

Culture

◄ **300s** Buddhism is introduced from China.

A.D. 300

Government

1392 The Choson Dynasty is established and rules until 1910.

History

660s The kingdom of Silla unifies the Korean Peninsula.
(Silla crown) ►

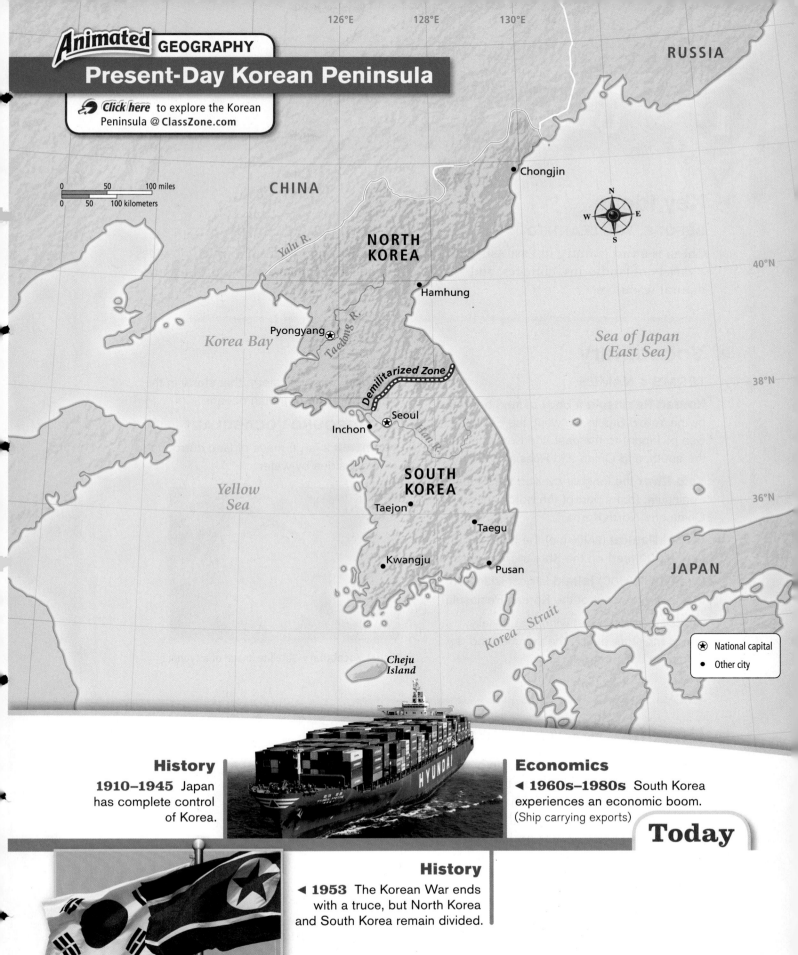

126°E   128°E   130°E

RUSSIA

CHINA

0   50   100 miles
0   50   100 kilometers

Yalu R.

NORTH
KOREA

• Chongjin

N
W   E
S

40°N

• Hamhung

Pyongyang ✪

Taedong R.

Korea Bay

*Sea of Japan
(East Sea)*

Demilitarized Zone

✪ Seoul

38°N

Inchon •

Han R.

*Yellow
Sea*

SOUTH
KOREA

Taejon •

• Taegu

36°N

Kwangju •

• Pusan

JAPAN

Korea Strait

*Cheju
Island*

✪ National capital
• Other city

History
1910–1945 Japan
has complete control
of Korea.

Economics
◄ **1960s–1980s** South Korea
experiences an economic boom.
(Ship carrying exports)

Today

History
◄ **1953** The Korean War ends
with a truce, but North Korea
and South Korea remain divided.

Reading for Understanding

▶ Key Ideas

BEFORE, YOU LEARNED

China is a vast country in East Asia with a variety of landforms, climates, and natural resources.

NOW YOU WILL LEARN

Korea lies on a peninsula, which provides a moderate climate and plentiful resources.

▶ Vocabulary

TERMS & NAMES

Korean Peninsula a body of land bordered by the Yellow Sea to the west, the East Sea (or Sea of Japan) to the east, the Korea Strait to the south, and China and Russia to the north

Yalu River the longest river on the Korean Peninsula; forms part of the border between China and North Korea

Mount Paektu (PAHK•too) the highest mountain (9,003 feet) on the Korean Peninsula

Cheju (CHEH•JOO) **Island** largest island off the southern coast of the Korean Peninsula

monsoon a seasonal wind that usually brings moist air during the summer and dry air during the winter

typhoon a tropical storm that starts in the western Pacific or Indian oceans

BACKGROUND VOCABULARY

peninsula a large mass of land surrounded on three sides by water

Visual Vocabulary satellite image of a typhoon

▶ Reading Strategy

Re-create the web diagram shown at right. As you read and respond to the **KEY QUESTIONS**, use the diagram to record main ideas about the physical geography of North Korea and South Korea. Add ovals or start a new diagram as needed.

 Skillbuilder Handbook, page R4

FIND MAIN IDEAS

Landforms — KOREA'S PHYSICAL GEOGRAPHY — Plants

Climate — Animals

Resources

GRAPHIC ORGANIZERS
Go to **Interactive Review** @ ClassZone.com

A Rugged Peninsula

Connecting to Your World

Have you ever seen a photograph of a sunrise over a mountain range, such as the Rockies or Appalachians in the United States? These pictures often convey a sense of calm and peace. Korea is dominated by mountainous terrain. The peaceful sunrises over its mountains have inspired people to call Korea the "Land of the Morning Calm." The peninsula's rocky landscape has played a large part in shaping the history and culture of the Korean people.

An Isolated Land

▼ KEY QUESTION What are some of the geographic features of the Korean Peninsula?

Korea is a **peninsula**, which means that it is surrounded on three sides by water: the East Sea (or Sea of Japan) to the east, the Yellow Sea to the west, and the Korea Strait to the south. China and Russia border Korea to the north. The **Korean Peninsula** has both isolated and protected its people. In fact, ancient Korea was called the "hermit kingdom." Today, the Korean Peninsula contains two nations—North Korea and South Korea. The tradition of isolation continues in North Korea, which has little contact with other nations.

Cheju Waterfall
According to legend, heavenly creatures bathed under this fall, which is surrounded by lush vegetation.

Mount Daedunsan
This mountain in South Korea is famous for its rocky cliffs.

The Korean Peninsula The map on the opposite page shows the bodies of water and landforms on the Korean Peninsula. As you have already learned, the Yellow Sea **A** is situated to the west of the peninsula. The Korea Strait lies between the peninsula's southern coast and the west coast of Japan. The eastern side of the Korean Peninsula borders the East Sea (also known as the Sea of Japan). The **Yalu River B**—known as the Amnok River in Korean—is the longest river on the peninsula. The Yalu and the Tumen rivers form the border between China and North Korea.

The rugged terrain of the Korean Peninsula consists of several mountain ranges. The Hamgyong (HAHM•GYUHNG) range extends along the peninsula's northern border and contains **Mount Paektu** (PAHK•too) **C**. At 9,003 feet, this peak is the highest on the peninsula. The Nangnim Mountains run from north to south through the center of North Korea. Farther south, the Taebaek (TAY•BACK) Mountains **D** run north to south along the eastern coast. Branching off from this range are the Sobaek Mountains, which extend across the center of South Korea.

More than 3,000 islands lie off the coasts of the Korean Peninsula. Many of them are small and uninhabited. But the largest, **Cheju** (CHEH•JOO) **Island E**, has a population of about 530,000. Cheju lies near the southern part of the peninsula and plays an active role in the culture and economy of South Korea.

Impact of Geography on Korea The isolation and protection provided by Korea's geography have allowed the Koreans to develop their own distinct culture. Of course, Chinese culture has had a strong influence. But Koreans have always adapted this culture to fit their own. Koreans even adapted the Chinese language to create their own, as you'll learn at left.

In general, Koreans have been content to remain in their land and follow their own way of life. However, maintaining a peaceful Korean state has not always been easy. Korea's aggressive neighbors, China, Japan, and Russia, have each attempted to control the peninsula. You will learn more about how these superpowers affected Korea's history in Section 2.

▲ **SUMMARIZE** Describe some of the geographic features of the Korean Peninsula.

CONNECT ⟶ Geography & Culture

The Hangul Alphabet

For over a thousand years, educated Koreans used a complicated writing system based on Chinese characters. Then in the 1440s, King Sejong, shown below, created a simple Korean writing script. The result was the hangul alphabet, which allowed uneducated Koreans to learn to read and write. The characters below express the word *hello*.

안녕하세요

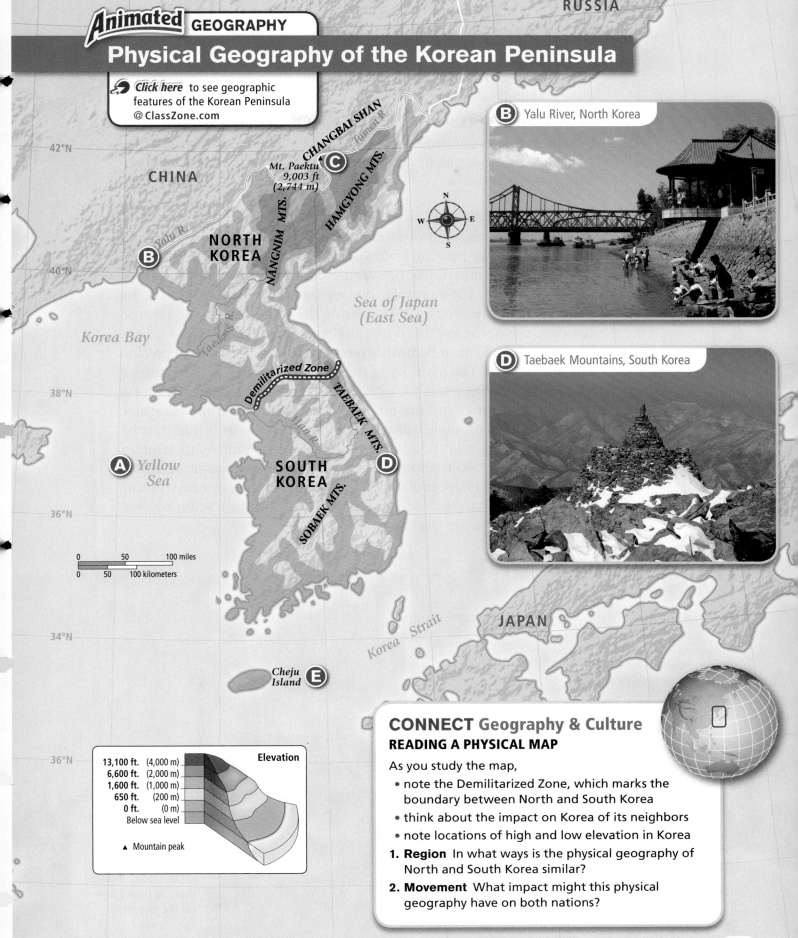

Physical Geography of the Korean Peninsula

Click here to see geographic features of the Korean Peninsula @ ClassZone.com

RUSSIA

CHINA

CHANGBAI SHAN

NORTH KOREA

Mt. Paektu 9,003 ft (2,744 m)

HAMGYONG MTS.

NANGNIM MTS.

Tumen R.

Yalu R.

Korea Bay

Taedong R.

Sea of Japan (East Sea)

Demilitarized Zone

TAEBAEK MTS.

Han R.

Yellow Sea

SOUTH KOREA

SOBAEK MTS.

B Yalu River, North Korea

D Taebaek Mountains, South Korea

N
W E
S

0   50   100 miles
0   50   100 kilometers

Korea Strait

JAPAN

Cheju Island **E**

Elevation

13,100 ft.   (4,000 m)
6,600 ft.   (2,000 m)
1,600 ft.   (1,000 m)
650 ft.   (200 m)
0 ft.   (0 m)
Below sea level

▲ Mountain peak

42°N
40°N
38°N
36°N
34°N
36°N

124°E   126°E   128°E   130°E   132°E

CONNECT Geography & Culture
READING A PHYSICAL MAP

As you study the map,

- note the Demilitarized Zone, which marks the boundary between North and South Korea
- think about the impact on Korea of its neighbors
- note locations of high and low elevation in Korea

1. **Region** In what ways is the physical geography of North and South Korea similar?

2. **Movement** What impact might this physical geography have on both nations?

Climate, Plants, and Animals

▼ **KEY QUESTION** What types of climates, plants, and animals are found on the Korean Peninsula?

The mountains of the Korean Peninsula and the seas that surround it both have a major impact on Korea's climate. This climate, in turn, has played a large role in determining the type of plant and animal life on the peninsula.

A Moderate Climate In general, the climate on the peninsula is moderate. Summer weather differs little throughout Korea, with average July temperatures ranging from 70°F to 80°F. But in the winter, the difference in temperature between North Korea and South Korea can be extreme. For example, the average January temperature in southeast Korea is around 35°F. During the same month, the average temperature in the northern mountains is only about –8°F.

Most of the Korean Peninsula receives around 40 inches of precipitation each year. The majority of this rain arrives during the summer monsoons. A **monsoon** is a seasonal wind that usually brings moist air during the summer and dry air during the winter. At times, summer monsoons help produce **typhoons**, fierce tropical storms that start in the western Pacific or Indian oceans. The Korean Peninsula is usually hit with one or two typhoons a year. Typhoons are similar to hurricanes, which you have probably heard about. Hurricanes are tropical storms that start in the northern Atlantic Ocean, the Caribbean Sea, or the eastern Pacific Ocean.

◄ COMPARING ► Climates

North Korea Winter in North Korea can be long, cold, and dry. **1. How do you think the winters affect the North Korean people?**

South Korea Spring temperatures average about 50°F in South Korea. **2. What impact does this climate appear to have on the country's vegetation?**

Plant and Animal Life The Korean Peninsula contains much diverse plant life, but the region's natural vegetation is largely forest. Today, forests cover about two-thirds of the land area of South Korea. Fir, spruce, pine, and elm trees grow in the northern and central parts of the country. Bamboo and evergreens grow along the southern coast.

The Korean Peninsula also has a wide variety of wildlife. Deer, mountain antelope, bears, and leopards make their home in mountainous areas and in the forests. Many types of birdlife also live on the peninsula, including herons, cranes, and wild pigeons. In addition, the peninsula is a popular stopover for ducks, wild geese, and swans migrating to Japan, Southeast Asia, and Australia.

As in much of the world, human activities have threatened the survival of wildlife on the Korean Peninsula, particularly in forested areas. People have cut down many of the trees for construction, heating, and cooking. This deforestation destroyed many of the animals' homes. Since the 1970s, however, strong efforts have been made to reforest the land. As a result, some animals that had been considered endangered are making a comeback. The black bear, for example, has returned to some remote mountain areas.

Some of the animals have been rescued by chance. In Section 2, you will learn about a wildlife preserve that accidentally developed along the border between North Korea and South Korea. This accidental preserve has become the Korean Peninsula's most important wildlife refuge.

Red-Crowned Crane In Korean culture, the red-crowned crane symbolizes happiness, good luck, and long life, and often appears in traditional paintings. **Why might a bird represent such positive attributes?**

 **CATEGORIZE** Tell what types of climates, plants, and animals are found on the Korean Peninsula.

Natural Resources

▼ **KEY QUESTION** How are the natural resources of North Korea and South Korea similar and different?

The rainfall and warm temperatures during the summer make Korea's climate ideal for growing rice. But the rocky terrain of the peninsula makes farmland scarce. Koreans have been able to squeeze tiny fields along hillsides by using terraced farming. Even so, the overall lack of good farmland has led Koreans to rely on other resources, including the abundant fish along the coastlines and mineral deposits.

Farmland and Agriculture The largest portion of farmland on the Korean Peninsula is found on the western and southern coastal plains. Because of overuse, however, the soil is not very fertile. To remedy this, farmers have extensively used irrigation and fertilizers.

Since most of the best farmland is located in South Korea, this nation has a much higher crop yield than North Korea. Rice is the most important crop in both North Korea and South Korea. These nations also grow wheat, potatoes, and barley. South Koreans, in addition, grow Chinese cabbage, melons, onions, and soybeans. Cheju Island is famous for its mandarin oranges. In fact, Cheju oranges constitute South Korea's major cash fruit crop.

Fishing The lack of usable land has affected Korea's fishing industry. Since the Korean Peninsula does not have enough land to raise much livestock, Koreans rely on fish as an important source of protein. As a result, the fishing industries of the Koreas have risen to keep up with the nutritional needs of the rising population. Both North Korea and South Korea have taken full advantage of their extensive coastal areas. In fact, South Korea has become one of the major deep-sea fishing countries of the world.

CONNECT   Geography & Culture

Women Divers of Cheju Island

For more than 1,500 years, the women divers, or *haenyo*, of Cheju Island have caught shellfish, squid, and sea urchins, such as the one shown here. This seafood has provided the main source of nourishment for themselves and their families. Their husbands often stay at home and watch the children.

The women divers work until they are well into their 60s—and beyond. They can plunge down to depths of 60 feet and stay underwater for three to five minutes. And all of this is done without the aid of any breathing equipment. This tradition of diving has been handed down from mother to daughter for generations.

CRITICAL THINKING

Make Inferences What inferences can you make about the women divers?

Mineral Resources The vast majority of mineral resources on the Korean Peninsula are in the north. In fact, North Korea has the largest magnesite deposit in the world. Other minerals include iron ore, coal, gold, lead, and zinc. North Koreans have taken advantage of these rich deposits by mining them extensively. Mineral resources in South Korea are few. However, the nation does have some large graphite and tungsten deposits.

Most of North Korea's electric power is produced by coal-burning plants. In contrast, the majority of electricity in South Korea is provided by petroleum-burning plants. However, this nation has to import all of its oil. As a result, the oil crisis of the 1970s hit South Korea hard. To reduce South Korea's dependency on oil, the government had built 20 nuclear power plants by 2006. By 2015, the government hopes to have about 30 such plants.

 COMPARE AND CONTRAST Explain how the natural resources of North Korea and South Korea are similar and different.

Minerals in the Koreas	
Minerals	**Uses**
Graphite	• pencils • applications that involve high heat
Magnesite	• flooring materials • fertilizers • bricks
Tungsten	• filament in light bulbs • heating element in electric furnaces
Zinc	• coating on iron and steel to protect from corrosion • batteries

Section 1 Assessment

ONLINE QUIZ For test practice, go to **Interactive Review** @ ClassZone.com

TERMS & NAMES

1. Explain the importance of
- Korean Peninsula
- Yalu River
- Mount Paektu
- Cheju Island

USE YOUR READING NOTES

2. Find Main Ideas Use your completed web to answer the following question:

What impact have people had on the vegetation on the Korean Peninsula?

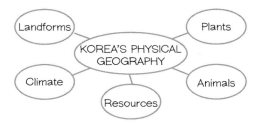

KEY IDEAS

3. What are some of the major mountain ranges of the Korean Peninsula?

4. Why did deforestation occur on the Korean Peninsula?

5. What have Korean farmers done to try to make their soil more fertile?

CRITICAL THINKING

6. Draw Conclusions How has the geography of the Korean Peninsula influenced Korea's culture?

7. Compare and Contrast How do the climates of North Korea and South Korea differ?

8. CONNECT to Today How has South Korea recently reduced its dependency on oil?

9. WRITING Compose an Essay Research and write an essay about the deep-sea fishing industry in South Korea. Include information about the types of ships used, the methods used to catch various fish, and the effect of this fishing on the environment.

Reading for Understanding

▶ Key Ideas

BEFORE, YOU LEARNED

Korea is surrounded by powerful neighbors, including China, Russia, and Japan.

NOW YOU WILL LEARN

The Korean Peninsula has been invaded by China, Russia, and Japan but has still maintained its cultural identity.

▶ Vocabulary

TERMS & NAMES

Three Kingdoms the three kingdoms that had formed on the Korean Peninsula by A.D. 300

Korean War (1950–1953) a conflict between North Korea and the Soviet Union on one side and South Korea, the United States, and the UN on the other

demilitarized zone a buffer zone between North Korea and South Korea

shamanism (SHAH•muh•NIHZ•uhm) a belief system in which a person called a shaman is believed to be able to communicate with spirits and heal the sick

celadon (SEHL•uh•DAHN) Korean ceramic pottery with a thin blue or green glaze

hanbok a traditional Korean costume

kimchi (KIHM•chee) a Korean dish made of pickled vegetables

REVIEW

Confucianism a belief system based on the teachings of Confucius

Buddhism a religion that began in India and is based on the teachings of Siddhartha Gautama

Visual Vocabulary *hanbok*

▶ Reading Strategy

Re-create the chart shown at right. As you read and respond to the **KEY QUESTIONS**, use the chart to summarize what you have learned about the history and culture of the Korean Peninsula.

 Skillbuilder Handbook, page R5

SUMMARIZE

KOREAN HISTORY	KOREAN CULTURE
The first state. . .	

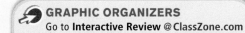

GRAPHIC ORGANIZERS
Go to **Interactive Review** @ ClassZone.com

Strong Traditions, Modern Innovations

Connecting to Your World

You have probably learned that the United States was torn apart by a civil war between the North and the South during the 1860s. After four years of fighting, the two sides reunited to form a stronger union. In the 1950s, Korea became a battleground for a war waged by the United States and the Soviet Union. The war pitted North Korea against South Korea. But this conflict had a different ending: North and South Korea remained divided. As you will see, however, the Korean Peninsula has been united for much of its history.

Korean History

▼ **KEY QUESTION** What are the major events in Korean history?

The first state on the Korean Peninsula was established around 2000 B.C. It took the name *Choson.* Around 108 B.C., China conquered the northern part of the peninsula. However, Korean tribes gradually won back the territory. In the northern area of the Korean Peninsula, several tribes united during the A.D. 100s and formed the state of Koguryo (KOH•gur•YOO). By about 300, two other states had been created on the peninsula. Historians refer to these states as the **Three Kingdoms**.

Koguryo Painting
A Korean noble-woman is waited on by her attendants in this fourth-century tomb mural painting.

Three Kingdoms Period The Three Kingdoms were Koguryo in the northeast, Paekche (PAHK•CHAY) in the southwest, and Silla (SIHL•uh) in the southeast. The kingdoms had much in common. For example, they all had a strong military system, which they used to help them expand their territory. In addition, each had powerful kings and aristocracies made up of tribal chiefs.

During the 660s, Silla conquered Paekche and Koguryo and took control of the entire peninsula. Unified Silla was broken apart by rebels in the 800s. But the state reunited around 935 and called itself *Koryo*. *Korea* comes from *Koryo*. In 1392, a general named Yi Song-gye became the ruler of Korea. He gave the country back its ancient name of Choson. The Choson Dynasty lasted until 1910, more than 500 years.

Japanese Conquest Starting in the 1600s, the rulers of the Choson Dynasty closed Korea to all foreigners. In 1876, however, Japan forced Korea to open a few ports to trade. Soon, the United States, Russia, and several European nations signed trade agreements with Korea. In 1904 and 1905, Japan fought Russia for control over Manchuria. Japan won the Russo-Japanese War and then attacked Korea. By 1910, the Japanese had gained complete control of Korea.

ANALYZING Primary Sources

The Proclamation of Korean Independence was published on March 1, 1919, during the Japanese occupation of Korea. It was inspired by the Fourteen Points of U.S. President Woodrow Wilson, which supported returning self-government to some occupied nations following World War I. The painting shown here depicts Japanese soldiers marching into Seoul.

> We have no desire to accuse Japan of breaking many solemn treaties since 1836, nor to single out specially the teachers in the schools or government officials who treat the heritage of our ancestors as a colony of their own, . . . finding delight only in beating us down and bringing us under their heel. . . . Our urgent need today is the settling up of this house of ours and not a discussion of who has broken it down, or what has caused its ruin.
>
> Source: Proclamation of Korean Independence

DOCUMENT–BASED QUESTION

What did the writers of this document probably hope to achieve?

During the Japanese occupation, Japan turned Korea into a colony to benefit its own interests. The Japanese government managed Korean farms and businesses and reduced the Koreans to low-paid workers in their own country. As the Japanese prepared for war during the 1930s, they tried to stamp out Korean culture. They even ordered Koreans to speak only Japanese and to take Japanese names. As World War II raged, Koreans were forced to help Japan's war effort and to endure many hardships. Japan's harsh rule is still a source of bitterness for many Koreans.

The Korean War Korea remained under Japanese rule until Japan was defeated in World War II in 1945. The Koreans wanted independence. But U.S. forces occupied southern Korea, and Soviet troops occupied the northern half. Soon, North Korea established a Communist government, and South Korea set up a republic.

In 1950, North Korean troops invaded South Korea, starting the **Korean War**. The Soviet Union had supplied North Korea with tanks, airplanes, and money in an attempt to take over the peninsula. South Korea fought back with Allied forces consisting of U.S. and UN troops. In time, China entered the war on the side of North Korea. You can follow the course of the war by studying the maps on this page. A cease-fire was declared in 1953, but no peace treaty was ever agreed on. In time, a 2.5-mile-wide buffer zone, called the **demilitarized zone** (DMZ), was set up. It separates North Korea and South Korea to this day.

The Allies lost about 500,000 troops, and the Communists lost around 1,500,000 troops. Civilian deaths were also very high. A total of about two million civilians died in North Korea and South Korea.

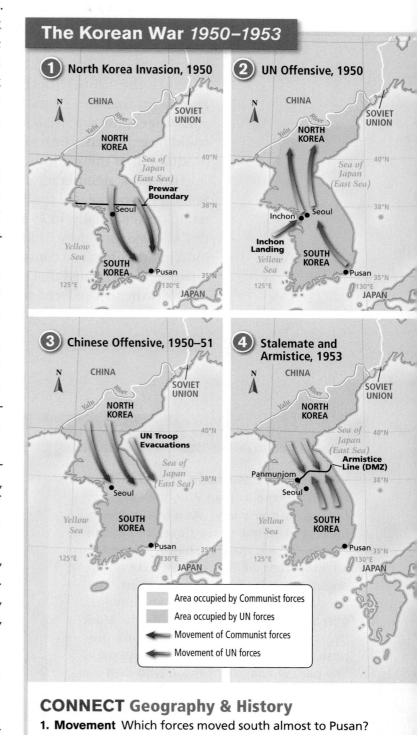

The Korean War *1950–1953*

1 North Korea Invasion, 1950

2 UN Offensive, 1950

3 Chinese Offensive, 1950–51

4 Stalemate and Armistice, 1953

Area occupied by Communist forces
Area occupied by UN forces
Movement of Communist forces
Movement of UN forces

CONNECT Geography & History

1. **Movement** Which forces moved south almost to Pusan?
2. **Region** Compare maps 1 and 4. Which side, if any, gained more territory?

Two Koreas In 1948, Kim Il Sung became North Korea's leader and continued to rule after the Korean War. Kim strove to make North Korea as self-sufficient as possible by emphasizing the development of heavy industry. He established a strict dictatorship. Kim died in 1994 and was succeeded by his son, Kim Jong Il. In the 2000s, North Korea started a nuclear weapons program, despite opposition from the United States, South Korea, and many other countries. North Korea has also been charged with numerous human rights violations.

Since the 1960s, South Korea has enjoyed an economic boom. The boom was due, in part, to financial aid from the United States and other countries. Also, South Korea began to produce goods that could be exported. The country used the resulting income to increase production of these goods.

However, democracy in South Korea has faced a rockier road. Several rulers violated the 1948 constitution and used the military to retain power. Finally, in 1987, South Korea adopted a new constitution that allowed for almost unlimited political freedom and granted greater individual rights. The constitution declared South Korea a democratic republic. It also stated that the country would seek reunification based on the principles of freedom and democracy. Some efforts have been made to reunify the two Koreas, as you will learn in Section 3.

▲ **SEQUENCE EVENTS** Discuss the major events in Korean history.

CONNECT ➤ History & Geography

Wildlife Preserve in the DMZ Since the end of the Korean War, the DMZ has been a no-man's-land. As a result, plants, birds, and animals have flourished in this region. In fact, the DMZ has developed into an important wildlife refuge. Extending about 150 miles from coast to coast, the zone has become home to many endangered animals, including the Asiatic black bears shown here. Some people have proposed turning the DMZ into a peace park. The park would honor those who died during the war and save the wildlife preserve.

CRITICAL THINKING
Make Predictions What might happen to the preserve if the two Koreas reunite?

To learn more about Yumi and her world, go to the **Activity Center** @ ClassZone.com

Hi! My name is Yumi. I am 14 years old and live in Seoul, the capital and largest city in South Korea. Seoul is a combination of old and new. For example, I live in a modern apartment complex, but nearby is Kyongbok, a medieval palace. My daily life also combines the old and new. Let me show you by describing a typical day.

In Korean, Yumi's name looks like this:

유미

6 A.M. Today, I am preparing for exams, so I get up early to study. Then I eat a traditional breakfast of rice, soup, kimchi, and fish. After breakfast, I ride my bike to school.

8 A.M.–3 P.M. At school, I study about new discoveries in science class and about my country's past in history class. Other courses include math and English. I eat a light lunch, which is provided by the school.

5 P.M. Sometimes, I spend a couple of hours after school with my friends. We go to shopping malls and play video games. But usually I have after-school classes in violin and English conversation.

7 P.M. I eat a traditional dinner with my family that includes rice and many *banchan* (side dishes). Then I study some more. When I can, I make time to watch my favorite TV show.

CONNECT to Your Life

Journal Entry Make a list of the recreational activities that you do on a regular basis. Then compare your activities with Yumi's. How are they different? How are they the same?

Haein-sa Temple This 8th-century temple houses the Tripitaka Koreana: woodblocks containing the most complete collection of Buddhist texts. **What do the woodblocks suggest about Buddhism in Korean culture?**

Preserving Korean Culture

▼ **KEY QUESTION** How have Koreans tried to preserve their distinct culture?

Over the past century, Korea has faced much adversity. But the Korean people are united by a common ethnicity and language—and the determination to preserve their culture.

Religious Beliefs The original belief system practiced on the Korean Peninsula is **shamanism**. A shaman is a person who is believed to be able to communicate with the spirit world and heal the sick. Another belief system, **Confucianism**, entered the peninsula around 100 B.C. from China. Confucianism stresses social order and good government and influences Korean society today.

Buddhism, an Indian religion that seeks to put an end to suffering, arrived during the A.D. 300s. It was the dominant religion in Korea for several hundred years. Today, many South Koreans still practice Buddhism. Christianity was introduced around 1784 and is South Korea's fastest-growing religion.

Many Koreans practice aspects of several religions. Because of this, South Korea has strong religious tolerance. North Korea, on the other hand, discourages any religious practice.

Korean Arts Buddhist influence can be seen in the many temples found throughout South Korea, such as the one above. These temples often contain stone towers called pagodas. They also include stone sculptures of Buddha.

Korean pottery has been strongly influenced by the Chinese. During the Koryo Dynasty, Korean artisans used Chinese techniques to develop a unique type of ceramic pottery called **celadon**. This pottery has a thin glaze that usually ranges in color from blue to green.

Celadon The ceramic pottery originated in China, but Korean potters made it their own. Even Chinese visitors remarked on the beauty of Korean celadon. ▶

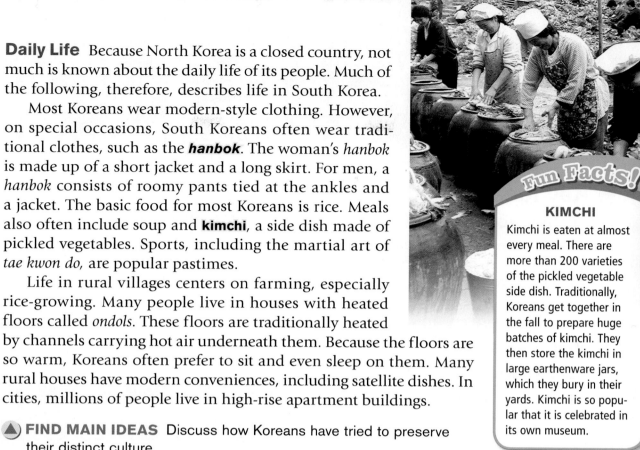

Daily Life Because North Korea is a closed country, not much is known about the daily life of its people. Much of the following, therefore, describes life in South Korea.

Most Koreans wear modern-style clothing. However, on special occasions, South Koreans often wear traditional clothes, such as the **hanbok**. The woman's *hanbok* is made up of a short jacket and a long skirt. For men, a *hanbok* consists of roomy pants tied at the ankles and a jacket. The basic food for most Koreans is rice. Meals also often include soup and **kimchi**, a side dish made of pickled vegetables. Sports, including the martial art of *tae kwon do,* are popular pastimes.

Life in rural villages centers on farming, especially rice-growing. Many people live in houses with heated floors called *ondols.* These floors are traditionally heated by channels carrying hot air underneath them. Because the floors are so warm, Koreans often prefer to sit and even sleep on them. Many rural houses have modern conveniences, including satellite dishes. In cities, millions of people live in high-rise apartment buildings.

 FIND MAIN IDEAS Discuss how Koreans have tried to preserve their distinct culture.

KIMCHI

Kimchi is eaten at almost every meal. There are more than 200 varieties of the pickled vegetable side dish. Traditionally, Koreans get together in the fall to prepare huge batches of kimchi. They then store the kimchi in large earthenware jars, which they bury in their yards. Kimchi is so popular that it is celebrated in its own museum.

Section 2 Assessment

ONLINE QUIZ
For test practice, go to
Interactive Review
@ ClassZone.com

TERMS & NAMES

1. Explain the importance of
- Three Kingdoms
- demilitarized zone
- celadon
- *hanbok*

USE YOUR READING NOTES

2. Summarize Use your completed chart to answer the following question:

Why did the Koreans deeply resent the Japanese occupation?

KOREAN HISTORY	KOREAN CULTURE
The first state. . .	

KEY IDEAS

3. What are some of the traits that the Three Kingdoms had in common?

4. How did Japan gain control over Korea?

5. What does life in rural villages center on?

CRITICAL THINKING

6. Make Inferences Do you think the Korean people benefited from the Korean War? Explain why or why not.

7. Sequence Events In what chronological order did major belief systems enter the Korean Peninsula?

8. CONNECT to Today Why do you think North Korea has recently started a nuclear weapons program?

9. TECHNOLOGY Create a Slide Show Using the Internet and your library, research the various artworks found in Buddhist temples, such as pagodas and sculptures. Then do a slide presentation that shows these works, and provide a brief history about each slide.

Reading for Understanding

▶ Key Ideas

BEFORE, YOU LEARNED

After the Korean War, the peninsula was divided into two countries: North Korea and South Korea.

NOW YOU WILL LEARN

North Korea and South Korea have very different government systems and economic structures.

▶ Vocabulary

TERMS & NAMES

totalitarian a type of government that controls every aspect of public and private life

Korean Workers' Party (KWP) a Communist political group that controls the government of North Korea

dictator a ruler who exercises complete political power

Kim Jong Il the leader of North Korea

chaebol (JEH•buhl) a family-owned conglomerate made up of related businesses

BACKGROUND VOCABULARY

conglomerate an organization made up of several companies in different businesses

Visual Vocabulary Samsung is a major *chaebol* in South Korea.

▶ Reading Strategy

Re-create the Venn diagram shown at right. As you read and respond to the **KEY QUESTIONS**, use the diagram to compare and contrast North Korea and South Korea.

 Skillbuilder Handbook, page R9

COMPARE AND CONTRAST

NORTH KOREA   BOTH   SOUTH KOREA

GRAPHIC ORGANIZERS
Go to **Interactive Review** @ ClassZone.com

Contrasting Countries

Connecting to Your World

Have you ever visited relatives in a nearby state? In the United States, making such a trip is pretty easy. However, similar visits have not been allowed between North Korea and South Korea for decades. When Korea split into two nations, many families were separated. As a result, Koreans could not visit relatives across the border at all. Recently, some movement between the two nations has been permitted, but only on a limited basis.

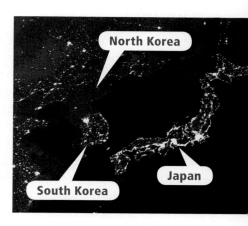

North Korea

South Korea

Japan

Satellite Image This nighttime image contrasts well-lit South Korea with the darkness of North Korea.

North Korea

▼ **KEY QUESTION** How are the government and economy of North Korea structured?

As you have learned, a Communist government was set up in North Korea that isolated its people from the rest of the world. As a result, most North Koreans have no contact with ideas that contradict their government. Also, North Korea became economically isolated, especially from the West. Instead of encouraging interaction with non-Communist economies, the government promotes a policy of *juche* (joo•cheh), or self-reliance.

North Korea May Day People hold colored placards to form a picture of Communist strength and victory in a show of national unity.

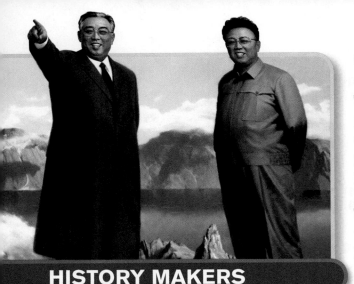

HISTORY MAKERS

Kim Jong Il born 1941

After Kim Il Sung (above left) died in 1994, his son, Kim Jong Il (above right), became the dictator of North Korea. Soon a cult developed within North Korea around the new leader. Official government accounts praised him as a godlike hero and created legends about his birth. To the outside world, however, Kim Jong Il is a secretive and dangerous figure who starves his people into submission. Above all, many regard Kim Jong Il's determination to develop nuclear weapons as a real threat to the United States and its allies.

ONLINE BIOGRAPHY
For more on the life of Kim Jong Il, go to the
Research & Writing Center @ ClassZone.com

Government North Korea is ruled by a highly centralized, totalitarian form of government. A **totalitarian** government controls every aspect of public and private life. The country does have a constitution, which, on paper, gives political power to the people. However, in reality, the people have almost no freedom. All of the power lies with a Communist group called the **Korean Workers' Party (KWP)**. This party controls elections and chooses who may run for office. The KWP itself is controlled by the chairman of the National Defense Commission. In effect, the chairman is a **dictator**, or a ruler who has complete political power. Since 1994, **Kim Jong Il** has been the chairman of the National Defense Commission and the dictator of North Korea. The country does have a law-making body called the Supreme People's Assembly. This legislature, though, has little power.

Since the early 2000s, the North Korean government has been dealing with an international dispute over its program to develop nuclear weapons. Many nations object to the program, but North Korea has refused to halt it. North Korea claims that it needs nuclear weapons to defend its people against possible aggressors.

Economy Like the government, all means of production in North Korea are controlled by the state. In addition, the economy stresses the good of the state over the welfare of the people. For example, the government spends huge amounts on military development. As a result, it has little money to invest in producing goods for its people.

The North Korean economy is also very isolated. True to its policy of self-reliance, the country has generally discouraged foreign investment. However, North Korea did accept economic aid from the former Soviet Union and from China.

North Korea's economic plans have not been a success. Since the late 1990s, the North Korean people have had one of the lowest standards of living in Asia. But hopeful signs have begun to emerge. During the last few years, South Korean businesses have started to move into North Korea. The money that these businesses make may help the North Korean people. The economic partnership may also help improve relations between the two countries.

Industries and Agriculture Throughout its history, North Korea has promoted heavy industry, especially for military production. Because of this, North Korea produces much military equipment, general machinery, steel, cement, textiles, and chemicals. The nation also heavily mines its many mineral deposits.

However, in the 1990s, the development of heavy industry in North Korea began to rapidly decline. One reason for this lies with the state's emphasis on military spending. North Korea spends so much on developing weapons that it does not have enough money to invest in its industrial equipment and infrastructure.

North Korea produces a variety of crops, including rice, barley, corn, wheat, and potatoes. Recently, though, crop production has fallen on hard times. During the mid-1990s, floods and droughts destroyed crops, causing thousands of people to starve to death. North Korean agriculture has never recovered. The lack of good farmland, the failures of state-run farms, and shortages of fertilizer and fuel have all added to the country's agricultural difficulties. In the early 2000s, North Korea has had to rely on aid from around the world to prevent its people from starving.

Fabric The production of textiles is an important industry in North Korea. The sales clerk shown here displays her colorful fabric in a Pyongyang department store.

▲ **EVALUATE** Discuss the structure of North Korea's government and economy.

CONNECT to Math

In the image below, a North Korean woman makes textiles for the trade market. Study the chart of North Korea's major trading partners, and then use the decimal numbers in it to play a rounding numbers matching game. Remember to round down any number that contains a decimal of 0.4 or less. Round up any number that contains a decimal of 0.5 or more.

North Korea's Major Trading Partners

3.8%   15.2%
6.0%
7.1%   39.0%
9.3%   19.6%

- ■ China
- ■ South Korea
- ■ Thailand
- ■ Japan
- ■ Russia
- ■ India
- ■ Others

Source: *KOTRA*, 2004

Activity

Rounding Numbers

1. Study the numbers in the box below. The numbers with decimals are taken from the trading partners pie chart.

2. Copy the Matching Game box on your paper.

3. Circle each number that contains a decimal. Then draw a line to match it with its rounded number.

Matching Game			
8	15.2	9	16
3	19.6	39.0	4
7	6	10	19
39	3.8	40	20
9.3	15	7.1	6.0

Voting South Koreans cast their ballots during the 2002 presidential election. **Does a similar election take place in North Korea?**

South Korea

▼ **KEY QUESTION** How do the government and economy of South Korea compare with those of North Korea?

In many ways, the government and economy of South Korea are the opposite of North Korea's government and economy. You can compare the two countries' governments in the feature below.

Government Like the United States, the South Korean government is divided into three branches—the executive, the legislative, and the judicial. The president heads the executive branch and serves a five-year term. He or she is chosen by popular election and cannot be reelected. The president appoints a prime minister, who handles the running of the government. South Korea's legislature has a single house called the National Assembly. Citizens elect the members of the assembly to four-year terms.

During the 1980s and 1990s, South Korea began to allow more political freedom. It developed a multiparty system. The country also allowed fairer elections and greater freedom for its people.

◄ COMPARING ◄ Korean Governments

NORTH KOREA

North Korean citizens elect the members of the Supreme People's Assembly. This body, however, is controlled by the National Defense Commission and the Korean Workers' Party.

CITIZENS
⬇ elect ⬇

SUPREME PEOPLE'S ASSEMBLY

controls ⬆   ⬆ controls

CHAIRMAN OF NATIONAL DEFENSE COMMISSION   controls ➡   KOREAN WORKERS' PARTY

SOUTH KOREA

South Korean citizens directly elect the president and the members of the National Assembly.

CITIZENS
elect

PRESIDENT   NATIONAL ASSEMBLY

appoints ⬇   ⬇ approves

SUPREME COURT

CRITICAL THINKING

1. **Compare and Contrast** How do the roles of chairman in North Korea and president in South Korea differ?

2. **Draw Conclusions** How much power do the people of North Korea have?

Economy After the Korean War, South Korea developed its economy with a series of five-year plans. The goal of these plans was to export goods and use the resulting income to increase production. The government expressed this approach through the slogan "Production, Exports, Construction!"

Soon South Korean businesses began to thrive. In fact, some companies expanded into family-owned conglomerates called **chaebols** (JEH•buhlz). A **conglomerate** is made up of several companies in different businesses. The businesses within a *chaebol* are related. For example, Samsung is one of South Korea's largest *chaebols*. It is made up of companies that produce electronic equipment such as televisions, microwave ovens, and computers.

Eventually, *chaebols* controlled much of South Korea's economy and greatly contributed to its growth. These organizations, though, had drawbacks. For instance, *chaebols* sometimes underpaid their workers, causing many to demand higher wages. Also, some *chaebols* made bad economic decisions that led to an economic downturn in 1997. After the government received foreign loans and closed poorly run businesses, the economy began to rebound. *Chaebols* continue to play a vital role in South Korea's economy today.

Industries and Agriculture South Korea has developed both heavy and light industries. Products include chemicals, steel, shipbuilding, automobiles, electronics, and telecommunications. You can learn about the locations of South Korea's industries by studying the map on this page.

South Korea's economy has shifted away from agriculture. And, as you have learned, South Korea's mountainous terrain does not provide much land for farming. Nevertheless, South Korean farms produce a variety of crops, including rice, root crops, barley, vegetables, and fruit.

▲ **COMPARE AND CONTRAST** Compare the government and economy of South Korea with those of North Korea.

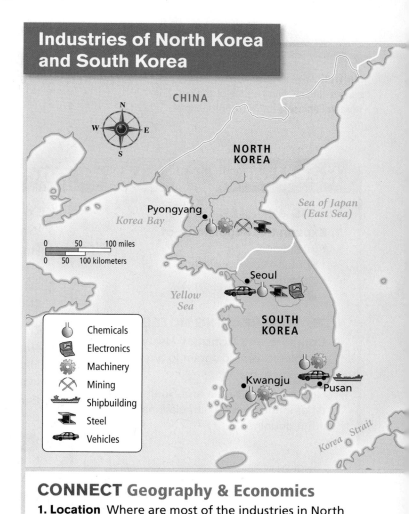

Industries of North Korea and South Korea

CHINA

NORTH KOREA

Sea of Japan (East Sea)

Pyongyang

Korea Bay

0   50   100 miles
0   50   100 kilometers

Seoul

Yellow Sea

SOUTH KOREA

Kwangju

Pusan

Korea Strait

Chemicals
Electronics
Machinery
Mining
Shipbuilding
Steel
Vehicles

CONNECT Geography & Economics

1. **Location** Where are most of the industries in North Korea and South Korea located?

2. **Region** What are North Korea's major industries?

Efforts Toward Reunification

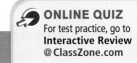 **KEY QUESTION** What steps have been taken toward the reunification of North Korea and South Korea?

Many obstacles remain before North Korea and South Korea can be reunited. For one thing, North Korea considers the South Korean government unlawful. Also, over the past decades, North Korea and South Korea have developed very different cultures.

But gradually, contacts between the two Koreas have increased. For example, more visits between family members have been allowed. Also, as you have already learned, a few South Korean businesses have moved into North Korea. The desire for reunification has even been reflected at the Olympic games. During the 2000, 2004, and 2006 games, North and South Korean athletes marched under the same flag during the opening ceremony. The two Koreas have agreed to compete as a single team in the 2008 Olympics.

FIND MAIN IDEAS Discuss the steps that have been taken toward the reunification of North and South Korea.

Unified Korea Flag Korean athletes carry a flag showing a map of the entire Korean Peninsula in the 2006 Olympics.

Section 3 Assessment

ONLINE QUIZ
For test practice, go to
Interactive Review
@ ClassZone.com

TERMS & NAMES

1. Explain the importance of
- totalitarian
- Korean Workers' Party
- dictator
- *chaebol*

USE YOUR READING NOTES

2. Compare and Contrast Use your completed Venn diagram to answer the following question:

How do North Korea and South Korea differ in their economic relationships with other countries?

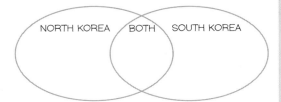

NORTH KOREA   BOTH   SOUTH KOREA

KEY IDEAS

3. What is *juche*?

4. How much power does the chairman of the National Defense Commission have in North Korea?

5. What have been some of the benefits and drawbacks of the *chaebols*?

CRITICAL THINKING

6. Recognize Bias and Propaganda Reread the History Makers on Kim Jong Il. How do official accounts of the leader reflect bias and propaganda?

7. Evaluate What might result from allowing the Korean people to travel freely within North and South Korea?

8. CONNECT to Today What message would North Korea and South Korea convey by competing in the Olympics as a single team?

9. ECONOMICS Research a *Chaebol* Choose a *chaebol* and research the type of products it makes and how well they sell in the United States. Summarize your findings in a one-paragraph report.

Interactive ⟵Review

Click here to complete these and other activities online @ ClassZone.com

CHAPTER SUMMARY

Key Idea 1
Korea lies on a peninsula, which provides a moderate climate and plentiful resources.

Key Idea 2
The Korean Peninsula has been invaded by China, Russia, and Japan but has still maintained its cultural identity.

Key Idea 3
North Korea and South Korea have very different government systems and economic structures.

For **Review and Study Notes**, go to **Interactive Review** @ ClassZone.com

NAME GAME

Use the Terms & Names list to complete each sentence on paper or online.

1. I am the highest mountain on the Korean Peninsula. __Mount Paektu__

2. I am the largest island off the coast of the Korean Peninsula. _____

3. I am the dictator of North Korea.
   _____

4. I am made up of the states of Koguryo, Paekche, and Silla. _____

5. I am the buffer zone between North Korea and South Korea. _____

6. I am the original belief system practiced on the Korean Peninsula. _____

7. I am a traditional Korean costume.
   _____

8. I am a Korean side dish. _____

9. I am the political group that controls the North Korean government. _____

10. I am a family-owned conglomerate of businesses. _____

Buddhism
chaebol
Cheju
conglomerate
demilitarized zone
hanbok
kimchi
Kim Jong Il
Korean Workers' Party
Mount Paektu
shamanism
Three Kingdoms

Activities

GeoGame

Use this online map to show what you know about the location, geographic features, and important places of the Korean Peninsula. Drag and drop each place name to its location on the map.

Geo GAME

North Korea

South Korea

demilitarized zone

Yalu River

Cheju Island

To play the complete game, go to **Interactive Review** @ ClassZone.com

Physical Geography of Korea

North Korea

Crossword Puzzle

Complete an online crossword puzzle to test your knowledge of Korean history and culture.

ACROSS
1. traditional Korean clothing

VOCABULARY

Explain the significance of each of the following.

1. Korean Peninsula
2. Mount Paektu
3. Cheju Island
4. Korean War
5. demilitarized zone
6. shamanism
7. *hanbok*
8. celadon
9. Three Kingdoms
10. *chaebol*

Explain how the terms and names in each group are related.

11. shamanism, Confucianism, and Buddhism
12. Korean Workers' Party, Kim Jong Il, and dictator

KEY IDEAS

1 A Rugged Peninsula

13. What bodies of water surround the Korean Peninsula?
14. What do the Yalu and Tumen rivers form?
15. How do summer monsoons affect the Korean Peninsula's climate?
16. How is the majority of the electricity produced in South Korea?

2 Strong Traditions, Modern Innovations

17. How did the Choson Dynasty isolate Korea?
18. How did the Korean War start?
19. What belief systems influence Korean society today?
20. What influences have inspired Korean arts?

3 Contrasting Countries

21. What is the role of the Korean Workers' Party in North Korea?
22. How is South Korea's government similar to the U.S. government?
23. What was the goal of South Korea's five-year economic plans?
24. How has the desire for the reunification of North and South Korea been reflected in the Olympics?

CRITICAL THINKING

25. **Compare and Contrast** Create a chart to compare and contrast the natural resources of North Korea and South Korea.

NORTH KOREA'S RESOURCES	SOUTH KOREA'S RESOURCES

26. **Evaluate** What steps has South Korea taken to overcome some of its problems?
27. **Make Inferences** Why do you think many South Koreans practice aspects of several religions?
28. **Identify Problems** What are some of the problems faced by North Korea?
29. **Connect Geography & Economics** How has North Korea's farmland affected its economy?
30. **Five Themes: Human-Environment Interaction** How have the geographic features of the Korean Peninsula affected this region's history?

Answer the ESSENTIAL QUESTION

How can North Korea and South Korea overcome their differences and live in peace?

Written Response Write a two- or three-paragraph response to the Essential Question. Use the rubric below to guide your thinking.

Response Rubric
A strong response will:
- identify the countries' differences and conflicts
- discuss the steps the two Koreas have taken toward overcoming these differences
- offer solutions about what more the two countries could do

LINE GRAPH

Use the graph to answer questions 1 and 2 on your paper.

Stock Market in South Korea

KOSPI (point)*

Year

*KOSPI—Korea's Stock Price Index

Source: Republic of Korea, Ministry of Finance and Economy

1. In what year did the stock market in South Korea reach its lowest level?

A. 1997
B. 1998
C. 2001
D. 2003

2. When did the stock market reach 850 points?

A. 1999
B. 2000
C. 2002
D. 2004

CHART

Examine the chart below. Use the information in the chart to answer questions 3 and 4 on your paper.

Spread of Chinese Influence A.D. 600–1400		
Korea	**Japan**	**Southeast Asia**
Buddhism	Buddhism	Buddhism
Writing system	Writing system	Ideas
Civil service	Printing	
Printing		
Porcelain		

3. Which aspect of Chinese culture was most widely spread?

A. writing system
B. printing
C. Buddhism
D. porcelain

4. Which region was most influenced by China?

A. Korea
B. Japan
C. Southeast Asia
D. They were all equally influenced by China.

GeoActivity

1. INTERDISCIPLINARY ACTIVITY–SCIENCE

With a small group, use appropriate resources to research the causes and effects of typhoons on the Korean Peninsula. Display your findings on a poster. Include pictures, charts, and captions that explain the causes and effects.

2. WRITING FOR SOCIAL STUDIES

Do you think North Korea should be allowed to develop a nuclear weapons program? Examine the conflicting viewpoints of North Korea and of the United States and others who oppose it. Write your opinion in a brief essay.

3. MENTAL MAPPING

Create an outline map of the Korean Peninsula and label the following:

• Yellow Sea
• East Sea
• Korea Strait
• Yalu River
• Cheju Island
• Mount Paektu
• Nangnim Mountains
• Taebaek Mountains

Japan

1
GEOGRAPHY

Land of the Rising Sun

2
HISTORY & CULTURE

Samurai to Animé

3
GOVERNMENT & ECONOMICS

Economic Giant

 ESSENTIAL QUESTION

How has Japan balanced its ancient traditions with its modern economy?

CONNECT Geography & History

Use the map and the time line to answer the following questions.

1. When did Heian become Japan's capital?

2. What is the capital of Japan today?

History

◄ **300s** The Yamato clan gains control of Japan. (Seventh-century ruler Shotoku Taishi)

A.D. 300

History

1100s Shogun rule is established. (Japan's first shogun, Minamoto no Yoritomo) ►

Government

◄ **794** Heian period begins, and the capital moves from Nara to Heian, modern Kyoto. (Phoenix Hall)

RUSSIA

Sea of Okhotsk

Kuril Islands (RUSSIA)

CHINA

NORTH KOREA

Sapporo

Hokkaido

Sea of Japan (East Sea)

Yellow Sea

SOUTH KOREA

Honshu

Shinano R.

Tone R.

JAPAN

Kawasaki ⊛ Tokyo
Kyoto Yokohama
Kobe Nagoya
Osaka

Hiroshima

Korea Strait

Kitakyushu
Fukuoka

Shikoku

Nagasaki

PACIFIC OCEAN

Kyushu

East China Sea

Ryukyu Islands

Scale
0 — 100 — 200 miles
0 — 100 — 200 kilometers

N
W E
S

⊛ National capital
• Other city

History
1941 Japan attacks Pearl Harbor, forcing the United States into World War II. (Japan's World War II naval battle flag) ▶

Today

Culture
◀ **1600s** Poetry called haiku develops. (Haiku poet Matsuo Basho)

Economics
1980 Japan becomes the largest producer of automobiles worldwide.

Reading for Understanding

▶ Key Ideas

BEFORE, YOU LEARNED

The Korean Peninsula is a ruggedly mountainous landmass in East Asia, bordered by China, Russia, and Japan.

NOW YOU WILL LEARN

The mountainous islands that make up Japan provide the country's people with scant living space, a varied climate, and limited resources.

▶ Vocabulary

TERMS & NAMES

Honshu Japan's largest and most populous island

Mount Fuji Japan's highest mountain peak

Kanto Plain the largest lowland of Japan, which extends from the Japanese Alps east to the Pacific

Hokkaido (hah•KY•doh) Japan's northern-most and second largest island

Kyushu (kee•OO•shoo) Japan's southernmost island and home to several large cities

Shikoku (shee•KAW•koo) Japan's smallest and least populated major island

Ring of Fire a geographic zone that extends along the rim of the Pacific Ocean and has numerous volcanoes and earthquakes

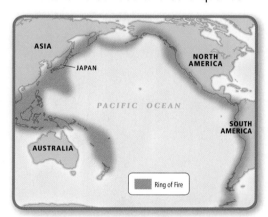

Visual Vocabulary Ring of Fire

▶ Reading Strategy

Re-create the chart shown at right. As you read and respond to the **KEY QUESTIONS**, use the chart to analyze the causes and effects of Japan's physical geography.

 Skillbuilder Handbook, page R8

ANALYZE CAUSES AND EFFECTS

PHYSICAL GEOGRAPHY	CAUSES AND/OR EFFECTS
Crowded Islands	
Located on Ring of Fire	
Varied Climate	
Limited Resources	
Abundant Wildlife	

 GRAPHIC ORGANIZERS
Go to **Interactive Review** @ClassZone.com

Land of the Rising Sun

Connecting to Your World

Think about the most beautiful scenery you've ever seen. You might recall majestic mountains, spectacular sunsets or sunrises, thundering waterfalls, or rapidly flowing rivers cutting through canyons. Japan possesses all of this natural beauty. Perhaps as a result, many of the Japanese people have a strong emotional bond with nature. In fact, the Japanese name for their country, *Nippon*, refers to nature. *Nippon* means "source of the sun" and is often translated as "Land of the Rising Sun."

Mountainous Islands

🔻 **KEY QUESTION** What are the main geographic features of Japan's four major islands?

Japan is made up of about 4,000 islands. It lies to the east of the Korean Peninsula, China, and Russia. The island nation is surrounded by the East Sea, or Sea of Japan, to the west and the Pacific Ocean to the south and east. The islands of Japan are actually the tops of a huge, mostly underwater, mountain range.

Cherry Blossoms Cherry trees from Japan blossom in Washington, D.C.

Mount Fuji A high-speed train runs past Mount Fuji.

JAPAN

▲ Mount Fuji

Major Islands Although Japan has thousands of islands, most of its people live on the four largest ones: Honshu, Hokkaido, Kyushu, and Shikoku. Locate the islands on the map on the opposite page.

- **Honshu** Ⓐ is Japan's largest island and is home to about 80 percent of its people. Honshu is a land of extreme elevations. The towering Japanese Alps run down the center of the island. Honshu also contains **Mount Fuji** Ⓑ, Japan's highest peak. The largest lowland of Japan, the **Kanto Plain** Ⓒ, extends from the Japanese Alps east to the Pacific.

- **Hokkaido** (hah•KY•doh) Ⓓ lies to the north and is the second largest of Japan's four major islands. It has many mountains and thick forests. This island is sparsely populated, but its long winters make it ideal for winter sports.

- **Kyushu** (kee•OO•shoo) Ⓔ is the southernmost of the major islands. A steep chain of mountains runs down the center of this island. The heavily populated northwestern plains are home to several large cities.

- **Shikoku** (shee•KAW•koo) Ⓕ is the smallest of Japan's main islands. Because almost all of Shikoku is covered with mountains, only about 3 percent of Japan's population lives there.

CONNECT **Geography & History**

Japan and the Ring of Fire

As you can see on the inset map on the opposite page, Japan is located along the **Ring of Fire**. This zone, which extends along the rim of the Pacific Ocean, has many active volcanoes and is subject to many earthquakes. Japan has about 80 active volcanoes and experiences about 1,500 earthquakes each year. Most of these earthquakes are minor—but not all. In 1923, the Great Kanto earthquake struck the Tokyo area, resulting in the deaths of about 140,000 people. The Kobe earthquake of 1995 killed about 6,000 people in that city. Some of the damage caused by the Kobe earthquake is shown here.

CRITICAL THINKING

Summarize What damage is apparent in this photograph of the Kobe earthquake?

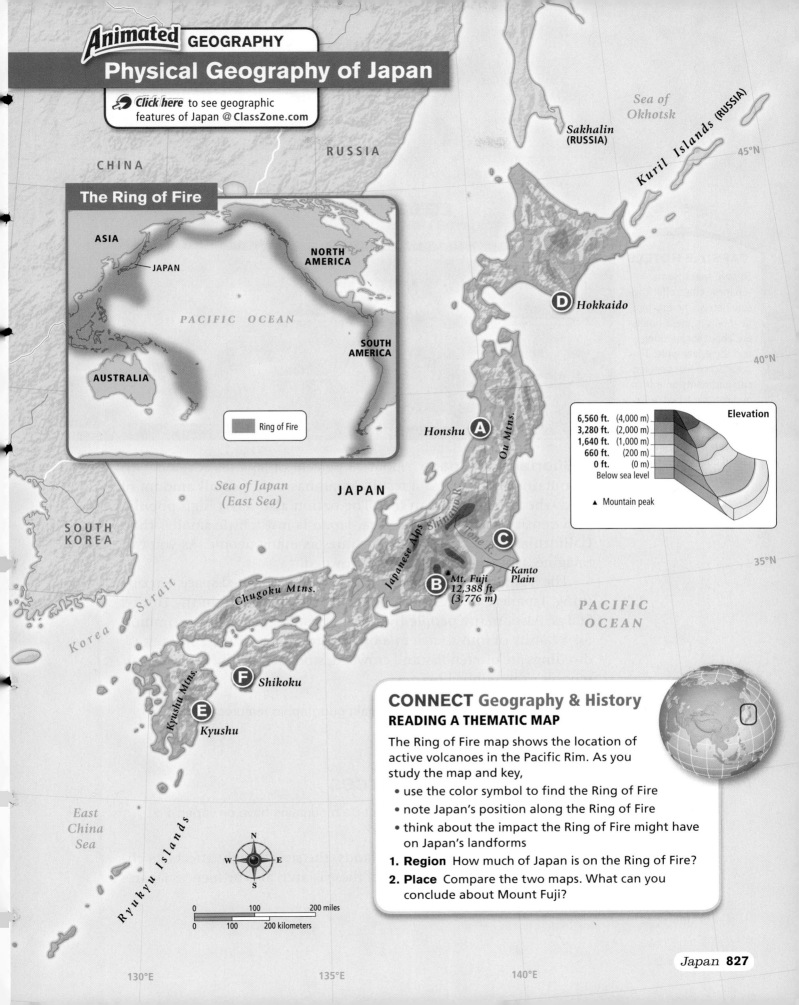

Physical Geography of Japan

Click here to see geographic features of Japan @ ClassZone.com

The Ring of Fire

ASIA

JAPAN

NORTH AMERICA

PACIFIC OCEAN

SOUTH AMERICA

AUSTRALIA

Ring of Fire

RUSSIA

CHINA

Sea of Okhotsk

Sakhalin (RUSSIA)

Kuril Islands (RUSSIA)

45°N

D Hokkaido

40°N

Sea of Japan (East Sea)

JAPAN

Honshu A

Ou Mtns.

Elevation

6,560 ft. (4,000 m)
3,280 ft. (2,000 m)
1,640 ft. (1,000 m)
660 ft. (200 m)
0 ft. (0 m)
Below sea level

▲ Mountain peak

SOUTH KOREA

Japanese Alps Shinano R. Tone R.

C

Kanto Plain

35°N

Mt. Fuji 12,388 ft. (3,776 m)

B

Chugoku Mtns.

Korea Strait

PACIFIC OCEAN

F Shikoku

Kyushu Mtns.

E

Kyushu

East China Sea

Ryukyu Islands

N
W   E
S

0   100   200 miles
0   100   200 kilometers

CONNECT Geography & History
READING A THEMATIC MAP

The Ring of Fire map shows the location of active volcanoes in the Pacific Rim. As you study the map and key,

- use the color symbol to find the Ring of Fire
- note Japan's position along the Ring of Fire
- think about the impact the Ring of Fire might have on Japan's landforms

1. **Region** How much of Japan is on the Ring of Fire?

2. **Place** Compare the two maps. What can you conclude about Mount Fuji?

130°E   135°E   140°E

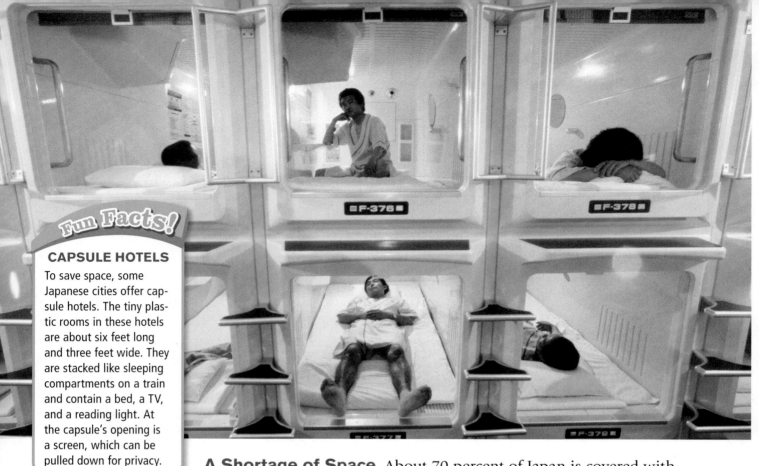

A Shortage of Space About 70 percent of Japan is covered with mountains and hills. As a result, Japan has only a small amount of land where its people can live. The nation also has a high population density. To give you an idea, Japan is just a little smaller than California, but it has about four times as many people. As you can imagine, Japanese cities are very crowded.

The Japanese have learned to adapt to their limited space. For one thing, Japanese homes tend to be smaller than those in the United States. Also, many people live in apartments. It is not uncommon for a family of four to live in a one-bedroom apartment. Since these dwellings are often noisy and crowded, students usually study at their schools or in public libraries.

▲ **SUMMARIZE** Describe the main geographic features of Japan's four major islands.

Climate and Resources

▼ **KEY QUESTION** What impact do mountains have on Japan's climate, resources, and wildlife?

Since Japan consists of many islands, the sea strongly affects its climate. The mountainous terrain of these islands also influences Japan's climate and its resources.

A Varied Climate The climates on the major islands are influenced by their latitudes and by the currents of the Pacific Ocean. The northern islands of Japan have generally cool weather, while the southern ones have a more tropical climate. The central islands have a moderate climate, with warm summers and mild winters. The mountains throughout the islands have colder temperatures because of their higher elevations. Most of Japan gets at least 40 inches of rain each year.

Resources and Wildlife Japan has deposits of coal, lead, and silver, but many of these are of poor quality. Forests are abundant, but they are located in remote mountain areas and are difficult to harvest. Not surprisingly, given its vast coastal waters, Japan looks to the sea for food. In fact, Japan has one of the largest fishing industries in the world.

Despite its dense human population, Japan has a great deal of wildlife, especially in regions that are thickly forested. Bears, wild boars, raccoon dogs, and deer can be found in these areas. Japan's wilderness also contains a large, shaggy-haired monkey called the Japanese macaque (muh•KAK).

Japanese Macaques
Also called snow monkeys, Japanese macaques live farther north than any other monkeys in the world.

 ANALYZE EFFECTS Discuss the impact of mountains on Japan's climate, resources, and wildlife.

Section 1 Assessment

ONLINE QUIZ
For test practice, go to
Interactive Review
@ ClassZone.com

TERMS & NAMES

1. Explain the importance of
- Honshu
- Mount Fuji
- Kanto Plain
- Ring of Fire

USE YOUR READING NOTES

2. Analyze Causes and Effects Use your completed chart to answer the following question:

Why does Japan have such limited living space?

PHYSICAL GEOGRAPHY	CAUSES AND/ OR EFFECTS
Crowded Islands	
Located on Ring of Fire	
Varied Climate	
Limited Resources	
Abundant Wildlife	

KEY IDEAS

3. On which two islands do most of the Japanese people live?

4. Why does Japan have so many earthquakes?

5. How does latitude affect Japan's climate?

CRITICAL THINKING

6. Evaluate What characteristics do the Japanese reveal in their ability to live on their crowded island nation?

7. Draw Conclusions What do you think is Japan's most important natural resource? Explain.

8. CONNECT to Today Subway employees push passengers into Tokyo subways and trains during rush hour. What does this tell you about the city?

9. WRITING Pen a Journal Entry Imagine that you are on a hike in the Japanese Alps. Write a journal entry about your experiences in these mountains. Record the sights you might see, the type of weather you might deal with, and the vegetation and wildlife you might encounter.

SECTION 2

Reading for Understanding

▶ Key Ideas

BEFORE, YOU LEARNED

Japan is a chain of islands that lies off the coast of China and the Korean Peninsula.

NOW YOU WILL LEARN

Over the centuries, Japan has adapted ideas and technologies from other lands and created a unique culture.

▶ Vocabulary

TERMS & NAMES

Heian (hay•ahn) **period** the era in Japanese history from A.D. 794 to 1185; arts and writing flourished during this time

samurai (SAM•uh•RY) professional soldiers of Japan

shogun the leader of the military government of Japan beginning in 1192

daimyo (DY•mee•OH) powerful samurai who became warrior-chieftains

Tokugawa Ieyasu (TOH•koo•GAH•wah EE•yeh•YAH•soo) shogun who unified Japan

Shinto Japan's original religion; involves worshiping gods believed to be found in nature

BACKGROUND VOCABULARY

clan a group of families related through a common ancestor

REVIEW

emperor a man who is the ruler of an empire

Visual Vocabulary statue of daimyo draped with war flag

▶ Reading Strategy

Re-create the time line shown at right. As you read and respond to the **KEY QUESTIONS**, use the time line to keep track of some of Japan's important historical and cultural events.

 See Skillbuilder Handbook, page R6

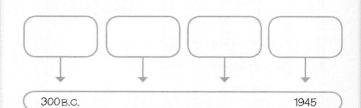

SEQUENCE EVENTS

300 B.C.   1945

🔁 **GRAPHIC ORGANIZERS**
Go to **Interactive Review** @ ClassZone.com

Samurai to Animé

Connecting to Your World

Have you ever played a video game or watched an animated film? If so, you have probably used a product from Japan. Japanese culture has strongly influenced culture in the United States and throughout the world. But the reverse has also been true. Hundreds of years ago, several cultures played an important role in shaping Japanese culture. In this section, you will learn what these cultures were and how they affected Japan.

Isolated Nation to World Power

▼ **KEY QUESTION** How did Japan change from an isolated nation to a world power?

The first influences on Japanese culture probably arrived from China and Korea around 300 B.C. At this time, Japanese families were organized into **clans**, who fought over land. Eventually, the Yamato family became the leading clan and established a member of its family as ruler, or **emperor**. The Yamato line of emperors continues to this day.

Video Games Only the United States sells more video games than Japan.

Influence from China Buddhism arrived in Japan from China. This statue of Buddha in Kyoto reflects China's influence.

831

Heian Period In the late 700s, the emperor moved his court from the capital of Nara to Heian (hay•ahn), which is modern Kyoto (kee•OH•toh). Heian remained the center of Japan's government for about 400 years. This era in Japanese history, which lasted from 794 to 1185, is called the **Heian period**.

Art and writing flourished during this period. Men and women of the nobility filled their days by painting and writing poetry and prose. In fact, one of the best accounts of Heian society was written by Lady Murasaki Shikibu (MOO•rah•SAH•kee SHEE•kee•boo). Her masterpiece, *The Tale of Genji*, is an account of the life of a prince in the emperor's court. The work is considered the world's first novel.

Samurai and Shoguns During the Heian period, the central government was relatively strong. However, by the mid-1000s, this power had begun to decrease. Wealthy clans bought large areas of land and set up private armies. The countryside became lawless and dangerous. As a result, smaller landowners sold parts of their land to strong warlords in exchange for protection. With more land, the lords gained more power. Soon, wars between rival lords became commonplace. To defend himself, each lord surrounded himself with a bodyguard of loyal warriors called **samurai** (SAM•uh•RY).

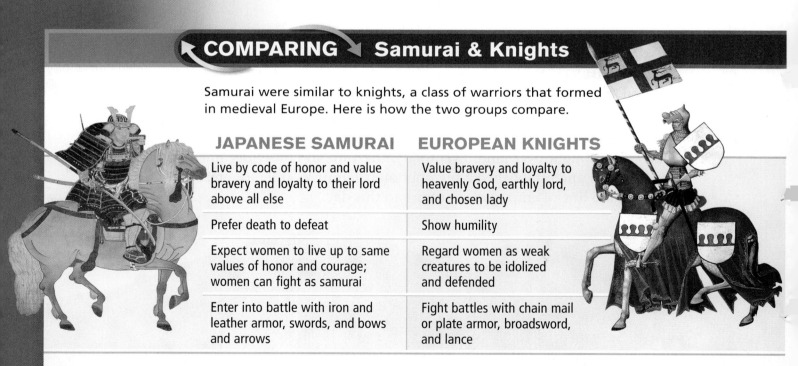

COMPARING Samurai & Knights

Samurai were similar to knights, a class of warriors that formed in medieval Europe. Here is how the two groups compare.

JAPANESE SAMURAI	EUROPEAN KNIGHTS
Live by code of honor and value bravery and loyalty to their lord above all else	Value bravery and loyalty to heavenly God, earthly lord, and chosen lady
Prefer death to defeat	Show humility
Expect women to live up to same values of honor and courage; women can fight as samurai	Regard women as weak creatures to be idolized and defended
Enter into battle with iron and leather armor, swords, and bows and arrows	Fight battles with chain mail or plate armor, broadsword, and lance

CRITICAL THINKING

Compare and Contrast What are some similarities and differences between Japanese samurai and European knights?

During the 1100s, two powerful clans fought for control—the Taira (TY•rah) and the Minamoto. Each clan had a large samurai army. After about 30 years of war, the Minamoto gained control. This clan set up a military government in Kamakura. In 1192, the leader of this government was given the title of **shogun**, which means "supreme general of the emperor's army." Although the emperor still reigned, the shogun held real power. This pattern of government, in which shoguns ruled through puppet emperors, lasted until 1867.

Unified Japan Between 1192 and 1600, Japan was torn by internal warfare. Peasants had to fight to defend their villages. Sometimes, they hired samurai to protect them. Very powerful samurai arose and became warrior-chieftains called **daimyo** (DY•mee•OH), who became lords in their own right. The daimyo formed armies and fought for military supremacy.

Finally, in 1600, a daimyo named **Tokugawa Ieyasu** (TOH•koo•GAW•wah EE•yeh•YAH•soo) restored order. Three years later, he became shogun and unified Japan. He then moved the capital to his base at Edo, a small fishing village that would later become the city of Tokyo.

The Tokugawa shogunate held power until 1868. During this time, Japan enjoyed a period of stability—and isolation. For more than 200 years, the country was closed to Westerners.

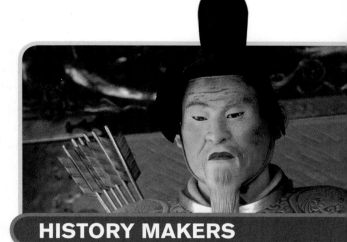

HISTORY MAKERS

Tokugawa Ieyasu 1543–1616

Tokugawa Ieyasu could be merciless in the defense of his clan. In the late 1500s, his wife and eldest son were accused of conspiring against the family. As a result, Ieyasu ordered his son to commit suicide and had his wife executed. He also never forgot a grudge. As an adult, he executed a prisoner who had insulted him in childhood. On the other hand, Ieyasu could also be kind and generous. He rewarded those who were loyal to him and even showed compassion to his enemies.

 ONLINE BIOGRAPHY
For more on the life of Tokugawa Ieyasu, go to the **Research & Writing Center** @ ClassZone.com

Himeji Castle Tokugawa Ieyasu's son-in-law built the castle after he helped win the battle that brought Ieyasu to power.

Rise of Modern Japan In 1853, the United States forced Japan to end its isolation. The government sent Commodore Matthew Perry to Japan with several warships to frighten the Tokugawa shogun. He soon agreed to open several Japanese ports to Western powers.

The Japanese people were angry that the shogun had given in to the foreigners' demands. As a result, the emperor was restored as head of government in 1868. The emperor chose the name *Meiji* (MAY•jee), which means "enlightened rule," for his reign. In an effort to counter Western influence, the emperor began a policy of modernization. Before long, Japan became a powerful nation.

As Japan's power grew, the nation sought to obtain an empire. In the early 1900s, Japan gained control of Korea. By 1937, Japan had invaded China and formed an alliance with Nazi Germany and Fascist Italy. Between 1939 and 1945, Japan joined and fought with these powers during World War II— and lost.

After the United States and the Allies won the war, they occupied Japan for several years and set up a democracy. In time, Japan developed into an economic superpower.

▲ **SUMMARIZE** Explain how Japan changed from an isolated nation to a world power.

Japanese Empire 1942

Map showing the Japanese Empire in 1942. Labels include: U.S.S.R., MONGOLIA, MANCHURIA, KOREA, JAPAN, CHINA, PACIFIC OCEAN, 30°N, Formosa, Wake Island, BURMA, Hainan, SIAM, FRENCH INDOCHINA, PHILIPPINES, Guam, MALAYA, Borneo, Equator, Gilbert Islands, 0°, DUTCH EAST INDIES, New Guinea, 120°E, AUSTRALIA, 150°E. Legend: — Areas controlled by Japan. Scale: 0 500 1,000 miles / 0 500 1,000 kilometers. Compass rose: N.

CONNECT Geography & History

1. **Location** What part of mainland China did Japan control?
2. **Region** What body of water borders all of the conquered territories?

Traditional and Modern Japanese Culture

▼ **KEY QUESTION** How does Japanese culture blend traditional and modern influences?

As you have learned, Japan has been isolated for long periods of time throughout its history. Because of this, 99 percent of the people who live there are of Japanese descent. Other groups include Chinese, Koreans, and the Ainu (EYE•noo). Some historians believe that the Ainu were Japan's original people. Most Ainu live on Hokkaido.

Japanese is the country's only official language. The written form reflects the influence of China on Japan. Chinese characters, called *kanji*, are used for nouns. Japanese characters, known as *kana*, can be used for changing nouns into adjectives and verbs.

Religious Traditions Japan's religious traditions also demonstrate China's influence—and Japan's ability to take in new ideas and make them its own. The two major religions of Japan are Shinto and Buddhism. **Shinto** is Japan's original religion and is rarely practiced anywhere else in the world. Followers of this belief worship many gods, called *kami*. These gods are believed to be found in aspects of nature, such as rivers, trees, and rocks.

Buddhism, which originated in India, spread from China to Japan during the 500s. A form of this religion, called Zen Buddhism, became important in Japan. Zen stresses strict discipline of the body and mind as the path to wisdom. Many Japanese use rituals from both religions in their daily lives.

Torii Gate Like all torii gates, this one on Miyajima Island near Hiroshima serves as an entry to a Shinto shrine. **How does the gate reflect the importance of nature in Shinto?**

Japanese Arts The arts in Japan blend traditional and modern influences. Kabuki is a traditional form of Japanese drama that features colorful costumes and an exaggerated acting style. Other traditional Japanese arts include flower arranging and the tea ceremony. Both reflect the importance of traditional Japanese virtues such as simplicity, discipline, and love of nature.

Modern arts are also popular in Japan. These include animated films called *animé*, which often feature characters with large, expressive eyes, and comic books called *manga*. Japan has many manga cafes, where people can read manga over a cup of tea or coffee.

CONNECT to Culture

Origami is an art form that involves folding paper into decorative shapes. Although origami started in China, it has thrived in Japan. One of the most popular origami shapes is the crane, shown here. The crane is considered a sacred bird in Japan. A finished sailboat is also shown.

Activity
Create an Origami Sailboat

Materials
• colored paper

1. With colored side down, fold your paper on line A–C. Open and fold point B to the diagonal crease. Then fold D to the crease.

2. Turn your paper around so that A is nearest to you. Fold A so that it meets points D and B. Then fold G–H up and crease on line E–F.

3. Finally, fold E–F up and crease on line G–H.

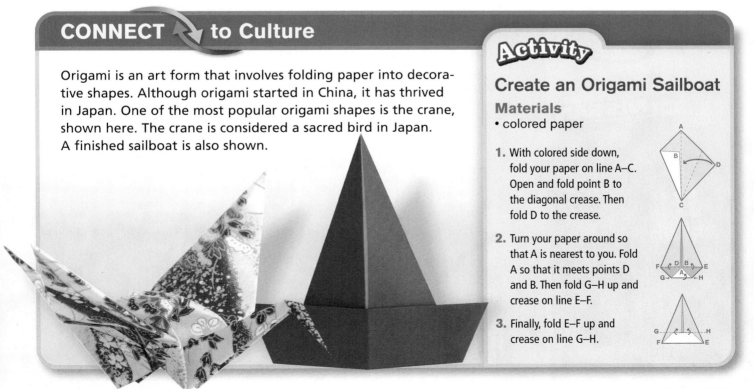

Japanese Literature

The earliest known Japanese poetry, called tanka, was the dominant verse form from the 700s until the 1500s. Tanka means "short songs" and consists of 31 syllables divided among five lines. During the Heian period, aristocrats routinely composed and exchanged tanka with their loved ones. In the 1600s, another type of poetry called haiku (HY•koo) developed. This verse has 17 syllables arranged in three lines. The following haiku is by Matsuo Basho, who is considered a master of the form.

Cool crescent moon

shining faintly high above

Feather Black Mountain

In addition to poetry, Japanese writers have made many contributions to fiction and drama. As you have learned, Lady Murasaki Shikibu is credited with writing the first novel. Zeami Motokiyo, who wrote in the late 1300s, is one of Japan's greatest playwrights.

Life in Japan

Because of Japan's shortage of living space, Japanese cities are very crowded. About three-fourths of the Japanese people live in cities. These urban areas are filled with dazzling, high-rise buildings, elegant department stores, and trendy shops. Even though the people live in small houses and apartments, overcrowding remains a constant problem. During rush hour, for instance, white-gloved employees push as many people into subways and trains as possible. Passengers have suffered broken bones from holding their arms in awkward positions in these cramped conditions.

Woodblock Print Haiku convey images of nature that are often illustrated with landscape prints.

Tokyo at Night Cars and people crowd the Ginza district in Tokyo, a popular area for entertainment and shopping.

In Japan's cities, most Japanese wear clothes that are similar to those worn in the United States. However, for special occasions, Japanese men and women might wear a traditional dress called a kimono. These garments are tied around the waist with a sash and are worn with sandals.

Although Western fast foods are popular in Japan, many Japanese still enjoy traditional fare, including rice with almost every meal. Other traditional foods include tofu (soybean curd cake) and sushi—vinegared rice usually topped with raw fish. Soups made with a soybean paste called *miso* are also popular.

You may be surprised to learn that the number one spectator sport in Japan is baseball. However, traditional sumo wrestling also has a wide following. Other popular traditional sports include *kendo* (fencing with bamboo sticks) and martial arts.

Japanese Baseball Japan won the first World Baseball Classic in 2006. Two of the players on the Japanese team played in the U.S. major leagues during the regular season.

 FIND MAIN IDEAS Describe how Japanese culture blends traditional and modern influences.

Section ❷ Assessment

ONLINE QUIZ
For test practice, go to
Interactive Review
@ ClassZone.com

TERMS & NAMES

1. Explain the importance of
- samurai
- shogun
- daimyo
- Shinto

USE YOUR READING NOTES

2. Sequence Events Use your completed time line to answer the following question:

During which period was the haiku developed?

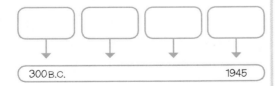

300 B.C.   1945

KEY IDEAS

3. How did the nobility fill their time during the Heian period?

4. Why did Japan begin to modernize during the mid- to late 1800s?

5. What is daily life like in Japanese cities?

CRITICAL THINKING

6. Make Inferences Why do you think the Japanese wanted to live in isolation from the West for so long?

7. Synthesize Reread the haiku in this section. How does the poem reflect the traditional Japanese values of simplicity, discipline, and love of nature?

8. **CONNECT to Today** What aspects of Japanese culture are popular in the United States today?

9. **TECHNOLOGY** **Give a Kabuki Slide Show** Research to learn about kabuki theater. Find pictures of costumes, make-up, and the set designs used. Then give a slide show about the drama form, using authentic kabuki music in the background.

Japan is a land of ancient traditions. But it is also an ultra-modern country, where new styles are set. Today, as you can see from these pictures, the past and present live side by side in Japan.

Traditional Japan

Since the 1600s, the Japanese people have enjoyed kabuki drama, with its colorful costumes and revolving stages. The dramas recall a time when the Japanese wore kimonos and musicians played a three-stringed instrument called the *shamisen*. In this traditional Japan, people have time to sit and reflect in the peaceful calm of a Zen garden.

Dress

Many different types of kimonos can be worn by men, women, and children.

Zen garden in Kyoto ▼

Entertainment

All of the roles in a kabuki drama are played by men.

Music

The sound of the *shamisen* is similar to that of a banjo.

Modern Japan

The worldwide popularity of animé attests to Japan's ability to set cultural trends. Other exports include karaoke and stylish, modern fashions. As you can see, modern life in Japan is also characterized by busy rush hours.

Dress

Today, Japanese fashion designers are copied throughout the world.

Crowded Tokyo subway ▼

Entertainment

Many animé films tell sophisticated stories about love, growing up, and female empowerment.

Music

In Japan, people can sing along with a karaoke player in public bars or in private shops.

CRITICAL THINKING

1. **Compare and Contrast** Select two corresponding images from traditional and modern Japan. How do they differ? What do they have in common?

2. **Analyze Causes** Why do you think animé and karaoke have become so popular in other countries?

Reading for Understanding

▶ Key Ideas

BEFORE, YOU LEARNED

Japanese culture blends traditional and modern elements.

NOW YOU WILL LEARN

The Japanese have drawn on their culture to create a modern government and become an economic giant.

▶ Vocabulary

TERMS & NAMES

militarism a government's aggressive use of its armed forces

Diet (DY•iht) Japan's law-making body, which consists of a House of Representatives and a House of Councillors

zaibatsu (ZY•baht•SOO) the large family-controlled banking and industrial groups that owned many companies in Japan before World War II

Junichiro Koizumi (JU•NEE•chee•roh KOH•EE•zoo•mee) Japan's prime minister from 2001 to 2006; Shinzo Abe became prime minister in 2006.

Visual Vocabulary The bombing of Pearl Harbor demonstrated Japanese militarism.

▶ Reading Strategy

Re-create the chart shown at right. As you read and respond to the **KEY QUESTIONS**, use the chart to jot down main ideas about Japan's government and economy.

 See Skillbuilder Handbook, page R4

FIND MAIN IDEAS

JAPAN'S GOVERNMENT	JAPAN'S ECONOMY
1.	1.
2.	2.
3.	3.

 GRAPHIC ORGANIZERS
Go to **Interactive Review** @ClassZone.com

Economic Giant

Connecting to Your World

You have probably seen stories on the news about people attempting to rebuild their homes in the wake of a disaster. In 2005, for example, the people of New Orleans faced this challenge after being hit by Hurricane Katrina. After World War II, Japan also faced horrible devastation. U.S. atomic bombs had reduced two cities, Hiroshima and Nagasaki, to rubble. Other cities had been hit hard by firebombing raids. But out of this destruction, Japan developed a modern government and a thriving economy.

Modernizing Japan's Government

▼ KEY QUESTION How did the new constitution of Japan make the nation more democratic?

For centuries, many Japanese had regarded their emperor as a divine figure. However, after Japan's defeat in World War II, the emperor denied any claim to divine origins. He also gave up his authority to rule and became a symbolic head of state. This change was just one of many in the process of making the Japanese government more democratic.

Legislature Japan's legislature meets in the National Diet Building in Tokyo. The emperor and empress of Japan are pictured in the oval portrait.

A New Constitution In 1947, Japan adopted a new constitution, which set up a parliamentary government. It also guaranteed the Japanese people many rights, including freedom of speech and religion and freedom of the press.

The new constitution prohibited Japan from having a military that can wage war. This policy was an intentional rejection of the militarism that led Japan into World War II. **Militarism** refers to a government's aggressive use of its armed forces. In 2004, however, this policy began to change when Japanese troops were sent to Iraq for humanitarian and construction work. It was the first time Japanese soldiers had entered an active foreign war zone since World War II.

Government Structure Japan's government is divided into three branches—executive, legislative, and judicial. The legislature consists of a law-making body called the **Diet** (DY•iht). Members of the Diet are elected by the Japanese people. The prime minister heads the executive branch and is chosen by members of the Diet. The judicial branch of Japan is headed by the Supreme Court.

🔺 **ANALYZE EFFECTS** Tell how Japan's new constitution made the nation more democratic.

COMPARING ↔ U.S. & Japanese Governments

U.S. GOVERNMENT
U.S. citizens elect representatives and the President for the national government.

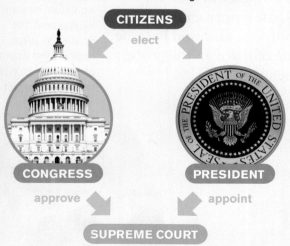

CITIZENS

elect

CONGRESS   PRESIDENT

approve   *appoint*

SUPREME COURT

JAPANESE GOVERNMENT
The members of the Diet are elected by the Japanese people. The emperor and the cabinet appoint the Supreme Court justices.

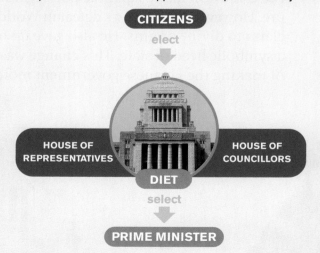

CITIZENS

elect

HOUSE OF REPRESENTATIVES   HOUSE OF COUNCILLORS

DIET

select

PRIME MINISTER

CRITICAL THINKING

Compare and Contrast How does the structure of Japan's government compare with that of the U.S. government?

Creating an Economic Powerhouse

▼ KEY QUESTION How did Japan create an economic powerhouse?

Like the government, Japan's economy was in chaos after World War II. Bombs had destroyed factories, and many people were unemployed. Despite all these problems, Japan managed to become an economic giant that is second only to the United States.

Japanese Companies and Workers Before the war, Japan's economy was run by large business groups called *zaibatsu* (ZY•baht•SOO). ***Zaibatsu*** were large, family-controlled banking and industrial groups. The Allies dissolved the *zaibatsu* after the war. However, groups composed of various businesses soon formed that were similar to the old *zaibatsu*. These groups pooled their resources to make investments in developing industries. Their cooperation greatly helped speed up Japan's economic growth.

CONNECT ➤ Economics & Culture

Recipe for Economic Success Much of Japan's success has to do with the country's emphasis on education and its willingness to reward hard work. The ability of the Japanese to adapt technologies and create new ones has also been an important ingredient.

Dedication Workers often put in 12-hour days. Many place the needs of the company before their own.

Adaptation The Japanese have always adapted to the influences of other cultures. Today, they often improve on imported technologies.

Innovation Japan has always pursued new ways of doing things. Japanese engineers lead the way in creating life-like robots.

CRITICAL THINKING
Evaluate How has the Japanese worker contributed to Japan's economic success?

Economic Miracle and Setbacks From the early 1950s to the early 1970s, Japan's economy skyrocketed. One reason for this economic boom was trade. Japan imported raw materials at low costs and exported manufactured goods. The nation also switched from producing products such as textiles to products such as electronics, which require fewer raw materials.

The success of the economy brought many social changes to Japan. Many people moved from rural areas to cities to work in factories and service industries. As a result, fewer people earned a living by farming. Some families saw their income doubling or tripling. In cities, the pressure to conform to traditional ways lessened. Because of this, young people often felt freer to develop their individuality.

By the 1990s, though, Japan's economy started to suffer some setbacks. The high price of Japanese products made them difficult to sell overseas. Also, Japanese industry faced stiff competition from low-cost businesses in developing nations. Soon, unemployment rose, and consumer spending declined. Many economists refer to the 1990s as Japan's "lost decade." In 2001, Prime Minister **Junichiro Koizumi** (JU•NEE•chee•roh KOH•EE•zoo•mee) made the economy his top priority. By 2006, many companies were again reporting record profits.

▲ **FIND MAIN IDEAS** Explain how Japan developed its economy.

ANALYZING Primary Sources

Junichiro Koizumi (born 1942) served as prime minister of Japan from 2001 to 2006. At one point, his popularity reached almost rock-star status. In this speech, he tried to inspire confidence in Japan's economic future.

> The top priority that I must address is to rebuild our economy and reconstruct our society into ones full of pride and confidence. . . . We must embrace difficulties ahead . . . and free ourselves of past limitations as we create an economic social structure befitting the 21st century in the spirit of "No fear, no hesitation, and no constraint."
>
> Source: Speech to the Diet, May 7, 2001, Junichiro Koizumi

DOCUMENT–BASED QUESTION

What does Koizumi think the Japanese must do to achieve economic reforms?

What the Economy Produces

▼ **KEY QUESTION** What are the major manufacturing, agricultural, and service industries of Japan?

As you have learned, Japan's economic strategy called for producing many high-quality products that could be made with materials imported for a low cost. As a result, the Japanese focused on making electronic equipment and automobiles.

Manufacturing During the 1950s, the Japanese got a foothold in the electronics industry by producing transistor radios. These small radios became very popular with young people, especially in the United States and Europe. Soon, the Japanese began to manufacture televisions, tape recorders, VCRs, and computers. Innovations in the manufacturing process spurred the development of electronics.

Innovations also helped the growth of Japan's auto industry. For example, as early as 1970, the Japanese used digital technology with assembly lines. The rise of the auto industry in Japan is incredible. In 1962, Japan was sixth in the world in automobile production. By 1967, it had overtaken West Germany to rank second. And then in 1980, Japan surpassed the United States to become the largest producer of automobiles in the world.

Agriculture As you may recall, Japan has little farmland. However, Japanese farmers have been able to make this land as productive as possible. First of all, it has helped that Japan's climate is ideal for growing certain crops, such as rice. In addition, farmers extensively use irrigation and fertilizers.

The primary crop by far is rice. Other products include eggs, potatoes, fruits, and vegetables. Japan, though, does need to import some agricultural products, such as animal feed, wheat, and beans.

Major Industries of Japan

- Chemicals
- High-tech
- Iron and steel
- Machinery
- Precision instruments
- Shipbuilding
- Textiles
- Vehicles

Sea of Okhotsk

Hokkaido

Sapporo

Sea of Japan (East Sea)

Honshu

Toyama

Tokyo

Nagoya

Kobe

Hiroshima

Osaka

Shikoku

Kyushu

PACIFIC OCEAN

CONNECT Geography & Economics

1. **Region** On which island are most of the industries located?
2. **Human-Environment Interaction** Why do you think shipbuilding is a major industry in Japan?

Tokyo Disneyland Tokyo Disneyland was the first Disney park to be built outside of the United States. It is one of the most visited theme parks in the world, attracting tourists from all over the globe.

Service Industries As manufacturing industries thrived in Japan, so too did the industries that served them. Banks, for example, have a lot of power in Japan. In fact, the Bank of Japan strongly influences the government's economic policies. Also, some of Japan's banks have a major impact on international banking.

In addition, Japan has many service industries that deal with entertainment, such as nightclubs, movie theaters, and restaurants. Although Western fast-food restaurants have become popular, traditional Japanese restaurants continue to attract many customers. Japan has a great variety of traditional eating places, including sushi restaurants. It also has a healthy tourist industry. Tourism was an important part of Junichiro Koizumi's policies. His efforts paid off. In 2005, Japan hosted more than 6 million visitors from overseas.

 SUMMARIZE Identify Japan's major manufacturing, agricultural, and service industries.

Section 3 Assessment

ONLINE QUIZ For test practice, go to **Interactive Review** @ ClassZone.com

TERMS & NAMES

1. Explain the importance of
- militarism
- Diet
- *zaibatsu*
- Junichiro Koizumi

USE YOUR READING NOTES

2. Find Main Ideas Use your completed chart to answer the following question:

What economic obstacles did Japan have to overcome after World War II?

JAPAN'S GOVERNMENT	JAPAN'S ECONOMY
1.	1.
2.	2.
3.	3.

KEY IDEAS

3. What does Japan's constitution prohibit?

4. How did the *zaibatsu* influence Japan's businesses after World War II?

5. What are Japan's major manufacturing industries?

CRITICAL THINKING

6. Form and Support Opinions Do you think Japan's constitution should be amended to allow the Japanese to wage war? Explain why or why not.

7. Analyze Effects How do you think families are affected by the long workdays put in by many Japanese employees?

8. CONNECT to Today What impact do Japanese products have on the everyday lives of Americans?

9. ECONOMICS Compare Cars Research a car produced by a Japanese company. Then research a comparable car made by a U.S. company. Compare the two cars and write a report including information on style, price, features, and consumer ratings.

Interactive ◀▶ Review

Click here to complete these and other activities online @ ClassZone.com

CHAPTER SUMMARY

Key Idea 1
The mountainous islands that make up Japan provide the country's people with scant living space, a varied climate, and limited resources.

Key Idea 2
Over the centuries, Japan has adapted ideas and technologies from other lands and created a unique culture.

Key Idea 3
The Japanese have drawn on their culture to create a modern government and become an economic giant.

 For **Review and Study Notes**, go to **Interactive Review** @ ClassZone.com

NAME GAME

Use the Terms & Names list to complete each sentence on paper or online.

1. I am Japan's highest mountain. <u>Mount Fuji</u> 🖐
2. I am the largest lowland of Japan._____
3. I am a powerful samurai who became a warrior-chieftain. _____
4. I am the shogun who unified Japan and moved the capital to Edo. _____
5. I am Japan's original religion. _____
6. I am the aggressive use of a government's armed forces. _____
7. I am Japan's law-making body, which consists of two houses._____
8. I am a large family-controlled business group that owned many companies in Japan before World War II. _____
9. I am Japan's largest and most populous island. _____
10. I am a period in Japanese history in which arts and writing flourished. _____

daimyo

Diet

Heian

Honshu

Kanto Plain

Junichiro Koizumi

militarism

Mount Fuji

Shinto

shogun

Tokugawa Ieyasu

zaibatsu

Activities

GeoGame

Use this online map to show what you know about Japan's location, geographic features, and important places. Drag and drop each place name to its location on the map.

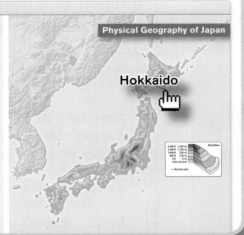

To play the complete game, go to **Interactive Review** @ ClassZone.com

Crossword Puzzle

Complete an online crossword puzzle to test your knowledge of Japan.

ACROSS
1. professional soldier of Japan

VOCABULARY

Explain the significance of each of the following.

1. Mount Fuji
2. Kanto Plain
3. Heian period
4. samurai
5. shogun
6. daimyo
7. Shinto
8. militarism
9. Diet
10. Junichiro Koizumi

Explain how the terms and names in each group are related.

11. samurai, shogun, and daimyo
12. Honshu, Hokkaido, Kyushu, and Shikoku

KEY IDEAS

1 Land of the Rising Sun

13. What geographic feature forms the islands of Japan?
14. What is the Ring of Fire?
15. How does the climate of Japan's mountains differ from other regions of Japan?
16. Where does Japan get much of its food?

2 Samurai to Animé

17. To which clan have Japanese emperors belonged throughout history?
18. How did the Tokugawa shogunate affect Japan's foreign relations?
19. What are the two major religions of Japan?
20. What is tanka poetry?

3 Economic Giant

21. What is the role of the Japanese emperor today?
22. What were the *zaibatsu*?
23. What social changes did Japan's booming economy bring to the country between the 1950s and the 1970s?
24. Why did Japan focus on producing electronic equipment and automobiles?

CRITICAL THINKING

25. **Compare and Contrast** Use a Venn diagram to compare Japan in the early 1900s before World War II with the country after the war.

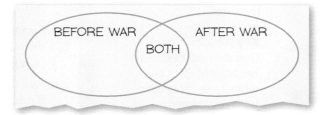

26. **Evaluate** How is the Japanese love of nature reflected in the country's culture?
27. **Form Opinions** Do you think the Tokugawa shogunate did more to help or to hurt Japanese society? Explain your answer.
28. **Make Inferences** Why do you think the Allies dissolved the *zaibatsu* after World War II?
29. **Connect Geography & Economics** How have Japan's natural resources affected its economy?
30. **Five Themes: Human-Environment Interaction** How has Japan's geography affected the way the Japanese live in cities?

Answer the ESSENTIAL QUESTION

How has Japan balanced its ancient traditions with its modern economy?

Written Response Write a two- or three-paragraph response to the Essential Question. Use the rubric below to guide your thinking.

Response Rubric
A strong response will:
- discuss the importance of Japan's cultural traditions
- explain how Japan has built up its strong economy
- emphasize Japan's ability to adapt to new ideas and changing times

STANDARDS-BASED ASSESSMENT

✓ **Test Practice**
- **Online Test Practice @ ClassZone.com**
- **Test-Taking Strategies and Practice** at the front of this book

THEMATIC MAP

Use the earthquake map to answer questions 1 and 2 on your paper.

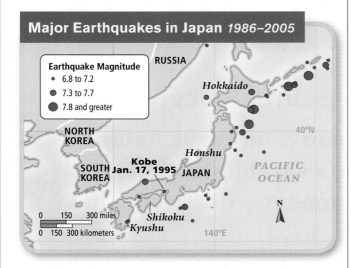

Major Earthquakes in Japan *1986–2005*

Earthquake Magnitude
- 6.8 to 7.2
- 7.3 to 7.7
- 7.8 and greater

RUSSIA
Hokkaido
NORTH KOREA
Honshu
Kobe Jan. 17, 1995
SOUTH KOREA JAPAN
40°N
PACIFIC OCEAN
Shikoku
Kyushu
140°E

0 150 300 miles
0 150 300 kilometers

PIE GRAPH

Use the pie graph on Japan's exports to answer questions 3 and 4 on your paper.

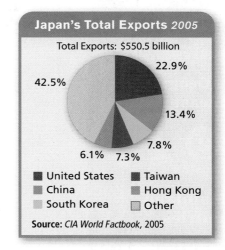

Japan's Total Exports *2005*

Total Exports: $550.5 billion

- 22.9%
- 42.5%
- 13.4%
- 7.8%
- 6.1%
- 7.3%

- ■ United States
- ■ China
- ■ South Korea
- ■ Taiwan
- ■ Hong Kong
- ■ Other

Source: *CIA World Factbook*, 2005

---

1. What was the magnitude of the 1995 earthquake in Kobe?

A. less than 6.8
B. 6.8 to 7.2
C. 7.3 to 7.7
D. 7.8 and greater

2. Near which island have most of the greatest magnitude earthquakes occurred?

A. Hokkaido
B. Honshu
C. Kyushu
D. Shikoku

3. Which country among those listed below is Japan's biggest export partner?

A. South Korea
B. China
C. United States
D. Taiwan

4. What percentage of Japan's total exports were sent to China?

A. 6.1 percent
B. 7.3 percent
C. 13.4 percent
D. 42.5 percent

GeoActivity

1. INTERDISCIPLINARY ACTIVITY–ART

With a small group, design and create a miniature Japanese Zen garden. Use your library and the Internet to research this art form. Find out about patterns used in gravel and what rocks can represent. Present your Japanese Zen garden to your class.

2. WRITING FOR SOCIAL STUDIES

Imagine that you are a tourist in a Japanese city. Write a diary entry describing a typical day. Discuss the crowds, the sights, the food, and the blend of old and new you witness.

3. MENTAL MAPPING

Create an outline map of Japan and label the following:

- Pacific Ocean
- East Sea
- Honshu
- Hokkaido
- Kyushu
- Shikoku
- Japanese Alps
- Kanto Plain

Southeast Asia

ESSENTIAL QUESTION

How can Southeast Asian nations establish stable governments and economies?

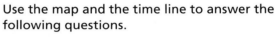

CONNECT Geography & History

Use the map and the time line to answer the following questions.

1. What two island chains are part of Southeast Asia?

2. Which Southeast Asian country was once known as Siam?

Culture
◄ **1300s** Muslim traders bring Islam to Indonesia.
(Mosque in Jakarta)

500

History
500s A people known as the Khmers establish an empire on the mainland peninsula.

History
1688 Siam, or present-day Thailand, begins to limit relations with Europeans.
(King Chulalongkorn of Siam) ►

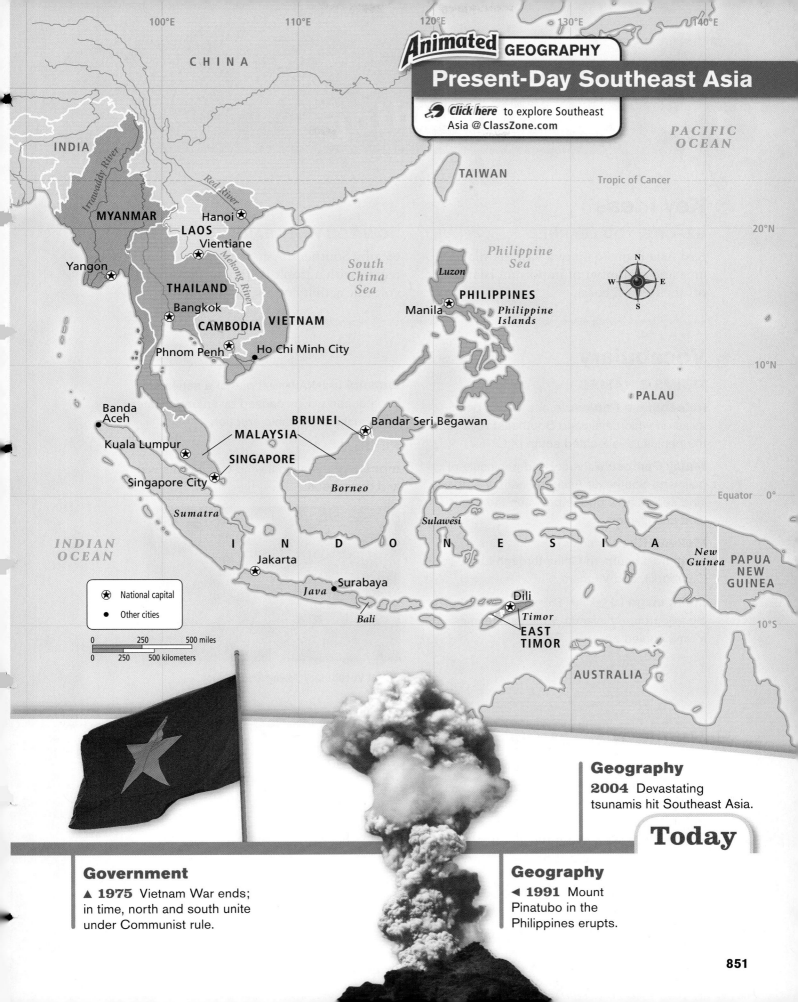

CHINA

INDIA

PACIFIC OCEAN

TAIWAN

Tropic of Cancer

Irrawaddy River

Red River

MYANMAR

Hanoi

LAOS

Vientiane

Yangon

Mekong River

THAILAND

Bangkok

CAMBODIA

VIETNAM

Phnom Penh

Ho Chi Minh City

South China Sea

Philippine Sea

Luzon

PHILIPPINES

Manila

Philippine Islands

20°N

10°N

PALAU

Banda Aceh

BRUNEI

Bandar Seri Begawan

MALAYSIA

Kuala Lumpur

SINGAPORE

Singapore City

Borneo

Sumatra

Sulawesi

INDIAN OCEAN

I N D O N E S I A

New Guinea

PAPUA NEW GUINEA

Equator 0°

Jakarta

Java

Surabaya

Bali

Dili

Timor

EAST TIMOR

10°S

AUSTRALIA

★ National capital
● Other cities

0 — 250 — 500 miles
0 — 250 — 500 kilometers

Geography
2004 Devastating tsunamis hit Southeast Asia.

Today

Government
▲ **1975** Vietnam War ends; in time, north and south unite under Communist rule.

Geography
◄ **1991** Mount Pinatubo in the Philippines erupts.

Reading for Understanding

▶ Key Ideas

BEFORE, YOU LEARNED

East Asia is made up of a vast mainland area and a number of important islands off the eastern coast.

NOW YOU WILL LEARN

Nearby Southeast Asia is a mountainous region with a tropical climate and much volcanic activity on its many islands.

▶ Vocabulary

TERMS & NAMES

Indochinese Peninsula one of two peninsulas on which mainland Southeast Asia lies; the peninsula is located south of China

Malay Peninsula the second peninsula of mainland Southeast Asia; the narrow strip of land serves as a bridge between the mainland and islands

Mekong River a major river that runs south from southern China through Laos, Cambodia, and Vietnam

archipelago (AHR•kuh•PEHL•uh•GOH) a set of closely grouped islands, which sometimes form a curved arc

tsunami (tsu•NAH•mee) one or a series of large ocean waves caused by an underwater earthquake or volcanic eruption

REVIEW

monsoon a seasonal wind that causes wet and dry seasons

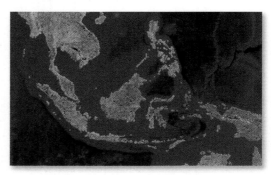

Visual Vocabulary Malay Archipelago

▶ Reading Strategy

Re-create the chart shown at right. As you read and respond to the **KEY QUESTIONS**, use the chart to jot down main ideas about Southeast Asia's geographic features, climate, plants, and animals.

 Skillbuilder Handbook, page R4

FIND MAIN IDEAS

	MAINLAND	ISLANDS
Geographic Features		
Climate		
Plants and Animals		

 GRAPHIC ORGANIZERS
Go to **Interactive Review** @ ClassZone.com

Physical Geography of Southeast Asia

Connecting to Your World

You may have heard of Mount St. Helens, the volcano that erupted in 1980 in the state of Washington. The blast killed 57 people and sent ash thousands of feet into the air. In 1991, a volcanic eruption that was ten times larger occurred on Mount Pinatubo in the Philippines. More than 300 people died in this eruption, and many thousands more lost their homes. In this section, you will learn why volcanic eruptions and other natural disasters occur frequently in Southeast Asia.

Mainland and Islands

▼ **KEY QUESTION** What are some of the advantages and disadvantages of Southeast Asia's physical geography?

Southeast Asia has two distinct subregions: the southeastern corner of the Asian mainland and a great number of islands. Both regions have many mountains. Most of the mountains on the islands were formed from volcanoes. Southeast Asia is part of the Ring of Fire, a zone of volcanoes around the rim of the Pacific Ocean. As a result, volcanic eruptions and earthquakes are common.

Island Nation A temple built in the 17th century to honor a Hindu water goddess floats on the water in Bali, one of the islands that makes up Indonesia.

853

Mekong River The Mekong River is the heart and soul of mainland Southeast Asia. Millions of people rely on the river for farming, fishing, water, and transport. **What does this Vietnamese farmer seem to be using the Mekong for?**

Peninsulas As shown on the map on the opposite page, mainland Southeast Asia lies on two peninsulas. The **Indochinese Peninsula Ⓐ** is located south of China. The **Malay Peninsula Ⓑ** is a narrow strip of land about 700 miles long. It serves as a bridge between the mainland and the islands.

The Indochinese Peninsula has a series of north-south mountain ranges separated by river valleys and lowlands. To the west of these mountains flows one of the world's great rivers—the **Mekong Ⓒ**. It runs south for about 2,600 miles from southern China through Laos, Cambodia, and Vietnam. The river opens onto a wide fertile delta on Vietnam's coast.

Island Chains Most of the islands of Southeast Asia are grouped into archipelagoes. An **archipelago** (AHR•kuh•PEHL•uh•GOH) is a set of closely grouped islands. The largest of these island groups is the Malay Archipelago, which includes Indonesia Ⓓ and the Philippines Ⓔ. Indonesia is made up of about 17,500 islands. Java, Sumatra, and Borneo are the most important islands. The Philippines lies to the north of Indonesia. This nation consists of about 7,100 islands. The largest and most important of these islands is Luzon.

Natural Disasters You have already learned about the volcanic eruption of Mount Pinatubo in 1991. An even greater disaster occurred on December 26, 2004, when a series of tsunamis hit many parts of Southeast Asia. A **tsunami** (tsu•NAH•mee) is a very large ocean wave caused by an underwater earthquake or volcanic eruption. The Asian tsunami, as the disaster was called, was one of the deadliest in modern history. The tsunamis were caused by an earthquake that released energy equal to about 23,000 atomic bombs.

▲ **ANALYZE EFFECTS** Describe some of the advantages and disadvantages of Southeast Asia's physical geography.

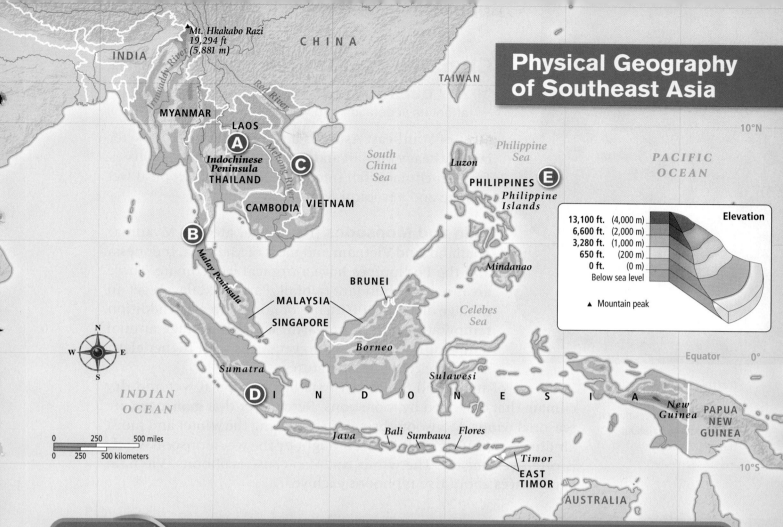

Physical Geography of Southeast Asia

Mt. Hkakabo Razi
19,294 ft
(5,881 m)

CHINA

INDIA

TAIWAN

MYANMAR

LAOS

Ⓐ

Indochinese
Peninsula
THAILAND

Ⓒ

South
China
Sea

Luzon

Philippine
Sea

PACIFIC
OCEAN

10°N

CAMBODIA   VIETNAM

PHILIPPINES Ⓔ

Philippine
Islands

Ⓑ

Malay Peninsula

Mindanao

MALAYSIA

BRUNEI

SINGAPORE

Celebes
Sea

Borneo

Sumatra

Sulawesi

INDIAN
OCEAN

Ⓓ I   N   D   O   N   E   S   I   A

Equator   0°

New
Guinea

PAPUA
NEW
GUINEA

N
W   E
S

Java   Bali   Sumbawa   Flores

Timor
EAST
TIMOR

10°S

AUSTRALIA

0   250   500 miles
0   250   500 kilometers

Elevation

13,100 ft.   (4,000 m)
6,600 ft.   (2,000 m)
3,280 ft.   (1,000 m)
650 ft.   (200 m)
0 ft.   (0 m)
Below sea level

▲ Mountain peak

CONNECT Geography & History

The 2004 Asian Tsunami On December 26, 2004, a 9.0-magnitude earthquake in the Indian Ocean triggered tsunamis up to 50 feet high. The gigantic waves caused devastating damage in many parts of Indonesia, southern Thailand, Sri Lanka, southern India, and elsewhere. The inset map shows the worst-affected areas. Besides taking more than 200,000 lives, the tsunamis also destroyed thousands of miles of coastline. The image here shows the devastation in Banda Aceh, a city in Sumatra.

CRITICAL THINKING

Draw Conclusions Study the large map above. Why do you think Sumatra and southern Thailand were especially affected by the tsunamis?

INDIA   MYANMAR

THAILAND

SOMALIA

SRI
LANKA

Banda Aceh

MALAYSIA

MALDIVES

INDONESIA

INDIAN
OCEAN

— Worst-affected Areas
◎ Earthquake Epicenter

90°E   100°E   110°E   120°E   130°E

Rafflesia The Rafflesia, which is native to Indonesia, is the world's largest flower. It can grow to be about three feet across.

Climate, Vegetation, and Wildlife

KEY QUESTION How does Southeast Asia's climate affect its vegetation and wildlife?

Most of Southeast Asia has a tropical climate characterized by heavy rainfall and generally warm temperatures. Tropical climates fall into two categories: a tropical wet climate and a tropical wet and dry climate.

Rain and Monsoons The coastal areas of Myanmar, Thailand, and Vietnam and most of Malaysia, Indonesia, and the Philippines have a tropical wet climate. These areas receive abundant rainfall. Parts of Malaysia get an average of about 100 inches of rain per year. In addition, temperatures are very warm, with an average annual temperature of 80°F. However, areas with higher elevation have cooler temperatures.

Much of mainland Southeast Asia has a tropical wet and dry climate that is shaped by monsoons. Remember that **monsoons** are seasonal winds. Monsoons bring dry air during the winter and moist air during the summer. Rainfall brought by the wet monsoon winds is often very heavy. The winds can also cause typhoons. Vietnam experiences about five typhoons each year.

◀ COMPARING ▶ Regional Rainfall

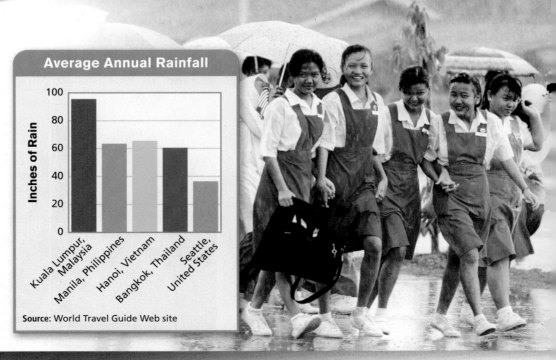

In the image shown here, Malaysian schoolgirls walk in the rain. As you can see in the graph, Malaysia receives more rain than any other country in Southeast Asia. Compare the amounts of rainfall received by these Southeast Asian cities with that received by Seattle, one of the rainiest cities in the United States.

CRITICAL THINKING

Compare and Contrast
Which three cities receive about the same amount of rainfall?

Average Annual Rainfall

Inches of Rain

100
80
60
40
20
0

Kuala Lumpur, Malaysia
Manila, Philippines
Hanoi, Vietnam
Bangkok, Thailand
Seattle, United States

Source: World Travel Guide Web site

Vegetation and Wildlife Southeast Asia's hot, humid climate supports tropical vegetation. In fact, Southeast Asia has one of the greatest varieties of vegetation on Earth. For example, it has a remarkable number of tree species. Tropical evergreen forests are situated in areas with much rainfall near the equator. Deciduous forests are common in the wet and dry climate zone. Teak, a wood used in shipbuilding and furniture, comes from these forests. Some unusual plants thrive in Southeast Asia. Many of these plants have strong-smelling flowers and fruits.

Southeast Asia also has thousands of varieties of birds and animals, and new species are still being discovered. In 2005, scientists found dozens of new plant and animal species in an isolated forest area of Indonesia. Not even people from nearby villages had ever visited the area. In addition, Southeast Asia is home to such large animals as the rhinoceros, tiger, and elephant. The orangutan is native to Indonesia and Malaysia.

Sumatran Rhinoceros
This small species of rhino has two horns and a coat of coarse hair. Most of these rhinos live in remote mountain areas of Indonesia.

 EVALUATE Explain how Southeast Asia's climate affects its vegetation and wildlife.

Section 1 Assessment

ONLINE QUIZ
For test practice, go to **Interactive Review** @ ClassZone.com

TERMS & NAMES

1. Explain the importance of
- Indochinese Peninsula
- Malay Peninsula
- Mekong River
- archipelago

USE YOUR READING NOTES

2. Find Main Ideas Use your completed chart to answer the following question:

Which Southeast Asian subregion receives more rainfall, the mainland or the islands?

	MAINLAND	ISLANDS
Geographic Features		
Climate		
Plants and Animals		

KEY IDEAS

3. Why are earthquakes and volcanic eruptions common in Southeast Asia?

4. Why is the Mekong an important river?

5. How do monsoons affect the climate of Southeast Asia?

CRITICAL THINKING

6. Make Inferences Based on the geographic features of Indonesia, what might be some of the major economic activities of this nation?

7. Draw Conclusions Why do you think new species of animals are still being discovered in Southeast Asia?

8. CONNECT to Today What do you think people in Southeast Asia could do to prevent a huge loss of life in the event of another tsunami?

9. TECHNOLOGY Create a Multimedia Presentation Create a multimedia presentation that shows how a volcano in the Ring of Fire forms and erupts. Use library and Internet sources. Include descriptions with your visuals.

Reading for Understanding

▶ Key Ideas

BEFORE, YOU LEARNED

Southeast Asia is made up of mainland countries and island chains.

NOW YOU WILL LEARN

The nations of mainland Southeast Asia have closely connected histories and diverse cultures.

▶ Vocabulary

TERMS & NAMES

Indochina the name for a former French colony in Southeast Asia made up of Cambodia, Laos, and Vietnam

Khmer (kmair) **Empire** an empire that began in the 500s and had gained control of much of mainland Southeast Asia by the 800s

colonialism the control by one power over a dependent area or people

Tet the Vietnamese New Year and most important holiday in Vietnam

Siam the former name of Thailand

constitutional monarchy a government in which the powers of the king or queen are limited by a constitution

Aung San Suu Kyi (awng sahn soo chee) leader of the democracy movement in Myanmar

microstate an independent country that is very small in area and population

Visual Vocabulary celebration of Tet

▶ Reading Strategy

Re-create the web diagram shown at right. As you read and respond to the **KEY QUESTIONS**, use a different copy of the diagram to summarize the history, government, economy, and culture of each mainland country.

 See Skillbuilder Handbook, page R5

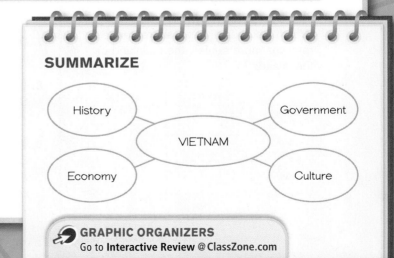

SUMMARIZE

History — Government — VIETNAM — Economy — Culture

GRAPHIC ORGANIZERS
Go to **Interactive Review** @ ClassZone.com

The Mainland Countries

Connecting to Your World

What have you already learned about the Vietnam War? Maybe you know that the war was fought between Communist and anti-Communist forces in North and South Vietnam. You might also know that the United States got involved in the conflict and that this involvement deeply divided the country. Vietnam is one of the mainland countries of Southeast Asia. In this section, you'll learn about the history and politics of mainland Southeast Asia and some of the causes that led to the Vietnam War.

Cambodia, Laos, and Vietnam

▼ **KEY QUESTION** How are the histories, cultures, and economies of Indochina connected?

Indochina is the name given to a former French colony made up of Cambodia, Laos, and Vietnam. Indochina got its name because of its location east of India and south of China. India and China have also had a strong influence on Indochinese culture. The Mekong River flows through Cambodia, Laos, and Vietnam, forming a highway that connects them. For centuries, this river has been used to transport goods and ideas. Not surprisingly, the histories of these nations are also closely connected.

Angkor Wat This temple in Cambodia was built in the 1100s as a Hindu temple but became a Buddhist temple about 100 years later. **Which two countries probably influenced the temple's religious uses?**

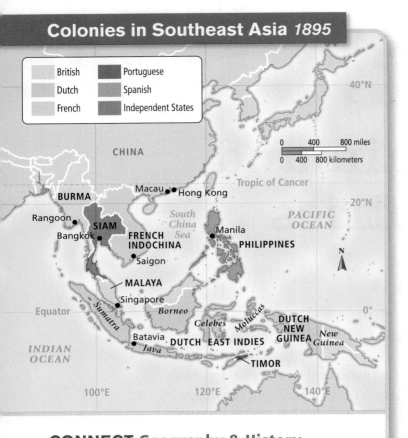

Colonies in Southeast Asia 1895

British
Dutch
French
Portuguese
Spanish
Independent States

0   400   800 miles
0   400   800 kilometers

CHINA

Macau • Hong Kong

Tropic of Cancer

40°N

20°N

BURMA

Rangoon •
SIAM
Bangkok •
FRENCH
INDOCHINA
Saigon •

South
China
Sea

Manila

PACIFIC
OCEAN

PHILIPPINES

N

MALAYA
Singapore

Sumatra

Borneo

Celebes

Moluccas

DUTCH
NEW
GUINEA

New
Guinea

0°

Equator

INDIAN
OCEAN

Batavia •
Java

DUTCH EAST INDIES

TIMOR

100°E   120°E   140°E

CONNECT Geography & History

1. **Location** What colony was controlled by France?
2. **Region** Which European country could access both the Indian and the Pacific oceans from its colony?

History and Government By the 800s, the **Khmer** (kmair) **Empire** had gained control of much of mainland Southeast Asia. The empire reached its peak around 1200. At different times, the Chinese also exerted political influence over parts of the mainland.

European colonists had been arriving in Southeast Asia since 1509. In the 1850s, France began to take control of Vietnam. The French also seized Laos and Cambodia. They took over the countries' political, economic, and social systems in order to obtain wealth, a policy called **colonialism**. By the 20th century, Europeans had colonized all of Southeast Asia except Siam (now Thailand).

In 1953, Laos and Cambodia gained their independence from France. The following year, a peace agreement ended fighting between Vietnam and France, dividing the country into a Communist north and a non-Communist south. But in 1957, a war between North Vietnam and South Vietnam broke out. In time, the fighting involved the United States and also spilled over into Cambodia and Laos. Finally, in 1975, South Vietnam was taken over by North Vietnam. Both Vietnam and Laos established Communist governments. Cambodia was ruled by a brutal Communist dictator until it became a democracy in 1993.

Culture and Economy More than 80 percent of the people in the three nations of Indochina live in rural areas. The majority of Indochinese practice Buddhism. They celebrate religious holidays as well as other traditional holidays. In Vietnam, the most important holiday is **Tet**, the Vietnamese New Year.

Laos and Cambodia have developing economies made up of small industries, such as clothing and textiles. Most of the people work as rice and peanut farmers. Vietnam, on the other hand, has one of the fastest-growing economies in the world. It is developing its oil industry and exports more coffee than any other country except Brazil.

▲ **EVALUATE** Explain how the histories, cultures, and economies of Indochina are connected.

THAILAND

Thailand

▼ **KEY QUESTION** What events in Thailand's past have helped the country prosper?

Thailand is one of the most prosperous countries in Southeast Asia. For most of its history, it was known as **Siam**. Some scholars believe that the word *Siam* means "golden." The nation changed its name to Thailand in 1949.

History and Government The first people to live in the region of Thailand called themselves the Thai, which means "free." The Thai remained free, even after the Europeans began to arrive in Southeast Asia in the 1500s.

In the mid-1800s, Thai leader King Mongkut began to modernize his country. He and his son, King Chulalongkorn, started schools, built railroads, and abolished slavery in Siam. Through their leaders' guidance, the Siamese people escaped the harsh treatment that many other Southeast Asians experienced under foreign control.

Thailand has been a **constitutional monarchy** since 1932, a government in which the powers of the king or queen are limited by a constitution. Thailand came under the control of Japan in 1941. After World War II, a series of military dictators ruled the country. In the mid-1970s, Thailand began to develop a more democratic government. This process was halted in 2006, however, when the military overthrew the prime minister.

Culture and Economy Most of Thailand's people live in rural areas. In the early 1960s, though, large numbers of Thai began to move to cities in search of work. By 2006, the capital city of Bangkok had over 9 million people.

Thai food, including a noodle dish called pad thai, has become very popular in the United States and other countries. In fact, Thai cuisine ranks as the fourth most popular in the world.

Nearly 50 percent of the workers in Thailand earn a living by farming or fishing. Rice, corn, and sugar cane are some of the crops grown. Thailand's industries produce automobiles, electronic equipment, clothing, and plastics. Tourism is also a booming industry.

▲ **DRAW CONCLUSIONS** Identify the events in Thailand's history that have helped the country prosper.

CONNECT ↻ **Geography & History**

Neutral Zone

Siam lay between British-controlled Burma (now Myanmar) and French Indochina. Siamese kings skillfully promoted their country as a neutral zone between the two powers. However, King Chulalongkorn was influenced by European architecture. He had the palace shown here decorated with marble imported from Italy.

MYANMAR

MALAYSIA

Myanmar and Malaysia

🔽 **KEY QUESTION** How do Myanmar and Malaysia compare?

Thailand's neighbors, Myanmar and Malaysia, present contrasting pictures. Malaysia has a thriving market economy and freely elected officials. However, Myanmar has widespread poverty and suffers under a military dictatorship.

History and Government In 1044, the Myanmar region united into a kingdom. Its people adopted Buddhism, which arrived from India. Since the main ethnic group of the kingdom was Burman, the region came to be called Burma. During the 1800s, Great Britain colonized Burma. Although Burma won its independence in 1948, it soon came under the control of a military dictator. In 1989, a new military government changed the country's name to Myanmar. A pro-democracy movement led by **Aung San Suu Kyi** (awng sahn soo chee) has struggled against this government ever since.

For hundreds of years, much of Malaysia was known as Melaka. This country was founded around 1400 and was strongly influenced by Arab Muslim traders. In the 1500s, Melaka came under the control of European colonizers and other rulers. Finally, in 1963, the states of Malay, Sabah, Sarawak, and Singapore united to form the Federation of Malaysia. Singapore left this group in 1965. Today, Malaysia is governed by a constitutional monarchy.

Culture and Economy Most of the people of Myanmar live in rural areas, while more than half the population of Malaysia lives in cities. About two-thirds of Myanmar's population are Burmese who practice Buddhism. Malaysia is ethnically much more diverse. About 60 percent of the people are Muslim.

Myanmar's economy is based on agriculture. Rice and teak are important crops. Malaysia, on the other hand, has an industrialized economy. The country produces a wide range of goods, including electronics and automobiles, which it trades on the international market.

🔺 **COMPARE AND CONTRAST** Compare and contrast Myanmar and Malaysia.

HISTORY MAKERS

Aung San Suu Kyi born 1945

Suu Kyi and other peace activists traveled throughout Myanmar, calling for democratic reforms and free elections. In 1989, after thousands of peaceful demonstrators had been shot and killed, Suu Kyi herself came face to face with an army unit that had been ordered to shoot her. At the last minute, however, an army major stepped in and withdrew the order. In 1991, while under house arrest, Suu Kyi's efforts to establish democracy in her country earned her the Nobel Peace Prize.

 ONLINE BIOGRAPHY
For more on the life of Aung San Suu Kyi, go to the
Research & Writing Center @ ClassZone.com

Singapore

 KEY QUESTION What type of economy and government does Singapore have?

Singapore is a densely populated island nation located at the southern tip of the Malay Peninsula. It is sometimes called a **microstate** because of its very small area—about 225 square miles. Singapore is a wealthy and powerful country. Its industrialized economy depends heavily on its exported goods, including electronics, chemicals, and clothing. In addition, the nation is a major financial center and has many banks and a stock exchange.

Officially, Singapore is a republic, but the government is dominated by one political party. This party limits freedom of speech and controls economic activities. Because Singapore favors order over liberty, the government enforces strict rules on its people. As a result, the country has a clean, corruption-free image throughout the world.

Singapore The Central Area district is the hub of economic activity in Singapore.

 SUMMARIZE Describe Singapore's economy and government.

Section 2 Assessment

ONLINE QUIZ For test practice, go to **Interactive Review** @ ClassZone.com

TERMS & NAMES

1. Explain the importance of
- Indochina
- Khmer Empire
- Siam
- Aung San Suu Kyi

USE YOUR READING NOTES

2. Summarize Use your completed web diagrams to answer the following question:

Which mainland countries appear to have the strongest economies?

KEY IDEAS

3. How did the war between North Vietnam and South Vietnam affect Indochina?

4. How did Siam avoid colonization?

5. What is the Federation of Malaysia?

CRITICAL THINKING

6. Identify Problems In your opinion, what are the most difficult problems facing the mainland countries of Southeast Asia?

7. Make Inferences What influences might account for the fact that about 60 percent of the population of Malaysia is Muslim?

8. CONNECT to Today How might colonialism have affected the ability of some Southeast Asian countries to establish stable governments and economies?

9. WRITING Write a Feature Article Imagine that you have been assigned to write a feature on the Vietnamese holiday of Tet. Research to find images and information on the holiday's history and traditions.

Reading for Understanding

▶ Key Ideas

BEFORE, YOU LEARNED

The mainland countries of Southeast Asia are a mix of rural and urban cultures and wealthy and poor economies.

NOW YOU WILL LEARN

Indonesia and the Philippines both have rich cultural traditions and long histories as centers of trade.

▶ Vocabulary

TERMS & NAMES

Bahasa Indonesia (bah•HAH•suh in•duh•NEE•zhuh) the language of Indonesia

shadow puppet traditional Indonesian art, in which puppets are handled from behind a screen lit by a bright light

Filipino an inhabitant of the Philippines

Ferdinand Marcos dictatorial president of the Philippines between 1965 and 1986

Corazon Aquino (uh•KEE•noh) politician who opposed Marcos and was president of the Philippines between 1986 and 1992

REVIEW

archipelago a set of closely grouped islands, which sometimes form a curved arc

Visual Vocabulary Ferdinand Marcos

▶ Reading Strategy

Re-create the chart shown at right. As you read and respond to the **KEY QUESTIONS**, use the chart to categorize facts about the history, government, culture, and economy of Indonesia and the Philippines.

 See Skillbuilder Handbook, page R7

CATEGORIZE

	INDONESIA	THE PHILIPPINES
History		
Government		
Culture		
Economy		

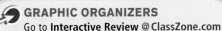
GRAPHIC ORGANIZERS
Go to **Interactive Review** @ ClassZone.com

SECTION 3
FOCUS ON

Indonesia and the Philippines

Connecting to Your World

If you wanted to travel to a friend's house, would you try to get there by boat? Probably not. Most Americans journey from one place to another by car, bus, or train. However, on the islands of Southeast Asia, people often travel by boat. As a result, the surrounding seas serve as a sort of highway connecting the islands in this region. The seas, though, have also made it difficult to unify the island nations of Southeast Asia.

Indonesia

KEY QUESTION What unites and divides the people of Indonesia?

Indonesia is an **archipelago** that stretches for about 3,200 miles and consists of more than 17,500 islands. As you have already learned, the main islands are Java, Sumatra, and Borneo. Some of the smaller islands are uninhabited, but others are densely populated. Java, for instance, contains about 60 percent of Indonesia's population. Many cities in Indonesia are huge. For example, Jakarta, the country's capital, has more than 8 million people. Indonesia is the fourth most populous country in the world.

Jakarta Jakarta has broad boulevards, but traffic is a problem. To reduce congestion, some roads are only open to vehicles carrying three or more passengers.

865

History and Government As early as 1000 B.C., the region of Indonesia had become a crossroads for trade. Over the years, many goods and ideas arrived from distant lands. Indian traders brought Hinduism, and traders from both India and China carried Buddhism. By the 1300s, Muslim traders from Arabia had introduced Islam.

During the 1500s, Portugal gained control of present-day Indonesia and set up trade. The Dutch took over in 1641. They established the Dutch East India Company, a group that dominated trade on most of the islands. Indonesia gained independence from the Dutch in 1949 but was controlled by a military regime for many years. Today, Indonesia is a republic. In 2004, it held its first direct presidential elections. The new president pledged to promote democratic reforms.

Culture and Economy Most of the people of Indonesia live in rural areas. The population of the country is one of the most ethnically diverse in the world. About 300 ethnic groups make this island nation their home and speak about 250 different languages. For years, Indonesia lacked a common language. Then in the late 1920s, the nation created a language called **Bahasa Indonesia** that helped unify the people. Cultural traditions also unite Indonesians. Traditional arts include **shadow puppets**, in which puppets, such as those below, are worked from behind a screen lit by a bright light **A**. On the other side of the screen, the audience sees the puppets as shadows **B**.

From 1987 to 1997, Indonesia's economy grew rapidly. Then the nation suffered a financial slump when its money became devalued and its stock market fell. Indonesia's economy is still recovering. Today, oil and natural gas produce the greatest wealth in Indonesia. In fact, it is the world's largest exporter of liquefied natural gas. Manufacturing is also a major activity. Nonetheless, fishing and farming are a huge part of the economy, employing about half of all Indonesians.

▲ **DRAW CONCLUSIONS** Identify some of the factors that unite and divide Indonesians.

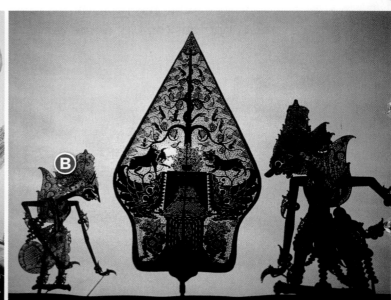

866

The Philippines

KEY QUESTION How has the Philippines improved its government and economy?

The Philippines is made up of around 7,100 islands, but only about 1,000 of them are inhabited. The nation is named for King Philip II of Spain, who sent explorers to the region during the 1500s. The people who live in the Philippines are called **Filipinos**.

History and Government Since ancient times, traders from China and the Malay region have had a strong influence on the culture of the Philippines. By the late 1500s, the Spanish Empire had colonized the Philippines. The Spanish controlled the area until 1898. After being defeated in the Spanish-American War, Spain handed control of the Philippines over to the United States. U.S. rule of the region lasted until 1946, when the Philippines gained its independence.

After independence, however, the country faced many economic problems. In 1965, **Ferdinand Marcos** became president and improved the economy. But in 1973, Marcos seized complete control of the government. **Corazon Aquino** (uh•KEE•noh) opposed Marcos during the 1986 election. Although the government declared that Marcos had won, many people suspected fraud. After much protest, Marcos left the country and Aquino took over as president. Today, the Philippines has a democratic government headed by a president.

 ONLINE PRIMARY SOURCE To read more of Aquino's speeches, go to the **Research & Writing Center** @ClassZone.com

ANALYZING Primary Sources

Corazon Aquino (born 1933) was married to Benigno Aquino, Jr., a political rival of Ferdinand Marcos. When her husband was assassinated in 1983, Aquino suspected that Marcos was behind the death. She ran against Marcos in 1986 and became the first woman president of the Philippines. In the following, Aquino describes her political philosophy.

> I don't have any formula for ousting [overthrowing] a dictator or building democracy. . . . All I can suggest is to forget about yourself and just think of your people. It's always the people who make things happen.
>
> Source: *Time Asia*, August 1999, article by Sandra Burton

DOCUMENT–BASED QUESTION
According to Corazon Aquino, who builds a democracy?

Rice Terraces in Luzon
Farmers first carved rice terraces into the mountains of Luzon about 2,000 years ago. The levels were reinforced with stone walls.

Culture and Economy Filipino culture blends Malay, Chinese, Spanish, and American influences. These influences can be seen in the country's languages and religions. The official languages of the country are Filipino and English. More than 80 percent of the people are Roman Catholic. In fact, the Philippines has more Christians than any other nation in Asia. Christianity was introduced when the Philippines became a Spanish colony. The country also has a large Muslim population. Forty-seven percent of the people live in cities. The largest city is the capital, Manila.

Traditionally, the economy of the Philippines has depended on farming. Over the last few decades, however, manufacturing and mining have developed significantly. Factories produce clothing, electronic goods, and wood products for export. The fertile volcanic soil of the islands helps farmers grow many crops, such as rice, sweet potatoes, bananas, and sugar cane. Kapok trees, which produce a fiber used for insulation and mattresses, are plentiful.

▲ **IDENTIFY SOLUTIONS** Explain how the Philippines has improved its government and economy.

Section 3 Assessment

ONLINE QUIZ
For test practice, go to
Interactive Review
@ ClassZone.com

TERMS & NAMES

1. Explain the importance of
- Bahasa Indonesia
- Filipino
- Ferdinand Marcos
- Corazon Aquino

USE YOUR READING NOTES

2. Categorize Use your completed chart to answer the following question:

What probably accounts for the great ethnic diversity in Indonesia?

	INDONESIA	THE PHILIPPINES
History		
Government		
Culture		
Economy		

KEY IDEAS

3. Why did Indonesia create a new language?

4. What problems did the Philippines face after gaining independence?

5. How did Corazon Aquino come to power?

CRITICAL THINKING

6. Make Inferences How did Corazon Aquino further the development of democracy in the Philippines?

7. Compare and Contrast How are the economies of Indonesia and the Philippines similar and different?

8. CONNECT to Today What do you think the people of Indonesia could do today to become a more united nation?

9. ART Draw a Shadow Puppet Using the Internet and library sources, find pictures of Indonesian shadow puppets. Then draw a shadow puppet of your own. Explain the role the puppet would play in a traditional performance.

Interactive ⟵ Review

Click here to complete these and other activities online @ ClassZone.com

CHAPTER SUMMARY

Key Idea 1
Southeast Asia is a mountainous region with a tropical climate and much volcanic activity on its many islands.

Key Idea 2
The nations of mainland Southeast Asia have closely connected histories and diverse cultures.

Key Idea 3
Indonesia and the Philippines both have rich cultural traditions and long histories as centers of trade.

For **Review and Study Notes**, go to **Interactive Review** @ ClassZone.com

NAME GAME

Use the Terms & Names list to complete each sentence on paper or online.

1. I am a narrow strip of land that serves as a bridge between the mainland and islands.
   Malay Peninsula _____

2. I was the dictatorial president of the Philippines between 1965 and 1986. _____

3. I am a very large ocean wave caused by an underwater earthquake or volcanic eruption.
   _____

4. I am a region that contains Cambodia, Laos, and Vietnam. _____

5. I had gained control of much of mainland Southeast Asia by the 800s. _____

6. I am the former name of Thailand. _____
   _____

7. I am a term for an independent country that is very small in area. _____

8. I am the leader of the pro-democracy movement in Myanmar. _____

9. I am the common language of Indonesia. _____
   _____

10. I am a set of closely grouped islands. _____
    _____

archipelago
Bahasa Indonesia
Indochina
Indochinese
    Peninsula
Khmer Empire
Malay Peninsula
Ferdinand Marcos
microstate
Siam
Aung San Suu Kyi
tsunami

Activities

Flip Cards

Use the online flip cards to quiz yourself on the terms and names introduced in this chapter.

Mekong River

?

a major river that runs south from southern China through Laos, Cambodia, and Vietnam

Crossword Puzzle

Complete an online crossword puzzle to test your knowledge of the history and culture of Southeast Asia.

ACROSS
1. the most important holiday in Vietnam

VOCABULARY

Explain the significance of each of the following.

1. Indochinese Peninsula
2. Malay Peninsula
3. Mekong River
4. Indochina
5. Khmer Empire
6. Siam
7. Aung San Suu Kyi
8. microstate
9. Bahasa Indonesia
10. Filipino

Explain how the terms and names in each group are related.

11. Indochina, Siam, and colonialism
12. Ferdinand Marcos and Corazon Aquino

KEY IDEAS

1 Physical Geography of Southeast Asia

13. Which island nations are located on the Malay Archipelago?
14. What causes a tsunami?
15. Which two types of climate predominate in Southeast Asia?
16. How does the climate in Southeast Asia affect its vegetation?

2 The Mainland Countries

17. What historical events have affected all of Indochina?
18. How did King Chulalongkorn modernize Siam?
19. What does Malaysia trade on the international market?
20. In what ways is the government of Singapore powerful?

3 Indonesia and the Philippines

21. What religions did traders bring to Indonesia?
22. Where do most of the people of Indonesia live?
23. Why did Ferdinand Marcos leave the Philippines?
24. What cultures have strongly influenced the Philippines?

CRITICAL THINKING

25. **Analyze Causes and Effects** Create a chart to identify the impact in Southeast Asia of colonization, the war between North and South Vietnam, and the Asian tsunami.

CAUSES	EFFECTS
Colonization	
War between North and South Vietnam	
Asian tsunami	

26. **Form Opinions** Why do you think Southeast Asia attracted so many colonists?
27. **Make Inferences** Why do you think Aung San Suu Kyi is considered a hero throughout much of the world?
28. **Draw Conclusions** How are Spanish and American influences reflected in Filipino culture?
29. **Five Themes: Location** How has Singapore's location benefited its economy?
30. **Connect Geography & Culture** Why do you think the tourism industry is booming in Thailand?

Answer the ESSENTIAL QUESTION

How can Southeast Asian nations establish stable governments and economies?

Written Response Write a two- or three-paragraph response to the Essential Question. Use the rubric below to guide your thinking.

Response Rubric
A strong response will:
- describe the governments and economies of the Southeast Asian nations today
- discuss the problems the nations have faced in the past
- detail the steps the nations are taking to improve their governments and economies

STANDARDS–BASED ASSESSMENT

THEMATIC MAP

Use the map to answer questions 1 and 2 on your paper.

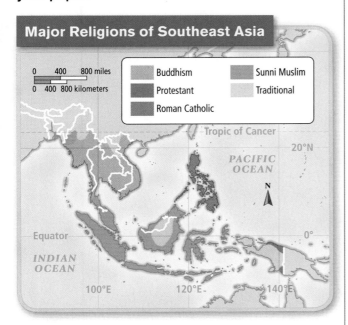

Major Religions of Southeast Asia

BAR GRAPH

Examine the bar graph below. Use the graph to answer questions 3 and 4 on your paper.

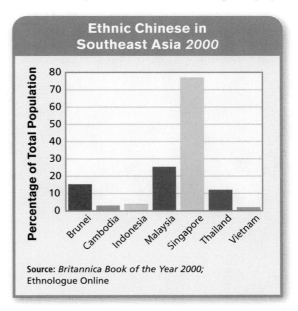

Ethnic Chinese in Southeast Asia 2000

Source: *Britannica Book of the Year 2000;* Ethnologue Online

1. What is the predominant religion of mainland Southeast Asia?

A. Roman Catholic   **C.** Traditional
B. Buddhism   **D.** Sunni Muslim

2. Which country has the largest population of Sunni Muslims?

A. the Philippines   **C.** Indonesia
B. Cambodia   **D.** Thailand

3. Which Southeast Asian nation has the highest percentage of ethnic Chinese?

A. Singapore   **C.** Indonesia
B. Malaysia   **D.** Thailand

4. What percentage of Vietnam's population is made up of ethnic Chinese?

A. 77.0   **C.** 12.1
B. 15.4   **D.** 1.5

GeoActivity

1. INTERDISCIPLINARY ACTIVITY–SCIENCE

With a small group, prepare a poster on tsunamis. Research to find information on the size and speed of the waves, how they are formed, and possible warning systems. Use pictures and diagrams to illustrate the information.

2. WRITING FOR SOCIAL STUDIES

Unit Writing Project Revisit your country slide show. To further convince your family to go to the country, write a detailed description of a place that best represents it. For Cambodia, for instance, you might write about Angkor Wat.

3. MENTAL MAPPING

Create an outline map of Southeast Asia and label the following:

- Pacific Ocean
- Mekong River
- Indochinese Peninsula
- Indochina
- Malay Peninsula
- Malay Archipelago
- Indonesia
- the Philippines

UNIT 9

Oceania and Antarctica

Why It Matters:

As modern technology shrinks our world, the people of the lands of Oceania have become much closer neighbors. Their lands include resources important to world trade. Their unique cultures add to the diversity of our world.

Two friends in Western Australia

CHAPTER 29 Australia and New Zealand

A War Canoe in the Solomon Islands

CHAPTER 30 Oceania and Antarctica

◄ Meet Mick

In this unit, you will meet Mick, a middle-school boy from the Outback in Australia. Learn more about him on **Worldster** @ClassZone.com

Use the Unit Atlas to learn about the geography of Oceania and Antarctica. As you study the maps in the atlas, notice geographic patterns and specific details about the two regions. Answer the questions on each map in your notebook.

As you study the graphs on this page, compare the landmass, population, islands, and volcanoes of Oceania and Antarctica with those of the United States. Then jot down the answers to the following questions in your notebook.

Comparing Data

1. How does the landmass of Oceania compare with that of the United States?

2. How much larger is the population of the United States than that of Oceania?

3. How does the South Island of New Zealand compare with the world's largest island?

4. How does the number of active volcanoes for this entire region compare to the United States?

Comparing Data

Landmass

Oceania
3,275,375 sq. mi.

Continental United States
3,165,630 sq. mi.

Antarctica
5,405,430 sq. mi.

Population

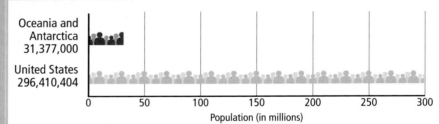

Oceania and Antarctica
31,377,000

United States
296,410,404

Population (in millions)

Islands

World's Largest	U.S. Largest		South Island, New Zealand	Tasmania
Greenland 839,999 sq. mi.	Hawaii 4,021 sq. mi.	New Guinea 341,631 sq. mi.	58,439 sq. mi.	26,383 sq. mi.

Volcanoes

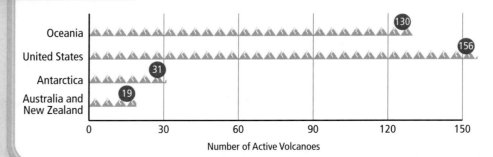

Oceania — 130

United States — 156

Antarctica — 31

Australia and New Zealand — 19

Number of Active Volcanoes

Population Density

120°E 140°E 160°E 180° 160°W 140°W

40°N

CHINA

JAPAN

PACIFIC OCEAN

MIDWAY IS. (U.S.)

Tropic of Cancer

HAWAII (U.S.)

20°N

PHILIPPINES

NORTHERN MARIANA IS. (U.S.)

WAKE I. (U.S.)

JOHNSTON ATOLL (U.S.)

GUAM (U.S.)

MARSHALL ISLANDS

PALAU

FEDERATED STATES OF MICRONESIA

Equator 0°

NAURU

KIRIBATI

INDONESIA

PAPUA NEW GUINEA

SOLOMON ISLANDS

TUVALU

TOKELAU (N.Z.)

SAMOA

FRENCH POLYNESIA (Fr.)

Darwin

VANUATU

WALLIS AND FUTUNA (Fr.)

AMERICAN SAMOA (U.S.)

COOK ISLANDS (N.Z.)

NEW CALEDONIA (Fr.)

FIJI

TONGA

NIUE (N.Z.)

20°S

PITCAIRN IS. (U.K.)

Tropic of Capricorn

AUSTRALIA

Brisbane

Perth

Persons per square mile

Sydney

Adelaide

Canberra

Over 520

Melbourne

260–519

130–259

INDIAN OCEAN

Auckland

NEW ZEALAND

Wellington

25–129

1–24

40°S

0

Christchurch

0   500   1,000 miles

0   500   1,000 kilometers

SOUTHERN OCEAN

THINK LIKE A GEOGRAPHER

1. **Place** Which island group is most densely populated?

2. **Human-Environment Interaction** How would you describe the population density pattern of Australia?

Climate

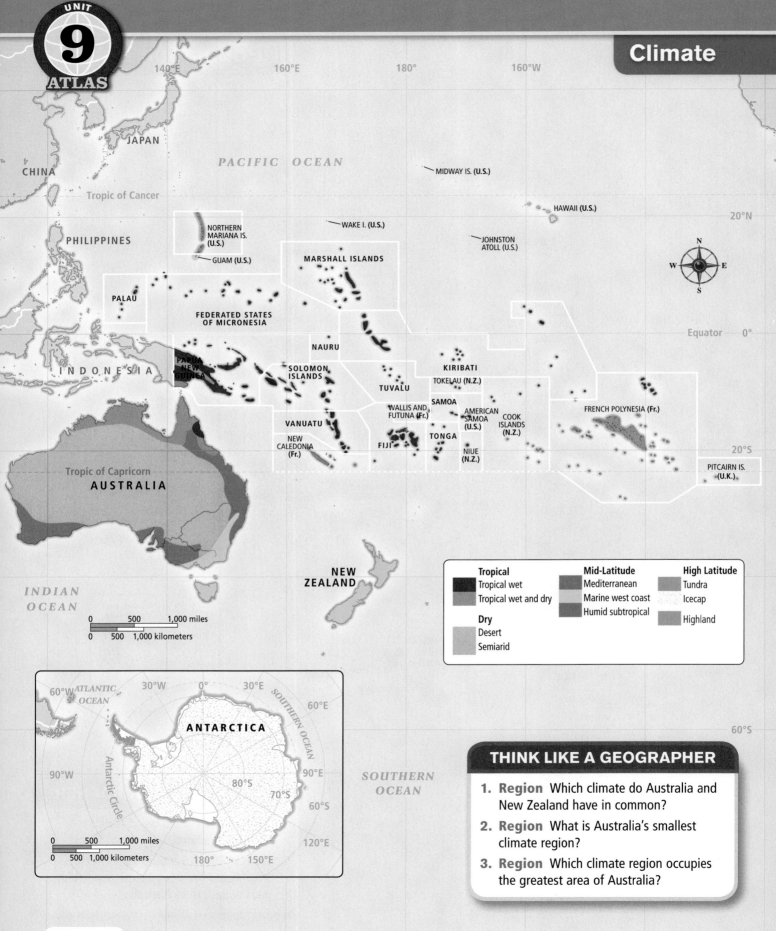

140°E 160°E 180° 160°W

JAPAN

CHINA

PACIFIC OCEAN

Tropic of Cancer

MIDWAY IS. (U.S.)

PHILIPPINES

NORTHERN
MARIANA IS.
(U.S.)

WAKE I. (U.S.)

HAWAII (U.S.)

JOHNSTON
ATOLL (U.S.)

20°N

GUAM (U.S.)

MARSHALL ISLANDS

PALAU

FEDERATED STATES
OF MICRONESIA

Equator 0°

INDONESIA

PAPUA
NEW
GUINEA

NAURU

SOLOMON
ISLANDS

TUVALU

KIRIBATI

TOKELAU (N.Z.)

SAMOA

WALLIS AND
FUTUNA (Fr.)

AMERICAN
SAMOA
(U.S.)

COOK
ISLANDS
(N.Z.)

FRENCH POLYNESIA (Fr.)

VANUATU

NEW
CALEDONIA
(Fr.)

FIJI

TONGA

NIUE
(N.Z.)

20°S

PITCAIRN IS.
(U.K.)

Tropic of Capricorn
AUSTRALIA

INDIAN
OCEAN

0   500   1,000 miles
0   500   1,000 kilometers

NEW
ZEALAND

Tropical
Tropical wet
Tropical wet and dry

Dry
Desert
Semiarid

Mid-Latitude
Mediterranean
Marine west coast
Humid subtropical

High Latitude
Tundra
Icecap

Highland

60°W ATLANTIC
OCEAN

30°W 0° 30°E

60°E

SOUTHERN OCEAN

ANTARCTICA

90°W 90°E

80°S

70°S

SOUTHERN
OCEAN

60°S

60°S

0   500   1,000 miles
0   500   1,000 kilometers

180° 150°E 120°E

THINK LIKE A GEOGRAPHER

1. **Region** Which climate do Australia and New Zealand have in common?

2. **Region** What is Australia's smallest climate region?

3. **Region** Which climate region occupies the greatest area of Australia?

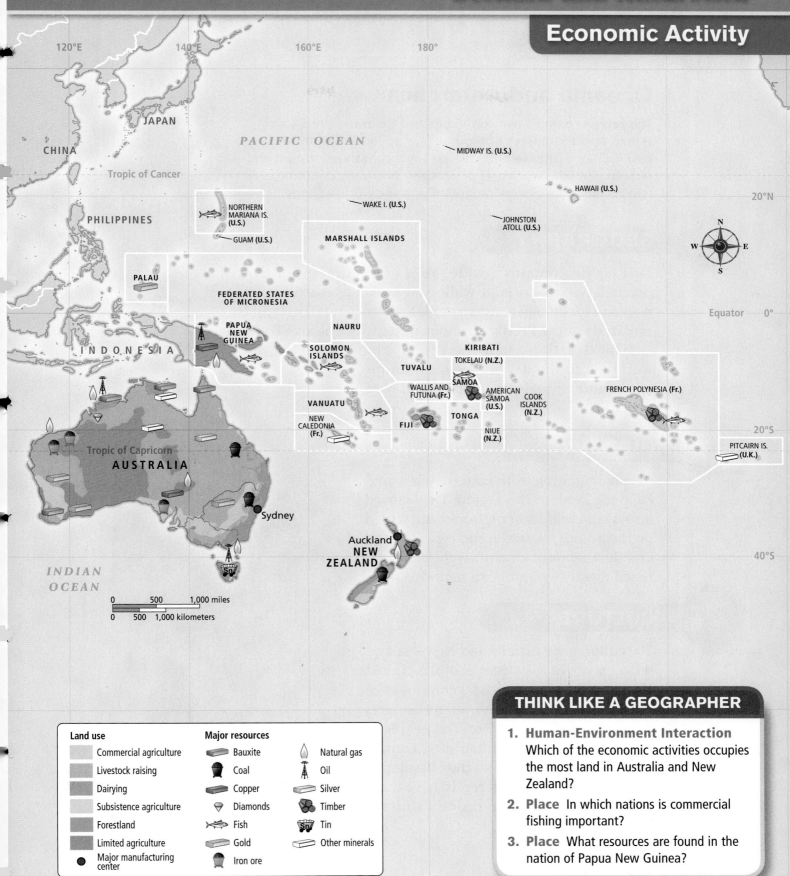

120°E 140°E 160°E 180°

JAPAN

PACIFIC OCEAN

MIDWAY IS. (U.S.)

CHINA

Tropic of Cancer

HAWAII (U.S.)

20°N

PHILIPPINES

WAKE I. (U.S.)

JOHNSTON ATOLL (U.S.)

NORTHERN MARIANA IS. (U.S.)

GUAM (U.S.)

MARSHALL ISLANDS

PALAU

FEDERATED STATES OF MICRONESIA

Equator 0°

INDONESIA

PAPUA NEW GUINEA

NAURU

KIRIBATI

TOKELAU (N.Z.)

FRENCH POLYNESIA (Fr.)

SOLOMON ISLANDS

TUVALU

SAMOA

WALLIS AND FUTUNA (Fr.)

AMERICAN SAMOA (U.S.)

COOK ISLANDS (N.Z.)

VANUATU

NEW CALEDONIA (Fr.)

FIJI

TONGA

NIUE (N.Z.)

20°S

PITCAIRN IS. (U.K.)

Tropic of Capricorn

AUSTRALIA

Sydney

Auckland
NEW ZEALAND

40°S

INDIAN OCEAN

0   500   1,000 miles
0   500   1,000 kilometers

Land use
- Commercial agriculture
- Livestock raising
- Dairying
- Subsistence agriculture
- Forestland
- Limited agriculture
- Major manufacturing center

Major resources
- Bauxite
- Coal
- Copper
- Diamonds
- Fish
- Gold
- Iron ore
- Natural gas
- Oil
- Silver
- Timber
- Tin
- Other minerals

THINK LIKE A GEOGRAPHER

1. **Human-Environment Interaction** Which of the economic activities occupies the most land in Australia and New Zealand?

2. **Place** In which nations is commercial fishing important?

3. **Place** What resources are found in the nation of Papua New Guinea?

Oceania and Antarctica

This region contains two continents and thousands of islands spread across hundreds of thousands of square miles of the Pacific Ocean. Until recently the area was considered distant and remote. But with electronic devices and fast transportation, even remote lands have been integrated into the world at large.

GEOGRAPHY

This region contains a wide range of physical geography. Australia is a vast dry land, while New Zealand has active volcanoes and earthquakes. Antarctica is a frozen desert. Thousands of islands in the Pacific are atolls or parts of volcanic cones.

The isolation from the rest of the world led to the development of unique plants and animals in Australia and New Zealand.

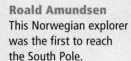

Roald Amundsen
This Norwegian explorer was the first to reach the South Pole.

HISTORY

People migrating from eastern Asia populated the lands of this region. They moved across land bridges or the ocean and settled on the islands. Australia and New Zealand and the islands of Oceania were later colonized mostly by European nations.

CULTURE

The cultures of Australia and New Zealand reflect some of the customs of the United Kingdom, which colonized them. However, their cultures also have many aspects unique to their way of life. The people of the islands of Oceania had little contact with the outside world so they developed their own ways. Only recently have these island cultures begun to connect with the outside world.

GOVERNMENT

Many of the countries of this region were colonies of European nations or the United States. Many of them gained their independence after World War II. The governments of the two largest nations, Australia and New Zealand, are linked to the United Kingdom. The governments of most of the nations are democratic.

ECONOMICS

Australia and New Zealand have well developed economies that focus primarily on producing raw materials such as wool, meat, and minerals. These products are traded in the international marketplace. Both Australia and New Zealand, along with the island nations of Oceania, have begun to expand their tourism industries.

Emperor Penguins
Colonies of many types of penguins are found in the Antarctic region.

Country Almanac

Click here to compare the most recent data on countries @ ClassZone.com

Unit Project

Illustrated Time Line

As you read this unit, look for a description of the migration of people across the region. Do research to find information about people settling the lands. Create an illustrated time line showing the arrival of different groups in the subregions and countries of Oceania.

Think About:

- the first people to arrive in the region
- European colonizers

Oceania and Antarctica

Many of the nations in this region are tiny. The smallest nation is Nauru, which covers only 8.2 square miles with about 13,000 people. The region of Oceania, on the other hand, is gigantic— 3,275,375 square miles and 32 million people.

Water Lily Water Lily on an island in Fiji

Australia

GEOGRAPHY
Capital: Canberra
Total Area: 2,967,909 sq. mi.
Population: 20,155,000

ECONOMY
Imports: machinery; chemicals; fuels; food
Exports: fuels; metals; textiles; food

CULTURE
Language: English
Religion: Catholic 27%; Protestant 37%; Orthodox 3%; no religion 16%

Fiji

GEOGRAPHY
Capital: Suva
Total Area: 7,054 sq. mi.
Population: 848,000

ECONOMY
Imports: fuels; machinery; textiles; animals
Exports: clothing; sugar; fish; gold

CULTURE
Language: English; Fijian; Hindustani
Religion: Christian 57%; Hindu 33%; Muslim 7%; nonreligious 1%

Kiribati

GEOGRAPHY
Capital: Tarawa
Total Area: 313 sq. mi.
Population: 103,092

ECONOMY
Imports: food; machinery; fuels
Exports: seaweed; fish; copra

CULTURE
Language: English
Religion: Catholic 55%; Protestant 37%; Mormon 3%; Baha'i 2%

Marshall Islands

GEOGRAPHY
Capital: Majuro
Total Area: 70 sq. mi.
Population: 59,071

ECONOMY
Imports: fuels; machinery; food
Exports: copra; coconut oil; aquarium fish

CULTURE
Language: Marshallese; English
Religion: Protestant 63%; Catholic 7%; Mormon 3%

Federated States of Micronesia

GEOGRAPHY
Capital: Palikir
Total Area: 271 sq. mi.
Population: 110,000

ECONOMY
Imports: food; fuels; machinery; tobacco
Exports: fish; bananas

CULTURE
Language: English; Trukese
Religion: Catholic 53%; Protestant 42%; Mormon 1%

Nauru

GEOGRAPHY
Capital: Yaren District
Total Area: 8 sq. mi.
Population: 13,048

ECONOMY
Imports: agricultural products
Exports: phosphate

CULTURE
Language: Nauruan; English
Religion: Protestant 54%; Catholic 28%

New Zealand

GEOGRAPHY
Capital: Wellington
Total Area: 103,738 sq. mi.
Population: 4,028,000

ECONOMY
Imports: machinery; petroleum; cars
Exports: beef; dairy products; wood

CULTURE
Language: English; Maori
Religion: Protestant 27%; Catholic 13%; no religion 27%

Palau

GEOGRAPHY
Capital: Koror
Total Area: 177 sq. mi.
Population: 20,303

ECONOMY
Imports: machinery; food; fuels; chemicals
Exports: high-grade tuna; clothing

CULTURE
Language: Palauan; English
Religion: Catholic 42%; Protestant & other Christian 30%; Modekngei 9%

Papua New Guinea

GEOGRAPHY
Capital: Port Moresby
Total Area: 178,704 sq. mi.
Population: 5,887,000

ECONOMY
Imports: petroleum; food; machinery
Exports: gold; petroleum; copper; logs

CULTURE
Language: English; Motu; Tok Pisin
Religion: Protestant 63%; Catholic 30%; traditional beliefs 4%; Baha'i 1%

Samoa

GEOGRAPHY
Capital: Apia
Total Area: 1,137 sq. mi.
Population: 185,000

ECONOMY
Imports: petroleum; machinery
Exports: fish; clothing; coconut products

CULTURE
Language: Samoan; English
Religion: Protestant 57%; Mormon 26%; Catholic 21%

Solomon Islands

GEOGRAPHY
Capital: Honiara
Total Area: 10,985 sq. mi.
Population: 478,000

ECONOMY
Imports: food; petroleum; machinery
Exports: timber; fish; cacao beans

CULTURE
Language: English
Religion: Protestant 74%; Catholic 11%; traditional beliefs 3%

Tonga

GEOGRAPHY
Capital: Nuku'alofa
Total Area: 289 sq. mi.
Population: 102,000

ECONOMY
Imports: food; fuels; machinery
Exports: squash; fish; vanilla beans

CULTURE
Language: Tongan; English
Religion: Free Wesleyan 41%; Catholic 16%; Mormon 14%

Tuvalu

GEOGRAPHY
Capital: Funafuti
Total Area: 10 sq. mi.
Population: 11,636

ECONOMY
Imports: food; fuels; machinery; metals
Exports: copra; stamps; handicrafts

CULTURE
Language: Tuvalan; English; Samoan
Religion: Church of Tuvalu 85%; Seventh-day Adventist 4%; Catholic 1%

Vanuatu

GEOGRAPHY
Capital: Port-Vila
Total Area: 4,710 sq. mi.
Population: 211,000

ECONOMY
Imports: machinery; food; chemicals; fuels
Exports: coconut oil; timber; beef; kava

CULTURE
Language: Bislama; French; English
Religion: Protestant 54%; Catholic 16%; traditional beliefs 4%; Baha'i 3%

Outrigger canoe The lands of Oceania were settled by people who came there in oceangoing outrigger canoes.

1

GEOGRAPHY

Unique Lands

2

FOCUS ON

Australia

3

FOCUS ON

New Zealand

CHAPTER 29 Australia and New Zealand

ESSENTIAL QUESTION

How has the human geography of Australia and New Zealand changed since European settlement?

CONNECT ➤ Geography & History

Use the map and the time line to answer the following questions.

1. Which body of water did Captain Cook cross to get from Australia to New Zealand?
2. What is the approximate location in latitude and longitude of the 2000 Olympic Games?

Culture

◀ **40,000 B.C.** Australia is gradually settled by aboriginal people. (Aboriginal art–Iguana painted on tree bark)

40,000 B.C.

Geography

1000 A.D. The Maori migrate to New Zealand from Polynesia.

Geography

1769–1770 Captain James Cook explores New Zealand and Australia for Great Britain. ▶

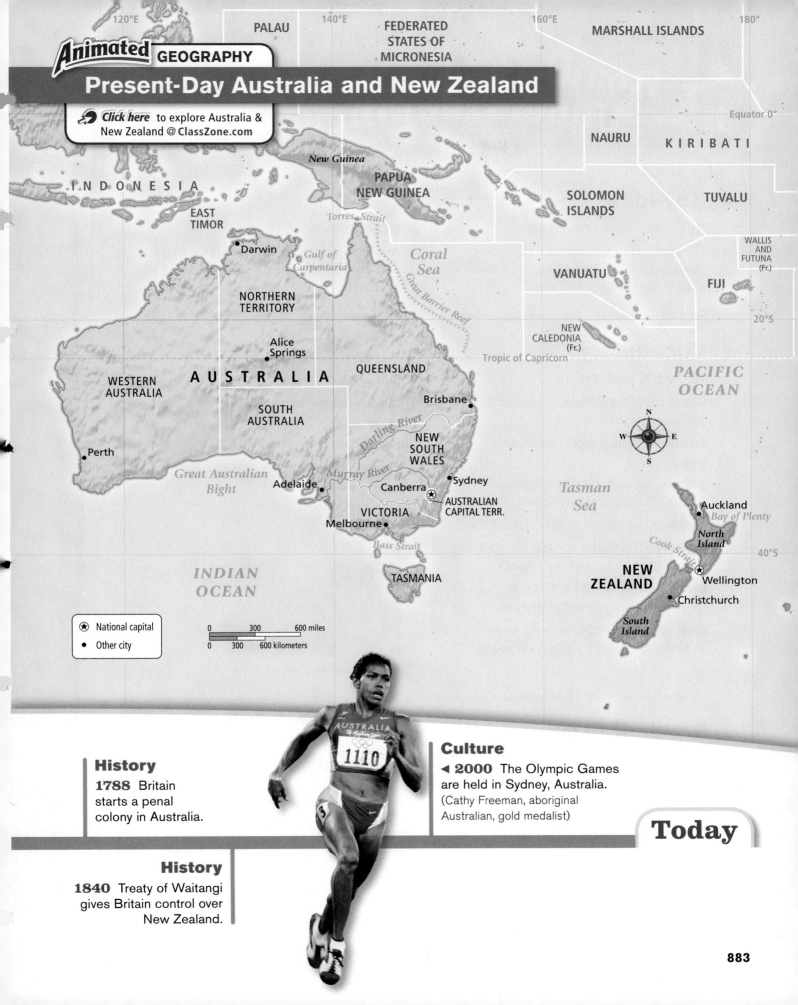

Present-Day Australia and New Zealand

Click here to explore Australia & New Zealand @ ClassZone.com

120°E   140°E   160°E   180°

PALAU

FEDERATED STATES OF MICRONESIA

MARSHALL ISLANDS

Equator 0°

NAURU

KIRIBATI

INDONESIA

New Guinea

PAPUA NEW GUINEA

SOLOMON ISLANDS

TUVALU

EAST TIMOR

Torres Strait

Coral Sea

VANUATU

WALLIS AND FUTUNA (Fr.)

FIJI

• Darwin

Gulf of Carpentaria

Great Barrier Reef

NEW CALEDONIA (Fr.)

20°S

NORTHERN TERRITORY

Tropic of Capricorn

PACIFIC OCEAN

WESTERN AUSTRALIA

Alice Springs

A U S T R A L I A

QUEENSLAND

SOUTH AUSTRALIA

Brisbane

Darling River

NEW SOUTH WALES

Tasman Sea

• Perth

Great Australian Bight

Murray River

Adelaide

Sydney

Canberra ⊛

AUSTRALIAN CAPITAL TERR.

Auckland •
Bay of Plenty

VICTORIA

Melbourne •

North Island

Cook Strait

40°S

INDIAN OCEAN

Bass Strait

TASMANIA

NEW ZEALAND

⊛ Wellington

• Christchurch

South Island

⊛ National capital
• Other city

0   300   600 miles
0   300   600 kilometers

N
W   E
S

History

1788 Britain starts a penal colony in Australia.

History

1840 Treaty of Waitangi gives Britain control over New Zealand.

AUSTRALIA

1110

Culture

◀ **2000** The Olympic Games are held in Sydney, Australia. (Cathy Freeman, aboriginal Australian, gold medalist)

Today

Reading for Understanding

▶ Key Ideas

BEFORE, YOU LEARNED

The nations of Southeast Asia face challenges with diverse cultures and with developing economies.

NOW YOU WILL LEARN

Australia and New Zealand have plant and animal life found nowhere else on Earth.

▶ Vocabulary

TERMS & NAMES

Great Dividing Range a range of low mountains in Australia

Southern Alps a mountain chain in New Zealand

geyser (GY•zuhr) a hot spring that shoots sprays of steam and boiling water into the air

Outback the interior region of Australia

Uluru (oo•LOO•roo) a spectacular rock out-cropping in the Australian Outback

Great Barrier Reef a 1,250-mile chain of coral reefs off the coast of Australia

marsupial (mahr•SOO•pee•uhl) an animal with an abdominal pouch to carry its young

BACKGROUND VOCABULARY

outcropping bedrock that rises above the soil

draft animal an animal used to pull a heavy load

Visual Vocabulary geyser

▶ Reading Strategy

Re-create the web diagram shown at right. As you read and respond to the **KEY QUESTIONS**, use the diagram to categorize important details about the physical geography of Australia and New Zealand.

 See Skillbuilder Handbook, page R7

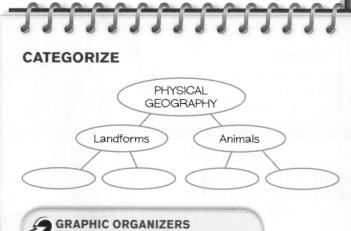

CATEGORIZE

PHYSICAL GEOGRAPHY

Landforms   Animals

GRAPHIC ORGANIZERS
Go to **Interactive Review** @ClassZone.com

Unique Lands

Connecting to Your World

In some ways, the first explorations of Australia and New Zealand by Europeans were like the first explorations of the moon. The explorers and astronauts had to cross enormous distances to their destinations and knew little about actual conditions in the unknown lands. The early European explorers in Australia found a land very different from their native countries of England and the Netherlands. Australia was a vast, dry region inhabited by many exotic creatures. Think about how strange it would be to encounter kangaroos, if you had never seen one before!

A girl and a wallaby

Landforms

▼ **KEY QUESTION** What are the landscapes of Australia and New Zealand like?

Australia is the world's smallest continent. Geographically, the continent consists of the island of Australia, the islands of New Zealand, Papua New Guinea, and several nearby islands. Australia is located about 7,000 miles southwest of North America. The continent of Australia is completely in the Southern Hemisphere. In fact, the continent is so far away from the other inhabited continents that it has developed some characteristics not found anywhere else in the world.

Uluru This enormous sandstone rock in the middle of the Australian desert is 5 miles around, and more than 1,100 feet high.

AUSTRALIA

○ Uluru
(Ayers Rock)

Mountains and Coastlands Australia has few highland areas and only one range of low mountains called the **Great Dividing Range Ⓐ**. This range lies on the eastern side of the continent. The area east of the range is quite hilly. See the map on the opposite page.

New Zealand consists of two main islands—North Island and South Island—and several smaller islands. Located on the volcanic Ring of Fire, much of the country is covered by mountains and hills. A mountain chain, the **Southern Alps Ⓑ**, runs down the middle of South Island. Seventeen peaks in this chain rise higher than 10,000 feet. Hundreds of rivers flow into narrow, deep-sided inlets created by melting glaciers. North Island has dense forests, active volcanoes, and many hot springs. Some hot springs called **geysers** (GY•zuhrz) shoot sprays of steam and boiling water into the air.

A Geyser Erupts New Zealand's location on the Ring of Fire makes geysers a part of the landscape. **What other physical features are found on the Ring of Fire?**

Deserts and Flatlands One-third of Australia is a low-lying desert region. The Great Dividing Range blocks moisture-bearing winds, making the interior dry. Australia has four major deserts, which range from sand to gravel and rock. Australians call the entire isolated region the **Outback**. Within the Outback is an immense rock **outcropping** called **Uluru** (oo•LOO•roo) Ⓒ, also called Ayers Rock. This enormous piece of red sandstone is 1.5 miles wide, 2.2 miles long, and rises more that 1,100 feet above the desert floor. Uluru is sacred to Australian native peoples.

The Great Barrier Reef One of Australia's most spectacular physical features is the **Great Barrier Reef Ⓓ**. The reef is located off the northeast coast of Australia and is a 1,250-mile chain of about 2,900 coral reefs formed by about 400 species of coral. Thousands of species of fish, mollusks, and sponges, as well as endangered green and loggerhead turtles, inhabit the reefs. Humpback whales also come to the reef's warm waters to bear their young. You can learn more about the reef in Animated Geography at the end of this section.

A Silvertip Shark Patrols the Great Barrier Reef Among many thousands of species of fish and animals found on or around the reef, the shark is one of the largest.

Ⓐ **COMPARE AND CONTRAST** Describe the landscapes of Australia and New Zealand.

Physical Geography of Australia & New Zealand

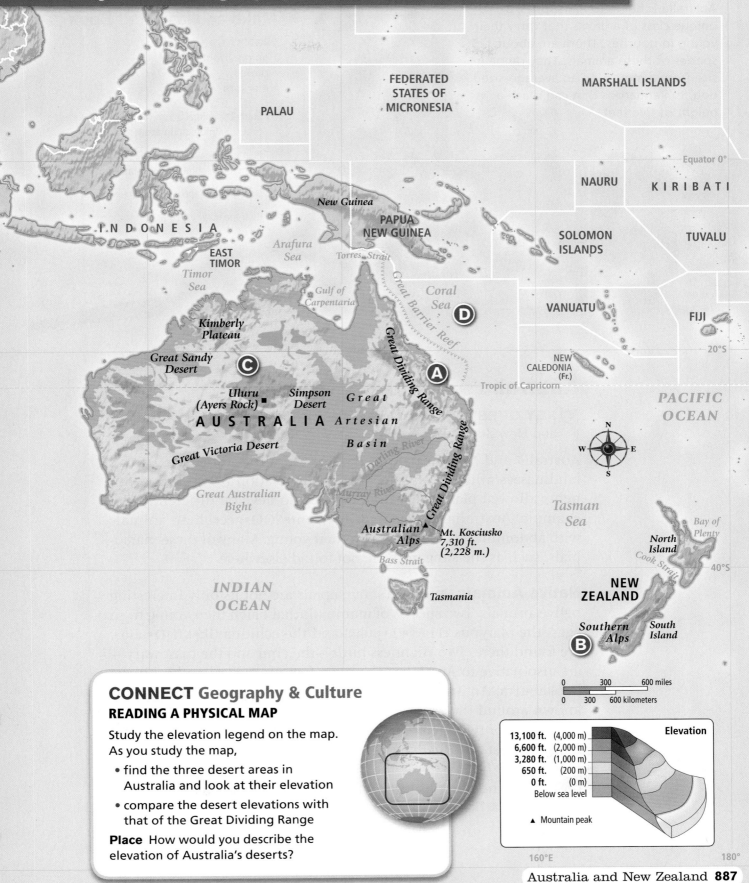

20°N

PALAU

FEDERATED STATES OF MICRONESIA

MARSHALL ISLANDS

Equator 0°

NAURU

KIRIBATI

New Guinea

PAPUA NEW GUINEA

SOLOMON ISLANDS

TUVALU

INDONESIA

EAST TIMOR

Arafura Sea

Torres Strait

Gulf of Carpentaria

Coral Sea

D

VANUATU

FIJI

20°S

Timor Sea

Great Barrier Reef

NEW CALEDONIA (Fr.)

Tropic of Capricorn

Kimberly Plateau

Great Sandy Desert

C

Uluru (Ayers Rock) ▪

Simpson Desert

AUSTRALIA

Great Dividing Range

A

PACIFIC OCEAN

Great Artesian

Basin

N
W E
S

Great Victoria Desert

Darling River

Great Dividing Range

Tasman Sea

North Island

Bay of Plenty

Cook Strait

Murray River

Great Australian Bight

Australian Alps

▲ Mt. Kosciusko 7,310 ft. (2,228 m.)

40°S

INDIAN OCEAN

Bass Strait

Tasmania

NEW ZEALAND

Southern Alps

South Island

B

CONNECT Geography & Culture

READING A PHYSICAL MAP

Study the elevation legend on the map. As you study the map,

- find the three desert areas in Australia and look at their elevation
- compare the desert elevations with that of the Great Dividing Range

Place How would you describe the elevation of Australia's deserts?

0   300   600 miles
0   300   600 kilometers

Elevation	
13,100 ft.	(4,000 m)
6,600 ft.	(2,000 m)
3,280 ft.	(1,000 m)
650 ft.	(200 m)
0 ft.	(0 m)
Below sea level	

▲ Mountain peak

160°E   180°

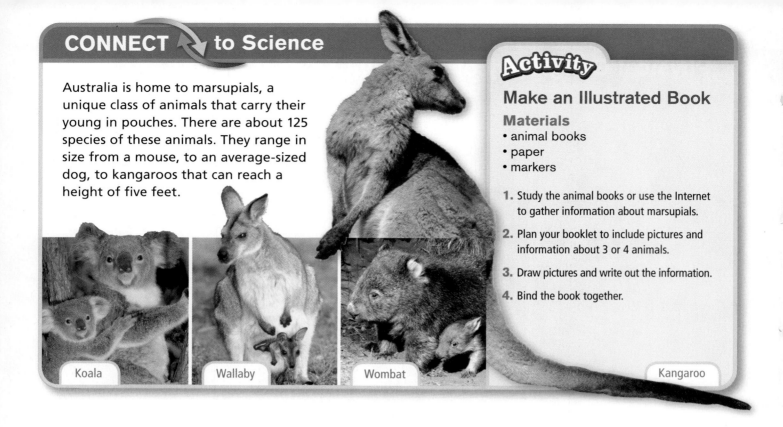

Australia is home to marsupials, a unique class of animals that carry their young in pouches. There are about 125 species of these animals. They range in size from a mouse, to an average-sized dog, to kangaroos that can reach a height of five feet.

Koala

Wallaby

Wombat

Kangaroo

Activity

Make an Illustrated Book

Materials
- animal books
- paper
- markers

1. Study the animal books or use the Internet to gather information about marsupials.

2. Plan your booklet to include pictures and information about 3 or 4 animals.

3. Draw pictures and write out the information.

4. Bind the book together.

Australia's Animals

▼ **KEY QUESTION** What types of animals are found only in Australia and New Zealand?

Australia and New Zealand separated from the rest of the Earth's landmasses millions of years ago. Their isolation from other continents allowed plants and animals there to develop differently. For example, Australia has **marsupials** (mahr•SOO•pee•uhlz), animals with abdominal pouches to carry their young. Many of these marsupials, such as the kangaroo, are not found elsewhere.

Native Animals Australia's marsupials are not its only interesting native animals. Two species of mammals that hatch their young from eggs, the platypus (PLAT•ih•puhs) and the echidna (ih•KIHD•nuh), are found there. Two flightless birds—the emu and the cassowary—are also native to Australia. The most famous Australian bird is the kookaburra. An Australian folk song celebrating the kookaburra is known around the world.

Except for two species of bats, New Zealand has no native mammals. Almost all other species were brought there. New Zealand's many native birds include the kiwi, the only bird in the world with nostrils on the tip of its bill. In fact, New Zealanders' slang term for themselves is "kiwi."

Non-Native Animals Over the years, many animals were brought to Australia and New Zealand. Geographers believe that the dingo, a doglike, meat-eating animal, probably came to Australia with the earliest settlers at least 3,500 years ago. More recent imports to both Australia and New Zealand are sheep, goats, cattle, and pigs. They were brought to establish farming and ranching operations.

Perhaps the most dramatic story of non-native animals concerns rabbits in Australia. In 1859, Thomas Austin released 24 rabbits into Australia so that he could hunt them. The rabbit population exploded because rabbits had few natural enemies. By 1900, Australia had more than a billion rabbits! The Australian government built a 2,000-mile fence to keep the rabbits from spreading. Rabbits destroyed crops and competed with grazing animals for grasslands. They are still a problem today, in spite of efforts to keep them under control.

SUMMARIZE Identify unique animals of Australia and New Zealand.

CONNECT Geography & Culture

Australia's Camels

Camels were introduced into Australia by explorers who used them to travel its deserts. Later, camels became farm animals. They also were used in construction projects as **draft animals**, animals used to pull heavy loads. When machines replaced camels, they were released into Australia's semiarid lands. Today, there are free-range camel herds in the Outback.

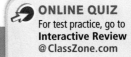

Section 1 Assessment

ONLINE QUIZ
For test practice, go to
Interactive Review
@ ClassZone.com

TERMS & NAMES

1. Explain the importance of
- Great Dividing Range
- Southern Alps
- Outback
- Great Barrier Reef

USE YOUR READING NOTES

2. Categorize Use your completed web diagram to answer the following question:

What physical features are found in New Zealand?

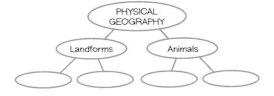

PHYSICAL GEOGRAPHY

Landforms   Animals

KEY IDEAS

3. What is the Australian Outback?

4. What are the two main islands of New Zealand?

5. Why did unique animal species develop in Australia and New Zealand?

CRITICAL THINKING

6. Find Main Ideas What is one of the many differences between the physical landscapes of Australia and New Zealand?

7. Analyze Causes and Effects What geographical factor accounted for the early isolation of Australia and New Zealand?

8. CONNECT to Today Why might governments want to limit the importation of non-native animals?

9. SCIENCE Draw a Species Map Research the plants and animals native to your state. Create an illustrated map showing five or six of these native species.

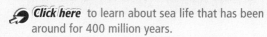

Click here to dive into the Great Barrier Reef
@ ClassZone.com

THE GREAT BARRIER REEF

The Great Barrier Reef is the grandest of all the coral reefs found in the ocean. Chains of coral reefs stretch 1,250 miles off the coast of Australia. The reef is home to thousands of species of plants and animals.

Click here to learn about sea life that has been around for 400 million years.

Click here Learn how the skeletons of millions of tiny animals and plants build a reef.

Click here to learn why the Great Barrier Reef is a World Heritage Area.

Map of Reef

Great Barrier Reef

Cairns

Townsville

PACIFIC OCEAN

N

AUSTRALIA

GeoActivity

Design a Conservation Poster Research the environmental threats to the Great Barrier Reef. Design a poster that encourages people to take care of the reef and avoid harmful practices.

Reading for Understanding

▶ Key Ideas

BEFORE, YOU LEARNED

Australia is home to unique animals and physical features.

NOW YOU WILL LEARN

Australia's history, culture, and economic life have been shaped by both aborigines and European immigrants.

▶ Vocabulary

TERMS & NAMES

James Cook a British explorer who claimed land in Australia

aborigine (ab•uh•RIHJ•uh•nee) an original inhabitant of Australia

penal colony a settlement that serves as a prison

Charles Perkins an aboriginal rights leader

BACKGROUND VOCABULARY

mechanized equipped with machines

REVIEW

hunter-gatherer a person who hunts animals and gathers plants for food

constitutional monarchy a government in which the powers of the king or queen are limited by a constitution

Visual Vocabulary Charles Perkins and aborigines

▶ Reading Strategy

Re-create the web diagram shown at right. As you read and respond to the **KEY QUESTIONS**, use the diagram to record main ideas and details about the history, culture, and economy of Australia.

 Skillbuilder Handbook, page R4

FIND MAIN IDEAS

History

Culture

AUSTRALIA

Economy

GRAPHIC ORGANIZERS
Go to **Interactive Review** @ClassZone.com

Australia

Connecting to Your World

Did you know that Australia is called "The Land Down Under"? It lies completely in the Southern Hemisphere. Its seasons are reversed from those in the Northern Hemisphere. So, people there go to the beach from December through March and often celebrate New Year's Day with a backyard barbecue. Now you will learn how similar and how different Australia is from North America.

History and Government

▼ **KEY QUESTION** How did the arrival of British settlers change life in Australia?

Early European explorers believed there was a "great southern land" somewhere in the vast area of the Pacific and Indian Oceans. In the 1600s, explorers investigated the west, southwest, and northwest coasts of Australia but found it a dry desert, worth little. Then in 1770, British sea captain **James Cook** claimed the fertile east coast for Britain. The European explorers were not the first people to arrive in this southern land. Peoples from Southeast Asia had migrated there across water and by a land bridge at least 40,000 years before.

Aboriginal Art
This modern wall mural is based on traditional aboriginal styles of painting.

Aborigines: The First Settlers The British called the first settlers of Australia **aborigines** (ab•uh•RIHJ•uh•neez), meaning "original inhabitants." They were **hunter-gatherers**, who spread across the vast island continent to hunt animals and gather plants for food. They lived in distinct groups that had their own languages. When European colonists arrived, over 300,000 aborigines lived on the continent.

British Colony In 1786, Britain established a **penal colony**, or prison settlement, in this remote land. Men and women who had been imprisoned in England were transported by ship to Australia. The first group arrived in 1788, complete with guards and their families. Over the years, a total of about 160,000 came.

In 1790, the British government began to offer land grants to settlers, army officers, and even freed convicts to help populate the land. Four colonies were set up along the coasts and one on the island of Tasmania. In 1851, gold was discovered. Thousands of people from around the world flocked to Australia, and the population tripled. Clashes broke out between aborigines and settlers over the ownership of land. Many aborigines were killed or driven into the Outback. In the later part of the 20th century, **Charles Perkins**, an aborigine himself, led the fight for aboriginal rights. Aborigines continue to struggle to regain lands taken from them by later immigrants.

HISTORY MAKERS

Charles Perkins 1936–2000

Charles Perkins, an important aboriginal leader, has been compared to U.S. civil rights leader Dr. Martin Luther King, Jr. Both of them worked for the rights of their people, and both led protests against racial discrimination.

Perkins was born on a reservation in the Outback and was sent away to school at age ten. There, he saw firsthand the unfair treatment of the aborigines. He was one of the first of his ethnic group to graduate from college. In 1984, Perkins became head of the Department of Aboriginal Affairs, the first aborigine to head a government department.

ONLINE BIOGRAPHY
For more on the life of Charles Perkins, go to the **Research & Writing Center @ ClassZone.com**

Independent Nation In 1901, Australia gained independence from Britain. The six colonies merged into a single government. Australia is a **constitutional monarchy**, a government in which the authority of the monarch is limited by a constitution. The monarch of the United Kingdom is Australia's monarch, but the monarch has little to do with running the government. An appointed governor general represents the monarch. The prime minister heads Australia's parliamentary-style government. The political party that wins the most seats in the two-house federal parliament selects the prime minister. All Australians 18 years of age and older are required to vote.

▲ **SUMMARIZE** Explain how the arrival of Europeans changed Australia.

U.S. GOVERNMENT

CITIZENS

elect

CONGRESS
enacts laws

PRESIDENT
acts as head of
government
and head of state

AUSTRALIAN GOVERNMENT

QUEEN OF ENGLAND
acts as head of state

appoints

GOVERNOR GENERAL
represents Queen

CITIZENS

elect

PARLIAMENT
enacts laws

selects

reports to

PRIME MINISTER
acts as head of government

CRITICAL THINKING

Compare and Contrast How does the Prime Minister's role differ from that of the U.S. president?

Aussie Culture

▼ **KEY QUESTION** What makes Australian culture unique?

Australia's distinctive culture has mainly been influenced by its earliest inhabitants, the aborigines, and its British settlers. Australia's isolation and its unusual plants and animals have also helped to develop a distinctive "Aussie" culture.

Aboriginal Heritage Each aborigine group had traditional lands that were defined by mountains, rivers, or lakes. Aborigines believe there is a close connection between people and the land, plants, and animals. This special relationship with the land forms the basis of their spiritual life. It helps them to understand and care for their environment.

Aboriginal people describe the creation of their land in a series of traditional stories known as "dreamtime" stories. The stories explain the lives of their ancestors and also the aborigines' relationship to the land. Often, the stories are linked to sacred sites, such as Uluru. Today, about 2 percent of the population is aborigine.

Modern Australia Australia is home to immigrants from many parts of the world. Most of these immigrant groups have only come since the end of World War II. About 20 percent of all Australians were born in other countries. However, Australia's early settlement was by immigrants who came from British Isles. Many elements of Australian culture are similar to the cultures of those countries. For example, English is the official language, and about 70 percent of the people are Christians.

About 85 percent of all Australians live in cities located in the southeastern quarter of the country. Sydney, Melbourne, and Brisbane are on the east coast. The capital, Canberra, is further inland. The rest of Australia is lightly populated, with most of the population living in coastal areas. Unlike cities in other countries you have studied, Australian cities have few apartment buildings. Most people live in single-family homes with small gardens.

The language spoken in Australia is English, but it has a unique vocabulary unfamiliar to those who do not live there. The language developed because the settlers had to describe unfamiliar animals and plants and unusual situations. Sometimes the settlers borrowed words from the aborigines, such as *kangaroo* and *koala*. Other words, such as *brumbies* for wild horses and *outback*, were invented by the settlers.

Sports and Entertainment Because of their country's generally sunny, warm climate, Australians enjoy outdoor sports and recreation. Australians like team games such as rugby and cricket, which were introduced by British settlers. A popular spectator game is Australian-rules football, a combination of soccer and rugby played on a cricket field. Australians also enjoy sun and surf activities. They are very proud of their world-class athletes in tennis, swimming, and golf. Australians have also won many Olympic medals in track and field events, swimming, and diving.

The film industry in Australia is more than 100 years old. In the early years, movies tried to create a separate Aussie identity by using themes from the country's history. In recent years, a number of Australian actors and directors have gained international fame for their acting and productions.

Living in the Bush Australians call the lightly populated interior of their country the Outback, or the bush. People in the bush frequently live on huge ranches called "stations." Neighbors may be many miles away. People living on these stations often have a small plane that they use the way most people use a car.

Children in the bush may live 200 miles from a school. These children are educated by correspondence schools and "schools of the air." They listen to instruction broadcast over two-way radio several times a week. At least once a week, most have an on-air private lesson with a teacher. Students receive their assignments by mail, complete them, and return them to the teacher. Today, they use e-mail and the Internet for their lessons as well.

▲ **FIND MAIN IDEAS** Explain why Australian culture is unique.

THE BOOMERANG

Aborigines of Australia created the boomerang. They used the curved, flat wooden stick to hunt animals, as a tool, and as a weapon in warfare. "Returning" boomerangs can be thrown into the wind, go hundreds of feet, and then return to the thrower. Today, the sports-loving Australians hold boomerang competitions.

Worldster
A Day in Mick's Life

To learn more about Mick and his world, go to the **Activity Center @ ClassZone.com**

G'day! My name is Mick. I am 13 years old and live with my family on a sheep station (you probably know it as a ranch) in the Outback of Australia. We Aussies call it "living in the bush." Sometimes I miss not being with other kids. But I play games and sports with my two sisters and my brothers. Let me tell you about my day.

To tell you about his day Mick might say:

"G'day, mates! Here's a Captain Cook (a look) at my day."

8 A.M. I get up, get dressed, and go have brekkie (breakfast). We usually eat eggs and snags (sausages) and put Vegemite (a yeast and vegetable spread) on our toast.

9 A.M.–3 P.M. Time for school. One room in our home is a school room for me and my brothers and sisters. We use computers and two-way radios to be in contact with our teacher, who is hundreds of miles away. Our mum helps us with our lessons.

4 P.M. I am going with my dad, who is flying our family's small plane over the station to check on our sheep. He lets me sit in the copilot seat and, sometimes, even take the controls.

6 P.M. My mum is grilling on the barbie (barbeque grill) tonight. After dinner, my family and I are going to watch our country's favorite sport, Australian-rules football, on the telly (television).

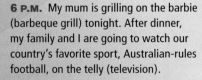

CONNECT to Your Life

Journal Entry Think about your school day. How is your school experience different from Mick's? What else is different about your life? Record your ideas in your journal.

A Well-Developed Economy

KEY QUESTION What are Australia's economic activities?

Australia has abundant mineral resources and productive agricultural lands. It also has a well-educated workforce. As a result, it is one of the world's wealthier nations. But unlike many of the developed nations, much of Australia's wealth comes from the processing of raw materials rather than the manufacturing of finished goods.

Opals The stones are valued for their fiery appearance. This photo shows a raw piece at right and a finished piece at left.

Economic Resources Raw materials needed in many different manufacturing processes and as energy sources are easily found in Australia. Coal, natural gas, and oil provide energy for the country. Natural gas is also exported. Minerals, such as copper, nickel, lead, and bauxite (used for producing aluminum), are in great supply. Gold, diamonds, and opals (a gemstone) are also found here.

In addition to its mineral resources, about 65 percent of Australia's land is suitable for agriculture. Most of the agricultural land is dry grazing land that supports large sheep and cattle ranches. Less than 10 percent of the agricultural land is cropland.

Economic Activities Mining and farming are important to Australia's economy. Large quantities of raw materials, such as coal,

COMPARING ◄ Economic Activities

Ranching Raising cattle and sheep is a major economic activity.

Opal Mining Australia's mines produce diamonds, lead, zinc, and opals for the world market.

Tourism Millions of people travel to Australia to visit unique parks.

petroleum, wheat, wool, meat, minerals, and gemstones, are exported. Australian exports are sold on the world market, but especially to Japan, China, and South Korea.

Because Australia was so far from other industrialized countries, it had to either make products locally or import them at great cost. So, Australia produces many of the goods that it needs. Such goods include automobiles, food products, iron and steel, textiles, and household appliances. It imports the machines used to make these products and also imports construction equipment and mining machines. Australia's farms are highly **mechanized**, or equipped with machines, so the demand for farm workers is small. In addition to wool and cattle hides, Australians also produce dairy products, sugar cane, and fruits such as bananas, pineapples, and apples.

Many Australians work in the tourism industry. The Great Barrier Reef and Australia's many beaches attract about 5 million visitors a year. The largest numbers of tourists come from Japan, New Zealand, and nations in Southeast Asia.

Australia's Top Export Markets

Country	Exports from Australia
China	wool, iron ore, copper, coal
Japan	coal, iron ore
New Zealand	motor vehicles, chemicals
South Korea	wheat, zinc, wool, beef, sugar
United States	beef, crude petroleum

Source: *Australian Government Bureau of Statistics 2005*

▲ **SUMMARIZE** Identify Australia's major economic activities.

Section 2 Assessment

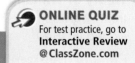

ONLINE QUIZ
For test practice, go to
Interactive Review
@ ClassZone.com

TERMS & NAMES

1. Explain the importance of
- James Cook
- aborigine
- penal colony
- Charles Perkins

USE YOUR READING NOTES

2. Find Main Ideas Use your completed web diagram to answer the following question:

How did immigration change the culture of Australia?

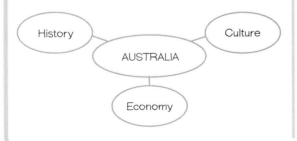

KEY IDEAS

3. What was the original reason for British colonization of Australia?

4. What are the two main cultural influences on Australia?

5. How do people in Australia make their living?

CRITICAL THINKING

6. Make Inferences How did European settlement influence Australia's development?

7. Analyze Cause and Effect What effect did Australia's location far from other inhabited areas have on its economic development?

8. CONNECT to Today How does the situation of the aborigines today compare to that of Native Americans?

9. WRITING **Create an Australian-English Dictionary** Use the Internet and library books to research Australian English. List ten unique Australian words and the word in American English that has the same meaning.

Reading for Understanding

▶ Key Ideas

BEFORE, YOU LEARNED

Life in Australia has been shaped by both aboriginal and European influences.

NOW YOU WILL LEARN

New Zealand's history, culture, and economy have been influenced by the Maori and European immigrants.

▶ Vocabulary

TERMS & NAMES

Maori (MOW•ree) a Polynesian people who were the first inhabitants of New Zealand

Polynesia islands of the central and southern Pacific

Treaty of Waitangi (WY•TAHNG•gee) a treaty between the British and the Maori signed in 1840

Pakeha (PAH•kee•HAH) a Maori word that means "white people"

hydroelectric power electricity produced by moving water

geothermal energy power produced by the internal heat of the Earth

REVIEW

geyser an erupting hot spring

Visual Vocabulary Maori in traditional costume

▶ Reading Strategy

Re-create the web diagram shown at right. As you read and respond to the **KEY QUESTIONS**, use the diagram to record important main ideas and details about the history, culture, and economy of New Zealand.

 Skillbuilder Handbook, page R4

FIND MAIN IDEAS

History — NEW ZEALAND — Culture

NEW ZEALAND — Economy

GRAPHIC ORGANIZERS
Go to **Interactive Review** @ ClassZone.com

New Zealand

Connecting to Your World

Imagine a place so far away that it would take you 17 hours to fly there from New York or 12 hours from Los Angeles. That place is New Zealand, about a thousand miles southeast of Australia and about 30 times smaller than Australia. Now imagine trying to find that small bit of land by ship in a vast ocean without good maps. That is what the earliest explorers had to do in their search for the southern islands. Their voyages took years to complete. But their discoveries expanded the knowledge of the planet and its people.

Waiting for a Flight Flight times to New Zealand from the United States are more than 12 hours.

History and Government

▼ **KEY QUESTION** How did the Maori lose control of New Zealand?

Earlier you read that two large islands—North Island and South Island—and several smaller outlying islands make up the country of New Zealand. The islands were inhabited mostly by birds until the **Maori** (MOW•ree) people migrated there some time between A.D. 950 and 1150. The Maori people came by canoes from other islands of **Polynesia**, which are in the central and southern Pacific Ocean.

Marlborough Sounds South Island, New Zealand

NEW ZEALAND

North Island
Marlborough Sounds
PACIFIC OCEAN
South Island

Maori Settlement The Maori called the land Aotearoa (ow•tay•ah•ROH•ah). It means "land of the long white cloud" and refers to the thick clouds and snow-capped mountains. The Maori, like the aborigines of Australia, were hunter-gatherers and fishers. They settled mainly on North Island and hunted a large flightless bird called the moa. By the 1500s, they had killed almost all of these birds. Over the years, the Maori learned to be farmers. They lived in separate tribes of about 500 members. Their culture was rich and included skilled woodcarvers who created wood sculptures using stone tools.

Maori Wood Sculpture Wood sculptures tell stories to the viewer. The surface carvings have specific meaning to those who can read them. The carvings tell the history of the Maori people.

Europeans began to arrive in the mid-1600s. A Dutch sea captain, Abel Tasman, stopped in the islands in 1642. Cartographers named the area *Nieuw Zeeland* after a territory in the Netherlands. English Captain James Cook came to the islands more than a hundred years later, in 1769. He was the first European to explore New Zealand and claimed it for Great Britain.

A British Colony Soon, other Europeans—sailors, explorers, and traders—stopped at the islands. In the late 1700s, about 100,000 Maori lived there. In 1814, British Protestant missionaries established the first European settlement on North Island. Because there was no official government, there was much lawlessness in New Zealand. The Maori and the settlers fought each other. The British colonists asked their government to come and establish law and order.

In 1840, Maori chiefs signed the **Treaty of Waitangi** (WY•TAHNG•gee) with Britain. It stated that the Maori accepted the British queen as their ruler in exchange for British protection. The British believed the treaty allowed them to control the land while protecting Maori rights. But the Maori thought that they still had control of the land and that the British were only minor officials. The difference in the understanding of the treaty terms caused problems. British settlers began buying land without Maori permission. Between 1845 and 1872, land wars broke out. When they were over, the British had control of the islands, and the Maori had suffered great losses. Today, Maoris make up about 15 percent of the population.

After gold was discovered in 1861, more settlers arrived. Like the Australian gold rush, many unsuccessful gold seekers did not have the funds to return home. So, they settled on the land and began farming or raising sheep or cattle.

Even though they were a British colony, the New Zealanders thought of themselves as a separate group. In 1907, they asked Britain to allow them to be a self-governing country.

Self-Government Today, New Zealand has a government similar to that of Australia. New Zealand is a constitutional monarchy. The monarch of the United Kingdom is head of state, but has little control. The monarch appoints a governor general, who also has little power. A parliamentary-style government is in place. The one-house parliament has 120 members. Seven seats in parliament are reserved for Maori members, but Maori may also be elected to other seats.

New Zealanders have always been concerned about equal rights for all citizens. The country was one of the first to guarantee women the vote, in 1893. (The United States did not guarantee this right to women until 1920.) The Maori continued to make efforts to get provisions of the Treaty of Waitangi to be enforced. In the 1990s, the Maori finally gained a settlement that provided land and money to the Maori people. New Zealand also provides many social services and old-age pensions for all its people.

▲ **ANALYZE CAUSE AND EFFECT** Explain how the British gained control of New Zealand.

ANALYZING Primary Sources

◀ *Present-day rally for Maori rights*

The Treaty of Waitangi was signed by Maori leaders and the British government on February 6, 1840. Under the treaty, Britain annexed New Zealand. Because the treaty was written in both Maori and English, each party interpreted the treaty terms differently. Below is a part of the treaty.

> Her Majesty the Queen of England confirms and guarantees to the Chiefs and Tribes of New Zealand and to the respective families and individuals thereof the full exclusive and undisturbed possession of their Lands and Estates Forests Fisheries and other properties which they may collectively or individually possess so long as it is their wish and desire to retain the same in their possession.
>
> Source: Government of New Zealand

DOCUMENT–BASED QUESTION
What right does the British government appear to be granting to the Maori?

Traditional Maori Costumes and Tattoos
Facial tattoos are common for both men and women.

Culture

▼ **KEY QUESTION** What have been the main influences on New Zealand's culture?

Most New Zealanders are descendants of early British colonists. All New Zealanders of European ancestry are called **Pakehas** (PAH•kee•HAHS), or white people, by the Maori. New Zealand's culture reflects both British and Maori influences. For example, English and Maori are official languages. New Zealand has an urban culture. Almost 85 percent of the people live in coastal cities, mainly on the North Island. In rural areas, most people live in small villages or on farms or ranches.

Maori Culture The Maori have worked hard to preserve their culture. They also have a good relationship with the *Pakehas*. But Maori leaders would like more opportunities for their people. The Maori have set up Web sites, cultural schools, and newspapers to help retain their culture. In recent years, they have filed claims in court to try to recover their traditional lands. One of the most distinctive aspects of Maori culture is body tattooing. The tattoos are signs of power and prestige. Most Maori follow traditional religious beliefs that honor ancestors and the natural environment.

Sports and Recreation Since most New Zealanders live no more than 80 miles from the sea, water sports such as swimming, sailing, surfing, and fishing are popular. Many families own a small beach house where they go on weekends. New Zealand's mild climate and its mountains, especially those on the South Island, make hiking, climbing, and camping year-round activities. Skiing and snowboarding are also popular. Team sports like rugby and cricket, borrowed from the British, are enjoyed by many.

Wellywood New Zealand's scenic mountains, beaches, forests, and pasturelands have become popular locations for international movie productions, as well as the country's own. In fact, the New Zealand film industry has become big business. It is called Wellywood because it has its headquarters in the capital city of Wellington, and also because it is compared to America's Hollywood. Large studios and technical-effects companies work together to produce a variety of films. One of the biggest projects in motion-picture history, the *Lord of the Rings* trilogy, was filmed in New Zealand.

▲ **SUMMARIZE** Explain the influence of geography on life in New Zealand.

Film Production in New Zealand

You probably know that J.R.R. Tolkien's *Lord of the Rings* takes place in Middle Earth. But did you know that Middle Earth was New Zealand? Director Peter Jackson selected 150 locations in his native country of New Zealand for the three films. New Zealand also supplied about 2,000 production people and thousands of minor performers.

CRITICAL THINKING

Make Inferences Why did the *Lord of the Rings* director choose to film in New Zealand?

a scene from Lord of the Rings ▶

An Economy Based on Land Resources

🔻 **KEY QUESTION** What are New Zealand's major economic activities?

New Zealand has a few mineral resources, and it also has good cropland and pastureland, abundant forests, and beautiful scenery. These land resources are the basis for New Zealand's economy. Many of New Zealand's goods are exported to Asia, Australia, Great Britain, and the United States.

Agriculture, Forestry, and Fishing Did you know that New Zealand has about 25 times as many sheep and cattle as people? Raised on rich pasturelands, these animals produce wool, meat, and dairy products in great quantities that are exported around the world. North Island forests provide timber for export. The fishing industry also supplies huge catches of fish and rock lobster.

Sheep New Zealand's economy relies heavily on the raising of sheep. **Why is New Zealand suited for sheep raising?**

Hydroelectric Plant
New Zealand relies heavily on this form of power. **What aspect of New Zealand's geography makes this possible?**

Manufacturing There has been a growing emphasis on manufacturing in New Zealand since the end of World War II. Since that time New Zealand has worked hard to build businesses in the country so that they would not need to import so many products. Today food products and manufactured goods, including automobiles, electronics, furniture, and metal products, are produced in New Zealand. Some textiles are produced because of the great quantities of wool available here. About 40 percent of the workforce is employed in manufacturing. Auckland, New Zealand's largest city, is the country's largest manufacturing center.

New Zealand has a very limited supply of petroleum. Its industrial production depends on the use of **hydroelectric power**, electricity produced by moving water. The many waterfalls in mountainous areas are some of the sources of hydroelectric power. About three-fourths of all power in New Zealand is created by moving water.

Geothermal energy, power produced by the internal heat of the Earth, is another source of power. Geothermal energy is generated by harnessing the steam or hot water in New Zealand's **geysers**. In some areas, engineers have drilled deep holes to release the underground steam that is then piped to stations to be converted to electricity.

 SUMMARIZE Identify the major economic activities of New Zealand.

Section ③ Assessment

ONLINE QUIZ
For test practice, go to **Interactive Review** @ ClassZone.com

TERMS & NAMES

1. Explain the importance of
- Maori
- Treaty of Waitangi
- *Pakeha*

USE YOUR READING NOTES

2. Find Main Ideas Use your completed web diagram to answer the following question:

In what ways have the Maori preserved their culture?

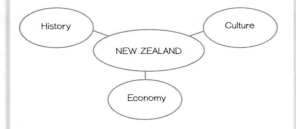

KEY IDEAS

3. Who were the first settlers of New Zealand and when did they arrive?

4. What was the purpose of the Treaty of Waitangi?

5. What are New Zealand's three major agricultural products?

CRITICAL THINKING

6. Analyze Cause and Effect What type of government developed in New Zealand? Why?

7. Evaluate How did New Zealand's physical geography contribute to its economic development?

8. CONNECT to Today Why might the government of New Zealand want to encourage the New Zealand film industry?

9. TECHNOLOGY Plan a Power Presentation Plan a power presentation about the cultural life of New Zealand. Include pictures and descriptions in your presentation.

Click here to complete these and other activities online @ ClassZone.com

CHAPTER SUMMARY

Key Idea 1
The nations of Australia and New Zealand have plant and animal life found nowhere else on earth.

Key Idea 2
Australia's history, culture, and economic life have been shaped by both aborigines and European immigrants.

Key Idea 3
New Zealand's history, culture, and economy have been influenced by the Maori and European immigrants.

For **Review and Study Notes**, go to **Interactive Review** @ ClassZone.com

NAME GAME

Use the Terms & Names list to complete each sentence on paper or online.

1. I am the interior desert region of Australia.
   _____Outback_____

2. I am an animal with an abdominal pouch.
   _____

3. I am descended from a Polynesian people that settled New Zealand._____

4. I worked to ensure that aborigines gained the rights they deserve._____

5. I am a mountain chain in New Zealand.
   _____

6. I am a British explorer who was one of the first Europeans to explore Australia._____

7. I am the islands of the central and southern Pacific. _____

8. I am an agreement between the British and the Maori. _____

9. I am an original inhabitant of Australia.
   _____

10. I am a settlement that serves as a prison.
    _____

aborigine
James Cook
geyser
Great Barrier Reef
Great Dividing Range
Maori
marsupial
Outback
Pakeha
penal colony
Polynesia
Charles Perkins
Southern Alps
Treaty of Waitangi

Activities

GeoGame

Use this online map to reinforce your understanding of the geography of Australia and New Zealand. Click and drag each place name to its location on the map.

Geo GAME

Australia

North Island

South Island

Tasman Sea

New Zealand

To play the complete game, go to **Interactive Review** @ClassZone.com

Australia and New Zealand

Australia

Crossword Puzzle

Complete an online crossword puzzle to test your knowledge of Australia and New Zealand.

Across
1. an animal with an abdominal pouch to carry its young

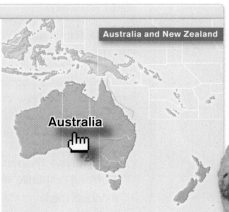

VOCABULARY

Explain the significance of each of the following.

1. geyser
2. marsupial
3. James Cook
4. penal colony
5. constitutional monarchy

Explain how the terms and names in each group are related.

6. Outback, Uluru, and Great Barrier Reef
7. Great Dividing Range and Southern Alps
8. aborigine and Maori
9. Maori, Treaty of Waitangi, and *Pakeha*
10. aborigine and Charles Perkins

KEY IDEAS

1 Unique Lands

11. Why did Australia and New Zealand develop unique plant and animal life?
12. What are the three distinct landforms of Australia?
13. What are the two main islands of New Zealand?
14. Why does New Zealand have so many mountains, geysers, and volcanoes?

2 Australia

15. When did the aborigines arrive in Australia and from what locations did they come?
16. What mineral drew Europeans to Australia in the 1800s?
17. What two peoples influenced Australia's culture?
18. What are five of Australia's major exports?

3 New Zealand

19. Who were the first settlers of New Zealand and from what locations did they come?
20. Why did the Treaty of Waitangi cause problems between the British and the Maori?
21. What are three elements of Maori culture?
22. What are New Zealand's most important natural resources?

CRITICAL THINKING

23. **Compare and Contrast** Create a table to compare and contrast Australia with New Zealand.

FEATURE	AUSTRALIA	NEW ZEALAND
geography		
first settlers		
European colonizer		

24. **Draw Conclusions** How do the landforms of Australia and New Zealand affect where people live?
25. **Connect to Economics** How important is trade to Australia and New Zealand?
26. **Five Themes: Movement** Why did it take so long for Europeans to settle Australia and New Zealand?
27. **Connect Geography & Culture** How did the arrival of British settlers affect the native peoples of Australia and New Zealand?

Answer the ESSENTIAL QUESTION

How has the human geography of Australia and New Zealand changed since European settlement?

Written Response Write a two- or three-paragraph response to the Essential Question. Be sure to consider the key ideas of each section as well as specific ideas about how life in Australia and New Zealand has changed from their earliest settlement. Use the rubric below to guide your thinking.

Response Rubric
A strong response will:
- discuss the first settlers in the region
- identify changes that occurred in culture and economics because of European settlement

Test Practice

- Online Test Practice @ ClassZone.com
- Test-Taking Strategies and Practice
  at the front of this book

TABLES

Use the chart to answer questions 1 and 2 on your paper.

World Production of Wool	
Country	Metric Tons
Australia	395,000
New Zealand	199,000
China	152,000
United Kingdom	42,000
South Africa	32,000
United States	10,000

Source: Commodity Research Bureau, *CRB Commodity Yearbook 2004*

1. Which country is the largest producer of wool in the world?

A. Australia   C. New Zealand
B. China   D. South Africa

2. How does U.S. wool production compare to the wool production of New Zealand and Australia?

A. They are about the same.
B. The United States produces more than New Zealand.
C. Australia produces less than the United States.
D. Australian and New Zealand produce more than the United States.

PRIMARY SOURCE

Read the primary source below and use context clues to answer questions 3 and 4 on your paper.

In 1812, the schooner *Parramatta* put into the Bay of Islands . . . for provisions and water. She was supplied by the natives [Maori] with potatoes, pork, and fish . . . and when they [Maori] required payment they were thrown overboard, fired at, and wounded. The schooner immediately [left] but was . . . driven on shore in a storm and the islanders revenged themselves by putting the crew to death.

Source: Committee of the Church of England Missionary Society, *Memorandum to the Earl of Bathhurst, Secretary of State of the Colonies,* 1817

3. The subject of this primary source is

A. a list of typical foods eaten by the Maori
B. a story about an early explorer of New Zealand
C. the relationship between European sailors and the Maori
D. missionaries in New Zealand converting Maoris

4. Does this quotation show evidence of a bias? Explain your answer.

GeoActivity

1. INTERDISCIPLINARY ACTIVITY–SCIENCE

With a small group, review New Zealand's energy sources. Choose either hydroelectric power or geothermal energy to research and create a museum-style display. Be sure that your display shows where the energy sources are located in New Zealand and how they work.

2. WRITING FOR SOCIAL STUDIES

Review information on the Maori attempts to regain their traditional lands. Form an opinion on the issue. Then write a paragraph supporting your opinion that could be posted on a Web log (blog).

3. MENTAL MAPPING

Create an outline map of Australia and New Zealand and label the following:

Australia
- Great Dividing Range
- Outback
- Tasmania

New Zealand
- North Island
- South Island
- Southern Alps

30 Oceania and Antarctica

 ESSENTIAL QUESTION

How do the regions of Oceania demonstrate cultural diffusion?

CONNECT Geography & History

Use the map and the time line to answer the following questions.

1. Which state of the United States is found in Oceania?

2. Which European nations who staked claims to islands in the Pacific still control them?

Geography

1521 Sailing under the Spanish flag, explorer Ferdinand Magellan reaches Guam. ▶

40,000 B.C.

History

c. 40,000 B.C. Settlers of Oceania come from Southeast Asia in outrigger canoes like the one above.

Culture

1800s European colonies are established on larger islands of Oceania.

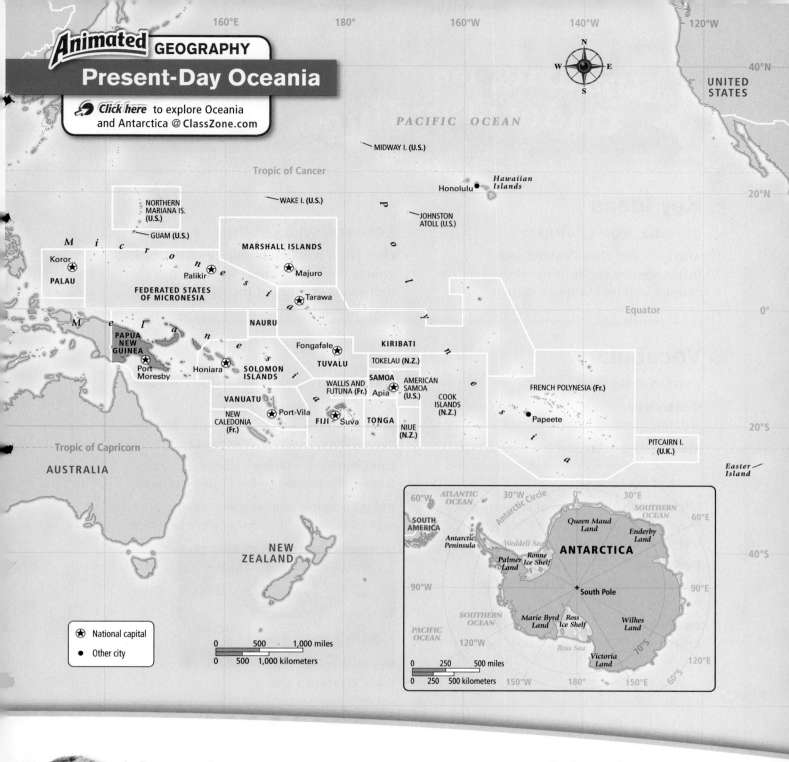

PACIFIC OCEAN

160°E · 180° · 160°W · 140°W · 120°W

40°N

UNITED STATES

Tropic of Cancer

MIDWAY I. (U.S.)

20°N

Hawaiian Islands
Honolulu

WAKE I. (U.S.)

JOHNSTON ATOLL (U.S.)

M i c r o n e s i a

NORTHERN MARIANA IS. (U.S.)

GUAM (U.S.)

Koror
PALAU

Palikir

MARSHALL ISLANDS

Majuro

FEDERATED STATES OF MICRONESIA

Tarawa

Equator 0°

P o l y n e s i a

M e l a n e s i a

NAURU

PAPUA NEW GUINEA
Port Moresby

Honiara

SOLOMON ISLANDS

Fongafale

TUVALU

KIRIBATI

TOKELAU (N.Z.)

WALLIS AND FUTUNA (Fr.)

SAMOA
Apia

AMERICAN SAMOA (U.S.)

COOK ISLANDS (N.Z.)

FRENCH POLYNESIA (Fr.)

Papeete

VANUATU

Port-Vila

NEW CALEDONIA (Fr.)

FIJI
Suva

TONGA

NIUE (N.Z.)

20°S

PITCAIRN I. (U.K.)

Tropic of Capricorn

AUSTRALIA

Easter Island

NEW ZEALAND

★ National capital
• Other city

0   500   1,000 miles
0   500   1,000 kilometers

ATLANTIC OCEAN

60°W · 30°W · 0° · 30°E

SOUTH AMERICA

Antarctic Circle

SOUTHERN OCEAN

60°E

Antarctic Peninsula

Weddell Sea

Queen Maud Land

Enderby Land

Palmer Land

Ronne Ice Shelf

ANTARCTICA

90°W

+ South Pole

90°E

PACIFIC OCEAN

SOUTHERN OCEAN

120°W

Marie Byrd Land

Ross Ice Shelf

Wilkes Land

40°S

Ross Sea

Victoria Land

70°S

120°E

0   250   500 miles
0   250   500 kilometers

150°W · 180° · 150°E

60°S

Geography
◀ **1911** Norwegian explorer Roald Amundsen is the first to reach the South Pole.

Culture
▼ **1959** Antarctic Treaty opens Antarctica to international scientific research.

Today

History
1941–1945 Islands of the Pacific are battlegrounds during World War II.

Reading for Understanding

▶ Key Ideas

BEFORE, YOU LEARNED

Australia and New Zealand were influenced by the cultures of their native peoples and by European settlers.

NOW YOU WILL LEARN

Oceania is home to hundreds of cultural groups living on islands spread across thousands of miles of the Pacific Ocean.

▶ Vocabulary

TERMS & NAMES

Oceania the region of the Pacific Ocean with thousands of islands

Melanesia a subregion of Oceania that includes islands northeast of Australia and south of the equator

Micronesia a subregion of Oceania that includes islands east of the Philippines and north of the equator

Polynesia a subregion of Oceania that includes islands of the central and southern Pacific

oceanic island an island rising from the deep sea floor on a volcanic foundation

coral island a type of oceanic island that is a coral reef

atoll a ring-shaped coral reef encircling a central lagoon with no inner island

trust territory a territory placed under the control of a country by the United Nations

pidgin a simple form of speech that is a mixture of words from two or more languages

Visual Vocabulary atoll

▶ Reading Strategy

Re-create the chart shown at right. As you read and respond to the **KEY QUESTIONS**, use the chart to compare and contrast details about the subregions of Oceania.

 Skillbuilder Handbook, page R9

COMPARE AND CONTRAST

MELANESIA	MICRONESIA	POLYNESIA
1.	1.	1.
2.	2.	2.
3.	3.	3.

 GRAPHIC ORGANIZERS
Go to **Interactive Review** @ ClassZone.com

Oceania: The Pacific World

Connecting to Your World

What do you think is the ideal climate? Many people believe that the climate and weather of the Pacific islands are ideal. The Pacific islands have a mild tropical climate with warm, but not too hot, temperatures. Gentle ocean breezes cool off the evenings, and sandy beaches are everywhere. In this section, you will study life in the Pacific islands and decide for yourself if they are your idea of a perfect place.

Three Subregions of Oceania

▼ KEY QUESTION What are the three subregions of Oceania?

Oceania is a region of the Pacific Ocean with thousands of islands. It stretches from Hawaii on the northeast, to Easter Island on the east, south to New Zealand, and west to the island of New Guinea. Geographers estimate there are between 20,000 and 30,000 islands in the Pacific Ocean. Some are just tiny specks in the vast ocean. Others are very large, such as Australia, a continent; New Zealand; and New Guinea, the second largest island in the world. Islands located close to Asia, such as the Philippines, Indonesia, and Japan, are not considered part of the region.

Easter Island Statues Hundreds of carved stone heads on this island look out over the Pacific Ocean.

PACIFIC OCEAN

SOUTH AMERICA

○ Easter Island

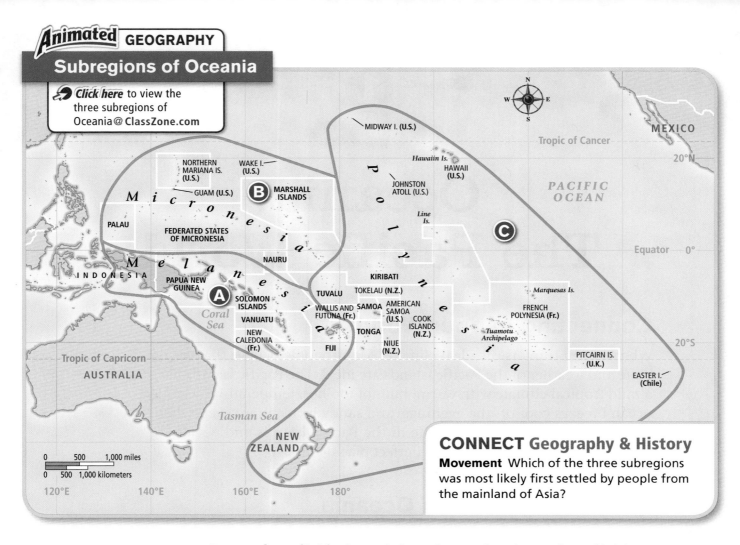

Click here to view the three subregions of Oceania @ ClassZone.com

MIDWAY I. (U.S.)

NORTHERN MARIANA IS. (U.S.)

WAKE I. (U.S.)

Micronesia

GUAM (U.S.)

B MARSHALL ISLANDS

PALAU

FEDERATED STATES OF MICRONESIA

NAURU

Melanesia

INDONESIA

PAPUA NEW GUINEA

A SOLOMON ISLANDS

VANUATU

NEW CALEDONIA (Fr.)

Coral Sea

TUVALU

WALLIS AND FUTUNA (Fr.)

FIJI

KIRIBATI

TOKELAU (N.Z.)

SAMOA

AMERICAN SAMOA (U.S.)

TONGA

COOK ISLANDS (N.Z.)

NIUE (N.Z.)

Polynesia

Hawaiin Is.

HAWAII (U.S.)

JOHNSTON ATOLL (U.S.)

Line Is.

C

Marquesas Is.

FRENCH POLYNESIA (Fr.)

Tuamotu Archipelago

PITCAIRN IS. (U.K.)

EASTER I. (Chile)

MEXICO

Tropic of Cancer

20°N

PACIFIC OCEAN

Equator   0°

20°S

Tropic of Capricorn

AUSTRALIA

Tasman Sea

NEW ZEALAND

0   500   1,000 miles
0   500   1,000 kilometers

120°E   140°E   160°E   180°

CONNECT Geography & History

Movement Which of the three subregions was most likely first settled by people from the mainland of Asia?

Geographers divide Oceania into three subregions. These divisions are based on the physical geography of the islands and the culture and ethnic backgrounds of the peoples living there. The subregions are Melanesia, Micronesia, and Polynesia.

Melanesia The islands of **Melanesia** Ⓐ are close to Southeast Asia, northeast of Australia, and south of the equator. The world's second largest island—New Guinea—is located here.

Micronesia As you might have guessed, **Micronesia** Ⓑ means "small islands." Most of the islands of Micronesia are small, low-lying coral islands found east of the Philippines and north of the equator.

Polynesia The third region, **Polynesia** Ⓒ, means "many islands." This subregion is the largest in Oceania. It covers thousands of square miles of the central and southern Pacific and stretches as far north as the Hawaiian Islands.

▲ **SUMMARIZE** Describe the subregions of Oceania.

CONNECT to Science

In Oceania, islands are constantly building and eroding. Islands can be created by natural forces. They are also subject to erosion and, thus, might disappear.

There are three types of islands in Oceania—continental islands, **oceanic islands** rising from the deep sea floor on a volcanic foundation, and **coral islands**, which are coral reefs. An **atoll** is a ring-shaped coral reef encircling a lagoon with no inner island. Below, see oceanic and coral islands.

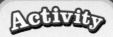

Activity

Make a Model

Materials
• modeling materials
• colored pencils or markers, paper

1. Study the diagrams below. Choose one of the two types of islands to create in three dimensions.

2. Using the illustrations below as a guide, create a series of 3–5 small models showing in more detail how the type of island you selected is formed.

3. Write a caption for each model.

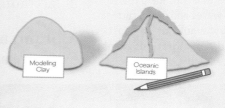

Oceanic Islands

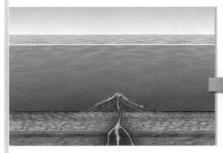

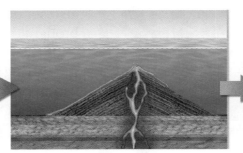

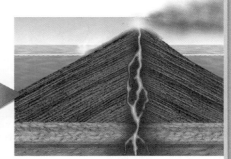

1. Magma sometimes erupts through cracks in the ocean floor.

2. Over time, layers of lava can build up to form a volcanic cone.

3. Some volcanic cones rise above sea level and become islands.

Coral Islands

1. Some corals form reefs on the sides of volcanic islands.

2. As the island erodes, the reef continues to grow upward.

3. In time, only the low islands of the reef remain.

History and Government

▼ KEY QUESTION Who settled the islands of Oceania?

The islands of Oceania were settled in three waves. The first peoples settled around 40,000 years ago on the islands of Melanesia and, later, those of Micronesia. Thousands of years later, groups from the settled islands moved east as far as Polynesia. In the 1800s, Europeans arrived in Oceania to establish colonies.

Oceania's First Settlers

The earliest settlers of Oceania probably moved across land bridges or came by large canoes from the mainland of Asia and from Indonesia. These people may have left crowded conditions where they lived to look for more land. As they moved, they took animals and plants with them to start their new lives. In this way, the environment of the Pacific islands was changed to accommodate the culture of the newcomers.

Colonization and Independence

The first European contact with Oceania was made by explorer Ferdinand Magellan, who reached Guam in 1521. Later, British and French explorers came to the islands, bringing traders and Christian missionaries and colonists. In time, the United States, Germany, and Japan also set up colonies. The colonizers brought their language and religions with them.

During World War II, the Allies fought the Japanese across the region of Oceania for control of the Pacific. After the war, people living on islands that were European colonies began to pressure the colonizers for self-rule. Some islands became trust territories administered by larger nations, such as the United States, New Zealand, Australia, and Britain. A **trust territory** is a territory placed under the control of another country by the United Nations. The countries prepared the territories to achieve self-government.

From 1962 to 1994, 12 islands or island groups were given independence. Some islands, such as French Polynesia, are still controlled by the original colonizers.

▲ FIND MAIN IDEAS Identify the groups that settled the islands of Oceania.

Navigation Chart Pacific Islanders used charts like this to record the patterns of waves and ocean currents. **How would these charts aid the migrations across the Pacific?**

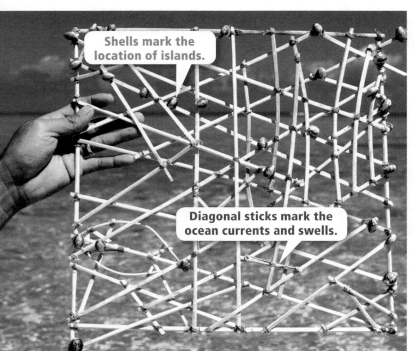

Shells mark the location of islands.

Diagonal sticks mark the ocean currents and swells.

Culture

▼ **KEY QUESTION** What are the cultures of Oceania like?

The many peoples of Oceania's small islands live a traditional way of life. Family and village are the focus of their lives. Most live in small farming or fishing villages, just as their ancestors did. Households include parents, grandparents, uncles, aunts, and cousins. They may occupy one house or a cluster of houses. A chief heads each village.

About one-third of the world's languages are spoken in Oceania. Scholars estimate about 1,000 languages are found there. About 740 are spoken in Papua New Guinea alone. With so many languages, communication between peoples in Oceania was difficult. So, a form of speech called pidgin developed. **Pidgin** is a mixture of two or more languages and is spoken by people with different native languages.

▲ **MAKE GENERALIZATIONS** Describe the cultures of Oceania.

CONNECT ▸ Geography & Culture

Pidgin

Melanesian pidgin is spoken widely in Oceania. Pidgin languages often are a combination of a Western language, such as English, French, or German, and the local language.

The language is quite colorful. Here is how a piano is described in Melanesian pidgin: "bigfala bokis garem plande tit, iu hitim hemi kraeout" (a big box with many teeth, when you hit it, it cries).

HIPPOCRENE CONCISE DICTIONARY
NEO-MELANESIAN DICTIONARY
NEW GUINEA PIDGIN-ENGLISH
Compiled by Friedrich Steinbauer

Section 1 Assessment

ONLINE QUIZ
For test practice, go to **Interactive Review** @ ClassZone.com

TERMS & NAMES

1. Explain the importance of
- Oceania
- Melanesia
- Micronesia
- Polynesia

USE YOUR READING NOTES

2. Compare and Contrast Use your completed chart to answer the following question:

In which of the subregions of Oceania would you find people who had traveled the farthest from Southeast Asia?

MELANESIA	MICRONESIA	POLYNESIA
1.	1.	1.
2.	2.	2.
3.	3.	3.

KEY IDEAS

3. What are the three subregions of Oceania?

4. How were the Pacific islands first settled?

5. What is the traditional way of life for Pacific Islanders?

CRITICAL THINKING

6. Draw Conclusions How did contact with Europeans and Americans affect the peoples of Oceania?

7. Understand Causes Why was it necessary to set up trust territories in Oceania?

8. CONNECT to Today Why might tourism be an important industry for the islands of Oceania to develop?

9. WRITING Prepare a Travel Brochure Select one of the nations of Oceania and prepare a travel brochure for tourists. Describe the nation's physical setting, climate, and attractions, and include pictures.

The entire population of Oceania, excluding Australia and New Zealand, is over 12 million. The population is spread out over thousands of square miles of the Pacific Ocean. Geographers divide the areas into three regions based on ethnic groups and on language.

Polynesia

Ancestors of Polynesians sailed across thousands of miles of the Pacific to settle these islands. Although the lands are widespread, the cultures of the subregion are similar in language, housing, and art forms. Tourism forms the basis of some economies.

POLYNESIA

▲ *A Polynesian man displays traditional tattoos from head to toe.*

French Polynesia ▼

Polynesian Work

A Polynesian works with an oyster to create a pearl for the pearl industry.

Micronesian Work

Ifalik Island fishermen bring in a catch. Many in Micronesia work in the fishing industry.

◄ A Micronesian child in traditional headdress and grass skirt gets ready for a special dance.

Micronesia

The oceanic islands in this subregion depend on agriculture for their economy. The coral islands have coconuts and fishing industries. The region was mostly under control of the United States as a group of trust territories.

Islands of Palau ▼

Melanesia

Hundreds of languages are spoken in this subregion, and the cultures are quite varied. Many of the people living here are subsistence farmers. The rugged lands are rich in minerals, which attracted European settlement.

MELANESIA

◄ A Melanesian tribesman wears a traditional headdress and boar's tusks for a ritual ceremony.

Melanesian Work

New Guinea lumbermen take advantage of the forests on the island.

CRITICAL THINKING

1. **Draw Conclusions** How do the islanders of Oceania use their environment to meet their needs?

2. **Form and Support Opinions** What challenges do you think the people of Oceania face?

Reading for Understanding

SECTION **2**

▶ Key Ideas

BEFORE, YOU LEARNED

Oceania has three distinct subregions, Melanesia, Micronesia, and Polynesia.

NOW YOU WILL LEARN

Antarctica has no permanent residents because it has such a harsh environment.

▶ Vocabulary

TERMS & NAMES

Transantarctic Mountains mountains that divide Antarctica into two parts

geographic South Pole the point where all lines of longitude meet

icecap a glacier that covers a large area

Antarctic Peninsula an S-shaped peninsula that is part of the Andes Mountain chain

ice shelf huge flat sheet of ice extending over the ocean, but attached to the land

iceberg a large piece of floating ice

Robert Scott a British polar explorer

Roald Amundsen Norwegian polar explorer who was the first to reach the South Pole

Antarctic Treaty an agreement signed in 1959 calling for the peaceful use of Antarctica

BACKGROUND VOCABULARY

ozone hole the seasonal thinning of a protective layer of atmospheric gas high above Antarctica

Visual Vocabulary iceberg

▶ Reading Strategy

Re-create the Venn diagram shown at right. As you read and respond to the **KEY QUESTIONS**, use the diagram to organize important details and draw conclusions about the physical geography of Antarctica.

 Skillbuilder Handbook, page R13

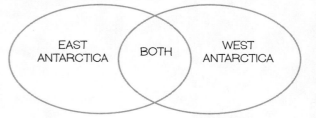

DRAW CONCLUSIONS

EAST ANTARCTICA BOTH WEST ANTARCTICA

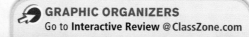
GRAPHIC ORGANIZERS
Go to **Interactive Review** @ClassZone.com

SECTION

2

FOCUS ON

Antarctica: A Frozen Desert

Connecting to Your World

You just learned about lands that have a climate many people believe to be ideal. Now try to imagine a place where the summer temperatures range from –30°F to 59°F. In the winter, it is so cold (–40°F to –100°F) that even a short exposure to the elements could mean certain death. This place is Antarctica—the land at the "bottom of the Earth."

Leopard Seal
Herds of leopard seals roam the Antarctic waters.

An Icy Landscape

▼ **KEY QUESTION** What are the physical features of East and West Antarctica?

Like Australia, Antarctica is an island continent. It is the world's fifth largest continent. It is the coldest, windiest, and most isolated continent, and one of the driest. Unlike other continents, Antarctica is buried under thousands of feet of ice. At its thickest point, the ice is around two miles deep. This ice-cover holds as much as 70 percent of the Earth's fresh water. Poking up through the ice are mountains. But just 2 percent of the land is ice-free. Even more floating ice surrounds Antarctica. Geographically, it is divided into sections, East Antarctica and West Antarctica.

Gentoo Penguins
An adult feeds a baby penguin at an Antarctic seashore.

Antarctica: Physical

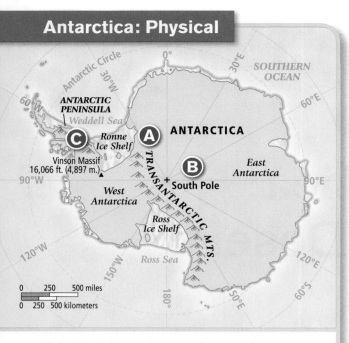

CONNECT Geography & History

1. **Location** At what point do the lines of longitude come together?
2. **Place** Which ocean surrounds the continent of Antarctica?

East Antarctica The **Transantarctic Mountains** Ⓐ run across the continent from the Ross Sea to the Weddell Sea. They divide Antarctica into two sections. Some mountain peaks in East Antarctica are higher than 14,000 feet. Dry, ice-free valleys are located within these mountains where glaciers were once found. What little snow falls is blown out of the valleys by the wind. Some of the valleys have frozen lakes. The eastern side of the continent is covered by a huge plateau, mountains, and the **geographic South Pole** Ⓑ. That is the point where all lines of longitude meet. The entire region is a cold, high, and dry land.

It is hard to believe that Antarctica, with its snow and ice, has a dry climate. However, desert climate is one in which precipitation is under 10 inches per year. Only a little more than six inches of snow falls in Antarctica each year. That makes it a polar desert. The yearly amount of precipitation in Antarctica is somewhat larger than the amount of rain that falls in Africa's Sahara desert. See the graphs below.

◄COMPARING ► Climate: Antarctica and Sahara

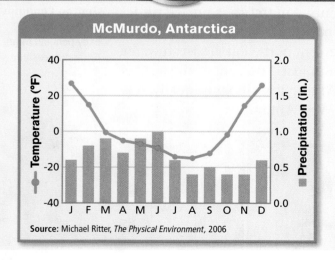

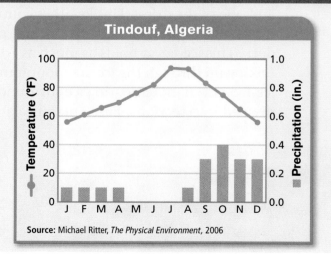

CRITICAL THINKING

Compare and Contrast How do the two regions compare in the amount of precipitation received each year?

West Antarctica The western side of Antarctica has a huge **icecap**, a glacier that covers a large area. The icecap links five off-shore islands into a frozen land of mountains, volcanoes, and the **Antarctic Peninsula ⓒ**. This S-shaped peninsula points toward South America and actually is a part of the Andes Mountain chain. The peninsula is the warmest, most ice-free region of Antarctica.

Ice Shelves and Icebergs The rugged coastline of Antarctica is marked by bays and channels. **Ice shelves** are huge, flat sheets of ice extending over the ocean, but attached to the land. In the summer, parts of these shelves break off and float away. These large floating pieces of ice are called **icebergs**. Antarctic icebergs are enormous, sometimes covering thousands of square miles. Their smooth, flat shape and massive size make them different from the usually smaller, peaked icebergs found in the Arctic.

🔺 **COMPARE AND CONTRAST** Describe how West Antarctica differs from East Antarctica.

Exploration of Antarctica

🔻 **KEY QUESTION** Why do scientists continue to explore Antarctica?

Geographers had long thought there might be a seventh continent, but it was not until 1820 that a Russian explorer probably made what was the first sighting of Antarctica. Soon, European explorers were trying to map the coastline and to sail completely around the island continent. By 1895, explorers thought about crossing Antarctica to reach the geographic South Pole.

The Race to the South Pole Early expeditions failed to reach the South Pole because of the extremely harsh conditions. Then, in 1911, two explorers—**Robert Scott** of Great Britain and **Roald Amundsen** of Norway—organized polar expeditions. Using dog sleds, Amundsen and his team reached the South Pole on December 14, 1911. Scott's team, which used ponies and motor-powered sleds, arrived on January 17, 1912. Unfortunately, all members of Scott's expedition froze to death on the return journey. An American admiral, Richard Byrd, led five expeditions to the continent between the late 1920s and the 1950s. Later expeditions used aircraft and satellites to photograph the continent's features.

Robert F. Scott The British explorer perished on his return trip from the South Pole.

Antarctica Territorial Claims

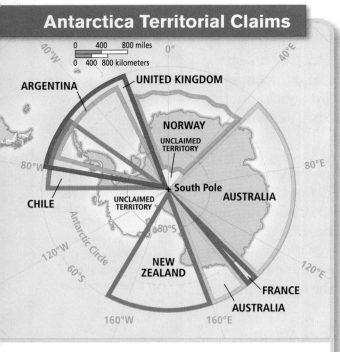

0 400 800 miles
0 400 800 kilometers

ARGENTINA   UNITED KINGDOM
NORWAY
UNCLAIMED TERRITORY
80°W   80°E
South Pole
CHILE   UNCLAIMED TERRITORY   AUSTRALIA
Antarctic Circle
120°W   120°E
60°S   80°S
NEW ZEALAND
FRANCE
AUSTRALIA
160°W   160°E

CONNECT Geography & History

1. **Place** Which three countries have overlapping claims?
2. **Place** Which of the nations making claims are not Antarctica's neighbors?

Scientific Outpost In 1957, a worldwide program of scientific investigation called the International Geophysical Year began. Sixty-seven countries agreed to conduct scientific experiments around the world and at science stations in Antarctica. When it ended, 7 of the 12 countries that had set up research stations in Antarctica claimed a part of the continent. Fearing attempts to use the land for military purposes, the nations later agreed to the **Antarctic Treaty** (1959). The treaty stated that Antarctica should be used for peaceful scientific research and the environment should be protected. Today, more than 25 countries have scientific outposts there. They study climate, animal behavior, earthquakes, solar radiation, and changes in the **ozone hole** (the seasonal thinning of a protective layer of atmospheric gas above Antarctica).

 MAKE INFERENCES Identify reasons why Antarctica continues to be explored.

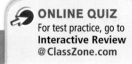

ONLINE QUIZ
For test practice, go to **Interactive Review** @ ClassZone.com

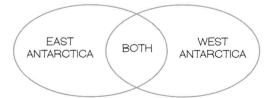

Section 2 Assessment

TERMS & NAMES

1. **Explain the importance of**
   - Transantarctic Mountains
   - geographic South Pole
   - Antarctic Peninsula
   - Antarctic Treaty

USE YOUR READING NOTES

2. **Draw Conclusions** Use your completed Venn diagram to answer the following question:

   Which physical features do both East and West Antarctica share?

   EAST ANTARCTICA   BOTH   WEST ANTARCTICA

KEY IDEAS

3. What physical feature divides Antarctica?
4. What is the warmest, most ice-free region of Antarctica?
5. Which explorer was the first to lead a successful expedition to the South Pole?

CRITICAL THINKING

6. **Find Main Ideas** What was the purpose of the Antarctic Treaty?
7. **Understand Effects** What might happen to Antarctica if global warming increases?
8. **CONNECT to Today** What might Antarctica be like today if the Antarctic Treaty had not prevented more land claims there?
9. **SCIENCE** **Create a Plant and Animal Life Poster** Use the Internet to research the plants and animals found on Antarctica and collect images. Then label and display them on a poster.

924 Chapter 30

CHAPTER SUMMARY

Key Idea 1
Oceania is home to hundreds of cultural groups living on islands spread across thousands of miles of the Pacific Ocean.

Key Idea 2
Antarctica has no permanent residents because it has such a harsh environment.

For **Review and Study Notes**, go to **Interactive Review @ ClassZone.com**

NAME GAME

Use the Terms & Names list to complete each sentence on paper or online.

1. I am the region in the Pacific Ocean with thousands of islands. _____Oceania_____

2. I am a ring of reefs around a lagoon. _____

3. I am the point where all lines of longitude meet. _____

4. I am a subregion of Oceania that includes islands of the central and southern Pacific and stretches north. _____

5. I am a glacier that covers a large land area. _____

6. I am a Norwegian polar explorer who was the first to reach the South Pole. _____

7. I am the mountains that divide Antarctica into two parts. _____

8. I am an agreement signed in 1959 calling for the peaceful use of Antarctica. _____

9. I am a subregion of Oceania that includes islands northeast of Australia and south of the equator. _____

10. I am a form of speech that is a mixture of words from two or more languages. _____

atoll
Roald Amundsen
Antarctic Peninsula
Antarctic Treaty
geographic South Pole
icecap
ice shelf
Melanesia
Micronesia
Oceania
pidgin
Polynesia
Robert Scott
Transantarctic Mountains
trust territory

Activities

Flip Cards

Use the online flip cards to quiz yourself on the terms and names introduced in this chapter.

oceanic island

an island created by volcanic action

Crossword Puzzle

Complete an online crossword puzzle to test your knowledge of Oceania and Antarctica.

ACROSS
1. a large piece of floating ice

VOCABULARY

Explain the significance of each of the following.

1. pidgin
2. Transantarctic Mountains
3. Antarctic Peninsula
4. geographic South Pole
5. Antarctic Treaty

Explain how the terms and names in each group are related.

6. oceanic island, coral island, and atoll
7. Melanesia, Micronesia, and Polynesia
8. Oceania and trust territory
9. icecap, ice shelf, and iceberg
10. Roald Amundsen and Robert Scott

KEY IDEAS

1 Oceania: The Pacific World

11. How is Oceania divided?
12. What were the three waves of settlement of the Pacific islands?
13. Why did Europeans come to Oceania?
14. What are the two traditional economic activities of the Pacific Islanders?
15. What is a trust territory?
16. Why did pidgin language develop?

2 Antarctica: A Frozen Desert

17. Why are their no permanent residents in Antarctica?
18. What are the two geographical divisions of Antarctica?
19. How are Antarctic icebergs formed?
20. Which European explorer was the first to reach the geographic South Pole?
21. What is the major activity conducted in Antarctica?
22. What is the purpose of the Antarctic Treaty?

CRITICAL THINKING

23. **Compare and Contrast** Create a table to compare and contrast the physical description, climate, population, and political status of Oceania and Antarctica.

CHARACTERISTICS	OCEANIA	ANTARCTICA
Physical Description		
Climate		
Population		
Political Status		

24. **Five Themes: Movement** Why was Antarctica the last continent to be discovered and explored?
25. **Make Generalizations** How has the world benefited from international cooperation in Antarctica?
26. **Connect to Economics** Why is the growth of the tourist industry important for the economies of the Pacific islands?
27. **Connect Geography & History** What happened to the colonies of Oceania after World War II?
28. **Connect Geography & Culture** What is distinctive about Oceania in terms of its languages?

Answer the
ESSENTIAL QUESTION

How do the regions of Oceania demonstrate cultural diffusion?

Written Response Write a two- or three-paragraph response to the Essential Question. Be sure to consider the key ideas of each section as well as basic ideas related to cultural diffusion. Use the rubric below to guide your thinking.

Response Rubric
A strong response will:
- point out the waves of settlers and colonizers in the region
- identify aspects of the culture that show changes

STANDARDS-BASED ASSESSMENT

 **Test Practice**

• Online Test Practice @ ClassZone.com
• Test-Taking Strategies and Practice
  at the front of this book

CHART

Use the chart to answer questions 1 and 2 on your paper.

Countries of Oceania		
Country	Date of Independence	Population (2005 Estimate)
Fiji	1970	905,949
Marshall Islands	1986	60,422
Nauru	1968	13,287
Palau	1994	20,579
Papua New Guinea	1975	5,670,544
Samoa	1962	176,908
Vanuatu	1980	208,754

Source: *CIA World Fact Book*, 2006

1. Which country was the first to gain independence?

A. Fiji   C. Papua New Guinea
B. Nauru   D. Samoa

2. Which is the smallest nation to gain independence?

A. Marshall Islands
B. Nauru
C. Palau
D. Vanuatu

CLIMATE GRAPH

Examine the climate graph below. Use the information in the graph to answer questions 3 and 4 on your paper.

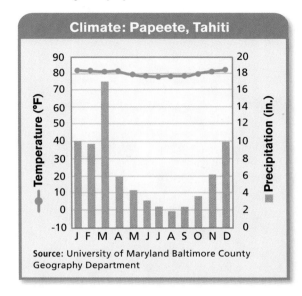

Climate: Papeete, Tahiti

Source: University of Maryland Baltimore County Geography Department

3. In which month does it rain the most?

4. Why would the month of August be a good time to visit Papeete?

GeoActivity

1. INTERDISCIPLINARY ACTIVITY–SCIENCE

With a small group, research the various types of ice formations found in Antarctica. Create a museum-style display of these formations. Be sure your display includes images of the formations, their names, and descriptions.

2. WRITING FOR SOCIAL STUDIES

Unit Writing Project After you have completed your illustrated time line showing the arrival of different groups in the region, add a series of newspaper headlines to the time line that also tell the story of migration in this region.

3. MENTAL MAPPING

Create an outline map of the southern Pacific and label the following:

• Melanesia   • Antarctica
• Micronesia   • Australia
• Polynesia   • New Zealand

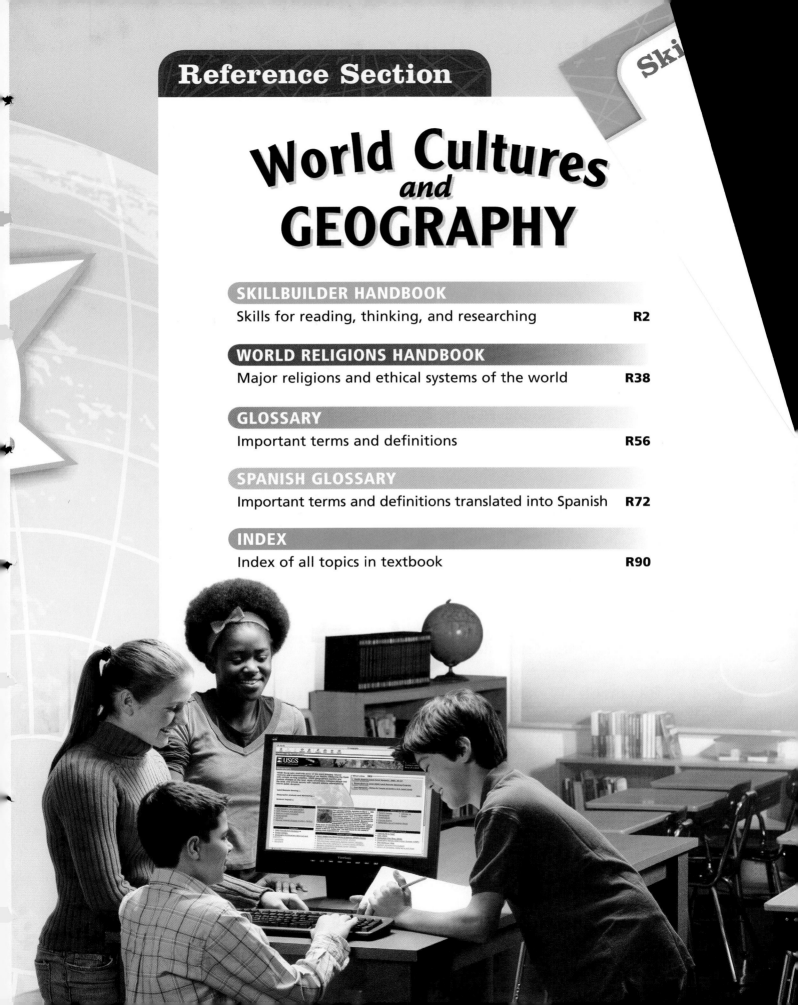

Reference Section

Ski

World Cultures
and
GEOGRAPHY

Contents

Reading and Critical Thinking Skills

Reading Maps, Graphs, and Other Visuals

Research, Writing, and Presentation Skills

Using the Internet

1.1 Taking Notes

Defining the Skill

When you **take notes,** you write down the important ideas and details of a passage. A chart or an outline can help you organize your notes to use in the future.

Applying the Skill

The following passage describes several different types of bodies of water. Use the strategies listed below to help you take notes on the passage.

How to Take and Organize Notes

Strategy 1 Look at the title to find the main topic of the passage.

Strategy 2 Identify the main ideas and details of the passage. Then summarize the main ideas and details in your notes.

Strategy 3 Identify key terms and define them. The term *hydrosphere* is shown in boldface type and highlighted; both techniques signal that it is a key term.

Strategy 4 In your notes, use abbreviations to save time and space. You can abbreviate words such as *gulf (G.)*, *river (R.)*, and *lake (L.)*, as long as you write the proper name of the body of water with the abbreviation.

---

1 BODIES OF WATER

2 All the bodies of water on Earth form what is called **3** the **hydrosphere**. The world's **2** oceans make up the largest part of the hydrosphere. Oceans have smaller regions. **2** Gulfs, such as the Gulf of Tonkin, and seas, such as the Sea of Japan, are extensions of oceans. Land partially encloses these waters.

2 Oceans and seas contain salt water, but most lakes and rivers contain fresh water. The water in rivers, such as the **2** Nile River in Africa, flows down a channel in one direction. This movement is the current. Lake water, such as that found in **2** Lake Victoria in Africa, can have currents too, even though the water is surrounded by land. Some lakes feed into rivers, and some rivers supply water to lakes.

Make a Chart

Making a chart can help you take notes on a passage. The chart below contains notes from the passage you just read.

2

Item	Notes
1. **3** hydrosphere	all water on Earth
a. oceans	salt water; largest part of hydrosphere
b. gulfs and seas	**4** G. of Tonkin; **4** S. of Japan; part of ocean
c. lakes and rivers	usually fresh water; **4** Nile R. flows; **4** L. Victoria surrounded by land

Practicing the Skill

Turn to Chapter 1, Section 2, "Technology Tools for Geographers." Read "The Science of Mapmaking," and use a chart to take notes on the passage.

1.2 Finding Main Ideas

Defining the Skill

A **main idea** is a statement that summarizes the subject of a speech, an article, a section of a book, or a paragraph. Main ideas can be stated or unstated. The main idea of a paragraph is often stated in the first or last sentence. If it is the first sentence, it is followed by sentences that support that main idea. If it is the last sentence, the details build up to the main idea. To find an unstated idea, use the details of the paragraph as clues.

Applying the Skill

The following paragraph provides reasons why Japan and Australia make such good trading partners. Use the strategies listed below to help you identify the main idea.

How to Find the Main Idea

Strategy 1 Identify what you think may be the stated main idea. Check the first and last sentences of the paragraph to see if either could be the stated main idea.

Strategy 2 Identify details that support the main idea. Some details explain that idea. Others give examples of what is stated in the main idea.

TRADING PARTNERS

Australia is an island. Japan is also an island, though much smaller than Australia. Australia is not as densely populated as Japan. 2 In Japan, an average of 881 people live in each square mile. Australia averages 7 people per square mile. 2 Australia has wide-open lands available for agriculture, ranching, and mining. 2 Japan buys wool from Australian ranches, wheat from Australian farms, and iron ore from Australian mines. To provide jobs for its many workers, 2 Japan developed industries. Those industries 2 sell electronics and cars to Australia. 1 Australia and Japan are trading partners because each has something the other needs.

Make a Chart

Making a chart can help you identify the main idea and details in a passage or paragraph. The chart below identifies the main idea and details in the paragraph you just read.

> **Main Idea:** Australia and Japan are good trading partners because each supplies something the other needs.
> **Detail:** Japan's population density is 881 people per square mile; Australia's is 7 per square mile.
> **Detail:** Australia has land, natural resources, and agricultural products.
> **Detail:** Japan buys wool, wheat, and iron ore from Australia.
> **Detail:** Japan has many industries.
> **Detail:** Australia buys electronics and cars from Japanese industries.

Practicing the Skill

Turn to Chapter 15, Section 1, "Sweeping Across Eurasia." Read "Human-Environment Interaction." Create a chart that identifies the main idea and the supporting details.

1.3 Summarizing

Defining the Skill

When you **summarize,** you restate a paragraph, passage, or chapter in fewer words. You include only the main ideas and most important details. It is important to use your own words when summarizing.

Applying the Skill

The passage below describes the origins of several state names in the United States. Use the strategies that follow to help you summarize the passage.

How to Summarize

Strategy ① Look for topic sentences stating the main idea or ideas. These are often at the beginning of a section or paragraph. Briefly restate each main idea in your own words.

Strategy ② Include key facts and any names, dates, numbers, amounts, or percentages from the text.

Strategy ③ After writing your summary, review it to see that you have included only the most important details.

STATES' NAMES

① The name of a state often comes from that state's geography. For example, ② the name for Montana comes from a Spanish word that means "mountainous."

① Other states are named after people who were in power at the time the area was explored or settled. ② A French explorer named Louisiana after the French king at the time, Louis XIV. The state of ② Georgia was named after King George II of England, who granted the right to start the colony.

① Still other states get their names from Native American tribes living in the area when Europeans arrived. ② Arkansas, Alabama, and Massachusetts were named for the Native American tribes living there.

Write a Summary

You should be able to write your summary in a short paragraph. The paragraph at right summarizes the passage you just read.

③ The names of states in the United States often came from geographical features, the names of people in power, or the names of Native American tribes.

Practicing the Skill

Turn to Chapter 6, Section 1, "Mountains, Prairies, and Coastlands." Read "Climates of Canada," and write a short paragraph summarizing the passage.

1.4 Sequencing Events

Defining the Skill

Sequence is the order in which events occur. Learning to follow the sequence of events through history will help you to better understand how events relate to one another.

Applying the Skill

The following passage explains the sequence of events that led to the U.S. Civil War. Use the strategies listed below to help you follow the sequence of events.

How to Find the Sequence of Events

Strategy ❶ Look for specific dates provided in the text. The dates may not always read from earliest to latest, so be sure to match an event with the date.

Strategy ❷ Look for clues about time that allow you to order events according to sequence. Words and phrases, such as *day*, *week*, *month*, or *year*, may help to sequence the events.

> **THE CIVIL WAR BEGINS**
>
> On ❶ December 20, 1860, South Carolina became the first state to secede, or leave the Union. Many others followed. In ❷ February of the next year, these states united to form the Confederate States of America, also called the Confederacy. Soon afterward, Confederate soldiers began seizing federal forts. By the time that Lincoln was sworn in as president on ❶ March 4, 1861, few southern forts remained in Union hands. The most important was Fort Sumter.
>
> On the morning of ❶ April 12, Confederate cannons began firing on Fort Sumter. The war between North and South had begun.

Make a Time Line

Making a time line can help you sequence events. The time line below shows the sequence of events in the passage you just read.

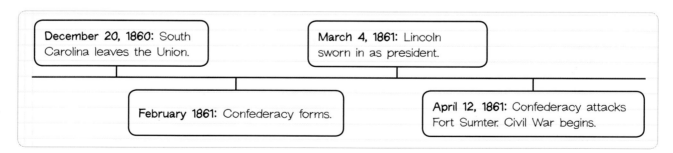

December 20, 1860: South Carolina leaves the Union.

February 1861: Confederacy forms.

March 4, 1861: Lincoln sworn in as president.

April 12, 1861: Confederacy attacks Fort Sumter. Civil War begins.

Practicing the Skill

Turn to Chapter 7, Section 4, "From Colonization to Independence." Read "Mexico's Path to Independence," and make a time line showing the sequence of events in the passage.

1.5 Categorizing

Defining the Skill

To **categorize** is to sort people, objects, ideas, or other information into groups, called categories. Geographers categorize information to help them identify and understand patterns in geographical data.

Applying the Skill

The following passage discusses the involvement of various countries in World War II. Use the strategies listed below to help you categorize information.

How to Categorize

Strategy ❶ First, decide what kind of information needs to be categorized. Decide what the passage is about and how that information can be sorted into categories. For example, look at the different ways countries reacted to World War II.

Strategy ❷ Then find out what the categories will be. To learn how countries reacted to the war, look for clue words such as *in response, some, other,* and *both.*

Strategy ❸ Once you have chosen the categories, sort information into them. Which countries were Axis Powers? Which were Allies? What about the ones who were conquered and those who never fought at all?

WORLD WAR II ALLIANCES

❶ During World War II, most countries around the world had to choose which side to take in the conflict. Some countries were conquered so quickly that they could not join either side. ❷ *Others* chose to remain neutral. ❷ Italy and Japan joined with Germany to form the Axis Powers. In 1939, Germany began the war by invading Poland. ❷ *In response,* Great Britain and France (the first two Allied Powers) declared war on Germany. Germany quickly conquered many countries, including Denmark, Norway, the Netherlands, Belgium, and France. ❷ During 1941, *both* the Soviet Union and the United States entered the war on the Allied side. ❷ Sweden and Switzerland remained neutral during the war.

Make a Chart

Making a chart can help you categorize information. The chart below shows how the information from the passage you just read can be categorized.

❸

Name of Alliance	Axis Powers	Allied Powers	Neutral
Countries	• Germany • Japan • Italy	• Great Britain • France • Soviet Union • United States	• Sweden • Switzerland

Practicing the Skill

Turn to Chapter 2, Section 1, "The Earth and Its Forces." Read "External Forces Shaping the Earth." Make a chart in which you categorize the external forces shaping Earth.

1.6 Analyzing Causes and Effects

Defining the Skill

A **cause** is an action that makes something happen. An **effect** is the event that is the result of the cause. A single event may have several causes. It is also possible for one cause to result in several effects. Geographers identify cause-and-effect relationships to help them understand patterns in human movement and interaction.

Applying the Skill

The following paragraph describes events that caused changes in the way of life of the ancient Maya people of Central America. Use the strategies below to help you identify the cause-and-effect relationships.

How to Analyze Causes and Effects

Strategy 1 Ask why an action took place. Ask yourself a question about the title and topic sentence, such as, "What caused Mayan civilization to decline?"

Strategy 2 Look for effects. Ask yourself, "What happened?" (the effect). Then ask, "Why did it happen?" (the cause). For example, "What caused the Maya to abandon their cities?"

Strategy 3 Look for clue words that signal causes, such as *caused*, *contributed to*, and *led to*.

---

1 DECLINE OF MAYAN CIVILIZATION

1 The civilization of the Maya went into a mysterious decline around A.D. 900. **2** Mayan cities in the southern lowlands were abandoned, trade ceased, and the huge stone pyramids of the Maya fell into ruin. No one really understands what happened to the Maya, but there are many theories.

3 Some believe that a change in climate *caused* the decline of Mayan civilization. Three long droughts between 810 and 910 meant that there was not enough water for Mayan crops. **2** As a result, the Maya abandoned their cities. **3** Other researchers believe that additional problems *contributed to* the crisis. They include overpopulation and warfare among the Mayan nobility.

Make a Diagram

Making a diagram can help you analyze causes and effects. The diagram below shows two causes and an effect for the passage you just read.

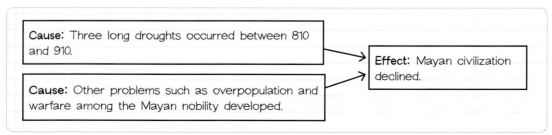

Cause: Three long droughts occurred between 810 and 910.

Cause: Other problems such as overpopulation and warfare among the Mayan nobility developed.

Effect: Mayan civilization declined.

Practicing the Skill

Turn to Chapter 29, Section 1, "Unique Lands." Read "Non-Native Animals." Then make a diagram about the causes and effects of Australia's rabbit population.

1.7 Comparing and Contrasting

Defining the Skill

Comparing means looking at the similarities and differences between two or more things. **Contrasting** means examining only the differences between them. Geographers compare and contrast physical features, regions, cultures, beliefs, and situations in order to understand them.

Applying the Skill

The following passage describes the Dead Sea, in southwest Asia, and the Red Sea, located between northeast Africa and southwest Asia. Use the strategies below to help you compare and contrast these two bodies of water.

How to Compare and Contrast

Strategy ❶ Look for two aspects of the subject that can be compared and contrasted. This passage compares the Red Sea and the Dead Sea, two salty bodies of water close to one another.

Strategy ❷ To find similarities, look for clue words indicating that two things are alike. Clue words include *both, together,* and *similarly.*

Strategy ❸ To contrast, look for clue words that show how two things differ. Clue words include *however, but, on the other hand,* and *yet.*

SALTY SEAS

❶ According to the Bible, God parted the Red Sea so Moses could lead his people across it. The Bible also mentions the Dead Sea, calling it the Salt Sea. The Dead Sea is one of the saltiest bodies of water in the world. ❷ *Similarly,* the Red Sea also has a high salt content. Many observers argue that the Dead Sea is not really a sea at all. It is more of a lake since it is fed by the Jordan River and is surrounded by land on all four sides. ❸ *On the other hand,* the Indian Ocean feeds the Red Sea. The Red Sea is also the larger of the two seas. It is 170,000 square miles, while the Dead Sea is under 400 square miles. ❷ *Both* bodies of water provide minerals for commercial use, especially salt.

Make a Venn Diagram

Making a Venn diagram can help you identify similarities and differences between two things. In the overlapping area, list characteristics shared by both subjects. Then, in the separate ovals, list the characteristics of each subject not shared by the other. This Venn diagram compares and contrasts the Red Sea and the Dead Sea.

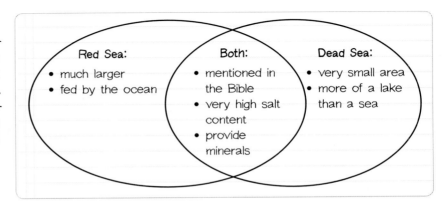

Red Sea:
- much larger
- fed by the ocean

Both:
- mentioned in the Bible
- very high salt content
- provide minerals

Dead Sea:
- very small area
- more of a lake than a sea

Practicing the Skill

Turn to Chapter 3, Section 3, "Resources and Economics." Read "Measuring Economic Development." Then make a Venn diagram showing similarities and differences between developed and developing nations.

1.8 Identifying Problems and Solutions

Defining the Skill

Identifying problems means finding and understanding the difficulties faced by a particular group of people during a certain time. **Identifying solutions** means understanding how people tried to remedy those problems. By studying how people solved problems in the past, you can learn ways to solve problems today.

Applying the Skill

The following passage describes the problems of floods and droughts in early Mesopotamia. Use the strategies listed below to find and understand these problems.

How to Identify Problems and Solutions

Strategy ❶ Look for the difficulties or problems faced by a group of people.

Strategy ❷ Consider how situations that existed at that time and place contributed to these problems.

Strategy ❸ Look for the solutions that people or groups employed to deal with the problems. Think about whether the solutions were good ones.

FLOOD AND DROUGHT IN MESOPOTAMIA

❶ In ancient Mesopotamia, farmers had to deal with both floods and droughts. They often had either too much rain or too little. ❷ If too much rain fell, the rivers might overflow and wash everything away. Too little rain also created difficulties. ❷ During a drought, the river levels dropped, making it hard to water crops.

❸ To combat the lack of rain, farmers in Mesopotamia eventually built canals to carry water from the river to the fields. Such a system is called irrigation. ❸ Farmers also built dams to hold back excess water during floods.

Make a Chart

Making a chart can help you identify information about problems and solutions. The chart below shows the problem, contributing factors, and solutions in the passage you just read.

❶ Problem	❷ Contributing Factors	❸ Solutions
Floods and droughts made farming difficult in Mesopotamia.	Too much rain caused floods that washed everything away. Droughts caused the river level to drop, making it hard to water crops.	Farmers built canals to carry water from the river to the fields. Farmers built dams to hold back excess water during floods.

Practicing the Skill

Turn to Chapter 2, Section 4, "Environmental Challenges." Read "Desertification." Then make a chart that summarizes the problem of desertification faced by many arid and semiarid areas and the solutions that people who live in these areas are applying.

1.9 Making Inferences

Defining the Skill

Inferences are ideas that the author has not directly stated. **Making inferences** involves reading between the lines to interpret the information you read. You can make inferences by studying what is stated and using your common sense and previous knowledge.

Applying the Skill

The passage below examines the great pyramids of ancient Egypt. Use the strategies below to help you make inferences from the passage.

How to Make Inferences

Strategy ① Read to find statements of facts and ideas. Knowing the facts will give you a good basis for making inferences.

Strategy ② Use your knowledge, logic, and common sense to make inferences that are based on facts. Ask yourself, "What does the author want me to understand?" For example, from the facts about the pyramids' purpose, you can make the inference that the Egyptians believed in life after death. See other inferences in the chart below.

> **THE PYRAMIDS OF EGYPT**
>
> One reason that ancient Egypt is famous is for its giant pyramids. ① The Egyptians built these magnificent monuments for their kings, or pharaohs. Each pyramid was a resting place where an Egyptian pharaoh planned to spend the afterlife. ① Overseers, who ran the construction of each pyramid for the pharaoh, managed the workers and tracked the supplies. The largest pyramid, built for Khufu, required workers to place 6.5 million tons of stone. ① Workers built these long-lasting structures with none of the modern cutting tools and machines that we have today.

Make a Chart

Making a chart can help you organize information and make logical inferences. The chart below organizes information from the passage you just read.

① Stated Facts and Ideas	② Inferences
Egyptians built their pyramids as resting places for their pharaohs in the afterlife.	Egyptians believed in life after death.
A staff oversaw construction of the project.	Pyramid building was a complicated task that required organization.
The Egyptians built the pyramids without modern equipment.	The Egyptians were skilled engineers and hard workers.

Practicing the Skill

Turn to Chapter 26, Section 3, "Contrasting Countries." Read "Economy" under "North Korea." Then use a chart like the one above to make inferences about the effect of North Korea's economy on its citizens.

1.10 Making Generalizations

Defining the Skill

To **make generalizations** means to make broad judgments based on information. When you make generalizations, you should gather information from several sources.

Applying the Skill

The following three passages contain views on the United States as a melting pot of different cultures. Use the strategies below to make a generalization about these ideas.

How to Make Generalizations

Strategy ❶ Look for information that the sources have in common. These three sources all look at the relationship of immigrants to the United States.

Strategy ❷ Form a generalization that describes this relationship in a way that all three sources would agree with. State your generalization in a sentence.

THE MELTING POT

At the turn of the century, ❶ many native-born Americans thought of their country as a melting pot, a mixture of people of different cultures and races who blended together by abandoning their native languages and customs.

—*The Americans*

❶ A nation, like a tree, does not thrive well till it is engrafted with a foreign stock.

—*Journals* (Emerson, 1823)

❶ The United States has often been called a *melting pot*. But in other ways, U.S. society is an example of *cultural pluralism*. . . . That is, large numbers of its people have retained features of the cultures of their ancestors.

—*World Book Encyclopedia*

Make a Diagram

Using a diagram can help you make generalizations. The diagram below shows how the information you just read can be used to generalize about immigrants' contributions.

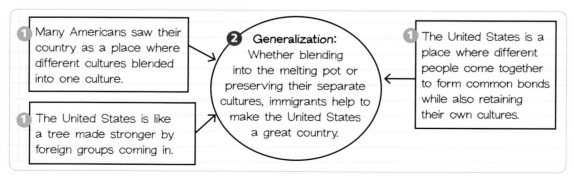

❶ Many Americans saw their country as a place where different cultures blended into one culture.

❷ Generalization: Whether blending into the melting pot or preserving their separate cultures, immigrants help to make the United States a great country.

❶ The United States is a place where different people come together to form common bonds while also retaining their own cultures.

❶ The United States is like a tree made stronger by foreign groups coming in.

Practicing the Skill

Turn to Chapter 19, Section 1, "Three Trading Empires." Read "European Imperialism," and study the chart on page 584. Also examine the map on page 579. Use a diagram to make a generalization about imperialism in Africa.

1.11 Drawing Conclusions

Defining the Skill

Drawing conclusions means analyzing what you have read and forming an opinion about its meaning. To draw conclusions, look at the facts and then use your own common sense and experience to decide what the facts mean.

Applying the Skill

The following passage presents information about Europe's mountain ranges. Use the strategies listed below to help you draw conclusions about their effects.

How to Draw Conclusions

Strategy 1 Read carefully to identify and understand all the facts.

Strategy 2 List the facts in a diagram and review them. Use your own experiences and common sense to understand how the facts relate to each other.

Strategy 3 After reviewing the facts, write down the conclusions you have drawn about them.

EUROPE'S MOUNTAIN RANGES

Mountains are a key landform in Europe. **1** The Alps stretch across eight countries in southern Europe. The mountain range affects travel within those countries. **1** The Pyrenees once formed a natural barrier between France and Spain. Europe also has several smaller mountain ranges.

Europe's mountain ranges separated the groups of people who settled the land thousands of years ago. **1** With the mountains in between them, many different cultures were able to develop in Europe. **1** Mountain ranges contain natural resources, such as timber. These resources also influenced where people chose to settle.

Make a Diagram

Making a diagram can help you draw conclusions. The diagram below shows how to organize facts to draw a conclusion about the passage you just read.

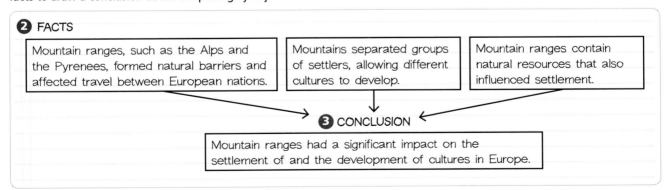

2 FACTS

| Mountain ranges, such as the Alps and the Pyrenees, formed natural barriers and affected travel between European nations. | Mountains separated groups of settlers, allowing different cultures to develop. | Mountain ranges contain natural resources that also influenced settlement. |

3 CONCLUSION

Mountain ranges had a significant impact on the settlement of and the development of cultures in Europe.

Practicing the Skill

Turn to Chapter 10, Section 2, "A Multicultural Society." Read "Africans." Then make a diagram to help you draw conclusions about African influences on Brazilian culture.

1.12 Making Decisions

Defining the Skill

Making decisions involves choosing between two or more options, or courses of action. In most cases, decisions have consequences, or results. Sometimes decisions may lead to new problems. By understanding how historical figures made decisions, you can learn how to improve your own decision-making skills.

Applying the Skill

The passage below explains the decision British Prime Minister Chamberlain faced when Germany threatened aggression in 1938. Use the strategies below to analyze his decision.

How to Make Decisions

Strategy ❶ Identify a decision that needs to be made. Think about what factors make the decision difficult.

Strategy ❷ Identify possible consequences of the decision. Remember that there can be more than one consequence to a decision.

Strategy ❸ Identify the decision that was made.

Strategy ❹ Identify actual consequences that resulted from the decision.

PEACE OR WAR?

In 1938, German leader Adolf Hitler demanded a part of Czechoslovakia. ❶ British Prime Minister Neville Chamberlain had to decide how to respond to that aggression. ❷ He could threaten to go to war, but he feared that Britain was not ready. ❷ If he gave Germany the region, he might avoid war, but he would be setting a bad example by giving in to a dictator. ❸ Chamberlain decided to give Germany what it demanded. In exchange, Hitler promised not to take any more land in Europe. ❹ Six months later, Germany took the rest of Czechoslovakia and later invaded Poland.

Make a Flow Chart

Making a flow chart can help you identify the process of making a decision. The flow chart below shows the decision-making process in the passage you just read.

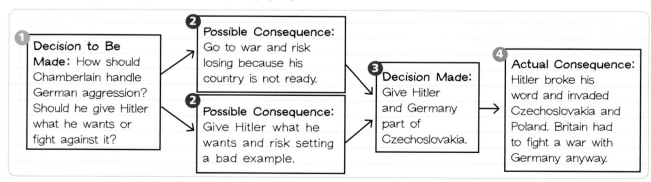

① **Decision to Be Made:** How should Chamberlain handle German aggression? Should he give Hitler what he wants or fight against it?

② **Possible Consequence:** Go to war and risk losing because his country is not ready.

② **Possible Consequence:** Give Hitler what he wants and risk setting a bad example.

③ **Decision Made:** Give Hitler and Germany part of Czechoslovakia.

④ **Actual Consequence:** Hitler broke his word and invaded Czechoslovakia and Poland. Britain had to fight a war with Germany anyway.

Practicing the Skill

Turn to Chapter 15, Section 2, "Governing a Vast Land." Read "Superpower and Collapse." Then make a flow chart to identify Gorbachev's policy decision and its consequences.

1.13 Evaluating

Defining the Skill

To **evaluate** is to make a judgment about something. Geographers evaluate the actions of people in history. One way to do this is to examine both the positives and the negatives of an action, and then decide which is stronger—the positive or the negative.

Applying the Skill

The following passage examines the rule of Mustafa Kemal of Turkey. Use the strategies listed below to evaluate the success of his reforms.

How to Evaluate

Strategy 1 Before you evaluate a person's actions, first determine what that person was trying to do. In this case, think about what Kemal wanted to accomplish.

Strategy 2 Look for statements that show the positive, or successful, results of his actions. For example, did he achieve his goals?

Strategy 3 Also look for statements that show the negative, or unsuccessful, results of his actions. Did he fail to achieve something he tried to do?

Strategy 4 Write an overall evaluation of the person's actions.

KEMAL RULES TURKEY

In 1923, Turkey became an independent republic. Mustafa Kemal became Turkey's first president. **1** Kemal wanted his nation to resemble European countries rather than its Islamic neighbors. Kemal quickly replaced Turkey's Islamic government with a nonreligious system. He also replaced the Arabic alphabet and the Islamic calendar with Western versions of each. **3** Kemal's actions drew protests from traditionalists. **2** However, Kemal's moves helped to modernize Turkey. **2** They also benefited women, who had lived with many restrictions under Islamic law. Women now had greater social freedom. They also could vote and run for political office.

Make a Diagram

Making a diagram can help you evaluate. List the positives and negatives of the person's actions and decisions. Then make an overall judgment. The diagram below shows how the information from the passage you just read can be evaluated.

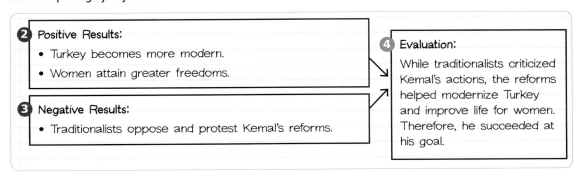

2 Positive Results:
- Turkey becomes more modern.
- Women attain greater freedoms.

3 Negative Results:
- Traditionalists oppose and protest Kemal's reforms.

4 Evaluation:
While traditionalists criticized Kemal's actions, the reforms helped modernize Turkey and improve life for women. Therefore, he succeeded at his goal.

Practicing the Skill

Turn to Chapter 11, Section 3, "The Middle Ages and Renaissance." Read "Forces of Change," and make a diagram to evaluate the decision to take part in the Crusades.

1.14 Distinguishing Fact from Opinion

Defining the Skill

Facts are events, dates, statistics, or statements that can be proved to be true. **Opinions** are judgments, beliefs, and feelings. By identifying facts and opinions, you will be able to think critically when a person is trying to influence your own opinion.

Applying the Skill

The following passage describes the church Hagia Sophia. It was one of the more notable structures in the development of Constantinople as the capital of the Byzantine Empire. Use the strategies listed below to distinguish facts from opinions.

How to Distinguish Fact from Opinion

Strategy ❶ Look for specific information that can be proved or checked for accuracy.

Strategy ❷ Look for assertions, claims, and judgments that express opinions. In this case, one speaker's opinion is addressed in a direct quote.

Strategy ❸ Think about whether statements can be checked for accuracy. Then, identify the facts and opinions in a chart.

> **HAGIA SOPHIA**
>
> ❶ Hagia Sophia was built between A.D. 532 and 537. The Byzantine emperor Justinian ordered that the cathedral be built on the site where an earlier church had burned down. ❶ The church is noted for its large central dome, which rises 185 feet above the ground. With numerous windows, arches, and vaults, the structure is hailed by many as an architectural masterpiece. ❷ Said one observer, "You would declare that the place is not lighted by the sun from without, but that the rays are produced from within."

Make a Chart

Making a chart can help you distinguish fact from opinion. The chart below analyzes the facts and opinions in the passage above.

Statement	❸ Can It Be Proved?	❸ Fact or Opinion
Hagia Sophia was built between A.D. 532 and 537.	Yes. Check historical documents.	fact
Hagia Sophia's dome is 185 feet high.	Yes. Check measurement records.	fact
The inside of Hagia Sophia is so beautiful that it appears to make its own sunlight.	No. This cannot be proved. It is what one speaker believes.	opinion

Practicing the Skill

Turn to Chapter 28, Section 2, "The Mainland Countries." Read "Singapore." Then make a chart like the one above in which you analyze key statements about Singapore to determine whether they are facts or opinions.

1.15 Analyzing Points of View

Defining the Skill

Analyzing points of view means looking closely at a person's arguments to understand the reasons behind that person's beliefs. The goal of analyzing a point of view is to understand different thoughts, opinions, and beliefs about a topic.

Applying the Skill

The following passage describes the difference between Native American and European attitudes about land use. Use the strategies below to help you analyze the points of view.

How to Analyze Points of View

Strategy ① Look for statements that show you a particular point of view on an issue. For example, Native Americans believed land should be preserved for the future. European colonists believed land could be owned and changed as desired.

Strategy ② Think about why different people or groups held a particular point of view. Ask yourself what they valued. What were they trying to gain or to protect? What were they willing to sacrifice?

Strategy ③ Write a summary that explains why different groups of people might have taken different positions on this issue.

> ### LAND USE
>
> Native Americans and Europeans had many conflicts because of differing ideas about land use. ① Most Native Americans believed that land must be preserved for future generations. They believed the present generation had the right to use land for hunting and farming. However, no one had the right to buy or sell land.
>
> In contrast, Europeans had a long history of taming wilderness and owning land. As a result, ① Europeans believed that they could buy land, sell it, and alter it. For example, if they wished to mine for gold underground, they could destroy landscape as they dug the mine. ① Europeans used land to make money.

Make a Diagram

Making a diagram can help you analyze points of view. The diagram below analyzes the different points of view of the Native Americans and the European colonists in the passage you just read.

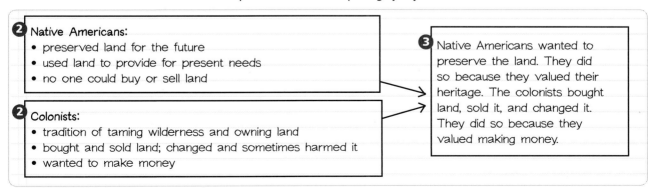

② Native Americans:
- preserved land for the future
- used land to provide for present needs
- no one could buy or sell land

② Colonists:
- tradition of taming wilderness and owning land
- bought and sold land; changed and sometimes harmed it
- wanted to make money

③ Native Americans wanted to preserve the land. They did so because they valued their heritage. The colonists bought land, sold it, and changed it. They did so because they valued making money.

Practicing the Skill

Turn to Chapter 22, Section 2, "Israel and the Palestinian Territories." Read "A New Israel" and "The Palestinian Territories." Make a diagram to analyze the different points of view of the Israelis and the Palestinians.

1.16 Recognizing Bias

Defining the Skill

Bias is a prejudiced point of view. Accounts that are biased tend to present only one side of an issue and reflect the opinions of the writer. Recognizing bias will help you understand how much to trust the primary and secondary sources that you find.

Applying the Skill

The following passage is from an 1883 speech in which Jules Ferry supported the French policy of imperialism. Use the strategies listed below to help you recognize bias in the passage.

How to Recognize Bias

Strategy ❶ Identify the author and examine any information about him or her. Does the author belong to a group, social class, or political party that might lead to a one-sided view of the subject?

Strategy ❷ Think about the opinions the author is presenting. Look for words, phrases, statements, or images that might convey a positive or negative slant.

Strategy ❸ Examine the evidence provided to support the author's opinions. Is the opinion correct? Would the same information appear in another account of the same event?

> ❶ **JULES FERRY ARGUES FOR FRENCH IMPERIALISM**
>
> Nations are great in our times only by means of the activities which they develop; . . . Something else is needed for France: . . . that ❷ she must also be a great country exercising all of her rightful influence over the destiny of Europe, that ❷ she ought to propagate [spread] this influence throughout the world and carry everywhere that she can ❸ her language, her customs, her flag, her arms, and her genius.
>
> —Jules Ferry, Speech Before the French National Assembly, July 28, 1883

Make a Chart

Making a chart can help you recognize bias in primary and secondary sources. The chart below analyzes the bias in the passage you just read.

Author	Jules Ferry
Occasion and Purpose	speech in front of the French National Assembly, arguing for France to practice imperialism
Tone	urging, superior
Slanted Language	"exercising all of her rightful influence;" "ought to propagate [spread] this influence"
Description of Bias	Ferry argues that France had the right and the obligation to practice imperialism and spread French control and culture to colonies around the world.

Practicing the Skill

Look through newspapers and news magazines to find an article related to geography. Then use a chart like the one above to analyze the article for bias.

1.17 Synthesizing

Defining the Skill

Synthesizing involves putting together clues, information, and ideas to form an overall picture. Geographers synthesize information in order to develop interpretations of important facts.

Applying the Skill

The following passage describes the agricultural revolution. The highlighting indicates the different kinds of information that will help you synthesize.

How to Synthesize

Strategy ❶ Look carefully for facts that will help you base your interpretations on evidence.

Strategy ❷ Look for explanations that link the facts together. This statement is based on the evidence of ancient tools mentioned in the next sentence.

Strategy ❸ Consider what you already know that could apply. Your knowledge will probably lead you to accept this statement.

Strategy ❹ Bring together the information you have about the subject. This interpretation brings together different kinds of information to arrive at a new understanding.

THE AGRICULTURAL REVOLUTION

❶ Flaked arrowheads found with mammoth bones at ancient sites suggest that some early people lived as big game hunters. ❷ After the big game became extinct, people shifted to hunting smaller game. They made tools, such as bows and arrows for hunting small game as well as baskets for collecting nuts.

About 10,000 years ago, people began to farm. ❸ The rise of agriculture brought tremendous change. More people lived in settled villages, and the storage of surplus food became more important. As their surplus increased, people had time to develop specialized skills and think about the world. ❹ From this agricultural base rose larger, more stable, and more complex societies.

Make a Diagram

Making a diagram can help you organize the facts, examples, and interpretations that you need to synthesize. The diagram below synthesizes the passage you just read.

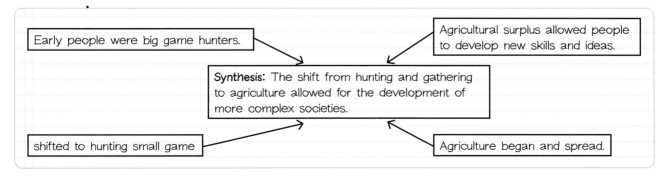

Practicing the Skill

Turn to Chapter 3, Section 2, "Why People Move." Read "Causes of Migration." Then use a diagram like the one above to form a synthesis about why people migrate.

2.1 Reading Maps: Physical

Defining the Skill

Physical maps represent the landforms, or physical features, on Earth's surface, such as mountains or bodies of water. By learning about the different elements of maps, it will be easier for you to read them.

Applying the Skill

A physical map of Peru is shown below. Use the strategies listed below to help you read the map.

How to Read a Physical Map

Strategy ❶ Read the title. This will tell you what place or region is represented by the map.

Strategy ❷ Look for the grid-lines that form a pattern of squares over the map. These numbered lines represent latitude (horizontal) and longitude (vertical). They indicate the location of the area on Earth.

Strategy ❸ Read the map legend. On a physical map, the legend often includes a scale to help you determine elevation as well as information about physical features.

Strategy ❹ Use the scale and the pointer or compass rose to determine distance and direction.

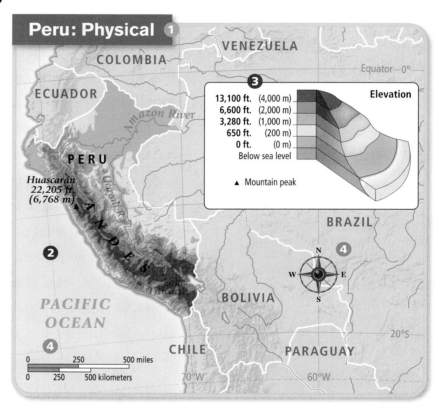

Make a Chart

Making a chart can help you organize the information given on a map. The chart below summarizes information about the physical map you just studied.

Title	Peru: Physical
Location	the Pacific coast of South America, near the equator and latitude 70° W
Legend Information	colors = elevation
Scale	1 in. = 500 miles, 5/8 in. = 500 km
Summary	Peru is located on the Pacific Ocean. The Andes run along the west coast, and the Amazon River and Ucayalí River flow through the country.

Practicing the Skill

Turn to Chapter 21, Section 2, "Physical Geography of South Asia." Study the physical map of South Asia on page 661. Make a chart to identify the information on the map.

2.2 Reading Maps: Political

Defining the Skill

Political maps represent political features of various places, such as national borders and capital cities. The countries on political maps are often shaded in different colors to make them easier to distinguish from each other.

Applying the Skill

A political map of Peru is shown below. Use the strategies listed below to help you read the map.

How to Read a Political Map

Strategy ❶ Read the title. This identifies the main idea of the map and will tell you what place or region the map represents.

Strategy ❷ Look for the grid-lines that form a pattern of squares over the map. These numbered lines represent latitude (horizontal) and longitude (vertical). They indicate the location of the area on Earth.

Strategy ❸ Read the map legend. The legend will help you to interpret the symbols on the map. On a political map, these symbols often include icons for major and capital cities.

Strategy ❹ Use the scale and the pointer or compass rose to determine distance and direction.

Make a Chart

Making a chart can help you organize the information given on a map. The chart below summarizes information about the political map you just studied.

Title	Peru: Political
Location	the Pacific coast of South America, near the equator and latitude 70° W
Legend Information	star icon = national capital; dot = other city
Scale	1 in. = 500 miles, 5/8 in. = 500 km
Summary	Peru, located on the Pacific Ocean, borders Ecuador, Colombia, Brazil, Bolivia, and Chile. Its capital is Lima.

Practicing the Skill

Turn to Chapter 26, "The Korean Peninsula," and study the political map of North and South Korea on page 795. Make a chart to identify the information on the map.

2.3 Reading Maps: Thematic

Defining the Skill

Thematic maps represent specific themes, or ideas. Climate, language, migration, population density, and economic activity maps are all different kinds of thematic maps.

Applying the Skill

The following map shows selected products of Mexico. Use the strategies listed below to help you read the map.

How to Read a Thematic Map

Strategy 1 Read the title. This identifies the theme of the map and will tell you what place or region is represented by the map.

Strategy 2 Some thematic maps have latitude (horizontal) and longitude (vertical) lines. They can help indicate the location of the area on Earth.

Strategy 3 Read the map legend. On a thematic map, the legend is very important because the colors and symbols on the map are specific to the theme. The legend will help you interpret them.

Strategy 4 Use the pointer or compass rose to determine direction. If the map has a scale, it can help you determine distance.

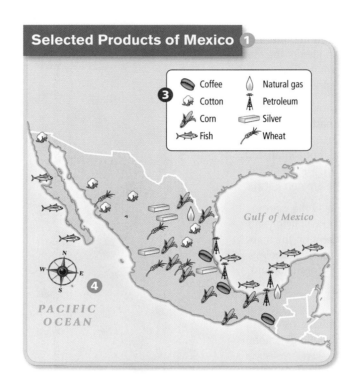

Selected Products of Mexico 1

Legend:
- Coffee
- Cotton
- Corn
- Fish
- Natural gas
- Petroleum
- Silver
- Wheat

Gulf of Mexico

PACIFIC OCEAN

Make a Chart

Making a chart can help you organize the information given on a map. The chart below summarizes information about the thematic map you just studied.

Title	Selected Products of Mexico
Location	Mexico, which borders the Pacific Ocean and the Gulf of Mexico
Legend Information	Icons represent specific products.
Summary	Mexico's different regions produce a variety of goods and crops, including coffee, corn, fish, petroleum, and silver.

Practicing the Skill

Turn to Chapter 12, Section 2, "Spain and Portugal." Study the map of the Iberian Peninsula on page 372, and make a chart to identify the information on the map.

2.4 Reading Maps: Cartograms

Defining the Skill

A **cartogram** takes statistical data and represents it visually in the form of a map. Rather than representing land area, a cartogram shows a different set of data about a country, such as population or gross domestic product. The size of the nations on the cartogram are adjusted to reflect the selected data for each one.

Applying the Skill

The following cartogram shows world population. Use the strategies listed below to help you read the cartogram.

How to Read a Cartogram

Strategy ① Read the title. This identifies the data and region represented by the cartogram.

Strategy ② Look at the sizes of the countries shown to see how they compare to each other. Cartograms adjust the sizes of countries to convey relative data. Because of this, the countries' shapes are altered.

Strategy ③ Compare the cartogram to a conventional map such as the world political map on pp. A16–A17. This will help you determine how much more or less of the selected data a particular country has by comparing its relative size on the cartogram to its size on the map.

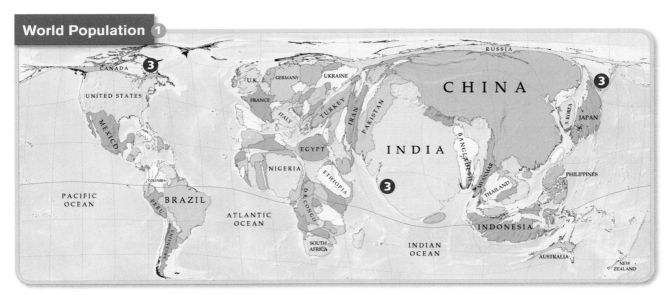

World Population ①

Make a Chart

Making a chart can help you organize the information given on a cartogram. The chart below summarizes information about the cartogram you just studied.

Title	World Population
Location	the world
Summary	Countries are shown either smaller or larger than their actual area depending on their population. For instance, India and Japan are shown larger than normal because they have high populations. Canada and Russia, which are more sparsely populated, are smaller than normal.

2.5 Reading Graphs and Charts

Defining the Skill

Graphs and charts translate information into a visual form. Graphs take numerical information and present it using pictures and symbols instead of words. Different kinds of graphs include bar graphs, line graphs, and pie graphs. Charts are created by simplifying, summarizing, and organizing information. This information is then presented in a format that is easy to understand. Tables and diagrams are examples of commonly used charts.

Applying the Skill

Use the strategies listed to read the graphs and chart on these pages.

How to Read Graphs

Strategy ❶ Read the title to identify the main idea of the graph. Ask yourself what kind of information the graph shows. Check the graph's source line to make sure the data is reliable.

Strategy ❷ Read the labels on the graph. Bar and line graphs have labels on their vertical axis and horizontal axis. Pie graphs have labels for each wedge of the pie. These labels tell you what data the graph represents.

Strategy ❸ Look at the graph. Try to find patterns, such as similarities and differences or increases and decreases.

Strategy ❹ Summarize the information shown on the graph. Use the title to help you focus on what information the graph is presenting.

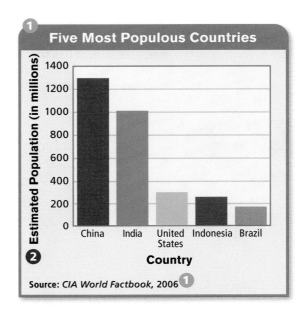

Five Most Populous Countries

Source: *CIA World Factbook*, 2006

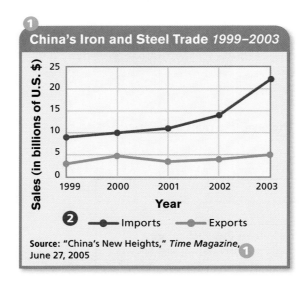

China's Iron and Steel Trade *1999–2003*

Source: "China's New Heights," *Time Magazine*, June 27, 2005

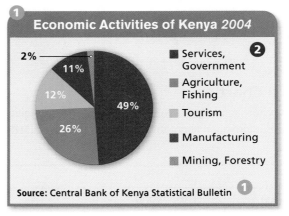

Economic Activities of Kenya *2004*

- Services, Government
- Agriculture, Fishing
- Tourism
- Manufacturing
- Mining, Forestry

Source: Central Bank of Kenya Statistical Bulletin

How to Read Charts

Strategy 1 Read the title to find out what the chart is about. Ask yourself what kind of information the chart shows.

Strategy 2 Read the headings to see how the chart is organized.

Strategy 3 Study the data in the chart to understand the facts that it was designed to show.

Strategy 4 Summarize the information shown in each part of the chart. Use the title to help you focus on what information the chart is presenting.

1 World Economic Development

2 Country	Status	GDP in US Dollars*	GDP/Person in US Dollars*	Infant Mortality per 1,000 Live Births	Life Expectancy at Birth	Literacy Rate (Percent)
3 Burkina Faso	developing	5.4 billion	1,300	91.35	48.9	26.6
India	developing	719.8 billion	3,400	54.63	64.7	59.5
Uruguay	developing	13.2 billion	9,600	11.61	76.3	98.0
Germany	developed	2.8 trillion	30,400	4.12	78.8	99.0
Japan	developed	4.9 trillion	31,500	3.24	81.3	99.0
United States	developed	12.5 trillion	42,000	6.43	77.9	99.0

Source: *CIA World Factbook*, 2006   * official exchange rate

Write a Summary

Writing a summary can help you understand the information contained in graphs and charts. The paragraph below summarizes information from the chart above.

4 The chart compares several indicators of economic development for three developing and three developed nations: Burkina Faso, India, Uruguay, Germany, Japan, and the United States. The developed nations have higher GDPs and literacy rates, longer life expectancies, and lower infant mortality than the developing nations. Of the countries shown, the United States has the highest GDP per person, Burkina Faso the lowest.

Practicing the Skill

Turn to Chapter 5, Section 3, "A Diverse Culture." Look at "Comparing Languages, Religion, and Ethnicity," and study the language chart and religion pie graph. Then write a paragraph each summarizing what you learned from the chart and the graph.

2.6 Interpreting Political Cartoons

Defining the Skill

Political cartoons express an opinion about a serious subject. A political cartoonist uses symbols, familiar objects, and people to make his or her point quickly and visually. Sometimes words used in the cartoon will help to clarify its meaning.

Applying the Skill

The cartoon below is about the competition between the Russian Empire and Great Britain over territory in Central Asia. Use the strategies listed below to help you interpret this and other political cartoons.

How to Interpret Political Cartoons

Strategy ❶ Identify the subject of the cartoon. Look at the cartoon as a whole. If the cartoon has them, read the title and caption.

Strategy ❷ Look for symbols that the cartoonist used to communicate ideas. The bear in this cartoon represents Russia. The lion is a symbol of Great Britain.

Strategy ❸ Analyze the other visual details of the cartoon. The man in the middle, wearing Central Asian dress, is crouching in fear as the bear and lion stare at him hungrily. This suggests that the Russian Empire and Great Britain are interested in devouring Central Asian territory.

PUNCH, OR THE LONDON CHARIVARI.—November 30, 1878.

❶ "SAVE ME FROM MY FRIENDS!"

Make a Chart

Making a chart can help you interpret a political cartoon. The chart below summarizes the information from the cartoon above.

Subject	competition between Russia and Great Britain over Central Asia
Symbols and Details	The bear, representing the Russian Empire, and the lion, symbolizing Great Britain, are circling their prey, a man representing Central Asia.
Message	Central Asia is afraid that its "friends," the Russian Empire and Great Britain, are going to take control of its territory.

Practicing the Skill

Turn to Chapter 20, "East, Central, and Southern Africa." Study the political cartoon on page 639. Use a chart like the one above to summarize information from the cartoon to help you interpret its meaning.

2.7 Creating a Map

Defining the Skill

When you **create a map,** you can choose what geographical information to include. You can show political information, such as the area covered by empires or countries. Your map can also be a thematic map, showing data on climates, population, or resources.

Applying the Skill

Below is a map that a student created that shows the vegetation zones of Africa. Use the strategies listed below to learn how to create your own map.

How to Create a Map

Strategy ❶ Select a title that identifies the map's geographical area and purpose.

Strategy ❷ Use dashes to draw latitude and longitude lines. Using these as a guide, draw the area you are representing.

Strategy ❸ Create a legend that identifies the map's colors or icons.

Strategy ❹ Draw the colors or icons on the map to show information.

Strategy ❺ Draw a compass rose and scale.

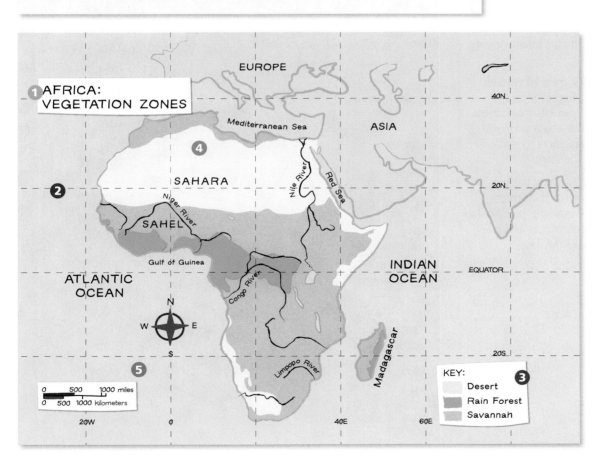

Practicing the Skill

Turn to Chapter 14, Section 2, "Hungary and the Czech Republic." Read "Government and Economics" under "Hungary." Using the map on page 325 as a guide, create a map of Europe showing Hungary's trading partners.

2.8 Creating a Model

Defining the Skill

When you **create a model,** you use information and ideas to show an event, situation, or place in a visual way. A model might be a poster or diagram that explains something. Or, it might be a three-dimensional model, such as a diorama, that depicts an important scene or situation.

Applying the Skill

The following sketch shows the early stages of a model of a feudal manor in Europe. Use the strategies listed below to help you create your own model.

How to Create a Model

Strategy ❶ Gather the information you need to understand the situation or event. In this case, you need to be able to show the parts of a manor and their uses.

Strategy ❷ Visualize an idea for your model. Once you have created a picture in your mind, make an actual sketch to plan how it might look.

Strategy ❸ Think of symbols you may want to use. Since the model should give information in a visual way, think about ways you can use color, pictures, or other visuals to tell the story.

Strategy ❹ Gather the supplies you will need. Then create the model. For example, you would need pictures of manors and art supplies to make this model.

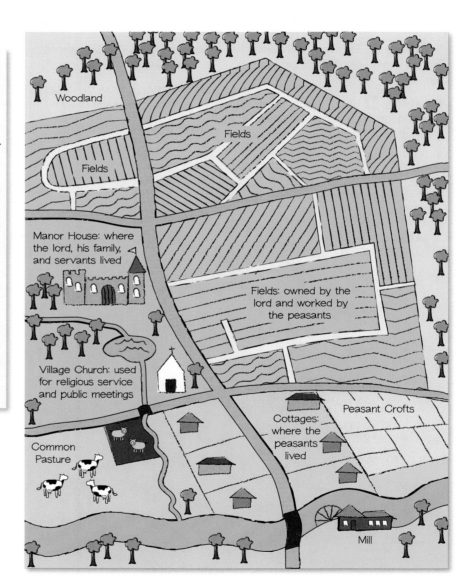

Woodland

Fields

Fields

Manor House: where the lord, his family, and servants lived

Fields: owned by the lord and worked by the peasants

Village Church: used for religious service and public meetings

Peasant Crofts

Cottages: where the peasants lived

Common Pasture

Mill

Practicing the Skill

Turn to Chapter 28, Section 3, "Indonesia and the Philippines." Read "Culture and Economy" under "Indonesia" and the text about shadow puppets in the "Fun Facts," and look at the images on page 866. Then create a model of a shadow puppet theater.

3.1 Outlining

Defining the Skill

Outlining is a method of organizing information. Once you have settled on a topic for a report or paper, you must do research. When you have all the information you need, then you have to organize it. An outline lists your report's main ideas in the order in which they will appear. It also organizes main ideas and supporting details according to their importance.

Applying the Skill

The outline at right is for a research report about the causes and effects of earthquakes. Use the strategies listed below to help you make an outline.

How to Outline

Strategy ① Read the main ideas of this report. They are listed on the left and labeled with capital Roman numerals. Each main idea will need at least one paragraph in your report.

Strategy ② Read the supporting ideas for each main idea. These are indented and labeled with capital letters. Notice that some main ideas require more supporting ideas than others.

Strategy ③ Read the supporting details in the outline. They are indented farther and labeled with numerals. Some supporting ideas will not have supporting details. It is not necessary to include every piece of information that you have. An outline is merely a guide to follow as you write your report.

Strategy ④ Reports can be organized in different ways. This report is arranged to show the causes and effects of earthquakes. The outline should clearly reflect the way the report is organized.

---

① I. Causes of Earthquakes
   A. Shifting tectonic plates
   ② B. Volcanoes
   C. Human activities
      ③ 1. Large underground nuclear explosions, deep mine excavations, and filling large reservoirs can all cause earthquakes.

II. Effects of Earthquakes
   A. Earthquakes usually do not kill people directly.
   B. Damage to natural features
      1. shifting of large blocks of Earth's crust
         a. can cause landslides
         b. can break down the banks of rivers and lakes and cause flooding
   C. Damage to man-made structures
      1. Ground shaking causes structures to sway, bounce, and possibly collapse.
   D. Cause other catastrophic events
      1. Fires
         a. San Francisco, 1906
      2. Tsunamis
         a. Indian Ocean, 2004

Practicing the Skill

Turn to Chapter 17, Section 2, "Human Beginnings in Africa." Read the section and gather information from it about hominid finds in Africa. Write an outline for a report about the topic using the correct outline form.

3.2 Writing for Social Studies

Defining the Skill

Writing is an important skill to learn. It allows you to communicate your thoughts and ideas. There are many different kinds of writing used in social studies.

Narrative Writing

Narrative writing tells a story. Some narratives are fictional, but historians and geographers write narratives about events that really happened. A narrative has three basic parts. The beginning sets the scene. The body presents a conflict. The resolution settles the conflict and ends the narrative. The sample below describes the volcano Krakatoa.

> One of the most destructive volcanic eruptions in recorded history happened in 1883, when two-thirds of the Indonesian island of Krakatoa was blown apart. The explosion sent volcanic ash 50 miles into the air. The surrounding area was plunged into darkness for two days. Krakatoa was uninhabited by humans, but the eruption buried all life on the island under a layer of ash. It took five years for plants and animals to thrive again on Krakatoa.

Persuasive Writing

Persuasive writing is writing whose purpose is to convince another person to adopt your opinion or position. People use persuasive writing for many reasons, such as convincing a government to adopt a proposal. Geographers and historians use persuasive writing to propose interpretations of facts. The sample below presents arguments for establishing a tsunami warning system in the Indian Ocean. The system began operations in 2006.

> In December 2004, a catastrophic tsunami struck Southeast Asia. Massive losses underline the need for a tsunami early warning system in the Indian Ocean. Such a system would predict and detect tsunamis and communicate warnings to the region's inhabitants. It will cost millions of dollars and require the cooperation of nations already monitoring seismic activity. However, many feel it is worth the effort to reduce destruction from tsunamis.

Expository Writing

Expository writing is meant to explain. It might examine a process or event, compare and contrast two different regions or civilizations, explain causes and effects, or explore problems and solutions. Expository writing has three main parts. The introduction states the main idea. The body supports the main idea with facts and examples. The conclusion summarizes the information and restates the main idea. In the sample below, the author explains some of the major causes of earthquakes.

> Earthquakes, the sudden movement of Earth's crust followed by a series of vibrations, have several causes. Most are caused by shifts in tectonic plates. Stress builds up along fault lines until it is finally released, making the ground shake. Earthquakes can also be triggered by the explosive action of a volcano. Human activities, such as deep mining, can prompt earthquakes as well. No matter the cause, earthquakes can have dramatic effects.

Applying the Skill

No matter what kind of writing you are doing—whether it is narrative, persuasive, or expository writing or something more complicated such as a research report—it needs to be clear, concise, and factually accurate. The strategies listed below will help you achieve your goal. The following passage is part of a larger research report about earthquakes. Notice how using these strategies helped the author convey information about the effects of earthquakes.

How to Write for Social Studies

Strategy 1 Focus on your topic. Be sure that you clearly state the main idea of your piece so that your readers know what you intend to say.

Strategy 2 Collect and organize facts and supporting details. Gather accurate information about your topic to support the narrative you are crafting or the point you are trying to make. Creating an outline can help you organize your thoughts and information.

Strategy 3 Write a first draft, using standard grammar, spelling, sentence structure, and punctuation. Proofread your writing. Make sure it is well organized and grammatically correct. Make any necessary revisions in your final draft.

EFFECTS OF EARTHQUAKES

1 Earthquakes usually do not kill people directly. Instead, most deaths and injuries occur as a result of damage to natural features and man-made structures. Earthquakes can also cause other catastrophes that harm people.

2 During an earthquake, large blocks of Earth's crust shift. These shifts can cause landslides or break down the banks of rivers and lakes and cause flooding. **2** The ground shaking that occurs during an earthquake can make buildings sway and bounce. The stress causes some buildings to collapse. All of these situations are dangerous for people.

Sometimes, earthquakes can cause other disasters, such as tsunamis or fires. **2** A 1906 quake in San Francisco started a fire that burned for three days. About 3,000 people died in this event. **2** An undersea earthquake caused the Indian Ocean tsunami in 2004, which claimed at least 280,000 lives.

Practicing the Skill

Turn to Chapter 11, Section 1, "Europe's Dramatic Landscape." Read "Europe's Resources." Then write a persuasive paragraph convincing European government leaders about the importance of developing renewable energy sources. Use the strategies listed above to help you make your paragraph clear and informative.

3.3 Forming and Supporting Opinions

Defining the Skill

When you **form opinions,** you interpret and judge the importance of events and people in history. You should always **support your opinions** with facts, examples, and quotations.

Applying the Skill

The following passage describes the impact of the policy of apartheid on South Africa. Use the strategies listed below to form and support an opinion about the policy.

How to Form and Support Opinions

Strategy ① Look for important information about the subject. Information can include facts, quotations, and examples.

Strategy ② Form an opinion about the subject by asking yourself questions about the information. For example, how important was the subject? How does it relate to similar subjects in your own experience?

Strategy ③ Support your opin- ions with facts, quotations, and examples. If the facts do not support the opinion, then rewrite your opinion so that it is supported by the facts.

THE POLICY OF APARTHEID

From the mid- to late-twentieth century, South Africa had a policy called apartheid, which separated whites and nonwhites. ① Nonwhites faced discrimination concerning where they could live, what jobs they could hold, and what they were taught in school. Many were forced to leave their homes and relocate in less desirable areas. Nonwhites' protests of these policies led to years of conflict. A number of nations also criticized apartheid. ① In 1985, the United States and Great Britain restricted trade with South Africa. In 1989, Frederik Willem de Klerk became president of South Africa. He opposed apartheid. His efforts helped to end the country's policy of segregation.

Make a Chart

Making a chart can help you organize your opinions and supporting facts. The following chart summarizes one possible opinion about the policy of apartheid in South Africa.

② Opinion	The policy of apartheid oppressed many South Africans and hurt the nation's economy.
③ Facts	Nonwhites faced discrimination concerning where they could live, what jobs they could hold, and what they were taught in school.
	Many nonwhites were forced to relocate in less desirable regions.
	Nations opposed to apartheid restricted trade with South Africa.

Practicing the Skill

Turn to Chapter 16, Section 1, "Center of a Landmass." Read "Human-Environment Interaction," and form your own opinion about Soviet projects in Central Asia. Make a chart like the one above to summarize your opinion and the supporting facts and examples.

3.4 Using Primary and Secondary Sources

Defining the Skill

Primary sources are materials written or created by people who lived during historical events. The writers might have been participants or witnesses. Primary sources include letters, journals, articles, and artwork. **Secondary sources** are materials that teach about an event, such as textbooks. When you research, you will use both kinds of sources.

Applying the Skill

The following passage uses primary and secondary sources to describe Kublai Khan's lifestyle. Use the strategies listed below to help you learn how to use these sources.

How to Use Primary and Secondary Sources

Strategy ❶ Distinguish secondary sources from primary sources. Most of the paragraph is a secondary source. The observation by Marco Polo is a primary source. The primary source supports the point the secondary source is making.

Strategy ❷ Determine the main idea of the secondary source. Look for details that support it.

Strategy ❸ Identify the author of the primary source and consider why the author produced it. Consider what the document was supposed to achieve. Is it credible? Is it promoting a particular viewpoint? In this case, Polo seems to be an objective observer.

LIFESTYLE OF KUBLAI KHAN

❶ Unlike his Mongol ancestors, Kublai Khan spent almost his entire life in China. ❷ He enjoyed living in the luxurious manner of a Chinese emperor. He maintained a beautiful summer palace at Shangdu, on the border between Mongolia and China. He also built a new square-walled capital at the site of modern Beijing. The size of Kublai's palace in Beijing greatly impressed the European traveler ❸ Marco Polo. "The whole building is at once so immense and so well constructed that no man in the world . . . could imagine any improvement in design or execution," Polo observed.

Make a Chart

Making a chart can help you assess information from primary and secondary sources. The chart below summarizes information from the passage above.

Questions	Answers
What is the main idea?	Kublai Khan enjoyed a life of luxury.
What are the supporting details?	He had a beautiful summer palace. He built a new capital in Beijing.
Who wrote the primary source?	Marco Polo
What can you tell about the primary source?	Polo appears to be an objective observer. The source seems credible.

Practicing the Skill

Turn to Chapter 21, Section 2, "Physical Geography of South Asia." Read "Monsoons" and the primary source on page 662. Make a diagram to summarize the information found in the sources and to help you read them.

3.5 Using a Database

Defining the Skill

A **database** is a collection of data, or information, that is organized so that you can find and retrieve information on a specific topic quickly and easily. Once a computerized database is set up, you can search it to find specific information without going through the entire database. The database will provide a list of all information in the database related to your topic. Learning how to use a database will help you learn how to create one.

Applying the Skill

The chart below is a database for famous mountains in the Eastern Hemisphere. Use the strategies listed below to help you understand and use the database.

How to Use a Database

Strategy ❶ Identify the topic of the database. The most important words in this title are *Mountains* and *Eastern Hemisphere*. These words were used to begin the research for this database.

Strategy ❷ Identify the kinds of data you need to enter in your database. These will be the column headings of your database. The key-words *Mountain, Location, Height,* and *Interesting Facts* were chosen to focus the research.

Strategy ❸ Identify the entries included under each heading.

Strategy ❹ Use the database to help you find information quickly. For example, in this database, you could search for "Mountains over 28,000 feet" to find a list of famous mountains that are more than 28,000 feet tall.

❶ FAMOUS MOUNTAINS OF THE EASTERN HEMISPHERE

❷ MOUNTAIN	LOCATION	HEIGHT ABOVE SEA LEVEL (FEET)	INTERESTING FACTS
❸ Dhaulagiri	Nepal	26,810	name means "White Mountain"
Everest	border of Nepal and China	❹ 29,035	tallest mountain in the world
Fuji	Japan	12,388	considered sacred by many Japanese
K2	Pakistan	❹ 28,250	second tallest mountain in the world
Khan-Tengri	border of China, Kazakhstan, and Kyrgyzstan	22,949	pyramid-shaped mountain is highest point in Kazakhstan
Xixabangma Feng (formerly Gosainthan)	China	26,291	Gosainthan means "place of God" in Sanskrit.

Practicing the Skill

Create a database of countries in Oceania that shows the name of each country, its capital, its land area, and its population. Use the information on pages 880 and 881 in the Unit 9 Atlas "Country Almanac" to provide the data. Use a format like the one above for your database.

3.6 Creating a Multimedia Presentation

Defining the Skill

Audio and video recordings, photographs, CD-ROMs, television, and computer software are all different kinds of media. To **create a multimedia presentation,** you need to collect information in different media and organize them into one presentation so that your audience watches, listens, and learns.

Applying the Skill

The photographs below show students using computers to create multimedia presentations. A multimedia presentation can incorporate computers, but it does not have to. Use the strategies listed below to help you create your own multimedia presentation.

How to Create a Multimedia Presentation

Strategy ① Identify the topic of your presentation and decide which media are best for an effective presentation. For example, you may want to use video or photographic images to show the dry character of a desert. Or, you may want to use CDs or audio tapes to provide music or to make sounds that go with your presentation, such as the sounds of a camel.

Strategy ② Research the topic in a variety of sources. Images, text, props, and background music should reflect the region and the historical period of your topic.

Strategy ③ Write the script for the presentation. You could use a narrator and characters' voices to tell the story. Primary sources are an excellent source for script material.

Strategy ④ Put together your presentation. Supplement your script with the images, props, music, and other media that you selected from your research. If you create your presentation on your computer, you can save the file for future viewing.

Practicing the Skill

Create a multimedia presentation about Red Square in Moscow, Russia. Turn to Chapter 15, Section 3, "Blending Europe and Asia," and look at the images on page 479 for ideas about what your presentation might include.

4.1 Using a Search Engine

Defining the Skill

Using a **search engine** can be a useful way to do research on the Internet. A search engine is a tool designed to find information on the Internet. There are billions of Web sites and documents available on the Internet. Using a search engine properly can help you sort through the vast amount of information.

Applying the Skill

The screen below shows a popular search engine. Use the strategies listed below to help you search the Internet.

How to Use a Search Engine

Strategy ❶ Brainstorm keywords to enter into the search engine. Make a list of possible search terms. It often helps to try to be specific. If your research topic is what careers geographers can have, try entering *careers in geography* instead of just *geography*. This will narrow the results to relevant information.

Strategy ❷ Many search engines will provide an excerpt of a Web site below the link to the site. Read these to help you determine if the Web site is relevant to your topic and worth visiting.

Strategy ❸ Click on the link to go to the Web site you are interested in exploring in depth. If you can, open the new Web site in a separate window, so that it is easier to come back to your original search.

Practicing the Skill

Choose a topic from Unit 1 that you would like to learn more about. Develop a list of keywords to help you search the Internet for information about that topic. Visit a search engine, and enter your keywords. Take a look at your search results, and consider which keywords were the most useful and why.

4.2 Evaluating Internet Sources

Defining the Skill

By **evaluating Internet sources** for credibility, you can make sure that you are only using the most accurate, reliable information as a resource.

Applying the Skill

The screen below shows a Web site about geography. Use the strategies listed below to learn how to assess its credibility.

How to Evaluate Internet Sources

Strategy ❶ Look at the Web site's Internet address. The three-letter code in it will help you determine who created the site. Almost anyone can set up a Web site with a ".com," or commercial, address. School Web sites use ".edu," or education, addresses. Addresses that end with ".org" are used by nonprofit organizations. Official government Web sites end in ".gov." These last three will often be more reliable than commercial Web sites.

Strategy ❷ Try to identify the author of the Web site and when it was last updated. This information does not always appear. Some sites are anonymous, or created by an unidentified author. You should not use these as sources because the information could be outdated, or the author might not know much about the Web site's topic.

Strategy ❸ Use another source to verify the information you find on the Internet. Online encyclopedias contain accurate information. Sources with .gov and .edu addresses are usually reliable. So is information from newspaper, magazine, and television news channel Web sites. Search several sites, and try to find two or three sources with the same information.

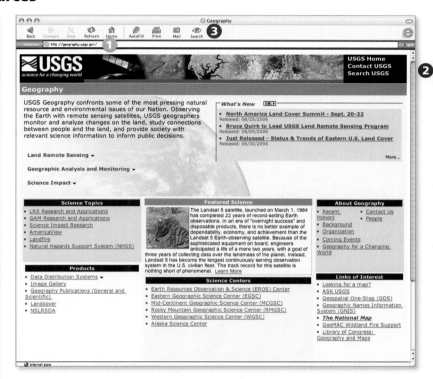

Practicing the Skill

Choose one of the Web sites that you found in your search from "Practicing the Skill" for "Using a Search Engine" on page R36 of this handbook. Evaluate the Web site to assess its credibility and its usefulness as a resource. Use the strategies listed above to help you.

World Religions and Ethical Systems

A Global View

A religion is an organized system of beliefs and practices, often centered on one or more gods. In this book, you have learned about many different religions and their impact on the world. Religions have guided people's beliefs and actions for thousands of years. They have brought people together. But they have also torn them apart.

Religions are powerful forces today as well. They affect everything from what people wear to how they behave. There are thousands of religions in the world. In the following pages, you will learn about five major religions: Buddhism, Christianity, Hinduism, Islam, and Judaism. You will also learn about Confucianism, an ethical system. Like a religion, an ethical system provides guidance on how to live your life. However, unlike religions, ethical systems do not center on the worship of gods. The chart on the opposite page shows what percentages of the world population practice the five major religions. The map shows where these religions are predominant or where they are practiced by significant numbers.

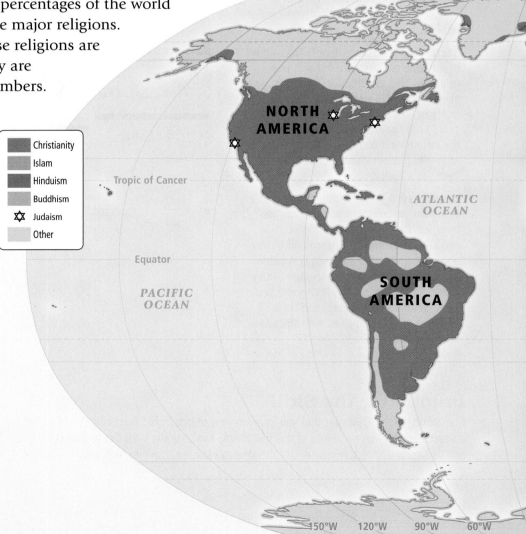

Christianity
Islam
Hinduism
Buddhism
✡ Judaism
Other

Tropic of Cancer

Equator

PACIFIC
OCEAN

NORTH
AMERICA

ATLANTIC
OCEAN

SOUTH
AMERICA

150°W   120°W   90°W   60°W

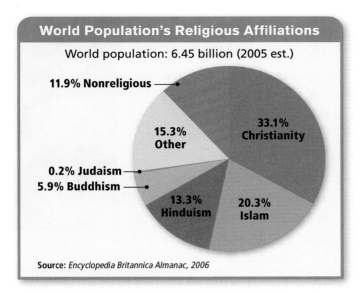

World Population's Religious Affiliations

World population: 6.45 billion (2005 est.)

- 11.9% Nonreligious
- 15.3% Other
- 0.2% Judaism
- 5.9% Buddhism
- 13.3% Hinduism
- 20.3% Islam
- 33.1% Christianity

Source: *Encyclopedia Britannica Almanac, 2006*

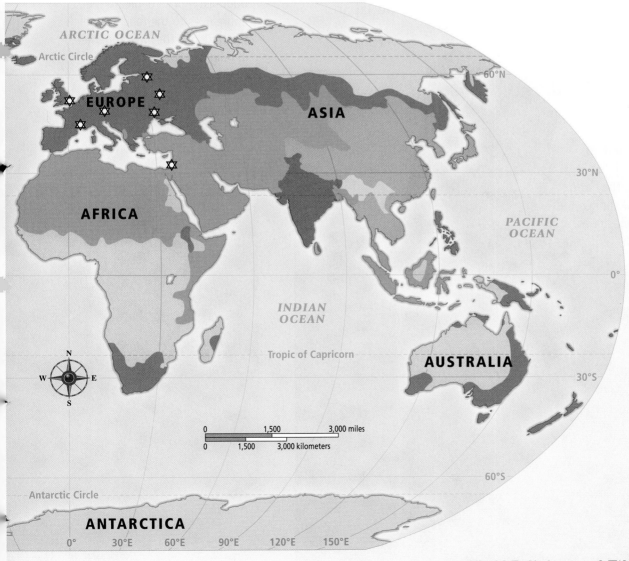

Buddhism

Buddhism began in India in the sixth century B.C. The religion was founded by Siddhartha Gautama (sihd•DAHR•tuh GOW•tuh•muh), who came to be known as the Buddha. *Buddha* means "enlightened one." He was born into a noble family but left home to search for enlightenment, or wisdom. The Buddha is said to have achieved enlightenment after long study. According to Buddhist tradition, he taught his followers that the way to end suffering was by practicing the Noble Eightfold Path. This path involved observing the following: right opinions, right desires, right speech, right action, right job, right effort, right concentration, and right meditation.

After the Buddha's death, Buddhism spread in India, Ceylon, and Central Asia. Missionaries spread the faith. Buddhist ideas also traveled along trade routes. The religion, however, did not survive on Indian soil. Today, most Buddhists live in Sri Lanka (formerly Ceylon), East Asia, Southeast Asia, and Japan.

▼ Monks
Buddhist monks dedicate their entire lives to the teachings of the Buddha. They live together in religious communities called monasteries. There, the monks lead lives of poverty, meditation, and study. In this photograph, Buddhist monks in Myanmar hold their begging bowls.

▼ Buddha
Statues of the Buddha, such as this one in Japan, appear in shrines throughout Asia. Buddhists try to follow the Buddha's teachings by meditating, a way of emptying the mind of thought. They also make offerings at shrines, temples, and monasteries.

Learn More About Buddhism

▲ **Pilgrimage**

For centuries, Buddhists have come to visit places in India and Nepal associated with the Buddha's life. These sites include the Buddha's birthplace and the fig tree where he achieved his enlightenment. Worshipers also visit the Dhamekha Stupa in Sarnath, India, the site of the Buddha's first sermon, shown here.

Symbol The Buddha's teaching, known as the dharma, is often symbolized by a wheel because his teaching was intended to end the cycle of births and deaths. The Buddha is said to have "set in motion the wheel of the dharma" during his first sermon.

Primary Source

The Buddha called his insight into the nature of suffering the Four Noble Truths. In the following selection, the Buddha tells his followers how they can end suffering and find enlightenment. The path involves understanding that life on Earth is brief and full of sadness. It also involves giving up selfish desire.

All created things are transitory [short-lived]; those who realize this are freed from suffering. This is the path that leads to pure wisdom.

All created beings are involved in sorrow; those who realize this are freed from suffering. This is the path that leads to pure wisdom.

All states are without self; those who realize this are freed from suffering. This is the path that leads to pure wisdom.

from the *Dhammapada*
Translated by Eknath Easwaran

Christianity

Christianity is the largest religion in the world, with about 2 billion followers. It is based on the life and teachings of Jesus, as described in the Bible's New Testament. Jesus, a Jew, taught many ideas from the Jewish tradition. Some biblical prophets had spoken of a day when a promised figure would come to save all of humankind. By the end of the first century A.D., many Jews and non-Jews had come to believe that Jesus was the one who would make this happen. Now called "Christians," they spread their faith throughout the Roman Empire.

Christians regard Jesus as the Son of God. They believe that Jesus entered the world and died to save humanity.

▼ Easter and Palm Sunday

On Easter, Christians celebrate their belief in Jesus' resurrection, or his being raised to heavenly life after he was put to death. The Sunday before Easter, Christians observe Palm Sunday. This day celebrates Jesus' triumphal entry into Jerusalem. Palm branches, like those carried in this procession in El Salvador, were spread before him.

▲ **Jesus and the Disciples**
Jesus' followers included 12 disciples, or pupils. Jesus passed on his teachings to his disciples. This painting from the 1400s shows Jesus with his disciples.

▼ **St. Paul's Cathedral**
Paul was a missionary who spread Christian beliefs throughout the Roman Empire. He started churches almost everywhere he went. Many churches today, such as this great cathedral in London, are named for Paul.

Symbol According to the New Testament, Jesus was crucified, or put to death on a cross. As a result, the cross became an important symbol of Christianity. It represents the belief that Jesus died to save humanity.

Primary Source

One of Jesus' most famous sermons is the Sermon on the Mount. In this talk, Jesus provided guidance to his followers. His words were written down in the New Testament, the part of the Bible that describes the teachings of Jesus. In the following verses, Jesus explains that people can be saved by opening their hearts to God and by treating others as they would like to be treated.

Ask, and it will be given you; seek, and you will find; knock, and it will be opened to you. For every one who asks receives, and he who seeks finds, and to him who knocks it will be opened. Or what man of you, if his son asks him for a loaf, will give him a stone? Or if he asks for a fish, will give him a serpent? If you then, who are evil, know how to give good gifts to your children, how much more will your Father who is in heaven give good things to those who ask him? So whatever you wish that men would do to you, do so to them; for this is the law and the prophets.

Matthew 7:7–12

Hinduism

Hinduism is a way of life guided by religious beliefs and practices that developed over thousands of years. Hindus believe that a supreme being called Brahman is the soul of the universe. The same presence, they believe, can also be found within each person. People can be freed from suffering and desires once they understand the nature of Brahman. The religious practices of Hindus include prayer, meditation, selfless acts, and worship of the various Hindu deities.

Today, Hinduism is the major religion of India and Nepal. It also has followers in Indonesia, Africa, Europe, and the Western Hemisphere.

▼ **Festival of Diwali**
Diwali, the Festival of Lights, is the most important festival in India. Diwali may have begun as a harvest festival in ancient India. Today, it marks the beginning of the year for many Hindus. They celebrate the festival by lighting candles and lamps, as shown in this photograph.

Learn More About Hinduism

▲ Deities

Brahman often takes the form of three deities in Hinduism. Brahma is the creator of the universe. Vishnu is its protector. Shiva is its destroyer. All three deities are represented in this sculpture.

▼ Brahmin Priest

Brahmin priests, like the one shown here, are among Hinduism's religious leaders. These priests take care of the holy images in temples and read from the religion's sacred books.

Symbol The syllable *Om* (or *Aum*) is often recited at the beginning of Hindu prayers. *Om* is the most sacred sound in Hinduism because it is believed to contain all other sounds. The syllable is represented by the symbol shown below.

Primary Source

Hinduism has many sacred texts. The Vedas, four collections of prayers, rituals, and other sacred texts, are the oldest Hindu scriptures. They are believed to contain all knowledge, past and future.

The *Bhagavad-Gita* is another sacred Hindu text. In this work, Vishnu takes on the personality of a chariot driver named Krishna. Krishna and the warrior Arjuna discuss the meaning of life and religious faith. In this selection, Krishna explains that Brahman cannot be destroyed.

> Weapons do not cut it,
> fire does not burn it,
> waters do not wet it,
> wind does not wither it.
>
> It cannot be cut or burned;
> it cannot be wet or withered;
> it is enduring, all-pervasive,
> fixed, immovable, and timeless.
>
> *Bhagavad-Gita* 2:23–24

Islam

Islam is a religion based on the teachings of the Qur'an, the religion's holy book. Followers of Islam, known as Muslims, believe that God revealed these teachings to the prophet Muhammad through the angel Gabriel around A.D. 610. Islam teaches that there is only one God—the same God that is worshiped in Christianity and Judaism. In Arabic, God is called Allah. Muslims also believe in the prophets of Judaism and Christianity. In fact, Muslims traditionally refer to Christians and Jews as "people of the book." That is because Christians and Jews have received divine revelations from scriptures in the Bible.

Today, most Muslims live in southwestern and central Asia and parts of Africa. Islam also has many followers in Southeast Asia. Muslims show their devotion by performing acts of worship known as the Five Pillars of Islam. These include faith, prayer, charity, fasting, and a pilgrimage to Mecca.

▼ The Dome of the Rock
The Dome of the Rock in Jerusalem is one of Islam's holiest sites. The rock on the site is the spot from which Muslims say Muhammad rose to heaven to learn Allah's will. With Allah's blessing, Muhammad returned to Earth to bring God's message to all people.

▲ Muslim Prayer
Five times a day—dawn, noon, mid-afternoon, sunset, and evening—Muslims face toward Mecca to pray. Like the people in this photograph, Muslims stop what they are doing when they hear the call to prayer. Everything comes to a halt—even traffic.

▼ Ramadan

During the holy month of Ramadan, Muslims fast, or do not eat or drink, from dawn to sunset. The family shown here is ending their fast. The most important night of Ramadan is called the Night of Power. This is believed to be the night the angel Gabriel first spoke to Muhammad.

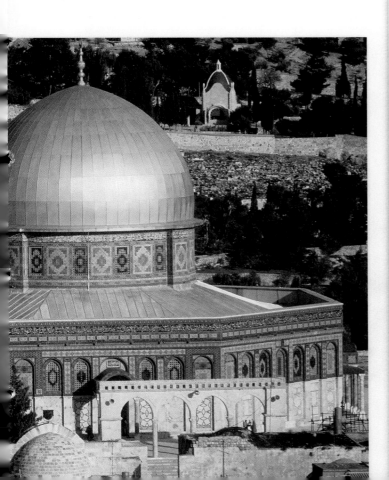

Learn More About Islam

Symbol The crescent moon has become a symbol of Islam. The symbol may be related to the new moon that begins each month in the Islamic lunar calendar.

Primary Source

The Qur'an is the spiritual guide for Muslims. It also contains teachings for Muslim daily life. The following chapter is called the Exordium (introduction). It is also called Al-Fatihah. Muslims recite this short chapter, as well as other passages from the Qur'an, when they pray.

In the Name of God, the Compassionate, the Merciful

Praise be to God, Lord of the Universe,
The Compassionate, the Merciful,
Sovereign of the Day of Judgment!
You alone we worship, and to You alone
   we turn for help.
Guide us to the straight path,
The path of those whom You have favored,
Not of those who have incurred Your wrath,
Nor of those who have gone astray.

Qur'an 1:1–6

Judaism

Judaism was the first major monotheistic religion—that is, based on the concept of one God. The basic teachings of Judaism come from the Torah, the first five books of the Hebrew Bible. Judaism teaches that a person serves God by studying the Torah and living by its teachings. The Torah became the basis for the civil and religious laws of Judaism. The followers of Judaism, or Jews, also believe that God set down many moral laws for all of humanity with the Ten Commandments.

Today, there are more than 15 million Jews throughout the world. Many live in Israel, where a Jewish state was created in 1948.

▼ Abraham

According to the Torah, God chose a Hebrew shepherd named Abraham to be the "father" of the Hebrew people. In the 19th century B.C., Abraham led his family to a land that he believed God had promised them. This painting illustrates their journey.

▲ Rabbi
Rabbis are the Jewish people's spiritual leaders and teachers. A rabbi often conducts the services in a synagogue, or Jewish house of worship. Like the rabbi shown here, he or she may also conduct the ceremony that marks Jewish children's entrance into the religious community.

▼ Western Wall
Many Jews make the pilgrimage to the Western Wall, shown here. The sacred wall formed the western wall of the courtyard of the Second Temple of Jerusalem. The temple was built in the second century B.C. The Romans destroyed it in A.D. 70.

Learn More About Judaism

Symbol The Star of David, also called the Shield of David, is a very important symbol of Judaism. The symbol honors King David, who ruled the kingdom of Israel about 1000–962 B.C.

Primary Source

The Book of Genesis is the first book of the Hebrew Bible and of the Torah. Genesis tells the history of the Hebrew people. It focuses on the individuals with whom God had a special relationship. In the following verses, God speaks to Abraham. His words express a promise of land and a special pledge to the Hebrew people.

Now the Lord said to Abram [Abraham], "Go from your country and your kindred and your father's house to the land that I will show you. And I will make of you a great nation, and I will bless you, and make your name great, so that you will be a blessing. I will bless those who bless you, and him who curses you I will curse; and by you all the families of the earth will bless themselves."

Genesis 12:1–3

Confucianism

Confucianism is an ethical system based on the teachings of the Chinese scholar Confucius. It stresses social and civic responsibility. Confucius was born in 551 B.C., during a time of crisis in China. He hoped his ideas and teachings would restore the order of earlier times to his society. But although Confucius was active in politics, he never had enough political power to put his ideas into practice. After his death, Confucius' students spread his teachings. As a result, his ideas became the foundation of Chinese thought for more than 2,000 years.

Today, Confucianism guides the actions of millions of Chinese people and other peoples of the East. It has also greatly influenced people's spiritual beliefs. While East Asians declare themselves to follow a number of religions, many also claim to be Confucians.

▼ **Temple**
Although Confucianism has no clergy or gods to worship, temples, like this one in Taiwan, have been built to honor Confucius. In ancient times, the temples provided schools of higher education. Today, many have been turned into museums.

◄ Confucius

Confucius believed that society should be organized around five basic relationships. These are the relationships between (1) ruler and subject, (2) father and son, (3) husband and wife, (4) elder brother and junior brother, and (5) friend and friend.

▲ Confucius' Birthday

Historians do not know for certain the day when Confucius was born, but people in East Asia celebrate his birthday on September 28. In Taiwan and China, it is an official holiday known as Teachers' Day. The holiday pays tribute to teachers because Confucius himself was a teacher. Here, students in Beijing take part in a ceremony honoring their teachers.

Learn More About Confucianism

Symbol The yin-and-yang symbol represents opposite forces in the world working together. Yin represents all that is cold, dark, soft, and mysterious. Yang represents everything that is warm, bright, hard, and clear. The yin-and-yang symbol represents the harmony that Confucius hoped to restore to society.

Primary Source

Confucius' teachings were collected by his students in a book called the *Analects*. In the following selections from the *Analects*, Confucius (called the Master) instructs his students about living a moral and thoughtful life.

The Master said: "Even in the midst of eating coarse rice and drinking water and using a bent arm for a pillow happiness is surely to be found; riches and honors acquired by unrighteous means are to me like the floating clouds." (7.16)

The Master said: "When I walk with two others, I always receive instruction from them. I select their good qualities and copy them, and improve on their bad qualities." (7.22)

The Master said: "The people may be made to follow something, but may not be made to understand it." (8.9)

from the *Analects*
Translated by Raymond Dawson

Other Important Religions

You have learned about the five major world religions. Now find out about some other important religions: Bahaism, Shinto, Sikhism, and Zoroastrianism. These religions are important both historically and because they have many followers today.

▼ Shinto
Shinto, meaning "way of the gods," is Japan's oldest and only native religion. Shintoists worship many gods, called *kami*. They believe that kami are spirits found in mountains, rivers, rocks, trees, and other parts of nature. Shintoists often worship the kami at shrines in their homes. They also celebrate the gods during special festivals, such as the one shown here. Today, there are about 3 million Shintoists, mostly in Japan.

▲ Bahaism
Bahaism (buh•HAH•IHZ•uhm) is a young religion, with more than 7 million followers throughout the world. It was founded in 1863 in Persia (modern-day Iran) by a man known as Bahaullah, which means "splendor of God" in Arabic. Followers believe that, in time, God will break down barriers of race, class, and nation. When this happens, people will form a single, united society. All of the Baha'i houses of worship have nine sides and a central dome, symbolizing this unity. The Baha'i house of worship shown here is located in Illinois.

◄ Sikhism

Sikhism was founded in India over 500 years ago by Guru Nanak. The religion's 24 million followers, called Sikhs, believe in one God. Like Buddhists and Hindus, Sikhs believe that the soul goes through repeated cycles of life and death. However, Sikhs do not believe that they have to live outside the world to end the cycle. Rather, they can achieve salvation by living a good and simple life. Uncut hair symbolizes this simple life. Many Sikh men cover their long hair with a turban, like the one worn by this man.

▲ Zoroastrianism

Zoroastrianism (ZAWR•oh•AS•tree•uh•NIHZ•uhm) was founded in ancient Persia around 600 B.C. by a prophet named Zoroaster. This prophet taught that Earth is a battleground where a great struggle is fought between the forces of good and the forces of evil. Each person is expected to take part in this struggle. At death, the Zoroastrian god, called Ahura Mazda (ah•HUR•uh MAZ•duh), will judge the person on how well he or she fought. This stone relief shows Ahura Mazda (*right*) giving the crown to a Persian king. Today, there are about 2.5 million Zoroastrians throughout the world.

Comparing World Religions and Ethical Systems

	Buddhism	Christianity	Hinduism	Islam	Judaism	Confucianism
Followers worldwide (estimated 2005 figures)	379 million	2.1 billion	860 million	1.3 billion	15.1 million	6.5 million
Name of god	no god	God	Brahman	Allah	God	no god
Founder	the Buddha	Jesus	no founder	no founder but spread by Muhammad	Abraham	Confucius
Holy book	many sacred books, including the Dhammapada	Bible, including Old Testament and New Testament	many sacred texts, including the Upanishads	Qur'an	Hebrew Bible, including the Torah	*Analects*
Clergy	Buddhist monks	priests, ministers, monks, and nuns	Brahmin priests, monks, and gurus	no clergy but a scholar class, called the ulama, and imams, who may lead prayers	rabbis	no clergy
Basic beliefs	• Followers can achieve enlightenment by understanding the Four Noble Truths and by following the Noble Eightfold Path of right opinions, right desires, right speech, right action, right jobs, right effort, right concentration, and right meditation.	• There is only one God, who watches over and cares for his people. • Jesus is the Son of God. He died to save humanity. His death and resurrection made eternal life possible for others.	• The soul never dies but is continually reborn until it becomes divinely enlightened. • Persons achieve happiness and divine enlightenment after they free themselves from their earthly desires. • Freedom from earthly desires comes from many lifetimes of worship, knowledge, and virtuous acts.	• There is only one God, who watches over and cares for his people. • Persons achieve salvation by following the Five Pillars of Islam and living a just life. The pillars are faith, prayer, charity, fasting, and pilgrimage to Mecca.	• There is only one God, who watches over and cares for his people. • God loves and protects his people but also holds people accountable for their sins and shortcomings. • Persons serve God by studying the Torah and living by its teachings.	• Social order, harmony, and good government should be based on strong family relationships. • Respect for parents and elders is important to a well-ordered society. • Education is important for the welfare of both the individual and society.

Source: *Encyclopedia Britannica Almanac, 2006*

Review

KEY IDEAS

Buddhism (pages R40–R41)

1. How did the Buddha believe that his followers could end their suffering?
2. How did Buddhism spread?

Christianity (pages R42–R43)

3. Why is Jesus important to the Christian religion?
4. What are some Christian beliefs?

Hinduism (pages R44–R45)

5. What is the importance of Brahman in Hinduism?
6. What three deities does Brahman often take the form of?

Islam (pages R46–R47)

7. How do Muslims believe the teachings of the Qur'an were revealed?
8. Why do Muslims traditionally refer to Christians and Jews as "people of the book"?

Judaism (pages R48–R49)

9. What does it mean to say that Judaism is a monotheistic religion?
10. What are the Ten Commandments?

Confucianism (pages R50–R51)

11. What did Confucius hope to restore?
12. What five relationships are important in Confucianism?

Other Important Religions (pages R52–R53)

13. How does Shinto differ from Bahaism, Sikhism, and Zoroastrianism?
14. How is Sikhism similar to Buddhism and Hinduism?

CRITICAL THINKING

15. **Compare and Contrast** What goal do Buddhists and Hindus share?
16. **Draw Conclusions** How does Islam affect the everyday lives of its followers?

INTERPRETING A PIE CHART

The pie chart below shows what percentages of the population of India practice the major religions. Use the pie chart to answer the following questions.

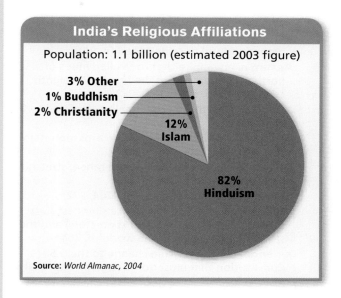

India's Religious Affiliations

Population: 1.1 billion (estimated 2003 figure)

3% Other
1% Buddhism
2% Christianity
12% Islam
82% Hinduism

Source: *World Almanac, 2004*

1. **What percentage of the people in India practice Hinduism?**

   A. 1 percent
   B. 2 percent
   C. 12 percent
   D. 82 percent

2. **Which religion is practiced by 12 percent of the population?**

   A. Buddhism
   B. Christianity
   C. Hinduism
   D. Islam

Glossary

A

aborigine (AB•uh•RIHJ•uh•nee) *n.* an original inhabitant of Australia (p. 892)

African National Congress (ANC) *n.* South African political party opposing apartheid (p. 624)

Afrikaner *n.* a South African of European ancestry who speaks a language called Afrikaans (p. 624)

agricultural revolution *n.* the shift from gathering food to raising food (p. 96)

Aksum *n.* an empire that controlled much of northern Ethiopia from the first to the eighth century A.D. (p. 606)

alpaca *n.* a South American mammal related to the llama (p. 272)

Alpine *adj.* having to do with the Alps mountain range (p. 382)

Alps *n.* Europe's tallest mountain range, stretching across southern Europe (p. 326)

altiplano *n.* a high plateau (pp. 204, 272)

Amazon River *n.* South America's longest river (about 4,000 miles, or 6,400 kilometers) and the second-longest river in the world (p. 204)

amendment *n.* a written change to the U.S. Constitution that must go through an approval process (p. 146)

Amundsen, Roald *n.* Norwegian polar explorer first to reach the South Pole (p. 920)

Anatolian peninsula *n.* in Southwest Asia between the Black Sea and Mediterranean Sea (p. 652)

ancestor *n.* an early relative (p. 544)

Andes Mountains *n.* a mountain range located on South America's west coast and extending the full length of the continent (p. 204)

animism *n.* the belief that spirits exist in animals, plants, natural forces, and ancestors (p. 544)

annex *v.* to add to an existing territory (p. 230)

Antarctic Peninsula *n.* an S-shaped peninsula that is part of the Andes Mountain chain (p. 920)

Antarctic Treaty *n.* an agreement signed in 1959 calling for the peaceful use of Antarctica (p. 920)

anthropologist (AN•thruh•PAHL•uh•jihst) *n.* a scientist who studies culture (p. 88)

apartheid (uh•PAHRT•hyt) *n.* the official policy of racial segregation practiced in South Africa from 1950 to 1991 (p. 624)

Appalachian (AP•uh•LAY•chee•uhn) **Mountains** *n.* a mountain chain in the Eastern United States, running parallel to the Atlantic Ocean (p. 122)

Aquino (uh•KEE•noh), **Corazon** *n.* politician who opposed Marcos and was president of the Philippines between 1986 and 1992 (p. 864)

Arabian Peninsula *n.* peninsula of Southwest Asia between the Red Sea and Persian Gulf (p. 652)

Aral Sea *n.* an inland body of water in Central Asia that has been steadily shrinking (p. 496)

archipelago (AHR•kuh•PEHL•uh•GOH) *n.* a set of closely grouped islands, which sometimes form a curved arc (pp. 198, 736, 852, 864)

artisan *n.* a worker skilled in making products or art with his or her hands (p. 254)

Aryan *n.* one of a group of Indo-European nomadic herders who are believed to have migrated to the Indian subcontinent (p. 698)

Ashanti (uh•SHAN•tee) *n.* a people of Ghana (pp. 580, 586)

Aswan High Dam *n.* a structure to control the floodwaters of the Nile River and provide electricity (p. 554)

Atlas Mountains *n.* series of mountain ranges stretching from Morocco to Tunisia (p. 568)

atmosphere *n.* the layer of gases that surround the Earth (p. 34)

atoll *n.* a ring-shaped coral reef encircling a central lagoon with no inner island (p. 912)

Aung San Suu Kyi (awng sahn soo chee) *n.* leader of the democracy movement in Myanmar (p. 858)

autonomy *n.* self-governance or independence (p. 376)

Aztec *n.* an early civilization in the Valley of Mexico (p. 212)

B

Bahasa Indonesia (bah•HAH•suh in•duh•NEE•zhuh) *n.* the common language of Indonesia (p. 864)

Baltic States *n.* Latvia, Lithuania, and Estonia, three countries that border the Baltic Sea (p. 424)

Bangalore *n.* south-central Indian city that is home to many high-tech industries (p. 716)

basin *n.* a region drained by a river system (p. 536)

Basque (bask) *n.* an ethnic group living in the western Pyrenees and along the Bay of Biscay in Spain and France; also the name of their language (p. 370)

Bechuanaland (bech•WAH•nuh•LAND) *n.* colonial name for Botswana (p. 630)

Bedouin *n.* an Arabic-speaking, traditionally nomadic people of Southwest Asia (p. 676)

Beirut *n.* capital of Lebanon and a center of banking and finance (p. 688)

Benelux (BEHN•uh•LUHKS) *n.* name for the economic union formed by Belgium, the Netherlands, and Luxembourg to ensure the fast and efficient movement of people, goods, and services within these nations (p. 376)

Berbers (BUR•buhrz) *n.* the original inhabitants of North Africa and the Sahara (p. 568)

Berlin Wall *n.* a wall built by East Germany's Communist government to close off East Berlin from West Berlin; torn down in 1991 (p. 382)

Bhagavad-Gita *n.* one of the sacred writings of Hinduism (p. 706)

Biafra (bee•AF•ruh) *n.* a largely Igbo region of Nigeria that declared its independence in 1967, but surrendered after losing a civil war with Nigeria in 1970 (p. 586)

bilingual *adj.* using or able to use two languages equally well (p. 164)

bipedal *adj.* walking on two feet (p. 544)

birth rate *n.* the number of births per 1,000 people per year (p. 58)

blues *n.* a type of music with lyrics that express sorrow, usually about problems in love or the hardships of life (p. 138)

Boer *n.* a Dutch colonist or descendant in South Africa (p. 624)

Bogotá *n.* capital city of Colombia (p. 266)

Bolívar, Simón (boh•LEE•vahr, see•MOHN) *n.* leader for independence in northern South America (pp. 220, 266)

Bolsheviks (BOHL•shuh•VIHKS) *n.* a group of revolutionaries who took control of the Russian government in 1917 (p. 468)

Bosniac *n.* an ethnic Muslim from Bosnia and Herzegovnia (p. 440)

bossa nova (BAHS•uh NOH•vuh) *n.* a jazz version of the samba, a Brazilian dance (p. 296)

Botero, Fernando *n.* Colombian artist known for portraits of people with exaggerated forms (p. 266)

boycott *v.* to stop buying and using products from certain sources as a way of protest (p. 304)

brain drain *n.* the loss of skilled workers who move in search of better opportunities (p. 424)

Brasília *n.* Brazil's current capital city (p. 290)

bread basket *n.* an abundant grain-producing region (p. 424)

Briton *n.* a British person (p. 408)

Buddha *n.* a name, meaning the "enlightened one," used for Siddhartha Gautama, the founder of Buddhism (pp. 698, 706, 774)

Buddhism *n.* a major world religion that began in India and is based on the teachings of Siddhartha Gautama (pp. 476, 698, 706, 774, 804)

Byzantine Empire *n.* the eastern half of the Roman Empire that survived for a thousand years after the fall of Rome (p. 362)

C

cabinet system *n.* a system of government that links the executive and legislative branches by choosing the prime minister and major department heads from the legislature (p. 176)

Cabral, Pedro Álvares *n.* Portuguese explorer who in 1500 claimed land that is now part of Brazil for Portugal (p. 290)

camel *n.* a humped mammal used in the desert as a pack animal and provider of meat, milk, and wool (p. 580)

Camp David Accords *n.* peace treaty negotiated by U.S. President Jimmy Carter, Egyptian President Anwar el-Sadat, and Israeli Prime Minister Menachem Begin between Egypt and Israel, signed at the U.S. presidential retreat in Maryland in 1979 (p. 562)

Canadian Shield *n.* a horseshoe-shaped, rocky plateau that covers much of eastern central Canada (p. 156)

Candomblé (kahn•duhm•BLEH) *n.* African religious practices that are mixed with Roman Catholic beliefs to produce a unique belief system (p. 296)

canopy *n.* the highest layer in a forest, formed by the treetops (p. 536)

Cape Colony *n.* South African land settled by Dutch colonists called Boers in the 1600s and 1700s (p. 624)

capoeira (KAP•oh•AY•ruh) *n.* a Brazilian dance combined with martial arts (p. 296)

Caracas *n.* capital city of Venezuela (p. 266)

carbon dioxide *n.* a gas composed of carbon and oxygen (p. 48)

Caribbean Community and Common Market (CARICOM) *n.* a trade organization of several Caribbean nations (p. 260)

Carthage (KAR•thihj) *n.* an ancient North African city-state (p. 568)

cartographer (kahr•TAHG•ruh•fur) *n.* a geographer who creates maps (p. 10)

Caspian Sea *n.* a large body of water bordering Russia to the south and situated between Transcaucasia and Central Asia (pp. 460, 496)

caste *n.* in India, a social class that a person belongs to by birth (p. 698)

cataract *n.* a high waterfall or rapids (p. 554)

Caucasus (KAW•kuh•suhs) **Mountains** *n.* a mountain range that runs between the Black Sea and the Caspian Sea (p. 496)

celadon (SEHL•uh•DAHN) *n.* Korean ceramic pottery with a thin blue or green glaze (p. 804)

Central America Free Trade Agreement (CAFTA) *n.* an agreement to promote trade between the United States and countries of Central America (pp. 254, 260)

Central Asia *n.* a region that contains the republics of Kazakhstan (KAH•zahk•STAN), Kyrgyzstan (KEER•gee•STAN), Tajikistan (tah•JIHK•ih•STAN), Turkmenistan (TURK•mehn•ih•STAN), and Uzbekistan (uz•BEHK•ih•STAN) (p. 496)

cession *n.* surrendered territory (p. 230)

chaebol (JEH•buhl) *n.* in Korea, a family-owned conglomerate made up of related businesses (p. 812)

Chang Jiang (chahng jyahng) *n.* the longest river in Asia, flowing through eastern China (p. 756)

Channel Tunnel *n.* the underwater railroad tunnel between France and England under the English Channel (p. 414)

Chechnya (CHEHCH•nee•uh) *n.* a largely Islamic republic in southwestern Russia that continues to fight for its independence (p. 486)

Cheju (CHEH•JOO) **Island** *n.* largest island off the southern coast of the Korean Peninsula (p. 796)

chinampas *n.* in Mexico, artificial islands used for farming (p. 212)

Christianity *n.* a monotheistic religion based on the life and teachings of Jesus of Nazareth and on the writings of the Christian Bible (p. 682)

Church of England *n.* the official church of England headed by the Archbishop of Canterbury (p. 408)

citizen *n.* a person who owes loyalty to a country and receives its protection (p. 78)

city-state *n.* a political unit made up of a city and its surrounding lands (pp. 334, 666)

Civil War (1861–1865) *n.* a conflict between the U.S. North and South over the issues of states' rights and slavery (p. 130)

civilization *n.* an advanced form of culture that developed in cities (p. 666)

clan *n.* a group of families related through a common ancestor (p. 830)

climate *n.* the typical weather conditions of a region over a long period of time (p. 40)

climatologist *n.* a geographer who studies climates (p. 16)

coalition *n.* an alliance or partnership, often a temporary one (p. 362)

Cold War *n.* a conflict between the United States and the Soviet Union after World War II that never developed into open warfare (p. 468)

colonia *n.* a neighborhood in Mexico (p. 236)

colonialism *n.* the control by one power over a dependent area or people (p. 858)

colony *n.* a group of people who settle a distant land but are ruled by their homeland, such as the United States; overseas territory ruled by a nation, such as Mexico from the 1500s to 1821 (pp. 130, 220)

Columbian Exchange *n.* the movement of plants and animals between Latin America and Europe after Columbus' voyage to the Americas in A.D. 1492 (p. 220)

Columbus, Christopher *n.* Italian navigator and explorer who sailed for Spain and explored the Caribbean and the coast of Central and South America (p. 370)

command economy *n.* an economic system in which the production of goods and services is decided by a central government (pp. 72, 424, 486, 512, 784)

commonwealth *n.* a self-governing political unit that is associated with another country (p. 260)

Commonwealth of Nations *n.* an association made up of the United Kingdom and many former British colonies (pp. 164, 400, 624)

communal *adj.* referring to shared ownership of property (p. 774)

communism *n.* a type of government in which the Communist Party holds all political power and controls the economy (pp. 78, 260, 424, 468, 764)

compulsory *adj.* required (p. 362)

Confucianism (kuhn•FYOO•shuh•nihz•uhm) *n.* a belief system based on the teachings of Confucius, a Chinese scholar (pp. 764, 774, 804)

conglomerate *n.* an organization made up of several companies in different businesses (p. 812)

Congo River *n.* Africa's second-longest river (p. 618)

conquistador (kahn•KWIHS•tuh•DAWR) *n.* Spanish word for "conqueror" (p. 220)

Constitution *n.* the document that is the basis for the U.S. government (p. 130)

constitution *n.* the set of laws and principles that defines the nature of a government (pp. 176, 230)

Constitution of 1917 *n.* Mexican constitution written during the revolution that is still in effect today (p. 230)

constitutional monarchy *n.* a government in which the powers of the king or queen are limited by the constitution (pp. 176, 414, 736, 858, 892)

continent *n.* one of seven large landmasses on the Earth's surface (pp. 26, 122)

Continental Divide *n.* a high ridgeline in the Rocky Mountains that divides east-flowing from west-flowing rivers (p. 122)

continental shelf *n.* the submerged land at the edge of a continent (p. 34)

Cook, James *n.* a British explorer who claimed land in Australia (p. 892)

coral island *n.* a type of oceanic island that is a coral reef (p. 912)

cottage industry *n.* a small business in which the workers manufacture items in their homes (pp. 716, 728)

coup (koo) *n.* military takeover (p. 586)

cuíca (KWEE•kuh) *n.* a friction drum used in the samba, a Brazilian dance (p. 296)

cultural blending *n.* something new created from combining the elements of two or more cultures (p. 138)

cultural hearth *n.* the heartland of a major culture; an area where a culture originated and spread to other areas (pp. 96, 212)

culture *n.* the shared attitudes, knowledge, and behaviors of a group (pp. 66, 88, 138, 212, 544)

cuneiform (KYOO•nee•uh•form) *n.* the first known writing system, which used wedge-shaped symbols and was developed in Sumer (p. 666)

cyclone *n.* a violent storm with fierce winds that rotate in a circular pattern like a hurricane (p. 658)

Cyrillic (suh•RIHL•ihk) **alphabet** *n.* the official writing system of Russia (p. 476)

czar (zahr) *n.* title for the rulers of Russia from the mid-1500s to the early 1900s (p. 468)

Czechoslovakia (CHEHK•uh•sluh•VAH•kee•uh) *n.* former country in Eastern Europe that existed from 1918 until 1993, when it split into the Czech Republic and Slovakia (p. 432)

D

daimyo (DY•mee•OH) *n.* in Japan, powerful samurai who became warrior-chieftains (p. 830)

Dao (DOW) *n.* according to the belief system of Daoism, a force that guides the whole universe (p. 774)

Daoism (DOW•IHZ•uhm) *n.* a Chinese belief system based on the idea of natural order in the world (p. 774)

database *n.* a collection of information that can be analyzed (p. 10)

Day of the Dead *n.* holiday to remember loved ones who have died (p. 236)

death rate *n.* the number of deaths per 1,000 people per year (p. 58)

debris (duh•BREE) *n.* the scattered remains of something broken or destroyed (p. 10)

Deccan (DEHK•uhn) **Plateau** *n.* a high area of land at the center of the Indian subcontinent (p. 658)

deforestation *n.* the cutting and clearing away of trees (p. 304)

degraded *adj.* of a lower quality than previously existed (p. 48)

delta *n.* the triangle-shaped deposit of rich soil at a river's mouth (p. 554)

demilitarized zone *n.* a buffer zone between North Korea and South Korea (p. 804)

democracy *n.* a government in which the citizens make political decisions, either directly or through elected representatives (p. 334)

demographer *n.* a geographer who studies the characteristics of human populations (p. 58)

demonstration *n.* a public gathering to protest a policy or action (p. 784)

dependency *n.* a place governed by a country that it is not officially a part of (p. 260)

deport *v.* to expel from a country (p. 424)

desert *n.* a region with plants specially adapted to dry conditions (p. 40)

desertification *n.* the change of fertile land to desert; the process in which farmland becomes less productive because the land is degraded (pp. 48, 536)

devolution *n.* the process of shifting some power from national to regional government (p. 414)

dictator *n.* a person with complete control over a country's government (pp. 254, 260, 266, 812)

dictatorship *n.* a state or government ruled by a leader with absolute power (pp. 78, 568)

Diet (DY•iht) *n.* Japan's law-making body, which consists of a House of Representatives and a House of Councillors (p. 840)

diffusion *n.* the spread of ideas, inventions, and patterns of behavior from one group to another (p. 96)

discrimination *n.* actions that might be hurtful to an individual or a group (p. 66)

diversity *n.* having many different ways to think or to do something, or a variety of people (p. 66)

Dom Pedro I *n.* Brazil's first Portuguese emperor; declared Brazil's independence from Portugal in 1822 (p. 290)

Dom Pedro II *n.* second emperor of Brazil, under whose rule slavery was abolished in Brazil in 1888 (p. 290)

domesticate *v.* to adapt or train plants or animals for human use (p. 544)

domestication *n.* the raising and tending of a plant or an animal to be of use to humans (p. 96)

dominion *n.* in the British Empire, a nation that is allowed to govern its domestic affairs (p. 164)

draft animal *n.* an animal used to pull a heavy load (p. 884)

drainage basin *n.* the area drained by a major river (p. 34)

Dravidian (druh•VIHD•ee•uhn) *n.* speakers of a language group found in India since the earliest times; mostly spoken in South India today (p. 698)

drought *n.* a long period of little or no rainfall (p. 594)

duchy (DUHCH•ee) *n.* the territory ruled by a duke or duchess (p. 376)

Dust Bowl *n.* a region of the U.S. Great Plains that suffered drought and suffocating dust storms in the 1930s (p. 130)

dynastic (dy•NAS•tihk) **cycle** *n.* in China, the pattern of the rise and fall of dynasties (p. 764)

dynasty (DY•nuh•stee) *n.* a family or group that rules for several generations, such as in China (pp. 554, 606, 764)

E

earthquake *n.* a sudden movement of the Earth's crust followed by a series of shocks (p. 26)

eclectic *adj.* made up of parts from a variety of sources (p. 432)

economic system *n.* a way people use resources to make and exchange goods (p. 72)

economy *n.* a system for producing and exchanging goods and services among a group of people (pp. 72, 304)

ecotourism *n.* travel to unique environments by people who take care to preserve them in their natural state (pp. 254, 736)

edible *adj.* fit for eating (p. 272)

emissions *n.* substances discharged into the air (p. 48)

emperor *n.* a ruler of an empire, which is a group of different territories or cultures led by a single all-powerful authority (pp. 764, 830)

empire *n.* a political system in which people or lands are controlled by one ruler (pp. 212, 220)

Enlightenment *n.* a philosophical movement in the 1600s and 1700s that was characterized by the use of reason and scientific methods (p. 350)

environment *n.* the physical surroundings of a location (p. 4)

equinox *n.* one of the two times a year when the sun's rays are over the equator and days and nights around the world are equal in length (p. 40)

Eritrea *n.* a former region of Ethiopia that became an independent country in 1993 (p. 606)

erosion *n.* the wearing away and movement of weathered materials by water, wind, or ice (p. 26)

escarpment *n.* a steep slope separating two flat areas of different heights (p. 536)

estancia (eh•STAHN•see•ah) *n.* large farm or ranch in Argentina (p. 280)

ethanol (EHTH•uh•NAWL) *n.* a liquid made by using a chemical process to convert sugar cane to a kind of alcohol that can be used for fuel (p. 304)

ethnic cleansing *n.* removing an ethnic or religious group from an area by force or the mass killing of members of such a group (p. 440)

ethnic group *n.* a group of people who share language, customs, and a common heritage (pp. 88, 476, 504)

Euphrates (yoo•FRAY•teez) **River** *n.* a river of Southwest Asia that flows from a plateau on the Anatolian peninsula to the Persian Gulf (p. 652)

Eurasia *n.* a term used to refer to a single continent made up of Europe and Asia (pp. 460, 496)

European Union (EU) *n.* an organization of European nations whose members cooperate on economic, social, and political issues (pp. 350, 362, 688)

Everglades *n.* a huge wetlands area of southern Florida (p. 122)

export *n.* a product or resource sold to another country (pp. 72, 304)

export *v.* to send something from one country to another (p. 146)

extended family *n.* the family unit that contains more relatives than just parents and children, including grandparents and other close family (p. 688)

F

famine *n.* a severe shortage of food that causes widespread hunger (pp. 594, 658)

fascism (FASH•IHZ•uhm) *n.* a political philosophy that promotes blind loyalty to the state and a strong central government controlled by a powerful dictator (p. 362)

fast *v.* to avoid eating, often for religious reasons (p. 728)

favelas (fuh•VEH•lahs) *n.* Brazilian name for the poor neighborhoods that surround the cities (p. 290)

federal republic *n.* form of government in which power is divided between a national government and state governments (p. 266)

federal system *n.* a government system in which powers are divided between the national and state or provincial governments (pp. 146, 176)

federation *n.* colonies, states, or countries that have joined together (p. 594)

Fertile Crescent *n.* a region stretching from the Persian Gulf northwest up the Tigris and Euphrates rivers and west over to the Mediterranean Sea (p. 666)

feudalism *n.* a political system in which lords gave land to vassals in exchange for services (p. 342)

fiesta *n.* a holiday celebrated with parades, games, and food (p. 236)

Filipino *n.* an inhabitant of the Philippines (p. 864)

First Nations *n.* organized cultural groups of Canada's native peoples (p. 164)

foreign investment *n.* money put into a business by people from another country (p. 512)

fossil *n.* remains of early life preserved in the ground (p. 544)

fossil fuels *n.* sources of energy from ancient plant and animal remains; includes fuels such as coal, oil, and natural gas (pp. 48, 326)

Fox, Vicente *n.* Mexican president from the National Action Party who was elected in 2000 (p. 230)

free enterprise *n.* an economic system in which businesses are free to operate without much government involvement (pp. 146, 176, 784)

French Revolution *n.* a conflict in France between 1789 and 1799 that ended the monarchy and led to changes in the way France was governed (p. 350)

G

Gaelic *n.* any of the Celtic family of languages spoken in Ireland or Scotland (p. 408)

Gandhi, Mohandas (GAHN•dee, MOH•hehn•DAHS) *n.* a 20th-century Indian who helped lead his country to independence by using nonviolent resistance to colonial rule (p. 698)

Ganges (GAN•JEEZ) **River** *n.* a river of South Asia that flows southeast from the Himalayas to the Bay of Bengal (p. 658)

García Márquez, Gabriel *n.* Colombian author and Nobel Prize winner (p. 266)

gaucho (GAOW•choh) *n.* Argentinian cowboy (p. 280)

Gautama, Siddhartha (GAW•tuh•muh, sihd•DAHR•tuh) *n.* the founder of Buddhism also known as the Buddha, or "enlightened one" (p. 774)

Gaza Strip *n.* a narrow territory along the Mediterranean Sea (p. 682)

Geographic Information Systems (GIS) *n.* a computer- or Internet-based mapping technology (pp. 10, 16)

geographic South Pole *n.* the point where all lines of longitude meet (p. 920)

geography *n.* the study of people, places, and environments (p. 4)

geomorphology (JEE•oh•mawr•FAHL•uh•jee) *n.* the study of how the shape of the Earth changes (p. 16)

geothermal energy *n.* power produced by the internal heat of the Earth (p. 900)

geyser (GY•zuhr) *n.* a hot spring that shoots sprays of steam and boiling water into the air (pp. 884, 900)

Ghana *n.* a West African kingdom between the A.D. 700s and the A.D. 1000s in what is now Mauritania and Mali; a modern country in West Africa (p. 580)

glacier *n.* a large, slow-moving mass of ice (p. 26)

global economy *n.* economy in which buying and selling occurs across national borders (pp. 146, 244)

Global Positioning System (GPS) *n.* a system that uses a network of Earth-orbiting satellites to pinpoint location (p. 10)

global warming *n.* an increase in the average temperature of the Earth's atmosphere (pp. 48, 304)

globe *n.* a model of the Earth in the shape of a sphere (p. 10)

glyph *n.* a carved or engraved symbol that stands for a syllable or a word (p. 212)

Gobi (GOH•bee) **Desert** *n.* a high desert in China and Mongolia (p. 756)

Golan Heights *n.* a region that was formerly part of southwest Syria that Israel has occupied since the 1967 war (p. 688)

golden age *n.* a period during which a society attains prosperity and cultural achievements (p. 698)

Good Friday Agreement *n.* an agreement between Northern Ireland's unionists and nationalists that set up a new government (p. 414)

Gorbachev (GAWR•buh•CHAWF), **Mikhail** *n.* Soviet leader from 1985 to 1991 who increased freedoms for the Russian people (p. 468)

government *n.* an organization set up to make and enforce rules for a society (p. 78)

Grand Canyon *n.* a deep gorge cut through northern Arizona by the Colorado River (p. 122)

Great Barrier Reef *n.* a 1,250-mile chain of coral reefs off the coast of Australia (p. 884)

Great Depression *n.* a period of severe economic decline from 1929 into the early 1940s (p. 130)

Great Dividing Range *n.* a range of low mountains in Australia (p. 884)

Great Lakes *n.* five lakes forming the largest group of freshwater lakes in the world (pp. 122, 156)

Great Plains *n.* a vast grassland in central North America (p. 122)

Great Wall *n.* a long, huge wall built over several centuries to keep nomads out of China (p. 764)

Great Zimbabwe *n.* an empire built by the Shona people from the first to the eighth century A.D. (p. 630)

Greater Antilles *n.* the northern largest Caribbean islands that include Cuba, Jamaica, Hispaniola (which includes Haiti and the Dominican Republic), and Puerto Rico (p. 198)

Green Revolution *n.* the use of special seeds, irrigation, fertilizers, and pesticides to produce high crop yields and food production (pp. 716, 728)

greenhouse effect *n.* the trapping of the sun's heat by gases in the Earth's atmosphere (p. 48)

greenhouse gas *n.* any gas in the atmosphere that contributes to the greenhouse effect (p. 48)

grid *n.* a network of horizontal and vertical lines that create squares or rectangles (p. 666)

griot (gree•OH) *n.* a West African storyteller (p. 544)

Gross Domestic Product (GDP) *n.* the total value of all the goods and services produced in a country in a year (pp. 72, 280)

ground water *n.* water found beneath the Earth's surface (p. 34)

guerrilla *n.* a member of an irregular army that operates in small bands (p. 630)

Gulf of Mexico *n.* an arm of the Atlantic Ocean that lies south of the United States (p. 122)

H

habitable lands *n.* lands suitable for human living (p. 58)

Hammurabi's Code *n.* one of the world's first law codes, compiled by the ruler Hammurabi (p. 666)

hanbok *n.* a traditional Korean costume (p. 804)

Harappan civilization *n.* an ancient civilization that developed along the Indus River (p. 666)

Hausa (HOW•suh) *n.* a people of northern Nigeria and southern Niger (p. 586)

Heian (hay•ahn) **Period** *n.* an era in Japanese history from A.D. 794 to 1185; arts and writing flourished during this time (p. 830)

Hidalgo, Miguel ("Father Hidalgo") *n.* father of Mexican independence (p. 220)

hieroglyphics *n.* an Egyptian writing system in which picture symbols stand for meanings or sounds (p. 554)

highlands *n.* mountainous or hilly sections of a country (pp. 198, 204)

Himalayas (HIHM•uh•LAY•uhz) *n.* the highest mountains in the world, which stretch along northern India, separating India from China and the rest of Asia (pp. 658, 756)

Hinduism *n.* the modern name for the major religion of India, which developed from Brahmanism (pp. 698, 706)

Hitler, Adolf *n.* German head of state from 1933 to 1945 (p. 382)

Hokkaido (hah•KY•doh) *n.* Japan's northernmost and second largest island (p. 824)

Holocaust *n.* the systematic murder of Jews and other minorities by the Nazis during World War II (pp. 350, 382, 682)

hominid *n.* a human primate; an early human (p. 544)

Honshu *n.* Japan's largest and most populous island (p. 824)

Horn of Africa *n.* a horn-shaped extension of land on the east coast of Africa (p. 606)

Huang He (hwahng huh) *n.* a river that flows from the Kunlun Mountains to the Yellow Sea (p. 756)

Hudson Bay *n.* a large inland sea to the north of the Canadian province of Ontario (p. 156)

hunter-gatherer *n.* a person who hunts animals and gathers plants for food (pp. 618, 892)

hydroelectric *adj.* having to do with electricity created by water-powered engines (p. 156)

hydroelectricity *n.* electric power generated by water (p. 304)

hydroelectric power *n.* electricity made by water-powered engines (pp. 326, 756, 900)

hydrologic cycle *n.* the circulation of water between the Earth, the oceans, and the atmosphere (p. 34)

I

ice shelf *n.* huge flat sheet of ice extending over a body of water, but attached to the land (p. 920)

iceberg *n.* a large piece of floating ice (p. 920)

icecap *n.* a glacier that covers a large area (p. 920)

icon *n.* religious image used by Orthodox Christians in their worship (p. 476)

Igbo (IHG•bo) *n.* a people of southeastern Nigeria (p. 586)

igloo *n.* a house made of snow (p. 170)

immigrant *n.* a person who leaves one area to settle in another (pp. 66, 130, 296, 408)

immigration *n.* process of coming to another country to live (p. 244)

imperialism *n.* the practice of one country controlling the government and economy of another country or territory (pp. 350, 400, 580)

import *n.* a product or resource that comes into a country (p. 72)

import *v.* to bring something from one country into another (p. 146)

Inca *n.* an early civilization in the Andes Mountains of Peru (p. 212)

indigenous *n.* native to a region (p. 272)

Indochina *n.* the name for a former French colony in Southeast Asia made up of Cambodia, Laos, and Vietnam (p. 858)

Indochinese Peninsula *n.* one of two peninsulas on which mainland Southeast Asia lies; the peninsula is located south of China (p. 852)

Indus River *n.* a river in South Asia that flows from the Himalayas to the Arabian Sea (p. 658)

Industrial Revolution *n.* the shift that began in Great Britain in the 1760s from making goods by hand to making them by machine (pp. 350, 400)

inflation *n.* a price increase or a fall in the purchasing power of money (p. 594)

infrastructure *n.* basic services a community needs, such as roads, railroads, water and power lines, schools, and post offices (p. 594)

innovation *n.* something new that is introduced for the first time (p. 96)

Interstate Highway System *n.* a network of more than 45,000 miles of roads that links every major U.S. city (p. 146)

Inuit (IHN•yoo•iht) *n.* the native peoples who inhabit the Arctic region of North America (p. 164)

Inuktitut (ih•NOOK•tih•tut) *n.* the language of the Inuit (p. 170)

Islam *n.* a monotheistic religion based on the teachings of Muhammad and the writings of the Qur'an, the Muslim holy book (pp. 476, 504, 562, 676)

isolate *v.* to cut off or set apart from a group (p. 334)

Istanbul *n.* the largest city of Turkey, formerly called Constantinople (capital of the Byzantine, or Eastern Roman, Empire) and originally called Byzantium in ancient times (p. 688)

isthmus *n.* strip of land that connects two landmasses (p. 198)

ivory *n.* the hard white substance that makes up an elephant's tusk (p. 618)

J

jaguar *n.* a large cat mainly found in Central and South America (p. 212)

jazz *n.* a type of music that developed from a blending of African rhythms, American band music, and the musical styles of African Americans and Europeans (p. 138)

jellaba *n.* a traditional Berber garment; a robe with full sleeves (p. 568)

Jerusalem (juh•ROO•suh•luhm) *n.* the current capital of Israel and an ancient city that is holy to Judaism, Christianity, and Islam (p. 682)

joropo (huh•ROH•poh) *n.* Venezuelan national folk dance (p. 266)

Juárez, Benito (1806–1872) *n.* Indian who became president and a Mexican national hero (p. 230)

Judaism (JOO•day•IHZ•uhm) *n.* the monotheistic religion of the Jews, based on the writings of the Hebrew Bible (pp. 476, 682)

K

Kalahari *n.* a desert in southern Africa (p. 630)

Kanto Plain *n.* the largest lowland of Japan, which extends from the Japanese Alps east to the Pacific (p. 824)

Kara Kum *n.* a huge desert that covers most of Turkmenistan (p. 496)

karma *n.* in Hinduism, the consequences of a person's actions in this life, which determine his or her fate in the next life (p. 706)

Kashmir *n.* a region in the northwest part of the Indian subcontinent; India and Pakistan dispute control of Kashmir (p. 716)

Kente cloth *n.* a brightly colored, woven cloth made by the Ashanti and Ewe peoples (p. 586)

Kenyatta, Jomo *n.* independent Kenya's first president (p. 612)

Khmer (kmair) **Empire** *n.* an empire that began in the 500s and had gained control of much of mainland Southeast Asia by the 800s (p. 858)

kibbutz (kih•BOOTS) *n.* a type of settlement in Israel in which the community shares all wealth and property (p. 682)

Kim Jong Il *n.* the Communist leader of North Korea (p. 812)

kimchi (KIHM•chee) *n.* a Korean dish made of pickled vegetables (p. 804)

King, William Lyon Mackenzie *n.* Canadian prime minister who led his country to independence (p. 164)

knight *n.* a vassal trained in combat who fought on behalf of lords (p. 342)

Koizumi, Junichiro (KOH•EE•zoo•mee, JU•NEE•chee•roh) *n.* Japan's prime minister from 2001 to 2006 (p. 840)

Kongo *n.* a member of a people living along the lower Congo River; a Bantu-speaking kingdom of the Congo River region arising in the 1300s (p. 618)

Korean Peninsula *n.* a body of land bordered by the Yellow Sea to the west, the East Sea (or Sea of Japan) to the east, the Korea Strait to the south, and China and Russia to the north (p. 796)

Korean War (1950–1953) *n.* a conflict between North Korea and the Soviet Union on one side and South Korea, the United States, and the UN on the other (p. 804)

Korean Workers' Party (KWP) *n.* a Communist political group that controls the government of North Korea (p. 812)

Kosovo *n.* a self-governing province within Serbia (p. 440)

Kurd *n.* a member of an ethnic group that does not have its own country but whose homeland lies in parts of Turkey, Iraq, and Iran (p. 676)

Kush *n.* an ancient Nubian kingdom in northern Sudan (pp. 554, 606)

Kyushu (kee•OO•shoo) *n.* Japan's southernmost island and home to several large cities (p. 824)

L

lacrosse *n.* a team sport invented by Native Americans (p. 170)

Lake Balkhash *n.* a lake in eastern Kazakhstan (p. 496)

land bridge *n.* dry land that appeared between Asia and Alaska during the Ice Age (p. 130)

land reform *n.* dividing up large plots of land to distribute land more evenly (p. 630)

landform *n.* a feature on the Earth's surface formed by physical force (p. 34)

landlocked *adj.* surrounded by land with no access to an ocean or sea (pp. 272, 280, 496, 728)

Landsat *n.* a series of information-gathering satellites that orbit above Earth (p. 10)

language *n.* human communication, either written, spoken, or signed (p. 88)

language family *n.* a group of languages that have a common origin (p. 88)

Latin America *n.* the region that includes Mexico, Central America, the Caribbean Islands, and South America (p. 198)

legislature *n.* the law-making body of a government (p. 716)

Leopold II *n.* King of Belgium, who was forced to give up his private ownership of the Congo Free State (p. 618)

Lesser Antilles *n.* the smaller Caribbean islands southeast of the Greater Antilles (p. 198)

Lewis and Clark Expedition *n.* a journey made by Lewis and Clark to explore the Louisiana Territory (p. 130)

lineage *n.* descent from an ancestor (p. 544)

literacy *n.* the ability to read and write (p. 138)

llama *n.* a South American mammal related to the camel (p. 272)

llanos (YAH•nohs) *n.* grasslands of South America's Central Plains (pp. 204, 266)

location analyst *n.* a person who studies an area to find the best location for a client (p. 16)

location *n.* an exact position using latitude and longitude, or a description of a place in relation to places around it (p. 4)

lord *n.* a powerful landowner (p. 342)

Louisiana Purchase *n.* the action by which President Thomas Jefferson bought the Louisiana Territory from France in 1803 (p. 130)

Loyalist *n.* a person who supported Great Britain during the American Revolutionary War (p. 164)

M

Maghrib (MUHG•ruhb) *n.* the Arab name for North Africa, which means "the West" (p. 568)

magma *n.* molten rock (p. 26)

Magna Carta *n.* a charter, or document, signed by England's King John in 1215 that limited the power of the monarch and guaranteed nobles basic rights (p. 400)

Magyar *n.* an ethnic Hungarian person or the Hungarian language (p. 432)

mainland *n.* the primary landmass of a continent or territory rather than its islands or peninsulas (p. 400)

Malay Peninsula *n.* the second peninsula of mainland Southeast Asia; the narrow strip of land that serves as a bridge between the mainland and islands (p. 852)

Mali *n.* a West African empire between the A.D. 1200s and the A.D. 1500s; a modern West African country (p. 580)

Mandela, Nelson *n.* South Africa's first African president (p. 624)

manifest destiny *n.* the idea that the United States should own all the land between, and even beyond, the Atlantic and Pacific Oceans (p. 130)

manor *n.* a noble's house and the villages on his land where the peasants lived (p. 342)

Mao Zedong (MOW dzuh•dahng) *n.* Communist leader of China from 1949 to 1976 (p. 764)

Maori (MOW•ree) *n.* a Polynesian people who were the first inhabitants of New Zealand (p. 900)

map *n.* a representation of a part of the Earth (p. 10)

maquiladora (mah•kee•la•DOHR•uh) *n.* factory in which materials are imported and assembled into products for export (pp. 244, 254)

Marcos, Ferdinand *n.* dictatorial president of the Philippines between 1965 and 1986 (p. 864)

market economy *n.* an economic system in which the production of goods and services is decided by supply and the demand of consumers (pp. 72, 146, 382, 424, 486, 512)

marsupial (mahr•SOO•pee•uhl) *n.* an animal with an abdominal pouch to carry its young (p. 884)

Marxist *n.* a person who supports the philosophy behind communism, including government ownership of the land and the means of production (p. 630)

Mau Mau *n.* a Kenyan independence movement that began in the 1940s (p. 612)

Maya *n.* an early civilization located in what is now the Yucatán Peninsula, Guatemala, and northern Belize (p. 212)

mechanized *adj.* equipped with machinery (pp. 304, 892)

medieval *adj.* from the Middle Ages (p. 342)

Mekong River *n.* a major river that runs south from southern China through Laos, Cambodia, and Vietnam (p. 852)

Melanesia *n.* a subregion of Oceania that includes islands northeast of Australia and south of the equator (p. 912)

Mercosur *n.* association of several South American countries to promote trade among the countries (p. 280)

Mesopotamia *n.* the land between the Tigris and Euphrates rivers (p. 666)

mestizo (mehs•TEE•zoh) *n.* person with mixed European and Native American ancestry (pp. 220, 254)

Mexican Revolution *n.* a fight for reforms in Mexico from 1910 to 1920 (p. 230)

Micronesia *n.* a subregion of Oceania that includes islands east of the Philippines and north of the equator (p. 912)

microstate *n.* an independent country that is very small in area and population (p. 858)

Middle Ages *n.* the period between the fall of the Roman Empire and the modern era, from about A.D. 476 to 1453 (p. 342)

Middle Kingdom *n.* an ancient Chinese name for China (p. 764)

migration *n.* the process of relocating to a new region (p. 66)

militarism *n.* a government's aggressive use of its armed forces (p. 840)

millet *n.* a grain raised in West Africa, often made into porridge (p. 594)

Milosevic, Slobodan (muh•LOH•suh•VICH, SLAW•baw•dahn) *n.* president of Serbia from 1989 to 1997 and of Yugoslavia from 1997 to 2000; a key figure in the ethnic conflicts in the Balkans in the 1990s (p. 440)

missionary *n.* a person sent to do religious work in another place (p. 88)

Mississippi River *n.* the largest river and chief waterway of the United States (p. 122)

Mobuto Sese Seko (moh•BOO•too SAY•say SAY•koh) *n.* dictator of the Democratic Republic of the Congo from 1965 to 1997 (p. 618)

modernize *v.* to accept new ways or ideas (pp. 562, 606)

monarch *n.* a king or queen who rules a country or territory (p. 716)

monarchy *n.* a type of government in which a ruling family headed by a king or queen holds political power (pp. 78, 334)

monotheism *n.* a belief in one god (p. 676)

monsoon *n.* a seasonal wind system that produces a wet or dry season in a region, sometimes with heavy rainfall (pp. 612, 658, 796, 852)

Moors *n.* the group of Muslims from North Africa who conquered Spain in the eighth century (p. 370)

mosaic *n.* a picture made by placing small, colored pieces of stone, tile, or glass on a surface (p. 266)

Mount Everest *n.* the world's tallest mountain, located in the Himalayas (p. 658)

Mount Fuji *n.* Japan's highest mountain peak (p. 824)

Mount Kilimanjaro *n.* the highest mountain in Africa, in northeast Tanzania (p. 536)

Mount McKinley (also called Denali) *n.* the tallest mountain of North America, located in Alaska (p. 122)

Mount Paektu (PAHK•too) *n.* the highest mountain (9,003 feet) on the Korean Peninsula (p. 796)

Muhammad (also spelled Mohammed) *n.* the founder and major prophet of Islam (p. 676)

multicultural *adj.* relating to or including many different cultures (p. 408)

multilingual *n.* able to speak many languages (p. 376)

multinational corporation *n.* a company that operates in more than one country (p. 146)

mummy *n.* a body prepared for burial according to ancient Egyptian practice (p. 554)

mural *n.* a wall painting (pp. 236, 296)

Musa, Mansa (moo•SAH, MAHN•sah) *n.* leader of the Mali empire from 1312 to about 1337 (p. 580)

Muslim *n.* a follower of Islam (pp. 504, 562, 676)

N

Nagorno-Karabakh (nuh•GAWR•noh-KARH•uh•BAHK) *n.* a province in Azerbaijan that Armenians believe should be a part of their country (p. 512)

National People's Congress (NPC) *n.* China's national law-making body (p. 784)

nationalism *n.* pride in and loyalty to one's nation (pp. 350, 362)

natural resource *n.* something that is found in nature that is necessary or useful to humans (p. 72)

neutrality *n.* a policy of not taking part in war (p. 382)

Nile River *n.* the longest river in the world, which empties into the Mediterranean Sea in northeast Egypt (pp. 536, 554)

nirvana *n.* in Buddhism, a state of wisdom that breaks the cycle of reincarnation (p. 706)

Nkrumah, Kwame (uhn•KROO•muh, KWAHM•eh) *n.* modern Ghana's first president (p. 586)

nomad *n.* member of a group who makes a living by herding animals and moving from place to place as the seasons change (pp. 96, 504)

nonviolent resistance *n.* a method of protest that draws attention to a problem without using violence (p. 698)

Nordic *adj.* relating to Scandinavia (p. 388)

North American Free Trade Agreement (NAFTA) *n.* agreement that reduced trade barriers among Mexico, Canada, and the United States (pp. 244, 254)

North Atlantic Drift *n.* warm ocean current that helps keep Europe's climate mild (p. 326)

North China Plain *n.* the fertile region between the Huang He and Chang Jiang rivers (p. 764)

Northern European Plain *n.* vast area of flat or gently rolling land from France to Russia (pp. 326, 376)

Nubia *n.* in ancient times, the Nile River valley of southern Egypt and northern Sudan (p. 554)

Nunavut (NOO•nuh•VOOT) *n.* a territory created in 1999 from the eastern part of the Northwest Territories and home to many Inuit (p. 156)

O

oasis *n.* fertile or green spot in a desert created by underground water coming to the surface (p. 652)

obelisk *n.* a pillar-shaped stone monument (p. 606)

Oceania *n.* the region of the Pacific Ocean with thousands of islands (p. 912)

oceanic island *n.* an island rising from the deep sea floor on a volcanic foundation (p. 912)

official language *n.* a language that by law must be used for government, business, and education (p. 138)

oligarchy (AHL•ih•GAHR•kee) *n.* a government ruled by a few powerful individuals (pp. 78, 334)

Olmec *n.* an early civilization along the Gulf Coast of what is now southern Mexico (p. 212)

ombudsman *n.* an official who investigates citizens' complaints against the government (p. 388)

one-crop economy *n.* an economy that depends on a single crop for income (pp. 260, 512)

Organization of the Petroleum Exporting Countries (OPEC) *n.* a group of oil-producing countries founded in 1960 (p. 676)

Orthodox Christianity *n.* the Eastern branch of Christianity that spread to Russia in the 900s and became the state religion (p. 476)

Ottoman Empire *n.* a Muslim empire based in Turkey that lasted from the 1300s to 1922 (pp. 676, 688)

Outback *n.* the interior region of Australia (p. 884)

outcropping *n.* bedrock that rises above the soil (p. 884)

ozone hole *n.* the seasonal thinning of a protective layer of atmospheric gas high above Antarctica (p. 920)

P

Pakeha (PAH•kee•HAH) *n.* a Maori word that means "white people" (p. 900)

Palestine Liberation Organization (PLO) *n.* a political group that claims to represent all Palestinians and to be working toward gaining an independent Palestinian nation (pp. 682, 688)

Palestinian territories *n.* the West Bank and Gaza Strip combined (p. 682)

Pampas *n.* grassy plains in south-central South America (pp. 204, 280)

Pan-Africanism *n.* a movement calling for the unity of all people of African descent (p. 580)

papyrus *n.* a paperlike material made from the stems of the papyrus reed (p. 554)

Parliament *n.* the national legislature of the United Kingdom (pp. 176, 400)

parliamentary *adj.* relating to a government with the parliament form of legislature (p. 716)

patrician (puh•TRIHSH•uhn) *n.* a wealthy landowner who held a high government position in ancient Rome (p. 334)

patrilineal *adj.* descent from father to father (p. 544)

patron *n.* a wealthy or powerful person who provides money, support, and encouragement to an artist or a cause (p. 342)

peacekeeping *n.* referring to military forces whose purpose is to prevent or end war (p. 688)

Peloponnesus (PEHL•uh•puh•NEE•suhs) *n.* the peninsula in southern Greece where Sparta was located (p. 334)

penal colony *n.* a settlement that serves as a prison (p. 892)

peninsula *n.* a body of land nearly surrounded by water (pp. 326, 796)

Perkins, Charles *n.* in Australia, an aboriginal rights leader (p. 892)

permafrost *n.* ground that is frozen throughout the year (p. 460)

persecution *n.* cruel treatment on the basis of religion, race, ethnic group, nationality, political views, gender, or class (p. 66)

Persia *n.* a historic region of Southwest Asia located mostly in what is now Iran (p. 676)

perspective *n.* a technique used by artists to give the appearance of depth and distance (p. 342)

Peter the Great *n.* a czar who ruled Russia from 1682 to 1725 and tried to make Russia more European (p. 468)

pharaoh *n.* a ruler of ancient Egypt (p. 554)

pidgin *n.* a simple form of speech that is a mixture of words from two or more languages (p. 912)

Piedmont (PEED•MAHNT) *n.* a hilly, upland region between the Appalachian Mountains and the coastal plain of the South (p. 122)

place *n.* a geographical term that describes the physical and human characteristics of a location (p. 4)

plantation agriculture *n.* the use of large farms to raise cash crops (p. 736)

plateau *n.* a high area of flat land (pp. 34, 198, 652, 756)

Plateau of Iran *n.* a high plateau in central and eastern Iran, surrounded by mountains (p. 652)

Plaza of the Three Cultures *n.* plaza in Mexico City that shows parts of Aztec, Spanish, and modern influences in Mexico (p. 236)

plebeian (plih•BEE•uhn) *n.* a commoner who was allowed to vote but not to hold government office in ancient Rome (p. 334)

polders (POHL•durz) *n.* land reclaimed by draining it of water with the use of a dam and pump (p. 376)

Polynesia *n.* a subregion of Oceania that includes islands of the central and southern Pacific (pp. 900, 912)

polytheistic *adj.* believing in many gods (p. 666)

population *n.* the number of people who live in a specified area (p. 58)

population density *n.* the average number of people who live in a certain area (p. 58)

porridge *n.* a soft food, made by boiling cereal grain in milk or water (p. 612)

precipitation *n.* falling water droplets in the form of rain, snow, sleet, or hail (p. 40)

prime minister *n.* the head of the cabinet and chief executive of government in a parliamentary system; for example, the head of the Canadian government (pp. 176, 716)

privatization (PRY•vuh•tih•ZAY•shuhn) *n.* the process of selling government-owned businesses to private individuals (p. 486)

privatize *v.* to sell government-owned businesses to private individuals (p. 512)

propaganda *n.* distorted or inaccurate information that is deliberately used to influence opinion (p. 476)

protectorate *n.* a weaker country or area controlled by a stronger country (p. 562)

Protestant *n.* a member of a Christian Church founded on the principles of the Reformation (p. 342)

province *n.* a governmental division like a state (pp. 156, 784)

Prussia *n.* the most powerful German state in the Holy Roman Empire (p. 382)

public education *n.* schooling that is paid for by the government (p. 138)

pull factor *n.* a reason that attracts people to another area (p. 66)

Punic (PYOO•nik) **Wars** *n.* wars fought between Rome and Carthage during the third and second centuries B.C. (p. 568)

push factor *n.* a reason that causes people to leave an area (pp. 66, 236)

Putin (POOT•ihn), **Vladimir** *n.* president of Russia who increased executive power in the 2000s (p. 486)

Pygmy *n.* a member of a people with an average height of less than five feet (p. 618)

pyramid *n.* an ancient Egyptian structure, built over or around a tomb (p. 554)

Q

quilombos (kih•LOHM•buhs) *n.* communities created by escaped African slaves (p. 296)

quinoa (kih•NOH•uh) *n.* a kind of weed from the Andean region that produces a small grain (p. 272)

quota *n.* a target amount for production (p. 618)

R

rain forest *n.* a broadleaf tree region in a tropical climate (pp. 204, 304)

Ramadan *n.* the ninth month of the Muslim calendar, during which Muslims fast from sunrise to sunset each day (p. 728)

rate of natural increase *n.* the death rate subtracted from the birth rate (p. 58)

raw material *n.* an unprocessed natural resource that will be converted to a finished product (p. 72)

Reconquista *n.* the successful effort by the Spanish to drive the Moors out of Spain (p. 370)

Red Sea *n.* a narrow sea that divides northeast Africa from the Arabian Peninsula (p. 606)

reform *n.* action to improve social or economic conditions (p. 784)

Reformation *n.* a movement in the 1500s to change practices in the Catholic Church (p. 342)

refugee *n.* a person who flees a place to find safety (pp. 66, 440)

region *n.* an area that has one or more common characteristics that unite or connect it with other areas (p. 4)

reincarnation *n.* the rebirth of a soul in another body (p. 706)

relief *n.* the difference in the elevation of a landform from its lowest point to its highest point (p. 34)

religion *n.* an organized system of beliefs and practices, often centered on one or more gods (p. 88)

remote sensing *n.* obtaining information about a site by using an instrument that is not physically in contact with the site (p. 10)

Renaissance (REHN•ih•SAHNS) *n.* a rebirth of creativity, literature, and learning in Europe from about 1300 to 1600 (p. 342)

renewable energy sources *n.* sources of energy able to be replaced through ongoing natural processes (p. 326)

representative democracy *n.* a type of government in which citizens hold political power through elected representatives (pp. 78, 146)

representative government *n.* a system of government with a legislature that is at least partly elected by the people (p. 400)

republic *n.* a government in which citizens elect representatives to rule in their name; another term for representative democracy (pp. 146, 334)

Republic of Texas *n.* constitutional government of Texas after independence from Mexico (p. 230)

reunify *v.* to bring something that has been separated back together (p. 382)

revolution *n.* the overthrow of a ruler or government; a major change in ideas (p. 230)

Rhodesia *n.* the colonial name for the countries that are today Zambia and Zimbabwe (p. 630)

rig *v.* to influence or fix the results of an election (p. 594)

Ring of Fire *n.* a geographic zone that extends along the rim of the Pacific Ocean and has numerous volcanoes and earthquakes (pp. 26, 824)

Rio de Janeiro (REE•oh day zhuh•NAYR•OH) *n.* Brazil's capital city from 1763 to 1960 (p. 290)

ritual *n.* a set of regularly followed ceremonies (p. 774)

Rivera, Diego *n.* famous muralist who painted the history of Mexico on the walls of the National Palace (p. 236)

Rocky Mountains *n.* a mountain range that extends about 3,000 miles from New Mexico to Alaska (p. 122)

Romance language *n.* any of the languages that developed from the Roman language, Latin, such as Spanish, Portuguese, French, Italian, and Romanian (p. 362)

Rose Revolution *n.* a peaceful uprising in Soviet Georgia that helped force a corrupt president to resign (p. 512)

Rosetta Stone *n.* an ancient Egyptian stone that provided a key to decipher hieroglyphics (p. 562)

Royal Canadian Mounted Police *n.* an organization of officers who were responsible for law enforcement in the Canadian West (p. 170)

rural *adj.* having to do with the countryside (pp. 58, 236)

Russification *n.* the effort to make countries occupied by the Soviet Union more Russian by replacing local languages and customs (pp. 424, 504)

S

Sadat, Anwar el- *n.* president of Egypt from 1970 to 1981 (p. 562)

safari *n.* an overland expedition for exploring, hunting, or photography (p. 612)

Sahara *n.* the world's largest desert (p. 536)

Sahel (suh•HAYL) *n.* a semiarid region just south of the Sahara (p. 536)

samba (SAM•buh) *n.* music and dance, with roots in African rhythms; the most famous form of Brazilian music worldwide (p. 296)

Sami *n.* people of northern Scandinavia who traditionally herd reindeer; also the name of their language (p. 388)

samurai (SAM•uh•RY) *n.* professional soldiers of Japan (p. 830)

San Martín, José de *n.* leader for independence in southern South America (pp. 220, 280)

sanction *n.* a penalty or pressure applied to a country for not obeying an order or law (p. 624)

Sanskrit *n.* an ancient language of India, first spoken by the Aryans (p. 698)

Santa Anna, Antonio López de (1794–1876) *n.* Mexican general, president, and leader of Mexican independence from Spain (p. 230)

savanna *n.* a vegetation region in the tropics or subtropics with a mix of grassland and scattered trees (pp. 40, 536)

scholar-official *n.* an educated person who worked in China's government (p. 764)

Scientific Revolution *n.* a major change in European thinking in the mid-1500s that led to the questioning of old theories (p. 350)

Scott, Robert *n.* a British polar explorer (p. 920)

seafaring *adj.* using the sea for transportation (p. 326)

secular *adj.* worldly or not related to religion (p. 342)

sediment *n.* pieces of rock in the form of sand, stone, or silt deposited by wind, water, or ice (p. 26)

segregation *n.* the policy of separating people of different races (p. 624)

seismic (SYZ•mihk) *adj.* having to do with earthquakes (p. 756)

Selassie, Haile (suh•LAS•ee, HY•lee) *n.* emperor of Ethiopia from 1930 to 1974 (p. 606)

self-rule *n.* independent government (p. 580)

self-sufficient *adj.* able to provide for one's own needs without outside help (p. 304)

selva *n.* Spanish name for the eastern Peruvian regions that contain rain forests (p. 272)

separatist *n.* a person who wants a region to break away from the nation it is a part of (pp. 164, 370)

serf *n.* in Europe, a person who lived and worked on the manor of a lord or vassal; in Russia, a peasant who is bound to the land (pp. 342, 468)

service industry *n.* an industry that provides services rather than objects (p. 254)

Seven Years' War (1756–1763) *n.* a conflict between Britain and France that was fought in North America, Europe, and India (p. 164)

shadow puppet *n.* traditional Indonesian art, in which puppets are handled from behind a screen lit by a bright light (p. 864)

shah *n.* title for the king of Persia or Iran (p. 676)

Shakespeare, William *n.* English playwright and poet during the late 16th and early 17th centuries (p. 408)

shamanism (SHAH•muh•NIHZ•uhm) *n.* a belief system in which a person called a shaman is believed to be able to communicate with spirits and heal the sick (p. 804)

Shi Huangdi (shee hwahng•dee) *n.* the first emperor to unify much of China (p. 764)

Shikoku (shee•KAW•koo) *n.* Japan's smallest and least populated major island (p. 824)

Shinto *n.* Japan's original religion; involves worshiping gods believed to be found in nature (p. 830)

shock therapy *n.* in Russia, term applied to Yeltsin's economic plan, which called for an abrupt shift from a command economy to a market economy (p. 486)

shogun *n.* the leader of the military government of Japan beginning in 1192 (p. 830)

Siam *n.* the former name of Thailand (p. 858)

Siberia *n.* a huge region in Asian Russia (p. 460)

Sierra Madre Occidental *n.* mountain range that runs from north to south down the western part of Mexico (p. 198)

Sierra Madre Oriental *n.* mountain range that runs from north to south down the eastern part of Mexico (p. 198)

Silk Roads *n.* major trade routes that ran from China to the rest of East Asia, through Central Asia, and into Europe (pp. 504, 774)

silt *n.* the fine, fertile soil carried by rivers and deposited on nearby lands (pp. 554, 666)

Solidarity *n.* Poland's first independent labor union, cofounded by Lech Walesa (p. 424)

solstice *n.* the time during the year when the sun reaches the farthest northern or southern point in the sky (p. 40)

Songhai (sawng•hy) *n.* an ancient West African empire, which was most powerful about A.D. 1500 (p. 580)

souk (sook) *n.* open-air market common in North Africa (p. 568)

Southern Alps *n.* a mountain chain in New Zealand (p. 884)

Southern Cone *n.* South American nations located in the cone-shaped southernmost part of South America (p. 280)

Soviet Union *n.* a Communist nation, consisting of Russia and 14 other states, that existed from 1922 to 1991 (p. 728)

spatial *adj.* referring to where a place is located and its physical relationship to other places, people, or environments (p. 4)

specialization *n.* a focus on producing a limited number of a specific product (p. 72)

squatter *n.* person who settles on unoccupied land without having legal claim to it (p. 236)

St. Lawrence Seaway *n.* a waterway made up of the St. Lawrence River, the Great Lakes, and several canals (p. 156)

stability *n.* durability; resistance to change (p. 586)

Stalin, Joseph *n.* a cruel 20th-century dictator who had millions of his political enemies executed (pp. 468, 512)

standard of living *n.* an economic measure relating to the quality and amount of goods available to a group of people and how those goods are distributed across the group (p. 432)

stateless societies *n.* groups that have no single authority, but make decisions based on compromise (p. 544)

steppe *n.* a grassy plain; in Russia, this area lies south of the taiga (p. 460)

Stone Age *n.* the earliest period of human culture, in which people used stone tools (p. 544)

strategic *adj.* relating to a plan of action designed to achieve a specific goal; in relation to the military, helpful in the fighting of a war (pp. 432, 728)

subcontinent *n.* a large landmass that is part of a continent but is considered a separate region (p. 658)

subsistence farming *n.* farming that produces just enough to feed the farmer's family, with little or nothing left over to sell (pp. 254, 586, 728, 736)

Sudan *n.* a country of northeast Africa, located south of Egypt (p. 562)

Suez Canal *n.* a waterway linking the Red Sea with the Mediterranean Sea (p. 562)

Sumer *n.* a region of city-states in Mesopotamia that was home to the first civilization (p. 666)

surveyor *n.* a person who maps and measures the land (pp. 10, 16)

sustainable *adj.* refers to using natural resources in such a way that they exist for future generations (p. 48)

Swahili *n.* an African language, commonly spoken in East Africa (p. 612)

T

taiga *n.* (TY•guh) a vast forest in Russia that lies south of the tundra (p. 460)

Taino (TY•noh) *n.* Indian group in the Caribbean islands (p. 260)

Taj Mahal *n.* a beautiful tomb in India built by the Mughal ruler Shah Jahan to honor his wife, who died in 1631 (p. 698)

Taklimakan (TAH•kluh•muh•KAHN) **Desert** *n.* the second largest sand desert in the world (p. 756)

Taliban *n.* a conservative Islamic group that took control of Afghanistan in the mid-1990s (p. 728)

technology *n.* people's application of knowledge, tools, and inventions to meet their needs (p. 96)

tectonic plate *n.* a large rigid section of the Earth's crust that is in constant motion (pp. 26, 198, 536)

territory *n.* a Canadian political unit that doesn't have enough people to be a province (p. 156)

Tet *n.* the Vietnamese New Year and most important holiday in Viet Nam (p. 858)

theocracy *n.* a government run by religious leaders (p. 676)

Three Gorges Dam *n.* a barrier built on the Chang Jiang to control floods (p. 756)

Three Kingdoms *n.* the three kingdoms that had formed on the Korean Peninsula by A.D. 300 (p. 804)

three-dimensional *adj.* describing an image in which there is a sense of depth and perspective (p. 4)

Tiananmen (tyahn•ahn•mehn) **Square** *n.* the location in Beijing, China, of a huge demonstration for democratic rights that occurred in 1989 (p. 784)

Tian Shan (TYAHN SHAHN) *n.* a mountain range that runs across Kyrgyzstan and Tajikistan (p. 496)

Tigris River *n.* a river of Southwest Asia that flows from a plateau on the Anatolian peninsula to the Persian Gulf (p. 652)

Tito, Josip Broz *n.* the Communist leader of Yugoslavia from 1953 to 1980 (p. 440)

Tokugawa Ieyasu (TOH•koo•GAH•wah EE•yeh•YAH•soo) *n.* shogun who unified Japan (p. 830)

Tolstoy (TOHL•stoy), **Leo** *n.* a 19th-century writer who is one of Russia's greatest novelists (p. 476)

totalitarian (toh•tal•ih•TAIR•ee•uhn) *adj.* referring to a type of government that controls every aspect of public and private life (pp. 468, 812)

tourism *n.* industry that provides services for travelers (p. 260)

Transantarctic Mountains *n.* mountains that divide Antarctica into two parts (p. 920)

Transcaucasia (TRANS•kaw•KAY•zhyuh) *n.* a region between the Black and Caspian seas that contains the republics of Armenia, Azerbaijan (AZ•uhr•by•ZHYAHN), and Georgia (p. 496)

transcontinental railroad *n.* a railroad that crosses a continent (p. 130)

trans-Saharan *adj.* across the Sahara (p. 580)

Treaty of Tordesillas (TAWR•day•SEEL•yahs) *n.* 1494 treaty between Spain and Portugal that gave Portugal control over land that is now Brazil (p. 290)

Treaty of Waitangi (WY•TAHNG•gee) *n.* a treaty between the British and the Maori signed in 1840 (p. 900)

trust territory *n.* a territory placed under the control of a country by the United Nations (p. 912)

tsunami (tsu•NAH•mee) *n.* a series of giant, destructive ocean waves caused by underwater earthquakes, volcanoes, or landslides (pp. 658, 736, 852)

tundra *n.* a cold, dry climate and vegetation adapted to the climate in the Arctic Circle; in Russia, located in the far north (pp. 156, 460)

typhoon *n.* a tropical storm that starts in the western Pacific or Indian oceans (p. 796)

tyrant *n.* someone who takes power illegally (p. 334)

U

Uluru (oo•LOO•roo) *n.* a spectacular rock outcropping in the Australian Outback (p. 884)

Union of Soviet Socialist Republics (USSR), or **Soviet Union** *n.* a nation with a Communist government created by the Bolsheviks in 1922; dissolved in 1991 (p. 468)

unwritten constitution *n.* a framework for government that is not a single written document but includes many different laws, court decisions, and political customs (p. 414)

Ural Mountains *n.* a north-south mountain range that forms the border between European and Asian Russia (p. 460)

urban *adj.* having to do with a city (pp. 16, 58, 236)

urban planner *n.* a person who creates plans for developing and improving parts of a city (p. 16)

urbanization *n.* growth in the number of people living in urban areas; the process of city development (pp. 58, 290)

V

vassal *n.* a less wealthy noble who paid taxes to and served a lord in exchange for land (p. 342)

Vatican *n.* the official residence of the pope in Vatican City, and the political and religious center of the Roman Catholic Church (p. 362)

Vedas *n.* ancient Sanskrit writings that are the earliest sacred texts of Hinduism (p. 698)

vegetation region *n.* an area that has similar plants (p. 40)

Velvet Revolution *n.* the peaceful protest by the Czech people that led to the smooth end of communism in Czechoslovakia (p. 432)

Victoria Falls *n.* a 355-foot waterfall on the Zambezi River in South Central Africa (p. 536)

Vikings *n.* a seafaring Scandinavian people who raided northern and western Europe from the 9th to the 11th century (p. 388)

volcano *n.* an opening in the Earth's crust from which molten rock, ash, and hot gases flow or are thrown out (p. 26)

Volga River *n.* the longest river in Europe, flowing through European Russia (p. 460)

W

Walesa, Lech (wah•LEHN•suh, lehk) *n.* Polish leader who cofounded Solidarity and served as president of Poland from 1990 to 1995 (p. 424)

weather *n.* the condition of the Earth's atmosphere at a given time and place (p. 40)

weathering *n.* the gradual physical and chemical breakdown of rocks on the surface of the Earth (p. 26)

welfare state *n.* a social system in which the government provides for many of its citizens' needs (p. 388)

West Bank *n.* a region west of the Jordan River (p. 682)

wind farm *n.* a power plant that uses windmills to generate electricity (p. 414)

X

Xi Jiang (she jyahng) *n.* a river in southeast China (p. 756)

Y

Yalu River *n.* the longest river on the Korean Peninsula; forms part of the border between China and North Korea; known as the Amnok River in Korean (p. 796)

Yeltsin (YEHLT•sihn), **Boris** *n.* president who abruptly transformed the Russian economy after the Soviet Union collapsed (p. 486)

Yoruba (YAWR•uh•buh) *n.* a people of southwestern Nigeria, parts of Benin, and Togo (p. 586)

Yugoslavia *n.* a country on the Balkan Peninsula from 1918 to 1991 (p. 440)

yurt *n.* a portable, tentlike structure used by the nomads of Central Asia (p. 504)

Z

zaibatsu (ZY•baht•SOO) *n.* large family-controlled banking and industrial groups that owned many companies in Japan before World War II (p. 840)

Zaire *n.* the Democratic Republic of the Congo's name between 1971 and 1997 (p. 618)

ziggurat (ZIG•oo•rat) *n.* a temple built atop a series of increasingly smaller platforms (p. 666)

Spanish Glossary

A

aborigine [aborigen] *s.* habitante originario de Australia (pág. 892)

African National Congress (ANC) [Congreso Nacional Africano] *s.* partido político sudafricano que se oponía al *apartheid* (pág. 624)

Afrikaner [afrikáner] *s.* sudafricano descendiente de europeos que habla un idioma denominado afrikáans (pág. 624)

agricultural revolution [revolución agrícola] *s.* el cambio de recolectar alimentos a cultivarlos (pág. 96)

Aksum *s.* imperio que controló la mayor parte del norte de Etiopía desde el siglo I hasta el siglo VIII a.C. (pág. 606)

alpaca *s.* mamífero suramericano de la misma familia que la llama (pág. 272)

Alpine [alpino] *adj.* relativo a la cadena montañosa de los Alpes (pág. 382)

Alps [Alpes, los] *s.* la cadena montañosa más alta de Europa, que se extiende por el sur de Europa (pág. 326)

altiplano *s.* meseta situada a gran altitud (págs. 204, 272)

Amazon River [río Amazonas] *s.* el río más extenso de Suramérica (aproximadamente 4,000 millas o 6,400 kilómetros) y el segundo más extenso del mundo (pág. 204)

amendment [enmienda] *s.* cambio realizado por escrito a la Constitución de EUA, que debe pasar un proceso de aprobación (pág. 146)

Amundsen, Roald *s.* explorador polar noruego, primero en llegar al Polo Sur (pág. 920)

Anatolian peninsula [península de Anatolia] *s.* en el sudoeste de Asia, entre el mar Negro y el mar Mediterráneo (pág. 652)

ancestor [ancestro] *s.* antepasado (pág. 544)

Andes Mountains [Cordillera de los Andes] *s.* cadena montañosa ubicada en la costa oeste de Suramérica, que se extiende a lo largo de todo el continente (pág. 204)

animism [animismo] *s.* creencia en la existencia de espíritus en los animales, plantas, fuerzas naturales y ancestros (pág. 544)

annex [anexar] *v.* añadir a un territorio existente (pág. 230)

Antarctic Peninsula [Península Antártica] *s.* península en forma de S que forma parte de la cadena de la cordillera de los Andes (pág. 920)

Antarctic Treaty [Tratado Antártico] *s.* acuerdo firmado en 1959 que acordó el uso pacífico de la Antártida (pág. 920)

anthropologist [antropólogo] *s.* científico que estudia la cultura (pág. 88)

apartheid [*apartheid*] *s.* política oficial de segregación racial establecida en Sudáfrica desde 1950 hasta 1991 (pág. 624)

Appalachian Mountains [montes Apalaches] *s.* cadena montañosa en el este de los Estados Unidos, que corre paralela al océano Atlántico (pág. 122)

Aquino, Corazon [Corazón Aquino] *s.* política que se opuso a Marcos y fue presidenta de las Filipinas entre 1986 y 1992 (pág. 864)

Arabian Peninsula [Península Arábiga] *s.* península del sudoeste de Asia, entre el mar Rojo y el golfo Pérsico (pág. 652)

Aral Sea [Mar de Aral] *s.* cuerpo de agua interior ubicado en Asia central que se está reduciendo de manera continua (pág. 496)

archipelago [archipiélago] *s.* conjunto de islas agrupadas, que a veces toma la forma de un arco curvo (págs. 198, 736, 852, 864)

artisan [artesano] *s.* trabajador hábil en fabricar con sus manos productos o arte (pág. 254)

Aryan [ario] *s.* uno de los grupos de pastores nómadas indoeuropeos, que se cree emigraron al subcontinente indio (pág. 698)

Ashanti [asante o ashanti] *s.* un pueblo de Ghana (págs. 580, 586)

Aswan High Dam [presa de Asuán] *s.* estructura para controlar las inundaciones del río Nilo y para proporcionar electricidad (pág. 554)

Atlas Mountains [montes Atlas] *s.* grupo de cadenas montañosas que se extiende desde Marruecos hasta Túnez (pág. 568)

atmosphere [atmósfera] *s.* capa de gases que rodea la Tierra (pág. 34)

atoll [atolón] *s.* arrecife de coral en forma de anillo que contiene una laguna central sin islas en su interior (pág. 912)

Aung, San Suu Kyi *s.* líder del movimiento democrático de Myanmar (pág. 858)

autonomy [autonomía] *s.* gobernabilidad propia o independencia (pág. 376)

Aztec [azteca] *s.* antigua civilización del valle de México (pág. 212)

B

Bahasa Indonesia [indonesio] *s.* lengua común de Indonesia (pág. 864)

Baltic States [Países Bálticos] *s.* Letonia, Lituania y Estonia, tres países cuyas costas dan al mar Báltico (pág. 424)

Bangalore [Bengaluru] *s.* ciudad en el sur de la región central de la India que alberga muchas industrias de tecnología de punta (pág. 716)

basin [cuenca] *s.* región drenada por un sistema fluvial (pág. 536)

Basque [vasco] *s.* grupo étnico que vive en los Pirineos occidentales y a lo largo del golfo de Vizcaya, en España y Francia; también el nombre de su idioma (pág. 370)

Bechuanaland [Bechuanalandia] *s.* nombre colonial de Botsuana (pág. 630)

Bedouin [beduino] *s.* pueblo de habla árabe y tradicionalmente nómada del sudoeste de Asia (pág. 676)

Beirut *s.* capital del Líbano y centro bancario y financiero (pág. 688)

Benelux *s.* nombre de la unión económica formada por Bélgica, los Países Bajos y Luxemburgo para asegurar la rapidez y la eficiencia en el movimiento de personas, bienes y servicios entre los tres países (pág. 376)

Berbers [bereberes] *s.* habitantes originarios del norte de África y el Sahara (pág. 568)

Berlin Wall [Muro de Berlín] *s.* muro construido por el gobierno comunista de Alemania Oriental para separar Berlín Oriental de Berlín Occidental; derribado en 1991 (pág. 382)

Bhagavad-Gita *s.* uno de los escritos sagrados del hinduismo (pág. 706)

Biafra *s.* región de Nigeria, habitada mayormente por igbos (o ibos), que declaró su independencia en 1967 pero se rindió después de perder una guerra civil con Nigeria en 1970 (pág. 586)

bilingual [bilingüe] *adj.* que usa o es capaz de usar correctamente dos idiomas (pág. 164)

bipedal [bípedo] *adj.* que camina en dos pies (pág. 544)

birth rate [tasa de natalidad] *s.* cantidad de nacimientos por año, por cada 1,000 personas (pág. 58)

blues [*blues*] *s.* tipo de música donde las letras de las canciones expresan congoja, habitualmente debido a problemas amorosos o a las penurias de la vida (pág. 138)

Boer [bóer] *s.* colono o descendiente de colonos holandeses de Sudáfrica (pág. 624)

Bogotá *s.* capital de Colombia (pág. 266)

Bolívar, Simón *s.* líder independentista del norte de Suramérica (págs. 220, 266)

Bolsheviks [bolcheviques] *s.* grupo de revolucionarios que tomó el control del gobierno de Rusia en 1917 (pág. 468)

Bosniac [bosnio] *s.* grupo étnico musulmán de Bosnia-Herzegovina (pág. 440)

bossa nova *s.* versión estilo *jazz* de la samba, un baile brasileño (pág. 296)

Botero, Fernando *s.* artista colombiano famoso por sus retratos de personas con figuras exageradas (pág. 266)

boycott [boicotear] *v.* dejar de comprar y de usar productos de ciertos orígenes, a modo de protesta (pág. 304)

brain drain [fuga de cerebros] *s.* pérdida de trabajadores calificados que emigran en búsqueda de mejores oportunidades laborales (pág. 424)

Brasília [Brasilia] *s.* capital actual de Brasil (pág. 290)

bread basket [granero] *s.* región de producción abundante de granos (pág. 424)

Briton [británico] *s.* natural de Gran Bretaña (pág. 408)

Buddha [Buda] *s.* palabra que significa "el iluminado", usada para denominar a Siddhartha Gautama, el fundador del budismo (págs. 698, 706, 774)

Buddhism [budismo] *s.* una de las principales religiones del mundo, que se inició en la India y se basa en las enseñanzas de Siddhartha Gautama (págs. 476, 698, 706, 774, 804)

Byzantine Empire [Imperio Bizantino] *s.* la mitad oriental del Imperio Romano, que sobrevivió más de mil años después de la caída de Roma (pág. 362)

C

cabinet system [sistema parlamentario] *s.* sistema de gobierno que vincula el poder ejecutivo y el legislativo a través de la elección de un primer ministro y varios ministros de la legislatura (pág. 176)

Cabral, Pedro Álvares *s.* explorador portugués que en el año 1500 reclamó como posesión portuguesa parte del territorio actual de Brasil (pág. 290)

camel [camello] *s.* mamífero con gibas en su dorso utilizado en el desierto como animal de transporte y para la producción de carne, leche y algodón (pág. 580)

Camp David Accords [Acuerdos de Camp David] *s.* tratado de paz entre Egipto e Israel, negociado por el presidente de EUA, Jimmy Carter, el presidente de Egipto, Anwar el-Sadat, y el primer ministro israelí, Menachem Begin, firmado en la residencia presidencial de Maryland, en 1979 (pág. 562)

Canadian Shield [escudo canadiense] *s.* planicie rocosa con forma de herradura que cubre gran parte del este de la región central de Canadá (pág. 156)

candomblé *s.* prácticas religiosas africanas que se mezclan con creencias católicas para crear un sistema único de creencias (pág. 296)

canopy [cubierta forestal] *s.* la capa superior de un bosque, formada por las copas de los árboles (pág. 536)

Cape Colony [Colonia del Cabo] *s.* territorio sudafricano donde se establecieron los colonos holandeses denominados bóers a fines del siglo XVII y principios del siglo XVIII (pág. 624)

capoeira *s.* danza brasileña combinada con artes marciales (pág. 296)

Caracas *s.* capital de Venezuela (pág. 266)

carbon dioxide [dióxido de carbono] *s.* gas compuesto de carbono y oxígeno (pág. 48)

Caribbean Community and Common Market (CARICOM) [Comunidad del Caribe] *s.* organización comercial de varias naciones del Caribe (pág. 260)

Carthage [Cartago] *s.* antigua ciudad estado del norte de África (pág. 568)

cartographer [cartógrafo] *s.* geógrafo que traza mapas (pág. 10)

Caspian Sea [Mar Caspio] *s.* gran cuerpo de agua en el límite sur de Rusia, ubicado entre Transcaucasia y Asia Central (págs. 460, 496)

caste [casta] *s.* en la India, clase social a la cual se pertenece desde el nacimiento (pág. 698)

cataract [catarata] *s.* salto grande de agua o rápidos (pág. 554)

Caucasus Mountains [cordillera del Cáucaso] *s.* cadena montañosa que se extiende entre el mar Negro y el mar Caspio (pág. 496)

celadon [porcelana *celadón*] *s.* cerámica vidriada de Corea con un barniz de brillo azul tenue o verde (pág. 804)

Central America Free Trade Agreement (CAFTA) [Tratado de Libre Comercio entre Estados Unidos y América Central] *s.* acuerdo para fomentar el comercio entre los Estados Unidos y los países de América Central (págs. 254, 260)

Central Asia [Asia Central] *s.* región que comprende las repúblicas de Kazajistán, Kirguistán, Tayikistán, Turkmenistán y Uzbekistán (pág. 496)

cession [cesión] *s.* territorio entregado (pág. 230)

chaebol [*chaebol*] *s.* en Corea, un conglomerado familiar que se compone de empresas afines (pág. 812)

Chang Jiang [Yangsté] *s.* el río más extenso de Asia, que fluye a través del este de China (pág. 756)

Channel Tunnel [*Eurotúnel*] *s.* túnel ferroviario entre Francia e Inglaterra que corre bajo el Canal de la Mancha (pág. 414)

Chechnya [Chechenia] *s.* república mayormente islámica del sudoeste de Rusia que continúa su lucha por la independencia (pág. 486)

Cheju Island [Isla de Jeju] *s.* la isla más grande de la costa sur de la península de Corea (pág. 796)

chinampas *s.* en México, islas artificiales utilizadas para la agricultura (pág. 212)

Christianity [cristianismo] *s.* religión monoteísta basada en la vida y las enseñanzas de Jesús de Nazaret y en las escrituras de la Biblia cristiana (pág. 682)

Church of England [Iglesia de Inglaterra o Anglicana] *s.* iglesia oficial de Inglaterra, cuya cabeza es el Arzobispo de Canterbury (pág. 408)

citizen [ciudadano] *s.* persona que debe lealtad a un país y recibe su protección (pág. 78)

city-state [ciudad estado] *s.* unidad política compuesta de una ciudad y las tierras a su alrededor (págs. 334, 666)

Civil War [Guerra Civil o de Secesión] (1861–1865) *s.* conflicto entre el Norte y el Sur de EUA sobre las cuestiones de los derechos de los estados y la esclavitud (pág. 130)

civilization [civilización] *s.* una forma de cultura avanzada que se desarrolló en las ciudades (pág. 666)

clan *s.* grupo de familias que tienen en común los mismos ancestros (pág. 830)

climate [clima] *s.* condiciones habituales del tiempo de una región durante un largo período de tiempo (pág. 40)

climatologist [climatólogo] *s.* geógrafo que estudia los climas (pág. 16)

coalition [coalición] *s.* alianza o asociación, habitualmente transitoria (pág. 362)

Cold War [Guerra Fría] *s.* conflicto entre los Estados Unidos y la Unión Soviética tras la Segunda Guerra Mundial, que nunca se desarrolló en forma de combate armado explícito (pág. 468)

colonia *s.* un vecindario de México (pág. 236)

colonialism [colonialismo] *s.* control de una potencia sobre un área o sobre personas que dependen de ella (pág. 858)

colony [colonia] *s.* grupo de personas que se asientan en una tierra lejana pero están gobernadas por su madre patria, como los Estados Unidos; territorio de ultramar gobernado por una nación, como México desde el siglo XVI hasta 1821 (págs. 130, 220)

Columbian Exchange [intercambio colombino] *s.* traslado de plantas y animales entre América Latina y Europa, después del viaje de Colón a América en 1492 d.C. (pág. 220)

Columbus, Christopher [Cristobal Colón] *s.* navegante y explorador italiano que navegaba al servicio de España y exploró el Caribe y las costas de América Central y de Suramérica (pág. 370)

command economy [economía planificada] *s.* sistema económico en donde la producción de bienes y servicios es decidida por un gobierno central (págs. 72, 424, 486, 512, 784)

commonwealth [mancomunidad] *s.* unidad política de gobierno autónomo que está asociada a otro país (pág. 260)

Commonwealth of Nations [Mancomunidad Británica de Naciones] *s.* asociación compuesta por el Reino Unido y muchas antiguas colonias británicas (págs. 164, 400, 624)

communal [comunal] *adj.* relativo a la posesión compartida de los bienes (pág. 774)

communism [comunismo] *s.* tipo de gobierno en donde el Partido Comunista posee la totalidad del poder político y controla la economía (págs. 78, 260, 424, 468, 764)

compulsory [obligatorio] *adj.* exigido (pág. 362)

Confucianism [confucianismo] *s.* sistema de creencias basado en las enseñanzas de Confucio, un sabio chino (págs. 764, 774, 804)

conglomerate [conglomerado] *s.* organización compuesta por varias empresas de diferentes industrias (pág. 812)

Congo River [río Congo] *s.* el segundo río más extenso de África (pág. 618)

conquistador s. explorador y guerrero español que llegó al continente americano en el siglo XVI (pág. 220)

Constitution [Constitución] *s.* documento que es la base del gobierno de los EUA (pág. 130)

constitution [constitución] *s.* conjunto de leyes y principios que definen la naturaleza de un gobierno (págs. 176, 230)

Constitution of 1917 [Constitución de 1917] *s.* constitución mexicana redactada durante la revolución que aún está en vigencia (pág. 230)

constitutional monarchy [monarquía constitucional] *s.* gobierno donde los poderes del rey o la reina están limitados por la constitución (págs. 176, 414, 736, 858, 892)

continent [continente] *s.* una de las siete enormes extensiones de tierra de la superficie de la Tierra (págs. 26, 122)

Continental Divide [divisoria continental] *s.* formación lineal a lo largo de las montañas Rocosas que divide las aguas que fluyen hacia el oeste de las que fluyen hacia el este (pág. 122)

continental shelf [plataforma continental] *s.* tierra sumergida al borde de un continente (pág. 34)

Cook, James *s.* explorador británico que reclamó tierras en Australia (pág. 892)

coral island [isla de coral] *s.* tipo de isla oceánica que es un arrecife de coral (pág. 912)

cottage industry [industria artesanal] *s.* pequeña empresa donde los trabajadores fabrican ítems en sus hogares (págs. 716, 728)

coup [golpe de Estado] *s.* toma del poder por parte de los militares (pág. 586)

cuíca s. zambomba utilizada en la samba, una danza brasileña (pág. 296)

cultural blending [mezcla cultural] *s.* algo nuevo que se crea al combinar los elementos de dos o más culturas (pág. 138)

cultural hearth [núcleo cultural] *s.* la zona central de una cultura importante; el área en la cual una cultura se originó y se expandió a otras áreas (págs. 96, 212)

culture [cultura] *s.* actitudes, conocimientos y comportamientos compartidos por un grupo de personas (págs. 66, 88, 138, 212, 544)

cuneiform [cuneiforme] *s.* el primer sistema de escritura conocido, que usaba símbolos en forma de cuña y fue desarrollado en Sumeria (pág. 666)

cyclone [ciclón] *s.* tormenta violenta de vientos feroces que rotan en una pauta circular como un huracán (pág. 658)

Cyrillic alphabet [alfabeto cirílico] *s.* el sistema oficial de escritura de Rusia (pág. 476)

czar [zar] *s.* título de los soberanos de Rusia desde mediados del siglo XVI hasta comienzos del siglo XX (pág. 468)

Czechoslovakia [Checoslovaquia] *s.* antiguo país de Europa del Este que existió desde 1918 hasta 1993, cuando se dividió en la República Checa y Eslovaquia (pág. 432)

D

daimyo [daimio] *s.* en Japón, samuráis poderosos que se convirtieron en caciques guerreros (pág. 830)

Dao [Tao] *s.* de acuerdo al sistema de creencias del taoísmo, una fuerza que guía todo el universo (pág. 774)

Daoism [taoísmo] *s.* sistema de creencias chino basado en la idea del orden natural del mundo (pág. 774)

database [base de datos] *s.* recopilación de información que puede analizarse (pág. 10)

Day of the Dead [Día de Muertos] *s.* día feriado para recordar a los seres queridos que han fallecido (pág. 236)

death rate [tasa de mortalidad] *s.* cantidad de muertes por año, por cada 1,000 personas (pág. 58)

debris [escombros] *s.* restos dispersos de algo roto o destruido (pág. 10)

Deccan Plateau [meseta de Decán] *s.* área elevada a gran altura en el centro del subcontinente indio (pág. 658)

deforestation [deforestación] *s.* tala y eliminación de árboles (pág. 304)

degraded [degradado] *adj.* de calidad menor a la que existía previamente (pág. 48)

delta *s.* depósito de tierra de forma triangular en la boca de un río (pág. 554)

demilitarized zone [zona desmilitarizada] *s.* zona de separación entre Corea del Norte y Corea del Sur (pág. 804)

democracy [democracia] *s.* gobierno en el cual los ciudadanos toman decisiones políticas, ya sea de manera directa o a través de los representantes que han elegido (pág. 334)

demographer [demógrafo] s. geógrafo que estudia las características de las poblaciones humanas (pág. 58)

demonstration [manifestación] s. reunión pública para protestar por una política o una decisión (pág. 784)

dependency [dependencia] s. lugar gobernado por un país del cual oficialmente no forma parte (pág. 260)

deport [deportar] v. expulsar de un país (pág. 424)

desert [desierto] s. región con plantas especialmente adaptadas a condiciones secas (pág. 40)

desertification [desertificación] s. transformación de tierra fértil en tierra desértica; proceso por el cual la tierra de cultivo pierde su productividad debido a que la tierra se degrada (págs. 48, 536)

devolution [traspaso] s. proceso por el cual se transfiere algo del poder del gobierno nacional al gobierno regional (pág. 414)

dictator [dictador] s. persona que tiene el control absoluto sobre el gobierno de un país (págs. 254, 260, 266, 812)

dictatorship [dictadura] s. estado o gobierno regido por un líder con poder absoluto (págs. 78, 568)

Diet [Dieta] s. organismo legislativo del Japón, que se compone de una Cámara de Representantes y una Cámara de Consejeros (pág. 840)

diffusion [difusión] s. propagación de ideas, inventos y pautas de conducta de un grupo a otro (pág. 96)

discrimination [discriminación] s. acciones que pueden herir a un individuo o a un grupo (pág. 66)

diversity [diversidad] s. tener muchas maneras diferentes de pensar o de hacer algo, o una variedad de personas (pág. 66)

Dom Pedro I [Pedro I] s. primer emperador portugués de Brasil; proclamó Brasil independiente de Portugal en 1822 (pág. 290)

Dom Pedro II [Pedro II] s. segundo emperador de Brasil; durante su reinado, en 1888, se abolió la esclavitud en Brasil (pág. 290)

domesticate [domesticar] v. adaptar o entrenar plantas o animales para uso de los seres humanos (pág. 544)

domestication [domesticación] s. cría y cuidado de una planta o un animal para ser de utilidad a los seres humanos (pág. 96)

dominion [dominio] s. en el Imperio Británico, nación a la que se le permite administrar sus asuntos internos (pág. 164)

draft animal [animal de carga] s. animal usado para jalar una carga pesada (pág. 884)

drainage basin [cuenca de drenaje] s. área drenada por un río principal (pág. 34)

Dravidian [lenguas drávidas] s. grupo de lenguas que se hablan en la India desde tiempos muy remotos; en la actualidad, se las habla principalmente en el sur de la India (pág. 698)

drought [sequía] s. largo período de escasa precipitación o carencia total de lluvia (pág. 594)

duchy [ducado] s. territorio regido por un duque o una duquesa (pág. 376)

Dust Bowl [Cuenca de Polvo] s. región de las Grandes Planicies de los EUA que padeció sequías y tormentas de polvo sofocantes durante la década de 1930 (pág. 130)

dynastic cycle [ciclo dinástico] s. en China, el patrón de caída y ascenso de las dinastías (pág. 764)

dynasty [dinastía] s. familia o grupo que gobierna durante varias generaciones, como en China (págs. 554, 606, 764)

E

earthquake [terremoto] s. movimiento repentino de la corteza terrestre seguido de una serie de sacudidas (pág. 26)

eclectic [ecléctico] adj. compuesto a partir de partes de diversos orígenes (pág. 432)

economic system [sistema económico] s. manera en que las personas usan los recursos para fabricar e intercambiar bienes (pág. 72)

economy [economía] s. sistema de producción e intercambio de bienes y servicios entre un grupo de personas (págs. 72, 304)

ecotourism [ecoturismo] s. viajes que algunas personas realizan a medio ambientes únicos, en los que se preocupan por preservarlos en su estado natural (págs. 254, 736)

edible [comestible] adj. apto para ser comido (pág. 272)

emissions [emisiones] s. sustancias liberadas en el aire (pág. 48)

emperor [emperador] s. líder de un imperio, que es un grupo de territorios o de culturas diferentes regido por una autoridad suprema (págs. 764, 830)

empire [imperio] s. sistema político en donde las personas o las tierras son controladas por un soberano único (págs. 212, 220)

Enlightenment [Ilustración] s. movimiento filosófico de los siglos XVII y XVIII que se caracterizó por el uso de la razón y los métodos científicos (pág. 350)

environment [medio ambiente] s. el entorno físico de una ubicación (pág. 4)

equinox [equinoccio] s. una de las dos ocasiones en el año en que los rayos del sol caen directamente sobre el ecuador y los días y las noches tienen la misma duración en todo el mundo (pág. 40)

Eritrea *s.* antigua región de Etiopía, que se convirtió en un país independiente en 1993 (pág. 606)

erosion [erosión] *s.* desgaste y movimiento de materiales desgastados por el agua, el viento o el hielo (pág. 26)

escarpment [escarpa] *s.* pendiente empinada que separa dos áreas llanas de diferente altura (pág. 536)

estancia *s.* hacienda o finca agrícola de gran tamaño de la Argentina (pág. 280)

ethanol [etanol] *s.* líquido que se obtiene mediante un proceso químico que convierte la caña de azúcar en un tipo de alcohol que se puede usar como combustible (pág. 304)

ethnic cleansing [limpieza étnica] *s.* eliminar un grupo étnico o religioso de un área a través de la fuerza o del asesinato en masa de los miembros del grupo (pág. 440)

ethnic group [grupo étnico] *s.* grupo de personas que comparten un idioma, costumbres y un patrimonio cultural común (págs. 88, 476, 504)

Euphrates River [río Éufrates] *s.* río del sudoeste de Asia que fluye desde una planicie de la península de Anatolia hasta el golfo Pérsico (pág. 652)

Eurasia *s.* término usado para designar a un único continente compuesto por Europa y Asia (págs. 460, 496)

European Union (EU) [Unión Europea (UE)] *s.* organización de naciones europeas cuyos miembros cooperan en asuntos económicos, sociales y políticos (págs. 350, 362, 688)

Everglades [los *Everglades*] *s.* área inmensa de terrenos pantanosos al sur de Florida (pág. 122)

export [exportación] *s.* producto o recurso vendido a otro país (págs. 72, 304)

export [exportar] *v.* enviar algo de un país a otro (pág. 146)

extended family [familia ampliada] *s.* unidad familiar que agrupa a otros familiares además de los padres y los hijos, incluyendo a los abuelos y a otros parientes cercanos (pág. 688)

F

famine [hambruna] *s.* escasez severa de alimentos que causa hambre generalizada (págs. 594, 658)

fascism [fascismo] *s.* filosofía política que fomenta la lealtad ciega hacia el estado y un fuerte gobierno central controlado por un dictador poderoso (pág. 362)

fast [ayunar] *v.* no comer, habitualmente por motivos religiosos (pág. 728)

favelas [*favelas*] *s.* término brasileño para designar a los vecindarios pobres que rodean las ciudades (pág. 290)

federal republic [república federal] *s.* forma de gobierno donde el poder está dividido entre un gobierno nacional y los gobiernos estatales (pág. 266)

federal system [sistema federal] *s.* sistema de gobierno donde los poderes están divididos entre el Estado nacional y los gobiernos provinciales o estatales (págs. 146, 176)

federation [federación] *s.* colonias, estados o países que se han unido (pág. 594)

Fertile Crescent [Creciente Fértil] *s.* región que se extiende desde el golfo Pérsico hacia el noroeste, hasta los ríos Tigris y Éufrates, y hacia el oeste, hasta el mar Mediterráneo (pág. 666)

feudalism [feudalismo] *s.* sistema político en el cual los señores feudales daban tierras a sus vasallos a cambio de servicios (pág. 342)

fiesta *s.* día feriado que se celebra con desfiles, juegos y comida (pág. 236)

Filipino [filipino] *s.* habitante de las Filipinas (pág. 864)

First Nations [Primeras Naciones] *s.* pueblos indígenas de Canadá organizados en grupos culturales (pág. 164)

foreign investment [inversión extranjera] *s.* dinero aportado a una empresa por personas de otro país (pág. 512)

fossil [fósil] *s.* restos de vida primitiva preservados bajo tierra (pág. 544)

fossil fuels [combustibles fósiles] *s.* fuentes de energía a partir de restos antiguos de animales y plantas; se incluyen los combustibles como el carbón, el petróleo y el gas natural (págs. 48, 326)

Fox, Vicente *s.* presidente mexicano perteneciente al Partido de Acción Nacional, elegido en 2000 (pág. 230)

free enterprise [libre empresa] *s.* sistema económico en el cual las empresas son libres de operar, con poca interferencia del gobierno (págs. 146, 176, 784)

French Revolution [Revolución Francesa] *s.* conflicto ocurrido en Francia, entre 1789 y 1799, que puso fin a la monarquía y produjo cambios en la manera de gobernar Francia (pág. 350)

G

Gaelic [gaélico] *s.* cualquiera de los dialectos de la familia de lenguas celtas habladas en Irlanda o Escocia (pág. 408)

Gandhi, Mohandas *s.* hindú del siglo XX que ayudó a obtener la independencia de su país usando la resistencia pacífica frente al dominio colonial (pág. 698)

Ganges River [río Ganges] *s.* río de Asia del Sur que fluye al sudeste desde los Himalayas hasta el Golfo de Bengala (pág. 658)

García Márquez, Gabriel *s.* autor colombiano ganador del Premio Nobel (pág. 266)

gaucho s. vaquero argentino (pág. 280)

Gautama, Siddhartha *s.* fundador del budismo, también conocido como Buda, o "el iluminado" (pág. 774)

Gaza Strip [Franja de Gaza] *s.* territorio estrecho que se extiende a lo largo del Mar Mediterráneo (pág. 682)

Geographic Information Systems (GIS) [Sistemas de Información Geográfica] *s.* tecnología de mapeo basada en las computadoras o Internet (págs. 10, 16)

geographic South Pole [Polo Sur geográfico] *s.* punto de encuentro de todas las líneas de longitud (pág. 920)

geography [geografía] *s.* estudio de las personas, los lugares y los medios ambientes (pág. 4)

geomorphology [geomorfología] *s.* estudio de cómo cambia la forma de la Tierra (pág. 16)

geothermal energy [energía geotérmica] *s.* energía producida por el calor interno de la Tierra (pág. 900)

geyser [géiser] *s.* manantial caliente que dispara chorros de vapor y agua hirviendo al aire (págs. 884, 900)

Ghana *s.* reino de África Occidental entre el siglo VIII y XI d.C. ubicado en lo que hoy es Mauritania y Malí; país moderno de África Occidental (pág. 580)

glacier [glaciar] *s.* gran masa de hielo de movimiento lento (pág. 26)

global economy [economía global] *s.* economía en la cual se compra y vende atravesando las fronteras nacionales (págs. 146, 244)

Global Positioning System (GPS) [Sistema de Posicionamiento Global] *s.* sistema que usa una red de satélites que orbitan la Tierra para dar una ubicación exacta (pág. 10)

global warming [calentamiento global] *s.* aumento de la temperatura promedio de la atmósfera terrestre (págs. 48, 304)

globe [globo] *s.* modelo de la Tierra con forma esférica (pág. 10)

glyph [glifo] *s.* símbolo tallado o grabado que representa una sílaba o una palabra (pág. 212)

Gobi Desert [Desierto de Gobi] *s.* desierto elevado en China y Mongolia (pág. 756)

Golan Heights [Altos de Golán] *s.* región que formaba parte del suroeste de Siria y que Israel ha ocupado desde la guerra de 1967 (pág. 688)

golden age [edad dorada] *s.* período durante el cual una sociedad alcanza prosperidad y realiza logros culturales (pág. 698)

Good Friday Agreement [Acuerdo de Viernes Santo] *s.* acuerdo entre los unionistas y nacionalistas de Irlanda del Norte que estableció un nuevo gobierno (pág. 414)

Gorbachev, Mikhail *s.* líder soviético de 1985 a 1991 que incrementó las libertades del pueblo ruso (pág. 468)

government [gobierno] *s.* organización establecida para crear y hacer cumplir las reglas de una sociedad (pág. 78)

Grand Canyon [Gran Cañón] *s.* barranco profundo que atraviesa el norte de Arizona excavado por el río Colorado (pág. 122)

Great Barrier Reef [Gran Arrecife de Coral] *s.* cadena de arrecifes de coral de 1,250 millas, cerca de la costa de Australia (pág. 884)

Great Depression [Gran Depresión] *s.* período de severo declive económico, desde 1929 hasta comienzos de la década de 1940 (pág. 130)

Great Dividing Range [Gran Cordillera Divisoria] *s.* cordillera de montañas bajas en Australia (pág. 884)

Great Lakes [Grandes Lagos] *s.* cinco lagos que forman el mayor grupo de lagos de agua dulce del mundo (págs. 122, 156)

Great Plains [Grandes Llanuras] *s.* grandes prados del centro de América del Norte (pág. 122)

Great Wall [Gran Muralla] *s.* muralla enorme y extensa construida en el transcurso de varios siglos para mantener a los nómadas fuera de China (pág. 764)

Great Zimbabwe [Gran Zimbabue] *s.* imperio erigido por el pueblo shona desde el siglo I hasta el siglo VIII d.C. (pág. 630)

Greater Antilles [Antillas Mayores] *s.* las islas más grandes del norte del Caribe, entre las que se incluyen Cuba, Jamaica, La Española (la cual incluye Haití y la República Dominicana) y Puerto Rico (pág. 198)

Green Revolution [Revolución Verde] *s.* uso de semillas especiales, irrigación, fertilizantes y pesticidas para lograr un elevado rendimiento de los cultivos y una gran producción de alimentos (págs. 716, 728)

greenhouse effect [efecto invernadero] *s.* retención del calor del sol producido por los gases de la atmósfera terrestre (pág. 48)

greenhouse gas [gas invernadero] *s.* cualquier gas de la atmósfera que contribuye al efecto invernadero (pág. 48)

grid [cuadrícula] *s.* red de líneas horizontales y verticales que crean cuadrados o rectángulos (pág. 666)

griot s. narrador de África Occidental (pág. 544)

Gross Domestic Product (GDP) [Producto Bruto Interno (PBI)] *s.* valor total de todos los bienes y servicios producidos por un país en un año (págs. 72, 280)

ground water [agua subterránea] *s.* agua que se encuentra debajo de la superficie terrestre (pág. 34)

guerrilla [guerrillero] *s.* miembro de un ejército irregular que opera en unidades militares pequeña (pág. 630)

Gulf of Mexico [Golfo de México] *s.* ensenada del océano Atlántico que se ubica al sur de los Estados Unidos (pág. 122)

H

habitable lands [tierras habitables] *s.* tierras apropiadas para ser habitadas por los seres humanos (pág. 58)

Hammurabi's Code [Código de Hammurabi] *s.* uno de los primeros códigos legales del mundo, compilado por el gobernante Hammurabi (pág. 666)

hanbok [*hanbok*] *s.* traje tradicional coreano (pág. 804)

Harappan civilization [civilización Harappa] *s.* civilización antigua que se desarrolló a lo largo del río Indo (pág. 666)

Hausa [hausa] *s.* un pueblo del norte de Nigeria y sur de Níger (pág. 586)

Heian Period [Período Heian] *s.* era de la historia japonesa desde 794 d.C. hasta 1185 d.C.; las artes y la escritura florecieron durante esta época (pág. 830)

Hidalgo, Miguel ("Padre Hidalgo") *s.* padre de la independencia mexicana (pág. 220)

hieroglyphics [jeroglíficos] *s.* sistema de escritura egipcio en el cual los símbolos pictográficos representan significados o sonidos (pág. 554)

highlands [tierras altas] *s.* regiones montañosas o accidentadas de un país (págs. 198, 204)

Himalayas [Himalayas] *s.* las montañas más altas del mundo, las cuales se extienden a través del norte de India, separando la India de China y del resto de Asia (págs. 658, 756)

Hinduism [Hinduismo] *s.* nombre actual para la religión principal de la India, la cual se desarrolló a partir del bramanismo (págs. 698, 706)

Hitler, Adolf *s.* jefe de estado alemán desde 1933 a 1945 (pág. 382)

Hokkaido *s.* isla más septentrional de Japón y segunda en tamaño (pág. 824)

Holocaust [Holocausto] *s.* asesinato sistemático de judíos y otras minorías por parte de los nazis durante la Segunda Guerra Mundial (págs. 350, 382, 682)

hominid [homínido] *s.* primate humano; ser humano primitivo (pág. 544)

Honshu *s.* la isla más grande y más poblada de Japón (pág. 824)

Horn of Africa [Cuerno de África] *s.* extensión de tierra con forma de cuerno en la costa este de África (pág. 606)

Huang He *s.* río que fluye desde las montañas Kunlun hasta el Mar Amarillo (pág. 756)

Hudson Bay [Bahía de Hudson] *s.* gran mar en el interior al norte de Ontario, provincia canadiense (pág. 156)

hunter-gatherer [cazador-recolector] *s.* persona que caza animales y recolecta plantas para obtener alimento (págs. 618, 892)

hydroelectric [hidroeléctrico] *adj.* relativo a la electricidad generada por motores que funcionan con agua (pág. 156)

hydroelectricity [hidroelectricidad] *s.* energía eléctrica generada por el agua (pág. 304)

hydroelectric power [energía hidroeléctrica] *s.* electricidad generada por motores que funcionan gracias a la fuerza del agua (págs. 326, 756, 900)

hydrologic cycle [ciclo hidrológico] *s.* circulación del agua entre la Tierra, los océanos y la atmósfera (pág. 34)

I

ice shelf [barrera de hielo] *s.* inmensa capa plana de hielo que se extiende sobre un cuerpo de agua, pero permanece unida a la tierra (pág. 920)

iceberg [glaciar] *s.* gran pedazo de hielo flotante (pág. 920)

icecap [casquete glaciar] *s.* glaciar que cubre un área extensa (pág. 920)

icon [ícono] *s.* imagen religiosa usada por los cristianos ortodoxos en su culto (pág. 476)

Igbo [igbo] *s.* pueblo del sureste de Nigeria (pág. 586)

igloo [iglú] *s.* vivienda hecha de nieve (pág. 170)

immigrant [inmigrante] *s.* persona que deja un área para habitar en otra (págs. 66, 130, 296, 408)

immigration [inmigración] *s.* proceso de ir a vivir a otro país (pág. 244)

imperialism [imperialismo] *s.* la práctica de un país de controlar el gobierno y la economía de otro país o territorio (págs. 350, 400, 580)

import [importación] *s.* producto o recurso que llega a un país (pág. 72)

import [importar] *v.* llevar algo de un país a otro (pág. 146)

Inca [inca] *s.* civilización antigua que se desarrolló en la Cordillera de los Andes, en Perú (pág. 212)

indigenous [indígena] *s.* nativo de una región (pág. 272)

Indochina [Indochina] *s.* nombre de una antigua colonia francesa del sureste de Asia constituida por Camboya, Laos y Vietnam (pág. 858)

Indochinese Peninsula [península de Indochina] *s.* una de las dos penínsulas en las que se ubica el sureste de Asia continental; la península está ubicada al sur de China (pág. 852)

Indus River [río Indo] s. río de Asia del sur que fluye desde los Himalayas hasta el Mar Arábigo (pág. 658)

Industrial Revolution [Revolución Industrial] s. cambio que comenzó en Gran Bretaña en la década de 1760 de producir bienes a mano a hacerlo mediante máquinas (págs. 350, 400)

inflation [inflación] s. aumento de los precios o caída del poder adquisitivo del dinero (pág. 594)

infrastructure [infraestructura] s. servicios básicos que necesita una comunidad, tales como carreteras, ferrocarriles, agua y líneas eléctricas, escuelas y oficinas de correos (pág. 594)

innovation [innovación] s. algo nuevo que es presentado por primera vez (pág. 96)

Interstate Highway System [Sistema de Carreteras Interestatales] s. red de más de 45,000 millas de carreteras que une a todas las ciudades principales de EUA (pág. 146)

Inuit [inuit] s. pueblos nativos que habitan la región ártica de América del Norte (pág. 164)

Inuktitut [inuktitut] s. idioma de los inuit (pág. 170)

Islam [islam] s. religión monoteísta basada en las enseñanzas de Mahoma y los escritos del Corán, el libro sagrado de los musulmanes (págs. 476, 504, 562, 676)

isolate [aislar] v. separar o apartar de un grupo (pág. 334)

Istanbul [Estambul] s. la ciudad más grande de Turquía, anteriormente llamada Constantinopla (capital del Imperio Bizantino, o Imperio Romano Oriental) y originariamente llamada Bizancio en la antigüedad (pág. 688)

isthmus [istmo] s. franja de tierra que conecta dos territorios (pág. 198)

ivory [marfil] s. sustancia dura y blanca de la que están hechos los colmillos de los elefantes (pág. 618)

J

jaguar s. felino de gran tamaño que habita principalmente en América Central y del Sur (pág. 212)

jazz [jazz] s. tipo de música que se desarrolló a partir de una mezcla de ritmos africanos, música estadounidense de orquesta y estilos musicales afroamericanos y europeos (pág. 138)

jellaba [chilaba] s. vestimenta tradicional bereber; túnica de mangas largas (pág. 568)

Jerusalem [Jerusalén] s. capital actual de Israel y ciudad antigua considerada sagrada por el judaísmo, el cristianismo y el islam (pág. 682)

joropo s. baile folklórico nacional de Venezuela (pág. 266)

Juárez, Benito (1806–1872) s. indio que se convirtió en presidente y héroe nacional mexicano (pág. 230)

Judaism [judaísmo] s. religión monoteísta de los judíos, basada principalmente en los escritos de la Biblia hebrea (págs. 476, 682)

K

Kalahari s. desierto del sur de África (pág. 630)

Kanto Plain [Planicie de Kanto] s. la llanura de Japón de mayor extensión, que se extiende desde los Alpes japoneses al este, hasta el Pacífico (pág. 824)

Kara Kum s. desierto inmenso que cubre la mayor parte de Turkmenistán (pág. 496)

karma s. en el hinduismo, las consecuencias de las acciones de una persona en esta vida, las cuales determinan su destino en la próxima vida (pág. 706)

Kashmir [Cachemira] s. región en la parte noroeste del subcontinente indio; India y Pakistán se disputan el control de Cachemira (pág. 716)

Kente cloth [tela kente] s. tela tejida de colores vivos, hecha por los pueblos ashanti y ewe (pág. 586)

Kenyatta, Jomo s. primer presidente después de la independencia de Kenia (pág. 612)

Khmer Empire [Imperio Khmer] s. imperio que comenzó en el siglo VI y había ganado el control de gran parte del sureste de Asia continental hacia el siglo IX (pág. 858)

kibbutz [kibutz] s. tipo de colonia agrícola de Israel en el que la comunidad comparte la riqueza y todos los bienes (pág. 682)

Kim Jong Il s. líder comunista de Corea del Norte (pág. 812)

kimchi [kimchi] s. plato coreano hecho de vegetales encurtidos (pág. 804)

King, William Lyon Mackenzie s. primer ministro canadiense que llevó a su país a la independencia (pág. 164)

knight [caballero] s. vasallo entrenado en el combate que peleaba en nombre de un señor feudal (pág. 342)

Koizumi, Junichiro s. primer ministro japonés de 2001 a 2006 (pág. 840)

Kongo [Congo] s. pueblo que habitaba a lo largo del río Congo; reino de habla bantú de la región del río Congo surgido en el siglo XIV (pág. 618)

Korean Peninsula [península de Corea] s. masa de tierra bordeada por el Mar Amarillo al oeste, el Mar del Este (o Mar del Japón) al este, el Estrecho de Corea al sur y China y Rusia al norte (pág. 796)

Korean War [Guerra de Corea] (1950–1953) *s.* conflicto entre Corea del Norte y la Unión Soviética por un lado, y Corea del Sur, los Estados Unidos y las Naciones Unidas por el otro (pág. 804)

Korean Workers' Party (KWP) [Partido Coreano de los Trabajadores] *s.* grupo político comunista que controla el gobierno de Corea del Norte (pág. 812)

Kosovo *s.* provincia autónoma dentro de Serbia (pág. 440)

Kurd [kurdo] *s.* miembro de un grupo étnico que no tiene su propio país pero cuya tierra natal se ubica en partes de Turquía, Irak e Irán (pág. 676)

Kush *s.* antiguo reino de Nubia ubicado en el norte de Sudán (págs. 554, 606)

Kyushu *s.* isla del extremo sur de Japón donde se hallan muchas ciudades grandes (pág. 824)

L

lacrosse [*lacrosse*] *s.* deporte de equipo inventado por los americanos nativos (pág. 170)

Lake Balkhash [lago Balkhash] *s.* lago del este de Kazakstán (pág. 496)

land bridge [puente terrestre] *s.* tierra firme que surgió entre Asia y Alaska durante la Edad de Hielo (pág. 130)

land reform [reforma agraria] *s.* acción de dividir grandes porciones de terreno para distribuir la tierra más equitativamente (pág. 630)

landform [accidente geográfico] *s.* rasgo de la superficie terrestre formado por la fuerza física (pág. 34)

landlocked [mediterráneo] *adj.* rodeado por tierra sin acceso a un océano o mar (págs. 272, 280, 496, 728)

Landsat [*Landsat*] *s.* serie de satélites que reúnen información y orbitan sobre la Tierra (pág. 10)

language [lenguaje] *s.* comunicación humana ya sea escrita, hablada o por señas (pág. 88)

language family [familia de lenguas] *s.* conjuntos de lenguas que derivan de una misma lengua originaria (pág. 88)

Latin America [Latinoamérica] *s.* región que incluye México, América Central, las islas del Caribe y Suramérica (pág. 198)

legislature [legislatura] *s.* organismo legislativo de un gobierno (pág. 716)

Leopold II [Leopoldo II] *s.* rey de Bélgica, obligado a entregar su propiedad privada del Estado Libre del Congo (pág. 618)

Lesser Antilles [Antillas Menores] *s.* las islas del Caribe más pequeñas ubicadas al sureste de las Antillas Mayores (pág. 198)

Lewis and Clark Expedition [Expedición de Lewis y Clark] *s.* viaje realizado por Lewis y Clark para explorar el Territorio de Luisiana (pág. 130)

lineage [linaje] *s.* descendencia de un ancestro (pág. 544)

literacy [alfabetización] *s.* la capacidad de leer y escribir (pág. 138)

llama *s.* mamífero suramericano emparentado con el camello (pág. 272)

llanos s. prados de las planicies centrales de Suramérica (págs. 204, 266)

location analyst [analista de ubicación] *s.* persona que estudia un área para encontrar la mejor ubicación para un cliente (pág. 16)

location [ubicación] *s.* posición exacta según la latitud y longitud, o la descripción de un lugar en relación a los lugares que lo rodean (pág. 4)

lord [señor] *s.* terrateniente poderoso (pág. 342)

Louisiana Purchase [Adquisición de Luisiana] *s.* acción por la cual el presidente Thomas Jefferson compró el Territorio de Luisiana a Francia en 1803 (pág. 130)

Loyalist [Leal] *s.* persona que apoyó a Gran Bretaña durante la Guerra Revolucionaria Norteamericana (pág. 164)

M

Maghrib [Magreb] *s.* nombre árabe de África del norte, que significa "el oeste" (pág. 568)

magma *s.* roca fundida (pág. 26)

Magna Carta [Carta Magna] *s.* carta, o documento, firmado por el rey Juan de Inglaterra en 1215 que limitaba el poder del monarca y le garantizaba derechos básicos a los nobles (pág. 400)

Magyar [magiar] *s.* persona de la etnia húngara o el idioma húngaro (pág. 432)

mainland [continente] *s.* masa terrestre principal de un continente o territorio, excluyendo a sus islas o penínsulas (pág. 400)

Malay Peninsula [península de Malaya] *s.* la segunda península del sureste de Asia continental; la franja estrecha de tierra que sirve como puente entre el continente y las islas (pág. 852)

Mali [Malí] *s.* imperio de África Occidental entre el siglo XIII d.C. y el siglo XVI d.C.; país actual de África Occidental (pág. 580)

Mandela, Nelson *s.* primer presidente africano de Sudáfrica (pág. 624)

manifest destiny [destino manifiesto] *s.* idea de que Estados Unidos debía poseer toda la tierra entre, e inclusive más allá de, los océanos Atlántico y Pacífico (pág. 130)

manor [finca solariega] *s.* casa del noble y las aldeas ubicadas en sus tierras donde vivían los campesinos (pág. 342)

Mao Zedong [Mao Tsé Tung] *s.* líder comunista de China entre 1949 y 1976 (pág. 764)

Maori [maorí] *s.* pueblo de Polinesia compuesto por los primeros habitantes de Nueva Zelanda (pág. 900)

map [mapa] *s.* representación de una parte de la Tierra (pág. 10)

maquiladora s. fábrica en la que los materiales son importados y ensamblados para producir bienes de exportación (págs. 244, 254)

Marcos, Ferdinand *s.* presidente dictatorial de las Filipinas entre 1965 y 1986 (pág. 864)

market economy [economía de mercado] *s.* sistema económico en el que la producción de bienes y servicios se determina según la oferta y la demanda de los consumidores (págs. 72, 146, 382, 424, 486, 512)

marsupial *s.* animal provisto de una bolsa abdominal para llevar a sus crías (pág. 884)

Marxist [marxista] *s.* persona que apoya la filosofía subyacente al comunismo, incluyendo la posesión de la tierra y de los medios de producción por parte del gobierno (pág. 630)

Mau Mau *s.* movimiento por la independencia de Kenia que comenzó en la década de 1940 (pág. 612)

Maya [maya] *s.* civilización antigua ubicada en lo que hoy es la Península de Yucatán, Guatemala y el norte de Belice (pág. 212)

mechanized [mecanizado] *adj.* equipado con maquinaria (págs. 304, 892)

medieval *adj.* relativo a la Edad Media (pág. 342)

Mekong River [río Mekong] *s.* río principal que corre hacia el sur, desde el sur de China a través de Laos, Camboya y Vietnam (pág. 852)

Melanesia *s.* subregión de Oceanía que incluye las islas al noreste de Australia y al sur del ecuador (pág. 912)

Mercosur *s.* asociación de varios países de Suramérica con el fin de promover el comercio entre los países (pág. 280)

Mesopotamia *s.* tierra entre los ríos Tigris y Éufrates (pág. 666)

mestizo s. persona con mezcla de ancestros europeos y americanos nativos (págs. 220, 254)

Mexican Revolution [Revolución Mexicana] *s.* lucha por lograr reformas en México entre 1910 y 1920 (pág. 230)

Micronesia *s.* subregión de Oceanía que incluye las islas al este de las Filipinas y al norte del ecuador (pág. 912)

microstate [microestado] *s.* país independiente con un área y una población muy pequeñas (pág. 858)

Middle Ages [Edad Media] *s.* período entre la caída del Imperio Romano y la Edad Moderna, desde aproximadamente el 476 d.C. hasta 1453 (pág. 342)

Middle Kingdom [Reino Medio] *s.* antiguo nombre chino de China (pág. 764)

migration [migración] *s.* proceso de trasladarse a una nueva región (pág. 66)

militarism [militarismo] *s.* uso agresivo de las fuerzas armadas por parte de un gobierno (pág. 840)

millet [mijo] *s.* grano cultivado en África Occidental, a menudo convertido en gachas (pág. 594)

Milosevic, Slobodan *s.* presidente de Serbia desde 1989 a 1997, y de Yugoslavia desde 1997 a 2000; una figura clave en los conflictos étnicos de los países balcánicos en la década de 1990 (pág. 440)

missionary [misionero] *s.* persona enviada para realizar trabajo religioso en otro lugar (pág. 88)

Mississippi River [río Misisipi] *s.* río más largo y vía fluvial principal de los Estados Unidos (pág. 122)

Mobuto Sese Seko *s.* dictador de la República Democrática del Congo desde 1965 a 1997 (pág. 618)

modernize [modernizar] *v.* aceptar nuevas costumbres o ideas (págs. 562, 606)

monarch [monarca] *s.* rey o reina que gobierna un país o territorio (pág. 716)

monarchy [monarquía] *s.* tipo de gobierno en el cual una familia gobernante encabezada por un rey o una reina ejerce el poder político (págs. 78, 334)

monotheism [monoteísmo] *s.* creencia en un solo dios (pág. 676)

monsoon [monzón] *s.* sistema de vientos estacionales que produce una estación húmeda o seca en una región, en ocasiones con lluvias intensas (págs. 612, 658, 796, 852)

Moors [moros] *s.* grupo de musulmanes de África del Norte que conquistó España en el siglo VIII (pág. 370)

mosaic [mosaico] *s.* imagen creada al colocar pequeñas piezas coloreadas de piedra, azulejo o vidrio sobre una superficie (pág. 266)

Mount Everest [Monte Everest] *s.* la montaña más alta del mundo, ubicada en los Himalayas (pág. 658)

Mount Fuji [Monte Fuji] *s.* la cumbre más alta de Japón (pág. 824)

Mount Kilimanjaro [Monte Kilimanjaro] *s.* la montaña más alta de África, al noreste de Tanzania (pág. 536)

Mount McKinley [Monte McKinley (también llamado Denali)] *s.* montaña más alta de América del Norte, ubicada en Alaska (pág. 122)

Mount Paektu [Monte Paektu] *s.* la montaña más alta de la Península Coreana (9,003 pies) (pág. 796)

Muhammad (Mohammed) [Mahoma] *s.* fundador y profeta principal del islam (pág. 676)

multicultural [multicultural] *adj.* relativo a muchas culturas diferentes o que las incluye (pág. 408)

multilingual [multilingüe] *s.* capaz de hablar muchos idiomas (pág. 376)

multinational corporation [corporación multinacional] *s.* compañía que opera en más de un país (pág. 146)

mummy [momia] *s.* cuerpo preparado para el entierro de conformidad con la antigua práctica egipcia (pág. 554)

mural *s.* pintura hecha sobre una pared (págs. 236, 296)

Musa, Mansa *s.* líder del Imperio Malí desde 1312 a 1337 aproximadamente (pág. 580)

Muslim [musulmán] *s.* seguidor del islam (págs. 504, 562, 676)

N

Nagorno-Karabakh [Nagorno Karabaj] *s.* provincia de Azerbaiyán sobre la que los armenios tienen reclamos territoriales, pues creen que debe ser parte de su país (pág. 512)

National People's Congress (NPC) [Congreso Nacional del Pueblo] *s.* organismo legislativo nacional de China (pág. 784)

nationalism [nacionalismo] *s.* orgullo por la propia nación y lealtad a ella (págs. 350, 362)

natural resource [recurso natural] *s.* algo que se halla en la naturaleza que es necesario o útil para los seres humanos (pág. 72)

neutrality [neutralidad] *s.* política de no tomar parte en la guerra (pág. 382)

Nile River [río Nilo] *s.* río más largo del mundo, que desemboca en el Mar Mediterráneo al noreste de Egipto (págs. 536, 554)

nirvana *s.* en el budismo, estado de sabiduría que rompe con el ciclo de la reencarnación (pág. 706)

Nkrumah, Kwame *s.* primer presidente de la actual Ghana (pág. 586)

nomad [nómada] *s.* miembro de un grupo que vive del pastoreo de animales y que se desplaza de un lugar a otro con el cambio de estación (págs. 96, 504)

nonviolent resistance [resistencia pacífica] *s.* método de protesta que atrae la atención hacia un problema sin usar la violencia (pág. 698)

Nordic [nórdico] *adj.* relativo a Escandinavia (pág. 388)

North American Free Trade Agreement (NAFTA) [Tratado de Libre Comercio de América del Norte] *s.* acuerdo que redujo las barreras comerciales aduaneras entre México, Canadá y los Estados Unidos (págs. 244, 254)

North Atlantic Drift [Corriente del Atlántico Norte] *s.* corriente oceánica cálida que ayuda a mantener moderado el clima de Europa (pág. 326)

North China Plain [Planicie del Norte de China] *s.* región fértil entre los ríos Huang He y Chang Jiang (pág. 764)

Northern European Plain [Planicie del Norte de Europa] *s.* área vasta de tierras llanas o de relieve leve que se extiende desde Francia hasta Rusia (págs. 326, 376)

Nubia *s.* en la antigüedad, el valle del río Nilo al sur de Egipto y al norte de Sudán (pág. 554)

Nunavut *s.* territorio creado en 1999 con la parte este de los Territorios del Noroeste, hogar de muchos inuit (pág. 156)

O

oasis *s.* sitio verde o fértil de un desierto, creado por aguas subterráneas que llegan a la superficie (pág. 652)

obelisk [obelisco] *s.* monumento de piedra con forma de columna (pág. 606)

Oceania [Oceanía] *s.* región del Océano Pacífico con miles de islas (pág. 912)

oceanic island [isla oceánica] *s.* isla que emerge del fondo del mar sobre una base volcánica (pág. 912)

official language [idioma oficial] *s.* idioma que de acuerdo con la ley debe ser usado en los asuntos del gobierno, los negocios y la educación (pág. 138)

oligarchy [oligarquía] *s.* gobierno regido por unos pocos individuos poderosos (págs. 78, 334)

Olmec [olmeca] *s.* civilización antigua a lo largo de la Costa del Golfo en lo que hoy es el sur de México (pág. 212)

ombudsman [defensor del pueblo] *s.* funcionario que investiga las quejas de los ciudadanos contra el gobierno (pág. 388)

one-crop economy [economía de monocultivo] *s.* economía que depende de un único cultivo para obtener ingresos (págs. 260, 512)

Organization of the Petroleum Exporting Countries (OPEC) [Organización de Países Exportadores de Petróleo (OPEP)] *s.* grupo de países productores de petróleo fundado en 1960 (pág. 676)

Orthodox Christianity [cristianismo ortodoxo] *s.* rama oriental del cristianismo que se difundió en Rusia en el siglo X y se convirtió en su religión oficial (pág. 476)

Ottoman Empire [Imperio Otomano] *s.* imperio musulmán basado en Turquía que duró desde el siglo XIV hasta 1922 (págs. 676, 688)

Outback [*outback*, desierto australiano] *s.* región interior de Australia (pág. 884)

outcropping [filón] *s.* afloramiento de una masa metalífera o pétrea que asoma a la superficie del terreno (pág. 884)

ozone hole [agujero de ozono] *s.* disminución estacional de una capa protectora de gas atmosférico que se encuentra por encima de la Antártida (pág. 920)

P

Pakeha s. palabra maorí que significa "gente blanca" (pág. 900)

Palestine Liberation Organization (PLO) [Organización para la Liberación de Palestina (OLP)] *s.* grupo político que dice representar a todos los palestinos y trabajar para la obtención de una nación palestina independiente (págs. 682, 688)

Palestinian territories [territorios palestinos] *s.* Cisjordania y la Franja de Gaza juntas (pág. 682)

Pampas *s.* llanuras cubiertas de pasto en la zona central del sur de Suramérica (págs. 204, 280)

Pan-Africanism [panafricanismo] *s.* movimiento que reclama la unidad de todas las personas de ascendencia africana (pág. 580)

papyrus [papiro] *s.* material semejante al papel hecho de los tallos de la caña de papiro (pág. 554)

Parliament [Parlamento] *s.* legislatura nacional del Reino Unido (págs. 176, 400)

parliamentary [parlamentario] *adj.* relativo a un gobierno que tiene un parlamento como poder legislativo (pág. 716)

patrician [patricio] *s.* terrateniente acaudalado que ocupaba un alto puesto gubernamental en la antigua Roma (pág. 334)

patrilineal *adj.* descendencia de padre a padre, o predominio de la línea paterna en una organización social (pág. 544)

patron [mecenas] *s.* persona acaudalada o poderosa que provee dinero, apoyo y ánimo a un artista o a una causa (pág. 342)

peacekeeping [fuerza de paz] *s.* relativo a las fuerzas armadas cuyo propósito es prevenir, evitar o poner fin a la guerra (pág. 688)

Peloponnesus [Peloponeso] *s.* la península del sur de Grecia donde se encontraba Esparta (pág. 334)

penal colony [colonia penal] *s.* asentamiento que sirve como prisión (pág. 892)

peninsula [península] *s.* una masa de tierra rodeada casi completamente por agua (págs. 326, 796)

Perkins, Charles *s.* en Australia, un líder de los derechos de los aborígenes (pág. 892)

permafrost [permahielo] *s.* suelo que se mantiene congelado a lo largo del año (pág. 460)

persecution [persecución] *s.* trato cruel por motivo de religión, raza, grupo étnico, nacionalidad, opiniones políticas, género o clase (pág. 66)

Persia *s.* región histórica del suroeste de Asia ubicada principalmente en lo que hoy es Irán (pág. 676)

perspective [perspectiva] *s.* técnica usada por los artistas para dar la impresión de profundidad y distancia (pág. 342)

Peter the Great [Pedro el Grande] *s.* zar que gobernó Rusia desde 1682 a 1725 y trató de hacerla más europea (pág. 468)

pharaoh [faraón] *s.* gobernante del antiguo Egipto (pág. 554)

pidgin [pidgin] *s.* forma simple de hablar que es una mezcla de palabras de dos o más idiomas (pág. 912)

Piedmont [piedemonte] *s.* región alta de montaña entre los montes Apalaches y la llanura costera del sur (pág. 122)

place [lugar] *s.* término geográfico que describe las características físicas y humanas de una ubicación (pág. 4)

plantation agriculture [agricultura de plantación] *s.* uso de grandes granjas para obtener cultivos comerciales (pág. 736)

plateau [meseta] *s.* área plana situada a considerable altura (págs. 34, 198, 652, 756)

Plateau of Iran [Meseta de Irán] *s.* meseta de altura ubicada en el este y en el centro de Irán, rodeada por montañas (pág. 652)

Plaza of the Three Cultures [Plaza de las Tres Culturas] *s.* plaza de la Ciudad de México que muestra partes de las influencias azteca, española y moderna en México (pág. 236)

plebeian [plebeyo] *s.* persona humilde a la que se le permitía votar pero no podía ocupar un cargo gubernamental en la antigua Roma (pág. 334)

polders [pólder] *s.* terreno pantanoso ganado al mar drenándole el agua con el uso de una presa y una bomba y que una vez desecado se dedica al cultivo (pág. 376)

Polynesia [Polinesia] *s.* subregión de Oceanía que incluye las islas del centro y del sur del Pacífico (págs. 900, 912)

polytheistic [politeísta] *adj.* que cree en muchos dioses (pág. 666)

population [población] *s.* número promedio de personas que viven en una área determinada (pág. 58)

population density [densidad de población] *s.* número promedio de personas que vive en una determinada área (pág. 58)

porridge [gacha] *s.* comida blanda que se prepara hirviendo granos de cereal en leche o agua (pág. 612)

precipitation [precipitación] *s.* agua que cae en forma de lluvia, nieve, aguanieve o granizo (pág. 40)

prime minister [primer ministro] *s.* jefe del gabinete y el funcionario principal del poder ejecutivo en un gobierno de sistema parlamentario; por ejemplo, el jefe del gobierno canadiense (págs. 176, 716)

privatization [privatización] *s.* el proceso de vender empresas que son propiedad del gobierno a individuos (pág. 486)

privatize [privatizar] *v.* vender empresas que son propiedad del gobierno a individuos (pág. 512)

propaganda *s.* información tergiversada o imprecisa que se usa deliberadamente para influenciar la opinión pública (pág. 476)

protectorate [protectorado] *s.* área o país más débil controlado por un país más fuerte (pág. 562)

Protestant [protestante] *s.* miembro de una iglesia cristiana basada en los principios de la Reforma (pág. 342)

province [provincia] *s.* división gubernamental similar a un estado (págs. 156, 784)

Prussia [Prusia] *s.* el estado alemán más poderoso del Sacro Imperio Romano (pág. 382)

public education [educación pública] *s.* educación que es financiada por el gobierno (pág. 138)

pull factor [factor de atracción] *s.* motivo que atrae a la gente a otra área (pág. 66)

Punic Wars [Guerras Púnicas] *s.* guerras entre Roma y Cartago durante los siglos III y II a.C. (pág. 568)

push factor [factor de exclusión] *s.* motivo que hace que la gente abandone un área (págs. 66, 236)

Putin, Vladimir *s.* presidente de Rusia que incrementó el poder ejecutivo en la década de 2000 (pág. 486)

Pygmy [pigmeo] *s.* miembro de un pueblo con una altura media aproximada de menos de cinco pies (pág. 618)

pyramid [pirámide] *s.* antigua estructura egipcia, construida sobre una tumba o cerca de ella (pág. 554)

Q

quilombos *s.* comunidades creadas por esclavos africanos fugitivos (pág. 296)

quinoa [quinua] *s.* tipo de planta de la región andina que produce semillas pequeñas comestibles (pág. 272)

quota [cupo] *s.* meta de la cantidad de producción (pág. 618)

R

rain forest [bosque tropical] *s.* región poblada de árboles en un clima tropical (págs. 204, 304)

Ramadan [ramadán] *s.* noveno mes del calendario musulmán, durante el cual los musulmanes ayunan todos los días desde el amanecer hasta la puesta del sol (pág. 728)

rate of natural increase [tasa de crecimiento natural] *s.* tasa de muertes restada de la tasa de nacimientos (pág. 58)

raw material [materia prima] *s.* recurso natural no procesado que será convertido en un producto acabado (pág. 72)

Reconquista *s.* esfuerzo exitoso realizado por los españoles para expulsar de España a los moros (pág. 370)

Red Sea [Mar Rojo] *s.* mar estrecho que separa el noreste de África de la Península Arábiga (pág. 606)

reform [reforma] *s.* acción de mejorar las condiciones sociales o económicas (pág. 784)

Reformation [Reforma] *s.* movimiento del siglo XVI que buscó cambiar las prácticas de la Iglesia Católica (pág. 342)

refugee [refugiado] *s.* persona que huye de un lugar para encontrar seguridad (págs. 66, 440)

region [región] *s.* área que tiene una o más características en común que la unen o conectan con otras áreas (pág. 4)

reincarnation [reencarnación] *s.* el renacimiento de un alma en otro cuerpo (pág. 706)

relief [relieve] *s.* diferencia en la elevación de un accidente geográfico desde su punto más bajo a su punto más alto (pág. 34)

religion [religión] *s.* sistema organizado de creencias y prácticas, a menudo centrado en uno o más dioses (pág. 88)

remote sensing [detección remota] *s.* obtención de información sobre un sitio mediante el uso de un instrumento que no está en contacto físico con el mismo (pág. 10)

Renaissance [Renacimiento] *s.* renacimiento de la creatividad, la literatura y el aprendizaje en Europa desde aproximadamente el siglo XIV hasta el siglo XVII (pág. 342)

renewable energy sources [fuentes de energía renovables] *s.* fuentes de energía que pueden ser reemplazadas a través de procesos naturales en curso (pág. 326)

representative democracy [democracia representativa] *s.* sistema de gobierno en el cual los ciudadanos ejercen el poder político a través de representantes elegidos (págs. 78, 146)

representative government [gobierno representativo] *s.* sistema de gobierno con una legislatura que es al menos en parte elegida por el pueblo (pág. 400)

republic [república] *s.* gobierno en el que los ciudadanos eligen representantes para que gobiernen en su nombre; otro término para la democracia representativa (págs. 146, 334)

Republic of Texas [República de Texas] *s.* gobierno constitucional de Texas luego de la independencia de México (pág. 230)

reunify [reunificar] *v.* volver a unir algo que había sido separado (pág. 382)

revolution [revolución] *s.* el derrocamiento de un gobernante o gobierno; un cambio importante en las ideas (pág. 230)

Rhodesia [Rodesia] *s.* nombre colonial de los países que hoy son Zambia y Zimbabwe (pág. 630)

rig [manipular] *v.* influenciar o arreglar los resultados de una elección (pág. 594)

Ring of Fire [Anillo de Fuego] *s.* zona geográfica que se extiende a lo largo del borde del Océano Pacífico y tiene numerosos volcanes y terremotos (págs. 26, 824)

Rio de Janeiro [Río de Janeiro] *s.* capital de Brasil desde 1763 a 1960 (pág. 290)

ritual *s.* conjunto de ceremonias llevadas a cabo regularmente (pág. 774)

Rivera, Diego *s.* muralista famoso que pintó la historia de México sobre las paredes del Palacio Nacional (pág. 236)

Rocky Mountains [Montañas Rocosas] *s.* cordillera que se extiende aproximadamente 3,000 millas desde Nuevo México hasta Alaska (pág. 122)

Romance language [lengua romance] *s.* cualquiera de las lenguas que se desarrollaron a partir de la lengua romana, el latín, tales como el español, el portugués, el francés, el italiano y el rumano (pág. 362)

Rose Revolution [Revolución de las Rosas] *s.* levantamiento pacífico en la Georgia soviética que contribuyó a forzar la renuncia de un presidente corrupto (pág. 512)

Rosetta Stone [Piedra Roseta] *s.* antigua piedra egipcia que proporcionó un código para descifrar los jeroglíficos (pág. 562)

Royal Canadian Mounted Police [Real Policía Montada de Canadá] *s.* organización de oficiales responsables del cumplimiento de la ley en el oeste canadiense (pág. 170)

rural *adj.* relativo al campo (págs. 58, 236)

Russification [rusificación] *s.* esfuerzo en hacer que los países ocupados por la Unión Soviética se volvieran similares a Rusia mediante la sustitución de los idiomas y costumbres locales (págs. 424, 504)

S

Sadat, Anwar el- *s.* presidente de Egipto desde 1970 a 1981 (pág. 562)

safari *s.* una expedición por tierra en la que se practica la exploración, la caza o la fotografía (pág. 612)

Sahara *s.* el desierto más grande del mundo (pág. 536)

Sahel *s.* región semiárida al sur del Sahara (pág. 536)

samba *s.* música y baile, con raíces en los ritmos africanos; el estilo de música brasileña más famosa en el mundo (pág. 296)

Sami [sami] *s.* pueblo del norte de Escandinavia que tradicionalmente arrea renos; también es el nombre de su idioma (pág. 388)

samurai [samuráis] *s.* soldados profesionales de Japón (pág. 830)

San Martín, José de *s.* líder de la independencia en el sur de Suramérica (págs. 220, 280)

sanction [sanción] *s.* castigo o presión aplicados a un país por no obedecer una orden o ley (pág. 624)

Sanskrit [sánscrito] *s.* idioma antiguo de la India, hablado por primera vez por los arios (pág. 698)

Santa Anna, Antonio López de (1794–1876) *s.* general mexicano, presidente y líder de la independencia mexicana de España (pág. 230)

savanna [sabana] *s.* región de vegetación en los trópicos o subtrópicos con una mezcla de pastizales y árboles dispersos (págs. 40, 536)

scholar-official [académico-funcionario] *s.* persona educada que trabajaba en el gobierno chino (pág. 764)

Scientific Revolution [Revolución Científica] *s.* cambio rotundo en el pensamiento europeo a mediados del siglo XVI que llevó al cuestionamiento de viejas teorías (pág. 350)

Scott, Robert *s.* explorador británico que recorrió el polo (pág. 920)

seafaring [marinero] *adj.* que usa el mar para transportarse (pág. 326)

secular *adj.* mundano, no relacionado con la religión (pág. 342)

sediment [sedimento] *s.* pedazos de roca en forma de arena, piedra o cieno depositados por el viento, el agua o el hielo (pág. 26)

segregation [segregación] *s.* política de separar a la gente de razas diferentes (pág. 624)

seismic [sísmico] *adj.* relativo a los terremotos (pág. 756)

Selassie, Haile *s.* emperador de Etiopía de 1930 a 1974 (pág. 606)

self-rule [gobierno autónomo] *s.* gobierno independiente (pág. 580)

self-sufficient [autosuficiente] *adj.* capaz de satisfacer las propias necesidades sin ayuda externa (pág. 304)

selva s. nombre que se le da en español a la región al este de Perú que contiene bosques tropicales (pág. 272)

separatist [separatista] s. persona que quiere que una región se separe de la nación de la que forma parte (págs. 164, 370)

serf [siervo] s. en Europa, persona que vivía y trabajaba en la finca de un señor feudal o de un vasallo; en Rusia, campesino atado a la tierra (págs. 342, 468)

service industry [industria de servicios] s. industria que provee servicios en lugar de objetos (pág. 254)

Seven Years' War [Guerra de los Siete Años] (1756–1763) s. conflicto entre Gran Bretaña y Francia cuyos combates tuvieron lugar en América del Norte, Europa y la India (pág. 164)

shadow puppet [títeres de sombras] s. arte tradicional indonesio, en el que se manejan títeres desde detrás de una pantalla iluminada por una luz brillante (pág. 864)

shah [sah] s. título del rey de Persia o Irán (pág. 676)

Shakespeare, William s. dramaturgo y poeta inglés de finales del siglo XVI y principios del siglo XVII (pág. 408)

shamanism [chamanismo] s. sistema de creencias en el cual una persona llamada chamán se supone dotada de poderes para comunicarse con los espíritus y sanar a los enfermos (pág. 804)

Shi Huangdi s. primer emperador en unificar gran parte de China (pág. 764)

Shikoku s. isla principal más pequeña y menos poblada de Japón (pág. 824)

Shinto [sintoísmo] s. religión original de Japón; involucra la adoración de dioses que se cree se hallan en la naturaleza (pág. 830)

shock therapy [terapia de choque] s. en Rusia, término dado al plan económico de Yeltsin, el cual exigía un cambio abrupto desde una economía dirigida a una economía de mercado (pág. 486)

shogun [sogún] s. líder del gobierno militar japonés que comenzó en 1192 (pág. 830)

Siam s. antiguo nombre de Tailandia (pág. 858)

Siberia [Siberia] s. inmensa región de Rusia asiática (pág. 460)

Sierra Madre Occidental s. cordillera que se extiende de norte a sur por la parte oeste de México (pág. 198)

Sierra Madre Oriental s. cordillera que se extiende de norte a sur por la parte este de México (pág. 198)

Silk Roads [Rutas de la seda] s. principales rutas de comercio que iban desde China hasta el resto del este de Asia, a través de Asia Central y hasta Europa (págs. 504, 774)

silt [cieno] s. suelo fértil y blando transportado por los ríos y depositado en los terrenos circundantes (págs. 554, 666)

Solidarity [Solidaridad] s. primer sindicato independiente de Polonia, cuyo cofundador fue Lech Walesa (pág. 424)

solstice [solsticio] s. época del año en la que el Sol alcanza en el cielo su punto extremo al norte o al sur (pág. 40)

Songhai s. antiguo imperio de África Occidental, que tuvo su mayor poderío alrededor del siglo XVI d.C. (pág. 580)

souk [zoco] s. mercado al aire libre común en África del Norte (pág. 568)

Southern Alps [Alpes del Sur] s. cadena montañosa de Nueva Zelanda (pág. 884)

Southern Cone [Cono Sur] s. naciones de Suramérica ubicadas en la parte con forma de cono del extremo sur de Suramérica (pág. 280)

Soviet Union [Unión Soviética] s. nación comunista, compuesta por Rusia y otros 14 Estados, que existió entre 1922 y 1991 (pág. 728)

spatial [espacial] adj. relativo a la ubicación de un lugar y a su relación física con otros lugares, personas o ambientes (pág. 4)

specialization [especialización] s. énfasis en producir una cantidad limitada de un producto específico (pág. 72)

squatter [ocupante ilegal] s. persona que se asienta en tierras sin ocupar sin tener un derecho legal sobre ellas (pág. 236)

St. Lawrence Seaway [vía marítima de San Lorenzo] s. vía fluvial compuesta por el río San Lorenzo, los Grandes Lagos y diversos canales (pág. 156)

stability [estabilidad] s. durabilidad; resistencia al cambio (pág. 586)

Stalin, Joseph s. cruel dictador del siglo XX que hizo ejecutar a millones de sus enemigos políticos (págs. 468, 512)

standard of living [estándar de vida] s. medida económica relativa a la calidad y cantidad de bienes disponibles para un grupo de personas y cómo se distribuyen esos bienes en el grupo (pág. 432)

stateless societies [sociedades sin estado] s. grupos que no tienen una autoridad única, sino que toman decisiones basadas en el acuerdo (pág. 544)

steppe [estepa] s. planicie cubierta de hierba; en Rusia, esta área se ubica al sur de la taiga (pág. 460)

Stone Age [Edad de Piedra] s. primer período de la cultura humana, en el que las personas usaban herramientas de piedra (pág. 544)

strategic [estratégico] *adj.* relativo a un plan de acción diseñado para alcanzar una meta específica; con relación a lo militar, de ayuda en la lucha de una guerra (págs. 432, 728)

subcontinent [subcontinente] *s.* gran masa de tierra que es parte de un continente pero se considera como una región separada (pág. 658)

subsistence farming [agricultura de subsistencia] *s.* agricultura que produce tan sólo lo suficiente para alimentar a la familia del agricultor, quedando poco excedente o nada para vender (págs. 254, 586, 728, 736)

Sudan [Sudán] *s.* país del noreste de África, ubicado al sur de Egipto (pág. 562)

Suez Canal [Canal de Suez] *s.* vía marítima que une el Mar rojo con el Mar Mediterráneo (pág. 562)

Sumer [Sumeria] *s.* región de ciudades-estado de la Mesopotamia que albergó a la primera civilización (pág. 666)

surveyor [agrimensor] *s.* persona que traza un mapa del terreno y lo mide (págs. 10, 16)

sustainable [sostenible] *adj.* relativo al uso de recursos naturales de tal manera que existan para las generaciones futuras (pág. 48)

Swahili [swahili] *s.* idioma africano, comúnmente hablado en África Oriental (pág. 612)

T

taiga *s.* extenso bosque de Rusia que se ubica al sur de la tundra (pág. 460)

Taino [taíno] *s.* pueblo indígena de las islas del Caribe (pág. 260)

Taj Mahal *s.* hermosa tumba que se halla en India, construida por el gobernante mogol Shah Jahan para honrar a su esposa, que murió en 1631 (pág. 698)

Taklimakan Desert [Desierto de Taklimakán] *s.* el segundo desierto de arena más grande del mundo (pág. 756)

Taliban [talibán] *s.* grupo islámico conservador que tomó el control de Afganistán a mediados de la década de 1990 (pág. 728)

technology [tecnología] *s.* aplicación del conocimiento, herramientas e inventos de las personas para satisfacer sus necesidades (pág. 96)

tectonic plate [placa tectónica] *s.* sección rígida de gran tamaño en la corteza terrestre que se encuentra en movimiento constante (págs. 26, 198, 536)

territory [territorio] *s.* unidad política canadiense que no tiene suficientes personas como para ser una provincia (pág. 156)

Tet *s.* año nuevo vietnamita y el feriado más importante en Vietnam (pág. 858)

theocracy [teocracia] *s.* gobierno regido por líderes religiosos (pág. 676)

Three Gorges Dam [Presa de las Tres Gargantas] *s.* barrera construida en el río Chang Jiang para controlar las inundaciones (pág. 756)

Three Kingdoms [Tres Reinos] *s.* los tres reinos que se habían formado en la Península de Corea hacia el año 300 d.C. (pág. 804)

three-dimensional [tridimensional] *adj.* que describe una imagen en la que hay un sentido de profundidad y perspectiva (pág. 4)

Tiananmen Square [Plaza Tiananmen] *s.* la ubicación en Pekín, China, de una inmensa manifestación a favor de los derechos democráticos que se realizó en 1989 (pág. 784)

Tian Shan *s.* cordillera que se extiende a través de Kirguistán y Tayikistán (pág. 496)

Tigris River [río Tigris] *s.* río del suroeste de Asia que fluye desde una meseta en la Península de Anatolia hasta el Golfo Pérsico (pág. 652)

Tito, Josip Broz *s.* líder comunista de Yugoslavia desde 1953 a 1980 (pág. 440)

Tokugawa Ieyasu *s.* sogún que unificó Japón (pág. 830)

Tolstoy, Leo *s.* escritor del siglo XIX que es uno de los más grandes novelistas rusos (pág. 476)

totalitarian [totalitario] *adj.* relativo a un tipo de gobierno que controla todos los aspectos de la vida pública y privada (págs. 468, 812)

tourism [turismo] *s.* industria que provee servicios para los viajeros (pág. 260)

Transantarctic Mountains [Montañas Transantárticas] *s.* montañas que dividen a la Antártida en dos partes (pág. 920)

Transcaucasia *s.* región entre los mares Negro y Caspio que comprende las repúblicas de Armenia, Azerbaiyán y Georgia (pág. 496)

transcontinental railroad [ferrocarril transcontinental] *s.* ferrocarril que cruza un continente (pág. 130)

trans-Saharan [trans-sahariano] *adj.* que atraviesa el Sahara (pág. 580)

Treaty of Tordesillas [Tratado de Tordesillas] *s.* tratado de 1494 entre España y Portugal que le dio a Portugal el control sobre la tierra que hoy es Brasil (pág. 290)

Treaty of Waitangi [Tratado de Waitangi] *s.* tratado entre los británicos y los maoríes firmado en 1840 (pág. 900)

trust territory [territorio en fideicomiso] *s.* territorio puesto bajo el control de un país por las Naciones Unidas (pág. 912)

tsunami [tsunami] *s.* serie de olas oceánicas gigantes y destructivas causadas por terremotos, volcanes o desplazamientos de tierras submarinos (págs. 658, 736, 852)

tundra *s.* clima seco y frío y vegetación adaptada a tal clima que se halla en el Círculo Polar Ártico; en Rusia, ubicada en el extremo norte (págs. 156, 460)

typhoon [tifón] *s.* tormenta tropical que comienza en los océanos Pacífico o Índico (pág. 796)

tyrant [tirano] *s.* alguien que toma el poder ilegalmente (pág. 334)

U

Uluru *s.* espectacular afloramiento rocoso en el desierto interior australiano (pág. 884)

Union of Soviet Socialist Republics (USSR), o **Soviet Union** [Unión de Repúblicas Socialistas Soviéticas (URSS), o Unión Soviética] *s.* nación con un gobierno comunista creada por los bolcheviques en 1922; disuelta en 1991 (pág. 468)

unwritten constitution [constitución no escrita] *s.* marco de gobierno que no es un único documento escrito sino que incluye muchas leyes diferentes, decisiones judiciales y costumbres políticas (pág. 414)

Ural Mountains [montes Urales] *s.* cordillera que se extiende de norte a sur y forma la frontera entre la Rusia europea y la asiática (pág. 460)

urban [urbano] *adj.* relativo a la ciudad (págs. 16, 58, 236)

urban planner [urbanista] *s.* persona que crea planes para desarrollar y mejorar partes de una ciudad (pág. 16)

urbanization [urbanización] *s.* crecimiento en el número de personas que viven en áreas urbanas; el proceso de desarrollo de las ciudades (págs. 58, 290)

V

vassal [vasallo] *s.* noble menos acaudalado que pagaba impuestos y servía a un señor feudal a cambio de tierras (pág. 342)

Vatican [Vaticano] *s.* la residencia oficial del Papa en la Ciudad de Vaticano y el centro político y religioso de la Iglesia Católica Romana (pág. 362)

Vedas *s.* antiguos escritos en sánscrito que son los primeros textos sagrados del hinduismo (pág. 698)

vegetation region [región de vegetación] *s.* un área que tiene plantas similares (pág. 40)

Velvet Revolution [Revolución de Terciopelo] *s.* protesta pacífica del pueblo checo que condujo al fin paulatino del comunismo en Checoslovaquia (pág. 432)

Victoria Falls [cataratas Victoria] *s.* cataratas de 355 pies de alto en el río Zambezi, en el sur de África Central (pág. 536)

Vikings [vikingos] *s.* pueblo marinero escandinavo que realizó incursiones en Europa occidental y del norte desde el siglo IX al siglo XI (pág. 388)

volcano [volcán] *s.* abertura en la corteza terrestre de la que fluyen o salen expelidos roca fundida, ceniza y gases calientes (pág. 26)

Volga River [río Volga] *s.* río más largo de Europa, que fluye a través de la Rusia europea (pág. 460)

W

Walesa, Lech *s.* líder polaco, cofundador de Solidaridad, que fue presidente de Polonia desde 1990 a 1995 (pág. 424)

weather [tiempo] *s.* la condición de la atmósfera terrestre en un momento y lugar dados (pág. 40)

weathering [desgaste] *s.* erosión física y química gradual de las rocas en la superficie de la Tierra (pág. 26)

welfare state [estado de bienestar] *s.* sistema social en el que el gobierno satisface muchas de las necesidades de sus ciudadanos (pág. 388)

West Bank [Cisjordania] *s.* región al oeste del río Jordán (pág. 682)

wind farm [parque eólico] *s.* central de energía que usa molinos de viento para generar electricidad (pág. 414)

X

Xi Jiang *s.* río en el sureste de China (pág. 756)

Y

Yalu River [río Yalu] *s.* el río más largo de la Península de Corea; forma parte de la frontera entre China y Corea del Norte; conocido como el río Amnok en coreano (pág. 796)

Yeltsin, Boris *s.* presidente que transformó abruptamente la economía rusa después del colapso de la Unión Soviética (pág. 486)

Yoruba [yoruba] *s.* pueblo del suroeste de Nigeria, parte de Benín y Togo (pág. 586)

Yugoslavia *s.* país en la Península de los Balcanes desde 1918 a 1991 (pág. 440)

yurt [yurta] *s.* estructura portátil semejante a una tienda usada por los nómadas de Asia Central (pág. 504)

Z

zaibatsu *s.* grandes grupos financieros e industriales controlados por familias que poseían muchas compañías en Japón antes de la Segunda Guerra Mundial (pág. 840)

Zaire *s.* nombre de la República Democrática del Congo entre 1971 y 1997 (pág. 618)

ziggurat [zigurat] *s.* templo construido encima de una serie de plataformas progresivamente más pequeñas (pág. 666)

Index

Page references in **boldface** indicate Key Terms & Names and Background Vocabulary that are highlighted in the main text.

Page references in *italics* indicate illustrations, charts, and maps.

E

S

Acknowledgments

Text Acknowledgments

Front Matter
Houghton Mifflin: Adaption of line graph from "Exports of English Manufactured Goods, 1700-1774," from *A History of World Societies,* Fifth Edition by John P. McKay, Bennett D. Hill, John Buckler, and Patricia Buckley Ebrey. Copyright © 2000 by Houghton Mifflin Company. All rights reserved. Used by permission.

Unit 1
Christian Science Monitor: Excerpt from "As English Spreads, Speakers Morph It Into World Tongue," by David Rohde from *Christian Science Monitor,* May 17, 1995. Copyright © 1995 by the *Christian Science Monitor.* Reprinted by permission of the *Christian Science Monitor* (www.csmonitor.com). All rights reserved.

Unit 3
John Bierhorst: Excerpt from "The Eagle On the Prickly Pear," from *The Hungry Woman* by John Bierhorst. Copyright © 1984 by John Bierhorst. Reprinted by permission of the author.

Rhett A. Butler: Excerpt from Interview with William F. Laurance by Rhett A. Butler. Copyright © 2006 by Rhett A. Butler. Reprinted by permission of Rhett A. Butler, mongabay.com.

Unit 4
Andreas Ramos: Excerpt from "A Personal Account of The Fall of the Berlin Wall," by Andreas Ramos from www.andreas.com/berlin.html. Copyright © by Andreas Ramos. Reprinted by permission of the author.

Unit 6
Atlantic Monthly: Excerpt from "An African Voice" interview with Chinua Achebe by Katie Bacon from *Atlantic Online,* August 2, 2000. Copyright © 2000 by *Atlantic Monthly.* Reprinted with permission of *Atlantic Monthly Online.*

Unit 7
Diablo Press: Excerpt from *India Emerges: A Concise History* by Steven Warshaw. Copyright © 1987, 1988 Diablo Press Inc. Reprinted by permission of Diablo Press Inc.

Newsweek: Excerpt from "A City That Echoes Eternity" by Kenneth Woodward, from *Newsweek,* July 24, 2000. Copyright © 2000 by *Newsweek.* Reprinted by permission of *Newsweek, Inc.* All rights reserved.

Unit 8
Shambhala Publications: "Cool crescent moon," by Bashō, translated from the Japanese by Sam Hamill. Copyright © 1998 by Sam Hamill. Reprinted by permission of Shambhala Publications, Inc.

Photography

Front Matter
cover *front to back* © Dennis Cox/Alamy; © Theo Allofs/zefa/Corbis; © Robert Fried/Alamy; © David Sanger Photography/Alamy; © Bruce Coleman Inc./Alamy; *background* © Adam Crowley/Getty Images; **Senior Consultants** *top* Photograph by Robert S. Bednarz; *center* Photograph by Marci Smith Deal; *bottom* Photograph by Inés M. Miyares; **Senior Consultants** *top* Photograph by Rob Caron; *center* Photograph by Erica Houskeeper; *bottom* Photograph by Joe Wieszczyk; **Student Panel** Photographs by Bac To Trong; **Contents in Brief** *top left* © Keren Su/Getty Images; *top center* © Corbis; *top right* © Beth Dixson/Getty Images; **Introduction to World Geography** *top left* © Joeseph Sohm-Visions of America/Getty Images; *top right* © Tibor Bognar/Alamy; **The United States and Canada** *top left* © Fridmar Damm/zefa/Corbis; *top center* © Getty Images; *second from top right* © Irwin Barrett/Getty Images; *top right* © Art Wolfe/Getty Images; **Latin America** *top left* © Getty Images; *top, reef* © Royalty-Free/Corbis; *top, small dolphin* © David Tipling/Alamy; *top, big dolphin* © Stuart Westmorland/Corbis; **Europe** *top left* © Simon Reddy/Alamy; *top right* © Bill Bachmann/Index Stock Imagery/Jupiter Images; **Russia and The Eurasian Republics** *top left* © Pavel Filatov/Alamy; *top center* © Pavel Filatov/Alamy; *top right* © Pavel Filatov/Alamy; *top right inset* © Royalty-Free/Corbis; **Africa** *top left* © Sylvia Cordaiy Photo Library Ltd./Alamy; *top center* © Joshua D. Polman/Alamy; *top right* © Stan Osolinski/Oxford Scientific/Jupiter Images; **Southwest Asia and South Asia** *top left* © Design Pics Inc./Alamy; *top center* © Dinodia Images/Alamy; *top right* © Michelangelo Gratton/Getty Images; **East Asia and Southeast Asia** *top left* © Jose Fuste Raga/Corbis; *top right* © Angelo Cavalli/Getty Images; **Oceania and Antarctica** *top left* © Chris Cheadle/Getty Images; *top center* © Peter Scoones/Getty Images; *top right* © David Tipling/Getty Images; **Features** *top* Confucius (551-479 B.C.). Scroll painting. Bibliotheque Nationale, Paris. Photo © Snark/Art Resource, New York; *bottom right* © Stockbyte Silver/Alamy; **Features** *top* © Rob Melnychuk/Getty Images; **Graphs, Tables, and Charts** © Gavriel Jecan/Corbis; **Reading for Understanding** *top* © Comstock Images/Alamy; **Geography Handbook** NASA Goddard Space Flight Center; **A11** *bottom left* © Getty Images; *top right* © Bruce Roberts/Photo Researchers, Inc.; *second from top right* © Frans Lanting/Corbis; *third from top right* © David R. Frazier/Photo Researchers, Inc.; **A12–13** Image created by Reto Stockli with the help of Alan Nelson, under the leadership of Fritz Hasler/NASA.

Unit 1 Opener
1 *top right* © Getty Images; *top left* © Digital Vision/Getty Images; *bottom right* © Peter Horree/Alamy; *bottom left* © Philip and Karen Smith/Getty Images.

Chapter 1
2-3 NASA Goddard Space Flight Center; **2** *bottom left* Strabo (1584). Engraving. The Granger Collection, New York; *bottom right* © Science Museum/Science and Society Picture Library; *top left* © Peter Horree/Alamy; **3** *bottom left* © Science Museum/Science and Society Picture Library; *bottom right* © Photolibrary/Alamy; *center right* © Peter Horree/Alamy; *center left* © Photo Researchers, Inc.; **5** *bottom* NASA; *top left* © Keren Su/Getty Images; *top center* © Corbis; *top right* © Beth Dixson/Getty Images; **6** *top* © Silvestre Machado/Getty Images; *second from top* © Gavin Hellier/Getty Images; *center* © Danita Delimont/Alamy; *second from bottom* © Lester Lefkowitz/Corbis; *bottom* © Phil Schermeister/Peter Arnold, Inc.; **7** *second from top* © David R. Frazier/Photo Researchers, Inc.; *center left* © Craig Lovell/Eagle Visions Photography/Alamy; *second from bottom* © Frans Lanting/Corbis; *bottom* © Bruce Roberts/Photo Researchers, Inc.; **8** © Mark Segal/Panoramic Images/NGSImages.com; **11** *center right* © The Image Works, Inc.; *bottom* © Rob Matheson/Corbis; *top left* © Keren Su/Getty Images; *top center* © Corbis; *top right* © Beth Dixson/Getty Images; **12** *bottom left* Strabo (1584). Engraving. The Granger Collection, New York; *bottom right* Horace L. Jones. trans., *The Geography of Strabo*, 8 vols. (New York: G.P. Putnam's Sons, (1917), vol. 1, pp. 451-455, 501-503, 277-385, passim; **13** *bottom center* © NASA/Angela King/Geology.com; *bottom right* © Max Dannenbaum/Getty Images; **14** *center* © David R. Frazier Photolibrary, Inc./Alamy; **15** © Craig Lovell/Eagle Visions Photography/Alamy; **16** © David Vaughan/Photo Researchers, Inc.; **17** *center* © Mark Gibson/Alamy; *bottom* © Mark Edwards/Peter Arnold, Inc.; *top left* © Keren Su/Getty Images; *top center* © Corbis; *top right* © Beth Dixson/Getty Images; **18** © Johnathan Smith; Cordaiy Photo Library Ltd./Corbis; **19** *top* © age fotostock/SuperStock; *bottom* © Jeff Greenberg/Alamy; **20** © Erin Cigliano; **21** *bottom left* © NASA/Angela King/Geology.com; *bottom right* © Scott Rothstein/ShutterStock; **22** © Scott Rothstein/ShutterStock.

Chapter 2
24 *bottom* The Granger Collection, New York; *top left* © Peter Horree/Alamy; **25** © Gary Braasch/Corbis; **26** © Gregory G. Dimijian, M.D./Photo Researchers, Inc.; **27** *bottom* © Roger Ressmeyer/Corbis; *top left* © Robert Glusic/Getty Images; *top center* © Getty Images; *top right* © Royalty-Free/Corbis; *top right inset* © Peter Arnold, Inc./Alamy; **31** *background* © George Steinmetz/Corbis; *bottom* © Roger Ressmeyer/Corbis; **32-33** © James Randklev/Getty Images; **33** © Corbis; **34** D. Brown/PanStock/Panoramic Images/National Geographic Image Collection; **35** *center right* NASA; *bottom* © David Lyons/Alamy; *top left* © Robert Glusic/Getty Images; *top center* © Getty Images; *top right* © Royalty-Free/Corbis; *top right inset* © Peter Arnold, Inc./Alamy; **36** © Scott T. Smith/Corbis; **38** Sitki Tarlan/Panoramic Images/National Geographic Image Collection; **39** © James D. Watt/Image Quest Marine; **40** © Jeff Lepore/Photo Researchers, Inc.; **41** *center right* © Jeff Schultz/AlaskaStock.com; *bottom* © Arend/Soucek/AlaskaStock.com; *top left* © Robert Glusic/Getty Images; *top center* © Getty Images; *top right* © Royalty-Free/Corbis; *top right inset* © Peter Arnold, Inc./Alamy; **43** *all* © Getty Images; © Getty Images; © Getty Images; **46** *center left* © Ed George/NGSImages.com; *bottom left* © Mark Moffett/Minden Pictures; **48** © Frank Kroenke/Peter Arnold, Inc.; **49** *bottom* © Knut Mueller/Peter Arnold, Inc.; *top left* © Robert Glusic/Getty Images; *top center* © Getty Images; *top right* © Royalty-Free/Corbis; *top right inset* © Peter Arnold, Inc./Alamy; **51** Fritz Reiss/AP/Wide World Photos; **52** © William Campbell/Corbis; **53** *center left* © Douglas Peebles/Corbis; *bottom right* Sitki Tarlan/Panoramic Images/National Geographic Image Collection; **54** NASA.

Chapter 3
56 *top left* © Peter Adams Photography/Alamy; *bottom left* Kuba mask. Kuba related peoples, Zaire. Wood, pigment. Private collection. Photo © Aldo Tutino/Art Resource, New York; *bottom right* © The British Museum/HIP/The Image Works, Inc.; **57** *center* NASA; *bottom left* © Gary Randall/Getty Images; *bottom center*

© First/zefa/Corbis; **58** © Royalty-Free/Corbis; **59** *bottom* © David Lawrence; *top left* © Joseph Sohm-Visions of America/Getty Images; *top right* © Tibor Bognar/Alamy; **60** © Art Kowalsky/Alamy; **61** © Peter Adams Photography/Alamy; **62** © PCL/Alamy; **64** *center left* © Dave G. Houser/Post-Houserstock/Corbis; *center right* © Australian Scenics; *bottom* © John Hay/Lonely Planet Images; **65** *center left* © Robin Moyer/OnAsia; *center right* © Dan Bigelow/Getty Images; *bottom* © Robert Harding Picture Library Ltd/Alamy; **66** © Yellow Dog Productions/Getty Images; *center right* © Alexander Walter/Getty Images; *bottom* The Granger Collection, New York; *top left* © Joeseph Sohm-Visions of America/Getty Images; *top right* © Tibor Bognar/Alamy; **68** The Granger Collection, New York; **69** Kuba mask. Kuba related peoples, Zaire. Wood, pigment. Private collection. Photo © Aldo Tutino/Art Resource, New York; **70** Brennan Linsley/AP/Wide World Photos; **71** © Beatrice Mategwa/Reuters/Corbis; **73** *bottom* © Photo Researchers, Inc.; **74** *top left* © Joeseph Sohm-Visions of America/Getty Images; *top right* © Tibor Bognar/Alamy; **75** Steve Raymer/National Geographic Image Collection; **76** © Sue Cunningham Photographic/Alamy; **77** © Authors Image/Alamy; **78** © Le Segretain Pascal/Corbis; **79** *top left* © Joeseph Sohm-Visions of America/Getty Images; *top right* © Tibor Bognar/Alamy; *center right* © Denise Kappa/ShutterStock; *bottom* © Marc Muench/Getty Images; **81** © Majid/Getty Images; **82** Gregory Bull/AP/Wide World Photos; **83** *bottom left* © Le Segretain Pascal/Corbis; *bottom right* © Dan Lamont/Corbis; **84** © Bettmann/Corbis.

Chapter 4

86 *bottom center* © The British Museum/Topham-HIP/The Image Works, Inc.; *bottom right* © Jane Sweeney/Lonely Planet Images; *top left* © Philip and Karen Smith/Getty Images; *bottom left* © Louis Fox/Getty Images; **87** Limestone tablet with Sumerian pictographic script. Symbol of the hand indicates the proprietor. End of 4th millenium. Mesopotamia. 5 x 4.2 cm. A) 19936. Louvre, Paris. Photo © Erich Lessing/Art Resource, New York; *bottom right* © Peter Horree/Alamy; *top left* © Nathan Benn/Corbis; *center* Benin aquamanile in the shape of a leopard (1700s). British Museum, London. Photo © Art Resource, New York; *top right* © Lowell Georgia/Corbis; **88** © Pascal Goetgheluck/Photo Researchers, Inc.; **89** *bottom* © David L. Brown/PanStock/Jupiter Images; *top left* © Joe Sohm/Pan America/Jupiter Images; *top center* © David Jones/Alamy; *top right* © Kevin Schafer/Alamy; **90** © Sergio Gaudenti/Kipa/Corbis; **91** *top left* © Rob Melnychuk/Getty Images; *top left* © Yellow Dog Productions/Getty Images; *top center* © Jeff Greenberg/PhotoEdit; *second from right* © Michael Newman/PhotoEdit; *bottom right* © Getty Images; **92** Boddhisatva Kuan-Yin (Avalokitesvara) (1271-1368 B.C.). Porcelain Ch'ing Pai ware with blue glaze. National Museum, Beijing. Photo © Erich Lessing/Art Resource, New York; **96** © Images&Stories/Alamy; **97** *center right* © Bill Bachman/Danita Delimont; *bottom* © Robert Azzi/Woodfin Camp and Associates, Inc.; *top left* © Joe Sohm/Pan America/Jupiter Images; *top center* © David Jones/Alamy; *top right* © Kevin Schafer/Alamy; **98** *left* Pot with handles, ribbon-ornaments and animal scenes. Baked clay with white incrustations. The Louvre, Paris. Photo © Erich Lessing/Art Resource, New York; *center* Basket woven with a killer whale crest. Spruce root. Museum of Anthropology, University of British Columbia, Vancouver, British Columbia, Canada. Photo © Werner Forman/Art Resource, New York; *right* Pouch (1800s). Mixed media. 30cm. Peabody Essex Museum, Salem, Massachusetts. Photo © Bridgeman Art Library; **100** © David Noble Photography/Alamy; **101** *bottom right* Limestone tablet with Sumerian pictographic script. Symbol of the hand indicates the proprietor. End of 4th millenium. Mesopotamia. 5 x 4.2 cm. A) 19936. Louvre, Paris. Photo © Erich Lessing/Art Resource, New York; *bottom left* © Pascal Goetgheluck/Photo Researchers, Inc.; *center left* © Dynamic Graphics Group/IT Stock Free/Alamy; **102** © J. Marshall - Tribaleye Images/Alamy.

Unit 2 Opener

105 *bottom left* © Galen Rowell/Corbis; *top right* © Royalty-Free/Corbis; *bottom right* © Robert Harding/Getty Images; **110** © Lee Snider/Corbis; **111** *top right* © Paul A. Souders/Corbis; *bottom* © JupiterMedia/Alamy; **113** © Royalty-Free/Corbis; **114** © Tom Walker/Getty Images; **115** © Buddy Mays/Corbis; **116** © Getty Images; **117** © franzfoto.com/Alamy; **118** © Joseph Van Os/Riser/Getty Images; **119** © Visual&Written SL/Alamy.

Chapter 5

120 *bottom left* © Lee Snider/Photo Images/Corbis; *bottom right* *Battle of Lexington* (about 1850), Alonzo Chappel. Photo © Bettmann/Corbis; *top left* © Bill Ross/Corbis; **121** *bottom left* The Granger Collection, New York; *bottom right* AP/Wide World Photos; **123** *center left* © Sean Daveys/Australian Picture Library/Corbis; *center right* © bilderlounge/Alamy; *bottom* © Christopher Talbot Frank/Photex/zefa/Corbis; *top left* © Fridmar Damm/zefa/Corbis; *top center* © Getty Images; *second from top right* © Irwin Barrett/

Getty Images; *top right* © Art Wolfe/Getty Images; **124** © Joseph Sohm/Corbis; **126** *top left* © David Muench/Corbis; *bottom right* © Tom Bean/Corbis; **127** *top right* © Royalty-Free/Corbis; *bottom left* © Tom Bean/Corbis; **128-129** *top* © Andrew Sacks/Corbis; *bottom* © Reinhard Eisele/Corbis; **128** *top inset* © Galen Rowell/Corbis; *center* © Luis Castaneda Inc./Getty Images; *bottom left* © Arthur Morris/Corbis; **129** *top* © Tom Bean/Corbis; *second from right* © William Manning/Corbis; *right* © Arthur Morris/Corbis; *bottom* © Marvin E. Newman/Getty Images; **131** *center right* © Veer; *bottom* © Robert Holmes/Corbis; *top left* © Fridmar Damm/zefa/Corbis; *top center* © Getty Images; *second from top right* © Irwin Barrett/Getty Images; *top right* © Art Wolfe/Getty Images; **133** *The Drafting of the Declaration of Independence* (1909), Jean Leon Germome Ferris. Painting. Photograph © PoodlesRock/Corbis; **135** © Francis G. Mayer/Corbis; **136** *top left* The Granger Collection, New York; *bottom* © Bettmann/Corbis; **137** © Corbis; **138** © Richard T. Nowitz/Corbis; **139** *center right* © David Katzenstein/Corbis; *bottom* © Alan Schein Photography/Corbis; *top left* © Fridmar Damm/zefa/Corbis; *top center* © Getty Images; *second from top right* © Irwin Barrett/Getty Images; *top right* © Art Wolfe/Getty Images; **140** © Veer; **141** © Rob Lewine/Corbis; **142** © Getty Images; **143** © Pictorial Press/Alamy; **144** © Natalie Fobes/Corbis; **145** © Paul. J. Sutton/Duomo/Corbis; **147** *bottom* © Roger Ressmeyer/Corbis; *top left* © Fridmar Damm/zefa/Corbis; *top center* © Getty Images; *second from top right* © Irwin Barrett/Getty Images; *top right* © Art Wolfe/Getty Images; **148** *top left* © Martin H. Simon/Corbis; *top center* © Corbis; *top right* © Brooks Kraft/Corbis; **150** © Chad Ehlers/Alamy; **151** © Francis G. Mayer/Corbis; **152** The Granger Collection, New York; **153** © Bettmann/Corbis.

Chapter 6

154 *bottom left* © David Sanger photography/Alamy; *bottom right* © Philip Gould/Corbis; *top left* © David Noton Photography/Alamy; **155** © Corbis; **156** © Kike Calvo/V&W/The Image Works, Inc.; **157** *bottom* © Ray Juno/Corbis; *top left* © Grant Taylor/Getty Images; *second from top left* © Corbis; *top center* © John Wang/Getty Images; *second from top right* © David Tipling/Alamy; *top right* © Bruce Heinemann/Getty Images; **158** *center left* © Ron Watts/Corbis; *bottom left* © Terrance Klassen/Alamy; *center right* © Ed Simpson/Getty Images; *bottom right* © Wolfgang Kaehler/Corbis; **160** © Rob Howard/Corbis; **161** © Terry W. Eggers/Corbis; **162** *bottom left* © Richard T. Nowitz/Corbis; **164** © Robert McGouey/Corbis; **165** *bottom* © Ron Watts/Corbis; *center right* © David Sanger photography/Alamy; *top left* © Grant Taylor/Getty Images; *second from top left* © Corbis; *top center* © John Wang/Getty Images; *second from top right* © David Tipling/Alamy; *top right* © Bruce Heinemann/Getty Images; **166** *bottom left* © John Farmer/Cordaiy Photo Library Ltd./Corbis; *John Cabot* (about 1450). Color print. Photo © Image Select/Art Resource, New York; *Jacques Cartier, Samuel de Champlain, Henry Hudson* © North Wind Picture Archives/Alamy; **167** © Bettmann/Corbis; **168** *bottom right* © Royalty-Free/Corbis; **169** © Ted Spiegel/Corbis; **170** *left* © Michael S. Yamashita/Corbis; *right* © Peter Arnold, Inc./Alamy; **171** *center left* © Paul A. Souders/Corbis; *bottom* © Wayne R. Bilenduke/Getty Images; *top left* © Grant Taylor/Getty Images; *second from top left* © Corbis; *top center* © John Wang/Getty Images; *second from top right* © David Tipling/Alamy; *top right* © Bruce Heinemann/Getty Images; **172** © Natalie Fobes/Corbis; **173** *top* © Bryan & Cherry Alexander Photography/Alamy; *bottom* © Corbis; **174** *top left* © Bryan & Cherry Alexander Photography/Alamy; *top center* © Alissa Crandall/Corbis; *second from right* © Wolfgang Kaehler/Corbis; *bottom right* © Bryan & Cherry Alexander Photography/Alamy; *bottom left* © Galen Rowell/Corbis; **175** © Wally McNamee/Corbis; **177** *bottom* © Andre Jenny/Alamy; *top left* © Grant Taylor/Getty Images; *second from top left* © Corbis; *top center* © John Wang/Getty Images; *second from top right* © David Tipling/Alamy; *top right* © Bruce Heinemann/Getty Images; **178** Jeff McIntosh/AP/Wide World Photos; **179** © Getty Images; **181** *bottom right* © David Sanger photography/Alamy; *bottom left* © Paul A. Souders/Corbis; **182** © Robert McGouey/Alamy.

Unit 3 Opener

185 *top right* © Peter M. Wilson/Alamy; *top left* © Ian Cumming/Axiom; *bottom left* © Mauritius/SuperStock; *bottom right* © Rachael Bowes/Alamy; **190-191** © Wide Group/Iconica/Getty Images; **191** © eStock Photo/Alamy; **193** © Larry Fisher/Masterfile; **194** © Andoni Canela/ASA/IPNstock; **195** © Carol Barrington/IPNstock.

Chapter 7

196 *bottom left* © Werner Forman/Corbis; *bottom right* Chalchihuitlicue. Sculpture. British Museum, London. Photo © Werner Forman/Art Resource, New York; *top left* © Dynamic Graphics Group/IT Stock Free/Alamy; **197** *bottom left* The Granger Collection, New York; *bottom right* The Granger Collection, New York; **199** *top left* © Royalty-Free/Corbis; *top center* © Getty Images; *bottom* © Toby Maudsley/Getty Images; *top waterfall* © imagebroker/Alamy;

top macaw © Getty Images; top leaves © Getty Images; **200** © Jeff Hunter/Getty Images; **201** © Danny Lehman/Corbis; **202** left © Getty Images; center © eStock Photo/Alamy; right © Robert Everts/Getty Images; **203** © Gail Shumway/Getty Images; **204** © Gary Cook/Alamy; **205** top left © Royalty-Free/Corbis; top center © Getty Images; bottom © Peter Adams Photography/Alamy; top waterfall © imagebroker/Alamy; top macaw © Getty Images; top leaves © Getty Images; **206** © Jay Dickman/Corbis; **208** © Keith Dannemiller/Alamy; **209** top left © Simon Littlejohn/Alamy; top right © Derrick Francis Furlong/Alamy; bottom left © Pixonnet.com/Alamy; bottom right © Jeremy Horner/Corbis; **210** © Hemis/Alamy; **211** © H. Sitton/zefa/Corbis; **213** top left © Royalty-Free/Corbis; top center © Getty Images; center right © SEF/Art Resource, New York; bottom © Vanni/Art Resource, New York; top waterfall © imagebroker/Alamy; top macaw © Getty Images; top leaves © Getty Images; **214** center left Photo by Fernando Rochaix, University of Texas/Courtesy of the Naachtun Archaeological Project; bottom left Drawing by Peter L. Mathews, La Trobe University, Australia/Courtesy of the Naachtun Archaeological Project; bottom center Photo by Fernando Rochaix, University of Texas/Courtesy of the Naachtun Archaeological Project; **215** center right © Loren McIntyre-Woodfin Camp/IPNstock; © Getty Images; center left © Werner Forman/Art Resource, New York; The Granger Collection, New York; left Detail of a page from the Codex Becker depicting two war-chiefs. Museum fuer Voelkerkunde, Vienna, Austria. Photo © Werner Forman/Art Resource, New York; **216** © Dagli Orti/Museo Ciudad Mexico/The Art Archive; **217** © Wolfgang Kaehler/Corbis; **218** bottom left © Danny Lehman/Corbis; **220** The Granger Collection, New York; **221** top left © Royalty-Free/Corbis; top center © Getty Images; top waterfall © imagebroker/Alamy; top macaw © Getty Images; top leaves © Getty Images; **222** © James Quine/Alamy; **223** Father Hidalgo at the Battle of Monte de las Cruces, 1810 (1865), Joaquin Ramirez. National Palace, Mexico City. Photo © Art Resource, New York; **224** © J. Marshall - Tribaleye Images/Alamy.

Chapter 8

228 bottom left Portrait of Emperor Maximilian of Mexico (1865), Albert Graefle. Museo Nacional de Historia, Castillo de Chapultepec, Mexico City. Photo © Schalkwijk/Art Resource, New York; bottom right The Granger Collection, New York; top left © Tom Bean/Getty Images; **229** bottom right © Reuters/Corbis; **231** center right Santa Anna (1849). Lithograph. Photo The Granger Collection, New York; bottom Encounter of the Armies (1964), David Alfaro Siqueiros. Mural. Museo Nacional de Historia, Castillo de Chapultepec, Mexico City. Photo © Schalkwijk/Art Resource, New York; top left © Macduff Everton/Getty Images; top center © blickwinkel/Alamy; pine © Getty Images; top right, large butterfly © Getty Images; top right, group of butterflies © Elvele Images/Alamy; **233** Benito Juarez (1870). Steel engraving. Photo The Granger Collection, New York; **234** Francisco "Pancho" Villa (1914). Oil over a photograph. Photo The Granger Collection, New York; **235** © Janet Schwartz/Getty Images; **236** © Tony Anderson/Getty Images; **237** bottom © Royalty-Free/Corbis; top left © Macduff Everton/Getty Images; top center © blickwinkel/Alamy; pine © Getty Images; top right, large butterfly © Getty Images; top right, group of butterflies © Elvele Images/Alamy; **238** left © John Mitchell Stock Photography, photographersdirect.com; right © Viviane Moos/Corbis; **239** Self Portrait with Changuito (1945), Frida Kahlo. Fundacion Dolores Olmedo, Mexico City. © Banco de Mexico Trust. Photo © Schalkwijk/Art Resource, New York; **240** top left © JupiterMedia/Alamy; center right © Danita Delimont/Alamy; bottom left © Danita Delimont/Alamy; bottom right © Spike Mafford/Getty Images; **241** © Henry Romero/Reuters/Corbis; **242** top right © Kathleen Finlay/Masterfile; center left © David Hiser/Getty Images; bottom right © Kayte Deioma Photography, photographersdirect.com; background © Irfan Parvez, http://pg.photos.yahoo.com/ph/iparvezfareast/my_photos; **243** top left © Steve Hamblin/Alamy; bottom © Russell Monk/Masterfile; center right © Rommel/Masterfile; background © Chris Barton Travel Photography/photographersdirect.com; **244** © Keith Dannemiller/Corbis; **245** bottom © Lynsey Addario/Corbis; top left © Macduff Everton/Getty Images; top center © blickwinkel/Alamy; pine © Getty Images; top right, large butterfly © Getty Images; top right, group of butterflies © Elvele Images/Alamy; **246** © Reuters/Corbis; **247** © Oxford Scientific/Jupiter Images; **248** © Tom Tracy Photography/Alamy; **249** bottom left Benito Juarez (1870). Steel engraving. Photo The Granger Collection, New York; bottom right © Tony Anderson/Getty Images; center left © Blend Images/Veer; **250** © Danita Delimont/Alamy.

Chapter 9

252 top left © Stuart Westmorland/Getty Images; bottom left © Royalty-Free/Corbis; bottom right © Bettmann/Corbis; **253** bottom left © Brian A. Vikander/Corbis; bottom right © Bettmann/Corbis; **255** center right © Stuart Westmorland/Getty Images; bottom

© Hemis/Alamy; top left © Getty Images; top, reef © Royalty-Free/Corbis; top, small dolphin © David Tipling/Alamy; top, big dolphin © Stuart Westmorland/Corbis; **257** © Matthew Johnston/Alamy; **258** © Mauritius/SuperStock; **259** top right © Justine Evans, photographersdirect.com; top © Kevin Schafer/Getty Images; **261** bottom © Look GMBH/eStock Photo; top left © Getty Images; top, reef © Royalty-Free/Corbis; top, small dolphin © David Tipling/Alamy; top, big dolphin © Stuart Westmorland/Corbis; **263** © Alejandro Ernesto/epa/Corbis; **265** © Bob Krist/Corbis; **267** bottom © Hisham Ibrahim/Getty Images; center left two © Pablo Corral V/Corbis; center right © age fotostock/SuperStock; top left © Getty Images; top, reef © Royalty-Free/Corbis; top, small dolphin © David Tipling/Alamy; top, big dolphin © Stuart Westmorland/Corbis; **268** Simon Bolivar. Painting. The Granger Collection, New York; **269** © Charles W Luzier/Corbis; **270** © Reuters/Corbis; **271** © Carl & Ann Purcell/Corbis; **273** center right © Michael J. P. Scott/Getty Images; bottom © Eye Ubiquitous/Corbis; top left © Getty Images; top, reef © Royalty-Free/Corbis; top, small dolphin © David Tipling/Alamy; top, big dolphin © Stuart Westmorland/Corbis; **274** © David Noton Photography/Alamy; **275** top left © Steve Vidler/eStock Photo; bottom right Victor R. Caivano/AP/Wide World Photos; **276** top left © Ed Kashi/Corbis; top center © Alistair Berg/Alamy; top right © Owen Franken/Corbis; **277** © Steve Vidler/eStock Photo; **278** background © Nik Wheeler/Corbis; top right © Stephen Frink/Corbis; center left © Ted Spiegel/Corbis; bottom right © Danita Delimont/Alamy; **279** top left © Robert Harding World Imagery/Corbis; center right © Pablo Corral V/Corbis; bottom left © Juniors Bildarchiv/Alamy; background © Fridmar Damm/zefa/Corbis; **281** center right © Hemis/Alamy; bottom © Jon Crwys-Williams/Alamy; top left © Getty Images; top, reef © Royalty-Free/Corbis; top, small dolphin © David Tipling/Alamy; top, big dolphin © Stuart Westmorland/Corbis; **282** bottom left © Chad Ehlers/Alamy; top left Jesus Inostroza/AP/Wide World Photos; **283** right © Danita Delimont/Alamy; top left © Claudia Raschke-Robinson/Just One Productions/The Kobal Collection; **284** © Richard Wareham Fotografie/Alamy; **285** bottom right © Michael J. P. Scott/Getty Images; **286** © Hemis/Alamy.

Chapter 10

288 top left © Theo Allofs/Getty Images; bottom left © Newberry Library/SuperStock; bottom center © Roger Day/Alamy; **289** bottom left © Luis Pacheco/Alamy; bottom right © Christian Liewig/Tempsport/Corbis; **290** Dom Pedro I of Brazil (1800s). Lithograph. The Granger Collection, New York; **291** top left © Panoramic Images/Getty Images; top right © Luiz C. Marigo/Peter Arnold, Inc./Alamy; top, ants © Digital Archive Japan/Alamy; top center © Getty Images; bottom © Ary Diesendruck/Getty Images; **292** © The Granger Collection, New York; **294** top left © ImageState/Jupiter Images; top right © Eduardo Garcia/SuperStock; **295** © Adrian Lascom/Alamy; **296** © Terry Winn Photography, photographersdirect.com; **297** top left © Panoramic Images/Getty Images; top right © Luiz C. Marigo/Peter Arnold, Inc./Alamy; top, ants © Digital Archive Japan/Alamy; top center © Getty Images; bottom © Edward Parker/EASI-Images/CFWiages.com/photographersdirect.com; **298** top right Cover Illustration from Tales of the Amazon: How the Munduruku Indians Live. Text © 1996 by Daniel Munduruku. Illustrations © 1996 by Laurabeatriz. First published in Canada by Groundwood Books Ltd. Reprinted by permission of the publisher.; bottom © Images&Stories, photographersdirect.com; **299** © James Davis Photography/Alamy; **300** top inset © Paulo Fridman/Corbis; top © Cassio Vasconcellos/Getty Images; **301** bottom left © Rick Gomez/Masterfile; second from top left © Julia Waterlow/Eye Ubiquitous/Hutchison; second from right © Martina Urban/Getty Images; bottom right © Rainer Raffalski Photography, photographersdirect.com; top left © David R. Frazier Photolibrary, Inc./Alamy; **302** left © Sue Cunningham Photographic/Alamy; inset Photograph by Ed-Imaging; **303** © Tom Cockrem Photography, photographersdirect.com; **305** top left © Panoramic Images/Getty Images; top right © Luiz C. Marigo/Peter Arnold, Inc./Alamy; top, ants © Digital Archive Japan/Alamy; top center © Getty Images; bottom © mediacolor's/Alamy; **306-307** bottom © Will and Deni McIntyre/Getty Images; **306** bottom inset © Stephen Ferry/Getty Images; top left © Reuters News Picture Archive; **307** top right © Paulo Backes Fotografia e Paisagismo, photographersdirect.com; bottom © Ricardo Beliel/BrazilPhotos/Alamy; bottom right © James Davis Photography/Alamy; **308** © Paulo Backes Fotografia e Paisagismo, photographersdirect.com; **309** bottom left © Roger Day/Alamy; bottom right © Lebrecht Music and Arts Photo Library/Alamy; center left © Creatas; **310** © The Granger Collection, New York.

Unit 4 Opener

313 top left © BL Images Ltd/Alamy; top right © David Sailors/Corbis; bottom left © Kieran Doherty/Reuters/Corbis; bottom right © William Manning/Corbis; **318** © Getty Images; **320** Peter Dejong/AP/Wide World Photos; **323** © Peter Adams Photography/Alamy.

Chapter 11

324 *top left* © nagelestock.com/Alamy; *bottom left* The Granger Collection, New York; *bottom right* © Metropolitan Museum of Art; **325** *bottom left Napoleon Crossing the Alps* (1801), Jacques Louis David. Oil on canvas. 259 cm x 221 cm. Chateaux de Malmaison et Bois-Preau, Rueil-Malmaison, France. Photo © Réunion des Musées Nationaux/Art Resource, New York; *bottom right* © First/zefa/Corbis; **326** © K. Yamashita/PanStock/Panoramic Images/NGSImages.com; **327** *center right* © Jon Arnold Images/Alamy; *bottom* © Nik Wheeler/Corbis; *top left* © Josef Beck/Getty Images; *top right* © Su Davies/Life File/Getty Images; *top swan* © David Martyn Hughes/Alamy; **328** © Paul Hardy/Corbis; **330** *left* © Hortus/Alamy; *second from left* © images-of-france/Alamy; *second from right* © Stan Kujawa/Alamy; *right* © Jorma Jaemsen/zefa/Corbis; **331** © Doug Houghton/Alamy; **332** © nagelestock.com/Alamy; **335** *center right* © Ted Russell/Getty Images; *bottom* © Frank Chmura/Panoramic Images/National Geographic Image Collection; *top left* © Josef Beck/Getty Images; *top right* © Su Davies/Life File/Getty Images; *top, swan* © David Martyn Hughes/Alamy; **336** *bottom* © Peter Grumann/Alamy; *bottom right* The Granger Collection, New York; **337** Detail from the Alexander battle. Mosaic. Museo Archeologico Nazionale, Naples, Italy. Photo © Erich Lessing/Art Resource, New York; **339** © Hideo Kurihara/Alamy; **340** *top right* Kleophrades Painter (500-490 B.C.). Attic red figure amphora. 37 cm. Antikensammlung, Staatliche Museen zu Berlin, Berlin, Germany. Photo © Bildarchiv Preussischer Kulturbesitz/Art Resource, New York; *center left* Greek hydria from Vulci (530 B.C.). Museo Nazionale di Villa Giulia, Rome. Photo © Scala/Art Resource, New York; *right mask* © Ancient Art and Architecture; *left mask* © The Lowe Art Museum, The University of Miami/Superstock; *bottom right* © Buddy Mays/Corbis; *background* © John Elk III/Lonely Planet Images; **341** *top left* Neptune Calming the Waves (1757), Lambert-Sigisbert Adam. Marble sculpture. Louvre, Paris. Photo © Giraudon/Bridgeman Art Library; *top right Breadseller in Public Square*, from *House of the Baker*. Fresco. Museo Archeologico Nazionale, Naples, Italy. Photo © Scala/Art Resource, New York; *bottom left* © Gianni Dagli Orti/Corbis; *background* © Art Kowalsky/Alamy; **343** *center right* © Royalty-Free/Corbis; *bottom* Detail from the Bayeux Tapestry (1000s). Wool embroidery on linen. Musee de la Tapisserie, Bayeux, France. Photo © Bridgeman Art Library; *top left* © Josef Beck/Getty Images; *top right* © Su Davies/Life File/Getty Images; *top, swan* © David Martyn Hughes/Alamy; **344** © Metropolitan Museum of Art; **346** © Jason Hawkes/Corbis; **347** *top right Mona Lisa* (1503-1506), Leonardo da Vinci. Oil on wood. 77 x 53 cm. Inv. 779. Louvre, Paris. Photo © Erich Lessing/Art Resource, New York; *bottom left* Maesta (Madonna Enthroned), Duccio di Buoninsegna. Museo dell'Opera Metropolitana, Siena, Italy. Photo © Scala/Art Resource, New York; *bottom right The Peasants' Wedding* (1568). Oil on oakwood. 114 cm x 164 cm. Kunsthistorisches Museum, Vienna, Austria. Photo © Erich Lessing/Art Resource, New York; **349** © akg-images; **351** *center right* © akg-images; *bottom An Experiment at the Accademia del Cimento*, Gaspero Martellini. Tribuna di Galileo, Museo della Scenza, Florence, Italy. Photo © Scala/Art Resource, New York; *top left* © Josef Beck/Getty Images; *top right* © Su Davies/Life File/Getty Images; *top, swan* © David Martyn Hughes/Alamy; **352** *top left* Execution of King Louis XVI of France (1793). Colored etching. Photo The Granger Collection, New York; *bottom right* Napoleon in Coronation Robe (1810), François Gerard. Oil on canvas 205 cm x 150.5 cm. Chateaux de Malmaison et Bois-Preau, Rueil-Malmaison, France. Photo © Réunion des Musées Nationaux/Art Resource, New York; **354** *left column, top* © Bettmann/Corbis; *left column, second from top* © Swim Ink 2, LLC/Corbis; *left column, second from bottom* © Corbis; *left column, bottom* © Bettmann/Corbis; *second column, top* © Hulton-Deutsch Collection/Corbis; *second column, second from top* © Swim Ink 2, LLC/Corbis; *second column, second from bottom* © Bettmann/Corbis; *second column, bottom* © Corbis; **356** © Photograph by Sharon Hoogstraten; **357** © Metropolitan Museum of Art; **358** © Photograph by Sharon Hoogstraten.

Chapter 12

360 *top left* © Rohan/Getty Images; *bottom left* Detail from Theodora's Court, bust of Theodora. S. Vitale, Ravenna, Italy. Photo © Scala/Art Resource, New York; *bottom right* The Taking of the Bastille, July 14, 1789 Anonymous French painter. Musée National du Chateau, Versailles, France. Photo © Erich Lessing/Art Resource, New York; **361** *bottom left* © Tom Stoddart Archive/Getty Images; *bottom right* © Suomen Kuvapalveluoy/Corbis; **363** *top left* © Adrian Neal/Getty Images; *top right* © Westend61/Alamy; *center right* Polynices and Eriphyle (about 450-440 B.C.). Red figure oinochoe. Louvre, Paris. Photo © Réunion des Musées Nationaux/Art Resource, New York; *bottom* © Roger Wood/Corbis; **364** © Sergio Pitamitz/Corbis; **365** © New York Times Co./Getty Images; **367** Luca Bruno/AP/Wide World Photos; **368** *center left* © Franco Origlia/Getty Images; *top right* © Gareth McCormack/Lonely Planet Images; *bottom* © Jose Fuste Raga/Corbis;

369 *top left* © MedioImages/Getty Images; *bottom left* © Robert Harding Picture Library Ltd/Alamy; *bottom* © Atlantide Phototravel/Corbis; **370** The Granger Collection, New York; **371** *top left* © Adrian Neal/Getty Images; *top right* © Westend61/Alamy; *center right* © Iraida Icaza/Getty Images; *bottom* © John Heseltine/Alamy; **372** © Pete Saloutos/Corbis; **373** Jon Dimis/AP/Wide World Photos; **374** Henry the Navigator (1400s), Nuno Goncalves. Museu Nacional de Arte Antiga, Lisbon, Portugal. Photo © Bridgeman-Giraudon/Art Resource, New York; **375** © Buddy Mays/Corbis; **376** © K. M. Westermann/Corbis; **377** *top left* © Adrian Neal/Getty Images; *top right* © Westend61/Alamy; *center right* © Wolfgang Rattay/Reuters/Corbis; *bottom* © Stock Connection/Jupiter Images; **378** Jacques Brinon/AP/Wide World Photos; **379** *right* © Angelo Cavalli/zefa/Corbis; *inset* © char abumansoor/Alamy; **380** *bottom center* © Brand X Pictures/Alamy; *bottom left* © Greg Stott/Masterfile; **381** © David Noble Photography/Alamy; **383** *top left* © Adrian Neal/Getty Images; *top right* © Westend61/Alamy; *bottom* © Josef Beck/Getty Images; **384** © Robert Maass/Corbis; **385** *bottom* © ImageState/Alamy; *center right* © David Bathgate/Corbis; **386-387** © Stefan Matzke/NewSport/Corbis; **387** © Denis Balibouse/Reuters/Corbis; **388** © Corbis; **389** *top left* © Adrian Neal/Getty Images; *top right* © Westend61/Alamy; *center right* © Nik Wheeler/Corbis; *bottom* © Chris Lisle/Corbis; **391** *bottom left* © Royalty-Free/Corbis; *top left* © Maskot; *second from top left* © P. Manner/zefa/Corbis; *second from right* © Jonathan Blair/Corbis; *bottom right* © FoodPix/Jupiter Images; **392** © Royalty-Free/Corbis; **393** © Nik Wheeler/Corbis; **394** © Rohan/Getty Images; **395** *bottom right* © Nik Wheeler/Corbis; **396** Detail from Theodora's Court, bust of Theodora. S. Vitale, Ravenna, Italy. Photo © Scala/Art Resource, New York.

Chapter 13

398 *bottom right* Signing the Magna Carta (1800s). Engraving. The Granger Collection, New York; *top left* © Kim Sayer/Corbis; *bottom left* © David Noble Photography/Alamy; **399** *bottom left* Factories: England (about 1850). Engraving. The Granger Collection, New York; *bottom right* © Tim Hawkins/Eye Ubiquitous/Corbis; **401** *bottom* © Panoramic Images/Getty Images; *top left* © Hideo Kurihara/Alamy; *top center* © images-of-france/Alamy; *top right* © Getty Images; *center right* © Peter Casolino/Alamy; **402** © PanStock/Jupiter Images; **403** *top* King William III and Queen Mary II. The Granger Collection; *bottom* © Swim Ink 2, LLC/Corbis; **404** © Hulton-Deutsch Collection/Corbis; **408** © Nathan Benn/Corbis; **409** *center right* © Daemmrich Bob/Corbis; *top left* © Hideo Kurihara/Alamy; *top center* © images-of-france/Alamy; *top right* © Getty Images; *bottom* © Panoramic Images/Getty Images; **410** © Grant Pritchard/britainonview; **411** *top* © Scott Barbour/Getty Images; *bottom* © Simon Reddy/Alamy; **412** *left* © Christian Liewig/Corbis; *right* © Steve C. Michell/epa/Corbis; **413** © Ashley Cooper/Corbis; **414** © Photo Researchers, Inc.; **415** *center right* © Tim Graham/Corbis; *bottom* © Julian Calder/Corbis; *top left* © Hideo Kurihara/Alamy; *top center* © images-of-france/Alamy; *top right* © Getty Images; **416** *second from right* © Sergio Pitamitz/zefa/Corbis; *left* © Free Agents Limited/Corbis; *second from left* © Photo 24/Brand X Pictures/Getty Images; *right* © Tim Graham/Corbis; **418** © qaphotos.com/Alamy; **419** © Robert Brook/Photo Researchers, Inc.; **420** © Visual Arts Library (London)/Alamy.

Chapter 14

422 *bottom left* Boar (400-300 B.C.). Bronze statuette. Hungarian National Museum, Budapest, Hungary. Photo © Erich Lessing/Art Resource, New York; *bottom right* © Bettmann/Corbis; *top left* © ML Sinibaldi/Corbis; **423** *bottom right* © James Reeve/Corbis; **425** *bottom* © Momatiuk-Eastcott/Corbis; *top left* © Simon Reddy/Alamy; *top right* © Bill Bachmann/Index Stock Imagery/Jupiter Images; **426** © Konrad Zelazowski/Alamy; **427** *bottom right* John Maniaci/Wisconsin State Journal/AP/Wide World Photos; *bottom* © Bernard Bisson/Corbis; **428** © Reuters/Corbis; **429** *hand with egg* © Jim Sugar/Corbis; *right egg* © Ingram Publishing/Alamy; *bottom* © Peter Turnley/Corbis; *left egg* © Hemera Technologies/Alamy; **430** © Tiit Veermae/Alamy; **431** © Peter Turnley/Corbis; **432** © Peter Turnley/Corbis; **433** *center right* © Stock Connection Distribution/Alamy; *bottom* © Panoramic Images/Getty Images; *top left* © Simon Reddy/Alamy; *top right* © Bill Bachmann/Index Stock Imagery/Jupiter Images; **434** *pepper* © imagebroker/Alamy; *can* © Danita Delimont/Alamy; *bottom left* © Catherine Karnow/Corbis; *bottom right* © Ivan Zupic/Alamy; **436** © Reuters/Corbis; **437** *top* © ML Sinibaldi/Corbis; *bottom* © Robert Harding World Imagery/Corbis; **438** *bottom left* © Jose Luis Pelaez Inc/Getty Images; *top left* © Janine Wiedel Photolibrary/Alamy; *top center* © David Young-Wolff/PhotoEdit; *top right* © Simon Reddy/Alamy; *bottom right* © Mario Ponta/Alamy; **439** *top* © Justin Leighton/Alamy; *top inset* © Motoring Picture Library/Alamy; **440** © Bettmann/Corbis; **441** *center right* AP/Wide World Photos; *bottom* © FAN travelstock/Alamy; *top left* © Simon Reddy/Alamy; *top right* © Bill Bachmann/Index Stock Imagery/Jupiter Images; **442** © Jon Hicks/Corbis; **443** © WoodyStock/Alamy; **444** © CapitalCity Images/Alamy; **445** © Bettmann/Corbis; **446** John Maniaci/Wisconsin State Journal/AP/Wide World Photos.

Unit 5 Opener
449 *bottom left* © 2004 Adrienne McGrath; *top right* © John Lamb/Getty Images; *bottom right* © Eitan Simanor/Alamy; **455** © Dean Conger/Corbis; **456** © Klaus Nigge/National Geographic/Getty Images; **457** © Sovfoto/Eastfoto, photographersdirect.com.

Chapter 15
458 *top left* © Ellen Rooney/Getty Images; *bottom left* © Diego Lezama Orezzoli/Corbis; *bottom right* © SIME s.a.s./eStock Photo; **459** *bottom right* The Granger Collection, New York; *bottom center* © Steve Allen Travel Photography/Alamy; *bottom left* © Corbis; **461** *bottom* © Ralph White/Corbis; *top left* © Pavel Filatov/Alamy; *top center* © Pavel Filatov/Alamy; *top right* © Pavel Filatov/Alamy; *top right inset* © Royalty-Free/Corbis; **462** © Boyd Norton; **463** *center left* © Michel Setboun/Corbis; *bottom left* © Carsten Peter/Getty Images; **464** © Bryan & Cherry Alexander Photography; **465** *top left* © Bryan & Cherry Alexander Photography/Alamy; *top right* © Pavel Filatov/Alamy; *bottom left* © Boyd Norton/Evergreen Photo Alliance; *bottom right* © Pat O'Hara/Corbis; **466** *bottom left* © Bryan & Cherry Alexander Photography/Alamy; © Peter Arnold, Inc./Alamy; *bottom right* © Bryan & Cherry Alexander Photography/Alamy; *top left* © Royalty-Free/Corbis; **469** *top left* © Pavel Filatov/Alamy; *top center* © Pavel Filatov/Alamy; *top right* © Pavel Filatov/Alamy; *top right inset* © Royalty-Free/Corbis; *bottom* © Gavin Hellier/Jon Arnold Images/Alamy; **470** © SuperStock; **471** © By courtesy of Sotheby's Picture Library, London; **473** © Bernard Bisson & Thierry Orban/Sygma/Corbis; **474** *top left* © JTB Photo/Alamy; **476** © Mark Sykes/Alamy; **477** *bottom* © Picture Contact/Alamy; *top left* © Pavel Filatov/Alamy; *top center* © Pavel Filatov/Alamy; *top right* © Pavel Filatov/Alamy; *top right inset* © Royalty-Free/Corbis; **478** © Reuters/Corbis; **479** *top right* © Mark Sykes/Alamy; *center inset* © Reuters/Corbis; *center left* © Douglas Armand/Getty Images; *background* © José Fuste Raga/zefa/Corbis; *bottom right* © AFP/Getty Images; **480** *bottom inset* © Franck Fife/AFP/Getty Images; **481** *bottom inset* © Lesegretain/Corbis; *bottom* © Pierre Perrin/Corbis; **482** *top* © 2006 Artists Rights Society (ARS), New York/ADAGP, Paris. Photo © Albright-Knox Art Gallery/Corbis; *bottom* © Kurov Alexander/Itar-Tass/Corbis; **483** © Thomas Johnson/Corbis; **484** *top left* © Bryan & Cherry Alexander; *background* © Marc Garanger/Corbis; *bottom right* © Nick Haslam/Alamy; *top right* © Jack Sullivan/Alamy; **485** *top left* © Iain Masterton/Alamy; *top right* © Peter Turnley/Corbis; *background* © Bryan & Cherry Alexander Photography/Alamy; *bottom left* © Steve Raymer/Corbis; *second from top left* © Iain Masterton/Alamy; **487** *center right* © Panov Alexei/ITAR-TASS/Corbis; *bottom* © Jeremy Nicholl/Alamy; *top left* © Pavel Filatov/Alamy; *top center* © Pavel Filatov/Alamy; *top right* © Pavel Filatov/Alamy; *top right inset* © Royalty-Free/Corbis; **488** *right* © Reuters/Corbis; **489** © Jeremy Nicholl/Alamy; **491** © SuperStock; **492** © Mark Sykes/Alamy.

Chapter 16
494 *top left* © Keren Su/China Span/Alamy; *bottom left* © Paul H. Kuiper/Corbis; *bottom right* Portrait of Timur (1780), Pierre Duflos. © Stapleton Collection/Corbis; **495** *left* © WorldSat International, Inc.; *right* © WorldSat International, Inc.; **497** *bottom* © Marc Garanger/Corbis; *top left* © Upperhall/Robert Harding World Imagery/Getty Images; *top right* © Imageshop/Alamy; *top right inset* © Creatas/Dynamic Graphics Group/Alamy; **498** © Jerry Kobalenko/Getty Images; **499** © Charles and Josette Lenars/Corbis; **500** *left* © Zurab Kurtsikidze/epa/Corbis; *right* © Tony Allen Photography, photographersdirect.com; **501** © Reuters/Corbis; **502** © AFP/Getty Images; **503** © Reuters/Corbis; **504** © Charles and Josette Lenars/Corbis; **505** *bottom* Temp. Credit: © Ludovic Maisant/Corbis; *top left* © Upperhall/Robert Harding World Imagery/Getty Images; *top right* © Imageshop/Alamy; *top right inset* © Creatas/Dynamic Graphics Group/Alamy; *center right* © Nevada Wier/Robert Harding Picture Library Ltd./Alamy; **506** © Robert Harding Picture Library; **507** *bottom left* © Titus Moser/Eye Ubiquitous/Hutchison; *center right* © Marco Brivio/Alamy; *bottom right* Robert Harding Picture Library; **508** © HIP-Archive/Topham/The Image Works, Inc.; **509** *bottom* © Simon Richmond/Lonely Planet Images; *top right* © Vladimir Sidoropolev Photography, photographersdirect.com; *center right* © Vladimir Sidoropolev Photography, photographersdirect.com; *bottom right* © James Strachan/Getty Images; **510** *top left* © Photo © 2004 Adrienne McGrath; *top left* © Eliane Farray-Sulle/Alamy; *second from top left* © Antoine Gyori/Corbis; *second from right* © Antoine Gyori/Corbis; *right* © Index Stock Imagery/Jupiter Images; **511** © Reuters/Corbis; **513** *bottom* © Alexey Panov/AFP/Getty Images; *top left* © Upperhall/Robert Harding World Imagery/Getty Images; *top right* © Imageshop/Alamy; *top right inset* © Creatas/Dynamic Graphics Group/Alamy; **514** Joseph Stalin (1935), Nikolaj Vasilevic Tomskij. Oil on canvas. © SuperStock; **515** © Sergei Karpukhin/Reuters/Corbis; **516** © Staton R. Winter/Getty Images; **517** *bottom left* © Marc Garanger/Corbis; *bottom right* Robert Harding Picture Library; **518** © Nevada Wier/Corbis; **519** © David Samuel Robbins/Corbis.

Unit 6 Opener
521 *top left* © Renee Lynn/Getty Images; *top right* © Royalty-Free/Corbis; *bottom left* © Remi Benali/Corbis; *bottom right* © W. Robert Moore/National Geographic/Getty Images; **522** © Getty Images; **527** © Peter Turnley/Corbis; **529** © blickwinkel/Alamy; **530-531** © Heinrich van den Berg/Gallo Images/Getty Images; **533** © Peter Johnson/Corbis.

Chapter 17
534 *top left* © Renee Lynn/Getty Images; *bottom left* © Gabriela Staebler/zefa/Corbis; *bottom center* © Bettmann/Corbis; *bottom right* © Javier Trueba/MSF/Photo Researchers, Inc.; **535** *bottom left* © Gianni Dagli Orti/Corbis; *bottom right* © Wildlife Art Ltd.; **536** © Kazuyoshi Nomachi/Corbis; **537** *center right* © Joe McDonald/Corbis; *bottom* © Index Stock/Alamy; *top left* © Getty Images; *top center* © John Conrad/Corbis; *top right* © James Warwick/Getty Images; **538** © ISS-NASA/Getty Images; **539** *left* © Images of Africa Photobank/Alamy; *right* © Torleif Svensson/Corbis; **540** *top left* © Stockbyte Silver/Alamy; **543** © George Steinmetz/Corbis; **545** *center right* © Tom McHugh/Photo Researchers, Inc.; *bottom* © BennettPhoto/Alamy; *top left* © Getty Images; *center left* © John Conrad/Corbis; *top right* © James Warwick/Getty Images; **546** *top left* © Patrick Robert/Corbis; *bottom left* © John Reader/Photo Researchers, Inc.; *bottom right* © Bettmann/Corbis; **547** © John Reader/Photo Researchers, Inc.; **548** © Carla Signorini/Images of Africa Photobank/Getty Images; *top right* © Michael Hart/Getty Images; *bottom left* © Bettmann/Corbis; **549** *center left* © Kazuyoshi Nomachi/Corbis; **550** *top left* © Torleif Svensson/Corbis; *bottom left* © Stockbyte Silver/Alamy.

Chapter 18
552 *top left* © Royalty-Free/Corbis; *bottom left* © Charles & Josette Lenars/Corbis; *bottom right* Selim I (1808), John Young. Watercolour on paper. Photo © Bridgeman Art Library; **553** *bottom left* © The Art Archive/Corbis; *bottom right* © Jonathan Blair/Corbis; **555** *bottom* © G.J. Owen; *top left* © Sami Sarkis/Getty Images; *top center* © Getty Images; *top right* © Sandi Ford/Alamy; **556** © Lloyd Cluff/Corbis; **557** *bottom left* © Historical Picture Archive/Corbis; *bottom* Photograph by Sharon Hoogstraten **558** © Frank Trapper/Corbis; **559** © Sandro Vannini/Corbis; **560** *top left* © Jean-Pierre Lescourret/Corbis; **562** © Jonathan Blair/Corbis; **563** *center right* © The Art Archive/Corbis; *bottom* © Jean Dominique DALLET/Alamy; *top left* © Sami Sarkis/Getty Images; *top center* © Getty Images; *top right* © Sandi Ford/Alamy; **564** *Mehemet Ali* (1800s), Louis Charles Couder. Oil on canvas. Chateau de Versailles, France. Photo © Bridgeman Art Library; **565** © Premium Stock/Corbis; **566** © Actual Films/Principe Productions; **567** © Wally Nell/epa/Corbis; **568** © Chris Lisle/Corbis; **569** *bottom* © Antoine Gyori/Corbis; *top left* © Sami Sarkis/Getty Images; *top center* © Getty Images; *top right* © Sandi Ford/Alamy; **570** *left* © Chris Lisle/Corbis; *right* © Roger Antrobus/Corbis; **571** *bottom* © Patrick Robert/Corbis; *top* © Digital Vision/Getty Images; *center* © Comstock Images/Jupiter Images; **572** © Peter Adams Photography/Alamy; **574** © K. M. Westermann/Corbis; **575** © Giraudou Laurent/Corbis; **576** © Lloyd Cluff/Corbis.

Chapter 19
578 *top left* © SuperStock; *bottom right* © David Jones/Alamy; *bottom left* © Art Wolfe/Getty Images; **579** *bottom* © Mary Evans Picture Library/Alamy; *bottom right* © Corbis; **581** *top left* © Sylvia Cordaiy Photo Library Ltd./Alamy; *top center* © Joshua D. Polman/Alamy; *top right* © Stan Osolinski/Oxford Scientific/Jupiter Images; *bottom* © Frans Lemmens/Getty Images; **583** Askia Muhammed. © Leo and Diane Dillon; **585** © Alain DeJean/Corbis; **586** © Robert Estall photo agency/Alamy; **587** *top left* © Sylvia Cordaiy Photo Library Ltd./Alamy; *top center* © Joshua D. Polman/Alamy; *top right* © Stan Osolinski/Oxford Scientific/Jupiter Images; *bottom* © Paul Almasy/Corbis; **589** *top left* © Greenpeace/Corbis; *bottom right* Saurabh Das/AP/Wide World Photos; **590** *bottom left* © Paul Almasy/Corbis; *bottom* © Digital Vision Ltd./SuperStock; **591** © Margaret Courtney-Clarke/Corbis; **592** *top left* © Robert Estall photo agency/Alamy; *top right* © Michael S. Lewis/Corbis; *center* © Yann Arthus-Bertrand/Corbis; *bottom right* © Gary Cook/Alamy; **593** *top left* © Julian Nieman/Alamy; *top right* © Gary Cook/Alamy; *center* © Yann Arthus-Bertrand/Corbis; *bottom left* © Stephanie Colasanti/Corbis; **594** © Peter Bowater/Alamy; **595** *top left* © Sylvia Cordaiy Photo Library Ltd./Alamy; *top center* © Joshua D. Polman/Alamy; *top right* © Stan Osolinski/Oxford Scientific/Jupiter Images; *center right* © Nik Wheeler/Corbis; *bottom* © Karsten Wrobel/Alamy; **596** © David C. Conrad; **597** *top left* © Mike Goldwater/Alamy; *top center* © Finbarr O'Reilly/Reuters/Corbis; *second from right* © Michael Dwyer/Alamy; *bottom right* © Daniel Berehulak/Getty Images; **598** *center left* © Luc Gnago/Reuters/Corbis; *bottom* © Patrick Robert/Corbis; **599** © Christian Liewig/Corbis; **600** © Charles and Josette Lenars/Corbis; **601** © Margaret Courtney-Clarke/Corbis; **602** © Robert Estall photo agency/Alamy.

Chapter 20

604 *top left* © Brian A. Vikander/Corbis; *bottom left* © Werner Forman/Corbis; *bottom right* © David Reed/Corbis; **605** *bottom left* © Marion Kaplan/Alamy; **606** © Pixtal/SuperStock; **607** *top left* © Mike Copeland/Getty Images; *top center* © Paul A. Souders/Corbis; *top right* © Art Wolfe/Getty Images; *center right* © J. P. De Manne/Robert Harding World Imagery/Getty Images; *bottom* © Robert Preston/ Alamy; **609** © Werner Forman/Corbis; **610** *bottom left* © imagebroker/ Alamy; *bottom right* © Stock Connection/Jupiter Images; **611** © Earl and Nazima Kowall/Corbis; **612** © age fotostock/SuperStock; **613** *top left* © Mike Copeland/Getty Images; *top center* © Paul A. Souders/ Corbis; *top right* © Art Wolfe/Getty Images; *center right* © Martin Harvey/Corbis; *bottom* © Images of Africa Photobank/Alamy; **614** *top left* © Charles O. Cecil/Alamy; *top right* © foodfolio/Alamy; **615** © Dylan Martinez/Reuters/Corbis; **616** © Marion Kaplan/Alamy; **617** © Gavriel Jecan/Corbis; **619** *top left* © Mike Copeland/Getty Images; *top center* © Paul A. Souders/Corbis; *top right* © Art Wolfe/Getty Images; *bottom* © David Wall/Alamy; **621** © Jacques Jangoux/Alamy; **622** *left* © Francisco Cruz/SuperStock; *center* © J. Marshall - Tribaleye Images/ Alamy; *right* © Robert Estall photo agency/Alamy; **623** Lionel Healing/ AFP/Getty Images; **625** *top left* © Mike Copeland/Getty Images; *top center* © Paul A. Souders/Corbis; *top right* © Art Wolfe/Getty Images; *center right* Naashon Zalk/AP/Wide World Photos; *bottom* © Eric Nathan/Alamy; **626** © David Turnley/Corbis; **627** AP/Wide World Photos; **628** *left* © Patrick Durand/Corbis; *right* © Charles O'Rear/ Corbis; **630** © David Reed/Corbis; **631** *top left* © Mike Copeland/Getty Images; *top center* © Paul A. Souders/Corbis; *top right* © Art Wolfe/ Getty Images; *bottom* © Patrick Ward/Corbis; **632** *bottom* © Robert Harding Picture Library Ltd/Alamy; *center right* Conical tower on the southern side of the great enclosure. The purpose is still shrouded in mystery. Marius Loots, South Africa; **633** © Anthony Bannister/Gallo Images/Corbis; **634** © Brian Seed/Alamy; **636** © Expuesto - Nicolas Randall/Alamy; **637** © Bernard Bisson/Corbis; **638** © Robert Harding Picture Library Ltd/Alamy; **639** © /politicalcartoons.com.

Unit 7 Opener

641 *top left* © Frans Lemmens/zefa/Corbis; *top right* © Medioimages/ Alamy; *bottom left* © Sheldan Collins/Corbis; *bottom right* © Jiri Rezac/Alamy; **642** © Getty Images; **646-647** © Jayanta Shaw/Reuters/ Corbis; **649** © Massimo Listri/Corbis.

Chapter 21

650-651 © Michael S. Yamashita/Corbis; **650** *top left* © Alistair Baird/Alamy; *bottom left* © Zen Icknow/Corbis; *bottom right* © Visual Arts Library (London)/Alamy; **651** *bottom right* © Gianni Dagli Orti/Corbis; **652** © Jeremy Horner/Corbis; **653** *center right* © Roger Wood/Corbis; *bottom* © Profimedia.CZ s.r.o./Alamy; *top left* © Design Pics Inc./Alamy; *top center* © Dinodia Images/Alamy; *top right* © Michelangelo Gratton/Getty Images; **654** © Ricki Rosen/Corbis; **656** *bottom* © Sindre Ellingsen/Alamy; **657** Burhan Ozbilici/AP/Wide World Photos; **659** *center right* © Arko Datta/Reuters/Corbis; *top left* © Design Pics Inc./Alamy; *top center* © Dinodia Images/Alamy; *top right* © Michelangelo Gratton/Getty Images; **660** *left* © Alistair Baird/ Alamy; *right* © David Samuel Robbins/Corbis; **662** © Rafiqur Rahman/ Reuters/Corbis; **663** © Anuruddha Lokuhapuarachchi/Reuters/Corbis; **664** *center left* © Reuters/Corbis; *bottom left* © Rafiqur Rahman/ Reuters/Corbis; **667** *second from center right* © Science Museum/ SSPL/The Image Works, Inc.; *center right* © Science Museum/SSPL/The Image Works, Inc.; *bottom* © Tor Eigeland/Alamy; *top left* © Design Pics Inc./Alamy; *top center* © Dinodia Images/Alamy; *top right* © Michelangelo Gratton/Getty Images; **668** *bottom* © Ali Jarekji/ Reuters/Corbis; *bottom left* © Peter Horree/Alamy; **669** © Gianni Dagli Orti/Corbis; **670** © JTB Photo/Alamy; **671** *bottom left* © Michael S. Yamashita/Corbis; *bottom right* © Visual Arts Library (London)/ Alamy; **672** © Michael S. Yamashita/Corbis.

Chapter 22

674 *top left* © Medioimages/Alamy; *bottom left* © Bojan Brecelj/ Corbis; *bottom right* © Peter Horree/Alamy; **675** *bottom left* © Trip/ Alamy; *bottom right* © W. Robert Moore/National Geographic/Getty Images; **676** © Popperfoto/Alamy; **677** *top left* © Tibor Bognár/Corbis; *top right* © Mike Hill/Oxford Scientific/Jupiter Images; *bottom* © George Steinmetz/Corbis; **678** © Dbimages/Alamy; **680** © Robert Patrick/Corbis; **681** © Paul Almasy/Corbis; **683** *top left* © Tibor Bognár/Corbis; *top right* © Mike Hill/Oxford Scientific/Jupiter Images; *center right* © Reinhard Krause/Reuters/Corbis; *bottom* © Annie Griffiths Belt/Corbis; **684** © Nina Large/ArenaPal/Topham/The Image Works, Inc.; **685** *left* © Royalty-Free/Corbis; *center* © Hanan Isachar/ Israel images/Alamy; *right* © Sandro Vannini/Corbis; **686** © Hanan Isachar/Israel images/Alamy; **687** © Douglas Kirkland/Corbis; **689** *top left* © Tibor Bognár/Corbis; *top right* © Mike Hill/Oxford Scientific/ Jupiter Images; *bottom* © Herbert Spichtinger/zefa/Corbis; **690** © Murat Taner/zefa/Corbis; **692** © Hemis/Alamy; **693** © Tim Graham/ Alamy; **694** © Herbert Spichtinger/zefa/Corbis.

Chapter 23

696 *top left* © Wolfgang Kaehler/Corbis; *bottom left* © Borromeo/ Art Resource, New York; *bottom right* © The British Library/HIP/The Image Works, Inc.; **697** *bottom left* © Pallava Bagla/Corbis; *bottom right* © Dinodia Images/Alamy; **699** *top left* © Gale Beery/Index Stock Imagery/Jupiterimages Corporation; *top center* © Getty Images; *top right* © blickwinkel/Alamy; *center right* © Maciej Wojtkowiak/Alamy; *bottom* © Grant Dixon/Lonely Planet Images/Getty Images; **700-701** © Historical Picture Archive/Corbis; **701** © The British Library/HIP/The Image Works, Inc.; **702** © Pallava Bagla/Corbis; **703** © Bettmann/ Corbis; **704** © Bettmann/Corbis; **705** AP/Wide World Photos; **706** © Burstein Collection/Corbis; **707** *top left* © Gale Beery/Index Stock Imagery/Jupiterimages Corporation; *top center* © Getty Images; *top right* © blickwinkel/Alamy; *center right* © Dinodia Images/Alamy; *bottom* © Michael S. Lewis/Corbis; **709** *bottom* © CMCD, Inc.; *inset top* © Jeremy Horner/Corbis; *inset bottom* © Lindsay Hebberd/Corbis; **710** *left* © Earl and Nazima Kowall/Corbis; *right* © Robert Wallis/ Corbis; **711** *center right* © DAMFX/The Kobal Collection; *bottom* © Arko Datta/Reuters/Corbis; **712** *bottom left* © Photosindia.com LLC/Alamy; *top left* © David H. Wells/Corbis; *top center* © Jonah Calinawan/Alamy; *second from right* © Dinodia Images/Alamy; *right* © Dinodia Photo Library; **713** © Kamal Kishore/Reuters/Corbis; **714** *center left* © David Samuel Robbins/Corbis; *top right* © Christine Osborne/Corbis; *background* © Stephanie Colasanti/Corbis; *bottom right* © Chris Lisle/Corbis; **715** © Kapoor Baldev/Corbis; *top right* © Robert Wallis/Corbis; *background* © Dinodia Images/Alamy; *bottom left* © Brian Lee/Corbis; **716** © Charles and Josette Lenars/ Corbis; **717** *top left* © Gale Beery/Index Stock Imagery/Jupiterimages Corporation; *top center* © Getty Images; *top right* © blickwinkel/ Alamy; *center right* © Stringer/India/Reuters/Corbis; *bottom* © John Peter Photography/Alamy; **718** © Getty Images; **720** © Pallava Bagla/ Corbis; **722** © Reuters/Corbis; **723** *bottom left* © Pallava Bagla/Corbis; *bottom right* © Dinodia Images/Alamy; **724** © Burstein Collection/ Corbis.

Chapter 24

726 *top left* © Casa Productions/Corbis; *bottom left* © Joe McDonald/ Corbis; *bottom center* © Reuters/Corbis; *bottom right* © Time Life Pictures/Getty Images; **727** *bottom left* © Dennis M. Sabangan/epa/ Corbis; *bottom right* © Gopal Chitrakar/Reuters/Corbis; **729** *top left* © Colin Monteath/Oxford Scientific/Jupiter Images; *top center* © Andy Rouse/Getty Images; *center right* © Michael Edwards/Getty Images; *bottom* © Michael S. Yamashita/Corbis; **730** © Reuters/Corbis; **732** *left* © Galen Rowell/Corbis; *right* © Tiziana and Gianni Baldizzone/Corbis; **733** © Liba Taylor/Corbis; **734** *top left* © Zohra Bensemra/Reuters/ Corbis; *top right* © Faisal Mahmood/Reuters/Corbis; *center* © Mian Khursheed/Reuters/Corbis; *bottom right* © Goran Tomasevic/Reuters/ Corbis; **735** *top left* © Jayanta Shaw/Reuters/Corbis; *top right* © Rafiqur Rahman/Reuters/Corbis; *center* © Rafiqur Rahman/Reuters/ Corbis; *bottom left* © Rafiqur Rahman/Reuters/Corbis; **736** © Chad Ehlers/Alamy; **737** *top left* © Colin Monteath/Oxford Scientific/Jupiter Images; *top center* © Andy Rouse/Getty Images; *center right* © Michael Edwards/Getty Images; *center right* © Sergio Pitamitz/zefa/ Corbis; © Eye Ubiquitous/Corbis; **738** *top* © Stock Connection/ Alamy; *bottom* © Keren Su/China Span/Alamy; **740** © Jeremy Horner/ Corbis; **741** *center left* © Image Source/Getty Images; *bottom right* © Reuters/Corbis; **742** © Chad Ehlers/Alamy; *bottom* © Keren Su/China Span/Alamy.

Unit 8 Opener

745 *top left* © Panorama Media (Beijing) Ltd./Alamy; *top right* © Jeremy Woodhouse/Getty Images; *bottom left* © Darby Sawchuck Photography, photographersdirect.com; *bottom right* © Tibor Bognár/Corbis; **751** © Arco Images/Alamy; **753** © Ingo Jezierski/Getty Images.

Chapter 25

754 *top left* © Getty Images; *bottom left* Confucius (551-479 B.C.). Scroll painting. Bibliotheque Nationale, Paris. Photo © Snark/Art Resource, New York; *bottom right* Qin Shi Huang (about 1900). Photo © HIP/Art Resource, New York; **755** *bottom left* © Luis Castaneda Inc/Getty Images; *bottom right* © Peter Adams/Getty Images; **756** © John Foster/Masterfile; **757** *top left* © Jose Fuste Raga/Corbis; *top right* © Angelo Cavalli/Getty Images; *bottom* © epa/Corbis; **758** *top left* © Royalty-Free/Corbis; *bottom* © ImagineChina; **760** The Granger Collection, New York; **761** *left* © Keren Su/China Span; *right* © Michael S. Yamashita/Corbis; **762** © China Photos/Reuters/Corbis; **763** Science Museum/Science and Society Picture Library; **765** *top left* © Jose Fuste Raga/Corbis; *top right* © Angelo Cavalli/Getty Images; *center right* Qin Shi Huang (about 1900). Photo © HIP/Art Resource, New York; © Juliet Coombe/Getty Images; **766** © Harvey Lloyd/Getty Images; **767** The Granger Collection, New York; **768** *left* Chinese coins with holes for stringing on cords. (tenth century B.C.) © Dagli Orti/The Art Archive; *top right* Marco Polo (1820) Line engraving. Italian. The Granger Collection; *top left* Banknote from Kublai Khan's first issue of banknotes. Private Collection/Photo © The Bridgeman Art Library; **769** *compass* © Science Museum/Science and Society Picture Library; *bottom left* Chinese map of the Eastern hemisphere (1790). Staatsbibliothek zu Berlin, Berlin, Germany. Photo © Bildarchiv Preussischer Kulturbesitz/Art Resource, New York; **771** © Yann Layma/Getty Images; **772** *top left* © Yann Layma/Getty Images; **775** *top left* © Jose Fuste Raga/Corbis; *top right* © Angelo Cavalli/Getty Images; *bottom* © ImagineChina; *center right* © Inga Spence/Index Stock Imagery, Inc.; **776** © ImagineChina; **779** © Bruce Connolly/Corbis; **780** *bottom left* © Jack Hollingsworth/Corbis; *top left* © Rick Lew/FoodPix/Jupiter Images; *second from top left* © Bruno Barbey/Magnum Photos; *second from top right* © Royalty-Free/Corbis; *bottom right* © ImagineChina; **782** *bottom* © Keren Su/Getty Images; *center left* © David Butow/Corbis; *top right* Photo © 2004 Adrienne McGrath; *bottom right* © Tom Nebbia/Corbis; **783** *bottom* © Didier Bauweraerts/Van Parys Media/Corbis; *top left* © Yann Layma/Getty Images; *top right* © ImagineChina; *bottom left* © Keren Su/China Span; **784** © Robin Moyer/OnAsia; **785** *top left* © Jose Fuste Raga/Corbis; *top right* © Angelo Cavalli/Getty Images; *center right* © Frederic J. Brown/AFP/Getty Images; *bottom* © Digital Vision/Getty Images; **786** *left* © Joseph Sohm/ChromoSohm Inc./Corbis; *bottom center* © Free Agents Limited/Corbis; *bottom right* © Photo 24/Brand X Pictures/Getty Images; **788** © Jon Hicks/Corbis; **789** © ImagineChina; **790** China Daily Information Corp/Reuters News Picture Archive; **791** *bottom right* Qin Shi Huang (about 1900). Photo © HIP/Art Resource, New York; **792** *top left* Confucius (551-479 B.C.). Scroll painting. Bibliotheque Nationale, Paris. Photo © Snark/Art Resource, New York.

Chapter 26

794 *bottom left* © JTB Photo/Alamy; *top left* © WizData,inc./Alamy; *bottom right* Gold crown from Ch'onmachong. Silla kingdom. National Treasure No. 188. National Kyongiu Museum, Republic of Korea; **795** *bottom left* © Bobby Yip/Reuters/Corbis; *bottom center* © Richard Hamilton Smith/Corbis; **796** NASA; **797** *center right* © Wolfgang Kaehler/Corbis; *bottom* © Trip/Alamy; *top left* © Andre Seale/Alamy; *top right* © blickwinkel/Alamy; *top right inset* © Gary Stones/Alamy; **798** © Craig J. Brown; **799** *top right* © JTB Photo/Alamy; *center right* © FAN travelstock/Alamy; **800** *left* © Jörén Gerhard/OnAsia; *right* © TongRo Image Stock/Alamy; **801** © Steve Kaufman/Corbis; **802** *bottom right* © David White/Alamy; *bottom* © Digital Archive Japan/Alamy; **804** © John Borthwick/Lonely Planet Images; **805** *bottom* © Werner Forman/Corbis; *top left* © Andre Seale/Alamy; *top right* © blickwinkel/Alamy; *top right inset* © Gary Stones/Alamy; **806** © Leonard de Selva/Corbis; **808** *bottom right* © Photojourneys, photographersdirect.com; *inset* © Claro Cortes IV/Reuters/Corbis; **809** *bottom left* © LWA/Dann Tardif/Getty Images; *top left* © Craig J. Brown; *top center* © Fotosearch Stock Photography; *second from right* © Jean Chung/OnAsia; *bottom right* © Chad Ehlers/Alamy; **810-811** Pear-shaped vase (1100s to 1200s). Korea. Celadon ceramic, with incrustations under "sanggam" glaze. Koryo period. Height 32.5 cm. Inv.: MG 18279. Musée des Arts Asiatiques-Guimet, Paris. Photo © Pascal Pleynet/Réunion des Musées Nationaux/Art Resource, New York; **810** *top left* © Chris Lisle/Corbis; *top right* © Chris Lisle/Corbis; **811** © KCNA/epa/Corbis; **812** © Christopher Farina/Corbis; **813** *center right* NASA; *bottom* © KCNA/epa/Corbis; *top left* © Andre Seale/Alamy; *top right* © blickwinkel/Alamy; *top right inset* © Gary Stones/Alamy; **814** © nichola west/Alamy; **815** *top right* © Tom Wagner/Corbis; *bottom* © Jeon Heon-Kyun/epa/Corbis; **816** © Chung Sung-Jun/Getty Images; **818** © Reuters/Corbis; **819** © John Borthwick/Lonely Planet Images; **820** © David White/Alamy.

Chapter 27

822 *top left* © Toyofumi Mori/Getty Images; *bottom left* Shotoku Taishi. Private Collection, Paris. Photo © Dagli Orti/The Art Archive; *bottom right* © Burstein Collection/Corbis; *bottom right* © Archivo Iconografico, S.A./Corbis; **823** *bottom left* © Tibor Bognar/Corbis; *bottom right* © Martin Plomer/Dorling Kindersley/Getty Images; **825** *top right* © Seth Rutledge/Alamy; *top center* © Yoshio Sawaragi/Dex Image/Jupiter Images; *top left* © C. Bowman/Robert Harding World Imagery/Getty Images; *center right* © Tim McGuire/Corbis; *bottom* © Free Agents Limited/Corbis; **826** © Reuters/Corbis; **828** © Roger Ressmeyer/Corbis; **829** © DLILLC/Corbis; **830** © Chris Lisle/Corbis; **831** *top right* © Seth Rutledge/Alamy; *top center* © Yoshio Sawaragi/Dex Image/Jupiter Images; *top left* © C. Bowman/Robert Harding World Imagery/Getty Images; *bottom* © Shin Terada, Sweetish Fotostage ST; *center right* © Royalty-Free/Corbis; **832** *left* Eisei-Bunko Museum; *right* Detail of Knight with green and white shields on red horse: Capodilista Codex. Manuscripts. Civic Library of Padua, Italy. Photo © SuperStock; **833** *top* © Ric Ergenbright/Corbis; *bottom* © Iain Masterton/Alamy; **835** *top* © Jon Hicks/Corbis; *bottom left* Photograph by Bac To Trong; **836** *top left* © Christie's Images/Corbis;

bottom © R. Ian Lloyd/Masterfile; **837** © Andy Rain/epa/Corbis; **838** *top right* © Royalty-Free/Corbis; *top left* © Michael Kim/Corbis; *background* © Catherine Karnow/Corbis; *bottom right* © Jack Fields/Corbis; **839** *top right* © Walt Disney Pictures/ZUMA/Corbis; *top left* © Masterfile; *background* © Douglas Armand/Alamy; *bottom left* © Barry Lewis/Corbis; **840** © Bettmann/Corbis; **841** *top right* © Seth Rutledge/Alamy; *top center* © Yoshio Sawaragi/Dex Image/Jupiter Images; *top left* © C. Bowman/Robert Harding World Imagery/Getty Images; *bottom* © Royalty-Free/Corbis; *bottom right* © Anonymous/Corbis; **842** *bottom left* © Free Agents Limited/Corbis; *bottom center* © Photo 24/Brand X Pictures/Getty Images; *bottom right* © Royalty-Free/Corbis; **843** *bottom left* © Tom Wagner/Corbis; *bottom center* © Reuters/Corbis; *bottom right* © Issei Kato/Reuters/Corbis; **844** © Issei Kato/Reuters/Corbis; **846** © Yuriko Nakao/Reuters/Corbis; **847** Eisei-Bunko Museum; **848** © Chris Lisle/Corbis.

Chapter 28

850 *top left* © Adam Deschamps/Alamy; *bottom left* © Jack Fields/Corbis; *bottom right* © Mary Evans Picture Library/The Image Works, Inc.; **851** *bottom left* © Neil McAllister/Alamy; *bottom right* © David Hodges/Alamy; **852** © Image Makers/Getty Images; **853** *top left* © Bruno Morandi/Robert Harding World Imagery/Getty Images; *top center* © Getty Images; *top right* © JTP Photo/Alamy; *bottom* © Getty Images; **854** © Hemis/Alamy; **855** © Mark Pearson/Alamy; **856** *top left* © Frans Lanting/Corbis; *bottom* © Tim Graham/Corbis; **857** © Terry Whittaker/Alamy; **858** © Chris Lisle/Corbis; **859** *top left* © Bruno Morandi/Robert Harding World Imagery/Getty Images; *top center* © Getty Images; *top right* © JTP Photo/Alamy; *bottom* © Gavin Hellier/Getty Images; **861** © Luca I Tettoni/Corbis; **862** Richard Vogel/AP/Wide World Photos; **863** © DigitalVision/eStock Photo; **864** © Ted Spiegel/Corbis; **865** *top left* © Bruno Morandi/Robert Harding World Imagery/Getty Images; *top center* © Getty Images; *top right* © JTP Photo/Alamy; *bottom* © Chris Tan/Getty Images; **866** *bottom right* © Free Agents Limited/Corbis; *bottom left* © David Hanson/Getty Images; **867** © Reuters/Corbis; **868** © Paul A. Souders/Corbis; **869** *bottom left* © Hemis/Alamy; *bottom right* © Chris Lisle/Corbis; **870** Richard Vogel/AP/Wide World Photos.

Unit 9 Opener

873 *bottom left* © Royalty-Free/Corbis; *top right* © Oliver Strewe/Lonely Planet Images; *bottom right* © Robert Harding Picture Library Ltd./Alamy; **878** The Granger Collection, New York; **879** © Bill Curtsinger/NGSImages.com; **880** © MedioImages/Getty Images; **881** © Owen Franken/Corbis.

Chapter 29

882 *top left* © Image Source/Alamy; *bottom left* Birem, Iguana of the Rocks, Midjau-Midjawu, group Gunwinggu. Aboriginal art, painted on Eucalyptus bark. Musée du Quai Branly, Paris. Photo © J. G. Berizzi/Réunion des Musées Nationaux/Art Resource, New York; *bottom right* The Granger Collection, New York; **883** © Duomo/Corbis; **884** © Nik Wheeler/Corbis; **885** *top left* © Jose Fuste Raga/Corbis; *center* © Matthew Noble/Alamy; *top right* © Dallas and John Heaton/Stock Connection; *bottom* © Charles and Josette Lenars/Corbis; *center right* © Paul A. Souders/Corbis; **886** *top left* © Nik Wheeler/Corbis; *bottom* © Jeff Hunter/The Image Bank/Getty Images; **888** *top* © Frans Lanting/Corbis; *left* © Juergen and Christine Sohns/Animals Animals - Earth Scenes; *center* © Gary Bell/zefa/Corbis; *right* © Dave Watts/Alamy; **889** © Hulton-Deutsch Collection/Corbis; **890** *center right* © Leonard Douglas Zell/Lonely Planet Images; *bottom left* © AM Corporation/Alamy; **892** © John Van Hasselt/Corbis; **893** *bottom* © Suzanne Long/Alamy; *top left* © Jose Fuste Raga/Corbis; *center* © Matthew Noble/Alamy; *top right* © Dallas and John Heaton/Stock Connection; **894** © John Van Hasselt/Corbis; **895** *left* © Free Agents Limited/Corbis; *right* © Photo 24/Brand X Pictures/Getty Images; **896** *top* © Norman Chan/ShutterStock; *bottom* © SCPhotos/Alamy; **897** *bottom left* © Royalty-Free/Corbis; *top left* © Royalty-Free/Corbis; *second from top left* © Mark Richards/PhotoEdit; *third from top left* © Phototake Inc./Alamy; *bottom right* © Paul A. Souders/Corbis; **898** *top left* © Paul A. Souders/Corbis; *left* © Dave G. House/Post-Houserstock/Corbis; *center* © Paul A. Souders/Corbis; *right* © Bill Bachman/Alamy; **900** © Mike Powell/Getty Images; **901** *top left* © Jose Fuste Raga/Corbis; *center* © Matthew Noble/Alamy; *top right* © Dallas and John Heaton/Stock Connection; *center right* © Laureen Middley/Getty Images; *bottom* © Panoramic Images/Getty Images; **902** © Werner Forman/Corbis; **903** © Neil Rabinowitz/Corbis; **904** © Chris Ballentine/Paul Thompson Images/Alamy; **905** *top right* © Pierre Vinet/New Line/Saul Zaentz/Wing Nut Films/The Kobal Collection; *bottom* © Paul Thompson/Eye Ubiquitous/Corbis; **906** © Anthony Cooper/Ecoscene/Corbis; **907** © Frans Lanting/Corbis; **908** © John Warden/Getty Images.

Chapter 30
910 © Bill Curtsinger/NGSImages.com; *bottom left* Owen Franken/ Corbis; *bottom* The Granger Collection, New York; **911** *bottom left* The Granger Collection, New York; *bottom right* © Danita Delimont/ Alamy; **912** © Paul Chesley/Getty Images; **913** *top left* © Chris Cheadle/Getty Images; *top center* © Peter Scoones/Getty Images; *top right* © David Tipling/Getty Images; *bottom* © Kevin Schafer/Getty Images; **915** © Jodi Cobb/NGSImages.com; **916** © NGSImages.com; **917** © Hippocrene Books; **918** *top right* © Gary Steer/Lonely Planet Images; *bottom left* © Jean-Bernard Carillet/Lonely Planet Images; *bottom right* © Wolfgang Kaehler/Corbis; *center* © Jean-Bernard Carillet/Lonely Planet Images; **919** *top left* © Anders Ryman/Corbis; *center right* © Jodi Cobb/NGSImages.com; *center* © Klaus Nigge/NGSImages.com; *center* © Tim Laman/NGSImages.com; **920** © Photo Researchers, Inc.; **921** *top left* © Chris Cheadle/Getty Images; *top center* © Peter Scoones/Getty Images; *top right* © David Tipling/ Getty Images; *center right* © Getty Images; *bottom* © Maria Stenzel/ NGSImages.com; **923** *center right* © Photo Researchers, Inc.; *bottom right* The Granger Collection, New York; **925** *top left* © Kevin Cooley/ Getty Images; *bottom left* © Jodi Cobb/NGSImages.com; **926** © Paul Chesley/Getty Images.

End Matter
R1 Photograph by Ed-Imaging; **R23** © Mark Newman/University of Michigan; **R26** © HIP-Archive/Topham/The Image Works, Inc.; **R35** *top* © Michael Newman/PhotoEdit; *bottom* © Bob Daemmrich/PhotoEdit; **R36** Screenshot © Google Inc. and is used with permission; **R37** Courtesy of USGS; **R40-R41** *top* © Lindsay Hebberd/Corbis; *bottom* © Dave Bartruff/Corbis; **R40** *bottom left* © Comstock; **R41** *top right* © David Samuel Robbins/Corbis; **R42-R43** *top* The Tribute Money, Masaccio (Maso di San Giovanni). S. Maria del Carmine, Florence, Italy. Photo © Scala/Art Resource, New York; **R42** *bottom left* Luis Romero/AP/Wide World Photos; **R43** *bottom left* © Angelo Hornak/ Corbis; *top right* © Comstock Images/Jupiter Images; **R44** © Reuters/ Corbis; **R45** *top left* Heads of Brahma, Vichnu and Shiva (late 800's). Phnom Bok (Siemreap). Musée des Arts Asiatiques-Guimet, Paris. Photo © Erich Lessing/Art Resource, New York; *bottom left* © Bennett Dean; Eye Ubiquitous/Corbis; *top right* © ArkReligion.com/Alamy; **R46-R47** © Richard T. Nowitz/Corbis; **R46** *bottom left* Muslim men praying in the street. Photo © Arthur Thévenart/Corbis; **R47** *top left* Jassim Mohammed/AP/Wide World Photos; *top right* © Michael S. Yamashita/Corbis; **R48-R49** *top* Photograph by Bill Aron; **R48** *bottom left* © The Art Archive/Corbis; **R49** *bottom left* © Christie's Images/ Corbis; *top right* © Nathan Benn/Corbis; **R50** *bottom* © Yoshio Tomii/ SuperStock Inc.; *top* © SuperStock Inc.; **R51** *left* © ImagineChina; *top right* Chinese ying and yang (200's). Roman. Mosaic. Archaeological Museum, Sousse, Tunisia. Photo © Dagli Orti/Art Archive; **R52-R53** © Bob Krist/Corbis; **R52** © Royalty-Free/Corbis; **R53** *top* © Chris Lisle/ Corbis; *center right* © Paul Almasy/Corbis.

Illustrations
Maps by Rand McNally **A14-A37**
All other maps, locators and globe locators by GeoNova LLC
Illustration by Nick Rotondo/Bizzy Productions **162-163**
Illustration by Peter Bull **218-219, 218** *both,* **474-475, 474, 560-561, 560** *center left,* **664-665, 890-891, 890** *top left*
Illustration by Peter Dennis **348**
Illustration by Ken Goldammer **A8-A9**
Illustration by Martin Hargraves **345**
Illustration by Michael Jaroszko **Graphs, Charts, and Tables, 558**
Illustration by Bob Kayganich **46-47, 46** *top left*
Illustration by Precision Graphics **28, 29, 37, 42, 50, 655, 659, 915** *both*
Illustration by Sebastian Quigley **772-773, 772** *both*
Illustration by Robert Sikora **406-407, 406** *both*
Illustration by Stephen R. Wagner **540**
All other illustrations by McDougal Littell/Houghton Mifflin Co.

The editors have made every effort to trace the ownership of all copyrighted material found in this book and to make full acknowledgment for its use. Omissions brought to our attention will be corrected in a subsequent edition.